# NEW REVISED
## *CAMBRIDGE*
# GED
## PROGRAM
## Comprehensive Book

**CAMBRIDGE** Adult Education
Globe Fearon Educational Publisher

Production Editors: **Shirley Hinkamp**
**Louise Capuano**
**Noël Vreeland Carter**
**Christine Mann**
**Linda Moore**
Interior Design: **LCI Designs**
Cover Design: **Karen Salzbach**
Illustrations: **Vantage Art**
Prepress Buyer: **Ray Keating**
Manufacturing Buyer: **Lori Bulwin**
Scheduler: **Leslie Coward**

©1993 by REGENTS/PRENTICE HALL
A Simon & Schuster Company
Englewood Cliffs, NJ 07632

Printed in the United States of America

10   9   8   7   6   5   4   3

ISBN   0-13-388752-9

Prentice-Hall International (UK) Limited, *London*
Prentice-Hall of Australia Pty. Limited, *Sydney*
Prentice-Hall Canada, Inc., *Toronto*
Prentice-Hall Hispanoamericana, S.A., *Mexico*
Prentice-Hall of India Private Limited, *New Delhi*
Prentice-Hall of Japan, Inc., *Tokyo*
Simon & Schuster Asia Pte. Ltd., *Singapore*
Editora Prentice-Hall do Brasil, Ltda., *Rio de Janeiro*

# New Revised Cambridge GED Program

<u>Executive Editor</u>
Mark Moscowitz

<u>Project Director/Senior Editor</u>
Robert McIlwaine

<u>Development Editor</u>

Julie Scardiglia

<u>Writers</u>

Beverly Ann Chin
Gloria Levine
Karen Wunderman
Stella Sands
Michael Ross
Alan Hines
Donald Gerstein

<u>Consultants/Reviewers</u>

Marjorie Jacobs
Cecily Bodnar
Diane Hardison
Dr. Margaret Tinzmann
Nora Chomitz
Bert C. Honigman
Sylvester Pues

<u>Photo Researchers</u>

Page Poore
Ellen Diamond

<u>Electronic Design</u>

Molly Pike Riccardi
Freddy Flake

# Contents

# *Introduction*

## WHAT IS THE GED?

The initials GED stand for General Educational Development. You may also have heard the tests referred to as the High School Equivalency Tests. The GED diploma is widely regarded as the equivalent of a high school diploma.

The GED is a way for millions of adults in the United States and Canada to get diplomas or certificates without returning to high school. Each year about half a million people take advantage of the opportunity to take the GED Tests.

## Who Recognizes the GED?

The GED is recognized by employers, unions, and state and federal civil services. Many vocational institutes, colleges, and universities accept students who have obtained a GED. All 50 states and parts of Canada use the GED Tests results to issue high school equivalency credentials. However, each state has its own standards for what constitutes a passing grade. For information on the requirements in your state, contact the High School Equivalency Program of the State Department of Education in your state capital.

## What Is Tested on the GED Tests?

The material found on the GED is based on the subjects covered in most high schools around the country. Thus you will be learning about the subject areas that you would be most likely to study if you attended four years of high school. However, the focus of the GED is not on content, but on *skills.* You will not have to memorize specific dates, names, and places. For example, whether you recall the day on which a battle was fought or the title of a novel is less important than whether you can read and understand a passage on history or literature.

The GED is actually five separate tests. With one exception, the tests are composed entirely of multiple-choice questions. The one exception is the 200-word essay that you will be required to write as part of the Writing Skills Test. The chart below describes the structure of the five tests:

## THE WRITING SKILLS TEST

The Writing Skills Test examines your knowledge of the conventions of written English and your ability to write.

## What Kind of Questions Are on the Writing Skills Test?

The Writing Skills Test is composed of two parts. Part I tests your knowledge of the conventions of written English: usage, sentence structure, and mechanics (punctuation, capitalization, and spelling). Part II tests your ability to write an expository essay.

In Part I, you will read paragraphs made up of 10 to 12 sentences. Each sentence in each paragraph will be numbered. You will be asked to locate and correct the errors in certain sentences.

In Part II, you will be asked to write an essay that states your opinion or provides an explanation about a certain topic. You will write a 200-word essay in which you support your opinion or defend your explanation with specific details. There are no "correct answers" for this sort of test. Your essay will be judged not for the opinion or explanation you give, but rather on the overall effectiveness of your argument. Your writing will be rated on whether it is clear, well-organized, and generally free of errors in usage, sentence structure, and mechanics.

As with the other GED tests, all of the 55 questions in Part I of the Writing Skills Test are in multiple-choice format.

## THE SOCIAL STUDIES TEST

The Social Studies Test examines your ability to understand, use, analyze, and evaluate social studies material: information from the fields of history, geography, economics, political science, and behavioral science.

## What Kind of Questions Are on the Social Studies Test?

When you take the test, you will read passages and answer questions, some of which test your understanding: you will be required to restate information, summarize ideas, or identify implications of the information given in the passages you read. Other questions will test your ability to use, analyze, and evaluate what you understand. You may read a passage that defines social studies terms and then be asked to choose examples that demonstrate the meaning of those terms. Or you may be given a passage from, say, a newspaper editorial, and be asked to distinguish facts from opinions, or to recognize a writer's assumption, or to distinguish the author's conclusion from the supporting evidence, or to identify a cause-and-effect relationship. Finally, you may read a passage that presents an argument about a social studies topic and then be required to decide how valid the argument is. You may be asked to decide whether the data presented proves what the author says it does. You may be asked to recognize the hidden values that are behind what the author writes.

About one third of the items are based on graphic material. The other two thirds are based on written material.

## THE SCIENCE TEST

The 66 items on the Science Test examine your ability to understand, use, analyze, and evaluate information from the life and physical sciences: biology, earth science, chemistry, and physics.

## What Kind of Questions Are on the Science Test?

As in the Social Studies Test, when you take the Science Test you will read passages and answer questions based on those passages. The questions will test your understanding and your ability to use, analyze, and evaluate what you understand. You may read a passage that describes a scientific phenomenon and then be asked to apply that information in a slightly different context. To do that, you will have to imagine how another situation might work, based on what you have been told about the first situation. Some questions will test your ability to distinguish facts from opinions, to distinguish facts and opinions from hypotheses, to recognize assumptions, to tell the difference between a conclusion and its supporting statements, or to identify cause-and-effect relationships. A passage may describe a scientific experiment. You may be asked to evaluate whether the data provided support a certain conclusion. About half the passages relate to biology; the others relate to the physical sciences: earth science, chemistry, and physics.

## THE INTERPRETING LITERATURE AND THE ARTS TEST

The Interpreting Literature and the Arts Test examines your ability to understand and analyze popular and classical literature and commentary about literature and the arts.

## What Kind of Questions Are on the Literature and the Arts Test?

Like the Social Studies and Science tests, the Interpreting Literature and the Arts Test will require you to read passages and answer questions that test your understanding and your ability to use and analyze what you understand. The passages you will read are all taken from actual published works. About half of the 45 questions will be based on popular literature—nonfiction, fiction, drama, and poetry (including song lyrics) recently written and widely enjoyed by today's readers. About one-fourth of the questions will be based on passages from classical literature—works that are considered to have earned a place in literary history. Finally, one-fourth of the questions will be based on commentary—writing about literature, theater, music, dance, film, and art.

## THE MATHEMATICS TEST

The Mathematics Test examines your ability to use arithmetic, algebra, and geometry to solve the kind of math problems that you are likely to encounter in your daily life or at work.

# What Kind of Questions Are on the Mathematics Test?

When you take the Mathematics Test, you will solve problems based on brief passages and graphic material. Solving some of the problems will require working through two or more steps. For example, you might be given information about two prospective jobs with different pay and different annual raises. You might also be told the cost of transportation to each job. Then you might be asked to calculate which job would net more money at the end of two years. To answer that question would require performing several different operations.

None of the questions will require that you use formulas you have memorized. If a question requires you to use a formula, it will be provided for you. About two-thirds of the problems are based on written passages. The other one-third are based on graphic material. You may be asked one or more questions about each of the pieces of graphic material. All of the items on the Mathematics Test are in multiple-choice format.

This book gives you a four-step preparation for taking the GED Tests.

## Step One: Prediction

In this first step, you will find the Predictor Tests. The tests are very much like the five actual GED Tests. However, with the exception of Part II of the Writing Skills Test, the Predictor Tests are only about half as long as the GED Tests. Taking the Predictor Tests will give you an idea of what the real GED Tests will be like. By evaluating your performance on the Predictor Tests, you will get a sense of your strengths and weaknesses in the areas of writing, social studies, science, literature, and mathematics. This information will help you to plan your studies accordingly.

## Step Two: Instruction

The instruction section is divided into five units. The first two units, *Unit I: Writing Skills, Part I: Grammar.* and *Unit II: Writing Skills, Part II: Essay Writing,* will help you learn the editing and essay writing necessary for passing the Writing Test of the GED. *Unit III: Readings in Social Studies and Science* will teach you the reading skills you need for all the passages on the GED. You will also be able to use these reading strategies in *Unit IV: Interpreting Literature and the Arts.* Unit IV will also give you instruction on reading the basic types of literature you will find on the Interpreting Literature and the Arts Test of the GED. *Unit V* is on *Mathematics.*

## Step Three: Practice

This section gives you valuable practice in answering the types of questions you will find on the actual GED Tests. The Practice Items section consists of GED-like questions grouped according to subject. This organization of the Practice Items section allows you to test your understanding of one branch of each subject at a time. Each group of Practice Items consists of the same number of items as are on the related GED Test. You can use your results to track your progress and to give you an idea of how prepared you are to take the real tests.

## Step Four: Simulation

Finally, a simulated version of all five of the GED Tests is offered. They are as much like the real tests as possible. The number of questions, their level of difficulty, and the way they are organized are the same as you will find on the actual tests. You will have the same amount of time to complete each test as you will have when you take the GED.

## Answers and Explanations

At the back of this book, you will find a section called Answers and Explanations. This section contains the answers to all the questions in the Previews, Lesson Exercises, Reviews, Chapter Quizzes, the Practice Items, and the Simulated Tests. The answer section is a valuable study tool: It tells you the right answer and explains why each answer is right. It shows solutions for mathematics problems. Entries in the answer section point out the writing, reading, or mathematics skill you need to answer an item successfully. In the New Revised Cambridge GED Program all answer keys have been greatly expanded to explain the thinking process involved in answering each question, so that you can develop the the thinking skills demanded by the GED exam.

Whether you are working with an instructor or alone, you can use this book to prepare for the GED Tests in the way that works best for you.

## Take a Glance at the Contents

Before doing anything else, look over the Contents and get a feel for this book. Leaf through the book to see what each section looks like.

## Take the Predictor Tests

Your performance and score on the Predictor Tests will be very useful to you as you work with the rest of this book. Taking the tests will help you identify your particular strengths and weaknesses. This will help you plan your course of study.

## Begin Your Instruction

After you have analyzed your strengths and weaknesses, you are ready to begin instruction. You can work through the instruction in many ways.

Your GED preparation will probably be most successful if you work on all five subjects of the tests at the same time. This way, you can make steady progress in each of the GED subjects throughout the period of your preparation.

At the beginning of each unit you will find a Progress Chart. As you complete an activity, such as a lesson exercise or a chapter quiz, you can record your performance on that chart. The chart allows you to see your progress from lesson to lesson. If you feel you are not making enough progress, you can vary your method of studying or ask your teacher for help.

## Use the Practice Items

At certain points in your instruction, you have choices: you can proceed from one chapter directly to the next or you can go to the Practice section to work on GED-like items in the part of a subject you have just studied. Thus you can get practice on GED-like items frequently during the course of your instruction. Or, if you wish, you can wait until you've finished a whole unit—or all five units— before you do the Practice Items.

## Take the Simulated Tests

Finally, once you have completed the Instruction and Practice sections of the book, you should take the Simulated Tests. These tests will help you assess how ready you are to take the actual tests.

## Try Your Best!

To attain a passing score on the GED Tests, you will probably need to have more than half of the items on each test correct. To give yourself a margin for passing, try to maintain a score of at least 80 percent correct as you work through this book. The Progress Charts and Performance Analysis Charts will help you compare your work with this 80 percent figure. If you maintain 80 percent scores, you are probably working at a level that will allow you to do well on the GED.

# NEW REVISED *CAMBRIDGE*

# GED

## PROGRAM
### Comprehensive Book

# Introduction

Imagine that you were going to take the GED Tests today. How do you think you would do? In which subjects and areas would you perform best, and which would give you the most trouble? The Predictor Tests that follow can help you answer those questions. They are called Predictor Tests because your test results can be used to predict where your strengths and weaknesses are in relation to the actual GED Tests.

You will find a Predictor Test for each of the five GED Tests: Writing Skills, Social Studies, Science, Interpreting Literature and the Arts, and Mathematics. The Predictor Tests are like the actual GED Tests in many ways. They will check your skills as you apply them to the kinds of passages you will find on the real tests. The questions are like those on the actual tests.

## How to Take the Predictor Tests

The Predictor Tests will be most useful to you if you take them in a manner similar to that in which the actual tests are given. If possible, complete each test in one sitting with as little distraction as possible. It probably is best to take only one per day. The Writing Skills Test has two parts, and it might be best if you took only one part at a time.

So that you have an accurate record of your performance, write your answers neatly on a sheet of paper, or use an answer sheet provided by your teacher. For Part II of the Writing Skills Test, plan and write your essay on fresh sheets of paper.

As you take each test, don't be discouraged if you find you are having difficulty with some (or even many) of the questions. The purpose of these tests is to help you identify your strengths and weaknesses. So relax. You will have plenty of opportunities to correct any weaknesses and retest them.

You may want to time yourself to see how long you take to complete each test. With the exception of the Writing Skills Predictor Test, each Predictor Test is about half as long as the actual GED Test for that subject. Part II of the Writing Skills Predictor Test is the same length as the GED. If you complete each Predictor Test in half the time allotted for the corresponding real GED Test, you are right on target. You will be told how much time you should allow at the beginning of each test. You shouldn't worry too much if it takes you longer.

When you are done with each Predictor Test, check your answers by using the answer section that begins on page 41. Put a check by each item you answered correctly.

## How to Use Your Score

On pages 57-59, you will find Performance Analysis Charts. Fill in the charts; they will help you find out which areas you are most comfortable with, and which give you the most trouble.

As you begin a chapter in the book, you may want to refer back to the appropriate Performance Analysis Chart to see how well you did in a specific area of a Predictor Test.

# PREDICTOR TEST 1
# Writing Skills, Part 1: Grammar

**TIME:** 38 minutes

**Directions:** The items in Part I of this test are based on a paragraph that contains numbered sentences. Some of the sentences may contain errors in sentence structure, usage, or mechanics. *A few sentences, however, may be correct as written.* Read each paragraph and then answer the nine to ten items that follow it. For each item, choose the answer that would result in the most effective writing of the sentence or sentences. The best answer must be consistent with the meaning and tone of the rest of the paragraph.

---

FOR EXAMPLE:

Sentence 1: **Although it may take only two hours to watch the average motion picture takes almost a year to make.**

What correction should be made to this sentence?

**(1)** replace *it* with *they*

**(2)** change *take* to *have taken*

**(3)** insert a comma after *watch*

**(4)** change *almost* to *all most*

**(5)** no change is necessary

The correct answer is **(3)**. In this example, a comma is needed after the clause *Although it may take only two hours to watch.*

---

Items 1 to 10 are based on the following paragraph.

(1) Now, as always, consumers must behave responsible in making their purchases. (2) There are many Consumer Commissions that check on products. (3) Some consumer groups are private. (4) Such as the one Ralph Nader formed. (5) Even with these groups, buyers must be watchful theirselves. (6) They cannot depend only on salesclerks, many stores are understaffed. (7) If items are not examined carefully when purchased, they may be disappointed later. (8) They must make sure that the packages have not already been opened. (9) Consumers must also check the labels for warranties, warnings, and how to care for the product. (10) When buying a toy for young children, consumers should check it's construction to make certain that it is safe for their youngsters. (11) In order to feel secure about a purchase, consumers must buy with care.

1. Sentence 1: **Now, as always, consumers must behave responsible in making their purchases**

   What correction should be made to this sentence?

   (1) change the spelling of *always* to *allways*
   (2) remove the comma after *always*
   (3) change *responsible* to *responsibly*
   (4) replace *their* with *there*
   (5) no correction is necessary

2. Sentence 2: **There are many Consumer Commissions that check on products.**

   What correction should be made to this sentence?

   (1) replace *there* with *they're*
   (2) change *are* to *is*
   (3) change the spelling of *Commissions* to *Comissions*
   (4) change *Consumer Commissions* to *consumer commissions*
   (5) insert a comma before *that*

3. Sentences 3 & 4: **Some consumer groups are private. Such as the one Ralph Nader formed.**

   Which of the following is the best way to write the underlined portion of these sentences? If you think the original is the best way, choose option (1).

   (1) private. Such as the one
   (2) private, such as the one
   (3) private; such as the one
   (4) private. For example, the one
   (5) private; for example, the one

4. Sentence 5: **Even with these groups, buyers must be watchful theirselves.**

   What correction should be made to this sentence?

   (1) change the spelling of *watchful* to *watchfull*
   (2) remove the comma after *groups*
   (3) change *watchful* to *watchfully*
   (4) replace *theirselves* with *themselves*
   (5) no correction is necessary

5. Sentence 6: **They cannot depend only on salesclerks, many stores are understaffed.**

   Which of the following is the best way to write the underlined portion of this sentence? If you think the original is the best way, choose option (1).

   (1) salesclerks, many stores
   (2) salesclerks many stores
   (3) salesclerks. Because many stores
   (4) salesclerks being that many stores
   (5) salesclerks because many stores

6. Sentence 7: **If items are not examined carefully when purchased, they may be disappointed later.**

   Which of the following is the best way to write the underlined portion of this sentence? If you think the original is the best way, choose option (1).

   (1) purchased, they may be
   (2) purchased. They may be

(3) purchased, buyers may be

(4) purchased, sales-clerks may be

(5) purchased, buyers would be

7. Sentence 8: **They must make sure that the packages have not already been opened.**

What correction should be made to this sentence?

(1) change *sure* to *surely*

(2) insert a comma after *that*

(3) change the spelling of *already* to *all ready*

(4) change *opened* to *open*

(5) no correction is necessary

8. Sentence 9: **Consumers must also check the labels for warranties, warnings, and <u>how to care for the product.</u>**

Which of the following is the best way to write the underlined portion of this sentence? If you think the original is the best way, choose option (1).

(1) how to care for the product.

(2) how the product must be cared for.

(3) care instructions for the product.

(4) there are ways of caring for the product.

(5) instructing how to care for the product.

9. Sentence 10: **When buying a toy for young children, consumers should check it's construction to make certain that it is safe for their youngsters.**

What correction should be made to this sentence?

(1) change the comma after *children* to a semicolon

(2) remove the comma after *children*

(3) change *it's* to *its*

(4) replace *their* with *there*

(5) no correction is necessary

10. Sentence 11: **In order to feel secure about a purchase, consumers must buy with care.**

If you rewrote sentence 11 beginning with

*Unless consumers buy with care,*

the next words should be

(1) in order to feel secure

(2) so that they will feel secure

(3) they may feel secure

(4) they may not feel secure

(5) the purchase may not feel secure

Items 11 to 19 are based on the following paragraph.

(1) The computer is an invention that affects my life in many ways. (2) Although we may not use computers at work, we have found them in many other places. (3) For example, computers are used to record the prices of groceries at stores, to provide us with cash at banks, and they also process our bills. (4) Many new cars use computers to check they're engines and recommend any needed changes. (5) One of the most common new uses of computers are handling long distance phone calls. (6) Many young children were used to working with computers in school. (7) Sometimes computers go down, but they usually work well. (8) Computers help us all by increasing the speed with which you can conduct business. (9) Computers are found throughout our lives. (10) We should learn more about them.

11. Sentence 1: **The computer is an invention that affects my life in many ways.**

What correction should be made to this sentence?

(1) replace *an* with *one*

(2) insert a comma before *that*

(3) change the spelling of *affects* to *effects*

(4) change *my life* to *our lives*

(5) no correction is necessary

12. Sentence 2: **Although we may not use computers at work, we have found them in many other places.**

What correction should be made to this sentence?

(1) insert a comma after *them*
(2) replace *Although* with *Because*
(3) remove the comma after *work*
(4) replace *have found* with *find*
(5) no correction is necessary

13. Sentence 3: **For example, computers are used to record the prices of groceries at stores, to provide us with cash at banks, and they also process our bills.**

Which of the following is the best way to write the underlined portion of this sentence? If you think the original is the best way, choose option (1).

(1) and they also process our bills.
(2) and our bills are processed by them.
(3) and the processing of our bills.
(4) and billing us.
(5) and to process our bills.

14. Sentence 4: **Many new cars use computers to check they're engines and recommend any needed changes.**

What correction should be made to this sentence?

(1) replace *they're* with *there*
(2) replace *they're* with *their*
(3) insert a comma before *and*
(4) change the spelling of *recommend* to *reccomend*
(5) no correction is necessary

15. Sentence 5: **One of the most common new uses of computers are handling long distance phone calls**

Which of the following is the best way to write the underlined portion of this sentence? If you think the original is the best way, choose option (1).

(1) are handling
(2) handled
(3) handle
(4) is handling
(5) were handling

16. Sentence 6: **Many young children were used to working with computers in school**

What correction should be made to this sentence?

(1) replace *were* with *are*
(2) change *used* to *use*
(3) insert a comma after *working*
(4) insert a comma after *computers*
(5) no correction is necessary

17. Sentence 7: **Sometimes computers go down, but they usually work well.**

Which of the following is the best way to write the underlined portion of the sentence? If you think the original is the best way, choose option (1).

(1) go down, but they usually work well.
(2) go down but they usually work well.
(3) go down but, they usually work well.
(4) go down. But they usually work good.
(5) go down, but, they usually work good.

18. Sentence 8: **Computers help us all by increasing the speed with which you can conduct business.**

What correction should be made to this sentence?

(1) insert a comma before *by*
(2) insert a comma before *with*
(3) replace *which* with *whom*
(4) replace *you* with *we*
(5) no correction is necessary

19. Sentences 9 & 10: **Computers are found throughout our lives. We should learn more about them.**

The most effective combination of sentences 9 and 10 would include which of the following groups of words?

(1) Computers are found throughout our lives, being that we should learn
(2) Computers are found throughout our lives, but we should learn

**(3)** Because computers are found throughout our lives, we should learn

**(4)** Unless computers are found throughout our lives, we should learn

**(5)** Computers are found throughout our lives, because we should learn

Items 20 to 28 are based on the following paragraph.

**(1)** Each one of you are facing important choices about your career. **(2)** While it may seem hard to decide. **(3)** There are some steps you can take to help you to choose. **(4)** First, make a list of your interests, achievements, and talents. **(5)** If your talents lie in one field, you can explore the different careers within that field. **(6)** Career choices in the medical field, for example, can include jobs as Doctors, physical therapists, nurses, or assistants. **(7)** After reading about several careers, one should try to talk to people who work in those careers. **(8)** These talks with workers can help you learn more about their jobs. **(9)** You can discuss the pros and cons of a job and learn about the required training. **(10)** Once you have learned about several careers, you can decide on a career more easily.

**20.** Sentence 1: **Each one of you are facing important choices about your career.**

What correction should be made to this sentence?

**(1)** replace *are* with *is*
**(2)** change *facing* to *faced*
**(3)** change the spelling of *important* to *importent*
**(4)** insert a comma after *choices*
**(5)** no correction is necessary

**21.** Sentences 2 & 3: **While it may seem hard to decide. There are some steps you can take to help you to choose.**

Which of the following is the best way to write the underlined portion of

these sentences? If you think the original is the best way, choose option (1).

**(1)** to decide. There are
**(2)** to decide; there are
**(3)** to decide, there are
**(4)** to decide and there are
**(5)** to decide so there are

**22.** Sentence 4: **First, make a list of your interests, achievements, and talents.**

What correction should be made to this sentence?

**(1)** replace *your* with *you're*
**(2)** change the spelling of *intrests* to *interests*
**(3)** remove the comma after *intrests*
**(4)** change the spelling of *acheivements* to *achievements*
**(5)** no correction is necessary

**23.** Sentence 5: **If your talents lie in one field, you can explore the different careers within that field.**

Which of the following is the best way to write the underlined portion of this sentence? If you think the original is the best way, choose option (1).

**(1)** field, you can
**(2)** field. You can
**(3)** field; you can
**(4)** field you can
**(5)** field so that you can

**24.** Sentence 6: **Career choices in the medical field, for example, can include jobs as Doctors, physical therapists, nurses, or assistants.**

What correction should be made to this sentence?

**(1)** remove the comma after *example*
**(2)** change *Doctors* to *doctors*
**(3)** remove the comma after *Doctors*
**(4)** insert a comma after *physical*
**(5)** change the spelling of *assistants* to *assistance*

**25.** Sentence 7: **After reading about several careers, one should try to talk to people who work in those careers.**

What correction should be made to this sentence?

**(1)** change the spelling of *several* to *severel*

**(2)** replace the comma after *careers* with a period

**(3)** replace the comma after *careers* with a semicolon

**(4)** replace *one* with *you*

**(5)** change the spelling of *people* to *peeple*

**26.** Sentence 8: **These talks with workers can help you learn more about their jobs.**

If you rewrote sentence 7 beginning with

*By talking with workers,*

the next words should be

**(1)** you can learn

**(2)** more is learned

**(3)** jobs are learned

**(4)** helps you learn

**(5)** in order for you to learn

**27.** Sentence 9: **You can discuss the pros and cons of <u>a job and learn</u> about the required training.**

Which of the following is the best way to write the underlined portion of this sentence? If you think the original is the best way, choose option (1).

**(1)** a job and learn

**(2)** a job, and learn

**(3)** a job and, learn

**(4)** a job; and learn

**(5)** a job so that you learn

**28.** Sentence 10: **Once you have learned about several careers, you can decide on a career more easily.**

If you rewrote sentence 10 beginning with

*Learning about several careers*

the next words should be

**(1)** once you have decided

**(2)** their own jobs will be decided

**(3)** in order to decide

**(4)** and deciding about their own jobs

**(5)** will help you to decide

Answers are on pages 41-42

# PREDICTOR TEST 1
# Writing Skills, Part II: Essay Writing

**TIME:** 45 minutes

**Directions:** This is a test to see how well you can write. In this test, you are asked to write an essay in which you present your opinions about an issue. In preparing your essay, you should take the following steps.

**Step 1.** Read all of the information about the topic. Be sure that you understand the topic and that you write about only the assigned topic.

**Step 2.** Plan your essay before you write.

**Step 3.** Use scrap paper to make any notes.

**Step 4.** Organize your essay into at least three paragraphs: introduction, body, and conclusion. Each paragraph should have a topic sentence and at least three supporting details.

**Step 5.** Write your essay on a separate sheet of paper.

**Step 6.** Read what you have written. Make sure that your writing is legible.

**Step 7.** Check your paragraphing, sentence structure, spelling, punctuation, capitalization, and usage; make any changes that will improve your essay.

## TOPIC

> Many employers now offer alternatives to the traditional workweek, such as working part time, working at home, and working flexible hours.
>
> Decide which type of work schedule you would pick if you had the choice. Write a composition of about 200 words explaining why this option would be the best for you. Be specific, and use reasons or examples in your explanation.

**When you take the GED test, you will have 45 minutes to write about the topic question you are assigned. Try to write the essay for this test within 45 minutes. Write legibly and use a ballpoint pen so that your writing will be easy to read. Any notes that you make on scrap paper will not be counted as part of your score.**

**After you complete this essay, you can judge its effectiveness by using the Essay Scoring Guide and Model Essays in the answer key to score your essay. They will be concerned with how clearly you make the main point of your essay, how thoroughly you support your ideas, and how clear and correct your writing is throughout the composition. You will receive no credit for writing about a question other than the one assigned.**

Answers are on pages 43-47.

**TIME:** 42 1/2 minutes

**Directions:** Choose the one best answer to each question.

Items 1 to 3 are based on the following figure.

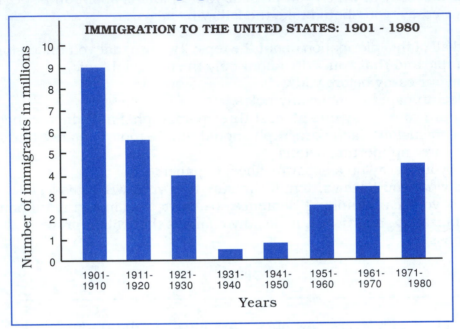

IMMIGRATION TO THE UNITED STATES: 1901 - 1980

1. According to the graph, during which of the following periods was immigration lowest?

   **(1)** 1931-1940
   **(2)** 1941-1950
   **(3)** 1951-1960
   **(4)** 1961-1970
   **(5)** 1971-1980

2. For which of the following years would a federal government study show the greatest need for increased jobs and housing for immigrants?

   **(1)** 1921-1930
   **(2)** 1941-1950
   **(3)** 1951-1960
   **(4)** 1961-1970
   **(5)** 1971-1980

3. How would you describe the pattern of immigration levels between 1901 and 1980?

   **(1)** steady increase
   **(2)** steady decrease
   **(3)** increase then decrease
   **(4)** decrease then increase
   **(5)** no increase or decrease

4. Property taxes help to pay for services that benefit property owners. These taxes are the main source of income for local governments. They are also used by some state governments. Which of the following would most likely be paid for by a property tax?

   **(1)** building a new nuclear submarine
   **(2)** building a new house
   **(3)** increasing the number of FBI agents
   **(4)** building new sidewalks
   **(5)** increasing the salaries of soldiers

Item 5 is based on the following figure.

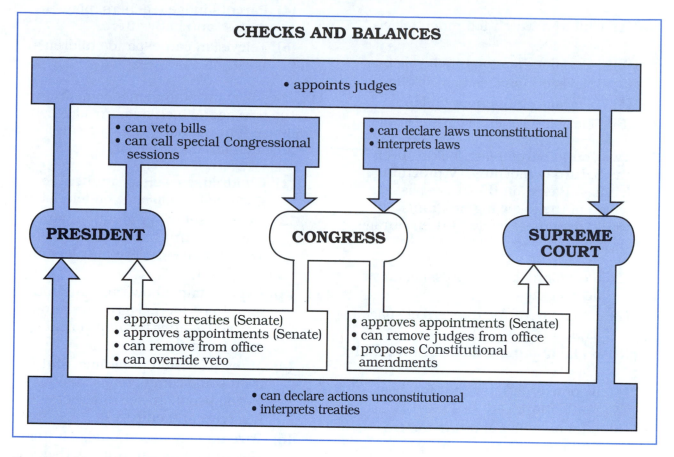

**CHECKS AND BALANCES**

- appoints judges

- can veto bills
- can call special Congressional sessions

- can declare laws unconstitutional
- interprets laws

**PRESIDENT**

**CONGRESS**

**SUPREME COURT**

- approves treaties (Senate)
- approves appointments (Senate)
- can remove from office
- can override veto

- approves appointments (Senate)
- can remove judges from office
- proposes Constitutional amendments

- can declare actions unconstitutional
- interprets treaties

5. President Reagan appointed Justice O'Connor, the first woman to sit on the Supreme Court. This appointment

(1) was not legal for President Reagan to make
(2) had to be approved by the Senate
(3) had to be approved by the Supreme Court
(4) did not have to be approved
(5) should have been made by Congress

Items 6 to 10 are based on the following passage.

Children, as well as adults, see a great deal of violence on television. Saturday morning cartoon programs show a violent act every two minutes. By high school graduation, an average youth has seen some 18,000 make-believe murders on television.

Some television critics worry that watching so much violence has negative effects on children. Experiments show that children tend to be more aggressive and overactive after viewing violence on television. Unfortunately, there are no conclusive studies on the effects of television violence after weeks, months, and years of viewing.

But even television critics agree that television is not all bad. Creative programs such as "Sesame Street" help children to develop basic skills. Many television programs, and even some commercials, allow young people to see different lifestyles and cultures. American children learn about life in faraway lands. Inner-city youths learn about the lives of farm children.

Clearly, television is a powerful influence on children. Parents may need to judge it just as carefully as they judge teachers, playmates, and babysitters.

**6.** Which of the following statements best summarizes the point of the passage?

**(1)** Children watch too much television.
**(2)** Television has too much violence.
**(3)** Television teaches basic skills.
**(4)** Television influences children.
**(5)** Television violence causes crime.

**7.** Two young parents are looking over the Saturday morning TV program listings. Based on the above passage, which of the following programs would they most likely NOT encourage their children to watch?

**(1)** a cartoon about expressing anger acceptably
**(2)** a film about the dangers of space exploration
**(3)** a film about animals in Africa and Asia
**(4)** a comedy-fantasy that teaches mathematics
**(5)** a fantasy film about monsters and laser weapons

**8.** Why would parents want their children to watch TV?

**(1)** It helps children have a more realistic view of the world.
**(2)** It teaches children fundamental skills for dealing with society's violence.
**(3)** It informs children of other people's ways of life.
**(4)** It introduces children to positive role models.
**(5)** It helps children to judge teachers, playmates and babysitters.

**9.** The author of the passage assumes, but does not state, which of the following ideas?

**(1)** Some critics are fearful of TV's effects on children.
**(2)** Most youngsters watch television.

**(3)** Violent programs can affect children's behavior.
**(4)** Parents judge teachers, playmates, and babysitters.
**(5)** Television can expand children's horizons.

**10.** The following statements come from the passage. Which one provides evidence that television-viewing can affect children's behavior?

**(1)** Children, as well as adults, see a great deal of violence on television.
**(2)** By high school graduation, an average youth has seen some 18,000 make-believe murders on television.
**(3)** Experiments show that children tend to be more aggressive and overactive after viewing violence on television.
**(4)** Many television programs, and even some commercials, allow young people to see different lifestyles and cultures.
**(5)** Parents may need to judge it [television] just as carefully as they judge teachers, playmates, and babysitters.

**11.** The largest of the seven continents is Asia with an area of 44,400,000 square kilometers. The next largest is Africa, followed by North America and South America. Antarctic is smaller than South America, but larger than Europe. Europe's area is over 10,000,000 square kilometers, and Australia's area is 8,500,000 square kilometers.
The size of each continent's population is influenced by many factors. Two of the most important factors are how large the continent is and what its climate is like. Which continent could be expected to have the smallest population?

**(1)** Antarctica
**(2)** Australia

**(3)** Europe

**(4)** North America

**(5)** South America

**12.** In 1776, Adam Smith wrote a book called *The Wealth of Nations*. Smith believed that governments should not control economic development. He thought producers should produce whatever they wanted. The goods should then be sold at whatever price people were willing to pay. The free marketplace would control production and prices.

According to Adam Smith's beliefs, which of the following would be the reason that the free marketplace would control price?

**(1)** Consumers would determine prices by either buying or refusing to buy goods.

**(2)** If left on their own, producers would charge reasonable prices.

**(3)** The producers would determine the price of goods according to their supply.

**(4)** The government sometimes would set price limits to assist economic development.

**(5)** The producers and consumers together would determine a fair price for all goods.

Items 13 and 14 are based on the following table.

| Population Changes in the Five Largest U.S. Cities | | | | | |
|---|---|---|---|---|---|
| | 1900 | 1950 | 1960 | 1970 | 1980 |
| Chicago | 1,700,000 | 3,600,000 | 3,550,000 | 3,369,000 | 3,000,000 |
| Houston | 44,000 | 596,000 | 940,000 | 1,200,000 | 1,600,000 |
| Los Angeles | 102,000 | 1,970,000 | 2,480,000 | 2,800,000 | 2,966,000 |
| New York | 3,437,000 | 7,890,000 | 7,780,000 | 7,895,000 | 7,071,000 |
| Philadelphia | 1,290,000 | 2,070,000 | 2,000,000 | 1,950,000 | 1,688,000 |

Source: U.S. Bureau of the Census

**13.** Which cities would city planners study to determine reasons for population increases since 1970?

**(1)** Chicago and Houston

**(2)** New York and Chicago

**(3)** Philadelphia and New York

**(4)** Houston and Los Angeles

**(5)** Philadelphia and Chicago

**14.** Based on the table, which area of the United States has shown a steady increase in population since the turn of the century?

**(1)** Northeast

**(2)** Southwest

**(3)** Southeast

**(4)** Midwest

**(5)** Northwest

Item 15 is based on the following cartoon.

It's not sex discrimination, dear. Your salaries are different because your jobs are different. You're a cleaning lady and he's a sanitation engineer.

THE BOSS

**15.** Which one of the following statements best explains the message of the cartoon?

(1) Cleaning ladies and sanitation engineers do the same jobs.

(2) Employees with different jobs earn different salaries.

(3) Men and women cannot perform the same tasks at work.

(4) Men are often paid more than women for the same jobs.

(5) Men and women have different titles for similar jobs.

Item 16 is based on the following quote.

"And so, my fellow Americans, ask not what your country can do for you—ask what you can do for your country. My fellow citizens of the world: Ask not what America will do for you, but what together we can do for the freedom of man."

John F. Kennedy

**16.** Which one of the following activities provides the best example of a response to the ideas expressed by John F. Kennedy?

(1) joining an organization to encourage foreign travel

(2) asking citizens of other countries to visit America

(3) asking for more freedom of movement for U.S. citizens

(4) welcoming a home for the disabled into your neighborhood

(5) working to reduce taxes on people in your income group

Items 17 to 21 are based on the following information.

Listed below are three types of political systems with brief descriptions of how power is distributed in them.

**1. Absolute Monarchy:** One person, the monarch, inherits power and rules for life. An absolute monarch has the power to make or change laws at any time he or she chooses.

**2. Constitutional Monarchy:** The monarch inherits power and rules for life but has limited power. The monarch can advise lawmakers, but laws are made by a group of people elected by the citizens of the nation, and the monarch cannot overrule these laws. In some countries, such a monarch has no power at all but is a national symbol rather than a real ruler.

**14**    Predictor Test

**3. Direct democracy:** All qualified citizens vote directly on every law and have some say in how the country is governed.

**4. Representative democracy:** Citizens elect people to represent them—that is, to express their political attitudes for them by passing or changing laws. Representative democracy is therefore sometimes called indirect democracy.

**5. Dictatorship:** One person takes total control of the country. The dictator has power over all laws and economic matters. Since dictators also try to control people's beliefs and values, citizens usually are not allowed to criticize the government.

**17.** A head of state wanted his policies to be carried on after his death. To assure that, he carefully directed his children's education. He was most likely head of what type of government?

(1) absolute monarchy
(2) constitutional monarchy
(3) direct democracy
(4) representative democracy
(5) dictatorship

**18.** After the government of a certain country is overthrown, the leader of the revolution arrests the country's elected representatives and potential opposition leaders. He declares himself the sole head of the government. He then takes control of the nation's television stations and closes down its newspapers. Which of the following names the type of political system the leader has set up?

(1) absolute monarchy
(2) constitutional monarchy
(3) direct democracy
(4) representative democracy
(5) dictatorship

**19.** The United States is an example of which type of political system?

(1) absolute monarchy
(2) constitutional monarchy
(3) direct democracy
(4) representative democracy
(5) dictatorship

**20.** Under which system would the people be most responsible for the laws enacted?

(1) absolute monarchy
(2) constitutional monarchy
(3) direct democracy
(4) representative democracy
(5) dictatorship

**21.** A country is governed by a young king who inherited his position from his deceased father. After a two-day national strike, he tried to outlaw labor unions but was unsuccessful because of certain laws. What type of government does he head?

(1) absolute monarchy
(2) constitutional monarchy
(3) direct democracy
(4) representative democracy
(5) dictatorship

Item 22 is based on the following passage.

"Just because my grandfather worked this farm and my father was a farmer here, it doesn't mean that I have to be a farmer, even though I am the only son. I don't like to work outdoors. I want to go to school to learn how to be an accountant. I know there are no accountants in my family, but I'm sure I can be one if I can find a way to afford college."

**22.** From what the speaker says, one of the most important values held by his family is

(1) money
(2) tradition
(3) education
(4) religion
(5) status

Items 23 to 26 are based on the following table.

| Employment Gains and Losses | |
|---|---|
| Five industries with the largest number of employment gains and five with the largest number of losses since 1980 | |
| | Jobs (in thousands) |
| **Gainers** | |
| Communication equipment | 119 |
| Electronic components/ accessories | 119 |
| Office and computing machines | 102 |
| Commercial printing | 71 |
| Miscellaneous plastics products | 71 |
| **Losers** | |
| Blast furnace and basic steel products | 245 |
| Construction and related machinery | 145 |
| Womens' and misses' outerwear | 50 |
| Plastics materials and synthetics | 43 |
| Footwear (except rubber) | 42 |

Source: Bureau of Labor Statistics, U.S. Department of Labor.

**23.** Based on the information in the table, which one of the following statements is true?

(1) Jobs that supply services rather than products are increasing.

(2) Communications, electronics, and computer industries have provided the most new jobs since 1980.

(3) It is easy to find a job making shoes.

(4) More people would rather be construction workers than steel-workers.

(5) The footwear industry has lost more jobs than the outerwear industry.

**24.** Based on the table, which of the following people would be most likely to enroll in a program offering job retraining?

(1) a teacher
(2) a commercial printer
(3) a producer of computers
(4) a worker in a telephone manufacturing facility
(5) a worker in a shoe factory

**25.** Which of the following statements CANNOT be justified from the information given in the table?

(1) Producers of office machines and computers have more new jobs available than producers of plastics materials and synthetics.

(2) Producers of communications equipment and electronic components have together gained more than 200,000 new jobs.

(3) More shoes are imported than are produced in the United States.

(4) Shoe factories have lost fewer jobs than commercial printers have gained.

(5) Producers of plastics products have gained jobs while producers of plastics materials have lost jobs.

**26.** Which of the following conclusions is best supported by the information in the table?

(1) The safest jobs are in the long-established skills areas.

(2) Most new jobs are being created by the newer technologies.

(3) It doesn't matter what you study in school if you want a secure job.

(4) Commercial printing has a doubtful future.

(5) Women's outerwear manufacturing has a bright future.

Item 27 is based on the following passage.

The First Amendment to the United States Constitution says:

"Congress shall make no law respecting an establishment of religion, or prohibiting the free exercise thereof; or abridging the freedom of speech, or of the press; or the right of the people to assemble, and to petition the government for a redress of grievances."

27. Which one of the following rights is not protected by the First Amendment?

   **(1)** freedom of speech
   **(2)** freedom of religion
   **(3)** the right to a jury trial
   **(4)** the right to protest to the government
   **(5)** freedom of the press

28. Population density refers to the number of people living in a certain amount of space. Populations are more dense in cities than in rural areas. Cities are often built in locations where goods and services can easily be transported. In the nineteenth century, where were populations densest in the United States?

   **(1)** in deserts
   **(2)** in mountainous areas
   **(3)** near waterways
   **(4)** in valleys
   **(5)** in plains areas

Items 29 to 32 are based on the following passage.

Before the Civil War the Northern and Southern states were like two different societies. The Northern states had many large cities. Most of the country's industry was located in the North. Many people lived in cities and worked in factories.

The Southern states consisted mainly of small towns and farms. Southern cities were small. There were few factories in the South. Most Southerners lived on farms and plantations. The South's economy was based mainly on cotton.

In 1824, the federal government raised the tax on imported goods. Southerners felt that this tax law favored Northerners. The South depended on the North and foreign producers for manufactured goods, and on the North for shipping and receiving its own goods. In addition, Southerners had to go to Northern banks for loans. Because they depended on the North, many Southerners felt their states were like colonies of the North.

29. Which one of the following statements best explains how the South's lack of industry affected its economic status?

   **(1)** The North had more cities than the South.
   **(2)** The South consisted mainly of small towns and farms.
   **(3)** The South felt it was a colony of the North.
   **(4)** The South depended on the North for manufactured goods.
   **(5)** The South felt that the tax on imported goods was unfair.

30. Which one of the following statements best explains why Southerners believed that taxes on imported goods were unfair to them?

   **(1)** Southerners provided cotton for the North.
   **(2)** The South had to import more goods than the North.
   **(3)** Southerners went to Northern banks for loans.
   **(4)** Only Southerners had to pay the taxes.
   **(5)** The Southern states had few big cities.

**31.** Which one of the following statements best reflects the main emphasis of the passage?

    **(1)** Economic differences between the North and the South played no role in the Civil War.

    **(2)** Economic differences between the North and the South centered on the issue of bank loans.

    **(3)** The North and the South developed into different kinds of societies with different economies and different economic needs.

    **(4)** The South's lack of industry caused the Civil War.

    **(5)** The North and the South were more alike than they were different.

**32.** The passage states that many Southerners felt their states were like colonies of the North. Which of the following statements gives the most likely cause for that feeling?

    **(1)** The South was economically dependent on the North.

    **(2)** The South was settled by people from the North.

    **(3)** The South had no banks of its own.

    **(4)** The North and the South were like different societies.

    **(5)** The South had to pay more import taxes than the North.

Answers are on pages 48-50.

**TIME**: 47 1/2 minutes

**Directions:** Choose the one best answer to each question.

Item 1 is based on the following passage.

A brewery worker lifts a 50-pound keg of beer onto a delivery truck. In doing so, the worker does 150 foot-pounds of work. Then the worker loads an identical keg onto a different truck. This time the worker does 200 foot-pounds of work.

1. Why does it take more work to lift the second keg?

   (1) The second truck is higher off the ground than the first.
   (2) The second keg contains more beer.
   (3) The man has gotten tired.
   (4) The first keg weighs less than the second.
   (5) Only the second lift requires energy.

2. Tides are the rise and fall of Earth's oceans, caused by the gravitational pull of the moon. The gravity of the planets affects Earth, too, but not as much as the moon's gravity. Larger bodies pull more strongly, but the planets' distances from Earth offset the effect of their sizes. Which of the following is true of the planets?

   (1) They are larger than the moon.
   (2) Some of them are larger than the moon; some are smaller.
   (3) They are smaller than the moon.
   (4) They are the same size as the moon.
   (5) Some of them are the same size as the moon.

Items 3 to 7 are based on the following passage.

Everywhere on Earth plants and animals are related to each other in food chains. Each organism's position in the chain is determined by two things: by what it eats and by what eats it.

Each organism in a food chain uses energy to sustain its life. It passes on some of that energy when it is eaten by the next link in the chain. At each step, less energy is available for use.

When a food chain is listed, arrows are used to show which way the energy passes.

The following explains the links in a simple food chain.

**1. Producer:** Most of these are green plants. They convert energy from the sun directly into nourishment.

**2. Primary Consumer:** These are animals that eat vegetable matter. When you eat a salad, you are a primary consumer.

**3. Secondary Consumer:** Secondary consumers eat primary consumers. You do this when you eat hamburger, which is made from cattle that have eaten grass and grain.

**4. Tertiary Consumer:** These are meat-eaters that eat secondary consumers. For example, large fish that eat small fish that in turn eat shellfish are tertiary consumers. So are humans in those cultures that eat dog meat or lion meat.

**5. Decomposer:** These are usually bacteria and fungi. They bring about the decay of dead organisms and break down their waste products. The breakdown substances are reused by the producers.

3. Consider this food chain: leaf→insect→fish→bird→human. Which link has the least available energy?

    (1) bird
    (2) fish
    (3) human
    (4) insect
    (5) leaf

4. Consider this chain: lettuce→rabbit→human. The human is a

    (1) producer
    (2) primary consumer
    (3) secondary consumer
    (4) tertiary consumer
    (5) decomposer

5. Consider this chain: grass →insect→bird→snake→bacteria. The snake is a

    (1) producer
    (2) primary consumer
    (3) secondary consumer
    (4) tertiary consumer
    (5) decomposer

6. Which kind of food-chain link is not shown in this chain? pond weed→minnow→bass→otter

    (1) producer
    (2) primary consumer
    (3) secondary consumer
    (4) tertiary consumer
    (5) decomposer

7. Vegetarians claim that they make more efficient use of the world's food resources than do those who eat meat. Which of these statements from the passage might they use to justify this claim?

    (1) Each organism's position in the chain is determined by what it

eats and by what eats it.
    (2) At each step, less energy is available for use.
    (3) Producers convert energy directly from the sun into nourishment.
    (4) Primary consumers eat vegetable matter.
    (5) The breakdown substances are reused by the producers.

Item 8 is based on the following diagram.

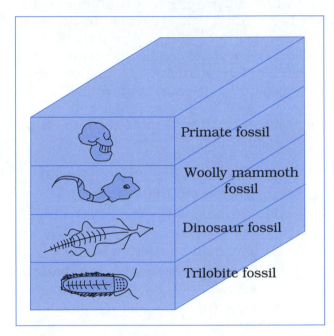

Younger rock layers and their fossils are usually found on top of older rock layers and their fossils. The diagram above shows a cross-section of rock from northern Canada. Trilobite fossils are remnants of organisms living in a tropical sea, whereas dinosaur and woolly mammoth fossils are those of organisms of the land.

8. The figure provides evidence to support which of the following conclusions?

    (1) The climate of northern Canada has remained essentially the same throughout Earth's history.
    (2) Northern Canada was once much drier than it is now.
    (3) Northern Canada has the kind of mild climate that allows many different animals to live together.

**(4)** Northern Canada used to be much cooler than it is now.

**(5)** The climate of northern Canada was radically altered by a period of cooling and drying.

Item 9 is based on the following passage.

The parts of a rosebush perform different services. The flower attracts insects by its bright color and sweet smell. This is how the plant reproduces, because the insects carry pollen from one place to another. The broad, flat leaves use the sun's energy to produce food, and exchange oxygen for carbon dioxide. The roots have many long branches which take minerals and water from the soil. The minerals and water are conducted to the leaves by the tubelike stem.

**9.** What does this passage tell us about rosebushes?

**(1)** Their color and scent are unimportant.

**(2)** Each part serves a life-sustaining function.

**(3)** The flower is the most important part.

**(4)** The flower is necessary for nutrition.

**(5)** Insects bring rosebushes food.

Items 10 to 12 are based on the following table.

| Gases in the Atmosphere (by percentage weight) | |
| --- | --- |
| Gas | Percent |
| Nitrogen | 78 |
| Oxygen | 21 |
| Argon | .9 |
| Carbon dioxide | .03 |
| Rare gases | .07 |

**10.** What percent of the atmosphere is made of the gas that sustains human and other animal life?

**(1)** 78

**(2)** 21

**(3)** 99

**(4)** .03

**(5)** 21.03

**11.** Which of the following statements cannot be concluded from the graph?

**(1)** Nitrogen and oxygen are the two most plentiful gases in the atmosphere.

**(2)** Carbon dioxide is not as important as oxygen for sustaining life.

**(3)** Gases in the atmosphere must be in relative balance to sustain life as we know it on earth.

**(4)** 1% of the earth's atmosphere is made up of carbon dioxide and rare gases.

**(5)** If the percentage of oxygen in the atmosphere were to decrease, human and animal life would be unaffected.

**12.** Carbon dioxide in the atmosphere tends to prevent heat from escaping. The percentage of $CO^2$ in the air has been changing. What might happen if its level reaches 5%?

**(1)** Continental coastlines would be unaffected.

**(2)** Areas now under water would become shores.

**(3)** Life on Earth would be largely unchanged.

**(4)** The polar icecaps would melt.

**(5)** Glaciers would grow larger.

**13.** When blood pressure is measured, two values result. The first value represents the force with which the heart pumps blood. It is the higher of the two numbers. The second, lower value indicates the flexibility of the arteries. Pulse pressure is the difference between the two. Thus, a person whose blood pressure reads 120 over 80 has a pulse pressure of 40.

Suppose the person's blood pressure is measured again a week later. The lower number is still 80, but the pulse pressure is 50. What would the reason be?

**(1)** The heart is damaged.
**(2)** The heart is pumping harder.
**(3)** The first value is lower than it was the last time.
**(4)** One of the readings must be wrong.
**(5)** The arteries have become less elastic.

**14.** A mitochondrion is a cell's "power-house." There are many in cells that need the highest level of energy for body work. Which of these body cells would have the most mitochondria?

**(1)** a blood cell
**(2)** a bone cell
**(3)** a muscle cell
**(4)** a nerve cell
**(5)** a skin cell

Items 15 to 18 are based on the following passage.

What causes an object to have a certain color? Light from the sun or an ordinary light bulb is white light. White light includes all the colors of the visible spectrum. The color of an opaque object is the color light it reflects. When white light falls on an opaque object, no light passes through it. Any light that falls on the object is either absorbed or reflected. An apple looks red because red light is reflected while the other colors are absorbed. A white object, then, reflects all colors and absorbs none. A black object absorbs all colors and reflects none.

Transparent objects, like tinted glass, acquire color somewhat differently because light passes through them. Light that falls on a transparent object is either absorbed or transmitted. The color of the object is the color of the light it transmits. Blue glass, for example, transmits only blue light. Clear glass transmits all colors and absorbs no color.

**15.** Which of the following statements explains why bananas are yellow?

**(1)** They absorb only yellow light.
**(2)** They absorb all of the white light.
**(3)** They reflect only yellow light.
**(4)** They reflect all of the white light.
**(5)** They transmit the yellow light.

**16.** In a dance concert, the only things on the stage that are blue are the dancers' shoes and gloves. In one scene the theater is dark. The audience should see hands and feet moving and nothing else. What color light should be directed at the stage?

**(1)** white
**(2)** black
**(3)** red
**(4)** blue
**(5)** yellow

**17.** If only green light is shone on a red apple, the apple looks black. Based on the information provided, which of the following statements best explains why this is so?

**(1)** The green light combines with red light to make black light.
**(2)** The apple absorbs the green light and reflects no light.
**(3)** The apple absorbs the green light and reflects black light.
**(4)** The apple cannot absorb green light, so it reflects no light.
**(5)** The apple reflects green light, which combines with black light.

**18.** A farmer notices that sunlight appears brighter in winter when his fields are snow-covered than in summer when the fields are lush and green. Based on the information provided, which of the following statements could explain his observation?

**(1)** Warm air makes sunlight look dimmer in summer than in winter.
**(2)** The field is closer to the sun in winter than in summer.

**(3)** White snow reflects more light than green plants do.

**(4)** Leaves on trees block the sunlight in summer.

**(5)** Plants use up the sunlight in photosynthesis.

19. Pollution makes the water of many lakes and streams in America unsafe for drinking. Among the pollutants are particles of solid waste, which stay suspended in the water. Temperature changes will not purify water of solid wastes. What might a city do to purify its water of solid wastes?

**(1)** Boil it.

**(2)** Freeze it.

**(3)** Let it settle.

**(4)** Filter it.

**(5)** Shake it.

20. The gene for brown eyes in humans is dominant, and the gene for blue eyes is recessive. A brown-eyed person has either two genes for brown eyes, or one for brown and one for blue. A blue-eyed person has only genes for blue eyes. Which of these couples will know the eye color of their children before birth?

**(1)** Father and mother are both brown-eyed.

**(2)** Father and mother are both blue-eyed.

**(3)** The father has brown eyes; the mother, blue.

**(4)** The mother has brown eyes; the father, blue.

**(5)** The parents already have one blue-eyed child.

Items 21 to 25 are based on the following passage.

Most animal circulatory systems have three main parts: the heart, the blood vessels, and the blood.

The heart is a pump that forces blood through the body. Bird hearts and mammal hearts have four chambers. The left and the right auricles are above the left and the right ventricles. Each auricle sends blood to the ventricle on its side of the heart. The ventricles send it to all the body's organs and parts.

The right auricle receives blood from all over the body. This blood is low in oxygen and carries waste products from the cells, such as carbon dioxide. The right ventricle sends the blood to the lungs, where it exchanges the waste gases for fresh oxygen. Then the blood flows to the left auricle, which sends it to the left ventricle. From the left ventricle it passes into the aorta, the largest artery in the body. One of the heart's valves ensures that the blood entering the aorta does not return to the heart. From the aorta it flows through other arteries throughout the body.

Because it has this complete separation, the bird heart and the mammal heart does the best job of keeping blood clean. Other animals lack the advantage of a four-chambered heart. Fish have only a single pump, which takes blood to the gills to regain oxygen. Amphibians, such as frogs and salamanders, have three-chambered hearts: two auricles above a single ventricle. Reptile hearts, such as snakes' and lizards', almost have four chambers, but the wall between the ventricles is not complete.

21. What is an artery?

**(1)** a blood vessel that takes blood away from the heart

**(2)** a blood vessel that carries blood to the heart

**(3)** a heart chamber below the auricles

**(4)** a heart chamber above the ventricles

**(5)** a valve under the left ventricle

22. A human heart suffers a break in the wall between its ventricles. What happens to the blood's oxygen concentration?

**(1)** It increases in the aorta.

(2) It increases in the left ventricle.

(3) It decreases in the right ventricle.

(4) It decreases in the left ventricle.

(5) It remains the same throughout.

23. Select the most powerful pumping chamber of the heart.

(1) aorta

(2) left auricle

(3) left ventricle

(4) right auricle

(5) right ventricle

24. A person has rheumatic fever as a child and suffers damaged heart valves. What problem is this person likely to have in later life?

(1) The blood moves freely from the

left ventricle to the aorta.

(2) Blood moves in the wrong direction.

(3) The heart lacks four full chambers.

(4) The heart will not pump blood.

(5) The lungs will not provide the blood with oxygen.

25. You are given a heart to study in biology lab. It is three-chambered. The best guess as to the animal it comes from is a

(1) cat

(2) fish

(3) lizard

(4) robin

(5) toad

Item 26 is based on the following diagram.

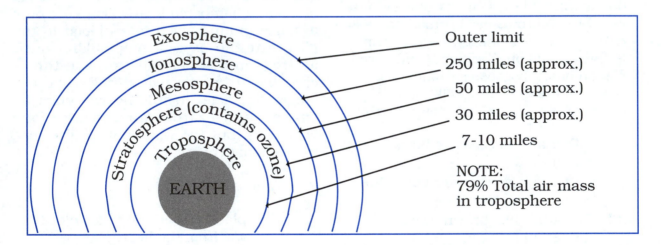

26. Pollution of the atmosphere is a threat to life on Earth. Air pollution affects which layer of the atmosphere most?

(1) exosphere

(2) ionosphere

(3) mesosphere

(4) stratosphere

(5) troposphere

Item 27 is based on the following passage.

Heat is transferred in three different ways:

1. **Conduction:** Heat is transferred through solids by conduction. Molecules in the solid vibrate more and more. The result is the transfer of heat through the solid.

2. **Convection:** Heat is transferred through liquids and gases by convection. Molecules in the liquid or gas move long distances giving off energy that causes heat.

**3. Radiation:** Radiation transfers heat in waves or particles. It usually travels from a source in straight lines and strikes matter—any liquid, solid, or gas. The matter heats as a result.

**27.** A pot of water on a gas stove is boiling. How is heat transferred to make the water boil?

(1) by conduction only
(2) by convection only
(3) by radiation only
(4) by both conduction and convection
(5) by both radiation and conduction

Items 28 and 29 are based on the following diagram.

CHEMICAL STRUCTURES OF THREE FUELS

```
      H  H  H
      |  |  |
  H—C—C—C—H
      |  |  |
      H  H  H
```
Propane

```
      H  H  H  H
      |  |  |  |
  H—C—C—C—C—H
      |  |  |  |
      H  H  H  H
```
Butane

```
      H  H  H  H  H
      |  |  |  |  |
  H—C—C—C—C—C—H
      |  |  |  |  |
      H  H  H  H  H
```
Pentane

**28.** C = 1 carbon atom. $H^2$ = 2 hydrogen atoms. Which fuel is represented by the formula $C^4H^{10}$?

(1) butane
(2) carbon
(3) hydrogen
(4) pentane
(5) propane

**29.** Each carbon atom weighs 12 units; each hydrogen atom, 1 unit. The weight of propane is 44. What is the weight of pentane?

(1) 14
(2) 17
(3) 58
(4) 72
(5) 204

**30.** Earth is about 5 billion years old. Fossil evidence shows that life started about 3 billion years ago. Since then, plants and animals have been evolving, continuously changing. For example, dinosaurs are gone, but new kinds of reptiles now exist. Once a life form becomes extinct, it never reappears.

Which is the most reasonable conclusion that can be drawn from this passage?

(1) Dinosaurs will return to Earth someday.
(2) No new fish species have developed since fish first appeared on Earth.
(3) Human evolution has stopped.
(4) Living organisms arose from a nonliving source.
(5) Living organisms are a very recent occurrence on Earth.

**31.** Your body needs to maintain fluid balance. Improper fluid balance can affect your blood pressure. When you eat food or drink liquids, your body gains fluids. It makes fluids by chemical reactions. It releases fluids through sweat, urine, and feces. If your salt intake is high, your body may retain fluids. That can make your blood pressure rise. Sometimes reducing salt intake is enough to make high blood pressure return to normal.

Following a doctor's orders, several patients went on a strict salt-free diet.

Later, the doctor read their blood pressures. Some patients had blood pressures that were still too high. The doctor told them to take medicine that would make them

(1) eat more salt
(2) eat less salt
(3) urinate more
(4) urinate less
(5) sweat less

Items 32 and 33 are based on the following chart.

| FOUR COMMON ROCK TEXTURES | | |
|---|---|---|
| Type of Texture | Description | Examples |
| Coarse-grained | Made up of visible grains or crystals | Granite<br>Marble<br>Sandstone |
| Fine Grained | Made up of microscopic grains or crystals | Limestone<br>Basalt |
| Glassy | Containing no mineral crystals at all | Obsidian |
| Layered | Made up of mineral crystals all lined the same direction | Slate<br>Schist<br>Sandstone |

Source: From Fariel et al., *Earth Science*. Menlo Park, Calif.: Addison-Wesley, 1984, page 86.

**32.** On a hike, you pick up a rock and can see mineral crystals in it. The rock's texture is not layered. It may be

(1) granite
(2) limestone
(3) basalt
(4) obsidian
(5) schist

**33.** Which of the following statements is supported by information from the chart?

(1) Granite rocks may have different textures.
(2) All rocks that have the same texture are indistinguishable.
(3) The same kind of rock may look very different because it can have different textures.
(4) Most rocks containing crystals are layered.
(5) Sandstone, a layered rock, cannot be made up of coarse grains that line up in different directions.

Answers are on pages 50-52.

**TIME:** 33 minutes

**Directions:** Choose the one best answer to each question.

Items 1 to 4 refer to the following passage.

### HOW DOES SAM PROVE HIS FRIENDSHIP?

Sam . . . stood gazing for a moment, stock-still, gaping. A boat was sliding down the bank all by itself. With a shout Sam raced
(5) across the grass. The boat slipped into the water.

"Coming, Mr. Frodo! Coming!" called Sam, and flung himself from the bank, clutching at the departing
(10) boat. He missed it by a yard. With a cry and a splash he fell face downward into deep swift water. Gurgling he went under, and the River closed over his curly head.

(15) An exclamation of dismay came from the empty boat. A paddle swirled and the boat came about. Frodo was just in time to grasp Sam by the hair as he came up,
(20) bubbling and struggling. Fear was staring in his round brown eyes.

"Up you come, Sam my lad!" said Frodo. "Now take my hand!"
"Save me, Mr. Frodo!" gasped
(25) Sam. "I'm drownded. I can't see your hand."

"Here it is. Don't pinch, lad! I won't let you go. Tread water and don't flounder, or you'll upset the
(30) boat. There now, get hold of the side, and let me use the paddle!"

With a few strokes Frodo brought the boat back to the bank, and Sam was able to scramble out, wet as a
(35) water-rat. Frodo took off the Ring and stepped ashore again.

Of all the confounded nuisances, you are the worst, Sam!" he said.

"Oh, Mr. Frodo, that's hard!" said
(40) Sam shivering. "That's hard, trying

to go without me and all. If I hadn't a guessed right, where would you be now?"

"Safely on my way."
(45) "Safely!" said Sam. "All alone and without me to help you? I couldn't have a borne it, it'd have been the death of me."

"It would be the death of you to
(50) come with me, Sam," said Frodo, "and I could not have borne that."

"Not as certain as being left behind," said Sam.

"But I am going to Mordor."
(55) "I know that well enough, Mr. Frodo. Of course you are. And I'm coming with you." . . .

"So all my plan is spoilt!" said Frodo. "It is no good trying to escape
(60) you. But I'm glad, Sam. I cannot tell you how glad. Come along! It is plain that we were meant to go together. We will go, and may the others find a safe road!
(65) Strider will look after them. I don't suppose we shall see them again."

"Yet we may, Mr. Frodo. We may," said Sam.

From THE FELLOWSHIP OF THE RING by J.R.R. Tolkien. Copyright 1965 by J.R.R. Tolkien. Reprinted by permission of Houghton Mifflin Company.

**1.** What is the "hard" thing to which Sam refers (lines 37-39)?

  **(1)** trying to swim
  **(2)** Frodo's wish to travel without him
  **(3)** the journey ahead of them
  **(4)** Frodo's angry speech at the shore
  **(5)** leaving Strider behind

2. Which of the following things would Sam be LEAST likely to do?

   **(1)** give first aid to a hurt friend
   **(2)** keep a lonely friend company
   **(3)** turn away from a neighbor in need
   **(4)** go into a burning building to save a friend
   **(5)** ask for help when he needed it

3. Why does Sam prefer going with Frodo to staying with the others?

   **(1)** He knows they do not want to go to Mordor.
   **(2)** He is afraid of Strider.
   **(3)** He knows they will be safer without him.
   **(4)** He is loyal to Frodo.
   **(5)** He knows they do not want to travel by boat.

4. Why is Sam's final comment effective in holding the reader's interest?

   **(1)** It seems to hint at a later part of the story.
   **(2)** It has a humor that breaks the tension of the moment.
   **(3)** It reveals Sam's secret fears about the journey.
   **(4)** It is in direct contrast with what Sam told Frodo earlier in the passage.
   **(5)** It dramatizes the seriousness of the moment.

Items 5 to 8 refer to the following passage.

### WHAT CAN BE DONE ABOUT UNEMPLOYMENT?

I remember the first time I looked for work. There were hundreds of classified ads in the paper under the Help Wanted heading and I figured it
(5)  was going to be easy.
     Well, it didn't take me long to find out that the number of Help Wanted pages in the classified section of the newspaper has very little to do with
(10) getting a job.
     First you count out all the ads looking for nuclear physicists, registered nurses, animal trainers and, if you don't know anything about
(15) computers, you count out the ads looking for computer programmers. I mention that because there seem to be a lot of ads for them these days. I don't know what they do but I
(20) assume it's a terrible job that doesn't pay much. If it wasn't, there wouldn't be so many ads for them under Help Wanted.
     As soon as you get some experi-
(25) ence looking in the classified section, you get discouraged. You begin to read the classifieds the way you read the phone book when you're looking for one number. You know
(30) all those hundreds of listings don't mean anything. You get to spot the ones looking for door-to-door salesmen to work on commission only. There's usually only one or two
(35) categories that mean anything to you and if anything is listed there, you're probably too late for it.
     Unemployment is as much of a mystery as cancer and almost as
(40) bad. I've never understood why there should be any real unemployment. Do we mean there isn't any work to be done anywhere in the country? Do we mean people have everything
(45) they want to eat? Everything they need by way of housing? All the clothes, cars and creature comforts they want? Of course not. Then why isn't there work for everyone?
(50)     What we need is a President who can figure out a way to match up those ten million unemployed with the ten million Help Wanted ads. And when that's done, I hope every
(55) one fires those miserable people in the personnel offices so they have to go out and look for work themselves.

**5.** It is evident from the passage that computer programmers

    **(1)** are readily available in a large supply
    **(2)** do not need a college education
    **(3)** are like nuclear physicists
    **(4)** have an interesting job
    **(5)** are in demand in today's economy

**6.** According to the author, why does unemployment continue?

    **(1)** Not enough careful thought has gone into a solution.
    **(2)** There are not enough jobs to go around.
    **(3)** Not enough people have the right kind of education.
    **(4)** Not enough people have the right kind of experience.
    **(5)** Newspapers don't run enough Help Wanted ads.

**7.** The author's attitude toward the classified ads is that they are

    **(1)** useless for most people
    **(2)** helpful for certain people
    **(3)** too abstract in their content
    **(4)** only for experienced people
    **(5)** difficult to understand

**8.** By the "mystery" of unemployment, the author means all of the following EXCEPT

    **(1)** The people who are unemployed should not complain about the types of jobs available because few jobs will give them everything they want in the way of clothes, cars and other creature comforts.
    **(2)** There probably are plenty of jobs for the unemployed in the construction industry because it is illogical to think that the housing needs of the nation have been satisfied.
    **(3)** There is no necessary unemployment since there are so many million Help Wanted ads all over the country.
    **(4)** There probably are many unfilled jobs in agriculture and related industries because the demand for food cannot have been completely satisfied.
    **(5)** There probably are many jobs for the unemployed because of the unfulfilled demands for clothing, automobiles and other consumer goods.

Items 9 to 11 refer to the following passage.

### HOW DOES EDDIE FEEL ABOUT CATHERINE'S NEW JOB?

BEATRICE: Go, Baby, set the table.
CATHERINE: We didn't tell him about me yet.
BEATRICE: Let him eat first, then
(5)    we'll tell him.Bring everything in. (*She hurries Catherine out.*)
EDDIE: (*sitting at the table*) What's all that about? Where's she goin'?
(10)  BEATRICE: Noplace. It's very good news, Eddie. I want you to be happy.
EDDIE: What's goin' on? (*Catherine enters with plates, forks.*)
(15)  BEATRICE: She's got a job.(*Pause. Eddie looks at Catherine, then back to Beatrice.*)
EDDIE: What job? She's gonna finish school.
(20)  CATHERINE: Eddie, you won't believe it—
EDDIE: No—no, you gonna finish school.What kinda job, what do you mean? All of a sudden you—
(25)  CATHERINE: Listen a minute, it's wonderful.
EDDIE: It's not wonderful. You'll never get nowheres unless you finish school. You can't take no
(30)    job. Why didn't you ask me before you take a job?
BEATRICE: She's askin' you now,

she didn't take nothin' yet.

(35) CATHERINE: Listen a minute! I came to school this morning and the principal called me out of the class, see? To go to his office.

EDDIE: Yeah?

(40) CATHERINE: So I went in and he says to me he's got my records, y'know? And there's a company wants a girl right away. It ain't exactly a secretary, it's a stenographer first, but pretty soon you

(45) get to be secretary. And he says to me that I'm the best student in the whole class—

BEATRICE: You hear that?

EDDIE: Well why not? Sure she's the

(50) best.

CATHERINE: I'm the best student, he says, and if I want, I should take the job and the end of the year he'll let me take the exami-

(55) nation and he'll give me the certificate. So I'll save practically a year!

EDDIE: *(strangely nervous)* Where's the job? What company?

(60) CATHERINE: It's a big plumbing company over Nostrand Avenue.

EDDIE: Nostrand Avenue and where?

CATHERINE: It's someplace by the

(65) Navy Yard.

BEATRICE: Fifty dollars a week, Eddie.

EDDIE: *(to Catherine, surprised)* Fifty?

(70) CATHERINE: I swear. *(Pause.)*

EDDIE: What about all the stuff you wouldn't learn this year, though?

CATHERINE: There's nothin' more to learn, Eddie, I just

(75) gotta practice from now on. I know all the symbols and I know the keyboard. I'll just get faster, that's all. And when I'm workin' I'll keep get-

(80) tin' better and better, you see?

BEATRICE: Work is the best practice anyway.

(85) EDDIE: That ain't what I wanted, though.

CATHERINE: Why! It's a great big company—

EDDIE: I don't like that neighborhood over there.

(90) CATHERINE: It's a block and half from the subway, he says.

EDDIE: Near the Navy Yard plenty can happen in a block and a half. And a plumbin' company!

(95) That's one step over the waterfront. They're practically longshoremen.

BEATRICE: Yeah, but she'll be in the office, Eddie.

(100) EDDIE: I know she'll be in the office, but that ain't what I had in mind.

BEATRICE: Listen, she's gotta go to work sometime.

(105) EDDIE: Listen, B., she'll be with a lotta plumbers? And sailors up and down the street? So what did she go to school for?

CATHERINE: But it's fifty a week,

(110) Eddie.

EDDIE: Look, did I ask you for money? I supported you this long I support you a little more. Please, do me a favor, will ya? I

(115) want you to be with different kind of people. I want you to be in a nice office. Maybe a lawyer's office someplace in New York in one of them nice buildings. I

(120) mean if you're gonna get outa here then get out; don't go practically in the same kind of neighborhood. *(Pause: Catherine lowers her eyes.)*

9. Catherine says she will be able to take the job and finish school because

(1) she is the best student in the whole class
(2) there is nothing more for her to learn
(3) the principal of the school likes her
(4) while working she will get better and better
(5) she can take an exam and graduate

10. According to the excerpt, Eddie does not want Catherine to take the job because

(1) she will not earn enough there
(2) it is too far away from their home
(3) she will be working with long-shoremen and sailors
(4) it will not help her achieve a better life
(5) she is too young to go to work

11. Which of the following does Eddie think is the most important thing to consider for Catherine's future?

(1) money
(2) education
(3) social status
(4) happiness
(5) efficiency

Items 12 to 16 refer to the following passage.

### WHAT HAS HAPPENED TO THE WALT DISNEY TRADITION?

When I was five years old, my parents took me out late one afternoon. It was already dark. We walked several blocks, or maybe we (5) took a bus—that part is fuzzy. Anyway, we entered a building that was also dark. It remained dark until the magic began.

Magic is what I associate with my (10) first movie. Of course, what I saw that night was a delight conjured by Walt Disney. It happened to be Bambi. My mother says that she used a package of tissues in that (15) hour. I only remember staring at all those wonderful talking animals and wishing that I could live in such a world.

Several weeks ago I turned on the (20) "Disney Sunday Movie" and saw all people—not animated characters; just people. Now, it's not that I object to real people. It's just that the Disney gold came from some (25) thing else. For example, I dimly remember a family I saw in a Disney movie years ago. I think there were two boys. But I can picture clearly the pair of raccoons that constantly (30) visited the family's back door. One day they got inside the house and into everything—the dishes, the flour, the cereal. It was wonderful fun.

(35) So, when I turned on that Sunday movie, I was disappointed. The title—"Help Wanted: Kids"—was promising; but neither the couple in need nor the horrible children avail- (40) able ever amounted to more than a poor try. Did this effort deserve the name "Disney"? Is the public so unimaginative today that it accepts this kind of movie over flights of (45) fancy? Or has the Master's wand passed on to less able hands, to those who will allow much to replace best? Gain and art are, at best, uneasy companions.

(50) I guess I'm lucky that I grew up with Donald and Jiminy and Sleepy and Doc. Oh, I'm sure that from time to time we'll be allowed another look at Cinderella's bird friends (55) sewing her ball gown and Mickey's enchanted brooms carrying bucket after bucket of water.But I'm still looking for that new masterpiece from the old magic lantern.

12. The author's concern is that recent Disney movies lack

(1) audience appeal
(2) creativity
(3) human characters

(4) financial support

(5) a true-to-life quality

**13.** How does the author use the word "wand" (line 45)?

(1) to remind the reader of the magicians in several Disney movies

(2) to show a contrast between fantasy movies and true-life adventures

(3) to symbolize the popularity of Disney movies

(4) to refer to plans for movies that went unfinished when Walt Disney died

(5) to symbolize the art of creative moviemaking

**14.** The final paragraph indicates the author's belief that

(1) animated characters are not believable

(2) Walt Disney made many popular movies

(3) memorable characters cannot be found in current Disney efforts

(4) the Disney studio is unwilling to show the classic animated movies to current audiences

(5) talking animals are the most memorable characters

**15.** What kind of people are most likely to identify with the author and her message?

(1) Disney studio executives

(2) people who work "behind the scenes" in the movie industry

(3) children, for whom the classic movies are new

(4) people who grew up with the classic Disney movies

(5) students of moviemaking

Items 16 to 20 refer to the following passage.

**WHY IS FELD INTERESTED IN MAX?**

A figure emerged from the snow and the door opened. At the counter the man withdrew from a wet paper bag a pair of battered shoes for repair.

(5) Who he was the shoemaker for a moment had no idea, then his heart trembled as he realized, before he had thoroughly discerned the face, that Max himself was standing

(10) there, embarrassedly explaining what he wanted done to his old shoes. Though Feld listened eagerly, he couldn't hear a word, for the opportunity that had burst upon

(11) him was deafening.

He couldn't exactly recall when the thought had occurred to him, because it was clear he had more

(15) than once considered suggesting to the boy that he go out with Miriam. But he had not dared speak, for if Max said no, how would he face him again? Or suppose Miriam, who

(20) harped so often on independence, blew up in anger and shouted at him for his meddling? Still, the chance was too good to let by: all it meant was an introduction. They

(25) might long ago have become friends had they happened to meet somewhere, therefore was it not his duty—an obligation—to bring them together, nothing more, a harmless

(30) connivance to replace an accidental encounter in the subway, let's say, or a mutual friend's introduction in the street? Just let him once see and talk to her and he would for

(35) sure be interested. As for Miriam, what possible harm for a working girl in an office, who met only loudmouthed salesmen and illiterate shipping clerks, to make the

(40) acquaintance of a fine scholarly boy? Maybe he would awaken in her a desire to go to college; if not—the shoemaker's mind at last came to grips with the truth—let her marry

(45) an educated man and live a better life.

When Max finished describing

what he wanted done to his shoes, Feld marked them, both with enor-
(50) mous holes in the soles which he pretended not to notice, with large white-chalk x's, and the rubber heels, thinned to the nails, he marked with o's, though it troubled him he might
(55) have mixed up the letters. Max inquired the price, and the shoemaker cleared his throat and asked the boy, above Sobel's insistent hammering, would he please step
(60) through the side door there into the hall. Though surprised, Max did as the shoemaker requested, and Feld went in after him. For a minute they were both silent, because Sobel had
(65) stopped banging, and it seemed they understood neither was to say anything until the noise began again. When it did, loudly, the shoemaker quickly told Max why he had asked
(70) to talk to him.
　　"Ever since you went to high school," he said, in the dimly-lit hallway, "I watched you in the morning go to the subway to school,
(75) and I said always to myself, this is a fine boy that he wants so much an education."
　　"Thanks," Max said, nervously alert. He was tall and grotesquely
(80) thin, with sharply cut features, particularly a beak-like nose. He was wearing a loose, long slushy overcoat that hung down to his ankles, looking like a rug draped over his
(85) bony shoulders, and a soggy, old brown hat, as battered as the shoes he had brought in.
　　"I am a business man," the shoemaker abruptly said to conceal his
(90) embarrassment, "so I will explain you right away why I talk to you. I have a girl, my daughter Miriam—she is nineteen—a very nice girl and also so pretty that everybody looks
(95) on her when she passes by in the street. She is smart, always with a book, and I thought to myself that a boy like you, an educated boy—I thought maybe you will be interest-
(100) ed sometime to meet a girl like this." He laughed a bit when he had finished and was tempted to say more

but had the good sense not to.
　　Max stared down like a hawk. For
(105) an uncomfortable second he was silent, then he asked, "Did you say nineteen?"
　　"Yes."
　　"Would it be all right to inquire if
(110) you have a picture of her?"
　　"Just a minute." The shoemaker went into the store and hastily returned with a snapshot that Max held up to the light.
(115) 　　"She's all right," he said.
　　Feld waited.
　　"And is she sensible—not the flighty kind?"
　　"She is very sensible."
(120) 　　After another short pause, Max said it was okay with him if he met her.
　　"Here is my telephone," said the shoemaker, hurriedly handing him a slip of paper. "Call her up. She
(125) comes home from work six o'clock."
　　Max folded the paper and tucked it away into his worn leather wallet.

*The First Seven Years,* Bernard Malmud
*Prentice Hall Literature, The American Experience,* 2nd ed., Copyright 1991, 1989, Englewood Cliffs, N.J. 07632

**16.** According to the excerpt, Max is most probably

　**(1)** a salesman
　**(2)** a college student
　**(3)** a person Miriam met accidentally
　**(4)** a homeless person
　**(5)** a school friend of Miriam's

**17.** Feld is afraid Miriam will reject Max because

　**(1)** she will think Max is unattractive
　**(2)** she will think Max is too poor
　**(3)** she doesn't like scholarly men
　**(4)** she wants to make her own choices
　**(5)** she is not interested in men

**18.** The description of Max presents him as

   **(1)** tall and impressive
   **(2)** thin but well-built
   **(3)** nervous and threatening
   **(4)** unattractive and poor
   **(5)** friendly but awkward

**19.** Feld's reaction to Max's shoes (lines 47-55) indicates that he

   **(1)** doesn't think the shoes need repairing
   **(2)** thinks Max is trying to take advantage of him
   **(3)** doesn't want to admit how poor Max is
   **(4)** has decided his plan about Miriam is a bad idea
   **(5)** thinks he is getting too old for shoemaking

**20.** Max's response to Feld's proposal is

   **(1)** hostile
   **(2)** eager
   **(3)** shocked
   **(4)** curious
   **(5)** indifferent

Items 21 to 23 refer to the following song lyrics.

### IS THE WORLD CHANGING FOR THE BETTER?

They paved paradise and put up a
    parking lot,
With a pink hotel, a boutique,
    And a swinging hot spot.
(5)  Don't it always seem to go
    That you don't know what
    you've got till it's gone?
They paved paradise and put up a
    parking lot.
(10) They took all the trees and put
    them in a tree museum,
    And they charged the people a dollar
    and a half
    Just to see 'em.
(15) Don't it always seem to go

That you don't know what
    you've got till it's gone?
They paved paradise and put up a
    parking lot.
(20) Hey, farmer, farmer, put away the
    D.D.T. now.
    Give me spots on my apples, but
    leave me the birds
    And the bees. Please!
(25) Don't it always seem to go
    That you don't know what
    you've got till it's gone?
    They paved paradise and put up a
    parking lot.

*Big Yellow Taxi* music and lyrics by Joni Mitchell. Copyright 1970 & 1974 by Siquomb Publishing Corp. Reprinted by permission of Warner Brothers Music.

**21.** What is paradise to the author?

   **(1)** a place where trees are put in museums
   **(2)** the unspoiled natural world
   **(3)** farmland
   **(4)** the afterlife
   **(5)** a hotel with a parking lot and nightclub

**22.** What would the author prefer to have instead of D.D.T.?

   **(1)** a boutique
   **(2)** trees
   **(3)** her music
   **(4)** a room at a pink hotel
   **(5)** spotted apples

**23.** Which of the following other topics probably would NOT be included in this song?

   **(1)** chemical dumping
   **(2)** protecting the whales
   **(3)** enlarging wildlife preserves
   **(4)** drug abuse
   **(5)** oil spills

Answers are on pages 52-55.

**TIME:** 45 minutes

**Directions:** Choose the one best answer to each question.

1. Sarah worked 10.75 hours overtime in one week. If she earns $9.00 per hour overtime, what was her overtime pay that week?

   **(1)** $6.00
   **(2)** $96.75
   **(3)** $145.13
   **(4)** $240.00
   **(5)** $336.75

2. Janet works part-time at a supermarket. Tuesday, she worked 2 2/3 hours. Thursday, she worked 3 3/4 hours. Saturday, she worked 6 1/2 hours. How many hours did she work altogether that week?

   **(1)** $11 \frac{1}{12}$
   **(2)** $11 \frac{1}{2}$
   **(3)** $12 \frac{11}{12}$
   **(4)** $13 \frac{3}{8}$
   **(5)** $14 \frac{5}{12}$

3. Debbie sells and services computers. She earns a 30% commission on her sales and is paid a salary for her service work. If c = her annual sales and s = her monthly salary, which of the following expressions shows her annual income?

   **(1)** $s = .3c$
   **(2)** $.3(s + c)$
   **(3)** $.3(12s + c)$
   **(4)** $12s + .3c$
   **(5)** $12(s + .3c)$

Items 4 and 5 are based on the following information.

One feature of adjustable-rate mortgages (ARMs) is rates that are adjusted annually. The length of a loan varies from bank to bank. Most banks offer them for lengths of 15, 17, 20, or 25 years.

4. If a bank sets its ARM rate at 120% of the prime lending rate, and the ARM rate is 9%, what is the prime rate?

   **(1)** 7.5%
   **(2)** 10.8%
   **(3)** 11.0%
   **(4)** 13.0%
   **(5)** Not enough information is given

5. If a $50,000 ARM loan is made at an average simple-interest rate of 10.5%, how much interest would be paid during the life of the loan?

   **(1)** $ 78,750
   **(2)** $ 89,250
   **(3)** $105,000
   **(4)** $525,000
   **(5)** Not enough information is given

Items 6 and 7 refer to the following figure.

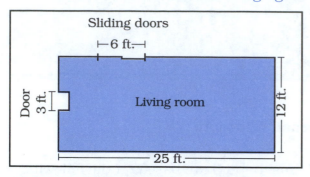

6. What is the minimum number of feet of baseboard needed for this room if none is needed for the doorways?

(1) 37
(2) 65
(3) 68
(4) 71
(5) 74

7. If 12" square floor tiles are sold in boxes of 25 each, how many boxes of tiles would be needed to cover the floor in this room?

(1) 12
(2) 65
(3) 74
(4) 300
(5) Not enough information is given.

Item 8 refers to the following table

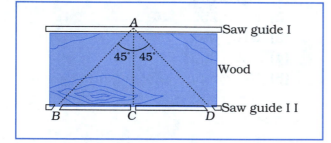

8. A carpenter wants to reuse a plank of wood. He wants to cut the end of the plank to be at a right angle to the length of the plank. Between which saw guides should he place his saw to cut the wood?

(1) A and B
(2) A and C
(3) A and D
(4) B and D
(5) C and D

9. The cost of a quart of milk is $.60 plus 2% sales tax in state A, $.59 plus 5% sales tax in state B, $.57 plus 4% sales tax in state C, and $.55 plus 9% sales tax in state D. Which of the following sequences correctly shows the order of states listed from the most expensive to the least expensive total cost of a quart of milk?

(1) A, B, C, D
(2) B, A, D, C
(3) D, B, C, A
(4) C, D, A, B
(5) Not enough information is given.

Item 10 refers to the following table.

| County | Marriages | Divorces |
|--------|-----------|----------|
| Albany | 293 | 172 |
| Carbon | 180 | 135 |
| Converse | 181 | 101 |
| Natrona | 801 | 698 |
| Washakie | 125 | 61 |

10. All the counties listed in the table had MORE marriages than divorces. In which county was the difference between the number of marriages and the number of divorces the smallest?

(1) Albany
(2) Carbon
(3) Converse
(4) Natrona
(5) Washakie

11. A mill produces bolts of a certain size. Quality-control standards allow the size of the bolts to vary, but none may be more than 15 ten-thousandths of an inch larger than the standard. Bolts that do not meet the standard

are rejected. If b represents the size of the bolt being measured and s represents the desired size, which formula should be used to determine which bolts should be rejected?

**(1)** b < s + .0015
**(2)** b > s + .0015
**(3)** b < s + .015
**(4)** b > s + .015
**(5)** b > .0015

Item 12 refers to the following table.

| Babies Born During One Week at Doctors Hospital | | |
|---|---|---|
| Day | Boys | Girls |
| Sunday | 5 | 2 |
| Monday | 0 | 8 |
| Tuesday | 6 | 7 |
| Wednesday | 4 | 4 |
| Thursday | 8 | 1 |
| Friday | 2 | 0 |
| Saturday | 7 | 9 |

**12.** According to the table, what was the average number of babies born per day?

**(1)** 4
**(2)** 5
**(3)** 7
**(4)** 8
**(5)** 9

**13.** One share of Brite Lighting, Inc. stock sold on Monday for $13.50. Tuesday it was down 50 cents. Wednesday it was up $1.25, and Thursday the price per share was the same. Friday it was down 75 cents. What was the closing price of the stock on Friday?

**(1)** $13.00
**(2)** $13.50
**(3)** $14.25
**(4)** $14.75
**(5)** $15.00

Item 14 refers to the following figure.

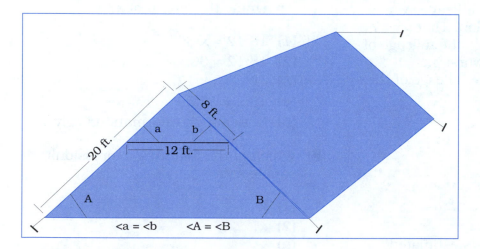

**14.** How many feet wide is the base of the tent?

**(1)** 13.3
**(2)** 24
**(3)** 28
**(4)** 30
**(5)** 40

**15.** The Nelsons are planning a two-week cross-country automobile trip. If they drive at an average speed of 53 miles per hour and drive 8 hours each day, how many miles will they travel altogether?

**(1)** 112
**(2)** 424
**(3)** 848
**(4)** 2968
**(5)** 5936

**16.** Jeff and Sally are planning the spring planting for their farm. Crops will be planted on 360 acres and will include twice as many acres of soybeans as wheat and three times as many acres of corn as wheat. Which equation should be used to determine the correct acreage for each crop? (w = the number of acres of wheat to be planted.)

**(1)** $w - 5 = 360$
**(2)** $w + 5 = 360$
**(3)** $w + 2w + 3w = 360$
**(4)** $3w - (2w + w) = 360$
**(5)** $3w \times 2w \times w = 360$

**17.** In a recent gas-mileage test, the car that had the best gas mileage averaged 56 miles per gallon. That was 7 miles less than 5 times the mileage of the car that had the worst gas mileage. What was the mileage of the worst car?

**(1)** 3.5
**(2)** 5.6
**(3)** 9.2
**(4)** 11.2
**(5)** 12.6

**18.** In July 1986, scientists estimated that the world's population had reached half the product of 4 times 2 billion increased by 2 billion. Which of the following expressions gives the 1986 world population?

**(1)** $2 + \frac{1}{2} (4 \times 2)$
**(2)** $\frac{2(4 \times 2)}{2}$
**(3)** $\frac{1}{2} (4 \times 2) + 2$
**(4)** $\frac{2(4 + 2)}{2}$
**(5)** $\frac{2 + (4 \times 2)}{2}$

Item 19 refers to the following figure.

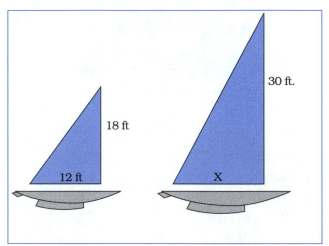

**19.** The height and the width of the smaller sail are 18 feet by 12 feet; the height and the width of the larger sail are 30 feet by x feet. If the two sails form similar triangles, which of the following proportions could be used to determine the length of x?

**(1)** 18:12 = x:30
**(2)** 18:12 = 30:x
**(3)** 18:30 = x:12
**(4)** 18:x = 12:30
**(5)** Not enough information is given.

**20.** Which of the following expressions equals $x^5/x^2$?

**(1)** $x^1$
**(2)** $x^3$
**(3)** $x^7$
**(4)** $x^{11}$
**(5)** Not enough information is given.

Item 21 refers to the following figure.

**21.**

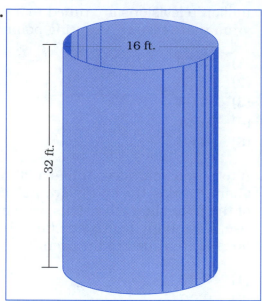

Assume that one bushel equals 1.25 cubic feet. To the nearest whole bushel, how many bushels of grain can be stored in the storage tank?

**(1)** 161
**(2)** 1286
**(3)** 1608
**(4)** 5145
**(6)** 6431

**22.** Three friends recently had dinner together in a restaurant and decided to split the $32.40 check plus a 15% tip evenly among themselves. How much money was paid by each of the three friends?

**(1)** $10.80
**(2)** $12.42
**(3)** $15.80
**(4)** $26.40
**(5)** $37.26

Item 23 refers to the following figure.

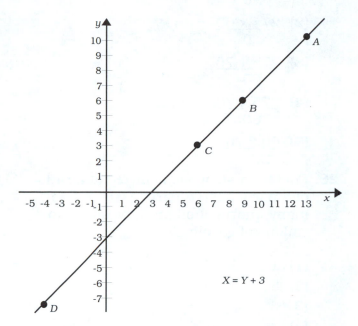

**23.** What is the slope of the line on the graph for points B (9,6) and C (6,3)? Refer to the formula on page 401.

**(1)** -1
**(2)** 1
**(3)** .5
**(4)** -.5
**(5)** 2

**24.** The ratio of hamburgers to hot dogs that were served at a school picnic was 7:4. If 245 hamburgers were served, how many hot dogs and hamburgers were served?

**(1)** 249
**(2)** 256
**(3)** 280
**(4)** 319
**(5)** 385

**25.** Amy types 70 words per minute. She has to type a 60-page report that contains, on the average, 275 words per page. Which of the following expressions shows the number of minutes that this should take her?

**(1)** $\dfrac{275 + 60}{70}$

**(2)** $\dfrac{275 \times 60}{70}$

**(3)** $\dfrac{275 + 70}{60}$

**(4)** $\dfrac{275 \times 70}{60}$

**(5)** $\dfrac{60 \times 70}{275}$

**26.** Fuel for a snowbile is mixed at a ratio of 3 parts oil to 8 parts gasoline. How many quarts of oil must be added to 4 gallons of gasoline?

**(1)** 1.5

**(2)** 3

**(3** 6

**(4)** 9

**(5)** 12

Items 27 and 28 are based on the following information.

Television ratings describe how popular shows are. Popularity can be expressed in two different ways.

(1) Rating Points
A rating point is the percent of *all televisions* tuned to a particular program. (*All* televisions includes those that are turned off.)

(2) Shares
A share is the percent of *all televisions in use* that are tuned to a particular program. (*All televisions in use* includes ONLY those televisions that are turned on.)

**27.** Assume that there are 83 million televisions in the United States and that

$\frac{1}{3}$ of them are turned on. How many million televisions are tuned to a program that receives 18 rating points?

**(1)** 3.74

**(2)** 6.50

**(3)** 14.94

**(4)** 16.61

**(5)** 21.69

**28.** A televised sports event has a 20% share. During the sports events, 45% of the 83 million televisions were in use. How many televisions (in millions) were tuned to the event?

**(1)** 7.47

**(2)** 9.00

**(3)** 16.60

**(4)** 23.00

**(5)** 37.35

Answers are on pages 55-56.

# ANSWERS AND EXPLANATIONS FOR THE PREDICTOR TESTS

# Writing Skills, Part 1

1. **(3)** *Usage/Adverb/Sentence Correction.* The adverb *responsibly* is needed to modify the verb phrase *must behave.*

2. **(4)** *Mechanics/Capitalization/Sentence Correction.* The words *consumer commissions* should not be capitalized since they refer to a general category and not a specific name.

3. **(2)** *Sentence Structure/Fragment/Sentence Revision.* The words *Such as the one Ralph Nader formed* are a fragment and must be joined to the previous sentence.

4. **(4)** *Usage/Pronoun Case/Sentence Correction.* There are no such words as *hisself* or *theirselves*; these reflexive pronouns are always written as himself and themselves.

5. **(5)** *Sentence Structure/Run-on/Sentence Revision.* A comma cannot join two independent sentences. Therefore, the second clause is made dependent on the first with the word *because.*

6. **(3)** *Usage/Vague Pronoun Reference/Sentence Revision.* It is not clear whether *they* refers to sales-clerks, to items or to buyers. (2) separates the complete thought of the sentence into a fragment *(If items are not examined carefully when purchased)* and an independent clause which lacks a complete thought. (5) changes the verb tense incorrectly.

7. **(5)** *Usage/Mechanics/Sentence Correction.* The sentence is correct as is.

8. **(3)** *Sentence Structure/Parallelism/Sentence Revision.* A series of items must use parallel, or similar, structure. Because *warranties* and *warnings* are nouns, the third item must be a noun also. *Instructions* is a noun.

9. **(3)** *Mechanics/Spelling/Sentence Correction.* The possessive form of *its* never takes an apostrophe. An apostrophe with *it's* always means *it is.*

10. **(4)** *Sentence Structure/Coordination & Subordination/Construction Shift.* When *unless* is used in one clause, the other clause states the opposite possibility. In order to retain the meaning of the original sentence, *they may not feel secure* is needed.

11. **(4)** *Usage/Pronoun Shift/Sentence Correction.* Throughout the paragraph, *our* and *we* are used. The first sentence must also use the plural *our lives.*

12. **(4)** *Usage/Tense Shift/Sentence Correction.* The verb tense of the second part of the sentence must conform to the verb tense of the first part, which is the present tense *(may not use)*. Also, the consistent verb tense of the entire passage is the present tense. (2) makes no sense and the other choices suggest incorrect changes in punctuation—(1) and (3)—or grammar—(5).

13. **(5)** *Sentence Structure/Parallelism/Sentence Revision.* Items written in a series require parallel structure. In this sentence, *to process our bills* is similar in structure to the two other phrases, *to record the prices* and *to provide us with cash.*

14. **(2)** *Mechanics/Spelling/Sentence Correction.* The possessive form *their* is needed before the word *engines*. The word *they're* means *they are*.

15. **(4)** *Usage/Subject-Verb Agreement/Sentence Revision. One* is the subject of the sentence (not *uses* or *computers*) and therefore a singular form of the verb is required. The passage as a whole is in the present tense, so (2) and (5) cannot be correct.

16. **(1)** *Usage/Tense Shift/Sentence Correction.* In order to maintain the same time sequence throughout the paragraph, the present verb *are* must be used.

17. **(1)** *Sentence Structure/Usage/Sentence Revision.* The original is correct. A comma is needed before the conjunction *but*, and the adverb *well* is needed to modify the verb *work*.

18. **(4)** *Usage/Pronoun Shift/Sentence Correction.* The paragraph has been written using the first person plural *we*. Therefore, the sentence is incorrect in shifting to the pronoun *you*.

19. **(3)** *Sentence Structure/Subordination/Construction Shift.* The best way of combining the two sentences is by making one sentence dependent on the other with the word *because*. The word *unless* would not provide the correct meaning.

20. **(1)** *Usage/Subject-Verb Agreement/Sentence Correction.* The subject *one* is singular and requires the singular verb *is*.

21. **(3)** *Sentence Structure/Fragment/Sentence Revision.* In order to avoid a fragment, the word group which begins with *while* must be joined to the main clause which begins with *there are*.

22. **(2)** *Mechanics/Spelling/Sentence Correction.* The word *interests* has three syllables.

23. **(1)** *Mechanics/Punctuation/Sentence Revision.* The original is correct. When a long, dependent word group introduces a sentence, it is set off with a comma.

24. **(2)** *Mechanics/Capitalization/Sentence Correction.* The term *doctors* is general and does not need to be capitalized.

25. **(4)** *Usage/Pronoun Shift/Sentence Correction.* The pronoun *you* should be used to refer to *the reader* and to maintain consistency throughout the paragraph.

26. **(1)** *Sentence Structure/Dangling Modifier/Construction Shift.* A noun, or pronoun, should be placed next to the phrase that modifies it. In this case you are the one who is talking with workers.

27. **(1)** *Mechanics/Punctuation/Sentence Revision.* When two verbs, *discuss* and *learn*, have the same subject, *you*, they should not be separated by a comma or other punctuation.

28. **(5)** *Sentence Structure/Subordination and Coordination/Construction Shift.* The phrase *learning about several careers* is the main subject of the sentence and requires the verb *will help* to follow it.

# Writing Skills, Part II

## Introduction to Holistic Scoring

The following GED Essay Scoring Guide provides a general description of the characteristics of GED essays that are scored by the Holistic Method.

### GED ESSAY SCORING GUIDE

Papers will show some or all of the following characteristics

*Upper-half papers make clear a definite purpose, pursued with varying degrees of effectiveness. They also have a structure that shows evidence of some deliberate planning. The writer's control of English usage ranges from fairly reliable at 4 to confident and accomplished at 6.*

**6** Papers scored as a 6 tend to offer sophisticated ideas within an organizational framework that is clear and appropriate for the topic. The supporting statements are particularly effective because of their substance, specificity, or illustrative quality. The writing is vivid and precise, though it may contain an occasional flaw.

**5** Papers scored as a 5 are clearly organized with effective support for each of the writer's major points. The writing offers substantive ideas, though the paper may lack the flair or grace of a 6 paper. The surface features are consistently under control, despite an occasional lapse in usage.

**4** Papers scored as a 4 show evidence of the writer's organizational plan. Support, though sufficient, tends to be less extensive or convincing than that found in papers scored as a 5 or 6. The writer generally observes the conventions of accepted English usage. Some errors are usually present, but they are not severe enough to interfere significantly with the writer's main purpose.

*Lower-half papers either fail to convey a purpose sufficiently or lack one entirely.*

*Consequently, their structure ranges from rudimentary at 3, to random at 2, to absent at 1. Control of the conventions of English usage tends to follow this same gradient.*

**3** Papers scored as a 3 usually show some evidence of planning or development. However, the organization is often limited to a simple listing or haphazard recitation of ideas about the topic, leaving an impression of insufficiency. The 3 papers often demonstrate repeated weaknesses in accepted English usage and are generally ineffective in accomplishing the writer's purpose.

**2** Papers scored as a 2 are characterized by a marked lack of development or inadequate support for ideas. The level of thought apparent in the writing is frequently unsophisticated or superficial, often marked by a listing of unsupported generalizations. Instead of suggesting a clear purpose, these papers often present conflicting purposes. Errors in accepted English usage may seriously interfere with the overall effectiveness of these papers.

**1** Papers scored as a 1 leave the impression that the writer has not only not accomplished a purpose, but has not made any purpose apparent. The dominant feature of these papers is the lack of control. The writer stumbles both in conveying a clear plan for the paper and in expressing ideas according to the conventions of accepted English usage.

**0** The zero score is reserved for papers which are blank, illegible, or written on a topic other than the one assigned.

Copyright 1985, GED Testing Service, September, 1985

Source: The 1988 Tests of General Educational Development: A Preview, American Council on Education, 1985. Used with permission.

## HOW TO SCORE YOUR ESSAY

The following six essays are designed to be used as models for the scoring of your essay. The essays are presented in order from the essay that deserves the lowest score (1) to the essay that deserves the highest score (6).

To score your essay, first compare your essay with the model essay that received a score of 1. If your essay is better than the 1 essay, compare it with the 2 essay and so on until you are able to decide where your essay fits when compared with the six model essays.

As you score your essay, read the character-trait analysis that follows each model essay. This analysis can help you to see how you might have improved your essay in order to have received a higher score.

## Model Essay—Holistic Score 1

**Exploring the options is a prewriting activity: These notes do not belong in the essay.**

Many of these choice are hard to make. Because they all look good. Someone wants to go to work at different times. Someone else wants to go to work at other times. Its good that employers gives that choice to workers. That way workers can work parttime if they want. They can also work at home too. What if a person wanted to work at home and take care of these children? That be good. Everybody could get some thing from that way. Many people would like working better if then.

**States the point of view: Undeveloped examples that do not support the point of view.**
**The point of view changes. Conclusion is vague.**

I think I would work flexible hours. That way I could work whenever I want. I would like to work early in the morning and get out early in the afternoon. That way I'd be home when my children got home from school. That would be good for them. I could work at home too. That way I'd be there for them. That is how I would choose it.

Character-Trait Analysis

1. The organization is poor.
2. The first paragraph does not belong in the essay. It could be used as a prewriting activity to explore the options.
3. The essay does not address the topic immediately. The point of view is given in the middle of the essay; it should be stated immediately.
4. The examples do not support the point of view. Working early in the morning and getting out early in the afternoon does not tell us why the writer would like flexible hours; it simply lists one type of schedule.
5. If the essay were longer, there would be more opportunity to develop the examples.
6. There are many serious errors in accepted English usage.

## Model Essay—Holistic Score 2

**States the point of view**

**Unsupported opinions, needs specific examples**

**Restates the point of view**

Many alternatives to employers jobs is good. My favorite is working flexible hours. Reasons is for people to work at different times is so they can do things they like to do. I would go to afternoon baseball games if I could. Movies are cheaper in the afternoon to but if you work a regular job you cant go then. Early bird dinner specials costs less to if you can get there soon enough. It would be easier to look for another job if you didn't like your job. It would be easier to go shopping or even getting to work could be easier if the roads weren't crowded. Anyway, I would like to work at flexible hours for many reasons. I could do what I want and I could still work.

Character-Trait Analysis

1. The organization is better than model essay 1. However, it is organized for the writer, not for the reader. Paragraphing would help this essay.

2. The point of view is stated immediately.

3. The conclusion follows a listing of unsupported opinions. Specific examples for the writer's point of view--such as, *I would like to be able to try the early bird dinner specials that many restaurants offer. But because I work a regular work day, I get home too late to do so. If I worked flexible hours, I could leave early enough to try them*—would strengthen this essay.

4. The essay should be longer to allow more space for specific examples.

5. Errors in accepted English usage interfere with the writer's purpose.

6. Because of the consistent point of view, this essay is better than the 1 essay. However, it lacks the depth and the sophistication of higher-scoring essays.

## Model Essay—Holistic Score 3

**States the point of view**

**Haphazard listing of ideas about the topic**

I would choose job sharing for my work schedule if I could because job sharing sounds like a good thing. It would let people share jobs. That way the employer can have a fresh person working all the time. That way he gets people who have lots of energy. It would make my job easier to do if I had someone else to do it with. I would like to share my job because of the extra time it would give me. The free time would let me do lots of things I don't have time to do now.

**Restates the point of view**

Sharing a job would give somebody else a job. Many people in today's world are out of jobs. Sharing would make two times as many jobs for the people out of work. That's another good thing about sharing jobs. Besides giving people more free time. People spend too much time at work anyway. That is not good. It would be better if people did not have to work too much. That's why I would choose job sharing if I could choose.

Character-Trait Analysis

1. The level of organization is similar to that of model essay 2. Better paragraphing might have brought the problems with the examples to the attention of the writer in time to correct them.

2. The supporting examples are too general. They are really a listing of ideas. *People spend too much time at work anyway* does not tell the reader why the writer would choose job sharing. For writing to be effective, it should use specific examples, not unsupported opinions.

3. The essay contains many sentence fragments: *Besides giving people more free time.* is one example. There are other problems with accepted English usage that interfere with the essay's effectiveness.

## Model Essay—Holistic Score 4

I would choose a traditional nine to five schedule if I had a choice about when I could work. I would select it so that I could have a steady income that I could count on. I do temporary work and can't count on where or when I will work or how much money I can make.

I would select it because I would like a regular job. I don't like working in a lot of different places, you meet a lot of people but you never get to know them. Working all day in one place lets you develop real friendships with people.

The other reason is that it costs more to do freelance or temporary work than it does to work full-time. I have to pay for my own health insurance and I don't get paid if I get sick. I also can't count on working every day, so I don't know how much money I've made each week until the end of the week.

There are advantages to working freelance, like having time off whenever I want it, but I would select a traditional nine to five job because of the friends I could make, the benefits I would get, and the extra money that I would make.

Character-Trait Analysis

1. The level of organization in this essay is very good.

2. It addresses the topic immediately and explains the writer's reasons for choosing this option. The point of view is clear.

3. The supporting examples are better than those in model essay 3. Notice the use of specific examples in the third paragraph of this essay. But the examples are not as convincing as those used in model essays 5 and 6. Check those essays for the use of specific examples that better illustrate the writer's point of view.

4. The ideas and the vocabulary in this essay are more sophisticated than those in essays 1, 2, and 3, but this essay lacks the depth of essays 5 and 6 .

## Model Essay—Holistic Score 5

If my employer offered alternatives to the traditional nine to five schedule, I would choose job sharing for two reasons. First, job sharing would make my job more secure. Second, job sharing would mean that I could work part-time.

Job sharing could ensure that I could keep my present job. I work full-time processing mail orders for a sportswear company. However, business has been slow lately and the company has been looking for ways to cut back. If I shared my job with a coworker, the company would save money and we could both keep jobs that we enjoy.

If I shared my job with a coworker, I would gain more time with my family, but I would also earn less money. I could not have a second car, and I would have to give up eating out and other luxuries. However, spending time with my family is more important to me than having these extras.

For the above reasons, job sharing is the type of work schedule that I would choose. Job sharing would allow me to work part-time at my present job. The decrease in income would be more than offset by the increase in both job security and in the amount of time that I would have to spend with my family.

Character-Trait Analysis

1. Both essays 4 and 5 have a very good level of organization. This essay's style indicates that the writer has had more practice writing this type of essay. See below.

2. This essay is more interesting to read than essay 4 because of the writer's command of the language and of a larger vocabulary.

3. The essay flows smoothly and has few problems with usage.

4. The examples used in this essay are good, but they are not as specific and vivid as those in essay 6. Therefore, this essay lacks the impact of essay 6.

## Model Essay—Holistic Score 6

**States the point of view and two reasons why the writer holds it**

If I could choose my own schedule, I would like to do free-lance work at home. As a free-lancer, I could adjust my work schedule according to my own energy levels and my family's needs.

**Elaborates on the first reason for the point of view with specific examples and contrasting details**

My concentration is best early in the morning and late at night. At about 10 a.m., I often start to get drowsy. Most nine to five jobs have a short coffee break at this point but I would like a longer break. If I were working at home I could put my work away and go out for an hour or two. That way, I would get some exercise and a change of scene, rather than a rushed cup of coffee and a donut.

**Elaborates on the second reason for the point of view with specific examples and contrasting details**

Having more time to spend with my preschooler would be another benefit of working at home. Whenever I chose, I could take a break and do something with my daughter. It would be wonderful to be able to put away a piece of frustrating work and make cookies with my child. I could enjoy having a relaxed lunch with her, rather than hurrying in the morning to make sandwiches for her to eat at daycare.

**Suggests and overcomes counterevidence; summarizes reasons; restates the point of view**

To get work done at home would require added self-discipline on my part and extra cooperation from my little girl, but the benefits would be worth the effort. Overall, working at home would be the type of schedule best suited to my energy peaks and family life.

Character-Trait Analysis

1. The essay shows a high level of organizational ability and a solid command of the English language.

2. The writer has a smooth and confident writing style. This comes from practicing the writing process.

3. The examples that support the writer's point of view are very specific and personal. They have a vivid, illustrative quality. For example, it is very easy to picture the *rushed cup of coffee and a donut* described in paragraph two. It is easy to see why the writer would choose to work at home, which would allow her *to get some exercise and a change of scene.*

4. This essay is not perfect. There are minor errors, such as those in punctuation, but they are not enough to detract from the overall effectiveness of this essay.

# Test 2 Social Studies

1. **(1)** *Comprehension/History.* In the graph, the shorter bars stand for the periods in which immigration was low. The shortest bar stands for the years 1931-1940, the decade with lowest immigration.

2. **(5)** *Application/History.* Because the level of immigration for 1971-1980 was about 4.5 million, the job and housing requirements would have been greatest.

3. **(4)** *Analysis/History.* Immigration was at a high point during the 1901-1910 period. It decreased to a low point during the 1930s and thereafter steadily increased.

4. **(4)** *Application/Economics.* Fire-fighting services are paid for by local governments and benefit property owners. Building a home is a private responsibility. The other choices include items that might be paid for by federal taxes. They do not benefit property owners more than non-property owners.

5. **(2)** *Application/Political Science.* Based on the chart, one of the functions of the Senate is to approve presidential appointments. Choices (1), (3), (4), and (5) are inaccurate.

6. **(4)** *Comprehension/Behavioral Science.* The main point of the passage is that television has a strong influence, both good and bad, on children. The passage indicates that television may show too much violence (2) and may also teach basic skills(3), but neither of these statements is the main point.

7. **(5)** *Application/Behavioral Science.* Since the main criticism of television mentioned in the passage is the possible negative effect on children of television violence, a story with laser weapons would be the least likely choice of the concerned parents of young children. The dangers of space exploration (2) would not consist of violence among humans, but rather of the threats to human life due to the lack of life-sup-porting atmosphere in outer space, or from the dangers of mechanical malfunction in the astronauts' equipment. There would be some violence among the animals of Africa and Asia (3), but these animals would not be role models the way violent humans would be, and the program's main interest probably would be in showing the ways the animals live in harmony with their natural environments. (1) concerns preventing violence and (4) contains no violence.

8. **(3)** *Analysis/Behavioral Science.* The third paragraph states that television allows young people to see and learn about different lifestyles and cultures. Nothing in the passage states or suggests the meanings in (1) and (2). The concern about violence on television clearly implies a concern that children will take violent people on television as role models; however, we are not told that the good kinds of television provide "positive role models," (4) only that they teach basic skills and an appreciation of different lifestyles. (5) misstates the last sentence, which is about the judgments of parents, not of children.

9. **(2)** *Analysis/Behavioral Science.* While the other choices are stated or implied, choice (2) is the assumption underlying the whole passage. The author says that children see a lot of violence on television and that television is a powerful influence on children. The author therefore must assume that most children watch television.

10. **(3)** *Evaluation/Behavioral Science.* The only alternative that offers evidence is choice (3). Experiments show behavior changes. None of the other choices mention behavior changes.

11. **(1)** *Analysis/Geography.* Although Antarctica is not the smallest continent, its population is the smallest. Antarctica's climate is too severe to support a large population.

**12. (1)** *Analysis/Economics.* The passage states that according to Adam Smith's beliefs goods would be sold at the price people—that is, consumers—are willing to pay for them. The passage nowhere says prices would be set by the reasonable decisions of producers (2), by producers according to the supply of goods (3), or by producers and consumers working together (5). (4) goes completely against Adam Smith's theory, which rejects government intervention in the economy.

**13. (4)** *Application/Geography.* Both Houston and Los Angeles have experienced population increases since 1970. In all other choices one or both of the cities have experienced a decrease in population during that time.

**14. (2)** *Analysis/Geography.* The table shows steady population growth since 1900 in Houston and Los Angeles, which are in the Southwest. Each city cited in other areas declined in population during at least two decades.

**15. (4)** *Analysis/Behavioral Science.* The main point of the cartoon is that because of sex discrimination, women are paid less than men even when both do the same job. Employers sometimes give men and women with the same job different titles to hide this kind of discrimination.

**16. (4)** *Application/History.* President Kennedy's speech called on Americans to act for the general good of their society rather than asking the U.S. government to do things for them. (3) and (5) both ask the government to do things for U.S. citizens, either all of them (3) or a special income group among them (5). (1) and (2) are actions that neither serve the country nor ask the country for anything, so both are irrelevant to the question. Only (4) describes an action that is motivated by a concern for serving a general public good rather than a personal interest.

**17. (1)** *Evaluation/Political Science.* An absolute monarch's child inherits leadership and power. An absolute monarch would be the leader most likely to try to influence the future through one of his children.

**18. (5)** *Application/Political Science.* Because the revolutionary leader has suppressed all debate and dissent, taken control of the country's media, and has declared himself "sole head," he has established a dictatorship.

**19. (4)** *Application/Political Science.* In the United States, citizens choose people to represent them. Other choices are inaccurate.

**20. (3)** *Evaluation/Political Science.* In a direct democracy the people vote on every law. They would be directly responsible for the laws they enacted.

**21. (2)** *Application/Political Science.* If a government is headed by a king, it is a monarchy. Since there are laws limiting the king's power, he heads a constitutional monarchy.

**22. (2)** *Evaluation/Behavioral Science.* The speaker is arguing against the expectation that he carry on the family tradition by becoming a farmer. He does not indicate anything about the family's opinions on money, religion, or status. Because there is no plan for his education, it must not be a very strong value.

**23. (2)** *Comprehension/Economics.* The table shows that the communication, electronic, and computer industries have provided the most new jobs since 1980.

**24. (5)** *Application/Economics.* Because the footwear industry has lost jobs, a worker in a shoe factory would be most likely to want job retraining. The other choices list jobs that are either not mentioned in the table or are in industries that have gained jobs.

**25. (3)** *Analysis/Economics.* The table does not provide the reasons industries have either gained or lost jobs.

**26. (2)** *Evaluation/Economics.* The only conclusion supported by the data in the table is that most new jobs are being created by the newer technologies: communications, electronics, and computers.

**27. (3)** *Comprehension/Political Science.* All of the rights listed are protected by the First Amendment, except the right to a jury trial. That right is not mentioned in the First Amendment.

**28. (3)** *Application/Geography.* In the United States through the last century, most transportation was by water. Towns and cities were built near waterways.

**29. (4)** *Comprehension/History.* The South's lack of industry made it depend on the North specifically for the manufactured goods it could not produce. This dependence was a direct effect of a cause—lack of industrialization. (2) is an effect of its lack of industry but describes an effect on its life-style rather than on its economic status. (1) describes an effect on the North of its having industry. (3) and (5) describe two attitudes which were effects of the South's economic dependence on the North; these attitudes cannot be the answer to the question because that status of economic dependence itself was caused by the South's lack of industry.

**30. (2)** *Analysis/History.* The passage states that the South lacked industry. It depended on the North and foreign producers for manufactured goods. The North did a lot of the manufacturing it needed for itself. The South would have to pay more import taxes than the North because it had to import more manufactured goods.

**31. (3)** *Comprehension/History.* The passage stresses the economic differences between the North and the South before the Civil War. These differences existed because the North and the South grew into two different kinds of societies. The North was more urban and industrial. The South was more rural and agricultural.

**32. (1)** *Analysis/History.* The South, primarily a producer of cotton, depended on the North for manufactured goods and services such as shipping and banking. Many Southerners felt that the North was prolonging this dependency, thus keeping the South economically weak.

**Test 3 Science**

**1. (1)** *Analysis/Physics. Work = Force x Distance.* Therefore, the first keg must have been lifted 3 feet and the second keg 4 feet (3 x 50 = 150; 4 x 50 = 200). If one is tired the work feels harder, but the same load moved over the same distance always equals the same work. Choices (2) and (4) are refuted by the word "identical." Every lift requires energy.

**2. (1)** *Comprehension/Physics.* The last sentence suggests that the planets are larger than the moon. It mentions the effect of the gravity of larger bodies. The word "but" indicates that the larger bodies referred to are the planets—all of them.

**3. (3)** *Comprehension/Biology.* Less energy is available at each successive link in the chain. Humans are the last link.

**4. (3)** *Application/Biology.* The human in this chain eats a primary consumer.

**5. (4)** *Application/Biology.* The snake eats the bird, which is a secondary consumer because it eats the insect.

**6. (5)** *Analysis/Biology.* The weed is a producer, the minnow a primary consumer, the bass a secondary consumer, and the otter a tertiary consumer. Only the decomposer is omitted.

**7. (2)** *Evaluation Biology.* Suppose a human being needs 2000 calories per day, and could get it by eating three pounds of vegetable food. But suppose a person eats meat instead. Then suppose that the animal whose flesh the person eats has to eat six pounds of plant material in order to pass on 2000 calories. The person uses up six pounds of vegetable food instead of three.

**8. (5)** *Evaluation/Earth Science.* Coral and ocean animals and reptiles live in hot, wet climates. The presence of fossils of these organisms in older (bottom) layers of rock shows that northern Canada was probably first covered by water, and then had a tropical climate. Fossils of the woolly mammoth in a more recent (closer to the top) layer indicate a change in climate from hot to cold. The presence of these and later primate fossils indicates that the region must also have become drier.

9. **(2)** *Comprehension/Biology.* Each function mentioned is necessary to the survival of the plant.

10. **(2)** *Comprehension/Chemistry.* Only oxygen, 21% of the atmosphere, sustains animal life.

11. **(3)** *Analysis/Chemistry.* (1) and (4) are factual summaries of information on the graphic. Nitrogen and oxygen make up 99% of the gases in the atmosphere (1) whereas carbon dioxide and rare gases make up only .10% (4). (2) is a logical conclusion from information on the graph: if carbon dioxide were more essential to sustaining life, it would exist in a higher percentage in the atmosphere. On the contrary, too much carbon dioxide or any other gas can greatly affect life. (5) is incorrect since oxygen is a necessary component for life and any decrease in it would affect human life. Since you know that the atmosphere is essential for sustaining life on earth, you can conclude (3).

12. **(4)** *Analysis/Earth Science.* There would be more carbon dioxide if the level reached 5%. More heat would be retained on and near Earth. The large masses of ice at the poles would melt, raising the sea level all over the world. Land now exposed would be underwater.

13. **(2)** *Comprehension/Biology.* Because the second number hasn't changed, the first must have increased by 10 to make the difference 50. Therefore, the heart has to be pumping harder.

14. **(3)** *Application/Biology.* Muscle cells are used in all movement. Movement is associated with the expenditure of energy.

15. **(3)** *Comprehension/Physics.* An opaque yellow object reflects yellow light and absorbs all other color light.

16. **(4)** *Application/Physics.* Blue light is reflected only by blue objects. The shoes and gloves would reflect blue light. Because nothing else on the stage is blue, nothing else would reflect any light; nothing else could be seen.

17. **(2)** *Analysis/Physics.* Because a red apple absorbs all color light except red, it absorbs the green light. In the absence of red light, there is no light for the apple to reflect, so the apple looks black.

18. **(3)** *Evaluation/Physics.* A white object reflects all the color of light, but a green object reflects only green light. Thus, there is more sunlight reflected by snow than by green plants. The additional reflected light would make sunlight appear brighter.

19. **(4)** *Application/Chemistry.* Only filtering will clean the water. Choices (1) and (2) are temperature changes; choices (3) and (5) will not work because suspended particles stay suspended.

20. **(2)** *Application/Biology.* Blue eyes is a recessive trait. So if both parents have blue eyes, they are both carrying genes for only blue eyes. They can have only blue-eyed children. The children of couples (1), (3), and (4) could have eyes of either color. A previous child's eye-color does not predict the eye-color of future brothers and sisters, so (5) is not correct.

21. **(1)** *Comprehension/Biology.* The third paragraph says the aorta and other arteries take blood from the heart to the rest of the body.

22. **(4)** *Analysis/Biology.* High-oxygen left-side blood will mix with low-oxygen right-side blood. This will dilute left-side oxygen levels.

23. **(3)** *Analysis/Biology.* The left ventricle's role is to pump blood throughout the body. All other heart chambers pump over much shorter distances. The aorta is not a heart chamber.

24. **(2)** *Analysis/Biology.* Paragraph 3 mentions the importance of the valve that lets blood into the aorta and not back into the heart.

25. **(5)** *Evaluation/Biology.* A toad, like its close relative the frog, is an amphibian.

26. **(5)** *Analysis/Earth Science.* The troposphere contains 79% of the air molecules around Earth, as one of the labels on

the diagram says. The item asks about air pollution. Air pollution affects the troposphere most because most of the air is in that layer.

27. **(4)** *Analysis/Physics.* The pot, a solid, heats by conduction; the water, a liquid, heats by convection. Choice (4) is the only alternative that mentions heat transference of both a solid and a liquid.

28. **(1)** *Application/Chemistry.* Count the atoms in the diagram. You will see that the butane molecule has 4 carbon atoms and 10 hydrogen atoms.

29. **(4)** *Analysis/Chemistry.* Pentane has 5 carbon atoms, each with a weight of 12, and 12 hydrogen atoms, each with a weight of 1. (5 x 12) + (1 x 12) = 72.

30. **(4)** *Evaluation/Earth Science.* Earth is older than the oldest evidence for life. Therefore, life may have developed from nonliving material. The other choices are contradicted by suggestions in the passage.

31. **(3)** *Analysis/Biology.* To lower blood pressure, body fluids must be released. Increasing urination releases more fluids. Choices (1), (4), and (5) would cause water retention. Choice (2) is incorrect because the patients are already on a salt-free diet.

32. **(1)** *Analysis/Earth Science.* According to the chart, crystals can be seen in coarse-grained rock, such as granite. Crystals cannot be seen in (2) limestone or (3) basalt without a microscope. There are no crystals in (4) obsidian. Choice (5) schist is layered.

33. **(3)** *Evaluation/Earth Science.* The chart shows sandstone as an example of both a coarse-grained and a layered rock. Therefore, the same rock may look different because of its different textures (3). The chart shows that granite has only a coarse texture (1). Rocks that have the same texture may look very different, such as marbles and sandstone which look nothing alike (2). All rocks contain crystals, so (4) is incorrect. (5) is also incorrect because sandstone is also listed as a coarse-grained rock.

## Test 4 Interpreting Literature and the Arts

1. **(2)** *Comprehension/Fiction.* Sam defines the "hard" thing when he says, "That's hard, trying to go without me and all." The other choices indicate things that may have presented some difficulty for Sam, but seeing Frodo try to leave alone is the only thing Sam admits is hard.

2. **(3)** *Application/Fiction.* In this passage, Sam makes it clear that he will go with Frodo, even though Frodo warns him, "It would be the death of you to come with me . . ." (lines 49-50). Sam is willing to risk all danger for the sake of his friend. Turning away from a neighbor in need—even if that neighbor, like Frodo, does not admit his need at first—would be completely out of character for Sam.

3. **(4)** *Comprehension/Fiction.* Sam never says that he wants to leave the others. He says only, "I'm coming with you" (lines 56-57), and he criticizes Frodo for trying to force him to do otherwise. He does not discuss the reasons for his loyalty, nor does the word "loyal" come up in his conversation. Instead, he states his decision to stay with Frodo as a fact, and he refuses to reconsider.

4. **(1)** *Analysis/Fiction.* Sam suggests to Frodo that they may see the other travelers again (line 67). This suggestion would make most readers wonder how events later in the plot might bring the travelers together. Most readers would want to read further to learn if Sam's suggestion turns out to be a prediction.

5. **(5)** *Comprehension/Nonfiction.* There is nothing stated in the passage about the training or education needed to become

a computer programmer; therefore, (2) is incorrect. In line 20 the author states computer programming is "a terrible job," so (4) is incorrect. Since there are a lot of ads for programmers (lines 17 - 18) there is a large demand or need for them (5). If there were a large number or supply of computer programmers, the Help Wanted pages would not have so many classified ads for them. Therefore, (1) is also incorrect.

6. **(1)** *Comprehension/Nonfiction.* The author raises the point in a series of questions (lines 42-49). The solution—a presidential plan (lines 50-53)—suggests that a proper solution will come about with proper planning. The implication is that unemployment has not been stopped because no one yet has given the problem the careful planning a solution would require. The author also implies that since he has given careful thought to the problem (lines 6-10), someone should be willing to give careful thought to a solution.

7. **(1)** *Comprehension/Nonfiction.* In the third paragraph, the author states about classified ads that "those hundreds of listings don't mean anything" and that "There's usually only one or two categories that mean anything to you and if anything is listed there, you're probably too late for it." (4) is wrong because he says in lines 24-26 that "As soon as you get some experience looking in the classified section, you get discouraged." Nothing stated supports the other choices.

8. **(1)** *Comprehension/Nonfiction.* The author says nothing about complaints of unemployed people about the types of jobs available to them. (2), (3) and (5) are restatements of questions the author raises in lines 42-49. (3) is implied by his statement in the first sentence of the last paragraph, which suggests that if there are ten million Help Wanted ads and ten million unemployed there is no necessary unemployment, only a lack of the proper plan to "match up" these unemployed with these jobs.

9. **(5)** *Comprehension/Drama.* Catherine says the principal is going to let her take an examination at the end of her first year of work and give her a graduation certificate. All the other choices are true restatements, but they are not the reason she will be able to take the job and finish school.

10. **(4)** *Analysis/Drama.* Eddie says "I want you to be with different kind of people" and he says "I mean if you're gonna get outa here then get out; don't go practically in the same kind of neighborhood." He is clearly impressed with the fifty dollars a week she will earn (NOTE: this play was written in the early 1950's), so (1) cannot be correct. His objection to the job is that it is too close to where Catherine lives, not too far away, so (2) is wrong. As for (3), he says that the plumbers she would work with are "practically longshoremen," not that she will work with longshoremen. His remark about "sailors up and down the street" in lines 106-107 clearly does not mean that she would be working with sailors but that the sailors might make approaches to her, a young and pretty woman, on the street. Therefore (3) is incorrect. Eddie never states or suggests she is too young to work, so (5) is wrong.

11. **(3)** *Comprehension/Drama.* Eddie's final speech in the excerpt shows that for him the most important thing for Catherine's future is not money (1), but rather, her chance to move out of her neighborhood and "be with different kind of people." His description of her new job's location, near their own neighborhood, shows that they live in a working-class neighborhood, "one step over the water front". He wants her to work in a "nice office," perhaps with lawyers, which indicates that he wants her to move from her working-class world into the so-called white-collar world or professional class. It is clear that he considers education (2) simply a necessary means to gaining this new social status (See lines 27-30: "You'll never get nowheres unless you finish school. You can't take no job."—meaning working-class job). As for efficiency (5), the comments about Catherine's stenographic skills and about her being the best in her whole class show that

her efficiency is also simply a way of lifting her into a higher social class. Everything Eddie says shows that he does not simply want Catherine to do whatever she thinks will make her happy (4). Catherine, like Eddie, equates happiness with success: she stresses making money and speeding up her education; he stresses improving her social status.

12. **(2)** *Comprehension/Commentary.* The point of this passage is that newer Disney productions fail to capture the magic of the classic movies. The author considers a "Disney Summer Movie" episode and concludes, ". . . the Disney gold came from something else" (line 24-25). She asks if the current movies are acceptable only to an unimaginative public (lines 42-45). She looks for a "new masterpiece" that has the Disney magic (lines 57-59)—and she has described that magic by discussing classic movies that have shown a lot of imagination, such as Bambi and Cinderella.

13. **(5)** *Analysis/Commentary.* The Master's wand" (line 45) is a metaphor, a figure of speech. It stands for all that made the name "Disney" special. The writer supports this metaphor by wondering if it has ". . . passed on to less able hands . . ." (line 46), to people who seem to carry on the Disney tradition but who do not have the imaginative craftsmanship shown in earlier Disney movies.

14. **(3)** *Comprehension/Commentary.* In the final paragraph the author names classic Disney characters and concludes with a wish for "new masterpieces" like the movies in which they appeared. Such a wish implies that no such characters exist in recent productions.

15. **(4)** *Analysis/Commentary.* The author's work is not technical; as such, it probably would be of little interest to people studying about or involved in the movie industry. It also deals with concepts of little interest to children. The author's tone is basically nostalgic. By wishing for a return to standards of the past, she probably is appealing to others who also wish to recapture the magic of their own youth.

16. **(2)** *Comprehension/Fiction.* Max is called "the boy" in line 16 and in lines 40-41 "a fine scholarly boy" who might "awaken in her (Miriam) a desire to go to college." Since Feld wants Miriam to "marry an educated man and live a better life" (lines 44-46), he would not want his daughter to marry a homeless person, so (4) cannot be correct. Since he has contempt for "loud-mouthed salesmen" (lines 37-38), (1) is wrong. Moreover, Max is clearly a customer, not a salesman. Feld is planning to have Max ask Miriam out precisely because Miriam has not met Max accidentally (line 30-31) or anywhere else, so (3) and (5) are incorrect.

17. **(4)** *Comprehension/Fiction.* Feld is afraid that "Miriam, who harped so often on independence," would get furious with him "for his meddling" (lines 19-22). Nothing in the excerpt supports the other choices.

18. **(4)** *Comprehension/Fiction.* Max is described as "grotesquely thin, with sharply cut features, particularly a beak-like nose" and as having "bony shoulders." (Grotesque means "distorted, strange and ridiculous") These details portray him as physically unattractive. Other details describe him as poor: his overcoat is described as "slushy," "looking like a rug" and his hat as "soggy," "old" and "as battered as the shoes he had brought in." He is described as tall, but not as impressive, so (1) is wrong; as thin, but with "bony shoulders," so (2) is wrong; as "nervously alert" but not as threatening, so (3) is wrong. All these details might suggest that he is awkward, but nothing in the excerpt suggests that he is friendly; therefore, (5) cannot be correct.

19. **(3)** *Comprehension/Fiction.* Max's shoes both have "enormous holes in the soles which he (Feld) pretended not to notice"—because they show how poor Max is. Feld also notices the "heels, thinned to the nails," of Max's shoes. Max's poverty is something Feld does not want to admit because it is a major flaw in his plan for Miriam to gain a better life by marrying Max. Since he notices the huge holes and worn heels of both shoes he cannot believe the

shoes need no repairs (1). As for (5), Feld is "troubled" when he thinks he might have mixed up the marks on the shoes (lines 00-00); he is not upset because he thinks he is too old to be a competent shoemaker but because he is nervous about making his proposal to Max. Nothing in the excerpt supports (3) and (4).

**20. (4)** *Comprehension/Fiction.* In his first reaction to Feld's proposal, Max "stared down like a hawk" (line 104) then asked questions about Miriam, requested a picture of her, and finally took her phone number. All these actions show curiosity. None of the other choices describe his response accurately.

**21. (2)** *Comprehension/Poetry.* The author defines paradise only by implying what it is not. It is not a place where land is paved over for parking lots, hotels, and such (lines 1-4). It is not a place where so many trees have been cut down that you must go to a museum to see a tree (lines 00-00). It is not a place where D.D.T. is used (line 00). In short, it is not a place that has been spoiled by people.

**22. (5)** *Comprehension/Poetry.* The author doesn't want to see birds and bees killed because farmers use D.D.T., an insecticide. She would rather have "spots on my apples" (line 22)—that is, fruit that doesn't look perfect—than risk killing animals such as birds and bees.

**23. (4)** *Application/Poetry.* In these verses the author talks about concern for nature. All of the choices except "drug abuse" continue the thought of protecting the natural environment.

---

*Test*

**5** # Mathematics

**1. (2)** *Arithmetic/Applications.*
10.75 x 9 = 96.75

**2. (3)** *Arithmetic/Applications.*

$2 \frac{2}{3} = 2 \frac{8}{12}$

$3 \frac{3}{4} = 3 \frac{9}{12}$

$6 \frac{1}{2} = 6 \frac{6}{12}$

$11 \frac{23}{12} = 12 \frac{11}{12}$

**3. (4)** *Algebra/Problem Solving.*
Because the salary (s) is monthly, it must be multiplied by 12. The annual sales (c) must be multiplied by .3 (30%) in order to determine Debbie's commission.

**4 (1)** *Arithmetic/Applications.*
$\frac{9}{1.20} = 7.5\%$

**5. (5)** *Arithmetic/Problem Solving.*
The amount of time for the loan is not given.

**6. (2)** *Arithmetic/Problem Solving.*
Find the perimeter of the room and subtract the width of the doorways.
(2 x 12) + (2 x 25) = 74
74 - 9 = 65

**7. (1)** *Arithmetic /Applications*
$A = lw$
A = 12 ft. x 25 ft.
A = 300 square feet
one 12" square tile = one 1 ft. square tile
300 square feet ÷ 1 square foot = 300 tiles
300 ÷ 25 = 12 boxes

**8. (2)** *Geometry/Applications.*
A right angle is a 90° angle and is indicated by A and C

**9. (2)** *Arithmetic/Problem Solving.*
B: .59 + 5% = .6195, or .62 to the nearest cent
A: .60 + 2% = .6120, or .61 to the nearest cent

D: .55 + 9% = .5995, or .60 to the nearest cent

C: .57 + 4% = .5928, or .59 to the nearest cent

**10.** **(2)** *Arithmetic/Applications.*

293 - 172 = 121 Albany County

180 - 135 = 45 Carbon County

181 - 101 = 80 Converse County

801 - 698 = 103 Natrona County

125 - 61 = 64 Washakie County

**11.** **(2)** *Algebra/Applications.*

15 ten-thousandths = .0015. > means greater than. Any bolt (b) larger than the desired size (s) + .0015 should be rejected.

**12.** **(5)** *Arithmetic/Problem Solving.*

Total babies born equals 63; 63/7 = 9

**13.** **(2)** *Arithmetic/Applications.*

$13.50 - .50 = $13 Tuesday

$13.00 + 1.25 = $14.25 Wednesday & Thursday

$14.25 - .75 = $13.50 Friday

**14.** **(4)** *Geometry/Problem Solving.*

Use similar sides to set up a ratio. If b = the base of the house, then 8:12 = 20:b.

**15.** **(5)** *Arithmetic/Applications.*

53 miles x 8 hours x 14 days = 5936

**16.** **(3)** *Algebra/Problem Solving.*

$w$ = wheat acres

$2w$ = soybean acres

$3w$ = corn acres

The total of those three numbers equals the total acres to be planted = 360.

**17.** **(5)** *Algebra/Problem Solving.*

Let $m$ = worst gas mileage.

$5m$ - 7 = 56

$5m$ = 63

$m$ = 12.6

**18.** **(5)** *Algebra/Applications.*

First find the product of 4 x 2 increased by 2, which equals 8 + 2 or 10. Now find half of 10 or divide 10 by 2. The result is 5 billion (5,000,000,000).

**19.** **(2)** *Geometry/Applications.*

To determine the correct proportion, compare the widths to the lengths.

$\frac{18}{12} = \frac{30}{x}$

**20.** **(2)** *Algebra/Applications.*

In $x_5/x_2$, x is the base in each term; 5 and 2 are the exponents. To divide, subtract exponents: 5 - 2 = 3.

**21.** **(4)** *Arithmetic/Problem Solving.*

First find the volume of the storage tank:

8 x 8 x 3.14 x 32 = 6430.72 cubic feet

Then divide the volume by 1.25:

$\frac{6430.72}{1.25}$ = 5144.576

The nearest whole number is 5145.

**22.** **(2)** *Arithmetic/Problem Solving.*

32.40 x 15% = 4.86

32.40 + 4.86 = 37.26

$\frac{37.26}{3}$ = 12.42

**23.** **(2)** *Geometry/Applications.* Solve the problem using the formula.

$s = \frac{Y^2 - Y^1}{x^2 - x^1}$

$s = \frac{6 - 3}{9 - 6}$

$s = \frac{3}{3} = 1$

**24.** **(5)** *Algebra/Problem Solving.*

7x = 245

x = 35

4(x) = 4(35) = 140 = number of hot dogs served

245 + 140 = 385 = total number of hot dogs and hamburgers served.

**25.** **(2)** *Algebra/Applications.*

The number of words per page (275) times the number of pages (60) divided by the number of words typed per minute (70) gives the number of minutes required to finish the report.

**26.** **(3)** *Arithmetic/Problem Solving.*

4 gallons = 16 quarts; 3:8 = 6:16

**27.** **(3)** *Arithmetic/Problem Solving.*

83 x .18 = 14.94

**28.** **(1)** *Arithmetic/Problem Solving.*

83 x .45 = 37.35

37.35 x .2 = 7.47

# Performance Analysis Charts for the Predictor Tests

**Directions:** Circle the number of each item that you got correct on each test. Count the number of item that you got correct on each row; count the number of items that you got correct in each column. Write the number of correct per row and column as the numerator in the fraction in the appropriate "Total Correct" box. (The denominators represent the total number of items in the row or column.) Write the grand total correct over the denominator in the lower right-hand corner of each chart. (For example, if you got 24 items correct in Writing Skills Part I, write 24 so that the fraction in the lower right-hand corner of that chart reads 24/28.)

# Test 1: Writing Skills, Part 1

| Item Type | Usage (page 64) | Sentence Structure (page 88) | Mechanics (page 102) | TOTAL CORRECT |
|---|---|---|---|---|
| Construction Shift | | 10, 19, 26, 28 | 12 | /5 |
| Sentence Correction | 1, 4, 7, 11, 16, 18, 20, 25 | | 2, 9, 14 22, 24 | /13 |
| Sentence Revision | 6, 15 | 3, 5, 8 13, 17, 21 | 23, 27 | /10 |
| Total Correct | /10 | /10 | /8 | /28 |

# Test 1: Writing Skills, Part II

**Directions:** After you have used the guidelines in the answer key to score your essay, make a record of your evaluation here.

Write the score for your essay in the box at the right.

List some of the strong points of your essay.

# Test 2: Social Studies

| Item Type | History (page 167) | Political Science (page 185) | Economics (page 193) | Geography (page 202) | Behavioral Sciences (page 208) | TOTAL CORRECT |
|---|---|---|---|---|---|---|
| Comprehension | 1, 29, 31 | 27 | 23 | | 6 | /6 |
| Application | 2, 16 | 5, 18, 19, 21 | 4, 24 | 13, 28 | 7 | /11 |
| Analysis | 3, 30, 32 | | 12, 25 | 11, 14 | 9, 15 | /9 |
| Evaluation | | 17, 20 | 26 | | 8, 10, 22 | /6 |
| Total Correct | /8 | /7 | /6 | /4 | /7 | /32 |

# Test 3: Science

| Item Type | Biology (page 222) | Earth Science (page 251) | Chemistry (page 263) | Physics (page 277) | TOTAL CORRECT |
|---|---|---|---|---|---|
| Comprehension | 3, 9, 13, 21 | | 10 | 2, 15 | /7 |
| Application | 4, 5, 14, 20 | | 19, 28 | 16 | /7 |
| Analysis | 6, 22, 23, 24, 31 | 12, 26, 32 | 11, 29 | 1, 17, 27 | /13 |
| Evaluation | 7, 25 | 8, 30, 33 | | 18 | /6 |
| Total Correct | /15 | /6 | /5 | /7 | /33 |

# Test 4: Interpreting Literature and the Arts

| Item Type | Nonfiction (page 288) | Fiction (page 312) | Drama (page 332) | Poetry (page 354) | Commentary (page 374) | TOTAL CORRECT |
|---|---|---|---|---|---|---|
| Comprehension | 5, 6, 7, 8 | 1, 3, 16, 17, 18, 19, 20 | 9, 11 | 21, 22 | 12, 14 | /17 |
| Application | | 2 | | 23 | | /2 |
| Analysis | | 4 | 10 | | 13, 15 | /4 |
| Total Correct | /4 | /9 | /3 | /3 | /3 | /23 |

# Test 5: Mathematics

| Item Type | Arithmetic (page 402) | Algebra (page 533) | Geometry (page 554) | TOTAL CORRECT |
|---|---|---|---|---|
| Comprehension (Skills) | | | | |
| Applications | 1, 2, 4, 7, 10, 13, 15 | 11, 18, 20, 25 | 8, 19, 23 | /14 |
| Analysis (Problem Solving) | 5, 6, 9, 12, 21, 22, 26, 27, 28 | 3, 16, 17, 24 | 14 | /14 |
| Total Correct | /16 | /8 | /4 | /28 |

*The page numbers in parenthesis indicate where in this book you can find the beginning of specific instruction about the various skills and fields and about the types of questions you encountered in the Predictor Tests. In mathematics, however, the items in the chart are classified as Skills, Applications, or Problem Solving. In the chapters in Unit V of this book, the three item types are covered in different levels:*

*Skill items are covered in Level 1;*
*Applications items are covered in Level 2;*
*Problem solving items are covered in Level 3.*

*For example, the skills needed to solve Item 20 are covered in Level 2 of Chapter 6 in Unit V. To locate in which chapter arithmetic items are addressed, reread the problems to see what kind of numbers (whole numbers, fractions, and so forth) are used and then go to the designated level of the appropriate chapter.*

# Writing Skills: Unit I

**Grammar** refers to usage, sentence structure, and mechanics (spelling, punctuation, capitalization) in writing. When you fill out a job application, work on a report at work, or write a business letter, you need to use correct grammar. Readers can understand your writing more easily if you use correct grammar. Readers also respect writers who use correct grammar.

## Prereading Prompt

Sometimes writing does not require correct grammar. For example, you don't have to worry about spelling and punctuation on your grocery list or for a quick note to your spouse. However, many situations exist which do require correct grammar. Make a list of situations in which you would want to use correct grammar in your writing.

# Grammar

## What is Grammar?

In the grammar lessons that follow, you will learn about

- **sentence structure**
- **usage**
- **mechanics**

You will discover

- how to correct fragments and run-on sentences and to combine parts of sentences correctly (sentence structure)
- how to correct problems with subject-verb agreement, verb tenses and pronoun references (usage)
- how to use spelling, punctuation, and capitalization rules (mechanics)

The GED Writing Skills Test contains a multiple-choice section that measures your ability to correct and **edit** errors in grammar. The grammar section contains several paragraphs of numbered sentences. Parts of sentences are underlined. Some of the test items ask you to decide whether an error in grammar exists in the underlined part. Some of the test items ask you to decide the best way to rewrite the underlined part to improve grammar and to improve meaning. From the multiple-choice option, you choose the answer that best corrects errors in the sentence structure, usage, and mechanics.

You will have seventy-five minutes to answer 55 test items Approximately one-third of the test items deal with sentence structure, one-third with usage, and one-third with mechanics.

Each skill begins with a preview and ends with a review. Previews and reviews are made up of items that test how well you apply your knowledge of specific aspects of the skill. **Previews** allow you to test your present knowledge. If you get 80% (8 of 10) correct in the preview, you may feel comfortable in skipping the lessons in that skill. If you get fewer than 80% of the items correct in either the preview or the review, then you should study all the lessons in that skill. At the end of each chapter, you can apply your knowledge on a Practice GED Test. The test items are in the same format as the real GED Test.

## Key Words

**Sentence Structure**—complete and correct sentences
**Edit**—to correct problems in mechanics
**Usage**—subject-verb agreement, verb tense and pronoun references
**Mechanics**—Spelling, punctuation, capitalization

# Unit I Progress Chart

## Writing Skills: Grammar

Use the following chart to keep track of your work. When you complete a lesson, circle the number of questions you answered correctly in the Lesson Exercise. The numbers in color represent scores at a level of 60% or better.

| Lesson | Page | | |
|---|---|---|---|
| | | **CHAPTER 1: Usage** | |
| | 64 | Skill 1: Subject Verb Agreement | |
| | 64 | Preview | 1 2 3 4 5 |
| 1 | 65 | Basic Rules of Subject-Verb Agreement | 1 2 3 4 5 6 7 8 9 10 |
| 2 | 69 | Interrupting Phrases | 1 2 3 4 5 |
| 3 | 70 | Inverted Sentence Structure | 1 2 3 4 5 |
| 4 | 72 | 'Here' and 'There' | 1 2 3 4 5 |
| 5 | 73 | Compound Subjects | 1 2 3 4 5 |
| | 74 | Review for Skill 1 | 1 2 3 4 5 6 7 8 9 10 |
| | 75 | Skill 2: Verb Tense | |
| | 75 | Preview | 1 2 3 4 5 |
| 1 | 75 | Verb Forms | 1 2 3 4 5 6 7 8 9 10 |
| 2 | 80 | Using Verb Tenses Correctly | 1 2 3 4 5 6 7 8 9 10 |
| | 81 | Review for Skill 2 | 1 2 3 4 5 6 7 8 9 10 |
| | 82 | Skill 3: Pronoun Reference | |
| | 82 | Preview | 1 2 3 4 5 |
| 1 | 82 | Pronoun Agreement: Number and Gender | 1 2 3 4 5 |
| 2 | 84 | Pronoun Agreement: Person | 1 2 3 4 5 |
| 3 | 85 | Relative Pronouns | 1 2 3 4 5 |
| 4 | 86 | Avoiding Unclear Pronoun References | 1 2 3 4 5 |
| | 87 | Review for Skill 3 | 1 2 3 4 5 6 7 8 9 10 |
| | | **CHAPTER 2: Sentence Structure** | |
| | 88 | Skill 1: Complete Sentences | |
| | 88 | Preview | 1 2 3 4 5 |
| 1 | 89 | Eliminating Sentence Fragments | 1 2 3 4 5 |
| 2 | 90 | Separating Run-On Sentence | 1 2 3 4 5 |
| 3 | 91 | Correcting Run-On Sentences | 1 2 3 4 5 |
| | 92 | Review for Skill 1 | 1 2 3 4 5 6 7 8 9 10 |
| | 93 | Skill 2: Sentence Construction: Coordination and Subordination | |
| | 93 | Preview | 1 2 3 4 5 |
| 1 | 93 | Equal Ideas: Coordination | 1 2 3 4 5 |

| Lesson | Page | | |
|---|---|---|---|
| 2 | 95 | Unequal Ideas: Subordination | 1 2 3 4 5 |
| | 97 | Review for Skill 2 | 1 2 3 4 5 6 7 8 9 10 |
| | 98 | Skill 3: Clear Sentences | |
| | 98 | Preview | 1 2 3 4 5 |
| 1 | 98 | Clarity of Thought | 1 2 3 4 5 |
| 2 | 100 | Parallel Structures | 1 2 3 4 5 |
| | 101 | Review for Skill 3 | 1 2 3 4 5 6 7 8 9 10 |
| | | **CHAPTER 3: Mechanics** | |
| | 102 | Skill 1: Capitalization | |
| | 102 | Preview | 1 2 3 4 5 |
| 1 | 103 | Proper Nouns and Proper Adjectives | 1 2 3 4 5 |
| 2 | 104 | Titles of People and Addresses | 1 2 3 4 5 |
| 3 | 105 | Days of the Week, Months of the Year, Holidays, Historical Time Periods, Historical Events, and Special Events | 1 2 3 4 5 |
| | 105 | Review for Skill 1 | 1 2 3 4 5 6 7 8 9 10 |
| | 106 | Skill 2: Punctuation | |
| | 106 | Preview | 1 2 3 4 5 |
| 1 | 106 | Commas Between Items in a Series | 1 2 3 4 5 |
| 2 | 108 | Commas after Introductory Elements | 1 2 3 4 5 |
| 3 | 109 | Commas with Sentence Interrupters | 1 2 3 4 5 |
| 4 | 110 | Avoiding Overuse of Commas | 1 2 3 4 5 |
| | 112 | Review for Skill 2 | 1 2 3 4 5 6 7 8 9 10 |
| | 112 | Skill 3: Spelling | |
| | 112 | Preview | 1 2 3 4 5 |
| 1 | 113 | Basic Spelling Rules | 1 2 3 4 5 |
| 2 | 115 | Possessives | 1 2 3 4 5 |
| 3 | 117 | Contractions | 1 2 3 4 5 |
| 4 | 119 | Frequently Confused Words | 1 2 3 4 5 |
| | 122 | Review for Skill 3 | 1 2 3 4 5 6 7 8 9 10 |

# CHAPTER 1
# Usage

## Objective

In this chapter you will learn about

- **subject-verb agreement**

- **verb tense**

- **pronoun reference**

## Skill 1
# Subject-Verb Agreement

### Preview

**Directions**: Edit the following sentences to correct all errors in subject-verb agreement. Not all of the sentences contain errors.

1. Women has many different jobs today.

2. Money problems, in addition to job stress, worries many women.

3. Across the country is many types of jobs.

4. There is many reasons for women to work.

5. Child care and flexible hours are important concerns for working women.

Check your answers. Correct answers are on page A-1. If you have at least four answers correct, do the Review for Skill 1 on page 74. If you have fewer than four answers correct, study Skill 1 beginning with Lesson 1.

# Basic Rules of Subject-Verb Agreement

Every sentence contains a subject and a verb. There are two basic rules of subject-verb agreement.

<u>Rule 1.</u> A SINGULAR SUBJECT MUST HAVE A SINGULAR VERB.

**Example:** A **dog barks** all night in my neighborhood.

<u>Rule 2.</u> A PLURAL SUBJECT MUST HAVE A PLURAL VERB

**Example:** **Dogs bark** all night in my neighborhood.

To use these rules, you must be able to identify the subject and the verb in each sentence. You must also be able to recognize the *singular* (one) and *plural* (more than one) forms of subjects and verbs.

## Subject

The subject of a sentence tells *who* or *what* the sentence is about. The subject is usually a noun or a pronoun. Most plural nouns end in **-s** or **-es**. The examples below show the singular and plural form of nouns.

| SINGULAR | PLURAL | SINGULAR | PLURAL |
|---|---|---|---|
| window | windows | baby | babies |
| desk | desks | party | parties |
| glass | glasses | wife | wives |
| lunch | lunches | shelf | shelves |

Some nouns have plural forms that do not end in **-s** or **-es**. Notice these singular nouns and their special plural forms.

| SINGULAR | PLURAL | SINGULAR | PLURAL |
|---|---|---|---|
| man | men | foot | feet |
| woman | women | tooth | teeth |
| child | children | goose | geese |
| | | mouse | mice |

A dictionary can help you correctly spell the plural form of nouns.

## Verb

The verb of the sentence says something about the subject. The verb can express a physical action, a feeling, or a mental action.

If the sentence has a singular noun as the subject, you must use a singular verb. Singular verbs usually end in **-s** or **-es** in the present tense. Notice the agreement of subjects and verbs in the chart below.

| SINGULAR | PLURAL |
|---|---|
| One **desk needs** a new drawer. | All **desks need** new drawers. |
| That **glass looks** clean. | These **glasses look** clean. |
| The **boy catches** the ball. | The **boys catch** the balls. |
| A **child walks** to school. | The **children walk** to school. |

When the subject of the sentence is the singular pronoun **he**, **she**, or **it**, you must use a singular verb. In the present tense, the singular verb for he, she, it, and the name of a singular person or thing always ends in **-s**.

**He washes** his shirt.
**She tastes** the soup.
**It rains** often in Seattle, Washington.
**Nancy needs** a new coat.
The city **skyline looks** beautiful at night.

When the subject of the sentence is the plural pronoun **we**, **you**, or **they**, you must use a plural verb.

**We wash** our clothes.
**You seem** happy today.
**They taste** the soup.

When the pronoun **I** is the subject of the sentence, the verb does not end in **-s**, even though I stands for one person and is a singular pronoun.

**I ride** a bus to work.
**I listen** to my radio.

The verbs **to be** and **to have** use special singular and plural forms. Notice the subject and verb agreement in the following chart.

| SINGULAR | PLURAL |
|---|---|
| **He is** a good customer. | **We are** ready to eat. |
| **She is** busy right now. | **They are** rarely late for work. |
| **It is** time to leave. | **You are** kind people. |
| **He was** happy to see me. | **We were** upset by the bad news. |
| **She has** a new coat. | **They have** a fair boss. |
| **It has** two pockets. | **You** players **have** a good team. |

Here is how the verbs *to be* and *to have* agree with the subject singular pronoun I.

**I am** thirty years old.
**I was** the last person in line.

In addition to the two basic rules of subject-verb agreement, here are other rules to help you determine whether a subject is singular or plural.

<u>Rule 3.</u> THE FOLLOWING INDEFINITE PRONOUNS ARE SINGULAR AND TAKE A SINGULAR VERB.

| | | | | |
|---|---|---|---|---|
| anyone | everyone | someone | one | no one |
| anybody | everybody | somebody | each | nobody |
| anything | everything | something | | |

**Example:** **Everybody seems** to have a cold.

**Example:** **Something is making** me sneeze.

<u>Rule 4.</u> THE FOLLOWING INDEFINITE PRONOUNS ARE PLURAL AND TAKE A PLURAL VERB.

| | | | |
|---|---|---|---|
| both | few | many | several |

**Example:** **Both are** good reasons for taking GED classes.

**Example:** **Many were** already registered for class.

<u>Rule 5.</u> THE FOLLOWING INDEFINITE PRONOUNS MAY BE EITHER SINGULAR OR PLURAL, DEPENDING ON HOW THEY ARE USED IN A SENTENCE.

| | | | | | |
|---|---|---|---|---|---|
| some | most | part | any | all | none |

**Example:** **Most** of the project **was completed.**

In the sentence above, **most** refers to a portion of the project, which is singular.

**Example:** **Most** of the missing pieces **were found**.

In the sentence above, **most** refers to **pieces**, which is plural.

<u>Rule 6.</u> THE FOLLOWING WORDS REFER TO A GROUP OF PEOPLE OR THINGS THAT ACT TOGETHER IN ONE UNIT. THESE WORDS ARE CALLED COLLECTIVE NOUNS. THEY USUALLY TAKE A SINGULAR VERB.

| | | | | | |
|---|---|---|---|---|---|
| army | audience | band | choir | class | club |
| committee | company | crowd | family | government | team |
| group | jury | panel | public | society | |

**Example:** The **company hires** women.
**Example:** The **band plays** marching music.

<u>Rule 7.</u> THE FOLLOWING WORDS ARE SINGULAR, EVEN THOUGH THEY APPEAR TO BE PLURAL AND THEY END IN **-S**. THESE WORDS TAKE SINGULAR VERBS.

civics      physics      economics      politics
mathematics      athletics      news      measles
mumps      United States

**Example:** The **United States is** made up of many ethnic groups.

**Example:** **Economics is** the study of the production and use of goods and services.

Rule 8. THE FOLLOWING WORDS ARE PLURAL IN MEANING AND TAKE A PLURAL VERB. THESE WORDS DO NOT HAVE A SINGULAR FORM.

scissors      pliers      shears      trousers
pants      jeans

**Example:** Those **jeans are** dirty.

**Example:** Where **are** my **scissors?**

## FIVE-STEP PROCESS TO CHECK SUBJECT-VERB AGREEMENT

As you edit sentences for subject-verb agreement, use this five-step process.

Step 1. Read the sentence and find the subject. Remember that the subject is who or what the sentence is about.

Step 2. Decide whether the subject is singular or plural.

Step 3. Locate the verb. Remember the verb tells something about the subject.

Step 4. Decide whether the verb is singular or plural.

Step 5. If the subject and the verb are both singular or both plural, they agree. If they do not agree, change the verb so that it agrees with the subject.Here is an example of how you can use this five-step process to decide whether the subject and verb agree in a sentence.

**Example:** The buses waits for people.

Step 1. The subject of the sentence is **buses**.

Step 3. The verb is **waits**.

Step 4. The verb ends in **-s** and is singular.

Step 5. The plural subject and the singular verb do not agree. The verb should be changed to the plural form **wait** so that it agrees with the plural subject **buses**.

**Edited:** The **buses wait** for people.

# Lesson 1 Exercise

**Directions**: Use the five-step process to decide whether or not the subject and verb agree in the sentences below. Change the form of the verb when necessary to correct all errors in subject-verb agreement. Not all of the sentences contain errors.

1. The weather reports says that it will probably rain tomorrow.
2. Everyone hope for clear skies for the picnic.
3. Most of the picnic posters has been made already.
4. Nobody believe it will rain.
5. Our team are practicing for the contest.
6. Athletics are not my strong point.
7. Your pants has some grease stains on them.
8. Jenny, you looks tired from running so fast.
9. All of our friends are cheering loudly.
10. I thinks our team will win the contest.

Answers are on page A-1.

## Lesson 2 — Interrupting Phrases

In many sentences, the subject does not appear next to the verb. Sometimes interrupting phrases separate the subject from the verb. An *interrupting phrase* is a group of words that has no subject or verb. The interrupting phrase breaks, or interrupts, the normal pattern of a subject immediately followed by a verb.

Even though a sentence contains an interrupting phrase, the verb must still agree with the subject.

The following sentence contains an interrupting phrase. Notice that the singular verb agrees with the singular subject.

**Example:**   The **noise** of the machines **is** very loud.

The subject of the sentence is **noise. Of the machines** is the interrupting phrase. The singular verb **is** agrees with the singular subject **noise**.

Here's another sentence that contains an interrupting phrase. This time, the interrupting phrase is set off by two commas.

**Example:**   The **doctor**, as well as the nurses, **talks** to me about my injury.

The subject of the sentence is **doctor. As well as the nurses** is the interrupting phrase. The singular verb **talks** agrees with the singular subject **doctor**.

Remember that interrupting phrases do not affect the subject-verb agreement. Before you use the five-step process from Lesson 1, cross out the interrupting phrases in the sentence. This will help you identify the subject of the sentence.

**Example:**  This stack of letters are ready for delivery.

The interrupting phrase is **of letters**.

Step 1.  The subject of the sentence is **stack**.

Step 2.  **Stack** is singular.

Step 3.  The verb is **are**.

Step 4.  The verb is plural.

Step 5.  The singular subject and the plural verb do not agree. The verb should be changed to the singular form **is** so that it agrees with the singular subject **stack**.

**Edited:**  This **stack** of letters **is** ready for delivery.

## Lesson 2 Exercise

**Directions**: Cross out the interrupting phrases and then use the five-step process to check subject-verb agreement. Correct any errors in subject-verb agreement. Not all of the sentences contain errors.

1. The package of cookies were bright green.
2. The cookies, in addition to the cake, was a treat for the children.
3. The children, together with the dog, want more cookies.
4. One of the packages of cookies have a special gift inside.
5. The plate of cookies sit on the table.

Answers are on page A-1.

## Lesson 3 — Inverted Sentence Structure

In most sentences, the subject comes before the verb. Occasionally, you will see sentences in which the subject comes after the verb. This pattern is called an *inverted sentence structure.*

The following examples have inverted sentence structure. Notice that the verb still agrees with the subject.

**Inverted:**  Next to the stores **is** the **parking lot**.

**Usual:**  The **parking lot is** next to the stores.

**Inverted:**  With a blizzard **come** slippery **roads**.

**Usual:**  Slippery **roads come** with a blizzard.

Questions have inverted sentence structure.

**Inverted:**    **Is** the **basket** of clothes too heavy for you?

**Usual:**    The **basket** of clothes **is** too heavy for you.

**Inverted:**    **Was** the **roll** of stamps in your desk?

**Usual:**    The **roll** of stamps **was** in your desk.

Before you use the five-step process to check subject-verb agreement, change the inverted sentence structure to the usual order. Continue to cross out any interrupting phrases that separate the subject from the verb.

**Example:**    Is the coats on this rack ready for the cleaners?

The usual order is **The coats on this rack is ready for the cleaners.**

The interrupting phrase is **on this rack.**

<u>Step 1.</u>  The subject of the sentence is **coats**.

<u>Step 2.</u>  **Coats** is plural.

<u>Step 3.</u>  The verb is **is**.

<u>Step 4.</u>  The verb is singular.

<u>Step 5.</u>  The plural subject and the singular verb do not agree.

The verb should be changed to the plural form **are** so that it agrees with the plural subject **coats**.

**Edited:**    **Are** the **coats** on this rack ready for the cleaners?

## Lesson 3 Exercise

**Directions**: Edit the following sentences for correct subject-verb agreement. Remember to put sentences in their usual order and to cross out interrupting phrases before you use the five-step process. Not all of the sentences contain errors.

1. At the trial were the jury.
2. Behind the defendant sits the family of the defendant.
3. Was the answers to the questions clearly heard?
4. Next to the judge stand the bailiff.
5. Does the reporters take pictures during the trial?

Answers are on page A-1.

# 'Here' and 'There'

Some sentences begin with the words **here** and **there**. While **here** and **there** may look like the subjects of sentences, they are not. **Here** and **there** are called *expletives* when they begin sentences as in the examples below.

**Example:**   Here **is** your **receipt**.

(**Receipt** is the subject. **Is** is the verb.)

**Example:**   There **is** good **reason** for traffic rules.

(**Reason** is the subject. **Is** is the verb.)

**Example:**   Here **are** our **petitions** to the mayor.

(**Petitions** is the subject. **Are** is the verb.)

**Example:**   There **are** many electrical **outlets** in the office.

(**Outlets** is the subject. **Are** is the verb.)

**Here** and **there** are never the subject of the sentence. When you see **here** and **there** at the beginning of a sentence, you must look at the noun that follows the verb to find the subject.

When you use the five-step process to check for subject-verb agreement, cross out **here** or **there** at the beginning of the sentence. Also cross out any interrupting phrases.

**Example:**   Here are a magazine with good recipes.

Notice that the plural verb **are** does not agree with the singular subject **magazine**. To correct the error, you must change the verb to **is**.

**Edited:**   Here **is** a **magazine** with good recipes.

## Lesson 4 Exercise

**Directions**: Edit the following sentences for correct subject-verb agreement. Remember to cross out the expletives and interrupting phrases. Not all of the sentences contain errors.

1. There is more than two million people living in Atlanta.
2. Here are the zip code for addresses in the downtown area.
3. There is many peach trees in Georgia.
4. Here is an article about the businesses in Atlanta.
5. There are many banks in that city.

Answers are on page A-1.

When a sentence contains more than one subject, the subjects are called *compound subjects.* Compound subjects are usually connected by words such as **and**, **or**, or **nor**.

The following three sentences contain compound subjects which are joined by the word **and**. Notice that a plural verb is used with compound subjects joined by **and**.

**Example:**   **Dusting and vacuuming** *keep* a home clean.

**Example:**   Regular **exercise and** good **diet** *prevent* many health problems.

**Example:**   Both **flowers and candy** *are* popular Valentine's Day gifts.

Compound subjects can also be joined by pairs of connective words such as **either . . . or**, **neither . . . nor**, or **not only . . . but also**. When compound subjects are joined by these pairs of words, the verb agrees with the subject that is closer to the verb.

**Example:**   Either the letters or the **package** *was mislabeled.*

**Example:**   Either the package or the **letters** *were mislabeled.*

**Example:**   Neither the passengers nor the **luggage** *arrives* on time.

**Example:**   Neither the luggage nor the **passengers** *arrive* on time.

**Example:**   Not only the computers but also the **printer** *was* broken.

**Example:**   Not only the printer but also the **computers** *were* broken.

As you use the five-step process to edit sentences for subject-verb agreement, look for compound subjects and the connective words. In the following sentence, the compound subject is **customers and store owner**. The singular verb must be changed to agree with the plural subject.

**Example:**   Both the customers and the store owner was pleased with the clearance sale.

**Edited:**   Both the **customers and** the **store owner** *were pleased* with the clearance sale.

## Lesson 5 Exercise

**Directions**: Edit the following sentences for subject-verb agreement. Not all of the sentences contain errors.

1. Jacquie and Connie are collecting donations for charity.
2. Neither Gordon nor Vance have any canned goods to donate.
3. Not only canned goods but also money are needed.
4. Either Jacquie or Connie are taking the canned goods to the donation center.
5. Both Salvation Army and Goodwill sells very inexpensive used clothing.

Answers are on page A-2.

## REVIEW FOR SKILL 1

**Directions**: Edit the following sentences to correct all errors in subject-verb agreement. Not all of the sentences contain errors.

1. Every April, Americans files their tax returns.
2. Federal taxes and state taxes is filed separately.
3. Do all states have an income tax?
4. Oscar and Ginny is organizing their financial records.
5. The box with the envelopes contain important receipts.
6. Under that box are the pamphlet with directions.
7. Most of the directions is easy to understand.
8. Here are the envelope with the medical receipts.
9. Neither the rent payments nor the apartment insurance are deductible.
10. No one like to pay higher taxes.

Check your answers. Correct answers are on page A-2. If you have at least eight answers correct, go to Skill 2. If you have fewer than eight answers correct, study Skill 1 beginning with Lesson 1.

# Verb Tense

## Preview

**Directions**: Edit the following sentences to correct all errors in verb tense or form. Not all of the sentences contain errors.

1.  Terence has drove to work without his lunch box.
2.  Later today, he will notice that his lunch is at home.
3.  In the last two weeks, he has forgot his thermos several times.
4.  Because he did not have his home-made lunch, he eats the cafeteria food.
5.  Tomorrow, he brought his lunch box and thermos.

Check your answers. Correct answers are on page A-2. If you have at least four answers correct, do the Review for Skill 2 on page 81. If you have fewer than four answers correct, study Skill 2 beginning with Lesson 1.

**Lesson**
**1**

## Verb Forms

## CATEGORIES OF VERB

When you are checking the correct use of the verb in a sentence, you need to identify the verb form. There are three categories of verbs: action verbs, linking verbs, and helping verbs.

## Action Verbs

An *action verb* shows either physical or mental action.

**Example:** The **machines cut** the material.

**Example:** Many **people think** about their future.

## Linking Verbs

A *linking verb* connects, or links, the subject of the sentence with a word or phrase that describes or renames the subject.

**Example:** The **soup is** thick and creamy.

**Example:** The **soup tastes** good.

**Example:** My **parents are** senior citizens.

**Example:** My **parents look** old.

The verb **to be**, as in two of the sentences above, is a common linking verb. Other verbs that can be used as linking verbs are listed below.

| | | | |
|---|---|---|---|
| appear | become | feel | look |
| seem | smell | sound | taste |

## Helping Verbs

The forms of the verb **to be** (**am**, **is**, **are**, **was**, **were**, **been**) are also often used in combination with other verbs. The forms of the verb **to have** (**has**, **have**, **had**) and the forms of the verb **to do** (**does**, **do**, **did**) are also common helping verbs. Other verbs are listed below.

| | | |
|---|---|---|
| can, could | may, might | must |
| shall, should | will, would | |

## Verb Tense

*Verb tenses* tell the time of the action. Verbs have three basic tenses: present, past, and future.

The three sentences below show the three main tenses of the verb **to work**.

**Present tense:** **Today**, the **employees work** a regular shift.

**Past tense:** **Yesterday**, the **employees worked** overtime.

**Future tense:** **Tomorrow**, the **employees will work** overtime.

The first sentence describes an action that is happening in the present. The second sentence describes an action that happened in the past. The third sentence describes an action that will happen in the future.

The present tense is also used to describe a general truth, as in the sentences below.

**Example:** Well-made **clothes last** longer than poorly made clothes.

**Example:** **Americans** usually **pay** their income taxes on April 15.

**Example:** **It snows** every winter.

The following chart shows the three basic tenses of verbs.

| TENSE | MEANING | VERB FORM | EXAMPLE |
|---|---|---|---|
| PRESENT | Something is happening now or is generally true. | Add **-s** or **-es** with singular | The man walks. She laughs. |
| | | Add no ending with plural nouns or with **we**, **they**, **you**, or **I**. | The men walk. They laugh. I smile. |
| PAST | Something happened in the past. | Add **-d** or **-ed** to the present tense. | The man walked. The men walked. She laughed. They laughed. |
| FUTURE | Something will happen in the future. | Add the helping verb **will** or **shall** to the present tense. | The man will walk. The men will walk. She will laugh. They shall laugh. |

## Principal Parts of Regular Verbs

The different tenses are formed from the principal parts of a verb. Every verb has three principal parts

| PRESENT | PAST | PAST PARTICIPLE |
|---|---|---|
| cook, cooks | cooked | have cooked, has cooked |
| wash, washes | washed | have washed, has washed |
| dry, dries | dried | have dried, has dried |
| taste, tastes | tasted | have tasted, has tasted |

Verbs like the ones above are called *regular verbs*. Regular verbs form their past tense by adding **-ed** or **-d** to the present tense. Regular verbs can form their past participle form by adding **have** (or **has**) to the past tense form.

**Example:** **I cooked** the meal for several hours.

**Example:** **I have cooked** the meal for several hours.

**Example:** **Hank washed** the vegetables.

**Example:** **Hank has washed** the vegetables.

# Principal Parts of Irregular Verbs

Many verbs form their past tense and the past participle in special ways. These verbs are called *irregular verbs*.

**Example:** The **customers ate** their lunch quickly.

**Example:** **They have eaten** all the potato chips.

**Example:** **Brad drank** his milk.

**Example:** **Julie has drunk** her coffee.

In the sentences above, the verbs **to eat** and **to drink** are irregular verbs. The past tense and past participles are formed in special ways.

Use the following list to learn the past tense and past participle forms of irregular verbs. The irregular verbs are grouped according to patterns.

| PRESENT | PAST | PAST PARTICIPLE |
|---|---|---|
| buy | bought | have bought |
| bring | brought | have brought |
| catch | caught | have caught |
| fight | fought | have fought |
| think | thought | have thought |
| | | |
| lay | laid | have laid |
| pay | paid | have paid |
| say | said | have said |
| | | |
| send | sent | have sent |
| bend | bent | have bent |
| sit | sat | have sat |
| | | |
| begin | began | have begun |
| drink | drank | have drunk |
| ring | rang | have rung |
| sing | sang | have sung |
| swim | swam | have swum |
| | | |
| blow | blew | have blown |
| grow | grew | have grown |
| know | knew | have known |
| throw | threw | have thrown |
| | | |
| break | broke | have broken |
| freeze | froze | have frozen |
| choose | chose | have chosen |
| speak | spoke | have spoken |
| steal | stole | have stolen |

| PRESENT | PAST | PAST PARTICIPLE |
| --- | --- | --- |
| forget | forgot | have forgotten |
| get | got | have gotten |
| do | did | have done |
| | | |
| drive | drove | have driven |
| eat | ate | have eaten |
| fall | fell | have fallen |
| fly | flew | have flown |
| give | gave | have given |
| go | went | have gone |
| see | saw | have seen |
| show | showed | have shown |
| take | took | have taken |
| tear | tore | have torn |
| wear | wore | have worn |
| write | wrote | have written |
| | | |
| become | became | have become |
| come | came | have come |
| run | ran | have run |
| | | |
| hit | hit | have hit |
| let | let | have let |
| put | put | have put |
| set | set | have set |

## Lesson 1 Exercise

**Directions**: Complete the following sentences by writing the past tense of the verb given in parentheses.

1. Last year, winter _____ very early. (come)
2. The cold wind _____ fiercely. (blow)
3. The lake in the park _____. (freeze)
4. The children _____ sleds downs the snow-covered hills. (ride)
5. Some children _____ snowballs at each other. (throw)

**Directions**: Complete the following sentences by writing the past participle form of the verb given in parentheses.

6. We have already _____ dinner. (eat)
7. Willie has _____ his second cup of coffee. (drink)
8. I have _____ to wash the dishes. (begin)
9. The children have _____ to bed. (go)
10. Jamie has _____ the dog for a walk. (take)

Answers are on page A-2.

# Using Verb Tenses Correctly

When you edit paragraphs for verb tenses, you need to read carefully to determine whether the action is present, past, or future. If you find verb tenses that are incorrect, you must edit the paragraph to make the tenses consistent throughout the paragraph. Here is a sample paragraph that contains errors in verb tense.

(1) Mel had a relaxing vacation. (2) Last week, he takes three days to visit his parents in Nevada. (3) He also sees his old friends. (4) His parents will want Mel to stay longer. (5) Mel needed to return to his job.

This paragraph is about an event that has already happened. All of the actions should use past tense verbs. Notice that Sentence 2 incorrectly uses the present tense **takes**. Sentence 3 incorrectly uses the present tense **sees**. There is also a verb-tense error in sentence 4 with the future tense **will want**.

Here is the edited paragraph with the correct tenses. Notice that all the tenses are consistently in the past tense.

(1) Mel **had** a relaxing vacation. (2) Last week, he **took** three days to visit his parents in Nevada. (3) He also **saw** his old friends. (4) His parents **wanted** Mel to stay longer. (5) Mel **needed** to return to his job.

When more than one verb appears in a sentence, you must also check for correct verb tense.

**Example:** The room **became** crowded as more people **arrived.**

The verb in the first part of the sentence, **became**, is in the past tense. The past tense verb is a clue to help you decide whether the verb tense in the second part of the sentence is correct. The verb, **arrived**, is also in the past tense. Since both verbs are in the past tense, the verb tenses in this sentence are consistent and correct.

Here is another example of a sentence with inconsistent verb tenses.

**Example:** Some guests brought salads, while other people make desserts.

This sentence is incorrect because the first part of the sentence is past tense (**brought**) and the second part of the sentence is present tense (**make**). When you edit the sentence, you should change the second verb to the past tense.

**Edited:** Some guests brought salads, while other people made desserts.

If the sentence expresses two actions that take place at different times, you may need to use two different verb tenses.

**Example:** The weather report predicts that this weekend will be very cold.

This sentence uses correct verb tenses. The prediction is made in the present. However, the prediction is made about a future event. Therefore, **will be** is the correct verb tense for the second verb in this sentence.

**Directions**: The following paragraph contains a mixture of present tense and past tense. Decide whether the present tense or the past tense is more appropriate. Then revise the paragraph so that all of the verb tenses are consistent. Not all of the sentences contain errors.

(**1**) Last year, Betty Ann Chow celebrates Christmas with her parents at their home. (**2**) When she visited her parents, she bring a fruit cake and cheese. (**3**) Mrs. Chow gives Betty Ann a warm sweater. (**4**) Mr. Chow bought his daughter a new pair of gloves. (**5**) After they exchanged gifts, they all go to church.

**Directions**: Choose the correct verb tense from the pair given in the parentheses.

6. Over the past decade, many people moved into the county, and the streets (will become, became) more crowded with cars.

7. If gasoline prices continue to go up next month, more people (rode, will ride) buses to work.

8. Because there was a water shortage, the county (issues, issued) restrictions on water usage.

9. When it rains, the reservoirs (store, stored) the water.

10. The county commissioners predicted that taxes (are, will be) increased.

Answers are on page A-2.

# REVIEW FOR SKILL 2

**Directions**: Edit the following paragraphs to correct all errors in verb tense. Not all of the sentences contain errors.

(**1**) Because people like warm weather, many Americans were moving to the southern states. (**2**) The southern states were places such as Florida, Arizona, New Mexico, and Texas. (**3**) These states are growing in population, while the northern states lost people.

(**4**) However, in the future, the increased population brought problems for local communities. (**5**) Some city planners are predicting that a severe housing shortage occurred. (**6**) Jobs were not available for people in the coming years. (**7**) As new families arrive in the community, more schools were needed.

(**8**) Many businesses welcome the population boom, but some local residents were worried about increased crime and taxes. (**9**) Some people do not want their community to grow too large. (**10**) The city planners listen carefully to the residents and discussed the problems of overpopulation.

Check your answers. Correct answers are on page A-3. If you have at least eight answers correct, go to Skill 3. If you have fewer than eight answers correct, study Skill 2 beginning with Lesson 1.

# Pronoun Reference

## Preview

**Directions**: Edit the following sentences to correct all errors in pronoun reference. Not all of the sentences contain errors.

1. Chesapeake Bay is located in Maryland, which is my home state.
2. Clams or oysters are delicious when it is fried.
3. When people eat fried chicken at picnics, you use your fingers.
4. Stella told Kathy that she made delicious clam chowder.
5. You would enjoy fishing because they are relaxing.

Check your answers. Correct answers are on page A-3. If you have at least four answers correct, do the Review for Skill 3 on page 87. If you have fewer than four answers correct, study Skill 3 beginning with Lesson 1.

Lesson

1

## Pronoun Agreement: Number and Gender

A *pronoun* is a word that refers to or replaces a noun or another pronoun. The word that the pronoun refers is called the *antecedent*. A pronoun must agree with its antecedent in number (singular or plural) and gender (sex).

**Example:** **Sophia** told **her** children that **she** would be home early.

The pronouns **her** and **she** refer to **Sophia. Sophia** is the antecedent for **her** and **she**.

Here is a chart that lists singular and plural pronouns.

|  | SINGULAR | PLURAL |
| --- | --- | --- |
| PERSONAL PRONOUNS | I, me, you, he, him, she,her, it, | we, you, they, us, them |
| POSSESSIVE PRONOUNS | my, mine, your, yours,his, hers, its | our, ours, your, yours, their, theirs |
| INDEFINITE PRONOUNS | anyone, anybody, everyone, everybody, several, many, no one, nobody, one, someone, somebody, each, either, neither | others, few, both, several, many |

These five rules can help you in the correct use of pronouns with their antecedents.

Rule 1. A SINGULAR ANTECEDENT REQUIRES A SINGULAR PRONOUN.

**Example:** **Hector** shook many hands as **he** campaigned in **his** neighborhood.

When a singular indefinite pronoun is the antecedent, the pronoun **his**, **her**, or **its** must be used.

**Example:** **Someone** left **his** gloves in the car.
*or*
**Example:** **Someone** left **her** gloves in the car.

When people write sentences, they often change the indefinite pronoun to another noun to avoid using **his** or **her**.

**Example:** **Everybody** brought **his** or **her** book to class.

**Example:** **People** brought **their** books to class.


Rule 2. A PLURAL ANTECEDENT REQUIRES A PLURAL PRONOUN.

**Example:** Many **workers** received **their** pay checks on Fridays.


Rule 3. WHEN A PRONOUN IS SEPARATED FROM ITS ANTECEDENT BY A PHRASE, THE PRONOUN MUST STILL AGREE WITH THE ANTECEDENT.

**Example:** **Ms. Makiko Omani**, one of Greg's closest friends, is noted for **her** skill in sewing.
(**Her** refers to Ms. Omani.)

Rule 4. A PLURAL PRONOUN IS USED TO REFER TO TWO OR MORE ANTECEDENTS THAT ARE JOINED BY **AND**.

**Example:** The **cab driver** and the **dispatcher** ate **their** lunches.

Rule 5. A SINGULAR PRONOUN IS USED TO REFER TO TWO OR MORE SINGULAR ANTECEDENTS THAT ARE JOINED BY **OR**.

**Example:** A **blouse or** a **shirt** is missing **its** button.

## Lesson 1 Exercise

**Directions:** Edit the following sentences to correct all the errors in pronoun-antecedent agreement. Not all of the sentences contain errors.

1. Many fathers make lunches for his children.
2. My mother baked bread for her family.
3. The container for the cookies is missing their cover.
4. The frying pan or the saucepan is missing their lid.
5. Andrew, one of the local electricians, brings their own lunch.

Answers are on page A-3.

# Pronoun Agreement: Person

In Lesson 1, you learned that pronouns must agree in number and gender with their antecedents. Pronouns must also agree with their antecedents in person. *Person* refers to the difference between the person who is speaking (*first person*: I), the person who is spoken to (*second person*: you), and the person being spoken about (*third person*: he, she, it). Pronouns must refer consistently to person.

Here is an example of an incorrect use of pronoun reference to person.

**Example:** People should wear seat belts if you don't want to be hurt in a car accident.

This sentence is incorrect because there is a shift from **people** (third person) to **you** (second person). To be consistent in pronoun person, change the pronoun **you** to **they** (third person).

**Edited:** **People** should wear seat belts if **they** don't want to be hurt in a car accident.

When you edit sentences for person, decide which person—first, second, or third—is appropriate for the meaning of the sentence. Then change the pronoun to make the person consistent. Do not shift from one person to another.

This chart will help you remember the different pronouns.

| | |
|---|---|
| FIRST-PERSON PRONOUNS | I, me, my, mine, we, us, our, ours |
| SECOND-PERSON PRONOUNS | you, your, yours |
| THIRD-PERSON PRONOUNS | he, him, his, she, her, hers, it, its, they, them, their, theirs |

## Lesson 2 Exercise

**Directions:** Edit the following sentences to correct all errors in pronoun shift. Not all of the sentences contain errors.

1. A balanced diet is important to our physical health as well as to our emotional health.
2. When people want to lose weight, you should exercise.
3. You should not go on a totally liquid diet if they have not talked with a doctor first.
4. When we drastically change our eating habits, you might feel anxious or tired.
5. A pregnant woman should talk with her doctor before they try to lose weight.

Answers are on page A-4.

Relative pronouns are words that introduce more information about a noun. The relative pronouns are **who**, **whom**, **which**, and **that**.

**Example:** **Helena**, **which** is the capital of Montana, can be very cold in the winter.

**Example:** **People who** enjoy their work are rarely late for their jobs.

The following chart can help you choose the correct relative pronoun.

| RELATIVE PRONOUN | REFERS TO |
| --- | --- |
| who, whom | people |
| which | animals, places, things |
| that | animals, places, things |

Read the following sentences. Which sentences need to be corrected for relative pronoun usage?

1. The car that skidded on the icy road hit a delivery truck.
2. The driver, which was badly shaken, sat in the disabled car.
3. The accident made several dents in the delivery truck, who had been freshly painted.

Sentence 1 is correct. The relative pronoun **that** refers to **car**.

Sentence 2 is incorrect. The relative pronoun **who** must be used to refer to **driver**.

**Edited:** The **driver**, **who** was badly shaken, sat in the disabled car.

Sentence 3 is incorrect. The relative pronoun **which** or **that** must be used to refer to **truck**.

**Edited:** The accident made several dents in the delivery **truck**, **which** had been freshly painted.

*or*

The accident made several dents in the delivery **truck that** had been freshly painted.

To determine whether you should use **who** or **whom**, substitute a personal pronoun for the relative pronoun. If you can substitute **I**, **we**, **he**, **she**, or **they** for the relative pronoun, then you should use **who**. If you can substitute **me**, **us**, **him**, **her**, or **them**, then you should use **whom**.

**Example:** Allyne (who, whom) I met at church, invited me to her home.

Since you would say "I met her at church," you should use **whom** for the relative pronoun.

**Edited:** **Allyne**, **whom** I met at church, invited me to her home.

**Example:** Allyne (who, whom) is a regular churchgoer, sings in the choir.

Since you would say "She is a regular churchgoer," you should use **who** in the sentence.

**Edited:**    **Allyne**, **who** is a regular churchgoer, sings in the choir.

## Lesson 3 Exercise

**Directions:** Edit the following sentences to correct all the errors in relative pronouns. Not all of the sentences contain errors.

1. The mountain range who stretches from Alaska to New Mexico is the Rocky Mountains.
2. Hikers which enjoy spectacular scenery like to camp in these mountains.
3. The snow that melts from the high mountains flows into the rivers.
4. Hikers often see animals who graze in the meadows.
5. One hiker who I admired had one artificial leg.

Answers are on page A-4.

**Lesson 4**

# Avoiding Unclear Pronoun References

## Vague References

When a pronoun does not clearly refer to an antecedent, the meaning of the sentence is vague or confusing.

**Vague:**    We wanted better working conditions which is why the strike occurred.

The relative pronoun **which** does not have a clear antecedent. To make the meaning clearer, you may need to remove the vague pronouns and rewrite the sentence.

**Clear:**    The strike occurred because we wanted better working conditions.

Here is another example of a sentence that contains a vague pronoun reference.

**Vague:**    In a recent survey, they said that the mayor probably would be re-elected.

The pronoun **they** does not have a clear antecedent. In the revised sentence, notice that **they** is removed in order to eliminate this vague reference.

**Clear:**    A recent survey said that the mayor would probably be re-elected.

## Ambiguous References

Sometimes sentence meanings are not clear because the pronoun can refer to more than one word in the sentence. When a pronoun can refer to more than one word in a sentence, the pronoun reference is ambiguous.

**Ambiguous:**     The teachers gave the students their books.

In this sentence, the pronoun **their** might refer to **teachers** or to **students**. The writer of this sentence needs to make the meaning clearer. If the writer meant that the books belonged to the teachers, the sentence could be rewritten this way:

**Clear:**     The teachers gave their books to the students.

If the writer meant that the books belonged to the students, the sentence could be rewritten this way:

**Clear:**     The students received their books from the teachers.

As you read the sentences, look carefully for pronouns that might refer to more than one word in the sentence.

## Lesson 4 Exercise

**Directions:** The following sentences contain vague or ambiguous pronoun references. Rewrite the sentences to make the meaning clear.

1. At work, they complained about the broken furnace.
2. The blizzard caused below-zero temperatures which is why the pipes froze.
3. On the radio, it said that the temperatures will continue to drop.
4. Mr. Nichols told Danny to check the pipes in his apartment.
5. Marcie helped Karen fill out her reports about the frozen pipes.

Answers are on page A-4.

## REVIEW FOR SKILL 3

**Directions:** Edit the following sentences to correct all errors in pronouns. You may need to rewrite sentences to make the meaning clear. Not all of the sentences contain errors.

**(1)** Mary Louise Bell wanted his own credit card. **(2)** She got an application form for a credit card from their bank. **(3)** Mary Louise asked her mother for her Social Security number. **(4)** The bank officer which ran a credit check on Mary Louise approved the credit card. **(5)** Mary Louise, who has been working full-time for two years, will receive her credit card next month.

6. Insurance agents talk with people in their offices.
7. Everyone should read their insurance policies carefully.
8. State Farm Insurance, one of the largest insurance companies, has their offices in this building.
9. When people want to buy life insurance, you should compare the prices and the benefits.
10. Ray Shapiro, who I have known for several years, is my insurance agent.

Check your answers. Correct answers are on page A-4. If you have fewer than eight answers correct, study Skill 3 beginning with Lesson 1.

# CHAPTER 2
# Sentence Structure

## Objective

In this chapter, you will learn about sentence structure

- **complete sentences**

- **coordination and subordination**

- **clear sentences**

## Skill 1

# Complete Sentences

### Preview

**Directions:** Edit the following items so that each item is a complete sentence. Add your own words as needed. Not all of the items are incomplete.

1. Because Marsha Chung was very helpful and friendly at the store.

2. She never called in sick she was always at work on time.

3. Marsha dressed neatly, her clothing was clean and pressed.

4. Marsha enjoyed her job; she liked her co-workers, too.

5. The manager who hired her.

Check your answers. Correct answers are on page A-5. If you have at least four answers correct, do the Review for Skill 1 on page 92. If you have fewer than four answers correct, study Skill 1 beginning with Lesson 1.

# Eliminating Sentence Fragments

Every sentence must contain three parts:

1. a subject
2. a verb
3. a complete thought

A group of words that does not contain all three things is called a *sentence fragment*. It is not complete.

**Fragment:** Registered to vote.

(missing a subject that answers *who*?)

**Sentence:** **Lester** registered to vote.

**Fragment:** A person with good work skills.

(missing a verb that describes the action of the subject)

**Sentence:** A person with good work skills **may qualify** for many jobs.

Even when a group of words contains a subject and a verb, the words may not express a complete thought.

**Fragment:** When you move to a new address.

Although this group of words has a subject (**you**) and a verb (**move**), it does not express a complete thought. What is happening when you move to a new address? To correct this sentence fragment, you must add more words to express the complete thought.

**Sentence:** When you move to a new address, you should notify the post office.

# Lesson 1 Exercise

**Directions:** Edit the following paragraph so that each item is a complete sentence. Add your own words as needed. Not all of the items are sentence fragments.

(**1**) When I installed the smoke alarm. (**2**) The package containing the directions. (**3**) The alarm should be checked every year. (**4**) Because batteries get old. (**5**) Smoke alarms which are a good safety measure.

Answers are on page A-5.

# Separating Run-On Sentences

Sometimes a writer expresses two complete thoughts as one sentence. When the writer does not separate the two complete thoughts with the correct punctuation, the result is a *run-on sentence*. Run-on sentences are confusing because the reader does not know where one complete thought ends and the second complete thought begins.

Read the example below. Can you separate the two complete thoughts?

**Run-on:**   Ted works at a nursing home helping senior citizens is a rewarding job.

The first complete thought is **Ted works at a nursing home**. The second complete thought is **Helping senior citizens is a rewarding job**.

A run-on sentence can be corrected by rewriting it as two separate sentences. A period is placed at the end of the first complete thought. A capital letter begins the second complete thought. Here is how the above run-on sentence can be edited.

**Edited:**   Ted works at a nursing home. Helping senior citizens is a rewarding job.

A run-on sentence also occurs when the writer incorrectly uses a comma to join two complete thoughts. When two complete thoughts are joined with only a comma and no connecting word, a *comma splice* occurs.

**Run-on:**   Mrs. Vashon is eighty years old, she has six grandchildren.

To correct a run-on sentence containing a comma splice, you can replace the comma with a period. Then you can rewrite the run-on sentence as two separate sentences.

**Edited:**   Mrs. Vashon is eighty years old. She has six grandchildren.

## Lesson 2 Exercise

**Directions:** Edit the following paragraph so that each sentence is a correct sentence. Not all of the items are run-on sentences.

(**1**) People should be aware of water pollution and their water consumption because water is an important natural resource. (**2**) Surface water is one source of water, ground water is another source of water. (**3**) Much of our water is polluted the pollution comes from many sources. (**4**) The government has agencies that monitor water pollution, the government also has stiff penalties for businesses that pollute the water. (**5**) Many industries are improving their water purification processes keeping the water clean is good business.

Answers are on page A-5.

# Correcting Run-On Sentences

In Lesson 2, you learned that you can correct a run-on sentence by rewriting it as two separate sentences.

There are three other ways you can correct a run-on sentence.

1. ELIMINATING A RUN-ON BY ADDING A COMMA AND A CONNECTING WORD

A comma and a connecting word (**and, but, or, nor, so, yet**) can be added after the first complete thought of the run-on sentence.

**Run-on:**   Max does the laundry Sally does the ironing.

**Edited:**   Max does the laundry**, and** Sally does the ironing.

**Run-on:**   Barbara drinks coffee she prefers tea.

**Edited:**   Barbara drinks coffee**, but** she prefers tea.

2. ELIMINATING A RUN-ON BY ADDING A SEMICOLON

A semicolon may be used after the first complete thought if the two complete thoughts are very closely related.

**Run-on:**   Dark colors can make a room seem smaller light colors can make a room appear larger.

**Edited:**   Dark colors can make a room seem smaller**;** light colors can make a room appear larger.

3. ELIMINATING A RUN-ON BY USING A SEMICOLON AND A CONNECTING WORD

   a. Sometimes the semicolon is used with a special kind of connecting word. In the following examples, notice that a semicolon separates the two complete thoughts. A comma follows the special connecting word in the second complete thought.

**Run-on:**   Suntan lotion helps a person tan gradually however sunscreen blocks the sun's rays and prevents sunburn.

**Edited:**   Suntan lotion helps a person tan gradually**; however,** sunscreen blocks the sun's rays and prevents sunburn.

**Run-on:**   I use suntan lotion when I work outside otherwise I would get a sunburn.

**Edited:**   I use suntan lotion when I work outside**; otherwise,** I would get a sunburn.

The special connecting words **however** and **otherwise** show the relationship of the second complete thought to the first complete thought.

b. Here is a list of other special connecting words that are often used with semicolons in front of them and commas after them.

1. *Words that add on a related sentence*: **furthermore**, **also**, **moreover**, **besides**, **in addition**, **for instance**, **for example**, **in fact**, **likewise**.

**Run-on:**     I don't like big cars, **besides**, they cost too much.

**Edited:**     I don't like big cars; **besides**, they cost too much.

2. *Words that add on a conclusion*: **therefore**, **thus**, **consequently**, **as a result**.

**Run-on:**     He bets a lot of money, **consequently** he is often broke.

**Edited:**     He bets a lot of money; **consequently**, he is often broke.

3. *Words that add on an opposing or opposite idea*: **however**, **on the contrary**, **nevertheless**, **on the other hand**, **instead**, **still**.

**Run-on:**     Maria likes her job, **however**, she wants to go to college.

**Edited:**     Maria likes her job; **however**, she wants to go to college.

## Lesson 3 Exercise

**Directions:** Edit the following items so that each item is a sentence. You may use any of the methods you have learned in this lesson or in Lesson 2.

1. About seventy percent of the Earth's surface is covered with water less than one percent is fresh water.
2. The average American uses nearly 125 gallons of water daily, most Americans do not realize how much water they use each day.
3. Colorado gets most of its water from snow, however, New York gets most of its water from rain.
4. Forests help water soak into the ground grass keeps the soil from washing away when it rains.
5. Chemicals from pesticides and fertilizers can pollute ground water therefore people should dispose of these chemicals in a safe manner.

Answers are on page A-5.

## REVIEW FOR SKILL 1

**Directions:** Edit the following paragraphs so that each sentence is correct. Add your own words as needed. Not all of the sentences contain errors.

(**1**) Advertisements for weight loss products that appear in many magazines. (**2**) Because people want to lose excess weight quickly. (**3**) Many weight loss products are ineffective, some products may even be harmful to some people. (**4**) People may lose weight however they regain weight as soon as they stop using the products. (**5**) People who want to lose weight.

(**6**) Last night, the power in the Kingsleys' home went off, but the battery-operated radio continued to work. (**7**) Jeff Kingsley thought there was a short circuit however Elaine Kingsley thought there was an overloaded circuit. (**8**) She found a flashlight, as a result they could see their way to the fuse box. (**9**) Elaine held the flashlight, Jeff reset the circuit breaker. (**10**) The power outage was caused by an overloaded circuit in fact the Kingsleys had plugged too many major appliances into the same outlet.

Check your answers. Correct answers are on page A-6. If you have at least eight answers correct, go to Skill 2. If you have fewer than eight answers correct, study Skill 1 beginning with Lesson 1.

# Skill 2

# Sentence Construction:

# Coordination and Subordination

---

## Preview

**Directions:** Edit the following items to correct all errors in sentence construction. Not all of the items contain errors.

1. Debts are difficult to pay off, on the contrary you should budget your money.

2. You do not have to pay interest if you pay the full balance each month.

3. Even though credit cards are convenient, I like shopping.

4. I have had a credit card since when I got my first full-time job.

5. Although I like to pay my bills on time, but I write checks for the bills as soon as I receive them.

Check your answers. Correct answers are on page A-7. If you have at least four answers correct, do the Review for Skill 2 on page 97. If you have fewer than four correct, study Skill 2 beginning with Lesson 1.

---

## Lesson 1

## Equal Ideas: Coordination

When you join two complete thoughts that are equal, you can use connecting words. Sometimes, connecting words are called *coordinators*.

This chart shows commonly used connecting words for equal ideas and their meanings. The coordinators **and**, **but**, **or**, **nor** and, **yet** take a comma when they join two complete thoughts in one sentence to make a compound sentence. The other connecting words in this chart take a semicolon in front of them and a comma after them.

| CONNECTING WORDS FOR EQUAL IDEAS | MEANING |
|---|---|
| and, besides, furthermore, also, in addition, likewise, moreover | add one idea to another |
| but, yet, however, instead, nevertheless, on the contrary, still, on the other hand | contrast one idea to another |
| therefore, consequently, thus, as a result, so | show cause and effect |
| for example, for instance, in fact, as a matter of fact | show a specific example |
| or, otherwise, either . . . or, neither . . . nor | express a choice between ideas |

When you use coordinators to join two complete and equal thoughts, remember the following points.

1. BE SURE THAT THE IDEAS IN A COMPOUND SENTENCE ARE RELATED.

Incorrect:  Rent is my biggest expense, and I like to go to the movies.

The unrelated ideas about the cost of rent and going to the movies do not belong in the same sentence.

Correct:  Rent is my biggest expense, **and** food is my next biggest expense.

*or*

Correct:  I like to go to the movies, **but** I do not like to pay high ticket prices.

2. BE SURE THAT THE COORDINATOR CLEARLY EXPRESSES THE MEANING OF THE  RELATIONSHIP BETWEEN THE TWO EQUAL IDEAS.

Incorrect:  Many people work overtime; however, some people do not get much vacation.

The ideas in this sentence are not in contrast to each other. Therefore, the connecting word **however** is incorrect.

Correct:  Many people work overtime; **however,** they may still earn too little to live comfortably.

Many people work overtime. **However,** they may still earn too little to live comfortably.

*or*

Correct:  Some people do not get much vacation; **however,** they may receive good pay.

Some people do not get much vacation. **However,** they may receive good pay.

**Directions:** Edit the following paragraph to correct errors in sentence construction. Add your own words as needed. Not all of the sentences contain have errors.

(**1**) Many household fires are caused by carelessness; however, smoking in bed is a primary cause of fires. (**2**) Overloaded electrical circuits can also cause a fire, but frayed extension cords can be dangerous. (**3**) Every home should have a fire extinguisher, on the contrary, a smoke detector is useful. (**4**) Old rags, newspapers, and magazines should not be placed near furnaces; furthermore, gasoline and paints should not be stored in hot, unventilated areas. (**5**) A fire can spread quickly; nevertheless, people should quickly evacuate the house.

Answers are on page A-7.

## Lesson 2

# Unequal Ideas: Subordination

Sometimes a sentence contains two ideas that are not of equal importance. One idea is more important than the other idea. The more important idea is called the *main idea*. The main idea is always a complete thought. The less important idea is called the *subordinate idea*. The subordinate idea is not a complete thought. If the subordinate idea is not joined to the main idea, the subordinate idea is a sentence fragment.

**Example:**  David Atsumi watched the evening news because he was interested in the election results.

The main idea, **David Atsumi watched the evening news,** is a complete thought. The subordinate idea, **because he was interested in the election results,** is not a complete thought. If it were not joined to the main idea, it would be a sentence fragment.

Here is another example of subordination.

**Example:**  When David went to the voting poll, he received a printed ballot.

The main idea, **he received a printed ballot,** is the complete thought. **When David went to the voting poll** is the subordinate idea.

The main idea may be the first or the second idea in the sentence. However, it is always a complete thought.

Words that join two ideas of unequal importance are called *subordinators.* Here is a list of common subordinators and their meaning.

| CONNECTING WORDS FOR UNEQUAL IDEAS: SUBORDINATORS | MEANING |
|---|---|
| after, as soon as, as long as, while, when, as, since, until, before, whenever | show time relationship |
| because, since, so that | show cause and effect |

| CONNECTING WORDS FOR UNEQUAL IDEAS: SUBORDINATORS | MEANING |
|---|---|
| if, unless | show possible condition |
| though, although, even though, whereas | show contrast |
| as though, as if | show likeness |
| where, wherever | show place |

## Four Rules for Using Subordination

When you use subordinators to join ideas of unequal importance in a sentence, remember the following rules.

**Rule1.** USE ONLY ONE SUBORDINATOR AT A TIME.

**Incorrect:** In Miami, many stores have signs in both English and Spanish since because many Hispanic people live in that city.

Use either **since** or **because**, but do not use both subordinators.

**Correct:** In Miami, many stores have signs in both English and Spanish because many Hispanic people live in that city.

**Rule 2.** BE SURE THAT THE TWO UNEQUAL IDEAS IN THE SENTENCE ARE RELATED.

**Incorrect:** Even though Arizona is a popular tourist state, José took a long vacation.

(The two ideas in the sentence do not relate to each other. Either the main idea or the subordinate idea must be changed so that the sentence makes sense.)

**Correct:** Even though Arizona is a popular tourist state, José decided to visit Texas.

**Correct:** Even though he does not have much money to travel, José took a long vacation.

**Rule 3.** DO NOT USE A COORDINATOR WHEN TWO IDEAS OF UNEQUAL IMPORTANCE ARE JOINED WITH A SUBORDINATOR.

**Incorrect:** Although the sky was overcast, but I still got a sunburn at the beach.

The subordinator **although** is used to join two ideas of unequal importance. Therefore, the coordinator **but** should not be used.

**Correct:** Although the sky was overcast, I still got a sunburn at the beach.

Rule 4. WHEN THE SUBORDINATE IDEA COMES AT THE BEGINNING OF THE SENTENCE, USE A COMMA TO SEPARATE THE SUBORDINATE IDEA FROM THE MAIN IDEA.

**Correct:**    If it rains today, we will cancel the picnic.

When the subordinate idea comes after the main idea, no comma is needed.

**Correct:**    We will cancel the picnic if it rains today.

## Lesson 2 Exercise

**Directions:** Edit the following items to correct all errors in sentence construction. Add your own words as needed. Not all of the sentences contain errors.

1. Although Victor likes his job, but he does not like to work overtime.
2. Whenever Victor had spare time he took GED classes.
3. He wanted to improve his reading skills so he could help his children with their homework.
4. Victor became interested in GED classes since when his son Manny entered first grade.
5. Because Manny enjoys school, a school bus picks up the children at eight every morning.

Answers are on page A-8.

## REVIEW FOR SKILL 2

**Directions:** Edit the following paragraphs to correct all errors in sentence construction. Add your own words as necessary. Not all of the sentences contain errors.

(**1**) Brenda's dishwasher made unusually loud noises whenever while the machine was operating. (**2**) Because Brenda was concerned about this problem she read the owner's manual.

(**3**) Although she put the utensils in the basket, but one spoon had dropped to the bottom of the dishwasher. (**4**) The spoon had caused lots of noise, but large pots and pans should be washed in the sink. (**5**) Brenda was relieved, because the spoon had not damaged the dishwasher.

(**6**) If a dishwasher is not loaded properly it may not clean dishes completely. (**7**) Large pieces of food should be removed from dishes since because food can cause drainage problems in the dishwasher. (**8**) Even though a dishwasher saves time, I still like to cook. (**9**) A dishwasher can also save energy because the machine can be turned off when it reaches the drying cycle. (**10**) When the dishwasher door is opened, but the dishes will air dry.

Check your answers. Correct answers are on page A-8. If you have at least eight answers correct, go to Skill 3. If you have fewer than eight answers correct, study Skill 2 beginning with Lesson 1.

# Clear Sentences

Lesson
1

## Clarity of Thought

Sometimes a sentence is grammatically correct, yet still unclear in its meaning. When a sentence is unclear, the lack of clarity is usually caused by one of these three problems.

1. UNCLEAR PRONOUN REFERENCES

As you learned in Chapter 1, pronouns should refer clearly to their antecedents.

**Unclear:**   Rosalind put a sign on the door. It was freshly painted.

In this example, does **it** refer to the **sign** or the **door**? If the writer meant that the sign was freshly painted, then the revised sentence might read:

**Clear:**   Rosalind put the freshly painted sign on the door.

If the writer meant that the door was freshly painted, the sentence might be rewritten:

Clear:      Rosalind put the sign on the freshly painted door.

There may be more than one way to correct an unclear pronoun reference. As you edit a sentence for clarity, try to make the sentence easy to read and understand.

## 2. MISPLACED MODIFIERS

Some sentences have unclear meanings because the parts of the sentence are not presented in a logical order. A word or group of words that describes a noun or verb is called a *modifier*. A modifier is *misplaced* when it is too far away from the noun or verb being described (modified). A clear sentence contains modifiers that are placed as near as possible to the words they describe.

Unclear:    Quinten left a bag at his friend's apartment full of candy bars.

Clear:      Quinten left a bag full of candy bars at his friend's apartment.

The phrase **full of candy bars** describes **bag**, not **his friend's apartment**.

Unclear:    The two men robbed the women wearing masks.

Clear:      The two men wearing masks robbed the women.

The phrase **wearing masks** describes **the two men**, not **the women**.

## 3. DANGLING MODIFIERS

Modifiers must clearly and logically describe the words they are near. When there is no word that can be modified logically, the modifier is called a *dangling modifier*. In other words, the modifier "dangles" because it cannot logically attach its description to the nearest word.

Incorrect:  Tired after a hard day at work, my hot shower relaxed me.

The modifier **Tired after a hard day at work** seems to describe **shower**. However, this modification is not logical. **My hot shower** cannot be tired, even though the modifier is located next to that word.

To correct a dangling modifier, rewrite the sentence so that the modifier comes immediately before or after the word it describes.

Correct:    Tired after a hard day at work, I took a relaxing hot shower.

Now the modifier, **Tired after a hard day at work**, correctly describes the next word, **I**.

Another way to correct this problem is to change the wording of the modifier.

Correct:    Because I was tired after a hard day at work, my hot shower
            relaxed me.

## Lesson 1 Exercise

**Directions:** Edit the following sentences to make clear sentences. Add your own words as needed. Not all of the sentences contain problems.

1. Watching a parade, the music of the marching bands was heard by the people.
2. People line the sidewalks eating cotton candy.
3. The floats are decorated with flowers filled with people.
4. Turning the corner, loud applause begins.
5. A clown with large shoes gives a balloon to a little girl.

Answers are on page A-9.

**Lesson 2**

# Parallel Structure

Read the following pair of sentences. What is the difference between the two sentences?

**1.** Carmen likes to walk, to swim, and dancing.

**2.** Carmen likes to walk, to swim, and to dance.

Sentence 1 uses the word **dancing**, whereas Sentence 2 uses **to dance**. Sentence 2 uses the correct form of the word. **To walk**, **to swim**, and **to dance** are all activities that have similar roles, or grammatical forms, in the sentence. When ideas have similar roles in a sentence, they should be worded in similar or parallel structures. Here are two other examples of sentences that do not contain parallel structure.

**1.** Laughing, smiling, and to joke are all signs that a person is happy.

In Sentence 1, the similar ideas are not expressed in parallel structure. Two ideas (**laughing** and **smiling**) end in **-ing**, but the third idea (**to joke**) does not. To correct this sentence for parallel structure, the sentence should be edited this way:

Correct: **Laughing**, **smiling**, and **joking** are all signs that a person is happy.

**2.** Before I go home, I need to shop for food, to get gas for the car, and my check needs to be deposited at the bank.

Sentence 2 contains two ideas that are parallel: **to shop for food** and **to get gas for the car**. However, the third idea, **my check needs to be deposited at the bank**, is not parallel. Here is how the sentence could be edited to correct the problem with structure:

Correct: Before I go home, I need **to shop for food**, **to get gas for the car**, and **to deposit my check at the bank**.

## THREE HINTS FOR CHECKING PARALLEL STRUCTURE

1. Look for a listing of ideas, things, or actions in the sentence. Connecting words (**and**, **but**, **or**) are frequently used.
2. Make sure each idea in the list is written in the same form.
3. If an idea is not written in the same form, change the form so that the idea is in parallel structure with the other ideas.

## Lesson 2 Exercise

**Directions:** Edit the following paragraph to make the sentences clear. Not all of the sentences contain problems.

(**1**) The Discovery Channel has television shows that are informative, interesting, and have educational value. (**2**) The nature programs are popular with people of all ages and backgrounds. (**3**) Some of the best programs show how endangered animals care for their young, how they protect themselves from predators, and that they sometimes lose the battle for survival. (**4**) Diving in the oceans, skiing down mountains, and when they explore deep caves are often shown on The Discovery Channel. (**5**) Watching modern explorers and to listen to their adventures is exciting.

Answers are on page A-9.

## REVIEW FOR SKILL 3

**Directions:** Edit the following paragraphs to make the sentences clear. Not all of the sentences contain problems.

(**1**) Benny put his hand by the window sill and felt the wind. It was cold. (**2**) Wanting to reduce heating bills, weatherstripping was added to the windows by Benny. (**3**) Heating bills are reduced when storm windows are installed drastically.(**4**) Benny also saved energy by setting his thermostat at 70 degrees and to wear a warmer sweater. (**5**) Benny also sleeps with a warm quilt on his bed made by his mother.

(**6**) Sue Ellen asked her roommate Alice to do her share of the cleaning in the apartment. (**7**) Irritated by her roommate's mess, the clothes and magazines were picked up by Sue Ellen. (**8**) A sweater lay on the floor that needed mending. (**9**) Sue Ellen swept the floors, vacuumed the rugs, and the bathroom needed cleaning. (**10**) Because Alice was not keeping the apartment clean, Sue Ellen asked her to move out.

Check your answers. Correct answers are on page A-9. If you have fewer than eight answers correct, study Skill 3 beginning with Lesson 1.

# CHAPTER 3
# Mechanics

## Objective

In this chapter you will learn about

- **capitalization**

- **punctuation**

- **spelling**

## Skill 1

# Capitalization

---

### Preview

**Directions:** Edit the following sentences to correct all errors in capitalization. Not all of the sentences contain errors.

1. Many people drink florida orange juice at breakfast.

2. Ivan thinks Winter is colder in Michigan than in Siberia.

3. Gretel works for frederick's bar and grill.

4. The restaurant is located at 245 riverside highway.

5. Sometimes, I enjoy taking my father to the restaurant for dinner.

Check your answers. Correct answers are on page A-10. If you have at least four answers correct, do the Review for Skill 1 on page 105. If you have fewer than four answers correct, study Skill 1 beginning with Lesson 1.

---

# Lesson 1 — Proper Nouns and Proper Adjectives

If a word begins with a capital letter, the word is considered *capitalized*. The first word of a sentence and the pronoun **I** are always capitalized. In addition, proper nouns and proper adjectives are always capitalized.

A *proper noun names* a specific person, place or thing.

| SPECIFIC PERSON | SPECIFIC PLACE | SPECIFIC THING |
|---|---|---|
| Martin Luther King, Jr. | South Carolina | Islam (religion) |
| Barbara Bush | Pacific Ocean | *TV Guide* (publication) |
| Ms. Fritz | Mount Rainier | Harst High School (building) |
| Dr. Drake | San Jose | Alcoholics Anonymous (organization) |
| | | Thanksgiving (holiday or special event) |

When a proper noun is used as an adjective, it is called a *proper adjective*:

- *American* music
- *Spanish* heritage
- *English* language
- *Japanese* imports
- *Buddhist* priest
- *Catholic* priest
- *Baptist* minister

**Example:** Every year, we see the **Christmas** tree in the park.

**Example:** Who is the captain of the California team this year?

**Example:** Steve's favorite food is **German** sausage.

**Example:** Have you eaten at the new **Mexican** restaurant?

Notice that the proper adjectives (**Christmas**, **California German**, and **Mexican**) are capitalized; however, the nouns they modify (tree, team, sausage, and restaurant) are not capitalized.

## Lesson 1 Exercise

**Directions:** Edit the following sentences to correct all capitalization errors. Not all of the sentences have errors.

1. One day, Doreen would like to visit hawaii.
2. She wants to see waikiki beach.
3. A popular tourist attraction is Volcanoes National Park.
4. Doreen also wants to eat authentic hawaiian food.
5. On her way to work, Doreen saw a poster of Oahu in the window of thompson's travel agency.

Answers are on page A-10.

Skill 1 Lesson 1: Capitalization   103

# Titles of People and Addresses

<u>Rule 1</u>. ALWAYS CAPITALIZE THE TITLE OF A PERSON WHEN IT IS PART OF THAT PERSON'S NAME.

Titles that are not used as part of a person's name are not capitalized.

**Example:**    At the meeting, **Senator Branco** smiled at the reporters.

Joyce Branco, a **senator** with a fine reputation, smiled at the reporters.

**Example:**    I visited **Uncle Mike** and **Aunt Betty** last summer.

I visited my **uncle** and **aunt** last summer.

**Example:**    We told **Mother** about our vacation plans.

She told her **mother** about our vacation plans.

<u>Rule 2.</u> CAPITALIZE THE NAMES AND ABBREVIATIONS OF SPECIFIC STREETS AND SPECIFIC HIGHWAYS. ALSO CAPITALIZE SPECIFIC REGIONS OF THE COUNTRY (the North, the South, the West, the East). But do not capitalize directions—north, south, west and east.

**Example:**    Lydia lives on the corner of **Oak Avenue** and **Madison Street**.

**but**:    The city map showed the names of **streets** and **avenues**.

**Example:**    Please deliver these flowers to 543 **Gore Rd**.

**but:**    Sherry parked her car on the side of the road.

**Example:**    Arnie's new apartment is on **South Martin Boulevard**.

During the Civil War, the **South** lost many soldiers.

**but:**    Rosie lives in the **south** part of town.

## Lesson 2 Exercise

**Directions:** Edit the following sentences to correct all capitalization errors. Not all of the sentences contain errors.

1.  When was the last time you talked to Mother?
2.  Phillip contributes money to the american heart association.
3.  Your father wants to meet you at the corner of south hawthorne road and pine avenue.
4.  He knows the President of the chicago lions club.
5.  I do not think Jeffrey Burns is related to senator Burns.

Answers are on page A-10.

Rule 1. CAPITALIZE THE DAYS OF THE WEEK, MONTHS OF THE YEAR, AND HOLIDAYS.

**Example:** Americans celebrate **Thanksgiving Day** on the fourth **Thursday** of **November**.

Do not capitalize the names of seasons.

**Example:** My favorite season is **autumn**; however, I also enjoy **spring**.

Rule 2. CAPITALIZE THE NAMES OF HISTORICAL EVENTS AND HISTORICAL TIME PERIODS. ALSO CAPITALIZE THE NAMES OF SPECIAL EVENTS.

**Example:** My family watched the movie about the **Civil War**.

**Example:** When I was a child, I enjoyed reading about the knights who lived during the **Middle Ages**.

**Example:** Because he liked sports, Chet watched much of the **Goodwill Games** on television.

## Lesson 3 Exercise

**Directions:** Edit the following sentences to correct all capitalization errors. Not all of the sentences contain errors.

1. In the United States, independence day is celebrated on July 4.
2. June 22 is the first official day of Summer.
3. Did you know that Mother's Day is the second sunday in may?
4. During the Dark Ages, many people died from tuberculosis and other diseases.
5. The auto races will be held in france this june.

Answers are on page A-10.

## REVIEW FOR SKILL 1

**Directions:** Edit the following sentences to correct all capitalization errors. Not all of the sentences contain errors.

1. In march, Oscars are awarded by the film industry
2. Sometimes, british actors and actresses receive awards.
3. Did you enjoy the movie about the american revolutionary war?
4. To my surprise, aunt Karen thought it was the best movie of the year.
5. She and I saw another good movie last saturday.
6. The movie was a comedy about a family's Summer vacation.

7. I think mother would have enjoyed that movie.

8. We saw Dr. Samuels at the Crystal Theater.

9. The theater is located on north vine avenue.

10. My apartment is only three blocks West of the theater.

Check your answers. Correct answers are on page A-10. If you have at least eight answers correct, go to Skill 2. If you have fewer than eight answers correct, study Skill 1 beginning with Lesson 1.

# *Skill* 2 Punctuation

---

## Preview

**Directions:** Edit the following sentences to correct all errors in punctuation. Not all of the sentences contain errors.

1. Three popular citrus fruits are, oranges, grapefruit, and, tangerines.

2. Robin likes different types of fruit, and makes tasty fruit salads.

3. When bananas are in season, Robin likes to make banana bread.

4. Fruits are a tasty, inexpensive, source of vitamins and minerals.

5. Fruits, an important part of a healthy diet are available all year.

Check your answers. Correct answers are on page A-11. If you have at least four answers correct, do the Review for Skill 2 on page 112. If you have fewer than four answers correct, study Skill 2 beginning with Lesson 1.

---

## *Lesson* 1 Commas Between Items in a Series

Many sentences contain words or phrases that are listed in a series. A series means that similar things are arranged one after another.

<u>Rule 1.</u> USE COMMAS TO SEPARATE THREE OR MORE ITEMS IN A SERIES.

**Example:** The American flag contains the colors of **red**, **white**, and **blue**.

**Example:** **Frying**, **broiling**, and **baking** are three types of cooking.

In the first example, the single words—**red**, **white**, and **blue**—are listed in a series. In the second example, the single words—**frying**, **broiling**, and **baking**—are listed in a series. Notice that commas are used after each item except the last one. Do not put a comma between the last item and the next word in the sentence.

**Incorrect:**  Frying, broiling, and baking, are three types of cooking.

Here is another example of how to use commas to separate items in a series.

**Example:**  Loran needs to **refill his blood-pressure prescription**, **buy toothpaste**, and **mail letters**.

In the example above, the three items in the series are **refill his blood-pressure prescription**, **buy toothpaste**, and **mail letters**.

Rule 2. USE COMMAS BETWEEN EACH ADJECTIVE WHEN THE ADJECTIVES MODIFY THE SAME NOUN.

**Example:**  The young girl had **small**, **delicate** hands.
**Example:**  **Large**, **cold**, **hard** chunks of ice fell from the roof.

In the first example, the adjectives **small** and **delicate** describe hands. In the second example, the adjectives **large**, **cold**, and **hard** describe chunks. Notice that a comma does not separate the last adjective from the noun.

**Incorrect:**  Large, cold, hard, chunks of ice fell from the roof.

Rule 3. DO NOT PUT A COMMA BETWEEN AN ADJECTIVE AND A NOUN WHEN THE ADJECTIVE MODIFIES THE NOUN.

**Incorrect:**  The car has a small, engine.

Rule 4. DO NOT USE A COMMA BETWEEN AN ADVERB AND AN ADJECTIVE WHEN THE ADVERB MODIFIES THE ADJECTIVE.

**Incorrect:**  The stove was terribly, hot.
**Incorrect:**  He is a very, kind man.

Rule 5. DO NOT USE A COMMA WHEN EACH OF THE ITEMS IN A SERIES IS JOINED BY A CONNECTING WORD, SUCH AS **AND** OR **OR**.

**Example:**  Would you like pie **or** cake **or** ice cream?

## Lesson 1 Exercise

**Directions:** Edit the following sentences to correct all punctuation errors. Not all of the sentences contain errors.

1. Linda Ronstadt, Sheena Easton, and Carly Simon, are three of Rhoda's favorite female singers.

2. On weekends, Rhoda cleans her apartment does her laundry and watches television.

3. She laughs at the funny, young, host of the talk show.

4. Many talk shows feature topics such as divorce or friendship or pet peeves.

5. Talk shows can be an entertaining, educational, experience.

Answers are on page A-11.

## Lesson 2 — Commas after Introductory Elements

<u>Rule 1.</u> USE A COMMA AFTER INTRODUCTORY WORDS, SUCH AS **HOWEVER**, **THEREFORE**, **OTHERWISE**.

**Example:** **However**, I will need to find day care for my children.

**Example:** **Therefore**, we must go on strike.

<u>Rule 2.</u> USE A COMMA AFTER INTRODUCTORY PHRASES.

**Example:** **On the other hand**, we did have a good time.

**Example:** **Looking through the magazine**, Mrs. Ying noticed an unusual picture.

<u>Rule 3.</u> USE A COMMA WHEN THE SUBORDINATE IDEA COMES BEFORE THE MAIN IDEA.

**Example:** **When you leave for work**, you should turn down the heat.

**Example:** **Because Raphael is ill**, Felipe must work by himself.

Do not use a comma to separate the main idea from the subordinate idea when the subordinate idea comes after the main idea.

**Incorrect:** Car engines are hard to start, when the weather is below zero degrees.

**Correct:** Car engines are hard to start when the weather is below zero degrees.

### Lesson 2 Exercise

**Directions:** Edit the following sentences to correct all punctuation errors. Not all of the sentences contain errors.

1. Because the tire pressure was low Donna added air to the tire.

2. She checked the wear on the tire tread before she went on her long trip.

3. Changing a flat tire on the interstate is a major hassle, when it is raining.

4. However you should not drive on a flat tire.

5. If a blow-out occurs at high speeds you could be involved in a serious accident.

Answers are on page A-11.

# Commas with Sentence Interrupters

When a group of words adds information that is not essential to the meaning of the sentence, that group of words is called a *sentence interrupter or a phrase in apposition*. The interrupter can be short or long; it can be as short as one word.

Use a comma before and after the sentence interrupter.

**Example:** Elton John, **a popular rock musician**, was interviewed by Connie Chung.

The interrupter—**a popular rock musician**—adds information that is not essential to the sentence. An interrupter is a common type of phrase that means almost the same thing as the noun it describes. Here are two more examples of this type of sentence interrupter.

**Example:** Andy Rooney, **who appears on 60 Minutes**, pokes fun at many pet peeves.

**Example:** The snake was attacked by a mongoose, **a weasellike animal**.

In the first example, the interrupter—**who appears on 60 Minutes**—does not add essential information to the sentence. Notice that commas are placed before and after the interrupter. In the second example, **a weasellike animal** is the interrupter. A comma separates the interrupter from the rest of the sentence.

Sometimes sentence interrupters are expressions that signal the reader to pause in the sentence. Commas are used before and after the sentence interrupter.

**Example:** Chocolate, **I think**, is the most popular flavor of ice cream.

**Example:** Vanilla, **on the other hand**, is my favorite ice cream.

In the above examples, **I think** and **on the other hand** do not add essential information to the sentence. The reader tends to pause while reading the interrupters.

Here is a list of common expressions that can be used as sentence interrupters.

| | | |
|---|---|---|
| I believe | on the contrary | after all |
| I think | on the other hand | by the way |
| I hope | incidentally | of course |
| I know | in my opinion | for example |
| I am sure | nevertheless | however |

**NOTE:** Do not use commas to set off information which is essential to the meaning of the sentence.

**Example:** **Your neighbor Polly** called to see how you were feeling.

In this example, the name of the neighbor—**Polly**—is needed to make the meaning clear. Without this essential information, the reader would not know which neighbor called.

**Example:** The **person who left the kittens in the alley** was not an animal lover.

The words **who left the kittens in the alley** add essential information to the sentence. The sentence is about the **person who left the kittens in the alley**, not about just "the person."

**Example:** The **company which donates the most money to the charity drive** will receive an award.

The words **which donates the most money to the charity drive** adds essential information. Without this essential information, the reader would not understand which company the sentence was about.

## Lesson 3 Exercise

**Directions:** Edit the following sentences to correct all punctuation errors. Not all of the sentences contain errors.

1. Seattle in my opinion is a nice city.
2. From the top of the Space Needle a popular tourist attraction a person can see all of Seattle.
3. Olympia which is the capital of Washington has fewer people than Seattle.
4. The mountain that overlooks the entire Seattle area is Mount Rainier.
5. Clouds however often cover the mountain.

Answers are on page A-11.

## Lesson 4 — Avoiding Overuse of Commas

Lessons 1 through 3 helped you understand when to use commas in sentences. This lesson will help you recognize when <u>not</u> to use commas.

<u>Rule 1</u>  DO NOT USE A COMMA BETWEEN THE SUBJECT AND VERB.

**Incorrect:** One of the highest-paid movie actors, is Tom Cruise.

**Correct:** One of the highest-paid movie actors is Tom Cruise.

<u>Rule 2.</u> DO NOT USE COMMAS WITH COMPOUND SUBJECTS OR WITH COMPOUND VERBS.

**Incorrect:** Candy, and cigarettes were highly prized gifts during World War II.

**Correct:** Candy and cigarettes were highly prized gifts during World War II.

| **Incorrect:** | Boxes of letters, and albums of pictures were stored in the attic. |
| **Correct:** | Boxes of letters and albums of pictures were stored in the attic. |

| **Incorrect:** | Brad wants a new car, but cannot afford one. |
| **Correct:** | Brad wants a new car but cannot afford one. |

| **Incorrect:** | Sheila types her reports, and proofreads them carefully. |
| **Correct:** | Sheila types her reports and proofreads them carefully. |

<u>Rule 3.</u> DO NOT USE A COMMA TO CONNECT TWO SENTENCES THAT ARE NOT JOINED BY A COORDINATOR.

| **Incorrect:** | Hazel is divorced, Carmen is married. |
| **Correct:** | Hazel is divorced, and Carmen is married. |
| **Correct:** | Hazel is divorced, but Carmen is married. |
| **Correct:** | Hazel is divorced. Carmen is married. |
| **Correct:** | Hazel is divorced; however, Carmen is married. |

<u>Rule 4.</u> DO NOT USE A COMMA AFTER A COORDINATOR THAT JOINS TWO COMPLETE THOUGHTS.

| **Incorrect:** | Nancy put the roast in the oven but, she forgot to set the timer. |
| **Correct:** | Nancy put the roast in the oven, but she forgot to set the timer. |

<u>Rule 5.</u> DO NOT USE A COMMA BEFORE THE WORD **BECAUSE**.

| **Incorrect:** | Rose left her job, because she did not get a raise. |
| **Correct:** | Rose left her job because she did not get a raise. |

## Lesson 4 Exercise

**Directions:** Edit the following sentences to correct all punctuation errors. Not all of the sentences contain errors.

1. Sunny beaches, and warm winters attract many tourists to Florida.
2. Many families visit Disney World a popular Florida attraction.
3. Other tourist attractions, are Busch Gardens, Sea World, and the Kennedy Space Center.
4. Orlando is one of the largest business centers of the state.
5. The tourists take photographs, and buy souvenirs.

Answers are on page A-11.

**Directions:** Edit the following sentences to correct all punctuation errors. Not all of the sentences contain errors.

1. Heroin, cocaine, and morphine, are narcotics.
2. Alcohol is also a drug but, it is not an illegal drug.
3. If you have a problem with drug addiction you should seek professional help.
4. However you must first recognize and acknowledge your problem.
5. Alcoholics Anonymous a self-help organization has a high success record.
6. One of the most popular beverages in America, is coffee.
7. Coffee, and tea contain caffeine.
8. People, who smoke cigarettes, have more health problems than people who do not smoke.
9. We do not mind people smoking in public, but we do not allow people to smoke in our home.
10. We do not like cigarette ashes on our polished, floor.

Check your answers. Correct answers are on page A-12. If you have at least eight answers correct, go to Skill 3. If you have fewer than eight answers correct, study Skill 2 beginning with Lesson 1.

*Skill* **3**

# Spelling

---

## Preview

**Directions:** Edit the following sentences to correct all errors in spelling. Not all of the sentences contain errors.

1. Russ washed the forks, spoons, and knifes.
2. Sometimes it's difficult to clean the pots and pans.
3. The childrens dishes are still on the table.
4. Russ is wipeing the table.
5. He couldn't here the baby crying.

Check your answers. Correct answers are on page A-12. If you have at least four answers correct, do the Review for Skill 3 on page 122. If you have fewer than four answers correct, study Skill 3 beginning with Lesson 1.

---

# Basic Spelling Rules

Spelling rules are based on the patterns of vowels and consonants in words. The *vowels* are **a**, **e**, **i**, **o**, **u**, and **y** when it appears in words like **cry** or **safety**. All the other letters of the alphabet are *consonants*.

Spelling rules are also based on the patterns of stressed and unstressed syllables. A *syllable* is a part of the word that makes a separate sound. A syllable always contains at least one vowel. Examples of one-syllable words are **try**, **home**, and **paint**.

A *stressed syllable* is the syllable that receives the most emphasis when you say the word. The syllable that does not receive the stress is called the *unstressed syllable*.

Examples of two-syllable words with the stress on the first syllable are **table**, **faithful**, and **tested**. Examples of two-syllable words with the stress on the second syllable are **machine**, **relax**, and **prefer**.

Examples of three-syllable words are **relaxing**, **decision**, and **computer**. In these words, the stress is on the second syllable.

**Comedy**, **interview**, and **minister** are examples of three-syllable words that have the stress on the first syllable.

Use the following rules to help you change singular nouns to plural nouns and to change verb forms.

## Noun Forms

Rule 1. IN GENERAL, PLURAL NOUNS ARE FORMED BY ADDING **-S** OR **-ES** TO SINGULAR NOUNS. PLURAL NOUNS ARE FORMED BY ADDING **-ES** TO SINGULAR NOUNS THAT END IN **-S**, **-X**, **-CH**, AND **-SH**.

| SINGULAR | PLURAL |
| --- | --- |
| desk | desks |
| gas | gases |
| tax | taxes |
| bench | benches |
| bush | bushes |

Rule 2. WHEN A SINGULAR NOUN ENDS IN A CONSONANT FOLLOWED BY **-Y**, THE PLURAL NOUN IS FORMED BY CHANGING THE **-Y** TO **-I** AND ADDING **-ES**.

| SINGULAR | PLURAL |
| --- | --- |
| cry | cries |
| party | parties |

When a singular noun ends in a vowel followed by **-y**, the plural noun is formed by just adding **-s**.

| SINGULAR | PLURAL |
| --- | --- |
| key | keys |
| relay | relays |

**Rule 3.** SOME NOUNS ARE THE SAME IN THE SINGULAR AND PLURAL FORM.

| SINGULAR | PLURAL |
| --- | --- |
| sheep | sheep |
| deer | deer |

**Rule 4.** WHEN A SINGULAR NOUN ENDS IN **-F**, THE PLURAL NOUN IS USUALLY FORMED BY CHANGING THE **-F** TO **-V** AND ADDING **-ES**. WHEN A SINGULAR NOUN ENDS IN **-FE**, THE PLURAL NOUN IS USUALLY FORMED BY CHANGING THE **-FE** TO **-VE** AND ADDING **-S**.

| SINGULAR | PLURAL |
| --- | --- |
| shelf | shelves |
| leaf | leaves |
| knife | knives |
| life | lives |

## Verb Forms

**Rule 5.** TO ADD **-ING** TO A VERB THAT ENDS IN **-E**, DROP THE FINAL **-E** BEFORE ADDING **-ING**.

| REGULAR FORM | **-ING** FORM |
| --- | --- |
| save | saving |
| write | writing |
| believe | believing |

**Rule 6.** TO ADD **-ING** OR **-ED** TO A ONE-SYLLABLE WORD THAT ENDS WITH A SINGLE VOWEL AND A SINGLE CONSONANT, DOUBLE THE FINAL CONSONANT BEFORE ADDING **-ING** OR **-ED**.

| REGULAR FORM | **-ING** FORM | **-ED** FORM |
| --- | --- | --- |
| plan | planning | planned |
| stop | stopping | stopped |
| stir | stirring | stirred |

**Rule 7.** TO ADD **-ING** OR **-ED** TO A TWO-SYLLABLE WORD THAT ENDS WITH A SINGLE VOWEL AND A SINGLE CONSONANT AND THAT HAS THE STRESS

ON THE SECOND SYLLABLE, DOUBLE THE FINAL CONSONANT BEFORE ADDING **-ING** OR **-ED**.

| REGULAR FORM | **-ING** FORM | **-ED** FORM |
|---|---|---|
| admit | admitting | admitted |
| occur | occurring | occurred |
| control | controlling | controlled |

## Lesson 1 Exercise

**Directions:** Edit the following sentences to correct all errors in spelling. Not all of the sentences contain errors.

1. Many single parents need child care for their babys.
2. Some parents are planing to look for second jobs.
3. One parent was saveing for new clothes for her child.
4. She admited that she did not want to ask for financial assistance.
5. Many local churches offered child care services for working parents.

Answers are on page A-12.

Lesson 2

# Possessives

The *possessive* form of a noun shows that something belongs to something or someone else. A possessive noun uses an apostrophe to show possession or ownership.

Rule 1.  TO FORM THE POSSESSIVE FORM OF A SINGULAR NOUN, ADD AN APOSTROPHE AND THE LETTER **-S** TO THE SINGULAR NOUN.

| SINGULAR NOUN | POSSESSIVE NOUN |
|---|---|
| Felix | Felix's smile |
| a reporter | a reporter's question |
| one doctor | one doctor's office |

To form the possessive of a singular noun that ends in **-s**, add an apostrophe and the letter **-s** to the singular noun.

| SINGULAR NOUN | POSSESSIVE NOUN |
|---|---|
| a dress | a dress's hem |
| an actress | an actress's picture |

Rule 2.  TO FORM THE POSSESSIVE FORM OF A PLURAL NOUN ENDING IN **-S**, ADD ONLY AN APOSTROPHE.

| PLURAL NOUN | POSSESSIVE NOUN |
|---|---|
| two books | two books' covers |
| some trucks | some trucks' engines |
| many cities | many cities' streets |

**Rule 3.**  TO FORM THE POSSESSIVE FORM OF A PLURAL NOUN THAT DOES NOT END IN **-S**, ADD AN APOSTROPHE AND THE LETTER **-S**.

| PLURAL NOUN | POSSESSIVE NOUN |
|---|---|
| children | children's toys |
| men | men's jackets |
| women | women's coats |
| mice | mice's nests |
| geese | geese's wings |

**Rule 4.**  DO NOT USE AN APOSTROPHE TO FORM THE POSSESSIVE FORM OF PRONOUNS.

**Examples:** This seat is mine.      This is my seat.

| | |
|---|---|
| That radio is hers. | That is her radio. |
| This hammer is his. | This is his hammer. |
| These towels are ours. | These are our towels. |
| The cat licks its paw. | The cats lick their paws. |
| Those tickets are theirs. | Those are their tickets. |
| These problems are yours. | You people have your problems. |
| This car is yours. | This is your car. |

## Lesson 2 Exercise

**Directions:** Edit the following sentences to correct all errors in spelling. Not all of the sentences contain errors.

1. Have you visited our citys museum?
2. One area displays childrens toys from the early nineteenth century.
3. Another area contains different types of men's hats and ladys gloves.
4. Gina's favorite display showed women's scarves and dresses.
5. The museum changes it's display every three months.

Answers are on page A-12.

# Lesson 3

## Contractions

A *contraction* is a word that is formed by combining two words into one word and by omitting one or more letters. An apostrophe takes the place of the omitted letters.

Here is a list of common contractions and the words that form them. Notice the use of the apostrophe in place of the omitted letters.

| COMPLETE FORM | CONTRACTION |
|---|---|
| I am | I'm |
| you are | you're |
| we are | we're |
| they are | they're |
| | |
| he is | he's |
| she is | she's |
| it is | it's |
| who is | who's |
| where is | where's |
| what is | what's |
| there is | there's |
| | |
| I will | I'll |
| you will | you'll |
| she will | she'll |
| he will | he'll |
| we will | we'll |
| they will | they'll |
| | |
| I would | I'd |
| you would | you'd |
| he would | he'd |
| she would | she'd |
| we would | we'd |
| they would | they'd |
| | |
| I have | I've |
| you have | you've |
| we have | we've |
| they have | they've |
| | |
| is not | isn't |
| are not | aren't |
| was not | wasn't |
| were not | weren't |

| COMPLETE FORM | CONTRACTION |
|---|---|
| have not | haven't |
| has not | hasn't |
| does not | doesn't |
| did not | didn't |
| | |
| would not | wouldn't |
| should not | shouldn't |
| could not | couldn't |
| cannot | can't |
| will not | won't |

Contractions are frequently confused with possessive pronouns. Be sure that you recognize the difference between **it's** and **its**, **who's** and **whose**, **you're** and **your**, and **they're** and **their**. Use an apostrophe only if you can put is in place of **'s** and **are** in place of **'re**.

| | |
|---|---|
| Contraction: | **It's** a hot summer day. |
| Possessive pronoun: | Put the letter back into **its** envelope. |
| | |
| Contraction: | **Who's** going to the football game? |
| Possessive pronoun: | I wonder **whose** gloves these are. |
| | |
| Contraction: | **You're** a great cook. |
| Possessive pronoun: | I always enjoy **your** letters. |
| | |
| Contraction: | I wonder what **they're** doing now. |
| Possessive pronoun: | **Their** time cards are still here. |

## Lesson 3 Exercise

**Directions:** Edit the following sentences to correct all errors in spelling. You may need to rewrite some words as contractions. Not all of the sentences contain errors.

1. Did'nt the Chinese introduce Marco Polo to spaghetti?
2. When you're body needs energy, you should eat pasta.
3. Lots of children think it's fun to eat spaghetti.
4. They suck the spaghetti strands into they're mouths.
5. My friends think Im a good Italian cook.

Answers are on page A-13.

Words that are pronounced the same way but that have different meanings and are spelled differently are called *homonyms*. Even though the words are correct when they are spoken, homonyms are spelling errors in writing.

**Incorrect:** Many people participated in the **piece** march.

**Correct:** Many people participated in the **peace** march.

In this pair of sentences, **piece** and **peace** are homonyms. Since the writer wants to say "absence of war," the correct spelling is **peace**. **Piece** means "a part of something."

The following sets of words are homonyms that are commonly confused.

**brake**      a device that stops a machine

**break**      to shatter into pieces; a pause

**Example:** The emergency **brake** held the car on the hill.

             If you drop a glass, it will **break** into many pieces.

             During her lunch **break**, Carla read a magazine.

**buy**      purchase

**by**      near; through the act of

**Example:** Can we afford to **buy** a new sofa?

             Amy lives **by** the theater.

             **By** lowering your thermostat, you reduce your heating bill.

**desert**      to leave; a dry area

**dessert**      final course of a meal

**Example:** A captain of a ship should never **desert** his crew.

             When you travel through a **desert**, take lots of water.

             Would you like cake or pie or custard for **dessert**?

**fair**      just; exhibit

**fare**      price of ticket

**Example:** The defendant wants a **fair** hearing at the trial.

             At the state **fair**, children enjoy the amusement rides.

             Senior citizens can ride the bus at a discounted **fare**.

| | |
|---|---|
| **for** | preposition |
| **four** | number 4 |

**Example:** This birthday card is **for** you.

The dining room table has **four** legs.

| | |
|---|---|
| **heal** | cure |
| **heel** | bottom of foot or shoe |

**Example:** This cast will allow the broken arm to **heal** correctly.

These new shoes gave me a blister on my right **heel**.

| | |
|---|---|
| **hear** | listen |
| **here** | this place; expletive |

**Example:** Speak loudly so that everyone can hear you.

Put the box **here**.

**Here** is today's mail.

| | |
|---|---|
| **hole** | opening |
| **whole** | entire amount |

**Example:** Did your dog dig a **hole** in my back yard?

Bret ate the **whole** pizza by himself.

| | |
|---|---|
| **meat** | flesh |
| **meet** | come together |

**Example:** The butcher helped us find inexpensive cuts of **meat**.

Ed and Phil will **meet** their wives at the cafe.

| | |
|---|---|
| **passed** | past tense of pass |
| **past** | time or event that has happened |

**Example:** Last week, I **passed** my driver's test.

In the **past**, pioneers lived in log cabins.

| | |
|---|---|
| **peace** | absence of war |
| **piece** | a part of something |

**Example:** Many countries want worldwide **peace**.

There is one **piece** of pizza left in the oven.

| | |
|---|---|
| **poor** | not rich |
| **pour** | to flow |

**Example:** Many **poor** people seek shelter at local charities.

Will you please **pour** the coffee into the mugs?

| | |
|---|---|
| **principal** | the head of a school; main |
| **principle** | basic law or belief |

**Example:** Ms. DeLarios is the **principal** of Walker High School.

Do you think illegal drugs are the **principal** cause of crime?

The scientist explained the **principles** of physics.

| | |
|---|---|
| **right** | correct; direction |
| **write** | compose |

**Example:** How many answers on the test did you get **right**?

After you pass Mason Avenue, turn **right** onto Carson Road.

Ken is going to **write** a memo to the supervisor.

| | |
|---|---|
| **steal** | take illegally |
| **steel** | a hard metal made from iron |

**Example:** The cashier was fired because he tried to **steal** money.

How much **steel** was used to build that skyscraper?

| | |
|---|---|
| **their** | possessive pronoun |
| **there** | that place; expletive |
| **they're** | contraction for "they are" |

**Example:** The carpenters take pride in **their** work.

Put the lumber over **there**.

**There** are five carpenters on this project.

**They're** going to build a new addition to the house.

| | |
|---|---|
| **threw** | past tense of throw |
| **through** | by means of |

**Example:** The pitcher **threw** the baseball to the catcher.

Otto took off his coat as he walked **through** the door.

| | |
|---|---|
| **to** | indicates direction |
| **too** | more than enough; extremely, very; also |
| **two** | the number 2 |

**Example:** Isaac is going **to** the store.

The soup is **too** salty.

Rita is coming, **too**.

I need **two** cans of beans.

| | |
|---|---|
| **wear** | have on |
| **where** | a place |

**Example:** Do you **wear** a uniform at work?

**Where** do you work?

| | |
|---|---|
| **weather** | climate |
| **whether** | if |

**Example:** The forecast said to expect rainy **weather** this week.

I wonder **whether** I should take an umbrella.

## Lesson 4 Exercise

**Directions:** Edit the following sentences for errors in homonyms. Not all of the sentences contain errors.

1. Do you know the principle cause of last week's accident?
2. We could here the crash from four blocks away.
3. The truck made a hole threw that wall.
4. Gene Mills, the driver, had just passed another car when his brakes failed.
5. Gene injured his heal when he slammed his foot against the brake pedal.

Answers are on page A-13.

## REVIEW FOR SKILL 3

**Directions:** Edit the following sentences to correct all errors in spelling. Not all of the sentences contain errors.

1. After she walked her dog, Paula DeSoto accidentally droped her keys into the bushes.
2. Her neighbor Rob Corwin offerred to help look for the keys.
3. Paula and Rob could'nt find the keys because the bushes were too thick.
4. However, Paula's dog Max went right to the keys and brought them to her.
5. The dog's tail wagged as Paula and Rob petted it's head.
6. Have you read the articles about our nations economy?

Chapter 3: Mechanics

**7.** Aren't you concerned about inflation and taxs?

**8.** The whole country seems to be worryed about the cost of food and gas.

**9.** I wonder weather my wages and my spouse's part-time job will be enough to meet our family's needs.

**10.** We're hopeing to save money to see us through next year.

Check your answers. Correct answers are on page A-13. If you have fewer than eight answers correct, study Skill 3 beginning with Lesson 1.

# Writing Skills: Unit II

**The Writing Process** is a series of steps used by writers to help them think about and improve their writing. It includes identifying your writing purpose and audience. Sometimes writing is personal and informal, such as when you write for yourself or to your family and very close friends. Sometimes writing is business-related, such as making a work order, filling out an accident report, or filing a grievance. For business-related writing, you need to spend more time thinking about your ideas, the order of the ideas, and your language. The audience or readers appreciate writing that contains clear ideas and that is logically organized.

## Prereading Prompt

Some people enjoy writing. They write letters to their family and friends. They make lists of things to do. They even write letters to complain about defective products or bad service. Other people feel embarrassed about their writing and think that they can't write. They avoid writing whenever they can.

Reflect on your feelings about writing. When do you enjoy writing? In what instances do you share your writing with someone else? Who is the person you trust to read your writing?

# The Writing Process

## What Is the Writing Process?

In the writing process lessons that follow, you will learn about

- **personal writing**
- **planning your writing**
- **writing, revising, and editing your writing**

You will discover

- how to keep a daily journal
- how to understand essay topics
- how to revise the ideas, organization, and language in your writing
- how to edit for mechanics

The GED Writing Skills Test includes an essay. This part of the test measures your ability to write an essay that explains your opinion on a general topic, which will be given to you. There is no "right" answer or opinion on the essay test. The topic will be broad. Your writing task is to explain your opinion on the assigned topic to other readers. You will have 45 minutes to write a 200 word essay.

Your essay will be evaluated by two readers on a scale of 0 to 6, your total score combining their two grades; for example, a 4 from one reader and a 5 from the other gives you a grade of 9. A zero grade is given if your essay is off the topic or is illegible. The evaluators look at your ability to present your ideas in an organized manner with logical reasons and clear examples. They also look for your ability to use correct grammar.

Unit II provides you with many opportunities to develop and practice your writing skills. Each chapter is divided into lessons, which present instruction, suggestions, and activities for writing. Chapter 1 begins with personal writing, and Chapters 2 and 3 help you practice writing essays for business-related writing and the GED test. When you work on revising and editing in Chapter 3, you may want to review the grammar you learned in Unit I.

As you work through this unit, you should ask another person (a friend or a teacher) to read and respond to your writing. Talking to another person can help you remember your purpose and audience for writing. Another person can also point out things—good points as well as weak points—that you might not see in your own writing.

## Key Words

**Audience**—readers for a piece of writing
**Revise**—to reread (and rewrite) your writing to improve ideas, organization, and language.

# CHAPTER 1
# Personal Writing

## Objective

In this chapter, you will learn how to

- **begin personal writing**

- **keep a daily journal**

- **enjoy your writing**

**Lesson 1**

## Personal Writing

Personal writing is like talking to yourself or to your close friends. When you do personal writing, you write your true feelings, thoughts, and ideas. The audience for the writing is you. Through personal writing, you can sometimes discover why you are worried, frustrated, or angry. Personal writing can also help you analyze your ideas and opinions. Some people discover that they can solve personal problems by writing about them.

By practicing personal writing, you can become more comfortable with writing. The more often you write, the more confident you will become in your ability to express your ideas on paper.

One way to practice personal writing is to start with free writing. In free writing, you write as quickly as possible about a topic and do not worry about correctness or neatness. You are the only person who will read this free writing. The quality of what you write is not important. However, writing quickly and freely is important. Think of free writing as stretching or warm-up exercises for your mind. You can start free writing for five minutes a day and gradually increase the time as you grow more comfortable with personal writing. Free writing is a good way to get into the habit of writing.

# Lesson 1 Activity

**Directions:** Select one of the following topics. Free write for five minutes. Remember to write as quickly as you can. Try not to stop until the five minutes are up. Do not worry about correctness or neatness.

Suggested Topics:

> a favorite possession
> things you like (dislike) about your job
> a person who is very special to you
> your pet peeves
> a favorite television show
> a favorite sport
> a special or recurring dream
> your goals in life
> things that are bothering you

Questions to Think About

1. Did you write as quickly as possible for five minutes?
2. How did you feel during this free writing?
3. Did you write honestly about your opinions and ideas?
4. Did you worry about correctness or neatness?

## Lesson 2 — Keeping a Daily Journal

A good place to keep your personal writing is in a daily journal. Keeping your writing in one place will help you see your growth as a writer. A journal can be a three-ring notebook or a spiral bound notebook.

As you develop the habit of personal writing in your daily journal, gradually increase your free writing to ten minutes a day. Choose different topics that are of interest to you. You can find topics in newspapers, magazines, television, and everyday life. In your journal, you can reflect on your work, your relationships, or experiences and events in your life. Since you are the audience, you can be honest about your personal thoughts and feelings.

Be sure to date your journal entries so that you can remember when you wrote them.

Here are some examples of daily journal entries. Each entry was written by a different person.

"May 5 . . . I really want to look for another job. I'm tired of working the graveyard shift. I never get to see my kids—they're sleeping when I go to work and they're getting ready for school when I come home."

"September 15 . . . I'm really worried about Nick. He's been really quiet these past weeks. I think something's wrong at work, but he won't tell me anything.

He probably doesn't want me to worry. Doesn't he know that it's better to tell me what's wrong than not to tell me? I've got to make him talk to me. Maybe I can help him with whatever's bothering him."

"December 10 . . . I hope Frank won't be called into active duty. His reserve unit was alerted yesterday. This oil crisis in the Middle East has gotten out of hand. I wish the countries would sit down, talk, and find a peaceful solution. I don't know how I'll manage if Frank gets called up."

"June 27 . . . Today was a very special day—my birthday. Jesse, Myron, and Glenda took me out to see 'Dances with Wolves.' I loved the movie! Rhonda sent me a card—I really miss her. It's too bad she had to move away last year. I wonder if she's seen the movie. I wish she could have been with us tonight. She always made me laugh. I hope she's doing okay in Texas."

These entries show the types of writing that might be found in a journal. Remember that you should write about topics that are of interest and importance to you. Do not worry about correctness or neatness because it is your personal writing. Since the writing is personal, no one should read your journal without your permission.

## Lesson 2 Activity

**Directions:** Begin keeping a daily journal today. Record the date of each entry. Select a topic listed below or choose a topic from Lesson 1. You may also choose your own topic. Try to free write for ten minutes. After you have written for ten minutes, reread your journal entry.

Suggested Topics:

     a recent event in your life
     how a political event affects you
     a problem in your family
     something that bothers or worries you
     something that you're proud of
     a relationship you're working on
     a goal you're working toward
     a person you admire and respect
     a situation that is unjust
     advice you need to follow

Questions to Think About

1. Did you feel comfortable writing for ten minutes?
2. Did you write honestly about your thoughts and feelings?
3. As you read your journal entry, did you think of other ideas about which to write?

# Enjoying Your Writing

As you practice personal writing, you will probably become more comfortable and confident in your writing. The following suggestions are other ways to make writing easy and enjoyable.

1. Find a quiet, comfortable place where you can write without being disturbed or distracted.
2. Try to maintain a good pace when you are writing.
3. Concentrate on your ideas, not on correctness.
4. Think of your journal writing as talking to yourself in the mirror. You can also imagine that you are talking with an understanding friend. Think of your writing as a conversation with that friend.

## Lesson 3 Activity

**Directions:** After you have made seven journal entries, reread each entry. For today's journal entry, write your response to the following topic: What I am learning from my journal.

Questions to Think About

1. Which entries are most interesting to read? Why?
2. Are the entries getting longer? More thoughtful? More honest?
3. Do you feel comfortable writing about your thoughts and feelings?

# CHAPTER 2
# Planning the Essay

## Objective

In this chapter, you will learn how to

- **plan an essay using the writing process**

- **understand essay topics**

- **generate ideas**

- **organize ideas**

**Lesson 1**

## The Writing Process

In Chapter 1, you practiced personal writing in a daily journal. Correctness and neatness are not important in personal writing since you are the only audience for the writing.

However, when you write for other people, you need to write more carefully. In order to communicate your ideas accurately to other people, you need to organize and explain your ideas. You also need to use appropriate language and correct spelling, punctuation, and usage.

As you prepare for the GED essay, you should practice writing on different topics. Keep in mind that your audience is other people who do not know what you think. The audience will look at your ability to explain your ideas clearly and to use correct language.

Knowing and using the three-step writing process can help you write effectively and prepare for the GED essay.

STEP 1.  PREWRITING

Prewriting, or planning, is the first step in the writing process. During this step, you select or are given a topic to write about. You think about the audience (readers) for your writing and your purpose for writing. You also generate and organize the ideas for your essay. In prewriting you also create a topic sentence that states your main idea about the subject.

STEP 2. WRITING

After you have generated your ideas, you write the essay, using ideas from your prewriting. Because the audience is people you do not know, you will use appropriate, businesslike language. Since the GED essay is a timed test, you probably will not have time to recopy your essay. Therefore, try to write as neatly as possible during this step. Writing on every other line gives you space to work on your writing as you move to the next step, revising and editing.

STEP 3. REVISING AND EDITING

When you have finished writing the draft, you need to rethink or revise your writing. During revising, you check the quality and logic of the ideas. You add information if it is needed as well as cross out any words or sentences that are not related to the topic or do not develop your main idea. You also change words that are vague or confusing or too informal. Finally, you edit or correct errors in usage, sentence structure, spelling, punctuation, and capitalization.

The three steps in the writing process can be used with any writing topic. The more you practice the writing process, the more comfortable you will feel with writing for an audience of other people.

During the GED essay test, you will have 45 minutes to write. As you practice writing for the GED essay, keep track of how much time you need for each step of the writing process. Different people need different amounts of time for the writing process. Below is a suggested schedule of how you might use the 45 minutes.

| | |
|---|---|
| Prewriting | 10 minutes |
| Writing | 25 minutes |
| Revising and Editing | 10 minutes |

## Lesson 1 Activity

When you took the Predictor Test, you wrote an essay. How many of the steps of the writing process did you use? Answer the following questions.

## Prewriting

1. How did you generate ideas before you began writing?
2. Did you organize your ideas before you began writing?
3. How much time did you spend on prewriting?

    **4.** Did you use your prewriting ideas as you wrote your essay?

    **5.** How much time did you spend writing the essay?

## Revising and Editing

    **6.** After you wrote the essay, did you read it again to see if the ideas made sense?

    **7.** Did you make any changes to make the ideas more understandable or to make the language more formal?

    **8.** Did you correct all errors in usage, sentence structure, spelling, punctuation, and capitalization?

    **9.** How much time did you spend on revising and editing?

Questions to Think About

    **1.** Whenever you answered "yes" to one of the questions, you identified a step of the writing process that you already use. Which steps of the writing process do you already use?

    **2.** Whenever you answered "no," you identified a step that you should learn to use. Which steps of the writing process do you need to learn and practice?

    **3.** Did you complete your writing process within the 45 minutes? As you continue to practice for the GED essay, keep track of the time you spend on each step of the writing process. The time will help you budget the 45 minutes you will have during the GED essay test.

---

## Lesson 2 — Understanding Essay Topics

When you take the second part of the GED Writing Skills Test, you will write an essay on a general topic. You will have 45 minutes to write an essay approximately 200 words long.

You need to understand the topic so that you can write a clear essay. Two people will read and rate your essay according to how well you wrote on the assigned topic. There is no right or wrong answer to the GED essay. When the people read your essay, they will be looking at your ability to (1) state your ideas, (2) support your ideas with reasons and examples, and (3) use correct grammar (usage, sentence structure, and mechanics).

When you are assigned a topic, it is important to take time to understand it. Understanding the essay topic is the first step in planning an essay.

Here is an example of an essay topic.

**TOPIC 1**—Television has been a part of American life for nearly 50 years. Some people think television has a negative effect on American families. Other people think television has a positive effect on American families.

Write an essay of about 200 words explaining whether you think television has a positive or a negative effect on American families. Support your opinion with reasons and examples.

After you have read the essay topic once, use these three steps to help you understand the essay topic.

**NOTE:** On the GED, you develop your essay by responding to a sentence in a short two-paragraph passage. This sentence is usually in the second paragraph.

1.   Underline the important or key words in the essay topic. Make sure you understand the key ideas of the topic.

2.   Make sure you understand your purpose in writing. Most GED essay topics will ask you to explain your opinion or to persuade the readers to agree with your opinion.

3.   Decide on your own point of view. Write one sentence that contains both the key ideas and your own point of view.

Remember that there is no right answer to the topic. What matters is how carefully you explain your opinion on the topic.

Let's apply these three steps to the sample topic.

1.   The key words in the essay topic are <u>television</u>, <u>positive</u> or <u>negative effect</u>, and <u>American families</u>. <u>Explaining</u> is another important word. <u>Nearly 50 years</u> is not an important idea.

2.   Your purpose in writing is to explain your point of view about whether television has a negative or a positive effect on American families.

3.   Write your opinion about the topic by completing the following statement: Television has a _____ effect on American families.

**NOTE:** You do not need to use the words "I think," "I feel," I believe," or "in my opinion" because an essay is understood to be a statement of your personal opinion.

Here are other topics that are similar to the GED topics. You should use these topics to practice your writing in Chapters 2 and 3.

**TOPIC 2**—Many of today's song lyrics contain strong language that refers to sex or violence. Some people want to have a rating system for records in order to protect young children. The rating system would be similar to the rating system used for movies. Other people think a rating system is unnecessary.

Do you agree or disagree with the idea of having a rating system for records? Write an essay of about 200 words explaining your point of view. Support your essay with reasons and examples.

**TOPIC 3**—Most people have an object or possession that is very special to them. For some people, the object is a piece of jewelry or clothing or furniture, a photograph, a book, or a toy.

Think of your favorite objects and select one object that has special meaning to you. In an essay of about 200 words, explain why this object is special. Include reasons that support your explanation.

**TOPIC 4**—Gambling and lotteries are controversial topics for many people. Some people think that gambling and lotteries are good sources of money for states. Other people think that gambling and lotteries encourage illegal activities.

Do you think gambling and lotteries are good ways for states to raise money? In an essay of about 200 words, explain your opinion and provide reasons that support your opinion.

**TOPIC 5**—The managers of a shopping mall are considering a policy that would ban smoking inside the enclosed area. This policy would require people to leave the mall in order to smoke. The managers will vote on the policy after they hear from the shoppers.

Imagine that you are a frequent shopper at this mall. Do you support this policy? In an essay, persuade the managers to pass (or not pass) this policy on smoking.

**TOPIC 6**—A recent newspaper editorial claimed that some people would rather receive welfare assistance than work. The editorial proposed that all able-bodied welfare recipients should be required to work four hours a day in order to participate in welfare programs. The work might involve picking up litter in public parks, delivering food to home-bound senior citizens, or being traffic guards at school crosswalks. The editorial asked readers to respond to its proposal.

Do you think able-bodied welfare recipients should or should not be required to work in order to participate in welfare programs? Write an essay of about 200 words that explains your opinion. Provide reasons and examples to support your opinion.

**TOPIC 7**—Recent surveys show that many teenagers do not take precautions when they engage in sex. Some high school counselors want to provide free condoms to students in order to reduce sexually transmitted diseases and unwanted pregnancies. The counselors want to hear parents' opinions about this idea.

Imagine that you are a parent of a teenager who attends this high school. Do you think high school counselors should or should not provide free condoms to teenagers? Write an essay of about 200 words that persuades the counselors to provide or not provide condoms to teenagers. Provide reasons and examples to support your view.

**TOPIC 8**—Life-support machines can prolong the lives of people who have no chance of recovery. Without the life-support machines, these people would die.

Should the families of dying people be allowed to take them off life-support machines and let them die? Write an essay of about 200 words that explains your opinion on the question. Provide reasons to support your opinion.

**TOPIC 9**—Religious groups are debating the changing role of women in today's churches. Some groups believe that women should be allowed to become priests or ministers. Other groups believe that only men should be priests or ministers.

Do you think women should be allowed to be priests? Write an essay of about 200 words that explains your opinion. Give reasons to support your opinion.

**TOPIC 10**—In some countries, men and women play equal roles in combat situations. However, in the United States, opinions differ on the role of women in combat. Some people believe that women should be allowed to assume the same duties and dangers in combat as men. Other people believe that women should not be allowed to participate in combat.

What is your opinion about women participating in combat? Write an essay that explains your opinion. Provide reasons and examples for your opinion.

**TOPIC 11**—Gun control is a nationally debated issue. Some people think strict gun control laws would reduce crime. Other people think gun control laws are unnecessary and ineffective.

Do you think gun control laws would reduce crime? Explain your opinion in an essay of about 200 words. Include reasons and examples to explain your opinion.

**TOPIC 12**—Many people feel that the death penalty should be used more often to deter murder. Other people feel that the death penalty is not an effective way to deter murder.

What are your feelings about the death penalty? Write an essay of about 200 words that explains why you feel the death penalty should or should not be used to deter murder. Include reasons and examples to support your opinion.

**TOPIC 13**—Some people like living in big cities such as New York, Los Angeles, and Houston. Other people prefer to live in rural farm areas.

If you had your choice of living anywhere in the United States, where would you choose to live? In an essay of about 200 words, name the city or town where you would choose to live. Provide reasons for your choice.

TOPIC 14—With more parents working and raising families, day care has become an important issue. Some people think that employers should provide day care. Other people think that day care is the responsibility of parents, not employers.

Do you think that employers should or should not be required to provide day care for employees? Write an essay of about 200 words that explains your opinion. Provide reasons and examples to support your opinion.

TOPIC 15—Rape is a serious crime that is receiving more coverage in the news. Newspaper and television reporters are debating whether they should or should not reveal the name of rape victims in news reports.

In an essay of about 200 words, give your opinion whether reporters should or should not reveal the name of rape victims. Support your opinion with reasons and examples.

TOPIC 16—Some school districts are thinking about changing to a 12-month school year for students. People in favor of the year-round school say that education will improve. People against year-round school say that teachers and students need a summer vacation.

What is your opinion on changing the public schools to a 12-month school year? Support your opinion with reasons and examples.

## Lesson 2 Activity

**Directions:** Select four different topics from this lesson and apply the three step process to those topics.

Questions to Think About

1. What words did you underline as key ideas in the essay topic?
2. What opinion did you decide to explain?
3. Did you write your opinion about the topic in one complete statement?

Lesson 3

# Generating Ideas

Now that you understand the essay topic, you need to generate the ideas you will use in your writing. By taking time to generate ideas before you write, you can write a better essay.

When you do your prewriting for the GED essay test, you should use a separate sheet of paper. Your prewriting pages will not be evaluated. The readers will look only at your essay, not at your prewriting.

Two ways of generating ideas are brainstorming and clustering.

## Brainstorming

When you brainstorm, you think of as many ideas as you can about your essay topic and write them down in a list as quickly as possible. When you are brainstorming, you do not worry about whether the ideas are good or bad or whether the ideas are spelled correctly. Remember, the purpose of brainstorming is to generate ideas about the topic as quickly as possible.

Here is an example of brainstorming on the sample topic of television's effect on American families. Notice that this writer has decided that television has a positive effect on American families.

*I THINK TELEVISION HAS A POSITIVE EFFECT ON AMERICAN FAMILIES BECAUSE*

*we learn about news events*
*good entertainment for whole family*
*programs for all ages*
*have a 19 inch tv set*
*can learn about elections*
*inexpensive entertainment*
*adults like dramas—LA Law, China Beach, In the Heat of the Night*
*teen shows—Whose the Boss, Fresh Prince of Bel-Air*
*my kids like cartoons, The Simpsons, Dinosaurs*
*too many commercials*
*good animal, nature shows on Discovery Channel*
*convenent entertainment—can stay home rather than go to theater*
*learn about strikes, crime, and natural disasters*
*educational programs for kids—Sesame Street and Reading Rainbow can learn new skills—cooking, drawing, foriegn language*

Notice that the brainstorming ideas are not written in sentences. Even though some ideas may not relate to the topic, no ideas are discarded at this time. Some words are misspelled or are not punctuated correctly. During brainstorming, you do not need to correct these errors.

## Clustering

Clustering is another prewriting strategy. Like brainstorming, you write as many ideas as you can and as quickly as you can. However, clustering helps you draw a picture so that you can see relationships among your ideas.

Here is an example of clustering made by another writer. Notice that this writer's opinion about the topic is written in the circle at the center of the paper. The other ideas come out of the center circle.

Notice that the clustering ideas are not written in sentences. As in brainstorming, no ideas are discarded at this time, and spelling errors are not important.

## Lesson 3 Activity

**Directions:** Select two of the topics you worked on in Activity 2. On one sheet of paper, brainstorm on one of the topics for five to ten minutes. Then, take another sheet of paper and cluster the second topic for five to ten minutes.

Questions to Think About

1. Which of the two prewriting strategies—brainstorming or clustering—generated more ideas for you?

2. Was ten minutes enough time for you to generate ideas? Did you still have more ideas to write?

# Organizing Ideas

After you have brainstormed or clustered your ideas on a topic, you need to organize the ideas. Organizing ideas during prewriting helps you decide which ideas to use (or not to use) in your essay.

Use the following four steps to organize your ideas for writing.

<u>Step 1.</u> Look at all of the ideas from your brainstorming or clustering. Cross out the ideas that do not relate to your writing purpose or to your opinion on the topic. Combine ideas that are similar in meaning.

<u>Step 2.</u> Arrange the ideas into groups. Give the groups titles. The titles will help you remember the main ideas or reasons that support your opinion. If you think of new ideas that relate to these main ideas, add them to your brainstorming or clustering.

<u>STEP 3</u> Decide which group of ideas should come first in your writing. Label that group as #1 to remind you to use these ideas in your first explanatory paragraph. Then, decide the order of the other groups of ideas and label them with the appropriate number.

<u>Step 4.</u> At the bottom of your brainstorming or clustering, write a short sentence for each major idea, in the order of the numbers you have given them.

Let's see how these steps are applied to the brainstorming list shown earlier.

# I THINK TELEVISION HAS A POSITIVE EFFECT ON AMERICAN FAMILIES BECAUSE

1    we learn about news events

2    good entertainment for whole family

     ~~programs for all ages~~

     ~~have a 19 inch tv set~~

1    can learn about elections

2    inexpensive entertainment

2    adults like dramas—LA Law, China Beach, In the Heat of the Night

2    teen shows—Whose the Boss, Fresh Prince of Bel-Air

2    my kids like cartoons, The Simpsons, Dinosaurs

     ~~too many commercials~~

3    good animal, nature shows on Discovery Channel

2    convenent entertainment—can stay home rather than go to theater

1    learn about strikes, crime, and natural disasters

3    educational programs for kids—Sesame Street and Reading Rainbow

3    can learn new skills—cooking, drawing, foriegn language


1. Television provides news.


2. Television provides convenient and inexpensive entertainment.


3. Television can be educational.

Step 1. Notice that this writer has drawn a line through **have a 19 inch tv set** and **too many commercials**. These ideas did not relate to the essay topic or to the writing purpose. The writer has crossed out **programs for all ages** because it is the same idea as **good entertainment for whole family**.

Step 2. This writer has formed three groups of ideas: news, entertainment, and education. Next to each idea, the writer has placed a number to show which group that idea belongs to.

Step 3. The numbers also show the order that this writer will use to support the point of view that television has had a positive effect on American families.

Step 4. At the bottom of the brainstorm list, the writer has written one sentence for each of the major reasons why television has a positive effect on American families.

This writer is ready to write the essay on the positive effect of television on American families.

Let's look at the way the other writer organizes ideas from the clustering.

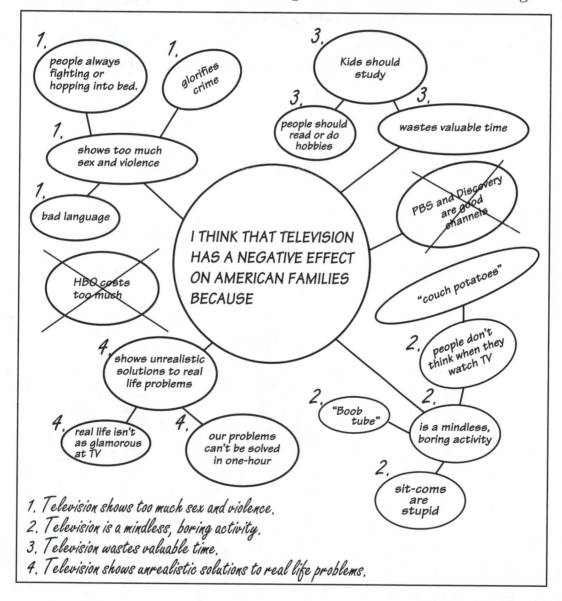

1. _Television shows too much sex and violence._
2. _Television is a mindless, boring activity._
3. _Television wastes valuable time._
4. _Television shows unrealistic solutions to real life problems._

Step 1. This writer has drawn a line through **PBS and Discovery are good channels** and **HBO costs too much** because these ideas do not support the writer's point of view on the negative effect of television.

Step 2. This writer has formed four groups of ideas: too much sex and violence; mindless, boring activity; wastes valuable time; and unrealistic solutions to real-life problems. Next to each idea is a number to show which group the idea belongs to.

Step 3. The numbers also show the order that the writer will use to support the opinion that television has a negative effect on American families.

Step 4. At the bottom of the clustering, the writer has written four sentences about the four main reasons why television has a negative effect on American families.

This writer is ready to write the essay on the negative effect of television on American families.

## Lesson 4 Activity

**Directions:** Use the four steps to organize your brainstorming and clustering ideas from the Lesson 3 Activity.

Questions to Think About

1. Did you eliminate ideas that are similar in meaning? Did you eliminate ideas that do not relate to the topic or to your writing purpose?
2. How did you decide on the groups of ideas?
3. How did you decide the order of the groups of ideas?
4. Did you write a short sentence for each major idea that supports your opinion on the topic?
5. Do you feel ready to write your essay?

# CHAPTER 3
## Writing, Revising and Editing the Essay

## Objective

In this chapter you will learn

- **how to write the essay**

- **how to revise the essay**

- **how to edit the essay**

## Lesson 1

## Writing the Essay

In Chapter 2, you learned how to understand the essay topic, how to generate ideas, and how to organize those ideas. Now it is time to write the essay.

During the GED test, you should plan to spend about 20 to 25 minutes writing the essay based on your prewriting. You should try to write about 200 words. However, the quality of your ideas and language are more important than the actual word count.

When you write the essay, skip a line between your writing so that you will have space to revise and edit your writing. You should use your best handwriting because you will not have time to recopy your essay. If you make a mistake while you are writing, draw a neat line through the mistake. You should also use formal language for this essay.

## Organization of the Essay

Your essay should be organized or arranged in three parts: the *introductory paragraph*, two to three *body paragraphs* (which make up the "body" of your essay), and the *concluding paragraph*. Each paragraph should be indented: that is, its first sentence should start approximately one inch to the right of the left margin.

The *introductory paragraph* rewords the topic, presents your opinion on the topic, and briefly states the major reasons in your argument.

The *body paragraphs* explain the reasons in more detail. Each paragraph in the body should contain one major reason.

The *concluding paragraph* should summarize your ideas and restate your opinion on the topic. You should not present any new reasons in this paragraph.

## Lesson 1 Activity

**Directions:** Select a writing topic from Chapter 2 and do the prewriting. If you wish, you may use one of the topics you have already brainstormed or clustered. Write the essay. Remember to skip lines and to use good handwriting.

Questions to Think About

1. How did you feel while you were writing the essay?
2. Did you use your prewriting ideas to help you write the essay?
3. How many words did you write? Were you near the 200 word guideline?
4. How much time did you spend on the actual essay writing (not including the prewriting)?

## Lesson 2
## Revising the Essay

*Revising* means to "re-see" or "re-think" the piece of writing. When you revise, you reread your essay to make sure that the ideas are organized. You also read to make sure that all the ideas support your topic and point of view.

During the GED Writing Skills Test, you may wish to revise and edit your essay at the same time. You should allow at least five to ten minutes during the test to revise and edit your writing.

However, as you do your own writing and prepare for the test, you may wish to work separately on revising and editing. Use the following questions to help you revise your essay.

## Revising Questions

1. Does the first (introductory) paragraph restate the topic, present your point of view about the topic, and briefly tell the major reasons for your point of view?
2. Does each of the following (body) paragraphs begin with a major reason for your point of view? Is each paragraph indented?
3. Do you give clear examples to support each of your reasons?
4. Does the last (concluding) paragraph restate the topic and summarize your point of view?
5. Do you use formal language in your writing?

Here is a sample essay based on the brainstorming list from Chapter 2. You may notice some errors in usage, sentence structure, capitalization, punctuation, or spelling in this essay. These errors will be discussed and corrected in the next lesson on editing. For now, let's use the revising questions to see how the writer makes changes to improve the organization and ideas of the essay.

Television has been a part of American life for nearly 50 years. I believe that television has had a positive effect on American families. Television provides American families with news, entertainment, and education.

Television provides news for Americans. When Americans watch the news on television, they see important local, national, and international events such as elections, strikes, crimes, and natural disasters. Knowing about these events makes people better.

Television provides an inexpensive and convenent form of entertainment. People do not have to pay for movie tickets at a theater, they can watch television in their homes. They provide entertainment for all members of the family. Adults like to watch shows like L.A. Law, China Beach, and In the Heat of the Night. Teens like Whose the Boss, and Fresh Prince of Bel-Air. My kids are hooked on cartoons, Dinosaurs, and The Simpsons.

Television can also be educational. The Discovery Channel has shows about animals, cultures, and regions of the world. Some people with hobbys watching programs that teach cooking, drawing. Young children learn the alphabet and numbers on Sesame Street and they learn good citizenship on Mr. Rogers Neighborhood. In fact, you can even learn another language by watching a foriegn language class on television.

Americans were fortunate to have television in their homes. As long as families have televisions, they will have access to news, entertainment, and education.

**REVISING QUESTION 1.** Does the first (introductory) paragraph restate the topic, present your point of view about the topic, and briefly tell the major reasons for your point of view?

In the first paragraph, the first sentence restates the topic, and the second sentence presents the writer's point of view on the topic. The third sentence gives the three major reasons. The first paragraph provides a good introduction to the essay.

**REVISING QUESTION 2.** Does each of the following (body) paragraphs begin with a major reason for your point of view? Is each paragraph indented?

In the second paragraph, the writer presents the first major reason—**Television provides news for Americans**. In the third paragraph, the second major reason—**Television provides entertainment**—is discussed. The third major reason—**Television can be educational**—is presented in the fourth paragraph. The last paragraph summarizes the writer's ideas and restates the writer's opinion on the topic. Each paragraph is indented.

**REVISING QUESTION 3.** Do you give clear examples to support each of your reasons?

At the end of the second paragraph, the writer noticed that the last sentence needed another word to make the meaning clearer. The writer decided to add the word **citizens** because good citizens watch the news.

In the fourth paragraph, the writer noticed that this sentence did not talk about education: **The Discovery Channel has shows about animals, cultures, and regions of the world.** The writer decided to add the words **that teach viewers**. The word **teach** refers to the paragraph's major idea, education. In that same paragraph, the writer thought of another example to go with **cooking** and **drawing**. The writer added **gardening** to the list of ideas.

In each of the body paragraphs, the writer provides clear examples to support the writer's point of view that television has a positive effect on American families.

**REVISING QUESTION 4.** Does the last (concluding) paragraph restate the topic and summarize your point of view?

The writer summarizes the topic and restates the point of view in the last paragraph. This paragraph is a good conclusion to the essay.

**REVISING QUESTION 5.** Do you use formal language in your writing?

The writer reread the essay and looked for words that were too informal. The last sentence of the third paragraph began with **My kids are hooked on**. The writer decided to change the words to **Children are entertained by**. These words are more formal, and they refer to the paragraph's major idea, entertainment.

Here is how the essay looks with the writer's revisions. Notice how the writer changed and added words to the essay. Because the writer skipped lines, the writer could easily make changes and add words during revision. The readers will be able to read and understand the changes in the essay.

Television has been a part of American life for nearly 50 years. I believe that television has had a positive effect on American families. Television provides American families with news, entertainment, and education.

Television provides news for Americans. When Americans watch the news on television, they see important local, national, and international events such as elections, strikes, crimes, and natural disasters. Knowing about these events makes people better *citizens* ∧.

Television provides an inexpensive and convenent form of entertainment. People do not have to pay for movie tickets at a theater, they can watch television in their homes. They provide entertainment for all members of the family. Adults like to watch shows like L.A. Law, China Beach, and In the Heat of the Night. Teens like Whose the Boss, and Fresh Prince of Bel-Air. ∧ *Children are entertained by* ~~My kids a hooked on~~ cartoons, Dinosaurs, and The Simpsons.

Television can also be educational. The Discovery Channel has shows ∧about *That teaches viewers* animals, cultures, and regions of the world. Some people with hobbys watching programs that teach cooking, drawing∧ *and gardening*. Young children learn the alphabet and numbers on Sesame Street and they learn good citizenship on Mr. Rogers Neighborhood. In fact, you can even learn another language by watching a foriegn language class on television.

Americans were fortunate to have television in their homes. As long as families have televisions, they will have access to news, entertainment, and education.

# Lesson 2 Activity

**Directions:** Use the questions in this lesson to revise your essay from Lesson 1.

Questions to Think About

1. Did you make any changes in the organization of your essay?
2. Did you make any changes or add any examples to make the ideas clearer?
3. Did you change any words to make the language more formal?
4. Which revising questions were most helpful to you?
5. How much time did you spend revising?

**Lesson 3**

# Editing the Essay

In Unit I, you learned about usage, sentence structure, and capitalization, punctuation, and spelling. When you edit an essay, you apply these grammar rules to your own writing. *Editing* means reading a piece of writing to correct problems in usage, sentence structure, capitalization, punctuation, and spelling.

During the GED test, be sure to spend at least five to ten minutes revising and editing your essay. Some writers like to revise and edit at the same time. Other writers like to revise and edit separately.

Use these questions to help you edit your essay.

## Usage

1. Do the subject and verb in each sentence agree?
2. Are the verb tenses correct and consistent throughout the essay?
3. Do all pronouns clearly refer to and agree with their antecedents?

## Sentence Structure

4. Are all sentences complete and correctly punctuated?
5. Are coordinators and subordinators used correctly?
6. Are all sentences written simply and clearly?

# Capitalization, Punctuation, Spelling

**7.** Are words capitalized correctly?

**8.** Are punctuation, especially commas and apostrophes, used correctly?

**9.** Are all words, especially homonyms, spelled correctly?

When you are editing your essay, you should make the corrections neatly and clearly so that the readers can easily read your writing. Drawing neat lines through misspellings and inserting correct spellings show that you know how to edit for the mechanics of writing.

Let's use the editing questions to understand how the writer edited the essay.

## Editing for Usage

In paragraph 3, the writer changed **They provide** to **Television provides**. It was not clear what the pronoun **They** referred to. When the writer replaced **They** with **Television**, the writer made the verb **provides** agree with **Television**.

When the writer reread this paragraph, the writer noticed the overuse of the words **show** and **like**. In the fourth sentence, the writer decided to replace **shows** with **dramas**. In the fifth sentence, the writer replaced **like** with **laugh with**. **Dramas** and **laugh with** are more colorful words than **shows** and **like**. **Dramas** and **laugh with** also relate to the idea of entertainment.

In paragraph 4, the last sentence used the pronoun **you**. The writer replaced **you** with **people**.

In paragraph 5, the writer noticed an incorrect verb tense in the first sentence. The writer changed **were** to **are** because the essay is written in the present tense. In the next sentence, the pronoun **they** could refer to **families** or **televisions**. The writer decided to change **they** to **Americans**.

## Editing for Sentence Structure

In paragraph 3, the writer found a run-on sentence: **People do not have to pay for movie tickets at a theater, they can watch television in their homes.** The writer decided to correct the run-on sentence by replacing the comma with a period and capitalizing **They**.

In the fourth paragraph, the writer noticed that the third sentence is a fragment. **Some people with hobbys watching programs that teach cooking, drawing, and gardening**. The writer corrected the fragment by changing the verb **watching** to **watch**. The sentence now reads: **Some people with hobbys watch programs that teach cooking, drawing, and gardening**. (Spelling will be corrected later.)

# Editing for Capitalization, Punctuation, and Spelling

In paragraph 3, the writer changed the spelling of **convenent** to **convenient**. The writer inserted a comma between **inexpensive** and **convenient**. The comma takes the place of **and. Inexpensive** and **convenient** describe **form**. The writer replaced **Whose** with **Who's** (**who's** means **who is**). The writer also removed the comma after **Boss.**

In paragraph 4, the writer changed the spelling of **hobbys** to **hobbies**. The writer inserted a comma after **Street** because **and** begins the second main idea. The writer put a comma after **drawing** because commas separate three or more items in a series. The writer added an apostrophe to **Mr. Rogers'** to show possession. The writer changed the spelling of **foriegn** to **foreign**.

Here is how this writer edited the essay on television. Notice the marks that the writer used to show corrections in spelling and punctuation. All of the changes are easy to read and understand.

---

Television has been a part of American life for nearly 50 years. I believe

that television has had a positive effect on American families. Television provides

American families with news, entertainment, and education.

Television provides news for Americans. When Americans watch the news on

television, they see important local, national, and international events, such as

elections, strikes, crimes, and natural disasters. Knowing about these events

             *citizens*

makes people better ∧.

                        ,          *convenient*

Television provides an inexpensive ∧ and ~~convenent~~ ∧ form of entertainment.

                                  . T

People do not have to pay for movie tickets at a theater, t∧hey can watch televi-

                  *Television*    *s*

sion in their homes. ~~They~~ ∧ provide ∧ entertainment for all members of the family.

             *dramas,*

Adults like to watch ∧ ~~shows~~ like L.A. Law, China Beach, and In the Heat of the

---

Night. Teens ~~like~~ *laugh with* ∧ ~~Whose~~ *Who's* ∧ the Boss and Fresh Prince of Bel-Air. ∧ *Children are entertained by* ~~My kids a~~

~~hooked on~~ cartoons, Dinosaurs, and The Simpsons.

Television can also be educational. The Discovery Channel has shows ∧*that teach viewers* about

animals, cultures, and regions of the world. Some people with ~~hobbys~~ *hobbies* ∧ watch

programs that teach cooking, drawing∧*,and gardening*. Young children learn the alphabet and

numbers on Sesame Street and they learn good citizenship on Mr. Rogers'∧

Neighborhood. In fact, you can even learn another language by watching a

∧*foreign* ~~foreign~~ language class on television.

Americans ∧*are* ~~were~~ fortunate to have television in their homes. As long as families have

television, ∧*Americans* ~~they~~ will have access to news, entertainment, and education.

**Directions:** Use the questions in this lesson to edit your own essay.

Questions to Think About

1. Did you make any corrections in usage?
2. Did you make any corrections in sentence structure?
3. Did you make any corrections in capitalization, punctuation, or spelling?
4. In which area(s) did you need to make the most corrections?
5. How much time did you spend in editing your essay?
6. What have you learned about writing an essay?
7. Do you feel proud of your writing efforts?

# Unit III

# READINGS IN SOCIAL STUDIES AND SCIENCE

Television news and talk shows, newspapers and magazines, even movies and novels constantly show us people of different nations, races and religions, both living in the United States and all around the world. The lives of all these people are shaped by the history of their group, by the land and climate of their native country, by the type of government under which and by all the beliefs and customs that define what is called their culture, or way of life—including food, dress, religion, sexual rules, art, music and sports. Social Studies is the study of all these different subjects. The content of science has just as great an influence on our daily lives. Nutrition, and health issues, such as pollution, AIDS, and the bad effects of smoking and fatty diets, have made nearly everyone more aware of biology (the study of the body) and of chemistry (the study of the basic composition, or makeup, of physical life). Controversies about nuclear power and nuclear weapons constantly bring physics (the study of energy and motion) into our lives.

The GED test covers the content areas of Social Studies in the following percentages: History, 25%; Economics, 20%; Political Science, 20%; Behavioral Science—which includes sociology, anthropology, and psychology—20%; and Geography, 15%. The exam tests the areas of science in these percentages: Biology, 50%; Earth Science, 20%; Chemistry, 20%; Physics, 10%.

The exam also covers reading skills in certain percentages. The questions in Social Studies and Science will be 20% *Comprehension* (the ability to understand details and summarize information), 30% *Application* (the ability to understand ideas and apply them to new situations), 30% *Analysis* (the ability to identify cause-and-effect relationships and to distinguish statements of fact from conclusions and underlying beliefs, and 20% *Evaluation* (the ability to judge whether statements are logical or have enough support, and how an author's values may have shaped them. Thirty percent of the questions in both Social Studies and Science will concern graphic material (tables, charts, and graphs.)

The two GED tests at the end of this book—the Practice Items and the Simulated Test—test these content areas and reading skills in the same percentages as on the GED exam.

To prepare you for these tests and for the GED, this unit integrates reading instruction and content material throughout. On the GED, you need only a knowledge of the basic concepts of Social Studies and Science; the exam tests your ability to read and think, not your recall of information. In every lesson of this unit, you will learn how to apply reading skills to content material in Social Studies and Science and how to use these skills to answer GED-type questions. A detailed answer key for each question will explain the thinking process needed to find the correct answer and why the incorrect answers are wrong. *Read the instructional answer keys carefully; they are the best way to teach yourself how to use reading skills to pass the GED.*

# Unit III  Progress Chart

# Readings in Social Studies and Science

Use the following chart to keep track of your work. When you complete a lesson, circle the number of questions you answered correctly in the Lesson Exercise. The numbers in color represent scores at a level of 60% or better.

| Lesson | Page | | |
|---|---|---|---|
| | | **CHAPTER 1: Social Studies** | |
| 1 | 156 | The Social Sciences that Make Up Social Studies | 1 2 3 |
| 2 | 161 | How Social Scientists Report Information | 1 2 3 4 |
| 3 | 167 | The Making of the United States | 1 2 3 |
| 4 | 172 | Regional Differences | 1 2 3 |
| 5 | 178 | Industrial Growth of the United States | 1 2 3 |
| 6 | 185 | Government and Political Science | 1 2 3 4 |
| 7 | 193 | Economics: Systems and Measures | 1 2 3 |
| 8 | 202 | Geography | 1 2 3 |
| 9 | 208 | Anthropology and Sociology | 1 2 3 |
| 10 | 214 | Psychology | 1 2 3 |
| | | **CHAPTER 2: Science** | |
| 1 | 222 | Cells—The Basic Units of Life | 1 2 3 |
| 2 | 226 | Reproduction and Heredity | 1 2 3 4 |
| 3 | 233 | The Systems of the Human Body | 1 2 3 |
| 4 | 240 | The Kingdoms and Systems of Nature | 1 2 3 |
| 5 | 246 | Behavior and Evolution | 1 2 3 |
| 6 | 251 | The Earth: Its Structure, Origin, and Place | 1 2 3 |
| 7 | 257 | The Earth: Its Atmosphere, Weather, and Climate | 1 2 3 |
| 8 | 263 | The Structure of Matter | 1 2 3 |
| 9 | 271 | Chemical Reactions and Energy | 1 2 3 |
| 10 | 277 | The World of Physics | 1 2 3 |

# CHAPTER 1

What *one* thing makes Earth different from all the other planets? *Life*. The life form that affects us most from day to day is human beings—people. Social studies is the study of people: where they live, how they live, what affects the way they live, and the groups in which they live.

Credit: Marc Anderson

## Prereading Prompt

"The social state is at once so natural, so necessary, and so habitual to man, that . . . he never conceives himself otherwise than as a member of a body." John Stuart Mill said this in the 19th century. If we could, how many of us would choose to live completely alone, cut off from friends and family? If people lived separately from each other, do you think human civilization would be where it is today?

154

# SOCIAL STUDIES

# Introduction to Social Studies

## What Is Social Studies?

Examining one major event of the 1990s can illustrate the ways social studies helps us understand our world. In 1990 and 1991, a stunned world watched as the countries of Central and Eastern Europe (East Germany, Czechoslovakia, and Hungary among others) fought for their freedom from the Soviet form of government. The free world cheered as millions of people gained their independence from governments that dictated how people must live. Finally, something happened that most of us thought we'd never see in our lifetime—the Soviet Union itself collapsed.

There are hundreds of questions to ask about this chain of events. What caused all these people to rebel against this form of government? Is there something in human nature that makes people need to be free? Will the transition to new governments be smooth, or will there be economic and personal hardship as people struggle to make order in their newfound freedom? What countries will now become friendly toward these newly free nations? Will people in these countries become depressed over losing the only way of life they've known? Or will they find new reasons for living now that they are free?

The more you learn about the events in Central and Eastern Europe, the more questions you will have. This is true of any event in any society. Social studies can help you find answers and make sense of all these complex issues. It can help you use the past to learn about the present, and it can organize information to give you a sense of order and place in a vast and ever-changing world.

## Key Words

**social studies**—a branch of study that examines people in society, both past and present

**society**—a group of people that shares a political and economic system, language, and history

# The Social Sciences That Make Up Social Studies

---

## Prereading Prompt

Very often, things that appear to have only one part are made up of many different, related parts, or branches. Even a simple object, such as a textbook, has a cover, chapters, a contents page, an index, and a glossary. This is also true of fields of study. Social studies is made up of several different, related fields of study called the social sciences.

---

## Key Words

**history**—the study of people and events in the past

**geography**—the study of the relationship between the Earth and its inhabitants

**economics**—the study of how a country's wealth is made and distributed

**political science**—the study of the world's governments

**behavioral science**—the study of why people act the way they do as individuals and in groups

The words *social* and *society* have a common Latin origin, meaning *partner* or *sharer*. The social sciences, therefore, are concerned with people and their relationships. Five main branches of study fall under the general heading of the social sciences: history, geography, economics, political science, and behavioral science.

The five social sciences are closely related. When you study one, such as history, you will almost certainly study another, such as political science or geography. Very likely, depending on the depth of your study, you will touch on all five branches to some degree. You can see how this would happen with a subject such as the American Civil War.

**History**, the record of actual events and people of a given time, would be your primary branch of study in this case. It is history—dates, names, and facts—that most of us think of when we think of social studies. In studying the history of the Civil War, you would learn about the people who played a major role in the events of the time: Abraham Lincoln, Stephen A. Douglas, Frederick Douglass, Ulysses S. Grant, Robert E. Lee, Nat Turner, and Dred Scott, to name just a few. You would also study the dates and details of specific battles in the war, with information as to why a given battle was a turning point for the North or another one was a terrific blow for the South. Since history includes the history of ideas, you also would study the fundamental contradiction of this great struggle: how a democratic society based on the idea of equality and justice for all was able to support an extensive slave system.

**Geography**, the study of physical features of the Earth and how these features affect people, played a major role in the Civil War. When learning about this period, you would probably learn facts related to this social science as well. For example, one of the key issues in the battle between the North and South—slavery—existed because the conditions in the South were well suited to agriculture. The rich soil and warm, moist climate were ideal for growing cotton and other crops, and this is how most Southerners made their living. In the North, the rocky soil and cooler climate made farming less profitable. As a result, the North became primarily an industrial region. The slavery issue, so central to the Civil War, developed out of the fact that the South needed inexpensive labor to work the land.

The South's need for inexpensive labor touches on another branch of the social sciences—**economics**, or the study of how people's wealth is made and distributed. The issues of the Civil War were in large part economic. The type of farming done in the South required huge numbers of people to plant and pick the crops. Farming would not have been profitable for Southerners if they had had to pay regular wages for this work. Though some slave owners freed their slaves before the war on moral grounds, most embraced slavery on economic grounds and therefore justified it morally. In the North, where the economy relied on industry, manufacturing generally did not require the huge numbers of workers that plantation farming did. Southerners supported slavery because their economy depended on it. If the abolitionists in the North had gotten their way, the economy of the South would have collapsed.

**Political science**, the study of government, is another branch of the social sciences you would study when looking at the Civil War. The power struggles of politics always influence the direction of history. In the election of 1860, the South threatened to leave the union if Lincoln, an antislavery candidate, was elected. This threat was not strong enough to keep Lincoln from being elected, and the Southern states did, in fact, leave the union and form their own government. The old government and the new went to battle, each with its own flag, laws, currency, and armies. Not until the end of the war did the United States become reunited.

In studying the Civil War, the three **behavioral sciences** would also help you understand what the conflict was all about. *Psychology*, the study of the mind, would give you insight into how it felt to be a Northerner or a Southerner. You might also learn about the mental anguish of President Lincoln, or the social—public rather than private—motives of generals Grant and Lee. *Sociology*, which is the study of the relationships people have with one another, could yield very interesting information about the effects of slavery on family life, or the unique relationship between slaves and their owners. Finally, *anthropology*, the study of groups of people, would be very useful in studying the Civil War. Using this behavioral science, you could analyze the cultural differences—differences in customs, beliefs, and lifestyles—between the North and the South.

# Using Context Clues

On the GED text, you may find that you do not know the meaning of all the words used. If you know how to use context clues, you will still be able to understand the material. When something is "in context," it is in surroundings that shape its meaning to some degree. These surroundings are the other words and sentences in the passage. They can help you find the meaning of an unfamiliar word or phrase.

Look again at the previous passage on the social sciences. Many of the words that might be unfamiliar, such as *sociology* and *anthropology*, are actually defined, or explained, immediately after they are used. This is one type of context clue: a **definition**.

When unfamiliar words are not directly defined, their meaning may be given indirectly by other words that come right after them and restate their meaning. Look at the last paragraph in the lesson above. Even if you didn't know the meaning of the phrase "cultural differences," you can understand it from the words right after it:—"differences in customs, beliefs, and lifestyles." This kind of clue is called a **paraphrase**.

Similar to paraphrase is **parallelism**. When two separate statements talk about the same thing in different words but mean the same thing, the statements are said to be parallel. In the fourth paragraph of the lesson, you are told that the "conditions" in the South were "well suited to agriculture." In the following sentence you are told that the South's soil and climate were "ideal for growing cotton and other crops." If you did not understand the word "agriculture," you could figure it out: "conditions" is parallel to "soil and climate" and "well suited" is parallel to "ideal"; therefore, agriculture must mean "growing cotton and other crops."

Now find the word *abolitionists* in paragraph five. This word refers to people whose point of view is *opposite* or *very different from* the point of view of the

Southerners in the sentence before it. That sentence tells you that Southerners supported slavery because their economy depended on it. You are told that the Southern economy would collapse if the "abolitionists" got their way. From this you can tell that abolitionists were people who wanted to do away with—abolish—slavery. This kind of clue is called **contrast**.

Now read the following paragraph and use context clues to answer the question.

> Most of the Civil War was fought on Southern territory. This should have been a tremendous asset to the Southerners, helping them to win the war. Southerners were familiar with the land; they were among their own people; they were accustomed to the hot weather; and they didn't have to move troops huge distances to fight battles. Unfortunately, this was not enough for them to win the war.

An *asset* is most likely

**(1)** a battle fought on home territory

**(2)** a disadvantage

**(3)** a military term meaning "successful battle"

**(4)** something that produces wealth

**(5)** something that is useful or valuable

The correct answer is (5). The phrase that follows this word tells you an asset *helped* the South win the war. Choice (1) is incorrect because it is too specific; it is only one thing that was an advantage to the South. There is no basis for choosing choice (2) because everything in the paragraph refers to things that *helped* the South. Choice (3) is not totally unreasonable, but the meaning is really too limited to make sense in this paragraph. You can rule out choice (4) because nothing in the paragraph refers to economics or making money.

# Lesson 1 Exercise

Items 1-3 are based on the following passage.

Laura Ingalls Wilder wrote a series of books that chronicles one family's life during the 1800s. The stories detail the daily events of their lives, focusing on the family's deprivation—they had little to live on—and their struggle to survive in the wilderness. These wonderful books, which were made into a popular TV series, *The Little House on the Prairie*, follow the family as they migrate by covered wagon from Wisconsin through Kansas, Minnesota, and finally into the Dakota Territory.

1. What is the most likely meaning of *chronicles* as used in this paragraph?

    (1) writes books
    (2) writes stories about family life
    (3) writes a series of books
    (4) records a history of events
    (5) writes stories for television

2. *Deprivation* probably means

    (1) a struggle for survival
    (2) a state or condition of poverty
    (3) an attempt to better one's life
    (4) a condition of sadness
    (5) the break-up of a family

3. The most likely meaning of the word *migrate* is

    (1) adjust to a new way of life
    (2) adjust to a new place
    (3) move from one country or region to another
    (4) take a long trip before returning home
    (5) coped with hardship

Answers are on page A-14.

## Lesson 2

# How Social Scientists Report Information

## Prereading Prompt

You probably see graphs every day in newspapers, magazines, and ads. Graphs give you a picture of collections of facts on a topic—the rise in the cost of living, the parts of a city budget, the different numbers of students getting GED diplomas in different states. Graphs are also widely used by social scientists. Learn about graphs—and statistics—in this lesson.

## Key Words

**quantified**—put into numbers

**statistics**—information in the form of numbers about a particular subject

Social scientists gather information by interviewing people and by doing studies. Scientifically controlled studies pull together all kinds of information, which is then **quantified**, or put into numbers. For example, the **population** of various states is information in the form of numbers.

**Statistics**—information in the form of numbers—can be used by scientists and organized so as to give more information. Social scientists use statistics to show trends in society, such as increases or decreases in the number and types of crime committed or the average income of various groups. By studying statistics, social scientists can examine the causes of problems and arrive at possible solutions.

When social scientists report information, they need a quick, clear way of showing and organizing statistics. **Graphs** are very useful for this purpose because they are pictures that show information. Three kinds of graphs are *bar graphs*, *circle graphs*, and *line graphs*.

## Bar Graphs

The figure below is a bar graph. As with any graph, the first thing you should do is read the title. The title indicates that this particular graph shows information on the amount of money people in Alphaville earn yearly and how much education these people have. The next thing you should look at in a bar graph is the **vertical axis**, the line that runs up and down the left side of the graph. On this graph, the vertical axis shows the *Average Income per Year*. Now look at the **horizontal axis**, which is the line that runs across the bottom of the graph. On this graph, the horizontal axis shows *Education Completed*. This graph combines two sets of statistics to show how much money people with a given level of education make in a year in Alphaville. To understand the graph, draw an imaginary line from the top of any bar to the vertical axis. For example, look at the bar for people completing high school. If you draw a line to the vertical axis, the line will fall just above $20,000. So high school graduates in Alphaville make an average of $21,000 a year.

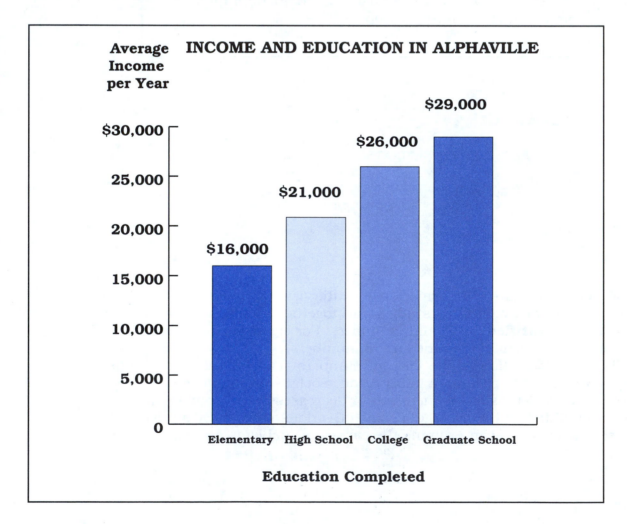

# Circle Graphs

A circle graph shows the parts of a circle like the pieces of a pie. Each part represents a percentage of the whole, the whole being 100%. Look at the circle graph that follows.

As always, first read the title of the graph. This one tells you that the graph contains information from the 1990 census. It shows the size of the various ethnic groups currently in the country. Now look at each "slice of the pie." Some, like the one labelled "White," are quite large. White people made up 80.3% of the U.S. population in 1990. Other parts of the circle are considerably smaller. Asians, for example, represent only 2.9% of the U.S. population. If you were told to add up the percentages in all the "slices" shown, the total would be 100% of the population of the United States.

Why put these statistics in the form of a circle graph? Quickly, without looking at the numbers, figure out which is the smallest ethnic group in the country. You should have immediately been able to locate the Native Americans as the smallest group. This is the beauty of information in graphic form. The statistics are organized in such a way that using them is greatly simplified.

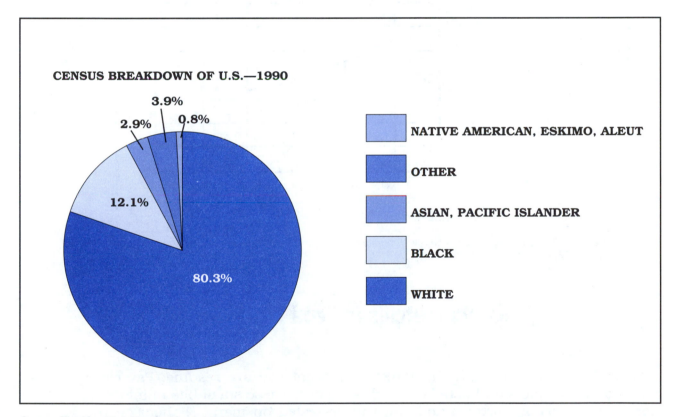

Source: The New York Times, March 11, 1991, page 1.

## Line Graphs

Like a bar graph, a line graph also uses a vertical axis and a horizontal axis. Look at the graph entitled "Crude Oil Production." Along the vertical axis, the production of oil is shown in millions of barrels per day. Along the horizontal axis, the years 1980-1984 are listed. Points are marked on the line to represent each year, and then those points are connected like a connect-the-dots game. The points on the graph show how many millions of barrels per day were produced in each year from 1980 to 1984. You find this number by drawing an imaginary line from the point out to the vertical axis. In 1980, for example, the point falls at about 27 million barrels per day. In 1984, it is about 16 million barrels per day. In addition to giving you this information, the line graph shows the general trend of oil production during these years. Simply by seeing the downward slope of the line you can tell that oil production decreased between 1980 and 1984.

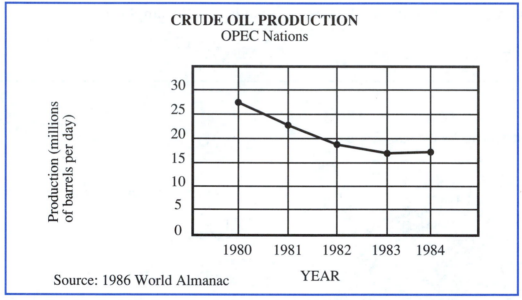

Source: 1986 World Almanac

## Finding Details in Text and Graphs

When you read a paragraph, think about what you are reading. Pay close attention to the facts and details in each sentence. These small bits of information can be very important, and you will be tested on many of them on the GED. When you read a passage of text, think about these questions: Who? What? Where? When? How? The answers to these questions will give you the details of the passage.

When you read a graph, notice its title, the description of each axis, and the statistics shown. When answering a detail question, go back to the text or graph to check your answer.

Read the following paragraph, look at the graph, and answer the questions. A time line is a graph that is usually laid out on a horizontal line. It shows a period of time during which certain events happened. The earliest date is on the left, and the most recent date is on the right. By examining the title and the other information given, you can see that this time line shows when the listed countries gained their independence. For example, the United States became independent in 1776. France did not become independent until 1789.Examine the time line carefully. Then try to answer the following questions from memory. Go back to the paragraph or the time line to check your answers. Use the paragraph to answer question 1 and the time line to answer question 2.

From *The Cambridge Comprehensive Program for the High School Equivalency Examination.* Copyright ©1987 Prentice Hall Regents.

1. According to the paragraph, the United States gained its independence

   (1) after France
   (2) at the same time as France
   (3) before France
   (4) in 1779
   (5) in 1789

The paragraph tells you the correct answer is (3). The United States became independent in 1776, thirteen years before France.

2. According to the time line, Paraguay became independent in

   (1) 1830
   (2) 1825
   (3) 1816
   (4) 1811
   (5) 1822

The correct answer is (4), 1811. Look at the data directly over the word *Paraguay* in the time line. You will see the date clearly marked.

Item 1 is based on the following paragraph.

> ...the speed at which the country's racial mix was altered in the 1980s was breathtaking, Census Bureau figures show. The rate of increase in the minority population was nearly twice as fast as in the 1970s. And much of the surge was among those of Hispanic ancestry, an increase of 7.7 million people or 56%, over 1980.

From *The New York Times*, Monday, March 11, 1991 Copyright ©1991 by The New York Times Company. Reprinted by permission.

1. According to the paragraph, the Hispanic population of the United States is currently

   (1) twice the size it was in the 1970s
   (2) 7.7 million
   (3) 56% larger than it was in the 1970s
   (4) 56% of the white population in the U.S.
   (5) 7.7 million greater than it was in 1980

Items 2 and 3 are based on the lesson selection and graph.

2. In paragraph 1, what does the word *quantified* mean?

   (1) put into effect
   (2) put into pictorial form
   (3) put into correct form
   (4) put into cause and effect
   (5) put into numerical form

3. According to the bar graph on page 162, what is the average yearly income of the holders of graduate school degrees in Alphaville?

   (1) $28,000
   (2) $29,000
   (3) $20,000
   (4) $18,000
   (5) $21,000

4. According to the line graph on page 164, crude oil production did not change between

   (1) 1980 and 1981
   (2) 1981 and 1982
   (3) 1982 and 1983
   (4) 1983 and 1984
   (5) 1982 and 1984

Answers are on page A-14.

# The Making of the United States

## Prereading Prompt

During a sporting event or other competition you usually want your class, school, or home team to win. People like to feel they belong to a group, and they like to see it succeed. This was the case when a group of English people settled in America in the 17th century. After a while, they no longer felt like English people, and they wanted what was best for their new country, not for England.

## Key Words

**majority rule**—following the decision reached by the largest number of people

**Boston Tea Party**—the incident in which colonists threw tea overboard in rebellion against new English taxes on tea and other goods

**Bill of Rights**—amendments to the Constitution that helped guarantee the rights of individuals

## From the Colonies to the Revolutionary War

In 1620, the Pilgrims came here from England in search of religious freedom. They landed at Plymouth, Massachusetts. On the voyage across the Atlantic, they drafted the Mayflower Compact. This agreement stated that the colonists would govern themselves by **majority rule**; they would vote on important decisions, and the idea voted for by the most people would be followed. This was the beginning of democracy in America.

By the 1700s, town meetings were being held in the New England colonies. People decided together on how things should be done in their communities. They even sent **representatives**, or people who would speak for them, when there were meetings of several colonies. At first, these attempts at self-rule did not cause a problem with England. England was having her own problems and was content to let the colonists handle their own affairs. However, this was to change in the latter part of the century. The French and Indian War, fought between England and France, put England deeply in debt. England was spending money to defend the colonies and felt justified in taxing them to raise money.

In 1765, the English crown put the **Stamp Act** into effect. It forced the colonies to pay a tax on all printed matter, from newspapers to legal documents. Documents are official papers, such as proof of ownership or proof of sale. When the colonists became angry about the Stamp Act, England **repealed** it, or did away with it. But in 1767, England put into effect the Townshend Acts, which placed new taxes on tea, glass, paint, and paper—things the colonists could not make for themselves and had to import from England. The colonists were so angered by this that they threw all the tea from English cargo ships into the Boston Harbor, an event which came to be known as the **Boston Tea Party**.

In response to the Boston Tea Party, England closed the port of Boston and cracked down on self-government in the Massachusetts colony. This made the colonists even angrier. They protested to England and formed an army. In 1775, fighting broke out, marking the beginning of the **Revolutionary War**. The colonists issued the **Declaration of Independence** in 1776. It contained many of the basic ideas that would form the backbone of government of the United States of America.

## States' Rights and the Federal Government

After seven years of fighting, the Revolutionary War was over. The colonies and England signed the **Treaty of Paris**, and the colonies became independent of England. The states were joined together by the **Articles of Confederation** in 1781. However, this was a weak contract. An example of this weakness was that Congress had the power to declare war but not to recruit an army.

The states were like separate countries; they taxed each others' goods, had different currencies, or money, and one state's laws could not be enforced in another state. The central government was very weak, and the states in different geographic areas had different problems and viewpoints.

In 1786, a group of farmers in Massachusetts took part in an uprising to protest government policies toward farmers in debt. This became known as **Shays's Rebellion**. The Articles of Confederation did not allow for the government to put down the rebellion, clearly demonstrating the need for a stronger central government. In response to this and many other problems, representatives from the states met in Philadelphia and drafted the **Constitution** in 1787. It was adopted in 1788.

Getting the Constitution **ratified**, or approved, was a true exercise in politics. There were numerous issues to be resolved, and numerous fears to be dealt with. For one thing, many people were afraid of a strong central government, fearing that individual freedoms would be sacrificed. Another major issue was how to fairly represent all the people and all the states in a federal government. The large states wanted representation based on population; this would give them an advantage because they had more people. The smaller states naturally thought this unfair and wanted each state to have equal representation regardless of its population.

These issues were settled through compromise. By the so-called **Connecticut Compromise**, the federal legislature would have *two* houses: the House of Representatives, in which representation is based on population; and the Senate, in which each state had two representatives, regardless of the population. Also, to calm fears that a strong federal government would take away individual rights and freedoms, there are ten **amendments**, or additions, to the original Constitution. These first ten amendments are known together as the **Bill of Rights**. They protect basic rights such as freedom of speech and religion, the right to a fair trial, and the right to demonstrate against the government.

# Restating Information: A Detail

Many of the questions on the GED will require you to answer questions based on facts—details—in a given passage. Usually, these details will not be given in the answers in the same words as they were in the passage you read. You will have to recognize the correct answer as a restatement of the information that was given. The information will be the same, but it will be written in different words.

When you read a sentence, think about the idea it expresses. Be sure you understand the idea. Turn it around in your mind and put it into your own words. If you can do this, you will be able to recognize that idea again, even if it is stated in other words.

Read the following passage about regional differences among the states. Pay close attention to the details.

> As the country grew, the Northeast developed an industrial and trading economy while the South exported more cash crops to Europe. In the West, cheap land encouraged many small family farms, which sold food to Northeastern cities. Northeastern states wanted tariffs, or fees, on goods being shipped into the country. This would protect growing American industries by making imported goods more expensive than those produced in America. Southern and Western states, which lacked factories of their own, didn't want tariffs. They wanted to be able to buy imported goods cheaply.

According to the information in the paragraph

(1) Northeastern states wanted people to buy cheap goods from Europe

(2) Southern states had many small family farms

(3) Northeastern states did not want European goods to be sold too cheaply in this country

(4) Southern states grew cotton and tobacco and often used slave labor to produce the crops

(5) Western states had many factories and produced large amounts of manufactured goods

Choice (3) is the correct answer. It is stated in the paragraph in the following words: "Northeastern states wanted tariffs, or fees, on goods being shipped into the country. This would protect growing American industries by making imported goods more expensive than those produced in America." Choice (1) is incorrect. Northeastern states were in competition with Europe in producing goods. If the European goods were cheaper, people would buy them instead of those produced by the Northeastern states. This is the opposite of what the paragraph states. Choice (2) is not mentioned in the paragraph. Western states, not Southern states, are described as having many small family farms. Choice (4) is true, but it is not mentioned in the paragraph. Choice (5) is untrue, and it is not stated in the paragraph.

## Lesson 3 Exercise

Items 1-3 are based on the following passage.

Several European countries looked to America to increase their wealth and power. Spain, France, and England were three of the powerful European nations that believed the New World—the Western Hemisphere—was full of opportunities. They sent explorers in search of these opportunities.

Spain first started colonies in South America and Mexico. In 1565, the Spanish explored Florida and started a colony in St. Augustine. Spain hoped to find gold in the New World and also wanted to own land there. It was also Spain's goal to convert, or change the religion of, the native populations to Catholicism.

In the 1600s, the French formed colonies in Canada and along the Mississippi River. They were interested in trading furs and fish. Although the French wanted to lay claim to the land, they were not interested in starting permanent colonies.

The English settled along the Eastern coast at about the same time. They founded their first permanent colony in Jamestown, Virginia, in 1607. They were also involved in exporting tobacco, cotton, fur, and timber. Holland and Sweden also established colonies along the Eastern seaboard in the 1600s. Settlements in Albany, the Hudson Valley, and Manhattan Island were established by the Dutch. Sweden had a settlement in Delaware. All of the Dutch settlements were surrendered to England in 1664 and renamed New York. The Swedish settlement also fell, first to the Dutch, and then to the English. By 1750, England had laid claim to the most land, with 1,250,000 settlers in English colonies.

1. According to the passage, what most interested the French in the New World?

   (1) agricultural opportunities
   (2) business and economic opportunities
   (3) carving out a piece of the new territory as their own
   (4) discovering gold
   (5) spreading their religion

2. According to the passage

   (1) the Dutch were not interested in establishing colonies in the New World
   (2) England was the first power to establish a colony in the New World
   (3) the Spanish were not interested in establishing colonies in the New World
   (4) Spain colonized Florida in the 16th century, earlier than any other nation
   (5) England claimed the colony on Manhattan Island from the Native Americans who lived there

3. According to the passage, which country was most aggressive in settling the New World?

   (1) England
   (2) Spain
   (3) France
   (4) Holland
   (5) Sweden

Answers are on page A-15.

# Regional Differences

## Prereading Prompt

Like arguments within a family, the disagreements that tore the nation apart during the Civil War were extremely painful. The stress and incredible hardship of the war almost destroyed our young nation.

## Key Words

**sectionalism**—identification with one's region rather than one's country

**secede**—withdraw from an organization or alliance

## Sectionalism: The Issues Leading to War

The 1800s brought growth and wealth to the young nation of the United States, but states in different sections found wealth through different means. The Northeast developed an industrial and trading economy. The South raised cotton and tobacco by using slave labor. The new West raised crops such as wheat and corn, which it sold for a profit to the Northeast. Each region had something the others needed, a system that worked quite well for a while.

A deep-seated conflict, however, threatened to destroy this national economic system. Slavery was considered necessary by many, if not most, Southerners for profitable farming in their region. On the many family farms of the North and West, on the other hand, a slave system did not make economic sense. Many in the North and West also thought slavery was a moral disgrace in a nation that claimed to be founded on the principle of individual freedom. Among these were people known as **abolitionists**, who wanted to quickly and completely do away with, or abolish, slavery.

These regional differences led to **sectionalism**: that is, people in each section of the country identified with the self-interest of their region, instead of the nation's self-interest; they made decisions about national issues based almost entirely on what would benefit their section alone. Northerners wanted to sell their manufactured goods for the most profit in America and Europe even if this made their products cost more in the South and West. Southerners wanted slavery to continue even in a democratic society so that they could get the most profit from their farming. Westerners wanted large amounts of federal money spent on roads and canals in their region, which would help them get their crops to market.

Sectionalism became even more deeply rooted when Andrew Jackson was elected president in 1828. Southerners and Westerners were angered when he enforced tariffs—taxes on foreign goods brought into the country. This made these foreign products more expensive. Northerners, however, favored these tariffs because they protected them from foreign competition which might offer the same goods at lower prices.

In 1854, the **Kansas-Nebraska Act** further divided the nation. Two new states—Kansas and Nebraska—were formed, and the people in these states were to decide the issue of slavery for themselves. Southerners and Northerners flocked to the new states, hoping to win the territory for their own causes. Slavery became the strongest issue dividing North and South.

In 1857, the Supreme Court attempted to settle this issue with the **Dred Scott Decision**. Dred Scott, a slave, had sued his owner for his freedom because he had been taken into free territory. He argued that this made him a free man. The Supreme Court, however, ruled that slaves—who were property, not citizens—were not allowed to sue. It further declared that Congress could not ban people from taking slaves into the new territories. This ruling favored the South and hurt the North, increasing the hatred between them.

By the election of 1860, these issues were so hot that an explosion seemed unavoidable. The explosion came when Abraham Lincoln, viewed by the South as an antislavery candidate, was elected president. The South **seceded**, or withdrew, from the Union. A new Southern government called the Confederate States of America was formed, with Jefferson Davis as President.

## The Civil War

In 1861, Confederate soldiers fired on federal troops at Fort Sumter, South Carolina, and the Civil War began. This was to be a war in which "brother fought against brother," a war that ripped the nation apart.

The **Union** had twice the population of the **Confederacy** and three-quarters of the total national wealth. It had more factories to produce weapons and more railroads to move troops and supplies. The Confederacy had the firm belief that its people were struggling fiercely to keep their way of life. Also, most of the battles were fought on Southern soil familiar to Confederates and populated by Southern loyalists hostile to "Yankee" soldiers. Each side had advantages and disadvantages, but the North's advantages were greater. Ultimately, in 1865, it was the North that won.

## Reconstruction

In 1863, slaves in the Confederate states had been freed by the **Emancipation Proclamation**. Slaves in the border states that were loyal to the Union were not freed. During Reconstruction, after the war, *all* the slaves were freed and given full constitutional rights. A few days after the end of the war, Lincoln was assassinated and Andrew Johnson became president. Congress forced a bitter South to accept military rule and changes in their state constitutions.

Many Northerners, called **carpetbaggers** by the South, moved into Southern states and became powerful influences in government and business. Some of these people were ruthless and dishonest, and the South resented their presence. Even though the war was over, many problems remained to be solved.

# Finding the Main Idea of a Paragraph

To find the **topic** of a group of details, you look for what they have in common. For example, suppose you read this list: cows, dogs, cats, tigers. You would summarize what it is about by saying that its topic is animals. To find the topic of a paragraph, read through it and ask yourself: What are all these sentences about? Look for any key words that are repeated. Then try to summarize what all the sentences are about.

Look at the first paragraph in this lesson. The second sentence tells you the Northeast developed an industrial and trading economy; the third sentence, that the South raised cotton and tobacco; the fourth, that the West raised crops such as wheat and corn. What are all these sentences about? The topic is: economic products of different sections of the United States. Look at the lesson's second paragraph. Its sentences tell us what the South, North, and West thought about slavery, so its topic is: attitudes toward slavery of sections of the United States. The sentences of the third paragraph tell you what each section wanted for itself economically. The paragraph's topic is: the different economic self-interests of the sections of the United States.

To find the **main idea** of a paragraph, you look for the most important thing that is said about the topic. The main idea is stated in a **topic sentence**, which often is at the beginning of the paragraph. However, it may be in the middle or at the end of the paragraph. The topic sentence of the lesson's second paragraph is its first sentence. The most important thing this paragraph says about its topic is that the different attitudes toward slavery created a deep conflict among the sections of the country, which threatened to destroy the national economic system. However, in the first paragraph, the main idea is stated partly in the first sentence and partly in the last sentence. Remember, the topic is: economic products of different sections of the United States. The most important thing said about this topic is that "different sections found wealth through different means" (first sentence) and "each region has something the others needed" (last sentence). On the other hand, the topic sentence of the third paragraph is its first sentence. The main idea is that the sections of the United States turned away from national self-interest to sectional self-interest—to sectionalism.

When you think you've found the main idea, check to see that all the other sentences in the paragraph support it. Try it with the following paragraph.

> African-American slaves gained their freedom in bits and pieces during the period of Reconstruction that followed the Civil War. The Emancipation Proclamation was a major step toward freedom, but it only freed slaves in the South. Three amendments to the Constitution were passed between 1865 and 1870; they abolished all slavery and gave former slaves citizenship and voting rights. Even so, many slaves were free in name only. Many could not find jobs, most had very little money, and almost all still bore the burden of having been slaves.

What is the main idea of this paragraph?

**(1)** Slaves gained their freedom slowly after the Civil War.

**(2)** The Emancipation Proclamation only partially freed the slaves.

**(3)** Despite their legal freedom, most former slaves lived in poverty during Reconstruction.

**(4)** Passing laws did very little for African-Americans after the Civil War.

**(5)** The Emancipation Proclamation was the most important step toward freedom for the slaves.

The correct answer is (1). The topic of this paragraph is the freeing of slaves after the Civil War. The most important thing said about the topic is: Slaves became free slowly, step by step, after the war. This idea is broad enough to cover all the other information in the paragraph. Choices (2) and (3) are details from the paragraph. Choice (4) is a statement that the paragraph does not support: Freedom from slavery and the gaining of citizenship and voting rights do not add up to "very little." Choice (5) is an opinion that is arguable, and it is not the main idea, but only one detail in the story of the gradual freeing of slaves after the Civil War.

Items 1–3 are based on the following passage.

The battle fought along the banks of Antietam Creek in Maryland on September 17, 1862, had a major impact on the course of the Civil War. It was led by the Confederacy, encouraged by its recent defeat of the Union Army in the Second Battle of Bull Run. Its purpose was to capture the federal Capitol at Washington, D.C. Under the leadership of General Robert E. Lee, the Confederate Army advanced into Maryland. They were met at Antietam by General George B. McClellan and the Federal Army. McClellan's troops successfully blocked Lee's advance, saving the Capitol and forcing the Confederates back into Virginia.

In losing the battle, the South was dealt a double blow. President Lincoln used the occasion of the Antietam victory to issue his Emancipation Proclamation. He announced that unless the Confederates surrendered by January 1, 1863, he would free slaves only in the South, not in the border states. Although Lincoln had long opposed slavery, the emancipation was more a political decision than a moral one; it put the South at a tremendous disadvantage in fighting the war.

It is estimated that 10,000 Confederate soldiers were killed or wounded at Antietam. The North suffered an even greater loss— 12,000 dead or wounded. The Battle of Antietam is remembered as the single bloodiest day in American combat history.

1. The main idea of the first paragraph is that

   (1) the Battle of Antietam had a major effect on the course of the Civil War
   (2) the Confederates thought they could win because they recently had won the Second Battle of Bull Run
   (3) The Federal Army won because of McClellan's superior leadership
   (4) the purpose of the battle was to take over the Capitol
   (5) the federal troops successfully blocked the advance of the Confederates

2. According to the second paragraph, what was the South's "double blow"?

   (1) sacrificing so many soldiers and losing the battle anyway
   (2) sacrificing so many soldiers only to have Lincoln make a decision based on politics, not morals
   (3) losing the battle and having Lincoln turn against them
   (4) losing the battle and having Lincoln free only Southern slaves
   (5) losing the battle and having to surrender by the end of the year

**3.** According to paragraph 3, what is Antietam's claim to history?

(1) 10,000 Southern soldiers were killed or wounded there.

(2) 12,000 Northern soldiers were killed or wounded there.

(3) 22,000 soldiers were killed or wounded there.

(4) The North had more casualties but won the battle anyway.

(5) The total casualties were greater than on any other day in U.S. history.

Answers are on page A-15.

# Industrial Growth of the United States

## Prereading Prompt

We are used to thinking of our major cities, such as New York, Los Angeles, and Chicago, as thriving urban centers. Millions of people live and work in these cities, businesses grow, many kinds of entertainment are available. This was not always the case. In 1880, only one quarter of the U.S. population lived in cities. What made millions of people pour into these urban centers?

## Key Words

**Industrial Revolution**—the change in an economy in which factories start to produce goods in great numbers

**the Great Depression**—the period of the 1930s when businesses failed, stock prices fell, banks closed, and millions were unemployed

## The Growth of Big Business

From the time of the Civil War until the end of the 1920s, manufacturing and business in the United States developed rapidly, which changed many aspects of American life. During the Civil War, there was a great need for weapons, ammunition, and uniforms. All these things had to be manufactured and distributed. Railroads were crucial for moving troops and supplies. Both the North and the South struggled to produce or buy what they needed. All this helped to advance the **Industrial Revolution** that was taking place here and in parts of Europe.

From 1865 on, factories sprang up to manufacture all kinds of products faster than they had ever been produced before. **Mass production** was becoming increasingly common: By this process, products were not produced one at a time, but were turned out in great numbers on an assembly line. The parts of the product moved along a conveyor belt past a line of workers. Each worker or group of workers performed one special set of tasks. As the parts of the product moved along the belt, more tasks were performed until the whole product was completed. This division of tasks among different workers is known as **division of labor**. By this process, the Industrial Revolution changed the nature of work.

The Industrial Revolution also changed people's daily lives. New machines and inventions were available to more people because their prices were lower. After World War I, middle-class Americans began buying automobiles, washing machines, vacuum cleaners, sewing machines, and radios. Laborsaving devices helped women do housework more quickly. More women took jobs outside the home, which further changed the lifestyles of both men and women.

## The New Immigration

In response to industry's need for workers, people moved from American farms and from Europe and Asia into American cities. As the Industrial Revolution progressed in the years after the Civil War, cities grew, railroads expanded, and people moved from farms to take jobs in factories. Business grew quickly and there was a need for more and more people to work in city factories. They didn't necessarily need special skills, just the willingness to work very hard.

In the late 1800s, millions of people came to the United States from eastern and southern Europe (Poland, Austria, and Italy) and from Asia (China) to fill these jobs. They were seeking freedom from oppression or a chance to work and feed their families. They joined the ranks of the millions of Americans who fled to the cities looking for work. Factory and business owners welcomed the cheap labor all these people provided.

## Reform Movements

Several movements that focused on protecting people from the abuses of big business emerged during this period. Work in many of the nation's factories was brutal and dangerous. Textile workers developed lung diseases from breathing dust and fiber all day. Coal miners died from cave-ins and gas in mine shafts. In one year, 195 steelworkers died in the mills of Pittsburgh alone. To add to the workers' difficulties, pay was low and workdays often as long as 12 to 14 hours. The workers had no power over the factory owners. If they threatened to quit, others were always ready to replace them. **Labor unions** began to form as early as the late 1700s. Their goals were to represent and protect the workers. The American Federation of Labor (AFL) was a confederation of already-existing labor unions founded in 1886 by Samuel Gompers.

The **Progressive Movement** tried to reform various industries and to improve the quality of American life. The rights of women and children became especially important to them. In 1911, for example, 146 young women who had been locked in their factory in New York City died in the *Triangle Fire*, which caused the state to approve factory safety laws. Children also worked in dangerous conditions in coal mines and tobacco and textile factories for as long as 12 hours a day, 6 days a week, and were unable to go to school. In 1900, nearly 2 million children under age 15 were at work. Child labor laws were passed, and women were finally given the right to vote with the passage of the Nineteenth Amendment in 1920. Children were guaranteed schooling by compulsory education laws.

Government also regulated business to protect consumers and small businesses. Antitrust laws were passed to prevent companies from forming **monopolies**. A monopoly occurs when one company controls an entire industry by driving all other companies out of business or by absorbing them. Monopolies allowed corporations to fix whatever prices they wanted because they had no competition. They also used their wealth to bribe legislatures so they could break laws freely. Laws also were passed to protect consumers from dangerous foods and drugs. Meatpacking companies at times used poisoned foods and even parts of rats in their canned meat. Drug companies sometimes used unsafe chemicals, and made false claims about their products. The Pure Food and Drug Act of 1906 stated that these products must be tested by the federal government before they could be sold.

## The Great Depression and the New Deal

During the 1920s, the United States experienced great prosperity. Business boomed and people speculated in the stock market. They bought shares in corporations **on margin**, that is, they borrowed money to buy shares, hoping their value would increase. For a while, that is exactly what happened. Then, in 1929, came the **stock market crash**. Stock prices fell drastically, and people lost their investments. Companies went out of business, banks closed, and great numbers of people were unemployed. It was the start of the **Great Depression**.

When Franklin Delano Roosevelt became president in 1933, he proposed a **New Deal** to help the country emerge from the Depression. Major legislation was passed to strengthen the banking system and regulate the stock market. The Social Security Act was passed in 1935, giving economic assistance to elderly people. The Works Progress Administration, the Civilian Conservation Corps, and the Tennessee Valley Authority were designed to provide jobs for the unemployed. By the beginning of the next decade, the United States was fighting World War II. Roosevelt's measures, combined with the massive war effort, helped turn the economy around.

## Finding the Main Idea of a Passage

In Lesson 4 you learned how to find the main idea of a paragraph: first, you find what the sentences of the paragraph are all about (the topic) and then you find the most important thing that is said about this topic (the main idea). To find the main idea of the passage, you follow the same method on a larger scale. You first find the main idea of each paragraph in the passage, and then find an idea that will cover all these ideas—the main idea of the passage.

Reading through a passage, you first want to see what it is generally about—its topic. But you also look for the topic sentence of each paragraph, the main idea of each paragraph. When you finish the passage, you should try to think of an idea that will cover all these ideas, that is, try to summarize the passage. Then look for a sentence in the passage that states this summary. That will be the topic sentence for the whole passage, which gives you the stated main idea of the passage.

Look at the first section of this lesson, entitled "The Growth of Big Business." The first paragraph tells us how the Civil War helped to advance the Industrial Revolution in the United States (the last sentence is the topic sentence). The second paragraph describes how the new manufacturing process of mass production changed the nature of work (the topic sentence is again the last sentence). The last paragraph tells us that the Industrial Revolution changed people's daily lives (the first sentence is the topic sentence). How do you summarize these main ideas? They all describe the ways the Industrial Revolution, coming out of the Civil War, changed American life. Is there a sentence that states this summary, covering all the main ideas? The first sentence in the passage does this: "From the time of the Civil War until the end of the 1920s, manufacturing and business in the United States developed rapidly, which changed many aspects of American life."

Read the following passage and try to find its main idea.

> Herbert Hoover won the election of 1928 but served only one term because of the Great Depression. Hoover, a Republic and a millionaire businessman, was perfectly suited to the mood of the times. The country was in a business boom, and Hoover promised to help it continue. He served from 1929 to 1933.
>
> But Hoover's popularity declined as times changed. When the Great Depression hit, Hoover felt sure things would improve in time. He did little to try to help the economy and the millions of unemployed. By the time he came up for reelection in 1932, people were desperate to see the economy improve. Hoover lost the election to Roosevelt.

Which of the following sentences best states the main idea of this passage?

**(1)** Hoover was elected in 1928 but lost four years later because of the Depression.

**(2)** Hoover was well suited to the mood of the times because people were desperate.

**(3)** Hoover tried to improve the economy in the Great Depression.

**(4)** Hoover became less popular when the Depression hit.

**(5)** Hoover lost the next election to Roosevelt.

Choice (1) is the main idea of the passage. It includes the most important ideas from both paragraphs: Hoover was elected in 1928; Hoover lost because of the Depression four years later. Choice (2) is false. It combines a detail from paragraph 1 and a detail from paragraph 2 to make a confusing statement. Hoover suited the mood of the times when the economy was prosperous; in the Depression, when people were desperate, he did not. (3) is also false. We are told "Hoover felt sure things would improve" in the Depression but "did little to try to help the economy." Choice (4) is the topic sentence of the second paragraph. (5) is a detail from the second paragraph.

## Lesson 5 Exercise

Item 1 is based on the following passage.

During the late 19th and early 20th centuries the American government adopted a **laissez-faire**, or "hands-off," policy toward business which led to social injustice and corruption. With business booming and the government looking the other way, there were huge fortunes to be made. J. P. Morgan and Andrew Carnegie made fortunes in steel, and John D. Rockefeller became the king of the oil industry. Power and money were concentrated in the hands of a few.

As big business got bigger, its morals got smaller. The giants of the big industries—railroads, steel, oil—grew even larger by forming trusts and monopolies. The reason for forming them was to own or control as many companies in a given industry as possible. This effectively eliminated competition. Once there was no competition, there was no limit to prices. With high prices, the rich got richer and the poor got poorer.

For the average industrial worker, living conditions were terrible, and working conditions were often worse. These were the days before overtime pay, minimum wage, and mandatory time off. The average worker put in 59 hours and made less then $10 a week, although many worked more than 70 hours and made even less.

Politics became corrupt also. City politicians took advantage of the poor by offering jobs in exchange for votes. Local governments, particularly in large cities like New York and Chicago, were controlled by small groups of people who used the government for profit.

1. Which of the following states the main idea of the passage?

   (1) *Laissez-faire* allowed big business to exploit workers in this period.

   (2) *Laissez-faire* policy created many social evils while creating wealth in this period.

   (3) In this period, the rich got richer and the poor got poorer.

   (4) The main effect of *laissez-faire* was elimination of economic competition.

   (5) Business in this period used government for profit.

Item 2 is based on the following passage.

By late 1890, one million women had taken jobs in factories in the United States. More women than men worked in the textile mills of New England and tobacco factories in the South. In New York City, women outnumbered men in the garment, or clothing, industry. During the 1800s, women had formed their own unions to work for better conditions, but none of these unions had lasted. Though women made up the majority of workers in some industries, their participation in the labor organizing movement was limited.

In 1900, men and women garment workers organized the International Ladies' Garment Workers Union, or ILGWU. In 1910, more than 20,000 women and men in the ILGWU struck. After several weeks, employers met their demands for better pay and shorter hours. This was a great victory for the union. The ILGWU became an important member of the AFL, the main American union organization. Along with other groups, the ILGWU tried to help women workers.

However, most women with factory jobs did not join unions. First, many of them were young and single and expected to marry and stop working. Second, many unions refused to accept women members. Third, even unions that accepted women did little to organize them. They often held meetings in saloons, which women could not enter.

Adapted from p. 476 of *The American Nation, Third Edition* by James West Davidson and John E. Batchelor. Copyright ©1991 Prentice-Hall, Inc..

2. Which of the following is the main idea of the passage?

(1) Organizing of women factory workers was successful mainly in the garment industry in this period.

(2) The failure of all-women unions in this period kept women from participating fully in the labor movement.

(3) Though women outnumbered men as factory workers in this period, unions failed to organize them adequately.

(4) Though women outnumbered men in some industries, they were not full-fledged members of the labor movement.

(5) Women's attitudes toward marriage and drinking, as well as male hostility, kept them from being active in the labor union movement.

Item 3 is based on the following passage.

The surge of new immigrants in the late 1800s encouraged *nativism*, a movement consciously hostile to immigrants. Nativists believed that the United States should favor native-born Americans' economic interests and social values over the interests and values of these newer Americans. They resented the new immigrants because they competed for jobs. Desperate for work, many newcomers were willing to accept low wages and harsh working conditions. When economic conditions worsened, antiforeign feelings became even stronger.

Many Americans also reacted negatively to the newcomers' unfamiliar customs and religious practices. The languages of southern Europe (such as Italian) and eastern Europe (such as Polish, Hungarian, or the Slavic languages) sounded strange to English-speaking Americans. Many Protestants were offended by Catholic festivals, such as saints' days. They also did not understand the traditional beards and head coverings worn by many eastern European Jews.

Outspoken prejudice and active discrimination against immigrants were widespread. Many American newspapers competed for readers by appealing to hostility toward these "foreign Americans." One editorial called them "an invasion of venomous reptiles ... who never did a day's work in their lives." Catholics could not find jobs in banks and offices. Jewish immigrants were excluded from the nation's better universities, restaurants, and hotels. In many industries, the most dangerous and low-paying jobs were called "foreign jobs." Anti-Chinese feeling became so violent that in 1882 Congress passed an exclusion act that stopped further immigration from China.

Adapted from pp. 150-152, *American Journey, The Quest for Liberty Since 1865* by James West Davidson, Mark H. Lytle, and Michael B. Stoff. Copyright © 1992 Prentice-Hall, Inc.

**3.** Which of the following is the main idea of the passage?

**(1)** Widespread discrimination against new immigrants by nativists in the 1800s kept the immigrants from getting decent work.

**(2)** A reaction against the strange foreign customs of the new immigrants in the 1800s was an even more important motive for nativist prejudice than the fear of competition over jobs.

**(3)** The willingness of the new immigrants in the 1800s to do poor-paying "dirty work" was the main reason nativists considered them strange and subhuman.

**(4)** Economic fear combined with social prejudice inspired nativists in the 1800s to discriminate actively against new immigrants.

**(5)** The nativist movement in the 1800s developed from economic fear to social prejudice to active discrimination in every phase of American life.

Answers are on page A-15.

# Government and Political Science

## Prereading Prompt

One way to look at systems of government is to think of them as experiments in human living. A system of government is devised by people to run a society, small or large. Some governments have people's best interests in mind, some don't. Similarly, sometimes they work, and sometimes they don't. Find out in this lesson what the differences are between systems of government.

## Key Words

**monarchy**—governmental power is concentrated in one person, who inherited the position

**dictatorship**—one person has total power and closely controls citizens' lives. Usually a dictatorship is not an inherited position.

**oligarchy**—rule by a small governing class of people

**democracy**—government in which the people exercise power either directly (a direct democracy) or through elected representatives (a representative democracy, or a republic)

## Types of Modern Government

Many nations have types of government that concentrate authority in a few people, or in one person, and give no power to the people. In a **monarchy**, the government's power is concentrated in one person. This individual is usually a king or a queen and achieves the position of monarch through inheritance—that is, from parents or some close family member such as an uncle or an aunt. An *absolute monarch* has complete authority to govern. Throughout history until the French and American revolutions in the late 18th century, most countries were ruled by such monarchs. A *constitutional monarch* has limited power and must work with other government officials, who really govern. Great Britain is the best-known constitutional monarchy. In a **dictatorship**, one person has total power and closely controls many aspects of the people's lives. Both the Nazi (National Socialist) government of Adolf Hitler in Germany (1933-1945) and the Communist dictatorship of Joseph Stalin in the old Soviet Union (1928-1953) sought total power over people's minds through constant propaganda and police-state terror. These were *totalitarian* dictatorships, in which the dictator became a god to be worshipped. Other dictators have used political terror while allowing traditional parts of society (industrialists, large landowners, churches) to keep some independent power. The governments of General Franco in Spain and General Pinochet in Chile were this type of dictatorship. In an **oligarchy**, a small governing class of the rich and powerful rules.

Unlike the forms of government already mentioned, a democracy allows its citizens to have a say in the government. In a **direct democracy**, all citizens of voting age have a direct say in running the government. They may or may not choose to exercise this right. Ancient Greece was a direct democracy, and early in U.S. history, towns had town meetings to decide important issues, which was a form of direct democracy. As the United States grew, however, **direct democracy** became impractical. Today, with a population of almost 250 million, it would be impossible for all eligible voters in America to have a direct say in government.

Most democratic nations are indirect democracies called **republics**. Like these nations, the United States is a **republic** or **representative democracy**; voters elect people to represent their views in the government. The representatives who are elected by the people then carry out government work that is based—ideally—on what the people want. One form of representative democracy is known as **parliamentary democracy**. Most European nations, Japan, Canada, and many South American countries are parliamentary democracies. In a parliamentary democracy, the head of state (the prime minister) is the leader of his or her party. Prime ministers are elected along with the members of parliament and must have the support of parliament. The parliamentary system is different from the system in the United States, in which the president and vice president are elected separately from the members of Congress and can come from a different party than the one that has a majority in Congress.

## The American Constitutional System

The American Constitution and our system of government are based on the theory that political power should not be concentrated in one person or group of people. The government of the United States of America is based on a **federal system**. In such a system separate states give up certain powers to a central government and keep other powers for themselves. Governors and state legislatures in all 50 states of the United States have powers independent of the central, **federal government** in Washington, D.C. States have their own laws and court systems. These are called **reserve powers**.

Power is also divided among the different parts of the federal government, as you can see in the chart "The System of Checks and Balances." This is called **the separation of powers**. Each part, or branch, of the national government has one kind of power and can control or limit the powers of the other two branches. The **legislative branch** creates, votes on, and passes bills which are intended to become new laws. The **executive branch** carries out the laws. When news reporters say "The U.S. government today acted on this issue," they usually mean the executive branch. The heads of the different departments— the Department of Defense (including the Army, Navy, and Air Force), the Health and Human Services Department (in charge of Medicare, Medicaid, and Social Security), the Justice Department (including all the federal courts and the F.B.I.), the State Department (which carries out foreign policy), and all the other executive departments—work directly for the president. These depart-

| The System of Checks and Balances | | |
|---|---|---|
| **President** | **Congress** | **Supreme Court** |
| **Powers** | **Powers** | **Powers** |
| 1. Enforces laws. <br> 2. Can veto bills. <br> 3. Appoints judges and other officials. <br> 4. Conducts foreign policy. <br> 5. Commander-in-Chief of Armed Forces | 1. Make laws. <br> 2. Can overide a president's veto <br> 3. Can impeach president. <br> 4. Approves president's appointments of judges and other officials. <br> 5. Approves treaties. <br> 6. Declares war. | 1. Interprets laws. <br> 2. Can declare laws unconstitutional. |
| **Controls** | **Controls** | **Controls** |
| 1. Can be removed by Congress (impeached). <br> 2. Congress can override veto. <br> 3. Appointments must be approved by Congress. <br> 4. Treaties must be approved by Congress. | 1. President can veto a bill passed by Congress. <br> 2. Laws passed by Congress can be declared unconstitutional by Supreme Court. | 1. Judges appointed for life by president. <br> 2. Appointments must be approved by Congress. <br> 3. Judges can be removed by Congress for improper behavior. |

are called *cabinet officers*. While the president can sign bills from Congress to make them laws officially, he can also cancel, or veto, them by refusing to sign them. The legislative branch can override such a *veto* if two-thirds of its members vote to do so. The **judicial branch** interprets laws. It can declare a law made by Congress or an act of the executive branch to be against the constitution—**unconstitutional**—and therefore illegal.

Power is also divided between the two parts of the legislative branch. In the **House of Representatives**, each state has a number of representatives (called *Representatives* or *Congressmen*) according to the size of its population. In the **Senate**, each state has two representatives (called *Senators*) regardless of the size of its population. The House system of representation favors states with big populations; the Senate system checks this power. Since all bills must be approved by both houses of Congress to become law, on most issues neither house can dominate the other.

## Political Science Statistics

Political science is the study of systems of government, but it is also the study of the inner workings of the political process. For a democratic government to function, politicians must know what people think and want. Politicians and social scientists alike need ways of getting this information. Some can be gleaned from the media—newspapers, magazines, TV. But the most direct way of getting such information is simply to ask people.

## Public Opinion Polls

"Whom do you favor for president?" "What was your income last year?" "How many children do you have?" "What is your religion?" Almost every area of life today has been studied by asking people such questions. Politicians and social scientists often conduct public opinion polls to find out not only what people think, but how they live.

We are all familiar with pre-election polls. Candidates use this information to guide their campaign strategies. They often gather statistics showing the ethnic, economic, and religious breakdown of the area in which they are campaigning. This enables them to tailor their campaign speeches to a specific group, helping them win votes. In Detroit, a candidate might address unemployment when talking to auto workers, whereas in a wealthier or more prosperous area, the focus would more likely be the capital gains tax.

## Statistical Studies

Statistical studies are ways of analyzing information to determine its meaning and usefulness. Social scientists apply mathematical formulas to determine the meaning and accuracy of information gathered through polls, interviews, and other kinds of surveys. For example, a statistical study can tell social scientists if an opinion poll has sampled enough people to accurately predict the opinions of the larger population it is supposed to represent. To be valid, the group being polled must reflect the entire population of the area being surveyed in terms of race, sex, and economic class.

## Finding a Detail in a Graphic

Charts, graphs, maps, and cartoons contain information that is as important as the information contained in written text. The difference is that specific pieces of information—details—are usually easier to spot in graphic form than in written text. To find a detail in a graphic, first be sure you understand what the graphic is illustrating. If the graphic has a title, read it. Then relate the title to the information in the graphic. For example, the graph below shows the money allowed for an imaginary city's budget. The pieces of the "pie" show where money is needed. Next to each color square is the percentage of the total money available that will be spent on that need. In this city, for example, "repairs to water system" take a mere 2% of the total budget. Road repairs get only a little more, with 5%.

Look at the graph carefully and then answer the question.

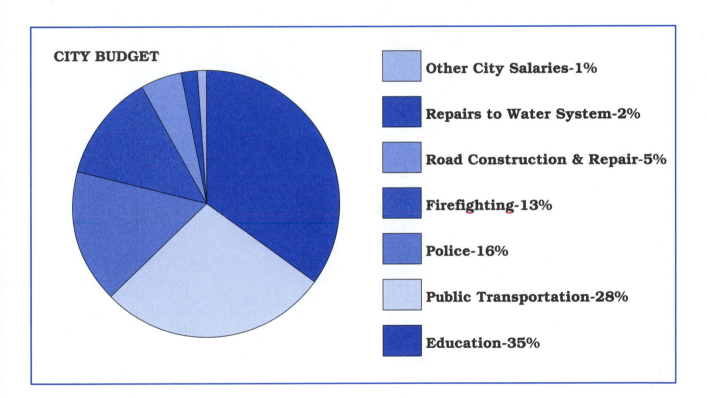

CITY BUDGET

Other City Salaries-1%

Repairs to Water System-2%

Road Construction & Repair-5%

Firefighting-13%

Police-16%

Public Transportation-28%

Education-35%

According to the graph, which statement below is accurate?

**(1)** More money is allotted for police than for public transportation.

**(2)** More money is allotted for repairs to the water system than for roads.

**(3)** Less money is allotted for education than for public transportation.

**(4)** Less money is allotted for police than for firefighting.

**(5)** Less money is allotted for roads than for firefighting.

The correct answer is (5). To answer the question correctly, you have to check each statement to see which service is actually receiving more money. The graph shows that road construction and repair is given 5% of the total budget, while firefighting receives 13% of the budget, so the statement in choice (5) is correct. For choices (1)-(4), the opposite of each statement is actually true, according to the graph.

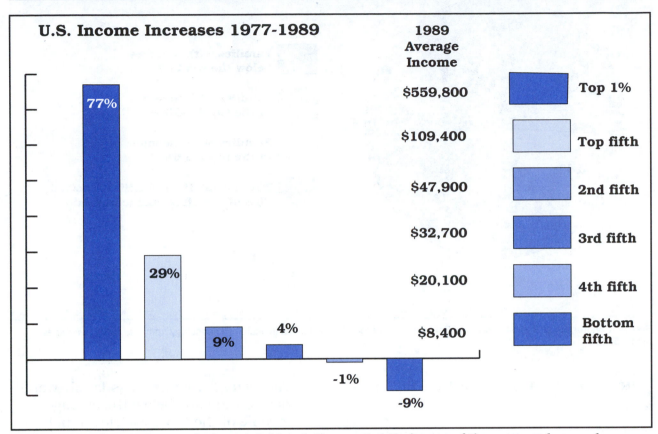

**U.S. Income Increases 1977-1989**

| 1989 Average Income | |
|---|---|
| $559,800 | Top 1% |
| $109,400 | Top fifth |
| $47,900 | 2nd fifth |
| $32,700 | 3rd fifth |
| $20,100 | 4th fifth |
| $8,400 | Bottom fifth |

77%

29%

9%

4%

-1%

-9%

**Note: The negative numbers on the bar graph (-1 and -9) mean that the income of these groups decreased.**

*The New York Times.* Copyright © 1991/92 by The New York Times Company. Reprinted by permission.

Items 1 and 2 are based on the bar graph.

1. Which of the following is NOT TRUE of the pretax income from 1977 to 1989 of the middle-class American family in the 3rd fifth?

   (1) Its income increased 73% less than the income of the richest 1% of Americans increased.

   (2) Its income increase was more than double the increase in the income of the poorest fifth of Americans.

   (3) Its income increased 25% less than the income of the top fifth of the American population increased.

   (4) Its income increased more than 4% more than the income of the 4th fifth increased.

   (5) Its income increased 5% less than the income of the 2nd fifth of the population increased.

2. Suppose you had an income in 1989 of $20,100. How much greater an increase in income would someone with an income of $109,400 have than you would have?

   (1) 29%
   (2) 25%
   (3) 73%
   (4) 20%
   (5) 30

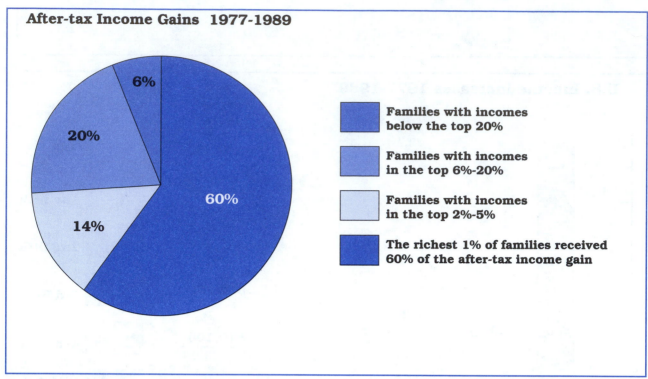

**After-tax Income Gains 1977-1989**

6%

20%

14%

60%

■ Families with incomes below the top 20%

■ Families with incomes in the top 6%-20%

□ Families with incomes in the top 2%-5%

■ The richest 1% of families received 60% of the after-tax income gain

Source: Congressional Budget Office and Paul Krugman of the Massachusetts Institute of Technology from *The New York Times*, March 5, 1991.

Items 3 and 4 are based on the circle graph.

3. If your income was below that of the richest 6-20% of Americans, how much less of the after-tax income gain would you get than this top 6-20%?

(1) 6%
(2) 14%
(3) 26%
(4) 54%
(5) 20%

4. The average middle-class family would have an income below the average income of the top 20%. How much less of an after-tax gain would this family receive than someone in the top 1%?

(1) 14%
(2) 20%
(3) 54%
(4) 8%
(5) 6%

Answers are on page A-16.

# Economics: Systems and Measures

## Prereading Prompt

All of us have our own way of managing money—setting priorities for shelter and food, trying to leave some for entertainment or savings. On a much larger scale, nations must also manage their spending. Governments use various systems to accomplish this purpose. Some attempt to closely control their nation's economy. Other believe that too much control can cause more problems. Learn more about these systems in this lesson.

## Key Words

**free-enterprise system**—system in which prices are set by supply and demand; consumers are free to buy what they choose

**welfare state services**—provision by the government of free or partially free health care, food, and housing for all people, paid for by taxes on the people

## Types of Economic Systems

The three main types of economic systems are **capitalism, socialism**, and **communism**. In a capitalist economy, most businesses are owned and run by private individuals or organizations. The production of goods and services is not under government control. Instead, businesses operate under a **free-enterprise system**; prices are set by supply and demand; consumers are free to buy what they choose. Consumers are people who buy or use goods and services. The United States is an example of a capitalist economy.

In a **socialist economy**, many businesses and industries are owned by the government. Generally, the people also pay very high taxes. This enables the government to provide **welfare state services**, or cradle-to-grave services, that give all people free or partially free health care, food, and housing. Sweden is a prime example of a socialist economy.

Under **communism**, the government owns all businesses and controls the distribution of goods and services. The government provides the same kind of services provided under socialism but is also involved in the control of all economic activity. Communist governments also control the information that is available to their people and to the world through newspapers, books, and TV. Until its break-up in 1991, the Soviet Union was a communist system.

None of these economic systems exists in pure form. For example, in so-called socialist England most businesses are privately owned. In the capitalist United States, most businesses operate under some kind of government control or legal regulation. In the old communist Soviet Union, some workers controlled businesses owned by the state.

## The Free-Enterprise System

In a free-enterprise system, citizens are free to produce and buy goods and services as long as they do so within the restrictions set by the government. Prices are determined by the **law of supply and demand**. Supply is the amount of available goods and services. Demand is how many people want to buy a particular product or service.

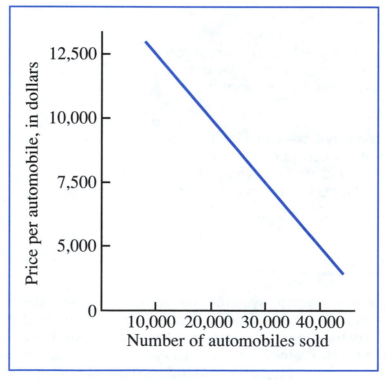

Source: From *New Revised Cambridge GED Program: Social Studies.*
Copyright © 1992 Regents/Prentice Hall.

The law of supply and demand states that when demand increases, supply increases; when demand decreases, supply decreases. Supply and demand also affect the price of goods. If the supply of an item is high, its price may fall, even if there is a great demand for it. Similarly, price can affect demand. In general, the higher the price of an item, the lower the demand for it.

By studying both supply and demand, businesses can determine an equilibrium point—the price at which consumers will buy exactly the amount supplied by the producer. Too much production can lead to a surplus of the product and cause prices to fall. Too little production can lead to shortages and cause prices to rise. The graph on the previous page illustrates this law.

## Business Cycles and the Federal Reserve System

Every capitalist economy regularly goes through **business cycles**; that is, economic "good times" of prosperity, when productivity and income are high, are followed by economic "bad times," when productivity and income are low. The bad time in a cycle is called a **recession**; if a recession is long and severe, it is called a **depression**. In recessions and especially in depressions, many businesses lay off workers or fail. In a situation of widespread unemployment and very low income, people can become homeless and even suffer from hunger. A return to prosperity from such an economic downturn is called a **recovery**.

To keep an economy healthy, governments try to prevent two economic "illnesses": inflation and unemployment. **Inflation** occurs when prices are very high and money decreases in value. Everything costs more and people have to pay more for the same amount of goods than they had been paying. Inflation often occurs during prosperity, when business is doing well and employment is high. **Unemployment** often occurs in recessions and depressions, when productivity and sales decline, and businesses lay off employees.

The U.S. government tries to prevent these two economic ills through the **Federal Reserve System**. Nicknamed "The Fed," it controls the supply of money in the U.S. economy in two ways: by a **reserve ratio** and by a **discount rate**. "The Fed" requires all the banks in the Federal Reserve System to keep— or reserve—a ratio or percent of their money deposits; they must not loan this money to other banks, businesses, or individuals. If "The Fed" sets a high reserve ratio, it has a **tight-money** policy, and there is less money available to borrow and use in the economy. If the reserve ratio is low, there is more money available and "The Fed" has an **easy-money** policy.

The Federal Reserve Bank also can make the money supply "tight" or "easy" by raising the interest rate it charges banks—the **discount rate**—for the money it loans to them. The banks then have to charge higher interest on loans to businesses and individuals, and fewer people can afford to borrow. Businessmen cannot afford loans to expand, or to start new businesses. Consumers cannot afford loans for major purchases, such as houses or cars. A low discount rate, makes loans easier to get. Tight-money policy is used to combat inflation. Easy-money policy is used to fight recessions and unemployment by stimulating economic growth.

# Two Economic Measures

The **Consumer Price Index** or **CPI** measures changes in the cost of living. It compares prices in different years of essential goods and services—food, clothing, housing, transportation, and so on.

Often—as in the table below—the base year used for comparisons is 1984 (1984 = 100). You can see that the average city dweller paid $123.5 for food in March 1989; the same amount of food cost only $100 in 1984. The CPI, therefore, shows that food cost almost 25% more in 1989 than in 1984.

| Consumer Price Index for all Urban Consumers (1984=100) | | |
|---|---|---|
| Group | March 1989 | March 1988 |
| All Items | 122.3 | 116.5 |
| Food | 123.5 | 115.9 |
| Alcoholic beverages | 121,8 | 117.4 |
| Apparel and upkeep | 119.3 | 114.3 |
| Total Housing | 121.5 | 117.0 |
|    Rent | 138.6 | 132.9 |
|    Gas & Elec. | 104.8 | 101.7 |
| Transportation | 111.9 | 106.5 |
| Medical Care | 146.1 | 136.3 |
| Entertainment | 124.7 | 119.0 |

Source: Department of Labor, Bureau of Labor Statistics

Another important economic statistic is the **Gross National Product** or **GNP**. This is the total value of everything produced and sold in a country during one year. If you buy a TV set or a shirt, or pay your utilities bill or get your car repaired, your purchases and payments are part of the U.S. GNP.

The GNP can be measured in **current dollars**, to show how much goods and services amount to according to the current value of the dollar. The GNP also can be measured in **constant dollars**—the value of goods and services according to the dollar's value in a base year. Using constant dollars helps account for inflation.

The graph on the facing page shows that between 1940 and 1970 the GNP rose from about 300 billion to around 1,000 billion (or 1 trillion) in constant dollars.

# Finding the Main Idea of a Graphic: Graphs

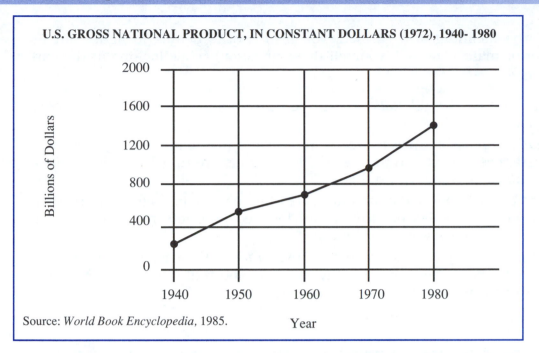

**U.S. GROSS NATIONAL PRODUCT, IN CONSTANT DOLLARS (1972), 1940- 1980**

Billions of Dollars

Year

Source: *World Book Encyclopedia*, 1985.

Graphs make pictures out of statistics to show you the way something is happening or changing, for instance, how the Consumer Price Index or Gross National Product has increased, or how many more hours people are working this year than last year.

To find the main idea of a graphic, look for the "big picture" that its details make—the main, or overall, idea they show. Ask yourself: What is the topic of the graph and what is its main point about this topic? Pay special attention to the title, which may help you find this main idea. Look at the GNP graph above and answer the following question.

The main point of the graph is that the U.S. Gross National Product

**(1)** can never decrease

**(2)** showed a fairly steady increase from 1940 to 1980

**(3)** in the year 2000 will be about $2,000 billion

**(4)** is not affected by inflation

**(5)** has doubled its rate of increase every 10 years from 1940 to 1980

(2) is the correct answer. If you cannot discover the "big picture" right away, you may want to find the main idea by eliminating the wrong answers. Check each answer choice against the graph to see which ones: (a) are false details; (b) are true details but are not big enough to be the main idea; (c) are "big ideas" the graph does not support. Choices (1) and (3) are big ideas with not enough support: From this graph you cannot tell if the U.S. GNP will "never decrease" or what it will be in the year 2000. (5) is a false detail: The GNP did double— approximately—from 1940 to 1950, but its rise was less than double from 1960 to 1970 and from 1970 to 1980. (4) makes no sense: The GNP shown on the graph is not affected by inflation because it is in constant dollars, but that is not the main point the graph makes about the U.S. GNP from 1940 to 1980.

# Finding the Main Idea of a Graphic: Cartoons

To find the meaning of a cartoon, you also use its details to figure out its main point or main idea. Ask yourself these questions while looking at the cartoon below.

**(1)** *What are the main details?* The three charts and the words shown in the "balloon."

**(2)** *What comparisons are made?* Comparisons are made among the three substances, showing that sales of illegal drugs are up while sales of alcohol and tobacco are down.

**(3)** *What is the main action or situation?* The speaker is suggesting to their audience that sales of alcohol and tobacco products might increase if these substances were made illegal.

**(4)** *Which answer gives the meaning of the cartoon?* Look for the answer that connects the details (and the way they are pictured) to the main action to express the meaning you see in the cartoon.

Source: *The Colorado Springs Gazette Telegraph*, May 30, 1990. Reprinted by permission of *The Colorado Springs Gazette Telegraph*.

Now try putting all this together to find the main idea of the cartoon. Look again at the cartoon and answer the question.

Which statement accurately reflects the main idea of the cartoon?

**(1)** Demand is determined by supply.

**(2)** Demand is determined by factors other than supply.

**(3)** Price is determined by supply.

**(4)** Price is determined by demand.

**(5)** Supply is determined by factors other than demand.

The correct answer is choice (2). The speaker in the cartoon is saying that making alcohol and cigarettes illegal will make more people buy alcohol and cigarettes. He wants us to believe that making these products illegal would make people want them more and there would be a higher demand for them. Choices (1) and (5) are not correct because the charts do not show anything about the supply of alcohol and tobacco, just a demand (that is, sales or consumption). Choices (3) and (4) can be eliminated because you have no basis for judging the prices of any of the substances shown.

Item 1 is based on the following graph.

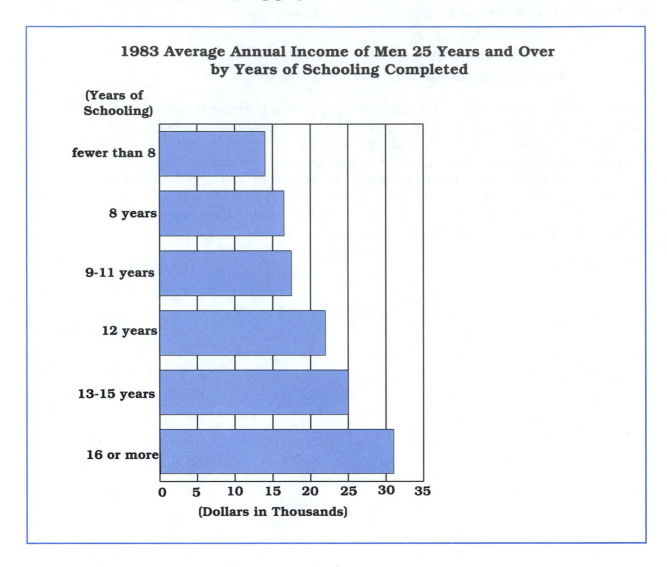

1983 Average Annual Income of Men 25 Years and Over
by Years of Schooling Completed

1. What is the main idea of the graph above?

   (1) The average annual income of men decreases with the amount of schooling they have had.

   (2) The number of years of schooling men complete varies with the income level of their families.

   (3) The average annual income of women with college degrees is higher than that of men without college degrees.

   (4) The average annual income of men increases with the years of schooling they have completed.

   (5) The yearly income of both men and women increases with the number of years of schooling they have completed.

Item 2 is based on the graph on page 194.

2. What is the main idea of the graph?

   (1) The price of cars varied as the number produced increased steadily.

   (2) The price of cars went up as more were sold.

   (3) The price of cars peaked at $12,500.

   (4) The price of cars went down as more units were produced.

   (5) The number of cars sold increased as the price per car came down.

Item 3 is based on the following political cartoon.

Source: From *PUCK,* August 20, 1913.

3. The main idea of this cartoon is that

   (1) the U.S. government and the U.S. banks need to be replaced

   (2) politicians and bankers always work together

   (3) the banks want to overthrow the U.S. government

   (4) political power hurts banking more than banking power hurts politics

   (5) political power corrupts banking and banking power corrupts politics

Answers are on page A-16.

# Lesson 8

# Geography

## Prereading Prompt

You are familiar with the neighborhoods you and your friends live in. Perhaps you have also traveled to different parts of the country, or even to foreign countries. No matter where you go, you notice how other places may be different from or similar to the place you are from. The weather, land, or amount of water may be different. All this is part of geography, the study of the Earth.

## Key Words

**landforms**—physical features of the land such as mountains, valleys, or plains

**latitude**—distance north or south of the equator

**longitude**—distance east or west of the prime meridian

**climate**—the general weather pattern in a geographic area

**ethnic group**—a group of people sharing racial, religious, and social characteristics

# Physical Geography

**Physical geography** deals with the physical forms of the Earth itself—the mountains, valleys, and flatlands that make up the shape of the land. These physical features are called **landforms**. **Topography** is a detailed description or representation of the landforms in a specific area. How high or low different landforms are can be shown on a topographical map, often by the use of different colors or shadings to indicate different elevations above sea level. The topography of an area is an essential part of the environment and has a strong influence on the way people live.

# Latitude and Longitude

If you look at a globe or a map of the world, you will see a line circling the Earth midway between the North and South poles. This imaginary line is the **equator**. The lines that run parallel to the equator are called lines of **latitude**. All areas above the equator are in the northern latitudes—the *Northern Hemisphere* ("hemisphere" means "half a sphere"). All areas below the equator are in the southern latitudes—the *Southern Hemisphere*. How far north or south of the equator a region lies is measured in degrees of latitude.

The **prime meridian** is an imaginary line that runs north to south through Greenwich, England. The lines that run parallel to the prime meridian are called lines of **longitude**. The prime meridian is at 0° longitude. Regions to the east of it are in the *Eastern Hemisphere*, and regions to the west of it are in the *Western Hemisphere*. How far east or west a region lies is measured in degrees of longitude.

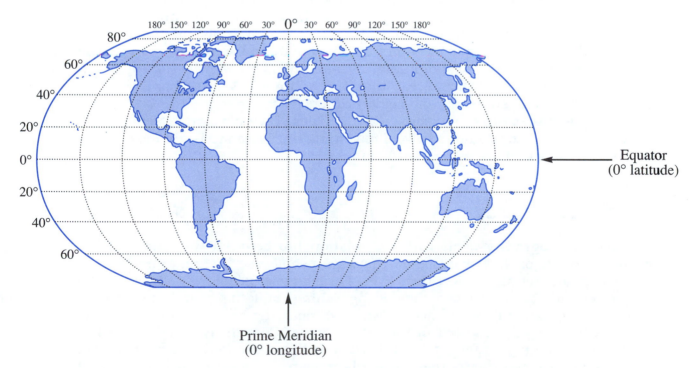

Equator (0° latitude)

Prime Meridian (0° longitude)

As you can see in the illustration, the lines of latitude and longitude cross each other to form an imaginary grid across the Earth. The point at which any line of latitude crosses a lone of longitude has two **coordinates**. One coordinate is the number of degrees latitude; the other coordinate is the number of degrees longitude. Coordinates can give the exact location of a given place. They are useful for locating and tracking large storms, such as hurricanes, and are also used for identifying the exact location of ships and planes as they travel.

## The Zones of Climate

Different regions of the Earth have different climate conditions. These regions are called zones of climate or **climatic zones**. A region's climate depends on many factors. In general, the closer a place is to the equator, the warmer is its climate. Near the equator are most of the world's jungles and rain forests, as well as some of its deserts.

The **tropics**, with their hot, wet, tropical climate, lie between two imaginary lines known as the **Tropic of Cancer** (23-1/2° north latitude) and the **Tropic of Capricorn** (23-1/2° south latitude). Most of the major countries of South America, Central America, and Africa are in the tropics. So are those in Southeast Asia (such as Vietnam, Thailand, the Philippines, and Indonesia), as well as much of India and parts of the Middle East. Caribbean islands such as Cuba, Jamaica, and the Bahamas are also in this **tropical zone**.

The two climatic zones above and below the tropics are the **temperate zones**. The northern temperate zone lies between the Tropic of Cancer and the *Arctic Circle* (near the North Pole). In this zone are found the United States, Russia, England, Europe, and Japan, as well as major parts of Canada, China, and the Middle East. The southern temperate zone lies between the Tropic of Capricorn and the *Antarctic Circle* (near the South Pole). In it are found Australia and the nations in southern South America such as Chile and Argentina. Both these temperate zones have four distinct seasons. Some of the areas in them are dry, or *arid*, others are *semi-arid,* and some are *marine*. The marine areas get a great deal of rainfall. Mountainous areas, which have a high elevation, are usually cooler. Areas that are far from any large body of water usually have hotter summers and colder winters.

The **arctic zones** are the regions near the poles. They have an extremely cold climate because they do not receive direct sunlight. These areas are mostly covered by ice caps and are very sparsely inhabited.

## Cultural Geography

**Cultural geography** deals with the relationship between the land and the people who live on it. It focuses on the ways people use the land and how its physical characteristics affect their lives. For example, people who live near the sea have traditionally earned their living fishing, building boats, and trading goods. The entire culture of people who live near the sea is centered on the water, a fact that is reflected in their daily living. Conversely, people who live inland on fertile plains farm the land. Their cultures are tied to farming, farm animals, and the weather of their particular region.

Cultural geographers also study the ethnic composition of populations and how these ethnic groups are distributed throughout the world. People in **ethnic groups** have certain racial, religious, and social traits in common.

For instance, cultural geographers may study different races in relation to their geographical origin. The world's population is divided into three broad racial groups. Each group consists of people with certain physical characteristics in common that include skin color, hair texture, and eye shape and color. The **Mongoloid race**, which originated in Asia, makes up 43% of the world's population. The Japanese and Chinese are members of this race. The **Caucasoid race**, which originated in Europe, makes up 33% of the world's population. Europeans and Americans of European descent are Caucasians. The **Negroid race**, which originated in Africa, makes up 24% of the world's population. Black Africans and African-Americans are members of this race.

People who share racial and ethnic ties also tend to share religious beliefs. Of the world's **major religions**, more people belong to **Christian** denominations than to any other. Over 1.5 billion Christians live throughout the world, on every continent and in almost every country. The next largest religion is **Islam**, with over 800 million followers (called Moslems or Muslims) throughout the world. The Arab countries of northern Africa and the Middle East are largely Moslem, and there are large populations of Moslems in southeastern Europe, Asia and North America. Many African-Americans follow Islam. The major religion of India is **Hinduism**. There are more than 600 million Hindus in India alone, with other large groups on other continents. Once the state religion of India, **Buddhism** is strong in Tibet, Mongolia, China, Korea, and Japan, with over 300 million followers.

Making inferences means finding information that is not directly stated in a passage. To do this, you have to use what *is* stated as a clue to help you figure out, or infer, what is not stated.

## Making Inferences

In the previous section on cultural geography you were told that shore-dwellers center their lives around fishing and boating. People who live inland center their lives around farming or industries that are not directly dependent on the ocean. Now suppose you were asked what the main food of inland farmers was. You could infer that inland farmers eat very little fish, because they don't have access to it. You could also infer that they eat a lot of fresh produce and meat from some farm animals.

Use the same skills to make inferences from a graphic. Look at the details that are given. Put them together to fill in the information that is *not* given. Try it with the following map and question.

*Remember:* An answer choice that restates a given detail is wrong for an inference question even if it restates the detail accurately, because you are being asked to make an inference, that is, to find an *unstated* meaning.

Based on the map, you can infer that people tend to live

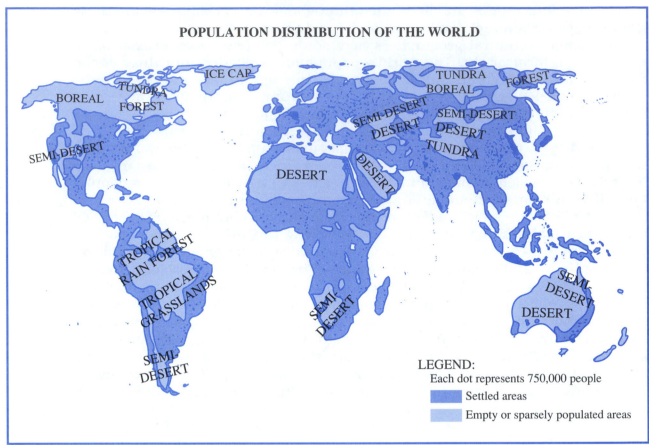

**POPULATION DISTRIBUTION OF THE WORLD**

LEGEND:
Each dot represents 750,000 people
■ Settled areas
▨ Empty or sparsely populated areas

Source: From *New Revised Cambridge GED Program: Social Studies.* Copyright ©1992 Regents/Prentice Hall.

Based on the map, you can infer that people tend to live

**(1)** outside of desert or tundra areas

**(2)** in the Eastern Hemisphere

**(3)** along the shoreline

**(4)** in regions that can supply food

**(5)** where it is warm

The correct answer is choice (4). The passage on cultural geography in the lesson tells you that people in coastal areas live off fish, and people in fertile inland areas live off farm animals and agriculture. Knowing this, look at the map. It shows that population concentration is heaviest on coasts (especially in the United States, England, Europe, China, and Japan). It is also heavy inland in these temperate zone nations—and in the tropic zone country of India. From this information, you can infer (4). The map also supports this inference by showing that deserts and areas in tropical forests or near the North Pole are not settled. Since you know that the climate in deserts and the tropics is extremely hot and that the climate near the poles is extremely cold, you can infer that these areas are hard to live in, and probably are not good sources of food. (1) is a true detail; it cannot be an inference because it is shown directly on the map. (2) and (3) are false details: they misstate what is shown on the map. Choice (2) might seem correct because there is more land area in the East than the West; the land in the West, however, is heavily populated. Choice (3) can be eliminated by looking at all the coastlines on the map that are *not* heavily populated, and by noticing that many people also live inland. Choice (5) is a false inference. You know that the climate gets colder as you get farther from the equator, yet the map shows that many people live in the areas far north and south of the equator in the temperate zones.

## Lesson 8 Exercise

Items 1 and 2 are based on the following passage.

Geography determines a country's natural resources. Coffee, sugar, and rubber trees don't grow in the temperate zones, where these products are in great demand. These trees do grow in countries in the tropics, however. On the other hand, there are relatively few oil fields in the tropics, while there are many in the temperate zones.

The imbalance of the world's natural resources has worked very much in favor of some nonindustrial Middle Eastern countries. Oil—so much in demand by the industrial world—is plentiful in the Middle East. Highly industrial countries, like Japan and those in Western Europe, have no oil of their own. They must depend solely on imported oil. This dependence has made Middle Eastern countries rich.

1. You can infer from this passage that

   (1) geography determines a country's natural resources
   (2) world trade makes it possible for countries to obtain resources that are not native to their region
   (3) the imbalance of natural resources has worked in favor of some countries
   (4) the industrial world takes advantage of nonindustrial nations
   (5) the temperate zones have more natural resources

2. You can infer from this passage that world trade is

   (1) more beneficial for developing (nonindustrial) nations than for industrial nations
   (2) more beneficial for industrial nations that for developing nations
   (3) mutually beneficial for both developing and industrial nations

   (4) not beneficial for developing and industrial nations
   (5) only moderately beneficial for developing nations

Item 3 refers to the map of latitude and longitude on page 203.

3. Looking at the map, you can infer that the climate in central Africa is probably most similar to that in

   (1) southern North America
   (2) central North America
   (3) central South America
   (4) northern South America
   (5) northern Africa

Answers are on page A-17.

# Lesson 9

# Anthropology and Sociology

## Prereading Prompt

You probably know your family's history and feel you are an important part of it. Your family, like others, is a group that is part of larger groups. The study of groups of people—their relationships and their place in a specific society—is the main concern of anthropology and sociology.

## Key Words

**sociology**—study of groups in society, their beliefs and relationships, and of social change

**physical anthropology**—study of the origins of the human race and the physical differences between racial groups

**cultural anthropology**—study of lifestyles, moral ideas, and beliefs of different societies

## Anthropology

The field of anthropology has two branches of study: **physical anthropology** and **cultural anthropology**. In general, physical anthropology deals with the origins of the human race and the physical differences between groups. Cultural anthropology is more concerned with the ways of life, values, and beliefs of various societies.

**208    Chapter 1: Social Studies**

How did the human race get to its current state of evolution? What effects have climatic conditions and other forces had on physical changes in body type, skin color, and facial structure? These are the kinds of questions **physical anthropologists** attempt to answer. Such scientific research helps us understand how geography helped create the different races. Members of the Negroid race, for example, have dark skin that developed in response to the intense sun in their original environment. Members of the Caucasoid race responded in kind to the *lack* of direct sunlight in the northerly latitudes. Their skin tends to be a pale pink and does not fare well in strong sunlight. As members of the races migrated to different regions, they developed physical traits to help them adjust to their new environments. Members of the Caucasoid race who migrated to areas with strong sunlight—around the northern shores of the Mediterranean, for example—tend to have a darker complexion that can withstand the sun's rays. Physical anthropologists can track the mass movements of various groups from one area to another by studying physical traits as well as the rates at which the different blood types appear in the races. This information is useful for piecing together the evolution of the species.

As their name suggests, the focus of **cultural anthropologists** is the culture of different groups and societies. All societies, and many groups within each society, have their own values, beliefs, and attitudes. Almost all societies have at least one religion, yet not all members of the society may subscribe to that religion, or to any religion at all. Societies also have different ways of celebrating occasions such as marriage and birth, and they also have different ways of observing death. The attitude toward children and the way they are raised is also particular to a given society. All of these are the concern of cultural anthropologists.

Underneath all of the specific attitudes, beliefs, and values of a society is its **creed**, the basic set of beliefs that supports all the other beliefs held by the society. In the United States, our basic creed, or fundamental belief, is that all people are created equal and should have equal opportunities. Much of our government, law, and day-to-day living is affected by this one idea. Clearly, all people in the United States do not believe in this creed, or we would not have racism and discrimination based on race, religion, or sex. Yet it is an underlying principle that holds our society together. In other countries, Moslem countries in the Middle East for example, religion is the basic creed that influences every part of the society. Cultural anthropologists study the creeds of the different societies in the world.

The tools of physical and cultural anthropologists are similar. Both collect information by living with people in society—observing, questioning, and formulating ideas about that society. They study their daily activities, ways of earning a living, eating habits, sexual customs, celebrations, architecture, clothing—anything that will help them find out who these people are. To study groups and societies that are no longer in existence—such as the ancient Greeks or cavemen—they may dig deep in the earth in search of ancient **artifacts** (objects made by humans such as cooking utensils, tools, weapons, and artworks) or **human remains** (human skeletons, or bodies turned to stone).

**Sociology** focuses on people in groups which are parts of the larger society. Society is made up of many smaller groups. For example, members of ethnic groups within a country share a common national heritage. In the United States, there are people of Italian, Irish, Polish, Greek, and Mexican heritage, to name just a few. Often people of a given ethnic background live in neighborhoods with others of the same background. In many cities, especially large ones such as New York and San Francisco, the result is communities called "Chinatown" and "Little Italy"—and other areas that are populated mainly by one cultural group.

People also frequently form groups with others who hold the same religious beliefs. The same society may include groups of Roman Catholics, Jews, Hindus, and Muslims (followers of Islam). People of the same ethnic background often share a common religion, as religion is an important part of most cultures.

Another kind of group is the **peer group**. This is made up of people who share a common age and way of life. Teenagers, for example, identify with other teenagers and adopt a mini-culture of their own. They dress similarly, listen to the same music, and often develop a way of speaking all their own.

The **socioeconomic group** is yet another way people identify with each other. Usually we refer to a lower, middle, and upper class when grouping people in this way. People in the same socioeconomic group share a similar income, standard of living, level of education, and level of occupation. In this country, it is possible to rise to a higher socioeconomic group by improving your income and in this way changing your lifestyle. Such change is known as **social mobility**.

Members of a society are expected to conform to certain standards of behavior, or **norms**. Behavior that doesn't conform to these standards is considered abnormal, or **deviant**. To ensure its survival, a society must transmit its values to its members—a process known as **socialization**. A number of social institutions perform the role of socializing people. These institutions include schools, churches and other houses of worship, and the family. Many sociologists believe that the family is the single most important factor in socialization. A child with a strong and supportive family will learn right from wrong and grow up to be a responsible member of society. The breakdown of the family is often blamed for the recent dramatic increase in crime and violence in American society.

## Inferring the Main Idea of a Paragraph

In Lesson 4, you learned how to find the stated main idea of a paragraph—the idea that is the most important thing said about the topic of the paragraph. After you find out the topic (what the paragraph is about), you look for the topic sentence—the one that states the main idea of the paragraph. This strategy is fine when there is a stated main idea, but sometimes the main idea is not stated. It has to be inferred. You have to figure out what is not stated from what *is* stated. To do this, first read the paragraph. Ask yourself: What is the most important idea expressed about the topic of this paragraph? Try to sum it up in one sentence. Does your sentence cover all of the important information stated in the paragraph?

Read the following paragraph. Then see which of the choices that follows it best covers the important information.

> Archaeologists search for objects left by previous societies. They dig to find the remains of houses, cooking utensils, tools, sculptures, and even human skeletons. Archaeologists then study the objects that people made and used. This is an important way of learning about other cultures, particularly those that existed before the invention of writing.

Which of the following sentences contains the unstated main idea of the paragraph?

**(1)** Archaeologists study the history of societies that no longer exist.

**(2)** Archaeologists must be trained to recognize important objects from the past and to approximate the dates of their origins.

**(3)** Archaeologists learn about the past by finding and studying the remaining parts of previous cultures.

**(4)** Archaeologists must know about human anatomy to understand the skeletons they unearth.

**(5)** Archaeologists travel to locations where people may have found objects from long ago and dig to find more.

Choice (3) is the correct answer. It covers all the important stated information in the paragraph. All the sentences in the paragraph support this sentence. Choice (1) is true, but it is too narrow; it doesn't cover everything because it doesn't explain the purpose of what archaeologists do: to help them understand past societies. Choices (2), (4), and (5) are not the main idea, although they are inferences you can make from details that are stated in the paragraph. If you are told that archaeologists study skeletons and other objects from the past, you can infer that they would need the knowledge and training mentioned in (2) and (4). Since societies from the past could be anywhere in the world, you can infer that they travel (5). However, none of these three inferences is big enough to be the main idea of the paragraph.

Item 1 is based on the following paragraph.

The numerous but incomplete studies that have been made of sexual harassment in the European Community countries have revealed that many women and some men suffer sexual harassment. The most frequent victims are those who are most vulnerable from a social or occupational point of view: women who are separated, divorced, or widowed, because their dependence on their jobs is greater and they have no protectors, or women who are new to their jobs or work part time. Members of groups that enjoy little social acceptance or integration—ethnic minorities, the disabled, lesbians—are also frequent victims of harassment. And studies show that women who are competing with men at fairly high levels of management, or who are in professions that are traditionally male, are more exposed than the average women to sexual harassment.

Carlota Bustelo, "'Sickness' of Sexual Harassment," *El Pais,* published in *World Press Review* in February 1992 © 1992

1. Which of the following contains the unstated main idea of the paragraph?

    (1) Sexual harassment in the European Community mainly victimizes people who are defenseless or threatening to men.

    (2) Sexual harassment in the European Community mainly victimizes groups who are unprepared for their new positions in the workplace.

    (3) Sexual harassment in the European Community is like that in the United States and the rest of the world.

    (4) Sexual harassment in the European Community mainly victimizes groups who have never been fully integrated in the society.

    (5) Sexual harassment in the European Community victimizes women competing with men at high levels more than any other group.

Item 2 is based on the following paragraph.

Rites of passage are rituals children go through in order to be accepted as adults by their society. Sometimes these rituals are tied to religion, as in the Jewish bar mitzvah, a religious ceremony in which 13-year-old boys are accepted as men. Many Jews also celebrate a female version of this ceremony, called the bat mitzvah in which 12-year-old girls are accepted as women. In American society, most rites of passage are not tied to religion. They may include such milestones as getting a driver's license, taking one's first alcoholic drink, and voting for the first time.

2. The inferred main idea of this paragraph is that

(1) most societies have some form of rites of passage

(2) rites of passage are rituals children go through to be accepted as adults

(3) in many cultures, the rites of passage are tied to religion

(4) American rites of passage are generally not tied to religion

(5) children who do not go through rites of passage do not reach maturity

Item 3 is based on the following paragraph.

Working women in India now number about 10 million, and women have entered all fields, from medicine to politics to piloting planes, yet sexual harassment is on the increase. It can be found as easily in a film studio as in a government office. Female workers in clerical jobs or in nursing often complain of harassment from supervisors or colleagues. Those in high-profile, glamorous occupations also receive unwanted male attention.

Source: Ranjana Sengupta, "A Symptom of Urban Anomie", *World Press Review*, February 1992. Originally published in *Indian Express*, New Delhi.

3. Which of the following contains the unstated main idea of this paragraph?

(1) About 10 million working women in India suffer sexual harassment in various fields of work.

(2) Working women in India in glamorous occupations suffer more sexual harassment than those in other kinds of work.

(3) Sexual harassment is the "price of admission" women in India must pay for working in mostly-male fields of work.

(4) As large numbers of women in India have entered the workforce, sexual harassment has increased in all fields of work.

(5) Sexual harassment of working women in India is due to the large number of them that have entered the workforce.

Answers are on page A-17.

# Psychology

## Prereading Prompt

You probably hear popular terms of psychology daily in conversation, on TV, or in movies, such as "anxiety," "neurotic," "repressed," or "conditioned." What do these terms mean to you? Have you ever observed someone's behavior and been unable to figure out the reasons behind it? Psychologists attempt to trace the causes of individual behavior, understand it, and, sometimes, change it. This lesson will tell you about two types of psychology.

## Key Words

**id**—the part of the unconscious mind that is responsible for our basic drives

**ego**—the logical, conscious part of the mind

**superego**—the largely unconscious part of the mind that carries moral standards

## Psychology

Psychology is one of the social sciences that studies human behavior. Unlike sociology and anthropology, it focuses on the individual. Psychologists attempt to understand the causes of behavior by analyzing the way the human mind works. Their work includes the study of normal behavior as well as the study of abnormal behavior and emotional illness.

# Psychoanalysis

Psychoanalysis is a means of treating people who have mental problems. A person who practices psychoanalysis—a specially trained doctor called a psychoanalyst—attempts to uncover long-forgotten or buried memories. The method was developed by Sigmund Freud in the late 19th century. At that time, Freud was a physician in Austria, working primarily with people who were paralyzed or blind. These people were special cases because there was no physical cause for their symptoms.

In the course of talking with some of these patients, Freud discovered that some of their symptoms began to disappear. Merely discussing some of their childhood traumas, or deeply disturbing experiences, seemed to help them. Freud reasoned that the cause of their symptoms was rooted in their minds, not in their bodies. The patients, of course, were unaware of this because the problems existed in the unconscious part of their minds. Painful childhood experiences had been **repressed**, or pushed out of sight, into this unconscious level of their minds. Yet the problems did not go away but expressed themselves as emotional disorders—such as extreme fears and hatreds, the inability to form love relationships, and self-destructive and even violent behavior. The problems might even express themselves indirectly as physical illnesses, such as blindness and paralysis. Freud worked to cure his patients by helping them bring their unconscious feelings and memories to a conscious level. Once they were brought to a conscious level, the patients could understand the causes of their problems and try to deal with them.

Freud believed that the human mind is made up of three parts: the id, the ego, and the superego. The **id** is part of the unconscious mind. It is responsible for all of the basic human drives for food and water, sex, and power. The **ego** is part of the conscious mind. It is usually logical and realistic, and in touch with the person's real situation. The ego helps people think clearly and make decisions. The **superego** is mainly unconscious. It contains the moral standards of society and people's deepest feelings about right and wrong. It is what most people refer to as their *conscience*.

In people who are mentally healthy, the id, ego, and superego work together in a balanced way. The drives of the id, such as sexual desire, are controlled by the ego and superego until they can be expressed in an appropriate way. People who cannot control their desires in an appropriate way are often prone to criminal behavior and violence. When looked at this way, all criminals can be said to suffer from emotional or mental illness.

# Behaviorism

**Behaviorism** is another school of psychology. This theory, unlike Freud's, is based on the idea that all human behavior is learned. If human behavior is learned, then it follows that it can be changed through training.

**Conditioning** is a method used by behaviorists to change behavior. A Russian scientist named Pavlov experimented with this method in the early 1900s. Knowing that animals salivate in anticipation of food, he tried to train a dog to salivate in response to something other than food, in this case, the sound of a bell. He did this by first training the dog to connect eating with the sound of the bell; each time the bell rang, the dog would be fed a tidbit. Eventually, the dog would salivate solely in response to the sound of the bell, even when no food was offered. This experiment led psychologists to believe that behavior can be controlled by forming connections, or **associations**, in the subject's mind.

In more recent times, a Harvard professor named B. F. Skinner carried Pavlov's experiments even further. He used a system of rewards to train animals. By giving his subjects bits of food (rewards) when they performed a desired behavior, he taught the animals to perform many behaviors on command. This principle of learning can be seen in everyday life. A parent will often reward a child for good behavior, thereby increasing the likelihood that the child will behave this way in the future.

Some behaviorists use punishment as well as reward in their learning experiments. Punishment is used to eliminate an undesirable or unwanted behavior. One form of punishment is mild electric shock. In experiments, each time an animal performs the unwanted behavior, a mild shock is administered. The shock is not strong enough to really hurt the animal, but it is unpleasant enough that the animal learns to avoid it by not repeating the behavior. This principle of learning has also been used by people without actually labelling it. When a child behaves in an undesirable way, a parent will often punish the child, making it less likely that the child will behave this way again.

The ideas in behaviorist theory are useful in everyday life, and most of us use them to some extent without even realizing it. The parent who gives praise and a big hug when a child has cleaned his room is using the principles of behaviorism. Likewise, the parent who yells at a child who has just drawn on the living room wall with a crayon is using another principle of behaviorism. Dog training is accomplished strictly with these theories of learning. By forming associations in the subject's mind, both reward and punishment cause learning to occur.

# Inferring the Main Idea of a Passage

Inferring the main idea of a passage is similar to inferring the main idea of a paragraph. The main idea will not be stated. You must put it together using the clues in the passage. Remember that the main idea of a passage must be broad enough to encompass the main ideas in all the paragraphs. On the other hand, the main idea cannot be vague. Although it is a general statement, it must refer clearly to the main ideas of all the paragraphs in the passage.

First read the entire passage. Then look for the main idea of each paragraph. If the main idea of some or all the paragraphs is not stated in a topic sentence, you must infer these before you can infer the main idea of the passage. Once you have all the main ideas of the paragraphs, you can put together a sentence that contains the main idea of the entire passage.

Read the following passage and then answer the question.

Carl Gustav Jung was a Swiss psychiatrist who was very interested in Freud's theories of the unconscious. The two men became friends and colleagues. However, they later disagreed on the importance of sexual drives in the conscious and unconscious mind. Freud believed sex was the primary motivation of human behavior, which Jung did not believe. This strong and basic disagreement caused Jung to break off his association with Freud.

Jung believed in a part of the mind he called the *collective unconscious*. According to his theories, this part of the mind holds a kind of racial memory through which the experiences of our ancestors affect us. He believed there are inborn patterns of behavior that affect everyone and are expressed in people's behavior and thoughts. These patterns have developed along with the human race. Jung's term for them is **archetypes**.

Which of the following is the inferred main idea of this passage?

**(1)** Jung developed a theory of the unconscious that did not include sexual drives.

**(2)** Jung was a Swiss psychiatrist who became famous because he disagreed with Freud over the importance of sexual drives.

**(3)** Jung believed that all human beings are influenced by archetypes that are formed over the centuries.

**(4)** Jung broke with Freud about the importance of sex and developed the theory of the collective unconscious.

**(5)** Jung's theory of the unconscious included more than Freud's theory of the unconscious.

(4) is correct. It is the only choice that covers the main ideas of both paragraphs. The first paragraph says that Jung was influenced by Freud and worked with him until he broke with Freud about the importance of sex as a basic motive of behavior. The second paragraph tells us that Jung developed a theory of a collective unconscious that was based on patterns of racial memory called archetypes. (2) gives only the main idea of the first paragraph, and (3) restates—not very completely—the main idea of the second paragraph. (1) and (5) make large inferences that have no support. Because Jung did not believe sex drives were as important as Freud believed they were does not mean he kept sex drives completely out of his concept of the collective unconscious. (5) cannot be the inferred main idea of the passage because it does not mention Jung's break with Freud over the importance of sex as a motive for behavior. (5) also assumes that Jung's concept of a racial memory covering centuries must necessarily "include more" than Freud's idea of the unconscious. However, since sex drives influence all kinds of relationships—with parents, children, friends—and affect all phases of life, the Freudian unconscious is likely to include as much as the Jungian unconscious.

Items 1 and 2 are based on the following passage.

All of us live with a certain amount of stress in our lives. When stress becomes extreme, however, we may feel as if we can't cope with it. A feeling of powerlessness may take over. This feeling is known as *anxiety*. The good news is that, as long as we can continue to control our anxiety and carry on our lives to our satisfaction, we can still be considered "healthy."

If anxiety does take control of us, however, we slip over the edge into what is known as *neurosis*. People suffering from neurosis cannot cope with their problems; they may even deny that they have problems at all. Emotional conflicts inside them get beyond their control, causing unnecessary conflicts with other people and upsetting their ability to work well or form close relationships. Their lives become confused and unhappy. They may develop bad habits such as alcoholism or drug abuse. This kind of self-defeating behavior signals deep problems that these neurotic people are unable to deal with on their own.

1. What is the unstated main idea of paragraph 1?

   (1) Anxiety is an unhealthy response to extreme stress.
   (2) Anxiety is a normal response to extreme stress.
   (3) Anxiety is an inability to cope with stress.
   (4) Anxiety is an inability to control our lives.
   (5) People cope with stress in different ways.

2. What is the unstated main idea of the entire passage?

   (1) Neurosis is an unhealthy response to anxiety.
   (2) Most people suffer from some form of neurosis.
   (3) Anxiety is normal unless it produces neurotic behavior.
   (4) Stress and anxiety can lead to neurotic problems such as alcoholism and drug abuse.
   (5) People whose anxiety has become neurotic should seek some kind of professional help.

Item 3 is based on the following passage.

To avoid feelings of anxiety, people develop *defense mechanisms*. Most of us have some defense mechanisms; they are called into use without our even realizing it. One defense mechanism is *denial*. Here's an example: A women has just broken off a long relationship with her boyfriend. A well-meaning friend asks her to dinner and a movie. She replies that she's fine, really, and besides, she's been so busy at work she hasn't even had time to think about her ex-boyfriend. In reality, this woman is lonely, hurt, depressed, and angry. She is denying her true feelings.

*Projection* is another defense mechanism. A person who projects is attributing his or her own feelings or desires to others. For example, a man would like to ask a woman out, but he can't because he's afraid of rejection. One night he says to his best friend, "Go on, ask her out. You know you want to." The man has projected his feelings for the woman onto his friend. As in the case of the woman using denial, the man is escaping his true feelings.

3. What is the unstated main idea of this passage?

   (1) Defense mechanisms help people to control emotional problems.

   (2) Denial and projection are the two main kinds of defense mechanisms.

   (3) Defense mechanisms are beyond the control of most people.

   (4) Denial and projection most often occur in people having difficulty with relationships.

   (5) Defense mechanisms are an undesirable response to anxiety.

Answers are on page A-18.

# CHAPTER 2

Science is the systematic study of all the physical things on Earth and in our universe. **Life sciences** study living things, such as animals and plants. **Physical sciences** study nonliving things, such as the composition and behavior of the Earth, of matter and energy, and of the basic substances in all things.

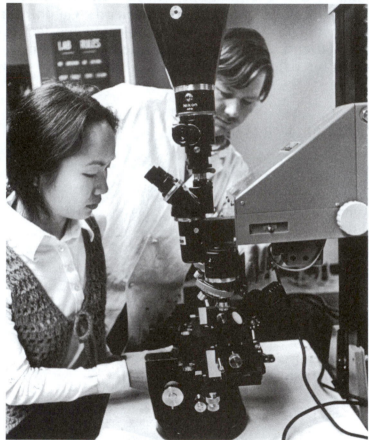

Credit: Laimute Druskis

## Prereading Prompt

The world we live in has been shaped in many ways by modern science. We all have some knowledge of scientific ideas and methods—from the tests or medicine a doctor gives us to the TV news about trips to outer space, new cures for diseases, new weapons, and other new machines. What recent changes caused by science can you think of?

# Science

# WHAT IS SCIENCE?

## Scientific Method

The scientific method is a way of gaining exact knowledge of the physical world. A thing observed by the senses is called a **phenomenon**; a scientifically tested observation is called a **fact**. The scientific method has six basic steps.

1. A new phenomenon is observed, or noticed.
2. A question about the observation is raised.
3. A possible answer, or explanation, called a **hypothesis**, is suggested.
4. An **experiment** is performed to test the hypothesis about the phenomenon.
5. Information from the experiment is examined.
6. A conclusion is reached about whether the hypothesis is true.

## Types of Modern Science

Because scientific knowledge is so vast, scientists today usually concentrate on one of the four main sciences:

**Biology**—the study of living things (animals and plants)
**Earth Science**—the study of our planet and its place in the universe
**Chemistry**—the study of what substances are made of and how they change
**Physics**—the study of how matter and energy are related

### Key Words

**hypothesis**—a possible answer to a scientist's question, which is tested in experiments

**theory**—a general explanation based on hypotheses that have been supported by the experiments used to test them

# Cells: The Basic Unit of Life

## Prereading Prompt

Think of what you already know about cells. What are they? What do they do? Ask yourself: How does a cell on my arm or my face depend on the sun to live? What can a plant do that I can't? Why is a cell considered alive, but a cloud is not? Read the passage to find out the characteristics of life.

## Key Words

**cell**—the smallest unit that has all the features of life

**nucleus**—the core or center of a cell

**photosynthesis**—process by which plants use sunlight to make food

## Cells: Their Structure and Function

Millions of living things have been examined by scientists and all of them have been found to contain at least one cell. Cells are the smallest things that carry on all the life processes. Tiny though cells are, they grow, they use energy, they respond to changes in their surroundings, and they reproduce themselves. In other words: If something's alive, it must have at least one cell, and if something's a cell, it must have all the characteristics of life.

Cells vary a great deal in size. Most cells are so small that you could put a million of them on the head of a pin. An exception is the yolk of a chicken egg, which is actually only one cell. **Microscopic organisms**—living things so small you need a microscope to see them—may be composed of only a few cells or even one cell. Large organisms are composed of many cells working together. Although the human body starts out as a single cell, by the time a person is grown, the body has more than a trillion cells.

The cell is like a factory, where each of its parts performs a specific function necessary to the life process. These functions consist of either building up or breaking down materials. Each animal cell is surrounded by a **cell membrane**, or outer surface, which holds it together and separates it from other cells. This membrane allows essential substances into the cell and keeps unwanted substances out. Most cells contain a **nucleus**, or core of the cell. The nucleus controls the activities in all the other cell parts, and contains chemicals that are necessary for reproduction.

The cell membrane encloses the **cytoplasm**, a watery material that surrounds the nucleus. The cytoplasm contains **organelles**, the structures that carry out the cell's functions: Fluid-filled organelles called **vacuoles** store food particles and waste material; hundreds of organelles called **mitochondria** take part in **cellular respiration**, the process in which energy in food is captured for use by the cell. **Centrioles**—in animal cells, not plant cells—are tiny bundles of tubes which take part in reproduction of the cell.

Plant cells have most of the same structures as animal cells except for centrioles. In addition, plant cytoplasm also contains vessels called **chloroplasts** that capture light energy and use it to make the cell's food. (Since animal cells cannot make food, they have no chloroplasts.) Plant cells also have a tough **cell wall** surrounding the cell membrane; the cell wall gives a plant its stiffness.

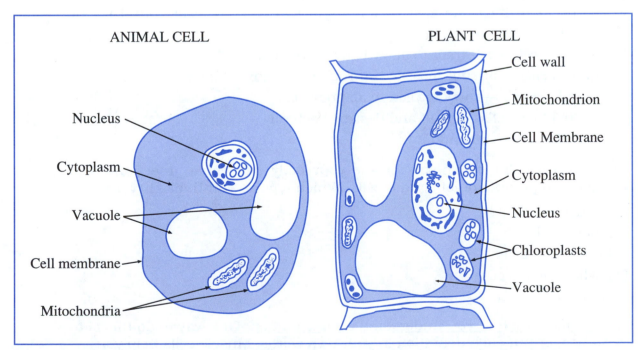

ANIMAL CELL            PLANT CELL

Nucleus · Cytoplasm · Vacuole · Cell membrane · Mitochondria

Cell wall · Mitochondrion · Cell Membrane · Cytoplasm · Nucleus · Chloroplasts · Vacuole

Source: From *New Revised Cambridge GED Program: Science* by Gloria Levine. Copyright ©1992 Regents/Prentice Hall.

## Cells and Energy

All of the life processes are powered by chemical reactions that take place in the cell. Some of the reactions break large materials into smaller ones. During this breakdown, energy is released for such activities as getting rid of waste or moving the cell around the body. Other reactions use energy to build small materials into larger ones needed for growth, repair, or reproduction. Some of these biological materials are: protein, carbohydrates, lipids, and nucleic acids. Both animal and plant cells do some building up and some breaking down.

Green plants capture the energy of sunlight during a process called **photosynthesis**. During photosynthesis, plants make a sugar called **glucose** by combining carbon dioxide and water in the presence of sunlight. The energy stored as food in glucose molecules may later be used by the green plant cell.

Only plants can make food, but an animal cell may use the food if the plant is eaten by an animal. The food particles must be digested until they are small enough to be taken into the cell.

Through a series of chemical changes, plant and animal cells break down glucose and release energy into the cell. Some of the energy is then trapped and used to build up materials that the cell needs. Most of the energy, however, is wasted as heat.

## Applying Information in Categories

When you apply general information, you show your understanding of it by using it in a new, specific situation. In the questions which follow, you will read lists of definitions or descriptions. In each question, you will be asked to decide which item on the list applies to a specific case.

Read the following general descriptions of five types of cells found in the human body.

**(1)** muscle cells—contract to allow body movement

**(2)** nerve cells—transmit messages through the body

**(3)** red blood cells—carry oxygen to all body cells

**(4)** white blood cells—engulf and destroy bacteria

**(5)** fat cells—store oil and fat

Suppose that tiny organisms invade your body and cause infection. Your body steps up production of certain cells. Which type do you think they are?

**(1)** muscle cells
**(2)** nerve cells
**(3)** red blood cells
**(4)** white blood cells
**(5)** fat cells

Step 1: Make sure that you understand each definition. One way to do this is to paraphrase, or put each definition in your own words: Muscle cells help you move; nerve cells send messages; red blood cells bring cells the oxygen they need; white blood cells destroy germs; fat cells store fat.

Step 2: Predict which definition fits the situation. The situation is: You have an infection. The definition which best matches this situation is (4). White blood cells get rid of bacteria, which can cause infection. It makes sense that your body would step up production of white blood cells if they were needed to fight incoming bacteria.

Step 3: Examine all the choices. Build a bridge of ideas between the general information about cells and each of the choices. Ask yourself: Would you need more muscle cells to fight an infection? Not necessarily. What about nerve cells? Probably not. Would you need more oxygen? No. Would you need extra fat cells? No. Your predicted choice (4) still seems like the best answer.

It is not necessary to memorize each description (what each cell does). The best strategy is to read the question carefully. Then look back at each of the descriptions in the list.

## Lesson 1 Exercise

Below are descriptions of five of the basic functions a cell must be able to perform if it is to stay alive.

(1) digestion—breaking down food into usable forms

(2) synthesis—making food into substances needed for growth

(3) excretion—getting rid of waste materials

(4) cellular respiration—releasing energy from foods

(5) reproduction—making more of its own kind

1. A laboratory technician looks through a microscope at some cells taken from a person's throat. She observes that one of the cells is splitting into two separate cells. What function is she observing?

(1) digestion
(2) synthesis
(3) excretion
(4) cellular respiration
(5) reproduction

2. A marine biologist takes a sample of water from a lake and examines it under a microscope. He observes a one-celled organism approach a food particle and surround it. This is probably the first step in which function?

(1) digestion
(2) synthesis
(3) excretion
(4) cellular respiration
(5) reproduction

3. A researcher examines some one-celled organisms under a microscope. She discovers that the organisms are giving off ammonia. The passage of ammonia out of the cell membrane is an example of

(1) digestion
(2) synthesis
(3) excretion
(4) cellular respiration
(5) reproduction

Answers are on page A-19.

# Reproduction and Heredity

## Prereading Prompt

Brainstorm all that you know about sexual reproduction in humans. Think of what you may know about the ways plants reproduce. How do bees and other insects help flowering plants reproduce? You probably know that you got your eye color and other characteristics from your parents. Read this lesson to learn more about how living things reproduce themselves.

## Key Words

**asexual reproduction**—formation of an offspring identical to the parent, from a part of the parent

**sexual reproduction**—formation of unique offspring by **two parents**

**heredity**—passage of traits from parents to offspring

## Asexual and Sexual Reproduction

**Asexual reproduction** is the formation of new cells or organisms from only one parent cell. **Sexual reproduction** is the formation of a new organism by uniting two cells. The cells in your human body reproduce themselves by asexual reproduction. Human beings reproduce themselves in their children by sexual reproduction.

You do not notice that the cells in your body are constantly dying because the body's cells are constantly making new cells to take the place of dying cells. Cells within a multicelled (many-celled) organism such as a human being, or the most familiar animals and plants, reproduce asexually in this way through a process known as **mitosis**. In mitosis, a cell divides to form two identical cells.

The process is similar when one-celled organisms such as the amoeba or paramecium reproduce. Such reproduction by splitting in half is called **fission**. It is considered **asexual reproduction** because it does not involve putting two parent cells together.

Some simple plants (such as yeasts) and animals (such as hydrae) develop small outgrowths, called **buds**, which split off into separate organisms. These new organisms are identical to the parent, but smaller. Even complex plants can sometimes reproduce asexually, with whole new plants developing from parts of a leaf, stem, or root.

**Sexual reproduction**, on the other hand, involves two parents. An **egg** cell from the female combines with a sperm cell from the male. This combination is called **fertilization**. But do you know how the egg and sperm cells form in the first place? They are formed by a process called **meiosis**.

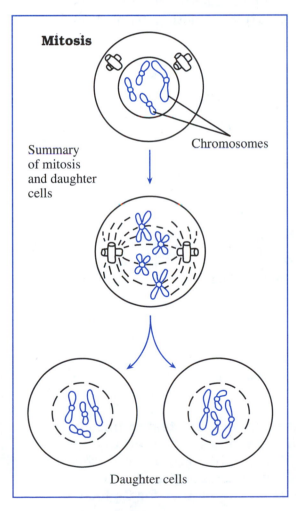

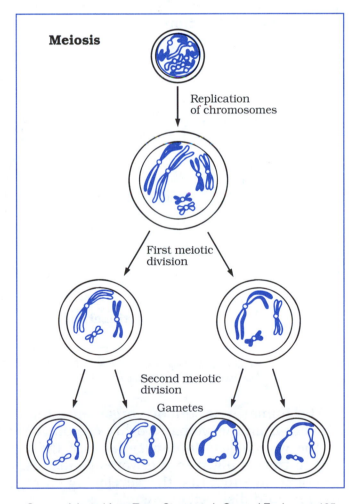

From *The Biology Coloring Book* by Robert Griffin. Copyright ©1986 by Coloring Concepts, Inc. Reprinted by permission of HarperCollins Publishers.

Source: Adapted from Tracy Storer et al, *General Zoology*, p. 195. Copyright ©1972 by McGraw-Hill, Inc. Adapted by permission of McGraw-Hill, Inc.

Like mitosis, **meiosis** is a process of cell division. A cell usually has one or more pairs of chromosomes in its nucleus. **Chromosomes** are small rod-like structures containing a chemical called *DNA* which makes up the **genes**. Genes in the chromosomes control the development of all the characteristics you get from your parents, such as hair color, eye color, skin color, and blood type. In meiosis, as in mitosis, each chromosome makes a duplicate of itself. In meiosis, however, unlike what happens during mitosis, the chromosomes split *twice*. Therefore the four new cells, known as **gametes**, have only half the normal number of chromosomes.

Sexual reproduction occurs when a gamete from a male unites with a gamete from a female, and a new cell is formed that has a complete number of chromosomes. This new cell is the **fertilized egg** or **zygote** from which a new plant or animal develops.

Where are the male and female parts of a flowering plant? If you have hay fever, you know about **pollen**. Those tiny particles which make you sneeze contain the male reproductive cells of the flower. Pollen from the **anther**, the male part of the plant, goes to the **stigma**, the female part of the plant, and then goes down the pollen tube to the **ovary**, which contains one or more little round **ovules**. Each ovule produces an egg cell, which the pollen fertilizes to form a tiny new plant. Other cells form a protective shell called a **seed** around this new plant. This whole fertilizing process is called **pollination** when it takes place inside one plant. When pollen from one plant fertilizes another plant, it is called **cross-pollination**.

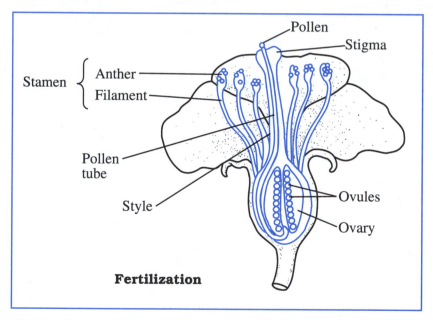

From *The Biology Coloring Book* by Robert Griffin. Copyright ©1986 by Coloring Concepts, Inc. Reprinted by permission of HarperCollins Publishers.

The human reproductive organs are the **ovaries** (female) and **testes** (male). The egg from the woman's ovary combines with the sperm from the man in one of the woman's **fallopian tubes** (see the figure above right). From there, the zygote travels down to the woman's **uterus**, a hollow, muscular organ. During the next nine months, the developing baby depends on the mother for its food, oxygen, and disposal of waste.

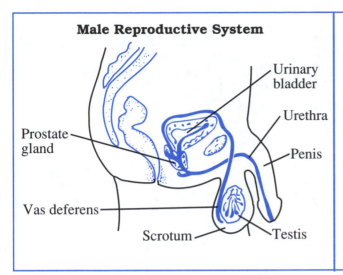

**Male Reproductive System**

Urinary bladder

Urethra

Penis

Prostate gland

Vas deferens

Scrotum

Testis

Source: Adapted from *Biology* by Peter Alexander et al. Copyright ©1986 Silver Burdett Company.

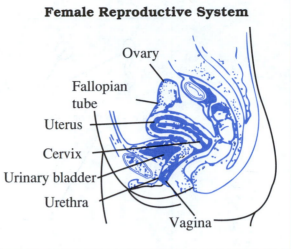

**Female Reproductive System**

Ovary

Fallopian tube

Uterus

Cervix

Urinary bladder

Urethra

Vagina

Source: Adapted from *Biology* by Kenneth R. Miller and Joseph Levine. Copyright ©1991 by Prentice-Hall, Inc.

## Genetics and Heredity

Why is it that an amoeba looks exactly like its parent but you don't look exactly like your parents? The reason is that the amoeba reproduces asexually. Each new amoeba has the *same* chromosomes as the single parent did, and therefore they look alike. During sexual reproduction of plants and animals, however, the offspring receive chromosomes from each of their two parents. These offspring have *different* combinations of chromosomes from their two parents, and therefore they do not look exactly like either parent or like each other. The story of how offspring receive traits from their parents is known as **genetics**.

In 1865, an Austrian monk named Gregor Mendel announced the first reliable laws of genetics, based on his work with pea plants. Mendel found that a pea plant with a short gene from one parent and a tall gene from the other always turned out to be tall. A pea plant with a short gene from each parent always turned out to be short. He concluded that tallness is a stronger trait than shortness. Scientists now call the "stronger" gene dominant, and the "weaker" one, recessive.

## Applying Information in Graphics

Complete the following comparison:

● is to ○ as HOT is to _____.

Given a list of choices, you would probably choose "COLD" as your answer because, like black and white, hot and cold are opposites. Some GED questions involve a similar task. They ask you to spot the correct comparison between information displayed in a graphic, and information in a different situation.

Examine the following graphic:

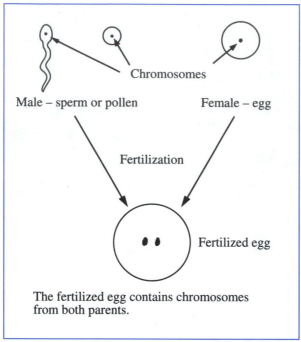

Chromosomes

Male – sperm or pollen

Female – egg

Fertilization

Fertilized egg

The fertilized egg contains chromosomes from both parents.

From *The Cambridge Comprehensive Program for the High School Equivalency Examination.* Copyright © 1987 Prentice Hall Regents.

Combining chromosomes as shown is most similar to what happens when a cook

**(1)** arranges three pancakes into a stack

**(2)** bakes two pieces of dough into one large biscuit

**(3)** mixes a cup of raisins with a cup of walnuts

**(4)** melts a chocolate bar and a stick of butter together

**(5)** whips a cup of sugar into a cup of cream

<u>Step 1: Make sure that you understand the graphic</u>. Look carefully at the drawings, arrows, and labels. The arrows on top show you that chromosomes are contained in both the sperm and egg. The arrows on the bottom show how the sperm and egg come together to make a fertilized egg. You can see that in the fertilized egg the chromosomes are still distinct and separate.

<u>Step 2: Examine all the choices.</u> Notice that you cannot predict the answer before looking at the choices. Build a bridge between the diagram and each of the choices about cooking. Ask yourself: Which example is most like fertilization, in which two parent cells join together, each contributing chromosomes to the fertilized egg? Stacking three pancakes (1) does not really combine things together at all; besides, the diagram shows only two cells combining. Baking two dough pieces together (2) would completely combine two things that are completely alike; the graphic shows two unlike things combining. (4) and (5) both show two unlike things *completely* combining. Only (3) describes two things that combine, but which share particles (like the chromosomes) that each thing had before and that remain separate and distinct after combining.

## Lesson 2 Exercise

Below is a chart showing some dominant (D) and recessive (R) traits.

Source: From *Blood and Guts: A Working Guide to Your Own Insides* by Linda Allison. A Brown Paper School Book. Copyright ©1976 by the Yolla Bolly. By permission of Little, Brown and Company.

1. Free earlobes (hanging from the ears and separated from the sides of the head) are dominant and attached earlobes (positioned flat against the sides of the head) are recessive. If earlobes were included on the chart, the artist might show

   (1) a girl with free earlobes (D) and a boy with free earlobes (R)
   (2) a girl with attached earlobes (D) and a boy with attached earlobes (R)
   (3) a girl with free earlobes (D) and a boy with attached earlobes (R)
   (4) a girl with free earlobes (D) and a girl with free earlobes (R)
   (5) a girl with attached earlobes (D) and a girl with attached earlobes (R)

2. Suppose you want to add tongue-rolling to the chart. How could you show that tongue-rolling, the ability to hold your tongue in a "U" shape, is dominant, and the inability to do so is recessive?

   (1) A woman who can roll her tongue (D) and a man who can't (R)
   (2) A woman who can't roll her tongue (R) and a man who can't (R)
   (3) A woman who can roll her tongue (D) and a man who can (R)
   (4) A man who can roll his tongue (D) and a man who can (R)
   (5) A man who can't roll his tongue (D) and a man who can (R)

3. Freckles are dominant. Which of the following would be the best way to illustrate this on the chart?

   (1) Two girls, (D) and (R): (D) has many more freckles.
   (2) Two boys, (D) and (R): (R) has very few freckles.
   (3) One boy (D), one girl (R): the boy has larger freckles.
   (4) One girl (D), one boy (R): the girl has larger freckles.
   (5) One boy (D), one girl (R): only the boy has freckles.

Item 4 is based on the fertilization diagram on p.230.

4. If the diagram showed a sperm with 24 chromosomes, how many dots would you see in the fertilized egg?

   (1) 2
   (2) 12
   (3) 24
   (4) 25
   (5) 48

Answers are on page A-19.

# The Systems of the Human Body

## Prereading Prompt

Do you know what the different parts of your brain do? You know that you need food and air to live. But do you know how the food you eat and the air you breathe get inside your body's cells?

## Key Words

**central nervous system**—the brain and spinal cord

**digestion**—breakdown of food into a form the body's cells can use

**respiration**—the body's intake of oxygen and release of carbon dioxide

**circulation**—movement of blood through the body

## Nervous System

Your body cannot do anything without some activity in the **central nervous system**. This is made up of the brain and spinal cord (see the diagram on the next page.) Whenever we think, remember, feel, imagine, or act, we rely on our brains. Our internal organ systems are under the brain's control, too.

If you could look underneath your skull at your brain, you would see a jellied gray mass of pressed-together coils, about the size of two fists pressed together and weighing about three pounds. This wrinkled globe is divided into two halves. For some reason, language and reasoning ability seem controlled mainly by the left side of the brain. The spatial skills we use when we draw a picture, or figure out which direction to take, seem to lie more in the right brain. Brain research also shows that the left side of the brain controls the right side of the body and the right brain controls the body's left side.

If you could shrink down to the level of cells in the brain, you would see billions of nerve cells webbed together in a pattern more complicated than that of any computer. These cells are passing many messages at once—electrical and chemical in nature—down through the spinal cord.

The **spinal cord** is that important nerve cord that lies protected by the backbone. It sends information not only from the brain to the muscles, but also from the sense organs (like the ears and nose) to the brain. People with spinal cord injuries may lose sensation in their limbs, and control over their muscles.

The **peripheral nervous system** is all of those nerves that connect the central nervous system with the outer parts of the body and the inner organs. It includes the nerves that control automatic activities like heart rate and digestion.

**The Nervous System**

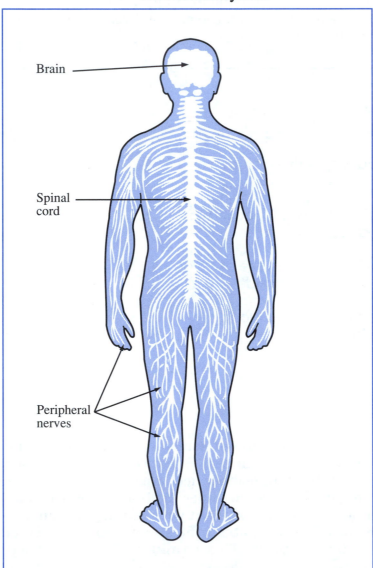

Source: Adapted from *Life Science* by Jill Wright et al. Copyright ©1991 by Prentice-Hall, Inc.

# Digestive System

In order for the body's cells to get nutrients and energy from food, it must be broken down small enough to fit into the cells. This process of breaking down food is called **digestion**. The mouth, stomach, and intestines are the major organs in the human digestive system (see the figure below). Once food is in your mouth, your teeth work to begin tearing and grinding it into smaller pieces. **Saliva** (spit) wets the food and starts breaking starches down into simpler sugars.

The pieces of food then travel down the tube called the **esophagus** to the stomach. In the stomach, substances called **acids** and **enzymes** break the food down into even smaller particles.

**The Digestive System**

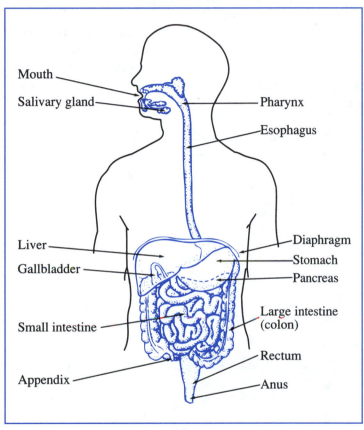

Source: Adapted from *Biology* by Kenneth R. Miller and Joseph Levine. Copyright ©1991 Prentice-Hall, Inc.

Partly liquid at that point, the food is then passed into the small intestine. This organ is coiled like a hose in the body. Stretched out, it is as long as four men lying end to end. As a result, there is plenty of time and space for digestion and absorption as food passes through the small intestine. In its walls, many tiny fingerlike structures, called **villi**, help mix the food while the walls contract in a churning motion, like that in a washing machine. The walls are also lined with cells that produce digestive juices. Additional digestive enzymes pass into the small intestine from the liver and pancreas. Once the food is digested, it is absorbed by passing through the intestinal wall into the bloodstream. Solid materials that can't be digested or used by the body pass into the large intestine. There they are stored until they pass out of the body. Other waste materials that result from various cell activities are dissolved in the blood. These are filtered out by two organs called the kidneys. Then a mixture of dissolved waste and water passes into the bladder. The mixture is stored there until it passes out of the body as urine.

## Circulatory System

After the digested food moves through the wall of the small intestine, it passes into very small blood vessels called **capillaries**. Some of these have walls that are only one cell thick, so it is easy for the food particles to enter and leave them. From these small vessels, the food passes into larger vessels which circulate blood around the body. Along the way, many food particles leave the blood and proceed into the cells that need nourishment.

A cell that has just received a delivery of food also needs oxygen to "burn" or oxidize the food. Oxidizing the food releases the energy the cell needs to survive. Like food, oxygen passes to the cells from the blood. The pump that keeps the blood moving is the **heart.** It is a muscular organ which is divided into two halves. Each half is divided into an upper and lower "room," or chamber.

**The Circulatory System**

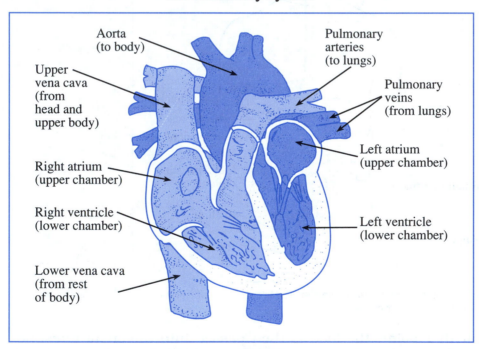

Source: From *New Revised Cambridge GED Program: Science* by Gloria Levine. Copyright ©1992 Regents/Prentice Hall.

Blood low in oxygen returns to the heart from the body through vessels called **veins**. The heart pumps the low-oxygen blood into the lungs, where it picks up oxygen. Then the oxygen-rich blood flows from the lungs back to the heart which pumps it out to the rest of the body through vessels called **arteries**. The heart plus the vessels carrying the blood make up the circulatory system.

## Respiratory System

**The Respiratory System**

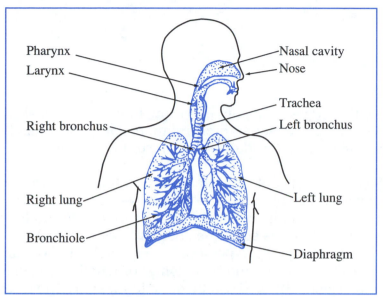

Source: Adapted from *Biology* by Kenneth R. Miller and Joseph Levine.
Copyright ©1991 by Prentice-Hall, Inc.

How does oxygen get into the **lungs** in the first place? After you breathe air in through your nose and mouth, it passes down the back of your throat to your windpipe and then into the two lungs. From there, as we have seen, oxygen passes into the blood, and circulates around the body. The blood also picks up waste materials from the cells. Remember the carbon dioxide the cell gives off when it oxidizes the food? It follows the reverse route from the oxygen we just followed: It passes out of the cell, into the blood, back to the lungs and out the nose or mouth. The pathway through which air passes into and out of the body is called the **respiratory system**.

# Recognizing Facts, Opinions, and Hypotheses

One type of question on the GED requires you to recognize the difference between facts, opinions, and hypotheses. To identify which is which, ask yourself: Is this something that can be proved by measurement or observation? If so, it is a fact. Is this someone's personal interpretation, a value or belief that cannot be proven? If so, it is an opinion. Is this an educated guess developed to explain observed facts, and then tested? If so, it is a hypothesis.

An advertisement for Rack-Up brand cigarettes states

A. Rack-Up has lower tar levels than most other cigarettes.

B. It has a rich, satisfying taste.

C. Rack-Up is the cigarette of choice among the choosiest smokers.

D. Smoking causes lung cancer, heart disease, and emphysema.

Which of the above statements is (are) most likely based on facts rather than on opinion?

(1) A only

(2) B only

(3) A and B only

(4) B and C only

(5) A and D only

<u>Step 1: Examine each of the four statements carefully.</u> In each case, ask yourself: Can this be proven or is it a personal interpretation? Only tar levels (A) and links between cigarette smoking and disease (D) can be proven.

<u>Step 2: Predict the answer.</u> Many people find items of this type—where you have to choose between various combinations of answers—confusing. You will be doing yourself a big favor if you figure out the answer BEFORE you look at the choices. Then all you have to do is skim the choices until you find the combination that matches yours. B and C are personal interpretations; we cannot measure whether the cigarette is "rich" and "satisfying" or whether the smokers who smoke it are the "choosiest." Studies can be done to measure the level of tar, and the relationship between smoking and disease, so statements A and D are most likely based on facts.

<u>Step 3: Examine the choices for the best answer.</u> Choice (5) is the one which matches your prediction (that statements A and D are the facts). The correct answer is (5).

## Lesson 3 Exercise

Items 1-3 are based on the following passage.

Researchers have noticed that people who tend to put on weight around their bellies are at higher risk for heart disease than are those who spread out in the thighs and buttocks. The observation has spurred scientists to wonder about the biochemistry of various fat deposits.

Dr. Richard Colby and his coworkers believe that each deposit has its own purpose. Some, like that bulging out from the belly, might be there as a quick energy source. This probably dates from the time when early humans needed to be able to fight or flee quickly. Other deposits, like those on the thighs, might be there for longer-term storage. These were probably useful to early humans during long periods when food was scarce.

Dr. Colby and other researchers have done many measurements of fat in various body areas. They have found that the fat under the skin of the stomach is especially sensitive to certain **hormones**, chemicals found in the body. This particular fat changes quickly when these hormones are released into the blood. The hormones can be useful in stimulating the body to act quickly. However, if the release continues too long, the end result can be high blood pressure and other heart problems.

From the New York Times News Service in *New London Day*, 11/19/90, page C1-2.

1. Which one of the following five choices is the central hypothesis of the study done by Dr. Colby and his coworkers?

   (1) Stomach fat responds differently to certain hormones than other types of fat do.
   (2) Excess stomach fat was probably more common among early men, who did the hunting, than among early women.
   (3) Stomach fat is more closely associated with heart disease than thigh fat is.
   (4) Fat in different areas of the body seems to serve different functions.
   (5) Thigh fat is not an undesirable type of fat to have.

2. Which one of the following five choices is a fact?

   (1) Abdominal fat responds differently to certain hormones than other types of fat do.
   (2) Excess abdominal fat was probably more common among early men, who did the hunting, than among early women.
   (3) Abdominal fat is more closely associated with heart disease than thigh fat is.
   (4) Fat in different areas of the body seems to serve different functions.
   (5) Thigh fat is not an undesirable type of fat to have.

3. Which one of the following five choices is best described as an opinion?

   (1) Abdominal fat responds differently to certain hormones than other types of fat do.
   (2) Excess abdominal fat was probably more common among early men, who did the hunting, than among early women.
   (3) Abdominal fat is more closely associated with heart disease than thigh fat is.
   (4) Fat in different areas of the body seems to serve different functions.
   (5) Thigh fat is not an undesirable type of fat to have.

Answers are on page A-19.

# The Kingdoms and Systems of Nature

## Prereading Prompt

How and why do scientists group living things? There has been a lot in the news lately about ecology and the environment. Do you know the connection between pollution and the "balance of nature"?

## Key Words

**ecosystem**—a system in nature in which plants and animals depend on each other for survival

**ecology**—the study of how organisms in an ecosystem depend on, and influence, each other

**food chain**—a system in nature in which each organism feeds on the organism just below it in the chain

## The Five Kingdoms of Living Things

From microscopic, single-celled organisms to human beings, there are billions of different life forms on Earth. Some scientists estimate that there are over a million types of insects alone. All of them share certain characteristics which have been discussed in earlier lessons, such as the ability to grow and reproduce.

In order to study these life forms carefully, however, scientists examine the differences among them as well as the similarities. To help in this task, scientists try to name each organism and **classify** it—place it in a category with other similar organisms. Without such a classification system, scientists studying living things would never be certain just which kind of group of animals was being discussed. The classification system also helps scientists figure out which living things evolved, or developed, over thousands of years, and from which other living things they evolved.

Look at the following classification chart.

| The Five Kingdoms | | |
|---|---|---|
| Kingdom | Description | Example |
| 1. Monera | One-celled; have no nuclei | Bacteria, blue-green algae |
| 2. Protista | One-celled; have nuclei | Protozoans, algae |
| 3. Fungi | Multicelled; have cell walls; cannot make food | Yeasts, molds, mushrooms |
| 4. Plantae (Plants) | Multicelled; have cell walls; use sunlight and chlorophyll to make food | Seeded plants, evergreens, ferns, mosses |
| 5. Animalia (Animals) | Multicelled; cannot make their own food; eat other organisms | Insects, reptiles, birds, mammals, fish, amphibians |

Each living thing belongs to a particular kingdom. Each kingdom contains living things that are alike in the most basic ways. For example, though plants vary greatly, almost all use photosynthesis to make food. Although animals vary even more, they are all multicelled and cannot make their own food. For this reason, plants and animals are grouped into separate kingdoms (**Plantae** and **Animalia**). Some organisms such as the mushrooms in your salad have cell walls, like many plants, but they cannot photosynthesize. As a result, scientists consider them in a kingdom of their own: **Fungi.** Scientists agree that one-celled organisms are neither plants nor animals, so they are divided into two kingdoms: **Monera** (without a nucleus) and **Protista** (with a nucleus).

## Ecosystems and Food Chains

You have seen how parts work together in a cell, how cells work together in an organ, how organs work together in a system, and how systems work together in one living thing. On an even larger scale, most living things depend on other living things for survival. For instance, animals depend on plants for food and oxygen. Plants depend on animals for waste material that they can convert into nutrients. Organisms depend on each other and interact with the living and nonliving things that surround them in areas of space known as **ecosystems**. An example of an ecosystem is a forest. Trees, plants, birds, insects, animals, bacteria, fungi, rocks, and soil are the parts of the ecosystem.

The organisms within an ecosystem each provide something that the others need. In the forest ecosystem, for instance, the trees and other plants supply food and shelter for such creatures as birds, insects, and small animals like squirrels and mice. These creatures, in turn, provide food for bigger creatures such as foxes or owls. The bacteria and fungi on the ground live off dead matter. They break it down into new soil which plants use.

Every living thing must be able to obtain energy from its environment to carry out the life processes. During photosynthesis, plants use the energy from sunlight to combine carbon dioxide and water into food. Plants are the food **producers** in nature. Animals get energy by eating plants, or by eating those organisms that eat plants. Animals are the **consumers** in nature—except where an animal "produces" food by being a meal for another animal that eats it. The flow of energy from the sun to producers to consumers is called a **food chain**.

The population size of each type of living thing is limited by the food energy available. At each level of a food chain, less energy is available because the more complex organisms require more energy to keep themselves alive. For instance, in the same area, a thousand shrubs and grasses may support only a hundred antelope. The hundred antelope in turn may support only ten lions. Similarly, you can provide more protein more cheaply for more people if you plant beans on an acre of land than if you graze cattle there.

## Ecological Balance

When all organisms in an ecosystem can survive by depending on each other, an ecological balance exists. When something occurs to throw off the balance, the survival of all the organisms is threatened. If the source of food in an ecosystem grows less, for instance, an imbalance will occur. All the populations that feed on that source will also decrease until a new balance is achieved. Similarly, if a population grows too quickly, members of the population will be competing for the same food. Those who can't get enough food will die of starvation. Again, this will occur until a new balance is reached.

An ecosystem's balance is delicate. If only one population in it is out of balance, the entire ecosystem can break down. Floods and other natural disasters can greatly harm an ecosystem. Human interference, too, can often cause an imbalance in the environment. For instance, pesticides used in agriculture may destroy insects that are harmful to crops. But those same insects provide food for other insects and for birds, which in turn provide food for larger animals. Every animal population in the ecosystem is therefore harmed by the insecticide. Likewise, when human beings cut down large sections of forests, they destroy not only trees, but also most of the populations that depend on the trees for food and shelter.

# Distinguishing Facts and Hypotheses in Graphics

In the last lesson, you answered questions about facts and hypotheses in passages. On the GED, similar questions may be asked about charts, maps, diagrams, and other graphics, as well.

Look at the following diagram of a field ecosystem.

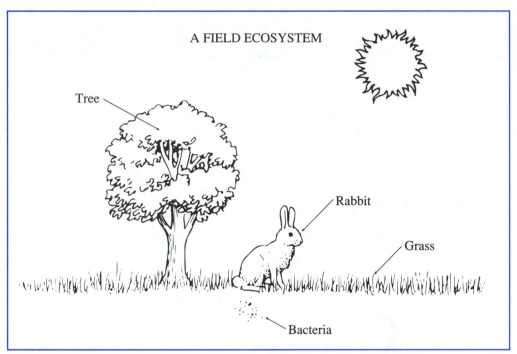

A FIELD ECOSYSTEM

Tree

Rabbit

Grass

Bacteria

Source: From *The Cambridge Comprehensive Program for the High School Equivalency Exam.* Copyright ©1987 by Prentice Hall Regents.

Which of the following is a *fact* supported by the diagram?

1. The grass in this ecosystem provides food and oxygen for the rabbit.
2. All life in the ecosystem would eventually die if all the bacteria suddenly died.
3. A recently observed decline in the number of trees is probably the result of eliminating too much bacteria.
4. In the future people will be more aware of the relationship between the ecosystem shown and their own.
5. The trees should be preserved rather than cut for lumber because of their importance to the ecosystem.

Step 1: Examine the graphic carefully. The label tells you that this is a "field ecosystem," so you know that the organisms in the picture depend on each other to live.

Step 2: Ask yourself: What do I already know about the information shown in the graphic? What are the relationships between the organisms labeled? How does the rabbit depend on the grass? What do bacteria do for the tree?

Step 3: Examine each of the five choices. In each case, ask yourself: Is this an observable fact which can be proven? Only (1) describes a fact. We can measure food and oxygen production by the grass and prove that it is used by the rabbit. (2) and (4) are predictions—opinions, not observed facts. (3) is a hypothesis (notice the use of "probably"); it is a suggested explanation for what has been observed. (5) is also an opinion. It may be your personal belief that conserving trees is of the utmost importance, but a person whose livelihood depends on the logging industry may feel differently.

## Lesson 4 Exercise

Questions 1-3 refer to the diagram below.

This diagram shows how DDT—an insecticide (insect-killer)—becomes more concentrated as it passes up a food chain from plant to top carnivore (meat-eater).

From *Science Matters: Achieving Scientific Literacy* by Robert M. Hazen and James Trefil. Copyright ©1991 by Robert M. Hazen and James Trefil. Used by permission of Doubleday, a division of Bantam Doubleday Dell Publishing Group, Inc.

1. Which of the following is a fact presented by the diagram?

    (1) DDT is more concentrated in a plant-eating squirrel than in a squirrel-eating owl.

    (2) DDT is more concentrated in the tree than in the squirrel which feeds off it because the tree is larger.

    (3) Birds have as high a concentration of DDT as other mammals.

    (4) The owl who eats a mouse gets a higher concentration of DDT than the mouse who eats grass.

    (5) The reason some hawks in this ecosystem have lower DDT concentrations than others is probably because they migrate to areas where DDT is not used.

2. Which of the following is a hypothesis based on the diagram—not an observed fact?

    (1) Owls and bobcats are meat-eaters.

    (2) The DDT passing from apples to mice is less concentrated than the DDT passing from mice to owls.

    (3) The bobcat who eats a squirrel absorbs a more concentrated poison than the squirrel who eats DDT-sprayed corn.

    (4) The decline in owl populations near some apple orchards is probably due to the use of DDT by the farmers.

    (5) DDT exists in less concentration in the squirrel than in the deer because the squirrel is smaller.

3. Which of the following is an opinion?

    (1) Use of DDT has been banned in the U.S.

    (2) Use of DDT should be banned throughout the world.

    (3) Some birds might be hurt less by DDT than others because they learn not to eat DDT-sprayed insects.

    (4) DDT is an undigestible poison which remains in the body of birds which absorb it.

    (5) Digestible insecticides would probably be less harmful to birds because they wouldn't build up in the eggs.

Answers are on page A-19.

# Behavior and Evolution

## Prereading Prompt

What is behavior? What do you already know about it from reading, watching TV, and observing? What is the current theory of "evolution"? Why is it causing so much controversy these days?

## Key Words

**behaviors**—observable ways an organism acts

**theory of evolution**—theory that each type of living thing alive today developed from a simpler form over many years

## Behavior

We have seen that all living things can respond to changes in their environment in ways that help them survive. Nonliving things react too, but they often react by changing permanently. If a fire is made near an ice cube, the ice cube melts. If a fire begins near a rabbit, on the other hand, the rabbit can move to keep from being killed. The heat and light from the fire are two examples of *stimuli*. A **stimulus** is anything in the environment which causes a living thing to act.

Both plants and animals respond to stimuli. Plant responses, which are called **tropisms**, you probably have often seen: a plant bending toward the light or growing its roots toward nutrients or water, or growing roots downward due to gravity. Even one-celled animal organisms such as the amoeba and paramecium respond to changes in the environment. For example, if you touch an amoeba lightly with a needle, it moves away. The actions that animals take in response to their environment are known as **behaviors**.

As we have seen, most animals have a nervous system which controls the animals' actions. Animals that have simple nervous systems—like the flatworm or starfish—are capable only of automatic, **reflex** action. Some human behaviors, too, are reflexes. For example, you react directly to a blast of cold air by shivering. Sometimes reflexes are linked together in a more complicated type of inborn behavior called an **instinct**. Behaviors like web-weaving in spiders and nest-building in birds are largely instinctive.

Many human actions, on the other hand, consist of a series of learned actions. Such a chain of learned behavior is called a **habit**. Did you have to think about what you were doing when you got dressed this morning? Probably not much. You have repeated that procedure so often that it has become a habit.

How does a human or other animal learn a new behavior? One way is by **trial and error**. Your cat, for example, may discover the right way to open a cabinet door after trying unsuccessfully in other ways to get at its cat food. The most complex form of learning is **insight** learning. By insight, some of the higher animals figure out how to solve a problem *without* using trial and error. For instance, a chimp in a cage where a bunch of bananas hangs overhead will figure out how to use a stick to knock them down.

## Evolution

Up until about 160 years ago, most people thought that living things remained the same over the years; thus, ancient ancestors must have looked like later forms. Then Charles Darwin (1809-1882) took a five-year sea voyage during which he carefully observed the plants, animals, and fossils on South America's coast. From these observations, he built on other scientists' ideas to form the **theory of evolution**, stating that each type of living thing develops gradually over time from simpler forms.

In any environment, there is a limited amount of food, water, and space. Darwin believed that living things tend to overbreed. For example, mice tend to produce more individuals than can survive in a certain environment. As a result, individual mice compete and there is "survival of the fittest" or **natural selection**. That is, those individuals that survive are those which are best suited or adapted to the environment. The mouse that runs slowly is more likely to be killed by a hunting fox than the speedy mouse. The slow mouse will probably not live long, but the fast mouse survives to reproduce a litter of fast mice.

Biologists have modified and added to Darwin's theory somewhat. They have discovered the actual material in the cell responsible for heredity—the genes or the chromosomes. They also have learned about **mutations** or sudden changes in the genes. While many mutations are harmful, occasionally one occurs that helps an organism fit better into its environment. Such favorable traits accumulate within a **species**, or group of organisms that interbreed. After many generations, the changes may result in the evolution of a new species.

Evolution is usually a very slow process because major changes in the environment tend to be drawn out over thousands of years. It may have taken an animal or a plant millions of years to evolve into its current state. What happens when the environment changes drastically and ecosystems are disrupted? For example, what happens when water and food sources dry up, or when long periods of cold settle in, or when human beings suddenly disrupt the environment? A species must have time to adapt to the new conditions. Those species that cannot adapt successfully die out, or become **extinct**—as the dinosaurs did. Many species have become extinct in recent years, such as the passenger pigeon. Some 240 others—such as the grizzly bear and California condor— are considered endangered species. And it is estimated that at this rate, 100,000 of the plants and species we know today may be gone within the next 10 years.

# Identifying Unstated Assumptions in Passages

An assumption is an idea that you take for granted without proof—an underlying belief. If you ask people about their assumptions, they are likely to say, "Of course! What else?" For example, someone who strongly recommends one diet instead of another has the assumption that dieting is important. Men arguing about which pitcher should be used assume that pitching will help their baseball team win. People who argue pro or con about rights—freedom of speech, women's rights, minority rights—assume that freedom is important and should be discussed.

Authors, too, make assumptions. On the GED, you will be asked to "read between the lines" to identify unstated assumptions. These assumptions may or may not be accurate. It is very important to avoid being swayed by inaccurate assumptions.

As you read the passage below, ask yourself what the writer wants the reader's attitude toward the early theory of evolution to be.

> Animal behaviors may be either inherited or learned. Inherited behavior is passed on through the genes and is practiced by every member of the species, usually helping the species survive. Learned behaviors may help an organism to survive in its environment, too. But scientific observation has shown that learned behaviors are not passed on through the genes. One early theory, however, claimed that learned behaviors play a role in evolution. According to this theory, short-necked animals might have evolved into giraffes by learning to stretch their necks to reach the leaves of trees. In this way, the results of this behavior might be passed on to future generations until eventually giraffes evolved.

The writer's main assumption in this passage is that scientific theory

**(1)** should not concern itself with learned behavior

**(2)** cannot understand much about inherited behavior

**(3)** should help the species it studies survive in its environment

**(4)** should be based on scientific observation

**(5)** should avoid controversial subjects such as evolution

Step 1: Figure out what *is* stated. A summary of the most important information in the passage might read: We know now that inherited behavior is passed down through the genes while learned behavior is not. An early theory described a learned behavior being passed on to offspring: Animals learned to stretch their necks, resulting in offspring with longer necks.

Step 2: Read between the lines. Before you look at the choices, you can come up with some ideas about the author's assumption. Ask yourself: What is a basic, unstated belief underlying what the author says in the passage? You can see that the author implies that the older theory is incorrect. The author states that from scientific observation we know that learned behavior is *not* passed on to offspring. He then says that the early theory claimed that longer necks developed by neck-stretching were, in fact, passed on. The theory was scientifically false: Why? What basic assumption about scientific theory does the author have? This assumption underlies his statements and what he wants you to think about them. He takes this underlying belief of his so much for granted that he does not bother to state it.

Step 3: Examine the choices. Choice (1) cannot be correct because the passage nowhere suggests that learned behavior should not be studied. Without such study, scientists would never have discovered that learned behavior could not be passed on through the genes. The passage suggests that science knows more about inherited behavior than any other kind, so (2) has no support. (3) confuses a statement in the passage, which says that some learned behaviors can help an organism survive, not that a scientific theory should give this help. (5) is a very large, unstated belief and so it could be an assumption, but it has no support. The early theory explains evolution incorrectly, but that does not suggest that the whole theory of evolution is wrong and should not be studied. (4) is the author's assumption: that scientific theory should be based on scientific observation. Such observation, he says, showed that learned behavior could not be passed on. If the early theory proved false, he assumes that it was not based on scientific observation.

# Lesson 5 Exercise

Questions 1-3 are based on the passage below.

> A certain species of poisonous toad lives in tropical South America. It competes for space and food with many nonpoisonous species. Nevertheless, all the toad populations in South America are kept generally in balance by animals that feed on poisonous and nonpoisonous toads alike.
>
> A proposal has been made to import some of the poisonous toads to Florida to control insects. Backers of the plan claim that the toads will flourish in the warm, moist climate. Some critics of the plan suggest that animals who feed on nonpoisonous toads may be endangered by feeding on the imported poisonous toads. However, experiments have shown that the animals that feed on Florida's nonpoisonous toads will avoid the South American ones because of their poison. Nevertheless, one scientist, Dr. Vaughn, opposes the plan to import the toads because he believes they might endanger the native toad species.

1. The writer reports experiments that have been done on animals that eat nonpoisonous toads. Which of the following is NOT an assumption made by the writer?

   (1) The results of the experiments are accurate.
   (2) Animals who feed on nonpoisonous toads will learn not to feed on the poisonous ones.
   (3) Behavior of toads in the real world can be predicted from behavior of toads in the experiment.
   (4) The balance among the toad populations in South America will be changed by the import of poisonous toads to Florida.
   (5) The imported toads would flourish because they would have few predators.

2. Which of the following is an unstated assumption of the supporters of the plan?

   (1) Introducing poisonous toads will affect the evolution of insects.
   (2) Protecting the native species of nonpoisonous toad is important.
   (3) Bringing in poisonous toads will endanger native animals who feed on nonpoisonous ones.
   (4) Controlling the number of insects will change the eating behavior of poisonous toads.
   (5) Reducing the number of insects will improve the quality of life for the human population of Florida.

3. Which of the following is an unstated assumption made by Dr. Vaughn?

   (1) The native toads will not be able to compete successfully with the imported toads.
   (2) Protecting the native toads is more important than protecting the predators.
   (3) Protecting the native toads is more important than protecting the poisonous ones.
   (4) Adding poisonous toads will result in an undesirable increase in the number of predators of native toads.
   (5) Adding poisonous toads will result in undesirable changes in the behavior of the insects.

Answers are on page A-20.

# Lesson 6

# The Earth: Its Structure, Origin, and Place In the Universe

## Prereading Prompt

Did you know that the Earth is layered like an onion? What is each layer like? How do you suppose the Earth came to have such a structure? What is Earth's "address" in space?

## Key Words

**crust**— the outermost layer of our planet Earth

**core**— the center of our planet Earth

**mantle**— the layer of Earth between the core and crust

**universe**— the mostly empty region that contains all that exists—from planets to star systems

## The Structure of the Earth

Earth has been slowly cooling since it was first formed. As the rocks and metals within the planet cooled, they formed into layers. The four layers of Earth, shown in the diagram on the next page, are different in temperature and in the type of materials they contain.

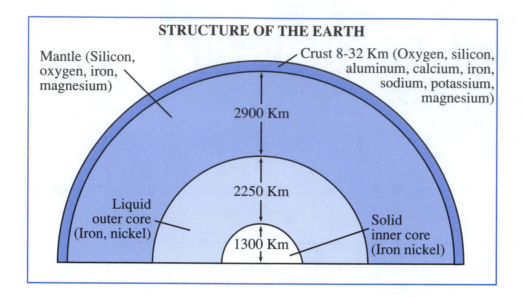

**STRUCTURE OF THE EARTH**

Mantle (Silicon, oxygen, iron, magnesium)

Crust 8-32 Km (Oxygen, silicon, aluminum, calcium, iron, sodium, potassium, magnesium)

2900 Km

2250 Km

1300 Km

Liquid outer core (Iron, nickel)

Solid inner core (Iron nickel)

The **crust** is the outermost layer of the Earth. The crust varies in thickness, from about 5 to 20 miles (8-32 kilometers) deep. We know most about the crust because it is on the crust that we and all living things exist. There are three main types of rock that make up Earth's crust: igneous, sedimentary, and metamorphic rock. Hot liquid rock, called **lava**, bursts out of hollow mountains (**volcanoes**), and reaches the Earth's surface; when it cools it forms **igneous rock**.

When particles of soil, sand, clay, mud, and living things are deposited in layers underwater, the layers are cemented together over time to form **sedimentary rock**. When rocks that are found deep within the crust are altered by its great heat and pressure, new **metamorphic rock** is made.

Beneath the crust is the **mantle**. This is a layer of heavy rocklike material about 1,800 miles (2900 kilometers) thick. A great deal of weight constantly pushes down on this layer. In fact, the pressure is more than what you would get if you put 12,500 cars on a dime. Temperature, too, increases dramatically the farther down into the Earth you go. The **core**, or center, of the Earth is thought to be made mostly of melted iron and nickel, with a rigid ball of iron and nickel in the middle.

## The Origin of the Earth

No one can say for certain how the universe began. A popular theory, however, suggests that it began in a "big bang" some 15 billion to 20 billion years ago. The **big bang theory** states that the universe was an incredibly dense clump of matter which then exploded and expanded outward. Over billions of years the force of gravity caused particles to cling to one another in larger and larger masses. About 4.6 billion years ago, one of the balls of melted metals and gases spun around until the surface began to cool. The surface of that ball, which we now know as Earth, formed a crust. The heavier metals remained in the center, while the lighter gases formed an envelope around the planet. This envelope is our atmosphere. Many scientists believe this theory because they can tell, by observing the light coming from certain stars to Earth, that these stars are going through this cooling process, too.

It is important to realize that the Earth *is still forming* and constantly changing. What causes these changes? Scientists have found that the crust, or outer surface of the Earth, is made up of broad **plates**. North America, South America, and the other huge land masses called **continents** have "roots" that go down 30-35 miles into the plates. The plates are constantly moving and colliding. These movements sometimes cause earthquakes to occur, volcanoes to erupt, or mountains to form.

In addition to plate movement, there are other influences which change the Earth. For instance, rocks are constantly being broken into small particles to form soil. Changing temperatures, freezing water, and plant growth all contribute to this breakdown, called **weathering**.

## The Position of Earth in the Universe

Where is our changing Earth located in the universe? Scientists' calculations of the volume of the universe show it to be much larger than anything we can imagine. It is so large that it must be measured in **light-years**. One light-year is the distance that light travels in one year—about 5.8 trillion miles. Most of our universe is empty space, containing no air or matter. Still, the universe contains millions of star systems—known as **galaxies**—that are incredibly large.

We live in the galaxy called the **Milky Way.** It is called that because it appears as a band of misty light in the sky at night. It includes our solar ("sun") system and a spiral-shaped group of about 120 billion stars. If you could look down on the entire Milky Way, you would see that our solar system is located out near one of its edges. All the stars you can see with the naked eye are in the Milky Way. If you started out at one end of the Milky Way, it would take 100,000 light-years to reach the other side.

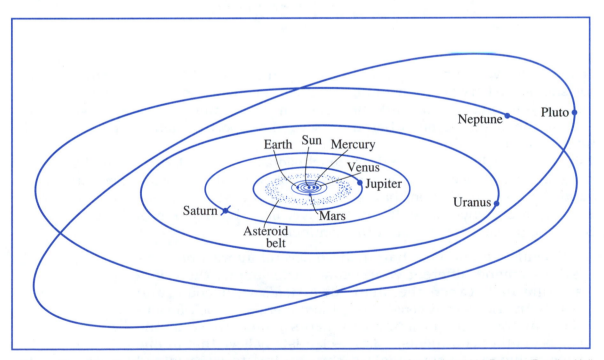

Source: From *New Revised Cambridge GED Program: Science* by Gloria Levine. Copyright ©1992 Regents/Prentice Hall.

Our **solar system** is made up of one star (the sun), nine planets, 44 moons, over 30,000 *asteroids* (small rocklike clumps of matter), over 100 billion *comets* (chunks of ice, dust, and gas), and about 1,500 *quasars* (bright, small, starlike objects). The Earth is the fifth largest planet in the solar system, and it is the third planet from the sun (see the diagram on the previous page). We are 93 million miles from the sun. It would take about 21 years to get there by jet. Our moon is 239,000 miles away from us—9 times the distance around our equator.

## The Motions of the Earth in Space

Imagine a rod through the Earth, going in at the North Pole and coming out at the South Pole. That imaginary rod is called the Earth's **axis**. Like a toy top, the Earth tilts on this axis as it **rotates**, or spins. The rotation of the iron core as the Earth spins makes the planet into a giant magnet. Like other magnets, the Earth has a north and south magnetic pole. It takes the Earth 24 hours to spin completely around one time. We see daylight when our part of the Earth is facing the sun. We have nighttime when our part of the Earth is turned away from the sun.

While the Earth is spinning, it is also moving in large circles. Like the other planets in the solar system, the Earth **revolves** around the sun. It takes the Earth 365 days (one year) to make one revolution. We experience summer when we are at the point in our journey around the sun when we tilt toward it, getting its most direct rays.

## Distinguishing Conclusions from Supporting Details in Passages

If a friend is late every time you agree to meet, you may reach the **conclusion** that he or she doesn't try very hard to be on time. A conclusion is a statement summarizing your main idea and the decision or opinion that you have reached. Your conclusion is often based on several supporting details or facts that point in a particular direction.

Writers use supporting details to draw conclusions. On the GED, you will be asked to distinguish between the supporting details an author uses to develop an idea and the final conclusion that is drawn. Ask yourself: Is this statement just one piece of evidence, or is it the final "verdict" the writer wants me to reach? Read the passage below about the continents.

> Scientists and others have noticed several interesting similarities among different continents. For example, there is a striking fit between the shape of Africa's west coast and South America's east coast. Also, the minerals in rock formations at the edges of many continents match those at the edges of other continents. Many scientists believe that at one time millions of years ago, all the continents were joined together in a single supercontinent, Pangaea.

Which of the following best states the central conclusion?

**(1)** There are both similarities and differences among the continents.

**(2)** The number of rock formations in some continents matches the number in others.

**(3)** The continents were once joined as a single continent.

**(4)** The shapes of Africa and South America suggest that they were once torn apart.

**(5)** The minerals at the edges of some continents match the minerals at the edges of others.

Step 1: Predict the conclusion. Ask yourself: What is the main idea about continents toward which the writer is building? The author is "making a case" for one huge continent. He gives details—about the coasts of continents fitting together, and about minerals providing evidence for a single giant continent—to support his case.

Step 2: Examine each choice. In each case, ask yourself: Is this a conclusion supported by the information—and not just a detail taken from the passage? (1) is wrong because the author mentions similarities but not differences. (2) is wrong because he mentions rock formations but says nothing about the number of them in different continents. (*NOTE:* Don't choose an answer just because it contains some of the wording of the original passage.) Choices (4) and (5) are not conclusions, but details that support (3). Choice (3), which matches your prediction, seems the likely answer.

Step 3: Choose the best answer—choice (3). (*NOTE:* Often—but not always—the conclusion is in the last line of the passage.)

## Lesson 6 Exercise

Questions 1-3 are based on the passage below.

Many Earth scientists believe that the Hawaiian Islands were created by a so-called hot spot beneath Earth's crust. According to these scientists, this spot is a point where melted rock from deep within the Earth rises close to the surface and repeatedly breaks through to create volcanoes. These volcanoes have formed the Hawaiian Islands. While this has been happening, however, the Pacific plate above the hot spot has been moving gradually toward the northwest. As it does so, it carries the islands with it. As each island moves off the hot spot, its volcanoes stop erupting, and the sea starts eroding the island away. The result is the geography of the islands as it appears today: The large and volcanically active island of Hawaii at the southeast end of the chain, and a string of smaller and smaller islands with inactive volcanoes leading away toward the northwest.

1. Which of the following is the conclusion drawn by the writer?

   (1) The appearance of the Hawaiian Islands chain is the result of the Pacific plate's movement over a hot spot.
   (2) The movement of a hot spot under the Pacific plate is the result of volcanic eruptions on the Hawaiian Islands.
   (3) The Hawaiian Islands move northwest as the Pacific plate on which they rest moves in that direction.
   (4) The island of Hawaii is the largest of a chain of inactive volcanoes which stretch northwest.
   (5) The movement of each island off the hot spot is the result of the sea's wearing away at the island.

2. Which of the following is a detail found in the passage?

   (1) The Pacific plate has been moving the hot spot toward the northwest.
   (2) The hot spot created eruptions of volcanoes by sending melted rock up to the Earth's crust.
   (3) The inactive volcanos will erupt once again when the plates begin to reverse the direction of their movement.
   (4) The volcanoes on the island of Hawaii at the southeast end of the chain still erupt.
   (5) The layout of the Hawaiian Islands would be different if the Pacific plate were moving southeast over the hot spot.

3. Which of the following is NOT a supporting detail in the passage?

   (1) Many scientists connect the formation of the Hawaiian Islands with a spot of melted rock.
   (2) The "hot spot" is a place where melted rock rises and breaks through the crust to form volcanoes.
   (3) Eventually the islands will move off the hot spot until they are no more.
   (4) The Pacific plate above the hot spot has been shifting slowly toward the northwest.
   (5) Active volcanoes become inactive as the island on which they lie moves off the hot spot.

Answers are on page A-21.

# Lesson 7

# The Earth: Its Atmosphere, Weather, and Climate

## Prereading Prompt

Have you heard about the greenhouse effect or the hole in the Earth's ozone layer? How are they harmful? What can we do?

What do you know about weather forecasting? What is the difference between weather and climate?

## Key Words

**atmosphere**—the envelope of air which surrounds Earth

**weather**—the condition of the atmosphere at a particular place for a short time

**climate**—the average weather of an area over a long time

## Earth's Atmosphere

The **atmosphere** is the envelope of air that surrounds Earth. It is about 350 miles thick and is held to the planet by **gravity**, the force inside the Earth that pulls all objects near it toward the Earth's surface. Most of the atmosphere is *nitrogen,* a gas used by plants to make protein, which all animals need in their diets. One-fifth of the atmosphere is *oxygen,* the part of the air that animals need to breathe and carry on the processes of life and which is needed to make fire. *Carbon dioxide,* essential for photosynthesis, as well as other gases such as argon, the gas used in light bulbs, are also in the atmosphere. Finally, the atmosphere contains large quantities of dust and water.

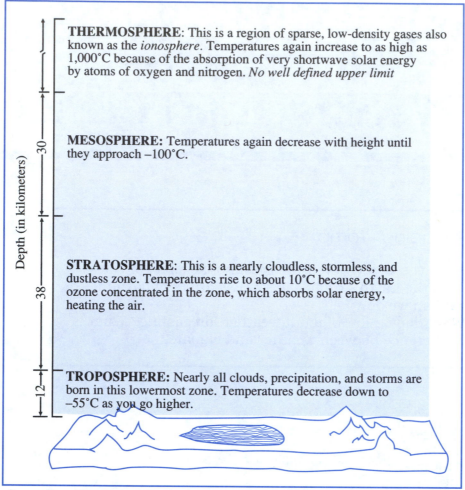

**THERMOSPHERE**: This is a region of sparse, low-density gases also known as the *ionosphere*. Temperatures again increase to as high as 1,000°C because of the absorption of very shortwave solar energy by atoms of oxygen and nitrogen. *No well defined upper limit*

**MESOSPHERE**: Temperatures again decrease with height until they approach −100°C.

**STRATOSPHERE**: This is a nearly cloudless, stormless, and dustless zone. Temperatures rise to about 10°C because of the ozone concentrated in the zone, which absorbs solar energy, heating the air.

**TROPOSPHERE**: Nearly all clouds, precipitation, and storms are born in this lowermost zone. Temperatures decrease down to −55°C as you go higher.

Depth (in kilometers)

30

38

12

Source: From *New Revised Cambridge GED Program: Science* by Gloria Levine. Copyright ©1992 Prentice Hall/Regents.

On the basis of temperature, the atmosphere is divided into four layers. The **troposphere** touches Earth and is the layer in which we live. Almost all weather takes place in the troposphere. Though the troposphere can be as much as 11 miles thick, most of the air it contains is within 3 miles of the planet's surface. Above the troposphere is the **stratosphere**. There we find a high concentration of **ozone**, a special form of oxygen. The stratosphere is warmed by chemical reactions occurring when ozone breaks down into oxygen. Above the stratosphere is the **mesosphere**, where air cools because there is no ozone. Above that is the **ionosophere**, where the air is very thin and cold. This is the layer which reflects radio waves back to the Earth and makes long-distance broadcasts possible. And finally, at the outer edge of the atmosphere lies the **thermosphere**. In the thermosphere, the layer the sun's rays first hit, air temperature rises again.

## Function of the Atmosphere

Earth, and life on Earth, would be very different without the atmosphere. In fact, there probably would be no life without it. It contains the oxygen, nitrogen, and carbon dioxide that living things require to carry on their life processes. The winds in the atmosphere carry heat and water around the globe. They also contribute to the wearing away, or erosion, of rock, which results in formation of soil. In addition, the atmosphere protects Earth against harmful elements from outer space. Particles in the upper atmosphere cause **meteoroids** (large chunks of matter from outer space) to burn up before they hit the ground. The ozone in the stratosphere filters out harmful **ultraviolet rays** or **radiation** from the sun. These UV rays are a type of light which, in large enough doses, can burn, cause skin cancer, and even blind people.

## Weather and Climate

Like everything else on Earth, the atmosphere is in a constant state of change. Changing conditions in the atmosphere are the main causes of weather and climate. **Weather** is the state of the atmosphere in a particular place and time. We might say that the weather today in San Juan, Puerto Rico, happens to be sunny and clear with temperatures in the 80s. **Climate** consists of the usual, prevailing weather conditions in a particular place over a long period of time. We say that the climate in the tropical region is hot and humid (moist). While there may be some days of cool, dry weather in the tropics, usually it is hot and humid there.

Both weather and climate are expressed in terms of temperature, **humidity** (how much moisture is in the air), air pressure, and wind. Weather and climate are affected by many things, but the most important factor is the sun. It is the sun's energy that **evaporates** water (changes it from liquid to gas), warms the air, and helps to cause winds.

The supply of fresh water on Earth is constantly being renewed through a process known as the **water cycle.** Heat from the sun causes the water droplets on the Earth's surface to evaporate. As the water vapor (mist) rises into the atmosphere, it cools. Clouds are produced as the water droplets **condense**—that is, return to their liquid form. Eventually, some of the droplets become heavy enough to fall to Earth as **precipitation** in the form of rain, snow, sleet, or hail.

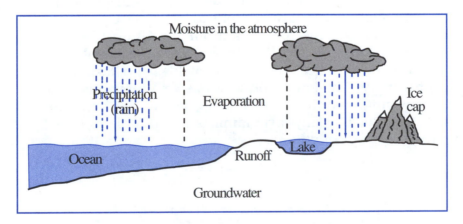

Source: From *New Revised Cambridge GED Program: Science* by Gloria Levine. Copyright ©1992 Prentice Hall/Regents.

Different parts of the Earth's surface absorb heat at different rates. Land warms up faster and cools down faster than the oceans. In addition, the equator receives more than twice as much sunlight as the poles do. These differences cause winds to flow. As air is heated by the sun, it becomes warmer and lighter and exerts less pressure. This heated air rises high into the atmosphere at the same time that the cooler, heavier air is falling. As the hot and cold air masses change places, they set up air currents called **convection currents**, which cause winds.

Convection currents interact with the Earth's rotation to create **prevailing winds**. These strong winds move across the whole globe, and are called "prevailing" because they prevail over, or dominate, other winds. The planet's spinning pushes winds to the east in the Northern Hemisphere and to the west in the Southern Hemisphere.

# Identifying Cause-and-Effect Relationships in Passages

You often try to find reasons or causes for the things that happen in your life. If you get sick, or your car stops running, you listen to the doctor or the auto mechanic as he or she explains what is causing these effects. You also try to predict the effects of many actions. When your boss announces a new policy, or you hear about a new law being passed concerning taxes or employment, you try to figure out what effects these actions will have on your life.

One important way that authors develop their ideas is by showing how one thing causes or results in another. You can identify a cause by asking yourself: What is causing this event—or events—to happen? You can identify an effect by asking yourself: What is the result—or results—of the action described? To understand a cause-and-effect connection, you should use what you read, the knowledge you may already have about the subject, as well as your common sense and imagination. Read the following passage.

> In the 1930s, a long dry spell hit much of the Great Plains. The area's normal climate, a mix of dry and wet conditions, was disrupted for several years by a stalled high-pressure system. This system brought prolonged clear skies. At the same time, it blocked the moist air from the Gulf of Mexico that normally brings rain to the Great Plains. Rain failed to fall, year after year. Wheat died in the fields, and farm animals went hungry. The bare ground was swept by winds that carried away millions of tons of topsoil, giving the area the name of "Dust Bowl." Many farm families left, unable to make a living under these conditions.

What was the cause of the dry spell?

**(1)** Little rain fell on the Great Plains for several years.

**(2)** The moist air from the Gulf of Mexico was cut off.

**(3)** Much of the wheat crop was lost due to lack of water.

**(4)** Millions of tons of topsoil were blown away.

**(5)** Many farm families left when their farms failed.

<u>Step 1: Determine what happened and why</u>. Ask yourself: What happened before the dry spell to cause it?

<u>Step 2: Predict an answer</u>. According to the passage, some sort of weather system blocked Gulf air, keeping it out of the Great Plains.

<u>Step 3: Examine the choices.</u> Choice (2) says pretty much the same thing as your prediction. The other choices are all details in the passage, but they don't explain why the dry spell happened. Instead, they tell what it was (1) and what were the results which followed—(3), (4), and (5).

<u>Step 4: Choose the best answer.</u> By process of elimination, choice (2) is the best answer.

---

### Tips on Finding the Cause for an Effect

- Look for an event that came before the effect.
- Don't assume that just because two events happen at about the same time, one necessarily caused the other.
- Instead, look for evidence that one event results from the other: The result is the effect; what makes it happen is the cause.

---

Questions 1-3 are based on the passage below.

Some mountain ranges create a weather effect called a "rain shadow." This effect occurs when moist air flowing across the range is forced upward by mountains. When the air rises, it cools, and the moisture in it condenses as rain or snow. As a result, the air that reaches the far side of the range is dry. Consequently, a desert may form on the far side of the mountain range.

**1.** Why does the moist air rise?

   **(1)** Moist air is heavier than dry air.

   **(2)** Moist air is pushed upward when it strikes mountains.

   **(3)** Moist air becomes cooler at higher altitudes.

   **(4)** The moisture in the air condenses as rain or snow.

   **(5)** The moisture on the far side of the mountains is less.

**2.** Which of the following is the final effect of the movement of moist air crossing over the mountains?

   **(1)** A wet area called the "rain shadow" forms on the mountains.

   **(2)** The air reaching the far side of the mountains is dry.

   **(3)** The air cools and condenses as it crosses the mountains.

   **(4)** Rain or snow falls on the near side of the mountains.

   **(5)** A desert develops on the far side of the mountains.

**3.** What causes the air on the far side of the mountain to be dry?

   **(1)** The mountain casts a shadow by blocking the sun.

   **(2)** The air is too warm for moisture to condense as rain.

   **(3)** The air loses moisture as it passes over the mountain.

   **(4)** The far side of the mountain is a desert.

   **(5)** The temperature is higher than on the near side.

Answers are on page A-21.

# The Structure of Matter

## Prereading Prompt

Every object around you—your cup, the coffee in it, the steam rising above it—is composed of matter. Just what is matter? What is it made of? Why is the cup hard and smooth and white while the coffee has different properties? What happens when matter changes from one state to another, say a solid to a liquid, or a liquid to a gas?

## Key Words

**atom**—the basic building block of matter

**nucleus**—center of an atom

**protons**—positively charged particles in a nucleus

**neutrons**—particles in a nucleus that have no electrical charge

**electrons**—negatively charged particles that circle the nucleus of an atom

**molecule**—two or more atoms bonded together

## Characteristics of Matter

Matter is any substance in the universe that has a given amount of material, or **mass**, and takes up space, or **volume.** Different kinds of matter have different kinds of tiny particles called **atoms**, in different arrangements. The atoms in a cup are different from the atoms in the coffee it holds.

## The Three States of Matter

Even the same kind of matter can occur in different forms or states. You probably already know about solids, liquids, and gases. **Solids** are hard things like ice cubes, pencils, and freeze-dried coffee. Perked coffee, paint, and vinegar are **liquids**, which you can pour. You probably can also think of many **gases**—from the steam rising over your coffee cup to the exhaust coming out of your car.

Sometimes matter changes from one state to another, as when a solid ice cube melts into a liquid puddle of water, which then evaporates into steam or mist, as a gas. In the solid state, matter has a definite shape and volume. In the liquid state, only volume is constant. The liquid takes on the shape of its container. In the gaseous state, neither shape nor volume is constant. A gas spreads out to fill the size and shape of its container.

## Physical and Chemical Properties of Matter

Different types of matter can be identified by different characteristics or properties. Properties that you can observe with your senses are called **physical properties**. These include size, shape, color, mass, texture, volume, taste, and smell. To describe some of the physical properties of a lump of sugar, you might say that it is white, sweet-tasting, and cube-shaped.

Matter can also be described in terms of chemical properties. **Chemical properties** describe how a substance will combine with other substances. When wood burns, it combines with oxygen to form new substances including ash and colorless, odorless gas. Wood's ability to combine with oxygen is an example of a chemical property.

## Physical and Chemical Changes in Matter

When only the physical properties of a substance change, the change is called a **physical change**. Mashing a potato changes the texture and shape of the potato. Even though the potato looks different, it is still potato.

However, when the identity of the substance is altered, the change is called a **chemical change**. Chemical changes produce new kinds of matter. If you leave the potato in the oven too long and burn it to a crisp, a new substance forms. The charred remains are no longer potato.

## Atoms and Molecules

If you took a sugar cube and started breaking it apart, eventually you would get down to the smallest particle of sugar. If you could divide that bit of sugar still further, you would find tiny particles called **atoms.** A trillion (one thousand billion) atoms could fit into the period at the end of this sentence. Only in recent years has science developed microscopes powerful enough to make atoms visible. We say that atoms are the basic building blocks of matter.

Small as it is, each atom contains even smaller particles. The center of an atom is called the **nucleus**. It contains **protons**, positively-charged particles, and **neutrons**, which have no electrical charge. Whirling around the nucleus at high speeds are clouds of negatively charged particles called **electrons**. The electrical attraction between the positively charged nucleus and the negatively charged electrons holds the whole system together. A given electron has a particular *energy level*, or area where it is most likely to be. An energy level can hold only a certain number of electrons (see figure above right).

Atoms combine in a process called **chemical bonding.** Any time atoms bond together, they form **molecules**. Sometimes the atoms are alike; sometimes they are not. In a molecule of oxygen, for example, there are two oxygen atoms. In a molecule of sugar, however, there are atoms of three kinds: carbon, hydrogen, and oxygen.

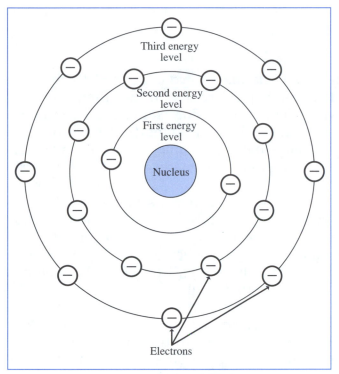

Source: From *The Cambridge Comprehensive Program for the High School Equivalency Examination.* Copyright ©1987 by Prentice Hall/ Regents

## Key Words

**element**—substance made up of only one type of atom

**compound**—substance containing two or more elements that have combined to form something new and different from the separate elements

## Elements and Compounds

**Elements** are made up of only one type of atom, and they cannot be broken down into simpler substances. Silver, silicon, oxygen, tin, and hydrogen are some common elements.

A **compound** is made up of two or more elements that combine. For instance, water is a compound. When hydrogen and oxygen atoms bond, or combine, to form a water molecule, they give the compound its "waterlike" properties. The elements hydrogen and oxygen are not altered themselves, but if they were separated again, the properties of each would be different from those of water.

## The Periodic Table

There are over 100 known elements. Scientists have organized them into a chart called the **periodic table**. The number of protons in an atom, known as its **atomic number**, determines what element it is. For example, all atoms that have just one proton are hydrogen atoms, while all atoms that have two protons are helium atoms. No two elements have the same atomic number. The **atomic weight** is the number of protons plus neutrons in an atom of each element.

The periodic table tells us more about an atom than its symbol and atomic number. The elements are also arranged in the table so that atomic number increases as you read from left to right. Interestingly, it turns out that elements in the same vertical column, or **group**, have similar chemical behavior and similar properties. For instance, copper (Cu), silver (Ag), and gold (Au) combine with other substances to form similar compounds. All the metals are on the left side of the table. **Metals** tend to be those elements that are shiny, that can be drawn out into thin wires, and that are good conductors of heat and electricity. All the **nonmetals**, except for hydrogen, are in the group on the right side of the table. These are elements that are not able to combine easily with other elements. Nonmetals tend to be poor conductors of electricity.

## Key Words

**mixture**—material created when two or more substances are mixed together but not chemically bonded

**solution**—mixture of one substance dissolved in another

## Mixtures and Solutions

Elements and compounds are called pure substances. A **pure substance** has only one kind of particle. It has constant properties throughout. Elements contain only one kind of atom, and compounds contain one kind of molecule. Elements and compounds are, therefore, pure substances. When two or more pure substances are mixed together, but are not chemically combined, the result is a **mixture**. The substances that are mixed keep their individual properties. For example, when you mix sugar with salt, the sugar crystals still taste sweet and the salt still tastes salty. Examples of some common mixtures include sand, spaghetti sauce, gasoline, and air.

# PERIODIC TABLE OF THE ELEMENTS

**Key**

| 6 | — Atomic number |
|---|---|
| **C** | — Element's symbol |
| Carbon | — Element's name |
| 12.011 | — Atomic mass |

1 — New designation
IA — Original designation

The new group designations are those assigned by IUPAC in 1984.

**Transition Metals** — groups 3 (IIIB), 4 (IVB), 5 (VB), 6 (VIB), 7 (VIIB), 8–10 (VIIIB), 11 (IB), 12 (IIB)

**Nonmetals** — groups 13 (IIIA) through 18 (VIIIA)

**Metals**

| Period | 1 (IA) | 2 (IIA) | 3 (IIIB) | 4 (IVB) | 5 (VB) | 6 (VIB) | 7 (VIIB) | 8 (VIIIB) | 9 (VIIIB) | 10 (VIIIB) | 11 (IB) | 12 (IIB) | 13 (IIIA) | 14 (IVA) | 15 (VA) | 16 (VIA) | 17 (VIIA) | 18 (VIIIA) |
|---|---|---|---|---|---|---|---|---|---|---|---|---|---|---|---|---|---|---|
| 1 | 1 H Hydrogen 1.00794 | | | | | | | | | | | | | | | | | 2 He Helium 4.003 |
| 2 | 3 Li Lithium 6.941 | 4 Be Beryllium 9.0122 | | | | | | | | | | | 5 B Boron 10.81 | 6 C Carbon 12.011 | 7 N Nitrogen 14.007 | 8 O Oxygen 15.999 | 9 F Flourine 18.998 | 10 Ne Neon 20.179 |
| 3 | 11 Na Sodium 22.990 | 12 Mg Magnesium 24.305 | | | | | | | | | | | 13 Al Aluminum 26.98 | 14 Si Silicon 28.086 | 15 P Phosphorus 30.974 | 16 S Sulfur 32.06 | 17 Cl Chlorine 35.453 | 18 Ar Argon 39.948 |
| 4 | 19 K Potassium 39.098 | 20 Ca Calcium 40.08 | 21 Sc Scandium 44.956 | 22 Ti Titanium 47.88 | 23 V Vanadium 50.94 | 24 Cr Chromium 51.996 | 25 Mn Manganese 54.938 | 26 Fe Iron 55.847 | 27 Co Cobalt 58.9332 | 28 Ni Nickel 58.69 | 29 Cu Copper 63.546 | 30 Zn Zinc 65.39 | 31 Ga Gallium 69.72 | 32 Ge Germanium 72.59 | 33 As Arsenic 74.922 | 34 Se Selenium 78.96 | 35 Br Bromine 79.904 | 36 Kr Krypton 83.80 |
| 5 | 37 Rb Rubidium 85.468 | 38 Sr Strontium 87.62 | 39 Y Yttrium 88.9059 | 40 Zr Zirconium 91.224 | 41 Nb Niobium 92.91 | 42 Mo Molybdenum 95.94 | 43 Tc Technetium (98) | 44 Ru Ruthenium 101.07 | 45 Rh Rhodium 102.906 | 46 Pd Palladium 106.42 | 47 Ag Silver 107.868 | 48 Cd Cadmium 112.41 | 49 In Indium 114.82 | 50 Sn Tin 118.71 | 51 Sb Antimony 121.75 | 52 Te Tellurium 127.60 | 53 I Iodine 126.905 | 54 Xe Xenon 131.29 |
| 6 | 55 Cs Cesium 132.91 | 56 Ba Barium 137.33 | 57 to 71 | 72 Hf Hafnium 178.49 | 73 Ta Tantalum 180.95 | 74 W Tungsten 183.85 | 75 Re Rhenium 186.207 | 76 Os Osmium 190.2 | 77 Ir Iridium 192.22 | 78 Pt Platinum 195.08 | 79 Au Gold 196.967 | 80 Hg Mercury 200.59 | 81 Tl Thallium 204.383 | 82 Pb Lead 207.2 | 83 Bi Bismuth 208.98 | 84 Po Polonium (209) | 85 At Astatine (210) | 86 Rn Radon (222) |
| 7 | 87 Fr Francium (223) | 88 Ra Radium 226.025 | 89 to 103 | 104 Unq Unnilquadium (261) | 105 Unp Unnilpentium (262) | 106 Unh Unnilhexium (263) | 107 Uns Unnilseptium (262) | 108 Uno Unniloctium (265) | 109 Une Unnilennium (266) | | | | | | | | | |

**Rare-Earth Elements**

**Lanthanoid Series**

| 57 La Lanthanum 138.906 | 58 Ce Cerium 140.12 | 59 Pr Praseodymium 140.908 | 60 Nd Neodymium 144.24 | 61 Pm Promethium (145) | 62 Sm Samarium 150.36 | 63 Eu Europium 151.96 | 64 Gd Gadolinium 157.25 | 65 Tb Terbium 158.925 | 66 Dy Dysprosium 162.50 | 67 Ho Holmium 164.93 | 68 Er Erbium 167.26 | 69 Tm Thulium 168.934 | 70 Yb Ytterbium 173.04 | 71 Lu Lutetium 174.967 |
|---|---|---|---|---|---|---|---|---|---|---|---|---|---|---|

**Actinoid Series**

| 89 Ac Actinium 227.028 | 90 Th Thorium 232.038 | 91 Pa Proactinium 231.036 | 92 U Uranium 238.029 | 93 Np Neptunium 237.048 | 94 Pu Plutonium (244) | 95 Am Americium (243) | 96 Cm Curium (247) | 97 Bk Berkelium (247) | 98 Cf Californium (251) | 99 Es Einsteinium (252) | 100 Fm Fermium (257) | 101 Md Mendelevium (258) | 102 No Nobelium (259) | 103 Lr Lawrencium (260) |
|---|---|---|---|---|---|---|---|---|---|---|---|---|---|---|

The symbols shown here for elements 104–109 are being used temporarily until names for these elements can be agreed upon.

Mass numbers in parentheses are those of the most stable or common isotope.

Source: From *Prentice Hall Physical Science* by Angela Bornn Bacher et al. Copyright ©1991, 1988 Prentice-Hall, Inc.

What happens if you stir a spoonful of sugar into a cup of hot tea? The solid sugar **dissolves** in the liquid tea. A more scientific way of putting this information is: A **solute** dissolves in the **solvent** to form a **solution.** The solution is *a special type of mixture*. The solid in this special type of mixture seems to disappear, unlike the solids in common mixtures, but actually it is still there, chemically unchanged.

Most common solutions consist of solids or liquids dissolved in liquids, with water as the solvent. Substances that will dissolve in water, such as sugar, salt, and carbon dioxide (to make carbonated water) are said to be soluble in water. Not everything is soluble in water, however. For example, oil is **insoluble** in water, which is why another solvent such as soap must be used to get oil stains out of clothing.

# Evaluating the Adequacy of Information in Passages

To evaluate something means to judge it. When an employer gives you an evaluation, the employer judges how well you have been doing your job.

About one out of four of the questions on the GED Science test will be evaluation questions. They will test your ability to go beyond comprehending and analyzing what you read to *judge* the accuracy—the adequacy and relevancy—of what you read. To evaluate the adequacy of information you judge whether the information in the passage gives adequate, or enough, support to the statement you are being asked about. Such information is *relevant* to the statement you are being asked about if it relates to, or connects to, it. If it doesn't, it is irrelevant. It may be accurate and true but it cannot give adequate support to the statement because it is about a different topic or answers a different question.

Some of the evaluation questions will ask you to recognize whether you have been given adequate information in a passage to justify drawing a particular conclusion. Politicians, advertisers, and others make a lot of grand claims; it is important to be able to distinguish those which are solidly supported from those which are not supported. With each answer choice, ask yourself: (1) Is there enough information to support this statement? (2) Is the information the right kind to support this statement? Put these questions to the test with the following exercise.

Elements can be combined with each other in countless ways to form chemical compounds that have properties and applications very different from their elemental raw materials. Nature and chemists have created millions of different chemicals. Some are very simple, like $H_2O$ (water) with two hydrogen atoms for every oxygen, or NaCl (table salt) with a one-to-one ratio of sodium and chlorine. Other compounds are exceedingly complex, combining a dozen or more different elements.

With only a few more than a hundred elements to play with, it might seem that the chemist's job of making new chemical combinations would be quickly exhausted. Not so. A million chemists could each make a new sample every day for a million years and still not come close to running out of things to try. Almost every aspect of modern life—food and clothing, transportation and communications, sports and entertainment—depends on the discoveries of chemistry.

The information in the passage most adequately supports which of the following statements?

**(1)** Without the work of chemists, we would have few of the necessities of life.

**(2)** Most of the things we use in modern life are products of simple chemical compounds.

**(3)** Because the number of chemical bonds is unlimited, the work of chemists will always be useful.

**(4)** Chemistry is concerned with creating new materials that have new properties and applications.

**(5)** The compounds $H_2O$ and NaCl are characteristic of the many products chemistry makes for our daily use.

Step 1: Examine the question to see exactly what it asks. Remember that some choices may have *some* support and still be wrong. You want the statement with the *most* support.

Step 2: Scan the choices. Try to find the statement with the most support. You also should try to eliminate clearly wrong statements. These may be completely false, or have some, but not enough, support. You might reject (1) as clearly wrong because "necessities of life" would include all kinds of food (vegetables, meat, fruit) as well as the oxygen we breathe, wool and cotton for clothes, and wood and stone for building—all things that chemists did not create.

Step 3: Examine the choices carefully and choose the best answer. Check the choices against statements in the passage to eliminate unsupported ones. You may have spotted (5) as clearly false when you scanned because $H_2O$ is water and NaCl is table salt, neither of which was invented by chemists. As for (2), the passage tells you that we depend on chemical discoveries for most of the things we use, but that some compounds are "exceedingly complex" and that chemists could make new combinations for millions of years. Therefore, there is no support for the idea that "simple chemical compounds" produce most modern products (2). Choice (4) is partly true but goes too far. From the lesson you know that chemistry is not concerned only with making new materials but also with discovering new knowledge about the structure and operation of nature. The passage, however, does support directly the idea that the work of chemists has unlimited usefulness: It says a million scientists could each invent a new chemical bond every day for a millions years and not run out of things to try. Together with the last sentence of the passage, this statement gives the most support to choice (3).

Questions 1 and 2 are based on the following passage.

A scientist examines two substances. Substance X is black. Substance Y has no color. X is soft and leaves a streak on paper. Y is hard and scratches anything, including glass. The surface of X is dull while the surface of Y is shiny. Y costs much more than X.

**1.** Which one of the following statements does the information in the passage best support?

**(1)** X and Y have different properties.

**(2)** X is an element and Y is a compound.

**(3)** X and Y have different types of atoms.

**(4)** X and Y are in different states.

**(5)** X and Y are composed of different elements.

**2.** The passage provides support for the belief that

**(1)** X is less useful than Y.

**(2)** Y is more common than X.

**(3)** Y is a metal.

**(4)** X is a nonmetal.

**(5)** X and Y are both solids.

Item 3 is based on the following passage.

Electrons orbit around the nucleus in specific ringed paths, as the planets circle around the sun. Each orbit, or level, has a different energy. The pathway closest to the nucleus, the inner orbit, has space for two electrons. Other orbits are usually complete when they contain eight electrons. If an atom has an incomplete outer orbit, it often becomes linked with another atom by a sort of "electron glue." Colliding atoms stick together by forming two types of chemical bonds. In one type, electrons are shared between two atoms. In the other, electrons are passed from one atom to another. In both types, the outer orbit becomes "complete" with eight electrons.

**3.** Which one of the following predictions is supported by the information in the passage?

Fluorine, which has seven electrons in its outer orbit

**(1)** will become useful as a fuel alternative

**(2)** will tend to form one type of bond as often as the other

**(3)** will give up its outer electrons easily

**(4)** will be heavier than most other gases

**(5)** will form chemical bonds easily

Answers are on page A-21

# Chemical Reactions And Energy

## Prereading Prompt

Brainstorm examples of one substance changing into another. Do you know what causes each change? How is energy involved? Can you name an acid, base, or salt you keep in your home?

## Key Words

**chemical reaction**—process in which electrons are transferred or shared between atoms and a new substance is formed

**reactants**— substances that enter into and are altered during a chemical reaction

**products**—substances that result from a chemical reaction

## Chemical Changes

In 1937 hundreds of people watched in horror as a hot-air balloon called the *Hindenburg* exploded in midair over New Jersey. The cause was a **chemical reaction**. A chemical reaction is a process in which the properties of substances change as new substances form. The hydrogen gas that held the balloon in the air combined with oxygen to form water. The reaction gave off a tremendous amount of energy.

Chemists write down chemical reactions in a kind of shorthand called a chemical equation. A chemical equation is useful because it gives the proportions of substances that allow the reaction to occur and the changes in energy that take place. The equation for what happened during the *Hindenburg* explosion is shown below:

$$2H_2 + O_2 \rightarrow 2H_2O + energy$$

This equation shows that two molecules of hydrogen and one molecule of oxygen will combine to form two molecules of water. In the equation, the substances at the beginning of the reaction, known as the **reactants**, are written on the left side. The substances that result from the reaction, known as the **products,** are written on the right side after the arrow. Hydrogen and oxygen are written as $H_2$ and $O_2$ because they are normally found in air as molecules consisting of two bonded hydrogen atoms and two bonded oxygen atoms.

In an equation, the number of atoms in the reactants must always equal the number of atoms in the product. This is because during a chemical reaction, atoms are *only rearranged* to form new substances. It is this rearrangement of atoms that gives the products of a reaction different properties from the reactants. *Matter is neither created nor destroyed.* This is the important **law of conservation of matter**.

Chemical reactions occur at different rates. The chemical reaction that causes a flashbulb to flash happens in less than a second, while the chemical reaction that produces rust can take weeks or even months. However, whenever a chemical reaction occurs, there is always a change in energy. The energy may be in the form of heat, light, or electric energy. When energy is given off, it is called an **exothermic reaction**. The *Hindenburg* explosion is an example of a reaction that gives off heat and light. A reaction that absorbs energy is called an **endothermic reaction**. Baking bread is an example of a reaction that absorbs heat. The process of photosynthesis, in which plants use energy from sunlight to make food, is also an endothermic reaction.

## Acids, Bases, and Salts

Would you drink acid? If your answer is no, you may be surprised to find that you eat and drink acids every day. Acids are found in oranges, lemons, grapes, apples, milk, tea, pickles, and vinegar. Most shampoo is also slightly acidic. Of course, some acids are strong and can burn holes in skin or clothes.

What do the acetic acid found in vinegar and the boric acid used to wash out eyes have in common? All **acids** are compounds that contain hydrogen. Acids tend to taste sour. They also turn litmus paper, a specially treated type of paper, from blue to red.

Bases are a group of compounds that act quite differently from acids. Lye, ammonia, soap, sea water, and eggs all contain common bases. **Bases** are compounds that contain *hydroxide*, an oxygen-hydrogen compound. Bases tend to taste bitter and feel slippery. They turn red litmus paper blue.

Chemists use the **pH scale** to indicate the strength of acids and bases. A substance with a pH of 7 is neutral. A pH below 7 indicates an acid and a pH above 7 indicates a base. The pH scale is often used in industry and farming. Certain crops, for instance, grow better in basic soil, while others do better in acidic or neutral soils.

The chemical reaction between an acid and a base is called **neutralization**. In every such reaction, one of the products is water. The other product is a **salt** formed from part of the acid and part of the base. The salt may be sodium chloride (ordinary table salt), sodium sulfate, or potassium chloride, or one of many other salts.

## Identifying Faulty Logic in Graphics

For some reason, we tend to accept the truth of a graphic more readily than we might accept a written statement. Maybe it has something to do with the principle that "a picture is worth a thousand words" or with the fact that we are bombarded by so many visual images in TV ads. In any case, it *is* important to judge the logic of the message conveyed by a drawing, graph, chart, or other graphic.

Iron mixed with sulphur (top) responds to magnetism (middle). Heat creates a new substance (below) that is non-magnetic.

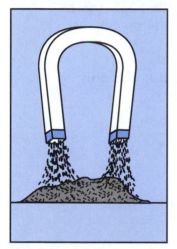

Which of the following statements is an example of *logical* reasoning about the diagram?

**(1)** The electrons in the iron-sulphur mixture have the same arrangement as they do in the new substance.

**(2)** The magnet caused a chemical change to occur.

**(3)** Heat created a new substance which was attracted by magnets.

**(4)** The iron-sulphur mixture would not have undergone a chemical change if it had not been heated.

**(5)** The iron-sulphur mixture would have become nonmagnetic over time.

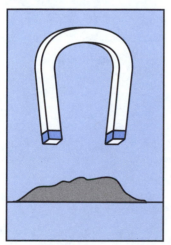

From *New Encyclopedia of Science*, Raintree, 1985. Copyright ©1985 Steck-Vaughn/Raintree.

Step 1: Examine the diagram carefully. Pay particular attention to labels. The caption tells you that the diagram shows three steps: The pile in the top drawing is a mixture of iron and sulphur. The middle drawing shows how a magnet attracts the mixture. The bottom drawing shows that after the mixture is heated, the magnet no longer attracts the substance.

Step 2: Figure out the main idea. What is the purpose of the diagram? Briefly, it shows that heating a mixture can change that mixture into a new, nonmagnetic substance.

Step 3: Examine each of the choices. This is one of those questions for which you cannot predict the answer before looking at all the choices. You are looking for the choice which is *logical*. You should eliminate all the choices which have holes in their reasoning. (1) is wrong because you can tell that a chemical reaction has occurred. The new substance has very different properties from the mixture; it is no longer magnetic. Your knowledge of chemical reactions tells you that when one substance changes into another, the pattern of electrons changes. As for (2), be careful not to assume that because one event comes before another, it *causes* the other. The magnet was used on the mixture some time before the chemical change, but the caption says that the heat "creates a new substance," that is, causes the change. (3) contradicts the evidence: You can see in the diagram that the new substance was *not* attracted by magnets. However, (4) makes sense. There is no evidence that anything but the heat caused the chemical change. It is logical to assume that without the heat, there would have been no change. (5) may or may not be true, but there is no evidence to support it.

Step 4: Choose the best answer. Choice (4) fits the question best. It is the only one of the five choices in which you *cannot* find a fault in the logic.

Questions 1-3 are based on the following advertisement.

*Note:* 1 percent milk is a low-fat milk; skim milk is also low in fat, since the cream in it has been removed.

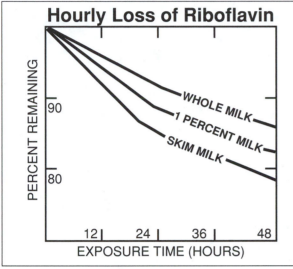

This shows milk's loss of riboflavin in plastic containers under fluorescent lights. Other tests show that milk loses even more of its vitamin A. (Source: "Protecting Your Milk from Nutrient Loss" by Dr. G.F. Senyk and Dr. W.F. Shipe, Department of Food Science, Cornell University.)

Fluorescent lights penetrate plastic milk containers and destroy important vitamins. But paper containers keep most harmful light out and more vitamins in.

Copyright ©1988 Paperboard Packaging Council. Used by permission.

1. Which of the following is most clearly faulty reasoning?

   (1) The plastic in plastic containers causes milk to lose riboflavin.

   (2) Exposure to fluorescent light causes milk to lose riboflavin.

   (3) Packaging milk in containers which reduce exposure to light might reduce loss of riboflavin.

   (4) Riboflavin has favorable effects on the body.

   (5) Paper cartons prevent the loss of Vitamin A.

2. Which of the following is the best example of *logical* reasoning about the information provided?

   (1) Since milk loses both vitamin A and riboflavin, dairies should be required to fortify milk with both vitamins.

   (2) Since all milk loses more vitamin A than riboflavin, skim milk can lose even more of its vitamin A in 24 hours than the loss shown on the graph.

   (3) Since whole milk starts out with more riboflavin than either skim milk or 1 percent milk have, it still has more riboflavin than the two other kinds of milk after 48 hours.

   (4) Since skim milk retains less riboflavin than whole milk or 1 percent milk, skim milk is the least healthy.

   (5) Since whole milk retains more riboflavin than skim milk or 1 percent milk, whole milk is the healthiest.

3. You logically can conclude from the graph that

   (1) the information is basically objective and unbiased because it is based on a scientific study by doctors

   (2) sunlight would produce a different effect on the milk than fluorescent light

   (3) the larger the plastic container of milk, the more rapid the loss of vitamins

   (4) milk also loses large amounts of vitamins A, C, and D when exposed to light

   (5) it is probable that 2 percent milk loses riboflavin when exposed to fluorescent light

Answers are on page A-22.

# The World of Physics

## Prereading Prompt

Why is the sky blue? Why are you able to see your reflection in a mirror? What makes a car go? We owe much of what we know about the way things around us work to physics.

## Key Words

**energy**—the ability to do work

**wave**—a special type of disturbance which passes through a substance and transfers energy

## PART 1: MOTION AND ENERGY

### Laws of Motion and Energy

The Earth revolving around the sun, a basketball falling through a hoop, and a car traveling along a city street all have one thing in common: They are all moving. A large part of physics deals with the study of motion.

The behavior of a moving object is described by three laws of motion set forth by Isaac Newton over 300 years ago. **Newton's first law of motion** is also known as the *law of inertia.* The law states that an object at rest will tend to stay at rest, and that *an object in motion will tend to continue in motion along a straight line,* unless acted upon by an outside force. If you take a ride on a roller coaster, you can feel inertia at work. As the roller coaster begins to move, you are pressed backward into your seat. This happens because your inertia works to keep you at rest. If the car stops abruptly, you will continue moving forward. Once you're moving, your inertia works to keep you in motion.

**Newton's second law of motion** states that *the force needed to move an object is directly proportional to the object's mass.* This means that the greater the mass of an object, the more force must be applied to change its state of motion. If you have ever tried to move a piano, you know that it takes considerably more energy to move it than to move a guitar. As you might expect, it also takes more force to stop a larger object than to stop a smaller one.

**Newton's third law of motion** states that *for every force, there is an equal and opposite force.* You can see how this principle works if you jump off a diving board. The downward push on the diving board results in an equivalent upward push that lifts you into the air.

## Potential Energy and Kinetic Energy

**Energy** is the ability to do work. One familiar form of energy is **kinetic energy**—the energy of motion. When a baseball player swings a bat, the bat has kinetic energy. When the bat strikes the ball, the bat does work by causing the ball to move in a different direction. Objects at rest also have energy—potential energy. **Potential energy** is energy of position, or stored energy. The baseball bat pulled back by the batter into a position to hit the ball has potential energy. Divers up on diving boards have potential energy; when they dive they have kinetic energy.

## Relationship Between Heat Energy and Mechanical Energy

One important type of kinetic energy is **heat energy**. Molecules in an object are in constant motion. When heat is applied to molecules, they gain energy and move faster. Therefore, an object's temperature is a measure of the average kinetic energy of its molecules.

Like all other forms of energy, heat has the ability to do work. In order to do work, heat must be converted into **mechanical energy**, the energy of a machine's moving parts. This energy conversion occurs when a car engine burns gasoline: The hot gases produced by the burning fuel apply energy to the pistons (discs), which move up and down in cylinders (hollow rods) in order to move the wheels of the car forward. The heat energy not converted to mechanical energy in this way is expelled as hot "exhaust" gases.

Mechanical energy also can be converted to heat energy through friction—the rubbing of one object against another. For example, the blades of an electric blender will feel warm after they have been in use for several minutes. Rubbing your hands together makes them warm.

## Two Laws of Thermodynamics

**Thermodynamics** is the study of the relationship between heat energy and mechanical energy. Thermodynamics is governed by two important scientific laws. The first is **the law of conservation of energy**: Energy is neither created nor destroyed. You see this law in action when you feel heat rising from your car engine. Not all of the engine's energy goes into moving your car, but this extra energy is not destroyed either. It is expelled into the air as heat energy. **The second law of thermodynamics** states that *heat will always move from a hotter object to a cooler one.* This law becomes obvious if you touch a hot stove—heat from the stove will quickly move to your hand. Note that the opposite is not true. Heat will not flow on its own from a colder object to a hotter one.

## PART 2: WAVES, SOUND, AND LIGHT

## Waves and the Behavior of Light

Imagine yourself at the beach watching a wave approach the shore. Now picture the wavelike motion of the water in your bathtub when you put your foot into one end. What these waves and all others have in common is that they are the *transmission of a disturbance that repeats its form across space and time.* All waves have an amplitude, a wavelength, and a frequency (see below).

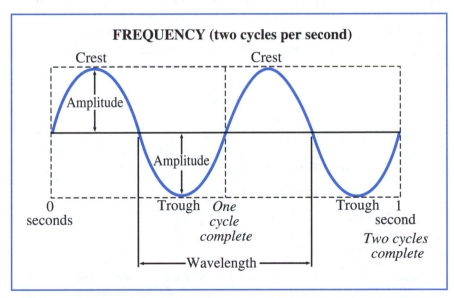

From *The New Revised Cambridge GED Program: Science* by Gloria Levine. Copyright ©1992 Prentice Hall/Regents.

**Amplitude** is the maximum distance the molecules of a wave are displaced from their normal rest position. The amplitude of an ocean wave would be its highest point above, or its lowest point below, the calm surface of the ocean. The high point in a wave is called a **crest**. The low point in a wave is called the **trough**. The distance from the rest position to the crest will always equal the distance from the rest position to the trough. A **wavelength** is the distance, in advance of a wave, from any point in its movement to the next point that has the same characteristics. The diagram shows a wavelength from one rest position to a similar rest position. The number of waves that pass a given point in a certain amount of time is called the **frequency** of the wave. For example, if two ocean waves, measured from crest to crest, pass a buoy in one second, the frequency of the wave is two per second.

## Wave and Sound

The **velocity** (speed in a given direction) of a wave is the product of the wavelength and frequency. The speed of a sound wave through a medium depends on the temperature and the density of the medium. Sound waves travel faster at higher temperatures and through more elastic materials. Iron and aluminum, both elastic metals, are good transmitters of sound; lead is dense and a poor transmitter. On the moon there is no sound, because the moon has no atmosphere to serve as a medium for transmitting sound waves.

## The Electromagnetic Spectrum

Light is made up of a stream of **photons**, or tiny packets of energy. Light waves are called **electromagnetic waves**. Scientists arrange these waves on a scale of decreasing wavelength and increasing energy and frequency. This scale is called the **electromagnetic spectrum** (see below). As you can see, only a very small part of this spectrum is visible to our eyes. All the other types of light cannot be seen and therefore make up the **invisible spectrum. Radio waves** have the longest wavelengths and the lowest frequencies in the electromagnetic spectrum. The highest-frequency radio waves are called **microwaves**. They are used mainly for communication, and for cooking. Short-wavelength

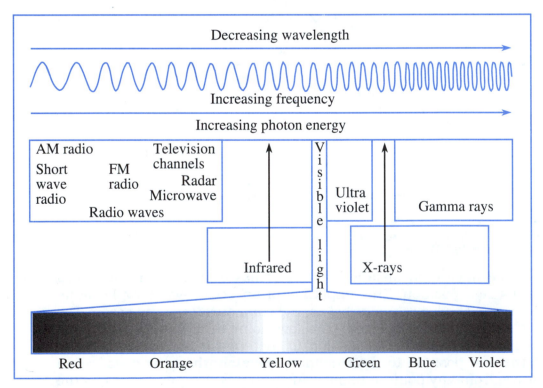

Source: Adapted from *Prentice Hall Physical Science*, p. 539, by Angela Bornn Bacher et al. Copyright ©1988 Prentice-Hall, Inc.

microwaves are used in radar to locate objects (such as airplanes or cars) and to determine their distance and speed. **Infrared rays** can be felt as heat from the sun, a light bulb, or a stove, while **ultraviolet rays** cause suntan and are used in food-processing plants to destroy germs. **X-rays** have so much energy they can be used to penetrate human skin and tissue in making pictures of our bone matter.

We know the different frequencies of visible light as the colors of the rainbow: red, orange, yellow, green, blue, and violet. The range of colors is called the **visible spectrum**, or just the spectrum. Frequency determines color. For example, red light has a slightly higher frequency than violet. Amplitude determines brightness. The greater the amplitude of a light wave, the brighter the light. In sunlight these colors are mixed together and we see them as white light.

## Reflection and Refraction

**Reflection** is the bouncing back of a wave when it hits a barrier that does not absorb the wave's energy. We see only transmitted and reflected light, not absorbed light. An apple appears red because it absorbs all colors except red. A white object reflects all colors of the spectrum, which when combined by our eyes appear white. A black object absorbs all colors and reflects none.

Each frequency **refracts**, or bends, at slightly different angles. This is what happens when light passes through a prism. A **prism** (see below) breaks up the frequencies of white light into the colors of the visible spectrum. Similarly, a rainbow is formed in the sky by the refraction of the sun's rays in falling rain or in mist.

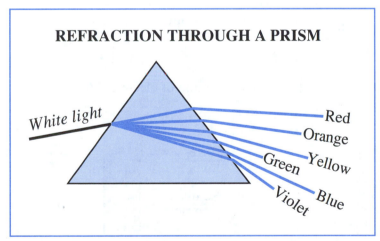

**REFRACTION THROUGH A PRISM**

Source: From *New Revised Cambridge GED Program: Science* by Gloria Levine. Copyright ©1992 Prentice Hall/Regents.

How much the light is refracted depends on the medium it is passing through because light, like all waves, travels at different speeds through different media. Because of refraction, an object under water often looks distorted when viewed through the water's surface. For instance, a fishing line under the surface of the water looks bent from above.

## Electricity

It may surprise you to learn that electricity is a basic property of all matter. Electricity is caused by the flow of electrons between atoms. This flow of electrons is called an **electric current.** Materials that allow electrons to move most freely are good **conductors.** Materials that slow down the flow of electrons within conductors are good **insulators.** Most metals are good conductors, especially wires made of copper, silver, and aluminum. Good insulators include rubber, plastic, wood, glass, and air. They keep electricity from escaping and giving people electrical shocks.

The most common type of electricity found in nature is called **static electricity.** Static electricity is the buildup of positive or negative charges on objects by the accumulation or loss of electrons. You can see static electricity at work if you dry your clothes in a dryer. As the clothes rub against each other, they exchange electrons. Some clothes build up positive charges by losing electrons, whereas others build up negative charges by gaining electrons. The opposite charges cause the clothes to stick to each other.

**Current electricity** is the controlled flow of electrons. One of the most dramatic examples is lightning, the sudden transfer of electrons between two clouds or between a cloud and Earth. Unlike the charges in static electricity, the charges in current electricity are continuously on the move.

In order for electricity to power appliances and do other useful work, it must be controlled. Take, for example, an electric light (see below).

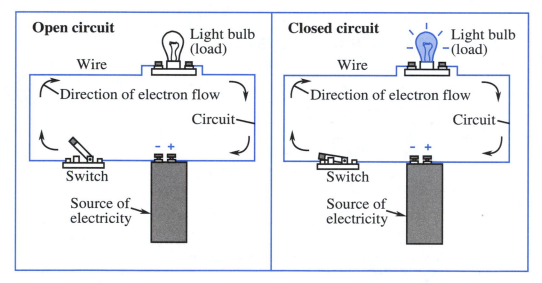

From *Prentice Hall Physical Science* by Angela Bornn Bacher et al, p. 456. Copyright © 1988, 1991 Prentice-Hall Inc.

Both ends of a conductor are connected to form a **circuit,** a complete, closed circular path for an electric current. The *source* provides the force needed to drive the electrons around the circuit. The *load* always offers resistance to the flow of electricity. As a result, electrical energy is converted into heat, light, or mechanical energy. As you can see, the source is the battery and the load is the light bulb. When the switch is turned off, the circuit becomes open; the current is broken and the light goes off. Electricity can flow only through a closed circuit.

## Magnetism

**Magnetism**, a force of pull and push, is a close relative of electricity. Like electricity, magnetism is a property of all physical things. Every magnet has two ends, called **poles**, from which the magnetic force extends. One pole is called the magnet's north pole, and the other its south pole. The magnetic force extends outward from the poles to create an area around the magnet where its magnetism can be felt. This area is called the **magnetic field**. What causes it? Scientists believe that magnetism is caused by the rotation of electrons within a substance. Every electron in every substance acts as a magnet.

If the north pole of one magnet is brought near the south pole of another magnet, the two poles will attract (pull) each other. If the north poles of two magnets are brought near each other, they will repel (push) each other. The same thing will happen if two south poles are brought together. These forces of attraction and repulsion are summed up by this rule: *Opposites attract; likes repel.* (see below).

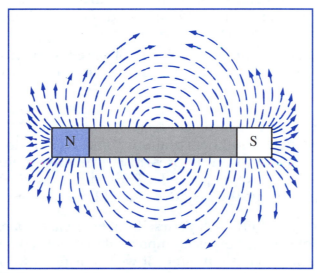

Source: Adapted from *Prentice Hall Physical Science* by Angela Bornn Bacher et al, p. 469. Copyright ©1991, 1988 Prentice-Hall Inc.

## Evaluating the Effect of Values On Information in Passages

What is most important to you? Each of us has a set of values, or priorities, that affect what we think and do. What authors write is affected by their values. On the GED, you may be asked to examine the values that shape written information. Once you are aware of these values, you are in a better position to judge whether you want to accept what you are being told.For example, as you read the statement below, think about how a real estate agency might try to "shape" the information provided by the Environmental Protection Agency (EPA).

> Can electricity cause cancer? The Environmental Protection Agency reports that some studies seem to link exposure to electromagnetic fields with increased risk of childhood leukemia and other cancers.

Which of the following statements would be most likely to appear in an ad paid for by a real estate agency?

**(1)** High-tension electric transmission lines carry large amounts of electricity over long distances. Homes, schools, and playgrounds should not be built anywhere near them.

**(2)** Electric distribution lines that carry current down local streets are far less powerful than those high-tension lines you see strung along high towers. The utility company can often bury these systems, but such rerouting is expensive.

**(3)** Shavers, hair dryers, can openers, and microwave ovens all generate powerful fields, and people should be careful to use them for only short periods of time.

**(4)** The EPA has put forward a serious government warning. Now is the time to rebuild your home so that your children spend the most time in rooms farthest from your street's electric distribution line.

**(5)** The EPA is unnecessarily frightening millions of parents. Buying a home near an electric distribution line is less hazardous than driving your child to school every day.

Step 1: Evaluate the source. The key words are "real estate agency." What is important to a real estate agency? You know that such agencies try to sell homes and property. Therefore, they want to present information in such a way as to make home-buying as attractive as possible. They would avoid or downplay any information that points out the negative side of home-buying.

Step 2: Examine each choice carefully. Ask yourself, in each case: Does this sound like someone to whom selling homes is important? (1) is the last thing a real estate agency would want to point out, since it would bring down the value of those homes they are trying to sell near power lines. (2) is a possibility. The statement de-emphasizes the problem and suggests a solution. Reject (3): Discouraging use of these household appliances would not encourage house-buying. (4) is not a good choice either, since it doesn't promote buying real estate. (It is the sort of statement you might expect in an ad for contractors who do remodeling.) (5) seems like the best answer. It downplays the danger and reassures the potential home-buyer.

Step 3: Choose the best answer. You have narrowed your choices down to two: (2) and (5). Looking more closely at choice (2), you may notice that the writer points out that the solution to the problem, while simple, is expensive. Real estate ads are not likely to point out additional expenses, which might frighten off potential buyers. By process of elimination, therefore, choice (5) is the best answer.

Questions 1-3 are based on the passage below.

Most people give very little thought to the cost of their refrigerator. After all, it is such a great improvement over an icebox! Experts on energy consumption, however, call the refrigerator an energy gulper. Automatic defrost is the cause of much of the high use of electricity by refrigerators. What's a person to do? Find the switch for automatic defrost and turn it off. Wipe the interior of the freezer with a paper towel dipped in vegetable oil. Next, stick sheets of clear wrapping plastic to the vegetable-oiled surface. Take the food out of the freezer, squirt hot water on the frosted areas with a turkey baster, and whole sheets of frost will peel right off with very little effort!

1. The writer is most likely

   (1) science adviser to the President
   (2) editor of a conservation newsletter
   (3) manufacturer of automatic defrost refrigerators
   (4) author of a historical research paper on kitchen appliances
   (5) writer of a column on "kitchen time-savers"

2. Which of the following statements best describes the author's point of view?

   (1) We would be better off using ice-boxes.
   (2) We should ban refrigerators without automatic defrost.
   (3) We should take the time to defrost refrigerators by hand.
   (4) We should accept that in today's busy world time is money.
   (5) We should conserve energy by spending a little more for refrigerators that have automatic defrosters.

3. Which of the following articles do you think the author would be *least* likely to recommend for "further reading"?

   (1) "Making Products Live Longer"
   (2) "Energy Efficiency of Popular Top-Freezer Refrigerators"
   (3) "The Rise and Fall and Rise of Energy Conservation"
   (4) "Say Good-Bye to Electricity Guzzlers"
   (5) "Remodeling for That Country Kitchen Look"

Answers are on page A-22.

# UNIT IV

# INTERPRETING LITERATURE AND THE ARTS

Literature consists of writing we enjoy which has a deeper and larger meaning than the writing we read for a practical purpose. It includes not only stories and poems but also factual reports and writing that expresses opinions about actual events. Such works of opinion, called articles or essays, are often about serious topics—politics, love, "the good life." Imaginative literature, on the other hand, gives us many different experiences. We respond to the ways a story reflects the world we live in and dramatizes feelings we have had. We also enjoy experiencing adventures and emotions that are beyond our experience, which the imaginations of writers give us in novels, plays, movies, and poems. Part of our sense of wonder is excitement at the authors' skill in making these imaginary things so real. Sometimes we respond simply to the beauty of the words and images. Commentary on the arts, as you will see, is written opinion about works of literature that is intended to help us understand their meaning and teach us how to judge their content and skill.

The reading passages in this section will prepare you for the Interpreting Literature and the Arts test by giving you a selection of the three types of literature that will appear on it: *Popular Literature*, which is high-quality writing by authors of the present time; *Classical Literature*, which is work by writers of the past that has a permanent value and interest; and *Commentary*, which consists of opinions on various kinds of literature and art—novels, plays, movies, television, concerts, architecture, and painting. On the Interpreting Literature and the Arts test, 50% of the passages will be popular literature; 25% will be classical literature; and 25% will be commentary.

Since Popular and Classical Literature include nonfiction, fiction, drama, and poetry, you will study these four types of literature in this section along with Commentary on the Arts. You will learn about the methods that writers use in each kind of literature, and also study each kind of writing in line with reading strategies you learned in the sections on Social Studies and Science—literal comprehension, inferential comprehension, application, and analysis. On the Interpreting Literature and the Arts test, 60% of the questions will be in literal and inferential comprehension; 15% will be application questions; and 25% will be analysis questions.

# Unit IV Progress Chart

## Interpreting Literature and the Arts

Use the following chart to keep track of your work. When you complete a lesson, circle the number of questions you answered correctly in the Lesson Exercise. The numbers in color represent scores at a level of 60% or better.

| | | | |
|---|---|---|---|
| | | **CHAPTER 1: Nonfiction** | |
| 1 | 290 | Literal Comprehension of Nonfiction | 1 2 3 |
| 2 | 296 | Inferential Comprehension of Nonfiction | 1 2 3 |
| 3 | 302 | Applying Ideas in Nonfiction | 1 2 3 |
| 4 | 306 | Analyzing Nonfiction | 1 2 3 |
| | | **CHAPTER 2: Fiction** | |
| 1 | 314 | Literal Comprehension of Fiction | 1 2 3 |
| 2 | 319 | Inferential Comprehension of Fiction | 1 2 3 |
| 3 | 324 | Applying Ideas in Fiction | 1 2 3 |
| 4 | 328 | Analyzing Fiction | 1 2 3 |
| | | **CHAPTER 3: Drama** | |
| 1 | 334 | Literal Comprehension of Drama | 1 2 3 |
| 2 | 339 | Inferential Comprehension of Drama | 1 2 3 |
| 3 | 344 | Applying Ideas in Drama | 1 2 3 |
| 4 | 349 | Analyzing the Effects of Language in Drama | 1 2 3 |
| | | **CHAPTER 4: Poetry** | |
| 1 | 356 | Literal Comprehension of Poetry | 1 2 3 |
| 2 | 361 | Inferring the Meaning of Figurative Language in Poetry | 1 2 3 |
| 3 | 365 | Applying Ideas in Poetry | 1 2 3 |
| 4 | 369 | Analyzing Poetry | 1 2 3 |
| | | **CHAPTER 5: Commentary on the Arts** | |
| 1 | 376 | Literal Comprehension of Commentary | 1 2 3 |
| 2 | 381 | Inferring the Meaning of Figurative Language in Poetry | 1 2 3 |
| 3 | 386 | Applying Ideas in Commentary | 1 2 3 |
| 4 | 390 | Analyzing Commentary | 1 2 3 |

# CHAPTER 1

Often when we think of literature, we think of imaginary people and imaginary situations. But what about the lives of real people, and their thoughts, ideas, and feelings? These, too, are a part of literature, a special type of literature called nonfiction. Nonfiction literature is created largely from facts or at times from a writer's opinions.

Credit: James K. Clark

## Prereading Prompt

Nonfiction literature is about actual people, events, or situations. Try to think of recent books or movies you have heard about that are nonfiction. What people, places, or situations in the news today might make good subjects for nonfiction literature? Is there some event from your own life that you think would make a good book or movie?

# Nonfiction

## What Is Nonfiction?

Nonfiction writing deals with actual people, places, and events. Most of the writing we read in newspapers, magazines, and textbooks is nonfiction. Nonfiction writers may try to report only the facts and include very little personal opinion, or they may present strong opinions about the facts. Blending facts with opinions—either the writers' own opinions or those of others—is a common characteristic of nonfiction.

Some nonfiction stands out because it does more than simply tell facts. Through skillful word choice, arrangement of details, and personal interpretation, nonfiction writers can create something of lasting value. If a work of nonfiction focuses on a subject that attracts readers because of its universal interest, then it is considered literature.

### Key Words

**biography**—a written work describing the life of a person

**autobiography**—a person's own account of his or her life

**article or essay**—an expression of a writer's thoughts and feelings on a subject, either formally or informally written

# Literal Comprehension of Nonfiction

## Prereading Prompt

When you read an article that really grabs your interest—about a scandal in Hollywood or about a hot political issue close to home—you ask yourself: What is this writer's main point? Knowing how to find the main idea of a passage in this way is very important for answering GED questions. You will learn how in this lesson.

## Key Words

**literal**—describing something that is expressed directly

**topic**—the subject of a piece of writing

**main idea**—the point the writer makes about a topic

**topic sentence**—a single sentence that states the main idea

**supporting details**— details that support the main idea

## What Is Literal Comprehension?

In daily conversation, you often express yourself directly. Authors, too, often state their ideas directly. Understanding what an author has directly told you is called **literal comprehension**.

## Finding the Topic and the Main Idea of a Paragraph

Every work of nonfiction you read has a topic. The topic is what the piece of writing is about. To find the topic of a nonfiction work, just ask yourself, "What is this piece of writing about? What are all the details about?" Usually, you need only look at the title or glance through the opening paragraphs to find the topic. A topic will be a general word or phrase like *inflation, marriage and divorce, high school sports, types of music*. What is the topic of the following paragraph?

### WHAT IS GOOD ABOUT CRAFT HOBBIES?

If you like to make things in your spare time and could use some extra money, you may want to sell your wares at craft fairs. Many people have hobbies such as woodworking, basketweaving, jewelry making, painting, flower arranging, stained glass making, and quilting, just to name a few. They set up shop on weekends in parks, churches, and school-yards.
(5)

The topic of this paragraph is

**(1)** hobbies that fill spare time

**(2)** hobby products that make money

**(3)** hobby products sold at craft fairs

**(4)** types of craft hobbies

**(5)** types of craft fairs

(3) is correct. The first sentence talks about things you might like to make in your spare time (that is, hobbies or hobby products) which you can sell at craft fairs. This is the general subject or topic of the whole paragraph. The rest of the paragraph consists of details that are part of this topic. The second sentence lists types of craft hobbies (choice 4). The last sentence lists types of craft fairs (choice 5) but says nothing about hobbies sold for money. The paragraph is clearly not about all hobbies (such as stamp collecting or gardening) but only about craft hobbies—and, in fact, craft hobbies that can be sold for money—so choices (1) and (2) are wrong.

The most important point a writer makes about a topic is called the **main idea**. It is often stated in a single sentence about the topic, called the **topic sentence**. To find the main idea, read the work carefully to find a sentence that answers the question, "What point is the author trying to make about the topic?" Answer the following question.

The main idea of the paragraph is that

    **(1)** hobbies are the best way to make money in your spare time

    **(2)** craft hobbies can be enjoyable and profitable

    **(3)** the number of craft fairs is growing in number

    **(4)** more people than ever before are making money from craft hobbies

    **(5)** the number of different types of craft hobbies is increasing

(2) is correct. This answer is a restatement of the first sentence of the paragraph, which is the topic sentence of the paragraph, the sentence that states the main idea. The main point the writer wants to make about craft hobbies is that they are something you can enjoy in your spare time and make money by selling. However, the writer does not say that craft hobbies are the best way to make money in your spare time—choice (1). There are also no statements in the paragraph like those in choices (3), (4), and (5). Notice that the statement of a main idea is usually a complete sentence, with a subject and verb, while the statement of a topic is usually a phrase or a word.

The details authors use to make the main idea convincing and effective are called **supporting details**. They may be examples, statistical proof, factual evidence, or strong reasons. In the previous paragraph, the supporting details are the types of craft hobbies listed in the second sentence and the different locations of craft fairs listed in the last sentence. These details are meant to support the main idea that craft hobbies are something many people enjoy and make money from doing.

## Finding the Topic and the Main Idea of a Passage

A *passage* is a series of paragraphs about the same topic. Remember that the main idea of a paragraph is the most important thing the writer says about the topic of the paragraph. Although a passage is often made up of several paragraphs, it has a single main idea, too. This main idea is general enough to cover all the other ideas in the passage.

Below are several sample questions about the topic and main idea of a passage that you could find on the Interpreting Literature and the Arts section of the GED:

- What main idea is stated in the passage?
- What sentence states the author's general attitude toward [the topic]?
- According to the passage, how is [the topic] explained?

Here's a strategy you can use to find the answer:

1.  Read the passage carefully, keeping the purpose question in mind. (The purpose question appears in capital letters at the beginning of the passage.) This question points you toward the passage's main idea.

2.  Identify the topic of the passage: What is it generally about?

3.  Look for the topic sentence of the passage—the sentence that states the main idea of the passage. Often it is somewhere in the first paragraph. If it is not there, it is likely to be in the last paragraph.

4. Look for the main idea of each paragraph as you read the passage. Try to see how these ideas are connected.

5. Look at the answer choices in the GED question and see if any of these choices states an idea big enough to cover all the main ideas in the passage. Test the main idea of the passage by making sure that the main idea of each paragraph supports it.

## Model Passage and Questions

The question below refers to the following passage. Use the strategy and see if you can identify what the main idea and supporting details are.

**WHAT ATTITUDE DO THE DANCERS HAVE TOWARD THE STAGEHANDS?**

The stagehands are the only "real" people backstage with us, and what a mixture they are—old and young, slim and rotund, married and single, bearded and clean-shaven. They drink, joke, laugh, watch the ball game or *Kojak*, and rush to
(5) the wings to pull at scenery, fix a blown-out light, or catch a debut.

We dancers are fairly unaware of them. They are the scenery, necessary and always there. A few of us talk and joke with them, and they are most sensitive and perceptive if
(10) they are "allowed" our friendship. They wink, hand out candy, comment on our new eyelashes, and catch us in the wings from a flying exit.

I've talked to many of them, and they all say the same two things—that we are all quite intimidating and quite beautiful,
(15) and that we live in a world of our own. They have never worked with such a strange group of dancers, all so young and dreamy and dedicated. They find us rather frightening and incomprehensible. The only contact that they have with many of us is in the form of complaints: the lights are too
(20) hot, there is too much snow, the stage is too slippery. We are true princesses. I suppose we are brought up this way.

From *Winter Season: A Dancer's Journal,* by Toni Bentley, Random House, © 1982.

According to the passage, how is the dancers' attitude toward the stagehands explained?

(1) Only a few stagehands are sensitive and perceptive.

(2) Dancers and stagehands never speak.

(3) Stagehands have never worked with such a strange group of dancers before.

(4) Dancers are fairly unaware of stagehands.

(5) Stagehands are necessary and always there.

The correct answer to the question is (4). Most sentences in the passage give supporting details that show that when dancers are backstage, they are fairly unaware of the stagehands. To the dancers, the stagehands "are the scenery," part of the background; they have contact with dancers only when the dancers complain. The dancers are "true princesses." (1) is wrong because the writer does not say this; she says only a few dancers talk to the stagehands, and that when they do, the stagehands are sensitive and perceptive. Since dancers complain to the stagehands, and a few chat with them, (2) is false. (3) explains the stagehands' attitude, not the dancers'. (5) is not a reason for the dancers to be unaware of the stagehands but a reason for them to be aware of them.

## Lesson 1 Exercise

Items 1 and 2 refer to the following paragraph. Choose the one best answer to each item.

### WHAT IMPORTANT QUALITIES SHOULD A WRITER POSSESS?

To create a market for your writing you have to be consistent, professional, a continuing writer—not just a one-article or a one-story or a one-book man. Those expert vendors, the literary agents, do not like to be bothered with a one-shot writer. No money in them. Agents like to
(5) help build a career, not light a flash in the pan. With one-shot writers, literary hucksters cannot pay their income taxes. Nor can publishers get their money back on what they lose on the first book. Even if you are a good writer, but not consistent, you probably will not get far. Color has nothing to do with writing as such. So I would say, in your
(10) mind don't be a colored writer even when dealing in racial material. Be a writer first. Like an egg: first, egg; then an Easter egg, the color applied.

From "Writers: Black and White," by Langston Hughes. Reprinted by permission of Harold Ober Associates Incorporated. Copyright © 1960 by American Society of African Culture.

1. Why does the author advise writers not to be "colored writers"?

   (1) It's harder to write about racial material.
   (2) There's no market for "colored writing."
   (3) Color has nothing to do with writing quality.
   (4) Agents won't work with them.
   (5) They're usually one–shot writers.

2. Which of the following best describes the main idea of the paragraph?

   (1) Agents like to help build the career of a writer.

   (2) Racial subjects are not very marketable.
   (3) One-shot writers don't make much money.
   (4) "Colored writers" are best able to write about racial material.
   (5) To be a successful writer you must be consistent.

Answers are on page A–24.

Item 3 is based on the following passage.

## WHAT CAN SCIENCE TELL US ABOUT DREAMS?

Scientific research has shown that dreams are not complete mysteries but instead make up a part of our mental life that has definite, observable characteristics. For instance, scientists have discovered that there is a close relationship between dreaming and the rhythms of
(5) sleep. Everyone passes through periods that include both deep and light sleep. For most people each period of sleep lasts about 1 1/2 to 2 hours. At the end of each period of sleep, a person has had a period of dreaming. Anyone who sleeps 8 hours a night has about five dream periods. Each dream period usually consists of several different
(10) episodes or adventures lasting anywhere from 5 to 50 minutes.

Researchers have also learned that eye movements are linked to dreaming. Rapid eye movement (REM) is a sign a person is dreaming. During a dream, the dreamer's eyes usually move rapidly back and forth behind closed eyelids. It is as if the dreamer was a spectator
(15) watching the events in the dream. Dreaming sleep is called REM sleep.

Research with blind people also shows the relationship between dreams and eye movements. When people have been blind all their lives, their eyes do not move when they dream. These people only feel or hear what is happening in their dreams.
(20) Scientists have also discovered that four out of every five dreams is in color. But people describe most dreams as gray or black and white. As dreams fade from memory they lose their color.

**3.** Which of the following best describes the author's attitude toward scientific research on dreams?

**(1)** Science has explained dreams as the result of eye movements during sleep.

**(2)** Science has shown that everyone's dreams are the same.

**(3)** Science has solved all the mysteries of dreams through observation.

**(4)** Science has observed basic characteristics of dreams.

**(5)** Science has shown the close relationship between dreams and the rhythms of sleep.

Answers are on page A–24.

# Inferential Comprehension of Nonfiction

## Prereading Prompt

If you see a letter carrier nervously hurry away from your neighbor's mailbox, you might conclude that she is trying to deliver the mail without being bitten by Arthur, your neighbor's cranky dog. Drawing conclusions from the clues you have been given about a situation is a common part of daily life. On the GED you may be asked to answer questions that show you understand the meaning of an author's main idea when it is not explained directly. You will learn how in this lesson.

## Key Words

**inference**—a conclusion drawn about the author's meaning by using information in the piece

**imply**—to suggest something without saying it directly

**point of view**—an author's opinion or attitude about a topic

## Making Inferences

In most nonfiction, the main idea is stated directly so that you immediately understand it. Sometimes, though, a writer does not tell you an idea directly. Instead, the author will **imply**, or suggest, an idea. You have to use his or her direct statements as clues to figure out this unstated meaning. In other words, you need to make connections between details to find the implied meaning. When you figure out an author's implied meaning in this way, you are inferring a meaning, or making an **inference**. This process is also called *inferential comprehension* or, more popularly, reading between the lines. Inferential comprehension is a higher-level reading skill than literal comprehension. You first must be able to understand what you read before you can find clues about the meaning that is between the lines.

Read the following paragraph and see if you can infer the answer to these questions: What does the word *extinct* mean? What does the word *vegetarians* mean? Why did the change of climate cause the dinosaurs to "become extinct"?

### WHY DID CHANGE OF CLIMATE MAKE DINOSAURS EXTINCT?

About 65 million years ago, dinosaurs became extinct. Some of these huge creatures were vegetarians that lived off plants. Scientists have some ideas about why these dinosaurs died out. One explanation is that the rise of moun-
(5) tain ranges caused the climate to change. The climate became too cold for many plants to grow. These dinosaurs could not survive.

If you do not know the meaning of the word *extinct*, you can infer it. By connecting details, you can see that "became extinct" is another way of saying "died out" and also the same as "could not survive." In the same way, you can infer that if these dinosaurs "lived off plants," *vegetarians* must be creatures that eat only plants for food—"eaters of vegetables."

Why the dinosaurs became extinct you can infer by finding a cause-and-effect relationship among stated details. If the vegetarian dinosaurs lived off plants, and the climate became too cold for many plants to grow, these dinosaurs must have died out because the climate change destroyed their source of food (plants). This is the unstated main idea of the paragraph: *dinosaurs died out because a climate change destroyed their food supply.*

## Inferring the Main Idea of a Paragraph or a Passage

Many inference questions on the Interpreting Literature and the Arts section of the GED will be like those above—questions about the meaning of a word or about the cause of some event. You also will be asked to infer other kinds of causes (which later lessons will discuss), such as the reason or motive for someone's action, or the attitude behind someone's statement. The answer may be the unstated main idea of a paragraph or it may be the author's whole attitude toward the topic—the main idea of the whole passage.

However, such GED questions about causes will not tell you whether the answer is stated in the passage or whether it is unstated. First try to remember the answer from your reading; if you can't remember it, look for the paragraph where you think the answer is. Here is a quick way to tell if the answer can be found directly in a paragraph or if you need to make an inference.

1. Scan the paragraph to see if the answer to the purpose question is stated directly. If no detail answers the question directly, go on to step 2.

**2.** Scan the paragraph to see if there are any clues that can help you answer the question by making an inference.

Here are some typical GED questions that may require you to infer the main idea of a paragraph, of several paragraphs, or of the whole passage.

- According to the article, what is the major reason for _____?
- The essay suggests that this kind of event/action will occur when _____
- According to the review, these people have the common characteristic of _____.

Here's a strategy you can use to find the answer to these questions when you need to infer the main idea of the whole passage:

**1.** As you read, try to identify the topic. Use the purpose question to help you.

**2.** Identify the main idea of each paragraph (the topic sentence of each paragraph).

**3.** Infer the main idea by putting the main ideas of all the paragraphs together and figuring out what important statement they are making about the topic.

> **REMINDER**: Before you read the passage: (1) read the purpose question and (2) read the questions and scan their answer choices. As you read the passage you can be looking for details that directly answer the questions and also for details you can put together to infer answers that are not stated.

## Inferring the Author's Point of View

If you read that the coach of a local basketball team has just put a strict code of conduct into effect, you can make a good guess why: He most likely feels that good manners and behavior help promote a positive team image.

In this example, you have inferred an opinion based on details. You do this almost every day, when you read an article or talk with people. From the details you read and hear, you make good guesses about how the person feels about various subjects or, in other words, what the author's **point of view** is.

On the Interpreting Literature and the Arts section of the GED Test, you may be asked to draw conclusions or infer the author's point of view. To do so, search for details, or clues, in the passage that suggest the author's opinion.

Here are several sample questions about inferring the author's point of view that might appear on the GED.

- The author believes that _____?
- Which of the following words best describes the author's attitude toward _____?
- With which of the following statements would the author agree?

In answering these questions, follow the steps outlined above for inferring the main idea of a paragraph or a passage. The answer to the question may be directly stated. If not, you may be able to infer it from several details in one paragraph or in several paragraphs.

## Model Passage and Question

Read this passage and the question that follows. Use the strategies just described to help you infer the unstated main idea and the author's point of view.

### WHAT DO HE AND HIS GIRLFRIEND FEEL ABOUT EACH OTHER?

When I came back from Europe I took a bus to Cleveland, where my new girl met me at the station. I had a silky-type moustache she hadn't seen before, and was more serious, but she was nervous and flustered to be driving a car on which
(5) her brother still owed three payments. Another thing was that the ring with the college seal I had given her when I left for Europe she had left in a washroom.

My new girl and her family lived on a big shaded lot, great for squirrels and birds. A dog named Sox barked and clawed
(10) at the screen when we came up the driveway. Her father, a law school professor, was sitting on the steps of the back porch, husking sweet corn. The day was a hot one, the windows of the house were open, the curtains tied back. From the window above the porch, a woman wearing a shower cap
(15) put out her head and spoke to all of us in a voice so calm it seemed disembodied. She hadn't expected a houseguest so early, she said, and leaned far out the window to shake a small rug.

My girl led me through the cool, dark house, taking the
(20) route that bypassed the kitchen, where the linoleum was covered with newspapers. Just the year before, I had come in through the kitchen, where her mother had been crouched, taking up the old papers and putting down new ones. Her parents had made the Grand Tour of Europe in the early
(25) twenties, coming back with the Dresden plates stored in the sideboard along with the goblets made in Venice. I was shown the room that had once been my girl's but was now her brother's. He had put up his tennis racquet, some Dartmouth pennants, and an Arabian sword in a scabbard. We stood fac-
(30) ing the rear dormer window, where a big fierce blue jay was hammering at the feed tray. The one thing I remember her saying to me was that she had lived most of her life in this room—could I imagine that? All I could think of at the time was how lucky she had been. That's how dumb I was.

Excerpt from *A Cloak of Light*, by Wright Morris Copyright © 1985 by Wright Morris. Reprinted by permission of HarperCollins Publishers.

Which of the following best describes the author's attitude about seeing his girl-friend again?

**(1)** They are returning to their life together as if they had never been apart.

**(2)** She is too caught up in her own life to care that he went to Europe.

**(3)** He realizes that she likes a secure family life more than he does.

**(4)** They both feel they may be on the verge of breaking up.

**(5)** They envy each other's different experiences in life.

(5) is correct. In a passage like this one that has so many unstated meanings, it may help to first eliminate answer choices that seem clearly wrong so you can zero in on the right answer. (1) cannot be right because details show that the man and woman both feel they are different than they were before he went to Europe (he has a new moustache she has never seen; she has lost the ring he gave her before he left). On the other hand, no detail suggests they feel so far apart that they are about to break up—choice (4). In fact, her showing him her family home and her room suggests she is trying to bring them closer. The details in the second paragraph do not suggest he likes a secure family life less than she does (3) since all the details seem positive in feeling. Her comment that "she had lived most of her life in this room—could I imagine that?" implies that she feels her life has been too limited; therefore, she *does* care that he went to Europe while she stayed home, and (2) cannot be right. (5) is the right answer because in the last sentence the author says he thought, when she made her comment, "how lucky she had been. That's how dumb I was." In other words, the two people envied each other's experiences in life.

## Lesson 2 Exercise

Items 1 through 3 refer to the following paragraph. Choose the one best answer to each item.

### WHY DOES IMAGINING THE GREAT PLAINS HELP HIM FALL ASLEEP?

Now, when I have trouble getting to sleep, I sometimes imagine that my bed is on the back of a flatbed pickup truck driving across the Great Plains. I ignore the shouts on the sidewalk and the bass vibrations from the reggae club across the street. The back of this truck has
(5)   sides but no top. I can see the stars. The air is cool. The truck will go nonstop for nine hours through the night. At first the road is as straight as a laser—State Highway 8, in North Dakota, say—where nothing seems to move except the wheels under me and the smell of runover skunks fading in and out in my nose. Then the road twists to
(10)  follow a river valley, and cottonwood leaves pass above, and someone has been cutting hay, and the air is like the inside of a spice cabinet. Then suddenly the wheels rumble on the wooden planks of a one-lane bridge across the River That Scolds at All the Others. Ever since the Great Plains were first called a desert, people have gone a long way
(15)  toward turning them into one. The Great Plains which I cross in my sleep are bigger than any name people give them. They are enormous,

bountiful, unfenced, empty of buildings, full of names and stories. They extend beyond the frame of the photograph. Their hills are hipped, like a woman asleep under a sheet. Their rivers rhyme. Their
(20) rows of grain strum past. Their draws hold springwater and wood and game and grass like sugar in the hollow of a hand. They are the place where Crazy Horse will always remain uncaptured. They are the lodge of Crazy Horse.

Excerpt from *Great Plains*, by Ian Frazier; published by Farrar, Straus, & Giroux, Inc. Copyright © 1989

1. What does the author mean when he says that the Great Plains "extend beyond the frame of the photograph"?

(1) Objects far away often appear close in this region.

(2) The region's size makes it too big to be experienced.

(3) The region is too undeveloped to show up well in photographs.

(4) Responses to the region cannot be captured in photographs.

(5) The plains are too empty to fill up a photograph.

2. Which of the following statements best summarizes the main idea of the excerpt?

(1) People have destroyed most of the beauty of the Great Plains.

(2) Civilization dulls the senses and the mind.

(3) Crowded cities don't allow people time to reflect.

(4) Dreams of the Great Plains create a desire to travel.

(5) The Great Plains inspire the imagination and emotions.

3. The author's attitude mainly comes from

(1) memories of people he met

(2) stories he heard

(3) memories of sounds, smells, and sights

(4) books he read

(5) photographs of the land

Answers are on page A–24.

# Applying Ideas in Nonfiction

## Prereading Prompt

If you know how to play one musical instrument, you can apply some of the same principles and learn how to play a second instrument. The knowledge you gained by planting your garden last year makes it easier for you to add new kinds of vegetables this year. You have probably experienced examples of applying information and ideas to new situations that are similar to these. Finding out how to use this skill will be helpful in answering questions on the GED Test.

## Key Words

**apply**—to take information and ideas from one situation and put them to some practical or specific use in another situation

## Applying Details and Main Ideas

When you use your knowledge in a new situation, you **apply** it. But before you can apply a skill, a strategy, or a piece of information to a new situation, you must first understand it. To answer application items on the GED, you have to use information and ideas from one nonfiction passage in another situation, different from the one in the text. Here are some sample questions about applying what you read that might appear on the Interpreting Literature and the Arts section of the GED.

- Which of the following do you think most likely happened next?
- The situation in the passage is like which of the following?

To answer any of these questions, read the passage, keeping the purpose question in mind. Pay close attention to details in the passage and look for the main idea.

## Applying the Author's Attitudes

In Lesson 2, you learned that certain details in a passage will give you clues about the author's attitude, or point of view. If you understand an author's point of view about a subject, you can sometimes predict how the author will feel about a different subject.

For example, suppose you read a magazine article written by a person who has dedicated her life to caring for others with AIDS. An application question on the GED might ask: How do you think the author feels about a national health care system?

To answer this type of question, think about the main idea the author has expressed and apply that idea to the new situation. In this example, you could guess that the author would be very aware of the burden an epidemic such as the AIDS epidemic places upon the health care system and society. She would probably want to see more funds available.

In the Interpreting Literature and the Arts section of the GED, you may be asked to take information from a passage and use it to predict the author's attitude in a new situation. Any time you say to yourself, "I wonder what the author would say about. . . ?," you are asking an application question, or applying what you read to a different situation. When you answer application questions, the key is understanding the principle behind the author's attitudes about the subject at hand.

Here are some sample questions about applying the author's attitudes that might appear on the GED.

- Would the author of the passage most likely enjoy_____?
- Which of the following ideas would the author most likely agree with?
- If the author lived in the South instead of the North, she would most likely_____?

## Model Paragraph and Question

Read the following excerpt and choose the best answer to the question.

### WHAT DOES THIS SLAVE LEARN ABOUT THE PATHWAY FROM SLAVERY TO FREEDOM?

Very soon after I went to live with Mr. and Mrs. Auld, she very kindly commenced to teach me the A, B, C. After I had learned this, she assisted me in learning to spell words of three or four letters. Just at this point of my progress, Mr.
(5)　Auld found out what was going on, and at once forbade Mrs. Auld to instruct me further, telling her, among other things, that it was unlawful, as well as unsafe, to teach a slave to read. . . . From that moment, I understood the pathway from

(10) slavery to freedom. It was just what I wanted, and I got it at a time when I the least expected it. Whilst I was saddened by the thought of losing the aid of my kind mistress, I was gladdened by the invaluable instruction which, by the merest accident, I had gained from my master. Though conscious of the difficulty of learning without a teacher, I set out with high

(15) hope, and a fixed purpose, at whatever cost of trouble, to learn how to read.

Excerpt from *Black Voices "Autobiography"* by Frederick Douglass. Published by New American Library, © 1968

Which of the following do you think most likely happened next to the author?

**(1)** Mrs. Auld secretly agreed to teach him to read in private.

**(2)** The author eventually stopped trying to learn how to read.

**(3)** Mr. Auld forbade his wife to teach the author further but allowed his slave to learn to read on his own.

**(4)** The author secretly continued to teach himself how to read.

**(5)** The author ran away and started a new life in a free state.

(4) is correct. The author says, "Though conscious of the difficulty of learning without a teacher, I set out with high hope, and a fixed purpose, at whatever cost of trouble, to learn how to read." This strong determination supports the author's will to learn how to read, even if he has to continue teaching himself. Choices (1) and (3) are incorrect because Mr. Auld strictly forbade the author's learning to read, and his wife would not likely disobey his wishes, nor would Mr. Auld agree to allow his slave to learn on his own. Choice (2) is not correct because the author has too much spirit and determination to simply give up, and choice (5) is incorrect because nothing in the paragraph suggests that he would want to run away because his mistress had stopped teaching him.

## Lesson 3 Exercise

Items 1 through 3 refer to the passage that follows. Choose the one best answer to each item.

### HOW DOES A FATHER TALK TO HIS SONS ABOUT DEATH?

The door to the room I shared with Priscilla was open when I came in, but I didn't go through that door that night. I went to my children's room. I stood above Justin, looking down at him. And then my son Nicholas began to moan, quietly at first. They did not know their

(5) grandfather was dead; they knew nothing about their grandfather. There would be time for that. I resolved to tell them what I could, and hoped they would want to know as much as I could tell. Nicholas cried out in his sleep, as he had so many times before, dragging me out of nightmares about his death with his own nightmares about his death,

(10) his dreams of cats with broken legs, broken-winged screaming birds, deer caught in traps, little boys hurt and crying, beyond the range of their parents' hearing. Sometimes I dreamt of my son bleeding to death from some simple wound I had neglected to learn to mend.

Now I smoothed his forehead as my father had smoothed mine when
(15) I was feverish. Justin breathed deeply. I crawled in bed beside my sweet Nicholas and took him in my arms and began to rock him in time to Justin's regular breaths. I stunk of whiskey and there was blood on my face from a fall leaving Kay's house, but I knew I couldn't frighten my son. He ceased moaning, and I rocked him in my arms till
(20) light came down on us, and he stirred awake in my arms as I, in his, fell into a sleep free of dreams.

Excerpt from *The Duke of Deception* by Geoffrey Wolff. Published by Random House copyright 1979. Used by permission.

1. If the author's sons asked to go visit their grandfather, the author would most likely

   (1) have Priscilla tell them that their grandfather had died
   (2) tell Justin in private that his grandfather had died and then have Justin tell Nicholas
   (3) ignore the question to avoid giving them an answer
   (4) tell his sons that their grandfather was sick in order to put off telling them that he had died
   (5) tell his sons gently but honestly about their grandfather's death

2. According to the passage, the author's response to his sons after his father's death is most similar to the response a defense attorney might have toward his or her client after

   (1) damaging courtroom testimony
   (2) winning the case
   (3) questioning a witness
   (4) jury selection
   (5) his or her closing argument

3. Which of the following types of events would the author be LEAST likely to take his sons to?

   (1) a baseball game
   (2) a bullfight
   (3) a movie
   (4) a funeral
   (5) a circus

Answers are on page A–25.

# Analyzing Nonfiction

## Prereading Prompt

**KISSING BANDIT LEAVES BRIDE AT THE ALTAR**

In the article that follows this newspaper headline, you would expect certain information. You would expect to learn the reason the Kissing Bandit didn't show up. You would also expect to learn more about the results of his absence. As you read, you would analyze, or examine, how effectively the author develops the reasons and results, or the cause-and-effect relationship, in his or her article. Knowing how to analyze a passage of nonfiction in this way is very important for answering GED questions. You will learn how in this lesson.

## Key Words

**analysis**—careful examination of the parts that make up a whole

**tone**—a manner of writing that expresses an author's basic attitude or feeling about a topic

**cause and effect**—the relationship between a reason and the results

# What Is Analysis?

When you analyze something, you look carefully at its parts to see what each one is and how they all fit together. On the Interpreting Literature and the Arts section of the GED, **analysis** questions test your ability to understand why an author uses a certain form, or structure, or uses a certain writing technique, or style, to create a certain effect in a passage. Rather than looking at what an author says or means (comprehension), or what the author might say about a different situation (application), you look at how the author says it, and why (analysis). Writers use different writing styles—formal or informal, simple or complicated. Authors also write with various purposes in mind: to report an event, to explain, to persuade, or to describe the way something looks.

Here are some sample analysis questions you might find on this section of the GED Test.

- Why did the author include (certain details) in the paragraph?
- What does the inclusion of (a specific detail) tell you about the author's opinion?
- The writing style used in this passage would also be effective in writing _____?

# Analyzing Cause–and–Effect Relationships

A **cause** is what makes something happen. It is the answer to the question "Why did this happen?" A cause can be a person's reason or motive for doing something, the answer to the question "Why did he/she do that?" The effect is whatever the cause makes happen. An **effect** is a result. It is the answer to the questions: "What happened?" or "What happened as a result of (the cause)?" You will find that a cause-and-effect relationship is often used by nonfiction writers in essays and articles. They often use cause and effect to explain an event to indicate how something should be done. Other nonfiction writers who want you to accept their opinions will use a cause–and–effect argument to persuade you that something happened for a certain reason and had certain results. Read the following paragraph and answer the question.

**HOW DID THE WAR OF 1812 CHANGE THE UNITED STATES?**

The War of 1812 helped to change the United States. During the war, the U.S. was unable to import goods from Britain. Therefore, Americans had to build their own factories and manufacture their own goods. The military victories also
(5)    resulted in the growth of national confidence and unity.

According to the excerpt, the War of 1812 changed the United States by

- **(1)** making Britain import goods from the United States
- **(2)** increasing the number of American military victories
- **(3)** making Americans build more factories
- **(4)** developing industry and nationalism
- **(5)** forcing the United States to import goods from Britain

(4) is correct. This question is asking you "What were the effects of the War of 1812 on the United States?" You must be sure to identify *all* the effects if there is more than one. Here, you must mention both of the effects of the war: the growth of industry (stated in sentence 3) and the growth of national confidence and unity (stated in sentence 4). Choice (3) mentions only one effect. The most important thing in cause–and–effect questions is to avoid confusing the cause–and–effect relationship. Both (1) and (5) make this error. The first two sentences tell us that the United States was changed because during the war the U.S. was unable to import goods from Britain, *not* that the U.S. was changed because it made Britain import goods from the U.S. (1), or because the war forced the U.S. to import goods from Britain (5). Many false answer choices on the GED mix up words and thoughts taken from a passage in this way. As for (2), the War of 1812 had the effect of developing nationalism, not the effect of increasing military victories. (2) is an example of the worst kind of error in understanding cause–and–effect relationships—mistaking a cause for an effect, or mistaking an effect for a cause. The victories were a cause of changes in the United States; (2) presents the victories as an effect, as one of the changes.

You will be able to analyze the cause-and-effect relationship in the structure of a passage more quickly if, before you read it, you look for key words and try to guess its topic. Remind yourself of what you may already know about the topic. When you recognize a key word, ask yourself what you know about it.

## Analyzing Tone

The way words are spoken can change their meaning. You use different **tones** when you speak. For example, when you are in a hurry, you probably ask a train ticket agent, "When is the next train leaving?" in a different tone than you do when you're in no rush at all. In the same way, a writer uses different tones to give different meanings to the things he or she wants to express.

An author's choice of words and phrasing—elements of tone—reflects the attitude he or she has about a particular subject. A writer might use different tones to communicate different ideas or to capture the reader's interest. Depending upon the purpose of a piece of writing—the information an author wishes to convey and how—he or she may opt for either a lighthearted tone or a more serious one.

In nonfiction, the tone of a piece of writing can be purely objective, or factual, as in a news article. This type of writing lacks emotion. The writer does not show his or her feelings about the topic, even if those feelings are strong—the tone is neutral.

In contrast, some nonfiction writing is subjective. That means it is based on a writer's thoughts and opinions. When a writer expresses his or her feelings about a topic, they are reflected in the tone of the writing.

Knowing how to identify tone is an important skill; if you miss the tone, you may miss the point of what you are reading. To figure out the tone of a passage, consider the kinds of words the writer uses and the things he or she chooses to tell about. The details within a passage will reveal what tone an author is using.

## Model Paragraph and Question

**WHAT IS MOST TROUBLING TO BEETHOVEN ABOUT HIS DEAFNESS?**

My ears whistle and buzz continually, day and night. I can say I am living a wretched life; for two years I have avoided almost all social gatherings because it is impossible for me to say to people: "I am deaf." If I belonged to any other profes-
(5) sion it would be easier, but in my profession it is an awful state, the more since my enemies, who are not few, what would they say? In order to give you an idea of this singular deafness of mine I must tell you that in the theatre I must get very close to the orchestra in order to understand the actor. If
(10) I am a little distant I do not hear the high tones of the instruments, singers, and if I be put a little farther away I do not hear at all. Frequently I can hear the tones of a low conversation, but not the words, and as soon as anybody shouts it is intolerable. It seems singular that in conversation there are
(15) people who do not notice my condition at all, attributing it to my absent-mindedness. Heaven knows what will happen to me. Vering says that there will be an improvement if no complete cure. I have often cursed my existence. Plutarch taught me resignation. If possible I will bid defiance to my fate,
(20) although there will be moments in my life when I shall be the unhappiest of God's creatures. . . . Resignation! What a wretched refuge—and yet the only one open to me. . . ."

Excerpt from *Beethoven: His Spiritual Development*, by J.W.N. Sullivan. Published by Vintage Books; copyright 1960.

How would you describe the tone of this passage?

**(1)** accepting

**(2)** angry

**(3)** confused

**(4)** melancholy

**(5)** patient

(4) is correct. Beethoven states that he is living "a wretched life" (line 2) and that "Heaven knows what will happen to me" (lines 16–17). He also says that, "at times, I shall be the unhappiest of God's creatures" (lines 20–21). These are the sentiments of a man who is quite melancholy, or sad. Choice (1) is incorrect because, although Beethoven speaks of resigning himself to his growing deafness, it's not something that he is really willing to accept ("Resignation! What a wretched refuge—"). Choice (2) is also incorrect; Beethoven may be angry about his fate, but anger is not the main tone of this passage. Choices (3) and (5) are not stated or suggested by any detail in the paragraph.

Items 1 through 3 refer to the following passage. Choose the one best answer to each item.

## WHY DID AIRPLANES BECOME EVIL IN THE GIRL'S IMAGINATION?

Last year I met a little Afghan girl, a refugee with her family in Pakistan. She had lived in a village that had water running through it from the mountains, and it had orchards and fields, and all her family and her relatives were there. Sometimes a plane crossed the sky from
(5) one of the larger cities of Afghanistan to another. She would run to the edge of the village to get nearer to that shining thing in the sky, and stand with her hands cradling her head as she stared up . . . up . . . up . . . Or she called to her mother, "An aeroplane, look!"

And then the Russians invaded, and one day the visiting aeroplane
(10) was a gunship. It thundered over her village, dropped its bombs and flew off. The house she had lived in all her days was rubble, and her mother and her little brother were dead. So were several of her relatives. And as she walked across the mountains with her father, her uncle, her aunt and her three surviving cousins, they were bombed by
(15) the helicopters and the planes, so that more people died. Now, living in exile in the refugee camp, when she thinks of the skies of her country she knows they are full of aircraft, day and night, and the little plane that flew over her village with the sunlight shining on its wings seems like something she once imagined, a childish dream.

From *"Observations"* by Doris Lessing. Copyright © 1987 Doris Lessing. Reprinted by permission of Jonathan Clowes Ltd., London, on behalf of Doris Lessing.

1. The tone of writing the author uses in this passage would probably NOT be effective for

   (1) a story about serial killings
   (2) a story about race discrimination
   (3) an obituary
   (4) a wedding announcement
   (5) a medical article

2. Which of the following first caused the girl's unhappiness?

   (1) the deaths of her mother and brother
   (2) the first flights of airplanes over her village
   (3) living in exile in the refugee camp
   (4) the deaths of her other relatives
   (5) the invasion by the Russian gunship

**3.** In the first paragraph of the passage, the author included the details of the girl's life before her village was bombed

(1) as a statement against the destructiveness of war

(2) to show how the girl's life was changed by the invading Russians

(3) to point out the misery of living in a refugee camp

(4) to show that the girl's life was not really changed by the bombing

(5) to show how easily childhood innocence is lost

Answers are on page A–25.

# CHAPTER 2

In fictional literature—often called "imaginative literature"—the people, events, and setting are created in the author's imagination. You might think of fiction as a kind of "movie in the author's mind" that you get to experience, too. Fictional literature, however, is more than mere imaginary writing. What makes a work of fiction a work of literature is that it contains insights and truths that give it an enduring, universal appeal.

Credit: Joyce Carol Oates, an American fiction writer, poet, and playwright from a working class background has written a book on boxing.

## Prereading Prompt

Almost every day you hear good stories, read them, or watch them on television and at the movies. What is it about them that keeps you on the edge of your seat and wanting to know how they will turn out? Is it a series of hair-raising events? Maybe it's the spectacular location. Understanding how these elements make a story fascinating is very important for answering GED questions.

# Fiction

## What Is Fiction?

Stories created from imagination have been around for just as long as people have. In prehistoric times, when people dreamed up myths and legends, they passed them on from one generation to another. With the development of writing, these stories were written down. More modern forms of telling stories include audio, video, and film. The people that appear in fiction and the experiences they have will often seem very true to life. **Fiction** often includes factual information, but its main focus is always on imagination.

Fictional literature always tells a story. *Plot* is the sequence of events, or what happens in the story. It is like a map that directs your journey through a story from beginning to end. The *characters* are the people who take part in the events in that story. *Setting* is the time, place, and surrounding circumstances in which the events in that story occur.

**Novels** and **short stories** are the two best-known forms of fictional literature. Novels are longer than short stories, but that's not the only difference. A novel usually tells a complicated story, and it can involve many characters. A short story is simpler and may focus on only a few characters.

### Key Words

**fiction**—a literary work portraying imaginary characters and events

**novel**—a long form of fiction with a complex plot

**short story**—a short form of fiction with fewer characters and a simpler plot than the novel

# Literal Comprehension of Fiction

## Prereading Prompt

When you read a story or watch a movie that is really involving, you may not be aware of it, but you continually ask questions, such as "Where is this taking place? Who are the people in the story? What will happen next?" Often, the author gives the answers to these questions directly. Knowing how to find the answers to these questions is very important for answering GED questions. You will learn how in this lesson.

## Key Words

**action**—what happens in a passage or story

**setting**—the time and place in which the events in a story occur

**narrative point of view**—the position from which a story is told

## Action, Plot, and Setting

To answer questions on the GED about the meaning of works of fiction, you must first have a clear idea of the **action**, or what is happening in the story. When reading about events in stories, keep in mind what you already know about cause–and–effect relationships and about logical ways of presenting ideas. When authors create stories, they put events together in sequences. A sequence consists of things put in a definite order according to logic, cause and effect, or time. In a story, events can be presented according to the order in which they happen in time, according to the way the sequence of causes and effects makes them happen, or according to the logical way the narrator understands them (say, a detective solving a case step by step). In some works of fiction, the author will go backwards in time to give you information about a character's past. This technique is sometimes called a "flashback," the name for such movements into the past in films. Most action in fiction, however, moves forward in time. The sequence of events in a fiction passage you will read on the GED makes up an action.

The way an author organizes a sequence of events in a full-length story or a novel is known as the **plot**. A plot can be a complex series of major and minor events and involve a great many characters, or the plot can be simple. It can involve only one character and one major action.

In fiction, just as in real life, events take place in certain settings. **Setting** is the time, place, and circumstance of the events in a story. Time refers to when the event takes place—the hour, day, month, or even the historical period. Place refers to where the action of the story happens. Circumstances are the determining events, for example, wartime, the Great Depression, famine, etc.

## Narrative Point of View

A story is always told by a narrator, the teller of the story, who may be a character within the story or the author himself or herself telling the story.

An author can choose to have the narrator relate the story from different points of view. In Lesson 2 of the last chapter, you learned that point of view is an author's opinion or attitude about a topic. **Narrative point of view**, however, is the method used to tell a story, that is, to narrate. There are two main kinds of narrative point of view: the first-person point of view and the third-person point of view.

In the third-person point of view, the narrator, or person telling the story, is not a character in the story, but the author. This third-person narrator is a "God-like" storyteller who knows everything, much more than any of the characters. Such a narrator can tell you what any of the characters is thinking and what is happening any time, anywhere, in the action. Long novels with many characters and complicated plots often use this narrative point of view.

In the first-person point of view, the narrator presents himself or herself as a character in the story, referring to himself or herself as "I." Using this point of view allows an author to address both the reader and the subject in a more direct, personal way, as if it were not fiction but an individual's true, factual story. A first-person narrator cannot go inside the minds of other characters but can still tell us a great deal about them. In the passage that follows from *The Joy Luck Club*, the narrator provides many details about how she thinks and feels. She also gives information about her father and her mother. You can get a clear picture of who these people are and their relationship to one another.

Items 1 and 2 refer to the following passage. See if you can find the answers that are the main action and the setting.

### WHEN DOES THIS WOMAN BEGIN TO FEEL CHINESE?

"Cannot be helped," my mother said when I was fifteen and had vigorously denied that I had any Chinese whatsoever below my skin. I was a sophomore at Galileo High in San Francisco, and all my Caucasian friends agreed: I was about

(5)  as Chinese as they were. But my mother had studied at a famous nursing school in Shanghai, and she said she knew all about genetics. So there was no doubt in her mind, whether I agreed or not: Once you are born Chinese, you cannot help but feel and think Chinese.

(10)  "Someday you will see," said my mother. "It is in your blood, waiting to be let go."

And when she said this, I saw myself transforming like a werewolf, a mutant tag of DNA suddenly triggered, replicating itself into a cluster of telltale Chinese behaviors, all those

(15)  things my mother did to embarrass me—haggling with store owners, picking her mouth with a toothpick in public, being color-blind to the fact that lemon yellow and pale pink are not good combinations for winter clothes.

But today I realize I've never really known what it means to

(20)  be Chinese. I am thirty-six years old. My mother is dead and I am on a train, carrying with me her dreams of coming home. I am going to China.

We are first going to Guangzhou, my seventy-two-year-old father, Canning Woo, and I, where we will visit his aunt,

(25)  whom he has not seen since he was ten years old. And I don't know whether it's the prospect of seeing his aunt or if it's because he's back in China, but now he looks like he's a young boy, so innocent and happy I want to button his sweater and pat his head. We are sitting across from each

(30)  other, separated by a little table with two cold cups of tea. For the first time I can ever remember, my father has tears in his eyes, and all he is seeing out the train window is a sectioned field of yellow, green, and brown, a narrow canal flanking the tracks, and three people in blue jackets riding an ox-driven

(35)  cart on this early October morning. And I can't help myself. I also have misty eyes, as if I had seen this a long, long time ago, and had almost forgotten.

1. What is the main action of the passage?

   (1) A girl is arguing with her mother.
   (2) A woman and her father are on a train trip.
   (3) A woman is comforting her sad father.
   (4) A nurse is explaining genetics to her daughter.
   (5) A girl tells her mother that she is not Chinese, but American.

2. What is the setting of the passage?

   (1) an early evening at home
   (2) a spring day in a car traveling through the Chinese countryside
   (3) a night on a train traveling through California
   (4) dusk on a train pulling into Hong Kong
   (5) a fall day on a train traveling through the Chinese countryside

The correct choice for question 1 is (2). The narrator tells us directly that she is on a train, going to China with her father. Choices (1) and (4) are incorrect because they are parts of a memory of a scene between the author and her mother. This scene took place in the past, before the current, main action of the passage. Choice (3) is incorrect because the narrator is aware of her father's emotions, but she does not try to comfort him. Choice (5) is incorrect because, again, the narrator said this to her mother in the remembered scene, which occurred before the main action of the passage, which is the train ride with her father.

The correct answer for the second question is choice (5). The narrator tells us that it is an early October morning. She also gives details about the Chinese countryside that she and her father view from the train window. Choice (1) is incorrect because the narrator tells us that it is during the day, and they are traveling on a train. Choice (2) is incorrect because we know that they are not in a car and that it is October. Choice (3) is incorrect because she tells us directly that it is day and they are traveling through China, not California. Choice (4) is incorrect because she tells us that it is early morning and they are traveling through the countryside, not into Hong Kong.

## Lesson 1 Exercise

Items 1 through 3 refer to the following passage. Choose the one best answer to each item.

### IS THIS MAN A THIEF?

The manager had appeared, and the clerk; and the events then happened with revolting and nauseating speed. Michael's hand was yanked from his pocket. The snakeskin box was pulled out by the detective, and identified by the manager and the clerk. They both
(5) looked at Michael with a queer expression, in which astonishment and contempt were mixed with vague curiosity.

"Sure that's ours," said the manager, looking slowly at Michael.

"I saw him pinch it," said the detective. "What about it?" He again smiled offensively at Michael. "Anything to say?"

(10) "It was all a joke," said Michael, his face feeling very hot and flushed. "I made a kind of bet with some friends . . . I can prove it. I can call them up for you."

The three men looked at him in silence, all three of them just faintly smiling, as if incredulously.

(15) "Sure you can," the detective said urbanely. "You can prove it in court . . . Now come along with me, mister."

Michael was astonished at this appalling turn of events, but his brain still worked. Perhaps if he were to put it to this fellow as man to man, when they got outside? As he was thinking this, he was firmly

(20) conducted through a back door into a dark alley at the rear of the store. It had stopped snowing. But the world, which had looked so beautiful fifteen minutes before, had now lost its charm. They walked together down the alley, the detective holding Michael's arm with affectionate firmness.

From "Impulse" by Conrad Aiken. From *The Short Stories of Conrad Aiken*; Copyright 1933, renewed © 1961 by author. Reprinted by permission of Brandt & Brandt Literary Agents, Inc.

1. The main action of the passage is

   (1) Michael's theft
   (2) Michael's self-defense
   (3) Michael's arrest
   (4) the detective taking Michael to court
   (5) the manager's and detective's accusations of Michael

2. What event took place just before the action of the passage begins?

   (1) The manager appeared.
   (2) Michael made a bet with his friends.
   (3) The clerk saw Michael steal the box.
   (4) The detective yanked Michael's hand from his pocket.
   (5) Michael took the snakeskin box.

3. Which of the following best describes the attitude of the three men toward Michael?

   (1) angry and threatening
   (2) cruel and brutal
   (3) frightened and embarrassed
   (4) suspicious and contemptuous
   (5) disgusted and revolted

Answers are on page A–25.

# Inferential Comprehension of Fiction

## Prereading Prompt

From stories you have read, you know that authors often imply information, that is, they sometimes do not state their ideas directly. Certain details about characters, setting, and the overall meaning of a story are like pieces of a jigsaw puzzle. When you read a story, you put these pieces together to understand what the author wants to get across. Finding out how to infer this information in a passage of fiction is important for answering GED questions. You will learn how in this lesson.

## Key Words

**theme**—the underlying, unifying idea in a work of literature

**conflict**—a major struggle or problem that one or more characters has to either face or overcome

**characterization**—the description of a character's physical traits, feelings, and attitudes

# Inferring Character and Setting

Do you ever practice the sport of people-watching? A favorite pastime in airports, malls, parks, ticket lines, and other public places is to sit or stand back and watch the world as it goes by. You may notice what people wear, what they do, and what they say to others. You draw conclusions about who they are, based on the clues they give you.

A writer's use of details to paint a picture of a character is called **characterization**. Most characterization requires the reader to make inferences from the details. It is true that sometimes a writer will tell you something about a character directly ("She was a bright person"). In fiction, however, just as in real life, the personality of a character is mostly revealed through particular words spoken, as by actions, thoughts, and feelings. When you put together details to infer a character's attitude about something, a feeling or a motive for saying or doing something, you are inferring character.

Some sample questions about inferring character on the GED are:

- The detail in line _____ indicates that the character's reaction is an attitude of _____ ?

- The remark in line 00 indicates that the character's intention/motive is _____?

- The character would like the other character to (do what action)?

Fiction writers may also imply where the action is happening—the **setting**. They expect you will discover this from the details they give. For example, if you read about creaking floors, dark and shadowy staircases, an eerie sound on the floor above, and a candle that suddenly goes out, you can guess that you are reading a passage that is set in a haunted house. Often the setting is suggested with one or two details—for example, the setting in the model passage in the last lesson.

## Inferring the Theme

Have you ever had an experience that has changed your way of thinking about something? For example, say that you have just met a man, and based on first impressions, you find that you don't particularly trust him. But then he chases you down the street to give you a $5 bill that you dropped. Later, you might tell another friend: "I judged him harshly because I didn't like the way he dressed. Appearances can be deceiving." Your words reveal that you have a new belief, or insight, about life.

Fiction writers use characters and their struggles to communicate their own beliefs and insights about life. The main idea that a writer communicates in a fictional work is called a **theme**. A theme usually expresses a general statement about life. In most fiction works, authors do not directly state their themes. You have to infer them by looking carefully at the details—especially the details about the characters' thoughts, words, and actions. Then, you have to think about what the author's basic attitude toward his subject is. One way to find the theme of a story is to figure out what the conflict, or struggle, is in the story. This conflict can be either internal (within the character) or external (between one character and another, between one character and society, or between one character and a force of nature).

Most questions on the Interpreting Literature and the Arts section of the GED will ask you the meaning of details about character, action, and setting. However, it will help you to answer these questions if you can infer the writer's main attitude toward the subject of the whole story. Pay attention to the purpose question before you start reading and as you read, ask yourself these questions:

• What is the main conflict, or struggle, in the story?
• What is the author's attitude toward the main character (or narrator)?
• What is the author's attitude toward the main action (or central conflict)?

## Model Passage and Question

Read the following passage. Review the purpose question and look for key words in the passage. Predict the underlying theme.

### WHAT DOES THE BOY FEEL ABOUT HIS FATHER?

Father was in the army all through the war—the first war, I mean—so, up to the age of five, I never saw much of him, and what I saw did not worry me. Sometimes I woke and there was a big figure in khaki peering down at me in the candle-
(5)  light. Sometimes in the early morning I heard the slamming of the front door and the clatter of nailed boots down the cobbles of the lane. These were Father's entrances and exits. Like Santa Claus he came and went mysteriously.

In fact, I rather liked his visits, though it was an uncom-
(10)  fortable squeeze between Mother and him when I got into the big bed in the early morning. He smoked, which gave him a pleasant musty smell, and shaved, an operation of astounding interest. Each time he left a trail of souvenirs—model tanks and Gurkha knives with handles made of bullet cases,
(15)  and German helmets and cap badges and button-sticks, and all sorts of military equipment—carefully stowed away in a long box on top of the wardrobe, in case they ever came in handy. There was a bit of the magpie about Father; he expected everything to come in handy. When his back was
(20)  turned, Mother let me get a chair and rummage through his treasures. She didn't seem to think so highly of them as he did.

From "My Oedipus Complex," by Frank O'Connor. Copyright 1930, 1952 by Frank O'Connor. Reprinted with permission from *The New Yorker*

What can you infer about the boy's attitude toward his father?

(1) He enjoys his father when he is around.
(2) He is scared of the things his father collects.
(3) He is angry that his father is not around more.

**(4)** He is bored by the hobbies his father has.

**(5)** He never gets a chance to see his father.

The correct answer is choice (1) The boy states that he rather liked his father's visits, and his "pleasant musty smell," and that he found his father's shaving "an operation of astounding interest" (lines 12–13). The boy also enjoyed rummaging through the father's "treasures" (lines 20–21). It is for this last reason that choice (2) is incorrect—the boy is not scared of the things his father collects but, rather, enjoys looking at them. Choice (3) is not correct because the narrator simply mentions that he "never saw much of him" (line 2), and not that he is angry about it. Choice (4) is incorrect because his father's hobbies are not mentioned in the passage, and choice (5) is not correct because it's obviously untrue.

## Lesson 2 Exercise

Items 1 through 3 refer to the paragraph below.

### WHY IS DON ANSELMO THE "GENTLEMAN OF RÍO EN MEDIO"?

There was a great deal of conversation, about rain and about his family. He was very proud of his large family. Finally we got down to business. Yes, he would sell, as he had agreed, for twelve hundred dollars, in cash. We would buy, and the money was ready. "Don Anselmo,"
(5) I said to him in Spanish, "We have made a discovery. You remember that we sent that surveyor, that engineer, up there to survey your land so as to make the deed. Well, he finds that you own more that eight acres. He tells us that your land extends across the river and that you own almost twice as much as you thought," He didn't know that. "And
(10) now, Don Anselmo," I added, "These Americans are *buena gente,* they are good people, and they are willing to pay you for the additional land as well, at the same rate per acre, so that instead of twelve hundred dollars you will get almost twice as much, and the money is here for you."
(15) The old man hung his head for a moment in thought. Then he stood up and stared at me. "Friend," he said, "I do not like to have you speak to me in that manner." I kept still and let him have his say. "I know these Americans are good people, and that is why I agreed to sell to them. But I do not care to be insulted. I have agreed to sell my house
(20) and land for twelve hundred dollars and that is the price."
I argued with him but it was useless. Finally he signed the deed and took the money but refused to take more than the amount agreed upon. Then he shook hands all around, put on his ragged gloves, took his stick and walked out with the boy behind him.

From Juan A. A. Sedillo, "Gentleman of Río en Medio," *New Mexico Quarterly*, 1939, reprinted in *Prentice–Hall Literature* (silver), pages pp. 87–88.

1. Don Anselmo's refusal of the extra money for the land suggests that he is

   (1) a man of honor
   (2) ignorant and easily tricked by the Americans
   (3) wealthy
   (4) bitter about the trick the Americans played
   (5) prejudiced against the Americans

2. The narrator would like Don Anselmo to

   (1) sell him the land instead of the Americans
   (2) hold out for even more money from the Americans
   (3) refuse the additional money
   (4) split the difference between the original and second prices with him
   (5) take the extra money

3. The author's attitude toward Don Anselmo is one of

   (1) embarrassment at his stubbornness
   (2) scorn at his foolishness

   (3) pride in his honor
   (4) sympathy for his situation
   (5) criticism of his ignorance

Answers are on page A–26.

# Applying Ideas in Fiction

## Prereading Prompt

Think of your favorite character in a fiction story or on television. What if you asked that person to help you solve a problem you're having right now? What would he or she say and do? Applying another person's attitudes to a new situation is something most of us daydream about at times. Finding out how to do this with characters in fictional literature is an important skill because it can help you understand more completely what you have read. In this lesson you will learn the skill of applying a character's or the author's attitude to a new situation.

## Applying the Attitude of an Author or of a Character

In the passage from "Gentleman of Río en Medio" that you read in Lesson 2, Don Anselmo refuses an offer of twice as much money for his land and house. Imagine that Don Anselmo had returned home and his neighbors had told him that he was foolish to refuse the money—especially since all the land is rightfully his. How would Don Anselmo respond to the neighbors? Most likely, he would have held his head high and said that he had made a bargain and his word cannot be broken—even if the situation changes in his favor.

On the GED test, you may be asked an application item that requires you to imagine how a character or the author of a fictional work would act in another situation. For this type of question you cannot simply go back and read the passage for an answer. as you would for comprehension items. Instead, you must find clues about the most likely choice in the specific details that the author has chosen to include.

Here's a strategy you can follow to find the answer.

1. Make a prediction based on your reading of the purpose question, the item, and the choices. This will give you an idea of what to look for when you read the passage.

2. Read the passage.

3. Study the events and the specific details that the author has chosen to include.

4. Finally, summarize the theme to yourself.

When you read the item and the choices again, you should be able to easily figure out the correct answer.

## Model Passage and Question

Read the following passage. See if you can find the answer to the question that applies the attitude of the character to a new situation.

### WHAT KIND OF PERSON IS JOAN?

Joan went to a school for models when she settled in the city, but it turned out that she photographed badly, so after spending six weeks learning how to walk with a book on her head she got a job as a hostess in a Longchamps. For the rest
(5) of the summer she stood by the hatrack, bathed in an intense pink light and the string music of heartbreak, swinging her mane of dark hair and her black skirt as she moved forward to greet the customers. She was then a big, handsome girl with a wonderful voice, and her face, her whole presence,
(10) always seemed infused with a gentle and healthy pleasure at her surroundings, whatever they were. She was innocently and hopelessly festive, and would get out of bed and dress at three in the morning if someone called her and asked her to come out for a drink, as Jack often did. In the fall, she got
(15) some kind of freshman executive job in a department store. They saw less and less of each other and then for quite a while stopped seeing each other altogether. Jack was living with a girl he had met at a party, and it never occurred to him to wonder what had become of Joan.

From "Torch Song" by John Cheever, from *Short Story Masterpieces*, Dell, 1954. Used by permission of Harcourt Brace Jovanovich.

If Joan were planning her week's vacation, which of the following options would she be most likely to decide upon?

(1) relaxing at home
(2) visiting her mother
(3) painting her apartment
(4) visiting nightclubs
(5) going on a camping trip

The correct choice is (4). Since the author gives details that show that Joan enjoys being around people and having a good time, we can imagine her wanting to experience the excitement of the city's nightlife. (1) and (3) are incorrect because we are told that Joan "would get out of bed and dress at three in the morning if someone called her and asked her to come out for a drink" (lines 12–14), which indicates she would not enjoy relaxing at home (1) or doing home repairs (3). (2) is incorrect, because the details about Joan do not suggest anything about the feelings she has for her family. Choice (5) is incorrect because Joan probably would be bored and restless on a camping trip, away from the

Items 1 through 3 refer to the following passage. Choose the one best answer to each item.

## WHAT IS THE NARRATOR'S ATTITUDE TOWARD THINKING?

Now and then a fellow gets to thinking. About all the sorrow and afflictions in this world; how it's liable to strike anywhere, like lightning. I reckon it does take a powerful trust in the Lord to guard a fellow, though sometimes I think that Cora's a mite overcautious, like she
(5) was trying to crowd the other folks away and get in closer than anybody else. But then, when something like this happens, I reckon she is right and you got to keep after it and I reckon I am blessed in having a wife that ever strives for sanctity and well-doing like she says I am.

Now and then a fellow gets to thinking about it. Not often, though.
(10) Which is a good thing. For the Lord aimed for him to do and not to spend too much time thinking, because his brain it's like a piece of machinery: it won't stand a whole lot of racking. It's best when it all runs along the same, doing the day's work and not no one part used no more than needful. I have said and I say again, that's ever living thing
(15) the matter with Darl: he just thinks by himself too much. Cora's right when she says all he needs is a wife to straighten him out. And when I think about that, I think that if nothing but being married will help a man, he's durn nigh hopeless. But I reckon Cora's right when she says the reason the Lord had to create women is because a man don't know
(20) his own good when he sees it.

From *As I Lay Dying*, by William Faulkner, Vintage Books, © 1987.

1. If the narrator was confronted with a large problem, he would most likely

   (1) think long and hard about it
   (2) think about it a little bit and then drop it
   (3) have a friend come up with a solution for him
   (4) collect information to help him solve it
   (5) ask advice of all his friends

2. If the narrator had a son who wanted to go to college, the narrator would most likely

   (1) feel proud
   (2) think it's a waste of time
   (3) think only women should go to college
   (4) say it's the Lord's will
   (5) not care one way or the other

3. If Darl wanted the narrator's advice on getting married, the narrator would be most likely to tell Darl to

   (1) go ahead and get married
   (2) think about it for a long time before he decides
   (3) get Cora's opinion
   (4) not get married
   (5) have a long engagement before getting married

Answers are on page A–26.

## Lesson 4

# Analyzing Fiction

## Prereading Prompt

Every day you get up, dress, comb your hair, and step out the door to face the world. The many details you attend to about your appearance, your manner, and your way of speech create an effect. They are your style. Fiction writers also create an effect by the many details and the kind of language they use. Figuring out the style—and how it works to create a tone or mood in a story—can help you analyze a work of fiction. Finding out how to do this is very important for answering GED questions. You will learn how in this lesson.

## Key Words

**mood**—a particular state of mind or feeling

**irony**—an effect created by a situation in which the outcome is different from what is expected; also, a statement in which the real meaning of the words is different from the meaning they at first appear to have

**sarcasm**—a type of irony in which the meaning of the words is the exact opposite of their usual meaning

## How Does an Author's Style Create a Tone or Mood?

**Style** is an author's characteristic way of writing. Just as the way you dress reflects your personality, an author's style reflects his or her personality. An author thinks about the appropriate style for a story, depending on the effect he or she desires to create. Is the story sad or humorous? Is it scary or tragic? Authors choose the details and the language—that is, create the style—that will convey the effect they want their stories to have when you read them. By this choice of words, they communicate a specific attitude toward their subject, a **tone**, the way people convey their feelings or thoughts on many subjects by their tone of voice. In these ways, style can create in the reader a **mood**—a particular state of mind or feeling—that will intensify the experience of the story.

Some sample analysis questions about style on the GED are:

- Why does the author mention (a certain detail)?
- The description of _____ is effective because it (makes what point or creates what response)?
- Why is the author's last sentence a good way to end the excerpt?
- Which of the following words best describes the mood of this excerpt?

One effect of style is called **irony**. Irony is essential to almost all fiction because it expresses the fundamental truth that appearance and reality are frequently two different things—that often the way things appear is not the way they really are. For example, the situation that seems safe is in fact dangerous, or the innocent-looking person is actually dishonest. Irony also expresses the sense that events often do not turn out as we expect. An example of an ironic situation would be the experience of a person who signs up for a dance audition and breaks a leg the day before. One kind of irony, which exists only in words, is **sarcasm**. In sarcasm the words mean the opposite of their usual meaning. Someone who says "I feel just great" when he or she feels terrible is being sarcastic. Often the tone of voice used in a sarcastic comment is the only clue to the speaker's true meaning.

## Model Passage and Question

Read the following passage and question. See if you can find the one best answer that analyzes the author's style.

### HOW DOES THE GRANDMOTHER PREPARE HERSELF FOR A CAR TRIP?

The next morning the grandmother was the first one in the car, ready to go. She had her big black valise that looked like the head of a hippopotamus in one corner, and underneath it she was hiding a basket with Pitty Sing, the cat, in it. She (5) didn't intend for the cat to be left alone in the house for three days because he would miss her too much and she was afraid he might brush against one of the gas burners. Her son, Bailey, didn't like to arrive at a motel with a cat.

She sat in the middle of the back seat with John Wesley

(10)  and June Star on either side of her. Bailey and the children's mother and the baby sat in front and they left Atlanta at eight forty-five with the mileage on the car at 55890. The grand-mother wrote this down because she thought it would be interesting to say how many miles they had been when they
(15)  got back. It took them twenty minutes to reach the outskirts of the city.

    The old lady settled herself, comfortably, removing her white cotton gloves and putting them up with her purse on the shelf in front of the back window. The children's mother
(20)  still had on slacks and still had her head tied up in a green kerchief, but the grandmother had on a navy blue straw sailor hat with a bunch of white violets on the brim and a navy blue dress with a small white dot in the print. Her col-lars and cuffs were white organdy trimmed with lace and at
(25)  her neckline she had pinned a purple spray of cloth violets containing a sachet. In case of an accident, anyone seeing her dead on the highway would know at once that she was a lady.

The author includes the last sentence to show that the old lady

**(1)** wants mainly to impress people with her superiority

**(2)** feels she is going to die soon

**(3)** is the only family member concerned with safety

**(4)** thinks of the trip as an adventure

**(5)** feels her family does not care what happens to her

(1) is correct. By including the last sentence, the author shows us that the grandmother's concern about her clothes and appearance—which is described in detail—is meant to impress people with the fact that she is a lady, even if she is lying dead on the highway. To take pride in her appearance after she is dead is ironic because she will not be alive to enjoy the impression she believes her well-dressed corpse will make. No details suggest she feels old, ill or in dan-ger, so (2) is wrong. The author gives us no information to make us believe (3), since driving safety is never mentioned. It is true that the grandmother's family pays no attention to her, but no detail suggests that she resents this; so (5) is incorrect. She does think of the trip as an adventure (4), but that is not the meaning of the last sentence.

Items 1 through 3 refer to the excerpt below. Choose the one best answer to each item.

## WHAT IS IT LIKE ON THE RIVER?

Going up that river was like traveling back to the earliest beginnings of the world, when vegetation rioted on the earth and the big trees were kings. An empty stream, a great silence, an impenetrable forest. The air was warm, thick, heavy, sluggish. There was no joy in the brilliance (5) of sunshine. The long stretches of the waterway ran on, deserted, into the gloom of overshadowed distances. On silvery sandbanks hippos and alligators sunned themselves side by side. The broadening waters flowed through a nob of wooded islands; you lost your way on that river as you would in a desert, and butted all day long against shoals, (10) trying to find the channel, till you thought yourself bewitched and cut off forever from everything you had known once—somewhere—far away—in another existence perhaps. There were moments when one's past came back to one, as it will sometimes when you have not a moment to spare to yourself; but it came in the shape of an unrestful (15) and noisy dream, remembered with wonder amongst the overwhelming realities of this strange world of plants, and water, and silence. And this stillness of life did not in the least resemble a peace. It looked at you with a vengeful aspect.

From *Heart of Darkness* by Joseph Conrad, W. W. Norton & Co., Inc., ©1986

1. Which of the following best describes the mood created in the excerpt?

   (1) menacing
   (2) angry
   (3) excited
   (4) peaceful
   (5) sad

2. The author begins the passage with the statement, "Going up that river was like traveling back to the earliest beginnings of the world" to emphasize that the river

   (1) was never visited by a human being before
   (2) was beautiful before human beings came
   (3) is a strange nonhuman world
   (4) is a world of giant plant life
   (5) is the most dangerous part of the world

3. The last sentence is an effective way to end the passage because it suggests that

   (1) the narrator is beginning to imagine things
   (2) there may be enemy humans along the river
   (3) the narrator is more lost than ever on the river
   (4) the jungle is full of animals
   (5) the narrator feels he is in danger

Answers are on page A–27.

# CHAPTER 3

**Drama** is a type of literature that tells a story through the speeches and actions of the characters alone—that is, drama usually has no narrator. We understand the characters from the statements they make directly to each other and by noticing details about their behavior and appearance.

Credit: Ballet Hispanico of NY photo by Tom Caravaglia

## Prereading Prompt

When you watch an exciting movie or a TV show you become involved with the characters and the problems that they face because they seem so real. Seeing a live play in a theater can be even more intense because you are so close to the action that you are almost a part of it. How do writers of dramatic literature make it seem as if you are experiencing an action in real life?

# Drama

## What Is Drama?

Throughout history, nearly every civilization has had some form of **drama**. It may have developed from ancient religious ceremonies that were performed to win favor from the gods. In these ceremonies, priests often pretended to be supernatural beings or animals. Sometimes, they imitated such actions as hunting. Stories grew up around some rites and lasted even after the ceremonies themselves had died out. These myths later formed the basis of much drama.

Drama shares some common elements with other types of literature. Like fiction, drama is a creation of the writer's imagination. Through plot, characters, setting, dialogue, and theme, it tells a story. But unlike other forms of literature, drama is written to be performed by actors and actresses.

Authors of plays, known as **playwrights**, create stories and characters with the intention of having them presented on a stage before an audience. A **play** is a work of drama written for the theater. Other types of plays may be intended for television (teleplay) or for film (screenplay). The written version of a play is often called a **script**.

As you read dramatic literature, try to "see" and "hear" what is taking place. The better able you are to imagine the action in your head, the better able you will be to understand the play.

---

### Key Words

**drama**—a type of literature that tells a story through the speech and actions of the characters in the story

**playwright**—an author of a play

**play**—a work of drama, meant to be performed

**script**—the written version of a play

---

# Literal Comprehension of Drama

## Prereading Prompt

Did you ever take part in a school play? Before you performed before an audience, chances are a director got all of the people in the play together to practice, or rehearse. The director may have explained the setting, the kind of character each person would play, how the characters would come on stage, and what they would do and say. The director was like a tour guide who mapped out the play. Written plays are also like guides. In this lesson, you will learn how to use the basic parts of plays to find out about the characters and action.

## Key Words

**dialogue**—what the characters in a work of literature say to each other

**stage directions**—the playwright's instructions about how the play should be performed or where the scenery should be placed

## Dialogue and Stage Directions

Because drama is written to be performed, it looks different on the page from other kinds of literature are printed. In a play, much of the story that is told appears in the form of **dialogue**, or conversation among the characters, and **stage directions**, the playwright's instructions about how the play should be performed.

In reading a work of drama, the character names next to the lines of dialogue always let you know who is speaking. Each character's words appear next to or below that character's name. The stage directions appear in italics, or parentheses, or both. Stage directions are important because they give you information about the setting and about the appearances, actions, and feelings of the characters. To find out the basic facts about the events, people, and setting of a play, you should read both the dialogue and stage directions.

## DIALOGUE

*(Joe and April sit down with their supper plates on the living room floor)*

APRIL: You came clear across the country to California for rain and left-overs.

JOE: It tastes great.

APRIL: Well. It makes me think of home, and my Aunt Peggy.

JOE: Old family recipe? What's in it?

APRIL *(hesitating)*: Chicken, catsup, and coke.

JOE: What?

APRIL: Coke—cola. Aunt Peggy puts it in everything. Cakes, salads. She says it gives stuff a zing.

JOE: I never heard of that.

APRIL: Gross, huh. It's an Arkansas thing.

From this brief scene, you learn a number of things. You find out that it is raining and that Joe and April are eating chicken. You also discover that they both have come to California from other places.

In plays, as in daily conversation, many of the dialogues state information directly. They can tell about events in the past or present, and hopes for the future.

Because playwrights cannot include long descriptive passages in their work, they must provide that description in some other way. Sometimes playwrights may include a narrator as a character who provides the necessary details or comments. More often, the playwright uses dialogue to provide the details.

When you read a play, try to picture how an actor might say the characters' words. For example, if a character is a shy man, the actor would most likely speak in a quiet and unassuming voice. By using your imagination in this way, you will make the play come alive as you read it.

## STAGE DIRECTIONS

Playwrights use stage directions to indicate a character's tone of voice, feelings, facial expressions, gestures, and actions. In the following excerpt, the playwright tells us in the stage directions that Martin *"paces several steps and falters, stops. He stands there."*

Stage directions can also explain the setting, that is, where and when the action takes place. Often the setting is stated very directly at the beginning of the play or scene, for example: *"The action takes place in the backyard of Joe Spara's house in Pittsburgh."* In the model passage below, the playwright uses details, such as "room," "bunk," and "khaki uniform," to show that the setting is an army barracks. At times, a conversation between characters may also reveal the time period and place of a play.

To answer literal comprehension questions on the GED about dialogue, first look to see if a line reference is given. Look at the line and the surrounding lines for the answer. If no line reference is given, look through the passage for key words from the question. For instance, in the model passage in this lesson, if the question asks, "Why does Richie want to make up a story," look for the words "make up a story" in Richie's dialogue. You will probably find the reason somewhere nearby.

## Model Passage and Questions

Look at the question and the passage below and see if you can figure out the one best answer to the literal comprehension question about dialogue.

### WHAT MISTAKE DOES MARTIN THINK HE HAS MADE?

(5) *(It is dusk as the lights rise on the room. Richie is seated and bowed forward wearily on his bunk. He wears his long sleeved, Khaki summer dress uniform. Behind him is Martin, a thin, dark young man, pacing, worried. A white towel stained red with blood is wrapped around his wrist. He paces several steps and falters, stops. He stands there.)*

RICHIE:  Honest to god, Martin, I don't know what to say anymore. I don't know what to tell you.

MARTIN:  *(beginning to pace again)*:  I mean it. I can't stand it. Look at me.

(10) RICHIE:  I know.

MARTIN:  I hate it.

RICHIE:  We've got to make up a story. They'll ask you a hundred questions.

MARTIN: Do you know how I hate it?

(15) RICHIE: Everybody does. Don't you think I hate it, too?

MARTIN: I enlisted, though. I enlisted and I hate it.

RICHIE: I enlisted, too.

MARTIN: I vomit every morning. I get the dry heaves. In the middle of every night. *(He flops down on the corner of Billy's bed and sits there,*
(20) *slumped forward, shaking his head.)*

RICHIE: You can stop that. You can.

MARTIN: No.

RICHIE: You're just scared. It's just fear.

MARTIN: They're all so mean; they're all so awful. I've got two years to go.
(25) Just thinking about it is going to make me sick. I thought it would be different from the way it is.

RICHIE: But you could have died, for god's sake. *(He has turned now; he is facing Martin.)*

MARTIN: I just wanted out.

(30) RICHIE: I might not have found you, though. I might not have come up here.

MARTIN: I don't care. I'd be out.

What lines of dialogue tell you how Martin physically reacts to being in the army?

**(1)** "I mean it. I just can't stand it. Look at me."

**(2)** "They're all so mean; they're all so awful."

**(3)** "I just wanted out."

**(4)** "I vomit every morning. I get the dry heaves. In the middle of every night."

**(5)** "I enlisted, though. I enlisted and I hate it."

(4) is correct. Martin describes directly his physical reactions to being in the army. In all the other choices he is not talking about his physical reactions, but is expressing his attitude toward being in the army: in (1) he is saying that he cannot stand the army; in (2) he is giving a reason why he does not like the officers and sergeants; in (3) he is telling Richie what he wants to do (get out of the army); and in (5) he is suggesting that he hates the army even more than Richie does because he entered the army voluntarily, by enlisting.

## Lesson 1 Exercise

Items 1 through 3 refer to the following excerpt. Choose the one best answer for each item.

### WHAT DOES PENNY THINK OF ESSIE'S DANCING?

ESSIE: *(fanning herself)*: My, that kitchen's hot.

PENNY *(finishing a bit of typing)*: What, Essie?

ESSIE: I say the kitchen's awful hot. That new candy I'm making—it just won't ever get cool.

(5) PENNY: Do you have to make candy today, Essie? It's such a hot day.

ESSIE: Well, I got all those new orders. Ed went out and got a bunch of new orders.

PENNY: My, if it keeps on I suppose you'll be opening up a store.

ESSIE: That's what Ed was saying last night, but I said No, I want to be a dancer. *(Bracing herself against the table, she manipulates her legs, ballet fashion.)*

(10) PENNY: The only trouble with dancing is, it takes so long. You've been studying such a long time.

ESSIE *(slowly drawing a leg up behind her as she talks)*: Only—eight—years. After all, mother, you've been writing plays for eight years. We started about the same time, didn't we?

(15) PENNY: Yes, but you shouldn't count my first two years, because I was learning to type.

1. Penny objects to Essie's dancing because she thinks

    (1) Essie can make more money opening a store
    (2) Essie's dance study is taking too much time
    (3) Essie's dance study takes time from her candy-making
    (4) Essie is not serious about being a dancer
    (5) Essie's husband, Ed, has new orders she has to fill

2. Penny thinks it is a bad day for Essie to make candy because

    (1) the candy takes too long to cool
    (2) Essie has too many new orders
    (3) the kitchen is too hot
    (4) the weather is uncomfortable
    (5) Essie needs to practice her dancing more

3. When she practices her dancing, Essie

    (1) fans herself
    (2) stops Penny from typing
    (3) braces herself against a table
    (4) eats candy
    (5) talks to Ed

Answers are on page A–27.

# Inferential Comprehension of Drama

## Prereading Prompt

Have you ever overheard two family members in an emotional discussion? Let's say it is Aunt Sally and your cousin Michael. "It's not only the hole in your ear," Aunt Sally argues. "No respectable boy ever wore one in my day!" From their behavior, conversation, and past actions, you can guess that Aunt Sally doesn't think her son should wear an earring. You use inference skills like these every day. Understanding how playwrights imply this type of information to form a clear picture of what is taking place can help bring the plays you read to life. Finding out how to do this is very important for answering GED questions. You will learn how in this lesson.

## Key Words

**motivation**—an outer influence or inner drive that moves a character to act or do something in a certain way

## Making Inferences in Drama

Playwrights sometimes convey details directly about character, setting, and theme through either stage directions or dialogue. However, you will find that this information is more often implied indirectly.

The reason for a character's behavior is called the character's **motivation**. The playwright cannot tell us directly about motivation the way the author of a piece of fiction might; he or she must show it to the audience indirectly through the words and actions of the characters. Watching the action, we infer the characters' motives from their behavior and dialogue.

These inferences, like those in fiction, consist of putting together details to find an unstated meaning. Also, like inferences in nonfiction, those in drama are based on a **cause-and-effect relationship**—a relationship in which one action causes another action in the dramatic situation. When a male character says something and a female character replies, we infer a certain attitude in him, which made him say what he said. We understand the woman's reply as a reaction to the man's statement and infer an attitude in her from what she says. Inferences like these, which you make constantly while watching movies or TV, are partly based on your ideas of cause and effect in people's interactions. You see that he is expressing some feelings toward her without saying them directly. You interpret that she likes his attitude toward her (or that she doesn't). Your knowledge of the way people interact gives you an idea of cause and effect in the behavior of people that helps you interpret dramas by making this kind of inference.

Most of the inference questions about drama on the GED will probably ask you to infer a character's attitude, or what causes an attitude, or what causes a change of attitude. These are all questions about motivation.

## Inferring Setting

When you read an excerpt from a play, you often will be told what the setting is. But you also may have to infer the setting from the characters' dialogue and actions. Imagine, for instance, that in a play it is a foggy night and a man and a woman are meeting on the deck of a boat. If the playwright wants the audience to know that the scene takes place in New York harbor, one character might point out how strange the Statue of Liberty looks in the fog. It would not be realistic to have a character say: "We are in the New York harbor tonight." Both characters already know that, and in real life, people are not likely to say something that they both know. Instead, the playwright has told the audience where the scene takes place in such a way that the information seems to come naturally. The playwright has implied the information without stating it directly.

When you are asked inference questions about the setting of a play on the GED test, ask yourself, "What words and actions show where the characters are?" If a specific line or name is mentioned in the question, find the line or word and look at the lines nearby for clues to the answer.

## Inferring Theme

From the chapters before this one, you learned that the theme of a literary work is an underlying truth about life that is expressed. The theme of a play can be conveyed by many aspects of the work—the title, the plot, the characters' dialogue and actions, the setting, and the mood. As you learned in regard to fiction, the theme of an imaginative work is often the same thing as the attitude of the author toward the action. The conflict among the characters and all the emotions dramatized are presented to you, the audience, to make you experience part of life from the writer's point of view. If you can summarize the main conflict and what the author seems to think about it, you will have formed a basic idea of the theme of the drama.

Doing this is similar to inferring the main idea of a passage, except that instead of factual statements, the details you are connecting for your summary are attitudes and actions of characters in a dramatic conflict.

The question refers to the excerpt below by Neil Simon. See if you can figure out the answer to the inference question about theme.

## WHAT HAS JUST HAPPENED TO EDNA AND MEL?

(Edna is holding the book upside down and shaking it, hoping some concealed item will fall out. It doesn't. Mel storms back into the living room.)

MEL: I hope they die. I hope the car they stole to get away in hits a tree and turns over and burns up and they all die!

(5) EDNA: You read about it every day. And when it happens to you, you can't believe it.

MEL: A television I can understand. Liquor I can understand. But shaving cream? Hair spray? How much are they going to get for a roll of dental floss?

(10) EDNA: They must have been desperate. They took everything they could carry. (Shakes the book one last time) They even found my kitchen money.

MEL: What kitchen money?

EDNA: I kept my kitchen money in here. Eighty-five dollars.

(15) MEL: In cash? Why do you keep cash in a book?

EDNA: So no one will find it! Where else am I gonna keep it?

MEL: In a jar. In the sugar. Some place they're not going to look.

EDNA: They looked in the medicine chest, you think they're not going to look in the sugar?

(20) MEL: Nobody looks in sugar!

EDNA: Nobody steals dental floss and mouthwash. Only sick people. Only that's who live in the world today. Sick, sick, sick people!

(She sits, emotionally wrung out. Mel comes over to her and puts his arm on her shoulder, comforting her.)

(25) MEL: It's all right . . . It's all right, Edna . . . As long as you weren't hurt, that's the important thing.

From *The Prisoner of Second Avenue* by Neil Simon. Copyright ©1972 by Neil Simon. Reprinted by permission of Random House, Inc.

What statement about life today does the scene between Mel and Edna suggest?

(1) Criminals are more violent than ever today.

(2) There is nothing logical about fate.

(3) Only sick people live in the world today.

(4) No part of life is safe from crime today.

(5) Crimes can be avoided by being alert.

The correct answer to the question is (4). The details show that Mel and Edna's home—and all their hiding places for money—have been broken into.

Even personal items of little apparent value, such as shaving cream, hair spray, and dental floss, have been stolen. Because of this, they both feel as though the world has become an unsafe place. While the burglars obviously broke into the apartment, there is no detail about violence and neither character mentions violence, so (1) is incorrect. (2) is too general and does not correspond to the details that are given. (3) is also wrong. True, Edna says that only sick people could have stolen such useless things as the robbers took, and that only sick people live in the world today (lines 20–21), but these are only her emotional statements. The subject of the scene is crime, not sickness in the world in general. (5) is incorrect because all the dialogue makes it clear that no amount of care or attention can prevent such crimes.

When you read dramatic literature, you do not have the advantage either of seeing a character's facial expressions or of hearing the rhythms or tones of that character's voice. So it is even more important when reading a play— instead of seeing it on stage—to be able to make logical guesses, or inferences, from the dialogue and stage directions.

## Lesson 2 Exercise

Items 1 through 3 refer to the following passage. Choose the one best answer to each item.

### WHAT KIND OF PERSON IS MARY TYRONE?

(She hears Edmund descending the stairs in the front hall. As he nears the bottom he has a fit of coughing. She springs to her feet, as if she wanted to run away from the sound, and goes quickly to the windows at right. She is looking out, apparently calm, as he enters from the front parlor, a book in one hand. She turns to him, her lips set in (5) a welcoming, motherly smile.)

MARY: Here you are. I was just going upstairs to look for you.

EDMUND: I waited until they went out. I don't want to mix up in any arguments. I feel too rotten.

MARY (almost resentfully): Oh, I'm sure you don't feel half as badly as you make (10) out. You're such a baby. You like to get us worried so we'll make a fuss over you. (Hastily) I'm only teasing, dear. I know how miserably uncomfortable you must be. But you feel better today, don't you? (Worriedly taking his arm) All the same, you've grown much too thin. You need to rest all you can. Sit down and I'll make you comfortable. (He sits down in the rocking chair and she puts a pillow behind (15) his back.) There. How's that?

EDMUND: Grand. Thanks, Mama.

MARY (kisses him—tenderly): All you need is your mother to nurse you. Big as you are, you're still the baby of the family to me, you know.

EDMUND (takes her hand—with deep seriousness): Never mind me. You take care (20) of yourself. That's all that counts.

MARY (evading his eyes): But I am, dear. (Forcing a laugh.) Heavens, don't you see

(25) how fat I've grown! I'll have to have all my dresses let out. *(She turns away and goes to the windows at right. She attempts a light, amused tone.)* They've started clipping the hedge. Poor Jamie! How he hates working in front where everyone passing can see him. There go the Chatfields in their new Mercedes. It's a beautiful car, isn't it? Not like our secondhand Packard. Poor Jamie! He bent almost under the hedge so they wouldn't notice him. They bowed to your father and he bowed back as if he were taking a curtain call. In that filthy old suit I've tried to make him throw away. *(Her voice has grown bitter.)* Really, he ought to have more (30) pride than to make such a show of himself.

From *Long Day's Journey into Night*, by Eugene O'Neill. Copyright © 1955 by Carlotta Monterey O'Neill. Yale University Press, 1971. Used by permission.

1. What can you infer about Mary from the stage directions at the beginning of the excerpt?

   (1) She is mainly interested in charming people.
   (2) She avoids anything unpleasant.
   (3) She is more ill than her son is.
   (4) She is basically a calm person.
   (5) She does not care for her son.

2. Mary's statements "Oh, I'm sure you don't feel half as badly as you make out" (line 9) and "But you feel better today, don't you?" (line 12) show that Mary's attitude toward Edmund is

   (1) encouraging
   (2) resentful
   (3) confused
   (4) detached
   (5) optimistic

3. Mary's reactions to what she sees out the window show that her main concern is

   (1) her husband's happiness
   (2) her son Jamie's response to her
   (3) the yard work the two men are doing
   (4) her family's social status
   (5) her own appearance

Answers are on page A–28.

# Applying Ideas in Drama

## Prereading Prompt

Have you ever seen a movie that brought tears to your eyes? Let's say you saw a movie about a child whose parents are killed in a plane crash. You might have thought about how you would feel if you were that child, or you might have imagined what it would be like if that child were your child. The situation might even have reminded you of another type of disaster that you or someone close to you experienced. Though you probably apply this knowledge to different situations in life all the time, figuring out how to do this in the plays you read is an important skill. On the GED, you may be asked to apply the attitude of a character or of a playwright to a new situation. You will learn how in this lesson.

## Applying the Characters' Attitudes

One way you can tell if a movie or a play is effective is to look around the theater and see how involved other audience members are. Are they "rooting" for a character, hoping that whatever he or she does will turn out for the best? Are they touched by an emotional situation the characters are going through? Chances are, the audience has become caught up in the story because the characters and their situations are ones to which most people can relate. There is some truth portrayed on stage or screen that sheds new light on the individual lives of the people sitting out in the darkened theater.

Another way to test the effectiveness of a dramatic work that you read is to think about the characters' personalities and philosophies, and then try to apply them to new situations.

In *Fences*, Rose and Troy discuss their son, who is about to go to college. Read this exchange and think about Troy's philosophy.

> ROSE: Cory done went and got recruited by a college football team.
>
> TROY: I told that boy about the football stuff. The white man ain't gonna let him get nowhere with that football. I told him when he first come to me with it. Now you come telling me he done went and got more tied up
> (5) in it. He ought to go and get recruited in how to fix cars or something where he can make a living.
>
> ROSE: He ain't talking about making no living playing football. It's just something the boys do. They gonna send a recruiter by to talk to you. He'll tell you he ain't talking about making no living playing football.
> (10) It's an honor to be recruited.
>
> TROY: It ain't gonna get him nowhere.

From *Fences,* by August Wilson. Copyright ©1986 by August Wilson. Used by permission of the New American Library, a division of Penguin Books, USA Inc.

Troy's basic point of view is that a person's background, race, and class determine what opportunities he or she can realistically expect in life. He so distrusts the motives of "the white man" that he believes a football scholarship to college is another means of exploiting black men; he does not believe his son can get any benefit from one. If you were to apply this attitude to other situations, you might expect that Troy wouldn't ask for a promotion at work because he would expect to be refused. He probably would consider any apparent favor from a white person to be insincere and reject it. His wife thinks their son can use the scholarship without trying to make a career of football. Because you know Troy's attitude on this topic, you can apply his point of view to other situations he might encounter.

## Applying the Playwright's and Characters' Attitude

The playwright's attitude about the conflict in a play is usually suggested by stage directions and by details in the dialogue. In the excerpt from *Fences* above, the playwright shows that both parents have different ideas about what is best for Cory, though they each have a concern for his future. The conflict between the two parents is the playwright's way of dramatizing the struggle of these people in their situation as black people living in a mainly white world. Though we can sympathize with Troy's attitude because we understand the pain that has caused it, we can also see that Rose's attitude sounds reasonable. We might infer from this that the playwright is dramatizing a conflict between Troy's emotional attitude and Rose's rational attitude. This playwright is so objective that different readers may side with different characters in this conflict.If, however, we feel that Rose's attitude is the one the playwright favors, and we were asked to apply the playwright's attitude to another situation, we might decide he would sympathize with any suffering person, but he would consider bitter attitudes like Troy's to be self-defeating. He would favor a rational attitude as a way of bettering one's life, even when there was reason to feel bitter from past experience.

On the Interpreting Literature and the Arts section of the GED Test, you may be asked application questions about the playwright's or characters' attitude in drama. As you learned in the previous chapters, application items test your ability to understand the main idea and details from one situation, then apply, or use, this information in a new context.

Read the passage below carefully with the purpose question and item following the passage in mind. Then ask yourself: What is the "old" situation that will help me understand the "new" situation? Read for information that will help you to build a "bridge" of ideas between the new situation in the item and the old situation in the passage.

## Model Passage and Question

Read the item and the passage below. Then try to figure out the one best answer to the application question.

### WHY DOES BIFF THINK HIS LIFE IS MIXED UP?

BIFF: I tell ya, Hap, I don't know what the future is. I don't know—what I'm supposed to do.

HAPPY: What do you mean?

(5)
BIFF: Well, I spent six or seven years after high school trying to work myself up. Shipping clerk, salesman, business of one kind or another. And it's a measly manner of existence. To get on that subway on the hot mornings in summer. To devote your whole life to keeping stock, or making phone calls, or selling or buying. To suffer fifty weeks of the year for the sake of a two-week vacation, when all you really desire is to
(10)
be outdoors with your shirt off. And always to have to get ahead of the next fella. And still that's how you build a future.

HAPPY: Well, you really enjoy it on a farm? Are you content out there?

BIFF (with rising agitation): Hap, I've had twenty or thirty different kinds of jobs since I left home before the war, and it always turns out the
(15)
same. I just realized it lately. In Nebraska when I herded cattle, and the Dakotas and Arizona, and now Texas. It's why I came home now, I guess, because I realized it. This farm I work on, it's spring there now, see? And they've got about fifteen new colts. There's nothing more inspiring or—beautiful than the sight of a mare and a new colt. Texas is
(20)
cool now, and it's spring. And whenever spring comes to where I am, I suddenly get the feeling, my God, I'm not gettin' anywhere! What the hell am I doing, playing around with horses, twenty-eight dollars a week! I'm thirty-four years old, I oughta be making my future. That's when I come running home. And now, I get here, and I don't know what
(25)
to do with myself. (After a pause) I've always made a point of not wasting my life, and everytime I come back here I know that all I've done is to waste my life.

HAPPY: You're a poet, you know that, Biff? You're a—you're an idealist!

BIFF: No, I'm mixed up very bad. Maybe I oughta get married. Maybe I
(30)
oughta get stuck into something. Maybe that's my trouble. I'm like a boy. I'm not married, I'm not in business, I just—I'm like a boy. . .

Which of the following would Biff be most likely to enjoy?

**(1)** a family reunion

**(2)** whitewater rafting

**(3)** a vacation at an expensive beach resort

**(4)** managing his own ranch

**(5)** having a family of his own

(2) is correct. It is easy to imagine Biff enjoying the thrill and risk of whitewater rafting. He would not become bored or have too much time to think about the problems in his life. (1) is incorrect because a family reunion would only remind Biff of the reasons why he thinks his life is wasted. (3) is incorrect because Biff doesn't seem to be the type of person who could relax very well on a vacation, and an expensive resort would put him in contact with people who probably would intimidate him. (4) is incorrect because he says he always grows restless when he stays too long anywhere; he probably would feel tied down if he had to manage his own ranch. While he directly states this in the dialogue, (5) is incorrect because all of the evidence he has given about himself shows that he would not be happy having a family of his own.

## Lesson 3 Exercise

Items 1 through 3 refer to the passage below. Choose the one best answer to each item.

### WHAT KEEPS SIBYL FROM BEHAVING LIKE A GROWN WOMAN?

*(She gently propels Sibyl to the sofa. Sibyl sits on the sofa at the left side. Miss Cooper sits upstage of Sibyl.)*

SIBYL: I'd like to be ordinary.

(5) MISS COOPER: I wouldn't know about that, dear. You see, I've never met an ordinary person. To me all people are extraordinary. I meet all sorts here, you know, in my job, and the one thing I've learned in five years is that the word normal, applied to any human being, is utterly meaningless. In a sort of way, it's an insult to our Maker, don't you think, to suppose that He could possibly work to any set pattern?

(10) SIBYL: I don't think Mummy would agree with you.

MISS COOPER: I'm fairly sure she wouldn't. Tell me—when did your father die?

SIBYL: When I was seven.

MISS COOPER: Did you go to school?

SIBYL: No. Mummy said I was too delicate. I had a governess some of the time, but
(15) most of the time Mummy taught me herself.

MISS COOPER: Yes, I see. And you've never really been away from her, have you?

SIBYL: Only when I had a job, for a bit. *(Proudly)* I was a salesgirl in a big shop in London—Jones & Jones. I sold lampshades. But I got ill, though, and had to leave.

(20) MISS COOPER *(Brightly)*: What bad luck! Well, you must try again some day, mustn't you?

SIBYL: Mummy says no.

MISS COOPER: Mummy says no. Well then, you must just try to get Mummy to say yes, don't you think?

(25) SIBYL: I don't know how.

MISS COOPER: I'll tell you how. By running off and getting a job on your own. She'll say yes quick enough then. *(She pats Sibyl's knee affectionately and rises.)* I have my menus to do.

From *Separate Tables* copyright ©1955 by Terence Rattigan by permission of Michael Imison Playwrights Ltd. 28 Almeida Street London N1 1TD

1. Which of the following situations is similar to the one Sibyl describes in the excerpt?

   (1) a man who uses his wife's temper as an excuse to stay at home each evening
   (2) a woman who diets although she does not need to
   (3) a man who takes a job that his wife disapproves of
   (4) a man who quits his job out of dislike of his boss
   (5) a woman who tells her mother she wants to think for herself

2. If Miss Cooper were a school teacher, which of the following would she be most likely to emphasize to her students?

   (1) paying attention to her as a teacher
   (2) fitting in with the other students
   (3) developing as individuals
   (4) obeying school rules
   (5) dressing appropriately

3. Which of the following scenes would be the least likely for the playwright to include in this play?

   (1) Sibyl's mother scolding Sibyl
   (2) Miss Cooper taking Sibyl shopping
   (3) Sibyl having dinner alone
   (4) Sibyl helping her mother clean house
   (5) Miss Cooper and Sibyl's mother singing around the piano

Answers are on page A–28.

# Analyzing the Effects of Language in Drama

## Prereading Prompt

Try watching television without the sound, and you will be amazed at how easily you can follow the action of the story. Or think of the many different ways you can say "Hello," and you might come up with dozens, depending upon your feelings and what you want to convey to the other person. In the same way, playwrights use a variety of techniques to let actors know how they should express themselves in a play. In addition to **language**, or the dialogue itself, playwrights use stage directions for **gestures** and tone to guide actors in creating a certain effect. Figuring out how this effect is created can help you analyze a work of drama. It is also important for answering GED questions. You will learn how in this lesson.

## Key Words

**gestures**—movements of the body meant to express ideas or emotions

## Analyzing the Playwright's Use of Language

Playwrights use a variety of techniques to help them convey their ideas. To portray their characters, they use not only what major actions the characters do (such as calling off a wedding, or changing sides in a dispute), and what they say directly (dialogue), but also specific gestures (physical actions such as opening a door, or moving toward or away from another character, or looking or not looking at someone).

When you read a play, you can know how the words are to be spoken only if such information is given in the **stage directions**. For example, if the stage directions say "*casually*," you know the character will speak without a great display of emotion. And if a characters exclaims, "How nice to see you" and the stage direction says "*(with a look of agitation)*," then you know that the character is actually irritated at that moment.

The **style of language** used by the characters in dialogue also reveals something about what each character is like and adds meaning to the work. The characters' speech should fit their background, age, education, and so on. For example, rough language might indicate that a character has a mean or violent nature; difficult, complicated words could suggest that a character is well educated or a show-off—or both!

**Gestures**, or bodily motions, can also add a level of meaning in a play. When you read a play, you must look closely at the stage directions to figure out the gestures and actions of the characters. These gestures and actions are important, since they often give you information about a character's feelings or personality. For example, a stage direction that states "*(without looking Henry in the eye)*" suggests that the character may be trying to hide something.

You will find that many of the techniques playwrights use are similar to those used in other types of literature. However, since plays are meant to be performed, it is important that you try to imagine the characters moving on a stage while you read. Think of it as creating a "movie in your mind." Picturing the movements, tone of voice, and facial expressions of the characters can add to the enjoyment and understanding of a play.

On the Interpreting Literature and the Arts section of the GED, you may be asked analysis questions about the effects a playwright achieves through language and gestures. When this happens, read the passage carefully, paying special attention to the stage directions. Keep the purpose question and items in mind as you read. After reading, return to the item and ask yourself these questions:

1. What does (this style of language, this gesture, this way of speaking) suggest? (For example, slamming the door would indicate anger, whereas carefully closing the door might suggest thoughtfulness, or shyness or timidity.)

2. How has the playwright used language to get across his or her ideas? (For example, a character who uses incorrect grammar and only very common words might be uneducated. A character who speaks very formally and uses difficult vocabulary might be highly educated.)

## Model Passage and Question

Read the item and the passage below. Then try to figure out the one best answer to each analysis question.

**WHAT IS BLANCHE'S VIEW OF LIFE?**

BLANCHE:  What's in your mind?  I see something in your eyes!

MITCH *(getting up)*:  It's dark in here.

BLANCHE:  I like it dark.  The dark is comforting to me.

MITCH:  I don't think I ever seen you in the light. *(Blanche laughs breath-*
(5)    *lessly)* That's a fact!

BLANCHE:  Is it?

MITCH:  I've never seen you in the afternoon.

BLANCHE:  Whose fault is that?

MITCH:  You never want to go out in the afternoon.

(10)   BLANCHE:  Why, Mitch, you're at the plant in the afternoon.

MITCH:  Not Sunday afternoon. I've asked you to go out with me sometimes on Sundays but you always make an excuse. You never want to
go out till after six and then it's always some place that's not lighted
much.

(15)   BLANCHE:  There is some obscure meaning in this but I fail to catch it.

MITCH:  What it means is that I've never had a real good look at you,
Blanche. Let's turn on the light here.

BLANCHE:  *(fearfully)* Light? Which light? What for?

MITCH:  This one with the paper thing on it. *(He tears the paper lantern*
(20)   *off the light bulb. She utters a frightened gasp.)*

BLANCHE:  What did you do that for?

MITCH:  So I can take a look at you good and plain!

BLANCHE:  Of course you don't really mean to be insulting!

MITCH:  No, just realistic.

(25)   BLANCHE:  I don't want realism. I want magic! *(Mitch laughs)* Yes, yes,
magic! I try to give that to people. I misrepresent things to them. I don't
tell truth, I tell what ought to be truth. And if that is sinful, then let me
be damned for it! Don't turn the light on!

*(Mitch crosses to the switch. He turns the light on and stares at her. She*
(30)   *cries out and covers her face. He turns the light off again.)*

MITCH:  *(slowly and bitterly)* I don't mind you being older than what I
thought. But all the rest of it—Christ! That pitch about your ideals
being so old-fashioned and all the malarkey that you've dished out all
summer. Oh, I knew you weren't sixteen any more. But I was fool
(35)   enough to believe you was straight.

BLANCHE:  Who told you I wasn't "straight"? My loving brother-in-law.
And you believed him.

From *A Streetcar Named Desire,* by Tennessee Williams. Copyright 1947 by Tennessee Williams. Reprinted by
permission of New Directions Publishing Corporation.

The playwright has Blanche say "Don't turn the light on!" to show that she

**(1)**  is afraid of the look in Mitch's eyes

**(2)**  thinks that Mitch's behavior is insulting

**(3)**  knows that Mitch has discovered she is not 'straight'

**(4)**  would rather live in dim light than in bright light

**(5)**  would rather live with illusions than with reality

(5) is correct. Blanche gives her view of life when she says, "I don't want realism. I want magic!" and when she says, "I don't tell truth, I tell what ought to
be truth." Her preference for illusions that are magical and beautiful rather

than for what is real is also suggested by a detail in the setting—the paper lantern she has put over the light bulb. Mitch's gesture of tearing off the lantern dramatizes his motivation in the entire scene: to make Blanche face reality.   Everything he says about Blanche's avoiding bright light leads up to his accusation that she is not "straight"—that is, honest. The main conflict is between Mitch's effort to expose Blanche to reality and Blanche's frightened resistance to this effort. (1), (2), and (4) are all details about Blanche's rejection of reality in favor of illusion, which is the theme of the scene. (3) is not true because at the moment she tells Mitch not to turn on the light, she does not know that he has found out she is not "straight."

## Lesson 4 Exercise

Items 1 through 3 refer to the following passage. Choose the one best answer to each question.

### WHY DOES BABE STICK HER HEAD IN THE OVEN?

MEG *(turns off the gas and moves Babe to a chair near the open door)*: Sit down. Sit down! Will you sit down!

BABE:  I'm okay. I'm okay.

MEG:  Put your head between your knees and breathe deep!

(5) BABE:  Meg—

MEG:  Just do it! I'll get you some water. *(She gets some water for Babe.)* Here.

BABE:  Thanks.

MEG:  Are you okay?

BABE:  Uh huh.

(10) MEG:  Are you sure?

BABE:  Yeah, I'm sure. I'm okay.

MEG *(getting a damp rag and putting it over her own face)*: Well, good. That's good.

BABE:  Meg—

MEG:  Yes?

(15) BABE:  I know why she did it.

MEG:  What? Why who did what?

BABE *(with joy)*: Mama. I know why she hung that cat along with her.

MEG:  You do?

BABE *(with enlightenment)*: It's 'cause she was afraid of dying all alone.

(20) MEG:  Was she?

BABE:  She felt so unsure, you know, as to what was coming. It seems the best thing coming up would be a lot of angels and all of them singing. But I imagine they have high, scary voices and little gold pointed fingers that are as sharp as

(25) blades and you don't want to meet 'em all alone. You'd be afraid to meet 'em all alone. So it wasn't like what people were saying about her hating that cat. Fact is, she loved that cat. She needed him with her 'cause she felt so all alone.

MEG: Oh, Babe . . . Babe. Why, Babe? Why?

(30) BABE: Why, what?

MEG: Why did you stick your head into the oven?

BABE: I don't know. I'm having a bad day. It's been a real bad day.

MEG: Babe, we've just got to learn how to get through these real bad days here. I mean, it's getting to be a thing in our family.

1. Babe's explanation of why her mother (lines 21–26) killed the cat is used by the playwright to show that Babe

   (1) hates her mother for killing the cat
   (2) is frightened and lonely like her mother
   (3) does not approve of her mother's suicide
   (4) is too much in shock to make sense
   (5) does not believe her mother went to heaven

2. Which of the following would NOT be a reason for the playwright to end the scene with the line, "I mean, it's getting to be a thing in our family"?

   (1) It stresses the link between Babe and her mother.
   (2) It relieves the tension of the scene with some humor.
   (3) It emphasizes Meg's down-to-earth personality.
   (4) It shows Meg does not consider this a serious suicide attempt.
   (5) It shows Meg's gentleness in dealing with her sister.

3. What does the gesture *"getting a damp rag and putting it over her own face"* suggest about Meg?

   (1) She is nearly as emotionally upset as Babe.
   (2) She cannot function well in the middle of a hot summer.
   (3) She wants Babe to feel sorry for her.
   (4) She wants to turn this into a humorous situation.
   (5) She had to put her own head in the oven to save Babe.

Answers are on page A–29.

# CHAPTER 4

Poetry is as old as history and as new as the latest hit tune. In the past when primitive people experienced war, a flood, or some other event that was important to them, they often made a record of it in a song. Today, poetry, as a record of thoughts and feelings, may be written down.

Credit: New York Convention & Visitors Bureau

## Prereading Prompt

If you have a choice between watching a movie or reading some poetry, which do you choose? Chances are, you choose the movie. But have you ever said to someone, "You're shaking like a leaf!" Do song lyrics go through your mind in the middle of the day? If so, you may have more of an appreciation for poetry than you think. Finding out the techniques poets use to express emotions and communicate ideas in fresh, original ways is a useful skill for answering GED questions. You will learn how in this chapter.

# Poetry

## What Is Poetry?

A poem can tell a story. It can express feelings about a person, place, object, or moment, or it can express ideas. Just as with a good song, it helps to hear a poem more than once to appreciate fully the way it expresses thoughts and feelings.

Just about any experience or observation is good subject matter for poetry—beautiful or ugly, strange or common, actual or imaginary. Often, an ordinary experience can make an interesting and unique poem because of the fresh angle in which the poet considers the subject matter.

Poets create **images**, or mental pictures, in a reader's mind. Sometimes a poet will write about a physical thing so that it expresses an idea or feeling in a powerful way, as when the young lover Romeo in Shakespeare's play says of his girlfriend, "Juliet is the sun." An image used in this way is called a **metaphor**. This metaphor expresses the lover's feeling that the woman he loves is the source of everything bright and beautiful in his life in the same way that the sun is the source of light and nourishment for every living creature in nature. As you can see, a metaphor involves a comparison—in this case, the young woman who is loved is compared to the sun. Poets can make metaphors out of anything to express their thoughts and feelings. Images and metaphors in poetry appeal to the mind, the senses, the emotions, and the imagination—all at the same time.

### Key Words

**image**—a mental picture of something or someone

**metaphor**—an image that compares an idea or emotion to a physical thing

# Literal Comprehension of Poetry

## Prereading Prompt

You probably know the words to many songs. A song's lyrics often express specific ideas about love, death, hope, and despair. You do not have to guess at the meaning of these songs: It is stated directly. Poems, like song lyrics, often use words that have a lot of emotional suggestions. Poets, like songwriters, often state the main idea of their poems directly, however, even though their words—and form—may express many other meanings indirectly. Knowing how to find the main idea in poetry is very important for answering GED questions. You will learn how in this lesson.

## Key Words

**rhyme**—a pattern of similar sounds in a poem usually appearing at the end of lines

**rhythm**—the flow or pattern of sounds in a piece of poetry, usually between sounds that are "heavy" (accented) and sounds that are "light" (unaccented)

**narrative poetry**—poetry that tells a story, with plot, characters, and dialogue

**lyric poetry**—poetry that expresses a thought or an intense emotion through images

## The Form of Poetry

You have probably noticed that poems appear in a different form than other kinds of written literature. The form of a poem is its outward arrangement, rather than its content or its subject matter. It is this feature—its form—that distinguishes a poem from a prose work. They are almost always written in **lines**— sometimes called poetic lines. A poetic line can have only so many words in it, unlike a sentence, which can have as many words as the writer wishes. These lines are usually divided into **stanzas**, or groups of lines.

Another characteristic of poetic lines is **rhythm**, the pattern of accented (emphasized) and unaccented (less emphasized) sounds. In these lines from "Annabel Lee," by Edgar Allan Poe, the heavy (or accented) sounds are in capital letters and underlined.

> It was <u>MANY</u> and <u>MANY</u> a <u>YEAR</u> a<u>GO</u>,
> In a <u>KING</u>dom <u>BY</u> the <u>SEA</u>,
> That a <u>MAID</u>en there <u>LIVED</u> whom <u>YOU</u> may <u>KNOW</u>
> By the <u>NAME</u> of <u>ANN</u>abel <u>LEE</u>;
> And this <u>MAID</u>en she <u>LIVED</u> with <u>NO</u> other <u>THOUGHT</u>
> Than to <u>LOVE</u> and be <u>LOVED</u> by <u>ME</u>.

Another characteristic that poems often have is **rhyme**, or words that have similar sounds. Rhyming words usually come at the end of lines. In the poem above, every other line rhymes. In the following poem, each pair of lines rhymes.

> What is Africa to <u>me</u>?
> Copper sun or scarlet <u>sea</u>,
> Jungle star or jungle <u>track</u>,
> Strong bronzed me, or regal <u>black</u>
> Women from whose loins I <u>sprang</u>
> When the birds of Eden <u>sang</u>?

From "Heritage" by Countee Cullen. Reprinted by permission of GRM Associates, Inc., Agents for the Estate of Ida M. Cullen. From the book *Colors* by Countee Cullen. Copyright ©1925 by Harper & Brothers; copyright renewed 1953 by Ida M. Cullen.

One of the beauties of poems is that you can usually read them quickly. They are like nuggets of thoughts or feelings. If you look at a newspaper photograph very closely, you see hundreds of little dots. Only when you "step back" from the composition of dots do you see the picture. Poetry shows you its meaning in a similar way. You may have to reread a poem to see its full meaning clearly and completely. However, you can experience much of its beauty and emotion the first time, as you can with a song you like.

## Finding Main Ideas and Details in Poems

Poems may not be written in the same way that other material you read is written, but that does not mean that the writing in poems is strange or vague. Do not let the form of poems keep you from seeing that poets make statements in their poems that are just as direct as the stated meaning in prose.

Many of the details in poems describe things clearly and exactly, just like details in a piece of fiction. You will find that often, the details poets choose are meant to help you imagine—or mentally see, hear, taste, touch, or smell—the images they want to create.

There are basically two types of poems. **Narrative poems** tell a story. Like novels and short stories in fictional literature, narrative poems have plot, characters, dialogue, and so on. Here's an example.

## WHAT DOES THE MILLWORKER THINK OF HER LIFE?

### Millworker

Now my grandfather was a sailor
He blew in off the water
My father was a farmer
And I, his only daughter
(5) Took up with a no good millworking man
From Massachusetts
Who dies from too much whiskey
And leave me these three faces to feed
Millwork ain't easy
(10) Millwork ain't hard
Millwork it ain't nothing
But an awful boring job
I'm waiting for a daydream
To take me through the morning
(15) And put me in my coffee break
Where I can have a sandwich
And remember
Then it's me and my machine
For the rest of the morning
(20) For the rest of the afternoon
For the rest of my life.

From "Millworker," by James Taylor. Copyright 1979 Country Road Music, Inc. All Rights Reserved. Used by permission.

**Lyric poems** are usually short and express a thought or an intense emotion. The following is a lyric poem by the French poet Arthur Rimbaud.

## WHAT DOES THE SPEAKER THINK OF SENSATIONS?

### Sensation

On blue summer evenings I'll go down the pathways
Pricked by the grain, crushing the tender grass—
Dreaming, I'll feel its coolness on my feet.
I'll let the wind bathe my bare head.

(5)
I won't talk at all, I won't think about anything.
But infinite love will rise in my soul,
And I'll go far, very far, like a gypsy,
Into Nature—happy, as if with a woman.

"Sensation" by Arthur Rimbaud, in *Sleeping on the Wing*, by Kenneth Koch and Kate Farrell (Vintage Books, 1982)

In the excerpt from "Millworker," James Taylor gives specific details about the life of a woman who works in a mill—where she came from, what she does during the day, how she feels, and what she dreams about. You do not have to infer these details. The sensation of experiencing nature on a cool summer evening is the intense emotion expressed in the poem by Arthur Rimbaud. He uses sensory details that help you to imagine yourself in the speaker's place.

## Model Question

The question below is based upon the poem by James Taylor above. Reread the poem. Then see if you can find the answer to the literal question about it.

Which of the following best describes the millworker's view of her life?

**(1)** Millwork is not hard work, but it is boring.

**(2)** I have to work in a bad job because I am a woman.

**(3)** Millwork is so boring that you begin to daydream.

**(4)** I ended up working in a mill because of my background.

**(5)** The mill job is boring, and I will have to do it until death.

The correct choice is (5). The speaker says that millwork is "an awful boring job" and in the last four lines says she will be doing it "For the rest of my life." (1) and (3) are incorrect because they are details, not the main idea. The speaker nowhere says or suggests that she is a millworker because she is a woman, so (2) is wrong. (4) is also incorrect because the speaker does not suggest that because her grandfather was a sailor and her father was a farmer she therefore ended up as a millworker.

On the Interpreting Literature and the Arts section of the GED test, you may be asked questions about the literal meaning of a poem. When this happens, first look at the title. Then you should be able to find a line or phrase in the poem that sums up the poet's thoughts and feelings about the subject. As with fiction literature, the details will help you understand the main idea more clearly.

Items 1 and 2 refer to the following poem. Choose the one best answer to each item.

### WHY DOES THE SPEAKER PITY THE IMMIGRANT?

### I Pity the Poor Immigrant

I pity the poor immigrant, who wishes he would have stayed home.
Who uses all his power to do evil, but in the end is left alone,
That man who with his fingers cheats, and who lies with every breath,
Who passionately hates his life and likewise fears his death.
(5) I pity the poor immigrant, whose strength is spent in vain,
Whose Heaven is like ironsides, whose tears fall like the rain,
Who eats but is not satisfied, who hears but does not see,
Who falls in love with wealth itself, and turns his back on me.
(10) I pity the poor immigrant, who tramples through the mud,
Who fills his mouth with laughing and who builds his town with blood,
Whose visions in the final end must shatter like the glass,
I pity the poor immigrant, when his gladness comes to pass.

From "Pity the Poor Immigrant" by Bob Dylan. Bob Dylan, Dwarf Music and B. Feldman & Co. Ltd., ©1968.

1. Which of the following best sums up "the poor immigrant" who is described in this poem?

   (1) someone who finds happiness through hard work
   (2) someone the speaker hates for leaving his native country
   (3) someone who makes himself unhappy trying to get rich
   (4) someone who does evil but is saved by heavenly love
   (5) someone who is strong and good but ends up a failure

2. The evil the speaker of the poem accuses "the poor immigrant" of committing against other people is

   (1) dishonesty
   (2) destroying property
   (3) hatred
   (4) starving people
   (5) killing loved ones

3. Which of the following best describes the main idea of the poem by Arthur Rimbaud on page 358?

   (1) Summer evenings are the most beautiful time of year.
   (2) Sensations of all kinds are better than thinking.
   (3) Infinite love is better than any sensations.
   (4) Dreams are the best source of sensations.
   (5) Experiences of nature are better than love or sensations.

Answers are on page A–29.

# Inferring the Meaning of Figurative Language in Poetry

## Prereading Prompt

Have you ever said something like this: "I'm so cold I feel like an ice cube"? Or "This cake is a brick"? Or maybe this: "The coffee was so strong that it got up and walked"? You probably use figures of speech every day. Poets, too, use figures of speech such as the examples above to get across their ideas and to delight their readers. Finding out how poets use figurative language is important for answering GED questions. You will learn how in this lesson.

## Key Words

**simile**—a comparison of two unlike things that uses "like" or "as"

**personification**—describing something nonhuman as if it were human

**symbol**—an object that represents not only itself but also an idea that is much broader in scope

One of the ways that poetry differs most from other *genres* (types or categories) of writing is in its reliance upon figures of speech, or figurative language, to express an author's thoughts. **Figurative language** is language that expresses additional or special meaning—meaning that is more than just the "dictionary definition" of the words. There are two kinds of figurative language.

A **simile** compares two unlike things by saying that one is *as* or *like* the other, as in this example:

> I wandered lonely as a cloud
> That floats on high o'er vales and hills …
> —William Wordsworth

A **metaphor** compares unlike things by saying the one is the other.

> My horse's eyes are made of big stars.
> His mane is made of short rainbows.
> —Anonymous: Native American (Navajo)

Similes and metaphors are most helpful in giving brief descriptions. This makes them especially suited to poetry, a form of writing that depends greatly on condensed language.

Another type of figure of speech that is often used in poetry is **personification**. Description of something nonhuman as if it were human, is called personification.

> The moon holds nothing in her arms
> —R. P. Lister

Obviously, the moon does not have arms. But here, something nonhuman—the moon—takes on human characteristics so that readers will more easily relate to the poet's ideas.

Poets often use symbols in their poems. A **symbol** is an object that represents not only itself but also an idea that is much broader in scope. The dove is an example of a familiar symbol. To many people around the world, it represents peace. This country's flag is another example of a symbol. It represents the United States of America, its government, and its people. Many religions have a symbol which contains a basic meaning of the faith: The symbol of Christianity is the cross; of Judaism, the Star of David; of Islam, the scimitar (curved sword) and star. A poet can make anything into a symbol—a tree, an animal, a part of the body, a road—and give it his or her original meaning.

On the Interpreting Literature and the Arts section of the GED test, you may be asked inference questions about figurative language in a poem. When this happens, be sure to first read the poem carefully. Look at the specific figure of speech in question. Then follow these steps:

*If the question is about a comparison*, try to picture what is being compared. By imagining the ideas in your mind, you will be better able to understand the meaning.

*If the question is about personification*, ask yourself, "What human qualities are being described? What do they reveal about the object?"

*If the questions is about a symbol*, ask yourself, "What does this symbol stand for? How is it described?"

## Model Passage and Question

Read the following passage. Then try to figure out the answer to the question, which asks you to interpret figurative language.

**HOW DOES THE POET DESCRIBE THE NIGHT?**

> Eagerly
> Like a woman hurrying to her lover
> Night comes to the room of the world
> and lies, yielding and content
> (5) Against the cool round face
> Of the moon.
> Night is a curious child, wandering
> Between earth and sky, creeping
> In windows and doors, daubing
> (10) The entire neighborhood
> With purple paint.
> Day
> is an apologetic mother
> Cloth in hand
> (15) Following after.

From "Four Glimpses of Night," by Frank Marshall Davis, in *Black Voices* (New American Library, 1968)

Which of the following best describes the way the poet presents "Day" in the poem?

**(1)** a mother who gave her child away

**(2)** a woman about to give birth

**(3)** a mother cleaning up after her child

**(4)** a woman with a cool round face

**(5)** a mother who wakes up early

(3) is correct. The personification of "Day" describes her as "an apologetic mother/Cloth in hand/Following after" the "Night," who as "a curious child" has painted "the entire neighborhood/With purple paint." Day is going to "clean up" after the Night by wiping away the "purple paint." The purple paint is the poet's metaphor for the color of the night at dawn, when the sky changes from the black of night to the purple of sunrise, just before full daylight arrives. No images in the poem suggest the meanings in the other answer choices. The image of the "cool round face" is used to describe the moon, not Day. It is true that Day *could* be compared to a mother who wakes up early (5), but the poem does not make this comparison.

It is more important to understand the meaning of any figure of speech than to identify the type of image it is because the GED will ask you only for the meaning of the figure of speech. However, the more familiar you are with the different kinds of figurative language the more comfortable you will feel.

# Lesson 2 Exercise

Items 1 through 3 refer to the following poem. Choose the one best answer to each item.

## WHAT DOES THE SPEAKER FEEL ABOUT DREAMS?

### Harlem

What happens to a dream deferred?
Does it dry up
like a raisin in the sun?
Or fester like a sore—
(5) And then run?
Does it stink like rotten meat?
Or crust and sugar over—
like a syrupy sweet?
Maybe it just sags like a heavy load.
(10) Or does it explode?

"Harlem" by Langston Hughes, from *The Panther and the Lash* by Langston Hughes, Copyright 1951 by Langston Hughes. Reprinted by permission of Alfred A. Knopf, Inc.

1. What idea is expressed in the last line?

    (1) Dreams can be destructive.
    (2) Unrealized dreams will die and disappear.
    (3) Unrealized dreams can produce violence.
    (4) Rotten dreams are the most explosive.
    (5) A dream is like a balloon too full of air.

2. Which of these words is used to describe the dream as having human qualities?

    (1) crust
    (2) fester
    (3) dry up
    (4) sags
    (5) explode

3. The dream is a symbol of

    (1) violence
    (2) anger
    (3) hope
    (4) disease
    (5) patience

Answers are on page A–29.

# Applying Ideas in Poetry

## Prereading Prompt

How would Robin Hood feel about an increase in income tax? How would Betsy Ross react to the late 20th century controversy over burning the flag? How would those two teenagers Romeo and Juliet resolve their problems if they lived in your community today? In this unit, you have learned how to apply information and ideas about literature to new situations. Poetry, just like other genres, can suggest a theme or an author's attitude that can be applied to another situation. Knowing how to take information from a poem and use it in a new context is important for answering GED questions. You will learn how in this lesson.

## Applying Themes and Details

Most poetic themes are universal. They are about human nature and human experience and therefore are themes that many people can identify with. As a result, it is often not difficult to "translate" the ideas of a poem into a variety of other situations.

The first step in answering an application item about a theme or a detail is to determine what the poet is saying. Then, apply that idea to the new setting. If a poet speaks of the beauty of a clear mountain stream, for example, you might assume that she would be in favor of strong controls to protect the environment.

Read this poem and think about the poet's attitude.

### Reflections

If the world looked in a looking glass,
It'd see back hate, it'd see back war and it'd see back sorrow,
It'd see back fear.
If the world looked in a looking glass, it'd run away with shame, and hide.

By Vanessa Howard, in *Globe Literature, Purple Level* (Globe Book Company, 1990)

The idea behind this poem is that the world is a place not of love but of hate. An application of that theme might be to look for something else that should be one way but upon reflection is really the opposite. The poet might express the same thought in words such as these:

> If television
> Had to watch television,
> It might doze off.

## Applying the Poet's Attitude

Recognizing the poet's attitude means thinking about both the theme of the poem and the details that support the idea. Sometimes the poet's attitude is clearly expressed as the theme of the poem; at other times, you must make inferences. If the poet makes use of a speaker, it is important to distinguish between the speaker's attitude and the poet's attitude.

If a theme of a poem is love of cities, you can apply the poet's attitude to situations apart from poetry. You can assume, for example, that if the poet were a photographer, she would be more likely to take photographs of urban scenes than she would of pastoral scenes.

## Model Passage and Question

Read the passage below. See if you can find the answer to the application item.

### WHAT DID THE STATUE OF LIBERTY TELL IMMIGRANTS?

> "Give me your tired, your poor,
> Your huddled masses yearning to breathe free,
> The wretched refuse of your teeming shore
> Send these, the homeless, tempest-tossed to me—
> (5) I lift my lamp beside the golden door!"

From "The New Colossus," by Emma Lazarus, in *Globe Literature, Red Level*, (Globe Book Company, 1990)

If the poet were living today, which of the following ideas would she most likely agree with?

**(1)** America is the only land of opportunity.
**(2)** Too many immigrants crowd into America today.
**(3)** We should screen people who come into our country.
**(4)** America should accept all immigrants in need.
**(5)** America can no longer be a home for different peoples.

The correct choice is (4). From the poet's attitude, you know that she would readily help anyone oppressed or in need, no matter what their background happened to be. (1) is incorrect because no comparison of America to other lands is stated or suggested. (2) is incorrect because America has always been made up of peoples from many different cultures. (3) is incorrect because all the lines in the poem insist on welcoming those in need, not those highly-qualified people who would be let into the country through screening. Choice (5) is incorrect because people from all over the world still continue to settle in America.

On the Interpreting Literature and the Arts section of the GED test, you may be asked to apply information from one situation to a new situation. The key to applying poetic themes and details is first to determine the ideas that a poet is expressing and then to consider those ideas at work in a new setting.

## Lesson 3 Exercise

Items 1 through 3 refer to the following poem. Choose the one best answer to each question.

### WHAT IS THE SIGNIFICANCE OF LIFE ON EARTH FOR THE UNIVERSE?

If this little world tonight
Suddenly should fall through space
In a hissing, headlong flight,
Shrivelling from off its face,
(5)  As it falls into the sun,
In an instant every trace
Of the little crawling things—
Ants, philosophers, and lice,
Cattle, cockroaches, and kings,
(10)  Beggars, millionaires, and mice,
Men and maggots all as one
As it falls into the sun . . .
Who can say but at the same
Instant from some planet far
(15)  A child may watch us and exclaim:
"See the pretty shooting star!"

"Earth," by Oliver Herford, *Globe Literature, Purple Level* (Globe Book Company, 1990)

1. If the speaker of the poem was confronted with loss of life caused by a forest fire, he probably would

   (1) say the human race could have prevented it

   (2) consider it a minor episode in the order of nature

   (3) tell children to enjoy it as a spectacle

   (4) say that all the life was about to die, anyway

   (5) predict that bigger forest fires would come

2. Which of the following best describes the poet's attitude in the poem?

   (1) From the point of view of the universe, life on Earth is insignificant.
   (2) The end of the world will make everything insignificant.
   (3) Children can often see what is significant.
   (4) A worldwide catastrophe in the nuclear age is unavoidable.
   (5) Lifeforms more advanced than humans inhabit the universe.

3. If the attitude the child expresses in the line "See the pretty shooting star!" was applied to a bad automobile accident, the child would most likely say

   (1) "Get the police to help everybody!"
   (2) "I didn't know such things could happen!"
   (3) "The world's really dangerous!"
   (4) "The blood is a nice bright red!"
   (5) "Everything's going to pieces!"

Answers are on page A–30.

# Analyzing Poetry

## Prereading Prompt

What happens when you are in a dark theater watching a movie and suddenly you hear the slow CRREAKKK!!! of a door . . . then footsteps? You probably expect that something scary is about to happen. When suspenseful music starts to play, then you know it's time to cover your eyes. Poets, like filmmakers, understand that their choice of words can create certain effects or moods. They use rhyme and sound repetition because it suggests certain ideas or emotions that enhance the meaning of the words. Knowing how to analyze the stylistic techniques a poet has used to create a mood in a poem is important in answering GED questions. You will learn how in this lesson.

## Key Words

**alliteration**—repetition of consonant sounds that appear at the beginning of words

**assonance**—repetition of vowel sounds in words

## Effects of Sound in Poetry

You have learned that a poem can create a mood through its presentation of images—in particular, through similes and metaphors. A poem can also create a mood through its patterns of sounds—both the kinds of sounds and the number of times certain sounds are repeated.

The repetition of sounds is a basic technique in poetry. Rhyme is one way to repeat sounds. Another common method is **alliteration**, the repetition of a consonant sound that comes at the beginning of words. Here's an example of alliteration from "The Raven," by Edgar Allan Poe:

> Deep into that darkness peering, long I stood there wondering, fearing,
> Doubting, dreaming dreams no mortals ever dared to dream before.

These lines create a mood of mystery and of fear of the unknown. This mood is mainly created by the images themselves—of looking deep into the dark, "fearing," and having dreams no human being ever dared to have before. But the repetition of the "d" sounds helps to create this mood, too, by the alliteration of "d" in "deep" and "darkness" in the first line, and by using the same alliteration in words in the second line that also express mystery and fear—"doubting," "dreaming," "dreams," and "dared."

The repetition of vowel sounds in words is called **assonance**. For example, in the words "met" and "neck," the vowel "e" has the same sound. Poets often use assonance to create a mood. Here is an example of assonance in "Ode to Melancholy," by John Keats.

> For shade to shade will come too drowsily,
> And drown the wakeful anguish of the soul.

The long, hollow sound of "ow" in "drowsily" is repeated in "drown" to make the reader experience more completely the description of someone sinking into a deep, heavy sleep. The lines tell us that this heavy sleep will "drown the wakeful anguish of the soul," in other words, that it will blot out the pain we suffer in our normal waking life. To suggest that only such heavy sleep can give us relief from the pain of life is a sad thought, and the mood of the lines darkens even more with the full "o"-sound in the last word, "soul."

## Model Passage and Question

Read the poems below. Then try to figure out the answer to the analysis questions.

**WHAT MEMORIES KEEP FLOODING BACK OVER THESE PEOPLE?**

### The Bean Eaters

> They eat beans mostly, this old yellow pair.
> Dinner is a casual affair.
> Plain chipware on a plain and creaking wood,
> (5) Tin flatware.
> Two who are Mostly Good.
> Two who have lived their day,
> But keep on putting on their clothes
> And putting things away.
> (10) And remembering . . .
> Remembering, with twinklings and twinges,
> As they lean over the beans in their rented back room that is full of beads
> and receipts and dolls and clothes, tobacco crumbs, vases and fringes.

"The Bean Eaters," by Gwendolyn Brooks copyright © 1991 by Gwendolyn Brooks, from *Blacks* published by Third World Press, Chicago, 1991)

Why are the last two lines an effective conclusion to the poem?

**(1)** They show how the old people keep thinking of the past.

**(2)** They make the old people seem even more unhappy.

**(3)** They show the old people really like expensive things.

**(4)** They show that the old people are planning to leave their rented room.

**(5)** They leave the reader wondering what will happen to them.

(1) is correct. In the lines just before the last two lines, the poet tells us that the old people keep "remembering/Remembering" as they sit in their rented back room full of all the things listed in the last two lines—things they keep for memory's sake. The old people are also called "Two who have lived their day (line 6)" which means they will tend to think of the past rather than the present. Since the things listed are the main pleasure of the old people, the things don't make them seem more unhappy (2), and since the things are ordinary, trivial things of no money-value, (3) cannot be true. Everything in the poem tells us that the old people are at the end of their lives, living in an unchanging routine (they "keep on putting on their clothes/And putting things away"); they will stay in their rented room until they die. Therefore, (4) and (5) are incorrect. Read the poem below. Then try to figure out the answer to the analysis question.

### WHAT IS GOD'S GRANDEUR LIKE?

### God's Grandeur

The world is charged with the grandeur of God.
It will flame out, like shining from shook foil;
It gathers to a greatness, like the ooze of oil
Crushed. Why do men then now not reck his rod?
(5)  Generations have trod, have trod, have trod;
And all is smeared with trade; bleared, smeared with toil;
And wears man's smudge and shares man's smell: the soil
Is bare now, nor can foot feel, being shod.

And for all this, nature is never spent;
(10)  There lives the dearest freshness deep down things;
And though the last lights off the black West went
Oh, morning at the brown brink eastward, springs—
Because the Holy Ghost over the bent
World broods with warm breast and with ah! bright wings.

"God's Grandeur," by Gerard Manley Hopkins (Oxford University Press, Inc. (N.Y., NY., 1973)

In lines 11–14, the poet contrasts "the last lights off the black West" with the "morning" to express the idea that

(1) human beings have destroyed the beauty of nature
(2) nature's beauty is unspoiled by human beings
(3) God's grandeur appears infrequently
(4) God's grandeur always triumphs in nature
(5) God shows his anger with man through nature

(4) is correct. In lines 9–10, the poet says that in spite of what men have done to dirty God's grandeur in nature (which he describes in lines 1–8), "nature is never spent; /There lives the dearest freshness deep down things." In lines 11–14, he contrasts darkness and light to express this idea. Sunset, when the "last lights off the black West went," is the image of what humans done to darken the beauty of nature. To show that God triumphs in nature in spite of what humans have done to spoil it, the poet compares His grandeur to the sun's light springing up over the "brown brink" of the Earth's horizon at the dawn of a new day. Therefore, it is clear that human beings have not destroyed nature's beauty, so (1) cannot be correct. However, lines 5–8 show that they have spoiled it in many ways, so (2) is wrong. (In fact, notice how the poet repeats "have trod, have trod, have trod," and how he uses the alliteration of "sm" sounds in "smeared" and "smudge" and "smell," to express disgust with what has been done to nature by "trade" (business) and "toil" (labor) in the polluted world of modern industry.) The poem begins by saying that "The world is charged with the grandeur of God"—meaning the world is filled with His grandeur as if with an electrical charge; since the poem ends by comparing this grandeur to dawn, which happens every day, His grandeur cannot appear infrequently; therefore, (3) cannot be correct. (5) is wrong because the image of the Holy Ghost expresses concern (it bends over the Earth with "warm breast") and positive feelings of hope and love ("ah! bright wings").

# Lesson 4 Exercise

Items 1 through 3 refer to the following poem. Choose the one best answer to each item.

## WHAT IS THE SPEAKER'S IDEA OF COURAGE?

### The Brave Man

The sun, that brave man,
Comes through boughs that lie in wait,
That brave man.

Green and gloomy eyes
In dark forms of the grass
(5) Run away.

The good stars,
Pale helms and spiky spurs,
Run away.

Fears of my bed,
(10) Fears of life and fears of death,
Run away.

That brave man comes up
From below and walks without meditation
That brave man.

"The Brave Man" by Wallace Stevens. From *Collected Poems* by Wallace Stevens. Copyright 1936 by Wallace Stevens and renewed 1964 by Holly Stevens. Reprinted by permission of Alfred A. Knopf, Inc.

1. The repetition of the line "Run away" is effective in making the reader feel that

   (1) the sun gets hotter as the day goes on
   (2) the speaker is afraid of the sun
   (3) the speaker identifies with the things that run away
   (4) the sun destroys everything in its path
   (5) the sun has no fear of anything

2. The tone of the fourth stanza—"Fears of my bed,/Fears of life and death,/Run away"–is

   (1) pessimistic
   (2) frightened
   (3) triumphant
   (4) sad
   (5) angry

3. Which of the following best describes the meaning of the statement in the last stanza that the sun "comes up/From below and walks without meditation/That brave man"?

   (1) True courage is something natural and instinctive.
   (2) Brave people are strong but not happy.
   (3) Brave people are often isolated and lonely.
   (4) True courage is a matter of attitude rather than action.
   (5) Brave people tend to be cruel.

Answers are on page A–30.

# CHAPTER 5

What do writers of commentary look for when they form their opinions? And how can you tell if they've effectively presented and defended those opinions? Critics and reviewers are people whose opinions qualify as commentary on the arts because they are experts in their fields. As such, they've learned how to support those opinions with their knowledge of their individual subject areas.

Credit: Miles Van der Rohe and Philip Johnson, Seagram Building, New York (1958)

## Prereading Prompt

One reviewer of a new movie may state: "It was awful. I didn't laugh once." Another reviewer may say: "What a movie! The special effects keep you on the edge of your seat!" Will you go? Usually, your decision depends on what you value most in a movie. Figuring out how writers of commentary carefully write their reviews to convince their audience to see things their way is important for answering GED questions. You will learn more about these techniques in this chapter.

# Commentary on the Arts

## What Is Commentary on the Arts?

**Commentary on the arts** is a type of nonfiction prose about literature and other kinds of creative works. As you examine the passages of commentary in this chapter, you will discover that commentary on the arts has three main purposes:

1. It *summarizes*, or provides information about art.
2. It *analyzes*, or shows how art achieves a particular effect.
3. It *evaluates*, or makes judgments about the value of art.

### About Which Arts is Commentary Written?

*Art* is sometimes defined as "the production of something beautiful." The arts, then, are the many ways in which artists create things of beauty to give pleasure to readers and viewers.

You have probably noticed that people often have different opinions about such things as movies or books. That's because they have different **standards** on which they judge something. Standards are a set of ideas about what makes something good or bad.

Some people write their opinions about various art forms as a profession. These people are called **critics** or **reviewers**. They might review:

- *literary arts*: nonfiction books, novels, short stories, poems, and plays in script form
- *visual arts*: painting, drawing, photography, architecture, and sculpture
- *performing arts*: music, dance, films, plays in performance, and television

On the *Interpreting Literature and the Arts* section of the GED test, you can expect about 25 percent of the items to be questions about commentaries on the arts. You will *not* be required to know anything in advance about the art forms these questions cover. To help you prepare, this chapter will focus on some of the elements that reviewers, critics, and authors use in developing their topics.

### Key Words

**commentary on the arts**—a written opinion about literature and other kinds of creative works

**standards**—a set of ideas about what makes something good and bad

375

# Literal Comprehension of Commentary

## Prereading Prompt

   If you tell a friend that she must hear your favorite singer's new album, she may say, "But I didn't like his first one." To convince her, you have to back up your opinion. You might mention the singer's fantastic voice, or the way he sings an oldie, or the terrific beat of a new song—any details that will help prove your point. Figuring out how critics express their opinions and then back them up with supporting details is a skill that will help you enjoy and better understand the commentary you read. Finding out how to do this is important for answering GED questions. You will learn how in this lesson.

## Key Words

**facts**—statements that can be proven to be true

**opinions**—statements that express the writer's beliefs or values but that cannot, or have not yet been proven to be true

## Reviews

   A **review** focuses on the author's opinion of a particular work of art—for example, a concert, a painting exhibition, or a play. It is the most common type of commentary on the arts. Reviews briefly describe the content of a piece and evaluate its strengths and weaknesses. Reviewers generally include the standards by which they judged the art work. Their purpose is to sway the reader's opinion. You will find reviews in newspapers and magazines—they are intended for the general reading public.

## Essays

Another important type of commentary is the **essay**. Most often, essays present a more in-depth analysis than reviews do, and authors of essays often assume that readers know something about the topic. An essay about the arts might be a comparison of two works of art or of two art forms. It might be an explanation of the meaning of a work of art. Some essays might, for example, analyze the latest trend in music or discuss the styles of new.film directors.

## Stated Main Ideas

Most critics want readers to understand their opinions easily. You will find that they usually state their views directly, rather than imply them. Many critics state their opinions rather early in their review; then they devote most of the review to explaining their reasons for holding these opinions. They usually present their main idea and supporting details in one of two ways:

- as a conclusion drawn from several broad statements, or
- as a contrast to ideas expressed early in the review.

It will help you to find the main idea more quickly in a GED question if, before you read it, you remind yourself what you may already know about the topic. For instance, in the model passage of this lesson, ask yourself: What do I already know about singers and jazz musicians?

## Supporting Details

**Facts** are statements that have been proven to be true. The facts that a critic introduces as supporting details can take the following forms:

- quotations from recognized experts
- statistics
- comparisons with similar works on which judgment has already been passed
- references to the plot or to other details in the work

An **opinion**, on the other hand, is a statement that expresses the writer's beliefs or values and that cannot be, or has not yet been, proven to be true. Commentary is considered effective if the author gives factual details that present a good defense of his or her opinion.

For example, an author who says of a television show, "This series was the most popular one on television in the past year" would not be offering strong support by saying, "My kids loved it." Rather than stating another opinion, the author should support his or her idea by stating a fact, such as how many viewers watched the series compared to how many viewers watched other television shows that year.

On the GED test, you may be asked literal comprehension questions about commentaries. When this happens, read the purpose question, the items following each passage, and then the passage itself. Keep these questions in mind. Look for a sentence that directly states the author's opinion. Then look for details, such as facts, that help support that opinion.

## Model Passage and Question

Read the item and the passage that follows. See if you can find the best answer to the literal comprehension question.

### WHY SHOULD THIS ALBUM BE TITLED *CONTRADICTIONS*?

*Compositions*, Anita Baker's fourth solo album, might better have been titled *Contradictions*. How can a singer as accomplished, talented and inquisitive as Baker make an album as relentlessly predictable as this one?

(5) Baker is without a doubt one of the most talented singers on the contemporary music scene. Like Marvin Gaye before her, she is a jazz artist masquerading as a pop singer. Her attention to detail, constant probing of melodies and the seemingly endless variety of approaches she brings to each (10) phrase gives her vocal performances genuine depth. Baker owes much to the late jazz singer Sarah Vaughan, whose throaty, full-bodied style is echoed in her own. But give Baker credit: Her no-nonsense style is devoid of the heavy affect that marred much of Vaughan's work.

(15) If Baker is potentially a singer for the ages, *Compositions* is an attempt to package her for the market of the moment. Unlike Baker's vocals, the arrangements lack identity. With the exception of two mid-tempo pieces, the album combines bland ballads and jazz-tinged flourishes to create upscale (20) make-out music.

A strong singer with as much style as Baker needs strong material, and the songs on *Compositions* are of mixed quality— which is particularly unfortunate because as the title indicates, Baker herself is responsible for most of the songwrit- (25) ing. The two best offerings, "Talk to Me" and "Soul Inspiration," are fine pop R&B ballads, good enough to guarantee the album's commercial success. But an artist of Anita Baker's abilities should have higher aspirations than that.

The critic wants readers to conclude that the album

**(1)** does not live up to Baker's potential as a singer

**(2)** does not present the singer's voice at its best

**(3)** will appeal only to people who like jazz

**(4)** presents the singer as a gifted songwriter

**(5)** reveals that the singer is imitating Sarah Vaughan

The correct choice is (1). In the first paragraph, the author states his main idea directly: Anita Baker is a very talented performer, but she has made an album that is "relentlessly predictable." Then he uses specific examples and comparisons to support that main idea. Choice (2) is incorrect because the author says the singer's vocal abilities are beautifully presented. Choice (3) is incorrect because the author states that the album is targeted for a broader audience. Choice (4) is incorrect because the author states that the songs written by the singer are not very noteworthy. Choice (5) is incorrect because the author says the singer's style overcomes some of the vocal problems he thinks Sarah Vaughan had and therefore is superior to Vaughn in some ways.

## Lesson 1 Exercise

Items 1 through 3 refer to the following passage. Choose the one best answer to each item.

### WHAT MAKES THIS MOVIE SO FRESH AND UNIQUE?

Hollywood's definition of a perfect couple is a man and a woman, one of whom is dead. How else to explain the wealth of ghostly love stories haunting the screen? Now, just six months after Richard Dreyfuss returned from heaven to snoop on his mate in *Always*, here's the
(5) ghostly Patrick Swayze mooning over his grieving girlfriend, Demi Moore, in *Ghost*. Swayze, a corporate banker, has just been killed by a New York mugger, but his spirit is still hanging around this Tribeca loft when he discovers Moore's life is in danger. How can he save her when he's immaterial? Enter Whoopi Goldberg as Sister Oda Mae Brown, a
(10) quack spiritual adviser. Imagine her surprise, after years of faking communication with the dead, when this white boy starts talking to her from beyond the grave, and won't leave her in peace until she gets involved in saving Demi—and helping Patrick track down the man who murdered him.
(15) A comedy, romance and supernatural thriller rolled into one, *Ghost* is a zippy hodgepodge that somehow manages to seem fresh even though it's built entirely out of borrowed parts. Screenwriter Bruce Joel Rubin is a clever magpie; he's raided every genre to create this seductive, funny hybrid, but he's done his job with a witty, light touch.
(20) *Ghost* becomes resistible only at the finish line, when the sappiness gets a bit out of control.

1. Which of the following statements best describes the critic's impression of the movie?

   (1) *Ghost* is a remake of other love stories with ghosts.
   (2) *Ghost* shows the lack of originality in current films.
   (3) *Ghost* mixes several types of movies in an entertaining way.
   (4) Ghost proves that a movie can be funny and scary.
   (5) Filmmakers use the supernatural when they have no new ideas.

2. Which of the following facts were used in the review?

   (1) Whoopi Goldberg's character is romantically involved with Patrick Swayze's character.
   (2) Patrick Swayze's character tracks down the man who murdered him.
   (3) The screenwriter also wrote *Always*.
   (4) Demi Moore's character is the comic element in the plot.
   (5) *Ghost* is a remake of another movie made in the 1940s.

3. Which of the following sentences supports the critic's main opinion of the movie?

   (1) Love stories with ghosts are popular now.
   (2) *Always* has the same plot.
   (3) The "perfect" couple in the movies changes each season.
   (4) The story contains a quack spiritual adviser.
   (5) *Ghost* becomes too sentimental at the end.

Answers are on page A–31.

# Inferential Comprehension of Commentary

## Prereading Prompt

Some people like rock music; others prefer easy listening. Some people enjoy action movies; others prefer comedies. Knowing the qualities that people like in art and literature is important. When someone makes a suggestion about what you might want to see or read, you will then immediately know on what basis they do so. You can then make intelligent choices for yourself. Inferring the basis of the critic's opinions is a skill that will help you enjoy the commentary that you read. Finding out how to do this is important for answering GED questions. You will learn how in this lesson.

## Key Words

**bias**—a personal attitude for or against something or someone; a mental leaning in one direction; a personal taste

**objectivity**—without bias; using facts and recognized standards to support ideas

## Bias

Writers of commentary usually have a background of special training and experience in evaluating the arts. They already have general opinions about what they like or dislike in art. You will find that in commentary written about literature and the arts, the personal tastes of critics are usually more obvious than those of other writers.

Although most commentary contains a stated main idea, occasionally the critic's main point must be inferred. If you understand the ways in which a particular passage may be colored by the critic's personal taste, you can begin to draw conclusions about the important ideas that the author wants to express. Knowing the critic's **bias**, or personal attitude or personal taste, will help you understand and judge reviews. This will help you decide for yourself if the review seems badly reasoned, or if you do not think his or her taste is like your own. In this way you can make the best use of reviews as guides to works of art and entertainment.

## Objectivity

In the last lesson, you learned that effective commentary depends upon factual support of the critic's opinion. The more that commentary is based upon recognized standards for quality in the arts—and the less it is based on the critic's personal tastes or opinion—the more **objective** it is considered to be.

If you read a commentary that begins "My own view is . . .," you know that you are about to learn the author's opinion and not fact. Even though the author is not objective, he or she may still have a valid point to make. The review may go on to explain why the author believes his or her opinion is correct. You can judge the validity of the point by examining how the views are supported—mostly by facts, or mostly by opinions.

Be careful not to accept a commentary merely because the critic has been objective, nor reject it merely because the critic reveals some personal bias. Instead, judge its effectiveness by the way the critic defends his or her opinion.

On the GED test, you may be asked inferential comprehension questions about commentary. When this happens, look for key words in the passage that relate to the question. For example, if you are asked to infer a reviewer's opinion of an actor's performance, look in the passage for the actor's name and words that relate to *performance* or *perform*. These words might tell how the reviewer thinks the actor performed, such as "brilliantly" or "charmingly." Read the sentences near the one in which the key words appear. Make a judgment about what the reviewer is saying about the actor's performance. Then see if your response is similar to one of the answer choices.

# Model Passage and Question

Read the item and the passage following. See if you can figure out the answer to the inferential comprehension question.

## WHAT MAKES DICK TRACY A CLASSIC "COMIC STRIP" MOVIE?

Right at the beginning, we see an old table radio and Dick Tracy's pale-yellow fedora, and we're back in the thirties—not the real thirties, of course, but the thirties that were experienced as myth even by people living then. *Dick Tracy* is an
(5) immense enlargement of Chester Gould's famous comic strip, yet it remains faithful to its odd glories. The comic-strip framework has been used as a license to go way beyond realism: At times we could be watching a gangster film from the early thirties but with everything slightly weird. On the radio,
(10) there is alarmed talk of thugs menacing newsdealers and shoeshine boys. Next, a starving little boy eats some scraps out of an ash can and runs down an alley; he enters a warehouse, hiding behind barrels, and sees a group of gangsters with freakishly puffy, misshapen faces playing poker under
(15) harsh light. The faces are grotesque but somehow strikingly human, almost sympathetic.

The perspectives are exaggerated, the colors primal pop. Human figures walk through Depression-era sets painted red and blue, and then, through the subtlest of special effects,
(20) the figures blend into drawn or miniaturized versions of big-city towers. Triumphantly stylized down to the smallest detail, *Dick Tracy* has been made with an enchanted love of color and design. There are lots of smooth, lacquered surfaces, a profusion of chrome and Formica and plastic, often
(25) overbright, as if lit by the excitement of what could be done with those materials when they were still new.

What can you assume the author thinks about the value of style in movies that are based on comic strips?

**(1)** A comic-strip film should have a style that remains accurate to the style of its source.

**(2)** The success of a movie relies primarily on its plot.

**(3)** Comic-strip characters dramatize the realities of their periods.

**(4)** The style of a comic-strip film should not only be faithful to its original source, but also enhance it.

**(5)** Stylized films distract from an audience's enjoyment.

(4) is correct. In his examples and other supporting details, the author suggests that Dick Tracy is successful because the filmmakers have made an "immense enlargement" (line 5) of the comic strip, while remaining faithful to the original source. (1) is incorrect because the author suggests that the original source should be the basis for a style that is not merely accurate but "larger than life." (2) cannot be true, since the author suggests that audiences go to

see comic-strip movies because they are interested primarily in the style and characters. The reviewer says the period of the 1930s we see in the movie is not the real 1930s "but the thirties that were experienced as myth even by people living then" (lines 3–4). Therefore, (3) is incorrect. (5) is incorrect because the reviewer suggests that he enjoys this movie because its exaggerated style is so inviting.

## Lesson 2 Exercise

Items 1 through 3 refer to the following passage. Choose the one best answer to each item.

### WHAT MADE FRANCIS BACON A FAMOUS PAINTER?

Francis Bacon is the Grand Old Man of British painting, and it might be expected that his survival to an eighth decade would prod someone to celebrate. So, even though New Yorkers last saw his work in 1975, when Henry Geldzahler brought it to the Metropolitan, we get another
(5) chance to see it this summer, in a show (organized by the Hirshhorn Museum) at the Museum of Modern Art. I hadn't noticed anyone waiting breathlessly for the sequel, but perhaps it's just me.

Bacon is one of those lucky painters who have had the consensus of history on their side from their first exhibition. One of the first pictures
(10) he sold (in 1948, two years after it was painted) went straight to the Modern and became everybody's image of postwar existential anguish. This is the famous meat-rack painting of slabs of butchered beef and strings of sausages draped like tinsel around a slack-jawed, black-robed authority figure whose eyes are shadowed by a black umbrella—
(15) a blind judge, if you will. The "judge" holds court in a sterile U.N.-style amphitheater you could associate with the trials of individual and collective guilt that preoccupied Europe after the Nazis fell. Modern life unfolds in a panorama of sterility and butchery, ruled by the terrifying figure of an eyeless justice who talks with bared teeth and who shields
(20) himself from the rain of Heaven with a proper bureaucratic umbrella. As a primal cry out of the crumbling London of the Blitz, this painting had no match in its time. Because it holds pride of place in MOMA'S collection, it has carried Bacon's reputation locally for decades.

**1.** In the first paragraph of the passage, what bias is the critic revealing?

**(1)** She thinks the painter is underrated.

**(2)** She thinks the painter is overrated.

**(3)** British painters are more interesting than American painters.

**(4)** Bacon's paintings disturb her.

**(5)** She thinks the painter's work has changed modern art.

2. How do you know that the critic is offering her opinion and not an entirely objective commentary?

(1) She ends the first paragraph with "perhaps it's just me."

(2) She gives facts about how different people have viewed Bacon's work.

(3) She concludes by stating why Bacon's reputation was made locally for decades.

(4) She discusses Bacon's place among other modern painters.

(5) She gives facts about Bacon's history.

3. Which of the following statements best expresses the main idea of the passage?

(1) Modern art after the war was effective because it shocked the public.

(2) The public cannot be objective about art that disturbs them.

(3) Bacon's art is overvalued because of its historical interest.

(4) Many artists do not achieve recognition until they reach an elderly age.

(5) Bacon's reputation has increased in recent years.

Answers are on page A–31.

# Applying Ideas in Commentary

## Prereading Prompt

You have already studied the application of ideas in the section of readings in social studies and science. It is just as valuable to know how to apply a writer's ideas in commentary on the arts. By knowing how a reviewer or critic reacts to one book or movie or play, you can make predictions about how he or she will react to other similar works of art. On the GED Test, you may be asked to apply main ideas, details, or the author's attitudes to new situations, and some of these will concern commentary on the arts. You will learn how to do this in this lesson.

## Applying Main Ideas and Details

As you have learned, one way to test your understanding of a writer's attitude is to see if you can predict accurately how he or she would react in a new situation—in other words, understand how the writer's attitude might be applied to a new situation.

The same method can be used in commentary. Let's say a reviewer enjoys a photographer's exhibition because of its many photographs of American public gardens. The reviewer might admire the way the photographer has captured the inventive uses of color and space. You might conclude that the reviewer would also enjoy abstract paintings which emphasize color and spatial designs. Another reviewer might feel that paintings should be representational—in other words, that the images should show objects you can recognize rather than abstract shapes. You might predict that this second reviewer would enjoy novels with realistic plots, while the first critic might prefer more experimental writing, or might like spectacles full of color and design, such as ballets or spectacular musicals.

## Applying the Author's Attitude

To determine the author's attitude in a commentary, you should determine the author's biases as well as his or her opinion.

For example, look again at the review of *Dick Tracy* in Lesson 2. The author's bias leans in favor of a strong style that heightens the style of the original source. Would he recommend a plain-looking restaurant that offers good food at a good price? Possibly, but not likely. Since he praises the movie's "immense enlargement," which goes "way beyond realism," you probably would predict that the reviewer would be more enthusiastic about fantasy in fiction and perhaps also new, experimental music.

On the GED test, you may be asked application questions about the main idea, details, or the author's attitude in commentary. When that happens, read the passage carefully with the question in mind. Try to find information that will help you "bridge" ideas between the new situation in the item and the old situation in the passage. Then narrow down the choices until you are satisfied that the answer you have chosen is the best one.

## Model Passage and Question

Read the item and the passage below and see if you can figure out the answer to the application question.

### WHY IS THE "GOOD WAR" AN INTERESTING BOOK?

Solemn-minded historians speak ill of oral history (history told as stories by those who were involved in the events), at least when it's published in book form. For them, oral history is self-serving and therefore suspect. It isn't history, it's the
(5) material of history; it must be analyzed and interpreted. And yet in the hands of a master interviewer and editor, oral history acquires a weight and perspective of its own. Studs Terkel knows very well that his books have less to do with "hard fact and precise statistics" than with memory, attitude,
(10) and aspiration.

It's this distinction that makes "The Good War" so interesting. (The title comes with quotation marks: they imply that Terkel reserves judgement as to how "good" World War II really was.) Terkel's book contains well over a hundred interviews
(15) with men and women of every social condition. It differs from the hundreds of personal accounts we have of that war, even from other collections of personal accounts, because he has invited his witnesses to speculate on the value of their experience, the value of the war itself.

From "What Did You Do in the War?" by Peter S. Prescott, *Newsweek*, October 15, 1984.

Which of the following television programs do you think the critic would most likely enjoy?

**(1)** a game show where the contestants have to reveal their most embarrassing moments

**(2)** a documentary about striking coal miners in the 1930s

**(3)** a mystery set in World War II

**(4)** a love story about a soldier and a Vietnamese woman

**(5)** home videos of the 1991 San Francisco earthquake

The correct response is (5). Home videos of the San Francisco earthquake would portray "real people" in much the same way that oral history reveals personal experiences by directly revealing them in their own words and actions. (1) is incorrect because the situation in which the revelations would be made—a TV show—probably is contrived to produce comedy for the audience, instead of giving personal experiences concerning history or social conditions. (2) is incorrect because a documentary would consist of material interpreted and shaped by the filmmaker. (3) and (4) are incorrect because both the mystery and the love story would be fiction, not direct factual statements by real people.

## Lesson 3 Exercise

Items 1 through 3 refer to the following passage. Choose the one best answer to each item.

### WHO MADE DANCE A RESPECTABLE PROFESSION FOR MEN?

Even thirty years ago ballet in this country was widely termed "the fairies' ball game," and most parents, particularly fathers, would rather see their sons enlist in the Foreign Legion than join a ballet class. It was the incredibly important social function of Edward Villella, along
(5) with his brilliant and close colleague Jacques d'Amboise, to do an enormous amount in breaking down the prejudice. Eddie and Jacques were not merely fantastic dancers (that, too, was essential), but they were regular guys.

Eddie went to Maritime College and boxed! Jacques looked like a
(10) basketball player, and they dated girls and got married! Regular—the kind of boys a son could bring home to his father. In 1968 NBC did a special on Villella called "Man Who Dances," which, with Gene Kelly's TV show of a decade earlier, "Dancing—A Man's Game," did an enormous amount to dispel prejudice against the male ballet dancer in this
(15) country and slowly to make the vexed question of a dancer's sexual preference as totally irrelevant as it is in football.

Villella's personal contribution to the development of that male image for the American dancer was terrific. He was simply a man who danced—and it was always his dancing that got across his message
(20) that men were natural dancers, and that to primitive man dancing was only a little less natural than hunting or praying, and closely related to both.

Reprinted by permission from "Edward Villella," by Clive Barnes, originally appearing *Dance Magazine,* November, 1989, page 114. © Copyright 1989.

1. The attitude of the author toward women entering a previously all-male profession probably would be

   (1) puzzled that the women would want to do such a thing
   (2) angry that the women would want to do such a thing
   (3) fearful of the conflict the women's action might cause
   (4) enthusiastic about the change the women were making
   (5) doubtful that the women would ever be accepted

2. Often in professional sports women athletes are paid less than men in the same sport because their ability to play and to attract ticket-buyers is said to be inferior to men's playing ability and popularity. If the author of the article were asked what he thought was the best way to break down this unfair practice, what do you think his advice to women athletes would be?

   (1) Demand new regulations that will make the pay fair for players of both sexes.
   (2) Refuse to play in major events until the pay is made fair for players of both sexes.
   (3) Gain equal pay by showing women can play as well as men.
   (4) Form a female athletes organization to negotiate higher pay.
   (5) Criticize the sexual attitudes of commentators on their sport.

3. Some modern choreographers have started to use break dancing, a kind of acrobatic street dancing, in combination with more traditional types of modern dance to create a new dance-form. What do you think the attitude of the author of the article would be toward this new dance-form?

   (1) hostile
   (2) encouraging
   (3) fearful
   (4) indifferent
   (5) bored

Answers are on page A–32.

# Analyzing Commentary

## Prereading Prompt

How many times have you successfully convinced someone to see a movie that you've seen? Or to read a book that you've enjoyed? Or watch a TV series that you think is outstanding? You have probably used the art of persuasion many times—perhaps without even knowing it! You have presented your opinion clearly, supported it effectively, and then summarized it neatly. Finding out how authors structure their arguments and use diction to persuade their readers is a useful skill that will help you better understand the commentary you read. Knowing how to analyze these elements is very important for answering questions on the GED test. You will learn how in this lesson.

## Key Word

**diction**—the particular choice of words an author uses to help emphasize his or her opinion

Part of what makes commentary so enjoyable is appreciating the skill with which an author has organized his or her argument. The most common structure for an argument is (1) *opinion*, (2) *support*, and (3) *conclusion*. Sometimes—particularly in longer passages of commentary—a critic will present the support, followed by his or her opinion, and then the conclusion. You have already learned that the most effective support of an argument comes from facts rather than opinions. The conclusion, then, comes in the form of a generalization or a restatement of the original point.

Here is an example of the elements in the structure of an argument:

**Opinion**   *The Butterfly Bandit* is a hilarious satire that is thoroughly enjoyable.

**Support**   It is well written. (opinion)
It has been on the New York Times Best Seller List for 43 weeks. (fact)
The plot is far-fetched, yet believable. (opinion)
It was given rave reviews by critics in the *New York Times*, *Sun-Times*, and *Boston Globe*. (fact)

**Summary**   This satire on the public's obsessions with crimes committed by weird, comical characters is so funny that you won't want to put it down.

As you read commentary, notice how the parts of the argument fit together. If you do not agree with the critic's conclusion, you should be able to think of a well-structured argument to support your view.

## Diction

As you have learned, the tone of a piece of writing shows the author's attitude toward his or her subject. Some commentaries may be formal or, in other words, serious in tone; others may be informal, or more personal or playful.

You will find that critics often use a particular choice of words, or **diction**, that helps emphasize the point they want to make. In commentary, diction may be used in several ways:

**Carefully chosen comparisons.**  For example: "[Dick Tracy is] tough and steely with Breathless [Mahoney], tender and tongue-tied with his girlfriend, the valiant and faithful Tess Truehart."

**Wordplay.**  For example: "Forget *Total Recall*." The effectiveness of wordplay usually depends upon how well the author's purpose suits the audience he or she is trying to reach.

**Descriptive language.**  An easy way to find out if a critic's opinion of a work of art is positive or negative is to look for the use of adjectives. (Remember that an adjective is a word that describes a person, place, object, or idea.) These adjectives might be used in reviews: brilliant, pretentious, gripping, unfocused, inspired, embarrassing. Some adjectives are complimentary. Others lead you to infer that the reviewer disapproves of the work of art.

Critics also choose their words to suit a given group of readers, or audience. For example, in order to appeal to experts, a critic might use many words that are understood only by readers who already know a great deal about the subject. On the other hand, the critic might use straightforward, everyday language to suit a more everyday audience. The effect is to gain the readers' confidence and to better prepare them to accept the critic's opinion.

On the Interpreting Literature and the Arts section of the GED test, you may be asked to analyze the structure of the argument or the diction in a commentary. To find an answer about the structure, look for the author's opinion, supporting details, and summary. (Be sure you are clear about whether the details are facts or opinions.) To find an answer about diction, look for the word or words in question and try to figure out what effect they are intended to have on the audience.

## Model Passages and Questions

Read the items and the passages below and try to figure out the answer to the analysis questions.

### WHAT IS THE LESSON OF SATYAJIT RAY'S CAREER?

Satyajit Ray's career in cinema is without doubt an example to all aspiring filmmakers. The trajectory of his work, however, holds a warning. The decision of the American Academy of Motion Picture Arts and Sciences to honor Ray

(5) with a special Oscar award for lifetime contribution to world cinema is as good an occasion as any to reflect on the genius of Ray, as well as on its pathetic degeneration.

Without the passionate struggle and integrity that went into the making of *Pather Panchali* (1954) and without the

(10) sensitivity that made *Charulata* (1965), Indian and world cinema would be poorer. Also, the recognition of cinema as a serious art form in India would have taken longer.

Ray stood alone, and it is in this isolation that we must search for the reasons for his creative decline. He worked in a

(15) climate that did not sustain the evolution of a truly alternative cinema. Ray himself never took an active part in promoting a healthy critical climate once he became established as a filmmaker.

He acquired a demigod status and took on the mantle of

(20) the infallible conscience and oracle of his times. His distance from life increased the more he was trapped in the cage of his creative arrogance. In such a situation, he could neither describe the world outside nor turn inward, the privilege that old age offers to the artist. Many artists use their advancing

(25) years to free themselves, to be more playful, to take risks with themselves and their expressive pursuits. Ray chose not to— his life thus remains for us an inspiration as well as a warning.

From "Reflections on Satyajit Ray," by Shuddhabrata Sengupta, from "Indian Express, New Delhi"; published in *World Press Review* Magazine in April 1992 © 1992.

The writer's argument that Ray's film work has declined is based on the idea that

**(1)** geniuses like Ray usually decline as they grow older

**(2)** Ray never took an active part in the world around him

**(3)** Ray became removed from life and egotistical

**(4)** Ray was unable to free himself from the poverty of India

**(5)** the Oscar recently awarded to Ray is a warning to filmmakers

(3) is correct. The writer of this essay believes that Satyajit Ray's movies have been great but have declined. He sees in Ray's career a lesson or warning for other filmmakers about what causes artists to decline. In several statements, he explains Ray's decline as a result of his "isolation" (line 13) and "distance from life" (lines 20-21) and also of his "demigod status" (line 19) and "his creative arrogance" (line 22). This idea of Ray's decline is restated in (3). The writer does not make the statement in (2); he says that Ray never took an active part in creating a "healthy critical climate" that might have stimulated him and kept his work great (lines 16-18). He also does not make the statements made in (1), (4), and (5).

## WHAT DO TV SITCOMS TELL US ABOUT AMERICAN FAMILY LIFE?

By the 1950's, television had established its role in reinforcing the values of family life. The ideological function of the sitcom [situation comedy]—then and now the dominant entertainment genre (there are no less than sixteen regularly
(5) scheduled sitcoms now running)—has remained constant. *From Father Knows Best* to *The Brady Bunch* to *Family Ties*, these scrubbed, well-functioning families have invaded living rooms and challenged us to measure up. They have presented images of family unity and harmony to a nation deep in
(10) the throes of domestic chaos and trauma.

Well before the advent of home TV, the divorce rate was soaring, juvenile delinquency and youthful rebellion were rampant, emotional distress and domestic violence were on the rise. But week after weeek, Americans sat rapt before
(15) their television screens watching Ward and June solve the current "problem with the Beaver [their son]" and retire safely behind their cheerfully shuttered windows.

To watch American sitcoms, then and now, is to enter an "America" in which adults spend virtually all their time in
(20) their well–appointed, commodity–filled kitchens and dens talking to and about their children, worrying over and solving their children's problems, successfully teaching their loving, respectful offspring moral lessons about honesty, tolerance, charity, and compassion. It is a world in which violence,
(25) drugs, racism and sexism barely exist; in which social issues of any kind, when they are raised at all, are seen to be quickly and easily solved in twenty–two minutes in the privacy of the family living room by fathers and mothers who still know best, with no help at all from government, schools, or
(30) social–service agencies.

From "A Family Affair" by Elayne Rapping. Reprinted by permission from *The Progressive*, 409 East Main St., Madison, WI 53703.

The author's reference to social issues that are "quickly and easily solved in twenty–two minutes (line 26) shows that she considers sitcoms to be

**(1)** a welcome relief from social problems

**(2)** an unreal response to social problems

**(3)** a quick, efficient approach to social problems

**(4)** an entertaining picture of social problems

**(5)** a temporary solution for social problems

(2) is correct. The author makes the reference to social problems that are "quickly and easily solved in twenty–two minutes" immediately after she lists several serious problems ("violence, drugs, racism, and sexism") that she clearly does not believe can be solved in "twenty–two minutes in the privacy of the family living room by fathers and mothers who still know best, with no help at all from government, schools, or social–service agencies" (lines 24–27). In the phrase quoted in the question, her diction is meant to make fun of the idea that such problems can be solved so quickly and easily. Her choice of words in this phrase expresses an attitude of disbelief and mockery toward the treatment of serious social issues on sitcoms. The whole passage expresses the same attitude: the first paragraph describes the unreal picture of "family unity and harmony" that sitcoms provide; the second paragraph describes the serious social problems that sitcoms ignore; the last paragraph makes fun of the over–simplified idea of problem solving that sitcoms create by ignoring these problems. Nothing in the passage supports any of the other choices.

Items 1 through 3 refer to the passage below. Choose the one best answer for each item.

### WHAT DOES THE REVIEWER THINK OF STEINEM'S BOOK?

For all those women who wailed "How could she do it?" when Gloria Steinem, the world's most famous feminist, began keeping company with demi-billionaire real estate developer and aspiring journalist Mort Zuckerman in the late '80s, *Revolution from Within: A Book of Self-*
(5) *Esteem* will serve as belated explanation.

When Steinem, now 57, pours a second cup of coffee and writes like she talks, there is no one more fascinating. The only comparable figure in public life is Ralph Nader, and he doesn't manage the trick of combining her monastic commitment with unapologetic glamour that gets
(10) her waved past the velvet ropes at clubs on both coasts. Strangers come up to her on the street and tell her, "You've changed my life," and cleaning women at the airport find a place for her to take a nap.

But we get too few glimpses of this person in the book who, despite all the self-actualization, writes as if she believes that what Julie
(15) Andrews or Mahatma Gandhi or the Gnostic Gospels have to tell us is more worthwhile than what makes her tick. Fortunately, one of the world's most interesting women is incapable of writing an uninteresting book, even when she summarizes most of the extant literature on the inner child. A $700,000 advance can buy a lot of self-esteem. But
(20) if that's not enough, if only the women whose lives were touched by Steinem were to buy the book, it would be a best seller. Here, Gloria, is $22.95. Buck up, and thanks for everything.

From "Even Feminists Get the Blues" by Margaret Carlson, *Time*, January 20, 1992. Copyright 1992 Time Inc. Reprinted by permission.

1. Judging from the author's tone, this review is probably most intended for

   **(1)** anti-feminists
   **(2)** women readers
   **(3)** feminists
   **(4)** gossip-column readers
   **(5)** male readers

2. The writer's response to Gloria Steinem's new book could be described as

   **(1)** loyal and supportive
   **(2)** surprised and hostile
   **(3)** disillusioned and bored
   **(4)** puzzled and angry
   **(5)** admiring and uncritical

3. The writing style used in this article would probably be most effective for

   **(1)** a guide to improving your self-image
   **(2)** a political article
   **(3)** a historical study of feminism
   **(4)** a biography of an artist
   **(5)** a book on how to succeed

Answers are on page A–32.

# Unit V

**Mathematics** consists of all the ways we use numbers to deal with the physical world. It is the way we understand and organize everything that can be measured by quantity. It is also used to describe all kinds of relationships between things as they exist in space together, move in relation to each other, or change in quantity over time.

## Prereading Prompt

You use math every day, probably much more than you realize. You add and subtract numbers to tell time, to pay a bill or calculate your gas mileage, to measure amounts for a recipe or for a customer's order. Do you know how you use multiplication and division when you figure how much "20% Off" is at a sale? Or when you compare the weights of packages of meat? Or when you figure out how much one drink in a six-pack costs? You use percents and decimals in such calculations, too. In this unit, you will practice basic problem-solving skills in math which you can use to pass the GED, and which also can help you on the job and in your daily life.

# Mathematics

## What is Mathematics?

### The Basic Types of Mathematics

The most basic type of mathematics is *arithmetic*, consisting of skills in addition, subtraction, multiplication, and division—skills you probably already use, with whole numbers, decimals, and percents. Another important type of math is *geometry*, the mathematics that deals with figures like squares, triangles, and rectangles, with the relationships between points and lines on a flat surface, and with amounts of space and distances around spaces. This unit also covers *graphs* (which you already have studied in Social Studies and Science) and skills in *algebra*, an advanced form of math used in engineering and science and which uses formulas you will study in earlier chapters of this unit.

### How the GED Tests the Types of Math

The GED Test in mathematics will test these content areas of math in the following percentages: 50% Arithmetic; 30% Algebra; 20% Geometry. 30% of all the questions on the test will involve graphs. On the test, you will have 90 minutes to do 56 multiple-choice questions.

### The Types of GED Math Questions

On the GED Math Test, your main task is to read carefully to see what each question is asking and apply the math skill needed to find the right answer. Figuring out which skill to use is as important as doing the computation accurately. Many questions are "word problems," which describe real-life practical problems that must be solved by mathematics. The test also includes a number of "setup questions," which ask you only to identify how you would set up the problem to solve it, without asking you for the actual solution. In this unit—and the two full GED tests in the back of the text—you will practice all the types of GED math problems.

### Key Words

**Mathematics**—the various sciences that use numbers to describe the physical world and to solve problems concerning quantities

**Word problem**—a mathematical question requiring the application of the appropriate math skill to the solution of a practical problem

# Unit V Progress Chart

# Mathematics

Use the following chart to keep track of your work. When you complete a lesson, circle the number of questions you answered correctly in the Lesson Exercise. The numbers in color represent scores at a level of 60% or better.

Lesson  Page

| | | |
|---|---|---|
| | 403 | **CHAPTER 1: Whole Numbers** |
| | 403 | Level 1: WHOLE-NUMBER SKILLS |
| | 403 | Preview 1 2 3 4 5 |
| 1 | 403 | Our Number System 1 2 3 4 5 6 7 8 9 10 |
| 2 | 404 | Addition of Whole Numbers 1 2 3 4 5 |
| 3 | 405 | Subtraction of Whole Numbers 1 2 3 4 5 6 7 |
| 4 | 406 | Multiplication of Whole Numbers 1 2 3 4 5 6 7 8 |
| 5 | 407 | Division of Whole Numbers 1 2 3 4 5 6 7 8 |
| | 409 | Level 2: WHOLE-NUMBER APPLICATIONS |
| 1 | 409 | Rounding Off 1 2 3 4 5 6 7 8 9 10 |
| 2 | 410 | Distance and Cost Formulas 1 2 3 4 5 6 |
| 3 | 413 | Powers and Roots 1 2 3 4 5 6 7 8 9 |
| 4 | 414 | Perimeter and Area of Polygons 1 2 3 4 5 6 |
| 5 | 418 | Volume 1 2 3 4 5 |
| 6 | 419 | Mean and Median 1 2 3 4 5 |
| | 422 | Level 3: WHOLE-NUMBER PROBLEM SOLVING |
| 1 | 422 | Setup Answers: Order of Operations 1 2 3 4 5 |
| 2 | 425 | Multistep Problems 1 2 3 4 5 6 7 8 |
| 3 | 427 | Estimating 1 2 3 4 5 |
| 4 | 429 | Item Sets 1 2 3 4 5 6 |

| | | |
|---|---|---|
| | 435 | **CHAPTER 2: Fractions** |
| | 435 | Level 1: FRACTION SKILLS |
| | 435 | Preview 1 2 3 4 5 |
| 1 | 435 | Reducing Fractions 1 2 3 4 5 |
| 2 | 436 | Raising Fractions to Higher Terms 1 2 3 4 5 |
| 3 | 437 | Mixed Numbers and Improper Fractions 1 2 3 4 5 6 7 8 9 10 |
| 4 | 438 | Adding Fractions and Mixed Numbers That Have Like Denominators 1 2 3 4 5 |
| 5 | 439 | Common Denominators 1 2 3 4 5 6 |
| 6 | 440 | Adding Fractions and Mixed Numbers That Have Unlike Denominators 1 2 3 4 5 |
| 7 | 441 | Subtracting Fractions and Mixed Numbers 1 2 3 4 5 6 7 8 |

Lesson  Page

| | | |
|---|---|---|
| 8 | 443 | Multiplying Fractions and Mixed Numbers 1 2 3 4 5 6 7 8 |
| 9 | 445 | Dividing Fractions and Whole Numbers 1 2 3 4 5 6 7 8 |
| | 447 | Level 2: FRACTION APPLICATIONS |
| 1 | 447 | Ratio 1 2 3 4 5 6 7 8 9 10 |
| 2 | 449 | Proportion 1 2 3 4 5 6 7 8 9 10 |
| 3 | 452 | Probability 1 2 3 4 5 |
| | 454 | Level 3: FRACTION PROBLEM SOLVING |
| 1 | 454 | Setup Problems 1 2 3 4 5 |
| 2 | 457 | Extraneous Information 1 2 3 4 5 |

| | | |
|---|---|---|
| | 462 | **CHAPTER 3: Decimals** |
| | 462 | Level 1: DECIMAL SKILLS |
| | 462 | Preview 1 2 3 4 5 6 7 |
| 1 | 462 | Reading and Writing Decimals 1 2 3 4 5 6 7 8 9 10 |
| 2 | 464 | Adding Decimals 1 2 3 4 5 |
| 3 | 465 | Subtracting Decimals 1 2 3 4 5 6 7 8 9 10 |
| 4 | 465 | Multiplying Decimals 1 2 3 4 5 |
| 5 | 467 | Dividing Decimals 1 2 3 4 5 |
| 6 | 468 | Interchanging Decimals and Fractions 1 2 3 4 5 6 7 8 9 10 |
| | 470 | Level 2: DECIMAL APPLICATIONS |
| 1 | 470 | Rounding Decimals 1 2 3 4 5 6 7 8 9 10 |
| 2 | 471 | Decimal Word Problems 1 2 3 4 5 |
| 3 | 472 | Metric Measurement 1 2 3 4 5 6 7 8 9 10 |
| 4 | 474 | Circumference and Area of Circles 1 2 3 4 5 6 7 8 |
| 5 | 476 | Volume of a Cylinder 1 2 3 4 5 |
| 6 | 477 | Comparing Decimals 1 2 3 4 5 |
| | 479 | Level 3: INSUFFICIENT DATA 1 2 3 4 5 |

| | | |
|---|---|---|
| | 484 | **CHAPTER 4: Percents** |
| | 484 | Level 1: PERCENT SKILLS |
| | 484 | Preview 1 2 3 4 5 6 7 |
| 1 | 484 | Interchanging Percents and Decimals 1 2 3 4 5 6 7 8 9 10 |

# Table of Measures
## U.S. Customary System

### Length

12 inches (in.) = 1 foot (ft.)
3 feet = 1 yard (yd.)
$16\frac{1}{2}$ feet = 1 rod (rd.)
$5\frac{1}{2}$ yards = 1 rod
5280 feet = 1 mile (mi.)
1760 yards = 1 mile

### Weight

16 ounces (oz.) = 1 pound (lb.)
2000 pounds = 1 short ton (sh. tn.)
2240 pounds = 1 long ton (l. tn.)

### Liquid

8 fluid ounces (fl. oz.) = 1 cup (c.)
2 cups = 1 pint (pt.)
2 pints = 1 quart (qt.)
4 quarts = 1 gallon

### Time

60 seconds (sec.) = 1 minute (min.)
60 minutes = 1 hour (hr.)
24 hours = 1 day (da.)
365 days = 1 year (yr.)

### Area

144 square inches = 1 square foot
(sq. in. or $in.^2$)      (sq. ft. or $ft.^2$)
9 square feet = 1 square yard (sq. yd. or $yd.^2$)
$30\frac{1}{2}$ square yards = 1 square rod (sq. rd. or $rd.^2$)
43,560 square feet = 1 acre (ac. or A)
4840 square yards = 1 acre
160 square rods = 1 acre
640 acres = 1 square mile (sq. mi. or $mi.^2$)

### Volume

1728 cubic inches = 1 cubic foot
(cu. in. or $in.^3$)      (cu. ft. or $ft.^3$)
27 cubic feet = 1 cubic yard (cu. yd. or $yd.^3$)

### Dry

2 pints (pt.) = 1 quart (qt.)
8 quarts = 1 peck (pk.)
4 pecks = 1 bushel (bu.)

# Abbreviations for Units of Measurement
## U.S. Customary System

### Length

inch(es) = in.
foot, feet = ft.
yard(s) = yd.
rod(s) = rd.
mile(s)* = mi.

*statute mile*

### Area

square inch = ($in.^2$) or sq. in.
square foot = ($ft.^2$) or sq. ft.
square yard = ($yd.^2$) or sq. yd.
square rod = ($rd.^2$) or sq. rd.
acre = ac. or A

### Volume

cubic inch = ($in.^3$) or cu. in.
cubic foot = ($ft.^3$) or cu. ft.
cubic yard = ($yd.^3$) or cu. yd.

### Weight

ounce = oz.
pound = lb.
short ton = sh. tn.
long ton = l. tn.

### Liquid

pint = pt.
quart = qt.
gallon = gal.

### Dry

pint = pt.
quart = qt.
peck = pk.
bushel = bu.

### Time

second = sec.
minute = min.
hour = hr.
day = da.
week = wk.
month = mo.
year = yr.

# Metric System

### Length

10 millimeters (mm) = 1 centimeter (cm)
10 centimeters = 1 decimeter (dm)
1000 meters = 1 kilometer (km)

### Weight (or Mass)

10 milligrams (mg) = 1 centigram (cg)
10 centigrams = 1 decigram (dg)
1000 grams = 1 kilogram (kg)

### Capacity

10 milliliters (ml) = 1 centiliter (cl)
10 centiliters = 1 deciliter (dl)
1000 liters = 1 kiloliter (kl)

# Formulas

| Description | | Formula |
|---|---|---|
| **AREA ($A$) of a:** | **square** | $A = s^2$, where $s$ = side |
| | **rectangle** | $A = lw$, where $l$ = length, $w$ = width |
| | **parallelogram** | $A = bh$, where $b$ = base, $h$ = height |
| | **triangle** | $A = \frac{1}{2}bh$, where $b$ = base, $h$ = height |
| | **circle** | $A = \pi r^2$, where $\pi$ = 3.14, $r$ = radius |
| **PERIMETER ($P$) of a:** | **square** | $P = 4s$, where $s$ = side |
| | **rectangle** | $P = 2l + 2w$, where $l$ = length, $w$ = width |
| | **triangle** | $P = a + b + c$, where $a$, $b$, and $c$ are the sides |
| | **circumference ($C$) of circle** | $C = \pi d$, where $\pi$ = 3.14, $d$ = diameter |
| **VOLUME ($V$) of a:** | **cube** | $V = s^3$, where $s$ = side |
| | **rectangular container** | $V = lwh$, where $l$ = length, $w$ = width, $h$ = height |
| | **cylinder** | $V = \pi r^2 h$, where $\pi$ = 3.14, $r$ = radius, $h$ = height |
| | **Pythagorean relationship** | $c^2 = a^2 + b^2$, where $c$ = hypotenuse, $a$ and $b$ are legs of right triangle |
| | **distance ($d$) between two points in a plane** | $d = \sqrt{(x_2 - x_1)^2 + (y_2 - y_1)^2}$, where $(x_1, y_1)$ and $(x_2, y_2)$ are two points in a plane |
| | **slope of a line ($m$)** | $m = \dfrac{y_2 - y_1}{x_2 - x_1}$, where $(x_1, y_1)$ and $(x_2, y_2)$ are two points in a plane |
| | **mean** | $= \dfrac{x_1 + x_2 + \ldots + x_n}{n}$, where the $x$'s are the values for which a mean is desired, and $n$ = number of values in the series |
| | **median** | = the point in an ordered set of numbers at which half the numbers are above and half the numbers are below this value |
| | **simple interest ($i$)** | $i = prt$, where $p$ = principal, $r$ = rate, $t$ = time |
| | **distance ($d$) as function of rate and time** | $d = rt$, where $r$ = rate, $t$ = time |
| | **total cost ($c$)** | $c = nr$, where $n$ = number of units, $r$ = cost per unit |

# CHAPTER 1
# Whole Numbers

Whole numbers are the foundation on which you build all your other mathematics skills. Mastering all the lessons in this chapter will make learning the other skills in this section quite a bit simpler.

## In this chapter you will learn to:

- Work with the number system and place value
- Add, subtract, multiply, and divide whole numbers
- Round whole numbers
- Use cost and distance formulas
- Find powers and square roots of whole numbers
- Find the perimeter and the area of plane figures
- Solve problems in item sets
- Write mathematical expressions in set-up solutions to problems
- Find the volume of solid figures
- Estimate
- Solve multistep problems

# Whole-Number Skills

## Preview

**Directions:** Solve each problem.

1. Identify the digit in the ten thousands place of 1,275,328.
2. Find the sum of 217, 1281, 323, and 89.
3. Find the difference between 2196 and 328.
4. Multiply 206 by 38.
5. Divide 1462 by 34.

Answers are on page A-33. If you have at least four answers correct, try the Chapter 1 Quiz on page 432. If you have fewer than four answers correct, study Level 1 beginning with Lesson 1.

## Our Number System

The number system we use is called a decimal system. It uses 10 different digits — 0, 1, 2, 3, 4, 5, 6, 7, 8, and 9. A digit is any number from 0 to 9. Each digit in a number has a value according to its **place** in the number. This value is called a **place value**. For instance, the digit 3 has the value of 30 in the number 32, but it has the value of 3 in the number 23. In other words, its value depends on its place in the number. In the number 32, 3 is in the tens place, so its value is 3 tens, or $3 \times 10$, or 30. In the ones place, its value is 3 ones, $3 \times 1$, or 3. At the top of page 404, look at the place value of the digits that make up the number 1,987,657,321.

## Place Values

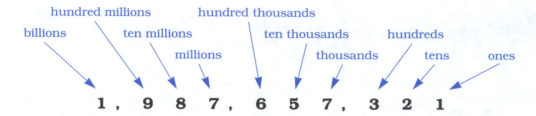

hundred millions

billions

ten millions

hundred thousands

ten thousands

hundreds

millions

thousands

tens

ones

**1 , 9 8 7 , 6 5 7 , 3 2 1**

Notice that 1 has the value of one billion in one place in the number and the value of 1 in another place. The number 7 has the value of 7 million in one place and 7 thousand in another place.

## Level 1, Lesson 1 Exercise

**Directions:** Name the place of the underlined digit.

1. 2̲47
2. 478̲0
3. 846̲
4. 675̲0
5. 6̲7,400

6. 1̲9,950
7. 44̲2
8. 7̲50,000
9. 4̲,846,500
10. 8̲,200,000,000

Answers are on page A-33.

## Lesson 2

# Addition of Whole Numbers

When you add, you combine numbers to find a **sum**, or total, of two or more numbers. Words that tell you to add in a problem are "and," "plus," and "altogether." For example: "How much is 4 and 6?" The addition or plus sign is +.

You can add numbers in any order: 4 + 6 is the same as 6 + 4. However, you must be careful to line up the numbers so that each digit is in the correct position for its place value.

## Level 1, Lesson 2 Exercise

**Directions:** Solve each problem.

1. Add 634, 13, and 8432.
2. Find the sum of 1589, 1420, and 1222.
3. Add: 195 + 6,708 + 21,213 + 45,931.

4. Find the sum of 252,189 and 12,745,923.
5. Add 1619, 8, and 419.

Answers are on page A-33.

# Subtraction of Whole Numbers

If you need to find how much more one number is than another, you subtract. The following words and phrases are used to indicate subtraction: difference; decrease; amount of increase; what's left or remains. A minus sign ( – ) is used to show a subtraction problem. In subtraction, unlike addition, you can subtract only two numbers at a time. When setting up a problem, always place the larger number on the top and make sure the digits in each column have the same place value.

Sometimes the digit in the top number in a column will be less than the digit in the bottom number. When this happens, you will need to borrow a unit from the next column to the left; this is the column with the next higher place value. Remember: When you borrow a unit it always has a value of 10. You add this 10 to the top digit so that you can subtract the bottom number from it.

**Example:** Subtract 7814 from 20,632.

**Step 1.** Because the 2 in the ones column is less than the 4, borrow 10 (1 ten) from the 3 in the tens column. This 3 in the tens column represents 30. The 2 becomes 12 (10 + 2) and the 3 becomes 2 (2 tens, or 20).

$$\begin{array}{r} {\scriptstyle 2\ 12} \\ 20,6\cancel{3}\cancel{2} \\ -\ 7,8\ 1\ 4 \\ \hline \end{array}$$

**Step 2.** Subtract 4 from 12 and write the answer in the ones column.

$$\begin{array}{r} {\scriptstyle 2\ 12} \\ 20,6\cancel{3}\cancel{2} \\ -\ 7,8\ 1\ 4 \\ \hline 8 \end{array}$$

**Step 3.** Repeat the process for each column, borrowing as needed.

$$\begin{array}{r} {\scriptstyle 1\ 10\quad 2\ 12} \\ \cancel{2}\ \cancel{0},6\ \cancel{3}\ \cancel{2} \\ -\ 7,8\ 1\ 4 \\ \hline 1\ 8 \end{array}$$

You can't subtract 8 from 6, so you look for the closest number to the left to borrow from. Since you cannot borrow from 0, the closest number you can borrow from is 2. You borrow 10 from 2: this changes the 2 to 1, and adds 10 to the 0, making it a 10.

**Step 4.** Borrow from this 10, changing it to 9 and adding the borrowed 10 to the 6, to make it 16. Now you can subtract the 8 from 16, and complete the problem.

$$\begin{array}{r} {\scriptstyle 1\ 9\ 16\ 2\ 12} \\ \cancel{2}\ \cancel{0},\cancel{6}\ \cancel{3}\ \cancel{2} \\ -\ 7,8\ 1\ 4 \\ \hline 1\ 2,8\ 1\ 8 \end{array}$$

## Level 1, Lesson 3 Exercise

**Directions:** Solve each problem. Set up correctly where needed.

1.  $\begin{array}{r} 852 \\ -361 \\ \hline \end{array}$

2.  $\begin{array}{r} 23,538 \\ -18,769 \\ \hline \end{array}$

3.  1059 – 328

4.  216 – 98

5.  Subtract 426 from 1005.

6.  How much is 8379 less than 13,328?

7.  Find the difference between 219 and 37.

Answers are on page A-33.

# Multiplication of Whole Numbers

Multiplication is a shortcut for addition. For example, if you wanted to add 4 + 4 + 4 + 4 + 4, you could multiply 5 × 4 instead of adding the five 4's. Words that indicate multiplication are "times" and "product." For example: "How much is 4 times 5?" or "Find the product of 4 × 5."

There are three ways to indicate multiplication: an ×, which is usually called "the multiplication sign," as in 4 × 5; a dot, as in 4 · 5; and parentheses, as in (4)(5). You can multiply numbers in any order: 4 × 5 = 5 × 4.

When you set up a multiplication problem, place the larger number on top. Using the digit in the ones column of the bottom number, multiply the top number starting with the digits in the ones column. Repeat for each column, working from right to left. Sometimes, you will have to carry as in addition.

**Example:** Multiply 835 by 4: 835 × 4.

$$\begin{array}{r} {\scriptstyle 1\,2} \\ 835 \\ \times \;\; 4 \\ \hline 3,340 \end{array}$$

When you multiply a multi-digit number by another multi-digit number, you multiply the top number by each digit in the bottom number. You start with the digit in the ones place and move right to left, column by column. You write your answer in the same column as the digit you are using to multiply. In multiplication, it is important to keep the digits with the same place value in the same column. When you have multiplied the top number by all digits in the bottom number, add the numbers together.

**Example:** Multiply 835 by 234: 835 × 234.

$$\begin{array}{r} 835 \\ \times \; 234 \\ \hline 3340 \\ 2505 \;\; \\ 1670 \;\;\; \\ \hline 195,390 \end{array}$$

## Level 1, Lesson 4 Exercise

**Directions:** Find each product. Be sure to set up the problems correctly where needed.

1. $\begin{array}{r} 53 \\ \times 4 \\ \hline \end{array}$

2. $\begin{array}{r} 321 \\ \times 44 \\ \hline \end{array}$

3. 140 · 2

4. 532 × 108

5. (79)(604)

6. (45)(397)

7. Multiply 3028 by 16.

8. What is the product of 163 times 129?

Answers are on page A-33.

When you need to find how many groups of one number are in another, you use division. For example, if you want to find how many groups of 2 are in 10, you divide 10 by 2. You can write this problem three different ways with math symbols: $10 \div 2$; $2\overline{)10}$; $\frac{10}{2}$. You read each of these as 10 divided by 2 or 2 divided into 10.

You can think of division as the opposite of multiplication. The number you use to divide is called the **divisor**. The number you are dividing is called the **dividend**. The answer is called the **quotient**.

$$\text{divisor} \quad 2\overline{)10}^{\;5\;\text{quotient}}_{\quad\text{dividend}}$$

**Example:** What is 234 divided by 6? (*or* what is $234 \div 6$?)

$$6\overline{)234}^{\;3}$$

**Step 1.** Estimate how many times the divisor (6) will go into the left-most digit of the dividend (2). Here, you can ask yourself how many 6's are in 2. The answer is none, so look at 23. Ask: how many 6's are there in 23? You know that $6 \times 3 = 18$ and $6 \times 4 = 24$. So $6 \times 4$ is too much. Enter the 3 on the answer line above the 3.

**Step 2.** Multiply the divisor times the quotient from the first division: $6 \times 3 = 18$. Write that answer under the part of the dividend you divided, and then subtract. Your answer is 5.

$$\begin{array}{r} 3 \\ 6\overline{)234} \\ -18 \\ \hline 5 \end{array}$$

**Step 3.** Bring down the next digit. Here the 4 comes down to make 54. Take your divisor into the new number. You know that 6 will divide evenly, 9 times, into 54 because $6 \times 9 = 54$. $54 \div 6 = 9$. Write the answer on the answer line, and multiply and subtract as you did above.

$$\begin{array}{r} 39 \\ 6\overline{)234} \\ -18 \\ \hline 54 \\ 54 \\ \hline 0 \end{array}$$

When you divide into every part of the dividend evenly in this way, you have nothing left over except 0. If your division does not come out evenly, it leaves a final number that is too small to divide into. This final leftover number is called a **remainder**. (You also can write your answer as 3 r 1.)

$$\begin{array}{r} 3, \text{ remainder } 1 \\ 3\overline{)10} \\ -9 \\ \hline 1 \end{array}$$

*Note:* Sometimes you cannot divide into a digit in the dividend because it is smaller than the divisor. You need to put a zero in the quotient and bring down the next digit of the dividend.

$$\begin{array}{r} 4 \\ 6\overline{)2412} \\ 24 \\ \hline 01 \end{array}$$

6 will not divide into 1.
Bring down 2 and divide.

$$\begin{array}{r} 402 \\ 6\overline{)2412} \\ 24 \\ \hline 12 \\ 12 \\ \hline \end{array}$$

# Dividing by a Two-Digit Number

Often on the GED test you will need to divide by a two-digit number. The process is the same as for a one-digit number. However, you need to estimate how many times your divisor will go into your dividend. To do this, you use only part of the divisor and part of the dividend.

**Example:** How many times does 72 go into 3247?

Step 1. Set up the problem.

$$72 \overline{)3247}$$

Step 2. We know that 72 will not go into 32, so ask yourself: How many times will 72 go into 324? Since you have not memorized the multiplication tables for 72, you will estimate. Think: How many times does 7 go into 32? $7 \times 4 = 28$. $7 \times 5 = 35$. Since 35 is larger than 32, we use 4. Write the 4 on the answer line in the proper place and multiply it by 72. $72 \times 4 = 288$. Write the number below the 324 and subtract. $324 - 288 = 36$.

$$72 \overline{)\begin{array}{r} 4 \\ 3247 \\ -288 \\ \hline 36 \end{array}}$$

Step 3. Bring the next digit down and divide again.

$$72 \overline{)\begin{array}{r} 4 \\ 3247 \\ -288 \\ \hline 367 \end{array}}$$

Think $7 \overline{)36} = ?$. $7 \times 5 = 35$. Use 5 for your estimate. Write the 5 on the answer line in the proper place and multiply it by 72: $72 \times 5 = 360$. Write the number below the 367 and subtract: $367 - 360 = 7$.

$$72 \overline{)\begin{array}{r} 45 \\ 3247 \\ -288 \\ \hline 367 \\ 360 \\ \hline 7 \end{array}}$$

Therefore, your answer is 45 r 7, or $45 \frac{7}{72}$.

When you are working with larger dividends, you bring down the next digit after each dividing, multiplying, and subtracting step until you have used all the digits.

Remember, you can check your work by multiplying.

## Level 1, Lesson 5 Exercise

**Directions:** Solve each problem. Set up correctly when necessary.

1. $20 \overline{)460}$

2. $8 \overline{)6992}$

3. $5 \overline{)32,945}$

4. $24 \overline{)3504}$

5. $85 \overline{)52,445}$

6. Divide 7084 by 36.

7. What is 19,584 divided by 204?

8. How many times does 196 go into 5096?

Answers are on pages A-33 and A-34.

# Whole Number Applications

**Level 2**

## Lesson 1

### Rounding Off

Sometimes you don't need to know the exact amount of something. Instead you are asked *about* or *approximately* how many, or how much, of something. For example, you might be asked about how many people live in your town. Instead of saying 52,825 people live there, you might round off to the nearest ten thousand and say about 50,000.

To round off a number, find the digit in the place to which you will round. Look at the digit to the right. If the digit to the right is 5 or greater, increase the digit in the place to which you will round by 1. If the digit to the right is 4 or less, leave the digit in the place to which you will round the same. Change each digit to the right of the digit to which you will round off to 0.

**Example 1:**  Round off 12,634 to the nearest ten.

| | |
|---|---|
| Step 1.  Find the digit in the place to which you will round. Here the 3 is in the tens place. | 12,6<u>3</u>4 |
| Step 2.  Look at the digit to the right of the 3. It is 4, so the 3 will be left the same. | 12,6<u>3</u>4 |
| Step 3.  Change the digit to the right of 3 to 0. The answer is 12,630. | 12,63<u>0</u> |

**Example 2:**  Round 14,785 to the nearest hundred.

| | |
|---|---|
| Step 1.  Find the digit in the place to which you will round. Here the 7 is in the hundreds place. | 14,<u>7</u>85 |
| Step 2.  Look at the digit to the right of the 7. It is 8, so the 7 must be increased by one. | 14,<u>7</u>85 |
| Step 3.  Change the 7 to 8 and change each digit to the right of it to 0. The answer is 14,800. | 14,<u>8</u>00 |

If the digit in the place to which you will round is 9 and it needs to be increased by one, you will need to change that digit to 0 and increase the digit to its left by one.

**Example 3:** Round 129,601 to the nearest thousand.

Step 1. Find the digit in the place to which you will round. Here the 9 is in the thousands place.    129,601

Step 2. Look at the digit to the right of the 9. It is 6, so the 9 must be increased by 1.    129,601

Step 3. Change the 9 to 10 and carry the 1 to the 2, which then becomes 3 (29 + 1 = 30). Change each digit to the right of the thousands place to 0. The answer is 130,000.    130,000

## Level 2, Lesson 1 Exercise

**Directions:** Round each number to the place indicated

1. 263 to the nearest ten
2. 1849 to the nearest hundred
3. 13,255 to the nearest hundred
4. 116,886 to the nearest ten thousand
5. 47,908 to the nearest hundred

6. 15,980 to the nearest hundred
7. 367,854 to the nearest hundred thousand
8. 89,928 to the nearest thousand
9. 89,982 to the nearest hundred
10. 1,543,229 to the nearest million

Answers are on page A-34.

# Lesson 2

# Distance and Cost Formulas

A formula gives the directions to find a certain result. It is like a recipe. The GED requires you to use a number of formulas. These formulas are printed on page 401. The first page of the GED math exam contains a formula sheet.

## Distance Formula

The distance formula is used to determine how far something travels. You must know the rate or speed and the amount of time. Multiplying these amounts will give you the distance.

The formula is written as:

$$d = rt$$

In this formula $d$ = distance, $r$ = rate, and $t$ = time. Two symbols next to each other in a formula mean you should multiply them together. The **rt** means you multiply the rate by the time.

**Example 1:** John drove 55 miles per hour for 6 hours. How many miles did he travel?

Step 1.  Put the values for the rate and time into the formula.

$d = rt$
$d = 55 \times 6$

Step 2.  *To find the distance:* Multiply.

$d = 55 \times 6 = 330.$

John traveled 330 miles.

If you know the distance traveled and either the rate or the time, you can find the missing amount by dividing the distance by the amount you know.

**Example 2:** Carol bicycled 36 miles in 4 hours. How many miles per hour did she travel?

Step 1.  Put the values into the formula.

$d = rt$
$36 = r \times 4$

Step 2.  *To find the value of* $r$: Since $36 = 4 \times r$, then $\frac{36}{4} = r$.

$4\overline{)36} = r$

Therefore $r = 9$ (Carol bicycled at 9 miles per hour).

$$\frac{9=r}{4\overline{)36}}$$
$$\underline{-36}$$

**Example 3:** Carol bicycled 36 miles at 9 miles per hour. How long did it take her to travel this distance?

Step 1.  Put the values into the formula.

$d = rt$
$36 = 9 \times t$

Step 2.  *To find the value of* $t$: Since $36 = 9 \times t$, then $\frac{7}{72} = t$.

$\frac{36}{9} = t$

$9\overline{)36} = t$

Therefore $t = 4$ (Carol took 4 hours to travel 36 miles).

$$\frac{4=t}{9\overline{)36}}$$
$$\underline{-36}$$

## Cost Formula

The cost formula is similar to the distance formula. To find the total cost of a number of units of similar items, multiply the number of units by the rate or cost for one unit.
The formula is written as:

$c = nr$

In this formula $c$ = total cost, $n$ = number of units, and $r$ = rate or cost per unit.

**Example 1:** A six-pack of soda costs $2. What is the total cost of 4 six-packs?

Step 1. Put the values for the number of units and the rate into the formula.

$$c = nr$$
$$c = 4 \times 2$$

Step 2. Multiply.

$$c = 8$$

The total cost of 4 six-packs is $8.

**Example 2:** If 4 six-packs cost $8, how much does one six-pack cost?

Step 1. Put the values into the formula.

$$c = nr$$
$$8 = 4 \times r$$

Step 2. *To find the value of* r : Since $8 = 4 \times r$, then $8 \div 4 = r$.

$$4\overline{)8} = r$$

Therefore $r = \$2$ (the cost per six-pack).

$$\begin{array}{r} 2 = r \\ 4\overline{)8} \\ 8 \end{array}$$

**Example 3:** If you spent $8 on soda and each six-pack cost $2, how many six-packs did you buy?

Step 1. Put the values into the formula.

$$c = nr$$
$$8 = n \times 2$$

Step 2. *To find the value of* n : Since $8 = n \times 2$, $8 \div 2 = n$.

$$2\overline{)8} = n$$

Therefore $n = 4$ (the number of six-packs).

$$\begin{array}{r} 4 = n \\ 2\overline{)8} \\ 8 \end{array}$$

## Level 2, Lesson 2 Exercise

**Directions:** Use the distance or cost formula to solve each problem. Depending on which amounts you are given, remember to multiply or divide.

1. Stephen jogs 6 miles per hour for 15 hours each week. What is the total number of miles he jogs?
2. If cherries cost $2 per pound, how much will 28 pounds cost?
3. George drove 570 miles in 6 days. How many miles did he drive per day?
4. Peter paid $21 for some pepperoni. If a pound of pepperoni costs $3, how many pounds did Peter purchase?
5. Jane paid $1000 for 40 tires. What did each tire cost?
6. Craig rode his bicycle 108 miles in 12 hours. At what rate, in miles per hour, did he ride?

Answers are on page A-34.

# Powers and Roots

Some formulas used to find measurements require the use of powers and roots. You will be working with these formulas in later parts of the mathematics unit.

## Powers

Powers or exponents are used to note how many times a number is multiplied by itself. For example, the three in $2^3$ tells you how many times to multiply 2 by itself.

$2^3 = 2 \times 2 \times 2 = 8$ (Think: $2 \times 2 = 4$; then $4 \times 2 = 8$).

$6^4 = 6 \times 6 \times 6 \times 6 = 1296$ (Think: $6 \times 6 = 36$; then $36 \times 6 = 216$; then $216 \times 6 = 1296$).

When the exponent is 2, you can say the number is *squared* or it is raised to the second power. When the exponent is 3, you can say the number is *cubed* or it is raised to the third power. When the exponent is 4 or greater, you say it is raised to that power. For example: $6^4$ is read as six raised to the fourth power; $4^5$ is read as four raised to the fifth power.

## Roots

You know that 5 squared is 25 ($5 \times 5 = 25$). Another way to say this is to say that 5 is the square root of 25. When you find the square root of a number, you find the number that is multiplied by itself to give you the original number. The sign for a square root is $\sqrt{\phantom{x}}$.

**Example 1:** Find the value of $\sqrt{49}$.

Step 1. Ask: What number times itself equals 49?

Step 2. Since $7 \times 7 = 49$, the square root of 49 is 7.     $\sqrt{49} = 7$

Keep in mind that although any number can be squared, not all numbers have an exact square root. For example, $2 \times 2 = 4$; but $\sqrt{2}$ cannot be determined exactly.

On the GED test, when you need to find the square root of a larger number, you can use a trial-and-error method.

**Example 2:** Find the square root of 169.

| | |
|---|---|
| Step 1. Estimate what number times itself might equal 169. This tells you that the square root of 169 is between 10 and 20. Try 15. | $10^2 = 100. \quad 20^2 = 400.$ <br><br> $15 \times 15 = 225.$ |
| Step 2. You now know the square root of 169 is between 10 and 15. Try 13. | $13 \times 13 = 169$ <br> $169 = 13^2$ |

**Directions:** For problems 1 to 7, find the value of each expression.

1. $8^2$      3. $7^3$      5. $3^4$      7. $\sqrt{64}$

2. $30^2$      4. $10^3$      6. $\sqrt{36}$

8. The square root of 23 is between which of the following pairs of numbers?

   (1) 1.2 and 2.3      (4) 5 and 6
   (2) 3 and 4          (5) 10 and 12
   (3) 4 and 5

9. The square root of 375 is between which of the following pairs of numbers?

   (1) 14 and 15      (4) 18 and 19
   (2) 15 and 16      (5) 19 and 20
   (3) 16 and 17

Answers are on page A-34.

# Lesson 4

# Perimeter and Area of Polygons

A polygon is a many-sided closed figure ("poly" means "many"). Three polygons with which you should be familiar are the rectangle, square, and triangle. Two helpful measurements of these polygons are **perimeter** and **area**. Formulas for these measurements are found on the formula page and in the examples below.

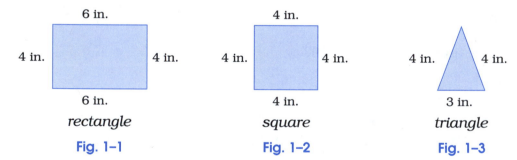

rectangle          square          triangle

Fig. 1–1          Fig. 1–2          Fig. 1–3

## Perimeter

The perimeter is the distance around a plane or flat figure. It is the total of the measurements of all the sides. If, for example, you wanted to fence a yard, you would need to know the perimeter of the yard in order to know how much fencing you would need. You would also need to know the perimeter of a photograph if you wanted to frame it. You can use a formula for finding the perimeter of a rectangle, a square, or a triangle.

**Example 1:** Find the perimeter of the rectangle in Figure 1–1.

Step 1. The formula for finding the perimeter of a rectangle is:

$P = 2l + 2w$ (where $P$ = perimeter, $l$ = length, and $w$ = width)

Set the problem up, substituting the measurement of the length, 6, for $l$, and the measurement of the width, 4, for $w$.

$P = 2l + 2w$
$P = (2 \times 6) + (2 \times 4)$

Step 2. Multiply.

$P = 12 + 8$

Step 3. Add the products.

$P = 20$

The perimeter of the rectangle is 20 inches.

**Example 2:** Find the perimeter of the square in Figure 1–2.

Step 1. The formula for finding the perimeter of a square is:

$P = 4s$ (where $s$ = the measurement of each side)

Set the problem up, substituting the measurement of each side, 4, for $s$.

$P = 4s$
$P = 4 \times 4$

Step 2. Multiply.

$P = 16$

The perimeter of the square is 16 inches.

**Example 3:** Find the perimeter of the triangle in Figure 1–3.

Step 1. The formula for finding the perimeter of a triangle is:

$P = a + b + c$ (where $a$, $b$, and $c$ = the measurements of the sides)

Set the problem up, substituting the measurements of the sides for $a$, $b$, and $c$.

$P = a + b + c$
$P = 4 + 4 + 3$

Step 2. Add the numbers.

$P = 11$

The perimeter of the triangle is 11 inches.

## Area

Area is the measurement of the space within a plane figure. If, for example, you wanted to carpet a room, you would need to know its area in order to know how much carpet you would need. Or, if you wanted to plant grass, you would need to know the area of the land needing seeds. Area is measured in square units, such as square inches, square feet, and square yards. The square unit you use for an area is determined by the units used to measure the sides of the figure. For example, if the sides are measured in yards, the area will be measured in square yards. Formulas are used for finding the area of rectangles, squares, and triangles.

**Example 1:** Find the area of the rectangle in Figure 1–1.

Step 1. The formula for finding the area of a rectangle is:

$A = lw$  (where $l$ = length and $w$ = width)

Set the problem up, substituting the measurements   $A = lw$
for the length and width for $l$ and $w$.                          $A = 4$ inches × 6 inches

Step 2. Multiply.                                                        $A = 24$ square inches

The area of the rectangle is 24 square inches, or 24 in.$^2$

**Example 2:** Find the area of the square in Figure 1–2.

Step 1. The formula for the area of a square is:

$A = s^2$  (where $s$ = the measurement of each side)

Set the problem up, substituting the measurement of    $A = s^2$
the side for $s$.                                                            $A = 4^2$

Step 2. Multiply.                                                        $A = 4 \times 4$
                                                                                $A = 16$ square inches

The area of the square is 16 square inches, or 16 in.$^2$

The formula to find the area of a triangle is:

$A = \frac{1}{2}bh$  (where $b$ = the measurement of the base and $h$ = the measurement of the height of the triangle; the height is measured in a straight line from the top of the triangle perpendicular to the base)

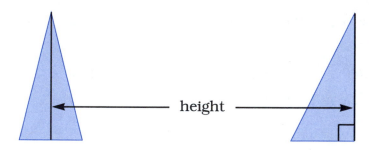

height

Fig. 1–4

The height of a triangle will not always be the same as that of a side. When it is not, you will be told the height. The formula indicates that you should multiply by $\frac{1}{2}$. That is the same as dividing by 2:

$10 \times \frac{1}{2} = 5$  *or*  $10 \div 2 = 5$

Therefore, the easiest way to use the formula is to first multiply the base times the height and then divide your answer by 2.

**Example 3:** Find the area of a triangle that has a base of 3 inches and a height of 6 inches.

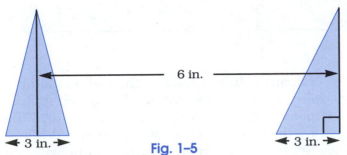

**Fig. 1–5**

Step 1. Set the problem up, substituting the measurements of the base and height for *b* and *h*.

$A = \frac{1}{2}bh$

$A = \frac{1}{2}(3 \times 6)$

Step 2. Multiply $3 \times 6$.

$A = \frac{1}{2}(18)$

Step 3. Divide the product by 2.

$2\overline{\smash{)}18}$ with quotient $9$

The area of the triangle is 9 square inches.

## Level 2, Lesson 4 Exercise

1. Find the perimeter and area of each polygon.

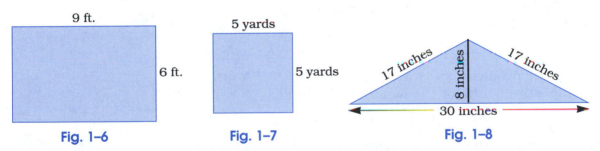

9 ft.    6 ft.    **Fig. 1–6**

5 yards    5 yards    **Fig. 1–7**

17 inches    8 inches    17 inches    30 inches    **Fig. 1–8**

*Directions for problems 2 to 6:* Decide which formula to use and solve each problem. Be sure to express your answers in the correct measurements.

2. David wants to fence his square backyard. If each side of the yard measures 45 feet, how many feet of fencing will he need?

3. Jonathan has to frame a rectangular picture. If the frame will measure 36 inches by 12 inches, assuming no waste, how many inches of framing will he need?

4. Find the perimeter of a triangular highway sign whose sides measure 5 feet, 6 feet, and 5 feet.

5. Cindy's rectangular living room measures 16 feet by 12 feet. What is the area of the room?

6. Pietro wants to cover a triangular plot of ground with sod. If its base is 20 feet and the height is 18 feet, how many square feet of sod does Pietro need?

Answers are on page A-34.

Volume is the measurement of space within a solid or three-dimensional figure, such as a cube. The volume of a milk container will be how much milk it can hold, for example. Volume is measured in cubic units. The cubic unit that you use for volume is determined by the units used to measure the sides of the figure. For example, if the sides are measured in yards, the volume will be measured in cubic yards. The volume formulas are given on the formula sheet. In this lesson, you will be finding volumes of rectangular containers and cubes. You will be working with the volume of cylinders in a later lesson.

To find the volume of a rectangular container or a cube, which is a rectangular container with equal sides, you multiply the length ($l$) by the width ($w$) and the height ($h$). This is written in formula form as:

$V = lwh$

Fig. 1–9

For a cube you may write the formula as:

$V = s^3$ (where $s$ = the measure of a side)

*cube*

Of course, the formula $V = lwh$ will work to find the volume of a cube as well.

**Example 1:**  Find the volume of the rectangular container in Figure 1–10.

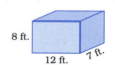

Fig. 1–10

8 ft.    12 ft.    7 ft.

Step 1. Set up the problem, substituting in the formula the measurements for the length, width, and height.

$V = lwh$
$V = 12 \times 7 \times 8$

Step 2. Multiply two of the measurements.

$12 \times 7 = 84$
$V = 84 \times 8$

Step 3. Multiply the product of the first two measurements by the third.

$84 \times 8 = 672$

The volume of the rectangular container is 672 cubic feet.

**Example 2:**  Find the volume of the cube in Figure 1–11.

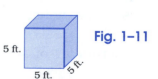

Fig. 1–11

5 ft.    5 ft.    5 ft.

Step 1. Set the problem up, substituting in the formula the side measurement for $s$.

$V = s^3$
$V = 5^3$

Step 2. Find the value of $5^3$.

$5 \times 5 = 25$
$25 \times 5 = 125$

The volume of the cube is 125 cubic inches.

**Directions:** Find the volume of the solids. Be sure to express your answers in cubic measurements.

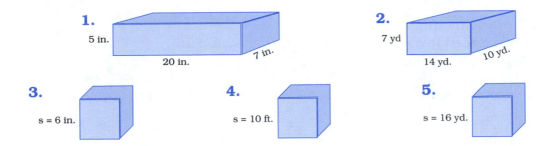

1. 5 in. 20 in. 7 in.

2. 7 yd 14 yd. 10 yd.

3. s = 6 in.

4. s = 10 ft.

5. s = 16 yd.

Answers are on page A-34.

## Lesson 6 — Mean and Median

To find the **mean**, or average, add up all the numbers in a series and divide by the total number of numbers you have. For example, the mean temperature for a week in Arizona is 86° if you divide the total of these daily temperatures by 7:

110°, 90°, 82°, 95°, 75°, 70°, 80°

On the other hand, the **median** shows the middle value of a series of numbers when the numbers are ordered from lowest to highest:

70°, 75°, 80°, <u>82°</u>, 90°, 95°, 110°

The median temperature for that week would be 82°.

Notice that the mean (average) and median here are not the same, even though the numbers used are identical.

## Finding the Mean

To find the mean (average) of a group of numbers, add the numbers together and divide the sum by the amount of numbers you added.

**Example 1:** Henry received the following scores on his GED test:

| *Subject* | *Score* |
|---|---|
| writing | 45 |
| social studies | 50 |
| science | 40 |
| literature | 47 |
| math | 43 |

What was his average score?

Step 1. Add the scores for the five tests.
The sum is 225.

$$\begin{array}{r} 45 \\ 50 \\ 40 \\ 47 \\ +\ 43 \\ \hline 225 \end{array}$$

Step 2. Count how many numbers you added together. Since you added five numbers, divide the sum of the numbers, 225, by 5.

$$5\overline{)225}^{\,45}$$

Henry's average score was 45.

## Finding the Median

To find a median, arrange the numbers from lowest to highest and locate the middle number. That is the median.

**Example 2:** Janet received the following scores on her GED test:

| Subject | Score |
|---|---|
| writing | 41 |
| social studies | 52 |
| science | 50 |
| literature | 37 |
| math | 45 |

Find her median test score.

Step 1. Arrange Janet's scores in order from lowest to highest.

37  41  45  50  52

Step 2. The score that is halfway between the two ends or has the same place when you count from both ends is the median. In this example, 45 is the third lowest score and the third highest score. It is the median.

37  41  <u>45</u>  50  52

*Note:* The mean score and the median score will not always be the same value. If you add all of Janet's scores and divide the sum by the number of scores, 5, you get 45. However, if her scores were, for instance, 25, 30, 45, 50, 60, the mean would be $210 \div 5 = 42$.

To find the median when you have an even number of values (for example: 11, 14, 15, 17, 19, and 21), simply find the average of the two middle values. To find the middle values, count the same number of places from each end of the series of numbers. 15 is the third from the lowest end, 17 is the third from the highest end, so they are the middle values.

$$\begin{array}{r} 15 \\ +\ 17 \\ \hline 32 \end{array} \qquad 2\overline{)32}^{\,16}$$

The median of this series of numbers is 16.

1. Find the mean of these numbers: 43, 42, 30, 50, 55.

2. Find the average of these numbers: 123, 421, 278.

3. Suzanne is a saleswoman and works on commission. On Monday, she earned $58; on Tuesday, she earned $62; on Wednesday, she earned $63; and on Thursday, she earned $33. What were her average daily earnings?

4. Arlene has been dieting for the past three months. The first month she lost 9 pounds, the second month, 10 pounds, and the third month, 8 pounds. What was her average monthly weight loss?

5. The members of the Johnson family have the following heights: 6 feet 1 inch; 5 feet 6 inches; 5 feet 9 inches; 5 feet 4 inches; and 5 feet 1 inch. What is the median height of the Johnson family?

Answers are on pages A-34 and A-35.

# Whole-Number Problem Solving

## Setup Answers: Order of Operations

Often on the GED you will not have to solve a word problem—you will only have to decide the proper way to solve it by showing how to set it up or write the expression for its solution.

To show a multistep setup you sometimes need to use parentheses.

**Example 1:** John and Lisa earn $255 and $325 per week. Which of the following expressions shows their combined annual income?

(1) $12(255 \times 325)$

(2) $52(255 + 325)$

(3) $\dfrac{(255 + 325)}{12}$

(4) $\dfrac{(255 + 325)}{52}$

(5) $\dfrac{(255 \times 325)}{52}$

Step 1. You add to find their combined weekly incomes.                    $255 + 325$

Step 2. To find the combined annual income, you multiply by 52, the number of weeks in a year.                    $52(255 + 325)$

To set up a multistep problem correctly, or recognize the correct expression for it, you need to know the correct **order of operations**.

First: Do all operations inside parentheses.

Second: Do all powers and square roots (if there are powers and square roots in the set-up).

Third: Do all multiplying and dividing.

Fourth: Do all adding and subtracting from left to right.

*Note:* To help memorize the order of operations, think of the phrase, "Please, Sir, Excuse My Dear Aunt Sally": parentheses, square roots, exponents, multiplication, division, addition, subtraction.

**Example 2:** Which of the following expressions represents the total combined area of the porch and yard minus the area of the walk?

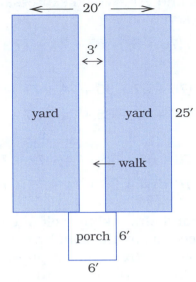

**(1)**  $6 + 6 \times 25 \times 20 - 3$

**(2)**  $6^2 + (25 \times 20) - (25 \times 3)$

**(3)**  $\dfrac{6^2 (20 \times 25)}{(25 \times 3)}$

**(4)**  $(6 + 6) + 25^2 - (3 \times 25)$

**(5)**  $6^2 + 25^2 + 20^2 - (25 \times 3)$

The correct answer is **(2)**. To find the correct expression, apply each formula for area.

Since the sides of the porch are equal, it is a square. The formula for the area of a square is $A = s^2$.      $A \text{ (porch)} = 6^2$

The yard and the walk are rectangles. The formula    $A \text{ (yard)} = 25 \times 20$
for the area of a rectangle is $A = lw$.      $A \text{ (walk)} = 25 \times 3$

The correct expression therefore is the following:     $6^2 + (25 \times 20) - (25 \times 3)$

To solve the problem, you would follow the order of operations:

<u>First:</u>  Do all operations inside parentheses.     $6^2 + (500) - (75)$

<u>Second:</u>  Do all powers and roots.     $36 + (500) - (75)$

<u>Third:</u>  Do all multiplying and dividing.     (there is none to do)

<u>Fourth:</u>  Do all adding and subtracting.     $536 - 75 = 461$ sq. ft.

## Level 3, Lesson 1 Exercise

**Directions:**  Select or write the proper expression for the following problems.

1.  Eric earns $145 and $85 weekly at his two part-time jobs. Which expression represents his annual income?

    **(1)**  $52(145 \times 85)$          **(4)**  $52(145 + 85)$

    **(2)**  $52 \times 145 \times 85$       **(5)**  $\dfrac{52(145 + 85)}{12}$

    **(3)**  $\dfrac{(145 + 85)}{52}$

**2.** The high temperatures for seven days in May were 76°, 67°, 65°, 74°, 77°, 75°, and 70°. Which expression shows the average or mean temperature for the seven days?

(1) $7(76 + 67 + 65 + 74 + 77 + 75 + 70)$

(2) $\dfrac{7}{(76 + 67 + 65 + 74 + 77 + 75 + 70)}$

(3) $\dfrac{(76 + 67 + 65 + 74 + 77 + 75 + 70)}{7}$

(4) $76 + 67 + 65 + 74 + 77 + 75 + 70 - 7$

(5) $76 + 67 + 65 + 74 + 77 + 75 + 70 \times 7$

**3.** Mr. and Mrs. Akbar took out a loan for a new car that costs $8600. They agreed to pay the loan by making 48 payments of $252 each. Which of the following expressions represents how much more than the price of the car the Akbars will pay for the loan?

(1) $48 \times 252 \times 8600$

(2) $48(252) - 8600$

(3) $\dfrac{8600 - (48 \times 252)}{12}$

(4) $(48 + 252) - 8600$

(5) $\dfrac{(48 \times 252)}{8600}$

**4.** A rectangular container which measures 3 feet long, 2 feet wide, and 4 feet high is half full. Which of the following expressions represents the volume (in cubic units) of the contents of the container?

(1) $\dfrac{(3 \times 2 \times 4)}{3}$

(2) $\dfrac{(3 \times 2 \times 4)}{2}$

(3) $2(3 + 2 + 4)$

(4) $3(3 \times 2 \times 4)$

(5) $\frac{1}{2}(3 + 2 + 4)$

**5.** The measure of each window in Joanne's house is 2 yards by 3 yards. The fabric she wants for window shades costs $4 per square yard. Which of the following expressions represents how much it will cost to make window shades for 12 windows?

(1) $4(2 + 3) \times 12$

(2) $\dfrac{12(2 \times 3)}{4}$

(3) $4(2 \times 3) \times 12$

(4) $2 + 3(4 \times 12)$

(5) $12(4 + 6)$

Answers are on page A-35.

To solve many of the problems on the GED test, you must use two or more operations. When you have such a problem: (1) identify the question you are being asked; (2) identify the information given to you; (3) identify the information you need; (4) decide what operations you will need to use; and (5) perform the operations in the correct order.

**Example 1:** Mary bought a compact disc for $9 and a cassette for $8. She paid for her purchase with a $20 bill. How much change did she receive?

Step 1. Identify the question you need to answer:
How much change did she receive?

Step 2. What information do you have? The cost of the disc ($9), the cassette ($8), and the amount she gave the clerk ($20).

Step 3. What information do you need to answer it? The total cost of her purchases and the amount with which she paid for it. (You know she paid $9 and $8 for her purchases and she paid for them with a $20 bill.)

Step 4. What operations will you need to perform to answer the question?

To find the total cost of her purchases, you add the cost of the two purchases.

$$\begin{array}{r} \$\ 9 \text{ compact disc} \\ +\quad 8 \text{ cassette} \\ \hline \$17 \end{array}$$

To find the change she received, you subtract to find the difference between the total cost and the amount of the bill she used to pay for the purchases.

$$\begin{array}{r} \$20 \text{ (amount of the bill)} \\ -\ \$17 \text{ (cost of purchases)} \\ \hline \$\ 3 \text{ (change)} \end{array}$$

**Example 2:** Find the area of the shaded portion of Figure 1–13.

Step 1. You must find the area of the outer, shaded portion of the figure.

Step 2. You know each side of the larger square measures 12 feet and each side of the smaller square measures 6 feet.

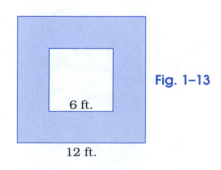

Fig. 1–13

6 ft.

12 ft.

Step 3. You need to know the area of each square and the difference between the two areas.

<u>Step 4.</u> You will have to find the areas and subtract to get the difference.

<u>Step 5.</u> Perform the operations.

*Larger square:*
$A = s^2$
$A = 12^2$
$A = 144$ square feet.

*Smaller square:*
$A = s^2$
$A = 6^2$
$A = 36$ square feet.

<u>Step 6.</u> Find the difference.

$$\begin{array}{r} 144 \text{ square feet} \\ - \ 36 \text{ square feet} \\ \hline 108 \text{ square feet} \end{array}$$

## Level 3, Lesson 2 Exercise

**Directions:** Solve each problem.

1. Dale bought items that cost $18, $9, and $7. How much change did he receive if he paid for them with a $50 bill?

2. Darlene earns $16,500 per year. Her employer deducts $2,100 per year for income and social security taxes. How much money does she have for other expenses each month? (What is her net monthly income?)

3. A community theater group presented a play, which cost it $480 to put on. If 300 people paid $4 each to attend it, how much money did the group make on its production?

4. Vance had $435 with him. He went to a feed store and bought 6 bags of feed costing $18 each. How much money did Vance have left?

5. Barbara is saving for a vacation trip that will cost $1344. She saves $28 a week. After saving for 32 weeks, how many more weeks will she need to save?

**Directions:** Find the area of the shaded part of each figure.

6.

4 yd.

13 yd.

12 yd.

28 yd.

7.

9 ft.

9 ft.

4 ft.

6 ft.

**8.**

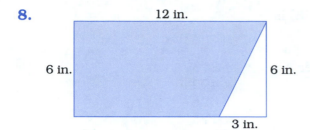

12 in.

6 in.        6 in.

3 in.

Answers are on page A-35.

## Lesson 3

## Estimating

Estimating is used when you don't need the exact amount for the answer to a problem. If you come across a question asking you "about how much" or "approximately how much" of something, you can estimate. Rounding numbers is a type of estimating.

**Example 1:** A park measures 813 feet by 492 feet. About how many square feet does it measure?

(1)  30,000
(2)  40,000
(3)  300,000
(4)  400,000
(5)  500,000

Step 1.  Round the numbers to the nearest hundred.          813 rounds to 800
                                                            492 rounds to 500

Step 2.  Multiply the rounded numbers.                          800
                                                              × 500
                                                            ─────────
                                                            400,000

The correct answer is **(4)**.

All the questions on the GED are multiple choice. While most ask for the exact answer, estimating can give you an idea of what the answer should be.

**Example 2:** A park measures 813 feet by 492 feet. How many square feet does it measure?

(1)  39,462
(2)  49,966
(3)  399,996
(4)  496,697
(5)  523,640

Step 1. Estimating as you did in the answer above tells you the answer should be about 400,000.

**Step 2.** Look over your answer choices. Answer **(3)** is closest to 400,000.

**Step 3.** Multiply to see if **(3)** is the correct answer.

The answer is 399,996 square feet, answer **(3)**.

$$\begin{array}{r} 813 \\ \times\,492 \\ \hline 1626 \\ 7317\phantom{0} \\ 3252\phantom{00} \\ \hline 399996 \end{array}$$

## Level 3, Lesson 3 Exercise

**Directions:** Estimate to solve each problem to the nearest round number.

1. A plane can carry 398 passengers. About how many passengers can 22 planes carry altogether?

2. On the New York Stock Exchange, 87,340 shares of a certain stock were traded by 982 brokers. What was the average number of shares each broker traded?

   **(1)** 80                **(4)** 900

   **(2)** 90                **(5)** 1000

   **(3)** 800

3. Assemblyperson Guerro's district contains 33 electoral precincts. There are 985 votes in each precinct. How many voters does Assemblyperson Guerro represent?

   **(1)** 10,000           **(4)** 40,000

   **(2)** 20,000           **(5)** 50,000

   **(3)** 30,000

4. Ann bought six blouses for $212. What was the average price of each blouse?

   **(1)** $20              **(4)** $50

   **(2)** $30              **(5)** $60

   **(3)** $40

5. Jake's game room measures 35 feet by 65 feet. What is its area?

   **(1)** 1200 square feet      **(4)** 1600 square feet

   **(2)** 1300 square feet      **(5)** 1800 square feet

   **(3)** 1400 square feet

Answers are on page A-35.

# Item Sets

On the GED test, you sometimes will need to solve two or more questions using information from the same text or from a table. You might not need all the information given to solve any particular question. For each question, you should determine what you are being required to answer, what information you must use to answer it, and what operations to use to answer the problem, and then solve it.

Examples 1 and 2 are based on the following paragraph:

The four members of the Alvarez family are taking a trip to Boston. They could take a plane, which would cost $158 round trip for each of the two adults and $98 for each of the two children. Instead of taking a plane, they could rent a car. The car rental would cost $43 per day with unlimited mileage for a two-door model. They would use the car for four days and spend about $200 for gas.

**Example 1:** What would the total cost of the plane tickets be?

Step 1. Determine the information you need to answer the question.

Adult tickets cost $158 and there are two adults. Children's tickets cost $98 each and there are two children.

Step 2. You can find the total cost of the adult tickets by multiplying the cost of one ticket by the number of adults needing tickets. Do the same for the children's tickets. Then add the two products.

Step 3. Solve the problem.

*Cost of adult tickets:*
$$\begin{array}{r} \$\ 158 \\ \times\ \ 2 \\ \hline \$\ 316 \end{array}$$

*Cost of children's tickets:*
$$\begin{array}{r} \$\ 98 \\ \times\ 2 \\ \hline \$\ 196 \end{array}$$

*Total cost:*
$$\begin{array}{r} \$\ 316 \\ +\ 196 \\ \hline \$\ 512 \end{array}$$

**Example 2:** The Alvarez family could rent a van for $58 a day. How much more would the car rental cost if they decide to rent the van instead of the two-door model?

Step 1. Determine the information you need to answer the question. First, you know from the paragraph that:

The Alvarez family would rent a vehicle for 4 days.

The two-door model costs $43 a day to rent.

However, this is not enough to answer the problem. Notice that the problem gives you the additional information you need: The van costs $58 a day to rent.

Step 2. Find the difference between the two costs by subtracting the daily rental cost of the two-door car from the daily rental cost of the van. Multiply by the number of days they will rent the car to find the difference for the trip.

*Difference in the daily rates:*

$ 58
– 43
$ 15

Step 3. Solve the problem.

*Total difference for the trip:*

$ 15
× 4
$ 60

Examples 3 and 4 are based on the following table:

### Jackson Family Food Expenses for Five Weeks

| | |
|---|---|
| Week 1 | $ 75 |
| Week 2 | 85 |
| Week 3 | 110 |
| Week 4 | 80 |
| Week 5 | 80 |

**Example 3:** For this five-week period, what is the mean amount the Jackson family spent for food per week?

Step 1. You need all the information from this table.

Step 2. You will have to find the total for the five weeks by adding, then divide by the number of weeks.

Step 3. Solve the problem.

*Total:*

110
85
80
80
+75
430

*Divide:*

$$5\overline{)430}\ \ \ 86$$

**Example 4:** How much more did the Jackson family spend for week 3 than in the week they spent the least amount for food?

Step 1. You know that in week 3 the Jacksons spent $110. The table tells you that the Jacksons spent the least amount for food in week 1, when they spent $75.

Step 2. You can find how much more was spent by subtracting.

Step 3. Solve the problem.

$110
– 75
35

Problems 1 to 3 are based on the following paragraph:

Steve has to make a decision: whether to continue his present part-time job and go to a community college at night, or whether to enroll in the work-study program at the community college. At his current job, he earns $8 per hour and works 30 hours per week. He spends $2 per day, Monday through Friday, on transportation. If he enrolls in the work-study program, he will be paid $4 per hour for 40 hours per week and receive free tuition. He would not have to pay for transportation either. If he keeps his part-time job, he will have to pay tuition of $40 per credit for 30 credits.

1. What is the difference between the two weekly wages?
2. If Steve works 50 weeks per year, how much would he earn annually in the work-study program if you include the tuition benefit?
3. Considering the hourly wages alone, how much more would Steve make per year if he stayed with his part-time job than from the work-study program? Assume that Steve would work 50 weeks per year in either job.

Items 4 to 6 are based on the following table:

| Longville Shopping Center | | |
|---|---|---|
| Store | Square Feet | Annual Rent |
| Boogie's | 1500 | $4 per square foot |
| Toner's | 1211 | $7 per square foot |
| Tim's | 2925 | $3 per square foot |
| Cowley's | 900 | $9 per square foot |

4. What is the annual rent for Boogie's?
5. If Tim's is shaped in a rectangle and the length is 65 feet, what does the width measure?
6. How much more is the annual rent for Toner's than for Cowley's?

Answers are on pages A-35 and A-36.

# Chapter 1 Quiz

1. The Ching family traveled 385 kilometers on the first day of their trip, 255 kilometers on the second day, 305 kilometers on the third day, and 628 kilometers on the fourth day. What is the total number of kilometers they traveled?

2. Jamel's restaurant check came to $28. He has $40. If he pays the bill and tips the waitress $5, how much money should he have left? Write the proper expression and solve the problem.

3. Ray calls an average of 15 people per hour in his telephone sales job. How many people does he call during a 40-hour workweek?

4. A fast-food restaurant serves 30 hamburgers and 20 cheeseburgers per hour. It is open 75 hours per week. How many hamburgers of both kinds does it serve per week? Write the proper expression and solve the problem.

5. Hank Ramirez drove his car at 53 miles per hour for 42 hours and 66 miles per hour for 11 hours. Rounded to the nearest ten, how many miles did he travel? Write the proper expression and solve the problem.

6. If one gallon of orange juice costs $3, how much do 8 gallons cost?

7. Find the value of $5^3$.

8. What is the square root of 841?

9. What is the perimeter of the rectangle?

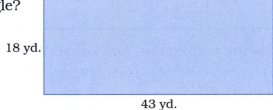

18 yd.

43 yd.

10. Find the area of this square.

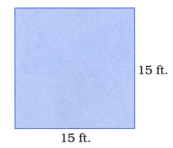

15 ft.

15 ft.

11. If filled to the top, how many cubic feet of sand will this sandbox hold?

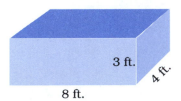

3 ft.

4 ft.

8 ft.

**12.** Paul wants to fence the border of his patio along the outside edge of the shaded portion. How many feet of fence does he need if the shaded portion measures 2 feet from the unshaded portion to outside on all sides?

**13.** He plans to seed the unshaded portion with grass. If he uses 1 pound of seed for every 10 square feet, how many pounds of grass seed does he need?

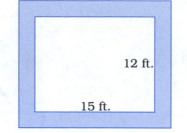

**14.** At $9 per square yard, how much will it cost to carpet this room?

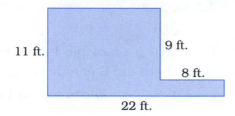

**15.** How much is a lot that measures 60 feet by 100 feet worth if the land is valued at $8 per square foot?

**16.** The Harris family bought a color television for $450. They paid $50 in cash and paid the balance in 10 equal monthly installments with no finance charge. What was the amount of each monthly payment?

**17.** Elaine mailed 4 books to her nephew. Each book weighed 2 pounds. If books cost $4 per pound to mail, how much postage did she have to pay in all?

Items 18 and 19 are based on the following paragraph:

Warren wants to buy a computer to replace his electric typewriter. One computer he likes costs $499, or for $275 more he can buy the same computer with a hard disk drive. He will also need a printer. He can buy a dot matrix printer for $239 but he likes a laser printer priced at $991. A black-and-white monitor costs $88 and a color monitor costs $342. He will also need word processing software. The program he likes costs $47.

**18.** If Warren purchases the computer with the hard disk drive, the dot matrix printer, the black-and-white monitor, and the word processing software, how much will it cost him?

**19.** The dot matrix printer A prints at a rate of 2 pages per minute. The laser printer B prints at a rate of 8 pages per minute. If Warren wants to print a 56-page report, how many more minutes will it take to print it on the dot matrix printer A than on the B printer. Write the proper expression and solve the problem.

**20.** The Johnson family spends $125 per week on food and $350 per month on rent. Write an expression that shows the total amount they spend on these items per year.

Answers are on page A-36.

# CHAPTER 2
# Fractions

Equal parts of a whole are called **fractions**. If you cut a pizza pie into 8 equal slices, each slice is a fraction of the whole pie. Since there are 8 equal parts, each fraction is written as $\frac{1}{8}$ — one part out of a total of 8. Two slices would be $\frac{2}{8}$; three, $\frac{3}{8}$; and so on. The whole would be $\frac{8}{8}$. Every whole thing divided into equal parts is written in this way, no matter how many parts there are. One car payment out of 60 payments on the whole cost of the car would be $\frac{1}{60}$ of the whole car payment.

## In this chapter, you will learn to:

- Reduce fractions to lowest terms
- Raise fractions to higher terms
- Change mixed numbers to improper fractions and improper fractions to mixed numbers
- Add and subtract mixed numbers and fractions
- Multiply and divide using fractions and mixed numbers
- Solve problems involving standard units of measurement, comparing and ordering fractions, tables, ratios, and probability
- Use ratios and proportions to solve word problems
- Identify the correct set-up for solving a problem
- Recognize extraneous information

## Preview

**Directions:**  Solve each problem. Be sure to express answers in lowest terms and change improper fractions to whole or mixed numbers.

1. Add $\frac{1}{4}$, $\frac{4}{6}$, and $\frac{7}{12}$.

2. Subtract $\frac{3}{5}$ from $\frac{14}{15}$.

3. Multiply $2\frac{5}{8}$ by $\frac{5}{9}$.

4. Divide $\frac{6}{11}$ by $\frac{21}{22}$.

5. Divide $4\frac{1}{5}$ by $1\frac{13}{15}$.

Check your answers on page A-36. If you have at least four answers correct, try the Chapter 2 Quiz on page 459. If you have fewer than four answers correct, study Level 1, beginning with Lesson 1.

## Lesson
### 1

# Reducing Fractions

Fractions show the relationship of parts to a whole. The top number is called the numerator. It represents the number of parts. The bottom number is called the denominator. It represents how many parts make up a whole.

<table>
<tr><td>numerator</td><td>part</td><td>$\dfrac{3}{4}$</td></tr>
<tr><td>denominator</td><td>whole</td><td></td></tr>
</table>

Most answers on the GED test will be reduced to lowest terms. If the numerator and denominator can be divided evenly by the same number, other than 1, the fraction can be reduced to simpler terms. It is helpful to find the highest number by which you can divide the numerator and denominator. If not, you will have to reduce again. If the numerator and denominator are both even numbers, they are divisible by 2. However, you still should find the highest possible number to divide by.

**Example:** Reduce $\frac{16}{24}$ to lowest terms.

Step 1. Find a number that divides evenly into both 16 and 24. The numbers that can divide 16 evenly are: 2, 4, 8, 16. The numbers that can divide 24 evenly are: 2, 4, 8, 12, 24. The numbers that can divide both numbers evenly are 2, 4, and 8.

Step 2. Use the highest common divisor, 8, and divide both 16 and 24.

$$\frac{16 \div 8}{24 \div 8} = \frac{2}{3}$$

*Note:* All numbers ending in 5 or 0 are divisible by 5. For example:

$$\frac{25}{30} \div \frac{5}{5} = \frac{5}{6}; \quad \frac{40}{45} \div \frac{5}{5} = \frac{8}{9}.$$

## Level 1, Lesson 1 Exercise

**Directions:** Reduce each fraction to lowest terms.

1. $\frac{5}{20}$   2. $\frac{6}{9}$   3. $\frac{56}{63}$   4. $\frac{15}{21}$   5. $\frac{275}{300}$

Answers are on page A-36.

Lesson 2

# Raising Fractions to Higher Terms

A fraction can also be raised to higher terms. The method is similar to reducing a fraction, except that instead of dividing both the numerator and denominator, you multiply them. You often need to raise fractions to higher terms to solve fraction addition and subtraction problems. Two or more fractions with the same value are called **equivalent fractions**.

**Example:** Raise the fraction $\frac{1}{2}$ to a fraction that has a denominator of 16.

Step 1. You can set up the problem by showing the original fraction to be equal to a fraction with the higher denominator and an unknown numerator.

$$\frac{1}{2} = \frac{?}{16}$$

Step 2. Multiply the denominator by 8.

$$\frac{1}{2} \times \frac{?}{8} = \frac{?}{16}$$

Step 3. Multiply the numerator by your division answer.

$$\frac{1}{2} \times \frac{8}{8} = \frac{8}{16}$$

**Directions:** Raise each fraction to higher terms by finding the missing numerator.

1. $\frac{1}{4} = \frac{?}{12}$    2. $\frac{1}{2} = \frac{?}{20}$    3. $\frac{2}{5} = \frac{?}{15}$

4. Increase $\frac{2}{3}$ to a fraction with a denominator of 24.

5. Raise $\frac{5}{6}$ to a fraction with a denominator of 30.

6. $\frac{3}{7}$ is equal to what fraction with a denominator of 35?

Answers are on page A-36.

## Lesson 3 — Mixed Numbers and Improper Fractions

A **mixed number** consists of a whole number and a fraction, such as $2\frac{1}{4}$. An **improper fraction** is one in which the numerator is equal to or greater than the denominator, such as $\frac{9}{4}$, which is equal to $2\frac{1}{4}$. An improper fraction in which the numerator and denominator are the same is equal to 1. For example, all these fractions equal 1:

$$\frac{2}{2} \qquad \frac{3}{3} \qquad \frac{5}{5} \qquad \frac{12}{12} \qquad \frac{20}{20} \qquad \frac{59}{59} \qquad \frac{321}{321}$$

To change an improper fraction to a whole or mixed number, divide the numerator by the denominator. If there is no remainder, the improper fraction becomes a whole number.

**Example 1:** Change $\frac{21}{7}$ to simpler terms.

Step 1. Divide 21 by 7.

Therefore $\frac{21}{7} = 3$

$$7\overline{)21} \quad \begin{array}{r} 3 \\ \underline{21} \\ 0 \end{array}$$

**Example 2:** Express $\frac{15}{6}$ in simpler terms.

Step 1. Divide 15 by 6.

$$6\overline{)15} \quad \begin{array}{r} 2 \text{ r } 3 = 2\frac{3}{6} \\ \underline{12} \\ 3 \end{array}$$

Step 2. Then reduce the $\frac{3}{6}$ to $\frac{1}{2}$ by dividing both the numerator and denominator by 3.

$$\frac{3}{6} \div \frac{2}{2} = \frac{1}{2}$$

Therefore $2\frac{3}{6} = 2\frac{1}{2}$

To change a mixed number to an improper fraction, multiply the whole number by the denominator and add that amount to the numerator.

**Example 3:** Change $5\frac{7}{8}$ to an improper fraction.

Step 1. Multiply the whole number, 5, by the denominator.

Step 2. Add 40 to 7, the numerator.

$$5\frac{7}{8} = \frac{?}{8}$$
$$5 \times 8 = 40$$
$$40 + 7 = 47$$
$$5\frac{7}{8} = \frac{47}{8}$$

**Directions:** Change each improper fraction to a whole or mixed number. Be sure to reduce any fraction to lowest terms if necessary.

1. $\frac{7}{7}$  2. $\frac{28}{4}$  3. $\frac{22}{10}$  4. $\frac{66}{9}$  5. $\frac{54}{8}$

**Directions:** Change each mixed number to an improper fraction.

6. $1\frac{1}{2}$  7. $2\frac{5}{6}$  8. $8\frac{3}{7}$  9. $4\frac{2}{5}$  10. $5\frac{11}{12}$

Answers are on page A-37.

**Lesson 4**

# Adding Fractions and Mixed Numbers That Have Like Denominators

To add fractions that have like denominators, add the numerators. Write the sum of the numerators over the common denominator. If the result is an improper fraction, change it to a whole or a mixed number. Remember to reduce fractions.

**Example 1:** Add $\frac{5}{8}$ and $\frac{7}{8}$.

<u>Step 1.</u> Add the numerators: $5 + 7 = 12$. Then write the total over the common denominator, 8.

<u>Step 2.</u> Change $\frac{12}{8}$ to a mixed number by dividing 12 by 8. You get $1\frac{4}{8}$.

$$\begin{array}{r} \frac{5}{8} \\ + \frac{7}{8} \\ \hline \frac{12}{8} = 1\frac{4}{8} = 1\frac{1}{2} \end{array}$$

<u>Step 3.</u> Reduce $\frac{4}{8}$ by dividing the numerator and the denominator by 4. The final answer is $1\frac{1}{2}$.

When adding mixed numbers, add the whole numbers separately. Then combine the fraction total with the whole-number total to get the final answer.

**Example 2:** Add $1\frac{5}{8}$ and $3\frac{7}{8}$.

<u>Step 1.</u> $1\frac{5}{8} + 3\frac{7}{8} = 4\frac{12}{8}$

<u>Step 2.</u> $\frac{12}{8} = 1\frac{4}{8} = 1\frac{1}{2}$

<u>Step 3.</u> $1\frac{1}{2} + 4 = 5\frac{1}{2}$

## Level 1, Lesson 4 Exercise

**Directions:** Solve each problem. Remember to express the answers in simplest form.

1. $\frac{3}{5} + \frac{1}{5}$  2. $\frac{7}{12} + \frac{11}{12}$  3. $6\frac{3}{8} + 7\frac{3}{8}$

4. $4\frac{7}{10} + 3\frac{3}{10}$  5. Find the sum of $12\frac{3}{10} + 9\frac{8}{10}$.

Answers are on page A-37.

# Common Denominators

To find a common denominator, you look for the lowest number that each denominator can divide into evenly. This number is called the **lowest common denominator**, or LCD.

You cannot add or subtract fractions with different denominators. That is like adding or subtracting apples and oranges. Before you add or subtract fractions, you must find and change the fractions to a **common denominator**.

First see if you can use one of the denominators in your addition or subtraction problem.

**Example 1:** Subtract $\frac{1}{8}$ from $\frac{3}{4}$.

Step 1. Set up the fractions for subtraction.

$$\frac{3}{4}$$
$$-\frac{1}{8}$$

Try 8, the larger denominator. Change the other fraction's denominator to 8.

$$\frac{3}{4} \times \frac{2}{2} = \frac{6}{8}$$

Step 2. Subtract the numerators of the fractions with this lowest common denominator, 8.

If this does not work, and the denominators of the fractions are small, try multiplying their denominators times each other.

**Example 2:** Find the LCD of $\frac{1}{3}$ and $\frac{3}{4}$ and add the fractions.

Step 1. Set up the fractions for addition.

$$\frac{1}{3}$$
$$+\frac{3}{4}$$

Multiply the denominators times each other.

$$3 \times 4 = 12$$

So 12 is your LCD.

Step 2. Change the fractions to equivalent fractions with the LCD and add the numerators of the fractions.

$$\frac{1}{3} \times \frac{4}{4} = \frac{4}{12} \qquad \frac{4}{12}$$
$$\frac{3}{4} \times \frac{3}{3} = \frac{9}{12} \qquad +\frac{9}{12}$$
$$\frac{13}{12} = 1\frac{1}{12}$$

Sometimes, to find the lowest common denominator, you will have to run through a series of multiples of each fraction in order to find the lowest number both denominators can divide into equally.

**Example 3:** Find the LCD for $\frac{3}{8}$ and $\frac{1}{6}$.

Step 1. Run through the multiples of each denominator.

*Multiples of 8:*
8, 16, 24, 32

24 is the lowest number both 8 and 6 can divide into evenly, so it is the LCD.

*Multiples of 6:*
6, 12, 18, 24

Sometimes, using multiples to find a common denominator can become too time-consuming. In that case, try multiplying the set of denominators by each other.

**Example 4:** Write equivalent fractions with a common denominator for $\frac{1}{5}$, $\frac{1}{6}$, and $\frac{1}{4}$, and then add the fractions.

Step 1. Multiply the denominators by each other.

$5 \times 6 \times 4$
$5 \times 6 = 30$
Use 120 as your common denominator. 
$30 \times 4 = 120$

Step 2. Find the equivalent fractions with the LCD of 120 and add the fractions. Then simplify the fraction in the answer.

$\frac{1}{5} \times \frac{24}{24} = \frac{24}{120}$

$\frac{1}{6} \times \frac{20}{20} = \frac{20}{120}$

$\frac{1}{4} \times \frac{30}{30} = \frac{30}{120}$

$\frac{74}{120} = \frac{37}{60}$

## Level 1, Lesson 5 Exercise

**Directions:** Find the LCD for each group of fractions. Change each fraction in the group to one with the LCD as the denominator.

1. $\frac{1}{3}$ and $\frac{2}{9}$

2. $\frac{2}{5}$ and $\frac{3}{8}$

3. $\frac{3}{4}$ and $\frac{5}{6}$

4. $\frac{1}{4}$ and $\frac{7}{10}$

5. $\frac{2}{3}$ and $\frac{9}{10}$

6. $\frac{1}{3}$, $\frac{5}{6}$, and $\frac{7}{8}$

Answers are on page A-37.

**Lesson 6**

## Adding Fractions and Mixed Numbers That Have Unlike Denominators

To add fractions or mixed numbers that have unlike denominators, first find the LCD. Change all fractions to equivalent fractions with the same LCD. Then follow the procedure for adding fractions that have like denominators.

**Example:** Find the sum of $3\frac{3}{4}$, $2\frac{1}{2}$, and $1\frac{2}{5}$.

Step 1. Find the LCD for $\frac{3}{4}$, $\frac{1}{2}$, and $\frac{2}{5}$. The lowest number that 4, 2, and 5 all divide into evenly is 20. Change each fraction to an equivalent fraction that has a denominator of 20.

$3\frac{3}{4} = 3\frac{15}{20}$

$2\frac{1}{2} = 2\frac{10}{20}$

$1\frac{2}{5} = 1\frac{8}{20}$

Step 2. Add the new numerators and put the sum over the common denominator, 20.

$\frac{33}{20}$

Step 3. Add the whole numbers to the sum of the fractions.

$$
\begin{array}{r}
3 \\
2 \\
1 \\
+ \ \dfrac{33}{20} \\
\hline
\end{array}
$$

Step 4. Simplify the mixed number:

$$6\dfrac{33}{20} = 7\dfrac{13}{20}$$

## Level 1, Lesson 6 Exercise

1. Add $\dfrac{2}{3}$ and $\dfrac{3}{4}$.

2. What is the total of $\dfrac{1}{2}$, $\dfrac{1}{4}$, and $\dfrac{5}{6}$?

3. What does $4\dfrac{1}{6}$ plus $8\dfrac{3}{8}$ equal?

4. What is the sum of $7\dfrac{2}{3}$ and $6\dfrac{1}{2}$?

5. Add $3\dfrac{4}{5}$ and $\dfrac{13}{15}$.

Answers are on page A-37.

## Lesson 7  Subtracting Fractions and Mixed Numbers

Just as in adding fractions, a common denominator is needed when fractions are subtracted. If the fractions have a common denominator, the difference between the fractions is found by subtracting the numerators and placing that result over the denominator. If the fractions do not have a common denominator, find one before subtracting the numerators. Express the answer in simplest form.

**Example 1:** Find the difference of $\dfrac{3}{4}$ and $\dfrac{2}{3}$.

Step 1. Set up the problem and change to the LCD, which is 12.

$$
\begin{array}{rcl}
\dfrac{3}{4} & = & \dfrac{9}{12} \\[2mm]
- \ \dfrac{2}{3} & = & \dfrac{8}{12} \\
\end{array}
$$

Step 2. Find the difference of the numerators. Place the result over the denominator. The answer is $\dfrac{1}{12}$.

$$
\begin{array}{rcl}
\dfrac{3}{4} & = & \dfrac{9}{12} \\[2mm]
- \ \dfrac{2}{3} & = & \dfrac{8}{12} \\
\hline
& & \dfrac{1}{12}
\end{array}
$$

When subtracting mixed numbers, find the LCD, if necessary, and subtract the whole numbers and the fractions separately.

**Example 2:** Find the difference between $10\dfrac{5}{6}$ and $2\dfrac{1}{9}$.

Set up the problem with the larger number on top. Find the LCD for the fractions and change the fractions to equivalent fractions with the LCD. Subtract the numerators. Then subtract the whole numbers.

$$
\begin{array}{rcl}
10\dfrac{5}{6} & = & 10\dfrac{15}{18} \\[2mm]
- \ 2\dfrac{1}{9} & = & 2\dfrac{2}{18} \\
\hline
& & 8\dfrac{13}{18}
\end{array}
$$

If you subtract a whole number from a mixed number, all you have to do with the fraction is bring it down in your answer. It is the same as subtracting 0 from another whole number except a fraction with a value of 0 is not written out.

**Example 3:** Subtract 2 from $15\frac{3}{4}$.

Step 1. Set up the problem with the larger number on top.

$$\begin{array}{r} 15\frac{3}{4} \\ -\ 2 \end{array}$$

Step 2. Bring the fraction down to the answer. Subtract the whole numbers.

$$\begin{array}{r} 15\frac{3}{4} \\ -\ 2 \\ \hline 13\frac{3}{4} \end{array}$$

To subtract a fraction or mixed number from a whole number, you must borrow from the whole number. To borrow, first reduce the whole number by 1. Then write the borrowed 1 as an equivalent fraction with the same denominator as the other fraction. *Remember:* a fraction with an equal numerator and denominator equals 1.

**Example 4:** Subtract $2\frac{3}{5}$ from 9.

Step 1. Set up the problem with the larger number on top.

$$\begin{array}{r} 9 \\ -\ 2\frac{3}{5} \end{array}$$

Step 2. Borrow from 9. Reduce the whole number, 9, by 1 and change the 1 to a fraction. 9 becomes $8\frac{5}{5}$.

$$\begin{array}{r} 9\ =\ 8\frac{5}{5} \\ -\ 2\frac{3}{5}\ =\ 2\frac{3}{5} \\ \hline 6\frac{2}{5} \end{array}$$

You also will have to borrow sometimes when subtracting mixed numbers. After finding the LCD, you may find the top fraction is smaller than the bottom fraction, and you will have to borrow from the whole number on top.

**Example 5:** $9\frac{1}{4} - 3\frac{4}{5}$.

Step 1. Set up the problem with the larger number on top. Find the LCD for $\frac{1}{4}$ and $\frac{4}{5}$. The lowest number that both 4 and 5 divide into equally is 20. Change both fractions to equivalent fractions that have denominators of 20.

$$\begin{array}{r} 9\frac{1}{4}\ =\ 9\frac{5}{20} \\ -\ 3\frac{4}{5}\ =\ 3\frac{16}{20} \end{array}$$

Step 2. Since you can't subtract $\frac{16}{20}$ from $\frac{5}{20}$, you need to borrow. Borrow a 1 from the 9. As you know, $1 = \frac{20}{20}$. Add the $\frac{20}{20}$ to the $\frac{5}{20}$ you have. The top number becomes $8\frac{25}{20}$.

$$\begin{array}{r} 9\frac{1}{4}\ =\ 9\frac{5}{20}\ =\ 8\frac{25}{20} \\ -\ 3\frac{4}{5}\ =\ 3\frac{16}{20}\ =\ 3\frac{16}{20} \end{array}$$

Step 3. Subtract the whole numbers and the fractions. Reduce the fraction if necessary.

$$\begin{array}{r} 8\frac{25}{20} \\ -\ 3\frac{16}{20} \\ \hline 5\frac{9}{20} \end{array}$$

1. $\frac{8}{9} - \frac{7}{9}$

2. $\frac{2}{3} - \frac{1}{6}$

3. $6\frac{4}{5} - 2\frac{1}{2}$

4. Subtract 5 from $7\frac{2}{5}$.

5. What is the difference between 11 and $2\frac{5}{6}$?

6. Find $8\frac{2}{5} - 1\frac{4}{5}$.

7. Take $6\frac{3}{4}$ away from $12\frac{2}{3}$.

8. What is $13\frac{1}{8}$ less $4\frac{7}{12}$?

Answers are on page A-37.

## Lesson 8    Multiplying Fractions and Mixed Numbers

In multiplication of fractions, you multiply the numerators together. Then you multiply the denominators. The **product**—or answer—is the product of the numerators over the product of the denominators. Then reduce the answer to lowest terms.

However, in the multiplication of fractions there is a shortcut called **canceling**. Canceling allows you to get your answer in lowest terms. When you use canceling, you have no need to reduce after multiplying.

To cancel, you look for the lowest number that will divide evenly into two or more fractions. Then multiply across—the numerators separately and the denominators separately—using the lower numbers.

**Example 1:** Find $\frac{3}{4} \times \frac{8}{9}$.

Step 1. Set up the problem. (Fraction multiplication problems are set up horizontally.)

$$\frac{3}{4} \times \frac{8}{9}$$

Step 2. Cancel: divide any numerator or denominator by the lowest number that will divide evenly into both. (3 will divide evenly into itself and into 9. 4 will divide evenly into itself and into 8.)

$$\frac{\overset{1}{\cancel{3}}}{\underset{1}{\cancel{4}}} \times \frac{\overset{2}{\cancel{8}}}{\underset{3}{\cancel{9}}}$$

Step 3. Multiply across, numerators times numerators and denominators times denominators.

$$\frac{\overset{1}{\cancel{3}}}{\underset{1}{\cancel{4}}} \times \frac{\overset{2}{\cancel{8}}}{\underset{3}{\cancel{9}}} = \frac{2}{3}$$

**Example 2:** Multiply $\frac{2}{7} \times \frac{7}{15} \times \frac{3}{8}$.

**Step 1.** Set up the problem and cancel. (2 will divide evenly into 8. 3 will divide evenly into 15. 7 will divide evenly into 7.)

$$\frac{\overset{1}{\cancel{2}}}{\underset{1}{\cancel{7}}} \times \frac{\overset{1}{\cancel{7}}}{\underset{5}{\cancel{15}}} \times \frac{\overset{1}{\cancel{3}}}{\underset{4}{\cancel{8}}}$$

**Step 2.** Multiply numerators times numerators and denominators times denominators.

$$\frac{\overset{1}{\cancel{2}}}{\underset{1}{\cancel{7}}} \times \frac{\overset{1}{\cancel{7}}}{\underset{5}{\cancel{15}}} \times \frac{\overset{1}{\cancel{3}}}{\underset{4}{\cancel{8}}} = \frac{1}{20}$$

When you multiply a fraction and a whole number, write the whole number as a fraction with the whole number as the numerator and a denominator of 1. Multiply as you would any other fraction.

**Example 3:** Multiply $\frac{7}{9} \times 6$.

**Step 1.** Set up the problem, writing 6 as the fraction $\frac{6}{1}$.

$$\frac{7}{9} \times \frac{6}{1} =$$

**Step 2.** Cancel.

$$\frac{7}{\underset{3}{\cancel{9}}} \times \frac{\overset{2}{\cancel{6}}}{1} =$$

**Step 3.** Multiply the numerators and multiply the denominators.

$$\frac{7}{\underset{3}{\cancel{9}}} \times \frac{\overset{2}{\cancel{6}}}{1} = \frac{14}{3} = 4\frac{2}{3}$$

When multiplying a mixed number with a fraction, a whole number or another mixed number, change the mixed number to an improper fraction.

**Example 4:** Find $\frac{3}{5} \times 7\frac{1}{2}$.

**Step 1.** Change $7\frac{1}{2}$ to an improper fraction.

$$7\frac{1}{2} = \frac{15}{2}$$

**Step 2.** Set up the problem and cancel.

$$\frac{3}{\underset{1}{\cancel{5}}} \times \frac{\overset{3}{\cancel{15}}}{2} =$$

**Step 3.** Multiply the numerators and multiply the denominators.

$$\frac{3}{\underset{1}{\cancel{5}}} \times \frac{\overset{3}{\cancel{15}}}{2} = \frac{9}{2} = 4\frac{1}{2}$$

## Level 1, Lesson 8 Exercise

**Directions:** Find the products. Remember to cancel.

1. $\frac{3}{4} \times \frac{1}{4}$    2. $\frac{2}{3} \times \frac{5}{9} \times \frac{3}{8}$    3. $\frac{3}{4} \times 8$    4. $2\frac{1}{2} \times \frac{4}{5}$

5. Find the product of $2\frac{1}{4}$ and $3\frac{1}{3}$.

6. Multiply $1\frac{2}{3}$ by 9.

7. Find the product of $1\frac{1}{6}$, $\frac{3}{7}$, and $4\frac{2}{3}$.

8. What is $3\frac{1}{5}$ times 6 times $1\frac{1}{4}$?

Answers are on page A-37.

# Dividing Fractions and Whole Numbers

When you divide with fractions and whole numbers, you invert the divisor and then multiply. **Invert** means to turn upside down, or reverse, the denominator and numerator. In a division problem set up horizontally, the divisor is the number to the right of the division sign. The answer to a division problem is called a **quotient**.

**Example 1:** Divide $\frac{2}{3}$ by $\frac{1}{6}$.

Step 1. Set up the problem horizontally.

$$\frac{2}{3} \div \frac{1}{6} =$$

Step 2. Invert the divisor and change the division sign to a multiplication sign.

$$\frac{2}{3} \times \frac{6}{1} =$$

Step 3. Cancel and multiply.

$$\frac{2}{\underset{1}{\cancel{3}}} \times \frac{\overset{2}{\cancel{6}}}{1} = \frac{4}{1} = 4$$

When dividing a fraction by a whole number, write the whole number as a fraction with a denominator of 1, invert and multiply.

**Example 2:** Divide $\frac{4}{7}$ by 16.

Step 1. Set up the problem, writing the 16 as $\frac{16}{1}$.

$$\frac{4}{7} \div \frac{16}{1} =$$

Step 2. Invert and change the division sign to a multiplication sign.

$$\frac{4}{7} \times \frac{1}{16} =$$

Step 3. Cancel and multiply. The quotient is $\frac{1}{28}$.

$$\frac{\overset{1}{\cancel{4}}}{7} \times \frac{1}{\underset{4}{\cancel{16}}} = \frac{1}{28}$$

When dividing by a mixed number, change the mixed number to an improper fraction, invert and multiply.

**Example 3:** Divide $1\frac{1}{3}$ by $2\frac{2}{9}$.

Step 1. Set up the problem.

$$1\frac{1}{3} \div 2\frac{2}{9} =$$

Step 2. Change the mixed numbers to improper fractions.

$$\frac{4}{3} \div \frac{20}{9} =$$

Step 3. Invert the divisor and then change the division sign to a multiplication sign.

$$\frac{4}{3} \times \frac{9}{20} =$$

Step 4. Cancel and multiply. The quotient is $\frac{1}{2}$.

$$\frac{\overset{1}{\cancel{4}}}{\underset{1}{\cancel{3}}} \times \frac{\overset{3}{\cancel{9}}}{\underset{5}{\cancel{20}}} = \frac{3}{5}$$

**Directions:** Find the quotients. Remember to invert and cancel. Express each answer in simplest form.

1. $\frac{1}{3} \div \frac{3}{4}$

2. $8 \div \frac{1}{2}$

3. $\frac{5}{6} \div 10$

4. $1\frac{2}{3} \div 3$

5. Divide $\frac{3}{5}$ by $5\frac{1}{4}$.

6. How many times does 4 go into $5\frac{1}{3}$?

7. Divide 5 by $4\frac{1}{6}$.

8. What is the quotient of $3\frac{1}{2}$ divided by $4\frac{5}{8}$?

Answers are on page A-38.

# Fraction Applications

## Ratio

A ratio is used to compare two numbers. A ratio can be written in several ways: as a fraction ($\frac{3}{5}$), using the word *to* (3 "to" 5), or using a colon (3:5).

When written as a fraction, the number being compared is the numerator and the number it is being compared to is the denominator.

**Example 1:** Gary used 5 gallons of gas to drive 75 miles. What is the ratio of miles to gallons for Gary's trip?

Step 1. Write the ratio using the terms you will compare. You are comparing the number of miles driven to the number of gallons of gas used. So write a fraction with 75 as the numerator and 5 as the denominator.

$$\frac{\text{miles}}{\text{gallons}} = \frac{75}{5}$$

Step 2. Reduce the fraction to lowest terms.

$$\frac{75 \div 5}{5 \div 5} = \frac{15}{1}$$

The ratio can be expressed as either $\frac{15}{1}$, 15 to 1, or 15:1. On the GED ratios can be expressed in any of these ways. What was actually found in Example 1 was the number of miles Gary drove on one gallon of gas, or the miles per gallon.

Sometimes a problem will require you to find the total or whole to which you are comparing a part.

**Example 2:** Irene budgets her monthly income as follows: $565 for rent and utilities; $250 for food and household expenses; $60 for transportation; $75 for entertainment; $50 for miscellaneous expenses; and $250 for savings. Assuming these budget items to take care of her total monthly income, what is the ratio of Irene's savings to her income?

**Step 1.** You were not given Irene's total monthly income, but you can add the budget items to find it.

$$\begin{array}{r} \$\ 565 \\ 250 \\ 250 \\ 75 \\ 60 \\ +\ 50 \\ \hline \$1250 \text{ total monthly income} \end{array}$$

**Step 2.** Write the ratio, savings to income.

$$\frac{\text{savings}}{\text{income}} = \frac{250}{1250}$$

**Step 3.** Reduce to lowest terms.

$$\frac{250 \div 250}{1250 \div 250} = \frac{1}{5} \quad \frac{\text{savings}}{\text{income}}$$

The ratio is $\frac{1}{5}$, 1 to 5, or 1:5. Irene saves $1 out of every $5 she earns.

## Level 2, Lesson 1 Exercise

**Directions:** Write a ratio to solve each problem.

1. The gas tank in David's pickup truck holds 22 gallons. The gas tank in his wife's car holds 10 gallons. What is the ratio of the smaller gas tank to the larger gas tank?

2. Last year, Josh ran 6 miles per hour in the marathon. This year, he ran 10 miles per hour. What is the ratio of Josh's running speed this year to his running speed last year?

3. Michele burns 3000 calories on days on which she goes to the gym. On days on which she does not go to the gym, she burns 2000 calories. What is the ratio of calories Michele burns on days she does not go to the gym to calories she burns on days she does go?

4. Oliver prepared a growing mixture that contained 2 parts topsoil, 1 part peat moss, and 1 part vermiculite. What is the ratio of topsoil to the total mixture?

5. Nancy answered 100 questions on a test. She had 20 incorrect answers. What is the ratio of her correct answers to the number of questions on the test?

Items 6 through 10 are based on the following:

Harry works in a factory which makes automobiles. A total of 3000 people work in the factory. Out of this many, 250 are managers, 100 work in the office, 750 work in part assembly, 500 work in painting, 200 work in the finishing department, 400 work in the warehouse, 300 work in maintenance, 150 are engineers, and 350 work in chassis assembly. The factory is located in a town with a population of 45,000.

6. What is the ratio of engineers to managers?

7. What is the ratio of total employees to the population of the town?

8. If all the employees except the managers, engineers, and office workers work on the factory floor, what is the ratio of factory floor workers to non-factory floor workers?

9. What is the ratio of warehouse workers to maintenance workers?

10. What is the ratio of chassis assemblers to the total employees?

Answers are on page A-38.

# Lesson 2

# Proportion

A proportion is an expression that shows two ratios (fractions) are equal. For instance, $\frac{2}{8} = \frac{1}{4}$ is a proportion. It is a mathematical expression that means "2 has the same relationship to 8 as 1 has to 4." You can solve many problems on the GED by using proportions. (Chapter 4 will show how to solve percent problems using ratio and proportion.)

In a correct proportion, multiplying the top number of one side of the proportion by the bottom number of the other side of the proportion will give the same result as multiplying the bottom number of the first side of the proportion by the top number of the other side. This is called **cross multiplying**. This means that if $\frac{a}{c} = \frac{b}{d}$, then $ad = bc$ ($a \times d = b \times c$). For example:

$$\frac{2}{8} = \frac{1}{4}$$
$$2 \times 4 = 1 \times 8$$
$$8 = 8$$

The products of such cross-multiplying are called **cross-products**. If a proportion is true, its cross-products are equal.

Cross multiplying is also used to find an unknown in a proportion. Many GED problems ask you to find an unknown. You can cross-multiply the ratios (fractions) of proportions to find the answers.

**Example 1:** In the proportion $\frac{4}{10} = \frac{6}{n}$, what is the value of $n$ ($n$ represents the missing number)?

Step 1. Cross multiply.

$$4n = 6 \times 10$$
$$4n = 60$$

Step 2. Then divide the numbers on the same side as the $n$ into the numbers on the other side of the equal sign.

$$n = \frac{60}{4} = 4\overline{)60}$$

$$\begin{array}{r} 15 \\ 4\overline{)60} \\ \underline{4} \\ 20 \\ \underline{20} \end{array}$$

449

# Proportion Word Problems

The proportion problems on the GED test will be word problems. Be sure to read each problem carefully in order to determine the correct relationship between numbers when you set up the proportion.

**Example 2:** A recipe for pancakes requires 2 cups of flour for 6 servings. If you want to make only 4 servings, how much flour should you use?

Step 1. Call the unknown amount of flour $f$. Determine the relationship between the numbers and write a correct proportion. Here is the way to write the proportion:

$$\frac{\text{larger amount of servings}}{\text{larger amount of flour}} = \frac{\text{smaller amount of servings}}{\text{smaller amount of flour}} \qquad \frac{6 \text{ servings}}{2 \text{ cups}} = \frac{4 \text{ servings}}{f \text{ cups}}$$

Step 2. Cross multiply.

$$6f = 2 \times 4$$
$$6f = 8$$

Step 3. Solve the problem. Change improper fractions to mixed numbers.

$$f = \frac{8}{6} = 1\frac{1}{3}$$

$1\frac{1}{3}$ cups of flour are used to make 4 servings.

When the problem involves a fractional amount, you use proportions in the same way you would with whole numbers. Change mixed numbers to improper fractions when necessary.

**Example 3:** If a map has a scale of 1 inch = 60 miles, what is the distance in miles of $2\frac{1}{2}$ inches on the map?

Step 1. The ratio of inches to miles on the map is 1 inch = 60 miles, or 1:60. Set up the proportion to find the number of miles $2\frac{1}{2}$ inches represents on the map.

$$\frac{\text{inches}}{\text{miles}} \quad \frac{1}{60} = \frac{2\frac{1}{2}}{n}$$

($n$ stands for the number of miles $2\frac{1}{2}$ inches represents on the map)

Step 2. Cross multiply to find the value of $2\frac{1}{2}$ inches. Change the mixed number to an improper fraction and the whole number to a fraction.

$$\frac{1}{60} = \frac{2\frac{1}{2}}{n}$$
$$n = \frac{60}{1} \times 2\frac{1}{2}$$
$$n = \frac{60}{1} \times \frac{5}{2}$$

Step 3. Cancel. Multiply numerators times numerators and denominators times denominators to find the value of $n$.

$$n = \frac{\overset{30}{60}}{1} \times \frac{5}{\underset{1}{2}} = \frac{150}{1}$$
$$n = 150 \text{ miles}$$

In some proportion problems, you have to change the ratios before you can solve the problem.

**Example 4:** Twice as many women as men work at Johnson's meat-packing plant. Altogether, 168 people work at the plant. How many of them are women?

Step 1. You are told that the ratio of men to women is 2:1. To find the actual number of women, you need a ratio of the number of women to the total number of workers. Add 2 and 1 to get the number for the total.

$$\begin{array}{r} 2 \text{ women} \\ + \ 1 \text{ man} \\ \hline 3 \text{ total} \end{array}$$

Step 2. Set up a proportion of the ratio of the number of women to the total number of workers.

$$\frac{\text{women}}{\text{total}} \quad \frac{2}{3} = \frac{n}{168}$$

Step 3. Cross multiply to find the number of women.

$$\frac{2}{3} = \frac{n}{168}$$
$$3n = 336$$
$$n = \frac{336}{3}$$
$$n = 112 \text{ women}$$

Always be sure you are putting the right ratios into your proportion. In the following example, you subtract the numbers you are given in order to get the ratio you need.

**Example 5:** Sam got 4 problems right out of 7 on a test with 35 questions. How many questions did he get wrong?

Step 1. 4 stands for the number right, and 7 stands for the total. Since the problem asks for the number wrong, subtract 4 from 7 to find the number wrong.

$$\begin{array}{r} 7 \text{ total} \\ - \ 4 \text{ right} \\ \hline 3 \text{ wrong} \end{array}$$

Step 2. Make a proportion with the ratio of the number wrong to the total. Put $n$ in the place of the number wrong, and put 35 in the place of the total.

$$\frac{\text{wrong}}{\text{total}} \quad \frac{3}{7} = \frac{n}{35}$$

Step 3. Cross multiply to find the number of questions Sam got wrong.

$$7n = 105$$
$$n = \frac{105}{7}$$
$$n = 15 \text{ questions wrong}$$

## Level 2, Lesson 2 Exercise

**Directions:** Use proportions to solve the following problems.

1. If a car used 8 gallons of gas on a 120-mile trip, how many gallons of gas will it use to travel 195 miles?

2. If $\frac{1}{2}$ inch represents a distance of 20 miles on a map, how many miles would 3 inches represent?

3. If you use 4 cups of water to cook 3 cups of cereal, how much water would you use to cook 2 cups of cereal?

4. The ratio of women to men in an office is 4:7. If there are 33 people in the office, how many are women?

5. The ratio of votes for the two candidates in an election was 2:5 for Bill Bartes as compared to Dan Dover. If Bill Bartes received 3000 votes, how many votes were cast in the election?

6. If Carl can clean his apartment in 2 hours, what part of it can he clean in 15 minutes?

   **(1)** $\frac{1}{2}$     **(2)** $\frac{3}{4}$     **(3)** $\frac{2}{3}$     **(4)** $\frac{1}{8}$     **(5)** $\frac{4}{5}$

7. There are 3 times as many men as there are women in the local doctor's club. The total membership is 80. How many members are women?

   **(1)** 20     **(2)** 30     **(3)** 40     **(4)** 50     **(5)** 60

8. It takes $2\frac{1}{4}$ yards of fabric to make one set of curtains. How many yards of fabric would you need to make 4 sets of curtains?

   **(1)** $8\frac{1}{2}$     **(2)** $6\frac{1}{4}$     **(3)** 9     **(4)** $8\frac{1}{4}$     **(5)** $7\frac{3}{4}$

9. The ratio of the number of problems Shirley got right to the number she got wrong was 7:2. There were 36 problems on the test. How many problems did she get right?

   **(1)** 20     **(2)** 22     **(3)** 24     **(4)** 28     **(5)** 32

10. A house owner wants to build an addition on top of his house. There is a local law against building houses too high in residential neighborhoods. He wants to find out how high his house is. He knows his flagpole is 20 feet high and casts a shadow 15 feet long at noon. The shadow of his house at noon is 30 feet. What is the height of his house in feet?

    **(1)** 40     **(2)** 45     **(3)** 50     **(4)** 60     **(5)** 65

Answers are on pages A-38 and A-39.

---

Lesson
3

# Probability

**Probability** is the chance that a given event will occur. For example, when you flip a coin, two kinds of events are possible: (1) heads will show, or (2) tails will show.

Probability can be expressed in fractions. The probability that heads will show when a coin is flipped is written as:

$$\frac{1 \quad \text{the number of heads on a coin (one kind of event)}}{2 \quad \text{the number of sides on a coin (all possible events)}}$$

The probability of heads in a coin flip is $\frac{1}{2}$. That means that if a coin is flipped, there is one chance in two that heads will show.

To show probability as a fraction, write the number of possibilities that one kind of event will occur as the numerator. Write the number of all possible events as the denominator.

Probability problems often involve picking an object from a group of similar objects without looking.

**Example 1:** There are 8 black checkers and 12 red checkers in a box. Bob picks a checker from the box without looking. What is the probability that it is a black checker?

Step 1. There are 8 chances of picking a black checker. Write 8 as the numerator.

$$\frac{8}{\phantom{8}} \qquad \text{one kind of event}$$

Step 2. Find the number of possible events: 8 black checkers + 12 red checkers = 20 checkers. Write 8 + 12 as the denominator. Add the terms in the denominator: 8 + 12 = 20.

$$\frac{8}{8+12} \qquad \text{all possible events}$$

$$\frac{8}{8+12} = \frac{8}{20}$$

Step 3. Reduce the fraction to lowest terms. There are 2 chances in 5 of picking a black checker.

$$\frac{8}{20} = \frac{2}{5}$$

**Example 2:** A bag contains 6 marbles. There are 3 red marbles, 2 yellow marbles, and 1 green marble in the bag. A red marble is picked from the bag and not replaced. What is the probability that the next marble, picked without looking, will be yellow?

Step 1. There are 2 yellow marbles in the bag. Write 2 as the numerator.

$$\frac{2}{\phantom{2}} \qquad \text{yellow marbles}$$

Step 2. How many marbles in all are left in the bag? 6 marbles − 1 red marble = 5 marbles. Use 5 as the denominator. There are 2 chances in 5 of picking a yellow marble.

$$\frac{2}{6-1} \qquad \text{total marbles}$$

$$\frac{2}{5}$$

Notice in Example 2 if the green marble had been picked from the bag first, there would be no green marbles in the bag. The probability of a green marble being picked as the next marble would be $\frac{0}{5}$ or no chance at all. A fraction with a numerator of 0 equals 0.

## Level 2, Lesson 3 Exercise

**Directions:** Find each probability. All picks are made without looking.

1. A purse contains two pennies, a dime and a nickel. What is the probability that the first coin taken from the purse will be the dime?

2. What is the probability of picking a pair of brown socks from a drawer that contains 2 pairs of black socks, 3 pairs of brown socks, and 4 pairs of white socks?

3. A carton contains 15 cans of tomato soup and 20 cans of chicken soup. What is the probability that the first can taken from the carton will be a can of tomato soup?

4. There were 5 red lollipops, 3 purple lollipops, and 2 green lollipops in a bag. Karen chose a purple lollipop. What is the probability the next person will pick a green one?

5. In a bag of 20 apples, 3 are bruised. What is the probability of picking an apple that is not bruised from the bag?

Answers are on page A-39.

# Level 3 Fraction Problem Solving

## Lesson 1 — Setup Problems

In Chapter 1, Level 3, Lesson 1, you were introduced to so-called "setup" problems on the GED, which do not ask you to find the answer to a problem: instead, they ask you to identify the operation needed to find the answer. To do this, you may have to apply your knowledge of fractions—of ratio, proportion and probability. You may also need to remember order of operations and formulas.

**Example 1:** Fred bought six boards that were each 9 feet long. Which of the following expressions represents the total length of the boards in yards?

(1) $\dfrac{(6 \times 9)}{36}$

(2) $\dfrac{(6 \times 9)}{3}$

(3) $3(6 \times 9)$

(4) $3 + 6 + 9$

(5) $3(6 + 9)$

Step 1. Multiply the number of boards times the length of each board in feet.
$6 \times 9 = 54$ feet

Step 2. Divide the total number of feet by 3 to get the total length of the boards in yards. (1 yard = 3 feet)
$\dfrac{54}{3} = 18$ yards

Therefore, the correct expression for these two operations is **(2)** $\dfrac{(6 \times 9)}{3}$.

To select the correct expression in this problem, you must apply your knowledge of order of operations and of units of measurement.

## Using Proportions in Setup Problems

Setting up a proportion from the data given in the word problem is often a quick and accurate way to find the correct expression in a GED setup question.

**Example 2:** Janet types 75 words per minute. Which of the following expressions tells you how long it would take her to type a report containing 8250 words?

**(1)** $8250 \times 75$

**(2)** $\dfrac{8250}{75}$

**(3)** $\dfrac{8250}{75 \times 60}$

**(4)** $\dfrac{8250 \times 75}{60}$

**(5)** $\dfrac{8250 \div 60}{75}$

Step 1. Set up the proportion to show the relationship among the facts in the problem.

$$\frac{\text{number of minutes}}{\text{number of words}} = \frac{1 \text{ min.}}{75 \text{ words}} = \frac{n \ (\text{minutes needed to type 8250 words})}{8250 \text{ words}}$$

Step 2. Cross-multiply to find the value of $n$.

$$\frac{1}{75} = \frac{n}{8250}$$

$$75n = 8250$$

Therefore, **(2)** is the correct answer: $8250 \div 75 = 110$ minutes.

$$n = \frac{8250}{75}$$

Note that some setup problems require only basic whole number operations, although most of the expressions offered as answers are fractions. For instance, you may be able to answer this problem by whole number operations.

Step 1. Set up problem:

$$\text{Total typing time for report} = \frac{\text{total words of report}}{\text{words typed per minute}} \qquad n = \frac{8250}{75}$$

Step 2. Divide word total by words typed per minute:

$$\frac{8250}{75} = 75\overline{)8250}$$

However, if you cannot see the whole number operation right away in a problem like this, a proportion may be useful.

## Level 3, Lesson 1 Exercise

**Directions:** Pick the setup that shows the correct solution to the problem. Remember to watch the signs and the order of operations carefully. Consult the formula page if you need to.

1. The workers at Green Gardens, Inc., can make 20 lawn mowers an hour. Which of the following expressions tells the total number of lawn mowers they can make working eight hours a day for five days a week?

**(1)** $\dfrac{(20 \times 8)}{5}$

**(2)** $\dfrac{(20 \times 5)}{8}$

**(3)** $\dfrac{(5 \times 8)}{20}$

**(4)** $20 \times 8 \times 5$

**(5)** $\dfrac{(20 + 8)}{5}$

2. For a circus performance, the ratio of the number of children's tickets sold to the number of adult tickets sold was 5:2. 630 children's tickets were sold. Which of the following expressions represents the <u>total</u> number of tickets sold?

**(1)** $\dfrac{5}{2} = \dfrac{630}{n}$

**(2)** $\dfrac{2}{5} = \dfrac{630}{n}$

**(3)** $\dfrac{5}{7} = \dfrac{630}{n}$

**(4)** $5n = 630$

**(5)** $\dfrac{n}{7} = \dfrac{5}{630}$

3. A box contains 15 green tennis balls, 12 orange tennis balls, and 9 white tennis balls. Which of the following expressions shows the probability that the first ball someone picks from the box will be green?

**(1)** $\dfrac{15}{12 + 9}$

**(2)** $\dfrac{15}{15 + 12 + 9}$

**(3)** $\dfrac{15 + 12 + 9}{15}$

**(4)** $\dfrac{12 + 9}{15}$

**(5)** $15(12 + 9)$

4. Bicycling burns off about 450 calories per hour. Which of the following expressions tells the number of hours required to burn off a pork chop which contains 310 calories and a glass of milk which contains 165 calories?

**(1)** $\dfrac{(310 + 450)}{165}$

**(2)** $310 + 165 + 450$

**(3)** $\dfrac{(310 + 165)}{450}$

**(4)** $\dfrac{(165 \times 450)}{310}$

**(5)** $\dfrac{(310 \times 165)}{450}$

5. A contractor must give an estimate for a new patio. The concrete slab he must pour measures $\frac{1}{6}$ yard by $3\frac{1}{6}$ yards by 6 yards. Concrete costs the contractor \$18 per cubic yard. Delivery costs \$25. Which of the following expressions represents his total cost estimate?

**(1)** $18(\frac{1}{6} + 3\frac{1}{6} + 6) + 25$

**(2)** $(\frac{1}{6} + 3\frac{1}{6} + 6)(18 + 25)$

**(3)** $18(\frac{1}{6} \times 3\frac{1}{6} \times 6) + 25$

**(4)** $(25 - 18)(\frac{1}{6} \times 3\frac{1}{6} \times 6)$

**(5)** $25(\frac{1}{6} + 3\frac{1}{6} + 6) + 18$

Answers are on page A-39.

# Extraneous Information

Not all the information given in a word problem is useful for solving the problem. In fact, sometimes useless information is placed in a problem in an attempt to throw you off the right course. To avoid this, always read the problem carefully, and decide what you are being asked to answer and what information is necessary in order to answer it.

**Example 1:** Daryl bought a coat on sale. The original price was $150. The sale price was $\frac{1}{5}$ off the original price. He paid sales tax of $10 and paid $15 for alterations. What was the sale price of the coat?

**Step 1.** You are asked to find the sale price of the coat. To answer the question, you need to know the original price, $150, and the discount, $\frac{1}{5}$ off. The cost of sales tax and alterations is extraneous information: You don't need to worry about it for this question.

**Step 2.** Multiply to find the amount the coat was discounted.

$$\overset{30}{\underset{1}{\cancel{150}}} \times \frac{1}{\underset{1}{\cancel{5}}} = \frac{30}{1}$$

**Step 3.** Subtract the discount from the original cost to find the sale price.

$$\begin{array}{r} 150 \\ -\ 30 \\ \hline 120 \end{array}$$

**Example 2:** Mike takes home $1400 a month. He pays $350 a month for rent, a $84 a month for car payments. What fraction of his monthly income goes to rent?

**Step 1.** The question asks you to compare Mike's rent to his monthly income. The $84 car payment is extraneous information.

**Step 2.** Make a fraction with the rent on top and the total monthly income on the bottom. Then reduce the fraction.

$$\frac{350}{1400} = \frac{1}{4}$$

## Level 3, Lesson 2 Exercise

**Directions:** Identify the extraneous information in each problem, then solve the problem.

1. Nick used $3\frac{1}{5}$ boxes of vinyl tiles. He had purchased 5 boxes of tiles at $15 each. If each box contained 20 tiles, how many tiles did Nick have left over?

**2.** Diane built a large storage shed. She purchased $1\frac{1}{2}$ pounds of 2-inch nails and $\frac{3}{4}$ pound of 3-inch nails at a price of $1 per pound. She used $\frac{5}{6}$ pound of 2-inch nails and $\frac{1}{2}$ pound of 3-inch nails. How many pounds of 2-inch nails did Diane have left?

**3.** Chuck manages a day care center. The number of children in attendance at the center ranges from 15 to 48, which is its capacity. Besides Chuck, four other people work at the day care center. The center is open for 16 hours a day, seven days a week. If the center has the maximum number of children in attendance $\frac{5}{8}$ of the time it is open, how many hours per week is the center at its maximum capacity?

**4.** Sylvia saved $5 on her grocery bill by using coupons. She was also given a refund of $1 for returning 20 deposit bottles. Her grocery bill came to $55 before the coupons were deducted. What fraction represents the coupon savings in relation to the original bill?

**5.** Conrad uses $1\frac{1}{4}$ cups of detergent to wash a load of clothes. He also used 1 capful of water conditioner and $\frac{1}{2}$ cup of bleach. If he does 3 loads of laundry per week, how many cups of bleach does he use in 4 weeks?

Answers are on page A-39.

# Chapter 2 Quiz

Solve each problem. Use the list of formulas when necessary.

1. There are 80 quarts of whole milk in a store, out of a total of 128 quarts of milk products. What is the ratio of the number of quarts of whole milk to the number of quarts of milk products?

2. If a map has a scale of 1 inch = 90 miles, what is the distance in miles between two cities $3\frac{1}{2}$ inches apart on the map?

3. The gas tank in Rachel's car holds 20 gallons. Before she started on a trip, the tank was $\frac{1}{4}$ full. If her car gets $16\frac{1}{2}$ miles per gallon, how far can she drive before her car runs out of gas?

4. Felix spends at least 30 hours per month volunteering at the hospital. He helped for $7\frac{1}{2}$ hours the first week of one month, $6\frac{3}{4}$ hours the second week, and $9\frac{1}{4}$ hours the third week. If he wishes to reach his goal of 30 hours, how much more time in hours and minutes must he volunteer?

5. Glenn has paid $\frac{5}{6}$ of his car loan. If the amount he borrowed was $3000, how much does he still owe?

6. There are 25 fiction books and 30 nonfiction books on a shelf. What is the probability of picking a fiction book from the shelf without looking at the titles?

Items 7 and 8 are based on the following partial list of ingredients for:

### Three-Grain Fruit Bread

| | |
|---|---|
| $8\frac{1}{2}$ cups of flour | $\frac{1}{3}$ cup skim milk powder |
| $2\frac{1}{4}$ cups of uncooked oatmeal | 3 cups fruit juice |
| $1\frac{3}{4}$ cups uncooked whole-wheat cereal | 1 cup yogurt |
| $1\frac{2}{3}$ cups cornmeal | |

7. The first five ingredients are dry and the last two are liquid. What is the ratio of dry to liquid ingredients?

8. Between cornmeal and whole-wheat cereal, which does the fruit bread contain more of?

9. At the factory where Patty works, the ratio of management to workers is 3:14. Including management, there are 340 people working at the factory. How many people work in management?

10. The ratio of the number of girls to the number of boys at the Morningside Day Care Center is 5:4. There are 84 boys enrolled at the center. How many children are there altogether?

11. Which of the following expressions gives the solution to $11:16 = n:4$?

(1) $\dfrac{(4 \times 11)}{16}$

(4) $\dfrac{4}{(11 \times 16)}$

(2) $\dfrac{(16 \times 11)}{4}$

(5) $\dfrac{(16 \times 4)}{11}$

(3) $16 \times 4 \times 11$

12. If health insurance benefits for an employee cost $42 per month and if the employee pays $\frac{2}{7}$ of the cost, which of the following expressions shows how much the employer pays?

(1) $42 + (42 \times \frac{2}{7})$

(2) $(42 \times \frac{2}{7}) - 42$

(3) $42 - (42 \times \frac{2}{7})$

(4) $(42 \times \frac{2}{7}) + 42$

(5) $\frac{2}{7} \times 42$

13. If Mark's salary is $2000 per month and he takes home $1500 after taxes, which of the following expressions shows the ratio of taxes Mark pays in relation to his salary before taxes?

(1) $\dfrac{2000 + 1500}{3500}$

(4) $\dfrac{2000 - 1500}{2000}$

(2) $\dfrac{2000 - 1500}{3500}$

(5) $\dfrac{1500}{2000}$

(3) $\dfrac{2000 + 1500}{2000}$

14. On a test, Rick got 6 problems wrong and 54 problems right. Of the total number of problems, he guessed the answers to 8 of them. What fraction of the problems did he get right? What information is extraneous?

15. The elementary schools in Greenport had a joint festival for three nights. Receipts on Monday were $2500; on Tuesday, $4850; and on Wednesday, $4200. The money was shared equally by five schools. Which of the following expressions tells the amount each school received?

(1) $\dfrac{(2500 + 4850 + 4200)}{5}$

(4) $\dfrac{(2500 + 4850 + 4200)}{3}$

(2) $5(2500 + 4850 + 4200)$

(3) $\dfrac{2500}{5 + 4850 + 4200}$

(5) $\dfrac{5}{(2500 + 4850 + 4200)}$

Answers are on pages A-39 and A-40.

# CHAPTER 3
# Decimals

We use decimals every day: on the odometer of a car, the scale and cash register in a grocery store, the gauge on a gas pump. The best-known decimals are those used to indicate the value of coins: any amount of change from a dollar, from 1 penny ($.01) to 99 cents ($.99), is a decimal amount, because those decimals are another way of writing fractions of $1.00. A decimal amount is always a fraction with a denominator of 100: .01 = $\frac{1}{100}$ and .99 = $\frac{99}{100}$.

---

## In this chapter you will learn to:

- Read and write decimals
- Add, subtract, multiply, and divide decimals
- Change decimals to equal fractions and fractions to equal decimals
- Round off decimals
- Solve word problems that involve decimals
- Use decimals in metric measurements
- Find circumference and area of circles, and volume of cylinders
- Compare and order decimals
- Identify problems that have insufficient data for solution

---

461

# Decimal Skills

---

## Preview

1. Write seven ten-thousandths as a decimal.
2. What is the sum of .431, .73, and .6?
3. What is the difference between .79 and .124?
4. What is the product of 2.5 and .43?
5. What is 1.261 divided by 9.7?
6. Change .68 to a fraction in lowest terms.
7. Change $\frac{1}{4}$ to a decimal.

Answers are on page A-40. If you have at least five correct, try the Chapter 3 Quiz on page 481. If you have fewer than five answers correct, study Level 1 beginning with Lesson 1.

---

Lesson

**1**

## Reading and Writing Decimals

A decimal is a fraction whose denominator is not written but is indicated by the position of the decimal point. Like a fraction, a decimal expresses a value less than 1. Unlike fractions, the denominators of decimals are limited to 10 or to powers of ten such as 100; 1,000; 10,000; and so forth. The decimal point separates the whole number from the decimal: All numbers to the left of the decimal point are whole numbers; all numbers to the right of the decimal point are decimals. The first number to the right of the decimal point is called a tenth; the second number, a hundredth—and so on. The place-value table summarizes the names of the decimal places as well as those of whole numbers.

| hundreds | tens | decimal point | tenths | hundredths | thousandths | ten-thousandths | hundred-thousandths | millionths | You read these numbers as: |
|---|---|---|---|---|---|---|---|---|---|
| | | . | 4 | | | | | | four tenths |
| | | . | 0 | 4 | | | | | four hundredths |
| | 4 | . | 0 | 0 | 4 | | | | four and four thousandths |
| 4 | 4 | . | 0 | 0 | 4 | 4 | | | forty-four and forty-four ten-thousandths |
| | | . | 0 | 0 | 4 | 0 | 4 | | four hundred four hundred-thousandths |
| | | . | 0 | 0 | 0 | 0 | 0 | 4 | four millionths |

A number that includes both a whole number and a decimal is called a **mixed decimal**. When reading a mixed decimal, instead of saying the whole number and the decimal, you can read the whole number, say "and" for the decimal point, and then read the digits of the decimal. For example, read 44.0044 in the table as "forty-four and forty-four ten-thousandths." You read 4.004 as "four and four thousandths."

The zeros between the decimal point and the other digits serve as place holders. It is the zero that makes .04 four hundredths instead of four tenths. Two zeros to the right of the decimal point make the decimal .004, or four thousandths. Zeros at the end of a decimal have no value and can be dropped. For example, the decimals .4, .40, and .400 have the same value because the zeros do not change the place value of the 4. The simplest way to express this value is .4.

Look at the ways the following decimals are written:

| Value | Decimal | Fraction Equivalent |
|---|---|---|
| nine hundredths | .09 | $\frac{9}{100}$ |
| thirteen thousandths | .013 | $\frac{13}{1000}$ |
| six ten-thousandths | .0006 | $\frac{6}{10,000}$ |
| six tenths | .6 | $\frac{6}{10}$ |

## Level 1, Lesson 1 Exercise

**Directions:** Match the number in the left-hand column with the words in the right-hand column.

1. 0.0075
2. 0.75
3. 100.01
4. 100.001
5. 0.075

a. seventy-five thousandths
b. one hundred and one thousandth
c. seventy-five ten-thousandths
d. one hundred and one hundredth
e. seventy-five hundredths

**Directions:** Express each value in decimal form.

6. seven and thirteen thousandths
7. twenty-seven ten-thousandths
8. ten and two hundred three millionths
9. thirteen hundredths
10. three hundred and seven tenths

Answers are on page A-40.

# Adding Decimals

To add decimals, be sure the decimal points are lined up. If all the decimals do not end at the same place, you can add zeros to those decimals that have the fewest number of places. That will help you keep the numbers in line in the columns. Once set up, add the same way you would a whole number. The decimal point is brought straight down.

**Example:** What is the sum of 25, .35, .7, and .984?

Step 1. Set up the problem. Be sure the decimal points are lined up and add zeros to keep the values in line. The whole number, 25, does not show a decimal point. With such a whole number, a decimal point is put after the ones place. Put the decimal in the answer directly below where it is in the problem.

```
         tens ones . tenths hundredths thousandths
        2 5 . 0 0 0
            . 3 5 0
            . 7 0 0
      +     . 9 8 4
```

Step 2. Add the columns straight down. Carry as needed.

```
           2   1
        2 5 . 0 0 0
            . 3 5 0
            . 7 0 0
      +     . 9 8 4
        2 7 . 0 3 4
```

## Level 1, Lesson 2 Exercise

**Directions:** Find the sums.

1. .19 + .8 + .326
2. $.73 + $.26 + $.11
3. .059 + .07 + .0694
4. 12 + .073 + .38
5. Find the sum of .6, .095, and .45.

Answers are on page A-40.

# Lesson 3

# Subtracting Decimals

To subtract decimals, follow the same rules for decimal placement as in addition. Always put the larger number on top. If the decimal of the top number has fewer places than the bottom number, add zeros to the top number. Subtract, borrowing as you would with whole number subtraction.

**Example:** Subtract 0.46 from 12.

**Step 1.** Set up the problem. Keep the decimal points in line and add zeros to the 12 to equal the number of decimal places in 0.46.

$$\begin{array}{r} 1\ 2\ .\ 0\ 0 \\ -\quad .\ 4\ 6 \\ \hline \end{array}$$

**Step 2.** Subtract. Borrow as needed.

$$\begin{array}{r} 9 \\ 1\quad \cancel{X}\ 1 \\ 1\ 2\ .\ \cancel{0}\ \cancel{0} \\ -\quad .\ 4\ 6 \\ \hline 1\ 1\ .\ 5\ 4 \end{array}$$

## Level 1, Lesson 3 Exercise

**Directions:** Find the difference for each problem.

1.  $\begin{array}{r} .7 \\ -\ .006 \\ \hline \end{array}$

2.  $\begin{array}{r} 30 \\ -\ .8 \\ \hline \end{array}$

3.  $\begin{array}{r} 39.1 \\ -\ .2 \\ \hline \end{array}$

4. $86.30 – $23
5. 5.004 – 1.999
6. What is the difference between 4.5 and 9.04?
7. Take .567 away from .8.
8. Subtract 32.32 from 189.11.
9. What is the difference between .43701 and 1.2953?
10. What does .6401 minus .39002 equal?

Answers are on page A-41.

# Lesson 4

# Multiplying Decimals

When multiplying decimals, do the computation as if the numbers had no decimals and you were multiplying whole numbers. When you have done the multiplication operations, you put in the decimal point. The decimal point's placement is determined by how many places there are to the right of the decimal in the numbers multiplied. First, find the total number of places by counting the decimal places in both the numbers multiplied. Then, for each place, count from right to left in the product, or answer. Place the decimal point there. When the product does not have enough places, zeros can be placed to the left of the product to make enough places.

**Example 1:** Find the product of .4 and .75.

Step 1. Set up the problem. You do not need to worry about keeping the decimal points in line.

$$
\begin{array}{r}
.75 \\
\times\ .4 \\
\end{array}
$$

Step 2. Multiply as if these were whole numbers. $75 \times 4 = 300$

$$
\begin{array}{r}
.75 \\
\times\ .4 \\
\hline
300 \\
\end{array}
$$

Step 3. Find the total number of decimal places in the two numbers that have been multiplied. Here it is three. Starting from the right, count three places to the left in the product. Drop the zeros to the right of the decimal number.

$$
\begin{array}{r}
.75 \\
\times\ .4 \\
\hline
.300 \\
\end{array} = .3
$$

**Example 2:** Find the product of .075 and .2.

Step 1. Set up the problem.

$$
\begin{array}{r}
.075 \\
\times\ .2 \\
\end{array}
$$

Step 2. Multiply as if these were whole numbers. $75 \times 2 = 150$

$$
\begin{array}{r}
.075 \\
\times\ .2 \\
\hline
150 \\
\end{array}
$$

Step 3. Find the total number of decimal places in the numbers that have been multiplied. Here it is four. Starting from the right count four places to the left. Since the product has only three digits, add a zero. Put in the decimal point. You can then drop the end zero.

$$
\begin{array}{r}
.075 \\
\times\ .2 \\
\hline
.0150 \\
\end{array} = .015
$$

## Level 1, Lesson 4 Exercise

**Directions:** Find the products. Be sure to place the decimal point in the proper place.

1. $9.6 \times 23$
2. $(.72)(.3)$
3. Multiply .705 by 5.
4. What is the product of 1.029 and .884?
5. Find the product of .678 times .14.

Answers are on page A-41.

# Dividing Decimals

When dividing with a decimal, you determine where the decimal will be placed before performing the division operations. When the divisor is a whole number, the decimal for the quotient is placed above the decimal of the dividend; in other words, you line up the decimal points. Dividing a whole number into a decimal is dividing a larger number into a smaller number.

## Dividing Decimals by Whole Numbers

**Example 1:** Divide .728 by 8

Step 1. Set up the problem. Place the quotient's decimal point directly above the decimal point in the dividend.

$$8\overline{)\overset{\centerdot}{.728}}$$

Step 2. Divide as you would if this were a whole number. Since 8 will not go into 7 at all, place a 0 above the 7, and take 8 into 72.

$$8\overline{)\overset{.091}{.728}}$$
$$\begin{array}{r} 72 \\ 8 \\ 8 \end{array}$$

## Dividing Decimals by Decimals

When the divisor has a decimal, move the decimal to the right as many places as are needed to make it a whole number. Then move the decimal in the dividend the same number of places. If the dividend does not have enough places to move the decimal point, add enough zeros to do it. Then put the decimal point in the quotient directly above the decimal point in the dividend.

**Example 2:** Divide 93.6 by .52

Step 1. Set the problem up.

$$.52\overline{)93.6}$$

Step 2. Move the decimal 2 places in the divisor. Move the decimal two places in the dividend, adding a zero. Put the decimal point in the quotient directly above the one in the dividend.

$$.52\overline{)9360.}$$

Step 3. Divide. Since the quotient is a whole number, the decimal point can be dropped.

$$52\overline{)\overset{180.}{9360.}}$$
$$\begin{array}{r} 52 \\ 416 \\ 416 \\ 0 \\ 0 \end{array}$$

**Directions:** Find the quotient.

1. $.4 \overline{\smash{)}.34}$    2. $6 \overline{\smash{)}1.26}$    3. $13 \overline{\smash{)}24.05}$    4. $.25 \overline{\smash{)}.1575}$
5. 75.4 divided by 5
6. .20 divided by .02
7. Divide .615 by .5.

Answers are on page A-41.

## Interchanging Decimals and Fractions

**Lesson 6**

A value less than a whole can be expressed either as a decimal or a fraction. Later, especially when you work with percents, you will often need to change between decimals and fractions.

## Changing Decimals to Fractions

To change a decimal to a fraction, write the digits in the decimals as the numerator. Write the name of the decimal—tenths, hundredths, thousandths, etc.—as the denominator. Then reduce the fraction.

**Example 1:** Change .08 to a fraction.

Write .08 as the numerator. The denominator is 100 because .08 has two places. Reduce $\frac{8}{100}$.

$$\frac{8}{100} = \frac{2}{25}$$

**Example 2:** Change 9.6 to a mixed number.

Write 9 as a whole number and 6 as the numerator. The denominator is 10 because 9.6 has one decimal place. Reduce $9\frac{6}{10}$.

$$9\frac{6}{10} = 9\frac{3}{5}$$

## Changing Fractions to Decimals

The line in a fraction means "divided by." For example, $\frac{7}{20}$ means "7 divided by 20." To change a fraction to a decimal, divide the numerator by the denominator. Put a decimal point and zeros to the right of the numerator.

**Example 3:** Change $\frac{9}{100}$ to a decimal.

Divide 7 by 20. Put a decimal point and zeros to the right of the 7. Bring the decimal point up into the answer.

$$
\begin{array}{r}
.35 \\
20\overline{)7.00} \\
6\;0 \\
\hline
1\;00 \\
1\;00 \\
\end{array}
$$

Some common decimal equivalents are as follows. You may want to memorize them.

$$\frac{1}{4} = .25 \qquad\qquad \frac{1}{3} = .33$$

$$\frac{1}{2} = .5 \qquad\qquad \frac{2}{3} = .67$$

$$\frac{3}{4} = .75 \qquad\qquad \frac{5}{6} = .83$$

## Level 1, Lesson 6 Exercise

**Directions:** Change each decimal to a fraction or a mixed number reduced to lowest terms.

1. .9     2. 18.375     3. 7.08     4. 6.4     5. .85

**Directions:**   Change each fraction to a decimal. Round off where necessary.

6. $\frac{7}{8}$     7. $\frac{4}{9}$     8. $\frac{8}{10}$     9. $\frac{7}{15}$     10. $\frac{9}{20}$

Answers are on page A-41.

# Level 2: Decimal Applications

## Lesson 1: Rounding Decimals

Decimals that carry into hundred-thousandths, millionths, and beyond represent very small amounts. When precision is necessary, a decimal to one of those places is helpful. However, decimals with several places can be hard to work with. When such precision is not necessary, rounding decimals will make a problem easier to solve. The rules for rounding decimals are almost the same as for rounding whole numbers. Find the place to which you are rounding; look at the digit to the right. If the digit to the right is less than 5, leave the place to which you are rounding the same. If the digit to the right is 5 or more, increase the place to which you are rounding by one. Instead of replacing the digits to the right of the number with 0s, as in whole numbers, drop those digits. Remember that when the digit that needs to be raised is 9, that 9 is changed to 0 and the digit to its left is increased by 1.

**Example 1:** Round 12.784 to the nearest tenth.

Step 1. Identify the digit in the tenths place.     12.7̲84

Step 2. Look at the digit to its right. Since it is 8, the digit in the tenths place, 7, will be increased to 8.     12.84

Step 3. Drop the digits to the right of the tenths place. 12.784 is rounded to 12.8.     12.8

**Example 2:** Round 1.714 to the nearest hundredth.

Step 1. Identify the digit in the hundredths place.     1.71̲4

Step 2. Look at the digit to its right. Since it is 4, the digit in the hundredths place will remain the same.

Step 3. Drop the digit to the right of the hundredths place. 1.714 is rounded to 1.71     1.71

**Example 3:** Round 3.89765 to the nearest hundredth.

Step 1. Identify the digit in the hundredths place.      3.8<u>9</u>765

Step 2. Look at the digit to its right. Since it is greater than 5, the digit in the hundredths place will change. However, since that digit is 9, it will be changed to 0, and the digit to its left, 8, will be increased by 1.      3.<u>90</u>765

Step 3. Digits to the right of the hundredths place and the 0 in the hundredths place can be dropped. 3.89765 rounded to the nearest hundredth is 3.9.      3.9

## Level 2, Lesson 1 Exercise

**Directions:** Round each number to the nearest tenth.

   **1.** .949     **2.** .371     **3.** 1.535     **4.** 10.061     **5.** 78.394

**Directions:** Round each number to the nearest hundredth.

   **6.** 5.8562   **7.** .7644     **8.** 23.7131     **9.** .5959     **10.** 8.1106

Answers are on page A-41.

# Decimal Word Problems

You have already had practice with word problems in Chapters 1 and 2. Word problems present situations in which you put the mathematics you have learned to practical use. When working a word problem, you should read the problem carefully to determine what the problem is asking you. You then need to decide which operation to use, set up the problem correctly, and solve it. Word problems requiring decimal skills often involve measurement or money.

**Example:** Cerra Machine Design used 22.5 ounces of copper to manufacture 8 rotors. To the nearest hundredth of an ounce, how much copper was needed to make each rotor?

Step 1. Determine what is being asked and decide which operation is needed. Here you are asked to find a per-unit amount, which requires division.

Step 2. Set up the problem.         $8\overline{)22.5}$

**Step 3.** Solve the problem. Add decimal places until the division results in no remainder.

$$
\begin{array}{r}
2.8125 = 2.81 \text{ oz.} \\
8\,)\overline{22.5000} \\
\underline{16}\phantom{.0000} \\
65\phantom{.000} \\
\underline{64}\phantom{.000} \\
10\phantom{.00} \\
\underline{8}\phantom{.00} \\
20\phantom{.0} \\
\underline{16}\phantom{.0} \\
40 \\
\underline{40}
\end{array}
$$

## Level 2, Lesson 2 Exercise

**Directions:** Solve each problem. Remember to read each problem carefully, determine what is being asked, and decide which operation to use.

1. Julia Piagga earns $10.80 per hour. How much does she earn in an 8-hour workday?

2. George Thompson paid $72.89 for 3.7 feet of gold tape. How much did the tape cost per foot?

3. The premium for Potaboc City's liability insurance was $119,583.54 the year before last, $142,568.45 last year, and $186,294.36 this year. What was the total cost of liability insurance for the three-year period?

4. At the end of the week, a tank held 374.2 gallons of fuel oil. It held 976.9 gallons at the beginning of the week. Assuming no fuel was wasted, how much fuel oil was burned for heat that week?

5. A truck rental firm charges $.89 per mile for use of one of its trucks. What would be the charge for 195 miles?

Answers are on pages A-41 and A-42.

**Lesson 3**

# Metric Measurement

Metric measurement is the standard system in most parts of the world. Its use has met limited acceptance in the United States, except in a few fields such as science and medicine.

The metric system has only three basic units of measurement:

1. The basic unit of length is the *meter*. A meter is a little longer than a yard. It is abbreviated as **m**.

2. The basic unit of weight is the *gram*. A gram is equal to about $\frac{1}{28}$ of an ounce. It is abbreviated as **g**.

3. The basic unit of volume is the *liter*. A liter is a little larger than a quart. It is abbreviated as **l**.

Units larger or smaller than the basic units are identified by prefixes. Changes in sizes of units increase or decrease by powers of 10. The Table of Measures on page 400 lists some of these units of measurement and their abbreviations. The most commonly used prefixes are:

| Prefix | Meaning |
|--------|---------|
| kilo (k) | 1000 |
| deci (d) | .1 |
| centi (c) | .01 |
| milli (m) | .001 |

For example, a kilometer (km) is 1000 meters. A centigram is one hundredth (.01) of a gram.

When changing units, the operations are the same as with the standard measurements; multiply to change a larger unit to a smaller unit and divide to change a smaller unit to a larger unit. However, because the operations use powers of ten, the multiplication or division can be done by moving a decimal point, adding zeros when necessary for proper place value. This is sometimes called quick multiplication and division.

When changing a larger unit to a smaller unit, find how many smaller units make up the larger unit and multiply by that amount. This example shows the quick multiplication method.

**Example 1:** Change 2.7 kilograms to grams.

Step 1. Find how many grams make up one kilogram.      1 kg = 1000 g

Step 2. Use quick multiplication to convert the         2,700
amount to grams. Count how many zeros there are
in 1000. There are three. Move the decimal point to     2.7 kg = 2700 g
the right the number of places equal to the number
of zeros. Here the decimal point will be moved three
places to the right. Since there is one digit to the
right of the decimal in 2.7, the other two places are
taken up by 0s.

When changing a smaller unit to a larger unit, find how many smaller units make up a larger unit and divide by that amount. This example shows the quick division method.

**Example 2:** Change 137 centimeters to meters.

Step 1. Find how many centimeters make up a meter.     100 cm = 1 m

Step 2. Use quick division to convert the amount to     137.
meters. Count how many zeros there are in the num-
ber by which you will divide. Here there are two        137 cm = 1.37 m
zeros in 100. Move the decimal two places to the left.

**Directions:** Use quick multiplication or division to solve each problem.

1. $134 \times 10$
2. $134 \div 10$
3. $987 \times 1000$
4. $.573 \div 10$
5. $452.214 \div 100$

**Directions:** Change each measurement to the other unit of measure. Consult the Table of Measures if necessary.

6. Change 17.21 meters to millimeters.
7. Change 3764 centimeters to meters.
8. Change .7 liters to centiliters.
9. Change 17 cg to grams.
10. Change 1.85 kg to grams.

Answers are on page A-42.

## Lesson 4

# Circumference and Area of Circles

A circle has curved sides, instead of straight lines like the figures with which you worked in Chapters 1 and 2. Every point on a circle's side is the same distance from the center. Because of these unique properties, working with circles is different from working with squares, rectangles, and triangles. Figure 3–1 shows some parts of a circle.

## Finding the Circumference of a Circle

**Fig. 3–1**

The **diameter (d)** of a circle is the straight-line distance from one edge of the circle through the center to the edge on the other side. The **radius (r)** is the straight-line distance from the center to the edge of the circle. For any circle, a diameter or a radius will always be the same length no matter where the points on the edge of the circle are. For any circle, the diameter is 2 times the length of its radius, and its radius is $\frac{1}{2}$ of its diameter.

$$d = 2r \qquad\qquad\qquad r = \frac{d}{2}$$

The **circumference (C)** of a circle is the distance around it, or its **perimeter**. To find the circumference, a number called π, the Greek letter **pi** (π), is used. π = 3.14. To find the circumference of a circle multiply the diameter by π, 3.14. This formula for circumference of a circle is listed in the formula table on page 401.

**C = πd**

**Example 1:** Find the circumference of a circle with a diameter of 10 feet.

Replace π with 3.14 and *d* with 10 ft. in the formula for the circumference of a circle. Multiply π times 10 to find *C*.

$C = \pi d$
$C = 3.14 \times 10$
$C = 31.4$ feet

**Example 2:** Find the circumference of a circle with a radius of 50 inches.

Step 1. Find the diameter of the circle.

$d = 2r$
$d = 2 \times 50$
$d = 100$ inches

Step 2. Replace π with 3.14 and *d* with 100 in the formula for the circumference of a circle. Multiply 100 times π to find *C*.

$C = \pi d$
$C = 3.14 \times 100$

## Finding the Area of a Circle

To find the area of a circle, multiply π by the radius squared. This formula is also listed on the formula page 401.

**A = πr²**

Remember that area is measured in square units, such as square inches, square feet, square yards, and square meters.

**Example 3:** Find the area of a circle that has a radius of 3 feet.

Step 1. Set up the problem using the formula.

$A = \pi r^2$
$A = 3.14 \times 3^2$

Step 2. Solve it.

$A = 3.14 \times 9$
$A = 28.26$ square feet

## Level 2, Lesson 4 Exercise

**Directions:** Items 1 to 3 are about a circle with a 6-inch diameter.

1. What is the radius of the circle?
2. What is its circumference?
3. What is its area?

**Directions:** Items 4 and 5 are about a circle with a 10-inch radius.

   **4.** What is its circumference?
   **5.** What is its area?

**Directions:** Solve each problem.

   **6.** Find the circumference of the circle in Figure 3–2.

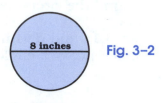

8 inches **Fig. 3–2**

   **7.** Find the area of the circle in Figure 3–3.

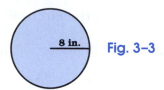

8 in. **Fig. 3–3**

   **8.** Find the circumference of the circle in Figure 3–4.

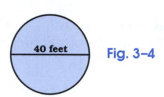

40 feet **Fig. 3–4**

Answers are on page A-42.

## Lesson 5 — Volume of a Cylinder

A cylinder is a three-dimensional figure that has straight sides and whose top and bottom are circles of equal radius. The soda pop can below is a cylinder. So is a water pipe or a drinking glass.

The size of a cylinder, like that of other three-dimensional figures, is determined by its volume and measured in cubic units. To find the volume of a cylinder, you multiply π by the radius ($r$) squared of an end by the height ($h$) of the cylinder. The formula, which is found in the Formula Table on page 401, is written as:

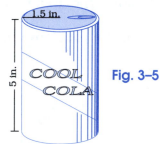

1.5 in.

5 in.

COOL COLA

**Fig. 3–5**

$$V = \pi r^2 h$$

**Example:** Find the volume of a can 5 inches high whose end has a radius of 1.5 inches.

Step 1. Using the formula, set the problem up.

$V = \pi r^2 h$
$V = 3.14 \times 1.5^2 \times 5$

Step 2. Solve by multiplying.

$V = 3.14 \times 2.25 \times 5$
$V = 35.325$ cubic inches

**Directions:** Find the volume of each cylinder. Be sure to express your answers in cubic units.

1. a 6-inch-high cylinder whose end has a 6-inch radius
2. a 12-foot-high cylinder whose end has a 4-foot diameter
3. a 7.5-meter-high cylinder whose end has a 10-meter radius
4. a 1-yard-high cylinder whose end has a .5-yard radius
5. a 20-centimeter-high cylinder whose end has an 8-centimeter radius.

Answers are on page A-42.

## Lesson 6

## Comparing Decimals

When comparing decimals, start with the tenths place and look at each place to the right until you are able to determine the relative size of the decimals. Adding zeros so that each decimal has the same number of places makes the process much easier.

**Example 1:** Which is larger, .706 or .7?

Step 1. Add zeros to .7 to give it the same number of places as .706.

$$.7 = .700$$
$$.706 = .706$$

Step 2. Compare the decimals. Both have the same digit in the tenths place. Look at the place to the right, the hundredths place. Again the decimals have the same digit. Look at the place to the right of the hundredths, the thousandths place. Here 6 is larger than 0. So .706 is larger than .7.

When ordering three or more decimals, the process is the same.

**Example 2:** Arrange .401, .4, and .41 in order from the smallest to the largest.

Step 1. Add zeros so that all the decimals have the same number of places.

$$.401 = .401$$
$$.4 = .400$$
$$.41 = .410$$

Step 2. Starting in the tenths place, compare. All the decimals have the same digit in that place. Look at the hundredths place. Here .410 is larger than the other two, but you are not able to tell which of the other two is larger. Look at the thousandths place. You are able to tell that .401 is larger than .400. From smallest to largest the decimals are ordered:  .4,  .401,  .410

**Directions:** Find the larger decimal in each set.

1. .51 *or* .501
2. .901 *or* .9001
3. .4 *or* .04

**Directions:** Arrange each set of decimals in order from the largest to the smallest.

4. .79, .7901, .7091, .791
5. .631, .6301, .6031, .63

Answers are on page A-42.

# Insufficient Data

Throughout the mathematics section of this book, it has been emphasized that when working with various types of word problems, you should read the question carefully, decide what you are being asked to answer, determine what information you need to answer and what operations you must perform, and then solve the problem. Some questions on the GED test do not have all the information to answer a question. On a multiple-choice question, one of the choices (probably choice 5) might be "Insufficient data is given to solve the problem." If you can't answer the problem with only the information contained in the problem, that is the correct answer. However, not all questions with this answer choice have insufficient data. Sometimes a choice is given to you to see if you can analyze the problem. You must make sure that there is insufficient data before picking that as your choice.

Examples 1 and 2 are based on the following:

Edna and Roger are planning to carpet three rooms of their apartment. The living room measures 16.5 feet by 18 feet. The dining room measures 11 feet by 9.5 feet. The guest room measures 10.5 feet by 8.5 feet, and the master bedroom measures 12.5 feet by 15 feet. They found carpeting they like that costs $11.50 per square yard.

**Example 1:** How many square feet larger is the master bedroom than the guest room?

**(1)** 98.25

**(2)** 89.25

**(3)** 57.5

**(4)** 38.75

**(5)** Insufficient data is given to solve this problem.

Step 1. Read the question carefully. You are being asked to compare the size of one room to another. You need to know the measurements of the rooms. Then you need to find the areas of the rooms and subtract. The information you need is in the problem:

The master bedroom measures 12.5' by 15'.

The guest room measures 10.5' by 8.5'.

Answer choice **(5)** is eliminated.

<u>Step 2.</u> Solve the problem.

Master bedroom: $A = 12.5 \times 15 = 187.5$
Guest room: $A = 10.5 \times 8.5 = 89.25$
$187.5 - 89.25 = 98.25$ square feet.

The correct answer is **(1)**.

**Example 2:** How much will carpeting the three rooms cost?

**(1)** $6828.12
**(2)** $5801.75
**(3)** $758.68
**(4)** $593.75
**(5)** Insufficient data is given to solve this problem.

Read the problem carefully. You are being asked to find the cost of carpeting three rooms. You are given the cost of the carpeting in square yards. The measurement of the rooms is given in feet. But wait, the paragraph tells you three rooms are to be carpeted. The measurements for four rooms are given. The paragraph does not tell which three rooms are to be carpeted. There is insufficient data to answer the question. The answer choice is **(5)**.

## Level 3 Exercise

**Directions:** Read each problem carefully. If there is enough information to solve the problem, then solve it. If there is insufficient data, tell what you would need to know in order to solve it.

1. Olga's children saved part of their lunch money to buy her a present. Juan saved $.25 per day. Sean and Ivan saved $.20 per day. How much did they save altogether for the present?

2. Elena bought a 250-milliliter bottle of cough-syrup for $3.99. Sales tax was $.24. She also bought 3 boxes of tissues at $1.19 each. Sales tax on each box was $.07. How much change did she receive from a $10 bill?

3. Feng Construction Company ordered 5 truckloads of concrete conduit at $9.50 per foot. How many feet of concrete did the company order?

4. Kwane Appliance ordered 120 televisions at $410 each and 40 stereos at $525 each. Shipping costs were $1.30 per pound. What was the total cost of the order?

5. Joe drove from his home to his grandmother's at an average speed of 59 miles per hour. He drove for 2 hours, rested, and then arrived at 5 p.m. How many miles is it from his home to his grandmother's?

Answers are on page A-42.

# Chapter 3 Quiz

**Directions:** Solve each problem. Use the Formula Table if needed. Items 12 to 15 require using skills practiced in earlier chapters.

1. Find the sum of 114.682 and 70.53.

2. What is the difference between 60.01 and 8.591?

Items 3 and 4 refer to the following table.

| Women's Olympic Downhill Skiing | | |
|---|---|---|
| Year | Skier | Time |
| 1960 | Biebl | 1 min. 37.60 sec. |
| 1964 | Hass | 1 min. 55.39 sec. |
| 1968 | Pall | 1 min. 40.87 sec. |
| 1972 | Nadig | 1 min. 36.68 sec. |
| 1976 | Mittermaier | 1 min. 46.16 sec. |
| 1980 | Moser | 1 min. 37.52 sec. |
| 1984 | Figini | 1 min. 13.36 sec. |

3. Arrange the winning speeds under 1 minute 40 seconds in order from the slowest to the fastest.

4. Arrange the years according to the winning speeds in order from fastest to the slowest.

5. Lee, George, Karen, and Jim shared the cost of a birthday party for Marie. They spent $125.35 for food, $56.76 for beverages, $14.60 for a cake, $9.85 for invitations and postage. Each person also spent $20 apiece for a present. What was each person's total expense for Marie's birthday?

6. Coaxial cable costs $3.65 per foot. To the nearest cent, how much does 3.9 yards cost?

7. Larry worked an average of 7.25 hours per day at $22.40 per hour in a 5-day workweek. His weekly paycheck showed $242 in deductions. What was his take-home pay for the week?

8. Casey spent 13.75 hours over two days writing a 33-page term paper. What was the average number of pages she wrote per hour (as a decimal)?

9. A rectangular room measures 14.25 feet by 12.75 feet. At $9.50 per square foot, what is the cost of carpeting the room to the nearest cent?

10. Oil Tank A is a cylinder 6.2 feet high with an end that has a radius of 5 feet. Oil Tank B is 6.9 feet high with an end that has a radius of 4.5 feet. Which tank holds more and by how many cubic feet?

11. What is the circumference of a circle that has a radius of .4 yards?

12. George pays $2.75 a day to park at his job. To drive to his job, he uses 6.5 gallons of gasoline a week, which he buys for $0.90 a gallon. What are his total transportation costs, including parking, for one 5-day work week?

    (1) $8.60
    (2) $14.65
    (3) $19.60
    (4) $20.25
    (5) Insufficient data is given to solve this problem.

13. Helen wants to paint a room whose walls measure 9 feet by 9 feet. She has paint that will cover 10 square yards per gallon. If she must buy the paint in one-gallon cans, how many cans of paint will she need to buy in order to paint the room?

    (1) 3
    (2) 4
    (3) 36
    (4) 40
    (5) Insufficient data is given to solve this problem.

14. Cheryl bought 3 pounds of pork at $1.29 a pound and 4 pounds of beef. What was the total cost of her purchases?

    (1) $9.03
    (2) $7.87
    (3) $5.16
    (4) $3.87
    (5) Insufficient data is given to solve this problem.

15. What is the perimeter of a rectangle with a length of 6.25 m?

    (1) 18.75 m
    (2) 15 m
    (3) 12.5 m
    (4) 6.25 m
    (5) Insufficient data is given to solve this problem.

Answers are on pages A-42 and A-43.

# CHAPTER 4
# Percents

Percent means hundredths. That simple rule is the key to working with percents. When you perform operations involving percents, you change the percent to a decimal or fraction. Then you work one of the operations you learned in Chapters 2 and 3.

The uses of percents include expressing the amount of interest you pay when you borrow money or earn when you invest it. Often discounts and commissions are expressed in percents. Also, percents are used to show what part of a group shares a common quality. For example, in opinion polls the share of people favoring one view is expressed as a percent.

## In this chapter you will learn to:

- Interchange percents, decimals, and fractions
- Recognize the components of percent problems
- Find a percent of a number
- Find what percent one number is of another
- Find a number when a percent of it is given
- Apply percent skills to word problems
- Use percent skills to compute interest
- Solve multistep problems that involve percents
- Find percent of increase and of decrease
- Use ratio and proportion to solve percent problems

# Level 1 Percent Skills

## Lesson 1 Interchanging Percents and Decimals

When changing a percent to a decimal, you divide by 100. You can use the quick division method explained in Chapter 3, Level 2, Lesson 3. To divide by 100 the quick way, simply move the decimal point two places to the left. Then drop the percent sign. If the percent is not written with a decimal point, remember the decimal point is to the right of the ones place.

**Example:** Change 10% to a decimal.

Step 1. Write the percent with the decimal point in the proper place.          10% = 10.%

**Step 2.** Do quick division by moving the decimal point two places to the left. Drop the percent sign. You should also drop the zero on the end.

$10.\% \div 100 = .10 = .1$

**Example 2:** Change $7\frac{1}{2}\%$ to a decimal.

**Step 1.** Change the fraction in the percent to a decimal. (Review Chapter 3, Level 1, Lesson 6 if you need to refresh your memory on how it is done.)

$7\frac{1}{2}\% = 7.5\%$

**Step 2.** Do quick division by moving the decimal point two places to the left and remove the percent sign. Notice you must add a zero in the tenths place as a place holder.

$7.5\% \div 100 = .075$

To change a decimal to a percent, multiply the decimal by 100 by using quick multiplication. This is done by moving the decimal point two places to the right. Then add a percent sign.

**Example 3:** Change .7 to a percent.

**Step 1.** Do the quick multiplication by moving the decimal two places to the right. Note that you must add a zero.

$.7(100) = 70$

**Step 2.** Add the percent sign.

$.7 = 70\%$

## Level 1, Lesson 1 Exercise

**Directions:** Change each percent to a decimal.

1. 29%
2. 3%
3. $1\frac{7}{10}\%$
4. .07%
5. 3.09%

**Directions:** Change each decimal to a percent.

6. .8
7. .05
8. .0396
9. 7.13
10. 30.001

Answers are on page A-43.

To change a percent to a fraction, drop the percent sign and write a fraction with the percent value as the numerator and a denominator of 100. Then reduce to lowest terms.

If the percent is written with a fraction or a decimal, you will need to take a preliminary step. If the percent includes a fraction value (e.g., $12\frac{1}{2}\%$), change the fraction value to a decimal (e.g., 12.5%) before placing the percent value in the numerator of the fraction. When the percent has a decimal (e.g., 12.5%), after writing the fraction with a denominator of 100 (e.g., $\frac{12.5}{100}$), add zeros to the denominator for every place to the right of the decimal, then remove the decimal point (e.g., $\frac{125}{1000}$).

**Example 1:** Change $1\frac{1}{4}\%$ to a fraction.

Step 1. Change the $\frac{1}{4}$ in the percent value to a decimal.    $1\frac{1}{4}\% = 1.25\%$

Step 2. Drop the percent sign. Write a fraction using the percent value as the numerator and 100 as the denominator.    $\frac{1.25}{100}$

Step 3. Add zeros to the denominator for each decimal place in the numerator. Drop the decimal point in the numerator.    $\frac{1.25}{100} = \frac{125}{10,000}$

Step 4. Reduce to lowest terms.    $\frac{125 \div 125}{10,000 \div 125} = \frac{1}{80}$

To change a fraction to a percent, multiply the fraction by 100. Add a percent sign. If the product is a mixed number, express the remainder as either a decimal or a fraction.

**Example 2:** Change $\frac{5}{6}$ to a percent.

Step 1. Multiply $\frac{5}{6}$ by 100.    $\frac{5}{\underset{3}{\cancel{6}}} \times \frac{\overset{50}{\cancel{100}}}{1} = \frac{250}{3}$

Step 2. Convert the improper fraction. Add a percent sign.

$$83\tfrac{1}{3}\%$$
$$3\overline{)250}$$
$$\underline{24}$$
$$10$$
$$\underline{9}$$
$$1$$

**Directions:** Change each percent to a fraction in simplest terms.

1. 96%    2. 14%    3. 62.5%    4. $56\frac{1}{4}\%$    5. 18.75%

**Directions:** Change each fraction to a percent.

6. $\frac{4}{15}$    7. $\frac{1}{8}$    8. $\frac{15}{16}$    9. $\frac{11}{40}$    10. $\frac{4}{5}$

Answers are on page A-43.

**Lesson 3**

## Common Equivalent Fractions, Decimals, and Percents

This table shows fractions, decimals, and percent equivalents you will often encounter on the GED and other situations where percents are used. Memorizing them will save you time.

| Percent | Decimal | Fraction | Percent | Decimal | Fraction |
|---|---|---|---|---|---|
| 90% | .9 | $\frac{9}{10}$ | 40% | .4 | $\frac{2}{5}$ |
| 87.5 or $87\frac{1}{2}\%$ | .875 | $\frac{7}{8}$ | 37.5 or $37\frac{1}{2}\%$ | .375 | $\frac{3}{8}$ |
| 80% | .8 | $\frac{4}{5}$ | $33\frac{1}{3}\%$ | .333* | $\frac{1}{3}$ |
| 75% | .75 | $\frac{3}{4}$ | 25% | .25 | $\frac{1}{4}$ |
| $66\frac{2}{3}\%$ | .667* | $\frac{2}{3}$ | 20% | .2 | $\frac{1}{5}$ |
| 62.5 or $62\frac{1}{2}\%$ | .625 | $\frac{5}{8}$ | $16\frac{2}{3}\%$ | .167* | $\frac{1}{6}$ |
| 60% | .6 | $\frac{3}{5}$ | 12.5 or $12\frac{1}{2}\%$ | .125 | $\frac{1}{8}$ |
| 50% | .5 | $\frac{1}{2}$ | 10% | .1 | $\frac{1}{10}$ |

\* Values rounded to the nearest thousandth.

## Level 1, Lesson 3 Exercise

Work on memorizing the above values. Have a fellow student, friend, or teacher quiz you orally on these values if you like.

Percent problems have three components: a **part**; a **rate**, or percent; and a **base**, or whole (the original amount). These components are related such that when you know two of the components, you can find the third.

Look at the following:

50 is 25% of 200.

In this sentence 50 is the part, 25% is the rate or percent, and 200 is the base or the whole. The statement can also be written:

25% of 200 is 50.

Here the components are the same, although the order has changed. Learning the components and being able to identify them will make working percent problems easier. Note that the whole or base in this type of sentence follows the word "of." You can also use the percent to help. If the percent is less than 100%, the part will be smaller than the whole.

100 is 50% of 200.

In the above sentence, the percent is less than 100%, because 100 is the part and 200 is the whole. However, look at this example:

100 is 200% of 50.

In the above sentence, the percent is more than 100%, because 100 is the part and 50 is the whole. When working word problems in the following lessons, a term representing the whole, such as "what number" or "the total," might follow the word "of" instead of the actual value.

## Level 1, Lesson 4 Exercise

**Directions:** For each statement, identify the part, rate or percent, and base or whole.

1.  5% of 250 is 12.5.
2.  300 is 10% of 3000.
3.  $33\frac{1}{3}$% of 300 is 100.
4.  93.6 is 15% of 624.
5.  175% of 18,960 is 33,180.

**Directions:** For each problem, tell which component you need to find to answer the question. Do not work the problem.

6.  What is 8% of 92?
7.  What percent of 86 is 43?
8.  75 is 10% of what number?
9.  45% of 4789 is what number?
10. 27 is what percent of 81?

Answers are on page A-43.

# Finding a Part of a Number

Multiply to find the part when you know the base and the rate. Use this formula:

part = rate × base

$$\boldsymbol{p = rb}$$

Before multiplying, change the rate from a percent to a fraction or a decimal. Some percents are easier to work as fractions; others, as decimals. *If you find in changing a percent into a decimal that you get two remainders that are the same, you should change the percent into a fraction instead.* Percents which contain $\frac{1}{3}$ ($33\frac{1}{3}$%), $\frac{2}{3}$ ($66\frac{2}{3}$%), or sixths ($\frac{1}{6}$ to $\frac{5}{6}$) are easier to use when converted to fractions.

**Example 1:** A piece of camera equipment costing $54 is marked down $23\frac{1}{3}$% on sale. What is the amount of the discount?

Step 1. Set up the problem.

$$p = rb$$
$$p = 23\frac{1}{3}\% \times \$54$$

Step 2. Change the percent (rate). $23\frac{1}{3}$% converts unevenly into the decimal (.233333 . . .) so you may want to use a fraction: $23\frac{1}{3} = \frac{70}{3}$

$$p = \frac{70}{3} \times \frac{54}{1}$$

Step 3. Multiply.

$$p = \frac{70}{{}_1 3} \times \frac{54^{18}}{1} = 1260$$

Mark off two decimal places from the right as you would if using a decimal.

$$p = \$12.60 \; \textit{amount of discount}$$

**Example 2:** Joe's mother gave him 70% of her inheritance of $900. How much did she give him?

Step 1. Set up the problem.

$$p = rb$$
$$p = 70\% \times \$900$$

Step 2. Change the percent. 70% changes evenly to the decimal .7.

$$p = .7 \times 900$$

Step 3. Multiply.

$$p = .7 \times 900 = 630.0$$
$$p = \$630$$

**Directions:** Find the part for each number.

1. $16\frac{2}{3}\%$ of 102

2. 90% of 81

3. 10% of 79

4. $87\frac{1}{2}\%$ of 776

5. $66\frac{2}{3}\%$ of 351

6. What is 4% of 234?

Answers are on page A-43.

**Lesson 6**

## Finding What Percent One Number Is of Another

When the percent is the unknown, we use this formula:

rate = part ÷ base

$$r = \frac{p}{b}$$

When you find what percent one number is of another, you compare a part to a whole (the whole = the base). First make a fraction with the part as the numerator and the whole as the denominator. Then change the fraction to a percent.
*In these problems, the base or whole usually follows the word **of**.*

**Example 1:** 18 is what percent of 24?

<u>Step 1.</u> Make a fraction with the part, 18, over the whole, 24, and reduce.

$$\frac{18}{24} = \frac{3}{4}$$

<u>Step 2.</u> Change $\frac{3}{4}$ to a percent.

$$\frac{3}{\underset{1}{\cancel{4}}} \times \frac{\overset{25}{\cancel{100}}\%}{1} = 75\%$$

In some problems, the whole you are comparing to the part may be smaller than the part.

**Example 2:** 42 is what percent of 30?

<u>Step 1.</u> Make a fraction with the part, 42, over the whole, 30, and reduce.

$$\frac{42}{30} = \frac{7}{5}$$

<u>Step 2.</u> Change $\frac{7}{5}$ to a percent.

$$\frac{7}{\underset{1}{\cancel{5}}} \times \frac{\overset{20}{\cancel{100}}\%}{1} = 140\%$$

**Directions:** Solve each problem.

1. What percent of 65 is 52?
2. What percent of 102 is 85?
3. 98 is what percent of 112?
4. 55 is what percent of 275?
5. 238 is what percent of 34?

Answers are on pages A-43 and A-44.

## Lesson 7

## Finding a Number When a Percent of It Is Given

Divide the part by the rate to find the base:

base = part ÷ rate

$$b = \frac{p}{r}$$

**Example 1:** 783 is 87% of what number?

Step 1. Set up the problem.

$$b = \frac{p}{r}$$
$$b = 783 \div 87\%$$

Step 2. Change the percent to a decimal and divide. Remember to move the decimal point in the divisor and dividend.

$$b = 783 \div .87$$
$$= .87\overline{)783.00}$$
$$b = 900$$

**Example 2:** 67% of what number is 146?

Step 1. Set up the problem.

$$b = \frac{p}{r}$$
$$b = 146 \div 67\%$$

Step 2. Change the percent to a fraction and divide.

$$67\% = .67 = \frac{2}{3}$$
$$b = 146 \div \frac{2}{3}$$
$$b = \frac{146}{1} \times \frac{3}{2} = 900$$

**Directions:** Solve each problem.

1. 22 is 22% of what number?

2. 1350 is 37.5% of what number?

3. 750 is 25% of what number?

4. 259 is $87\frac{1}{2}$% of what number?

5. 120 is $66\frac{2}{3}$% of what number?

Answers are on page A-44.

## Word Problems Involving Percent

As with any other word problem, when you are given a word problem involving percents, read the problem carefully. Remember that there are only three basic types of percent problems: find the part, find the rate, or find the base. Decide which of the three types of problems it is, select the information you need to solve the problem, set the problem up using the right formula and solve it. Remember: the number that comes after the word "of" in a question is usually the base.

**Example 1:** Sheila is buying a reduction valve that retails for $39.75. She is given a professional discount of 8% off that price. How much money will she save?

Step 1. You are being asked to find a part, 8% of 39.75. Set up the problem using the correct formula.

$$p = rb$$
$$p = 8\% \times 39.75$$

Step 2. Change 8% to a decimal and multiply.

$$p = .08 \times 39.75$$
$$p = \$3.18$$

**Example 2:** The net profit in 1990 at Baffle Industries was $385,000. In 1989, it was $350,000. What percent of 1989's profit was 1990's profit?

Step 1. You are being asked to find the rate. Before setting up the problem, determine which number is the base and which is the part. Remember that the base is the original amount. Now you can tell that 350,000 is the base and 385,000 is the part.

Step 2. Set up the problem, using the proper formula.

$$r = \frac{p}{b}$$
$$r = \frac{385,000}{350,000}$$
$$r = \frac{385,0\cancel{0}\cancel{0}\cancel{0}}{350,0\cancel{0}\cancel{0}\cancel{0}} \quad \textit{(reduce by 1000)}$$

Step 3. Divide.

$$r = 350\overline{)385.0}$$
$$\phantom{r = 350)}\underline{350}$$
$$\phantom{r = 350)}350$$
$$\phantom{r = 350)}\underline{350}$$

$$r = 1.1$$

Step 4. Change the quotient to a percent.

$1.1 \times 100\% = 1.10 = 110\%$

**Example 3:** It rained for 12 days during Norma's vacation; this was 80% of her vacation time. How long was her vacation?

Step 1. You are being asked to find the base; 12 is 80% of what number? Set the problem up using the correct formula.

$$b = \frac{p}{r}$$
$$b = 12 \div 80\%$$

Step 2. Change 80% to a decimal. Divide.

$$b = 12 \div 80\% \text{ or } .80\overline{)12.00}$$
$$b = 15 \text{ days}$$

## Level 2, Lesson 1 Exercise

**Directions:** Solve each problem. For problems 1–3, the correct formula is given. For problems 4–10, read carefully to determine the proper formula to use.

1. If 12% of Neri Productions' output of 9850 door hinges was defective, how many defective door hinges were produced? Use the formula: $p = rb$.

2. Mary received patents on 9 of her 15 inventions. What percent of her inventions were patented? Use the formula: $r = \frac{p}{b}$.

3. The bank requires a 10% down payment on a 30-year mortgage on a home. Ayesha made a minimum down payment of $12,000. What was the price of her home? Use the formula: $b = \frac{p}{r}$.

4. Alex completed 81 assemblies, which was 90% of the output of the best worker. What was the best worker's output?

5. A used automobile costs $5500. If the sales tax rate is 8%, how much tax must be paid on the purchase of the automobile?

6. Leo increased the number of cattle on his farm from 52 to 65. What percent of the size of his former herd is the size of his current herd?

7. Gotham's 1980 population of 3,005,000 had increased by 12% by 1990. How many more people were living in Gotham in 1990?

8. Gilberta Sutton's daily diet provides 70% of the 2400 calories she used to get. How many calories per day does her current diet supply?

9. After processing 35 applications, Martha learned that this was only $83\frac{1}{3}$ % of the number received that day. What was the total number that was received?

10. Rathmullan Associated bought a property for $297,000 and sold it for $341,550. What percent of the original price was the sale price?

Answers are on page A-44.

## Lesson 2

# Simple Interest

**Interest** is a fee paid for using money. When you borrow money or buy something on credit, you pay interest. When you deposit money in a savings account, the bank uses your money and pays you interest. The amount of interest paid is called the *part* in percent problems. It is determined by three factors:

- the amount of money borrowed, which is called the **principal**, serves as the base in percent problems
- the **rate**, which is the percent at which the interest is paid, and
- the amount of **time** for which the money is used. (**Note:** *Time in interest problems is always expressed in years and parts of years. For instance, 6 months could be expressed as .5 years or $\frac{1}{2}$ year.*)

This is called **simple interest**. To find the amount of simple interest, use the following formula:

interest = principal × rate × time (in years)

$$i = prt$$

**Example 1:** Find the interest for 3 years on a $20,000 note at 10% annual interest.

Step 1. Set up the problem using the formula.

$i = prt$
$i = 20,000 \times 10\% \times 3$
$i = 20,000 \times .1 \times 3$
$i = 2000 \times 3 = 6000$

When the time is expressed in months or months and years, be sure to change the time to years.

**Example 2:** Find the interest that is due on a 6-month, $4000 loan at 11% annual interest.

Step 1. Convert the months to years.

6 months = $\frac{6}{12}$ = $\frac{1}{2}$ year

Step 2. Set up the problem using the formula. Since you are using a fractional value for the years, write the percent as a fraction also.

$i = prt$
$i = 4000 \times \frac{11}{100} \times \frac{1}{2}$

Step 3. Multiply.

$i = \frac{\overset{40}{\cancel{4000}}}{1} \times \frac{11}{\underset{1}{\cancel{100}}} \times \frac{1}{2}$

$i = \frac{440}{2} = 220$

**Directions:** Change the number of months to years.

1. 2 months
2. 3 months
3. 4 months
4. 60 months
5. 54 months

**Directions:** Find the amount of interest on each loan.

6. a $5000 loan at 9% annual interest for 2 years.
7. a $1750 loan at 12% annual interest for 1 year.
8. a $200 loan at 11% annual interest for 9 months.
9. a $750 loan at 18% annual interest for 30 months.
10. a $2000 loan at $7\frac{1}{2}$% annual interest for 2 years.

Answers are on page A-44.

# Problem Solving That Involves Percents

Level 3

## Lesson 1

## Multistep Percent Problems

Although all percent problems involve finding either the part, rate, or base, some problems require several steps: You may have to add or subtract before, or after, you do a percent calculation. Or you may have to do several percent calculations and add or subtract after each one. You will be able to do these problems by using the percent formula correctly at each step.

Reading carefully, as always, will help you decide what you are being asked, what information you need to use, and what operations you need to perform with that information.

## Adding or Subtracting Before You Do a Percent Operation

**Example 1:** If 19 of every 25 new customers who came to Julia's Diner because of an advertisement came back for a second time, what percent did not return?

**Step 1.** You are to find the rate of customers who did not return. You know the base is 25, but to find the part that did not return you need to subtract from 25 the customers that returned, 19.

$$25 - 19 = 6$$

**Step 2.** Set up the problem using the correct formula.

$$r = \frac{p}{b}$$

$$r = \frac{6}{25}$$

**Step 3.** Divide. Convert the quotient to a percent.

$$r = 25\overline{)6.00} = .24$$

$$r = 24\%$$

**Example 2:** Of the new customers that Julia's Diner has attracted this week, 16 were from the neighborhood and 10 were from the next town. The customers this week totaled 120. What percent of this total were new customers?

Step 1. You are to find what percent of the base (the total of all customers) the part is. The part is the total of new customers. Add the two figures for new customers.

$16 + 10 = 26$

Step 2. Set up the problem using the correct formula.

$r = \dfrac{p}{b}$

$r = \dfrac{26}{120}$

Step 3. Divide and convert the quotient to a percent.

$r = 120\overline{)26.00} = .216$

$r = 22\%$

## Adding or Subtracting After You Do a Percent Operation

**Example 3:** Harry has saved $1400 for a new stereo system. This is 80% of his goal. How much more must he save to reach his goal?

Step 1. You are given a part and the rate. You can use this information to find the base. Set up the problem using the correct formula.

$b = \dfrac{p}{r}$

$b = \dfrac{1400}{80\%}$

$b = \dfrac{1400}{.80}$ or $.80\overline{)1400}$

Step 2. Divide to find the base (the total he needs to save).

$b = 1750$

Step 3. Subtract the part from the base to find how much more he needs to save.

$$\begin{array}{r} \$1750 \\ -1400 \\ \hline \$\ 350 \end{array}$$

**Example 4:** If the sales tax on a $60 jacket is 4%, what is its total price including the tax?

Step 1. You are to find the part (the amount of the tax) and add it to the base (before-tax price). Set up the formula.

$p = rb$

$p = 4\% \times 60 = .04 \times 60$

Step 2. Multiply and add the product (the part) to the base.

$p = .04 \times 60 = 2.40$

$$\begin{array}{r} \$60.00 \\ +\ 2.40 \\ \hline \$62.40\ \textit{total cost of coat} \end{array}$$

# Adding or Subtracting After Each Percent Operation

**Example 5:** When Linda got laid off at the Daily News, she took a job at Karl Printers with a salary that was 5% less than her salary at the Daily News, which was $18,000. She has just received a 3% raise. What is her present salary at Karl Printers?

Step 1. First find the part, 5% of $18,000. Set up the problem using the correct formula.

$p = rb$

$p = 5\% \times 18{,}000$

Step 2. Change the percent to a decimal and multiply.

$p = .05 \times 18{,}000$

$p = 900$

Step 3. Subtract the part from the base to find her salary at Karl Printers before her raise.

$$\begin{array}{r} \$18{,}000 \\ -\quad 900 \\ \hline \$17{,}100 \end{array}$$

Step 4. Find the amount of her raise. Her raise is 3% of $17,100, so you are finding the part.

$p = rb$

$p = 3\% \times 17{,}100$

$p = .03 \times 17{,}100$

$p = \$513$

Step 5. Add the part (513) to the base (17,100) to get her present salary after her raise.

$$\begin{array}{r} \$17{,}100 \\ +\quad 513 \\ \hline \$17{,}613 \end{array}$$

## Level 3, Lesson 1 Exercise

**Directions:** Solve each problem.

1. Shelley budgets $50 each week for expenses. One week she spent $10 for transportation and $23 for food. What percent of her weekly budget was left?

2. By waiting for a sale and using her employee discount, Marcia bought an outboard motor for $220, which is 55% of its original price. How much of a discount did she receive?

3. Ajax Hardware is selling $200 drills at 20% off. The sales tax is 5%. What does a drill cost?

4. An auctioneer's fee for selling a painting is $2\frac{1}{2}\%$ of the price for which it is sold. If the auctioneer earned $68.75 for selling a painting, how much should the seller receive?

5. Over the holidays Georgia gained 8 pounds, which is 8% of her former weight. Then she went on a diet and lost 10% of her new weight. What is her weight after her diet?

Answers are on page A-44.

# Percent Increase and Percent Decrease

**Percent increase** and **percent decrease** are used in science and business to reflect change. For example, you can find how much a temperature or a price goes up or down in relation to the original number.

   Percent increase and percent decrease problems are multistep problems. You first subtract to find the *actual* increase or decrease. Then use the formula $r = p \div b$ to find what percent the increase or decrease is of the original number.

**Example 1:** After 6 months of advertising, Julia's average daily number of customers rose from 275 to 330. What percent increase was this?

Step 1. Subtract to find the actual increase.              $330 - 275 = 55$

Step 2. Use the formula $r = p \div b$ to find the percent       $r = p \div b$
increase of the original amount.

$r = 55 \div 275$

$r = .2$

$r = 20\%$

   Remember, be sure to read word problems carefully. Sometimes it is not readily apparent what you are being asked to find.

**Example 2:** The Goal Line Shop advertises a $13.99 football on sale for $9.99. To the nearest percent, what is the discount rate?

Step 1. What is the problem asking you to find?
When working with money, **discount rate** is another       $13.99
way of saying percent decrease. Subtract to find the        $-\ \ 9.99$
actual decrease.                                            $\overline{\$\ \ 4.00}$

Step 2. Use the formula $r = p \div b$ to find the percent       $r = p \div b$
decrease of the original amount.

$r = \$4.00 \div \$13.99$

$r = .2859$

$r = .29$

$r = 29\%$

## Level 3, Lesson 2 Exercise

**Directions:** Find each percent of increase or percent of decrease. Be sure to read each problem carefully.

1. The average daily number of customers at Valley View Shopping Mall rose from 15,280 to 17,572. What was the percent of increase of customers?

2. Sales of crops on Bernice's farm dropped from $84,490.00 to $78,575.70. By what percent did the sales decrease?

**3.** The population of Palmetto rose from 25,900 to 31,080. By what percent did the population increase?

**4.** A scarf priced regularly at $15.00 is on sale for $9.00. What is the percent of its discount?

**5.** The Sound Store purchased speakers for $46 per pair. The speakers were sold for $115 per pair. By what percent did the store mark up the price?

Answers are on pages A-44 and A-45.

## Lesson 3

# Using Ratio and Proportion with Percent Problems

You can use the ratio and proportion setup to solve percent problems, no matter which of the three parts is missing (the percent or rate, the part, or the base or whole original amount). Applying the ratio and proportion method to percent problems would look like this:

$$\frac{\text{rate, or percent (\%)}}{100} = \frac{\text{part}}{\text{base, or whole (original amount)}}$$

Look at the following examples:

## Finding the Part by Using Proportions

**Example 1:** If a store is having a 25% sale on all winter merchandise, how much discount would you receive on a jacket which sells for $140?

Step 1. Set up the proportion.

$$\frac{25}{100} = \frac{p}{140} \; (= \text{part})$$

Step 2. Cross-multiply.

$$25 \times 140 = 100p$$
$$3500 = 100p$$

Step 3. Solve the problem. Divide both sides by 100 to solve for $p$.

$$\frac{3500}{100} = \frac{100p}{100}$$
$$\$35 = p \text{ (part)}$$

## Finding the Base or Whole by Using Proportions

**Example 2:** If a store is having a 25% sale on all winter merchandise and you receive a $35 discount off the price of a jacket, what is the original price of the jacket (before the sale)?

Step 1. Set up the proportion.

$$\frac{25}{100} = \frac{35}{b} \; (= \text{base})$$

Step 2. Cross-multiply.

$$25b = 3500$$

Step 3. Solve the problem. Divide both sides by 25 to solve for $b$.

$$\frac{\overset{1}{\cancel{25}}b}{\underset{1}{\cancel{25}}} = \frac{\overset{140}{\cancel{3500}}}{\underset{1}{\cancel{25}}}$$

$$b = \$140$$

**Example 3:** A store is having a sale on all winter merchandise. You will receive $35 off a jacket priced at $140. What is the percent discount you will receive?

Step 1. Set up the proportion.

$$\frac{r}{100} = \frac{35}{140}$$

Step 2. Cross-multiply.

$$140r = 3500$$

Step 3. Divide both sides by 140 to solve for $r$ (or cancel zeros and divide 350 by 14).

$$14\cancel{0}r = 350\cancel{0}$$

$$r = 14\overline{)350} = 25 \text{ or } 25\%$$

## Level 3, Lesson 3 Exercise

**Directions:** Solve the following problems using proportions.

1. Jack's Electronics is selling $320 VCRs at 20% off. What is the discount on the VCRs?

2. Janice earns $200 a week as a computer operator. Taxes take 30% of her weekly income. How much tax does she pay weekly?

3. Harry's company health policy paid 60% of his dental bill. If the policy paid $30, what was the original amount of the bill?

4. Apply Clothing is selling blouses for 20% off. If the discount on the blouses is $15, what was the original price?

5. Janice bought a sweeter for $45 that was originally priced at $75. What was the percent of discount?

Answers are on page A-45.

# Chapter 4 Quiz

**Directions:** Solve each problem.

1. Which of the following does not have the same value as the others?
   **(1)** .5
   **(2)** $\frac{5}{10}$
   **(3)** 50%
   **(4)** .05
   **(5)** 0.50

2. Which of the following does not have the same value as the others?
   **(1)** $\frac{2}{5}$
   **(2)** $\frac{4}{5}$
   **(3)** 40%
   **(4)** .4
   **(5)** $\frac{4}{10}$

3. Which of the following is not equal to 60%?
   **(1)** $\frac{6}{10}$
   **(2)** $\frac{3}{5}$
   **(3)** .06
   **(4)** $\frac{60}{100}$
   **(5)** 0.60

4. Radio advertising attracted $5\frac{1}{2}$% of the first 600 customers of Instabell Answering Service. How many of the 600 were not attracted by this advertising?

5. What is the total cost of a coat priced at $78.70 if the sales tax is 7%?

Question 6 refers to the graph on the right.

Student Survey

6. This graph shows the results of a survey that asked 100 high school students to list their favorite fast food. How many students preferred pizza?
   **(1)** 22
   **(2)** 38
   **(3)** 24
   **(4)** 48
   **(5)** 72

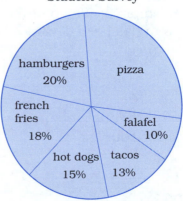

7. Fatima is driving to Denver. She has driven 392 miles already, which is 28% of the distance. How many more miles does she have to drive to reach Denver?

8. Mark has a $2500 municipal bond that earns $7\frac{1}{2}$% annual interest. How much interest does it earn in 18 months?

9. Kareen buys onions at a cost of $15 per hundred-pound sack. He sells them for $.40 per pound. What percent of the selling price is his cost?

10. If 51 of the 340 runners in the United Charities Marathon were first-time runners, what percent had run before?

11. 3819 candidates for election were endorsed by the Good Government Coalition. This was 57% of all candidates. How many candidates ran?

12. On an "Everything Must Go" sale, José saved $18 on a shirt originally marked at $24. Which of the following expressions shows the percent the shirt was marked down?

    (1) $\frac{18}{24}$

    (2) $24 \times 18 \times 100$

    (3) $\frac{(100 \times 18)}{24}$

    (4) $\frac{24}{(100 \times 18)}$

    (5) $100(24 - 18)$

13. 147 people from a neighborhood organization attended a meeting at city hall. They represent 87.5% of the organization's members. Which of the following expressions shows how many members there are in the organization?

    (1) $147 \times 87.5$

    (2) $\frac{(100 \times 147)}{87.5}$

    (3) $\frac{87.5}{(100 \times 147)}$

    (4) $\frac{87.5 \times 147}{100}$

    (5) $\frac{100}{87.5 \times 147}$

14. The currency in Honduras is based on the lempira. The lempira last year was devalued and went from its original 4 lempiras for one U.S. dollar to this year's 6 lempiras. Which of the following expressions show by what percent the lempira has been devalued?

    (1) $\frac{(6 \times 100)}{4}$

    (2) $\frac{4}{(6 \times 100)}$

    (3) $6 - 4 \times 100$

    (4) $\frac{6 \times 4}{100}$

    (5) $\frac{400}{6}$

**15.** 783 people attended a New Year's Eve ball. That number represented 87% of all invited guests. Which of the following expressions shows how many guests were invited to the ball?

(1) $\dfrac{(.87 \times 100)}{783}$

(2) $(.87 \times 783)100$

(3) $\dfrac{100 \times 783}{87}$

(4) $\dfrac{87}{100 \times 783}$

(5) $\dfrac{783 \times .87}{100}$

**16.** Bill receives a 10% commission on the clothing he sells. On Monday he sold a coat priced at $100, a suit priced at $250, and a sweater priced at $75. His daily salary is $80. Which of the following expressions shows how much he earned altogether on Monday?

(1) $10.(80 \times 100 + 250 + 75)$

(2) $\dfrac{80(100 + 250 + 75)}{.10}$

(3) $.10(100 + 250 + 75) + 80$

(4) $\dfrac{(100 + 250 + 75 + 80)}{.10}$

(5) $.10(100 + 250 + 75 + 80)$

**17.** George bought a $10,000 bond that pays interest at an annual rate of interest of 6%. Which expression below shows how many dollars he will receive as a quarterly interest payment?

(1) $\dfrac{10,000 \times 6}{4}$

(2) $\dfrac{10,000 \times 0.06}{4}$

(3) $10,000 \times 6 \times 4$

(4) $\dfrac{10,000 \times 4}{6}$

(5) $\dfrac{10,000 \times 4}{0.06}$

**18.** Find the interest on $600 at 8.5% annual interest for one year and six months.

**19.** The Chinese restaurant raised its prices 5%. It charges a 2% service charge for deliveries. How much would a $7.95 dinner cost at the new prices if it was delivered to Janet's house?

**20.** Lawrence took out a 2-year loan of $5000 at an annual rate of interest of $5\frac{1}{2}\%$. Which expression below shows how much interest he would pay?

(1) $2(5000 \times .055)$

(2) $5000 \times .055 + 2$

(3) $.055 (5000 \times 2)$

(4) $.5 \times 5000 \times 2$

(5) $2(5000 \times .5)$

Answers are on pages A-45 and A-46.

# CHAPTER 5
# Graphs

A **graph** is a diagram that shows the relationship among several items. Graphs are often used to present information in newspapers and magazines and on computer screens.

## In this chapter you will learn to:

- Read and interpret tables
- Read and interpret circle graphs
- Read and interpret bar graphs
- Read and interpret line graphs

## Preview

1. For the table in Figure 5–2 on page 507, list the top batters from best to worst according to their percent of hits per time at bat.

2. Based on the circle graph in Figure 5–3 on page 509, how much more of each dollar is invested in real estate than in all the other categories combined?

3. Look at the bar graph in Figure 5–4 on page 510. What was the percent increase in the number of subscribers between 1970 and 1982?

4. Look at the line graph in Figure 5–5 on page 511. How much did net farming income increase between 1983 and 1984?

5. Use the information in the line graph in Figure 5–5 on page 511 to find the yearly average of net income from farming for the years 1975 to 1984.

Answers are on page A-46. If you have at least four answers correct, try the Chapter 5 Quiz on page 513. If you have fewer than four answers correct, study this chapter beginning with Lesson 1.

# Tables

A **table** consists of numbers or other data that are shown in columns and rows in order to compare the data or to read it more easily. The title and key of a table tell you what the table is about. The column heads tell you what data is contained in a column. Sometimes there are heads for the rows across, also. A **symbol** is a sign, such as an asterisk, a star, a dot, or a cross-mark that stands for a word or idea. Graphs, tables, and charts often use symbols. The table in Figure 5–1 shows the schedule of buses to New Town.

| Old Town – New Town Bus Schedule* | | | | | | | |
|---|---|---|---|---|---|---|---|
| | A.M. | | | P.M. | | | |
| Old Town | 5:30 | 6:30 | 10:00 | 12:30 | 1:30** | 4:00 | 8:30 |
| Big Town | 6:10 | 7:10 | 10:40 | 1:10 | 2:10** | 4:40 | 9:10 |
| High Town | 6:30 | 7:30 | 11:00 | 1:30 | 2:30** | 5:00 | 9:30 |
| East Town | 6:45 | 7:45 | *** | 1:45 | 2:45** | 5:15 | 9:45 |
| New Town | 7:15 | 8:15 | *** | 2:15 | 3:00** | 5:45 | 10:15 |

\* Weekdays only—see weekend and holiday schedule for other times.

\*\* Reservations only.

\*\*\* Bus ends at High Town.

Fig. 5–1

**Example 1:** You want to know when the 6:30 a.m. bus from High Town arrives in New Town. Look down the column for the number next to New Town: 7:15 a.m. is the arrival time of the 6:30 a.m. bus from High Town.

**Example 2:** When does the last morning bus from Old Town arrive in New Town? The answer is 8:15, when the 6:30 bus arrives. The 10:00 bus from Old Town stops in High Town. The key tells you that the symbol \*\*\* means, "Bus ends at High Town."

**Example 3:** If you had to meet a friend in East Town at 2:45 on Saturday which bus would you take? Answer: none on the table. The symbol \* tells you that this schedule does not list weekend times.

Fractions or percents are used sometimes to compare data given in tables.

| Home-Team Batting Record* | | |
|---|---|---|
| Name | Hits | Times at Bat |
| Alberto | 24 | 60 |
| Elizabeth | 35 | 70 |
| John | 30 | 54 |
| Roger | 27 | 63 |

\* top batters only

Fig. 5–2

**Example 4:** What fraction (or percent) of the times at bat did Alberto get a hit?

Step 1. Read the table to find the information you need: Alberto got 24 hits in 60 times at bat.

Step 2. Write the relationship between these two in fraction form.

$$\frac{\text{hits}}{\text{at bats}} = \frac{24}{60}$$

Step 3. Reduce the fraction to lowest terms.

$$\frac{24 \div 12}{60 \div 12} = \frac{2}{5}$$

Alberto got a hit $\frac{2}{5}$ of his times at bat.

Step 4. If the question asked for the percent of hits in Alberto's times at bat, you would change the fraction to a decimal and then a percent.

$$\frac{2}{5} = .4 = 40\%$$

## Lesson 1 Exercise

**Directions:** Use the Home-Team Batting Record table to answer the following questions.

1. If William got 32 hits in 72 times at bat, how much higher was his percent of hits in times at bat than Alberto's percent of hits?

2. If Victoria got 9 hits in 24 times at bat who had a better percent of hits per time at bat, Elizabeth or Victoria?

**Directions:** Use the Old Town–New Town bus schedule to answer the following questions.

3. How long does the trip by reserved bus take from Old Town to New Town? How long do nonreserved buses take?

4. Which two towns are closest together?

5. If you were supposed to meet a friend at the bus station in East Town at 4:45 and took the 4:40 bus from Big Town, how many minutes late would you be?

   (1) 5
   (2) 10
   (3) 15
   (4) 20
   (5) 30

Answers are on page A-46.

# Circle Graphs

A **circle graph** shows the parts that make up a whole. A circle graph is divided into pie-shaped pieces that stand for percents or for parts of a dollar. The pieces of a circle graph add up to 100%.

To understand a circle graph, read the title of the graph and the labels for each part carefully.

The following example is based on the circle graph in Figure 5–3. The graph shows how each dollar that is invested in the farming sector is used. It shows how many cents out of each dollar are invested in various assets.

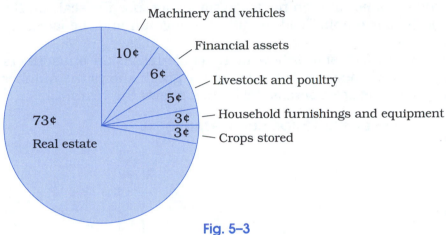

**DOLLAR INVESTMENT IN THE FARMING SECTOR**

Fig. 5–3

**Example:** What percent of the dollar is invested in crops stored?

Step 1.  Find the amount spent on crops stored:          $.03

Step 2.  Change $.03 to a percent. Since the graph           100
represents $1.00, or 100 cents, multiply by 100.          × .03
                                                      3.00%, or 3%

## Lesson 2 Exercise

**Directions:**  Items 1 to 5 refer to the circle graph in Figure 5–3.

1.  What percent of the dollar is invested in financial assets and in real estate combined?

2.  What category has twice as much of each dollar invested as is invested in livestock and poultry?

3.  What percent of the dollar is NOT invested in livestock and poultry and in crops stored?

4. What percent of each dollar is invested in machinery and vehicles and in household furnishings and equipment combined?

5. If the total investment in livestock and poultry is approximately $49 billion, what is the total dollar investment in the farming sector?

Answers are on page A-46.

**Lesson 3**

# Bar Graphs

A **bar graph** uses rectangles to compare quantities. The length of each rectangle is proportional to the size of the quantity it represents. Rectangles may run vertically or horizontally. To find the amount each rectangle stands for, use the scale on the side or the bottom of the bar graph. Read the title of the graph and the labels on each scale carefully.

The bar graph in Figure 5–4 shows how many cable-television subscribers there were in selected years. The scale at the left of the graph shows the number of subscribers in millions. The scale across the bottom shows the years.

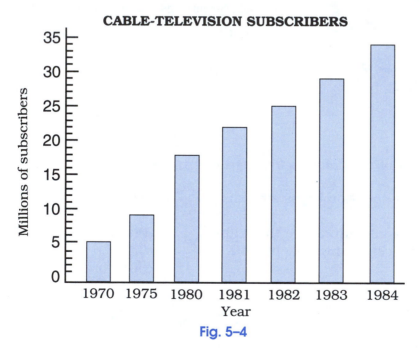

**Fig. 5–4**

**Example:** How many cable-television subscribers were there in 1975?

<u>Step 1.</u> Find the year on the scale at the bottom of the graph. Follow the rectangle above *1975* to the top.

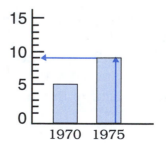

<u>Step 2.</u> Look directly to the left at the vertical scale. Each line stands for 1 million subscribers. The rectangle above *1975* ends one line below *10 million.* There were 9 million subscribers.

510    Chapter 5: Graphs

**Directions:** Items 1 to 5 are based on the bar graph in Figure 5–4.

1. How many cable-television subscribers were there in 1970?
2. In which year was the number of subscribers 22 million?
3. Between which two years was there an increase of 5 million subscribers?
4. The number of cable-television subscribers in 1970 was what fraction of the number of subscribers in 1982?
5. What was the percent increase in the number of subscribers between 1970 and 1984?

Answers are on page A-46.

**Lesson 4** — **Line Graphs**

**Line graphs** are usually used to report changes over a period of time. A line connects the points on the graph that report amounts and points in time. The vertical scale usually expresses the amount of the thing being measured. The horizontal scale usually shows points in time. If the line rises from left to right, it shows an increase or an *upward trend*. A line that falls from left to right shows a decrease or a *downward trend*.

The example is based on the line graph in Figure 5–5.

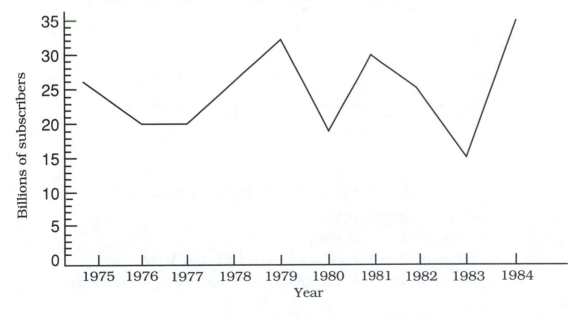

**NET INCOME OF FARM OPERATORS FROM FARMING**

Fig. 5–5

**Example:** What was the net income from farming in 1978?

Step 1. Find the year on the horizontal scale at the bottom of the graph. Then follow the line marked *1978* straight up to the point at the top.

Step 2. Look straight across to the vertical scale. You should be two lines above the $25 billion mark. The net income from farming in 1978 was $27 billion.

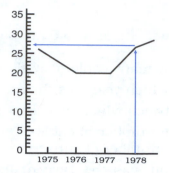

## Lesson 4 Exercise

The line graph in Figure 5–6 shows a comparison between the number of gas wells and the number of oil wells that were drilled between 1974 and 1984. Notice that there are two lines: one shows the number of oil wells that were drilled; the other shows the number of gas wells that were drilled.

**GAS WELLS AND OIL WELLS DRILLED, 1974-1984**

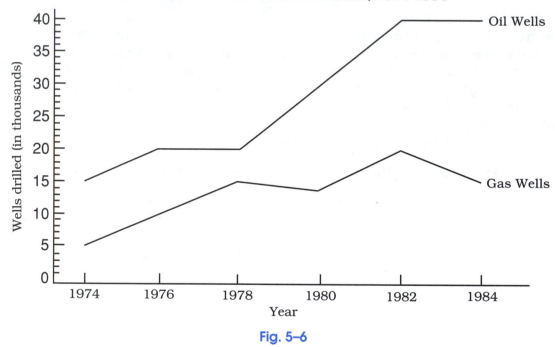

**Fig. 5–6**

**Directions:** Items 1 to 5 are based on the line graph in Figure 5–6.

1. How many oil wells were drilled in 1980?
2. How many gas wells were drilled in 1974?
3. How many gas wells and oil wells combined were drilled in 1984?
4. Between which years did the number of gas wells drilled show a downward trend?
5. In which year was the gap between the number of gas wells and the number of oil wells that were drilled the smallest?

Answers are on page A-46.

# Chapter 5 Quiz

**Directions:** Items 1 to 5 refer to the circle graphs in Figure 5–7.

**DISTRIBUTION OF FAMILIES BY NUMBER OF CHILDREN**

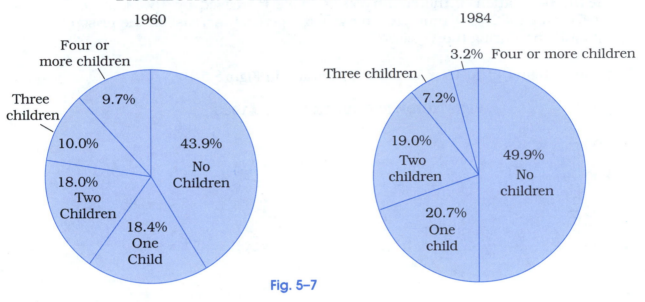

Fig. 5–7

1. What percent of the families in 1960 had one or more children?
2. What category showed the greatest change between 1960 and 1984?
3. What category showed the least change between 1960 and 1984?
4. By how many percentage points did the number of families having three or more children decrease from 1960 to 1984?
5. The 1984 U.S. population included approximately 62 million families. How many families in 1984 had no children?

**Directions:** Items 6 to 10 refer to the bar graph in Figure 5–8.

**FEDERAL AND STATE PRISONERS, 1965-1984**

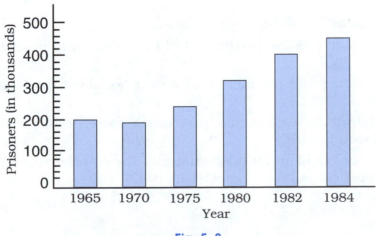

Fig. 5–8

6. In what year did the federal and state prison population first exceed 300,000?

7. Between what years did the federal and state prison population show a decline?

8. To the nearest 100,000, what was the increase in the federal and state prison population between 1980 and 1984?

9. Between 1970 and 1982, the federal and state prison population increased by approximately what percent?

10. If the population of the country as a whole increased by 13% between 1970 and 1982, how much greater was the percent increase in the prison population during those years?

**Directions:** Items 11 to 15 refer to the line graph in Figure 5–9.

**PESTICIDE PRODUCTION, 1970-1983**

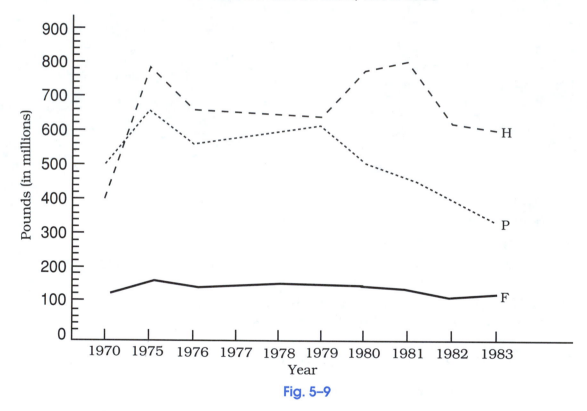

Fig. 5–9

11. What is the unit of measure of the vertical scale?

12. After 1975, in what year was the production of herbicides and pesticides most nearly equal?

13. Between what years does the production of pesticides show the longest downward trend?

14. To the nearest hundred million pounds, how much more herbicide than pesticide was produced in 1980?

15. To the nearest hundred million pounds, what was the combined production of herbicides, pesticides, and fungicides in 1982?

Answers are on pages A-46 and A-47.

# CHAPTER 6
# Algebra

Algebra is an advanced form of mathematics in which symbols play an important part. The formulas you have used in earlier chapters are a form of algebra. Algebra is useful when working in the science and engineering fields.

## In this chapter you will learn to:

- Use a number line
- Add, subtract, multiply, and divide signed numbers
- Add, subtract, multiply, and divide monomials
- Solve one-step and multistep equations
- Solve inequalities
- Multiply binomials
- Factor trinomials
- Translate words into algebraic expressions and equations
- Solve algebra setup problems

# Algebra Skills

---

## Preview

**Directions:** Solve each problem.

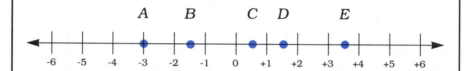

1. Which point represents $\frac{-3}{2}$ on the number line above?

2. $(+8) + (-4) - (-10) + (+3) =$

3. $-6 \times \frac{3}{8} =$

4. $(-4ac^2) + (18ac^2) =$

5. $+20a^5 \div -2a^3 =$

Answers are on page A-47. If you have at least four answers correct, try the Chapter 6 Quiz on page 538. If you have fewer than four answers correct, study Level 1 beginning with Lesson 1.

The following figure is called a **number line**:

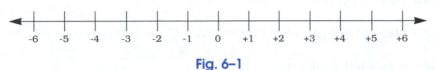

Fig. 6–1

Notice that the number line has numbers on both sides of the zero. The numbers to the right of the zero are positive numbers. They are sometimes noted with a plus sign. When a number has no sign, it is positive also. The numbers to the left of the zero are called negative numbers. Negative numbers are always noted with a minus sign. You might be familiar with negative numbers from reading the temperature on a thermometer. In fact, a thermometer is a type of number line. Very cold days have a temperature of below zero. For example:

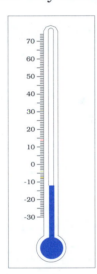

Fig. 6–2

This thermometer shows a temperature of 12 below zero, or –12 degrees.

Notice also the number line has arrows on each end. This indicates that the number line continues in both directions to infinity—that is, it continues without end.

The value of a point on a number line is determined by its position on the line in relation to zero.

Use the following number line for examples 1 and 2:

Fig. 6–3

**Example 1:** Which point has a value of –3 on the number line?

Step 1. Look to the left of 0 and locate negative 3 (–3).

Step 2. Read the letter which represents that point. The answer is A.

 Points on a number line are not always whole number values. A point can be a fraction, decimal, or mixed number.

**Example 2:** What are the values of point B and point C on the number line?

Step 1. Find the points labeled B and C.

Step 2. Find the values of the points. Point B is halfway between –1 and –2. It has a value of $-1\frac{1}{2}$ or –1.5. Point C is halfway between +1 and +2. It has a value of $+1\frac{1}{2}$ or +1.5.

## Level 1, Lesson 1 Exercise

**Directions:** For problems 1–5, mark each value on the number line.

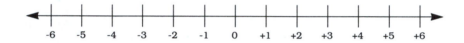

1. +3
2. –2
3. $-\frac{1}{2}$
4. +5.75
5. $+2\frac{1}{4}$

**Directions:** Choose the correct letter on the number line for each corresponding value below.

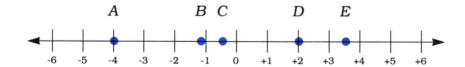

6. +2
7. –4
8. +3.5
9. $-\frac{7}{6}$
10. –.5

 Answers are on page A-47.

# Adding and Subtracting Signed Numbers

Negative and positive numbers are also called **signed numbers**. When adding and subtracting signed numbers, it is most important to watch the signs and to know what to do with them. As the examples illustrate, adding signed numbers sometimes requires subtraction skills and subtracting signed numbers sometimes requires addition skills.

When adding two numbers with the same sign, add the values and use the same sign for the sum.

**Example 1:** Add (–9) and (–4).

Step 1. Add the values. $\qquad$ $9 + 4 = 13$

Step 2. Because both numbers are negative, the $\qquad$ $(–9) + (–4) = –13$
sum is a negative number. Use the proper sign.

When adding two numbers with different signs, find the difference of the values of the two numbers by subtracting and use the sign of the larger number for the sum.

**Example 2:** Find the sum of (–20) and (+13).

Step 1. Find the difference of the two values. $\qquad$ $20 – 13 = 7$

Step 2. Use the sign of the larger number for the sum. $\quad$ $(–20) + (+13) = –7$
Because 20 is larger than 13, the sum is a negative
number.

When you have a group of signed numbers to add, find the total of the positive numbers and the total of the negative numbers. Then add these totals as you would two signed numbers with different signs.

**Example 3:** $(+5) + (–2) + (+8) + (–7) + (+3) = ?$

Step 1. Find the total of the positive numbers. $\qquad$ $5 + 8 + 3 = 16$

Step 2. Find the total of the negative numbers. $\qquad$ $(–2) + (–7) = (–9)$

Step 3. Find the difference between the two totals. $\qquad$ $16 – 9 = 7$

Step 4. Because the total of the positive numbers is $\qquad$ $(+5) + (–2) + (+8) + (–7) +$
larger than the total of the negative numbers, the sum $\quad$ $(+3) = (+16) + (–9) = +7$
is positive.

To subtract signed numbers, change the sign of the number being subtracted to the opposite sign and change the operation sign from subtraction to addition. Then add, following the rules for signed numbers.

**Example 4:** Find (+5) – (–8).

Step 1. Change the sign of the number being subtracted and the operation sign from subtraction to
addition.

(+5) – (–8) = (+5) + (+8)

Step 2. Add following the rules for adding signed numbers.

(+5) + (+8) = +13

**Example 5:** Find 6 – (–9).

Step 1. Change the sign of the number being subtracted and the operation sign from subtraction to
addition.

6 + (+9)

Step 2. Add following the rules for adding signed
numbers.

6 + (+9) = +15

**Example 6:** Find (–12) – (–18).

Step 1. Change the sign of the number being subtracted and the operation sign from subtraction to
addition.

(–12) + (+18)

Step 2. Add following the rules for adding signed
numbers.

(–12) + (+18) = +6

**Example 7:** Find (–5) – (–5) + (–1) + (+9) – (+3) – (+6) + (+2).

Step 1. Change the signs of the numbers being subtracted and the operation signs from subtraction to
addition.

(–5) + (+5) + (–1) + (+9)
+ (–3) + (–6) + (+2)

Step 2. Add following the rules for adding signed
numbers. Total the positive numbers.

5 + 9 + 2 = 16

Step 3. Total the negative numbers.

(–5) + (–1) + (–3) +
(–6) = –15

Step 4. Find the difference between the two totals.

16 – 15 = 1

Step 5. Since the total of the positive numbers is
larger, the answer has a plus sign.

(–5) + (+5) + (–1) + (+9)
+ (–3) + (–6) + (+2) = +1

**Directions:** Solve each problem.

1. (+4) + (+8)
2. (−10) + (−20)
3. (+14) + (−16)
4. (−9) − (+13)
5. (+4) − (−2) + (+6)
6. (−15) + (+3) + (−6) + (+7)
7. (+4) − (−8)
8. (−9) − (+6)
9. (−13) − (+3) + (−16)
10. (+3) − (−2) − (−20)

Answers are on page A-47.

---

## Lesson 3 — Multiplying and Dividing Signed Numbers

The rules for multiplying or dividing signed numbers are simple. If both numbers have the same sign, the answer is positive. If the numbers have different signs, the answer is negative.

**Example 1:** Multiply $(−12) \times (−2)$.

Step 1. Multiply the numbers. $\qquad\qquad\qquad\qquad$ $12 \times 2 = 24$

Step 2. Look at the signs the numbers have. Since $\qquad$ $(−12) \times (−2) = +24$
both are the same, the answer is positive.

**Example 2:** Find the quotient of $\frac{(−84)}{(+7)}$.

Step 1. Divide the numbers. $\qquad\qquad\qquad\qquad$ $\frac{84}{7} = 12$

Step 2. Look at the signs the numbers have. Since $\qquad$ $\frac{(−84)}{(+7)} = −12$
they are different, the answer is negative.

When you need to work a multiplication or division problem with more than two signed numbers, count the number of negative numbers in the problem. If there is an odd number of negative numbers, the answer is negative. If there is an even number of negative numbers, the answer is positive.

**Example 3:** Find $(+4) \times (-3) \times (-5) \times (-1)$.

Step 1. Multiply as if the numbers were not signed.    $4 \times 3 \times 5 \times 1 = 60$

Step 2. Count how many numbers are negative.    $(+4) \times (-3) \times (-5) \times (-1)$
Since three of the numbers are negative and three is    $= -60$
an odd number, the answer is negative.

**Example 4:** Find $\dfrac{(-3)(-1)(+5)(-2)}{(-10)}$ .

Step 1. Perform the operations as if the numbers    $3 \times 1 \times 5 \times 2 = 30$
were not signed.    $\dfrac{30}{10} = 3$

Step 2. Count how many numbers are negative.    $\dfrac{(-3)(-1)(+5)(-2)}{(-10)} = +3$
Since four of the numbers are negative and four is
an even number, the answer is positive.

## Level 1, Lesson 3 Exercise

**Directions:** Solve each problem.

1. $(+3)(-9)$    2. $-5(-5)$    3. $(+7)(+9)$    4. $\dfrac{(+50)}{(-5)}$    5. $(17)(-8)$

6. $\dfrac{(104)}{(-13)}$    7. $\dfrac{40}{+10}$    8. $\dfrac{(-6)(-3)}{10}$    9. $(-2)(4)(-5)(-3)$    10. $\dfrac{(6)(+1)(-2)(-3)}{2}$

Answers are on page A-47.

# Lesson 4  Adding and Subtracting Monomials

Algebra uses expressions to show mathematical relationships. An algebraic expression contains a combination of letters and numbers. $x + y$ is an expression that shows the sum of two numbers. $cd$ is an expression that shows the product of two numbers.

Algebraic expressions are made up of terms. A term is not separated by a + or – sign. A **monomial** is an expression that contains only one term. $9m$ is a monomial. $-12pq$ is a monomial. And $c^2$ is also a monomial. A **coefficient** is the number in front of a monomial. The **variables** are the letters. In the expression $9m$, the coefficient is 9, and the variable is $m$. In the expression $-12pq$, $-12$ is the coefficient, and $pq$ are the variables. In the expression $c^2$, the coefficient is 1 even though the 1 is not written, and $c$ is the variable.

Monomials that are like terms can be combined through addition or subtraction. The process is similar to adding or subtracting fractions with common denominators. When you combine (add or subtract) fractions with common denominators, you combine only the numerators. When you combine monomials which are like terms, you combine only the coefficients. Also, the rules for adding and subtracting signed numbers apply to combining monomials.

**Example 1:** $14y^2 + 3y^2$

Step 1. Since the monomials are like terms, you can combine them. Add the coefficients.

$14 + 3 = 17$

Step 2. The answer is written as the sum of the coefficients with the original variable and exponent.

$14y^2 + 3y^2 = 17y^2$

**Example 2:** Simplify $(7x^2y) - (2x^2y) + (-3x^2y)$.

Step 1. Note that all three monomials are like terms; they can be combined into one term.

Step 2. Combine the coefficients using the rules for adding and subtracting signed numbers.

$(+7) - (+2) + (-3) =$
$(+7) + (-2) + (-3) =$
$+7 + (-5) = +2$

Step 3. The answer is written as the sum of the coefficients with the original variables and exponents.

$(7x^2y) - (2x^2y) + (-3x^2y) = 2x^2y$

## Level 1, Lesson 4 Exercise

**Directions:** Simplify each expression.

1. $19x + 7x$
2. $(4b^2) + (13b^2)$
3. $(2abc) + (abc)$
4. $(13n^2) - (4n^2)$
5. $(-8s^3) - (+4s^3)$
6. $(+13b^2c^2) - (-13b^2c^2)$
7. $(-9.5a) + (10.2a) - (a)$
8. $(8st) - (+3st) + (-14st)$
9. $(c) - (-4c) - 4c$
10. $(10p^5q^7) + (p^5q^7) - (-9p^5q^7)$

Answers are on page A-47.

## Lesson 5 — Multiplying and Dividing Monomials

Monomials do not have to be like terms to be multiplied or divided. When multiplying monomials:

- multiply the coefficients, using the rules for multiplying signed numbers,
- add the exponents of similar bases (remember, a variable without a written exponent has an exponent of 1), and
- combine the results from the coefficients and all variables to show the product.

**Example 1:** Find $(-6x^2)(-3x^3)$.

Step 1. Multiply the coefficients. $\qquad -6 \times -3 = +18$

Step 2. Add the exponents. $\qquad x^2 \times x^3 = x^{2+3} = x^5$

Step 3. Combine the results to show the product. $\qquad (-6x^2)(-3x^3) = +18x^5$

**Example 2:** Find $(5q^2r)(-2q^5r^2s)$.

Step 1. Multiply the coefficients. $\qquad 5 \times (-2) = -10$

Step 2. Add the exponents of like variables.
$$q^2 \times q^5 = q^{2+5} = q^7$$
$$r \times r^2 = r^{1+2} = r^3$$

Note that the variable $s$ appears in only one monomial.

Step 3. Combine the results to show the product.
$$(5q^2r)(-2q^5r^2s) = -10q^7r^3s$$

When dividing monomials:

- divide the coefficients,
- subtract the exponents of like variables, and
- combine the results to show the quotient.

**Example 3:** Find $\dfrac{18s^5t^2}{-6s^2}$

Step 1. Divide the coefficients. $\qquad \dfrac{18}{-6} = -3$

Step 2. Subtract the exponents of like variables. $\qquad s^5 \div s^2 = s^{5-2} = s^3$

Notice that the divisor does not contain a variable $t$.

Step 3. Combine the results to show the exponent. $\qquad \dfrac{18s^5t^2}{-6s^2} = -3s^3t^2$

The rules of signed numbers apply when subtracting the exponents and it is possible to have a negative number in an exponent. A base with an exponent of zero is equal to 1. For example: $5^0 = 1$; $x^0 = 1$.

**Example 4:** Divide $25p^3s^5$ by $5p^5s^5$.

Step 1. Divide the coefficients.

$25 \div 5 = 5$

Step 2. Subtract the exponents.

$p^3 \div p^5 = p^{3-5} = p^{-2}$

$s^5 \div s^5 = s^{5-5} = s^0$

Step 3. Combine the results. Since $s^0 = 1$, it does not have to be written in the answer.

$\dfrac{25p^3s^5}{5p^5s^5} = 5p^{-2}$

## Level 1, Lesson 5 Exercise

**Directions:** Simplify each expression.

1. $2t^3 \times 2t^2$

2. $(3ab)(5ab^2)$

3. $(-3x)(4xy)(-3y)$

4. $\dfrac{y^4}{y^2}$

5. $\dfrac{-6s^6}{2s^2}$

6. $\dfrac{(32x^5)}{(-8x^3)}$

7. $2a \times \dfrac{2b}{4ab}$

8. $\dfrac{6(3x^6y^4z^6)}{3(4x^4y^4z^3)}$

9. $(4 \times 5a^2b^3)(2 \times 7b^2c)$

10. $\dfrac{20x^2}{-2x^3}$

Answers are on pages A-47 and A-48.

# Level 2

# Algebra Applications

## Lesson 1 — Solving One-Step Equations

Think: What number plus 5 equals 8?

You might have quickly subtracted in your head 5 from 8 to come up with the answer, 3. This is how an equation is solved.

An **equation** is an algebraic statement using numbers and math symbols which shows that two amounts are equal. If the above were written as an equation with x representing the unknown number, it would look like this:

$$x + 5 = 8$$

To solve an equation, you must keep both sides balanced. If you do an operation to one side of the equation, that is, to one side of the equal sign, you must do exactly the same operation to the other side. For example, you would solve the above equation by subtracting 5 from each side:

$$x + 5 - 5 = 8 - 5$$
$$x = 3$$

As you can see, to solve an equation with an addition sign, you subtract. This is called using the **inverse operation**.

- The inverse of addition is subtraction.
- The inverse of subtraction is addition.
- The inverse of multiplication is division.
- The inverse of division is multiplication.

By using the inverse operation, the variable representing the unknown number will be alone on one side of the equation. The other side will be the value of the unknown. In a one-step equation, it will take one inverse operation to find the solution.

**Example 1:** Solve $25x = 100$. Since 25 is the number on the side with the unknown, use 25 on both sides of the equation.

Step 1. Here $x$ is multiplied by 25. The inverse of multiplication is division. Divide both sides of the equation by 25.

$$\frac{25x}{25} = \frac{100}{25}$$

**Step 2.** Perform the division on both sides. $25x$ divided by 25 equals $x$; 100 divided by 25 equals 4: $\qquad x = 4$

**Example 2:** Solve $c - 8 = 10$.

**Step 1.** The inverse of subtraction is addition. Add 8 to each side of the equation. $\qquad c - 8 + 8 = 10 + 8$

**Step 2.** Perform the addition on both sides. $\qquad c = 18$

**Example 3:** Solve $\frac{1}{3}p = 36$.

**Step 1.** Set up the problem.

$$\frac{1}{3}p = 36$$

**Step 2.** Solve the problem, using the inverse operation of division. Remember that when dividing fractions, you invert and multiply.

$$\frac{\frac{1}{3}p}{\frac{1}{3}} = \frac{36}{\frac{1}{3}}$$

$$\frac{1}{\cancel{3}_1} \times \frac{\cancel{3}^1}{1}p = \frac{36}{1} \times \frac{3}{1}$$

$$p = \frac{36}{1} \times \frac{3}{1}$$

$$p = 108$$

## Level 2, Lesson 1 Exercise

**Directions:** Solve each equation.

1. $9x = 72$
2. $g + 20 = 64$
3. $c - 14 = 39$
4. $\dfrac{b}{5} = 30$

5. $32 = y + 7$
6. $\dfrac{1x}{2} = 6$
7. $42 = x - 1$
8. $x - 18 = 108$

Answers are on page A-48.

---

**Lesson 2**

# Solving Multistep Equations

Often, solving an equation will require more than one step. Such equations might have parentheses. They may require more than one inverse operation to get the variable by itself. When confronted with a multistep equation, work the problem in this order:

1. Do the operations required by the parentheses first.
2. Combine the separated unknowns.

3. Do the inverse operations requiring subtraction or addition.
4. Do the inverse operations requiring division or multiplication.

**Example 1:** Solve $5(x + 1) = 20$.

Step 1. Do the operation required by the parentheses.

$$5(x + 1) = 20$$
$$5x + 5 = 20$$

Step 2. Do the inverse operation requiring subtraction.

$$5x + 5 - 5 = 20 - 5$$
$$5x = 15$$

Step 3. Do the inverse operation requiring division.

$$\frac{5x}{5} = \frac{15}{5}$$

$$\frac{^1 5x}{5_1} = \frac{15^3}{5_1}$$

$$x = 3$$

## Unknowns on the Same Side of an Equation

When the unknown appears in two terms on the same side of the equation, use the rules for addition and subtraction of monomials to combine the terms.

**Example 2:** Solve $4x + 2x - 6 = 18$.

Step 1. Add the monomials on the left side of the equation.

$$4x + 2x - 6 = 18$$
$$6x - 6 = 18$$

Step 2. Add 6 to both sides.

$$6x - 6 + 6 = 18 + 6$$
$$6x = 24$$

Step 3. Divide each side by 6 to find the value of $x$.

$$\frac{6x}{6} = \frac{24}{6}$$

$$x = 4$$

## An Unknown on Both Sides of the Equation

When the variable appears on both sides of the = sign, use inverse operations to combine the variables. Remember that you want the unknowns on one side and numbers on the other side.

**Example 3:** Solve the equation $5x + 30 = 8x$.

Step 1. To get the variables on one side, subtract $5x$ from both sides.

$$5x - 5x + 30 = 8x - 5x$$
$$30 = 3x$$

Step 2. Divide both sides by 3. The solution is 10.

$$\frac{30}{3} = \frac{3x}{3}$$

$$10 = x$$

**Directions:** Solve each equation.

1. $3n + 5n = 40$
2. $8t + 12 = 2t - 6$
3. $2(y + 10) = 38$
4. $3x - 4 - x = 16$
5. $9s - 27 = 3s + 27$
6. $p + 2(p + 5) = 22$
7. $5b - 5 = 0$
8. $3(k + 7) + 7 = 80 + k$
9. $2(3b - 15) = 3(11 - b)$
10. $25a - 193 = 17a + 71$

Answers are on page A-48.

**Lesson 3**

# Solving Inequalities

Inequalities show the relationship between one number and another. There are four types of inequalities, each represented by a symbol:

**Less than** is represented by the symbol **<**.

> If 5 is less than 6, it is shown as $5 < 6$.
> In the expression $t < 6$, $t$ represents any number that is less than 6.

**Greater than** is represented by the symbol **>**.

> If 6 is greater than 5, it is shown as $6 > 5$.
> In the expression $t > 5$, $t$ represents any number that is greater than 5.

**Less than or equal to** is represented by the symbol ≤.

> If $t$ is less than or equal to 80, it is shown as $t \leq 80$.
> In this expression, $t$ represents 80 or any number less than 80.

**Greater than or equal to** is represented by the symbol ≥.

> If $t$ is greater than or equal to 80, it is shown as $t \geq 80$.
> In this expression, $t$ represents 80 or any number greater than 80.

If you have trouble remembering what each symbol represents, remember that the pointed end of the symbol points to the smaller value.

Solving for the unknown in inequalities is similar to solving equations. Inverse operations are used: Whatever is done to one side of the inequality is done to the other side to keep the relationship constant.

**Example 1:** Solve $n - 2 < 5$.

Step 1. Add 2 to both sides of the inequality.

$n - 2 + 2 < 5 + 2$

$n < 7$

Step 2. Substitute any number less than 7 to verify your solution.

$6 - 2 < 5$

$4 < 5$

**Example 2:** Is 4 one of the solutions for the inequality $3d - 26 \leq 1$?

Substitute 4 for $d$ and simplify the inequality.

$3(4) - 26 \leq 1$

$12 - 26 \leq 1$

$-14 \leq 1$

## Level 2, Lesson 3 Exercise

**Directions:** Solve each inequality.

1. $4y - 10 \geq 14$
2. $5t + 2 > 12$
3. $9v - 2 \leq 25$

**Directions:** Answer each question using the substitution method shown above.

4. In the inequality $13d - 4 > 22$, is 1 part of the set of solutions for $d$?
5. In the inequality $5m + 3 \geq 33$, is 6 part of the set of solutions for $m$?

Answers are on page A-48.

# Lesson 4 — Multiplying Binomials

A binomial is an algebraic expression that has two terms, such as $5x + 8$, $c - 6$, and $t^2 + 2$. To multiply binomials, each term of one binomial is multiplied by each term in the other binomial.

**Example 1:** Multiply $(3x - 8)(2x + 2)$.

Step 1. Set up the problem.

$$\begin{array}{r} 3x - 8 \\ \times\, 2x + 2 \end{array}$$

Step 2. Multiply the top terms by +2. Review the rules for multiplying signed numbers if you need to. $2 \times -8 = -16$; $2 \times 3x = 6x$. Enter these results beneath the answer line.

$$\begin{array}{r} 3x - 8 \\ \times\, 2x + 2 \\ \hline 6x - 16 \end{array}$$

**Step 3.** Multiply the top terms by $2x$. $2x \times -8 = -16x$; $2x \times 3x = 6x^2$. Enter these results so that the terms that can be combined are in a column.

$$
\begin{array}{r}
3x - 8 \\
\times\ 2x + 2 \\
\hline
6x - 16 \\
6x^2 - 16x \\
\end{array}
$$

**Step 4.** Add each column.

$$
\begin{array}{r}
3x - 8 \\
\times\ 2x + 2 \\
\hline
6x - 16 \\
6x^2 - 16x \\
\hline
6x^2 - 10x - 16 \\
\end{array}
$$

**Example 2:** Find $(c - 6)(c + 6)$.

**Step 1.** Set up the problem.

$$
\begin{array}{r}
c - 6 \\
\times\ c + 6 \\
\hline
\end{array}
$$

**Step 2.** Multiply the top terms by $+6$.

$$
\begin{array}{r}
c - 6 \\
\times\ c + 6 \\
\hline
6c - 36 \\
\end{array}
$$

**Step 3.** Multiply the top terms by $c$.

$$
\begin{array}{r}
c - 6 \\
\times\ c + 6 \\
\hline
6c - 36 \\
c^2 - 6c \\
\end{array}
$$

**Step 4.** Add the columns. Note that $6c$ and $-6c$ in the middle column cancel each other out, leaving $c^2 - 36$.

$$
\begin{array}{r}
c - 6 \\
\times\ c + 6 \\
\hline
6c - 36 \\
c^2 - 6c \\
\hline
c^2 + 0 - 36\ =\ c^2 - 36 \\
\end{array}
$$

## Level 2, Lesson 4 Exercise

**Directions:** Multiply these binomials.

1. $3t + 4$
   $\times\ t - 6$

2. $x - 5$
   $\times\ x + 5$

3. $(2b - 3)(3b - 4)$

4. $(c + 3)(c + 3)$

5. $(4a + 6)(2a - 3)$

Answers are on pages A-48 and A-49.

**Lesson 5**

# Factoring Trinomials

**Factors** are numbers that multiply together to give another number. For example, 2 and 3 are factors in the expression: $2 \times 3 = 6$. 6 and 1 are also factors of 6.

A **trinomial** is an algebraic expression that has three terms. The type of trinomial you will have to factor on the GED test will look like this:

$x^2 + 9x + 20$.

It has an unknown squared, an unknown with a coefficient, and a number.

To factor a trinomial into a pair of binomials that equal it when multiplied, first find the factors of the number that is alone. In the trinomial above, the number is 20. Then determine which pair of factors, when added together, would equal the coefficient of the variable, or the middle term. In the trinomial above, the middle term is $9x$, the coefficient is 9, and the variable is $x$.

**Example 1:** Factor $x^2 + 9x + 20$.

Step 1. Find the factors of 20 which add up to 9.

$$1 \times 20 = 20$$
$$2 \times 10 = 20$$
$$4 \times 5 = 20 \quad 4 + 5 = 9$$

Step 2. The factors of this trinomial are:

$$(x + 4)(x + 5)$$

When the number or last term is negative, one factor is negative and one is positive. The number of the middle term will determine which is negative.

**Example 2:** Factor $p^2 + 4p - 12$.

Step 1. Find the factors of $-12$ that add up to 4.

$$-2 \times 6 = -12$$
$$-2 + 6 = 4$$

Step 2. The factors of the trinomial are:

$$(p - 2)(p + 6)$$

When the number of the middle term is negative and the number is positive, both numbers in the factor are negative.

**Example 3:** Factor $y^2 - 10y + 16$.

Step 1. Find the factors of 16, when using pairs of negative numbers which add up to the negative 10.

$$-2 \times -8 = 16$$
$$-2 + (-8) = -10$$

Step 2. The factors of the trinomial are:

$$(y - 2)(y - 8)$$

Step 3. Check your work.

$$
\begin{array}{r}
y - 2 \\
y - 8 \\
\hline
- \quad 8y + 16 \\
y^2 - \ 2y \\
\hline
y^2 - 10y + 16
\end{array}
$$

## Level 2, Lesson 5 Exercise

**Directions:** Factor each trinomial.

**1.** $a^2 + 9a + 18$   **2.** $b^2 - 7b - 30$   **3.** $c^2 - 5c - 36$   **4.** $d^2 - 10d + 24$   **5.** $e^2 + 12e + 20$

Answers are on page A-49.

# Level 3

# Algebra Word Problems

## Lesson 1

# Writing Algebraic Expressions and Equations

You have had practice translating words into mathematical expressions in the earlier chapters. Sometimes an algebraic expression is necessary to solve a word problem. Remember to look for and identify key words to determine what operation to use. Here is a chart to help:

| | |
|---|---|
| **Addition** | **Subtraction** |
| $x + 6$ can be expressed as: | $n - 8$ can be expressed as: |
| $\quad x$ increased by 6 | $\quad n$ decreased by 8 |
| $\quad$ the sum of $x$ and 6 | $\quad n$ diminished by 8 |
| $\quad$ 6 more than $x$ | $\quad$ 8 less than $n$ |
| $\quad$ 6 and $x$ combined | $\quad$ 8 subtracted from $n$ |
| | |
| **Division** | **Multiplication** |
| $\frac{b}{5}$ can be expressed as: | $2a$ can be expressed as: |
| $\quad b$ divided by 5 | $\quad$ 12 times $a$ |
| $\quad$ the quotient of $b$ divided by 5 | $\quad$ twice $a$ |
| $\quad$ one-fifth of $b$ | $\quad a$ multiplied by 2 |
| $\quad$ 5 into $b$ | $\quad$ the product of $a$ and 2 |

**Example 1:** Write an algebraic expression for the phrase 4 times the sum of 6 and a number.

Step 1. Identify the key terms. *Times* means to multiply. *Sum* means to add.

Step 2. Determine to which values these operations will be applied. You are given two numbers and an unknown. The 4 will be used to multiply the sum of the unknown and the 6. Let $n$ stand for the unknown. Write an expression to show the sum of $n$ and 6.

$$n + 6$$

Step 3. To show that the sum is being multiplied by 4, place $n + 6$ inside parentheses; write the 4 outside.

$$4(n + 6)$$

**Level 3, Lesson 1: Writing Algebraic Expressions and Equations** 533

The same process can be used to set up equations to solve word problems. Look for key words such as "is," "equals," "total," "altogether," and "result" to determine where the equal sign is placed.

**Example 2:** Heather bought one wrench and one screwdriver. The screwdriver cost $7 and her bill totaled $16. What was the price of the wrench?

Step 1. Identify the key terms. The "and" in "one wrench and one screwdriver," and "totaled" in "her bill totaled," tell you to add the amounts represented by these items.

Step 2. You have the price of the screwdriver and the total price. You need to find the price of a wrench. Label this unknown value $w$. $w$ plus 7 equals 16. Write this in equation form.

$$w + 7 = 16$$

Step 3. Solve the equation.

$$w + 7 - 7 = 16 - 7$$
$$w = 9$$

The price of one wrench is $9.

**Example 3:** Suppose Heather bought two hammers and one screwdriver. The screwdriver cost $7 and the total bill was $23. What was the price of one hammer?

Step 1. You have the price of the screwdriver ($7) and the total price ($23). You need to find the price of one hammer. Label this unknown $n$.
$2n$ plus 7 equals 23. Write this as an equation.

$$2n + 7 = 23$$

Step 2. Solve the equation.

$$2n + 7 - 7 = 23 - 7$$
$$2n = 16$$
$$n = \frac{16}{2}$$
$$n = 8$$

One hammer costs $8.

## Level 3, Lesson 1 Exercise

For Items 1 to 6, write an algebraic expression. Use $x$ for the unknown when the question does not assign another letter for the unknown.

1. The sum of eight and a number, all multiplied by six

2. Three divided into the quantity of a number increased by seven

3. If Jim drives at an average speed of $r$ miles per hour, how far will he drive in four hours?

4. Let $g$ stand for Larry's gross salary. Larry's employer deducts 22% of Larry's salary for taxes. Write an expression for the amount of the deduction. (*Hint:* Change the percent to a decimal.)

5. Three times a number added to five times the number equals 24.

6. Twelve is the result of a number divided by eight.

7. Romana is three times older than Chris. Romana is 87. Which of the following represents Chris's age (if $x$ = Chris's age)?

    **(1)** $3x - 87$

    **(2)** $3x = 87$

    **(3)** $x = 87 - 3$

    **(4)** $x = 3(87)$

    **(5)** $\dfrac{87 - x}{3}$

8. Josh bought 4 books, each costing the same amount. The total price including $3 sales tax came to $51. How much did each book cost?

9. Seventy-seven workers at a factory participated in a bonus-sharing plan. The plan included a $4 per worker donation made by the factory to a charity of the worker's choice. Each worker's share of the total bonus plan was $100.00. How much of the total plan was paid directly to all the workers?

10. Karen drove the same number of miles each of the first three days of her trip. The fourth day she drove 364 miles. If she drove a total of 1255 miles, how many miles did she drive each of the first three days?

Answers are on page A-49.

## Lesson 2

# Algebra Setup Problems

On some GED questions, the correct answer will be expressed as an algebraic expression. You will need to use to your skills in reading algebra word problems and writing algebraic expressions but won't have to find a solution.

**Example 1:** Joe works 4 hours less than twice the number of hours Carlos works per week. If $n$ represents the number of hours Carlos works, which expression shows the number of hours Joe works?

    **(1)** $n - 4$

    **(2)** $4 - 2n$

    **(3)** $2n - 4$

    **(4)** $2n$

    **(5)** $4n$

You are told that the number of hours Joe works is, first, *twice* or *two times* the number of hours Carlos works, which indicates multiplication: $2 \times n$, or $2n$. Second, you are told that the total number of hours Joe works is four *less than twice* Carlos's hours. This means you subtract 4 from $2n$.

$$2n - 4$$

So **(3)** is the answer.

**Example 2:** Marie had $x$ amount of money on Friday. On Saturday, she spent $9 for a movie, snacks, and gas. If she used one half of the remaining money to pay a loan, which expression shows the amount of money she repaid on the loan?

**(1)** $2(x + 9)$    **(2)** $\dfrac{x}{(9 - 2)}$    **(3)** $\dfrac{(x - 9)}{2}$    **(4)** $x - 2 + 9$    **(5)** $\dfrac{x}{(2 - 9)}$

<u>Step 1.</u> A careful reading of this problem shows that you first must subtract what Marie spent from the amount she started with. This is expressed as: $\qquad\qquad x - 9$

<u>Step 2.</u> The amount left over is then divided by one half, or 2. To show this, place the amount left over in parentheses and show the result being divided by 2. $\qquad \dfrac{(x - 9)}{2}$

The correct answer is **(3)**.

Be careful not to be confused by **irrelevant information** in a setup word problem.

**Example 3:** Milly's weight at birth doubled at 5 months and tripled at one year of age. Which of the following expressions represents her approximate weight at one year old, if her weight at birth is $x$ pounds?

**(1)** $x$    **(2)** $x + 3$    **(3)** $x + 5$    **(4)** $2x$    **(5)** $3x$

You are asked to find Milly's weight at one year of age. You are told that her weight at one year of age is triple, or three times, her weight at birth, which is $x$. Her weight at one year is therefore $3x$. (Answer **(5)** is correct.) The fact that Milly's birth weight doubled at 5 months is irrelevant. Therefore the numbers 2 (for doubling) and 5 have no meaning for the problem, and answers **(3)** and **(4)** should be eliminated immediately.

## Level 3, Lesson 2 Exercise

**Directions:** Choose the expression that shows the correct setup for solving each problem.

1. There are 15 more women than men at the Wednesday night exercise class at the Greenport Community Center. Altogether, there are 47 people in the class. Which of the following expressions represents the total number of people, if $x$ equals the number of men?

   **(1)** $\dfrac{x + x + 15}{47}$

   **(2)** $x + 15 + 47$

   **(3)** $x + x + 15$

   **(4)** $x(x + 15)$

   **(5)** $47(x + 15)$

2. Carl weighs 65 pounds more than his wife, Cindy. Their son, Todd, weighs 115 pounds. Which of the following expressions shows the average weight of Carl, Cindy, and Todd? $x$ represents Cindy's weight.

   (1) $(2x + 180)$

   (2) $\dfrac{2x}{3} + 180$

   (3) $\dfrac{(2x + 180)}{3}$

   (4) $2x + 65$

   (5) $3(2x + 80)$

3. Altogether, Jim, Carmen, and George spent 95 hours campaigning for their friend Ed, who was running for state assemblyman. Both men also worked 40 hours each at their regular jobs during the campaign. Carmen worked 5 hours more than Jim, and George worked twice as long as Carmen. Which of the following expressions represents the number of hours George worked on the campaign if $x$ equals the number of hours Jim campaigned?

   (1) $x + 5$

   (2) $2(x + 5)$

   (3) $95 - 40$

   (4) $2x + 5 - 40$

   (5) $x + x + 5$

4. An amateur team gave a dinner to raise money. Tickets were $5 each. After subtracting expenses of $118, enough tickets were sold to raise $357. Which expression represents the amount raised after expenses if $x$ stands for the number of tickets sold?

   (1) $357 - 118 = x$

   (2) $5x - 118 = 357$

   (3) $\dfrac{357 - x}{5} = 118$

   (4) $\dfrac{5 - 118}{x} = 357$

   (5) $357 - 5x = 118$

5. It will cost $375 to charter a bus for a 15-member team. The team has only $265. Which expression represents the amount each team member will have to contribute to pay the bill? ($x$ represents the amount each team member must pay.)

   (1) $\dfrac{375}{15} = 265x$

   (2) $15x - 265 = 375$

   (3) $265 + 15x = 375$

   (4) $265 - 15x = 375$

   (5) $\dfrac{x}{15} + 265 = 375$

Answers are on page A-49.

# Chapter 6 Quiz

1. Which letter represents $\frac{-7}{6}$ on the number line?

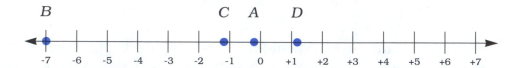

2. $(+14) - (-4) + (-8) - (+2) =$

3. $(+\frac{1}{3})(-18)(+4)(-3) =$

4. Simplify $(-10m^2n^2)(+10mn)(-3m^3n^2)$.

5. Solve for $b$: $46 - 3b = 7b + 6$.

6. Solve for $x$: $8x + 5 = 3(x - 5)$.

7. Solve for $n$: $12n + 3 \geq 2n + 23$.

8. Solve for $w$: $\frac{2w}{3} + 14 < 26$.

9. Write an algebraic expression: Eight less than one-half of a number.

10. Five times a number decreased by sixteen equals two more than three times the number. Find the number.

11. Multiply $(4c - 8)$ by $(2c + 6)$.

12. $(k - 11)(k + 11)$

13. Factor: $j^2 - j - 20$.

14. Hal, Phil, and Chris painted a house together. Hal worked three hours more than Phil. Chris worked two hours more than Hal. Altogether they worked 17 hours. How long did each one work?

15. Mr. and Mrs. Nash and their daughter Sally shared the driving on a trip to see relatives. Sally drove three hours more than Mrs. Nash, and Mr. Nash drove twice as many hours as Sally. They drove 33 hours altogether. How many hours did Mr. Nash drive?

16. Company A employs 30 more than three times as many employees as Company B. Which of the following expressions shows the total number of employees of the two companies? $b$ represents the number of employees of Company B.

    (1) $3b(b + 30)$

    (2) $3b + 30$

    (3) $3(b + 30)$

    (4) $3b + 30 + b$

    (5) $2b + 30$

**17.** In a miniature golf game, Suzanne had 3 more strokes than Gail. Ann scored twice as many strokes as Suzanne. If their scores total 246 strokes, which equation would show how many strokes Gail scored? $g$ represents the number of strokes Gail had.

**(1)** $3g + 9 = 246$

**(2)** $3(g + 9) = 246$

**(3)** $g + 3(2g + 3) = 246$

**(4)** $2g + 3 + 2(g + 3) = 246$

**(5)** $2(g + 2g + 3) = 246$

**18.** Joe is a plumber. He makes $3 an hour more than his assistant Phil. On a job on which they each spent ten hours, they made $350. Which of the following expressions represents their total wages, if $x$ stands for Phil's hourly wage?

**(1)** $\dfrac{x + x + 3}{350}$

**(2)** $10x + 10(x + 3) = 350$

**(3)** $10(x + 3) + x = 350$

**(4)** $\dfrac{350}{10(x + 3)}$

**(5)** $\dfrac{10(x + 3)}{350}$

**19.** Juan's take-home pay is five times the amount his employer takes out of his gross pay. Juan's gross weekly pay is $324. Which of the following expressions represents his gross weekly pay, if $x$ equals the amount the employer takes out?

**(1)** $x + 5x$

**(2)** $x + x + 5$

**(3)** $324 - x$

**(4)** $\dfrac{324}{5x - x}$

**(5)** $\dfrac{5x - x}{324}$

**20.** Barbara is three times as old as Lisa. The difference between their ages is 24 years. Find their ages.

**21.** Ted made a sandwich which had a total of 520 calories. The bread made up 130 calories and mayonnaise made up 105 calories. He used 3 slices of meat. How many calories per slice did the meat have?

**22.** Marie has been on a diet for 6 months and has lost 25 pounds. During the first 3 months, she lost some weight. During the last three months, she lost the same amount plus 3 more pounds. How much weight did she lose during the last 3 months?

**23.** A tenants' organization is lobbying members of the city council to vote against a proposed citywide rent increase of $50 per month for a studio apartment, $75 per month for a one-bedroom apartment, and $100 per month for a two-bedroom apartment. Which expression below shows how much rent Paul and Lisa will pay each week for their one-bedroom and studio apartments?

**(1)** $x + 125$

**(2)** $\dfrac{(x + 125)}{4}$

**(3)** $\dfrac{x + 75}{2}$

**(4)** $\dfrac{(x + 125)12}{4}$

**(5)** $(x + 75 + 50)4$

**24.** Dorothy, who makes curtains for a living, makes $4 an hour more than her helper, Ann. Dorothy and Ann each worked 25 hours on a job for which they earned $500 altogether. How much does Dorothy make in an hour?

**25.** Giorgio can type 4 times as fast as Chan. Together they can type 230 words a minute. Which of the following expressions shows how to find how fast Chan types? (*c* represents his typing speed.)

**(1)** $5c = 230$

**(2)** $230 - 5 = c$

**(3)** $230 + c = 4$

**(4)** $4c = 230$

**(5)** $\dfrac{c}{5} = 230$

Answers are on pages A-49 and A-50.

# CHAPTER 7
# Geometry

Geometry is a branch of mathematics that involves the measuring of lines, angles, surfaces, and three-dimensional figures. You have already learned several geometric concepts in this book. You have found the perimeter and area of squares, rectangles, triangles, and circles. You have also found the volume of cubes, rectangular solids, and cylinders.

In this chapter, you will become familiar with other geometric ideas which you need for the GED test. You will learn many new terms in this chapter. Take the time to memorize the terms you do not already know.

## In this chapter you will learn about:

- Points, lines, and planes
- The different types of angles
- The properties of pairs of angles
- The relationship between parallel lines and transversals
- The different types of triangles and their special properties
- Congruent triangles
- Similar triangles
- The Pythagorean relationship
- Plotting lines on a graph
- Calculating slope
- Finding the distance between points

# Geometry Skills

## Preview

1. In Figure 7–1, if lines $\overline{AB}$ and $\overline{CD}$ are in the same plane and do not intersect, what kind of lines are they?

**Fig. 7–1**

2. What kind of angle is shown in Figure 7–2?

3. How many degrees are there in the angle in Figure 7–2?

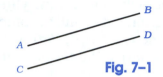

**Fig. 7–2**

4. In Figure 7–3, $\angle a = 110°$. What does $\angle b$ measure?

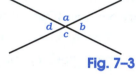

**Fig. 7–3**

5. Which angles are equal to $\angle c$ in Figure 7–4?

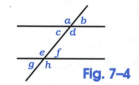

**Fig. 7–4**

6. If the vertex angle of an isosceles triangle is 76°, how many degrees does each base angle measure?

7. In Figure 7–5, $\angle a = 45°$ and $\angle b = 85°$. Find the measure of $\angle c$.

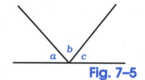

**Fig. 7–5**

Answers are on page A-50. If you have at least six correct, try the Chapter 7 Quiz on page 561. If you have fewer than six answers correct, study Level 1 beginning with Lesson 1.

# Points, Lines, and Planes

The geometry in this chapter and on the GED test is called **plane geometry**. It is concerned with only two dimensions, instead of three dimensions. While the figures used in this type of geometry may have a width and length, they have no depth. In other words, these figures, or planes, are completely flat!

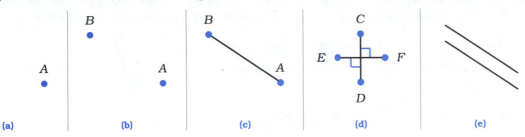

Fig. 7–6

A specific location within this plane is called a **point**. Often in drawings, points are labeled by a letter. In Figure 7–6(a), the point is labeled *A*.

In Figure 7–6(b), a second point is labeled *B*. The shortest distance between these two points is called a **line**. In Figure 7–6(c), a line has been drawn connecting these points. This line can be called *AB*.

When two lines in a plane cross each other, they **intersect**, as when two streets cross. Two intersecting lines form an angle. When two lines intersect at an angle of 90°, they are called **perpendicular lines**. In Figure 7–6(d), lines *CD* and *EF* are perpendicular; notice that the ⌐ symbol is used to show that these lines are perpendicular.

It is also possible for two lines in the same plane to never intersect. These lines are called **parallel**. Sometimes parallel lines will be designated by a // symbol as in Figure 7–6(e).

## Level 1, Lesson 1 Exercise

**Directions:** Match the terms with the definitions.

1. perpendicular lines
2. point
3. plane
4. parallel lines
5. line

a. an area with an infinite width and length but no height
b. lines in the same plane that never intersect.
c. one specific spot in a plane
d. lines that intersect at a right angle
e. the shortest distance between two points

Answers are on pages A-50 and A-51.

## Lesson 2

# Relationships of Angles

## Complementary Angles

Angles that combine to form a right angle are called **complementary angles**. The sum of the measurements of the angles will equal 90°. This property can be used to find the measure of one angle when the measure of the other is known.

**Example 1:** In Figure 7–7, ∠DEF = 67°. ∠DEF and ∠GEF are complementary angles. What does ∠GEF measure?

**Fig. 7–7**

<u>Step 1.</u> You know that the sum of both angles equals 90°.

<u>Step 2.</u> Find the difference between 90° and the measure given of ∠DEF to find the measure of ∠GEF.

90° – 67° = 23°

∠GEF = 23°

## Supplementary Angles

Angles that combine to form a straight angle are called **supplementary angles**. The sum of the measurement of the angles will equal 180°. As with complementary angles, you can find the measurement of one angle when the measurement of the other is known.

**Example 2:** In Figure 7–8, find the measurement of ∠HJL. ∠LJK = 33° and is a supplementary angle with ∠HJL.

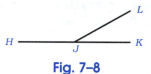

**Fig. 7–8**

<u>Step 1.</u> You know the sum of both angles equals 180°.

<u>Step 2.</u> Find the difference between 180° and the measurement given of ∠LJK to find the measurement of ∠HJL.

180° – 33° = 147°

∠HJL = 147°

## Vertical Angles

Angles formed by intersecting lines and which are opposite to each other, as in Figure 7–9, are equal. They are called **vertical angles**.

**Example 3:** ∠MQP = 85°. Find the measurement of the other angles.

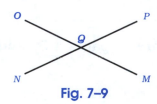

**Fig. 7–9**

<u>Step 1.</u> ∠*MQP* and ∠*NQO* are vertical angles. Since ∠*MQP* = 85°, ∠*NQO* = 85°.

<u>Step 2.</u> ∠*MQP* and ∠*MQN* are supplementary angles.     180° – 85° = 95°
∠*MQN* = 95°

<u>Step 3.</u> ∠*MQN* and ∠*PQO* are vertical angles. Since ∠*MQN* = 95°, ∠*PQO* = 95°.

## Corresponding Angles

When parallel lines are cut by a third line, the resulting angles have special relationships. The line cutting through the parallel lines is called a **transversal**.

In Figure 7–10, *AB* and *CD* are parallel lines. Because the transversal *EF* cuts through both lines the same way due to the parallelism, some of the angles formed by the intersection of *AB* and *EF* are equal to the angles formed by the intersections of *CD* and *EF*. The equal angles that are in the same relative position are called corresponding angles. Corresponding angles are equal. In Figure 7–10, the following are pairs of corresponding angles:

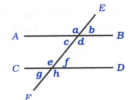

∠*a* and ∠*e*

∠*b* and ∠*f*

∠*c* and ∠*g*

∠*d* and ∠*h*

**Fig. 7–10**

For examples 4 and 5, ∠*a* = 110°.

**Example 4:** What is the measurement of ∠*h*?

<u>Step 1.</u> Find the corresponding angle to ∠*a* in the angles formed by *CD* and *EF*. Here it is ∠*e*.

<u>Step 2.</u> Since ∠*a* measures 110°, and ∠*e* is the corresponding angle, ∠*e* = 110°.

<u>Step 3.</u> ∠*e* and ∠*h* are vertical angles. Vertical     ∠*h* = 110°
angles are equal.

**Example 5:** What is the measurement of ∠*g*?

<u>Step 1.</u> Find the corresponding angle to ∠*a* in the angles formed by *CD* and *EF*. Again, it is ∠*e*.

<u>Step 2.</u> Since ∠*a* measures 110°, and ∠*e* is the corresponding angle, ∠*e* = 110°.

<u>Step 3.</u> ∠*e* and ∠*g* are supplementary angles. Find     180° – 110° = 70°
the difference between 180° and the measurement of     ∠*g* = 70°
∠*e* to find the measurement of ∠*g*.

**Directions:** Items 1 through 5 refer to Figure 7–11. ∠h = 65°.

1. Find the measurement of ∠d.
2. Find the measurement of ∠f.
3. ∠i corresponds to what angle?
4. What ∠ is vertical to ∠c?
5. What is the measurement of ∠b?

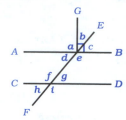

**Fig. 7–11**

Answers are on page A-51.

---

# Lesson 3

# Triangles

A triangle is a closed, three-sided plane figure. You should be somewhat familiar with triangles already. You learned how to find the area and perimeter of triangles in Chapter 1. The sum of the measures of the three angles inside any triangle is 180°. A triangle is referred to by the letters representing each of its points. The triangle in Figure 7–12(a) is referred to as △ABC.

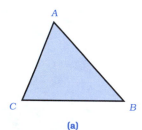

(a)

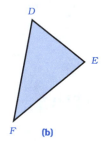

(b)

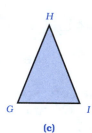

(c)

**Fig. 7–12**

Triangles have names based on the properties of their sides and angles.

In Figure 7–12(b), △DEF has no equal sides or angles. It is called a **scalene triangle**.

In Figure 7–12(c), △GHI has two equal sides and two equal angles. It is called an **isosceles triangle**. GH and HI are the equal sides. ∠G and ∠I are called the base angles and are equal. ∠H is called the vertex angle.

△JKL in Figure 7–13 has three equal sides and three equal angles. It is called an **equilateral triangle**. Each angle in an equilateral triangle measures 60°. This is because the sum of the angles is 180° and 180° ÷ 3 = 60°. Note that an equilateral triangle also has the properties of an isosceles triangle.

△MNP in Figure 7–13 is a **right triangle**. ∠P is a right angle: It has 90°. The side opposite the right angle in a right triangle is called the **hypotenuse**. The other two sides are called **legs**. If the other two angles in a right triangle each measure 45°, then the right triangle is also an isosceles triangle.

In any triangle, not just a right triangle, the longest side is opposite the largest angle.

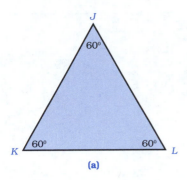

(a)

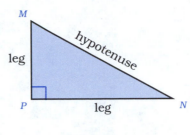

Fig. 7–13

(b)

**Example:** In △PQR in Figure 7–14, PQ = QR. If ∠P = 32°, what does ∠Q measure?

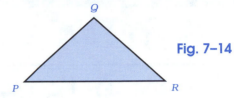

Fig. 7–14

Step 1. Determine what type of triangle this is. Since two sides are equal, it is an isosceles triangle.

Step 2. ∠P is a base angle. The other base angle is ∠R. ∠R = ∠P.

$\angle R = 32°$

Step 3. ∠P + ∠R + ∠Q = 180°

$32° + 32° + \angle Q = 180°$

Step 4. ∠Q = 180° − 64°

$\angle Q = 116°$

## Level 1, Lesson 3 Exercise

1.  In △ABC, ∠C = 40°. AB is perpendicular to AC. Find the measurement of ∠B.
2.  In △DEF, ∠D = 45° and ∠F = 35°. Find the measurement of ∠E.
3.  △GHI is isosceles. GH = HI. ∠H = 72°. Find the measurement of the base angles.
4.  In △JKL, ∠K = 55°. ∠J is 10° larger than ∠K. How large is ∠L?
5.  In triangle MNO, ∠O = 120° and ∠M = 26°. Find the measure of ∠N.

Answers are on page A-51.

# Level 2

# Geometry Applications

## Lesson 1 — Congruent and Similar Triangles Congruence

**Congruent triangles** are triangles that have the same shape and same size. When triangles are congruent, the corresponding sides and corresponding angles are equal.

In Figure 7–15, $\triangle ABC$ is congruent to $\triangle DEF$. Side $AB = DE$, $BC = EF$, and $AC = DF$. Also $\angle A = \angle D$, $\angle B = \angle E$, and $\angle C = \angle F$. Note, however, that congruent triangles are not always drawn to look exactly alike.

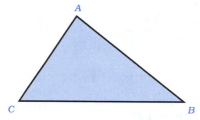
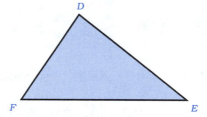

**Fig. 7–15**

**Example 1:** In Figure 7–16, $\triangle GHI$ and $\triangle JKL$ are congruent. $\angle G = \angle J$, $\angle I = \angle L$, and $\angle H = \angle K$. What side of $\triangle JKL$ equals 8 inches?

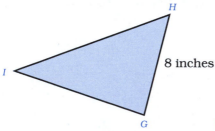
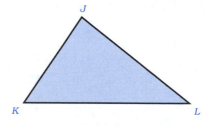

8 inches

**Fig. 7–16**

<u>Step 1.</u>  Identify the side on $\triangle GHI$ that equals 8 inches.     $GH = 8$ inches

<u>Step 2.</u>  Use tick marks to show similar sides and angles (see Figure 7–17). Since $\angle I = \angle L$ and $GH$ is opposite $\angle I$, the side opposite $\angle L$, $KJ$, corresponds to the side opposite $\angle I$, $GH$. $KJ$ measures 8 inches.

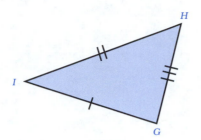

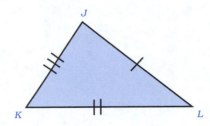

**Fig. 7-17**

## Similarity

   **Similar triangles** are triangles that have corresponding angles that are equal and corresponding sides that are proportional in length.
   In Figure 7–18, $\triangle STU$ is similar to $\triangle PQR$. Each side of $\triangle STU$ is twice the length of the corresponding side of $\triangle PQR$. If you know the length of two sides of $\triangle STU$, and the length of one corresponding side of $\triangle PQR$, you can use the proportion formula you learned in Chapter 2 to find the length of the corresponding side in $PQR$.

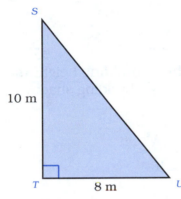

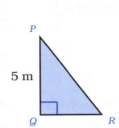

**Fig. 7-18**

**Example 2:** $ST = 10$ m, $TU = 8$ m. $\angle S = \angle P$. If $PQ = 5$ m, find the length of $QR$.

Step 1. Determine which sides correspond to each other. Since $\angle T = \angle Q$ and $\angle S = \angle P$, $ST$ corresponds to $PQ$ and $TU$ corresponds to $QR$.

Step 2. Set up a proportion reflecting this relationship.

$$\frac{ST}{TU} = \frac{PQ}{QR}$$

$$\frac{10}{8} = \frac{5}{QR}$$

Step 3. Cross-multiply and solve.

$$10 \times QR = 8 \times 5$$
$$10QR = 40$$
$$QR = \frac{40}{10} = 4$$

   Often on the GED test, the similarity is shown by using real objects, as illustrated in Figure 7–19.

building

**Example 3:** The building in Figure 7–19 casts a shadow 48 feet long at the same time that the flagpole casts a shadow 12 feet long. The flagpole is 18 feet tall. How tall is the building?

RPH Tower

48 ft.

flagpole

18 ft.    12 ft.

**Fig. 7–19**

Step 1. By connecting the top of the objects with the end of their shadows, triangles are formed. Determine which sides of the triangle correspond. The length of the building shadow corresponds to the length of the flagpole shadow. The building height corresponds to the flagpole height.

Step 2. Set up a proportion reflecting this relationship.

$$\frac{\text{flagpole height}}{\text{flagpole shadow}} = \frac{\text{building height } (b)}{\text{building shadow}}$$

$$\frac{18}{12} = \frac{b}{48}$$

Step 3. Cross-multiply and then divide to solve.

$$18 \times 48 = 12 \times b$$

$$864 = 12b$$

$$\frac{864}{12} = b$$

$$72 = b$$

**Example 4:** In Figure 7–20, $\triangle JMN$ is similar to $\triangle JKL$. Find the measurement of side $KL$.

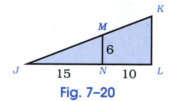

**Fig. 7–20**

Step 1. Find the length of $JL$.

$$JL = JN + NL = 15 + 10 = 25$$

Step 2. Determine the corresponding sides and set up the proportion.

$$\frac{MN}{JN} = \frac{KL}{JL}$$

$$\frac{6}{15} = \frac{KL}{25}$$

Step 3. Cross-multiply and then divide to solve.

$$6 \times 25 = 15 \times KL$$

$$150 = 15KL$$

$$\frac{150}{15} = \frac{KL}{15}$$

$$10 = KL$$

**Example 5:** Find the length of segment $XY$ in Figure 7–21.

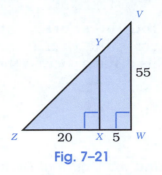

**Fig. 7–21**

**Step 1.** First note that $\triangle XYZ$ and $\triangle VWZ$ are similar. $\angle ZWV$ and $\angle ZXY$ are right angles. $\angle VZW$ and $\angle XZY$ are vertical angles and are equal. Therefore, $\angle ZYX$ and $\angle ZVW$ are equal.

**Step 2.** Determine the corresponding sides and set up the proportion.

$VW$ corresponds to $XY$ and $XZ$ corresponds to $WZ$.

$$\frac{XY}{55} = \frac{20}{25}$$

**Step 3.** Cross-multiply and then divide to solve.

$$XY \times 25 = 55 \times 20$$
$$25XY = 1100$$
$$XY = \frac{1100}{25}$$
$$XY = 44$$

## Level 2, Lesson 1 Exercise

**Directions:** Problems 1–5 refer to Figures 7–22 to 7–26.

1. In Figure 7–22, $\triangle ABC$ and $\triangle DEF$ are similar. $CA = FD$ and $CB = EF$. Which angle $= \angle B$?

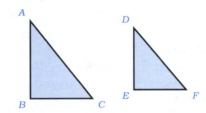

**Fig. 7–22**

2. How tall is the fence in Figure 7–23?

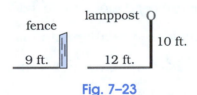

fence

lamppost

9 ft.    12 ft.    10 ft.

**Fig. 7–23**

3. How tall is the tree in Figure 7–24?

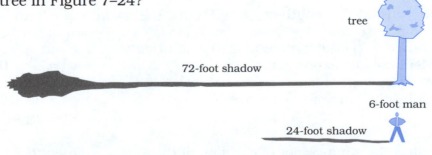

tree

72-foot shadow

6-foot man

24-foot shadow

**Fig. 7–24**

**4.** Find the shortest straight-line distance across the river (Fig. 7–25). *JK* represents this distance across the river.

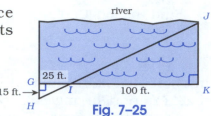

**Fig. 7–25**

**5.** Find the length of *DE* in Figure 7–26.

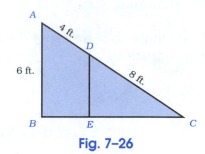

Answers are on page A-51.

**Fig. 7–26**

## Lesson 2 — The Pythagorean Relationship

The Pythagorean Relationship is a formula for finding the length of a side of a right triangle when the other two are known. The relationship was discovered in about 550 B.C. by a Greek mathematician named Pythagoras, for whom the relationship is named. Before proceeding, you might want to review the lesson on finding square roots in Chapter 1.

Look at the triangle in Figure 7–27. Side *AC* is the hypotenuse (the side opposite the right angle) and sides *AB* and *BC* are the legs. The relationship among the sides may be expressed in this way:

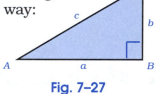

*For any right triangle, the square of the hypotenuse (the side opposite the right angle) is equal to the sum of the squares of the other two sides.*

**Fig. 7–27**

The Pythagorean relationship may be written as

$c^2 = a^2 + b^2$ (where $c$ = hypotenuse and $a$ and $b$ are the legs)

To solve problems that concern right triangles, substitute values for the letters in the equation to find the lengths of the sides of the triangle.

**Example 1:** Find the length of *AC* in Figure 7–27, where $a = 8$ and $b = 15$.

Step 1. Since *AC* is the hypotenuse, the solution to the problem may be expressed as:

$$c^2 = 8^2 + 15^2$$

Step 2. Find the sum of the squares.

$$c^2 = 64 + 225$$
$$c^2 = 289$$

Step 3. Find the square root of the sum of the legs.

$$c = \sqrt{289}$$
$$c = 17$$

**Example 2:** Find the length of $\overline{DE}$ in Figure 7–28.

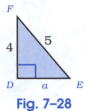

**Fig. 7–28**

Step 1. $\overline{DE}$ is a leg of the right triangle. If the length of $\overline{DE}$ = $a$, then:

$$5^2 = a^2 + 4^2$$

Step 2. Find the difference of the squares.

$$25 = a^2 + 16$$

Step 3. Subtract 16 from both sides of the equation to solve for $a^2$.

$$25 - 16 = a^2 + 16 - 16$$
$$9 = a^2$$

Step 4. Find the square root of 9.

$$9 = a^2$$
$$3 = a$$

## Level 2, Lesson 2 Exercise

**Directions:** Items 1 to 5 refer to Figures 7–29 to 7–32. Use the Pythagorean Relationship to solve each problem.

1. Find the length of $\overline{AB}$ in Figure 7–29.
2. Find the length of $\overline{DF}$ in Figure 7–30.

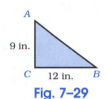

**Fig. 7–29**

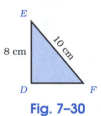

**Fig. 7–30**

3. How far away from the building is the base of the ladder in Figure 7–31?

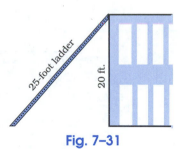

**Fig. 7–31**

4. The Millers drove 36 miles north and 15 miles east. What is the straight-line distance from their starting point?
5. How long is the guy wire in Figure 7–32?

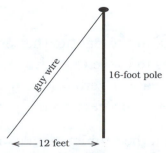

Answers are on page A-51.

**Fig. 7–32**

Coordinate geometry is similar to working with the map of a town. Many towns are plotted with a major street running north to south, and a major street running east to west. The two main streets meet in the middle of town. In coordinate geometry, instead of two major streets on a map, there is a $y$-axis, which runs up and down (or north to south), and an $x$-axis, which runs left and right (or east to west) on a graph (see Figure 7–33).

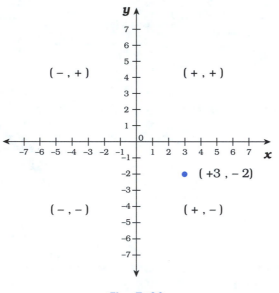

Fig. 7–33

- Places to the right of the zero on the $x$-axis are positive.
- Places to the left of the zero on the $x$-axis are negative.
- Places above zero on the $y$-axis are positive.
- Places below zero on the $y$-axis are negative.

Points on the coordinate map are similar to addresses on the town map. A point is identified first by its $x$ location and then by its $y$ location.

## Plotting Points

Look at Figure 7–33 again. The position of any point on the graph can be labeled by two numbers that are called **coordinates**. The coordinates are placed inside parentheses.

The *first* coordinate tells how far to the *left* or to the *right* of zero the point is placed. The *second* coordinate tells how far *above* or *below* zero the point is placed. For example, the point (+3, –2) is 3 spaces to the right of 0 and 2 spaces below 0, as shown in Figure 7–33.

**Example 1:** What are the coordinates of point *A* and point *B* on the graph in Figure 7–34?

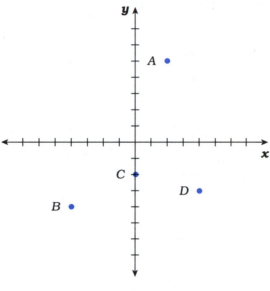

**Fig. 7–34**

| Point *A* |
|---|
| 2 spaces to the *right* of zero (+2) |
| 5 spaces *above* zero (+5) |
| Point *A* is at (+2, +5). |

| Point *B* |
|---|
| 4 spaces to the *left* of zero (–4) |
| 4 spaces *below* zero (–4) |
| Point *B* is at (–4, –4) |

**Example 2:** What are the coordinates of point *C* and point *D* on the graph in Figure 7–34?

| Point *C* |
|---|
| at zero (0) |
| 2 spaces *below* zero (–2) |
| Point *C* is at (0, –2) |

| Point *D* |
|---|
| 4 spaces to the *right* of zero (+4) |
| 3 spaces *below* zero (–3) |
| Point *D* is at (+4, –3) |

**Directions:** Find the coordinates of each point on the graph in Figure 7–35.

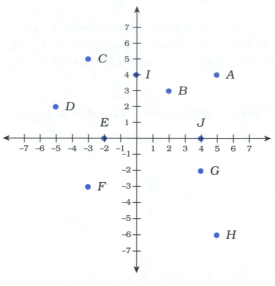

**Fig. 7–35**

| | | | | |
|---|---|---|---|---|
| 1. A | 2. B | 3. C | 4. D | 5. E |
| 6. F | 7. G | 8. H | 9. I | 10. J |

Answers are on page A-51.

## Lesson 2

# Slope

The slope of a line on a graph is the measure of its slant, or angle of inclination. The amount of slope in a line has a number value. You read the direction of a line from the left to right, starting from its x-axis position. If its x-axis position is above the zero on the y-axis, it goes "downhill": It has a negative slope. If its x-axis position is below the zero on the y-axis, it goes "uphill": It has a positive slope. Figure 7–36 shows three lines with different types of slope.

Line A goes uphill from left to right and has a positive slope.

Line B goes downhill from left to right and has a negative slope.

Line C goes straight across, parallel to the x-axis, with no slant and has a zero slope.

The following formula is used to find the value of slope. It is included on your formula list on page 401.

$$m = \frac{y_2 - y_1}{x_2 - x_1}$$

$m$ is the symbol mathematicians use to denote slope and $(x_1, y_1)$ and $(x_2, y_2)$ are used to denote two points on the line.

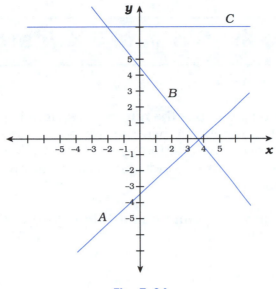

Fig. 7–36

You do not need a picture of the graph to find the slope if you have the coordinates of two points.

**Example 1:** What is the slope of the line containing the points (+2, +2) and (+3, +4)?

Step 1. Put the coordinates into the formula.
$(x_1, y_1) = (+2, +2)$ and $(x_2, y_2) = (+3, +4)$

$$m = \frac{y_2 - y_1}{x_2 - x_1}$$

$$m = \frac{+4 - (+2)}{+3 - (+2)}$$

Step 2. Solve for $m$.

$$m = \frac{2}{1} = 2$$

**Example 2:** Find the slope of a line containing the points (–5, +1) and (–3, –2)

Step 1. Put the coordinates into the formula. In this example, the second set of coordinates listed in the question is used as $(x_1, y_1)$. The first set of coordinates is used as $(x_2, y_2)$.

$$m = \frac{y_2 - y_1}{x_2 - x_1}$$

$$m = \frac{-2 - (+1)}{-3 - (-5)}$$

Step 2. Solve for $m$.

$$m = \frac{-3}{2}$$

## Level 3, Lesson 2 Exercise

**Directions:** Find the slope of the line containing the points with these coordinates.

1. (5, 3) and (0, 1)
2. (2, 2) and (3, –2)
3. (–2, –2) and (4, 2)

4. (–3, 2) and (2, –5)
5. (3, 4) and (4, 0)

Answers are on page A-51.

# Finding the Distance Between Points

The distance between two points on a graph is the number of spaces between them. Distance is expressed as a positive number. When the two points have either the same $x$ or $y$ coordinate, the distance can be found by counting the spaces. When the points are on opposite sides of an axis, count the distance to and from each point to the axis and add the amounts.

**Example 1:** Find the distance between points $A$ and $B$ in Figure 7–37.

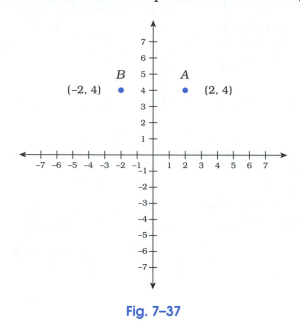

**Fig. 7–37**

Step 1. $A$ and $B$ have the same $y$ coordinate. Locate points $A$ and $B$ on the $x$ axis. Point $B$ is at –2, and point $A$ is at 2.

Step 2. Count the spaces between points $A$ and $B$:      4 spaces

When points don't have the same $x$ or $y$ coordinates, you use the following formula to calculate the distance between the two points.

$$d = \sqrt{(x_2 - x_1)^2 + (y_2 - y_1)^2}$$

where $d$ = distance;

$x_1$ and $y_1$ = the coordinates of one point;

$x_2$ and $y_2$ = the coordinates of the other point.

**Example 2:** Find the distance between points $C$ and $D$ in Figure 7–38.

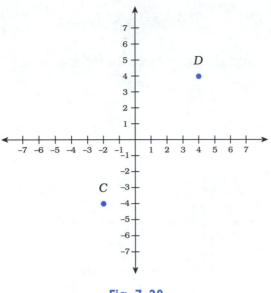

**Fig. 7–38**

Step 1. The coordinates for point $C$ are $(-2, -4)$. The coordinates for point $D$ are $(4, 4)$.

Step 2. Place these values in the formula.

$$d = \sqrt{(x_2 - x_1)^2 + (y_2 - y_1)^2}$$
$$d = \sqrt{(4 - (-2))^2 + (4 - (-4))^2}$$

Step 3. Solve for $d$.

$$d = \sqrt{6^2 + 8^2}$$
$$d = \sqrt{36 + 64}$$
$$d = \sqrt{100}$$
$$d = 10$$

Sometimes the formula will result in a number that cannot be calculated to an exact square root. When that happens, express the answer with the square root sign.

**Example 3:** Find the distance between two points with coordinates $(-5, 4)$ and $(3, 1)$.

Step 1. Place the values into the formula.

$$d = \sqrt{(x_2 - x_1)^2 + (y_2 - y_1)^2}$$
$$d = \sqrt{(3 - (-5))^2 + (1 - 4)^2}$$

Step 2. Solve for $d$.

$$d = \sqrt{8^2 + (-3)^2}$$
$$d = \sqrt{64 + 9}$$
$$d = \sqrt{73}$$

$\sqrt{73}$ cannot be calculated to an exact number; leave the result as it is.

**Directions:** Using Figure 7–39, find the distances as indicated.

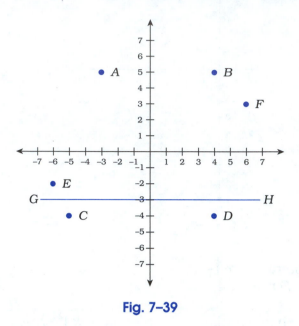

**Fig. 7–39**

1. What is the distance from point $A$ to point $B$?
2. Find the distance between point $C$ and point $D$.
3. What is the perpendicular distance from point $A$ to line $GH$?
4. What is the distance from point $E$ to point $F$?
5. What is the distance between points with coordinates of $(1, 1)$ and $(-1, -1)$?

Answers are on page A-52.

# Chapter 7 Quiz

1. Angles that combine to form a right angle are what kind of angle?

2. Angles that combine to form a straight line are what kind of angle?

3. What is the supplement of a 79° angle?

4. Find the measurement of ∠BAC (Fig. 7–40).

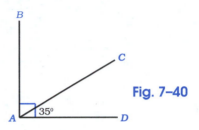

**Fig. 7–40**

5. ∠a = 115°. What is the measurement of ∠f (Fig. 7–41)?

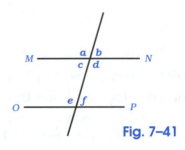

**Fig. 7–41**

6. What is the measurement of the third angle in a triangle if the other two measure 80° and 55°?

7. In an isosceles triangle, if the vertex angle measures 110°, what is the measure of each base angle?

8. If ∠D = ∠A, what kind of triangles are these (Fig. 7–42)?

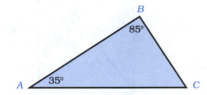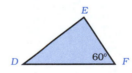

**Fig. 7–42**

9. What is the shortest distance from the radio tower to the farm (Fig. 7–43)?

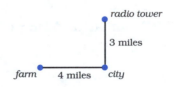

**Fig. 7–43**

**10.** Which point has the coordinates of (2, –3) (Fig. 7–44)?

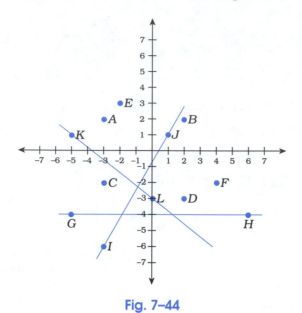

Fig. 7–44

**11.** What is the distance from point *E* to point *F*?

**12.** Which line on this graph has zero slope?

**13.** Find the slope of a line that contains the points (–3, 2) and (2, –5).

**14.** A man who is 6 feet tall casts a 2-foot shadow at the same time that a building casts an 18-foot shadow. How tall is the building?

**15.** In a line, $y = .5x - 4$; what is the $y$ coordinate when $x = -8$?

**16.** What is the slope of a line that contains points (–5, –4) and (5, 1)?

**17.** Gary bicycled 10 miles west and 24 miles south. What was the straight line distance from his starting point?

**18.** What is the length of diagonal line *LK* (Fig. 7–45)?

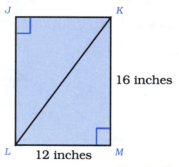

Fig. 7–45

**19.** Is △*ABC* similar to △*DEF* (Fig. 7–46)?

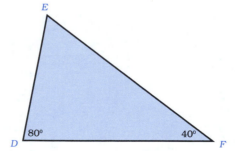
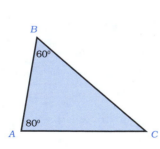

Fig. 7–46

**20.** $\angle M = \angle P$ and $\angle O = \angle R$. $MO = 30$, $NO = 18$, and $PR = 25$. Find $QR$. (See Fig. 7–47.)

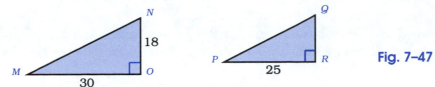

Fig. 7–47

**21.** A 5-foot vertical pole casts a shadow 3 feet long at the same time that a building casts a shadow 72 feet long. How tall is the building? (To solve this problem, draw a picture to show that the ground, the height of each object, and an imaginary line from the top of each object to the ground form similar triangles.)

**22.** $\angle B$ and $\angle D$ are each 90°, $\angle A = \angle E$, $AB = 10$ feet, $BC = 3$, and $CD = 24$ feet. $DE$ is the distance across a river. Find the measurement of $DE$. (See Fig. 7–48.)

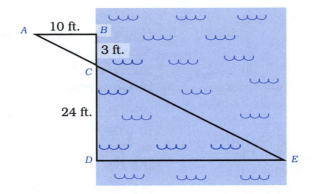

Fig. 7–47

**23.** The legs of a right triangle measure 36 inches and 48 inches. Find the length of the hypotenuse.

**24.** In this right triangle, what is the length of side $AB$ (Fig. 7–49)?

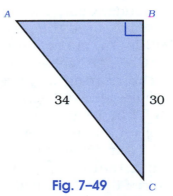

Fig. 7–49

**25.** Figure $MNOP$ is a rectangle. Side $MP$ is 15 feet long, and the diagonal distance $MO$ is 17 feet long. Find the measurement of $OP$. (See Fig. 7–50.)

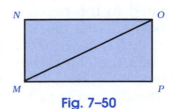

Fig. 7–50

Answers are on page A-52.

# PRACTICE ITEMS 1
# Writing Skills, Part I: Grammar

**Directions:** The items in Part I of this test are based on paragraphs that contain numbered sentences. Some of the sentences may contain errors in sentence structure, usage, or mechanics. A few sentences, however, may be correct as written. Read each paragraph and then answer the items that follow it. For each item, choose the answer that would result in the most effective writing of the sentence or sentences. The best answer must be consistent with the meaning and tone of the rest of the paragraph.

Items 1 to 9 are based on the following paragraphs.

(1) Since the 1970s, people with physical and other disabilities have moved into the mainstream of American life. (2) They have shown skeptics that they can lead full lives, for example, by winning Olympic gold medals, writing books, and serving in Congress. (3) The gains made by other minorities have inspired the disabled to demand equal access to jobs, education, and to get more housing.

(4) For example, hearing-impaired students at Gallaudet College in Washington, D.C., successfully used the protest tactics of the 1960s to make changes. (5) Gallaudet College was founded as a school for the hearing impaired. (6) Its presidents have always been people who could hear. (7) In 1988, students rejected the choice of yet another president who is not deaf. (8) Their demonstrations attracted national attention. (9) As a result, Gallaudet hired there first deaf president.

(10) Federal and local governments also have responded to the needs of the disabled. (11) Barriers that blocks full access to public facilities have been removed. (12) People in wheelchairs now can use ramps instead of stairs, and elevators often have Braille numbers to designate the floors.

1. Sentence 2: **They have shown skeptics that they can lead full lives, for example, by winning Olympic gold medals, writing books, and serving in Congress.**

   Which of the following is the best way to write the underlined portion of the sentence? If you think the original is the best way, choose option (1).

   **(1)** skeptics that they can lead full lives,
   **(2)** skeptics that the disabled can lead full lives,
   **(3)** skeptics, that the disabled can lead full lives,
   **(4)** skeptics that they, the disabled, can lead full lives.
   **(5)** skeptics that they can lead full lives

2. Sentence 3: **The gains made by other minorities have inspired the disabled to demand equal access to jobs, education, and to get more housing.**

   What correction should be made to this sentence?

   **(1)** change *minorities* to *Minorities*
   **(2)** insert a comma after *gains*
   **(3)** change *have* to *has*

**(4)** change *to get more housing* to *housing*

**(5)** no correction is necessary

3. Sentence 4: **For example, hearing-impaired students at Gallaudet college in Washington, D.C., successfully used the protest tactics of the 1960s to make changes.**

What correction should be made to this sentence?

**(1)** change *Collage* to *collage*

**(2)** change *D.C.* to *d.c.*

**(3)** change *college* to *College*

**(4)** insert a comma after *students*

**(5)** remove the comma after *Washington*

4. Sentence 5 and 6: **Gallaudet College was founded as a school for the hearing impaired. Its presidents have always been people who could hear.**

The most effective combination of sentences 5 and 6 would include which of the following groups of words?

**(1)** impaired although its

**(2)** impaired but their

**(3)** impaired, however, its

**(4)** impaired, and its

**(5)** impaired and their

5. Sentence 7: **In 1988, students rejected the choice of yet another president who is not deaf.**

Which of the following is the best way to write the underlined portion of the sentence? If you think the original is the best way, choose option (1).

**(1)** president who is not

**(2)** president who was not

**(3)** President who is not

**(4)** President who was not

**(5)** president whose not

6. Sentence 9: **As a result, Gallaudet hired there first deaf president.**

What correction should be made to this sentence?

**(1)** remove the comma after *result*

**(2)** change *president* to *President*

**(3)** change *there* to *its*

**(4)** change *there* to *their*

**(5)** no change is necessary

7. Sentence 10: **Federal and local governments also have responded to the needs of the disabled.**

What correction should be made to this sentence?

**(1)** change *goverments* to *governments*

**(2)** change *local* to *Local*

**(3)** change *goverments* to *Goverments*

**(4)** change *have* to *has*

**(5)** No change is necessary

8. Sentence 11: **Barriers that blocks full access to public facilities have been removed.**

Which of the following is the best way to write the underlined portion of the sentence? If you think the original is the best way, choose option (1).

**(1)** that blocks full access to

**(2)** that blocks full access on

**(3)** who blocks full access to

**(4)** that block full access to

**(5)** which blocked full access to

9. Sentence 12: **People in wheelchairs now can use ramps instead of stairs, and elevators often have Braille numbers to designate the floors.**

What correction should be made to this sentence?

**(1)** remove the comma after *stairs*

**(2)** insert a comma after *ramps*

**(3)** change *Braille* to *braille*

**(4)** change *and* to *but*

**(5)** no correction is necessary

Items 10 to 19 are based on the following paragraph.

(1) Someday accompanying your application for a job, you may be writing a business letter. (2) Without knowing exactly who will receive and read your letter. (3) You probably understand how important it is to write a neat, clear letter you may not realize how important it is to choose an appropriate greeting. (4) When in doubt, research shows, when you do choose a greeting, you should avoid the phrases *Dear Sirs* and *Gentlemen*. (5) A study using 75 letters of application for a university job were done. (6) Of the 28 applicants who used masculine greetings, none were chosen as a finalist for the job. (7) Every one of the 11 finalists for the position was from the group that found a way to avoid masculine greetings. (8) Each of the finalists uses a neutral greeting, such as *Dear Committee Members* or *To Whom It May Concern*. (9) Why should the form of the greeting make such a difference? (10) Masculine greetings are read by female employers, at times, and they may be annoyed by them. (11) In any case, you should find a neutral greeting because of you want to make a good first impression.

**10.** Sentence 1: **Someday accompanying your application for a job, you may be writing a business letter.**

If you rewrote sentence 1 beginning with
*Someday you may be writing a business letter*
the next words should be

**(1)** for a job

**(2)** to a job

**(3)** for application

**(4)** to accompany

**(5)** that accompanied

**11.** Sentence 2: **Without knowing exactly who will receive and read your letter.**

What correction should be made to this sentence?

**(1)** replace *Without knowing* with *You may not know*

**(2)** change the spelling of *receive* to *recieve*

**(3)** insert a comma after *receive*

**(4)** replace *your* with *you're*

**(5)** no correction is necessary

**12.** Sentence 3: **You probably understand how important it is to write a neat, clear letter you may not realize how important it is to choose an appropriate greeting.**

What correction should be made to this sentence?

**(1)** change the spelling of *probably* to *probally*

**(2)** change *understand* to *understands*

**(3)** insert a comma after *letter*

**(4)** replace *letter you* with *letter. You*

**(5)** replace *it is to choose* with *is your choice of*

**13.** Sentence 4: **When in doubt, research shows, when you do choose a greeting, you should avoid the phrases *Dear Sirs* and *Gentlemen*.**

If you rewrote sentence 4 beginning with *Research shows that*, the next word should be

**(1)** when

**(2)** unless

**(3)** however

**(4)** because

**(5)** since

**14.** Sentence 5: **A study using 75 letters of application for a university job were done.**

What correction should be made to this sentence?

**(1)** Change *using to uses*

**(2)** insert a comma after *job*

**(3)** change *were to was*

**(4)** change the spelling of *application* to *apliccation*

**(5)** no correction is necessary

15. Sentence 6: **Of the 28 applicants who used masculine <u>greetings, none were chosen</u> as a finalist for the job.**

Which of the following is the best way to write the underlined portion of this sentence? If you think the original is the best way, choose option (1).

**(1)** greetings, none were chosen

**(2)** greetings none were chosen

**(3)** greetings. None were chosen

**(4)** greetings, none was chosen

**(5)** greetings: none was chosen

16. Sentence 8: **Each of the finalists uses a neutral greeting, such as *Dear Committee Members* or *To Whom It May Concern*.**

What correction should be made to this sentence?

**(1)** replace *Each* with *All*

**(2)** insert a comma after *finalists*

**(3)** change *uses* to *used*

**(4)** change the spelling of *Committee* to *Comittee*

**(5)** Change *Members* to *members*

17. Sentence 9: **Why should the form of the greeting make such a difference?**

What correction should be made to this sentence?

**(1)** replace *should* with *had*

**(2)** insert a comma after *greeting*

**(3)** change *make* to *makes*

**(4)** change the spelling of *difference* to *diffarence*

**(5)** no correction is necessary

18. Sentence 10: **Masculine greetings are read by female employers, at times, and they may be annoyed by them.**

If you rewrote sentence 10 beginning with
*Perhaps masculine greetings*
the next word should be

**(1)** annoy

**(2)** at

**(3)** read

**(4)** to

**(5)** they

19. Sentence 11: **In any case, you should find a neutral <u>greeting because of you want</u> to make a good first impression.**

Which of the following is the best way to write the underlined portion of this sentence? If you think the original is the best way, choose option (1).

**(1)** greeting because of you want

**(2)** greeting because of one wants

**(3)** greeting. Because of you want

**(4)** greeting because you want

**(5)** greeting. Because you want

Items 20 to 28 are based on the following paragraph.

(1) If you buy a computer, you may want to join a club known as a user Group. (2) All members of the group use the same type of computer. (3) There are several advantages, to being part of a user group. (4) You can borrow programs from other members. (5) You may be able to copy a program you have borrowed and keep the copy for yourself. (6) If you are having a problem with your machine, you may find an other member who has already solved that very problem. (7) Others will trade notes with you about new software additions on the market, often there is a user group newsletter. (8) In the newsletter, one will find useful information about special software deals

and computer shows, among other items of interest. (9) To locate the user group that is nearest for your type of computer, check with your local computer dealer. (10) The dealer will either direct you to a nearby group or provide you with the phone number of a national user group manager. (11) The dues you pay are usually well worth the money you save, the knowledge you gain, and making friends.

20. Sentence 1: **If you buy a computer, you may want to join a club known as a user Group.**

    What correction should be made to this sentence?

    **(1)** replace *If* with *Since*
    **(2)** replace *buy* with *by*
    **(3)** remove the comma after *computer*
    **(4)** change *join* to *have joined*
    **(5)** change *Group* to *group*

21. Sentence 3: **There are several advantages, to being part of a user group.**

    What correction should be made to this sentence?

    **(1)** change the spelling of *There* to *They're*
    **(2)** change *are* to *is*
    **(3)** change the spelling of *advantages* to *advantiges*
    **(4)** delete the comma after *advantages*
    **(5)** no correction is necessary

22. Sentence 5: **You may be able to copy a program you have borrowed and keep the copy for yourself.**

    If you rewrote sentence 5 beginning with
    *Having borrowed a program,*
    the next word should be

    **(1)** you
    **(2)** yourself
    **(3)** one
    **(4)** copy
    **(5)** copying

23. Sentence 6: **If you are having a problem with your machine, you may find an other member who has already solved that very problem.**

    What correction should be made to this sentence?

    **(1)** change the spelling of *an other* to *another*
    **(2)** insert a comma after *member*
    **(3)** change *who* to *which*
    **(4)** change *has* to *have*
    **(5)** change the spelling of *already* to *all ready*

24. Sentence 7: **Others will trade notes with you about new software additions on the <u>market, often</u> there is a user group newsletter.**

    Which of the following is the best way to write the underlined portion of the sentence? If you think the original is the best way, choose option (1).

    **(1)** market, often
    **(2)** market often
    **(3)** market so often
    **(4)** because often
    **(5)** market. Often

25. Sentence 8: **In the newsletter, <u>one will find useful information</u> about special software deals and computer shows, among other items of interest.**

    Which of the following is the best way to write the underlined portion of the sentence? If you think the original is the best way, choose option (1).

    **(1)** one will find useful information
    **(2)** one will find information that is useful
    **(3)** one found useful information
    **(4)** you will find useful information
    **(5)** you will find information which is useful

**26.** Sentence 9: **To locate the <u>user group that is nearest</u> for your type of computer, check with your local computer dealer.**

Which of the following is the best way to write the underlined portion of this sentence? If you think the original is the best way, choose option (1).

**(1)** user group that is nearest
**(2)** user group, that is nearest
**(3)** user group who is nearest
**(4)** user group, which is nearest
**(5)** nearest user group

**27.** Sentence 10: **The dealer will either direct you to a nearby group or provide you with the phone number of a national user group manager.**

What correction should be made to this sentence?

**(1)** change *nearby* to *near-by*
**(2)** change *provide* to *provides*
**(3)** change the spelling of *either* to *ether*
**(4)** change *national* to *National*
**(5)** no correction is necessary

**28.** Sentence 11: **The dues you pay are usually well worth the money you save, the knowledge you gain, and making friends.**

What correction should be made to this sentence?

**(1)** change *you pay* to *one pays*
**(2)** change the spelling of *knowledge* to *knowlege*
**(3)** insert a comma after *pay*
**(4)** remove the comma after *gain*
**(5)** change *making friends* to *the friends you make*

Items 29 to 37 are based on the following paragraph.

(1) It pays to do some research before buying a new car. (2) On one hand, car prices are offen inflated by expensive options. (3) Sometimes dealers add such extras as cassette players or floor mats, although these items cost fairly little to install, the dealers may charge car buyers an exorbitant amount. (4) It certainly make sense to wait and put in a radio or a car alarm later if you will save thousands of dollars by doing so. (5) On the other hand, a relatively low car price at the cost of safety. (6) Find out how the car you are considering does on crash tests. (7) In these tests, dummies were fastened into the two front seats. (8) It is driven at 35 miles per hour into a wall. (9) Their condition is examined. (10) A prediction is made about whether actual passengers would have been severely injured, or killed. (11) It is likely that you will often travel at 35 miles per hour or more therefore you probably do not want a car that fails the test. (12) Learn all you can about the various American and foreign cars on the market so that you can exercise good judgment in how you spend your money.

**29.** Sentence 2: **On one hand, car prices are offen inflated by expensive options.**

What correction should be made to this sentence?

**(1)** remove the comma after *hand*
**(2)** change *are* to *is*
**(3)** change the spelling of *offen* to *often*
**(4)** insert a comma after *inflated*
**(5)** change *options* to *Options*

**30.** Sentence 3: **Sometimes dealers add such extras as cassette players or floor mats, although these items cost fairly little to install, the dealers may charge car buyers an exorbitant amount.**

Which of the following is the best way to write the underlined portion of the sentence? If you think the original is the best way, choose option (1).

**(1)** mats, although these items cost
**(2)** mats. Although these items cost
**(3)** mats, but these items cost
**(4)** mats although these items, cost
**(5)** mats, because these items cost

**31.** Sentence 4: **It certainly make sense to wait and put in a radio or a car alarm later if you will save thousands of dollars by doing so.**

Which of the following is the best way to write the underlined portion of the sentence? If you think the original is the best way, choose option (1).

**(1)** make sense to wait and put
**(2)** make sense waiting and putting
**(3)** make sense to wait, and put
**(4)** makes sense to wait and put
**(5)** make sense to wait. And put

**32.** Sentence 5: **On the other hand, a relatively low car price at the cost of safety.**

What correction should be made to this sentence?

**(1)** replace *On the other hand* with *However*
**(2)** remove the comma after *hand*
**(3)** insert *may come* after *price*
**(4)** replace *at the cost of* with *costing*
**(5)** replace *hand, a* with *hand. A*

**33.** Sentence 7: **In these tests, dummies were fastened into the two front seats.**

What correction should be made to this sentence?

**(1)** remove the comma after *tests*
**(2)** change *dummies* to *Dummies*
**(3)** change *were* to *are*
**(4)** insert a comma after *two*
**(5)** no correction is necessary

**34.** Sentences 8 and 9: **It is driven at 35 miles per hour into a wall. Their condition is examined.**

The most effective combination of sentences 8 and 9 would include which of the following groups of words?

**(1)** After the dummies' condition
**(2)** After the car is driven
**(3)** After their condition
**(4)** After driving them
**(5)** After they drive

**35.** Sentence 10: **A prediction is made about whether actual passengers would have been severely injured, or killed.**

Which of the following is the best way to write the underlined portion of the sentence? If you think the original is the best way, choose option (1).

**(1)** been severely injured, or killed.
**(2)** been severely injured or killed.
**(3)** severely been injured, or killed.
**(4)** been injured, severely, or killed.
**(5)** severe injuries, or death.

**36.** Sentence 11: **It is likely that you will often travel at 35 miles per hour or more therefore you probably do not want a car that fails the test.**

Which of the following is the best way to write the underlined portion of the sentence? If you think the original is the best way, choose option (1).

**(1)** more therefore you probably do not want

**(2)** more, therefore you probably did not want

**(3)** more therefore you probably did not want

**(4)** more; therefore, you probably do not want

**(5)** more and therefore, you probably did not want

**37.** Sentence 12: **Learn all you can about the various American and foreign cars on the market so that you can exercise good judgment in how you spend your money.**

What correction should be made to this sentence?

**(1)** change *American* to *american*

**(2)** change *foreign* to *Foreign*

**(3)** change the spelling of *exercise* to *exercize*

**(4)** change *spend* to *spends*

**(5)** no correction is necessary

Items 38 to 47 are based on the following paragraph.

(1) Many jobs involving more writing than they appear to at first glance. (2) For example, the position of national park ranger. (3) Many people look into ranger jobs because they want to work outdoors. (4) They learn that they must first take a test given by the U.S. park service. (5) Many applicants take the test and the finalists are the applicants with excellent scores. (6) The fortunate few which are chosen as rangers soon discover how much paperwork they must do. (7) You must keep records of guests' names, payments, campsite numbers, and departure dates. (8) Daily schedules of activitys need to be posted. (9) Displays in the park museums change, and they must relabel them. (10) Job duties also include writing comments for slide shows typing lists of park rules, and even filling out police reports. (11) Of course, park rangers do get to work outdoors, but they usually spend some time each day at their desks.

**38.** Sentence 1: **Many jobs involving more writing than they appear to at first glance.**

What correction should be made to this sentence?

**(1)** insert *are* after *jobs*

**(2)** change *involving* to *involve*

**(3)** insert a comma after *writing*

**(4)** replace *than* with *then*

**(5)** change the spelling of *appear* to *appeer*

**39.** Sentence 2: **For example, the position of national park ranger.**

Which of the following is the best way to write the underlined portion of this sentence? If you think the original is the best way, choose option (1).

**(1)** For example, the

**(2)** For example; the

**(3)** For example the

**(4)** One good example, is the

**(5)** One good example is the

**40.** Sentence 4: **They learn that they must first take a test given by the U.S. park service.**

What correction should be made to this sentence?

**(1)** change *learn* to *learns*

**(2)** insert a comma after *test*

**(3)** change *U.S.* to *u.s.*

**(4)** change *park service* to *Park Service*

**(5)** no correction is necessary

**41.** Sentence 5: **Many applicants take the test and the finalists are the applicants with excellent scores.**

If you rewrote sentence 5 beginning with
*Since many applicants take the test*

the next words should be

**(1)** applicants who
**(2)** therefore the applicants
**(3)** so the
**(4)** only those with
**(5)** many finalists

42. Sentence 6: **The fortunate few which are chosen as rangers soon discover how much paperwork they must do.**

    What correction should be made to this sentence?

    **(1)** change the spelling of *fortunate* to *fortunat*
    **(2)** replace *which* with *who*
    **(3)** change *are* to *is*
    **(4)** insert a comma after *rangers*
    **(5)** replace *they* with *one*

43. Sentence 7: **You must keep records of guests' names, payments, camp-site numbers, and departure dates.**

    Which of the following is the best way to write the underlined portion of this sentence? If you think the original is the best way, choose option (1).

    **(1)** You must keep
    **(2)** You must have kept
    **(3)** He must be keeping
    **(4)** She must keep
    **(5)** A ranger must keep

44. Sentence 8: **Daily schedules of activitys need to posted.**

    What correction should be made to this sentence?

    **(1)** change the spelling of *activitys* to *activities*
    **(2)** change the spelling of *schedules* to *scheduals*
    **(3)** insert a comma after *activitys*
    **(4)** change *need* to *needs*
    **(5)** no correction is necessary

45. Sentence 9: **Displays in the park museums change, and they must relabel them.**

    If you rewrote sentence 9 beginning with
    *Rangers must relabel changing*
    the next word should be

    **(1)** park
    **(2)** museums
    **(3)** displays
    **(4)** in
    **(5)** and

46. Sentence 10: **Job duties also include writing comments for slide shows typing lists of park rules, and even filling out police reports.**

    Which of the following is the best way to write the underlined portion of this sentence? If you think the original is the best way, choose option (1).

    **(1)** shows typing lists
    **(2)** shows. Typing lists
    **(3)** shows and typing lists
    **(4)** shows, typing lists
    **(5)** shows, typed lists

47. Sentence 11: **Of course, park rangers do get to work outdoors, but they usually spend some time each day at their desks.**

    Which of the following is the best way to write the underlined portion of this sentence? If you think the original is the best way, choose option (1).

    **(1)** outdoors, but
    **(2)** outdoors. But
    **(3)** outdoors but
    **(4)** outdoors but,
    **(5)** outdoors so

Items 48 to 55 are based on the following paragraphs.

(1) By the 1960s, the movie industry was in decline and recently films have made a comeback. (2) One change was the multi-theater. (3) In the past, a movie house one large auditorium showing one movie. (4) The multi-theater divides the space into as many as a dozen smaller theaters were different films are shown. (5) An equally dramatic breakthrough for films was the videocassette recorder, or VCR. (6) People with VCRs could now rent films, and watch them at home.

(7) At the same time that VCRs were gaining popularity cable television systems developed. (8) Dozens of channels became available to cable subscribers. (9) Cable networks sprang up to provide anything from round-the-clock news to religious broadcasting and sports programming.

(10) Popular music, too, grows in technological wizardry. (11) The music of the 1950s seemed tame; simple electric guitars were almost antique in contrast to newer instruments. (12) By the 1970s, rock musicians had adapted the new technology of super amplifiers and music synthesizers to their music.

48. Sentence 1: **By the 1960s, the movie industry was in decline and recently films have made a comeback.**

Which of the following is the best way to write the underlined portion of this sentence? If you think the original is the best way, choose option (1).

(1) decline and recently
(2) decline, so recently
(3) decline while recently,
(4) decline; nevertheless, recently
(5) decline, however, recently

49. Sentence 3: **In the past, a movie house one large auditorium showing one movie.**

What correction should be made to this sentence?

(1) change *showing* to *showed*
(2) insert *was* after *house*
(3) insert *is* before *one*
(4) insert *has been* before *one*
(5) insert commas after *house* and *auditorium*

50. Sentence 4: **The multi-theater divides the space into as many as a dozen smaller theaters were different films shown.**

What correction should be made to this sentence?

(1) change *divides* to *divided*
(2) change *shown* to *showing*
(3) insert a comma after *space*
(4) change *were* to *where*
(5) no correction is necessary

51. Sentence 5: **An equally dramatic breakthrough for films was the videocassette recorder, or VCR.**

If you rewrote sentence 5 beginning with
*The videocassette recorder*
The next words would be

(1) ,or VCR, was
(2) or VCR, was
(3) or VCR is
(4) was an equally
(5) or VCR, had been

52. Sentence 6: **People with VCRs could now rent films, and watch them at home.**

What correction should be made to this sentence?

(1) insert an apostrophe before the *s* in *VCRs*
(2) change the *them* to *it*
(3) remove the comma after *films*
(4) insert a comma after *VCRs*
(5) no correction is necessary

**53.** Sentence 7: **At the same time that VCRs were gaining popularity cable television systems developed.**

Which of the following is the best way to write the underlined portion of the sentence? If you think the original is the best way, choose option (1).

(1) were gaining popularity cable television
(2) gained popularity cable television
(3) gained popularity, cable television
(4) was gaining popularity, cable television
(5) were gaining popularity, cable television

**54.** Sentence 9: **Cable networks sprang up to provide anything from round-the-clock news to religious broadcasting and sports programming.**

What correction should be made to this sentence?

(1) change sprang to are springing

(2) change sprang to sprong
(3) change networks to Networks
(4) insert a comma after broadcasting
(5) no correction is necessary

**55.** Sentence 10: **Popular music, too, grows in technological wizardry.**

Which of the following is the best way to write the underlined portion of the sentence? If you think the original is the best way, choose option (1).

(1) music, too, grows
(2) music, too, grew
(3) music, too grew
(4) music too, grew
(5) music, too, is growing

Answers are on pages A-53-A-57.

# Performance Analysis Chart

**Directions:** Circle the number of each item that you got correct on the Practice Items. Count how many items you got correct in each row; count how many items you got correct in each column. Write the amount correct per row and column as the numerator in the fraction in the appropriate "Total Correct" box. (The denominators represent the total number of items in the row or column.) Write the grand total correct over the denominator 55 at the lower right corner of the chart. (For example, if you got 50 items correct, write 50 so that the fraction reads 50/55.)

| Item Type | Usage (page 64) | Sentence Structure (page 88) | Mechanics (page 102) | TOTAL CORRECT |
|---|---|---|---|---|
| Construction Shift | 18, 34, 45 | 4, 10, 13 22, 41, | 51 | /9 |
| Sentence Correction | 6, 14, 16, 27, 33, 42, 50, 54 | 2, 9, 11, 12, 28, 32, 38, 49, 52 | 3, 7, 17, 20, 21, 23, 29, 37, 40, 44 | /27 |
| Sentence Revision | 1, 5, 8, 15, 25, 26, 31, 43, 55 | 19, 24, 30, 36, 39, 48 | 46, 47, 53, 55 | /19 |
| Total Correct | /20 | /20 | /15 | /55 |

*The page numbers in parentheses in the column headings indicate where in this book you can find the beginning of specific instruction about the areas of grammar and about the types of questions you encountered in the Practice Items.*

**Directions:** This is a test to see how well you can write. In this test, you are asked to write an essay in which you present your opinions about an issue. In preparing your essay, you should take the following steps.

**Step 1.** Read all of the information about the topic. Be sure that you understand the topic and that you write about only the assigned topic.

**Step 2.** Plan your essay before you write.

**Step 3.** Use scrap paper to make any notes.

**Step 4.** Write your essay on a separate sheet of paper.

**Step 5.** Read what you have written. Make sure that your writing is legible.

**Step 6.** Check your paragraphing, sentence structure, spelling, punctuation, capitalization, and usage; make any changes that will improve your essay.

## TOPIC

In many jobs, when employees reach a certain age, they must retire. Some people are against having a mandatory retirement age, and others feel that there are reasons to support a required retirement age.

Decide whether you agree or disagree that people should be required to retire from their jobs when they reach a certain age. Write an essay, approximately 200 words long, that presents your opinion about this issue. Be specific, and use examples to support your point of view.

When you take the GED test, you will have 45 minutes to write about the topic question you are assigned. Try to write the essay for this test within 45 minutes. Write legibly and use a ballpoint pen so that your writing will be easy to read. Any notes that you make on scrap paper will not be counted as part of your score.

After you complete this essay, you can judge its effectiveness by using the Essay Scoring Guide and Model Essays in the answer key to score your essay. They will be concerned with how clearly you make the main point of your essay, how thoroughly you support your ideas, and how clear and correct your writing is throughout the composition. You will receive no credit for writing about a question other than the one assigned.

Answers are on pages A-56–A-57.

# Writing Skills, Part II

**Directions:** After you have used the guidelines in the answer key to score your essay, make a record of your evaluation here.

Write the score for your essay in the box at the right.

List some of the strong points of your essay.

List some of the weak points of your essay.

List improvements that you plan to make when you work on your next essay.

**Directions:** Choose the one best answer to each question.

## History

Items 1 to 3 are based on the following paragraph.

In 1777, the Second Continental Congress submitted the Articles of Confederation to the states for ratification. They went into effect in 1781. Under the Articles, a unicameral congress had the power to make war and peace, but it lacked the power to tax, to raise a national army, or to regulate international trade. Each state was equally represented in Congress. There was no provision for a federal judiciary, and the executive consisted of a committee of states, representing all thirteen former colonies.

1. The system of government under the Articles of Confederation resembled that which was to follow under the Constitution in that

    (1) the executive appointed heads of government departments
    (2) the national court could strike down legislative acts
    (3) the legislature was divided into two houses
    (4) the states were represented in the national government
    (5) the national government could impose tariffs on foreign goods

2. Which of the following statements best characterizes government under the Articles of Confederation?

    (1) The national government delegated a certain amount of power to the states.
    (2) The power of the national government was limited and decentralized.

    (3) The executive was given more extensive powers than the legislature.
    (4) The government was based on the principle of no taxation without representation.
    (5) The national government was granted direct authority over citizens.

3. In view of the kind of government established by the Articles of Confederation, which of the following would have most likely occurred?

    (1) The government had problems raising funds to pay Revolutionary War troops who were owed money.
    (2) Southern trade with the British West Indies prospered because of congressional funding.
    (3) The new government arm put down a rebellion of Massachusetts farmers who wanted to stop foreclosure of mortgages.
    (4) Congress placed a tax on imported goods to help new industries in the Northern states.
    (5) Property qualifications for voting were dropped.

Item 4 is based on the following cartoon.

4. Which of the following statements best summarizes the cartoonist's attitude toward President Andrew Jackson?

   (1) Andrew Jackson was being admired for rising above his somewhat uncouth frontier background.

   (2) The president was being criticized for abusing the power of his office.

   (3) Jackson was being praised for remaining aloof from government controversies and disputes.

   (4) The president was being presented as a loyal supporter of the British monarchy.

   (5) President Jackson was being accused of taking on regal airs and ignoring the common folk who elected him.

Item 5 is based on the following paragraph.

When the leaders of the major powers met at Yalta in 1945, although the Cold War had not yet started, there was already considerable distrust among them. In discussing the organization of the United Nations, they reached a compromise concerning the U.N. Security Council. Any permanent member of the Security Council would have the right to veto a decision that did not meet with its approval. (The major powers were to be the permanent members of the Security Council; other members were to serve on a rotating basis.)

5. Which of the following statements best explains why the veto was acceptable to the major powers?

   (1) The leaders believed in the principle of majority rule.

   (2) The uncertainties of postwar cooperation made it necessary for each of the great powers to protect its own interests.

   (3) The major powers were suspicious of the small powers.

   (4) The strongest nations were the best guardians of world peace.

   (5) The great powers thought it would be easy for them to agree on important issues.

Items 6 to 8 are based on the following passage.

After the Civil War there emerged two views concerning the conditions under which Southern states would be readmitted to the Union. Under the president's Ten Percent Plan, all Confederates, other than high military and civil officers, could be pardoned by taking an oath of loyalty to the Constitution and swearing to accept the abolition of slavery. If they did so, all property they had possessed, other than slaves, would be restored to them. After 10 percent of the 1860 voters in a state had sworn allegiance, these voters could write a new state constitution and send members to Congress.

Congressional proposals were more severe and called for more changes. The First Reconstruction Act divided the South into five military districts governed by generals. Constitutional conventions were to be held in each state. For purposes of electing delegates to these conventions and of holding subsequent elections, all adult males were to be given suffrage, with the exception of Confederates who had held public office before the war. The state governments that would be elected under the new constitutions had to ratify the recently proposed Fourteenth Amendment, which extended citizenship to blacks and granted them equal protection under the law. Only then would military rule be ended and the states readmitted.

Reconstruction initially proceeded under the Ten Percent Plan. But by 1867 congressional Reconstruction held sway.

6. Which of the following provisions were common to both presidential and congressional plans for Reconstruction?

   (1) military control of the South until new state constitutions had been written
   (2) prohibition of slavery and restrictions on certain high-ranking Confederates
   (3) citizenship and voting rights for blacks
   (4) restoration of property to Southerners and federal assumption of Southern debt incurred during the war
   (5) assistance for freed slaves and prohibition of sharecropping

7. Which of the following was the most likely effect of the Ten Percent Plan on freed blacks?

   (1) their admission into the electorate in large numbers

   (2) their return to former conditions of servitude
   (3) the passage of state laws restricting their rights
   (4) the election of black legislators on state and federal levels of government
   (5) a vast improvement in their standard of living

8. Which of the following is not a fact but an opinion about Reconstruction stated in the passage?

   (1) Both plans for readmitting the South to the Union called for Southerners to accept the end of slavery.
   (2) Both plans called for the establishment of new constitutions in the Southern states.
   (3) The president's plan of Reconstruction was more lenient than the congressional plan for readmitting the South to the Union.
   (4) The president's plan did not consider slavery to be a major social evil, while the congressional plan did.
   (5) The congressional plan of Reconstruction was more severe than the Ten Percent Plan.

Item 9 is based on the following cartoon.

McCutcheon in the Chicago Tribune

9. Which of the following conclusions is best supported by the information suggested by this early World War I cartoon?

   (1) European nations depended on American trade for their survival.

   (2) The American government's position of neutrality was not anchored in public support.

   (3) The U.S. government insisted that the warring nations transport American purchases in their own ships.

   (4) Great Britain respected American neutrality.

   (5) American neutrality policy was almost certainly doomed to failure.

Items 10 to 12 are based on the following passage.

Farmers, many of whom had heavy debts, wanted higher prices for their crops and a reduction of mortgage payments on their lands. Businesses wanted high tariffs to protect their products from foreign competition, a steady supply of labor, and a sound currency to support continued investment. Most middle-class Americans wanted the value of their savings, insurance, and investments to be secure. Workers, who were generally on fixed wages, wanted their wages to have the purchasing power to supply them with life's necessities.

Against this background, the 1896 presidential campaign between Democrat William Jennings Bryan and Republican William McKinley was fought over the issue of the free and limited coinage of silver. Free silver would have had an inflationary effect on the economy: With more money in circulation, the real value of the dollar would go down and prices would rise. The anti-silverite candidate, McKinley, won the election. However, the advocates of free silver found their problems eased by the discovery of gold in Alaska and elsewhere and its introduction into the U.S. economy.

**10.** Which of the following best explains why McKinley won the 1896 Presidential election?

**(1)** The free silver policy put more money in circulation, causing inflation, which frightened the majority of people.

**(2)** Workers in the Northeast refused to unite with farmers in the Midwest, which led to Bryan's defeat.

**(3)** Businessmen, workers, and middle-class citizens all opposed free silver for reasons of financial security.

**(4)** The majority of Americans feared the free silver policy would make farm goods too expensive.

**(5)** The majority of people counted on gold rather than silver to solve the economic problems of the time.

**11.** Which of the following groups was most likely to support the free-silver policy of the Democratic Party in 1896?

**(1)** workers on fixed wages

**(2)** middle-class Americans concerned about their savings

**(3)** industrialists needing investors

**(4)** consumers seeking low-priced commodities

**(5)** farmers faced with high mortgage rates

**12.** Which of the following statements best describes the impact of the discovery of gold on the American economy?

**(1)** It increased the money supply.

**(2)** It reduced the cost of living.

**(3)** It upset the balance of trade.

**(4)** It benefited people living on fixed incomes.

**(5)** It threw the country into a depression.

Item 13 is based on the following information.

In 1774, Parliament passed the Coercive Acts, closing the port of Boston. The acts also permitted the royal governor of Massachusetts to appoint members to local councils and juries and to control the agendas of town meetings. The colonists perceived these acts as denying them certain freedoms to govern themselves—freedoms they had enjoyed for more than a hundred years. In response, they organized a meeting of delegates to seek ways to protect their traditional rights as Englishmen. The meeting became known as the First Continental Congress. The Congress issued a Declaration of Resolves, which was sent to George III.

**13.** Based on the passage, which of the following would most likely be found in the Declaration of Resolves?

**(1)** assertions of independence from Britain

**(2)** demands for the restoration of colonial self-government

**(3)** arguments that the British Empire be dissolved

**(4)** discussion of how colonial rights should differ from the rights of Englishmen

**(5)** recognition of the need for colonial contributions to the cost of defending the British Empire

Items 14 and 15 are based on the following cartoon.

**14.** Which of the following statements best describes the message conveyed by the cartoon?

**(1)** Eastern and Western leaders are racing to see who will be first to control the spread of nuclear weapons, and Third World countries will judge who the winner is.

**(2)** Nuclear weapons are like a genie in a bottle.

**(3)** Leaders of the Soviet Union and the United States are forcing nuclear weapons on reluctant Third World countries.

**(4)** Leaders of the East and West are trying to limit the nuclear arms race while Third World nations are seeking to develop their own nuclear weapons.

**(5)** The superpowers and the Third World nations are working together to "bottle up" nuclear arms.

**15.** Which of the following statements is best supported by the cartoon?

   **(1)** Cooperation between the super-powers could successfully end the arms race.

   **(2)** The major problem of arms control is the spread of nuclear weapons to the developing countries.

   **(3)** The nuclear arms race has shifted the balance of power to the Third World.

   **(4)** Nuclear warfare is probably inevitable.

   **(5)** No Third World nation as yet has nuclear arms.

Items 16 and 17 are based on the following passage.

In 1895, Cuban rebels rose up against their Spanish colonial rulers. A sensationalist press and the blowing up of the U.S. battleship *Maine* in the Havana harbor stirred Americans to demand that the government declare war against Spain. For several years, President McKinley withstood the war fever, but in 1898, he finally asked Congress for a declaration of war. The Teller Amendment was attached to that declaration. It pledged the United States to support not only freedom from Spain but an independent government in Cuba. The United States easily won the Spanish-American War, and Cuba was freed from Spanish control.

In 1902, the Platt Amendment was passed by Congress as part of an army appropriations bill. Under strong pressure from the United States, the Cubans included its content in their new constitution. The measure limited Cuba's right to conduct international relations, to borrow money, or to yield territory to foreign powers. It empowered the United States to intervene in Cuba for the protection of "life, property, and individual liberty." And it allowed the United States to lease a naval base at strategically important Guantanamo Bay.

**16.** Based on the passage, which of the following statements best describes the relationship between the Teller and Platt amendments?

   **(1)** The Platt Amendment implements the provisions of the Teller Amendment.

   **(2)** The two amendments have little in common.

   **(3)** The provisions of the Platt Amendment contradict those of the Teller Amendment.

   **(4)** The two amendments together formed the basis for early 20th-century U.S. foreign policy regarding the Western Hemisphere.

   **(5)** Both amendments changed provisions of the U.S. Constitution.

**17.** Which of the following conclusions is best supported by the passage?

   **(1)** Between 1895 and 1902, imperialists were becoming less powerful in the U.S. government.

   **(2)** In 1902, a goal of U.S. foreign policy was to make Cuba an American sphere of influence.

   **(3)** In 1902, a major concern of U.S. foreign policy was improving relations with Latin American governments.

   **(4)** By late 1898, the Spanish-American War had become unpopular in the United States.

   **(5)** From 1898 to 1902, the influence of American business interests in Cuba declined.

## Geography

Items 18 and 19 are based on the following map.

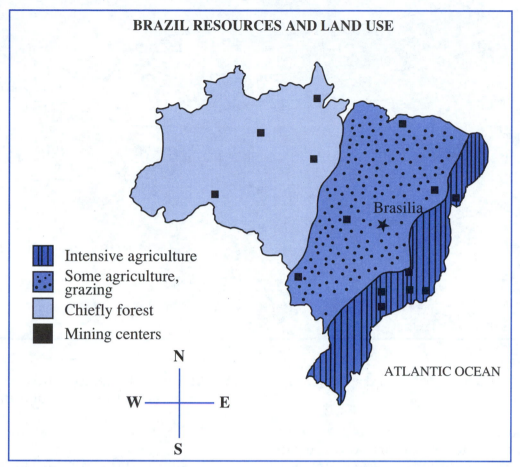

**BRAZIL RESOURCES AND LAND USE**

Intensive agriculture
Some agriculture, grazing
Chiefly forest
Mining centers

Brasilia

ATLANTIC OCEAN

N
W — E
S

18. Based on the data in the map, which part of Brazil would likely have the lowest population density?

   **(1)** the northwest
   **(2)** the northeast
   **(3)** the Atlantic coast
   **(4)** the southeast
   **(5)** the center

19. Which of the following statements about Brazil is supported by the map?

   **(1)** Brazil mainly exports agricultural products.
   **(2)** One of the chief obstacles to Brazil's growth is its lack of resources
   **(3)** Much of Brazil's land remains underused.
   **(4)** Brazil's resources are inadequate in view of its large population.
   **(5)** Farmers and mining companies must often compete for the same land.

20. Head-link cities link a country to the rest of the world. Which of the following statements do NOT describe the activities of a head-link city?

   **(1)** The city of Lagos served to give British colonists access to the interior of Nigeria.
   **(2)** Australia's agricultural products are shipped out of Sydney, destined in particular for Western Europe.
   **(3)** Much of the oil used by Dutch industries passes through the port of Rotterdam.
   **(4)** Many American goods are exported through New York.
   **(5)** The major link for transportation of goods between the Eastern states and the Midwest is provided by Chicago.

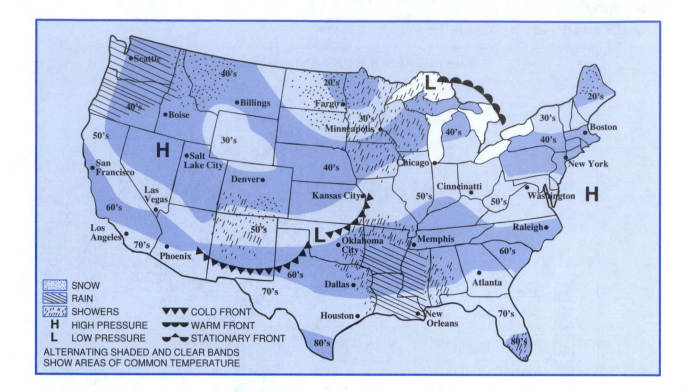

SNOW
RAIN
SHOWERS
H HIGH PRESSURE
L LOW PRESSURE
▼▼▼ COLD FRONT
●●● WARM FRONT
🔺▲ STATIONARY FRONT
ALTERNATING SHADED AND CLEAR BANDS
SHOW AREAS OF COMMON TEMPERATURE

**Items 21 to 23 are based on the following passage.**

Accurate weather forecasting is made possible by studying information about atmospheric conditions at several places. In the United States, weather data are gathered from more than 300 local weather stations. These data include temperature, air pressure, precipitation, and winds. They are used to prepare a daily weather map. Very often, information about sky conditions, air masses, and fronts is also included. So a weather map is a "picture" of weather information.

The information on weather maps is often recorded in the form of numbers, symbols, or lines. Symbols are used to show wind speed and direction, cloud cover, precipitation, position and direction of fronts, and areas of high pressure and low pressure. The symbols found on official weather bureau weather maps are used by all nations. However, these symbols may differ from those used on the simplified weather maps often shown in newspapers.

**21.** What was the temperature in Memphis on this particular day?

**(1)** 60's
**(2)** 40's
**(3)** between the 40's and 60's
**(4)** 50's
**(5)** impossible to determine

**22.** You can conclude that this is a map for which of the following months?

**(1)** January
**(2)** August
**(3)** May
**(4)** March
**(5)** September

**23.** Which of the following places would have the best weather for a 20-mile marathon?

**(1)** Memphis
**(2)** Houston
**(3)** Boston
**(4)** Kansas City
**(5)** San Francisco

Item 24 is based on the following map.

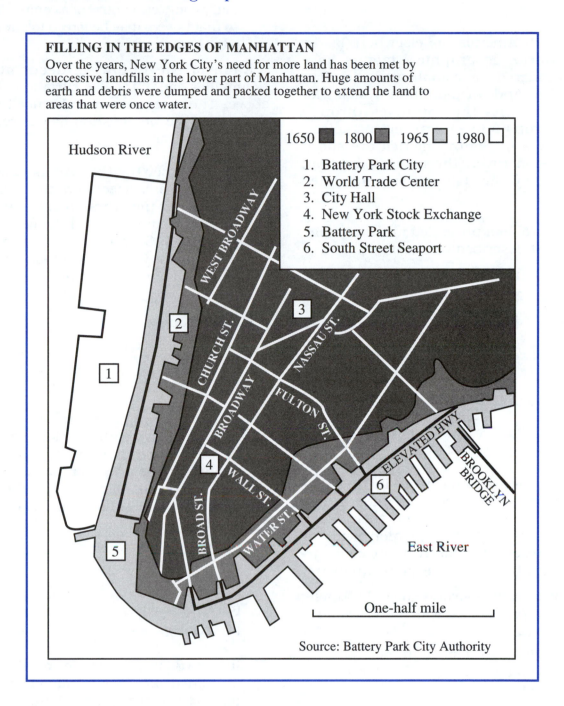

**FILLING IN THE EDGES OF MANHATTAN**

Over the years, New York City's need for more land has been met by successive landfills in the lower part of Manhattan. Huge amounts of earth and debris were dumped and packed together to extend the land to areas that were once water.

Hudson River

1650 ■ 1800 ■ 1965 □ 1980 □

1. Battery Park City
2. World Trade Center
3. City Hall
4. New York Stock Exchange
5. Battery Park
6. South Street Seaport

WEST BROADWAY

CHURCH ST.

BROADWAY

NASSAU ST.

FULTON ST.

WALL ST.

BROAD ST.

WATER ST.

ELEVATED HWY

BROOKLYN BRIDGE

East River

One-half mile

Source: Battery Park City Authority

**24.** A visitor to New York City in 1850 would not have found

**(1)** a view of the East River from Water St.

**(2)** the entire present-day length of Wall St.

**(3)** the site of the New York Stock Exchange

**(4)** Battery Park

**(5)** the intersection of Fulton and Church streets

Item 25 is based on the following information.

In South America, as elsewhere in the Third World, geographical factors have often hindered, or complicated, development. The Andean mountain system, for example, splits the countries through which it runs into several regions apiece. Most rivers in South America are short; the Amazon River, the major exception, flows largely through sparsely inhabited jungle.

**25.** The problem presented in the passage is best described as one of

(1) insufficient natural resources
(2) geographic isolation
(3) low population densities
(4) lack of navigable rivers
(5) extreme climatic conditions

## Economics

Items 26 to 29 are based on the following information.

Competition among firms in the marketplace is the basic element underlying a capitalist economy. However, there are a number of situations in which firms or other entities are able to limit competition. Listed below are five such situations.

**monopoly**—firm is the only supplier of a product for which there is no substitute

**oligopoly**—a small number of firms dominate the market for a product

**cartel**—firms or other entities act together to regulate production and prices of their products, in order to eliminate competition and/or raise prices

**trust**—firms formally merge by means of a common board of trustees for one company, which manages the member companies in such a way as to eliminate competition

**corner**—firms or individuals gain virtually complete control of a commodity, so that buyers may be forced to pay exorbitant prices.

Each of the following descriptions exemplifies one of the five situations listed above. The categories may be used more than once, but no question has more than one best answer.

**26.** In its infancy the U.S. automobile industry comprised more than 80 firms. Over the years, mergers and failures greatly reduced the field. By the early 1960s, three firms accounted for about 90 percent of total sales. This situation involves a(n)

(1) monopoly
(2) oligopoly
(3) cartel
(4) trust
(5) corner

**27.** In 1973 a group of major oil-producing nations were able, in large part by deliberately restricting output, to quadruple the price per barrel commanded by oil, all within the short space of six months. This situation involves a(n)

(1) monopoly
(2) oligopoly
(3) cartel
(4) trust
(5) corner

**28.** In the 1880s John D. Rockefeller combined various oil companies under the control of one large company he created for this purpose. This situation involves a(n)

(1) monopoly
(2) oligopoly
(3) cartel
(4) trust
(5) corner

**29.** If numerous electric companies serviced an area, the result would be inefficiency and higher, not lower, costs. Thus, state and local governments allow service to be handled by a single firm, although under the supervision of a public utility commission. This situation involves a(n)

**(1)** monopoly
**(2)** oligopoly
**(3)** cartel
**(4)** trust
**(5)** corner

Items 30 and 31 are based on the following graph

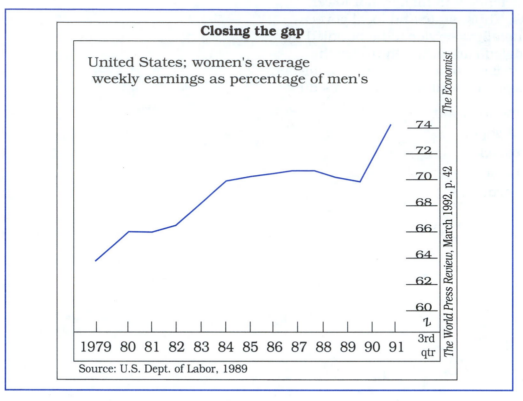

**Closing the gap**

United States; women's average weekly earnings as percentage of men's

*The Economist*

*The World Press Review, March 1992, p. 42*

74
72
70
68
66
64
62
60
%

1979  80  81  82  83  84  85  86  87  88  89  90  91

3rd qtr

Source: U.S. Dept. of Labor, 1989

**30.** Based on the graph, which of the following statements is true?

   **(1)** Women are now receiving equal pay for equal work.
   **(2)** During the past 12 years, women's earnings have increased more than decreased.
   **(3)** Since 1989 women's percentage of weekly earnings has risen greatly.
   **(4)** Prior to 1980 women were earning only 50 percent of what men were earning.
   **(5)** If the trend continues, by the year 2000 women's and men's weekly earnings will be equal for equal work.

**31.** According to the graph, in 1989 if a man and a woman were working the same job, the woman could expect to earn on the average 70 percent of what the man made. In which of the following jobs would you most likely find this difference in earnings?

   **(1)** receptionist
   **(2)** U.S. Postal Service letter carrier
   **(3)** doctor
   **(4)** machinist
   **(5)** dentist

Items 32 to 35 are based on the following passage.

   Dramatic changes have been taking place in industry in the United States over the last few decades—changes that have great significance for the nation's work force. Manufacturing industries (that is, industries that produce goods) have run into troubling times. Industries that produce services, on the other hand, have undergone an explosive growth.

   There are several factors contributing to this shift from a manufacturing to a service economy. A very important factor is that U.S. companies in all industries—including manufacturing industries—are taking advantage of technological advances that allow them to work more efficiently. This technology often requires service workers, such as computer programmers. A number of developments that are social, rather than strictly economic, also contribute. For example, the growing number of old people in America means there is a growing need for service workers in the health care field.

But, as already suggested, there is another factor behind the shift: The manufacturing sector has failed to expand. The main reason for this lack of expansion is that U.S. manufacturing companies, once dominant, have in recent decades had trouble competing with their foreign counterparts. They have lost a good part of their markets to Japanese and Western European companies in particular.

**32.** Based on the passage, those entering the labor force could be advised to consider all the following careers except

    **(1)** computer programmer
    **(2)** social worker
    **(3)** textile worker
    **(4)** car mechanic
    **(5)** hair stylist

**33.** Based on the passage, which of the following could best be cited as a small example of why the manufacturing sector has no longer been expanding rapidly?

    **(1)** An English visitor to the United States buys a raincoat in New York City but selects one made in South America.
    **(2)** A restaurant owner in Detroit buys all vegetables for her menu from a store in Canada.
    **(3)** An American manufacturing company decides to build its new plant in Taiwan instead of in the United States.
    **(4)** A family in St. Louis, Missouri, buys an automobile made in West Germany as the family vehicle.

    **(5)** An established New York manufacturer of men's hats ceases production because the market for hats has shrunk.

**34.** Which of the following conclusions can be drawn from the manufacturing industry's increasing use of new technologies?

    **(1)** The need for manufacturing workers will probably increase again.
    **(2)** The U.S. manufacturing industries will regain their competitiveness.
    **(3)** More U.S. manufacturing industries will cooperate with Japanese and Western European companies to produce goods.
    **(4)** The manufacturing sector will begin to grow faster than the service sector.
    **(5)** The manufacturing sector will produce more goods with fewer workers.

**35.** On the basis of the passage, it can be concluded that the number and kinds of jobs available for U.S. workers in the years to come will be affected by all of the following EXCEPT

    **(1)** developments in the economies of other countries
    **(2)** developments in American society
    **(3)** technological changes
    **(4)** government legislation regulating business
    **(5)** the kinds of decisions made by U.S. businesses

Items 36 and 37 are based on the following graph

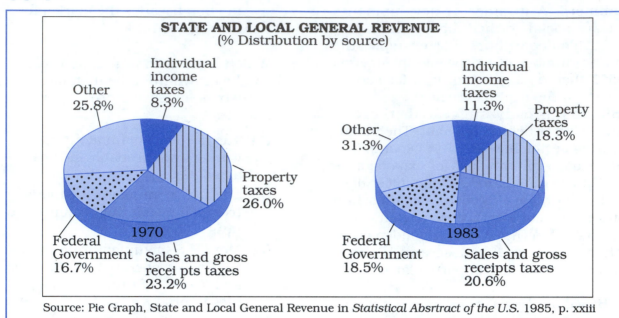

**STATE AND LOCAL GENERAL REVENUE**
(% Distribution by source)

Other 25.8%
Individual income taxes 8.3%
Property taxes 26.0%
1970
Federal Government 16.7%
Sales and gross receipts taxes 23.2%

Individual income taxes 11.3%
Property taxes 18.3%
Other 31.3%
1983
Federal Government 18.5%
Sales and gross receipts taxes 20.6%

Source: Pie Graph, State and Local General Revenue in *Statistical Absrtract of the U.S.* 1985, p. xxiii

**36.** The source of state and local general revenues that showed the greatest decline between 1970 and 1983 was

**(1)** federal government outlays
**(2)** property taxes
**(3)** sales and gross receipts taxes
**(4** individual income taxes
**(5)** other sources

**37.** Which of the following factors might partially explain why one source of state and local revenues exhibited a greater decline than any other between 1970 and 1983?

**(1)** rising unemployment rates
**(2)** reduced use of state and local highways
**(3)** fewer housing starts and more abandoned buildings
**(4)** higher sales taxes
**(5)** mandated cuts in the federal budget

## Political Science

Items 38 and 39 are based on the following passage.

When Congress sends the president a bill, or proposed law, that displeases him, he has two alternatives to signing it. First, he may veto the bill—that is, return it to Congress with a message explaining his objections. Congress will often try to write bills in a way that will be acceptable to the president, since overriding a veto requires a two-thirds vote of both houses. Alternatively, instead of vetoing a bill, the president may let it sit on his desk and do nothing with it. If Congress adjourns within ten days, the bill will not become a law. This is called a pocket veto.

Often Congress will attach riders, or extraneous provisions, to bills the president thinks are important. The president, unlike many state governors, does not have an item veto, the power to strike out those parts of a bill he does not like. He must accept or reject the entire measure, for he lacks the power to edit what Congress has written.

**38.** Which of the following statements is implied in the passage?

   **(1)** Presidents are more powerful than state governors.

   **(2)** Bills become law when the president signs them.

   **(3)** Presidents propose laws.

   **(4)** Bills automatically become laws once they reach the president.

   **(5)** Presidents have unlimited veto power.

**39.** Which of the following is NOT a conclusion you can draw from the passage?

   **(1)** Overriding a veto is more difficult than writing a bill acceptable to the president.

   **(2)** Congress tries to force the president to approve legislation he dislikes by attaching riders to bills he favors.

   **(3)** Many state governors have more extensive veto powers than the president has.

   **(4)** The only way Congress can overcome a presidential veto is by a two-thirds vote for the bill that has been vetoed.

   **(5)** The pocket veto allows the president to cancel a bill without stating his reasons for doing so.

Item 40 is based on the following information.

Ranked in order of importance, education, income, and age are the most influential factors in determining whether people will vote in elections. The more education people have, the more likely they are to vote. Those with higher incomes and higher-status careers are more inclined to vote than those with lower incomes or lower-status jobs. Older people (with the exception of the aged and infirm) are more apt to vote than younger people. Racial minorities turn out in lower numbers at the polls than whites do.

**40.** Which of the following statements is best supported by the passage?

   **(1)** Those who most need help from government are most likely to vote.

   **(2)** Nonvoting is a random behavior.

   **(3)** Voting is unrelated to sociological factors such as class and wealth.

   **(4)** Dynamic leadership would get nonvoters to vote.

   **(5)** A significant portion of the population is underrepresented in the U.S. government.

Items 41 and 42 are based on the following paragraph.

The Supreme Court exercises judicial review; that is, it determines whether acts of the Congress are constitutional. This raises the question of how the Constitution should be interpreted. Throughout American history to the present, there have been two basic views. Strict constructionists hold that the Constitution should be interpreted narrowly according to the intent of its framers and literally according to the words the framers used. This view has been used to justify the status quo. Loose constructionists claim that the document should be interpreted broadly according to the general purposes of the framers and that its words should be understood within a modern context. This view has adapted the Constitution to shifting national needs.

**41.** Which of the following statements is NOT an implication of the strict constructionist perspective?

   **(1)** The Constitution's words have the same meaning for all time.

   **(2)** The Court should follow the dictates of public opinion.

   **(3)** The intent of the framers can be readily discovered.

   **(4)** The framers intended their words to be taken at face value.

   **(5)** The needs and interests of the nation are unchanging.

**42.** Which of the following excerpts from judicial opinions is most in keeping with the loose constructionist view?

   **(1)** "The Constitution speaks not only in the same words but with the same meaning and intent with which it spoke when it came from the hands of the Framers."—Chief Justice Taney

   **(2)** "[T]he judicial branch has only one duty—to lay the article of the Constitution which is invoked beside the statute which is challenged and to decide whether the latter squares with the former."—Justice Roberts

   **(3)** "A Constitution that is viewed as only what the judges say it is is no longer a constitution in the true sense."—Attorney General Meese

   **(4)** "However, the Constitution does not vest in this Court the authority to strike down laws because they do not meet our standards of desirable social policy, 'wisdom,' or `common sense.'"—Chief Justice Burger

   **(5)** "We must never forget that it is a constitution we are expounding...[a] constitution intended to endure for ages to come, and consequently to be adapted to the various crises of human affairs."—Chief Justice Marshall

Items 43 and 44 are based on the following paragraphs.

According to the Constitution, when government officials are formally accused of having committed "high crimes and misdemeanors," they are impeached before the House of Representatives. Then they are tried in the Senate, a procedure which determines their guilt or innocence. An important test of the proper use of this congressional power came with the proceedings against President Andrew Johnson in 1868. Johnson was impeached by an opposition House, on the grounds that he had violated the Tenure of Office Act. But the reasons for his impeachment were in fact largely political, and he was acquitted of the charges. To the present, a total of 65 people have appeared in impeaching proceedings before the House of Representatives. Of these, only 14 have been impeached and 5 convicted. When officials are found guilty, they are removed from office.

**43.** Which of the following statements is supported by the passage?

   **(1)** A finding of guilt in the congressional procedure requires even stronger evidence than is required for a finding of guilt in a criminal case.

   **(2)** Impeachment is similar to an indictment because it determines whether or not there is probable cause for a trial.

   **(3)** After the House of Representatives impeached a governmental official, that person is removed from office.

   **(4)** Removal from office is an option that may be exercised when a government official is found guilty of "high crimes and misdemeanors."

   **(5)** Congress has made frequent use of its power to impeach and try government officials.

**44.** Which of the following statements best describes the purpose of the impeachment process?

   **(1)** to rid the government of incompetent officials

   **(2)** to remove members of the opposition party from government

   **(3)** to deny seats to unqualified members of Congress

   **(4)** to make government officials loyal to Congress

   **(5)** to find a remedy for officials who abuse their power

Items 45 and 46 are based on the following graph.

**CONTRIBUTIONS TO CONGRESSIONAL CANDIDATES**

PACs are Political Action Committees or sections of business, labor, professional, of other interest groups that raise funds to be contributed to candidates or political parties

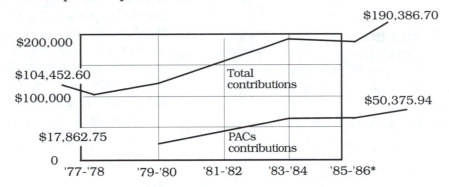

\* The latest figures are only through Sept. 30.
Source: Federal Election Commission
Source: Graph, "Campaign Costs Climb", *USA Today*, March 18, 1987, p. 4A

**45.** Which of the following statements about campaign contributions between 1977-1978 and 1985-1986 is not supported by the graph?

**(1)** Contributions to congressional campaigns increased significantly.

**(2)** PAC contributions more than doubled.

**(3)** Average PAC contributions provided about a fourth of the money raised by candidates during the last year shown on the graph.

**(4)** The sharpest increases of both PAC and non-PAC contributions occurred between 1979 and 1984.

**(5)** Contributions from other sources increased at a faster rate from 1977-1978 to 1985-1986 than contributions from PACs.

**46.** Which of the following statements is best supported by the data in the graph?

**(1)** PACs are the main source of campaign contributions.

**(2)** PACs are exerting too much influence on votes in Congress.

**(3)** Congressional campaigns are becoming so expensive that only the rich can afford to run for office.

**(4)** Campaign law limits on PAC contributions need to be rewritten.

**(5)** PACs are playing a greater role in the financing of political campaigns.

**47.** In many states, there are a number of mechanisms by which voters can play an active role in the law-making process at the state and local levels. One such mechanism is the referendum. The referendum enables voters to accept or reject proposed legislation. Which of the following actions offers the best example of participation in a referendum?

**(1)** circulating a petition to put on the ballot an amendment to the U.S. Constitution extending the debt limit

**(2)** pressing a lever in a voting booth to indicate support of a measure requiring the fluoridation of water

**(3)** signing a petition to remove a local judge from office

**(4)** selecting one of two nominees to run as the party's candidate

**(5)** writing a letter to a senator asking for a change in the speed limit on federal highways

Items 48 to 51 are based on the following information.

The U.S. Constitution contains a series of principles which form the basis of American government. Listed below are five of these principles and brief statements defining them.

**separation of powers**—the powers of government are divided among branches, such as a legislature, an executive, and courts, to prevent public offices or officials from becoming too powerful

**federalism**—the national government shares power with state governments

**republicanism**—the people govern themselves, rather than being ruled by a hereditary monarch or aristocracy

**democracy**—voters freely and openly elect public officials to make laws

**checks and balances**—each of the three branches of the government can limit and/or offset the actions of the others, so that no one branch becomes too powerful and each can share in some activities of the others

Each of the following specific provisions of the U.S. Constitution illustrates one of the basic principles described. Choose the principle that is most likely to apply in each example. The principles may be used more than once in the set of items, but no one question has more than one best answer.

**48.** Article 1, Section 6 of the Constitution prohibits senators and representatives from holding any other public office in the government while they are serving in Congress and prevents people who are holding other public offices from serving in Congress at the same time. This is an example of the principle of

**(1)** separation of powers
**(2)** federalism
**(3)** republicanism
**(4)** democracy
**(5)** checks and balances

**49.** Article 2, Section 2 of the Constitution gives the president the power to make treaties, to appoint ambassadors, and to name judges to the Supreme Court subject to the advice and consent of the Senate and the approval of two-thirds of the senators. This is an example of the principle of

**(1)** separation of powers
**(2)** federalism
**(3)** republicanism
**(4)** democracy
**(5)** checks and balances

**50.** Article 1, Section 9 of the Constitution prohibits the government from granting titles of nobility to Americans and prevents American citizens from accepting aristocratic titles from foreign governments without the consent of Congress. This is an example of the principle of

**(1)** separation of powers
**(2)** federalism
**(3)** republicanism
**(4)** democracy
**(5)** checks and balances

**51.** Article 5 of the Constitution specifies that constitutional amendments must be proposed by two-thirds of both houses of Congress or two-thirds of the state legislatures and must be ratified by three-quarters of state legislatures or of special state conventions called for the purpose of ratification. This is an example of the principle of

**(1)** separation of powers
**(2)** federalism
**(3)** republicanism
**(4)** democracy
**(5)** checks and balances

## Behavioral Science

Items 52 and 53 are based on the following passage.

Research on newborns shows that they have very different temperaments. Infants differ from one another in many ways, including the length of their attention span, their level of activity, how responsive they are to new stimuli, and how adaptable they are. Follow-up research has shown that these differences remain throughout childhood.

Only research suggests that temperament is not the only major factor influencing a child's development. From infancy on, the way the parents respond to their child's temperament can also be very important. Consider a child who feels uncomfortable in new situations. Parents' understanding of this fact and supportiveness of the child in such situations can help her or him become well-adjusted and happy. If, on the other hand, parents fail to understand and put pressure on her or him, she or he might, as a result, withdraw further.

**52.** A parenting manual influenced by the research cited might advise parents of infants to

   **(1)** try to know and understand their infant as an individual
   **(2)** establish and maintain regular routines for their infant
   **(3)** let instinct guide them in providing care for their infants
   **(4)** be well–informed about current research in child development
   **(5)** have control over their children's behavior

**53.** People have often debated whether heredity (nature) or family situation and other environmental factors (nurture) primarily influence human development. Which of the following claims is best supported by the research cited in the passage?

   **(1)** Nature is the primary influence on human development.
   **(2)** Nurture is the primary influence on human development.
   **(3)** Nature and nurture, acting together, are both primary influences on development.
   **(4)** The relative importance of nature and nurture will depend on the particular society.
   **(5)** Neither nature nor nurture can be considered a primary influence on development; other factors are more important.

Item 54 is based on the following information.

There are several basic research methods in behavioral science, including field studies, experiments, and surveys. In a survey, for example, people are asked about their opinions or behavior. Each method produces a different kind of data. Therefore, the method used in a study will depend on the hypotheses to be tested.

**54.** Which of the following hypotheses could best be tested using a survey?

   **(1)** People unconsciously react toward strangers in different ways, depending on the strangers' appearance.
   **(2)** People pride themselves on being independent, but often their actions are governed by a desire to conform to their peers.
   **(3)** Over the past 100 years, the crime rate in the United States has risen dramatically.
   **(4)** Most Americans believe that stronger gun control legislation is needed.
   **(5)** There is little real possibility of a nuclear war.

Items 55 to 58 are based on the following graph.

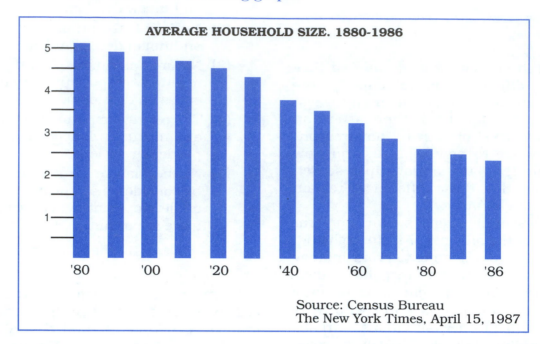

AVERAGE HOUSEHOLD SIZE. 1880-1986

Source: Census Bureau
The New York Times, April 15, 1987

The Census Bureau defines a household as all the people who live together in a house or apartment, whether or not they are related by blood or marriage.

**55.** Which of the following statements is best supported by the information in the graph?

**(1)** The trend toward a decrease in average household size has reversed itself in recent years.

**(2)** The trend toward a decrease in average household size appears to be continuing.

**(3)** Household size remains stable during periods of economic depression, when available income is smaller.

**(4)** The increase in the population of the United States has led to a decrease in average household size.

**(5)** One-person households, although common today, were virtually nonexistent in 19th-century America.

**56.** The decrease in household size over the last 100 years is a product of many demographic causes. Which of the following is NOT a cause?

**(1)** Families are having fewer children.

**(2)** The percentage of the nursing home population has increased.

**(3)** immigration to the United States has steadily decreased.

**(4)** The number of single-parent households has increased.

**(5)** More adults are choosing to live alone.

**57.** On the basis of the data in the figure, what advice might a market researcher offer a client?

**(1)** Use more TV advertising to market your product.

**(2)** Adapt your packaging to attract younger buyers.

**(3)** Target your products to a middle-class audience.

**(4)** Assign sales people to market your product house-to-house.

**(5)** Package your products for home consumption in smaller units.

**58.** The data in the figure ultimately reflect the personal decisions of many individuals regarding the lifestyle they prefer, etc. Each decision involves judgments and values as well as assessments of economic and social conditions. An emphasis on which of the following values would likely contribute to the trend shown in the graph?

(1) loyalty to friends and family
(2) personal and collective security
(3) personal rights and freedom
(4) cooperation with others
(5) fear of loneliness and isolation

Items 59 to 62 are based on the following article.

An increasing amount of sociological, psychological, and political research into how citizens decide to cast their ballots is confirming what astute politicians already knew: personality matters. In recent elections in particular, traditional concerns such as a candidate's stand on the issues, party affiliation, voting record, and philosophy have often seemed less important than questions about what kind of person the candidate is.

Many psychologists think the phenomenon is on the rise because of television. The camera brings viewers so close to politicians that they react on a personal and emotional level, rather than analyze the issues involved.

The University of Michigan's Institute for Social Research has documented the declining importance of party affiliation over the past three decades. Its surveys show that the proportion of people voting a straight ticket has dropped from nearly two-thirds in 1960 to only a third today.

In 1980 the Institute asked voters to name the principal character traits of each of the six leading presidential contenders, and then to explain how they felt about each contender. These character judgments proved much more reliable than party affiliation or issues in predicting who a voter would support.

Adapted from "Winning Hearts Not Minds," *Discover*, @SE:(1) Nov. 1984.

59. Based on the article, which response to a televised debate among presidential candidates best illustrates the impact of television on voter behavior? I won't vote for a candidate who

(1) has little experience in foreign affairs
(2) has taken stands against the working man
(3) isn't a member of my party
(4) doesn't come across as a strong leader
(5) wants to spend so much money on defense

60. Which of the following is NOT a conclusion of the research discussed in the article?

(1) Television has had a major impact on the way people vote.
(2) In recent elections, party affiliation has become less important to voters.
(3) A candidate's political beliefs and program are still the top concern of today's voters.
(4) In recent elections, voters have been focusing increasingly on candidates' personalities.
(5) Character judgments that individual voters have made proved to be better indicators of how they would vote than either issues or party affiliation.

61. Which of the following statements is best supported by research presented in the article?

(1) Voters are no longer interested in candidates' voting records and stands on issues.
(2) Television is responsible for voters' focusing on personality rather than issues.
(3) Voters are better able to get an accurate sense of candidates' personalities than of their stands on issues.

**(4)** The proportion of voters voting on straight party lines has declined.

**(5)** The proportion of eligible voters who actually vote has been declining in recent elections.

**62.** Based on the article, it can be argued that a potential threat to democracy in America lies in

**(1)** declining voter turnout

**(2)** excessive media influence

**(3)** failure of voters to sufficiently inform themselves about the candidates

**(4)** the failure of the two-party system

**(5)** the increasing role of money in determining the outcomes of elections

Item 63 is based on the following passage.

Propaganda is the deliberate dissemination of the message of an interest group. Propagandists seek to shape public opinion by focusing the public's attention on one view or choice to the exclusion of all others. Messages are designed to appeal to the audience's values and attitudes and thus to influence opinion in the desired direction.

**63.** Which of the following statements is supported by ideas in the passage?

**(1)** Propaganda messages are untrue.

**(2)** Advertising is a form of propaganda.

**(3)** Debate and discussion are tools of the propagandist.

**(4)** The opinions of experts are not used by propagandists.

**(5)** Propaganda has no place in a democratic society.

Item 64 is based on the following graph.

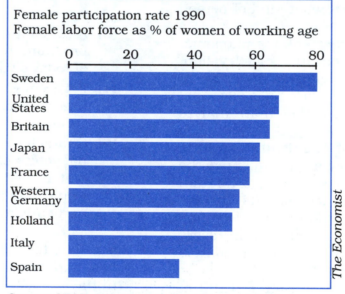

**Closing the gap**

Female participation rate 1990
Female labor force as % of women of working age

Source: OECD, U.S. Department of Labor *1989

**64.** Which of the following would be the best reason to explain why such a large percentage of Swedish women, compared to women of other countries, are participating in the work force?

**(1)** Prices in Sweden are so high that women must work to help support their families.

**(2)** Swedish families have more affordable and available day care.

**(3)** There are more single-parent families in Sweden.

**(4)** Sweden does not have a public welfare program for mothers with young children.

**(5)** Unemployment is higher in Sweden than in other countries.

Answers are on pages A-58-A-64.

# PRACTICE ITEMS 2: Social Studies

## Performance Analysis Chart

**Directions:** Circle the number of each item that you got correct on the Practice Items. Count how many items you got correct in each row; count how many items you got correct in each column. Write the number correct per row and column as the numerator in the fraction in the appropriate "Total Correct" box. (The denominators represent the total number of items in the row or column.) Write the grand total correct over the denominator 64 at the lower right corner of the chart. (For example, if you got 57 items correct, write 57 so that the fraction reads 57/64.)

| Item Type | History (page 167) | Political Science (page 185) | Economics (page 193) | Geography (page 202) | Behavioral Sciences (page 208) | TOTAL CORRECT |
|---|---|---|---|---|---|---|
| Comprehension | 1, 2, 4 6, 13, 14 | 41, 44, 45 | 30, 36 | 21 | 60 | /13 |
| Application | | 42, 47, 48, 49, 50, 51 | 26, 27, 28, 29, 31, 32, 33 | 20, 24 | 52, 54, 57, 59 | /19 |
| Analysis | 3, 5, 7, 8, 10, 11, 12, 16, | 38, 39 | 34, 35, 37 | 18, 22, 25 | 56, 58, 63, 64 | /20 |
| Evaluation | 9, 15, 17 | 40, 43, 46 | | 19, 23 | 53, 55, 61, 62 | /12 |
| Total Correct | /17 | /14 | /12 | /8 | /13 | /64 |

*The page numbers in parentheses above the column headings indicate where in this book you can find the beginning of specific instruction about the various fields of social studies and about the types of questions you encountered in the Practice Items.*

# PRACTICE ITEMS 3
## Science

**Directions:** Choose the one best answer to each question.

## Biology

Items 1 to 4 are based on the following passage.

Normal blood contains trillions of small, round cells called red blood corpuscles. These corpuscles carry oxygen from the lungs to your body. They are able to do this because they are spotted with molecules of a chemical called hemoglobin. Hemoglobin forms a loose bond with oxygen where oxygen is plentiful, and releases oxygen where there is little available.

In people with a condition called sickle-cell anemia, the hemoglobin is slightly different. Molecules of sickle-cell hemoglobin do not remain separate when they lose their oxygen as normal hemoglobin molecules do. Instead, they stick to one another, forming long, stiff rods or spirals. The rods push the red blood cell into a shape similar to a crescent moon, or sickle.

Sickle-shaped cells tend to clog the tiny blood vessels called capillaries. The body reacts to the blockage by trying to destroy the clogged cells. Soon, more red corpuscles are being destroyed than are being made by the body. The number of red blood cells in the blood drops. The sufferer becomes anemic, often feeling great pain. The condition may cause death.

Scientists first suspected that sickle-cell anemia was hereditary when they found that in the United States it tended to strike people whose ancestors came from Africa. Later research showed that the sickle-cell trait was common in central Africa, southern Italy and Sicily, Greece, Turkey, and parts of India.

1. At which body site would you expect to find the most hemoglobin bound to oxygen?
   (1) capillaries
   (2) heart
   (3) lungs
   (4) muscles
   (5) nose

2. When a person's sickle cell capillaries become clogged, which of the following most likely results?
   (1) a heart attack
   (2) a stroke
   (3) death
   (4) high blood cholesterol
   (5) fatigue and discomfort

3. All of the following characterize healthy hemoglobin molecules except
   (1) they are shaped in stiff spirals
   (2) they are found in the blood
   (3) they do not join tightly with oxygen
   (4) they carry oxygen
   (5) they are chemicals

4. From the information provided, which of the following persons is most likely have sickle cell anemia if his/her parents both carried the disease?
   (1) a South African child
   (2) a Hindu woman
   (3) a second-generation Greek-American
   (4) a Native American
   (5) a northern Italian farmer

Item 5 refers to the following passage and diagram.

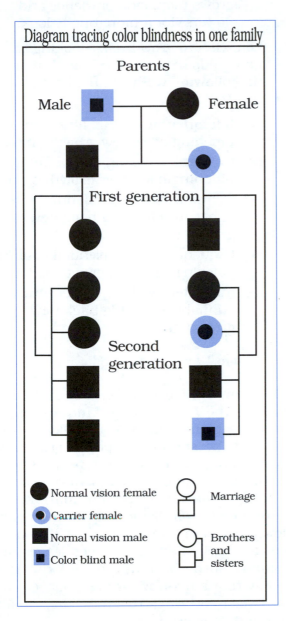

Diagram tracing color blindness in one family

Parents

Male  Female

First generation

Second generation

● Normal vision female

◉ Carrier female

■ Normal vision male

▣ Color blind male

○ / □ Marriage

○ / □ Brothers and sisters

Do you know the eye color of your grandparents, great-grandparents, and great-great-grandparents? Most people don't know the physical traits of their ancestors. However, by studying large numbers of people, scientists have found patterns of inheritance for traits such as eye color and color blindness.

5. Which of the following statements is best supported by the information in the diagram?

(1) Females who are color blind pass the gene along only to their daughters.

(2) Color blindness is a common phenomenon.

(3) Males inherit color blindness, and females pass along the trait.

(4) Color blindness can occur only in the second generation of children.

(5) Color blindness can be either inherited at birth or developed later in life.

6. Activity is a characteristic of life. Every living organism has the ability to react to the environment. The reactions are called behavior. Animal behavior may be either learned or inherited. A learned behavior is an activity that comes from experience. An inherited behavior is passed on through the genes. Which of the following is an inherited behavior?

(1) the ability to speak English

(2) the ability to blink

(3) the ability to write

(4) the ability to make friends

(5) the ability to raise children

7. A homeowner is trying to grow a lawn, but her front yard and backyard are both on the side of a hill and erosion (the gradual wearing away of the Earth's surface) is a problem. The woman seeds both yards with Kentucky bluegrass, which grows well in the area. Then she rakes the front yard in order to cover the seed. Before she has time to rake the back yard, it suddenly rains very heavily. Two weeks later the back yard is green with seedlings, while the front yard has only a few blades of grass. Which of the following factors is probably responsible for the difference in the growth of the grass?

- **(1)** the amount of rain
- **(2)** the type of soil
- **(3)** the type of seed
- **(4)** the amount of sunlight
- **(5)** rate of erosion

Item 8 is based on the following figure.

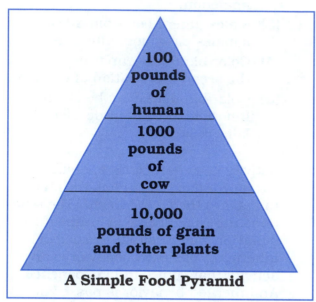

**A Simple Food Pyramid**

*(pyramid labels: 100 pounds of human / 1000 pounds of cow / 10,000 pounds of grain and other plants)*

**8.** A large amount of useful energy is lost with each step up a food pyramid. Thus 10,000 pounds of grains and other plants produces only 1,000 pounds of cow, and so on. Based on this information, which of the following would be the most efficient way for a country with a limited amount of farmland to feed a large number of people?

- **(1)** Produce food grains and livestock in the proportions depicted by the figure.
- **(2)** Produce exactly equal amounts of food grains and livestock.
- **(3)** Concentrate on raising livestock.
- **(4)** Concentrate on growing food grains.
- **(5)** Stop growing food grains.

**9.** The results of an experiment using marigolds are as follows:

- **A.** A marigold plant that is not given water droops and wilts.

- **B.** A marigold plant kept in the shade doesn't grow as well as one in the sun.

- **C.** A marigold plant in which the new growth is pinched back on top grows more side branches and flowers, for a more bushy look.

You wish to grow bushy-looking marigolds in a window box. Which of the following will yield the best results?

- **(1)** infrequent watering, little sunlight, pinching back new growth on top
- **(2)** frequent watering, little sunlight, pinching back new growth on top
- **(3)** frequent watering, plentiful sunlight, not pinching back new growth on top
- **(4)** frequent watering, plentiful sunlight, pinching back new growth on top
- **(5)** infrequent watering, plentiful sunlight, pinching back new growth on top

Items 10 to 13 refer to the following passage.

Plants, like animals, begin life as zygotes, the fusion of egg and sperm. In flowering plants, the egg is called a stigma, and the sperm is a pollen grain. The pollen is usually transferred to the stigma by the wind or by insects in a process called pollination. After pollination, the fertilized egg cell divides again and again, slowly becoming an embryo. At this point the embryo is made up of seed leaves and a stem. Both the embryo and the food supply that surrounds it are enclosed in a hard seed covering. Together, these make up the plant's seed.

When conditions—such as light, temperature, and moisture—are right for growing, the seed germinates. The cells in the embryo that make up the roots absorb water rapidly until they burst out of the seed coat. The roots grow down toward water and nutrients. The rest of the plant arches until it points toward the sun. The seed leaves begin to make food for the plant. After the first leaves mature, the seed leaves usually wither and fall off.

Many flowering plants reproduce asexually or vegetatively as well. Some send out runners on which a small, new plant forms. Plants that can reproduce in this way include strawberries and spider plants. Plants such as the African violet, coleus, and geranium can reproduce through cuttings placed in water. The cuttings grow roots and eventually new leaves.

10. The juicy white fruit of an apple surrounds the tiny embryo of the apple plant. What function does the fruit serve?

    (1) protection
    (2) water absorption
    (3) pollination
    (4) food supply
    (5) seed covering

11. Some people are allergic to the pollen grains of certain plants. Their allergies flare up at a certain time of the year. This is probably the time when plants to which they are allergic are

    (1) reproducing
    (2) germinating
    (3) growing
    (4) dividing to become embryos
    (5) maturing

12. For a plant species, what is the advantage of producing small, light grains of pollen?

    (1) The pollen grains tend to fertilize the plant's own stigma, ensuring reproduction.
    (2) The pollen grains are more easily transferred from plant to plant, ensuring genetic variation.
    (3) The pollen grains require little energy to produce, so the plant can make more of them.
    (4) The pollen grains are easily hidden within the flower, so they are not disturbed by animals.
    (5) The pollen grains are able to be transported long distances, so the plants spread across an ever-widening territory.

13. Which of the following statements about the offspring of vegetative reproduction is the most accurate?

    (1) The offspring have few commercial uses.
    (2) The offspring require fewer nutrients than plants grown from seeds.
    (3) The offspring are genetically identical to the parent plant.
    (4) The offspring become seeds before growing into mature plants.
    (5) The offspring will not grow into flowering plants.

14. A biochemist has discovered that water hyacinths will absorb and store dangerous chemicals found in water, including mercury and lead. One of the advantages of using hyacinths is that they reproduce very quickly. Through vegetative reproduction, one plant can make up to 65,000 new plants in a year. When one plant has absorbed all the chemicals it can, it is removed, and new ones quickly take its place. Which of the following is NOT a possible use of the biochemist's discovery?

    (1) beautify polluted water
    (2) clean up waterways to make them suitable for boating
    (3) purify drinking water
    (4) purify fishing ponds
    (5) decrease the amount of harmful chemicals in the environment

Items 15 and 16 are based on the following passage.

In times of severe cold, animals may hibernate for days or weeks at a time. Their body temperature drops, and they breathe only a few times a minutes. A hibernating animal uses the fat stored in its body for nourishment.

In times of extreme heat, other animals estivate. Just as with hibernating animals, the body functions of estivating animals slow down almost to a stop. To an observer, the animal appears to be either in a deep sleep or dead.

15. Which of the following facts about hibernation probably does not increase the animal's chances for survival?

    (1) The animal's temperature drops.
    (2) The animal breathes only a few times a minute.
    (3) The animal exists on body fat.
    (4) The animal cannot move around.
    (5) The animal stays underground for weeks at a time.

16. Which of the following is an accurate generalization about hibernation and estivation?

    (1) Both help protect the animal from predators.

(2) Both use more energy than when the animal is awake.
(3) Both are a response to winter.
(4) Both are a response to summer.
(5) Both are a response to extreme temperature changes.

17. When a person has a stroke and loses her ability to talk, what part of the brain is affected?

    (1) the medulla
    (2) the right side of the brain
    (3) the cerebellum
    (4) the cerebrum
    (5) the top of the brain

Item 17 refers to the following figure.

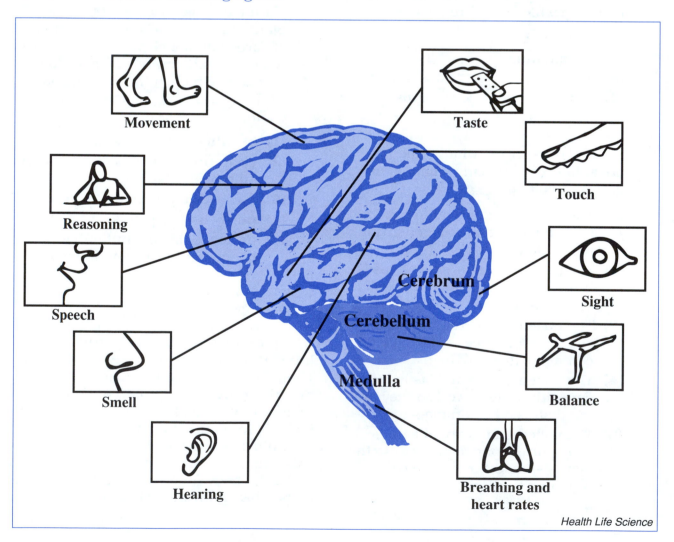

Health Life Science

**18.** Animals tend to adapt to the environment around them. On land, the only way for an animal to obtain food is to move about, so land animals are generally mobile. In the sea, by contrast, certain animals attach themselves as young adults to a rock or the ocean floor. They rarely, if ever, move about. These include sponges, corals, and oysters. Why is this adaptation successful in a marine environment?

**A.** Marine animals conserve energy by remaining still.

**B.** Marine animals make food from the sunlight that filters down through the water.

**C.** Adult marine animals no longer require food.

**D.** Marine animals are nourished by elements in the ocean floor.

**E.** Marine animals can wait for edible plants and small animals to be brought to them by the motion of the water.

**(1)** A and C only
**(2)** B only
**(3)** C only
**(4)** D only
**(5)** A and E only

## Items 19 and 20 are based on the following chart.

You don't just eat to stop your stomach from rumbling. You eat to stay alive. The foods you eat contain nutrients, chemical substances that are needed by your cells. Nutrients provide energy and help to build and repair body cells. Nutrients also help to keep your body healthy and functioning properly. There are six major groups of nutrients. This chart shows the six types of nutrients your body needs, their sources, and the simplest units of each nutrient.

| Nutrient | Source | Simplest Units |
|---|---|---|
| Carbohydrates | | Simple sugars |
| Fats | | Fatty acids and glycerol |
| Proteins | | Amino acids |
| Water | | Water |
| Minerals | | Minerals |
| Vitamins | | Vitamins |

*Health Life Science*

**19.** Based on the information in this chart, which of the following statements is correct?

   **(1)** Fatty foods are bad for your health.
   **(2)** Fish is the highest source of protein.
   **(3)** You can get water in your diet by drinking soda.
   **(4)** Bananas are a source of simple sugars.
   **(5)** Shellfish provide all the necessary minerals your body needs.

**20.** Which of the following statements is best supported by the information provided in the chart?

   **(1)** Most of the nutrients you need to keep healthy can be obtained by eating a diet rich in fruits and vegetables.
   **(2)** To stay healthy you should eat a balanced diet that contains fruits, vegetables, meat, and cereals.
   **(3)** Eating a fat-free diet is essential to a healthy, energetic body.
   **(4)** The Japanese diet, which consists of fresh vegetables, fish, and rice, is very nutritional.
   **(5)** Americans are relying less on meat as their main source of protein because of its high fat content.

Items 21 to 23 refer to the following graph.

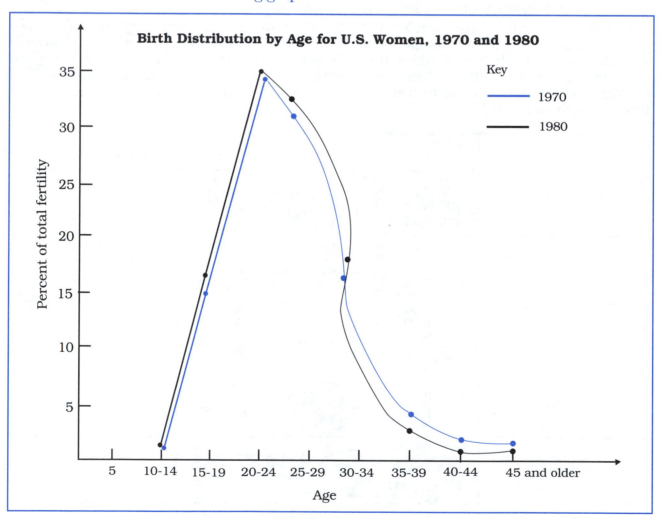

**21.** The largest share of births each year in the United States is to women between the ages of

   **(1)** 10 and 14
   **(2)** 15 and 19
   **(3)** 20 and 24
   **(4)** 25 and 29
   **(5)** 30 and 34

**22.** Young women give birth to more males than females. In higher age groups, the percentage of males born declines. This information and the graph will support which of the following conclusions?

   **(1)** Male babies are tougher than female babies.
   **(2)** The actual number of boys born to women in their later teens was greater in 1970 than in 1980.
   **(3)** In both years shown, the actual number of boys born to women in their later teens was greater than the number of boys born to women in their early 30s.
   **(4)** Natural selection favors young boys over young girls.
   **(5)** The number of girls born in the United States increased from 1970 to 1980.

**23.** Which of the following conclusions can be drawn from the graph?

   **(1)** The fertility rate is rising because more women are living longer lives.
   **(2)** The fertility rate of the U.S. population is dropping.
   **(3)** During the 1970s, the average American woman was between 20 and 24 years old.
   **(4)** The number of births to American women aged 20 to 24 was the same in 1980 as it was in 1970.
   **(5)** The age group of American women with the largest share of births was about the same in 1980 as it was in 1970.

Items 24 to 28 refer to the following passage.

How do you judge which foods and how much of them you should eat? One way is to follow the U.S. Department of Agriculture's (U.S.D.A.) seven dietary guidelines for Americans. These are:

**1.** Eat a variety of foods. Your body needs amino acids from proteins, essential fatty acids from vegetable oils and animal fats, and vitamins and minerals. Your diet should also include energy sources such as carbohydrates, fats, and proteins.

**2.** Maintain your ideal weight. Being too fat and being too thin are both associated with increased health risks. A good way to maintain a healthy weight is not to eat past the point where you are full, and to exercise several times a week.

**3.** Avoid too much fat, saturated fat, and cholesterol. The U.S.D.A. advises choosing lean meat, fish, poultry, and dry beans and peas as protein sources. Limit the amount of butter, cream, eggs, and fats you eat.

**4.** Eat foods with adequate starch and fiber. Complex carbohydrate foods such as grains, legumes, fruits, and vegetables contain many essential nutrients, and ounce for ounce, contain half the calories fats do.

**5. and 6.** Avoid too much sugar and sodium.

**7.** If you drink alcohol, do so in moderation. Alcoholic beverages are high in calories and low in nutrition.

**24.** Which of the following snack foods best meets the dietary guidelines?

   **(1)** air-popped popcorn
   **(2)** ice cream
   **(3)** potato chips
   **(4)** cake
   **(5)** cookies

**25.** Which of the following dairy foods best meets the dietary guidelines?

**(1)** four ounces of ice cream (3 grams protein, 9 grams fat, .035 grams sodium)

**(2)** one ounce of American cheese (6 grams protein, 7 grams fat, .390 grams sodium)

**(3)** six ounces of fruited yogurt (7 grams protein, 5 grams fat, .095 grams sodium)

**(4)** six ounces of plain yogurt (7 grams protein, 3 grams fat, .125 grams sodium)

**(5)** six ounces of whole milk (6 grams protein, 6 grams fat, .125 grams sodium)

**26.** Which of the following breakfast cereals best meets the dietary guidelines?

**(1)** a cereal containing 2 grams of protein, 12 grams of complex carbohydrates, and 14 grams of sugar per serving

**(2)** a cereal containing 4 grams of protein, 17 grams of complex carbohydrates, and 1 gram of sugar per serving

**(3)** a cereal containing 2 grams of protein, 23 grams of complex carbohydrates, and 12 grams of sugar per serving

**(4)** a cereal containing 2 grams of protein, 12 grams of complex carbohydrates, and 5 grams of sugar per serving

**(5)** a cereal containing 4 grams of protein, 8 grams of complex carbohydrates, and 9 grams of sugar per serving

**27.** A study of a large group of vegetarians found that they live at least seven years longer than the general American population. The group tended to have low rates of heart disease, diabetes, and cancers of the lungs and colon. In addition to their eating a diet rich in vegetables and fruits,

following which other U.S.D.A. guideline could be the reason for their good health?

**(1)** They limited their consumption of alcoholic beverages to only beer and wine.

**(2)** They exercised on a regular basis.

**(3)** They did not take drugs.

**(4)** They did not smoke.

**(5)** They ate plenty of fruits and vegetables.

**28.** An overweight friend announces that he is on a new "miracle" diet. He tells you that the diet calls for avoiding vegetables, fruits, breads, and other starches, since these are fattening. The diet replaces these with meat and other protein sources. Would you advise your friend to continue this diet; and on which guideline(s) are you basing your judgment?

**(1)** No, because he is violating guidelines 1 and 4.

**(2)** No, because he is violating guideline 2.

**(3)** No, because he is violating guidelines 5 and 6.

**(4)** Yes, because he is following guideline 5.

**(5)** Yes, because he is following guidelines 2 and 4.

**29.** Foxes that live in the Arctic region are predators that feed principally on lemmings, a type of small rodent. From time to time, usually when food supplies have been reduced by overgrazing, the lemming population declines. When this happens, the foxes go hungry, and their numbers diminish. Eventually, however, with the lemmings no longer numerous, the plants that make up their food supply can once again grow abundantly. Then the lemmings, no longer threatened by many foxes, can again increase their numbers. Eventually the foxes, with more lemmings to feed on, also increase in number and the cycle begins again. If the relationship between foxes and lemmings is a typical one, which of the following conclusions can be drawn about predator/prey relationships in the wild?

**(1)** Predators safeguard their food supply by limiting the number of prey they eat.

**(2)** Predators will eventually eliminate any given population of prey.

**(3)** Populations of predators and prey tend to evolve in a way that keeps the numbers of each type of animal in balance.

**(4)** As the number of prey animals decreases, predators become more numerous.

**(5)** As the number of prey animals increases, predators become less numerous.

**30.** Which of the following is the human being's attempt to protect nature's predator/prey relationship?

**(1)** issuing fresh-water fishing licenses

**(2)** establishing international fishing territories

**(3)** limiting the length of the deer-hunting season and the number of deer that can be shot

**(4)** establishing national camp-grounds in bear territory

**(5)** declaring certain animals "endangered species"

**31.** The placenta is the organ of exchange between an embryo and its mother. Nutrients and oxygen from the mother's blood diffuse across the placenta into the embryo's blood. In turn, carbon dioxide and other wastes from the embryo diffuse into the mother's blood.

Which of the following statements explains how drugs in the mother's blood can harm her baby?

**(1)** Drugs deplete the oxygen in the mother's blood, and thus the baby's.

**(2)** Drugs deplete the nutrients in the mother's blood, and thus her baby's.

**(3)** Drugs cross from the mother's blood to the baby's blood through the placenta, affecting the baby directly.

**(4)** Drugs slow down the diffusion of carbon dioxide from the baby's blood into the mother's blood, so that the baby's blood contains too much CO2.

**(5)** Drugs affect the rate at which the mother removes wastes from the baby, so that the baby is poisoned.

**32.** Scientists rely on a variety of clues in determining evolutionary history. They look at similarities and differences in modern-day organisms, as well as the fossil record. A similarity at the cellular level often indicates that two quite different organisms shared a common ancestor.

Which of the following is the best indication that mosses and trees may have evolved from a common green algal ancestor?

**(1)** All three live in forests.

**(2)** All three require water to live.

**(3)** All three are eaten by animals.

**(4)** All three possess chlorophyllis a and b in their cells and store food as starch.

**(5)** All three are land dwellers.

Item 33 is based on the following paragraph and graphic.

**Preventing the spread of disease**

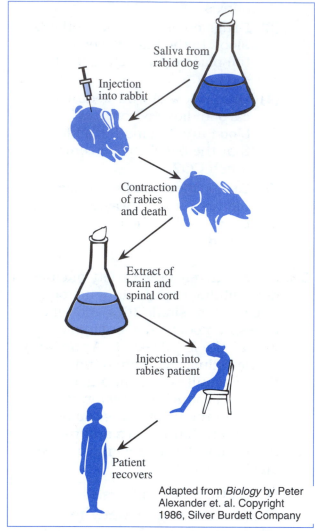

Saliva from rabid dog

Injection into rabbit

Contraction of rabies and death

Extract of brain and spinal cord

Injection into rabies patient

Patient recovers

Adapted from *Biology* by Peter Alexander et. al. Copyright 1986, Silver Burdett Company

People can acquire active immunity, which prevents their getting a disease, by being exposed to a disease or by being vaccinated. Vaccination is the injection of weakened or dead pathogens or their toxins into a healthy person. The person's body reacts by making antibodies, which give the person immunity to the disease. The substance used in the vaccination is called a vaccine. The figure shows the major steps in the development and use of a vaccine. The captions under each picture explain the steps in the process.

33. If some day a vaccine for AIDS is developed and given to a person, at what step would the person begin building a defense to the disease?

   **(1)** when the person tests HIV positive

   **(2)** after the person has full-blown AIDS

   **(3)** when the person tests HIV negative

   **(4)** after the person receives the vaccine

   **(5)** after the vaccine is injected into the rabbit

## Earth Science

34. A solar eclipse occurs when the moon passes directly between the sun and Earth. The moon casts a shadow over a small area on the daylight side of Earth, and for a short time this small area cannot see the sun.
Which of the following statements about a solar eclipse is true?

   **(1)** A solar eclipse affects only the part of Earth that is already in darkness.

   **(2)** A solar eclipse affects all parts of Earth equally.

   **(3)** During a solar eclipse, Earth is between the sun and the moon.

   **(4)** A solar eclipse affects only a small part of Earth.

   **(5)** A solar eclipse affects areas that are on opposite sides of Earth.

## Items 35 to 38 are based on the following maps and information.

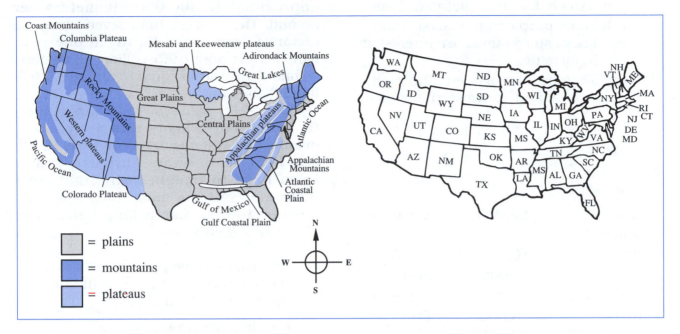

The shape of Earth's surface is called its topography. Earth's topography consists of three main landscape types: plains, mountains, and plateaus.

Plains are flat areas that are not very high above sea level. Plains in the interior of continents are somewhat higher than coastal plains. Mountains have elevations of 600 or more meters above sea level. Plateaus also have elevations of 600 or more meters, but they are not considered mountains because their surfaces are fairly flat.

The map above left shows the topography of the United States. The map above right is given to help you identify the states.

**35.** Two states that have similar landscape types are

  **(1)** California and Texas
  **(2)** Maine and Florida
  **(3)** Oregon and Indiana
  **(4)** North Carolina and Alabama
  **(5)** Idaho and Texas

**36.** A person is warned by a doctor not to live at any elevation higher than 600 meters. Which of the following locations would most likely be suitable as a place for this person to live?

  **(1)** Denver, Colorado
  **(2)** Phoenix, Arizona
  **(3)** Reno, Nevada
  **(4)** Boise, Idaho
  **(5)** Baton Rouge, Louisiana

**37.** Water flowing off the western slopes of the Appalachian Mountains would most likely eventually flow into which of the following?

  **(1)** the Atlantic Ocean
  **(2)** the Great Lakes and the Gulf of Mexico
  **(3)** the Great Lakes only
  **(4)** the Pacific Ocean
  **(5)** the western plateaus

**38.** The Midwestern states and the Atlantic coast states are noted for farming. According to the information provided, which of the following statements would best explain this fact?

  **(1)** High elevations are best suited to farming.
  **(2)** The best soils are found in areas that are mountainous.

**(3)** The largest areas of rich soil are usually found in plains regions.

**(4)** Many people in the coastal and Midwestern states are interested in farming.

**(5)** There is a lot of open land in the coastal and Midwestern states.

Item 39 is based on the following information and chart.

| Color | Temperature (C°) | Example |
|---|---|---|
| Blue or blue-white | 35,000 | Oridani |
| White | 10,000 | Sirius |
| Yellow | 6,000 | Sun |
| Red-orange | 5,000 | Centauri B |
| Red | 3,000 | Proxima |

The color of a star can help scientists determine its temperature. The following chart shows the average temperatures of different-colored stars.

**39.** Based on the chart, which of the following statements is true?

**(1)** The brighter a star is, the hotter its temperature.

**(2)** The more closely a star resembles the sun, the hotter its temperature.

**(3)** The more red in color a star is, the cooler its temperature.

**(4)** The more white in color a star is, the cooler its temperature.

**(5)** The nearer to the sun a star is located, the hotter its temperature.

Items 40 to 43 are based on the following passage.

Distances on Earth can be measured in meters or kilometers (1 kilometer = 1000 meters). In space, however, distances are often too great to be measured in kilometers. As a result, scientists use a unit of distance called the light-year to measure distances in space.

A light-year is the distance light travels in one year. Light travels at a speed of approximately 300,000 kilometers per second. This is more than seven times the distance around the Earth. In one year, light travels about 9.5 trillion kilometers, so one light-year is equal to about 9.5 trillion kilometers.

The nearest star system to ours is a little more than 4 light-years away. Some distant star systems are more than 12 billion light-years away. Although it may seem hard to imagine, the light from those star systems must have begun its journey toward Earth long before our planet was even formed.

**40.** According to the passage, which of the following quantities would be measured in light-years?

**(1)** distance around Earth

**(2)** distance between two continents

**(3)** distance between two star systems

**(4)** time needed to travel around Earth

**(5)** time needed to travel between two star systems

**41.** According to the information provided, light from the star system closest to Earth would

**(1)** take less time to reach us than light from the sun

**(2)** take about the same time to reach us as light from the sun

**(3)** take twice as long to reach us as light from the sun

**(4)** take about one year to reach us

**(5)** take more than four years to reach us

**42.** When you look into the night sky and see a star that is 1000 light-years away, which of the following are you actually seeing?

**(1)** the star as it appears at the moment you see it

**(2)** the star as it appeared one year ago

**(3)** the star as it appeared 1000 years ago

**(4)** a star that no longer exists

**(5)** one of the most distant stars in the universe

**43.** It can be concluded from the passage that the age of Earth is

**(1)** about the same as the age of the nearest star

**(2)** much less than the age of the nearest star

**(3)** about 12 billion years

**(4)** considerably less than 12 billion years

**(5)** considerably more than 12 billion years

**44.** Earth scientists disagree about just how much petroleum is left on Earth. Some say that given our present rate of use, we have only enough petrole-um to last until the year 2020. Others claim that we have enough to last until the year 2330. All agree, however, that eventually the world will experience a serious petroleum shortage. Based on the passage, which of the following represents an opinion rather than a statement of fact?

**(1)** There is a limited amount of petroleum on Earth.

**(2)** Much of the petroleum on Earth has already been used up.

**(3)** Earth scientists are concerned about the world's petroleum supply.

**(4)** By the year 2021, the world's petroleum supply will be gone.

**(5)** Earth scientists' estimates of how long our petroleum will last vary by 300 years.

## Chemistry

Item 45 refers to the following figure, in which cysteine and glycine, two amino acids, combine to form a dipeptide, one of the peptide linkages in protein

Cysteine          Glycine                    Dipeptide          Water

**45.** If the above reaction is a typical one, which of the following can be assumed?

**(1)** A peptide linkage cannot be broken.

**(2)** All dipeptides have the same molecular weight.

**(3)** All dipeptides have the same amino acid sequence.

**(4)** Every amino acid has the same number of atoms, although they are arranged in different configurations.

**(5)** Water is produced every time a peptide linkage is formed.

**46.** Proteins are arranged in complex shapes that are related to their functions. The action of enzymes, for example, depends on their having binding sites that attract and match sites on certain other molecules. Enzymes increase the rate of specific chemical reactions in the cell. So when an enzyme binds to the molecule for which it is designed, it speeds up the particular reaction in which that molecule is involved.
Which of the following conclusions about enzymes can be drawn from the passage?

(1) Most enzymes can bind to several different molecules.
(2) Changing an enzyme's shape will change its function.
(3) Changing an enzyme's shape will not change its function.
(4) The effect of the enzyme depends on the temperature at which the reaction takes place.
(5) Too many enzymes can slow down a reaction.

**47.** A balanced chemical equation is one in which the number of atoms on the left side equals the number of atoms on the right side. Which of the following is a balanced equation?

(1) $Na + HOH > NaOH + H_2$
(2) $Na + 2HOH > NaOH + H_2$
(3) $2Na + 3HOH > 2NaOH + H_2$
(4) $2Na + 2HOH > 2NaOH + H_2$
(5) $3Na + 3HOH > 3NaOH + H_2$

**48.** The basic particles of an atom are protons, neutrons, and electrons. Each proton has a charge of +1. Each electron has a charge of -1. Neutrons have no electric charge.
An atom with 10 protons, 8 neutrons, and 10 electrons loses 2 electrons. The charge of the atom is now equal to which of the following?

(1) -8
(2) -2
(3) 0
(4) +2
(5) +10

Items 49 and 50 are based on the following graph.

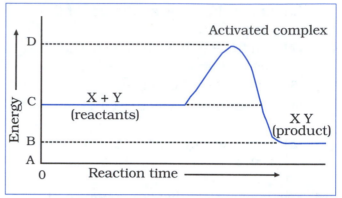

A certain amount of energy is necessary for a chemical reaction to occur. Once this energy is reached, the reactants form a temporary, high-energy arrangement called an activated complex. The products then form from the activated complex. The graph above shows the energy changes during the burning of graphite, a form of pure carbon.

**49.** When graphite is burned, the two reactants first form an activated complex; then, after burning, the $CO_2$ (carbon dioxide) is produced. Based on this information and on the graph, which of the following statements must be true?

(1) The reaction uses more energy than it gives off.
(2) There is more energy in the $CO_2$ than there was in the graphite and oxygen.
(3) There is the same amount of energy in the $CO_2$ as there was in the graphite and oxygen.
(4) Energy is absorbed in the creation of $CO_2$.
(5) There is less energy in the $CO_2$ than there was in the graphite and oxygen.

**50.** Which of the following statements best accounts for the change in energy level from point D in the activated complex to point B in the product, $CO_2$?

(1) Energy is absorbed during the reaction by the activated complex.

(2) Energy is gained by $CO_2$.

(3) Energy is given off in the burning of graphite.

(4) Energy is regained by the reactants.

(5) Energy is lost in forming the activated complex.

**51.** The boiling point of a substance is the temperature at which it changes from a liquid into a gas. The boiling point of water is 100°C. The boiling point of benzene is 80°C. The boiling point of chloroform is 60°C.

A chemist has a mixture of water, benzene, and chloroform. The chemist heats the mixture to a temperature of 85°C. The benzene and chloroform boil off, leaving the water. Which of the following conclusions does this experiment support?

(1) A chemist can take advantage of different boiling temperatures to separate substances in a compound.

(2) A chemist can take advantage of different boiling temperatures to separate substances in a mixture.

(3) Benzene and chloroform cannot be separated.

(4) A chemical reaction can be used to separate substances with different boiling temperatures.

(5) Substances with different boiling temperatures will not react with each other.

**52.** Baking powder contains the compound sodium bicarbonate. When baking powder is added to bread dough, the sodium bicarbonate reacts with acid to produce a gas, carbon dioxide. It is the carbon dioxide that causes bread to rise as it is being baked.

According to the passage, which of the following statements must be true?

(1) Bread dough contains at least one substance that is acidic.

(2) Bread dough contains oxygen.

(3) Bread dough cannot absorb carbon dioxide.

(4) Bread contains a mixture of gases.

(5) Bread rises more quickly when salt is present.

Items 53 to 55 are based on the following passage.

Carbon-14 is a radioactive form of the element carbon. When an element is radioactive, its atoms undergo spontaneous decay at a fixed rate. This fixed rate is called the half-life. The half-life of an element is the amount of time it will take for half of the atoms of that element to decay.

The half-life of carbon-14 is 5730 years. This means that after 5730 years, a 10-gram sample of carbon-14 will contain 5 grams of carbon-14 and 5 grams of a non-radioactive substance. In another 5730 years, the 5 grams will be reduced to 2.5 grams, and so on. Scientists can use the radioactive properties of carbon-14 to date the remains of ancient organisms. Every organism contains a certain amount of carbon-14 when it is alive. Once the organism dies, however, the carbon-14 begins to decay. By comparing the amount of carbon-14 present in the remains of an organism with the amount of carbon-14 known to have been present in the living organism, scientists can determine the approximate age of the remains.

**53.** According to the passage, carbon-14 is useful in dating the remains of ancient organisms mainly because it

(1) decays at a fixed rate
(2) is a form of the element carbon
(3) is present in dead organisms
(4) has a mass number of 14
(5) is present in only a few organisms

54. A radioactive form of the element iodine has a half-life of eight days. If scientists examine a 40-gram sample of radioactive iodine, how many grams will they find of a nonradioactive substance after eight days?

(1) 20 grams
(2) 10 grams
(3) 5 grams
(4) 8 grams
(5) 0 grams

55. Which of the following statements about carbon-14 can be inferred from the passage?

(1) Scientists know how much carbon-14 was present in ancient organisms when they were alive.
(2) Scientists do not know why living organisms contain carbon-14.
(3) The half-life of carbon-14 varies from one organism to another.
(4) Organisms alive today do not contain carbon-14.
(5) Scientists are presently doing research to learn more about carbon-14.

Item 56 is based on the following diagram.

56. Which of the following examples demonstrates the property of light that is shown by the picture?

(1) Swimming pools look shallower than they are.
(2) The curved lens of a magnifying glass makes a spider look larger than it is.
(3) A prism changes the direction of a light beam.
(4) An oar of a boat looks broken in the water.
(5) When you look into a mirror and wink your right eye, your left eye seems to wink back.

57. Centripetal force acts on an object moving in a circle, which tends to pull it toward the center of its circular path, and in this way keeps it moving in a circle about the center.
Which of the following does NOT describe centripetal force acting on an object?

(1) driving your car around a corner
(2) whirling a ball on the end of a string
(3) speed skating around an ice rink
(4) putting on your brakes as you bike downhill
(5) turning on a rotating sprinkler system

Items 58 to 61 are based on the following information.

What makes popcorn pop? At first glance, a kernel of popcorn looks just like a grain of ordinary corn. But a kernel of popcorn has two special features: a thick outer coat and a tiny bit of water inside the kernel.

When popcorn is heated, the water changes into steam. As the steam gets hotter and expands, pressure builds up inside the kernel. The kernel's thick outer coat keeps the steam inside until just the right moment. Then, all of a sudden, the coat gives way to the pressure and the kernel pops open. The white "fluff" that you see is the white pulp of the kernel that has reacted to the heat and sudden explosion.

**58.** According to the passage, which of the following events takes place before popcorn pops?

**(1)** White pulp in the kernel changes into steam.

**(2)** Water in the kernel combines with oxygen in the air.

**(3)** Air in the kernel suddenly expands.

**(4)** Water in the kernel changes into steam.

**(5)** Oxygen in the kernel explodes.

**59.** Which of the following actions would make popcorn pop faster?

**(1)** Add water to the popcorn.

**(2)** Leave the popcorn uncovered.

**(3)** Grease the pot containing the popcorn.

**(4)** Add salt to the popcorn.

**(5)** Raise the temperature of the popcorn.

**60.** A teacher wishes to use popcorn to demonstrate a scientific rule. Which of the following rules could be demonstrated?

**(1)** As pressure increases, volume decreases.

**(2)** As volume decreases, pressure decreases.

**(3)** As temperature increases, pressure decreases.

**(4)** As temperature increases, pressure increases.

**(5)** As temperature increases, volume decreases.

**61.** An uncovered jar of popcorn has been left on a shelf for several months. When the popcorn is heated, it does not pop. Which of the following statements best explains why this has happened?

**(1)** Insects have eaten away the hearts of the kernels.

**(2)** Exposure to air has dried out the kernels.

**(3)** Oxygen from the air has reacted chemically with the white pulp in the kernels.

**(4)** Moisture from the air has made the kernels soggy.

**(5)** The kernels have germinated into seedlings.

**62.** An iron bar may be magnetized by stroking it with a magnet. The magnets cause the tiny magnetic domains in the bar to line up in the same direction. In other words, all the north poles face in one direction, and the south poles face in the opposite direction. In unmagnetized iron, the north and south poles are arranged randomly.

If a magnetized iron bar is heated to the point that its molecules are rearranged, which of the following statements will be true when it cools?

**(1)** The north and south poles will have switched positions.

**(2)** The position of the magnetic domains will be unchanged.

**(3)** The magnetic domains will rotate to face perpendicular to their former position.

**(4)** The bar will no longer be a magnet.

**(5)** The bar's magnetic field will be greater than Earth's magnetic field.

Items 63 and 64 are based on the following graph.

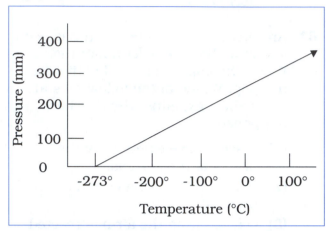

This graph represents the relationship between temperature and pressure for a gas kept at constant volume inside a sealed container.

**63.** According to the graph, which of the following statements describes how pressure changes with temperature?

**(1)** Pressure steadily decreases as temperature increases.

**(2)** Pressure steadily increases as temperature increases.

**(3)** Pressure remains constant as temperature increases or decreases.

**(4)** Pressure sometimes increases and sometimes decreases as temperature increases.

**(5)** Pressure remains constant at low temperatures but increases sharply at high temperatures.

**64.** Which of the following would you expect to happen if the sealed container were opened and the heated gas suddenly increased in volume?

**(1)** The pressure of the gas would stay the same.

**(2)** The pressure of the gas would increase.

**(3)** The temperature and pressure of the gas would both stay the same.

**(4)** The temperature and pressure of the gas would both increase.

**(5)** The pressure of the gas would decrease.

Items 65 and 66 are based on the following information.

The behavior of gases is often described by various gas laws. Below are brief descriptions of four of these laws.

**(1) Avogadro's hypothesis** —In two equal volumes of gas at the same temperature and pressure, there are the same number of molecules (regardless of what type of gas they are).

**(2) Boyle's law**—The volume of a fixed amount, or mass, of gas varies inversely with pressure of the gas. In other words, at constant temperature, the volume of a gas will decrease when the pressure on it increases, and the volume of a gas will increase when the pressure on it decreases.

**(3) Charles's law**—When the pressure is constant, the volume of a gas varies directly with the temperature. In other words, at constant pressure, the volume of a gas will increase as the temperature increases, and it will decrease as the temperature decreases.

**(4) Ideal gas law**—An "ideal gas" will behave according to Boyle's law with respect to volume and pressure if temperature is kept constant. Real gases, however, depart more or less from the law. The product of the pressure and volume of a gas is a constant that depends only upon the temperature.

**65.** During an operation, a small metal cylinder supplies enough oxygen for the patient to breathe for three hours. How could such a small container hold so much oxygen? The law that explains why it was so easy to fill the little tank with plenty of oxygen by adding pressure is

**(1)** Avogadro's hypothesis
**(2)** Boyle's law
**(3)** Charles's law
**(4)** Charles's law and Boyle's law
**(5)** Ideal gas law

**66.** Suppose you have two containers of the same size side by side on a table. If you fill one with chlorine gas and the other with helium, you will find that the chlorine-filled container is heavier. But the number of molecules in both containers is the same according to

**(1)** Avogadro's hypothesis
**(2)** Boyle's law
**(3)** Charles's law
**(4)** Avogadro's hypothesis and Charles's law
**(5)** Ideal gas law

Answers are on Pages A-65–A-69.

# PRACTICE ITEMS 3: SCIENCE

## Performance Analysis Chart

**Directions:** Circle the number of each item that you got correct on the Practice Items. Count how many items you got correct in each row; count how many items you got correct in each column. Write the number correct per row and column as the numerator in the fraction in the appropriate "Total Correct" box. (The denominators represent the total number of items in the row or column.) Write the grand total over the denominator 66 at the lower right corner of the chart. (For example, if you got 60 items correct, write *60* so that the fraction reads 60/66.).

| Item Type | Biology (page 222) | Earth Science (page 251) | Chemistry (page 263) | Physics (page 277) | TOTAL CORRECT |
|---|---|---|---|---|---|
| Comprehension | 3, 9, 16, 19, 21, 31 | 39, 40, 41 | 53 | 58, 63 | /14 |
| Application | 6, 8, 10, 14, 17, 24, 25, 26, 30, 32, 33 | 36 | 47, 48, 49, 54 | 56, 57, 62, 65, 66 | /21 |
| Analysis | 1, 2, 7, 11, 12, 15, 18, 23, 27, 29 | 34, 35, 37, 42, 43, 44 | 45, 46, 50, 52, 55 | 59, 60, 61, 64 | /23 |
| Evaluation | 4, 5, 13, 20, 22, 28 | 38 | 51 | | /8 |
| Total Correct | /33 | /11 | /11 | /11 | /66 |

*The page numbers in parentheses above the column headings indicate where in this book you can find the beginning of specific instruction about the various fields of science and about the types of questions you encountered in the Practice Items.*

**Directions:** Choose the one best answer to each question.

## Nonfiction

Items 1 to 4 are based on the following passage.

### WHAT DO INTELLIGENCE TESTS PROVE?

What is intelligence, anyway? When I was in the army I received a kind of aptitude test that all soldiers took and, against a normal of 100, scored

(5)  160. No one at the base had ever seen a figure like that and for two hours they made a big fuss over me. (It didn't mean anything. The next day I was still a buck private with KP

(10) as my highest duty.)

All my life I've been registering scores like that, so that I have the complacent feeling that I'm highly intelligent, and I expect other people

(15) to think so, too. Actually, though, don't such scores simply mean that I am very good at answering the type of academic questions that are considered worthy of answers by the people

(20) who make up the intelligence tests— people with intellectual bents similar to mine?

For instance, I had an auto-repair man once, who, on these intelligence

(25) tests, could not possibly have scored more than 80, by my estimate. I always took it for granted that I was far more intelligent than he was. Yet, when anything went wrong with my

(30) car I hastened to him with it, watched him anxiously as he explored its vitals, and listened to his pronouncements as though they were divine oracles—and he always fixed

(35) my car.

Well, then, suppose my auto-repair man devised questions for an intelligence test. Or suppose a carpenter did, or a farmer, or, indeed almost

(40) anyone but an academician. By every one of those tests, I'd prove myself a moron. And I'd be a moron, too. In a world where I could not use my academic training and my verbal tal-

(45) ents but had to do something intricate or hard, working with my hands, I would do poorly. My intelligence, then, is not absolute but is a function of the society I live in and of the fact

(50) that a small subsection of that society has managed to foist itself on the rest as an arbiter of such matters.

From Isaac Asimov, "What Is Intelligence, Anyway?"
*Psychology Today,* 1975.

1. Which of the following best states the author's view concerning intelligence tests?

   **(1)** No one is better at them than he is.
   **(2)** They test only a certain kind of intelligence.
   **(3)** The information they provide is totally inaccurate.
   **(4)** People who do well on them are usually very successful.
   **(5)** Farmers usually do better on them than carpenters.

2. Which of the following words is the best synonym for *aptitude* (line 3)?

   **(1)** mathematical
   **(2)** military
   **(3)** difficult

**(4)** intelligence

**(5)** general

3. If the author were to suggest an aptitude test for a plumber, whom would he probably recommend to write it?

   **(1)** other plumbers

   **(2)** the people who make up other intelligence tests

   **(3)** himself

   **(4)** companies that manufacture plumbing supplies

   **(5)** the military

4. The author's writing style can best be described as

   **(1)** formal

   **(2)** impartial

   **(3)** full of double meanings

   **(4)** academic

   **(5)** conversational

Items 5 to 8 are based on the following passage.

### WHAT IS IT LIKE TO BE A NONCONFORMIST?

What I must do is all that concerns me, not what the people think. This rule, equally arduous in actual and in intellectual life, may serve for the
(5) whole distinction between greatness and meanness. It is harder because you will always find those who think they know what is your duty better than you know it. It is easy in the
(10) world to live after the world's opinion; it is easy in solitude to live after your own; but the great man is he who in the midst of the crowd keeps with perfect sweetness the indepen-
(15) dence of solitude.

For nonconformity the world whips you with its displeasure.

The other terror that scares us from self-trust is our consistency; a
(20) reverence for our past act or word because the eyes of others have no other data for computing our orbit

than our past acts, and we are loath
(25) to disappoint them.

But why should you keep your head over your shoulder? Why drag about this corpse of your memory, lest you contradict somewhat you
(30) have stated in this or that public place? Suppose you should contradict yourself; what then? It seems to be a rule of wisdom never to rely on your memory alone, scarcely even in
(35) acts of pure memory, but to bring the past for judgment into the thousand-eyed present, and live ever in a new day.

From Ralph Waldo Emerson, *Self-Reliance*

5. Which of the following best sums up the main idea of the essay?

   **(1)** You should behave like everyone else.

   **(2)** Knowing your own mind is the first step to trusting yourself.

   **(3)** Your decisions should be guided by your trust in yourself.

   **(4)** Your present actions should be consistent with your past actions.

   **(5)** Living alone is the best way to live.

6. By referring to memory as a "corpse," (line 28) the author is implying that

   **(1)** he is losing his memory

   **(2)** the dead have no memory

   **(3)** we should remember and honor the dead

   **(4)** we should not dwell on past events

   **(5)** monuments are not always appropriate

**7.** What two things does the author say are impediments to our own self-reliance?

(1) love of solitude and the desire to be consistent

(2) the opinions of others and desire to be consistent

(3) the forgetfulness of human nature and the opinions of others

(4) the inability to compute data and the tendency to contradict yourself

(5) the fear of living alone and the forgetfulness of human nature

**8.** For which of the following would this essay be appropriate

**a.** a high school workshop on drug and alcohol abuse

**b.** seminar for young artists

**c.** a training session for nurses

(1) **a** only

(2) **b** only

(3) **a** and **b**

(4) **a** and **c**

(5) **b** and **c**

Items 9 to 12 are based on the following passage.

### WHAT ARE THE BENEFITS OF SYNTHETIC FOOD?

Let us imagine the day when a country's economy is based on the manufacture of synthetic food instead of on traditional methods of
(5)  food production. A few huge factories sited in different parts of the country where coal and petroleum are to be found prepare all the food required by the population.
(10)  Altogether, these factories occupy barely a few hundred square miles. Agriculture, with its need for a vast labor force and its limited capacity for progress, has been abolished,
(15)  with the exception perhaps of market gardens and horticulture.

There is no longer any need for the vast industry which formerly provided agriculture with its equip-
(20)  ment—tractors, machines, tools. Nor for the metal used in making them, nor for the fuel used to power them. Nor for chemical fertilizers, pesticides, etc. A large pro-
(25)  portion of the population previously engaged in these industries and in agriculture itself is thus freed for more productive work. Only a minute part of this manpower is
(30)  needed for the production of synthetic food.

The old food industry gives way to an entirely new industry, infinitely more compact. No more bad years,
(35)  poor harvests, unproductive land. No more calamitous losses due to climate, natural catastrophes, parasites, plant diseases, all of which today still take their toll on a consid-
(40)  erable part of every harvest.

All the conditions are to hand for the transformation of villages into towns and towns into garden cities. Food products, ready to eat, pack-
(45)  aged or tinned like the products on sale today, but with the fundamental difference that they contain the normal amount of vitamins and have the highest nutritive value, have
(50)  only to be heated.

The appearance of these dishes leaves nothing to be desired. With a standard composition (proteins, carbohydrates, fats, salts, vitamins)
(55)  adapted to each age need, these foods are the best source of health and energy the human system can have, infinitely better, at all events, than the best natural products.
(60)  No more obesity, no more fatty degeneration of the heart, liver and other complaints of the kind. At the least sign of physical abnormality, special diets can be composed with
(65)  more or less of one or another ingredient.

Vast tracts of land previously reserved for crop growing give way progressively to forests and parks.

(70) The silting and drying up of rivers is stopped and the abundance of food products leads to the solution of the world shortage of drinking water which at present is steadily worsen-

(75) ing.

The society of the future gains on all fronts: economic, social and also moral, as the slaughter of animals, a cruel vestige of the past, is progres-

(80) sively done away with.

From Alexander Nesmeyanov and Vassily Belikov (*Unesco Courier*, March 1969)

9. What does the author mean by "synthetic" food?

   **(1)** 100 percent natural foods
   **(2)** food grown on experimental farms
   **(3)** foods cultivated from the ocean
   **(4)** food manufactured from chemicals
   **(5)** organically grown food high in nutrition

10. Which of the following is NOT one of the benefits of synthetic foods mentioned in the article?

    **(1)** reduction of manpower used in agriculture
    **(2)** freedom from effects of weather on crops
    **(3)** reduction in individual food consumption
    **(4)** elimination of health problems due to fat consumption
    **(5)** use of farming land for parks and forests

11. The writers might use the same reasoning to argue for

    **(1)** no preservatives or additives in food
    **(2)** plastic clothing and accessories
    **(3)** hand-made furniture

    **(4)** increased agricultural production
    **(5)** communal living, eating, and working

12. Which of the following best describes the tone of the passage?

    **(1)** bored
    **(2)** optimistic
    **(3)** resigned
    **(4)** ironic
    **(5)** pessimistic

## Fiction

Items 13 to 16 are based on the following passage.

### DO CHEE AND OLD MAN FAT AGREE ABOUT WORKING THE LAND?

Chee rode the first part of the fifteen miles to Red Sands expectantly. The sight of sandstone buttes near Cottonwood Spring reddening in the

(5) morning sun brought a song almost to his lips. He twirled his reins in salute to the small boy herding sheep toward many-colored Butterfly Mountain, watched with

(10) pleasure the feathers of smoke rising against tree-darkened western mesas from the hogans sheltered there. But as he approached the familiar settlement sprawled in

(15) mushroom growth along the highway, he began to feel as though a scene from a bad dream was becoming real.

Several cars were parked around

(20) the trading store, which was built like two log hogans side by side, with red gas pumps in front and a sign across the tar-paper roofs: Red Sands Trading Post—Groceries—

(25) Cold Drinks—Sandwiches—Indian Curios. Back of the trading post an unpainted frame house and out-buildings squatted on the drab, tree-less land. Chee and the Little One's

(30) mother had lived there when they

stayed with his wife's people. That was according to custom—living with one's wife's people—but Chee
(35) had never been convinced that it was custom alone which prompted Old Man Fat and his wife to insist that their daughter bring her husband to live at the trading post.
(40)     Beside the post was a large hogan of logs, with brightly painted pseudo-Navajo designs on the roof— a hogan with smoke-smudged windows and a garish blue door which
(45) faced north to the highway. Old Man Fat had offered Chee a hogan like this one. The trader would build it if he and his wife would live there and Chee would work at his forge, mak-
(50) ing silver jewelry where tourists could watch him. But Chee had asked instead for a piece of land for a cornfield and help in building a
(55) hogan far back from the highway and a corral for the sheep he had brought to this marriage. . . .
    Chee's lips tightened as he began to look around for Old Man Fat.
(60) Finally, he saw him passing among the tourists collecting coins.
    Then the Little One saw Chee. The uncertainty left her face, and she darted through the crowd as her
(65) father swung down from his horse. Chee lifted her in his arms, hugging her tight. While he listened to her breathless chatter, he watched Old Man Fat bearing down on them,
(70) scowling.
    As his father-in-law walked heavily across the graveled lot, Chee was reminded of a statement his mother sometimes made: "When you see a
(75) fat Navajo, you see one who hasn't worked for what he has."

From Juanita Platero and Siyowin Miller, "Chee's Daughter," *Common Ground*, Vol. 8, Winter 1948 (American Council for Nationalities Service).

**13.** Chee and Old Man Fat are

  **(1)** Chinese

  **(2)** brothers

  **(3)** Navajo

  **(4)** tourists

  **(5)** ranchers

**14.** What do lines 43-45 show about Chee's feelings toward Old Man Fat?

  **(1)** Chee respects him.

  **(2)** Chee was happy to see him.

  **(3)** Chee worked for Old Man Fat.

  **(4)** Chee did not see him often.

  **(5)** Chee did not really like Old Man Fat.

**15.** Why is the phrase "familiar settlement sprawled in mushroom growth along the highway" (line 14 to 16) effective in conveying Chee's feelings about Red Sands?

  **(1)** It emphasizes Chee's love of nature.

  **(2)** It suggests that Red Sands is like a beautiful plant.

  **(3)** It makes Red Sands seem like an ugly thing.

  **(4)** It captures the sensations of a bad dream.

  **(5)** It distances the reader by describing Red Sands in an unusual way.

**16.** Which statement might reflect the authors' attitude toward the American farm crisis of the 1980s?

  **(1)** The farmers should sell their land.

  **(2)** The farmers should be respected and helped.

  **(3)** Farmers should be given job training for factory jobs.

  **(4)** Large corporations should buy the farmland.

  **(5)** Farmers should handle the crisis without any outside help.

Items 17 to 20 refer to the following passage.

## WHAT IS IT LIKE IN AN OPEN BOAT AT SEA?

None of them knew the color of the sky. Their eyes glanced level, and were fastened upon the waves that swept toward them. These waves
(5) were of the hue of slate, save for the tops, which were of foaming white, and all of the men knew the colors of the sea. The horizon narrowed and widened, and dipped and rose,
(10) and at all times its edge was jagged with waves that seemed thrust up in points like rocks.

Many a man ought to have a bathtub larger than the boat which
(15) here rode upon the sea. These waves were most wrongfully and bar- barously abrupt and tall, and each froth top was a problem in small boat navigation.
(20) The cook squatted in the bottom and looked with both eyes at the six inches of gunwale which separated him from the ocean. His sleeves were rolled over his fat forearms,
(25) and the two flaps of his unbuttoned vest dangled as he bent to bail out the boat. Often he said: "Gawd! That was a narrow clip." As he remarked it he invariably gazed eastward over
(30) the broken sea.

The oiler,[1] steering with one of the two oars in the boat, sometimes raised himself suddenly to keep clear of water that swirled in over
(35) the stern. It was a thin little oar and it seemed often ready to snap.

The correspondent, pulling at the other oar, watched the waves and wondered why he was there.
(40) The injured captain, lying in the bow, was at this time buried in that profound dejection and indifference which comes, temporarily at least, to even the bravest and most enduring
(45) when, willy nilly, the firm fails, the army loses, the ship goes down. The mind of the master of a vessel is rooted deep in the timbers of her, though he command for a day or a
(50) decade, and this captain had on him the stern impression of a scene in the grays of dawn of seven turned faces, and later a stump of a top- mast with a white ball on it that
(55) slashed to and fro at the waves, went low and lower, and down. Thereafter there was something strange in his voice. Although steady, it was deep with mourning,
(60) and of a quality beyond oration or tears.

"Keep 'er a little more south, Billie," said he.

" 'A little more south,' sir," said
(65) the oiler in the stern.

A seat in this boat was not unlike a seat upon a bucking bronco, and, by the same token, a bronco is not much smaller. The craft pranced
(70) and reared, and plunged like an ani- mal. As each wave came, and she rose for it, she seemed like a horse making at a fence outrageously high. The manner of her scramble
(75) over these walls of water is a mystic thing, and, moreover, at the top of them were ordinarily these problems in white water, the foam racing down from the summit of each wave,
(80) requiring a new leap, and a leap from the air. Then, after scornfully bumping a crest, she would slide, and race, and splash down a long line and arrive bobbing and nodding
(85) in front of the next menace.

"The Open Boat" by Stephen Crane, in *Prentice Hall Literature, The American Experience* (Prentice Hall, Inc., Englewood Cliffs, NJ, 1991, 1989

**17.** The captain feels "dejection and indif- ference" (lines 40-43) because he

(1) has lost his ship
(2) is injured
(3) wonders why he is there
(4) has lost his sense of direction
(5) is worried about the men in the boat

1. **Oiler:** The person responsible for oiling machinery in the engine room of a ship.

**18.** The author says "None of them knew the color of the sky" in line 1 to indicate that the men

   **(1)** are blinded by sea water
   **(2)** have lost there sense of color
   **(3)** are confusing the colors of the sea and the sky
   **(4)** are looking only at the sea
   **(5)** are drowning

**19.** The boat's action on the waves is compared to

   **(1)** a bathtub
   **(2)** a seat on a bucking bronco
   **(3)** a losing army
   **(4)** a topmast on a sinking ship
   **(5)** a horse trying to jump a fence

**20.** Which of the following best expresses the theme of the passage?

   **(1)** Extreme situations bring out hidden strengths in human beings.
   **(2)** Nature can paralyze any human being with terror.
   **(3)** Life is a constant struggle against unpredictable forces.
   **(4)** Danger reveals the same basic traits in all human beings.
   **(5)** Hostile natural forces reduce all people to an animal level.

Items 21 to 24 are based on the following passage.

### WHAT DID GRANDFATHER SAY AS HE DIED?

I am not ashamed of my grandparents for having been slaves. I am only ashamed of myself for having at one time been ashamed. About
(5) eighty-five years ago they were told that they were free, united with others of our country in everything pertaining to the common good, and, in everything social, separate like the
(10) fingers of the hand. And they believed it. They exulted in it. They stayed in their place, worked hard, and brought up my father to do the same. But my grandfather is the
(15) one. He was an odd old guy, my grandfather, and I am told I take after him. It was he who caused the trouble. On his death-bed he called my father to him and said,
(20) "Son, after I'm gone I want you to keep up the good fight. I never told you, but our life is a war and I have been a traitor all my born days, a spy in the enemy's country ever
(25) since I give up my gun back in the Reconstruction. Live with your head in the lion's mouth. I want you to overcome 'em with yeses, undermine 'em with grins, agree 'em to death
(30) and destruction, let 'em swoller you till they vomit or bust wide open." They thought the old man had gone out of his mind. He had been the meekest of men. The younger chil-
(35) dren were rushed from the room, the shades drawn and the flame of the lamp turned so low that it sputtered on the wick like the old man's breathing. "Learn it to the young-
guns," he whispered fiercely; then he died.
(40)    But my folks were more alarmed over his last words than over his dying. It was as though he had not
(45) died at all, his words caused so much anxiety. I was warned emphatically to forget what he had said and, indeed, this is the first time it has been mentioned outside the
(50) family circle. It had a tremendous effect upon me, however. I could never be sure of what he meant. Grandfather had been a quiet old man who never made any trouble, yet
(55) on his deathbed he had called himself a traitor and a spy, and he had spoken of his meekness as a dangerous activity. It became a constant puzzle which lay unanswered in the
(60) back of my mind.

21. What does Grandfather mean when he says, "Live with your head in the lion's mouth" (lines 26-27)?

    (1) retreat from the enemy
    (2) become a spy and a traitor
    (3) overcome the enemy through violence
    (4) place yourself in constant danger
    (5) live in the wild

22. Grandfather called himself a traitor and a spy (lines 22-24) because he

    (1) fought in the Civil War
    (2) did not stay in his place and work hard
    (3) was ashamed of being a slave
    (4) caused trouble for the family by going insane
    (5) did not stand up against the white man's oppression

23. If Grandfather relived his life today, his life-long behavior most likely would make him

    (1) become a union organizer
    (2) go into politics
    (3) work in a civil rights organization
    (4) become a journalist
    (5) work in a service occupation

24. Why might the author have situated Grandfather on his death bed?

    (1) to describe the poverty and despair of the family
    (2) to show that the family was not alarmed over his dying
    (3) to cause the narrator to feel guilty and uncomfortable
    (4) to represent the social weakness of slaves
    (5) to emphasize the importance of Grandfather's last words

## Drama

Items 25 to 27 are based on the following passage.

### DOES CALIGULA WANT TO BE A GOD ON EARTH?

CALIGULA: What's the use of the amazing power that's mine, if I can't have the sun set in the east, if I can't reduce the sum of suffering
(5) and make an end of death? No, Caesonia, it's all one whether I sleep or keep awake, if I've no power to tamper with the scheme of things.
(10) CAESONIA: But that's madness, sheer madness. It's wanting to be a god on earth.
CALIGULA: So you, too, think I'm mad. And yet—what is a god that I
(15) should (wish to be his equal? No, it's something higher, far above the gods, that I'm aiming at, longing for with all my heart and soul. I am taking over a kingdom where the
(20) impossible is king.
CAESONIA: You can't prevent the sky from being the sky, or a fresh young face from aging, or a man's heart from growing cold.
(25) CALIGULA (*with rising excitement*): I want ...I want to drown the sky in the sea, to infuse ugliness with beauty, to wring a laugh from pain.
CAESONIA (*facing him with an*
(30) *imploring gesture*): There's good and bad, high and low, justice and injustice. And I swear to you these things will never change.
CALIGULA (*in the same tone*): And
(35) I'm resolved to change them ... I shallmake this age of ours a kingly gift—the gift of equality. And when all is leveled out, when the impossible has come to earth and the
(40) moon is in my hands—then, perhaps, I shall be transfigured and the world renewed; then men will die no more and at last be happy.

From Albert Camus, *Caligula*, trans. Justin O'Brien (New York: International Creative Management, 1961)

**25.** What does Caligula desire?

   **(1)** to beautify the earth as an artist

   **(2)** to end equality and be king of a large empire

   **(3)** to be a spokesman for minorities and equal rights

   **(4)** to enjoy life more and dream of the impossible

   **(5)** to eliminate all differences and rule over nature itself

**26.** Which of the following most likely describes the author's purpose for including the phrase "or a man's heart from growing cold" in Caesonia's speech (lines 22-24)?

   **(1)** to imply that the world is a cold place in which to live

   **(2)** to emphasize Caligula's desire to overcome death

   **(3)** to give the reader a sense of the numerous tasks Caligula faces

   **(4)** to reveal Caesonia's cynical nature

   **(5)** to suggest Caesonia's concern over Caligula's attitude

**27.** What do the stage directions (line 29-30) reveal about Caesonia's feelings?

   **(1)** They show that she agrees with Caligula.

   **(2)** They show that she is laughing at Caligula.

   **(3)** They illustrate her anger.

   **(4)** They show that she is begging Caligula to give up his ideas.

   **(5)** They illustrate her love for Caligula in the way she looks at him.

Items 28 to 30 are based on the following passage.

## WHAT DILEMMA DOES KEN FACE AS A PARALYZED INVALID?

KEN: I am serious you know ... about deciding to die.

DR. SCOTT: You will get over the feeling.

(5) KEN: How do you know?

DR. SCOTT: But if we acted on your decision now, there wouldn't be an opportunity for you to accept it.

(10) KEN: I grant you, I may become lethargic and quiescent. Happy when a nurse comes to put in a new catheter, or give me an enema, or to turn me over. These (15) could become the high spots of my day. I might even learn to do wonderful things, like turn the pages of a book with some miracle of modern science, or to type (20) letters with flicking my eyelids. And you would look at me and say "Wasn't it worth waiting?" and I would say: "Yes" and be proud of my achievements. Really proud. I (25) grant you all that, but it doesn't alter the validity of my present position.

DR. SCOTT: But if you became happy?

(30) KEN: But I don't want to become happy by becoming the computer section of a complex machine. And morally, you must (accept my decision.

(35) DR. SCOTT: Not according to my morals.

KEN: And why are yours better than mine?

From Brian Clark, *Whose Life Is It Anyway?* (Chicago: Dramatic Publishing Company, 1978)

**28.** What does Ken mean by "becoming the computer section of a complex machine" (lines 31-32)?

    **(1)** becoming the victim of himself

    **(2)** being the "guinea pig" of medical research

    **(3)** being the thinking part of his life-support systems

    **(4)** "selling out" to the establishment

    **(5)** training to be a computer analyst

**29.** Which of the following best expresses Ken's attitude toward moral standards?

    **(1)** Individual moral rights are to be respected by all.

    **(2)** Morality should have no place in life-and-death decisions.

    **(3)** There is one "universal" morality.

    **(4)** A good, moral life leads to happiness.

    **(5)** Upstanding morals lead to high achievement.

**30.** The exchange of dialogue in this passage suggests that

    **(1)** Dr. Scott will discharge Ken

    **(2)** Ken will recover

    **(3)** Dr. Scott and Ken will become friends

    **(4)** Ken will learn to type

    **(5)** the conflict between Ken and Dr. Scott will continue

## Poetry

Items 31 to 33 are based on the following poem.

### WHAT KIND OF LIFE HAS MOTHER HAD?

### Mother to Son

    Well, Son, I'll tell you;
    Life for me ain't been no crystal stair.
    It's had tacks in it,
(5)    And splinters,
    And boards torn up,

    And places with no carpet on the floor,
    Bare.
(10)    But all the time
    I'se been aclimbin' on
    And reachin' landin's,
    And turning corners,
    And sometimes goin' in the dark
(15)    Where there ain't been no light.
    So boy, don't you turn back.
    Don't yet set down on the steps
    'Cause you finds it's kinder hard.
    Don't you fall now
(20)    For I'se still goin', Honey,
    I'se still climbin'
    And Life for me ain't been no crystal stair.

From Langston Hughes, "Mother to Son" (New York: Alfred A. Knopf, 1926, 1954)

**31.** According to the poem, what does the mother conclude about her life?

    **(1)** She is going to keep trying no matter how difficult it is.

    **(2)** She is going to turn over her struggle to her son.

    **(3)** Her life is too difficult to try to continue.

    **(4)** She is going to make more money from now on.

    **(5)** She has achieved everything she wanted to.

**32.** Based on the mother's statement to her son, you can infer that the son

    **(1)** was determined never to be a quitter

    **(2)** was a failure in his career

    **(3)** was tempted to quit and needed encouragement

    **(4)** had never known defeat

    **(5)** had acquired great wealth

**33.** Which of the following best describes the tone of this poem?

    **(1)** angry

    **(2)** bitter

**(3)** encouraging

**(4)** happy

**(5)** depressed

Items 34 to 36 are based on the following poem.

## HOW DO WORDS AFFECT THE PERSON IN THIS POEM?

He ate and drank the precious
words.
His spirit grew robust;
He knew no more that he was poor,
Nor that his frame was dust.
(5)     He danced along the dingy days,
And this bequest of wings
Was but a book. What liberty
A loosened spirit brings!

From Emily Dickinson, *The Poems of Emily Dickinson*
(Cambridge, Mass.: The Belknap Press of Harvard
University Press, 1951)

**34.** The poem tells us that the person is

**(1)** eating

**(2)** drinking

**(3)** growing

**(4)** flying

**(5)** reading

**35.** What does the first line of the poem imply?

**(1)** The man was poor and hungry.

**(2)** The man had just learned to read.

**(3)** The words were difficult to swallow.

**(4)** The words were like food to a hungry man.

**(5)** The man was reading at the table.

**36.** The tone of this poem is

**(1)** angry

**(2)** joyous

**(3)** somber

**(4)** funny

**(5)** frightened

## Commentary

Items 37 to 41 are based on the following passage.

## WHAT ARE THE EFFECTS OF TELEVISION ON CHILDREN?

Concern about the effects of television on children has centered almost exclusively upon the contents of the programs children
(5)     watch. Social scientists and researchers devise experiments...to determine whether watching violent programs makes children behave more aggressively, or conversely,
(10)    whether watching exemplary programs encourages "prosocial" behavior in children. Studies are conducted to discover whether television commercials make children greedy
(15)    and materialistic or, as some have suggested, generous and spiritual. Investigators seek to discover whether stereotypes on television affect children's ways of thinking,
(20)    causing them to become prejudiced, or open-minded, or whatever....
    Preschool children are the single largest television audience in America, spending a greater number
(25)    of total hours and a greater proportion of their waking day watching television than any other age group. According to one survey made in 1970, children in the 2-5 age group
(30)    spend an average of 30.4 hours each week watching television, while children in the 6-11 group spend 25.5 hours watching. The weekly average for adult viewers in 1971 was 23.3
(35)    hours. Another survey made in 1971 documented a weekly viewing time of 34.56 hours for preschool boys and 32.44 hours for preschool girls. Still other surveys suggest figures up to
(40)    54 hours a week for preschool viewers. Even the most conservative estimates indicate that preschool children in America are spending more than a third of their waking hours

(45) watching television.

What are the effects upon the vulnerable and developing human organism of spending such a significant proportion of each day engaging
(50) in this particular experience? How does the television experience affect a child's language development for instance? How does it influence his developing imagination, his creativi-
(55) ty? How does the availability of television affect the ways parents bring up their children? Are new child-rearing strategies being adopted and old ones discarded because
(60) the television set is available to parents for relief? Is the child's perception of reality subtly altered by steady exposure to television unrealities? How does watching television
(65) for several hours each day affect the child's abilities to form human relationships? What happens to family life as a result of family members' involvement with television?
(70) Though there may never be clearcut and final answers to these questions, the very fact that they are rarely raised, that the experience... is rarely considered, signals the dis-
(75) torted view American parents take of the role of television in their children's lives.

From Marie Winn, *The Plug-In Drug: Television, Children and the Family* (New York: Bantam Books, 1977)

**37.** According to the excerpt, the older television watchers are, the

   **(1)** more television they watch
   **(2)** more susceptible they are to television's influence
   **(3)** less they watch television
   **(4)** less they are affected by television
   **(5)** more they are able to distinguish between good and bad programming

**38.** How might "exemplary programs" encourage "prosocial behavior in children" (lines 10-12)?

   **(1)** by providing good role models for children to follow
   **(2)** by discouraging children from following social norms
   **(3)** by instructing children how to fight authority
   **(4)** by showing common social experiences
   **(5)** by showing the problems of underprivileged children

**39.** Which of the following questions about reading behavior would the author of this passage be most interested in?

   **(1)** What type of book do people most like to read?
   **(2)** What age groups are most likely to read westerns?
   **(3)** How do ghost stories affect people's beliefs in the supernatural?
   **(4)** Do people who read a lot have greater imaginations than people who seldom read?
   **(5)** Do surveys of television-watching influence the producers of television shows to change the content of their programs?

**40.** In the last sentence of the passage (lines 69-76), the author reveals that she thinks American parents

   **(1)** want clear-cut and final answers to questions about television's effect on children
   **(2)** ask important questions about television's effect on children
   **(3)** watch television too much themselves
   **(4)** are rarely considered when television and children are discussed
   **(5)** seldom question the effect of television on their children

**41.** The tone used in the excerpt would be least effective in which of the following?

   **(1)** news report

**(2)** political speech

**(3)** magazine article

**(4)** personal letter

**(5)** sociology textbook

Items 42 to 45 are based on the following passage.

### WHAT DID MARTHA GRAHAM CONTRIBUTE TO DANCE?

Martha Graham, like the Colorado River, seems too small to have changed the face of the world. On stage, magnified by the passion of

(5) her dancing, Graham was a figure as monumental as the tragic heroines she portrayed; in her living room, surrounded by art objects gathered during a lifetime of travel-

(10) ing, she is a tiny, fine-boned woman with a rich, seductive voice and dark eyes deep enough to hold the answers to all the questions in the universe.

(15) The Colorado River required eons in which to carve out the Grand Canyon; Graham has needed only fifty-nine years since making her first independent work of choreogra-

(20) phy to reshape the art of dance. At ninety-one, she ranks with Picasso, Stravinsky, and Joyce as an artist who formed the taste, the vision, and the style of the twentieth centu-

(25) ry—who changed the way we see the world. She not only altered the subject matter of dance, she devised and codified a technique that has become as widely recognized and

(30) used as the academic technique of ballet. She has commissioned major composers and sculptors to provide music and decor for her works; she has invented a complete dance-thea-

(35) ter that, for all its opulence, admits no extraneous elements. Moreover, she has created an image of modern dance that still holds the popular imagination....

(40) "Life today is nervous, sharp, zigzag," she asserted in 1929. "It

often stops in midair. That is what I aim for in my dances." Graham was a rebel then: modern dance was an

(45) angry, young art; ballet was the aging, effete enemy—an adversary to be raged against. The real problem with ballet, the choreographer said recently, was that "back then, it was

(50) pretty terrible ballet; it was face-tious. I had to find something to dance about, and the about was myself and the world around me."

That need set Graham—and a few

(55) of her contemporaries—apart and led to the development of modern dance as a major art form. It is an art invented in the United States and exported to the world—a distinc-

(60) tion shared only with jazz.

Joseph H. Mazo. *Horizon*, October 1985

**42.** According to the excerpt, Graham was innovative because she

**(1)** utilized movements from ballet in modern dance

**(2)** expressed the attitudes of her time in unique movement

**(3)** was the first woman choreographer

**(4)** used fluid movements which were often compared to rivers

**(5)** was the peer of Stravinsky and Picasso

**43.** According to the essay, Graham developed modern dance because she had a need to

**(1)** form the taste of the twentieth century

**(2)** find answers to questions about the universe

**(3)** make dance express her life and her world

**(4)** work with composers and sculptors

**(5)** become a monumental figure in the arts

**44.** Based on the excerpt's description of Graham's style, which of the following types of music would be most appropriate to accompany her choreography?

**(1)** soft rock

**(2)** medieval chants

**(3)** jazz

**(4)** military march

**(5)** heavy metal

**45.** Why is the writer's opening image of the Colorado River effective in conveying Martha Graham's accomplishments?

**(1)** It evokes the fluid movement of Graham's choreography.

**(2)** It introduces a dramatic situation at the beginning of the text.

**(3)** It emphasizes the power and impact of Graham on the dance world.

**(4)** It introduces a note of humor and irony.

**(5)** It provides a scene of "nature" to reflect Graham's "organic" dance philosophy.

Answers are on pages A-70-A-73.

# PRACTICE ITEMS 4:
## Interpreting Literature and the Arts

# Performance Analysis Chart

**Directions:** Circle the number of each item that you got correct on the Practice Items. Count how many items you got correct in each row; count how many items you got correct in each column. Write the number correct per row and column as the numerator in the fraction in the appropriate "Total Correct" box. (The denominators represent the total number of items in the row or column.) Write the grand total correct over the denominator 45 at the lower right corner of the chart. (For example, if you got 40 items correct, write 40 so that the fraction reads 40/45.)

| Item Type | Nonfiction (page 288) | Fiction (page 312) | Drama (page 332) | Poetry (page 354) | Commentary (page 374) | TOTAL CORRECT |
|---|---|---|---|---|---|---|
| Comprehension | 1, 2, 5, 6, 7, 9, 10 | 13, 14, 17, 18, 19, 21, 22 | 25, 28, 29, 30 | 31, 32, 34, 35 | 37, 38, 40, 42, 43, 45 | /28 |
| Application | 3, 8, 11 | 16, 23 | | | 39, 44 | /7 |
| Analysis | 4. 12 | 15, 20, 24 | 26, 27 | 33, 36 | 41 | /10 |
| Total Correct | /12 | /12 | /6 | /6 | /9 | /45 |

*The page numbers in parentheses above the column headings indicate where in this book you can find the beginning of specific instruction about the various types of literature and commentary and about the types of questions you encountered on the Practice Items.*

# PRACTICE ITEMS 5
# Mathematics

**Directions:** Choose the one best answer to each question. Formulas you may need are given on page 401.

## Arithmetic Items

Item 1 is based on the following figure.

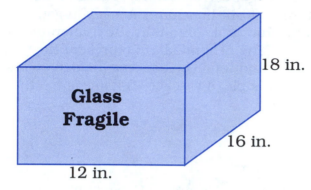

Glass
Fragile

18 in.

16 in.

12 in.

**1.** Which expression represents the volume of this packing box in cubic inches?

(1) 12 + 16 + 18
(2) 2(12 + 16 + 18)
(3) 12(16 + 18)
(4) (12)(16)(18)
(5) (18)(12 + 16)

**2.** Annette earned $12,480 last year. What was her weekly salary?

(1) $ 240.00
(2) $ 249.60
(3) $ 648.96
(4) $1040.00
(5) $3120.00

**3.** A box of Krunch-o-Wheats weighs $1\frac{1}{2}$ pounds. How much does a case containing 24 boxes weigh?

(1) 12 pounds
(2) 16 pounds
(3) $24\frac{1}{2}$ pounds
(4) 25 pounds
(5) 36 pounds

**4.** A grocery store offered eggs on sale for $.79 per dozen, and an additional $.30 saving by use of a coupon from its advertisement. Which of the following expressions would show the cost per egg, including the use of the coupon?

(1) $\frac{.79 - .30}{12}$

(2) $\frac{(.79 - .30)}{12}$

(3) $\frac{.79 + 30}{12}$

(4) $\frac{.79}{12 - .30}$

(5) $\frac{.79}{12}$

**5.** To reach work, Deborah rides the subway, which travels at 35 miles per hour. She rides for 30 minutes and then walks at 4 miles per hour for 20 minutes. Which of the following expressions would show the distance Deborah travels to work?

(1) (35 x 4) x 30
(2) 35/2 + 4
(3) $(35 \times \frac{1}{2}) + (4 \times \frac{1}{3})$
(4) (35 + 4)(30 + 20)
(5) (35 x 30) + (4 x 20)

Items 6 and 7 are based on the following information.

The Herreras bought a sofa for $795, a loveseat for $550, and a chair for $340. Their salesperson earned a 12% commission on this sale.

**6.** How much commission did the salesperson earn on this sale?

**(1)** $ 95.40
**(2)** $140.42
**(3)** $168.50
**(4)** $202.20
**(5)** Insufficient data is given to solve the problem.

**7.** This week the furniture store put the sofa on sale for 20% off. How much would the Herreras have paid if they had bought the sofa, love seat, and chair this week?

**(1)** $ 337
**(2)** $1049
**(3)** $1348
**(4)** $1526
**(5)** $1575

**8.** It takes Laura $\frac{3}{4}$ of an hour to mow her front lawn. What part of her front lawn can she cut in the 20 minutes she has before she must pick up her children from school?

**(1)** $\frac{1}{4}$

**(2)** $\frac{1}{3}$

**(3)** $\frac{4}{9}$

**(4)** $\frac{1}{2}$

**(5)** $\frac{3}{4}$

Item 9 is based on the following figure.

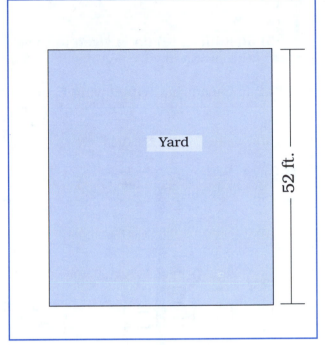

Yard

52 ft.

**9.** Which of the following expressions could you use to find the length of this yard if it has an area of 3328 square feet?

**(1)** $n = 52 \times 3328$
**(2)** $3328n = 52$

**(3)** $n = \frac{52}{3328}$

**(4)** $n = \frac{3328}{52}$

**(5)** Insufficient data is given to solve the problem.

**10.** Joe is buying a van that costs $18,000. If sales tax is 7%, what is the total cost of the van?

**(1)** $ 1,260
**(2)** $16,740
**(3)** $19,260
**(4)** $25,000
**(5)** $30,600

**11.** Anne is sewing skirts for her daughter's choir. If each skirt requires $1\frac{1}{2}$ yards, how many yards of material does she need?

**(1)** $1\frac{1}{2}$

**(2)** $4\frac{1}{2}$

**(3)** 6

**(4)** 15

**(5)** insufficient data is given to solve the problem.

Item 12 is based on the following figure.

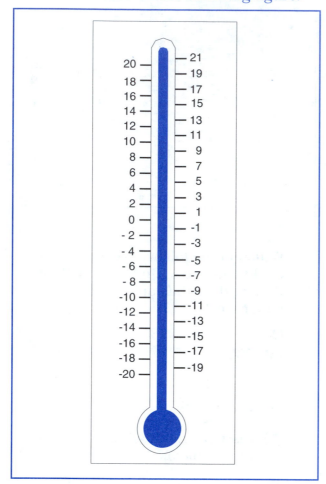

**12.** If the temperature was -10° and it warmed up 5°, to which point on the thermometer would the mercury rise?

**(1)**   5

**(2)** -15

**(3)**   0

**(4)**  -5

**(5)**  10

Item 13 is based on the following figure.

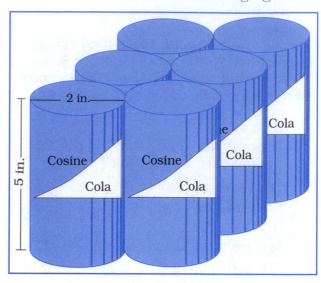

**13.** Which expression represents the volume of a six-pack of Cosine Cola?

**(1)** $6\,(3.14)(1)(5)^2$

**(2)** $6\,(3.14)(1)^2(5)$

**(3)** $6\,(3.14)^2(5)^2$

**(4)** $6\,(3.14)^2 2(5)$

**(5)** $6\,(3.14)(4)^2(5)$

**14.** At the end of a trading day, the prices of these five stocks changed in the following ways.

Stock A $+ \frac{1}{4}$

Stock B $- \frac{1}{2}$

Stock C $- \frac{1}{8}$

Stock D $\quad \frac{7}{8}$

Stock E $+ \frac{3}{4}$

Which of the following sequences correctly lists the changes in stock prices from the greatest to the least?

**(1)** A,B,C,D,E

**(2)** B,C,A,E,D

**(3)** C,B,A,D,E

**(4)** D,E,B,A,C

**(5)** E,B,D,C,A

**15.** Which of the following candy purchases would cost the LEAST: 9 pieces of bubble gum at $.05 each, 13 jelly beans at $.03 each, one candy bar at $.40, or 7 sour balls at $.06 each?

**(1)** bubble gum

**(2)** jelly beans

**(3)** candy bar

**(4)** sour balls

**(5)** Insufficient data is given to solve the problem.

Item 16 is based on the following graph.

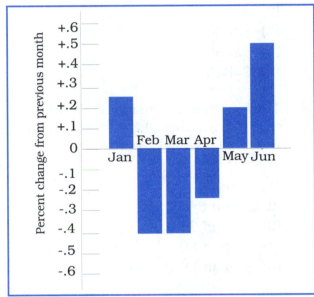

**16.** According to the graph, by about how much more did the Consumer Price Index change from the previous month in June than from the previous month in May?

**(1)** .2%

**(2)** .25%

**(3)** .3%

**(4)** .5%

**(5)** .7%

**17.** When home computers first hit the market, a computer with 4 kilobytes of memory cost $500 and up. Today, a 64-kilobyte computer can be pur-

chased for less than $150. How can the memory of the new computers be expressed in terms of the old memory?

**(1)** $4^1$

**(2)** $4^2$

**(3)** $4^3$

**(4)** $4^4$

**(5)** $4^5$

**18.** Light travels at a speed of $1.86 \times 10^5$ miles per second. How many miles can light travel in a second?

**(1)** 1.86000

**(2)** 186

**(3)** 18,600

**(4)** 186,000

**(5)** 18,600,000

**19.** Earl's Tree-Trimming Service had daily incomes during the first five days of October of $624, $547, $763, $436, and $925. What was Earl's average daily income for this period?

**(1)** $ 624

**(2)** $ 659

**(3)** $ 763

**(4)** $3295

**(5)** Insufficient data is given to solve the problem.

**20.** Helen received a catalog in the mail. It stated that 400 people, picked at random from those sending an order to the company, would win a prize. Which expression shows the probability of Helen's winning a prize if she is one of 2,000,000 people who send an order?

**(1)** $\dfrac{2{,}000{,}000}{400}$

**(2)** $\dfrac{2{,}000{,}000 - 400}{400}$

**(3)** $\dfrac{400}{2{,}000{,}000}$

**(4)** $\dfrac{2{,}000{,}000 - 400}{2{,}000{,}000}$

**(5)** $\dfrac{2{,}000{,}000 = 400}{2{,}000{,}000}$

**21.** Nora borrowed $5000 at 6% simple interest for one year. How much interest will she pay if she repays the loan in 6 months?

(1) $150
(2) $180
(3) $300
(4) $500
(5) $600

**22.** Marcus walks at an average speed of 4 mph for 2 hours every day. What is the total number of miles Marcus walks in one week?

(1) 14
(2) 20
(3) 28
(4) 40
(5) 56

Item 23 is based on the following graph.

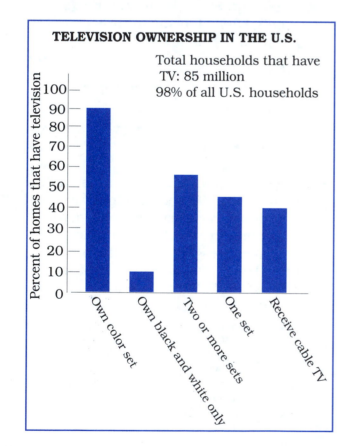

TELEVISION OWNERSHIP IN THE U.S.

Total households that have TV: 85 million
98% of all U.S. households

Percent of homes that have television

Own color set
Own black and white only
Two or more sets
One set
Receive cable TV

**23.** Approximately how many million homes have only one television set?

(1) 8.5
(2) 38.25
(3) 44.1
(4) 76.5
(5) 83.3

**24.** Paula plans to donate 6% of her annual income in equal amounts to her five favorite charities. If Paula earns $24,000 this year, how much will she donate to each charity?

(1) $ 288
(2) $1440
(3) $2000
(4) $2880
(5) $4800

**25.** The length of each side of a square that has an area of 30 square inches is between which two numbers of inches?

(1) 3 and 4
(2) 5 and 6
(3) 29 and 31
(4) 89 and 90
(5) 899 and 901

Item 26 is based on the following graph.

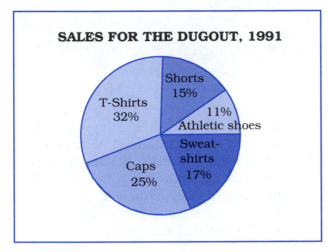

**SALES FOR THE DUGOUT, 1991**

Shorts 15%
T-Shirts 32%
11% Athletic shoes
Sweat-shirts 17%
Caps 25%

26. Approximately how many times as much money did The Dugout make in sales from T-shirts than from athletic shoes?

    (1)   2
    (2)   3
    (3)   11
    (4)   32
    (5)   Insufficient data is given to solve the problem

Item 27 is based on the following table.

| Mon | Tue | Wed | Thu | Fri | Sat |
|-----|-----|-----|-----|-----|-----|
| 84  | 72  | 80  | 93  | 102 | 148 |

27. Which expression shows the mean number of cars serviced daily?

    (1) $84 + 72 + 80 + 93 + 102 + 148 + 6$
    (2) $84 + 72 + 80 + 93 + 102 + 148 - 6$
    (3) $6(84 + 72 + 80 + 93 + 102 + 148)$
    (4) $\dfrac{6}{84 + 72 + 80 + 93 + 102 + 148}$
    (5) $\dfrac{84 + 72 + 80 + 93 + 102 + 148}{6}$

28. Raul bought six 50-pound bags of dog food and three 10-pound bags of puppy chow for his kennel. What was the total amount Raul paid for the pet food?

    (1) $ 48
    (2) $ 60
    (3) $300
    (4) $330
    (5) Insufficient data is given to solve the problem.

29. The Swansons are planning to drive to Florida for their vacation, a distance of 750 miles. If they will average 50 miles per hour, how many hours will it take them to drive this distance?

    (1)   7.5
    (2)   10
    (3)   12
    (4)   15
    (5)   20

## Algebra Items

30. For every $25 that the Shipleys spend for clothing, they spend $45 for entertainment. If the Shipleys spent $4000 for clothing in one year, how much did they spend for entertainment?

    (1) $3600
    (2) $4800
    (3) $5000
    (4) $7200
    (5) $8000

31. A triangular lot has a perimeter of 300 meters. Two sides measure 75 meters and 100 meters. What is the length of the third side in meters?

    (1) 100
    (2) 125
    (3) 175
    (4) 235
    (5) 475

32. Which of the following expressions is equal to $8d - h + 3h + 2d$?

    (1) $7d + 5h$
    (2) $10d + 2h$

**(3)** $10d + 3$

**(4)** $12dh$

**(5)** $12d^2h^2$

33. A movie theater sells adults' tickets for $4.00 and children's tickets for $2.50. If $a$ = the adults' tickets and $c$ = the children's tickets that are sold for a show, which of the following expressions would give the amount of money the theater received?

   **(1)** $4a + 2.5c$

   **(2)** $4a - 2.5c$

   **(3)** $\frac{a}{4} + \frac{c}{25}$

   **(4)** $(a + 4)(c + 2.5)$

   **(5)** $ac(4 + 2.5)$

34. Marcia has $200-deductible automobile insurance. Her insurance company will pay 80% of the amount that she is charged for repairs that exceed $200. If $r$ = the cost of car repairs, which of the following expressions would give the amount of money that the insurance company should pay her?

   **(1)** $.8(r + 200)$

   **(2)** $.8(r - 200)$

   **(3)** $.8r - 200$

   **(4)** $.8r + 200$

   **(5)** Insufficient data is given to solve the problem.

35. Find the value of $s(s - w) + w$, if $s = 7$ and $w = 4$.

   **(1)** 7

   **(2)** 16

   **(3)** 19

   **(4)** 25

   **(5)** 49

36. A restaurant usually charges three times the cost of the ingredients needed to make an item. Which of the following equations could be used to find the cost of the ingredients for an item priced at $4.95?

   **(1)** $3 = 4.95 + c$

   **(2)** $3c = 495$

   **(3)** $\frac{c}{3} = 4.95$

   **(4)** $495 - c = 3$

   **(5)** $\frac{4.95}{3} = c$

37. At a furniture-store sale, a couch can be purchased for half price when a dinette set is purchased at regular price. Which of the following expressions would show the total cost of a dinette set and a couch, if $s$ = the price of the dinette set and $c$ = the regular price of the couch?

   **(1)** $2(s + c)$

   **(2)** $s + 2c$

   **(3)** $\frac{s + c}{2}$

   **(4)** $\frac{s + 2}{c}$

   **(5)** $s + \frac{c}{2}$

38. Angie exercises for one hour every day. She does aerobics for twice as long as she warms up and cools down. How many minutes does she do aerobics each day?

   **(1)** 15

   **(2)** 20

   **(3)** 30

   **(4)** 40

   **(5)** 45

39. The ratio of rye grass seed to bluegrass seed in a bag of grass seed is 9:4. If the bag contains 24 pounds of bluegrass seed, how many pounds does the bag weigh?

   **(1)** 6

   **(2)** 10.7

   **(3)** 30

   **(4)** 54

   **(5)** 78

**40.** As a clothing salesclerk, Beth earns 30% commission on her sales. What were her sales, $s$, the week she earned $480?

(1) $ 686
(2) $1440
(3) $1600
(4) $2080
(5) Insufficient data is given to solve the problem.

**41.** Which of the following values of $k$ is part of the solution set to $3k + 1 < 13$?

(1)  2
(2)  4
(3)  5
(4) 10
(5) 12

**42.** Eric's son weighs 20 pounds less than his daughter. If Eric's son and daughter weigh a total of 70 pounds, how many pounds does Eric's son weigh?

(1)  5
(2) 25
(3) 45
(4) 50
(5) 65

**43.** As a heating company estimator, Juan estimates whether houses can efficiently use the Enermizer II furnace. To estimate, Juan uses the expression $1500 > f > 950$, in which $f$ = the square footage of a house. According to the expression, which of the following houses can use the Enermizer II?

HOUSE DIMENSIONS IN FEET
A   30 x 40
B   35 x 20
C   40 x 42
D   45 x 30
E   40 x 40

(1) A only

(2) B only
(3) A and E
(4) A and D
(5) B and C

**44.** Sarah bought 9 yards of lace trim for $29.61. What did the lace cost per yard?

(1) $2.69
(2) $3.00
(3) $3.29
(4) $9.97
(5) Insufficient data is given to solve the problem.

**45.** Phonograph records are produced in two speeds, 33 and 45 revolutions per minute (RPM). If a song requires 297 revolutions to be played at 33 RPM, which expression represents how many revolutions, r, it would take at 45 RPM?

(1) $r = 297 \times 33$
(2) $r = 297 \times 45$
(3) $r = \frac{297 \times 45}{33}$
(4) $r = \frac{297 \times 33}{45}$
(5) $r = \frac{33 \times 45}{297}$

**46.** Which of the following expressions is equal to $(y + 9)(y - 5)$?

(1) $45y^2$
(2) $y^2 - 4y + 45$
(3) $y^2 + 4y - 45$
(4) $y^2 + 4y + 45$
(5) $y^2 - 4y - 45$

## Geometry Items

Item 47 is based on the following figure.

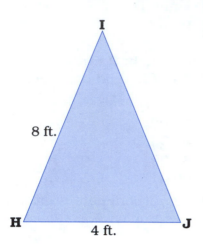

**47.** Triangle HIJ is an isosceles triangle. What is its perimeter in feet?

**(1)** 12
**(2)** 16
**(3)** 20
**(4)** 24
**(5)** Insufficient data is given to solve the problem.

Item 48 is based on the following figure.

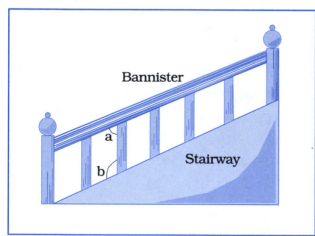

**48.** If the banister is parallel to the stairway and if angle a = 54°, then what must be the measure of angle b?

**(1)** 36°
**(2)** 54°
**(3)** 90°
**(4)** 126°
**(5)** 180°

Item 49 is based on the following figure.

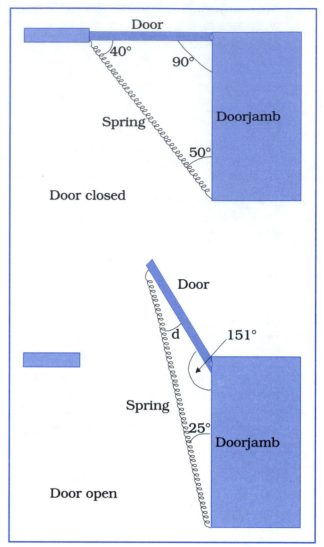

**49.** When the door is open, angle d would measure how many degrees?

**(1)** 4°
**(2)** 10°
**(3)** 14°
**(4)** 20°
**(5)** 25°

Item 50 is based on the following figure.
(side view of house)

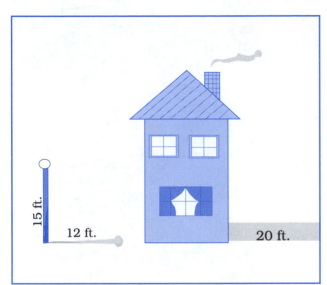

**50.** A homeowner wants to find the height of her house. She knows the lamppost by her driveway is 15 feet tall. When the lamppost casts a shadow that is 12 feet long, the house casts a shadow that is 20 feet long. Which expression can she use to find the height of her house?

**(1)** $\frac{15}{12} = \frac{h}{20}$

**(2)** $\frac{15}{12} = \frac{20}{h}$

**(3)** $\frac{15}{20} = \frac{12}{n}$

**(4)** $\frac{20}{12} = \frac{15}{h}$

**(5)** $\frac{20}{15} = \frac{h}{12}$

Item 51 is based on the following figure.

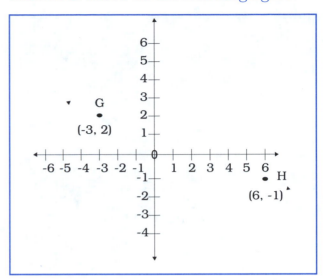

**51.** What is the slope of line GH?

**(1)** $-3$

**(2)** $-\frac{1}{3}$

**(3)** $-\frac{1}{5}$

**(4)** $\frac{1}{3}$

**(5)** $5$

**52.** Pam's round wading pool has a radius of 6 feet. Her parents want to build a round cover that has a 6-inch overlap. What would be the diameter of the cover in feet?

**(1)** $6\frac{1}{2}$

**(2)** $7$

**(3)** $12$

**(4)** $12\frac{1}{2}$

**(5)** $13$

Item 53 is based on the following figure.　　Item 54 is based on the following figure.

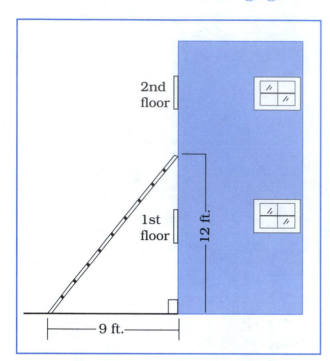

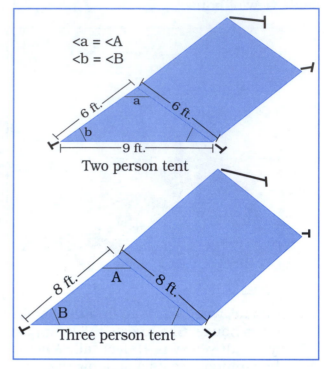

**53.** Merv will use an extension ladder to wash the second-story windows on his house. If he places the base of the ladder 9 feet from the house, how many feet should he extend his ladder?

**(1)** 　9
**(2)** 　12
**(3)** 　15
**(4)** 　21
**(5)** 108

**54.** How many feet wide is the base of the three-person tent?

**(1)** 　6
**(2)** 12
**(3)** 13.5
**(4)** 15.5
**(5)** 18.75

Item 55 is based on the following figure.

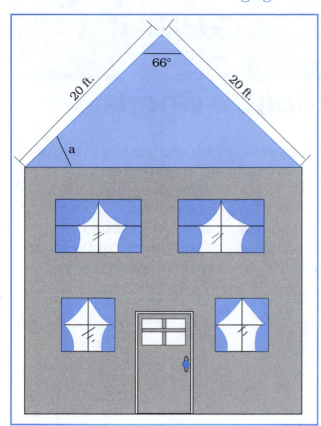

**55.** What is the measurement in degrees of angle *a*?

(1)  12
(2)  33
(3)  46
(4)  57
(5)  66

Item 56 is based on the following figure.

Mt. Burn is due north of Mt Green.
Mt. Blue is due west of Mt. Green.

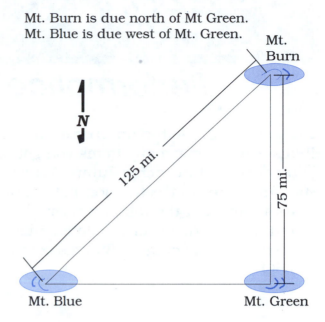

**56.** Using the Pythagorean Theorem, what is the distance in miles from Mt. Green to Mt. Blue?

(1)  $125 + 75$
(2)  $125^2 - 75^2$
(3)  $\sqrt{125 - 75}$
(4)  $\sqrt{125^2 + 75^2}$
(5)  $\sqrt{125^2 - 75^2}$

Answers are on pages A-74-A-77.

# PRACTICE ITEMS 5: MATHEMATICS

## Performance Analysis Chart

**Directions:** Circle the number of each item that you got correct on the Practice Items. Count how many items you got correct in each row; count how many items you got correct in each column. Write the number correct per row and column as the numerator in the fraction in the appropriate "Total Correct" box. (The denominators represent the total number of items in the row or column.) Write the grand total correct over the denominator 56 at the lower right corner of the chart. (For example, if you got 48 items correct, write 48 so that the fraction reads 48/56)

| Item Type | Arithmetic (page 402) | Algebra (page 533) | Geometry (page 554) | TOTAL CORRECT |
|---|---|---|---|---|
| Comprehension (Skills) | 12 | 32, 35 | 48, 49, 55 | /6 |
| Application | 2, 3, 17, 18, 20, 22, 25 | 31, 36, 41, 43, 46 | 47, 51 | /14 |
| Analysis (Problem Solving) | 1, 4, 5, 6, 7, 8, 9, 10, 11, 13, 14, 15, 16, 19, 21, 23, 24, 26, 27, 28, 29, 30 | 33, 34, 37,38, 39, 40,42, 44, 45 | 50. 52, 53, 54, 56 | /36 |
| Total Correct | /30 | /16 | /10 | /56 |

*The page numbers in parentheses above the column headings indicate where in this book you can find the beginning of specific instruction about the areas of grammar and about the types of questions you encountered in the Practice Items.*

**TIME:** 75 minutes

**Directions:** The items in Part I of this test are based on paragraphs that contain numbered sentences. Some of the sentences may contain errors in sentence structure, usage, or mechanics. *A few sentences, however, may be correct as written.* Read each paragraph and then answer the eight to ten items that follow it. For each item, choose the answer that would result in the most effective writing of the sentence or sentences. The best answer must be consistent with the meaning and tone of the rest of the paragraph.

FOR EXAMPLE:

Sentence 1:   **Although it may take only two hours to watch the average motion picture takes almost a year to make.**

What correction should be made to this sentence?

(1) replace *it* with *they*
(2) change *take* to *have taken*
(3) insert a comma after *watch*
(4) change *almost* to *all most*
(5) no change is necessary

The correct answer is (3). In this example, a comma is needed after the clause *Although it may take only two hours to watch.*

Items 1 to 9 are based on the following paragraph

(1) Payment by credit card became a popular substitute for payment with cash or check. (2) It is important to think carefully about your choice and how you use credit cards. (3) Before one applies for a card, find out each company's finance charge. (4) This charge, a portion of the unpaid balance, added to your bill each month. (5) You will be considering different cards. (6) Think about how widely it is accepted. (7) Not every type of credit card is accepted by every store. (8) Some companies give a donation to a certain organization, such as the Sierra club, if you buy their card. (9) Other companys give you credit toward buying specified items every time you use your card. (10) Once you do choose one, put the account number and emergency phone number in a safe place. (11) The card may be lost or stolen. (12) Finally, each time you are tempted to pay with plastic, remember that the convenience does have it's cost.

1. Sentence 1: **Payment by <u>credit card became</u> a popular substitute for payment with cash or check.**

   Which of the following is the best way to write the underlined portion of this sentence? If you think the original is the best way, choose option (1).

   **(1)** credit card became
   **(2)** Credit Card became
   **(3)** credit card, became
   **(4)** credit card become
   **(5)** credit card has become

2. Sentence 2: **It is important  to think carefully about your choice and how you use credit cards.**

   What correction should be made to this sentence?

   **(1)** change the spelling of *carefully* to *carefuly*
   **(2)** insert a comma after *choice*
   **(3)** replace *and* with *or*

   **(4)** replace *how you use* with *use of*
   **(5)** no correction is necessary

3. Sentence 3: **Before one applies for a card, find out each company's finance charge.**

   What correction should be made to this sentence?

   **(1)** replace *one applies* with *you apply*
   **(2)** change *applies* to *applied*
   **(3)** remove the comma after *card*
   **(4)** change *company's* to *Company's*
   **(5)** change the spelling of *company's* to *companies*

4. Sentence 4: **This charge, a portion of the unpaid <u>balance, added</u> to your bill each month.**

   Which of the following is the best way to write the underlined portion of this sentence? If you think the original is the best way, choose option (1).

   **(1)** balance, added
   **(2)** balance added
   **(3)** balance, adding
   **(4)** balance, is added
   **(5)** balance is added

5. Sentence 6: **Think about how widely it is accepted.**

   What correction should be made to this sentence?

   **(1)** replace *accepted* with *excepted*
   **(2)** change *it is* to *each card*
   **(3)** change *it is* to *they were*
   **(4)** insert *it* after *about*
   **(5)** no correction is necessary

6. Sentence 8: **Some companies give a donation to a certain organization, such as the Sierra club, if you buy their card.**

   What correction should be made to this sentence?

**(1)** remove the comma after *organization*

**(2)** change *Sierra* to *sierra*

**(3)** change *club* to *Club*

**(4)** replace *if* with *even if*

**(5)** no correction is necessary

7. Sentence 9: **Other companys give you credit toward buying specified items every time you use your card.**

What correction should be made to this sentence?

**(1)** change the spelling of *specified* to *spesified*

**(2)** change the spelling of *companys* to *companies*

**(3)** insert a comma after *items*

**(4)** change *use* to *used*

**(5)** replace *your card* with *it*

8. Sentences 10 and 11: **Once you do choose one, put the account number and emergency phone number in a safe place. The card may be lost or stolen.**

The most effective combination of sentences 10 and 11 would include which of the following groups of words?

**(1)** choose one, the card

**(2)** the account number because the card

**(3)** in a safe place, so the card

**(4)** in a safe place for the card

**(5)** in a safe place, for the card

9. Sentence 12: **Finally, each time you are tempted to pay with <u>plastic, remember that the convenience does have it's cost.</u>**

Which of the following is the best way to write the underlined portion of this sentence? If you think the original is the best way, choose option (1).

**(1)** plastic, remember that the convenience does have it's cost

**(2)** plastic remember that the convenience does have it's cost

**(3)** plastic, remember that the convenience does have its cost

**(4)** plastic, remembering that the convenience does have its cost

**(5)** plastic, remember that the convenience does have their cost

Items 10 to 17 are based on the following paragraph.

(1) Although it may be inconvenient to write a thank-you note after a job interview, the effort is worth the bother. (2) Many employers say that they are impressed by applicants who take the time to write a note of thanks. (3) These applicants are demonstrating that they have an important job skill, the ability to treat others with consideration. (4) The note that is clear and concise as well as effectively written shows that the writer has good communication skills. (5) By arriving in the mail soon after your meeting, the interviewer is prompted to think about you again. (6) The more he or she think about you, the better your chances. (7) The note can be used such that you emphasize, correct, or add to what you have already said. (8) You can ask questions in the letter to get information you still need. (9) For example, you were told that the job starts right after Memorial Day, but one sees a July starting date listed. (10) Clear up confusion by asking for the correct date in your thank-you note. (11) You received added attention along with your answer. (12) Take a moment to write a thank-you note shortly after you leave a job interview, the effort may get you the job.

10. Sentence 1: **Although it may be inconvenient to write a thank-you note after a job interview, the effort is worth the bother.**

If you rewrote sentence 1 beginning with *It may be inconvenient to write a thank-you note after a job interview,* the next word should be

**(1)** but
**(2)** and
**(3)** or
**(4)** for
**(5)** because

11. Sentence 3: **These applicants are demonstrating that they have an important job skill, the ability to treat others with consideration.**

    What correction should be made to this sentence?

    **(1)** change *are* to *is*
    **(2)** remove the comma after *skill*
    **(3)** change the spelling of *ability* to *abilaty*
    **(4)** change *others* to *other's*
    **(5)** no correction is necessary

12. Sentence 5: **By arriving in the mail soon after your <u>meeting, the interviewer</u> is prompted to think about you again.**

    Which of the following is the best way to write the underlined portion of this sentence? If you think the original is the best way, choose option (1).

    **(1)** meeting, the interviewer is prompted
    **(2)** meeting the interviewer is prompted
    **(3)** meeting, the interviewer, is prompted
    **(4)** meeting, the thank-you note prompts the interviewer
    **(5)** meeting, thoughts about you are prompted

13. Sentence 6: **The more <u>he or she think about you,</u> the better your chances.**

    Which of the following is the best way to write the underlined portion of this sentence? If you think the original is the best way, choose option (1).

    **(1)** he or she think about you

**(2)** he, or she think about you
**(3)** he or she thinks about you
**(4)** they think about you
**(5)** they thought about you

14. Sentence 7: **The note can be used such that you emphasize, correct, or add to what you have already said.**

    What correction should be made to this sentence?

    **(1)** replace *such that you* with *to*
    **(2)** change the spelling of *emphasize* to *emphisize*
    **(3)** remove the comma after *emphasize*
    **(4)** change *add* to *adding*
    **(5)** replace *you have* with *one has*

15. Sentence 9: **For example, you were told that the job starts right after Memorial Day, but one sees a July starting date listed.**

    What correction should be made to this sentence?

    **(1)** change *Day* to *day*
    **(2)** remove the comma after *example*
    **(3)** change the spelling of *perhaps* to *purhaps*
    **(4)** replace *one sees* with *you see*
    **(5)** change *July* to *july*

16. Sentence 11: **You received added attention along with your answer.**

    What correction should be made to this sentence?

    **(1)** change the spelling of *received* to *recieved*
    **(2)** change *received* to *will receive*
    **(3)** insert a comma after *attention*
    **(4)** change *your* to *you're*
    **(5)** change the spelling of *answer* to *anser*

17. Sentence 12: **Take a moment to write a thank-you note shortly after you leave a job interview, the effect may get you the job.**

What correction should be made to this sentence?

**(1)** insert a comma after *note*

**(2)** change *leave* to *left*

**(3)** replace *interview, the* with *interview. The*

**(4)** replace *the* with *so this*

**(5)** no correction is necessary

Items 18 to 25 are based on the following paragraph.

(1) The Internal Revenue Service, like other agencies handling a lot of information, uses computers widely. (2) It all starts with the income tax return you are supposed to put in the mail by the deadline in April its destination depends on your location. (3) For instance, if you live in New York city, you send your return to Holtsville, New York. (4) Workers at the Internal Revenue Servise Center type information from your return into a computer, which checks your addition and subtraction. (5) The computer then searches a data base, a computerized library, for storing large amounts of information. (6) There are many kinds of information in the data base about each American citizen. (7) For example, your bank sends information to the IRS about interest you make on your savings account. (8) Your employer sends salary information, and information about your car registration is sent by the Department of Motor Vehicles. (9) The computer looks through the data base. (10) It searches for information that should be reported on your tax forms. (11) If you have reported your earnings correctly, either your payment check or a refund check.

**18.** Sentence 1: **The Internal Revenue Service, like other agencies handling a lot of information, uses computers widely.**

What correction should be made to this sentence?

**(1)** change the spelling of *Service* to *Servise*

**(2)** change *Service* to *service*

**(3)** change the spelling of *a lot* to *alot*

**(4)** change *uses* to *use*

**(5)** no correction is necessary

**19.** Sentence 2: **It all starts with the income tax return you are supposed to put in the mail by the deadline in April its destination depends on your location.**

What correction should be made to this sentence?

**(1)** change *starts* to *start*

**(2)** change *April* to *april*

**(3)** insert a comma after *April*

**(4)** change *April its* to *April. Its*

**(5)** change *its* to *it's*

**20.** Sentence 3: **For instance, if you live in New York city, you send your return to Holtsville, New York.**

What correction should be made to this sentence?

**(1)** remove the comma after *instance*

**(2)** replace *you live* with *one lives*

**(3)** change *city* to *City*

**(4)** change *send* to *sent*

**(5)** replace *your return* with *them*

**21.** Sentence 4: **Workers at the Internal Revenue Servise Center type information from your return into a computer, which checks your addition and subtraction.**

What correction should be made to this sentence?

**(1)** change the spelling of *Servise* to *Service*

**(2)** change *Center* to *center*

**(3)** remove the comma after *computer*

**(4)** replace *which* with *who*

**(5)** change *checks* to *checked*

**22.** Sentence 5: **The computer then searches a data base, a computerized library, for storing large amounts of information.**

What correction should be made to this sentence?

**(1)** change *searches* to *searched*

**(2)** remove the comma after *library*

**(3)** replace *data base, a* with *data base A*

**(4)** change the spelling of *amounts* to *amountes*

**(5)** put a comma after *then*

**23.** Sentence 8: **Your employer sends salary information, and <u>information about your car registration is sent by the Department of Motor Vehicles.</u>**

Which of the following is the best way to write the underlined portion of this sentence? If you think the original is the best way, choose option (1).

**(1)** information about your car registration is sent by the Department of Motor Vehicles

**(2)** the Department of Motor Vehicles sends car registration information

**(3)** information about your car registration, by the Department of Motor Vehicles

**(4)** They know about your car registration from the Department of Motor Vehicles

**(5)** it is sent by the Department of Motor Vehicles, about your car

**24.** Sentences 9 and 10: **The computer looks through the data base. It searches for information that should be reported on your tax forms.**

The most effective combination of sentences 9 and 10 would include which of the following groups of words?

**(1)** It looks through the data base, and

**(2)** The computer searches the data base for information

**(3)** and it searches for information

**(4)** or it searches for information

**(5)** The information that should be reported

**25.** Sentence 11: **If you have reported your earnings correctly, either your payment check <u>or a refund check.</u>**

Which of the following is the best way to write the underlined portion of this sentence? If you think the original is the best way, choose option (1).

**(1)** or a refund check.

**(2)** nor a refund check.

**(3)** or a check is refunded.

**(4)** or a refund check is processed.

**(5)** or a refund check are processed.

Items 26 to 33 are based on the following paragraph.

(1) More people than ever are interested in higher education. (2) The number of people taking the GED Tests has risen. (3) An unfortunate result, has been the increase in diploma mills offering worthless degrees. (4) The American Council on Education reporting that there are now several hundred of these phony schools in existence. (5) Many advertised in well-known magazines and newspapers. (6) You can avoid wasting time, energy, and money on a useless degree. (7) Watch out for any school whose address changes frequently. (8) Beware if catalogs do'nt mention facilities such as libraries and laboratories. (9) Catalogs should describe degree requirements, they shouldn't stress the appearance of diplomas. (10) Neither you nor anyone else need to remain in doubt about the quality of a program. (11) To find out whether a school has official accreditation, write to the American Council on Education, One Dupont Circle, N.W., Washington, D.C. 20036.

**26.** Sentences 1 and 2: **More people than ever are interested in higher education. The number of people taking the GED Tests has risen.**

The most effective combination of sentences 1 and 2 would include which of the following groups of words?

(1) education, the number
(2) education because the number
(3) education, as a result, the number
(4) education; as a result, the number
(5) education; in addition, the number

27. Sentence 3: **An unfortunate result, has been the increase in diploma mills offering worthless degrees.**

What correction should be made to this sentence?

(1) remove the comma after *result*
(2) change *has* to *have*
(3) change the spelling of *increase* to *increse*
(4) insert a comma after *mills*
(5) replace *offering* with *who offer*

28. Sentence 4: **The American Council on Education reporting that there are now several hundred of these phony schools in existence.**

What correction should be made to this sentence?

(1) change *American* to *american*
(2) replace *reporting* with *reports*
(3) replace *there* with *they're*
(4) change *are* to *is*
(5) change the spelling of *existence* to *existance*

29. Sentence 5: **Many advertised in well-known magazines and newspapers.**

Which of the following is the best way to write the underlined portion of this sentence? If you think the original is the best way, choose option (1).

(1) advertised in well-known magazines
(2) advertised in magazines that are well-known
(3) advertising in well-known magazines

(4) advertise in well-known magazines
(5) advertises in well-known magazines

30. Sentence 8: **Beware if catalogs do'nt mention facilities such as libraries and laboratories.**

What correction should be made to this sentence?

(1) replace *do'nt* with *don't*
(2) change *mention* to *mentioned*
(3) change the spelling of *facilities* to *fasilities*
(4) insert a comma after *facilities*
(5) change the spelling of *laboratories* to *labratories*

31. Sentence 9: **Catalogs should describe degree requirements, they shouldn't stress the appearance of diplomas.**

Which of the following is the best way to write the underlined portion of this sentence? If you think the original is the best way, choose option (1).

(1) requirements, they
(2) requirements they
(3) requirements; they
(4) requirements, so they
(5) requirements, because they

32. Sentence 10: **Neither you nor anyone else need to remain in doubt about the quality of a program.**

What correction should be made to this sentence?

(1) insert a comma after *you*
(2) replace *nor* with *or*
(3) change *need* to *needs*
(4) change the spelling of *doubt* to *doute*
(5) no correction is necessary

33. Sentence 11: **To find out whether a school has official accreditation,**

write to the American Council on Education, One Dupont Circle, N.W., Washington, D.C. 20036

What correction should be made to this sentence?

**(1)** remove the comma after *accreditation*

**(2)** change the spelling of *Council* to *Counsel*

**(3)** change *Circle* to *circle*

**(4)** replace *write* with *a letter should be written*

**(5)** no correction is necessary

Items 34 to 41 are based on the following paragraph.

(1) Job hunting is something what you will probably do more than once. (2) Either because they choose to change jobs, or because it is a necessity, many workers change jobs. (3) Since most of today's new jobs are created in the service industries many job hunters will find service job openings. (4) Service jobs included a wide range of positions, from nursing aides to stockbrokers. (5) Although it may be fairly easy to get a service job, it is often difficult to find career ladders. (6) Career ladders are steps for working up to higher wages. (7) Some service jobs, such as industry positions for Nurses and cafeteria workers, pay fairly well from the start. (8) The problem with these jobs, however, are that they are disappearing. (9) Because of financial problems many American companies are having, not only factory workers but also the employees who serve them are losing their jobs. (10) Many job hunters are attempting to get jobs in the growing field of technology. (11) You may be among those who are taking classes to prepare for the level of reading and writing skills such jobs demand. (12) Time spent in such classes is time well spent; even if this is one's first job hunt, it probably will not be your last.

**34.** Sentence 1: **Job hunting is something what you will probably do more than once.**

What correction should be made to this sentence?

**(1)** replace *what* with *that*

**(2)** change *do* to *done*

**(3)** insert a comma after *do*

**(4)** replace *than* with *then*

**(5)** change the spelling of *once* to *ones*

**35.** Sentence 2: **Either because they choose to change jobs, or because it is a necessity, many workers change jobs.**

If you rewrote sentence 2 beginning with *Many workers change jobs, either by* the next words should be

**(1)** their choice

**(2)** choosing to change

**(3)** choice or

**(4)** changing choices

**(5)** necessary change

**36.** Sentence 3: **Since most of today's new jobs are created in the service industries many job hunters will find service job openings.**

Which of the following is the best way to write the underlined portion of this sentence? If you think the original is the best way, choose option (1).

**(1)** industries many job hunters will find

**(2)** industries. Many job hunters will find

**(3)** industries; many job hunters will find

**(4)** industries, many job hunters will find

**(5)** industries many job hunters found

**37.** Sentence 4: **Service jobs <u>included a wide range of positions, from</u> nursing aides to stockbrokers.**

Which of the following is the best way to write the underlined portion of this sentence? If you think the original is the best way, choose option (1).

**(1)** included a wide range of positions, from

**(2)** included a wide range of positions from

**(3)** including a wide range of positions, from

**(4)** included a wide range of positions; from

**(5)** include a wide range of positions, from

**38.** Sentences 5 and 6: **Although it may be fairly easy to get a service job, it is often difficult to find career ladders. Career ladders are steps for working up to higher wages.**

The most effective combination of sentences 5 and 6 would include which of the following groups of words?

**(1)** service jobs, steps

**(2)** career ladders, steps

**(3)** difficulty in finding steps

**(4)** find career ladders that are steps

**(5)** and career ladders are steps

**39.** Sentence 7: **Some service jobs, such as industry positions for Nurses and cafeteria workers, pay fairly well from the start.**

What correction should be made to this sentence?

**(1)** remove the comma after *jobs*

**(2)** change *Nurses* to *nurses*

**(3)** change the spelling of *cafeteria* to *cafateria*

**(4)** change *pay* to *pays*

**(5)** no correction is necessary

**40.** Sentence 8: **The problem with these jobs, however, are that they are disappearing.**

What correction should be made to this sentence?

**(1)** remove the comma after *jobs*

**(2)** change *are that* to *is that*

**(3)** replace *that* with *because*

**(4)** change *are disappearing* to *had disappeared*

**(5)** change the spelling of *disappearing* to *disapearring*

**41.** Sentence 12: **Time spent in such classes is time well <u>spent; even if this is one's</u> first job hunt, it probably will not be your last.**

Which of the following is the best way to write the underlined portion of this sentence? If you think the original is the best way, choose option (1).

**(1)** spent; even if this is one's

**(2)** spent even if this is one's

**(3)** spent, even if this is one's

**(4)** spent. Even if this is one's

**(5)** spent; even if this is your

Items 42 to 48 are based on the following paragraph.

(1) Computers are increasingly being used in the practice of medicine. (2) When doctors work with computers, they are less likely to forget important details. (3) To prepare for a patient's visit physicians can have computers retrieve patient records from a data base, or information storehouse. (4) Mr. Jones, for example, may have an appointment with dr. Smith for a routine blood pressure check. (5) Dr. Smith can get a computer report of relevant information about Mr. Jones, such as medications he takes and his recent blood pressure readings. (6) Another patient may make an unscheduled visit to see the doctor because a problem that has just developed. (7) The computer can scan thousands of patients' records for infor-

mation about people with similar symptoms. (8) No longer does doctors have to look through pages and pages of records for the information they need. (9) No longer do they need to rely on their own experience with a limited number of patients when making a decision about treatment. (10) Doctors can use computers to provide improved health care in many ways, and just one of these is putting medical records into data bases.

**42.** Sentence 2: **When doctors work with computers, they are less likely to forget important details.**

Which of the following is the best way to write the underlined portion of this sentence? If you think the original is the best way, choose option (1).

(1) computers, they are
(2) computers they are
(3) computers, it is
(4) computers; they are
(5) computers; it is

**43.** Sentence 3: **To prepare for a patient's visit physicians can have computers retrieve patient records from a data base, or information storehouse.**

What correction should be made to this sentence?

(1) replace *patient's* with *patience*
(2) insert a comma after *visit*
(3) replace *can have* with *had*
(4) replace *computers* with *them*
(5) change *retrieve* to *retrieving*

**44.** Sentence 4: **Mr. Jones, for example, may have an appointment with dr. Smith for a routine blood pressure check.**

What correction should be made to this sentence?

(1) remove the comma after *Jones*
(2) remove *may*
(3) replace *may have* with *had*
(4) change *dr.* to *Dr.*
(5) insert a comma after *Smith*

**45.** Sentence 6: **Another patient may make an unscheduled visit to see the doctor because a problem that has just developed.**

Which of the following is the best way to write the underlined portion of this sentence? If you think the original is the best way, choose option (1).

(1) doctor because a problem that
(2) doctor, because a problem that
(3) doctor because of a problem that
(4) doctor, because of a problem that
(5) doctor, about a problem that

**46.** Sentence 7: **The computer can scan thousands of patients' records for information about people with similar symptoms.**

What correction should be made to this sentence?

(1) change *patients'* to *patient's*
(2) replace *records for* with *records; for*
(3) replace *information about* with *information. There are*
(4) change the spelling of *similar* to *similer*
(5) no correction is necessary

47. Sentence 8: **No longer does doctors have to look through pages and pages of records for the information they need.**

What correction should be made to this sentence?

(1) change *does* to *do*
(2) change *doctors* to *Doctors*
(3) replace *through* with *threw*
(4) change *they need* to *one needs*
(5) no correction is necessary

48. Sentence 10: **Doctors can use computers to provide improved health care in many ways, and just one of these is putting medical records into data bases.**

If you rewrote sentence 10 beginning with *Putting medical records into data bases is just one of* the next words should be

(1) many ways
(2) these computers
(3) the computers
(4) the doctors
(5) the records

Items 49 to 55 are based on the following paragraphs.

(1) In the years since the civil rights movement of the 1960s, some signs have suggested progress toward racial equality. (2) However, African Americans continue to face racism and discrimination. (3) In 1988, a study found that banks make it harder for blacks to get home mortgages, even if they were successful members of the middle class.(4) Another study showed that black business owners had greater difficulty in getting loans to help them expand.

(5) Many of the African American leaders which once championed desegregation and voting rights have turned to economic goals. (6) The National Association for the Advancement of Colored People (NAACP) has a special program called "fair share."

(7) Under this program, the NAACP negotiates with major companies to increase minority hiring and the use of minority contractors. (8) What worries civil rights leaders most is the increasing gap between the black middle class and the black "underclass." (9) As more blacks have gone to college, the percentage of blacks in professional, technical, and managerial jobs has rose sharply. (10) Yet more than 30% of black families, including 45% of black children remain below the poverty line. (11) Also, the median family income of blacks today is between 50 and 60% of the income of the median family of whites.

49. Sentence 1: **In the years since the civil rights movement of the 1960s, some signs have suggested progress toward racial equality.**

Which of the following is the best way to write the underlined portion of this sentence? If you think the original is the best way, choose option (1).

(1) 1960s, some signs have suggested
(2) 1960s some signs have suggested
(3) 1960's some signs have suggested
(4) 1960s, some signs suggested
(5) 1960s some signs suggested

50. Sentence 3: **In 1988, a study found that banks make it harder for blacks to get home mortgages, even if they were successful members of the middle class.**

What correction should be made to this sentence?

(1) change *were* to *are*
(2) change the spelling of *successful* to *sucessful*
(3) insert *more* before *harder*
(4) change *make* to *made*
(5) no correction is necessary

**51.** Sentence 5: **Many of the <u>African American leaders which once</u> championed desegregation and voting rights have turned to economic goals.**

Which of the following is the best way to write the underlined portion of this sentence? If you think the original is the best way, choose option (1).

**(1)** African American leaders which once championed

**(2)** African American leaders which once champion

**(3)** African-american leaders who once championed

**(4)** African American leaders who once championed

**(5)** African American leaders who once have championed

**52.** Sentence 6: **The National Association for the Advancement of Colored People (NAACP) has a special program called "fair share."**

What correction should be made to this sentence?

**(1)** change *has* to *had*

**(2)** change *NAACP* to *Naacp*

**(3)** change *"fair share"* to *"Fair Share"*

**(4)** change *"fair share"* to *"Fare Share"*

**(5)** no correction is necessary

**53.** Sentence 8: **What worries civil rights leaders most is the increasing gap between the black middle class and the black "underclass."**

If you rewrote sentence 8 beginning with The increasing gap between the black middle class and black "underclass" the next words should be

**(1)** are what worries

**(2)** are what gives

**(3)** will be a worry of

**(4)** has worried

**(5)** is what worries

**54.** Sentence 9: **As more blacks have gone to college, the percentage of blacks in professional, technical, and managerial jobs has rose sharply.**

What correction should be made to this sentence?

**(1)** change *rose* to *risen*

**(2)** remove the comma after *college*

**(3)** change *has* to *have*

**(4)** change *gone* to *went*

**(5)** no correction is necessary

**55.** Sentence 10: **Yet more than 30% of black <u>families, including 45% of black children remain</u> below the poverty line.**

Which of the following is the best way to write the underlined portion of the sentence? If you think that the original is the best way, choose option (1).

**(1)** families, including 45% of black children remain

**(2)** familiys, including 45% of black children remain

**(3)** families including 45% of the black children, remain

**(4)** families, including 45% of black children, remain

**(5)** families including 45% of black childrens remain

Answers are on pages A-78-A-80.

**TIME:** 45 minutes

**Directions:** This is a test to see how well you can write. In this test, you are asked to write an essay in which you present your opinions about an issue. In preparing your essay, you should take the following steps.

**Step 1.** Read all the information about the topic. Be sure that you understand the topic and that you write about only the assigned topic.

**Step 2.** Plan your essay before you write.

**Step 3.** Use scrap paper to make any notes.

**Step 4.** Write your essay on a separate sheet of paper.

**Step 5.** Read what you have written. Make sure that your writing is legible.

**Step 6.** Check your paragraphing, sentence structure, spelling, punctuation, capitalization, and usage; make any changes that will improve your essay.

**TOPIC**

> Technology has been responsible for many changes in how we live our lives, including changes in how we spend our free time. Think about how you spend your free time.
>
> Write an essay, approximately 200 words long, explaining how technology has affected the way you spend your free time. Be specific and use examples to support your explanation.

**When you take the GED test, you will have 45 minutes to write about the topic question you are assigned. Try to write the essay for this unit test within 45 minutes. Write legibly and use a ballpoint pen so that your writing will be easy to read. Any notes that you make on scrap paper will not be counted as part of your score.after you complete this essay, you can judge its effectiveness by using the Essay Scoring Guide and Model Essays in the answer key to score your essay. They will be concerned with how clearly you make the main point of your essay, how thoroughly you support your ideas, and how clear and correct your writing is throughout the composition. You will receive no credit for writing about a question other than the one assigned.**

**TIME:** 85 minutes
**Directions:** Choose the one best answer for each question.

Items 1 and 2 are based on the following paragraph.

The impact of the Western frontier on American life has been subject to considerable debate among historians. Frederick Jackson Turner claimed that 19th-century westerners contributed qualities such as nationalism, resourcefulness, and individualism to American society. Turner argued that the westerner had to think and act in innovative, radically different ways, in order to meet the new and challenging conditions of the frontier. Many modern historians disagree with these claims, maintaining that the West was essentially conservative and simply sought to achieve the eastern goals of prosperity and success through access to open lands.

1. Which of the following developments associated with the West best supports Turner's thesis?

   (1) community barn-raising and land-clearing enterprises
   (2) disputes between farmers and cattlemen over land enclosure
   (3) the Midwest inventions of barbed wire, the steel plow, and the reaper
   (4) the rise of the Grange and other farm organizations
   (5) the national government's great giveaways of land to railroads

2. All of the following statements are likely explanations of why westerners were more nationalistic than easterners EXCEPT:

   (1) As recent arrivals on an ever-moving frontier, westerners lacked their own local traditions and therefore tended to give their loyalty to Washington.
   (2) People in the West needed U.S.-government-sponsored improvements in transportation for access to eastern markets.
   (3) Westerners were dependent on the national government for protection from Indians.
   (4) Westerners distrusted the eastern establishment and its control of the financial and political centers of power.
   (5) From their interior position, westerners were insulated from and resented European ideas and influences.

Item 3 is based on the following graph.

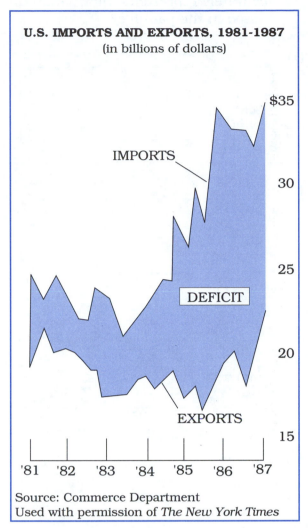

**U.S. IMPORTS AND EXPORTS, 1981-1987**
(in billions of dollars)

IMPORTS

$35

30

DEFICIT

25

20

EXPORTS

15

'81  '82  '83  '84  '85  '86  '87

Source: Commerce Department
Used with permission of *The New York Times*

3. Which of the following generalizations is supported by information provided in the graph?

(1) Imports tend to increase when exports decrease.

(2) A trade deficit exists when imports increase.

(3) A trade deficit exists when imports decrease.

(4) A trade deficit increases when the gap between imports and exports widens.

(5) A trade deficit occurs if there is a difference in value between exports and imports.

Item 4 is based on the following paragraph.

*Ethnocentrism* is the tendency of people to view their culture as superior to other cultures. Often ethnocentrism simply reflects people's positive feelings about their own culture. It can, however, be the basis for an aggressive and militaristic national policy toward other nations or cultures.

4. In which of the following American policies did ethnocentrism play a central role?

(1) **Good Neighbor Policy**—a policy of nonintervention in Latin America, based on the view that Latin Americans should settle their own affairs

(2) **Open Door Policy**—a policy according to which all nations would be assured equal trading rights in China, based on the view that open trade would bring greater profits to all

(3) **Manifest Destiny**—a policy of westward expansion, based on the view that the United States had a mandate to carry its civilizing influence across the continent

(4) **Truman Doctrine**—a commitment to lend economic and military assistance to countries threatened by totalitarian regimes, based on the idea that such aid could help these countries preserve their freedom

(5) **Monroe Doctrine**—a policy to keep out of European affairs and to keep Europeans out of the affairs of North and South America, based on the desire to keep Europe from further colonization of the Americas

Items 5 to 7 are based on the following passage.

Pollsters have been assessing Americans' feelings about public issues for some time. For example, the Harris Survey has been measuring the sense of "alienation," or powerlessness, since the 1960s. The pollsters define this indicator as the feeling that there are two systems of justice—one for those who are insiders in Washington, Wall Street, and corporate America, and another for ordinary citizens.

The results of these polls are troubling. In 1966, 29 percent of Americans felt alienated. From 1966 through 1972, the percentage of people who had this feeling rose steadily. In 1973, in the wake of the Watergate disclosures, a solid majority had a sense of powerlessness. In the years since, the alienation index has only once dropped below 50 percent of those polled and has reached as high as 65 percent.

Some analysts believe that the strong feeling of alienation indicates the remoteness individuals feel from the decision-making processes in the major institutions that affect their lives.

5. Which of the following statements best summarizes the main idea of the passage?

   (1) Pollsters have traced changes in the feeling of alienation.
   (2) Watergate was a key event in that it solidified high levels of alienation.
   (3) "Alienation" refers to the feeling that the ordinary citizen is powerless and receives different treatment from those who are in power.
   (4) In recent decades, the feeling of alienation has become widespread among Americans.
   (5) Alienation may, in the final analysis, be related to a feeling of remoteness from decision-making processes.

6. Which of the following figures most accurately represents information discussed in the passage?

(1)
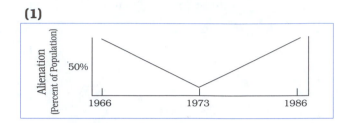

(2)
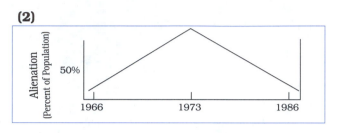

(5)
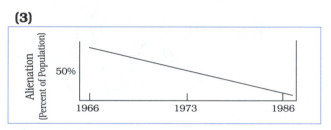

(1)

(4)
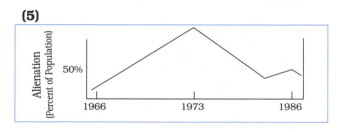

7. Which of the following steps would be most likely to contribute to the resolution of the problem discussed in the passage?

   (1) establishing a high-level commission to investigate wrongdoing in the business and financial communities

**(2)** attempting to get more of the public to vote

**(3)** establishing a regular forum in which citizens can speak directly with government leaders

**(4)** encouraging greater press coverage of inside events concerning Washington and Wall Street

**(5)** including more civics content in elementary and high school curricula

Item 8 is based on the following paragraph.

During Jefferson's administration the government employed 2,120 people in its various departments. Today, there are approximately five million employees working in about 2,000 departments, bureaus, agencies, government corporations, and commissions. In his study of bureaucracy, political scientist Herbert Kaufman traced 175 agencies for a 50-year period ending in 1973. He found that all but 27 of these agencies had survived and that 246 new agencies had been added to work in the same fields.

**8.** Which of the following statements about government bureaucracy is best supported by the passage?

**(1)** By and large the bureaucracy is efficiently organized and operated.

**(2)** The bureaucracy is in no way affected by political shifts the nation undergoes.

**(3)** The eventual need for a larger bureaucracy was foreseen by the founding fathers.

**(4)** As government has assumed more responsibility, government has become more bureaucratized.

**(5)** Division of labor and specialization of function are methods government bureaucrats tend to ignore.

Item 9 is based on the following passage.

On March 25, 1911, just before quitting time, wisps of smoke were the first warning of a terrible fire at the Triangle Shirtwaist Factory in New York City. The fire broke out in the lofts, where the cloth was stored. As the fire swept through the lint-filled air to the eighth- and ninth-floor sewing rooms, panic spread. Within moments, the upper stories were a raging inferno. Five hundred workers, most of them young immigrant women, raced for the exits.

Some exit doors were locked shut. The bosses wanted to keep the seamstresses in and union organizers out. Some of the doors opened only inward, in direct violation of the fire code. The stampede of terrified workers ran headlong into the doors, sealing them with the weight of their bodies. Elevators broke down. All but one of the fire escapes collapsed from the heat.

Firefighters arrived within minutes, but their ladders were too short to reach the top stories. Desperate women, their hair ablaze, threw themselves from windows rather than be burned alive.

**9.** From the passage it can be concluded that the Triangle Shirtwaist Factory tragedy, in which nearly 150 workers died, was mainly caused by

**(1)** a lack of modern firefighting equipment

**(2)** unsafe working conditions

**(3)** the bosses, who locked exit doors to keep organizers out

**(4)** the owner of the factory, who wanted to collect insurance money

**(5)** the panic of the immigrant workers

Items 10 to 12 are based on the following paragraph.

The Electoral College system is the result of a compromise worked out at the Constitutional Convention. Many delegates felt a matter as important as the election of the president should be put in the hands of Congress. However, there was also fear that this would result in congressional domination of the president. Thus, the Electoral College system was devised. Under this system, states are granted a number of electors proportionate to their representation in Congress, adjusted every ten years to take population shifts into account. Initially, electors were often chosen by state legislatures. Today, of course, they are chosen by the voters and are pledged to support a certain candidate. A candidate either wins all the state's electoral votes or none. When the Electoral College meets, if no candidate receives a majority of the electoral vote, the election is thrown into the House of Representative.

10. Which of the following statements is supported by the passage?

(1) Small states often have a more important role than big states in the election of a president.

(2) Voting in the Electoral College is weighted in favor of the 13 original states.

(3) Well-populated states have more influence than sparsely populated states in the Electoral College.

(4) Agricultural states are more important than industrial states in presidential elections.

(5) Each of the 50 states is given equal weight in the Electoral College.

11. Which of the following offers the best summary description of the Electoral College system?

(1) secret balloting
(2) popular voting
(3) convention balloting
(4) primary elections
(5) indirect election

12. Based on the passage, which of the following statements is the most likely reason for our having an Electoral College instead of having popular elections in which the people vote directly for their favorite candidate?

(1) In early presidential elections, a property qualification reduced the number of eligible voters.

(2) The framers feared too much democracy.

(3) The president and Congress were to be elected at the same time.

(4) A two-party system was not anticipated when the Constitution was written.

(5) State legislatures were empowered to elect senators.

Item 13 is based on the following paragraph.

In today's world, innovation—finding different and better ways to do things—may be necessary in order to compete successfully and to generate sales in new markets. The United States leads the world in innovations, but it seems to be losing ground to Japan and to West Germany. One indicator of the problem is the number of patents applied for. In 1971 there were 56,000 applications for U.S. patents; in 1983 there were only 33,000, and an increasingly larger share of the applications were made by foreign interests.

13. Based on the passage, the United States may lose some of its share of world markets unless it takes which of the following steps?

(1) denies foreign interests the right to secure U.S. patents

(2) expands sales and promotion efforts in the U.S.

(3) invests more money in research and development

(4) reduces patent fees

(5) models its economic system more closely on those of West Germany and Japan

Items 14 and 15 are based on the following map.

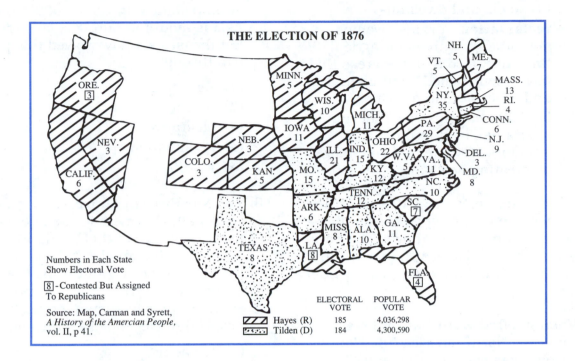

THE ELECTION OF 1876

Numbers in Each State
Show Electoral Vote

⑧ - Contested But Assigned
To Republicans

Source: Map, Carman and Syrett,
*A History of the Amercian People,*
vol. II, p 41.

| | ELECTORAL VOTE | POPULAR VOTE |
|---|---|---|
| Hayes (R) | 185 | 4,036,298 |
| Tilden (D) | 184 | 4,300,590 |

**14.** Which of the following statements summarizes the information presented in the map?

**(1)** Third-party candidates played a role in the election of 1876.

**(2)** The popular vote and the electoral vote were both won by the same candidate.

**(3)** Tilden's support was based mainly in Northern states.

**(4)** Hayes won the popular vote by only a narrow margin.

**(5)** The popular vote and the electoral vote were not won by the same candidate.

**15.** Which of the following statements best explains the election results displayed on the map?

**(1)** Although the election was close, the outcome was clear.

**(2)** Hayes won because he was assigned all the contested states.

**(3)** The balance of power in the election was held by U.S. territories.

**(4)** The American electorate perceived definite differences between the two candidates for president.

**(5)** Tilden captured mainly those states that were less populated and therefore had fewer electoral votes.

Items 16 to 20 are based on the following information.

As the world population continues to grow, its demands for food, materials, and space put a greater and greater strain on the environment. Humans have therefore been forced to find ways to turn unproductive land into land that can be put to use to satisfy our needs. This often involves large and dramatic alterations of the landscape. Listed below are five ways in which humans commonly alter the environment to make it more productive.

**(1)** **terracing**—cuts "steps" into steep slopes of land to create flat surfaces that can be cultivated

**(2)** **irrigation**—provides water for agricultural use through dams and canals

**(3) clearance**—removes natural vegetation to provide areas for crops, livestock, and dwellings

**(4) reclamation**—drains swamps and other wet areas for agricultural use; also restores areas that have been spoiled by industrial and other human activities

**(5) landfill**—extends coastline and riverbanks by dumping large amounts of waste and soil, thereby creating new land

Each of the following descriptions exemplifies one of the types of alterations of the landscape listed above. The categories may be used more than once, but no question has more than one best answer.

16. When the first European settlers arrived in North America, they found huge forests covering the land. The settlers made this land fit for large-scale cultivation through

(1) terracing
(2) irrigation
(3) clearance
(4) reclamation
(5) landfill

17. The island of Manhattan in New York City is in great demand as an area for business and residence. Because space is so limited, the city has increased the land available for construction through

(1) terracing
(2) irrigation
(3) clearance
(4) reclamation
(5) landfill

18. There is a great demand for rice in Southeast Asia. Rice can grow only in swampy lands, but most of Southeast Asia is mountainous. The farmers of Southeast Asia have solved this problem through

(1) terracing
(2) irrigation
(3) clearance
(4) reclamation
(5) landfill

19. The Nile River in Africa tends to flood seasonally. Farmers in the river valley take advantage of this by planting in the rich sediments left behind when the flood recedes. But during the rest of the year the river does not provide enough water to sustain crops. This problem has been solved through

(1) terracing
(2) irrigation
(3) clearance
(4) reclamation
(5) landfill

20. In various parts of the world forests have been destroyed by the practice of slash-and-burn agriculture. In many such areas, reforestation efforts are currently under way. These are attempts to alter the environment through

(1) terracing
(2) irrigation
(3) clearance
(4) reclamation
(5) landfill

Items 21 and 22 are based on the following graph.

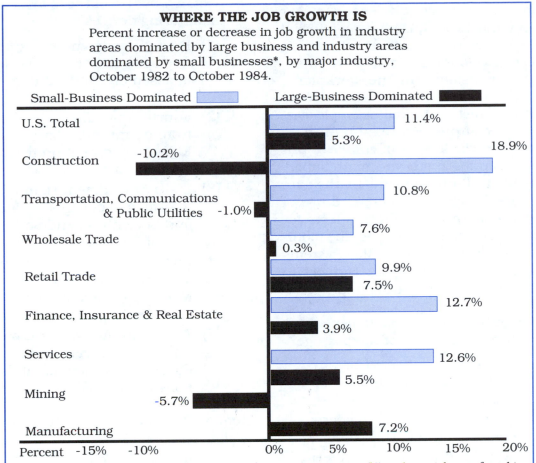

**WHERE THE JOB GROWTH IS**

Percent increase or decrease in job growth in industry areas dominated by large business and industry areas dominated by small businesses*, by major industry, October 1982 to October 1984.

Small-Business Dominated ☐     Large-Business Dominated ■

U.S. Total: 11.4% / 5.3%

Construction: 18.9% / -10.2%

Transportation, Communications & Public Utilities: 10.8% / -1.0%

Wholesale Trade: 7.6% / 0.3%

Retail Trade: 9.9% / 7.5%

Finance, Insurance & Real Estate: 12.7% / 3.9%

Services: 12.6% / 5.5%

Mining: -5.7%

Manufacturing: 7.2%

Percent  -15%  -10%  0%  5%  10%  15%  20%

*An industry is dominated by small business if 60 percent or more of its sales or jobs are found in businesses that employ fewer than 500 workers. Most major industries are partly dominated by large firms and partly dominated by small firms. In construction, for example, small firms do most of the home-building; large firms build most offices, roads, bridges, and so forth. The proportion of small businesses is so tiny in the mining and manufacturing industries, however, that those industries are considered to be totally dominated by large businesses.
Source: U.S. Small Business Administrtaion, Office of Advocacy.

**21.** Which of the following industries showed amounts of job growth for its large- and small-business-dominated areas that were most like the corresponding figures for the United States as a whole?

**(1)** wholesale trade

**(2)** retail trade

**(3)** finance, insurance, and real estate

**(4)** services

**(5)** manufacturing

**22.** Which of the following statements is supported by the information presented?

**(1)** No major industry with a small-business component deviated from the overall job-growth pattern of greater increases in areas dominated by small business

**(2)** Total job growth was sufficient to accommodate almost all new entrants into the labor force.

**(3)** Small businesses created more jobs than large businesses.

**(4)** Large construction firms lost business to foreign competitors.

**(5)** Overall, the construction industry experienced an increase in the number of jobs.

Items 23 to 25 are based on the following paragraph.

Recent years have witnessed major breakthroughs in testing and monitoring technology. There is concern, however, that these developments may have undesirable repercussions in the workplace, particularly in view of growing employer willingness to test and monitor employees. Thus, for example, Professor Alan F. Westin has stated: "Issues of employee privacy are becoming more and more important to 100 million workers in the late 1980s. These range from increased use of drug, psychological, and honesty tests for job applicants to the use of machine monitoring of employees using office systems technology. . . ." (*Columbia University Record* 12, February 27, 1987, p. 6)

**23.** Which of the following statements best describes the purpose of the passage?

   **(1)** to discuss some recent breakthroughs in testing and monitoring technology

   **(2)** to advocate the use of modern technology in the workplace

   **(3)** to show the necessity to screen job applicants

   **(4)** to show why privacy in the workplace has become an important concern

   **(5)** to reveal the intrusion of government in people's lives

**24.** Which of the following may prove to be the least likely response to these threats to privacy?

   **(1)** making the public more aware of the dangers of testing and monitoring

   **(2)** negotiating by unions to get employers to minimize their use of testing and monitoring

   **(3)** writing limits on testing and monitoring into employee contracts

   **(4)** banning testing and monitoring technology

   **(5)** passing laws to restrict the use of testing and monitoring

**25.** Which of the following amendments to the U.S. Constitution may have been violated by use of these tests and monitoring devices?

   **(1)** First Amendment guarantees of free speech, a free press, freedom of assembly, and freedom to petition

   **(2)** Fourth Amendment protection from unauthorized searches and Fifth Amendment protection from self-incrimination

   **(3)** Sixth Amendment rights to be informed of charges against one and Seventh Amendment guarantees of jury trials

   **(4)** Eighth Amendment bans on cruel and unusual punishment and Ninth Amendment powers reserved to the people

   **(5)** Thirteenth Amendment bans on involuntary servitude and Fourteenth Amendment definitions of citizenship

Item 26 is based on the following paragraph.

Much economic competition in the United States is based on price. But companies also engage in nonprice competition. Such competition, for example, involves attracting customers by running advertising campaigns people will remember. Advertisements attempt to associate the product with an image that people find desirable. Advertising is by no means the only way of achieving this association. Packaging and labeling are equally crucial to establishing the right "image." They should also differentiate the product from its competitors, making it stand out in people's minds.

**26.** Which of the following would be the best title for this passage?

    **(1)** Pricing Your Competitors Out of the Market

    **(2)** How to Run Your Business

    **(3)** Some Psychological Tools of Competition

    **(4)** Developing Effective Advertisements

    **(5)** Differentiate and Succeed

**27.** During the first quarter of the 20th century, reporters revealed that some of the nation's largest businesses had engaged in corrupt practices and had made shady deals with one another at the expense of the public. Reformers set out to get the government to remedy the situation. Which of the following actions probably occurred as a result?

    **(1)** Congress legalized union organization and collective bargaining.

    **(2)** For a more flexible currency, the government abandoned the gold standard.

    **(3)** Businesses were given subsidies to make their goods more competitive with goods manufactured abroad.

    **(4)** Tariffs on imports were raised to new heights.

    **(5)** To prevent monopolies and foster competition, antitrust laws were passed.

Item 28 is based on the following paragraph.

The Arctic Ocean separates the Soviet Union from North America. Both the Soviet Union and the United States view the Arctic as vital to their national security. The Soviet Union has many military bases on its northern edge, along the Arctic coast. The United States has bases in Alaska. Its allies have bases in Canada, Iceland, and Norway. Beneath the polar ice cap, nuclear submarines constantly patrol icy waters.

**28.** The passage implies that both the United States and the Soviet Union believe the Arctic Ocean is vital to national security because

    **(1)** numerous military bases are located there

    **(2)** it is the only place where nuclear submarines can be used

    **(3)** the Arctic contains a number of scarce resources

    **(4)** both the United States and the Soviet Union border on the Arctic Ocean

    **(5)** the Arctic Ocean has many important transportation routes

Item 29 is based on the following paragraph.

Japan's economic success has been attributed to a number of factors. One often-mentioned factor is the "team spirit" of Japanese workers. Another is Japan's willingness to abandon previously successful areas, such as textiles, in which developing nations now produce and sell goods more cheaply. At the same time, Japan has made sizeable investments in areas such as computers that are becoming increasingly important in today's world. Moreover, by saving an average of about 20 percent of their income, Japanese households have provided the capital needed for investments.

**29.** Based on the passage, which of the following is a factor that has contributed to Japan's economic growth?

    **(1)** the failure of other nations to compete successfully with Japan in any area that it enters

    **(2)** the free-spending habits of Japan's citizens, which have greatly stimulated the demand for goods

    **(3)** the ability to import and master the technology of other nations

    **(4)** the growth of trade unions and their assumption of a major role in the decision making process

    **(5)** the ability to base investment decisions on accurate assessments of the changing global economy

Items 30 and 31 are based on the following cartoon.

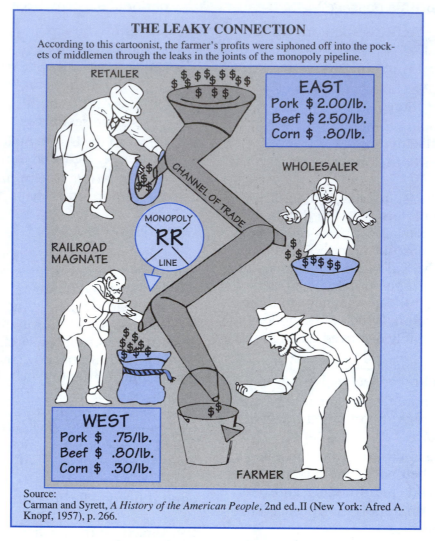

**THE LEAKY CONNECTION**

According to this cartoonist, the farmer's profits were siphoned off into the pockets of middlemen through the leaks in the joints of the monopoly pipeline.

RETAILER

EAST
Pork $ 2.00/lb.
Beef $ 2.50/lb.
Corn $ .80/lb.

CHANNEL OF TRADE

WHOLESALER

MONOPOLY
**RR**
LINE

RAILROAD MAGNATE

WEST
Pork $ .75/lb.
Beef $ .80/lb.
Corn $ .30/lb.

FARMER

Source:
Carman and Syrett, *A History of the American People*, 2nd ed.,II (New York: Afred A. Knopf, 1957), p. 266.

**30.** Which of the following statements is best supported by the cartoon?

(1) Farmers are suffering because harvest are poor due to drought.

(2) High mortgage rates on farmland are absorbing the farmers' profits.

(3) Agricultural surpluses are driving down farm prices.

(4) Farmers are not to blame if consumers pay high prices for food.

(5) Farmers are victims of inflationary fiscal policies.

**31.** Based on the cartoon, which of the following policies would prove most beneficial to farmers?

(1) price supports for their crops

(2) antitrust and railroad regulatory legislation

(3) lower mortgage interest rates

(4) lower tariff rates to open foreign markets

(5) technological improvements to get crops to market before they spoil

Items 32 to 34 are based on the following paragraph.

We hold these truths to be self-evident, that all men are created equal, that they are endowed by their Creator with certain unalienable rights, that among these are life, liberty and the pursuit of happiness. That to secure these rights, governments are instituted among men, deriving their just powers from the consent of the governed,—That whenever any form of government becomes destructive of these ends, it is the right of the people to alter or to abolish it, and to institute new government, laying its foundation on such principles and organizing its powers in such form, as to them shall seem most likely to effect their safety and happiness. Prudence, indeed, will dictate that governments long established should not be changed for light and transient causes; and accordingly all experience hath shown, that mankind are more disposed to suffer, while evils are sufferable, than to right themselves by abolishing the forms to which they are accustomed. But when a long train of abuses and usurpations, pursuing invariably the same object evinces a design to reduce them under absolute despotism, it is their right, it is their duty, to throw off such government, and to provide new guards for their future security.—Such has been the patient sufferance of these colonies; and such is now the necessity which constrains them to alter their former systems of government. The history of the present King of Great Britain is a history of repeated injuries and usurpations, all having in direct object the establishment of an absolute tyranny over these states.

**32.** According to the Declaration of Independence, which of the following is the final effect of depriving people of freedom, rights, and feelings of contentment?

(1) The people will be strong and endure the injustices.

(2) The people will organize massive protests and strikes.

(3) The people will immigrate to a freer country.

(4) The people will overthrow the government and form a better one.

(5) The people will get the help of another country to overthrow the government.

**33.** According to the excerpt, the King of England's actions knowingly resulted in

(1) unjustly oppressing the colonists

(2) the creation of a tyrannical new American government

(3) the unification of all colonies in the British Empire

(4) his removal from the throne

(5) the passage of new laws which protected the rights of the colonies

**34.** Supporting which of the following would be most consistent with the political beliefs of the writers of the Declaration of Independence?

(1) the independence of Angola when it was a Portuguese colony

(2) the Pro-Choice movement to defend a woman's right to abortion

(3) an African-American separatist movement

(4) the South's secession from the United States in 1860

(5) capital punishment for murder

Items 35 and 36 refers to the map below.

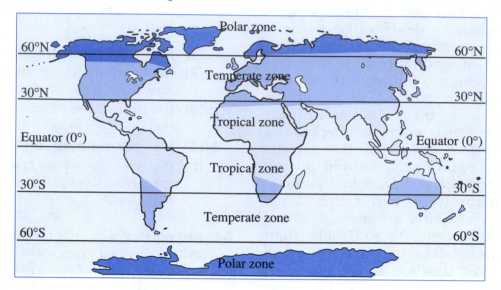

**35.** Which of the following can be inferred from the map?

(1) The average temperature in the southern temperate zone is around 60 degrees.

(2) No humans live in either polar zone.

(3) Countries within the same zone have similar climates.

(4) On any given day, it is never hotter in a tropical zone than in a temperate zone.

(5) All countries within the northern temperate zone have exactly the same climate.

**36.** Which of the following countries would you visit if you like a very hot, sunny climate?

(1) South Africa

(2) the United States

(3) northern Brazil

(4) China

(5) Southern Australia

Items 37 to 40 are based on the following passage.

In 1933, when President Franklin D. Roosevelt took office, the nation was in the throes of a severe economic depression. After the stock market crashed in 1929, corporations began to face bankruptcy since they could no longer sell their output, no matter how much they lowered their prices, nor could they raise money for new production. Twelve million Americans lost their jobs, and more than one million homeless people took to the road. Tens of thousands of mortgages were foreclosed; many savings accounts and the banks that had held them were wiped out. National income was more than halved.

To meet these difficulties, the Roosevelt administration proposed a New Deal, an unprecedented series of programs with three main goals: relief, recovery, and reform. "Relief" meant helping individuals in need, while "recovery" entailed aiding farmers, business people, and workers in order to lift the nation out of the Depression. Finally, "reform" meant government action to eliminate abuses in the economy and, through a range of new programs, to prevent future depressions. In short, the New Deal attempted to get the economy going again. Government officials promised to take steps to solve the nation's ills.

37. Based on the passage, which of the following statements best explains what caused the Great Depression of the 1930s?

   (1) Businesses raised their prices so high that people could not afford to buy their products, and, to make up their losses, corporations raised their prices even higher.
   (2) Labor unions demanded wages that were so high that companies could not afford to pay them, so businesses fired some of their workers, resulting in massive unemployment.
   (3) Businesses, lacking capital from a collapsed stock market, laid off workers to lower costs, but these workers then lacked purchasing power, so business output went unsold, leading to further layoffs.
   (4) Banks attempted to force businesses and individuals to whom they loaned money to accept unfavorable terms, but this move eventually backfired, resulting in numerous bank failures and a contraction of the economy.
   (5) Millions of Americans lost their jobs, and more than a million homeless people took to the road.

38. Which of the following government programs is the best example of a New Deal relief measure?

   (1) **The Glass-Steagall Act**, which separated commercial and investment banking and set up federal insurance to guarantee bank deposits up to a maximum amount
   (2) **The Agricultural Adjustment Act**, which subsidized farmers to withdraw acreage from production so that crop prices would be raised
   (3) **The Revenue Act**, which raised income taxes for corporations and individuals in the upper brackets to a historic level
   (4) **The Works Progress Administration,** which employed Americans from many walks of life in cultural and construction projects
   (5) **The Wagner Act**, which guaranteed collective bargaining and set up a National Labor Relations Board to supervise disputed union elections

39. Which of the following does the author of this passage value most?

   (1) the federal government's intervention in times of crisis to help people
   (2) a balanced budget at any cost
   (3) the state government's intervention to help its residents
   (4) a socialist economic system
   (5) cooperation between business and the federal government to solve the country's economic problems

40. According to the passage, which of the following is an opinion rather than a fact about the historical period when Roosevelt became president?

   (1) There were over 900,000 homeless people.
   (2) People lost the money they had deposited in banks.
   (3) Thousands of Americans were unemployed.
   (4) The economy collapsed from corporate abuses.
   (5) The Gross National Product was more than halved.

Items 41 and 42 are based on the following table.

**SOCIAL READJUSTMENT SCALE**

| LIFE EVENT | LIFE CHANGE UNITS |
|---|---|
| Death of one's spouse | 100 |
| Divorce | 73 |
| Marital separation | 65 |
| Jail term | 63 |
| Death of a close family member | 63 |
| Personal injury or illness | 53 |
| Marriage | 50 |
| Being fired at work | 47 |
| Marital reconciliation | 45 |
| Retirement | 45 |
| Change in the health of a family member | 44 |
| Pregnancy | 40 |
| Sex difficulties | 39 |
| Gain a new family member | 39 |
| Business readjustment | 39 |
| Change in one's financial state | 38 |
| Death of a close friend | 37 |
| Change to a different line of work | 36 |
| Change in number of arguments with spouse | 35 |
| Mortgage over $10,000 | 31 |
| Foreclosure of a mortgage or loan | 30 |
| Change in responsibilities at work | 29 |
| Son or daughter leaving home | 29 |
| Trouble with in-laws | 29 |
| Outstanding personal achievement | 28 |
| Wife beginning or stopping work | 26 |
| Beginning or ending school | 26 |
| Change in living conditions | 25 |
| Revision of personal habits | 24 |
| Trouble with one's boss | 23 |
| Change in work hours or conditions | 20 |
| Change in residence | 20 |
| Change in schools | 20 |
| Change in recreation | 19 |
| Change in church activities | 19 |
| Change in social activities | 18 |
| Mortgage or loan of less than $10,000 | 17 |
| Change in sleeping habits | 16 |
| Change in number of family get-togethers | 15 |
| Change in eating habits | 15 |
| Vacation | 13 |
| Christmas | 12 |
| Minor violations of the law | 11 |

Holmes and Rahe, The Social Readjustment Rating Scale, in *Journal of Psychosomatic Research*, Pergamon Press

**41.** The Life-Change Units in the table are based on the amount of stress that a change produces. Which of the following would produce the most stress for a person?

(1) being dismissed from one's job
(2) breaking one's leg

(3) birth of a child
(4) sickness of one's wife
(5) death of a brother

**42.** According to the table, which of the following would be least stressful?

(1) a change in work shift
(2) a vacation to the Pacific Northwest
(3) a husband moving out of his wife's and his apartment
(4) a $10,500 mortgage
(5) conviction for assault and battery

Items 43 to 45 are based on the following information.

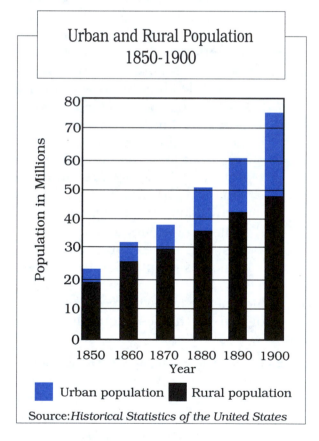

Urban and Rural Population 1850-1900

Source: *Historical Statistics of the United States*

Industrial expansion fueled the explosive growth of cities after the Civil War. Manufacturers built most of their new plants in cities in order to be near workers and transportation. This created new jobs, which, in turn, drew even more people into the cities. As newspaper editor Horace Greeley said, "We cannot all live in cities, yet nearly all seem determined to do so."

**43.** From the graph you can conclude that from 1850 to 1900

   **(1)** urban and rural populations were growing at the same rate
   **(2)** the population in the cities was growing at a faster rate than that in the countryside
   **(3)** the population in the countryside was outstripping that in the cities
   **(4)** Northeast city populations were growing at the fastest rate of all urban areas
   **(5)** the rural population in the U.S. was declining

**44.** The urban boom was strongest first in the Northeast. Which of the following is the most likely explanation for this phenomenon?

   **(1)** The climate was suitable for businessmen.
   **(2)** Most people had relatives and friends living in the Northeast.
   **(3)** The Northeast had the largest rural population in the U.S.
   **(4)** The Northeast had the most factories and access to transportation.
   **(5)** All railroads which transported workers and products throughout the U.S. led to and from the Northeast.

**45.** Which of the following would be the least likely reason for a business person to build a factory in a major city?

   **(1)** the arrival of millions of immigrants
   **(2)** high unemployment
   **(3)** low taxes
   **(4)** access to railroads
   **(5)** unpredictable climate

**46.** In 1899, Secretary of State John Hay sent notes to the five nations that had secured special military and trading rights in China, thus carving out spheres of influence for themselves. He urged that the territorial integrity of China be preserved and the business of all countries be welcomed. Which of the following situations would have met with Hay's approval?

   **(1)** Roosevelt, Churchill, and Stalin's informal agreement at the Yalta Conference at the end of World War II about which countries the Big Three would each view as under their influence
   **(2)** the 1973 OPEC oil boycott against the United States and Western European nations because they had sided with Israel in the Yom Kippur War earlier that year
   **(3)** Woodrow Wilson's Fourteen Points, which urged self-determination, equal trading rights for all nations, and an internal organization to guarantee the political independence of member states
   **(4)** Japan's proposal for a Greater East Asia Co-Prosperity Sphere of the early 1940s, which was to give Japan economic control over other nations in Asia
   **(5)** the Roosevelt Corollary to the Monroe Doctrine, stating that the United States would intervene in Latin America to collect debts due to European nations, but that the creditors themselves were not to do so

Item 47 is based on the following paragraph.

In 1940, before the United States entered World War II, President Roosevelt traded 50 aged U.S. destroyers for bases owned by the British in a simple exchange of notes with British government officials. Fearful of the delay that Senate approval of a treaty might have involved, President Roosevelt in effect found a quick way to help an embattled ally fighting for its survival. The agreement he made is considered a legitimate exercise of presidential power. The Constitution vests the president with primary responsibility for the conduct of foreign affairs even though Congress must fund foreign policy activities and assent to formal treaties.

**47.** Which of the following statements best describes the basis of the president's authority to arrange such a deal with Britain?

**(1)** The president is empowered to enter into executive agreements with other nations.

**(2)** The Constitution charges the president with responsibility to negotiate treaties subject to senatorial approval.

**(3)** The president is empowered to see that the laws are faithfully executed.

**(4)** The president may ask Congress to declare war against an enemy of the United States.

**(5)** Acts of the federal government are considered the supreme law of the land.

Item 48 is based on the following paragraph.

In all societies people exchange goods and services. In simple societies, however, exchanges are not economic transactions, but reciprocal gift-giving. A gift requires a return gift. Social events of almost every kind—from marriage to the planting of a garden—initiate gift-giving between families, clans, villages, or other social groups. A group often gains in status by returning a gift of greater value than one received.

**48.** Which of the following statements is best supported by the information in the passage?

**(1)** Calculations of profit and loss are basic to gift exchange.

**(2)** A primary purpose of exchange is to establish or maintain relationships among groups.

**(3)** Calculation of the value of gifts is forbidden in gift exchange.

**(4)** Only a few members of society are allowed to participate in gift exchange.

**(5)** The main purpose of gift exchange is to give people the opportunity to show off.

Items 49 to 53 are based on the following paragraph.

Most people obey the basic rules of their communities not only because they will be punished if they do not, but also because they believe the rules to be legitimate. People may believe rules are legitimate for a number of reasons. The following are principal types of reasons for which people believe rules are legitimate.

(1) **tradition**—belief that rules are legitimate because they have been passed down from generation to generation

(2) **emotion**—belief that rules are legitimate simply because the individual has a strong feeling that the rules and the overall model of society must be right

(3) **charisma**—belief that rules are legitimate based on faith in the leader who has established them

(4) **value principles**—belief that rules are legitimate because they are based on fundamental ethical or religious principles

(5) **lawfulness**—belief that rules are legitimate because they have been established through a legal process that is legitimate

Each of the following situations exemplifies one of the five bases for legitimacy of rules listed above. The types may be used more than once, but no question has more than one best answer.

**49.** A group adopts a constitution which sets forth a simple majority vote of the community as necessary for enacting a law. A law popular with only a small majority is nevertheless obeyed. In this example, the basis for belief in the legitimacy of the law is probably

**(1)** tradition

**(2)** emotion

**(3)** charisma

**(4)** value principles

**(5)** lawfulness

**50.** A country has been governed by a single leader during the entire 20 years of its independence. Opposition politicians, who were already frustrated by the leader's popularity, now strenuously object to a new law that limits opposition parties. Nonetheless, much of the public supports the law. In this example, the basis for the public's belief in the legitimacy of the law is probably

**(1)** tradition

**(2)** emotion

**(3)** charisma

**(4)** value principles

**(5)** lawfulness

**51.** A group passes a resolution urging its members to refuse to comply with a new law requiring registration for the draft. They argue that participation in the military runs counter to the group's belief in nonviolence. The members of the group overwhelmingly obey the resolution. The basis for their belief in its legitimacy is probably

**(1)** tradition

**(2)** emotion

**(3)** charisma

**(4)** value principles

**(5)** lawfulness

**52.** When a monarch dies, his oldest son, who is next in line of succession, is proclaimed king. The public mourns the king and prepares for his son's coronation. The basis for their belief in the proclamation's legitimacy is probably

**(1)** tradition

**(2)** emotion

**(3)** charisma

**(4)** value principles

**(5)** lawfulness

**53.** A community is formed around a leader who preaches that the world as we know it is about to end. A skilled orator with a magnetic personality, he promises a new and better world to people who abide by his prophecy and by the rules of his community. The basis for members' belief in the legitimacy of the rules of the community is probably

**(1)** tradition

**(2)** emotion

**(3)** charisma

**(4)** value principles

**(5)** lawfulness

**54.** During the 1830s, South Carolina Senator John C. Calhoun proposed the controversial doctrine of nullification. He argued that a state had the power to declare an act of Congress null and void. South Carolina put this doctrine into effect when it passed an ordinance annulling the Tariffs of 1828 and 1832 and prohibiting the collection of duties in South Carolina ports. However, the threat of President Andrew Jackson's Force Bill was sufficient to get the ordinance rescinded. Which of the following examples most closely carries out Calhoun's concept of nullification?

**(1)** the Senate's rejection of the treaty establishing the League of Nations

**(2)** President Truman's veto of the Taft-Hartley Act, which restricted and regulated unions

**(3)** Soviet use of its veto power when the UN Security Council resolved to send a mediator to settle the Indian-Pakistani dispute over Kashmir

**(4)** the Supreme Court's finding in the Dred Scott case that the Missouri Compromise of 1820 was unconstitutional

**(5)** Southern state conventions repealing the U.S. Constitution and declaring their secession from the Union

Item 55 is based on the following cartoon.

*"These weren't damaged in riots–they went to pieces years before."*

**55.** This 1967 cartoon was drawn in the aftermath of riots in Detroit, Newark, and other American cities during the administration of President Lyndon Johnson. Based on the cartoon, what was the main cause of the riots?

**(1)** Opposition to the Vietnam War led to riots and demonstrations as youths protested being drafted to fight in Southeast Asia.

**(2)** In spite of the civil rights movement, many American blacks felt that little had been done to improve the quality of their lives.

**(3)** American blacks protested their exclusion from the political process.

**(4)** Racism on the part of blacks and whites had taken a violent turn.

**(5)** Slum clearance programs sparked opposition from those who would be displaced by urban renewal.

Item 56 is based on the following graphs.

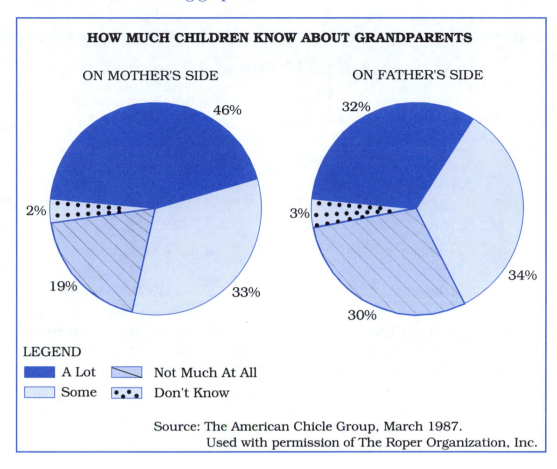

**HOW MUCH CHILDREN KNOW ABOUT GRANDPARENTS**

ON MOTHER'S SIDE

46%
2%
19%
33%

ON FATHER'S SIDE

32%
3%
30%
34%

LEGEND

■ A Lot    ▨ Not Much At All
□ Some    ⦿ Don't Know

Source: The American Chicle Group, March 1987.
Used with permission of The Roper Organization, Inc.

56. Which of the following statements might explain the pattern shown in the two graphs?

(1) Children tend to be closer to, and talk more with, their mother than their father.

(2) Children more often live closer to their father's parents than their mother's parents.

(3) Children today generally know little about grandparents on either side of the family.

(4) Children tend to know more about their mother's parents than about their father's.

(5) Children today only rarely see their grandparents.

Item 57 is based on the following table.

## Breakdown of payments made in selected years on a 20-year mortgage for $10,000 at 10 percent

| Year | Payments made over the year | Interest paid over the year | Principle (amount of loan) repaid over the year | Equity |
|------|------|------|------|------|
| 1 | 1,158 | 993 | 165 | 165 |
| 2 | 1,158 | 975 | 183 | 349 |
| 5 | 1,158 | 912 | 246 | 1,020 |
| 10 | 1,158 | 753 | 405 | 2,698 |
| 15 | 1,158 | 491 | 667 | 5,458 |
| 19 | 1,158 | 164 | 994 | 8,902 |
| 20 | 1,158 | 60 | 1,908 | 10,000 |

**57.** Which of the following statements about repayment of mortgages is true based on the information provided in the table?

(1) Calculations of equity are based on interest paid plus principal repaid.

(2) The principal to be paid in any given year will vary with the total amount paid during the year.

(3) Much of the interest will generally be repaid during the first ten years of repayment.

(4) Total interest payments can approach but cannot exceed total principal payments.

(5) The interest to be paid in any given year will vary with the amount of the loan still outstanding.

Item 58 is based on the following paragraph.

From 1860 to 1890, when white settlers moved to the Great Plains to farm the land, they came into conflict with the nomadic Plains Indians. White hunters killed off the buffalo which provided Plains Indians with food, clothing, and shelter. The U.S. cavalry destroyed the Indians' ability to defend their territory and then forced the survivors to move to reservations where they were expected to become farmers.

**58.** Which of the following statements is supported by the passage?

(1) White settlers initially tried to coexist with the Indians.

(2) Whites failed to understand or respect Indian culture and lifestyle.

(3) The Great Plains was the area of the U.S. in which there was most conflict between Native Americans and white settlers.

(4) Settlers destroyed the ecology of the Great Plains.

(5) The Native Americans eventually abandoned their culture and way of life.

Items 59 and 60 are based on the following graph.

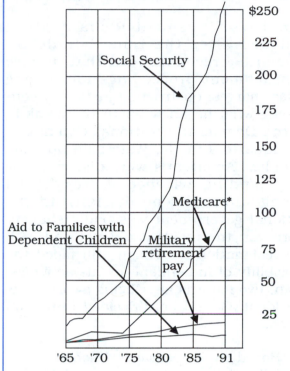

**GROWING ENTITLEMENT SPENDING**

Benefits paid in four federal entitlement programs, in billions of dollars by fiscal year.

(Figures for 1986 through 1991 are estimates from President Reagan's budget proposal)

Social Security

Medicare*

Aid to Families with Dependent Children

Military retirement pay

$250
225
200
175
150
125
100
75
50
25

'65   '70   '75   '80   '85   '91

*Medicare payments (health care for retired people) began in 1966

Source: From Burns, Peltason, and Cronin, Government By the People (Englewood Cliffs: Prentice Hall, Inc.,1987), p. 549. Used with permission.

**59.** Which of the following conclusions is supported by the information presented in the graph?

**(1)** The birth rate is soaring.

**(2)** The unemployment rate is shrinking.

**(3)** The American population is aging.

**(4)** Enrollment in the armed services is declining.

**(5)** Hospital costs are being brought under control.

**60.** Which of the following statements is best supported by the information in the graph?

**(1)** Private charities are assuming more responsibility for the nation's needy, reducing federal expenditures.

**(2)** Until the Great Depression, the federal government did little to aid the needy.

**(3)** Most federal entitlement programs are administered by state and local governments.

**(4)** The elderly probably have more interest group support pressuring Congress than do the young and the poor.

**(5)** Poverty programs perpetuate poverty and create a culture of poverty.

Items 61 and 62 are based on the following passage.

*Gross national product* (GNP) is essentially the market value of all goods and services produced by a nation during a specified period of time (for example, a year). The goods and services produced fall into two basic categories. Consumer goods and services—for example, televisions and haircuts—are used by individuals or households to meet their needs and wants. Capital (or "investment") goods and services are used in, or necessary to, the production of other goods. Machines, roads, and even maintenance work on office computers are examples of capital goods and services.

Both consumer goods/services and capital goods/services may be public as well as private. That is, the government purchases both consumer goods and services—for example, the services of public school teachers—and capital goods and services—for example, roads, dams, and sewage treatment plants.

By adding all public and private expenditures on both capital and consumer goods and services, we can obtain the GNP. Trends in the GNP are important data for economists and policymakers alike.

**61.** Which of the following is an example of a public consumer good/service?

**(1)** a car
**(2)** a factory building
**(3)** a highway system
**(4)** firefighters' services
**(5)** income tax preparers' services

**62.** Data that economists and policymakers might want to obtain about a country include (A) the overall level of activity of the economy, (B) the level of expenditures on various kinds of goods and services, and (C) the extent to which goods and services are distributed equally among the population. What could they learn about by looking at the country's GNP?

**(1)** A only
**(2)** B only
**(3)** C only
**(4)** A and B
**(5)** A, B, and C

Item 63 is based on the following paragraph.

In 1974, President Richard Nixon resigned after the House Judiciary Committee recommended that he face impeachment proceedings for, among other charges, obstructing justice by concealing what he knew about the break-in at the Democratic National Committee Headquarters in the Watergate building complex. Americans were disturbed by the mounting evidence of presidential wrongdoing, and public faith in the national government was badly shaken. Moreover, the incident did not end with the resignation, as Nixon still faced the possibility of indictment for his activities. Then, two months after being sworn in as president, Gerald Ford decided to pardon Nixon.

**63.** Based on the passage, which of the following statements best explains President Ford's decision?

**(1)** his belief that Nixon was innocent
**(2)** Nixon's request for clemency
**(3)** pressure from leading Republicans
**(4)** the need to regain the republic's confidence in government
**(5)** a lack of evidence concerning Nixon's role in Watergate

Item 64 is based on the graph below.

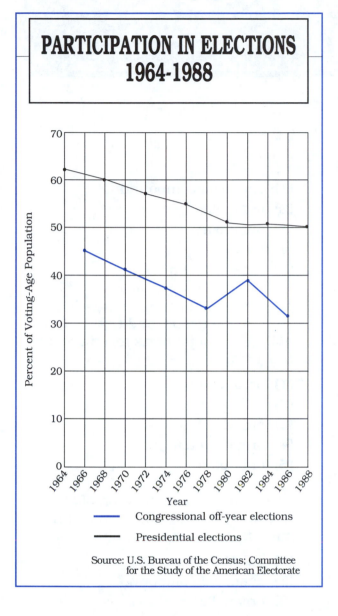

## PARTICIPATION IN ELECTIONS 1964-1988

Percent of Voting-Age Population

Year

—— Congressional off-year elections

—— Presidential elections

Source: U.S. Bureau of the Census; Committee
for the Study of the American Electorate

Answers are on pages A-83-A-89

**64.** Which of the following statements summarizes the information in the graph?

**(1)** There were more people voting in presidential than congressional elections in 1964.

**(2)** There has been a steady decrease in the number of people voting in presidential elections.

**(3)** There have been increases and decreases in the number of voters participating in congressional elections.

**(4)** Although more voters participate in presidential elections than in congressional elections, the numbers of people participating in both elections has shown an overall decline.

**(5)** There has been a steady decline in both presidential and congressional elections from 1964 to 1988.

# SIMULATED TEST 3
## Science

**TIME:** 90 minutes

**Directions:** Choose the one best answer to each question.

Items 1 to 4 refer to the following passage.

Living matter may be classified into different levels according to its complexity of organization. The lowest level consists of subatomic particles such as electrons, protons, and neutrons. These make up atoms, which in turn form more complex combinations called chemical compounds. Chemical compounds are not living themselves; in fact, many of the common compounds in the human body are found in both living and nonliving matter. Water is an example of such a compound.

In living matter, chemical compounds often combine to form microscopic bodies called organelles. These organelles are contained within the cells and carry out each cell's life processes.

Many cells function on their own. Unicellular organisms such as bacteria make up the majority of life on Earth. Other cells combine to form multicellular organisms. Multicellular organisms such as the human body include several levels of organization. The first is the tissue, a group of cells that are similar in structure and function. An example of a tissue is the nerves. Different tissues may join and work together, form ing an organ such as the stomach. Groups of organs and tissues may, in turn, be united in an organ system. For example, the nervous system, which coordinates all body activities, consists of the brain, the spinal cord, and the nerves.

1. An amoeba is a one-celled protozoan able to move, feed, and reproduce itself. The amoeba is a(n)

   (1) chemical compound
   (2) organelle
   (3) organism
   (4) tissue
   (5) organ system

2. The heart is made up of muscle tissues, nerve tissue, and tissues that hold the various parts together. The heart is a(n)

   (1) organelle
   (2) cell
   (3) organ
   (4) organ system
   (5) organism

3. Table salt is a combination of atoms necessary for life, although it is not alive itself. Table salt is a(n)

   (1) subatomic particle
   (2) chemical compound
   (3) organelle
   (4) cell
   (5) organism

4. A dog is a combination of many cells working together and forming an independent being. A dog is a(n)

   (1) tissue
   (2) organ
   (3) organ system
   (4) unicellular organism
   (5) multicellular organism

Items 5 and 6 refer to the following passage.

An important part of the water cycle is the release of water into the atmosphere by plants and animals. This process is called transpiration. Both plants and animals use some of the water they take in for their life processes and then transpire the rest.

In plants, transpiration takes place through tiny pores in the leaves. Animals transpire in different ways. People give off water through pores in the skin. Dogs and other mammals release moisture by panting. The moisture carries heat away from the body and thus also acts as a cooling-off mechanism.

**5.** Why do desert plants, such as cactuses, have few or no leaves?

    **(1)** to increase the rate of transpiration

    **(2)** to decrease the rate of transpiration

    **(3)** to increase the rate at which photosynthesis takes place

    **(4)** to decrease the rate at which photosynthesis takes place

    **(5)** to discourage animals from eating them

**6.** Which of the following would most increase the relative humidity (amount of moisture in the air) in a room?

    A. increase the number of animals

    B. decrease the number of animals

    C. increase the number of leafy plants

    D. decrease the number of leafy plants

    **(1)** A only

    **(2)** A and D only

    **(3)** A and C only

    **(4)** C only

    **(5)** B and C only

Item 7 refers to the following diagram.

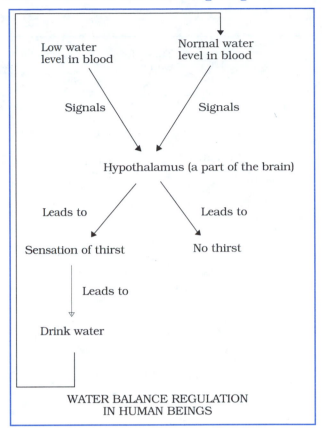

WATER BALANCE REGULATION
IN HUMAN BEINGS

**7.** A stimulus is an internal or external change in the environment. What is the direct stimulus for the thirst you feel on a hot day?

    **(1)** low water level in blood

    **(2)** the hypothalamus

    **(3)** sensation of thirst

    **(4)** a drink of water

    **(5)** the sun

**8.** The region of the atmosphere in which we live is called the troposphere. The troposphere extends an average of 12 kilometers above Earth's surface. As altitude increases in the troposphere, the air becomes colder and less dense. Based on this information, a person climbing Snowcap Mountain (elevation = 4.1 km) in July should be equipped with which of the following?

    **(1)** sunscreen and extra oxygen

    **(2)** protection against snow and rain

    **(3)** raingear and extra oxygen

    **(4)** extra food and sunscreen

    **(5)** warm clothing and extra oxygen

Items 9 to 11 are based on the following diagram.

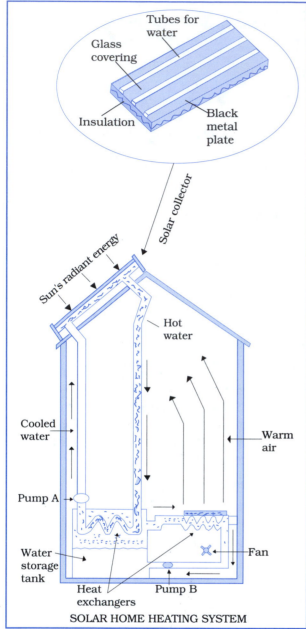

Glass covering
Tubes for water
Insulation
Black metal plate

Solar collector

Sun's radiant energy

Hot water

Cooled water

Warm air

Pump A

Water storage tank

Fan

Heat exchangers

Pump B

SOLAR HOME HEATING SYSTEM

**9.** Which of the following statements best summarizes the process of solar heating shown in the diagram?

**(1)** Heat from the sun is circulated through the hours by a pump and pipes and then moved to a storage tank.

**(2)** Water heated by the sun is stored in a tank and then warm air is blown through the house.

**(3)** Water heated by the sun in a

solar collector is transferred to a storage tank and then moved through pipes to heat the house.

**(4)** Water is pumped from a storage tank into a solar collector and then is moved back into the storage tank.

**(5)** A fan circulates warm air through the house after water has been heated by the sun.

**10.** A camper wishes to use solar energy to heat some water. For the best results, which of the following set-ups should be used?

**(1)** a black metal pot wrapped in a towel and covered with a piece of clear plastic food wrap

**(2)** a shiny aluminum pot covered with a piece of black cardboard

**(3)** a white pot wrapped in a towel and covered with a piece of clear plastic food wrap

**(4)** an all-glass pot surrounded by newspaper and covered with a shiny metal cover

**(5)** a black metal pot left uncovered and wrapped in aluminum foil

**11.** In an old-fashioned hot-water heating system, water heated in a boiler is moved through pipes to heat the house. Which of the following statements correctly compares a hot-water heating system to a solar heating system?

**(1)** A solar heating system and a hot-water heating system are exactly alike.

**(2)** The sun is to a solar heating system as a boiler is to a hot-water heating system.

**(3)** A water storage tank is to a solar heating system as a boiler is to a hot-water heating system.

**(4)** The function of a heat exchanger is the same for both systems.

**(5)** A solar collector is to a solar heating system as a boiler is to a hot-water heating system.

Evidence suggests that cocaine use dates back more than 3000 years. In Peru, where the coca plant grows, Inca Indians used to travel with a bag of coca leaves; 85-100 g of leaves would be chewed daily. In times of great physical exertion, additional leaves were chewed to increase stamina. The use of coca was tied into most religious practices of the Incas. Priests chewed leaves from the coca plant to achieve a meditative state. Later, Inca priests chewed coca to enhance their ability to prophesize. It was common for the Incas to bury their dead with coca leaves to assist the deceased in the final journey.

**12.** Coca drinks can be classified as a mild type of drug. Habitual cola drinkers can develop a mild psychological and perhaps physical dependency. Which of the following statements from the passage supports the idea that a Coca-Cola drink is a stimulant?

(1) Priests chewed coca leaves to achieve a meditative state.

(2) Inca priests chewed coca to enhance their prophesizing skills.

(3) Coca leaves were placed in the coffins of the dead to speed up their journey to heaven.

(4) Indians chewed coca leaves to give them more energy when working.

(5) Indians always traveled with coca leaves.

**13.** Leaves that turn yellow or orange in autumn have actually contained that color throughout the summer. However, in summer you cannot see the yellow or orange because the green pigment in chlorophyll hides it. Chlorophyll absorbs sunlight, providing the energy leaves need to produce sugar during photosynthesis. In autumn, the chlorophyll decays.

When this happens, the yellow or orange color becomes visible, changing entire forests into beautiful displays of "fall foliage." Which of the following is true regarding a tree with orange or yellow leaves in the fall?

(1) The tree is not carrying on photosynthesis at this time.

(2) The leaves are absorbing sunlight to use as energy in the spring.

(3) The tree is preparing for an active period of growth.

(4) The leaves appeared orange and yellow in the summer as well.

(5) The leaves formed new pigments as the chlorophyll decayed.

Items 14 and 15 are based on the following paragraph.

In the early 1980s the government of Canada began a program to kill wolves in British Columbia. The program was based on arguments that failure to thin out the wolf population would threaten the populations of the animals on which the wolves feed. These prey animals—caribou, moose, and mountain sheep—are popular targets for hunters in the area. The program's backers believe that pressure on the prey populations by both hunters and wolves may lead to the prey animals' extinction. To prevent this from happening, they say that human management of the wolf population is necessary to keep wolves and prey in balance. Opponents of the program disagree that human management is required, citing studies of an island on which a wolf pack and prey populations have maintained an approximate balance since the 1930s.

**14.** Which of the following titles best fits the passage?

(1) Hunting Game in Canada

(2) Controversy over Canadian Program to Kill Wolves

(3) Human Management of Animal Species

**(4)** How to Manage a Wolf Population

**(5)** Save the Wolf Campaign

15. Which of the following facts supports the argument of those who wish to thin out the wolf population?

   **(1)** From 1975 to 1985, all the prey populations decreased by large numbers.

   **(2)** Hunting accounts for more animal kills than the wolves do.

   **(3)** If left to themselves, prey and predator populations tend to achieve a rough balance.

   **(4)** Canada has more wolves than any other country.

   **(5)** The prey populations have declined because of severe weather conditions.

Items 16 to 20 refer to the following passage.

In the 19th century, the English naturalist Charles Darwin put forth a theory to explain how organisms evolve—that is, change and develop over time. From extensive observations, Darwin concluded that most species would multiply extremely rapidly if not kept in check by natural conditions or predators. Darwin also noticed that the size of the population of a given species tends to remain the same over long periods of time. From these two observations, Darwin concluded that not all members of a species survive to reproduce. Each individual must struggle to exist.

Darwin also observed that individuals of the same species have a wide variety of different traits. Based on this fact, he suggested that certain traits might make some individuals more successful than others in the struggle for existence. Individuals with these "favorable" traits would be more likely to survive and reproduce, thus passing the traits on to the next generation. Darwin's ideas were called the theory of natural selection. However, the theory was incomplete because Darwin could not explain the mechanism by which traits are inherited. In his day, the fact that genes contain hereditary information was not generally understood.

Scientists today generally support the theory of natural selection, but they believe that it operates on the genetic variations that appear among members of a species population. In each generation, different combinations of genes from parents produce new traits in the offspring. By natural selection, organisms with favorable traits are more likely than others to survive and reproduce, and thus these traits are spread throughout the species population.

16. According to Darwin, an elephant with a favorable trait would

   **(1)** be less likely to survive and reproduce

   **(2)** be able to acquire other favorable traits such as a longer trunk

   **(3)** lose against other elephants in the struggle for existence

   **(4)** be more likely to survive and reproduce, passing the trait on to offspring

   **(5)** be able to pass on acquired traits to offspring

17. Which of the following concepts is the main difference between Darwin's theory and the modern theory of evolution?

   **(1)** natural selection

   **(2)** inheritance of acquired traits

   **(3)** not all individuals survive to reproduce

   **(4)** individuals with favorable traits produce relatively more offspring

   **(5)** natural selection acts on genetic variations

18. Which of the following statements best explains why Darwin's theory did not go far enough in its explanation of how species develop?

   **(1)** Natural selection operates through the struggle for existence.

   **(2)** He did not include God's role in the development of different species.

**(3)** His work could be applied to animals but not to humans.

**(4)** Not all members of a species will reproduce.

**(5)** He did not know how traits are inherited from parents' genes.

**19.** Which of the following most determines the speed at which a species evolves?

**(1)** the rate at which the species reproduces

**(2)** the number of other members of the same species

**(3)** the size of the species population

**(4)** the attraction between males and females of the same species

**(5)** the average number of offspring produced by the species

**20.** Which of the following examples would NOT support Darwin's theory of evolution?

**(1)** An "odd-ball" variation in a species may survive while the majority of the species becomes extinct.

**(2)** A species may die out because its environment undergoes an extreme change.

**(3)** A large number of animals in a species may die every year during breeding season although the species stays the same size as a group.

**(4)** Each new generation has new traits that may help some offspring survive.

**(5)** Useful traits developed by the efforts of one generation may be passed on to its offspring to help them survive.

**21.** A type of magnet called an electromagnet can be made by wrapping coils of wire around a piece of iron and then passing an electric current through the wire. The electromagnet acts as a magnet only while the current is running. Its magnetism disappears as soon as the current is turned off, but it returns when the current is turned back on.

A manufacturer of heavy machinery equips a machine with a powerful electromagnet. For which of the following tasks would the machine be most effective?

**(1)** welding together pieces of metal

**(2)** picking up pieces of scrap metal and then depositing them in a refuse container

**(3)** transporting heavy objects long distances

**(4)** making magnets out of iron

**(5)** increasing the ability of a wire to conduct electric current

**22.** A National Academy of Sciences report on passive cigarette smoking states that the risk of lung cancer is about 30 percent higher for a non-smoking spouse of a smoker than for a nonsmoking spouse of a nonsmoker. It also states that respiratory infections such as pneumonia and bronchitis occur more often in children of smokers than in children of nonsmokers.

Which of the following generalizations can be made about inhaling the cigarette smoke of others?

**(1)** A smoker is harming his or her own health.

**(2)** Inhaling the smoke of others has no effect on a nonsmoker.

**(3)** Inhaling the smoke of others is a health hazard to a nonsmoker.

**(4)** Smokers contract more respiratory infections than nonsmokers.

**(5)** Children of smokers are more likely to try cigarettes themselves.

**23.** Recent experiments conducted on laboratory animals have shown that exposure to large amounts of ozone gas may cause cancer. Ozone, which pollutes the atmosphere when hydrocarbons from fossil fuels combine with nitrogen oxide, has already been known to cause headaches and breathing difficulties.

Based on the information provided, which of the following statements represents a hypothesis rather than a fact or an opinion?

**(1)** The link between ozone and cancer is pure speculation.

**(2)** Hydrocarbons from fossil fuels cause air pollution.

**(3)** Ozone can cause headaches and breathing difficulties.

**(4)** Exposure to large amounts of ozone can cause cancer.

**(5)** There is no conclusive evidence that ozone causes cancer.

Items 24 and 25 are based on the following portion of the Periodic Table of the Elements.

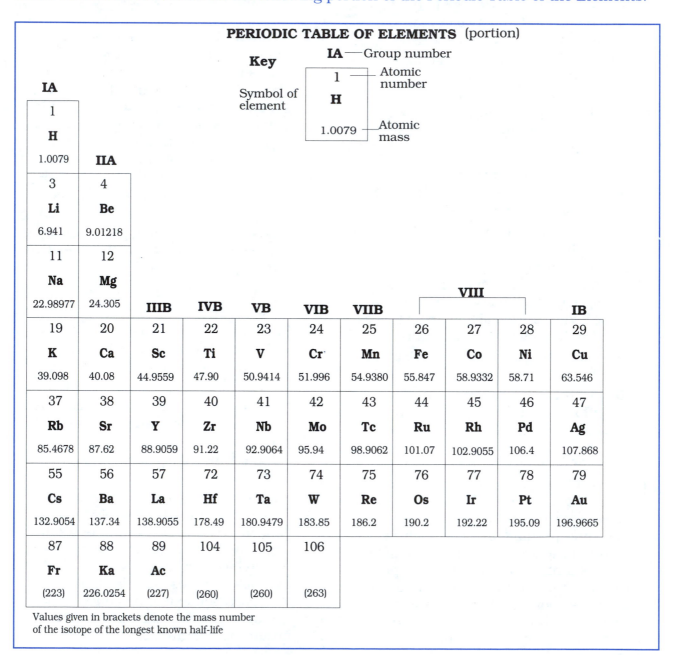

**PERIODIC TABLE OF ELEMENTS** (portion)

Values given in brackets denote the mass number of the isotope of the longest known half-life

The Periodic Table shows the symbol for each element, the atomic number, and the atomic mass. Atomic number and atomic mass increase as one moves from left to right and from top to bottom across the table. All of the elements in this portion of the table have metallic properties.

24. A manufacturer of electronics equipment needs a fairly heavy substance with metallic properties to use in making a part for an audio receiver. Which of the following would be the least likely substance to use?

    (1) tungsten (W)
    (2) sodium (Na)
    (3) platinum (Pt)
    (4) copper (Cu)
    (5) nickel (Ni)

25. Lithium (Li), Sodium (Na), potassium (K), rubidium (Rb), cesium (Cs), and francium (Fr) are all soft, silvery metals with low melting points, and all are highly reactive toward water and oxygen. This information supports which of the following statements?

    (1) Elements with similar chemical and physical properties are placed in the same horizontal row ("period") in the Periodic Table.
    (2) Elements with similar chemical and physical properties have similar atomic numbers.
    (3) Elements with similar chemical and physical properties have similar atomic masses.
    (4) Elements with similar chemical and physical properties are placed in the same vertical column ("group") in the Periodic Table.
    (5) Similarity of chemical and physical properties is not important in the organization of the Periodic Table.

26. Three basic natural laws governing the behavior of objects in motion were first expressed almost 300 years ago by the English mathematician Isaac Newton. The first law states in part that an object in motion will continue moving in a straight line in an unchanging direction unless acted upon by an outside force, such as gravity, the pull of objects toward the center of the Earth.

Which of the following is an example of the law of motion described above?

    (1) An automobile starts up from a complete stop.
    (2) A stone dropped from a high tower speeds up as it falls to the ground.
    (3) A golf ball rolls to a stop just inches from the hole.
    (4) An arrow shot straight up into the air stops rising and falls back to the ground.
    (5) A gun recoils backward after shooting a bullet.

27. Weathering of rock can take place by carbonation. Carbonation occurs when carbon dioxide in the air dissolves in rain, forming carbonic acid. although this acid is not harmful to plants and animals, it slowly dissolves rocks such as limestone and feldspar. Which of the following situations most closely resembles the weathering of rock by carbonation?

    (1) A stomach remedy reacts with excess stomach acid to produce a salt and carbon dioxide.
    (2) Carbon dioxide from automobile exhaust contributes to air pollution.
    (3) A piece of chalk (limestone) placed in a glass of carbonated water is gradually eaten away by bubbles of carbon dioxide.
    (4) Sulfur dioxide gas from factories dissolves with rainwater to form acid rain.
    (5) Two different rocks in the same climate weather very differently depending on which minerals are present in each rock.

**28.** Silver tarnishes when it reacts with sulfur. A rubber band wrapped around silver causes tarnishing because vulcanized rubber contains sulfur. Silver will also be tarnished by contact with hydrogen sulfide, which oxidizes to produce sulfur. Hydrogen sulfide is present in certain foods such as egg yolks and in small quantities in the atmosphere.

In order to keep silverware free from tarnish, a person should

**(1)** clean it with a sulfur-containing compound and then store it in an air-tight container

**(2)** leave it untouched for several hours after use and then clean it and store it in an open container

**(3)** expose it to hydrogen and oxygen and then store it in an open container

**(4)** clean it immediately after use and then store it in rubber casing

**(5)** clean it immediately after use and then store it in an air-tight container

Items 29 to 32 are based on the following passage.

What is heat? Until a few hundred years ago, scientists believed that heat was a mysterious fluid called caloric. Caloric was thought to be invisible, weightless, and capable of flowing from hotter objects to colder ones.

The scientists who finally challenged this idea were an American known as Count Rumford and an Englishman named James Prescott Joule. Rumford, working in 1798, and Joule, working about 40 years later, performed experiments that showed that objects in motion produce heat. You can see for yourself that this is true by rubbing your hands briskly together several times and noticing how quickly they become warm.

Because Rumford and Joule observed that energy of motion was converted into heat, they concluded correctly that heat must also be a form of energy. Thus the transfer of heat from one object to another is not the flow of a mysterious fluid, but a transfer of energy.

Heat will always move from a hotter substance to a colder substance. When hot and cold water are mixed together, the hot water will give up heat to the cold water. This happens because the molecules of hotter substances have more energy than the molecules of colder substances. As the two substances come in contact with each other, the hotter molecules collide with the colder molecules, transferring some of their energy in the process. Thus a mixture of hot and cold water in equal amounts will come to a temperature that is just about in between the original temperatures of the hot and cold water.

**29.** Which of the following statements is not true of heat?

**(1)** It can be produced by motion.

**(2)** It is invisible.

**(3)** It is a fluid.

**(4)** It flows from hotter objects to colder objects.

**(5)** It is a form of energy.

**30.** Which of the following demonstrates objects in motion producing heat?

**(1)** an iron

**(2)** the tires of a bicyclist pedaling up a hill

**(3)** a pen

**(4)** a runner jogging

**(5)** a stove heated to 350 degrees

**31.** An athlete sliding too quickly down a rope experiences a rope burn. Which of the following statements explains why this happens?

**(1)** Heat in the rope is converted into energy.

**(2)** Some of the energy of the slide is converted into heat.

**(3)** Energy in the rope is converted into heat.

**(4)** The motion of the rope produces heat.

**(5)** Molecules in the rope transfer energy to molecules in the athlete's hand.

**32.** Which of the following conclusions is supported by the passage?

**(1)** Molecules in hot water have twice as much energy as molecules in cold water.

**(2)** The amount of energy transferred in a molecular collision is always the same.

**(3)** The properties of heat are similar to those of a liquid.

**(4)** Energy can change from one form to another.

**(5)** A transfer of energy always involves a transfer of a fluid.

Items 33 to 35 are based on the following.

The human body is made up of several systems that function together. Listed below are definitions of some of the system.

**excretory system**—gets rid of both solid and liquid waste. The bladder, kidneys, and large intestines are involved in this system.

**locomotion system**—consists of muscles that are attached to a skeleton made up of bones inside the body. This system gives the body shape and support and enables us to move.

**endocrine system**—is made up of organs that send off chemicals called hormones into the body. These hormones pass into the blood or other fluids and affect particular organs or sometimes the whole body.

**digestive system**—breaks down food. The mouth, stomach, and intestines are the major organs involved in digesting food.

**respiratory system**—passes air in and out of the body. Your nose, mouth, and lungs are the main parts of your body involved in respiration.

For each of the following items, choose the definition that best describes the situation.

**33.** Whenever you walk into a restaurant, sit down, and order and chew your food, an important system of your body is working. Which system enables you to do all these things?

**(1)** excretory system
**(2)** locomotion system
**(3)** endocrine system
**(4)** digestive system
**(5)** respiratory system

**34.** Many long-distance joggers report that they experience a "runner's high." While they are exercising, their adrenal glands produce chemicals to give them the energy their bodies need. Which system of the body is producing adrenaline?

**(1)** excretory system
**(2)** locomotion system
**(3)** endocrine system
**(4)** digestive system
**(5)** respiratory system

**35.** The muscles and saliva in your mouth help you to chew and swallow your food. Eventually the food passes into and through the intestinal wall into the bloodstream. Which system of your body is involved in this process?

**(1)** excretory system
**(2)** locomotion system
**(3)** endocrine system
**(4)** digestive system
**(5)** respiratory system

Item 36 refers to the following paragraph and graphic.

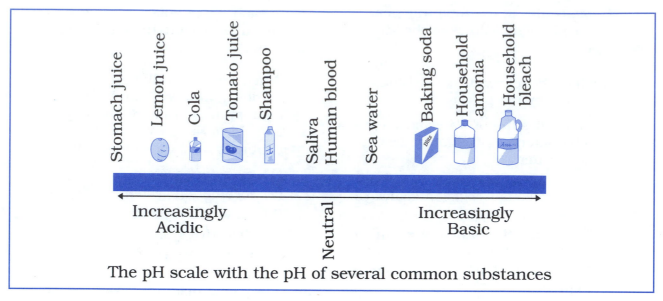

The pH scale with the pH of several common substances

Scientists have devised a scale for measuring how acidic or basic various solutions are. This scale, called the pH scale, indicates the concentration of hydrogen ions. The pH scale ranges from 0 to 14. Any solution with a pH of 7 is neutral; the number of hydrogen ions equals the number of hydroxide ions. A solution with a pH below 7 is acidic; the number of hydrogen ions is greater than the number of hydroxide ions. A solution with a pH above 7 is basic; the number of hydroxide ions is greater than the number of hydrogen ions. The lower the pH number, the more acidic is the solution. The higher the number, the more basic is the solution.

36. Which of the following conclusions can be supported by the diagram?

(1) Some substances are neither acidic nor basic.

(2) Basic substances will not produce ulcers.

(3) Tomato juice is highly acidic.

(4) Many people brush their teeth with baking soda because it is a basic.

(5) In an acidic substance, the number of hydroxide ions is greater than the number of hydrogen ions.

Item 37 is based on the following passage and graphic.

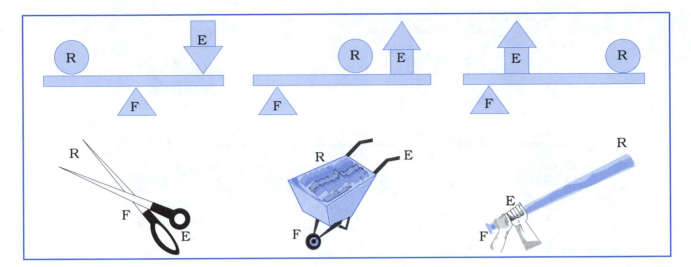

On the job and in our daily lives, we often use simple machines, such as levers, pulleys, and gears, to increase forces and make our work easier. Common examples of levers are the crowbar we use to jack up our cars to change a flat tire, the bottle opener used to pry off a bottle top, and the wheelbarrow used to move heavy loads.

A lever is a bar that is free to move about a fixed point. The fixed point is called the fulcrum. A pair of scissors is an example of a lever. The fulcrum is the center of the scissors, where the two blades are connected. The object to be cut exerts the resistance force. The effort force is exerted by the person using the scissors.

**37.** The passage provided adequate information to explain

**(1)** how gears work

**(2)** why people use levers

**(3)** the similarities among levers, pulleys, and gears

**(4)** how to use all common levers

**(5)** how levers help us do work in the most efficient way possible

Items 38 to 41 are based on the following passage.

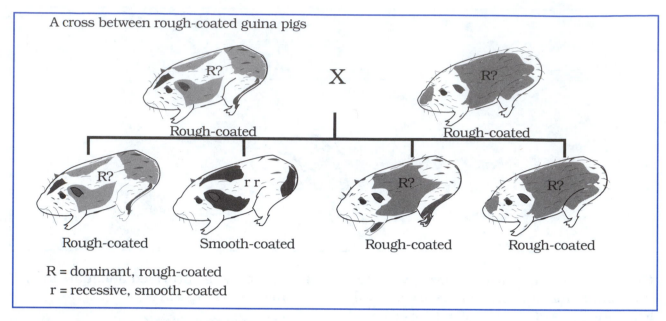

A cross between rough-coated guina pigs

Rough-coated X Rough-coated

Rough-coated   Smooth-coated   Rough-coated   Rough-coated

R = dominant, rough-coated
r = recessive, smooth-coated

Among living things, researchers have found thousands of traits that are *inherited*, or passed on from parents to their young. A feature that a living thing can pass on to its young is called a **trait**. In humans, you have surely noticed that eye color, hair color, facial features, and body build can be inherited by children from their parents. The passing of traits from parents to their young is called **heredity**. The branch of biology dealing with the study of heredity is **genetics**.

The foundation for the modern study of genetics was laid by an Austrian monk, Gregor Mendel (1822-1884). From his experiments, Mendel discovered that every inherited trait is determined by two genes. The offspring receives one gene from each parent. He concluded that genes are either dominant (symbolized by a capital letter) or recessive (a small letter). The dominant gene expresses itself in the offspring, whereas the recessive gene is not expressed. It is visible in the offspring only when the latter inherits two recessive genes.

**38.** If the two rough-coated guinea pigs in the diagram mate, what percentage of the offspring will be smooth-coated?

**(1)** 100%
**(2)** 50%
**(3)** 75%
**(4)** 25%
**(5)** 0%

**39.** If a rough-coated guinea pig (RR) mates with a smooth-coated guinea pig (rr), what will be the genetic combinations of the offspring?

**(1)** RR, RR, rr, rr
**(2)** Rr, rr, RR, rr
**(3)** rr, RR, RR, Rr
**(4)** rr, Rr, Rr, Rr
**(5)** Rr, Rr, Rr, Rr

**40.** When an offspring has an appearance different from the parents, neither of the inherited genes is dominant. Mendel found that when red flowers (AA) were crossed with white flowers (aa), neither the red nor white gene was dominant. Which of the following provides evidence for this?

**(1)** A flower with one red gene and one white gene is neither red or white but pink.

**(2)** Two red flowers will produce a red flower.

**(3)** Two white flowers will produce a white flower.

**(4)** A white flower and a red flower will usually produce a red flower.

**(5)** A white flower and a red flower will occasionally produce a white flower.

**41.** A dark-skinned father and a light-skinned mother will have a child whose skin color is between those of the parents. Two parents whose skin color is between dark and light can produce children whose skin color may be dark, light, or in between. A student argues that if one parent has light-colored skin and one parent has dark-colored skin, none of the children can have light-colored skin because the gene for dark-colored skin is dominant. What is incorrect about this argument?

**(1)** The gene for medium-colored skin is dominant over the gene for dark-colored skin.

**(2)** A dominant gene will determine a trait only 50% of the time.

**(3)** The gene for light-colored skin is dominant.

**(4)** A gene for dark-colored skin could mutate into one for light-colored skin.

**(5)** Neither the gene for light-colored skin nor the gene for dark-colored skin is dominant.

Items 42 to 46 are based on the following passage.

If you suspend an iron bar magnet horizontally from a string, one end of the magnet will always point north. This happens because a magnetic field surrounds Earth.

The region that is subject to Earth's magnetic field is called the magneto-sphere. The magnetosphere, which extends beyond Earth's atmosphere, is made up of charged particles blown out from the sun by the solar wind.

The magnetic forces that surround Earth are strongest near the poles. Earth's magnetic poles, however, do not coincide exactly with Earth's geographic poles. The north magnetic pole is located in northeastern Canada, about 1600 kilometers from the geographic North Pole. The south magnetic pole is located south of Australia, near the Antarctic Circle.

Scientists do not know exactly why Earth behaves like a magnet. For many years it was believed that Earth's magnetism was due to the presence of dense iron in the planet's inner core. In recent years, however, that idea has been challenged. Many scientists now believe that Earth's magnetism is caused by giant belts of electric current in the atmosphere and in Earth's crust.

**42.** The best title for this passage would be which of the following?

**(1)** How to Use a Magnet

**(2)** The Mysterious Solar Wind

**(3)** Magnetic Properties of Earth

**(4)** Iron and Magnetism

**(5)** Why Is Earth a Magnet?

**43.** The passage suggests that a relationship exists between which of the following two factors?

**(1)** magnetic properties and electricity

**(2)** composition of Earth's inner core and electricity

**(3)** location of Earth's magnetic poles and composition of Earth's inner core

**(4)** the solar wind and the properties of magnets

**(5)** location of the magnetosphere and composition of Earth's crust

**44.** A compass consists of a magnetized needle that is free to move. A person using a compass to find true direction should be most concerned about which of the following factors?

**(1)** the material composing the compass needle

**(2)** the location of Earth's magnetic north pole with respect to Earth's geographic north pole

**(3)** the difference between the compass and a bar magnet

**(4)** the effect of electric current on the compass

**(5)** the composition of Earth's inner core

**45.** In the passage, which of the following pieces of information is presented as a hypothesis rather than fact?

**(1)** the location of Earth's magnetic poles

**(2)** the location of Earth's magnetosphere

**(3)** the composition of Earth's magnetosphere

**(4)** the reason for Earth's magnetic properties

**(5)** the composition of Earth's inner core

**46.** The author of the passage does not provide data or evidence to support the assertion that

**(1)** the magnetic north pole is not located at the geographic North Pole

**(2)** a magnetic field surrounds Earth

**(3)** Earth exerts magnetic forces on magnets

**(4)** Earth's magnetism is caused by bands of electric current in the atmosphere

**(5)** the magnetic south pole is not located at the geographic South Pole

Items 47 to 50 are based on the following information.

Five types of chemical reactions are described below.

**(1)** **synthesis**—a reaction in which two substances combine to form a new substance (A + B = C)

**(2)** **decomposition**—a reaction in which a compound is broken down into two or more simpler substances (C = A + B)

**(3)** **single replacement**—a reaction in which one element is replaced by another in a compound (AX + C = CX + A)

**(4)** **double replacement**—a reaction in which the elements of the reacting compounds change places (AB + XY = AY + XB)

**(5)** **no reaction**—the substance or substances involved remain chemically unchanged

Each of the following items describes an example of one of the five types of reactions listed above. For each item, choose the reaction type that best describes the procedure. Any type may be used more than once.

**47.** When hydrochloric acid (HCl) is mixed with sodium hydroxide (NaOH), table salt (sodium chloride, NaCl), and water ($H_2O$ or HOH) are formed. This procedure is an example of

**(1)** synthesis
**(2)** decomposition
**(3)** single replacement
**(4)** double replacement
**(5)** no reaction

**48.** Passing an electric current through water ($H_2O$) results in the release of oxygen gas (O) and hydrogen gas ($H_2$). This procedure is an example of

**(1)** synthesis
**(2)** decomposition
**(3)** single replacement

**(4)** double replacement

**(5)** no reaction

**49.** Sulfuric acid ($H_2SO_4$) is poured onto a piece of zinc ($Z_n$). Hydrogen gas ($H_2$) is released into the air as a salt called zinc sulfate ($ZnSO_4$) forms. This procedure is an example of

**(1)** synthesis

**(2)** decomposition

**(3)** single replacement

**(4)** double replacement

**(5)** no reaction

**50.** One metal can replace another metal in a compound provided that the replacing metal is more active than the metal being replaced. Four metals in order of decreasing activity are lithium (Li), potassium (K), sodium (Na), and magnesium (Mg). Suppose that sodium (Na) is mixed in solution with lithium chloride (LiCl). The result would be an example of

**(1)** synthesis

**(2)** decomposition

**(3)** single replacement

**(4)** double replacement

**(5)** no reaction

**51.** A magazine article on beef contains the following statements:

(A) Beef is a source of protein, thiamin, riboflavin, niacin, vitamin B-12, iron, and zinc.

(B) Many consumers believe that beef contains high levels of fat and cholesterol.

(C) Meat labeled "lean" or "low-fat" has no more than 10 percent fat.

(D) Beef tastes better than other sources of protein.

Which of the above statements is most likely based on opinion rather than on fact?

**(1)** A and B only

**(2)** B only

**(3)** B and D only

**(4)** A and C only

**(5)** C and D only

Item 52 is based on the following diagram and information.

The diagram illustrates a phenomenon of sound waves called the Doppler Effect. When a moving object such as the train emits a sound such as a whistle, the sound waves spread out in all directions. However, the forward motion of the train compresses the sound waves ahead of the train. The more compressed the sound

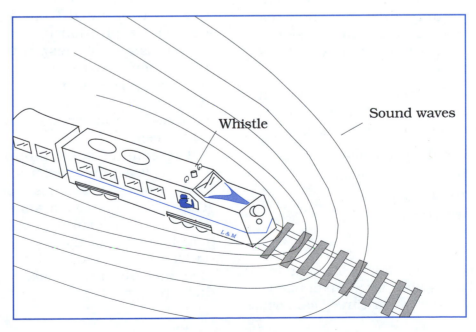

Whistle

Sound waves

waves are, the higher the pitch of the sound. As a result, if you were standing ahead of the train, you would hear the whistle as a very high-pitched sound.

**52.** What change would you hear in the sound of the whistle as the train passed by where you were standing?

   **(1)** The pitch would sound higher because you would be hearing sound waves that were more compressed.

   **(2)** The pitch would sound higher because you would be hearing sound waves that were less compressed.

   **(3)** The pitch would sound the same.

   **(4)** The pitch would sound lower because you would be hearing sound waves that were more compressed.

   **(5)** The pitch would sound lower because you would be hearing sound weaves that were less compressed.

**53.** Your immune system protects you by differentiating between your cells and foreign substances. Each cell has a unique chemical marker made up of a pattern of molecules at its surface. Because your particular gene combination is unique, the marks on your body cells differ from those on foreign substances. If the immune system detects a foreign mark, it will attack the substance.

Which of the following substances in your body is not likely to trigger an attack by your immune system?

   **(1)** your red blood cells

   **(2)** staphylococcal bacteria

   **(3)** house dust

   **(4)** pollen grain

   **(5)** polio virus

**54.** In general, a mammal's life span is related to its body size. Small mammals live only two or three years while

an elephant may live for 60 years. Which of the following mammals most likely has the shortest life expectancy?

   **(1)** a goat

   **(2)** a horse

   **(3)** a rabbit

   **(4)** a rat

   **(5)** a whale

Items 55 to 58 are based on the following information.

All living organisms need energy to carry out life processes. Organisms use the chemical energy that is stored in food, usually in the form of carbohydrates. The breakdown of food and the release of energy take place in individual cells through a process called cellular respiration.

During cellular respiration, the energy released by the breakdown of food molecules is used to convert adenosine diphosphate (ADP) into adenosine triphosphate (ATP). The high-energy ATP is then sent to whatever part of the cell needs energy. At that point, the ATP is converted back into ADP, releasing the stored energy to be used for cell activities. The leftover ADP may be reused by the cell.

There are two ways a cell can respire. Most organisms—like you—need oxygen for respiration to take place. Cells get the oxygen they need from air and water. Cellular respiration that uses oxygen is known as **aerobic respiration.** In aerobic respiration, most of the energy stored in glucose is released. A small amount of waste products—some water and carbon dioxide—also forms and must be expelled by the cell.

The cells of some simple organisms, such as yeast and bacteria, release energy by a process that does not use oxygen. That process is called **anaerobic respiration.** In this form of respiration, only a small amount of the energy that is stored in food is released, and more waste products (usually carbon dioxide gas and alcohol) are formed.

**55.** Which of the following processes is least important during periods of intense physical activity?

(1) the release of energy from glucose
(2) the conversion of ADP to ATP
(3) the conversion of ATP to ADP
(4) cellular respiration
(5) digestion of a large, recently eaten meal

**56.** Which of the following best explains why aerobic respiration of glucose is about 18 times more efficient than anaerobic respiration of glucose?

(1) The presence of oxygen allows the glucose to be completely broken down during aerobic respiration.
(2) ADP cannot be reused following anaerobic respiration as it can after aerobic respiration.
(3) Energy is released quickly during aerobic respiration.
(4) The glucose used in aerobic respiration comes from a more pure source than that used in anaerobic respiration.
(5) Individual cells are more efficient at aerobic respiration than at anaerobic respiration.

**57.** Biology is concerned with the study of life. Chemistry is the study of what matter is made of and how atoms change and combine into molecules. Earth science is the study of the Earth, planets, stars, and the forces that act upon them. Physics is the study of different forms of energy and matter. Which branches of science might be concerned with the material in the passage?

(1) chemistry and physics only
(2) chemistry and Earth science only
(3) biology and physics only
(4) biology, Earth science, and chemistry only
(5) biology, chemistry, and physics only

**58.** Scientists believe that the first living organisms evolved in an atmosphere without oxygen. Which of the following conclusions follows from this belief?

(1) Aerobic respiration evolved earlier than anaerobic respiration.
(2) Anaerobic respiration evolved earlier than aerobic respiration.
(3) Anaerobic respiration is a favorable genetic trait.
(4) Aerobic respiration is more efficient than anaerobic respiration.
(5) Organisms that depend on aerobic respiration will quickly die in an atmosphere without oxygen.

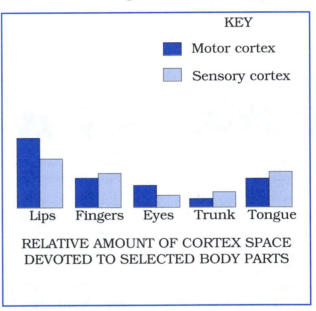

RELATIVE AMOUNT OF CORTEX SPACE DEVOTED TO SELECTED BODY PARTS

Item 59 is based on the following graph and information.

The sensory cortex is the part of the brain that receives signals from the skin, bones, joints, and muscles. The motor cortex moves the muscles.

**59.** Which of the following conclusions can be drawn from the graph?

(1) The two cortexes make up the largest part of the brain.
(2) The motor cortex is located opposite the sensory cortex in the brain.
(3) The sensory cortex and the motor cortex do not receive signals from the same body parts.

**(4)** The motor cortex is larger than the sensory cortex.

**(5)** The amount of cortex space devoted to a body part is related to how the part is used, not to the size of the part.

Items 60 and 61 are based on the following passage and diagrams.

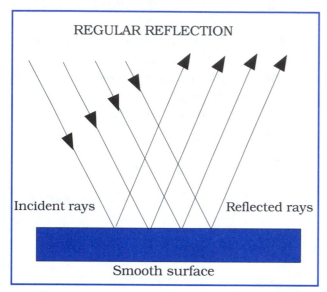

REGULAR REFLECTION

Incident rays          Reflected rays

Smooth surface

What happens to light when it strikes the surface of an object? Some of the light is absorbed by the object. The remaining light bounces off the surface of the object. Light that bounces off the surface of an object is said to be reflected.

The type of surface that light strikes determines the kind of reflection that is formed. No matter what type of surface light strikes, however, the angle formed by the incident ray and the normal equals the angle formed by the reflected ray and the normal. This is the law of reflection.

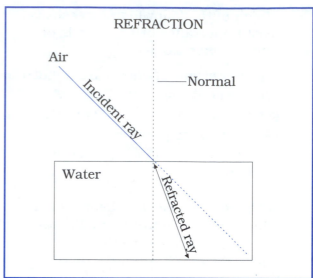

REFRACTION

Air

Incident ray

Normal

Water

Refracted ray

Light does not bend as it travels through a medium. Light travels in straight lines. What happens then when light passes from one medium to another? When light passes at an angle from one medium to another—air to water, glass to air, for example—it bends. The bending of light occurs because the speed of light changes according to the medium in which it is traveling. The bending of light due to a change in its speed is called refraction.

**60.** Which of the following represents a summary of the information provided?

    **(1)** Light travels in waves.

    **(2)** Reflection occurs when light strikes a surface and bounces back.

    **(3)** Refraction is the bending of light as it passes from one medium to another.

    **(4)** Reflection and refraction are two properties of light.

    **(5)** Light waves act in predictable ways.

**61.** A straw placed in a glass of water looks bent. Which of the following statements could explain why this happens?

    **(1)** Light is refracted as it passes from the air to the water.

    **(2)** Light is reflected from the surface of the glass.

    **(3)** The curved surface of the glass distorts the light as it hits the straw.

**(4)** Water molecules surrounding the straw are bent as light passes through them.

**(5)** Water reflects light, while glass refracts light.

62. Coal and other industrial fuels contain sulfur impurities. When these fuels are burned, sulfur released into the air combines with oxygen and water to form acids. These acids eventually mix with rainwater to form acidic rain. Not all scientists agree that acid rain is harmful to the environment. Yet surely when rainwater becomes an acidic as vinegar, plants and animals will suffer.
Which of the following statements represents the author's opinion?

**(1)** Scientists disagree about the effects of acid rain.

**(2)** Acid rain is caused by the careless burning of fuels by industry.

**(3)** Acid rain can have approximately the same acidity as vinegar.

**(4)** Industrial use of coal and other fuels pollutes the atmosphere.

**(5)** Acid rain poses a threat to living things.

Item 63 is based on the following information.

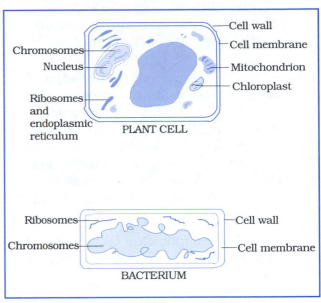

63. You are told that a particular cell that you are studying is either a bacterium or a plant cell. Which of the following observations would immediately tell you that the cell is a bacterium?

**(1)** The cell has no nucleus.

**(2)** The cell has a cell wall.

**(3)** The cell has a cell membrane.

**(4)** The cell has a chromosome.

**(5)** The cell contains chloroplasts.

64. The molecular formula for a compound tells how many of each type of atom are present in each molecule of the compound. For example, the molecular formula for methane, $CH_4$, indicates that one molecule of methane contains one carbon atom and four hydrogen atoms. The molecular formula for ethanol, $C_2H_6O$, could be used to determine each of the following EXCEPT

**(1)** the ratio of carbon atoms to hydrogen atoms in each molecule

**(2)** the number of each element present in the ethanol

**(3)** the arrangement of the atoms in each molecule

(4) the ratio of carbon atoms to oxygen atoms in each molecule

(5) the number of hydrogen atoms in the compound of ethanol

65. Scientists have proof that groups of songbirds have their own particular dialects. As a result of their studies, some researchers have hypothesized that the female cowbird listens to the dialect in choosing her mate; males who do not know the proper dialect include newcomers to the area and those too young to mate.

Which of the following facts about the female cowbird supports this hypothesis?

(1) She dislikes newcomers as mates.
(2) She teaches her dialect to her young.
(3) Young cowbirds don't sing as well as adult cowbirds.
(4) She mates only with cowbirds that know her dialect.
(5) She learns her dialect before becoming old enough to mate.

66. A rainbow is a natural phenomenon created when sunlight strikes water droplets suspended in the air. As the light passes through the droplets, different wavelengths are separated from each other. Our eyes perceive the results as the different colors of the rainbow.

A rainbow is evidence for which of the following statements about light?

(1) Lightwaves do not need a medium such as air through which to travel.
(2) Light is a type of energy.
(3) White light actually contains light of many different colors.
(4) Some types of light, such as infrared, are not visible under ordinary circumstances.
(5) Light may bend when passing through water.

Answers are on pages A-90-A-94.

**TIME:** 65 minutes
**Directions:** Choose the one best answer for each question.

Items 1 to 4 are based on the following passage.

### WHY ARE THE EVERTONS MOVING TO MEXICO?

"Let's stop and ask the way," says Sara, "while there is still daylight." And, as they take a diagonal course across a cleared space of land, she
(5) and her husband notice how the flat, pale rays from the west have lengthened the shadows of a row of tattered cornstalks, stunned survivors of the autumn harvest.
(10) But the owner of this field, the crooked fig tree, and the bent plowshare dulled by weeds and weather is nowhere in sight.

Richard points to a drifting haze.
(15) "There's some smoke from a cooking fire." But it turns out to be only a spiral of dust whirling behind an empty dam.

"We won't get to Ibarra before
(20) dark," says Sara. "Do you think we'll recognize the house?"

"Yes," he says, and without speaking they separately recall a faded photograph of a wide, low
(25) structure with a long veranda in front. On the veranda is a hammock woven of white string, and in the hammock is Richard's grandmother, dressed in eyelet embroidery and
(30) holding a fluted fan. Beyond is a tennis court and a rose garden.

Five days ago the Evertons left San Francisco and their house with a narrow view of the bay in order to
(35) extend the family's Mexican history and patch the present onto the past.

To find out if there was still copper underground and how much of the rest of it was true, the width of sky,
(40) the depth of stars, the air like new wine, the harsh noons and long, slow dusks. To weave chance-and-hope into a fabric that would clothe them as long as they lived.

(45) Even their closest friends have failed to understand. "Call us when you get there," they said. "Send a telegram." But Ibarra lacks these services. "How close is the airport?"
(50) and to avoid having to answer, the Evertons promised to send maps.

"What will you do for light?" they were asked. And, "How long since someone lived in the house?" But
(55) this question collapsed of its own weight before a reply could be composed.

Every day for a month Richard has reminded Sara, "We mustn't
(60) expect too much." And each time his wife has answered, "No." But the Evertons expect too much. They have experienced the terrible persuasion of a great-aunt's recollec-
(65) tions and adopted them as their own. They have not considered that memories are like corks left out of bottles. They swell. They no longer fit.

From Harriet Doerr, *Stones for Ibarra* (New York: Viking Penguin, 1984), pages 2-3

**1.** Which of the following best describes the Evertons?

**(1)** spontaneous thrill-seekers

**(2)** pessimistic wanderers

**(3)** brave adventurers

**(4)** antisocial recluses

**(5)** idealistic dreamers

**2.** Which of the following best describes Ibarra?

**(1)** It is a medium-sized town.

**(2)** It is a popular vacation spot with tourists.

**(3)** It lacks many modern conveniences.

**(4)** It resembles San Francisco in the style of its buildings.

**(5)** It is an abandoned industrial site.

**3.** When the author states that the Evertons "have not considered that memories are like corks left out of bottles" (lines 68-69), she means that the Evertons

**(1)** do not know that the weather in Mexico can be very hot and dry

**(2)** have not considered that the great-aunt's memories may not be accurate

**(3)** may not remember the directions to Ibarra

(4) have not considered that the Mexicans may not like them

**(5)** have not considered that their new life in Mexico will not have the luxuries of home

**4.** What is the author's purpose in using the present tense in telling of the Evertons' move?

**(1)** It allows the author to predict events later in the story.

**(2)** It emphasizes the Evertons' simple life in Mexico.

**(3)** It brings the action closer to the reader.

**(4)** It conveys the detached attitude of the author.

**(5)** It emphasizes the Evertons' spontaneous decision to move.

Items 5 to 7 are based on the following poem.

**WHAT IS THE SUBJECT OF THIS POEM?**

*Fog*
The fog comes
on little cat feet
It sits looking

over harbor and city
(5) on silent haunches
and then moves on

Carl Sandburg, "Fog," in *Chicago Poems* (New York: Holt, Rinehart and Winston, 1916)

**5.** Which of the following statements best summarizes the poet's description of fog?

**(1)** The fog blows swiftly over the city and the harbor.

**(2)** The harbor and the city have been covered with fog for days.

**(3)** The fog is black.

**(4)** One can see the shapes in the fog.

**(5)** The fog approaches slowly and quietly and leaves the same way.

**6.** The "little cat feet" (line 2) is best interpreted as

**(1)** the feet of pedestrians walking in the haze

**(2)** animals scurrying for shelter from the weather

**(3)** wisps of mist leading the fog into the city

**(4)** black soot carried in the fog

**(5)** short gusts of wind that accompany the fog

**7.** Why is the image of a cat effective in a description of fog?

**(1)** Fog tickles like a cat's whiskers.

**(2)** Fog looks like a slinking cat.

**(3)** Fog is as cool as a cat's nose.

**(4)** Fog moves in a catlike way.

**(5)** Fog feels as soft as a cat's fur.

Items 8 to 11 are based on the following passage.

## WHAT DOES BLANCHE THINK OF STELLA'S HOME?

BLANCHE: You sit down, now, and explain this place to me! What are you doing in a place like this?

STELLA: Now, Blanche—

(5) BLANCHE: Oh, I'm not going to be hypocritical, I'm going to be honestly critical about it! Never, never, never in my worst dreams could I picture—Only Poe! Only Mr. Edgar

(10) Allan Poe!—could do it justice! Out there I suppose is the ghoul-haunted woodland of Weir! (*She laughs*).

STELLA: No honey, those are the L &

(15) N tracks.

BLANCHE: No, now seriously, putting joking aside. Why didn't you tell me, why didn't you write me, honey, why didn't you let me

(20) know?

STELLA: (*carefully, pouring herself a drink*): Tell you what Blanche?

BLANCHE: Why, that you had to live in these conditions!

(25) STELLA: Aren't you being a little intense about it? It's not that bad at all! New Orleans isn't like other cities.

BLANCHE: This has got nothing to

(30) do with New Orleans. You might as well say—forgive me, blessed baby! (*She suddenly stops short*) The subject is closed!

STELLA: (*a little drily*): Thanks.

(35) (*During the pause, Blanche stares at her. She smiles at Blanche.*)

BLANCHE: (*looking down at her glass, which shakes in her hand*): You're all I've got in the world, and you're

(40) not glad to see me!

STELLA: (*sincerely*): Why, Blanche, you know that's not true.

BLANCHE: No?—I'd forgotten how quiet you were.

(45) STELLA: You never did give me a chance to say much, Blanche. So I just got in the habit of being quiet around you.

BLANCHE: (*vaguely*): A good habit to

(50) get into . . . (*then, abruptly*) You haven't asked me how I happened to get away from the school before the spring term ended.

STELLA: Well, I thought you'd volun-

(55) teer that information—if you wanted to tell me.

BLANCHE: You thought I'd been fired?

STELLA: No, I—thought you might

(60) have—resigned . . .

BLANCHE: I was so exhausted by all I've been through my—nerves broke. (*Nervously tamping cigarette*) I was on the verge of—luna-

(65) cy, almost! So Mr. Graves—Mr. Graves is the high school superintendent—he suggested I take a leave of absence. I couldn't put all of those details into the wire . . .

From *A Streetcar Named Desire*, by Tennessee Williams. Copyright 1947 by Tennessee Williams. Reprinted by permission of New Directions Publishing Corporation.

**8.** What is Blanche's opinion of her sister Stella's apartment?

**(1)** Stella's apartment is as bad as Blanche expected it to be from Stella's letters to her.

**(2)** Stella's apartment is worse than the bad apartments she's seen in other cities.

**(3)** Stella's apartment, like New Orleans, is as bad as she expected.

**(4)** Stella's apartment, like New Orleans, is not as bad as she expected.

**(5)** Stella's apartment is worse than she ever could have imagined it would be.

**9.** Which of the following is the reason Blanche gives for visiting Stella at this time?

**(1)** Blanche likes New Orleans as a city.

**(2)** Blanche's school let out before the end of spring term.

**(3)** Blanche has only Stella as a loved one in the world.

**(4)** Blanche was fired from her job.

**(5)** Blanche had a nervous breakdown.

**10.** Stella does not talk much with Blanche because

**(1)** She thinks Blanche is not looking well

**(2)** she is sorry she did not write to Blanche

**(3)** she is not glad to see Blanche

**(4)** she is waiting for Blanche to say why she has come

**(5)** she never talks much when she is with Blanche

**11.** Stella feels that Blanche's attitude toward her lifestyle is

**(1)** envious

**(2)** unobservant

**(3)** frightened

**(4)** unfair

**(5)** insincere

Items 12 to 17 are based on the following passage.

### ACCORDING TO JOYCE CAROL OATES, WHAT FUNCTION DOES BOXING SERVE?

Not all boxing fans are hard-drinking, cigar chewing, heavyset guys yelling themselves hoarse in a crowded arena. Picture instead a
(5) soft-spoken, frail-looking woman with the dignity of a Princeton professor, which is what she is. You might not think that one of our most prolific novelists would have the
(10) time to develop a passion for pugilism. But Joyce Carol Oates is as hooked on boxing as Marianne Moore was on the Brooklyn Dodgers.

Boxing, Oates argues, is "a cele-
(15) bration of the lost religion of mas-
culinity, all the more trenchant for its being lost." The 48-year-old novelist writes about the sport as a way of honoring her working-class back-
(20) ground. She comes, she says, from "a world in which a man who wouldn't fight another man would be characterized as a coward. In other classes, he would simply get a
(25) lawyer."

. . . The book is part prose poem, part history lesson. Oates rapidly sketches boxing's past, starting with its Greco-Roman origins as gladiato-
(30) rial homicide, and works on up to the present, pausing over the intro-
duction of the referee in the late 19th century. The "third man in the ring," she notes, is what "makes
(35) boxing possible." Otherwise, "the spectacle of two men fighting each other unsupervised in an elevated ring would seem hellish, if not obscene—life rather than art."
(40) Considered as theater, Oates writes, a boxing match is a "dialogue of split-second reflexes," whose "text is improvised in action." Considered as a political parable, it is "a strik-
(45) ing, if unintended, image of the political impotence of most men," who can't hit "the legitimate objects of their anger."

. . . Oates acknowledges that she
(50) started "On Boxing" with a feminist preconception. "I was interested in the sociology of masculine violence, and then I got more sympathetic with it, and saw it as really inevitable
(55) and quite natural." To those who favor abolishing the sport, she would point out that some fighters feel in more danger on the streets than in the ring. Boxing is their
(60) ticket out of the ghetto, a way to dis-
cipline aggression for the sake of something large—and potentially lucrative. . . . As for the fight fan's of view, Oates gives the
(65) floor to Emily Dickinson, whose view of great poetry applies at ring-

side: "You know it's great when it takes the top of your head off."

From "The Novelist at Ringside" (a review of Joyce Carol Oates's *On Boxing*), Newsweek, March 9, 1987, page 68

**12.** Joyce Carol Oates's attitude toward the referee is that he is

(1) a man who would not fight another man

(2) a necessary evil in boxing

(3) a part of the Roman origin of boxing

(4) a necessity for making boxing an art

(5) a part of life rather than art in boxing

**13.** Which of the following is NOT one of Oates's defenses of boxing?

(1) It is a way to gain wealth for many young men from the inner city.

(2) Some fighters feel it is no more dangerous than many city streets.

(3) It is a part of a lost religion of masculinity.

(4) It is part of the sociology of masculine violence.

(5) It is a way to discipline aggression for a larger purpose.

**14.** Oates's idea of boxing as a "political parable" (lines 43-48) is that it

(1) is improvised in action through reflexes

(2) is hellish, if not obscene, in its violence

(3) hits the legitimate objects of men's anger

(4) lets powerless men express their anger

(5) is a striking image of most men's lives

**15.** Joyce Carol Oates impresses the reader with the importance of boxing by

(1) comparing it to various forms of art

(2) criticizing boxing fans

(3) emphasizing the role of the referee

(4) mentioning its history

(5) describing the reflexes of boxers

**16.** Calling boxing "gladiatorial homicide" (lines 29-30) is a reference to

(1) the popularity of professional boxers today

(2) the lack of safety precautions for boxers

(3) the commitment of professional boxers to their sport

(4) the historical origins of boxing

(5) the carnival atmosphere at many boxing matches.

**17.** With which of the following statements would Joyce Carol Oates probably agree?

(1) Children should not be disciplined when they misbehave.

(2) All violent sports should be banned.

(3) Funding for school athletic programs should be reduced.

(4) Human beings are not aggressive by nature.

(5) Participation in school sports is a healthy expression of competitive instinct.

Items 18 to 20 are based on the following poem.

**WHY DOES THE POET THINK GOD MIGHT BE LONELY?**

*The Preacher Ruminates Behind the Sermon*

I think it must be lonely to be God.
Nobody loves a master. No. Despite
(5)   The bright hosannas, bright dear-
Lords, and bright
Determined reverence of Sunday eyes.

Picture Jehovah striding through the hall
(10)   Of His importance, creatures run
ning out

From servant-corner to acclaim, to shout
(15)  Appreciation of His merit's glare.
But who walks with Him?—dares to take His arm,
To slap Him on the shoulder, tweak His ear,
(20)  Buy Him a Coca-Cola or a beer,
Pooh-pooh His politics, call Him a fool?
Perhaps—who knows?—He tires of looking down.
(25)  Those eyes are never lifted. Never straight.
Perhaps sometimes He tires of being great
In solitude. Without a hand to hold.

Gwendolyn Brooks, "The Preacher Ruminates Behind the Sermon," in Black Voices: Poetry (New York: Abraham Chapman, 1968), page 462

**18.** Which of the following questions does the poem address?

**(1)** Who can understand what God is like?

**(2)** Who dares to question the ways of God?

**(3)** Why does God allow people to suffer?

**(4)** Does God really care about the details of our daily lives?

**(5)** Does God ever feel lonesome?

**19.** Be referring to "bright hosannas, bright dear-Lords, and bright/Determined reverence (lines 3-5), the poet implies that

**(1)** God does not notice the praise that comes from His worshippers

**(2)** God deserves the best that His worshippers can offer

**(3)** a lot of religious devotion is forced, not sincere

**(4)** worship is most meaningful to elderly people

**(5)** everyone worships God in his or her own way

**20.** Based on the poem, of which of the following churches would the poet most likely approve?

**(1)** one that has elaborate, dignified worship services

**(2)** one that is actively involved in social programs within the community

**(3)** one that is actively involved in community politics

**(4)** one that makes its members feel that they are friends of God

**(5)** one that supports a great number of missionaries

Items 21 to 25 are based on the following passage.

### WHAT HAPPENED WHEN CHARLEY LOCKJAW DIED?

Charles Lockjaw died last summer on the reservation. He was very old—a hundred years, he had claimed. He still wore his hair in
(5)  braids, as only the older men do in his tribe, and the braids were thin and white. His fierce old face was like a withered apple. He was bent and frail and trembling, and his
(10)  voice was like a wailing of the wind across the prairie grass. . . .

Old Charley died in his sleep in the canvas-covered tepee where he lived in warm weather. In the winter
(15)  he was crowded with the younger ones among his descendants in a two-room log cabin, but in the summer they pitched the tepee. Sometimes they left him alone there,
(20)  and sometimes his great-grandchildren scrambled in with him like a bunch of puppies.

His death was no surprise to anyone. What startled the Indian agent
(25)  and some of Charley's own people, and the white ranchers when they heard about it, was the fact that some of the young men of the tribe sacrificed a horse on his grave.
(30)  Charley wasn't buried on holy

ground; he never went near the mission. He was buried in a grove of cottonwoods down by the creek that is named for a dead chief. His lame (35) great-grandson, Joe Walking Wolf, and three other young Indians took this horse out there and shot it. It was a fine sorrel gelding, only seven years old, broke fairly gentle and (40) nothing wrong with it. Young Joe had been offered eighty dollars for that horse.

The mission priest was disturbed about the killing of the horse, justifi- (45) ably suspecting some dark pagan significance, and he tried to find out the reason the young men killed it. He urged Joe's mother, Mary, to find out, but she never did—or if she did, (50) she never told. Joe only said, with a shrug, "It was my horse."

The white ranchers chuckled indulgently, a little shocked about the horse but never too much upset (55) about anything Indians did. The rancher who told the story most often and with most interest was the one who had made the eighty-dollar offer to Joe Walking Wolf. Joe had (60) said to him, "Ain't my horse." But Joe was the one who shot it on old Charley's grave, and it didn't belong to anyone else.

But the Indian agent guessed (65) what had been going on. He knew more about Indians than the Federal Government required him to know. The horse was not government property nor the tribe's common proper- (70) ty; everybody knew it belonged to Joe. The agent did not investigate, figuring it was none of his business.

That was last summer, when old Charley died and the young men (75) took the horse out to where he was buried.

From Dorothy Johnson, "Scars of Honor," in *Argosy* (McIntosh and Otis, Inc., 1950)

21. What reason did Joe give to the white rancher for refusing to sell Charley's horse?

   (1) He planned to donate it to the mission in memory of his great-grandfather.
   (2) He wanted more money than the rancher was willing to pay.
   (3) He thought that the horse was part of the tribe's common property.
   (4) He would never let a white man ride the horse.
   (5) He said that the horse was not his to sell.

22. Based on the passage, one can assume that the death of the horse

   (1) had a ritual significance for the younger Indians
   (2) must have been an accident
   (3) had some dark, pagan significance
   (4) earned Joe Walking Wolf eighty dollars
   (5) represented a form of revenge for the young men

23. The mission priest's reaction to the event is somewhat similar to a tourist's reaction to

   (1) ethnic dances
   (2) a bullfight
   (3) a safari
   (4) a local festival
   (5) native handicrafts

24. The reader becomes aware of the irony in the great-grandson's name when it is revealed that the young man

   (1) is a half-breed
   (2) is lame
   (3) is illegitimate
   (4) loves to race horses
   (5) loves to hunt wolves

**25.** The attitude of the Indian agent toward the shooting of the horse would be best described as

**(1)** ignorant
**(2)** contemptuous
**(3)** understanding
**(4)** puzzled
**(5)** amused

Items 26 to 29 are based on the following passage.

## WHAT DID THE SPEAKER DO WHILE IN PRISON?

Estebita made our nights pleasanter by telling us in amazing detail about movies he'd seen. He was very frail, but his voice was extremely

(5) powerful, so even from behind the steel plates of his cell he could be heard by everyone. The place, all closed with metal doors, had good acoustics.

(10) Estebita gave such richness to his stories, so many details, that even today I confuse them with movies I've actually seen.

My will to survive grew stronger;

(15) my determination became as steely as my cell walls.

In spite of my weakness, I would lie on the floor and move my body to help my circulation. I did yoga exer-

(20) cises in meditation and concentration. I knew darkness could damage my vision. There were small holes in the iron sheet over the window. In the afternoon when the sheet had

(25) cooled, I would use first one eye and then the other, and look through the holes toward the blue sky and the green hills. I did these visual exercises daily, and believe I owe my

(30) sight to them.

There were men whose vision was permanently affected by those years in darkness.

I would put my ear against the

(35) metal plate to try to hear whether the guards were walking by. The only opening at the door was at the bottom, where there was about a half-inch space between the floor and the bars. If you squeezed

(40) against the floor a yard from the door, you might see a little piece of the hallway. (It was while lying face down on the floor, to take advantage of the ghastly waxen light that

(45) filtered into the hallway under the main gate, that I wrote the first notes about my ordeal.) The guards constantly walked by on tiptoe, sliding along the walls, so they could

(50) overhear our conversations. Sometimes Political Police officers did the same thing. We used a slang which was a crazy mixture of English, French, and Spanish and

(55) words we invented ourselves so they couldn't understand us.

We never knew who might be walking the hallways.

From Armando Valladares, *Against All Hope: The Prison Memoirs of Armando Valladares*, translated by Andrew Hurley (New York: Alfred A. Knopf, Inc., 1986)

**26.** That the prison had good "acoustics" (lines 8-9) means that

**(1)** the building was heavily guarded and locked
**(2)** the light in the halls was very bright
**(3)** the men entertained themselves
**(4)** the food was good
**(5)** sound traveled well in the building

**27.** Which of the following titles best expresses the main idea of this passage?

**(1)** The Determination to Live
**(2)** How Political Prisoners Are Tortured
**(3)** Spanish Prisons
**(4)** Defeated by the Enemy
**(5)** Estebita the Storyteller

**28.** If the speaker were stranded on a desert island, he would most likely

   **(1)** do exercises in meditation and concentration

   **(2)** give up hope of being rescued

   **(3)** not want to return to civilization

   **(4)** figure out how to find food and shelter

   **(5)** lead a carefree life in the sun

**29.** The speaker helps the reader to imagine what prison life was like by

   **(1)** repeating Estebita's stories

   **(2)** explaining the political background of his imprisonment

   **(3)** providing many descriptive details about his life in prison

   **(4)** including lengthy passages of dialogue

   **(5)** expressing his anger and frustration in short speeches to the other prisoners

Items 30 to 33 are based on the following passage.

### ARE THE RICH ALWAYS HAPPY?

"It is only on the surface that the rich seem to be happy," said Elena Ivanovna. "Every man has his sorrow. Here my husband and I do not
(5) live poorly, we have means, but are we happy? I am young, but I have had four children; my children are always being ill. I am ill, too, and constantly being doctored."
(10) "And what is your illness?" asked Rodion.

"A woman's complaint. I get no sleep; a continual headache gives me no peace. Here I am sitting and
(15) talking, but my head is bad, I am weak all over, and I should prefer the hardest labor to such a condition. My soul, too, is troubled; I am in continual fear for my children, my
(20) husband. Every family has its own trouble of some sort; we have ours. I am not of noble birth. My grandfa-

ther was a simple peasant, my
(25) father was a tradesman in Moscow; he was a plain, uneducated man too, while my husband's parents were wealthy and distinguished. They did not want him to marry me,
(30) but he disobeyed them, quarreled with them, and they have not forgiven us to this day. That worries my husband; it troubles him and keeps him in constant agitation; he loves
(35) his mother, loves her dearly. So I am uneasy, too, my soul is in pain."

Peasants, men and women, were now standing around Rodion's hut and listening. Kozov came up, too,
(40) and stood twitching his long, narrow beard. The Lytchkovs, father and son, drew near.

"And say what you like, one cannot be happy and satisfied if one
(45) does not feel in one's proper place," Elena Ivanovna went on. "Each of you has his strip of land, each of you works and knows what he is working for; my husband builds
(50) bridges—in short, everyone has his place, while, I, I simply walk about. I have not my bit to work. I don't work, and feel as though I were an outsider. I am saying all this that
(55) you may not judge from outward appearances; if a man is expensively dressed and has means it does not prove that he is satisfied with his life." She got up to go away and took
(60) her daughter by the hand.

From Anton Chekov, "The New Villa," in *The Witch and Other Stories* (London: David Garnett and Chatto and Windus, Ltd. Publishers, 1946).

**30.** According to Elena a person might feel "in one's proper place" (line 45) by

   **(1)** staying in the social class into which one is born

   **(2)** having a good education

   **(3)** marrying into a respectable family

   **(4)** working hard at one's personal goals

   **(5)** being in good health

**31.** What is Elena's attitude toward wealth?

   **(1)** She despises wealth and would prefer to be poor.

   **(2)** She is very happy being wealthy and not having to work.

   **(3)** She is embarrassed by her wealth and resents the peasants for making her feel uncomfortable.

   **(4)** She resents her husband for coming from a wealthy family.

   **(5)** She would gladly trade her wealth for good health and a purpose in life.

**32.** What is Elena's "illness" (line 10)?

   **(1)** loss of both vision and hearing

   **(2)** headaches and asthma

   **(3)** tuberculosis

   **(4)** sleeplessness and a stomach ulcer

   **(5)** weakness, headaches, and sleeplessness

**33.** The gathering of peasants around Rodion's hut (lines 37-42) lets the reader know that

   **(1)** Elena is about to leave her husband and children

   **(2)** Elena is moving her listeners to anger, not sympathy

   **(3)** they agree with the husband's parents' opinion of Elena

   **(4)** Elena's words are a lesson for everyone

   **(5)** only poor people have problems

Items 34 to 36 refer to the following passage.

### WHAT IS IT LIKE TO BE ELEVEN?

What they don't understand about birthdays and what they never tell you is that when you're eleven, you're also ten, and nine, and eight, and
(5) seven, and six, and five, and four, and three, and two, and one. And when you wake up on eleventh birthday you expect to feel eleven, but you don't. You open your eyes and every
(10) thing's just like yesterday, only it's today. And you don't feel eleven at all. You feel like you're still ten. And you are—underneath the year that makes you eleven.

(15) Like some days you might say something stupid, and that's the part of you that's still ten. Or maybe some days you might need to sit on your mama's lap because you're scared,
(20) and that's the part of you that's five. And maybe one day when you're all grown up maybe you will need to cry like if you're three, and that's okay. That's what I tell Mama when she's
(25) sad and needs to cry. Maybe she's feeling three.

Because the way you grow old is kind of like an onion or like the rings inside a tree trunk or like my little
(30) wooden dolls that fit one inside the other, each year inside the next one. That's how being eleven years old is.

You don't feel eleven. Not right away. It takes a few days, weeks
(35) even, sometimes even months before you say Eleven when they ask you. And you don't feel smart eleven, not until you're almost twelve. That's the way it is.

(40) Only today I wish I didn't have only eleven years rattling inside me like pennies in a tin Band-Aid box. Today I wish I was one hundred and two instead of eleven because if I
(45) was one hundred and two I'd have known what to say when Mrs. Price put the red sweater on my desk. I would've known how to tell her it wasn't mine instead of just sitting
(50) there with that look on my face and nothing coming out of my mouth.

"Whose is this?" Mrs. Price says, and she holds the red sweater up in the air for all the class to see.
(55) "Whose? It's been sitting in the coatroom for a month."

"Not mine," says everybody. "Not me."

"It has to belong to somebody," (60) Mrs. Price keeps saying, but nobody can remember. It's an ugly sweater with red plastic buttons and a collar and sleeves all stretched out like you could use it for a jump rope. It's (65) maybe a thousand years old and even if it belonged to me I wouldn't say so.

Maybe because I'm skinny, maybe because she doesn't like me, (70) that stupid Sylvia Saldivar says, "I think it belongs to Rachel." An ugly sweater like that, all raggedy and old, but Mrs. Price believes her. Mrs. Price takes the sweater and puts it (75) right on my desk, but when I open my mouth nothing comes out.

"That's not, I don't, you're not ... Not mine," I finally say in a little voice that was maybe me when I was (80) four.

"Of course it's yours," Mrs. Price says. "I remember you wearing it once." Because she's older and the teacher, she's right and I'm not.

(85) Not mine, not mine, not mine, but Mrs. Price is already turning to page thirty-two, and math problem number four. I don't know why but all of a sudden I'm feeling sick inside, like (90) the part of me that's three wants to come out of my eyes, only I squeeze them shut tight and bite down on my teeth real hard and try to remember today I am eleven, eleven. (95) Mama is making a cake for me for tonight, and when Papa comes home everybody will sing Happy birthday, happy birthday to you.

But when the sick feeling goes (100) away and I open my eyes, the red sweater's still sitting there like a big red mountain. I move the red sweater to the corner of my desk with my ruler. I move my pencil and (105) books and eraser as far from it as possible. I even move my chair a little to the right. Not mine, not mine, not mine.

In my head I'm thinking how long (110) till lunchtime, how long till I can take the red sweater and throw it over the schoolyard fence, or leave it hanging on a parking meter, or bunch it up into a little ball and toss (115) it in the alley. Except when math period ends Mrs. Price says loud and in front of everybody, "Now, Rachel, that's enough," because she sees I've shoved the red sweater to (120) the tippy-tip corner of my desk and it's hanging all over the edge like a waterfall, but I don't care.

"Rachel," Mrs. Price says. She says it like she's getting mad. "You put (125) that sweater on right now and no more nonsense."

"But it's not—"

"Now!" Mrs. Price says.

This is when I wish I wasn't (130) eleven, because all the years inside of me—ten, nine, eight, seven, six, five, four, three, two, and one—are pushing at the back of my eyes when I put one arm through one (135) sleeve of the sweater that smells like cottage cheese, and then the other arm through the other and stand there with my arms apart like if the sweater hurts me and it does, all (140) itchy and full of germs that aren't even mine.

That's when everything I've been holding in since this morning, since when Mrs. Price put the sweater on (145) my desk, finally lets go, and all of a sudden I'm crying in front of everybody. I wish I was invisible but I'm not. I'm eleven and it's my birthday today and I'm crying like I'm three in (150) front of everybody. I put my head down on the desk and bury my face in my stupid clown-sweater arms. My face all hot and spit coming out of my mouth because I can't stop (155) the little animal noises from coming out of me, until there aren't any more tears left in my eyes, and it's just my body shaking like when you have the hiccups, and my whole (160) head hurts like when you drink milk too fast.

But the worst part is right before the bell rings for lunch. That stupid Phyllis Lopez, who is even dumber (165) than Sylvia Saldivar, says she remembers the red sweater is hers! I take it off right away and give it to her, only Mrs. Price pretends like everything's okay.

(170) Today I'm eleven. There's a cake Mama's making for tonight, and when Papa comes home from work we'll eat it. There'll be candles and presents and everybody will sing (175) Happy birthday, happy birthday to you, Rachel, only it's too late.

I'm eleven today. I'm eleven, ten, nine, eight, seven, six, five, four, three, two, and one, but I wish I was (180) one hundred and two. I wish I was anything but eleven, because I want today to be far away already, far away like a runaway balloon, like a tiny *o* in the sky, so tiny-tiny you (185) have to close your eyes to see it.

"Eleven", by Sandra Cisneros, from *Woman Hollering Creek and Other Stories* (Random House, Inc., New York, 1991)

**34.** Which of the following summarizes the narrator's main point?

(1) Younger parts of yourself come out when you are in pain.

(2) In unfair situations, children feel like suffering adults.

(3) Children are always helpless against authority figures.

(4) A birthday can be as painful as any other day in your life.

(5) Getting older can expose you to more pain than you suffered at a younger age.

**35.** The narrator hated the sweater she was forced to accept because

(1) it didn't belong to her but to "stupid Phyllis Lopez"

(2) it had been sitting in the coatroom for a month

(3) it was ugly, old, and uncomfortable

(4) it was forced on her by a lie from "stupid Sylvia Saldivar"

(5) it was a sweater made for a three year old

**36.** The image of "a runaway balloon" in the last sentence is an effective way to end the passage because it emphasizes the narrator's desire

(1) to get to her birthday party

(2) to be one hundred and two years old

(3) to relive the day as a three–year–old

(4) to run away from school

(5) to forget her birthday

Items 37 to 41 are based on the following passage.

### HOW DID THE BEATLES' MUSIC SET A STANDARD?

Recently, I watched a television documentary on the Beatles—those mop-haired boys from Liverpool who changed pop music, moving their (5) songs forward on a rock beat but giving the music strange harmonies and haunting melodies. Song after song catches the emotions and the imagination through a mixture of (10) lyric lines and poetry. I wondered what was different about them and if the Beatles really sounded as different to our generation as heavy metal does to today's youngsters.

(15) The difference seems to be that the Beatles and their imitators were concerned with music. Heavy metal—with its synthesizers; electronic guitars; electronic drums; and (20) amplifiers, mixers, tweeters, woofers, and whatever other effect— is about sound, not music. Perhaps that's an artificial distinction, since music was historically defined by its (25) uses: *musica divina* or *musica sacra* was church music; *musica vulgaris* was secular and had no

sound restrictions.

Whatever the definitions, there is (30) something profoundly disturbing about heavy metal, just as there was something tremendously engaging about the Beatles and the music of the sixties. The group expressed and (35) reflected the spirit of their time, but most of all, they were good. When they played on Ed Sullivan's famous variety show on February 9, 1964, to an audience of seventy million— (40) 60 percent of all American television viewers—the Beatles had stolen most of the hearts of American pop fans. Even if the critics were almost forced not to like them, the public (45) did. They had a natural grace and charm, and they were obviously enjoying themselves and hoping that the fun would last....

The new recording technologies (50) were increasingly used by the Beatles, but they were enhancers rather than an end in themselves. When one listens to heavy metal and searches for something at its core, (55) all one hears is the throb of the technology hyping the beat. And in most pop rock, synthesized hand-claps and artificial impulses (provid- ing the acoustic equivalent of the (60) zaps of an electric game gallery) take the place of melody and harmony. The quest seems to be anarchist: today technology, tomorrow nothing but a barren landscape. (65) Perhaps we will find some undis- covered riches in today's pop just as we have in the pop classics of the past. But for the moment, I'm con- tent to listen to my old Beatles (70) records and happily remember those wonderful songs.

From Peter J. Rosenwald, ``Strawberry Fields Forever,'' *Horizon*, March 1985

**37.** According to the critic, what is the main difference between the Beatles' music and heavy metal?

**(1)** One appeals to the older genera- tion; the other appeals to the younger generation.

**(2)** One is concerned with music; the other is concerned with sound and technology.

**(3)** One is accepted by most music critics; the other is not.

**(4)** One is concerned with melody; the other is concerned with harmony.

**(5)** One reflects the spirit of its time; the other makes predictions about the future.

**38.** By stating ``today technology, tomor- row nothing but a barren landscape'' (lines 56-57) the critic predicts that

**(1)** computers, not people, soon will be writing the most popular music

**(2)** society will lose its interest in all forms of music

**(3)** melody and harmony will be lost to electronic sounds

**(4)** advances in technology will lead to better music

**(5)** advances in technology will kill composers' interest in attempting new musical styles

**39.** According to lines 40-48, American pop fans loved the Beatles mainly because they were

**(1)** musically talented

**(2)** young and funny

**(3)** musically original

**(4)** musically natural

**(5)** appealing and entertaining

**40.** Which of the following techniques does the critic use to support his views?

a. examples

b. quotations from musical authorities
c. historical references
d. disproving opposing opinions

(1) a and c
(2) a and d
(3) b and c
(4) a, b, and d
(5) b, c, and d

**41.** This critic might be expected to compare the changes in musical styles to the

(1) growth in popularity of personal computers
(2) development of modern dance from classical ballet
(3) movement from rhymed poetry to unrhymed poetry
(4) political upheavals in third-world countries
(5) increased use of special effects in movies

Items 42 to 45 are based on the following passage.

## WHAT IS THE PROBLEM FACED BY AFRICA'S RHINO POPULATION?

Wars, drought, a human population explosion and simple greed have all conspired against Africa's animals. The black rhino, a lumber-
(5) ing prehistoric tank that has survived for more than 70 million years, is already extinct in most parts of the continent. "No elephant is safe in Africa," says professional big-game
(10) hunter Robin Hurt in Tanzania. "Now if there are any survivors, they are cowering, frightened, in the deepest forest." Pessimists predict that wild Africa will soon become
(15) little more than a string of glorified safari parks as the true wilderness shrivels and the animals die out. The process is already under way in some of the continent's most
(20) popular game-viewing regions. "A few decades ago Africa was a sea of wild animals surrounding a few islands of humans," says Hurt. "Today the reverse is true."
(25) Poaching is one of the biggest threats—and it has decimated Africa's rhino population. As late as 1970, a healthy population of 65,000 was scattered throughout
(30) east, central and southern Africa. Today 4,500 rhinos are left, living in tiny groups that could die out unless they are immediately protected.
(35) It is a cruel trick of nature that rhinos are easy targets for poachers. Despite a keen sense of smell, they have poor eyesight, and many are so docile that a poacher adept at imitat-
(40) ing animal sounds can call a rhino to its death. They are also creatures of habit and must drink daily. Often a poacher can stake out a watering hole to find ready prey. The
(45) prize is the rhino's horn. Prices have soared from $17 per pound wholesale in the early 1970s to $300 per pound in the main markets in North Yemen, where rhino horn is
(50) used to make dagger handles, and in Asia, where it is used to make traditional medicines. The trade is illegal almost everywhere, but the laws are rarely enforced, and
(55) traders continue to sell as much as the poachers can provide.

From "Africa: The Last Safari?" *Newsweek*, August 18, 1986, pages 40-41

**42.** What is the main reason that poachers hunt rhinos?

(1) Tourists come to Africa to hunt wild game.
(2) Museums often ask for a variety of African animals for their natural-history displays.
(3) Local farmers want revenge for the damage that rhinos do to crops.
(4) Local craftspeople want to use rhinoceros hide to make souvenirs for tourists.

**(5)** High prices are paid for rhinoceros horn.

**43.** According to the passage, what is the probable future of African wildlife?

**(1)** Animals bred in zoos will gradually repopulate the African plains.

**(2)** Most animals will escape from wildlife parks.

**(3)** Wildlife population will continue to decline.

**(4)** Only the elephants will survive.

**(5)** Pollution will destroy most African wildlife.

**44.** Based on the excerpt, which of the following would the author be most likely to recommend?

**(1)** more zoos

**(2)** more safari parks

**(3)** more wilderness areas

**(4)** more game wardens

**(5)** more game laws

**45.** Which of the following is NOT a reason that the rhinos are an easy target for poachers?

**(1)** They cannot see well.

**(2)** They must drink water every day.

**(3)** They are easily tricked.

**(4)** They often visit the same places.

**(5)** They have a poor sense of smell.

Answers are on pages A-95-A-99.

# SIMULATED TEST 5
# Mathematics

**TIME:** 90 minutes

**Directions:** Choose the one best answer to each question. Formulas you may need are given on page 401.

Item 1 is based on the following figure.

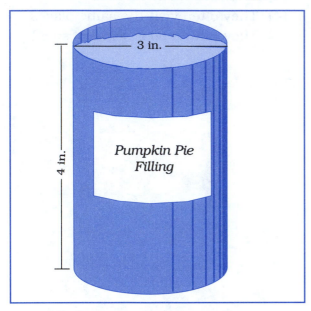

**1.** Which expression shows the approximate volume in cubic inches of the can of pie filling?

**(1)** $(3.14)(3)^2(4)$
**(2)** $(3.14)(3)(4)$
**(3)** $(3.14)(1.5)(4)$
**(4)** $(3.14)(1.5)^2(4)$
**(5)** $(3.14)(4)^2(1.5)$

**2.** The ride from Capital City to Rockville by train takes 50 minutes. If the train's average speed is 90 miles per hour, what is the distance in miles between the two cities?

**(1)** 40
**(2)** 75
**(3)** 90
**(4)** 140
**(5)** 450

**3.** What is the average number of miles per gallon (MPG) of the Wabash family's vehicles?

VEHICLE MPG

| | |
|---|---|
| Station wagon | 15 |
| Sedan | 22 |
| Pickup truck | 19 |
| Recreation vehicle | 8 |
| Motorcycle | 39 |

**(1)** 19
**(2)** 20.6
**(3)** 23.5
**(4)** 103
**(5)** Insufficient data is given to solve the problem.

**4.** Harvey is a leasing agent for a building that is 6 tenants more than 65% occupied. Which of the following expressions would indicate the number of tenants in the building if $u$ = the total number of units in the building?

**(1)** $.65(6) + u$
**(2)** $.65(u + 6)$
**(3)** $.65(u - 6)$
**(4)** $.65u - 6$
**(5)** $.65u + 6$

**5.** The Donovans are moving into a new house that measures 1500 square feet. That is 75 square feet more than 3 times the size of the apartment they shared when they were first married. How many square feet did their apartment measure?

**(1)** 250
**(2)** 475

**(3)** 500

**(4)** 525

**(5)** 1425

Item 6 is based on the following figure.

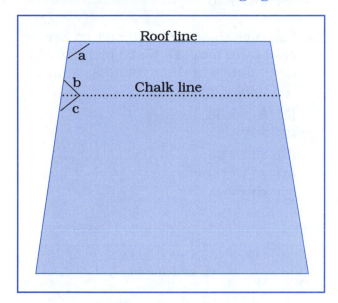

Roof line

a

b  Chalk line

c

Item 7 is based on the following figure.

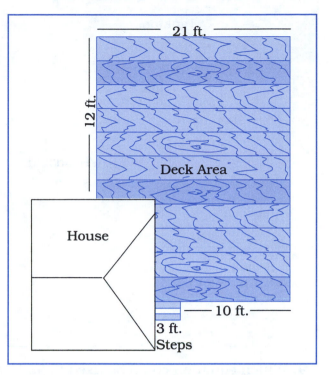

21 ft.

12 ft.

Deck Area

House

3 ft.
Steps

10 ft.

**6.** The chalk line is parallel to the roofline. If angle *a* measures 100°, what is the measure of angle *b*?

**(1)** 60°

**(2)** 80°

**(3)** 90°

**(4)** 100°

**(5)** Insufficient data is given to solve the problem.

**7.** How many square feet of wood will be needed for the floor of the deck?

**(1)** 120

**(2)** 156

**(3)** 252

**(4)** 372

**(5)** Insufficient data is given to solve the problem.

**8.** Sue, Peg, and Marie work together making wooden toys to sell at craft shows. They make $20 profit per train and $5 profit per puzzle. If they sell 18 trains and 60 puzzles and split the profits evenly, which of the following expressions shows the dollars of profit each person would get?

**(1)** 3(18 x 20 + 60 x 5)

**(2)** 18(20) + 60(5)

**(3)** 18(20) + 18(5)

**(4)** $\dfrac{18(5) + 60(20)}{3}$

**(5)** $\dfrac{18(20) + 60(5)}{3}$

Item 9 is based on the following figure.

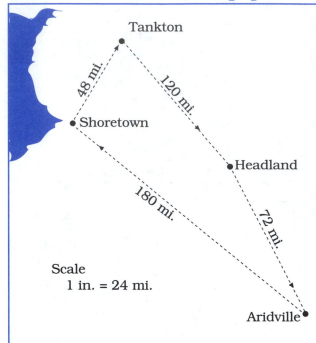

Tankton

48 mi.

120 mi.

Shoretown

Headland

180 mi.

72 mi.

Scale
1 in. = 24 mi.

Aridville

9. Which equation could be used to find how many inches on the map separate Shoretown and Aridville?

(1) $\frac{1}{24} = \frac{n}{180}$

(2) $\frac{1}{24} = \frac{180}{n}$

(3) $\frac{1}{180} = \frac{n}{24}$

(4) $\frac{24}{1} = \frac{n}{180}$

(5) $\frac{24}{180} = \frac{n}{1}$

Items 10 and 11 are based on the following information.

Bank credit cards are a convenient and a popular method of payment. Annual interest rates for purchases that have been made with bank credit cards vary, however. In Tompkinsville, bank A charges 10% interest, bank B 15% interest, bank C 16% interest, and bank D 18% interest. In addition, each bank charges a $25 annual fee for its card.

10. Bud charged a $588 couch on his card from bank B. If he pays for the couch in a year, how much interest will he pay?

(1) $ 49.98
(2) $ 70.56
(3) $ 88.20
(4) $499.80
(5) $676.20

11. Maria charged $29 and $84 on her card from bank D. If she plans to pay her balance in three months, what is the total she must pay?

(1) $   5.09
(2) $ 28.34
(3) $115.83
(4) $118.09
(5) $133.34

Item 12 is based on the following graph.

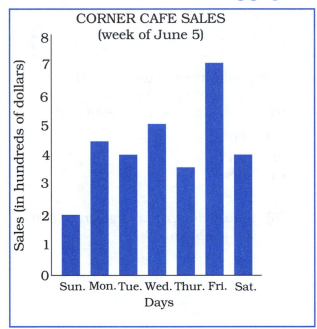

CORNER CAFE SALES
(week of June 5)

Sales (in hundreds of dollars)

Days

12. How many dollars greater were the sales on Friday than on Sunday?

(1)     5
(2)     9
(3)   30
(4) 500
(5) 900

**13.** What is the value of point *P*?

> **(1)** -5
> **(2)** -4
> **(3)** -3
> **(4)** 3
> **(5)** 4

**14.** A 20% discount is being offered on a coat that regularly sells for $150. What is the sale price of the coat?

> **(1)** $ 20
> **(2)** $ 30
> **(3)** $120
> **(4)** $130
> **(5)** $180

Items 15 and 16 are based on the following figure.

**15.** What is the slope of line *EF*?

> **(1)** $\frac{1}{4}$
> **(2)** $\frac{1}{2}$
> **(3)** 2
> **(4)** 4
> **(5)** 8

**16.** What is the distance from (0, 0) to point *B*?

> **(1)** $\sqrt{16}$
> **(2)** $\sqrt{64}$
> **(3)** $\sqrt{81}$
> **(4)** $\sqrt{90}$
> **(5)** Insufficient data is given to solve the problem.

**17.** Don sold two lots for $20,000 and $25,000. If his real estate broker earns an 8% commission on these sales, how much commission must Don pay his broker?

> **(1)** $ ,400
> **(2)** $1,600

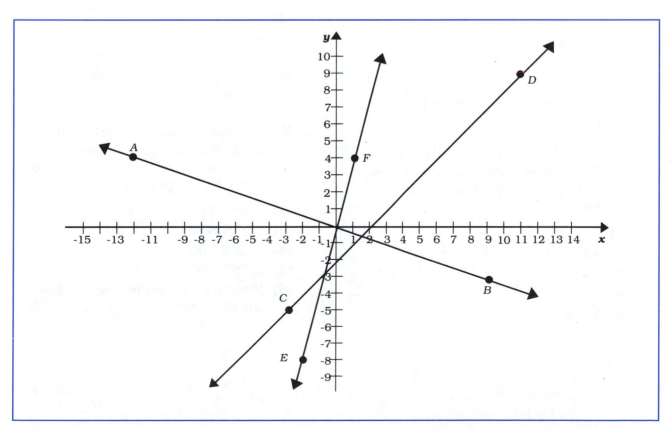

**(3)** $ 2,000
**(4)** $ 3,600
**(5)** $36,000

18. Which of the following expressions equals $(z + 7)(z - 1)$?

(1) $z^2 - 6z - 6$
(2) $z^2 - 6z - 7$
(3) $z^2 + 6z - 7$
(4) $z^2 + 7z + 7$
(5) $z^2 + 7z + 7$

19. Jill needs to buy 50 donuts to serve at an office meeting. If the donuts are priced at $3.00 per dozen, how much will this cost her?

(1) $   7.20
(2) $  12.00
(3) $  12.50
(4) $  15.00
(5) $150.00

Item 20 is based on the following figure.

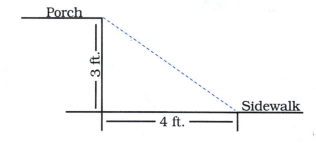

Porch

3 ft.

4 ft.

Sidewalk

20. If a stairway is to be built from the porch to the sidewalk, which expression shows how many feet long it will be?

(1) $\sqrt{4 + 3}$
(2) $\sqrt{4^2 + 3^2}$
(3) $\sqrt{4^2 + 3}$
(4) $\sqrt{4^2 - 3^2}$
(5) $\sqrt{4^2 \times 3^2}$

Items 21 refers to the following figure.

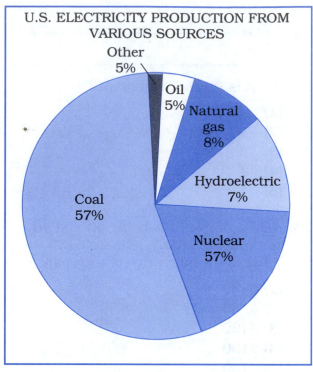

U.S. ELECTRICITY PRODUCTION FROM VARIOUS SOURCES

Other 5%
Oil 5%
Natural gas 8%
Hydroelectric 7%
Coal 57%
Nuclear 57%

21. If 7.36 million tons of coal were mined, how many million tons were used in the production of electricity?

(1) 1.67
(2) 3.07
(3) 4.19
(4) 7.73
(5) Insufficient data is given to solve the problem.

22. If 2,310,000 million kilowatt hours of electricity were produced, how many million kilowatt hours were produced by hydroelectric power?

(1)   292,370
(2)   378,840
(3)   623,700
(4)   3,788,400
(5) Insufficient data is given to solve the problem.

**23.** It usually takes three employees $7\frac{1}{2}$ hours to stock the shipment of parts that arrives weekly at Best Auto Supply. When the employees take a lunch break at the end of 5 hours, what part of this job will they have completed?

(1) $\frac{2}{5}$

(2) $\frac{1}{2}$

(3) $\frac{3}{5}$

(4) $\frac{2}{3}$

(5) $\frac{3}{4}$

Item 24 is based on the following figure.

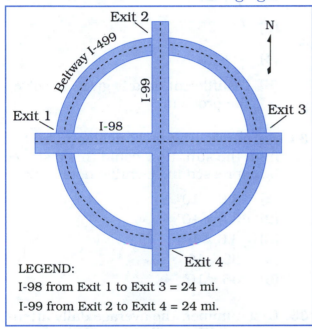

LEGEND:
I-98 from Exit 1 to Exit 3 = 24 mi.
I-99 from Exit 2 to Exit 4 = 24 mi.

**24.** How many miles long is the beltway?

(1) 37.68

(2) 75.36

(3) 87.24

(4) 113.04

(5) 150.72

**25.** Sixty people work at Plastico. If four times as many people work in the factory as work in the office at Plastico, how many people work in the factory?

(1) 12

(2) 45

(3) 48

(4) 75

(5) Insufficient data is given to solve the problem.

**26.** Factor $s^2 - 9s + 18$.

(1) $(s - 3)(s - 6)$

(2) $(s + 3)(s - 6)$

(3) $(s - 3)(s + 6)$

(4) $(s + 3)(s + 6)$

(5) $(s - 3)(s + 3)$

**27.** Anita mailed 10 packages, each costing $p$ in postage. She paid with a $20 bill and received $1.46 change. Which equation should be used to determine the cost of mailing one package?

(1) $10p = 1.46$

(2) $10 - 20p = 1.46$

(3) $10p - 20 = 1.46$

(4) $20p - 10 = 1.46$

(5) $20 - 10p = 1.46$

**28.** The square root of 53 is between which two numbers?

(1) 5 and 6

(2) 6.8 and 6.9

(3) 7 and 8

(4) 8 and 9

(5) 52 and 54

Item 29 is based on the following figures.

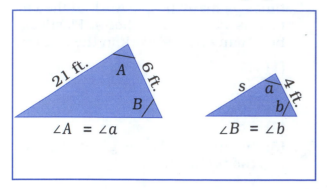

∠A = ∠a       ∠B = ∠b

**29.** How many feet long is side *s*?

(1) 14
(2) 15
(3) 17
(4) 21
(5) 24

**30.** Find the value of $\frac{v(v-w)}{w}$ if $v = 10$ and $w = 4$.

(1) $-2\frac{2}{5}$

(2) $1\frac{1}{2}$

(3) 6

(4) 15

(5) 24

**31.** The weekly commissions Derek earned as a salesperson in February were $232.58, $310.41, $298.27, and $356.25. Which of the following expressions shows Derek's average weekly commission in February?

(1) $232.58 + 310.41 + 298.27 + 356.25$
(2) $4 \times (232.58 + 310.41 + 298.27 + 356.25)$
(3) $232.58 + 310.41 + 298.27 + 356.25 - 4$
(4) $\frac{(232.58 + 310.41 + 298.27 + 356.25)}{2}$

(5) $\frac{(232.58 + 310.41 + 298.27 + 356.25)}{4}$

**32.** Twice the time it takes Joe to ride his bicycle to work, *r*, is still 5 minutes faster than the time it takes him to walk. If it takes him 45 minutes to walk to work, which of the following equations could be used to find how many minutes it takes him to ride?

(1) $r + 5 = 45$
(2) $r - 5 = 45$
(3) $2r + 5 = 45$
(4) $2r - 5 = 45$
(5) $2r - 45 = 5$

**33.** Paul spends $25 less than $\frac{3}{7}$ of his salary on rent. If *s* = his salary, which of the following expressions shows his rent?

(1) $\frac{3s}{7} - 25$

(2) $\frac{3s}{7} + 25$

(3) $\frac{7s}{3} - 25$

(4) $\frac{7s}{3} + 25$

(5) Insufficient data is given to solve the problem.

**34.** Mercury's orbit is 36 million miles from the sun. How could this distance be expressed in scientific notation?

(1) $3.6 \times 10^6$
(2) $3.6 \times 10^7$
(3) $3.6 \times 10^8$
(4) $36 \times 10^6$
(5) $36 \times 10^8$

**35.** Last summer, the average daily attendance at Waterville State Park was 542 children, 460 adults, and 315 senior citizens. This summer, the average daily attendance stayed the same except for adults, which increased 15%. What was the total average daily attendance this summer?

(1) 529
(2) 1071
(3) 1317
(4) 1332
(5) 1386

Items 36 and 37 refer to the following figure.

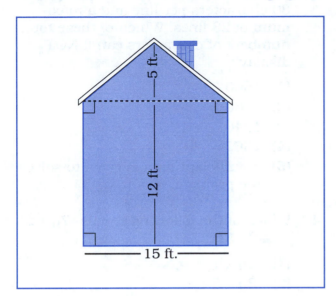

**36.** How many square feet of siding will be needed to cover this side of the house?

(1)  37.5
(2) 142.5
(3) 180.0
(4) 217.5
(5) 255.0

**37.** If covering the house with aluminum siding would cost $1.75 per square foot and painting it would cost $.75 per square yard, which of the following equations could be used to find the cost per square yard of having the house covered with aluminum siding?

(1)  $\frac{.75}{1} = \frac{n}{9}$

(2)  $\frac{.75}{9} = \frac{n}{1}$

(3)  $\frac{1.75}{1} = \frac{n}{3}$

(4)  $\frac{1.75}{1} = \frac{n}{9}$

(5)  $\frac{1.75}{9} = \frac{n}{1}$

**38.** Which of the following expressions would show the cost per tea bag, including a 4.5% sales tax, of a 48-bag box of tea that costs $5.78?

(1)  $\frac{5.78}{48}$

(2)  $\frac{.045\,(5.78)}{48}$

(3)  $\frac{.45\,(5.78)}{48}$

(4)  $\frac{1.045\,(5.78)}{48}$

(5)  $\frac{1.45\,(5.78)}{48}$

Item 39 is based on the following figure.

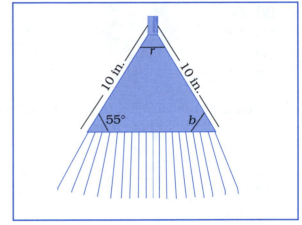

**39.** In the above drawing of a rake, what is the measure in degrees of angle $r$?

(1)   55
(2)   70
(3)   90
(4)  110
(5) Insufficient data is given to solve the problem.

**40.** Pat has 100 feet of fencing which she plans to put completely around her rectangular garden. If she wants to make the garden 30 feet long, what is the maximum width in feet her garden could be?

(1) 20
(2) 30
(3) 40
(4) 65
(5) 70

**41.** What does $\frac{32a^8b^7c^6}{8a^2b^7c^3}$ equal?

(1) $4a^4c^3$
(2) $4a^6c^3$
(3) $4a^{10}b^{14}c^9$

**(4)** $8a^4c^2$

**(5)** $16a^6c^3$

**42.** Orange-juice concentrate is mixed at a ratio of one part juice to three parts water. How many ounces of water should be used for an 18-ounce can of orange juice?

**(1)** 6

**(2)** 36

**(3)** 48

**(4)** 54

**(5)** 72

**43.** A box that measures 4 feet by 4 feet by 8 feet could hold how many cubic feet?

**(1)** 16

**(2)** 32

**(3)** 48

**(4)** 128

**(5)** Insufficient data is given to solve the problem.

**44.** Geraldine drives a truck for $m$ hours per week. If her average speed is 50 miles per hour, which of the following expressions would give the number of miles she drives in a week?

**(1)** $\frac{m}{50}$

**(2)** $\frac{50}{m}$

**(3)** $50m$

**(4)** $\frac{50m}{5}$

**(5)** $\frac{50m}{7}$

**45.** Jeremy runs for 45 minutes at 11 miles per hour 5 days per week. How many miles does he run in a week?

**(1)** 41.25

**(2)** 45.25

**(3)** 49.5

**(4)** 55.00

**(5)** 82.5

**46.** Jack's computer screen can display 80 characters per line and a maximum of 23 lines. Which of these total numbers of characters can it NOT display?

**(1)** 1600

**(2)** 1760

**(3)** 1840

**(4)** 1860

**(5)** Insufficient data is given to solve the problem.

**47.** Which of the following equals $-7g + 2h - (-4g) - 3h$?

**(1)** $-3g - h$

**(2)** $-3g + 5h$

**(3)** $3g - 5h$

**(4)** $-11g + h$

**(5)** $11g - h$

Item 48 is based on the following figure.

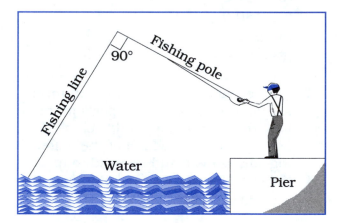

**48.** At what angle in degrees is the fishing line entering the water?

**(1)** 30

**(2)** 45

**(3)** 60

**(4)** 90

**(5)** Insufficient data is given to solve the problem.

**49.** Jan bought 15 yards of denim on sale. She plans to use this to make vests for the 6 members of her son's model railroad club. Which of the following expressions could Jan use to find the number of yards, $y$, she could possibly use for each vest?

**(1)** $6y < 15$

**(2)** $6y \leq 15$

**(3)** $6y \geq 15$

**(4)** $\frac{y}{6} \leq 15$

**(5)** $\frac{y}{6} > 15$

Item 50 is based on the following figure.

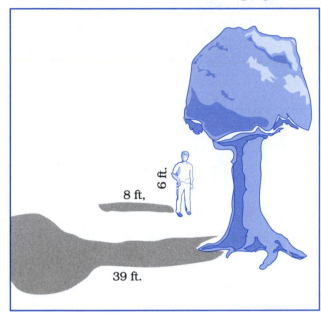

8 ft,

6 ft.

39 ft.

**50.** Martin is curious about how tall the old tree in his backyard is. Martin is 6 feet tall. If Martin casts a shadow that is 8 feet long at the same time the tree casts a shadow that is 39 feet long, which of the following equations could Martin use to find the height of the tree?

**(1)** $\frac{6}{8} = \frac{n}{39}$

**(2)** $\frac{6}{8} = \frac{39}{n}$

**(3)** $\frac{6}{39} = \frac{n}{8}$

**(4)** $\frac{8}{n} = \frac{6}{39}$

**(5)** $\frac{39}{8} = \frac{6}{n}$

**51.** Cara quit her job for a better one. If that year she earned $q$ at the first job and $b$ at the second job, which of the following expressions would give her average weekly salary?

**(1)** $\frac{(q + b)}{52}$

**(2)** $\frac{(q - b)}{52}$

**(3)** $\frac{52}{(q + b)}$

**(4)** $\frac{52}{(q - b)}$

**(5)** $\frac{52}{(q + b)}$

**52.** At a recent farm-association dinner, a drawing for 10 door prizes was held. Winners had to be present for the drawing, which was the last item of business. A total of 643 people attended the meeting, but some left early. What were the chances that someone who stayed would win a prize?

**(1)** $\frac{10}{643}$

**(2)** $\frac{2}{177}$

**(3)** $\frac{10}{585}$

**(4)** $\frac{58}{643}$

**(5)** Insufficient data is given to solve the problem.

**53.** Beth is planning to spend $40 on a wedding gift for her niece. Which of the following items that her niece has selected could she choose?

A. 4 bath towels at $8.99 each

B. 3 place settings of stainless at $15.00 each.

C. 1 dozen crystal glasses at $4.00 each

D. 2 pillows at $19.00 each

**(1)** A only

**(2)** D only

**(3)** A or D

**(4)** B or D

**(5)** A, C, or D

Item 54 is based on the following figure.

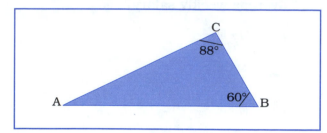

**54.** What is the measure of angle A?

**(1)** 32°

**(2)** 52°

**(3)** 60°

**(4)** 48°

**(5)** Insufficient data is given to solve the problem.

**55.** The base of a 1-gallon can of paint has a radius of 3 inches. The following lengths and widths describe the dimensions of the bottoms of cardboard cartons. Which carton could be used to ship six 1-gallon cans?

**(1)** 6 inches by 9 inches

**(2)** 12 inches by 18 inches

**(3)** 18 inches by 6 inches

**(4)** 18 inches by 18 inches

**(5)** 36 inches by 3 inches

Answers are on pages A-100–A-103.

**56.** A well-known singer was offered $15,000,000 to appear in 3 television commercials for a soft-drink company. If each commercial requires 8 hours of the singer's time to produce, how much will the singer make per hour?

**(1)** $   487,500

**(2)** $   600,000

**(3)** $   625,000

**(4)** $1,875,000

**(5)** $5,000,000

# Performance Analysis Charts for the Simulated Tests

**Directions:** Circle the number of each item that you got correct on each test. Count the number of items you got correct in each row; count the number of items you got correct in each column. Write the correct number per row and column as the numerator in the fraction in the appropriate "Total Correct" box. (The denominators represent the total number of items in the row or column.) Write the grand total correct over the denominator in the lower right corner of the chart. (For example, if you got 49 items correct in Writing Skills Part I, write 49 so that the fraction reads 49/55.)

## SIMULATED TEST 1: WRITING SKILLS Part I

| Item Type | Usage (page 64) | Sentence Structure (page 88) | Mechanics (page 102) | TOTAL CORRECT |
|---|---|---|---|---|
| Construction Shift | 35 | 8, 10, 24, 26, 38, 48, 53 | | /8 |
| Sentence Correction | 3, 5, 15, 16, 18, 32, 40, 47, 54 | 2, 14, 17, 19, 28, 34, 46 | 6, 7, 11, 20, 21, 22, 27, 30, 33, 43, 39, 44, 52 | /29 |
| Sentence Revision | 1, 13, 29, 37, 42, 50, 51 | 4, 12, 23, 25, 31, 41, 45 | 9, 36, 49, 55 | /18 |
| Total Correct | /17 | /21 | /17 | /55 |

*The page numbers in parentheses above the column headings indicate where in this book you can find the beginning of specific instruction about the various aspects of writing skills in Part 1 and about the types of questions you encountered in the Simulated Test.*

# WRITING SKILLS, PART II

**Directions:** After you have used the guidelines in the answer key to score your essay, make a record of your evaluation here.

Write the score of your essay in the box at the right.
List some of the weak points of your essay.

List improvements that you plan to make when you work on your next essay.

# SIMULATED TEST 2: SOCIAL STUDIES

| Item Type | History (page 167) | Political Science (page 185) | Economics (page 193) | Geography (page 202) | Behavioral Sciences (page 208) | TOTAL CORRECT |
|---|---|---|---|---|---|---|
| Comprehension | 9, 14 | 11, 23, 28, 47, 64 | 21, 26, 29, 57 | | 5, 6, 42 | /14 |
| Application | 38, 46, 54 | 25 | 13, 31, 61, 62 | 16, 17, 18, 19, 20, 36 | 4, 7, 41, 49, 50, 51, 52, 53 | /22 |
| Analysis | 2, 15, 27, 37, 40, 43, 44, 45, 55, 63 | 12, 32, 33 | 59 | 35 | 56 | /16 |
| Evaluation | 1, 39, 58 | 8, 10, 24, 34 | 3, 22, 30, 60 | | 48 | /12 |
| Total Correct | /18 | /13 | /13 | /7 | /13 | /64 |

*The page numbers in parentheses above the column headings indicate where in this book you can find the beginning of specific instruction about the various fields of social studies and about the types of questions you encountered in the Simulated Test.*

# SIMULATED TEST 3: SCIENCE

| Item Type | Biology (page 222) | Earth Science (page 251) | Chemistry (page 263) | Physics (page 277) | TOTAL CORRECT |
|---|---|---|---|---|---|
| Comprehension | 6, 7, 14, 16, 17, 22, 38, 54, 63 | 9, 42, 43 | | 29, 52, 60 | /15 |
| Application | 1, 2, 3, 4, 5, 33, 34, 35, 53 | 8, 10, 27 | 24, 47, 48, 49, 50 | 21, 26, 30 | /20 |
| Analysis | 13, 18, 19, 39, 51, 56, 57, 58, 59 | 11, 23, 44, 45 | 28, 62, 64 | 31, 61 | /18 |
| Evaluation | 15, 20, 40, 41, 55, 65 | 46 | 12, 25, 36 | 32, 37, 66 | /13 |
| Total Correct | /33 | /11 | /11 | /11 | /66 |

*The page numbers in parentheses above the column headings indicate where in this book you can find the beginning of specific instruction about the various fields of science and about the types of questions you encountered in the Simulated Test.*

# SIMULATED TEST 4: INTERPRETING LITERATURE AND THE ARTS

| Item Type | Nonfiction (page 288) | Fiction (page 312) | Drama (page 332) | Poetry (page 354) | Commentary (page 374) | TOTAL CORRECT |
|---|---|---|---|---|---|---|
| Comprehension | 26, 27, 42, 43, 45 | 1, 2, 3, 21, 22, 30, 32, 34, 35 | 8, 10 | 5, 6, 18, 19 | 13, 14, 16, 37, 38, 39 | /26 |
| Application | 28, 44 | 23 | | 20 | 17, 41 | /6 |
| Analysis | 29 | 4, 24, 25, 31, 33, 36 | 9, 11 | 7 | 12, 15, 40 | /13 |
| Total Correct | /8 | /16 | /4 | /6 | /11 | /45 |

*The page numbers in parentheses above the column headings indicate where in this book you can find the beginning of specific instruction about the various kinds of literature and about the types of questions you have encountered in the Simulated Test.*

# SIMULATED TEST 5: MATHEMATICS

| Item Type | Arithmetic (page 402) | Algebra (page 533) | Geometry (page 554) | TOTAL CORRECT |
|---|---|---|---|---|
| Comprehension (Skills) | 13, 34 | 30, 41, 47 | 39, 54 | /7 |
| Application | 1, 7, 9, 10, 18, 24, 28, 31, 46 | 26, | 6, 15, 16, 48 | /14 |
| Analysis (Problem Solving) | 2, 3, 8, 11, 12, 14, 17, 21, 22, 23, 35, 36, 37, 38, 43, 45, 52, 53, 56 | 4, 5, 19, 25, 27, 32, 33, 42, 44, 49, 51 | 20, 29, 40, 50, 55 | 35 |
| Total Correct | /30 | /15 | /11 | /56 |

The page numbers in parentheses above the column headings indicate where in this book you can find the beginning of specific instruction about the various skills and fields and about the types of questions you encountered in the Simulated Test. In mathematics, however, the items in the chart are classified as Skills, Applications, or Problem Solving. In the chapters in Unit V of this book, the three item types are covered in different levels:

Skill Items are covered in Level 1.
Applications items are covered in Level 2.
Problem Solving items are covered in Level 3.

For example, the skills needed to solve Item 4 are covered in Level 3 of Chapter 6 in Unit V. To locate in which chapter arithmetic items are addressed, reread the problem to see what kind of numbers (whole numbers, fractions, and so forth) are used and then go to the designated level of the appropriate chapter.

# Answer Key: Unit 1

## CHAPTER 1

### SKILL 1, PREVIEW

1. Women have many different jobs today.

   (Change has to have to agree with women.)

2. Money problems, in addition to job stress, worry many women.

   (Change worries to worry to agree with money problems.)

3. Across the country are many types of jobs.

   (Change is to are to agree with types.)

4. There are many reasons for women to work.

   (Change is to are to agree with reasons.)

5. Child care and flexible hours are important concerns for working women.

   (Correct.)

### SKILL 1, LESSON 1 EXERCISE

1. The weather reports say that it will probably rain tomorrow.

   (Change says to say to agree with weather reports.)

2. Everyone hopes for clear skies for the picnic.

   (Change hope to hopes to agree with everyone. Everyone is singular.)

3. Most of the picnic posters have been made already.

   (Change has to have to agree with most. Most is plural because it refers to posters.)

4. Nobody believes it will rain.

   (Change believe to believes to agree with nobody. Nobody is singular.)

5. Our team is practicing for the contest.

   (Change are to is to agree with team.)

6. Athletics is not my strong point.

   (Change are to is to agree with athletics. Athletics is singular.)

7. Your pants have some grease stains on them.

   (Change has to have to agree with pants.)

8. Jenny, you look tired from running so fast.

   (Change looks to look to agree with you. You refers to Jenny, a singular subject.)

9. All of our friends are cheering loudly.

   (Correct.)

10. I think our team will win the contest.

    (Change thinks to think to agree with I.)

### SKILL 1, LESSON 2 EXERCISE

1. The package of cookies was bright green.

   (Change were to was to agree with package.)

2. The cookies, in addition to the cake, were a treat for the children.

   (Change was to were to agree with cookies.)

3. The children, together with the dog, want more cookies.

   (Correct.)

4. One of the packages of cookies has a special gift inside.

   (Change have to has to agree with one.)

5. The plate of cookies sits on the table.

   (Change sit to sits to agree with plate.)

### SKILL 1, LESSON 3 EXERCISE

1. At the trial were the jury.

   (Change were to was to agree with jury.)

2. Behind the defendant sits the family of the defendant.

   (Correct. Sits agrees with the collective noun family, which is singular.)

3. Were the answers to the questions clearly heard?

   (Change was to were to agree with answers.)

4. Next to the judge stands the bailiff.

   (Change stand to stands to agree with bailiff.)

5. Do the reporters take pictures during the trial?

   (Change Does to Do to agree with reporters.)

### SKILL 1, LESSON 4 EXERCISE

1. There are more than two million people living in Atlanta.

   (Change is to are to agree with people.)

2. Here is the zip code for addresses in the downtown area.

   (Change are to is to agree with zip code.)

3. There are many peach trees in Georgia.

   (Change is to are to agree with trees.)

4. Here is an article about the businesses in Atlanta.

   (Correct.)

5. There are many banks in that city.

   (Correct: are agrees with banks, which is plural.)

## SKILL 1, LESSON 5 EXERCISE

1. Jacquie and Connie are collecting donations for charity.

   (Correct.)

2. Neither Gordon nor Vance has any canned goods to donate.

   (Change have to has to agree with Vance.)

3. Not only canned goods but also money is needed.

   (Change are to is to agree with money.)

4. Either Jacquie or Connie is taking the canned goods to the donation center.

   (Change are to is to agree with Connie.)

5. Both Salvation Army and Goodwill sell very inexpensive, used clothing.

   (Change sells to sell to agree with Salvation Army and Goodwill.)

## REVIEW FOR SKILL 1

1. Every April, Americans file their tax returns.

   (Change files to file to agree with Americans.)

2. Federal taxes and state taxes are filed separately.

   (Change is to are to agree with federal taxes **and** state taxes.)

3. Do all states have an income tax?

   (Correct. Have agrees with states, which is plural.)

4. Oscar and Ginny are

organizing their financial records.

   (Change is to are to agree with Oscar **and** Ginny.)

5. The box with the envelopes contains important receipts.

   (Change contain to contains to agree with box.)

6. Under that box is the pamphlet with directions.

   (Change are to is to agree with pamphlet.)

7. Most of the directions are easy to understand.

   (Change is to are to agree with most. Most is plural because it refers to directions.)

8. Here is the envelope with the medical receipts.

   (Change are to is to agree with envelope.)

9. Neither the rent payments nor the apartment insurance is deductible.

   (Change are to is to agree with apartment insurance.)

10. No one likes to pay higher taxes.

    (Change like to likes to agree with no one.)

## SKILL 2, PREVIEW

1. Terence has driven to work without his lunch box.

   (Change drove to driven. Past participle is needed.)

2. Later today, he will notice that his lunch is at home.

   (Correct.)

3. In the last two weeks, he has forgotten his thermos several times.

   (Change forgot to forgotten. Past participle is needed.)

4. Because he did not have his home-made lunch, he ate the cafeteria food.

(Change eats to ate. Past tense is needed to make verb tense consistent.)

5. Tomorrow, he will bring his lunch box and thermos.

   (Change brought to will bring. Future tense is needed.)

## SKILL 2, LESSON 1 EXERCISE

1. Last year, winter came very early.

   (Past tense of come)

2. The cold wind blew fiercely.

   (Past tense of blow)

3. The lake in the park froze.

   (Past tense of freeze)

4. The children rode sleds down the snow-covered hills.

   (Past tense of ride)

5. Some children threw snowballs at each other.

   (Past tense of throw)

6. We have already eaten dinner.

   (Past participle of eat)

7. Willie has drunk his second cup of coffee.

   (Past participle of drink)

8. I have begun to wash the dishes.

   (Past participle of begin)

9. The children have gone to bed.

   (Past participle of go)

10. Jamie has taken the dog for a walk.

    (Past participle of take)

## SKILL 2, LESSON 2 EXERCISE

1. Last year, Betty Ann Chow celebrated Christmas with her parents at their home.

   (Change celebrates to celebrated. Past tense is needed because Last year sets the verb tense for the paragraph.)

2. When she visited her parents, she brought a fruit cake and cheese.

   (Change bring to brought. Past tense is needed.)

3. Mrs. Chow gave Betty Ann a warm sweater.

   (Change gives to gave. Past tense is needed.)

4. Mr. Chow bought his daughter a new pair of gloves.

   (Correct.)

5. After they exchanged gifts, they all went to church.

   (Change go to went. Past tense is needed.)

6. Over the past decade, many people moved into the county, and the streets became more crowded with cars.

   (Past tense became is needed because of the first verb, moved.)

7. If gasoline prices continue to go up next month, more people will ride buses to work.

   (Future tense will ride is needed because of the words next month.)

8. Because there was a water shortage, the county issued restrictions on water usage.

   (Past tense issued is needed because of the first verb, was.)

9. When it rains, the reservoirs store the water.

   (Present tense store is needed because of the first verb, rains.)

10. The county commissioners predicted that taxes will be increased.

   (Future tense will be is needed. The prediction is for the future.)

REVIEW FOR SKILL 2

1. Because people like warm weather, many Americans are moving to the southern states.

   (Change were to are. Present tense is needed.)

2. The southern states are places such as Florida, Arizona, New Mexico, and Texas.

   (Change were to are. Present tense is needed.)

3. These states are growing in population, while the northern states are losing people.

   (Change lost to are losing. Present tense is needed to agree with are growing.)

4. However, in the future, the increased population will bring problems for local communities.

   (Change brought to will bring. Future tense is needed.)

5. Some city planners are predicting that a severe housing shortage will occur.

   (Change occurred to will occur. Predict means to guess the future.)

6. Jobs will not be available for people in the coming years.

   (Change were not to will not be. In the coming years means in the future.)

7. As new families arrive in the community, more schools are needed.

   (Change were to are. The verb arrive is present tense.)

8. Many businesses welcome the population boom, but some local residents are worried about increased crime and taxes.

   (Change were to are. The verb welcome is present tense.)

9. Some people do not want their community to grow too large.

   (Correct.)

10. The city planners listen carefully to the residents and discuss the problems of overpopulation.

   (Change discussed to discuss. The first verb, listen, is present tense.)

SKILL 3, PREVIEW

1. Chesapeake Bay is located in Maryland, which is my home state.

   (Correct.)

2. Clams or oysters are delicious when they are fried.

   (Change it is to they are to agree with oysters.)

3. When people eat fried chicken at picnics, they use their fingers.

   (Change you and your to they and their to agree with people.)

4. Stella told Kathy that Kathy made delicious clam chowder.

   (Replace she with Kathy to make the pronoun reference clear.)

5. You would enjoy fishing because it is relaxing.

   (Replace they are with it is. It refers to fishing.)

SKILL 3, LESSON 1 EXERCISE

1. Many fathers make lunches for their children.

   (Change his to their to agree with fathers.)

2. My mother baked bread for her family.

   (Correct.)

3. The container for the cookies is missing its cover.

(Change their to its. Its refers to container.)

4. The frying pan or the sauce pan is missing its lid.

(Change their to its. A singular pronoun is needed because or joins frying pan and sauce pan.)

5. Andrew, one of the local electricians, brings his own lunch.

(Change their to his to agree with Andrew.)

## SKILL 3, LESSON 2 EXERCISE

1. A balanced diet is important to our physical health as well as our emotional health.

(Correct.)

2. When people want to lose weight, they should exercise.

(Change you to they to agree with people.)

3. You should not go on a totally liquid diet if you have not talked with a doctor first.

(Change they to you to agree with you.)

4. When we drastically change our eating habits, we might feel anxious or tired.

(Change you to we to agree with we.)

5. A pregnant woman should talk with her doctor before she tries to lose weight.

(Change they try to she tries to agree with woman.)

## SKILL 3, LESSON 3 EXERCISE

1. The mountain range which stretches from Alaska to New Mexico is the Rocky Mountains.

or: The mountain range that stretches from Alaska to New Mexico is the Rocky Mountains.

(Replace who with which or that to agree with mountain range.)

2. Hikers who enjoy spectacular scenery like to camp in these mountains.

or: Hikers that enjoy spectacular scenery like to camp in these mountains.

(Replace which with who or that to agree with hikers.)

3. The snow that melts from the high mountains flows into the rivers.

(Correct.)

4. Hikers often see animals that graze in the meadows.

or: Hikers often see animals which graze in the meadows.

(Replace who with that or which.)

5. One hiker whom I admired had one artificial leg.

(Change who to whom because you would say "I admired him.")

## SKILL 3, LESSON 4 EXERCISE

Answers may vary in this exercise.

1. At work, employees complained about the broken furnace.

or: At work, people complained about the broken furnace.

(Replace they with employees or people.)

2. The pipes froze because the blizzard caused below- zero temperatures.

or: The blizzard's below-zero temperatures caused the pipes to freeze.

(Replace which with more specific wording.)

3. The radio announcer said that the temperatures will continue to drop.

(Replace it with radio announcer.)

4. Mr. Nichols told Danny to check the pipes in Danny's apartment.

(Replace his with Danny's to make the pronoun reference clear.)

5. Marcie worked with Karen to fill out Karen's reports about the frozen pipes.

(Replace her with Karen's to make the pronoun reference clear.)

## REVIEW FOR SKILL 3

1. Mary Louise Bell wanted her own credit card.

(Replace his with her to agree with Mary Louise Bell.)

2. She got an application form for a credit card from her bank.

(Replace their with her to agree with she.)

3. Mary Louise asked for her Social Security number from her mother.

(Rewrite the sentence so that her refers to Mary Louise.)

4. The bank officer who ran a credit check on Mary Louise approved the credit card.

(Replace which with who to agree with bank officer.)

5. Mary Louise, who has been working full-time for two years, will receive her credit card next month.

(Correct.)

6. Insurance agents talk in their offices with people.

(Rewrite the sentence so that their refers to insurance agents.)

7. People should read their insurance policies carefully.

(Replace everyone with people.)

8. State Farm Insurance, one of the largest insurance companies, has its offices in this building.

(Replace their with its to agree with State Farm Insurance.)

9. When people want to buy life insurance, they should compare the prices and the benefits.

(Replace you with they to agree with people.)

10. Ray Shapiro, whom I have known for several years, is my insurance agent.

(Change who to whom because you would say "I have known him.")

# CHAPTER 2

<u>SKILL 1, PREVIEW</u>

Answers may vary in this preview.

1. Because Marsha Chung was very helpful and friendly at the store, she was nominated for the Employee of the Year Award.

(Fragment did not express a complete thought. Words must be added to express a complete thought.)

2. She never called in sick. She was always at work on time.

or: She never called in sick; she was always at work on time.

(Run-on sentence can be corrected by inserting a period or a semicolon.)

3. Marsha dressed neatly. Her clothing was clean and pressed.

or: Marsha dressed neatly; her clothing was clean and pressed.

(Comma-splice error can be corrected by replacing the comma with a period or with a semicolon.)

4. Marsha enjoyed her job; she liked her co-workers, too.

(Correct.)

5. The manager who hired her was pleased with her work.

(Fragment did not contain a verb. A verb must be added to make a sentence.)

<u>SKILL 1, LESSON 1 EXERCISE</u>

Answers may vary in this exercise.

1. When I installed the smoke alarm, I placed it near the kitchen.

(Fragment did not express a complete thought. Words must be added to express a complete thought.)

2. The package containing the directions was red and white.

(Fragment did not contain a verb. A verb must be added to make a sentence.)

3. The alarm should be checked every year.

(Correct.)

4. Because batteries get old, I plan to replace them every year.

(Fragment did not express a complete thought. Words must be added to express a complete thought.)

5. Smoke alarms, which are a good safety measure, should be installed.

(Fragment did not contain a verb. A verb must be added to make a sentence.)

<u>SKILL 1, LESSON 2 EXERCISE</u>

1. People should be aware of water pollution and their water consumption because water is an important natural resource.

(Correct. When the main idea comes before the subordinate idea, no comma is needed between the two ideas.)

2. Surface water is one source of water. Ground water is another source of water.

(Comma-splice error can be corrected by replacing the comma with a period.)

3. Much of our water is polluted. The pollution comes from many sources.

(Run-on sentence can be corrected by inserting a period after **polluted**.)

4. The government has agencies that monitor water pollution. The government also has stiff penalties for businesses that pollute the water.

(Comma-splice error can be corrected by replacing the comma with a period.)

5. Many industries are improving their water purification processes. Keeping the water clean is good business.

(Run-on sentence can be corrected by inserting a period after **processes**.)

<u>SKILL 1, LESSON 3 EXERCISE</u>

1. About seventy percent of the Earth's surface is covered with water. Less than one percent is fresh water.

or: About seventy percent of the Earth's surface is covered with water, but less than one percent is fresh water.

or: About seventy percent of the Earth's surface is covered with water; however, less than one percent is fresh water.

(Run-on sentence can be corrected

[a] by inserting a period, or

[b] by inserting a comma and adding a coordinator, or

[c] by inserting a semicolon and adding a connecting word. A comma must be used after the connecting word.)

2. The average American uses nearly 125 gallons of water daily. Most Americans do not realize how much water they use each day.

or: The average American uses nearly 125 gallons of water daily, but most Americans do not realize how much water they use each day.

or: The average American uses nearly 125 gallons of water daily; however, most Americans do not realize how much water they use each day.

(Run-on sentence can be corrected

[a] by inserting a period, or

[b] by inserting a comma and adding a coordinator, or

[c] by inserting a semicolon and adding a connecting word. A comma must be used after the connecting word.)

3. Colorado gets most of its water from snow. However, New York gets most of its water from rain.

or: Colorado gets most of its water from snow;

however, New York gets most of its water from rain.

(Run-on sentence can be corrected

[a] by inserting a period, or

[b] by inserting a semicolon. A comma must be used after *however.*

4. Forests help water soak into the ground. Grass keeps the soil from washing away when it rains.

or: Forests help water soak into the ground, and grass keeps the soil from washing away when it rains.

or: Forests help water soak into the ground; likewise, grass keeps the soil from washing away when it rains.

(Run-on sentence can be corrected

[a] by inserting a period, or

[b] by inserting a comma and adding a coordinator, or

[c] by inserting a semicolon and adding a connecting word. A comma must be used after the connecting word.)

5. Chemicals from pesticides and fertilizers can pollute ground water. Therefore, people should dispose of these chemicals in a safe manner.

or: Chemicals from pesticides and fertilizers can pollute ground water; therefore, people should dispose of these chemicals in a safe manner.

(Run-on sentence can be corrected

[a] by inserting a period, or:

[b] by inserting a semicolon. A comma must be used after *therefore.*)

Answers may vary in this review.

1. Advertisements for weight loss products that appear in many magazines do not always express the complete truth.

(Fragment did not express a complete thought. Words must be added to express a complete thought.)

2. Because people want to lose excess weight quickly, they believe these false advertisements.

(Fragment did not express a complete thought. Words must be added to express a complete thought.

3. Many weight loss products are ineffective. Some products may even be harmful to some people.

or: Many weight loss products are ineffective, and some products may even be harmful to some people.

(Run-on sentence can be corrected

[a] by replacing the comma with a period, or

[b] by adding a coordinator after the comma.)

4. People may lose weight. However, they regain weight as soon as they stop using the products.

or: People may lose weight; however, they regain weight as soon as they stop using the products.

(Run-on sentence can be corrected

[a] by inserting a period after <u>weight</u> and inserting a comma after <u>however,</u> or:

[b] by inserting a semicolon after <u>weight</u> and inserting a comma after

however.)

5. People who want to lose weight need to learn to eat sensibly.

   (Fragment did not express a complete thought. Words must be added to express a complete thought.)

6. Last night, the power in the Kingsleys' home went off, but the battery-operated radio continued to work.

   (Correct.)

7. Jeff Kingsley thought there was a short circuit; however, Elaine Kingsley thought there was an overloaded circuit.

   or: Jeff Kingsley thought there was a short circuit. However, Elaine Kingsley thought there was an overloaded circuit.

   (Run-on sentence can be corrected

   [a] by adding a semicolon after circuit and inserting a comma after however, or

   [b] by inserting a period after circuit and inserting a comma after however.)

8. Elaine found a flashlight; as a result, they could see their way to the fuse box.

   or: Elaine found a flashlight. As a result, they could see their way to the fuse box.

   (Run-on sentence can be corrected

   [a] by replacing the comma with a semicolon after flashlight and inserting a comma after result, or

   [b] by replacing the comma with a period after flashlight and inserting a comma after result.)

9. Elaine held the flashlight.

Jeff reset the circuit breaker.

or: Elaine held the flashlight, and Jeff reset the circuit breaker.

(Run-on sentence can be corrected

[a] by replacing the comma with a period,

or:

[b] by adding a coordinator after the comma.)

10. The power outage was caused by an overloaded circuit; in fact, the Kingsleys had plugged too many major appliances into the same outlet.

or: The power outage was caused by an overloaded circuit. In fact, the Kingsleys had plugged too many major appliances into the same outlet.

(Run-on sentence can be corrected

[a] by inserting a semicolon after circuit and inserting a comma after fact,

or:

[b] by inserting a period after circuit and inserting a comma after fact.)

## SKILL 2, PREVIEW

Answers may vary in this preview.

1. Debts are difficult to pay off. Therefore, you should budget your money.

   or: Debts are difficult to pay off; therefore, you should budget your money.

   (Replace on the contrary with therefore to show clear meaning.)

2. You do not have to pay interest if you pay the full balance each month.

   (Correct. No comma is

needed when the subordinate idea follows the main idea.)

3. Even though credit cards are convenient, they may lead a person to buy more than is necessary.

   (The two unequal ideas need to be related. Rewrite the sentence, keeping either the subordinate idea or the main idea.)

4. I have had a credit card since I got my first full-time job.

   (Use only one subordinator at a time. Remove the subordinator when.)

5. Because I like to pay my bills on time, I write checks for the bills as soon as I receive them.

   (Replace although with because to show the clear relationship between the subordinate idea and the main idea. Remove the coordinator but because it is not used to join subordinate ideas.)

## SKILL 2, LESSON 1 EXERCISE

Answers may vary in this exercise.

1. Many household fires are caused by carelessness; in fact, smoking in bed is a primary cause of fires.

   (Replace however with a connecting word that shows a specific example: in fact, for example, for instance, as a matter of fact. Insert a comma after the connecting word.)

2. Overloaded electrical circuits can also cause a fire, and frayed extension cords can be dangerous.

   (Replace but with and. The second idea does not contrast the first idea.)

3. Every home should have a fire extinguisher. Furthermore, a smoke

detector is useful.

(Replace on the contrary with a connecting word that adds another main idea: furthermore, and, in addition, moreover.)

4. Old rags, newspapers, and magazines should not be placed near furnaces; furthermore, gasoline and paints should not be stored in hot, unventilated areas.

(Correct. The second idea adds meaning to the first idea.)

5. A fire can spread quickly; therefore, people should quickly evacuate the house.

(Replace nevertheless with a connecting word that shows cause and effect: therefore, consequently.)

## SKILL 2, LESSON 2 EXERCISE

Answers may vary in this exercise.

1. Although Victor likes his job, he does not like to work overtime.

(Do not use a coordinator when two unequal ideas are already joined by a subordinator.)

2. Whenever Victor had spare time, he took GED classes.

(When a subordinate idea begins a sentence, use a comma to separate the subordinate idea from the main idea.)

3. He wanted to improve his reading skills so he could help his children with their homework.

(Correct. When the subordinate idea comes after the main idea, no comma is needed to separate the two ideas.)

4. Victor became interested in GED classes when his son Manny entered first grade.

(Do not use two subordinators. Remove since.)

5. Because Manny enjoys school, Manny wants Victor to come to Parents' Night next week.

or: Because the school is far away, a school bus picks up the children at eight every morning.

(Sentence contained two unrelated ideas. Rewrite the sentence, keeping either the subordinate idea or the main idea.)

## REVIEW FOR SKILL 2

Answers may vary in this review.

1. Brenda's dishwasher made unusually loud noises whenever the machine was operating.

or: Brenda's dishwasher made unusually loud noises while the machine was operating.

(Use only one subordinator at a time. Remove while or whenever.)

2. Because Brenda was concerned about this problem, she read the owner's manual.

(When a subordinate idea begins a sentence, use a comma to separate the subordinate idea from the main idea.)

3. Although she put the utensils in the basket, one spoon had dropped to the bottom of the dishwasher.

(Do not use a coordinator to join two unequal ideas. Remove but.)

4. The spoon had caused lots of noise, but luckily no damage was done.

(Sentence contained two unrelated ideas. Rewrite, keeping either the first idea or the second idea.)

5. Brenda was relieved because the spoon had not damaged the dishwasher.

(No comma is needed between the main idea and the subordinate idea when the main idea comes first. Remove the comma.)

6. If a dishwasher is not loaded properly, it may not clean dishes completely.

(When a subordinate idea begins the sentence, use a comma to separate the subordinate idea from the main idea.)

7. Large pieces of food should be removed from dishes because food can cause drainage problems in the dishwasher.

or: Large pieces of food should be removed from dishes since food can cause drainage problems in the dishwasher.

(Use only one subordinator at a time. Remove because or since.)

8. Even though a dishwasher saves time, people still have to scrub pots and pans.

(Sentence contained two unrelated ideas. Rewrite, keeping either the first or the second idea.)

9. A dishwasher can also save energy because the machine can be turned off when it reaches the drying cycle.

(Correct. A comma is not needed when the subordinate idea comes after the main idea.)

10. When the dishwasher door is opened, the dishes will air dry.

(Remove but. Do not use a coordinator to join unequal ideas.)

1. Running down the street, the dog chased the ball.

   (Rewrite sentence so that <u>Running down the street</u> describes <u>dog</u>, not <u>ball</u>.)

2. The dog likes to chase balls, to dig holes, and to bark at squirrels.

   (Parallel structure is needed. Change <u>barking</u> to <u>to bark</u>.)

3. Chattering and squeaking, the squirrels run away from the dog. (Rewrite sentence so that <u>chattering</u> **and** <u>squeaking</u> describes <u>squirrels</u>, not <u>dog</u>.)

4. The dog chews its bone, wags its tail, and begs for its food.

   (Parallel structure is needed. Change **to** <u>wag</u> to <u>wags</u>.)

5. Sleeping on the rug, the dog seems tired but happy.

   (Correct. <u>Sleeping on the rug</u> describes <u>dog</u>.)

## SKILL 3, LESSON 1 EXERCISE

1. Watching a parade, the people heard the music of the marching bands.

   (Rewrite sentence so that <u>Watching a parade</u> describes <u>people</u>, not <u>music</u>.)

2. People eating cotton candy line the sidewalks.

   (Rewrite sentence so that <u>cotton candy</u> describes <u>people</u>, not <u>sidewalks</u>.)

3. The floats filled with people are decorated with flowers. (Rewrite sentence so that <u>filled with people</u> describes <u>floats</u>, not <u>flowers</u>.)

4. Turning the corner, the band hears loud applause.

   (Rewrite sentence so that <u>turning the corner</u>

describes the <u>band</u>.)

5. A clown with large shoes gives a balloon to a little girl.

   (Correct.)

## SKILL 3, LESSON 2 EXERCISE

1. The Discovery Channel has television shows that are informative, interesting, and educational.

   (Replace **have educational value** with <u>educational</u> to make the structure parallel.)

2. The nature programs are popular with people of all ages and backgrounds.

   (Correct.)

3. Some of the best programs show how endangered animals care for their young, how they protect themselves from predators, and how they lose the battle for survival.

   (Replace <u>that they sometimes lose the battle for survival</u> with <u>how they lose the battle for survival</u>.)

4. Diving in the oceans, skiing down mountains, and exploring deep caves are often shown on The Discovery Channel.

   (Replace <u>when they explore deep caves</u> with <u>exploring deep caves</u>.)

5. Watching modern explorers and listening to their adventures is exciting.

   (Replace <u>to listen to</u> with <u>listening</u>.)

## REVIEW FOR SKILL 3

1. Benny put his hand by the window sill and felt the wind. The window sill was cold.

   (Replace <u>it</u> with <u>window sill</u>.)

2. Wanting to reduce heating bills, Benny added

weatherstripping to the windows.

   (Rewrite the sentence so that <u>Wanting to reduce heating bills</u> describes <u>Benny</u>, not <u>weatherstripping</u>.)

3. Heating bills are drastically reduced when storm windows are installed.

   (Rewrite sentence so that <u>drastically</u> describes <u>are reduced</u>.)

4. Benny also saved energy by setting his thermostat at 70 degrees and wearing a warmer sweater.

   (Replace <u>to wear</u> with <u>wearing</u>.)

5. Benny also sleeps on his bed with a warm quilt made by his mother.

   (Rewrite sentence so that <u>made by his mother</u> describes <u>quilt</u>, not <u>bed</u>.)

6. Sue Ellen asked her roommate Alice to do Alice's share of the cleaning in the apartment.

   (Replace <u>her</u> with <u>Alice's</u> to make the meaning clear.)

7. Irritated by her roommate's mess, Sue Ellen picked up the clothes and magazines.

   (Rewrite sentence so that <u>Irritated by her roommate's mess</u> describes <u>Sue Ellen</u>, not <u>clothes</u>.)

8. A sweater that needed mending lay on the floor.

   (Rewrite sentence so that <u>that needed mending</u> describes <u>sweater</u>, not <u>floor</u>.)

9. Sue Ellen swept the floors, vacuumed the rugs, and cleaned the bathroom.

   (Replace <u>the bathroom needed cleaning</u> with <u>cleaned the bathroom</u>.)

10. Because Alice was not keeping the apartment

clean, Sue Ellen asked her to move out.

(Correct.)

## CHAPTER 3

### SKILL 1, PREVIEW

1. Many people drink Florida orange juice for breakfast.

   (Capitalize proper adjectives.)

2. Ivan thinks winter is colder in Michigan than in Siberia.

   (Do not capitalize seasons.)

3. Gretel works for Frederick's Bar and Grill.

   (Capitalize proper nouns, in this case, the name of a specific place.)

4. The restaurant is located at 245 Riverside Highway.

   (Capitalize names of highways.)

5. Sometimes, I enjoy taking my father to the restaurant for dinner.

   (Correct.)

### SKILL 1, LESSON 1 EXERCISE

1. One day, Doreen would like to visit Hawaii.

   (Capitalize proper nouns.)

2. She wants to see Waikiki Beach.

   (Capitalize proper nouns.)

3. A popular tourist attraction is Volcanoes National Park.

   (Correct.)

4. Doreen also wants to eat authentic Hawaiian food.

   (Capitalize proper adjectives.)

5. On her way to work, Doreen saw a poster of Oahu in the window of

Thompson's Travel Agency.

(Capitalize proper nouns.)

### SKILL 1, LESSON 2 EXERCISE

1. When was the last time you talked to Mother?

   (Correct.)

2. Phillip contributes money to the American Heart Association.

   (Capitalize proper nouns, in this case, the name of a specific organization.)

3. Your father wants to meet you at the corner of South Hawthorne Road and Pine Avenue.

   (Capitalize names of streets.)

4. He knows the president of the Chicago Lions Club.

   (Do not capitalize titles that are not part of a person's name. Capitalize the name of an organization.)

5. I do not think Jeffrey Burns is related to Senator Burns.

   (Capitalize title when it is part of a person's name.)

### SKILL 1, LESSON 3 EXERCISE

1. In the United States, Independence Day is celebrated on July 4.

   (Capitalize holidays.)

2. June 22 is the first official day of summer.

   (Do not capitalize seasons.)

3. Did you know that Mother's Day is the second Sunday in May?

   (Capitalize days of week and months.)

4. During the Dark Ages, many people died from tuberculosis and other diseases.

   (Correct. Capitalize historical time periods.)

5. The auto races will be held in France this June.

   (Capitalize names of special events, countries, and months.)

### REVIEW FOR SKILL 1

1. In March, Oscars are awarded by the film industry.

   (Capitalize months of year.)

2. Sometimes, British actors and actresses receive awards.

   (Capitalize proper adjectives.)

3. Did you enjoy the movie about the American Revolutionary War?

   (Capitalize historical events.)

4. To my surprise, Aunt Karen thought it was the best movie of the year.

   (Capitalize Aunt when used as part of that person's name.)

5. She and I saw another good movie last Saturday.

   (Capitalize days of week.)

6. The movie was a comedy about a family's summer vacation.

   (Do not capitalize seasons.)

7. I think Mother would have enjoyed that movie.

   (Capitalize Mother.)

8. We saw Dr. Samuels at the Crystal Theater.

   (Correct.)

9. The theater is located on North Vine Avenue.

   (Capitalize names of streets.)

10. My apartment is only three blocks west of the theater.

    (Do not capitalize a direction.)

1. Three popular citrus fruits are oranges, grapefruit, and tangerines.

   (Do not use commas before the first items in a series or before the last item in a series. Remove commas after <u>are</u> and <u>and</u>.)

2. Robin likes different types of fruit and makes tasty fruit salads.

   (Do not use a comma with compound verbs. Remove comma after <u>fruit</u>.)

3. When bananas are in season, Robin likes to make banana bread.

   (Correct.)

4. Fruits are a tasty, inexpensive source of vitamins and minerals.

   (Do not use commas to separate the adjective from the noun it describes. Remove comma after <u>inexpensive</u>.)

5. Fruits, an important part of a healthy diet, are available all year.

   (Use commas to separate interrupters. Insert a comma after <u>diet</u>.)

SKILL 2, LESSON 1 EXERCISE

1. Linda Ronstadt, Sheena Easton, and Carly Simon are three of Rhoda's favorite female singers.

   (Do not use a comma after the last item in the series. Remove comma after <u>Carly Simon</u>.)

2. On weekends, Rhoda cleans her apartment, does her laundry, and watches television.

   (Use commas to separate items in a series. Insert commas after <u>apartment</u> and after <u>laundry</u>.)

3. She laughs at the funny,

young host of the talk show.

   (Do not separate the last adjective from the noun it describes. Remove comma after <u>young</u>.)

4. Many talk shows feature topics such as divorce or friendship or pet peeves.

   (Correct.)

5. Talk shows can be an entertaining, educational experience.

   (Do not separate the last adjective from the noun it describes. Remove comma after <u>educational</u>.)

SKILL 2, LESSON 2 EXERCISE

1. Because the tire pressure was low, Donna added air to the tire.

   (Use a comma when the subordinate idea comes before the main idea. Insert a comma after <u>low</u>.)

2. She checked the wear on the tire tread before she went on her long trip.

   (Correct. When the subordinate idea comes after the main idea, no comma is needed.)

3. Changing a flat tire on the interstate is a major hassle when it is raining.

   (Do not use a comma to separate the main idea from the subordinate idea when the subordinate idea comes after the main idea. Remove the comma after <u>hassle</u>.)

4. However, you should not drive on a flat tire.

   (Use a comma after introductory words. Insert a comma after <u>However</u>.)

5. If a blow-out occurs at high speeds, you could be involved in a serious accident.

   (Insert a comma after

<u>speeds</u>. A comma is needed when the subordinate idea comes before the main idea.)

SKILL 2, LESSON 3 EXERCISE

1. Seattle, in my opinion, is a nice city.

   (Use commas to separate sentence interrupters. Insert commas before and after <u>in my opinion</u>.)

2. From the top of the Space Needle, a popular tourist attraction, a person can see all of Seattle.

   (Use commas to separate sentence interrupters. Insert commas before and after <u>a popular tourist attraction</u>.)

3. Olympia, which is the capital of Washington, has fewer people than Seattle.

   (Use commas to separate sentence interrupters. Insert commas before and after <u>which is the capital of Washington</u>.)

4. The mountain that overlooks the entire Seattle area is Mount Rainier.

   (Correct. <u>That overlooks the entire Seattle area</u> is essential to the meaning of <u>mountain</u>— and the meaning of the whole sentence. Therefore, it should not be set off by commas.)

5. Clouds, however, often cover the mountain.

   (Use commas to separate sentence interrupters. Insert commas before and after <u>however</u>.)

SKILL 2, LESSON 4 EXERCISE

1. Sunny beaches and warm winters attract many tourists to Florida.

   (Do not use a comma with compound subjects. Remove comma after <u>beaches</u>.)

2. Many families visit Disney World, a popular Florida attraction.

   (Insert a comma after <u>World</u>. A comma is needed to separate the sentence interrupter.)

3. Other tourist attractions are Busch Gardens, Sea World, and the Kennedy Space Center.

   (Do not use a comma to separate the subject from the verb. Remove the comma after <u>attractions</u>.)

4. Orlando is one of the largest business centers of the state.

   (Correct.)

5. The tourists take photographs and buy souvenirs.

   (Do not use a comma with compound verbs. Remove the comma after <u>photographs</u>.)

## REVIEW FOR SKILL 2

1. Heroin, cocaine, and morphine are narcotics.

   (Do not use a comma after the last item in a series. Remove comma after <u>morphine</u>.)

2. Alcohol is also a drug, but it is not an illegal drug.

   (Do not use a comma after the coordinator in a compound sentence. Remove comma after <u>but</u>. Use a comma before the coordinator in a compound sentence. Insert a comma after <u>drug</u>.)

3. If you have a problem with drug addiction, you should seek professional help.

   (Use a comma when the subordinate idea comes before the main idea. Insert a comma after <u>addiction</u>.)

4. However, you must first recognize and acknowledge your problem.

   (Use a comma after introductory words. Insert a comma after <u>However</u>.)

5. Alcoholics Anonymous, a self-help organization, has a high success record.

   (Use commas around sentence interrupters that are not essential to the meaning of the sentence. We know which organization Alcoholics Anonymous is without the sentence interrupter. Insert commas before and after <u>a self-help organization</u>.)

6. One of the most popular beverages in America is coffee.

   (Do not use a comma to separate the subject and verb. Remove the comma after <u>America</u>.)

7. Coffee and tea contain caffeine.

   (Do not use a comma with compound subjects. Remove comma after <u>coffee.</u>.)

8. People who smoke cigarettes have more health problems than people who do not smoke.

   (Do not use commas to separate essential information from the sentence. Remove commas before and after <u>who smoke cigarettes</u>.)

9. We do not mind people smoking in public, but we do not allow people to smoke in our home.

   (Correct.)

10. We do not like cigarette ashes on our polished floor.

    (Do not use a comma to separate the adjective from the noun it describes. Remove comma after <u>polished</u>.)

## SKILL 3, PREVIEW

1. Russ washed the forks, spoons, and knives.

   (Change the spelling of <u>knifes</u> to <u>knives</u>.)

2. Sometimes it's difficult to clean the pots and pans.

   (Correct.)

3. The children's dishes are still on the table.

   (Insert an apostrophe to show plural possession.)

4. Russ is wiping the table.

   (Change the spelling of <u>wipeing</u> to <u>wiping</u>.)

5. He couldn't hear the baby crying.

   (Change the spelling of <u>here</u> to <u>hear</u>.)

## SKILL 3, LESSON 1 EXERCISE

1. Many single parents need child care for their babies.

   (Change the spelling of <u>babys</u> to <u>babies</u>.)

2. Some parents are planning to look for second jobs.

   (Change the spelling of <u>planing</u> to <u>planning</u>.)

3. One parent was saving for new clothes for her child.

   (Change the spelling of <u>saveing</u> to <u>saving</u>.)

4. She admitted that she did not want to ask for financial assistance.

   (Change the spelling of <u>admited</u> to <u>admitted</u>.)

5. Many local churches offered child care services for working parents.

   (Correct.)

## SKILL 3, LESSON 2 EXERCISE

1. Have you visited our city's museum?

   (Change <u>citys</u> to <u>city's</u>.)

2. One area displays children's toys from the early

nineteenth century.

(Change <u>childrens</u> to <u>children's</u>.)

3. Another area contains different types of men's hats and ladies' gloves.

(Change <u>ladys</u> to <u>ladies'</u>.)

4. Gina's favorite display showed women's scarves and dresses.

(Correct.)

5. The museum changes its display every three months.

(Change <u>it's</u> to <u>its</u>.)

## SKILL 3, LESSON 3 EXERCISE

1. Didn't the Chinese introduce Marco Polo to spaghetti?

(Change <u>Did'nt</u> to <u>Didn't</u>.)

2. When your body needs energy, you should eat pasta.

(Replace <u>you're</u> with <u>your</u>.)

3. Lots of children think it's fun to eat spaghetti.

(Correct.)

4. They suck the spaghetti strands into their mouths.

(Replace <u>they're</u> with <u>their</u>.)

5. My friends think I'm a good Italian cook.

(Change <u>Im</u> to <u>I'm</u>.)

## SKILL 3, LESSON 4 EXERCISE

1. Do you know the principal cause of last week's accident?

(Replace <u>principle</u> with <u>principal</u>.)

2. We could hear the crash from four blocks away.

(Replace <u>here</u> with <u>hear</u>.)

3. The truck made a hole through that wall.

(Replace <u>threw</u> with <u>through</u>.)

4. Gene Mills, the driver,

had just passed another car when his brakes failed.

(Correct.)

5. Gene injured his heel when he slammed his foot against the brake pedal.

(Replace <u>heal</u> with <u>heel</u>.)

## REVIEW FOR SKILL 3

1. After she walked her dog, Paula DeSoto accidentally dropped her keys into the bushes.

(Change the spelling of <u>droped</u> to <u>dropped</u>.)

2. Her neighbor Rob Corwin offered to help look for the keys.

(Change the spelling of <u>offerred</u> to <u>offered</u>.)

3. Paula and Rob couldn't find the keys because the bushes were too thick.

(Change <u>could'nt</u> to <u>couldn't</u>.)

4. However, Paula's dog Max went right to the keys and brought them to her.

(Correct.)

5. The dog's tail wagged as Paula and Rob petted its head.

(Change <u>it's</u> to <u>its</u>.)

6. Have you read the articles about our nation's economy?

(Change <u>nations</u> to <u>nation's</u>.)

7. Aren't you concerned about inflation and taxes?

(Change the spelling of <u>taxs</u> to <u>taxes</u>.)

8. The whole country seems to be worried about the cost of food and gas.

(Change the spelling of <u>worryed</u> to <u>worried</u>.)

9. I wonder whether my wages and my spouse's part-time job will be

enough to meet our family's needs.

(Replace <u>weather</u> with <u>whether</u>.)

10. We're hoping to save money to see us through next year.

(Change the spelling of <u>hopeing</u> to <u>hoping</u>.)

# Answer Key: Unit III

## Chapter 1: Social Studies

### Lesson 1 Exercise

1. **(4)** *Comprehension/ American History.* The passage states that the series *"chronicles one family's* life." The sentence that follows the use of this word defines the word by saying "The stories detail the daily events of their lives...." This is another way of saying that the series records a history of events. Choices (1), (2), and (3) could not be correct because if you substituted them for the word *chronicles*, the sentence would read "... wrote a series of books that writes books [or: that writes stories about family life, or: writes a series of books]." The only basis for choosing (5) is that the passage does mention that the series was made into a TV show. However, this meaning would not make sense in the sentence in which the word appears, so choice (5) is also incorrect.

2. **(2)** *Comprehension/ American History.* The phrase immediately following the use of the word deprivation gives its **definition:** having little to live on. From this phrase, you are made to understand that the family lived with very little— in a state of poverty. You can eliminate choice (1) because the passage says "and their struggle to survive," indicating that their struggle to survive is something different from their deprivation. The passage doesn't discuss the family's attempt to better their lives (3), or that they are sad (4), or that the family had trouble staying together (5), so these three choices can be eliminated.

3. **(3)** *Comprehension/ American History.* The fact that the sentence says they "migrate by covered wagon" indicates that they went or moved somewhere. The sentence further tells you exactly where they went from and to. The passage does not discuss the family's adjustment to a new life or a new place, so choices (1) and (2) are incorrect. Choice (4) is not specific enough, since it says nothing about going west. The paragraph also says nothing about the familys' returning home. Choice (5) can be eliminated because it would make the sentence mean that the family coped with hardship by traveling from Wisconsin to the Dakotas.

### Lesson 2 Exercise

1. **(5)** *Comprehension/ Political Science.* The paragraph states that there was an increase of 7.7 million Hispanic people from 1980 to 1990. Choice (1) cannot be correct because the paragraph does not tell you how large the population was in 1970. Choice (2) is incorrect because the paragraph says there was an increase of 7.7 million, not that that's how many people there were. Choice (3) is incorrect because the paragraph says there was a 56% increase over 1980, not 1970. There is no basis for choosing (4), as the paragraph does not address the total number of whites in the United States.

2. **(5)** *Comprehension/ Political Science.* The text says that information that is quantified is put into numbers. Choice (5) uses slightly different words to say the same thing. There is no basis in the text surrounding the word quantified to choose answers (1), (2), (3), or (4).

3. **(2)** *Comprehension/ Behavioral Science.* A line drawn from the top of the graduate-school bar to the vertical axis intersects with $29,000. In this case, the graph also indicates the numbers on top of the bars. Choice (1) is close, but since the numbers are given at the top of the bars, you know that it cannot be correct. Choice (3) might be acceptable for high school, but the question asks for graduate school, and again, the numbers are actually given on top of the bars. Choice (4) cannot be correct because none of the bars represents this figure. Choice (5) is incorrect because it is the figure for high school, not grad-

uate school.

4. **(4)** *Comprehension/ Economics.* The line showing crude oil production is horizontal between 1983 and 1984, indicating no change in production. All the other choices cover periods in which there was a decrease.

## Lesson 3 Exercise

1. **(2)** *Comprehension/ American History.* The third paragraph tell you that the French "were interested in trading furs and fish." These are business and economic opportunities, as stated in choice (2). The passage says nothing about the French being interested in farming, so choice (1) can be eliminated. The paragraph specifically states that the French were not interested in starting permanent colonies, so choice (3) is incorrect. Choices (4) and (5) are mentioned with regard to the Spanish in paragraph 2, but not the French.

2. **(4)** *Comprehension/ American History.* To answer this question correctly, you would have to look at the dates of colonization for each country in the passage. The earliest date of colonization is 1565, by Spain in Florida. This date is in the 16th century. All other areas were colonized in the 1600s( or 17th century). You would know choice (2) was incorrect if you had compared the dates of colonization, as mentioned above. Choice (1) is incorrect because the last paragraph clearly states that Holland did establish colonies. Choice (3)

is incorrect because the second paragraph tells you that Spain wanted to own land in the New World. Choice (5) is incorrect because the text says England won Manhattan Island from the Dutch, not from Native Americans.

3. **(1)** *Comprehension/ American History.* The last sentence of the passage says that England owned the most land and had the most settlers in the New World. The paragraph containing that sentence also discusses England's battles to conquer colonies already established by other countries. There is no mention of other countries engaging in war to win already-established colonies. All these facts point to England as being most aggressive. You can, therefore, rule out the remaining choices.

## Lesson 4 Exercise

1. **(1)** *Comprehension/ American History.* To find the main idea, look for the topic sentence—the sentence that contains the single most important idea in the paragraph. In this case, the first sentence is the topic sentence. It tells you the name of the battle, where it was fought, when it was fought, and that it had a major impact on the course of the war. Choices (2) to (5) contain specific details about the battle, but they are too narrow to be main ideas.

2. **(4)** *Comprehension/ American History.* To answer this question, you have to find the details that support the topic sentence. The question itself gives you the main

idea—that the South was dealt a double blow. In paragraph two, the two important details—the two blows to the South—are that the South lost the battle, and that Lincoln freed only Southern slaves. In choice (1), it's true that these are both blows, but this paragraph does not mention the loss of Southern soldiers. Choice (2) doesn't make sense because it doesn't say what Lincoln's decision was. Choice (3) is incorrect because the paragraph states that Lincoln was already pro-Union; he didn't suddenly turn against the South. Choice (5) is incorrect because you know that the Emancipation Proclamation was issued and the Confederates did not surrender.

3. **(5)** *Comprehension/ American History.* This is a case where the topic sentence is the last sentence of the paragraph. Choice (5) clearly states that there were more casualties than on any other day in U.S. warfare—another way of saying that the battle is remembered as the single bloodiest day in American combat history. Choices (1) to (3) are details supporting the topic sentence. Choice (4) is true, but it is not the main idea of the paragraph.

## Lesson 5 Exercise

1. **(2)** *Comprehension/ American History.* This idea is stated in the first sentence of the passage. It is the only choice that covers the main ideas of all the paragraphs. Its reference to "social evils" covers paragraphs 2 and 3 and its reference to

"wealth" covers the first paragraph. (1) is the main idea of the third paragraph. The main idea of the second paragraph is that big business gained an unfair share of wealth through monopolies; (4) restates this idea but overstates it by saying that elimination of competition is "the main effect" of laissez-faire. (3) is a detail supporting the main idea of the second paragraph. (5) is the main idea of the last paragraph.

2. **(4)** *Comprehension/ American History.* This answer is a restatement of the topic sentence of the passage, which is the last sentence of the first paragraph. It is the only statement that covers all the main ideas of the passage. The first paragraph describes how women outnumbered men in some industries and how all-women unions failed. The other two paragraphs describe how women participated in the labor movement in a limited way. (3) may sound right at first, but it is untrue to say that "women outnumbered men as factory workers" (that is, in *all* industries). Though organizing women in the garment industry was a success, we do not know if it was the main such success in this period; therefore, (1) is incorrect. (2) and (5) make cause-and-effect statements with no support: We have no reason to believe that the failure of all-women unions, or women's attitudes toward marriage and drinking, were the major causes of their limited participation in the labor movement.

3. **(4)** *Comprehension/*

*American History.* Only (4) covers the main ideas of all three paragraphs. The first paragraph covers the nativists' economic fear of the new immigrants in the competition for jobs; the second paragraph, their social prejudices against the immigrants' customs and religious practices; and the third paragraph, the active discrimination against the new immigrants. (1) states only a detail in the last paragraph. (2) incorrectly restates the main idea of the second paragraph: social prejudice against "strange foreign customs" as a motive for nativist feelings was as important as but not more important than economic fear. (3) is an opinion without support, and (5) is a cause-and-effect statement without support.

## Lesson 6 Exercise

1. **(2)** *Comprehension/ Political Science.* The income of the poorest Americans, the bottom fifth, actually *decreased* 9%; therefore, the 4% increase of the typical middle-class family, the third fifth, was *more* than double the income change of the bottom fifth. All the other choices state details that are shown on the graph. (4) is correct because the income of the 4th fifth also decreased—by 1%—which means that the 3rd fifth's income increase exceeded the 4th fifth's income increase by more than 4% (if the 4th fifth had no decrease or increase it would have had 0% income change, and the 3rd fifth would have exceeded it by 4%).

2. **(5)** *Comprehension/ Political Science.* The graph shows that someone with an average income of $20,100 is in the 4th fifth and suffered an income decrease of 1%. The top fifth increased its income by 29%, so it gained a total of 30% more than the 4th fifth.

3. **(2)** *Comprehension/ Political Science.* The graphs shows that those in the top 6 to 20% received 20% of the after-tax income gain and that those below the 6 to 20% group received 6% of the after-tax income gain. Therefore, a person below this top group would get 14% (20% minus 6%) less of an after-tax income gain than someone in the top group.

4. **(3)** *Comprehension/ Political Science.* The graph shows that the average middle-class family was in the group that got an after-tax income gain of 6%. The top 1% got an after-tax income gain of 60%. The average middle-class family therefore got 54% (60% minus 6%) less of an after-tax income gain than the top 1% received.

## Lesson 7 Exercise

1. **(4)** *Comprehension/ Economics.* The graph clearly demonstrates that annual income increases each time more years of schooling are completed. Choice (1) is incorrect because it says the exact opposite of what the graph shows. Choice (2) is wrong because the graph gives no information on the income level of the families from which these men came. Choices (3) and (5) are

both incorrect because they mention women; the title of the graph indicates that this study was done only on men.

2. **(5)** *Comprehension/ Economics.* The steady downward slope of the line shows that more cars were sold as the price of the cars dropped. Choice (1) is incorrect for several reasons: to say the price varied is meaningless (did it go up or down?); and the graph does not address the number of cars produced, just those sold. Choice (2) is incorrect because it says the opposite of what the graph shows. Choice (3) is a detail supporting the main idea. Choice (4) is incorrect because the graph does not address the number of cars produced.

3. **(5)** *Comprehension/ Economics.* The hand representing the banks is shown squashing the Capitol, and the hand representing politics is trying to grab the banks. Each is seen attacking the other. The main action of the cartoon does not suggest choice (1), so it is incorrect. The action also shows something quite different from choice (2), so it is incorrect. Choices (3) and (4) are incorrect because they mention only one or the other as being hurt or wanting to overthrow the other one. The cartoon shows both being damaged equally. Therefore, (5) is the correct answer.

## Lesson 8 Exercise

1. **(2)** *Comprehension/ Geography.* The passage tells you that different countries have different natural resources and

that some of these resources are in demand in places where they do not naturally occur. From this (and perhaps your previous knowledge) you can infer that world trade enables countries to obtain resources that are not native to their region. Choices (1) and (3) are details that are stated in the paragraph, so they cannot be inferences. Choice (4) is an interesting idea, but it is not dealt with in this paragraph. In fact, the statement that the Middle Eastern countries have grown rich by selling oil to industrial nations might lead you to infer just the opposite of (4). Nothing in the excerpt suggests (5).

2. **(3)** *Comprehension/ Geography.* The passage states that industrial countries import, or buy, foreign oil from the Middle Eastern countries, who have become rich by selling their oil. You are also told that countries in the tropics grow products—coffee, sugar, rubber—for which countries in the temperate zones have a "great demand." From these statements you can infer that trade between these countries around the world benefits all of them, those who buy and those who sell. (4), therefore, is a false inference. There also is no basis for inferring that world trade is more beneficial for one or the other type of country, so choices (1) and (2) can be eliminated. Choice (5) is a false detail, contradicted by the statement in the second paragraph that trade in oil has made Middle Eastern nations rich.

3. **(4)** *Comprehension/ Geography.* Based on your prior knowledge of where continents are, the lesson's instruction, and the map, you can infer that as a general rule areas in the same latitudes have similar types of climate. Of the choices given, the only area that falls roughly within the same latitude as central Africa is northern South America.

## Lesson 9 Exercise

1. **(1)** *Comprehension/ Behavioral Science.* The paragraph discusses three groups of people who are victims of sexual harassment in the European Community. Only choice (1) covers all three groups. We are told that "the most frequent victims are those who are most vulnerable from a social or occupational point of view": These are, first, single women who need their jobs and "have no protectors," or who are new to their work or working part time; and second, groups whom society does not accept completely for reasons of prejudice—"ethnic minorities, the disabled, lesbians." The third group are women competing with men in high-level jobs or in previously all-male professions. Choice (1) refers to the first two groups as the "defenseless" and to the third group as those who are "threatening to men." (4) and (5) mention only one group each and are therefore details. (2) refers only to women "new to their jobs"—so it is part of a detail. Also, nothing supports the idea that all women new to their work are "unpre-

pared" for it. (3) is an opinion that may be true but has no support in the paragraph.

2. **(1)** *Comprehension/ Behavioral Science.* The passage describes the rites of passage in two cultures, mentioning that generally children go through rites of passage in order to be accepted as adults by their society. From this you can infer that most societies have some form of rites of passage. Choices (2), (3), and (4) restate details about these rites in the paragraph. There is no support for (5): A child who for some reason did not go through a rite of passage could still grow to maturity and have adult or mature attitudes, although he or she might not be accepted fully by members of his/her group or society. To "not reach maturity" also suggests that such a child might die before reaching adulthood, which makes no sense.

3. **(4)** *Comprehension/ Behavioral Science.* The two most important details in the paragraph are the large numbers of women who have entered the workforce in India and the increase in sexual harassment of these women. When you summarize the main idea of the paragraph for yourself, you need to cover both these points. The other answer choices are either incorrect details or incorrect summaries. (1) and (2) are false restatements of details. The paragraph does not say that all 10 million working women are victims of sexual harassment, or that women in glamorous occupations experience more harassment than any other group. (3) and (5) are false summaries; they are opinions based on unsupported cause-and-effect arguments. (3) suggests that because women are entering previously male fields, they must let men harass them as a "price of admission." (5) declares that sexual harassment is caused by the large numbers of women entering the workforce. Nothing in the paragraph supports these two opinions.

## Lesson 10 Exercise

1. **(2)** *Comprehension/ Behavioral Science.* Since people are considered healthy as long as they are dealing with their problems, you can infer that anxiety is a normal response to stress. This is the most important idea stated in the paragraph. All the details in the paragraph contradict choice (1), so it can be eliminated. (3) and (4) are false restatements of information in the paragraph. We are told that anxiety makes us feel "as if" we can't cope with stress, but that it is possible "to control our anxiety and carry on our lives." Choice (5) can be inferred but it does not mention anxiety or state the main point about it, so it cannot be the main idea of the paragraph.

2. **(3)** *Comprehension/ Behavioral Science.* This sentence contains the main idea from both paragraphs and so qualifies as the main idea of the passage. Choice (1) is only the inferred main idea of the second paragraph. (2) is a false inference; even if it had support, it could not be the main idea of the passage, because neurosis is discussed only in paragraph 2. (5) is wrong for the same reason. (4) is an acceptable inference from both paragraph but its focus on alcoholism and drugs is too narrow. The passage as a whole does not emphasize these bad habits, but rather emphasizes neurosis ("self-defeating behavior") and anxiety.

3. **(5)** *Comprehension/ Behavioral Science.* The passage states that people develop defense mechanisms in response to anxiety, and it states that people who use defense mechanisms are escaping their true feelings. From this you can infer that defense mechanisms are an undesirable response to anxiety. Choice (1) is incorrect because both paragraphs make it clear that defense mechanisms are ways in which people avoid, rather than control, their emotional problems. (3) is a restatement of a detail—the second sentence of paragraph 1. Choices (2) and (4) cannot be inferred on the basis of the two examples in the passage. They also are not the main idea of the passage.

# Chapter 2: Science

## Lesson 1 Exercise

1. **(5)** *Application/Biology.* When a cell splits, it makes another cell of its own kind. The technician didn't observe food particles (involved in Choices 1, 2, 3) or waste (Choice 3).

2. **(1)** *Application/Biology.* Engulfing a food particle is the first step in breaking it down (digestion, Choice 1). The food will later power the other four processes (Choices 2-5).

3. **(3)** *Application/Biology.* Excretion is the only process in the list which describes a substance inside of the cell being sent outside. All of the other choices describe processes which go on inside of the cell. (Don't be fooled by choice (5). Even if you didn't know that the ammonia made by the cell is a poisonous waste, you can figure out that it is not more of the cells "own kind.")

## Lesson 2 Exercise

1. **(3)** *Application/Biology.* Since we have been given no information that the trait is sex-linked, the sex of the people shown doesn't matter. The chart always shows one individual with the dominant trait (D) and one with the recessive trait (R). There is only one situation where the person labeled D has the dominant trait (free earlobes) and the one labeled R has the recessive trait (attached earlobes)—Choice (3).

2. **(1)** *Application/Biology.* The sex of the people doesn't matter, the person labeled (D) must have the dominant trait—tongue rolling ability, and the person labeled (R) must have the recessive trait—inability to tongue-roll.

3. **(5)** *Application/Biology.* Since freckles are dominant, only the person labeled (D) should have freckles. The chart tells you that if a trait is dominant it will cancel out completely the other, recessive trait in the parent organism. (Remember that the lesson told you that Mendel discovered that the tall pea-plant gene did this to the short pea-plant gene.) Therefore (1), (2), (3) and (4) are wrong.

4. **(5)** The diagram shows what you are told in the lesson: the fertilized egg receives the same number of chromosomes from each parent as each parent has. If the sperm had 24 chromosomes, the egg also would have 24, and the fertilized egg therefore would have 48.

## Lesson 3 Exercise

1. **(4)** *Analysis/Biology.* Choice (4) restates the topic sentence of the second paragraph ("Dr. Richard Colby and his coworkers believe that each (fat) deposit has its own purpose."), which is the main hypothesis. You know it is an hypothesis because the word "believe" is used in the quoted statement about Colby's main idea. Also, in the paragraph "probably" and "might" are used in the key statements about the two kinds of fat.(3) is a statement of fact, not an hypothesis. Nothing supports (2): we are told thigh fat and abdominal fat probably had different functions in early human times, but

not that one was more common than the other. (1) confuses a statement in the third paragraph that hormones can make stomach fat respond quickly. (5) is an opinion with no support in the passage.

2. **(3)** *Analysis/Biology.* The first sentence of the passage states that researchers have observed "that people who tend to put on weight around their bellies are at higher risk for heart disease than are those who spread out in the thighs and buttocks." The response of fat under the stomach-skin to hormones, discussed in the last paragraph, provides more evidence to support the association of this kind of fat with "high blood pressure and other heart problems." None of the other choices is a statement of fact supported by scientific observation and experimental proof. (See the answer key to question 1.for detailed comment on these choices.)

3. **(5)** *Analysis/Biology.* Choice (5) is an opinion. The use of "probably" in (2) and "seem" in (4) indicate that they are hypotheses—educated guesses—rather than opinions, which are statements of personal belief without any solid evidence behind them. Whether thigh fat is undesirable is a matter of personal opinion. A fashion model might think so, but many other men and women might disagree for any number of personal reasons.

## Lesson 4 Exercise

1. **(4)** *Analysis/Biology.* The

diagram together with its caption shows that concentration of DDT increases as it passes up the food chain from the grass-eating mouse to the mouse-eating owl. Perhaps the best way to find this answer is to eliminate the choices that are incorrect. The diagram shows just the opposite of (1) because the owl is further up the food chain. (2) and (3) are based on faulty logic. (2) is wrong because no information on the graph tells you that larger organisms have a higher concentration of DDT than smaller ones; concentration depends on their position in the food chain, not size. (3) is too big a generalization. Owls have a higher concentration of DDT than some mammals— the squirrel, mouse and deer— but not more than the bobcat. The word "birds" in (3) is too general also, since the owl eats other mammals, whereas many other birds eat seeds and plants, which would place them further down the food chain. (5) is clearly an hypothesis (notice the use of "probably") and is therefore not a fact.

2. **(4)** *Analysis/Biology.* Statement (4) is an hypothesis because it is a possible explanation of an observed fact, the decrease in the owl populations near some apple orchards. Choice (1) is clearly shown as a detail on the diagram. Choices (2) and (3) are also facts based on information in the diagram: the concentration of DDT increases as it passes up the chain; owls and bobcats are higher than squirrels and

mice. (5) is a false inference because nothing in the diagram or its caption suggests that the size of the organism makes the concentration of DDT higher or lower.

3. **(2)** *Analysis/Biology.* The word "should" gives a clue that whether to ban or not to ban is a matter of personal belief. Choices (1) and (4) are observed, measurable facts. Choices (3) and (5) are hypotheses: notice the use of "might" in (3) and "probably" in (5), which are typical of hypotheses. As hypotheses, (3) and (5) are "educated guesses" which attempt to explain facts.

## Lesson 5 Exercise

1. **(4)** *Analysis/Biology.* Since the author refers to the experiments as scientific evidence and does not bother to support them with arguments or statements of fact, his assumption must be that the experiments are (1) accurate and (3) can predict toad behavior in the real world.(2) is a specific prediction based on the experiment, which logically follows from these two assumptions; it cannot be an assumption, anyway, because it is stated. (5) follows logically from (2): if animals who feed on non-poisonous toads avoid eating poisonous toads, poisonous toads will have fewer predators. However, (4) is NOT an assumption of the passage. Nothing stated suggests this possible effect of importing the toads to Florida. Since the South American toads of both kinds probably will continue to reproduce at the same rate, and the ani-

mals that feed on both kinds will continue to keep up the balance between them, no change in the South American toad population is likely.

2. **(5)** *Analysis/Biology.* Although the writer doesn't talk about the reasons for wanting to control insects, we know from experience that these reasons include human disease, discomfort, and loss of crops. We assume that the supporters of the plan want to reduce insects to improve living conditions for humans. Supporters of the plan do NOT seem concerned about the native frog, because the danger to Florida frogs is raised as an issue only by Dr. Vaughn, an opponent of the plan. So, (2) is wrong. Nothing suggests they are concerned about the number of native animals, either, since possible danger to them from the imported frogs is immediately contradicted by reference to a scientific experiment. So (3) is wrong. Supporters assume that the eating behavior of poisonous frogs will affect the number of insects, not the reverse (4).

3. **(1)** *Analysis/Biology.* We are told that Dr. Vaughn thinks importing the poisonous toads will endanger the native toads. We need to figure out assumption underlying his statement. Choices (3) and (5) can be eliminated immediately: (5) is wrong because changes in the behavior of insects are nowhere suggested to be a danger to native toads. The idea of (3) "protecting the poisonous ones (toads)" is not even

mentioned. We are told that the experiment showed that predators of native toads would avoid poisonous ones, but that does not mean that the number of predators would increase; so (2) cannot be his assumption. However, if he feels the poisonous toads will endanger the native non-poisonous ones, he must assume (1)— that the native toads will not be able to compete successfully with the imported ones.

## Lesson 6 Exercise

1. **(1)** *Analysis/Earth Science.* All of the details support the idea that the geography of the islands is related to the movement of the plate over the hot spot. Choice (2) is a conclusion, but not one supported by the evidence. Choice (3) is true, but only a detail. (4) is wrong because Hawaii is a volcanically active island, not "the largest of a chain of in active volcanoes".(5) reverses the cause-and-effect.statement in the passage, which says that the wearing away of the island results from the island's movement off of the hot spot.

2. **(4)** *Analysis/Earth Science.* This information is found in the last line of the passage. Choices (1) and (2) sound like information in the passage, but they are *incorrect* restatements. The passage says that "the Pacific plate above the hot spot has been moving gradually toward the northwest"—not that the hot spot has been moving northwest (1). (2) reverses what the passage says: that the hot spot was cre-

ated by melted rock rising toward the surface of earth to create volcanoes. Choice (5) is a logical conclusion from the information given, but it is not the supporting detail for which the question asks.

3. **(3)** *Analysis/Earth Science.* All the choices except (3) are pieces of information found in the passage. Choice (3) is a conclusion which might be drawn from the information given.

## Lesson 7 Exercise

1. **(2)** *Analysis/Earth Science.* We are told that "moist air flowing across the range is forced upward by mountains." The cooling of the air (3), the condensation of the air's moisture into rain and snow (4), and the dryness of the air on the far side of the mountain (5) are all *results* of the air's rising, not a cause of its rising. By remembering that gravity pulls heavy things down, not up, you can tell that (1) could not be a cause for the air to rise; besides, nothing in the passage suggests this reason.

2. **(5)** *Analysis/Earth Science.* The passage describes the series of causes-and-effects in the movement of moist air up over mountains; the last effect or result in this series is the creation of a desert. The cooling and condensation of the moist air (3) is the cause of the effects in (1) and (2)—and (1) and (2) are restatements of the same event, the falling of rain and snow up in the mountains. This event causes (2), the dry air, which causes the final

effect or result, the desert (5).

3. **(3)** *Analysis/Earth Science.* The air loses moisture *before* it reaches the far side; this loss causes the air on the far side to be dry. (4) reverses the true cause-and-effect relationship: the dry air creates the desert; the desert is not a cause of the dry air. (1) suggests that "blocking the sun" with the "rain shadow" is what causes the air to be dry, when in fact the falling rain and snow cause it to be dry..(The heat of the sun would actually make the air dry.) The passage contradicts (2); if it were true it would be a cause for the air to stay moist, not become dry. Nothing supports (5); besides, a higher temperature would not necessarily make the air dry.

## Lesson 8 Exercise

1. **(1)** *Evaluation/Chemistry.* We are told that X and Y differ in color, hardness, and shine. The information contradicts (4); both sound like solids. Although X and Y are different in many ways, there is no evidence to support (2), (3), or (5); in fact, both X and Y could easily be carbon.

2. **(5)** *Evaluation/Chemistry.* Information points to the idea that both are solids (definite shape and volume). We only know that Y is more expensive than X, which may or may not mean that it is less common than X. However, X may be every bit as useful. So reject (1) and (2). We know that metals often shine, but that does not

mean that everything that shines is metal, so reject (3). There is no evidence at all for (4).

3. **(5)** *Evaluation/ Chemistry.* The information about energy orbits (eight electrons fills most orbits) supports the idea that flourine would probably form bonds easily: It lacks only one electron to fill its outer orbit. There is no evidence at all for (1) and (4); what evidence there is points away from (2) and (3). The flourine atom only needs one electron, so it would be likely to draw that one electron from another atom—forming a bond easily—rather than give up its seven electrons to form a bond.

## Lesson 9 Exercise

1. **(1)** *Evaluation/ Chemistry.* Be careful not to assume that since two things occur together, or nearly so, that one causes the other. Plastic may be RELATED to riboflavin loss, but the caption for the picture tells you that it is the light passing through the plastic which causes the loss. (2) is the main point of the graphic and (3) is the broader point the advertisers want to make. (4) is an inference you can logically make: if riboflavin were not good for your body, why would the advertisers try to convince you that loss of riboflavin is something to avoid? The graph's caption tells you that "milk loses even more of its vitamin A" from the effects of fluorescent light; since paper cartons prevent this loss, (5) is a logical deduction based on this information.

2. **(2)** *Evaluation/ Chemistry.* The graph shows the loss of riboflavin by skim milk after 24 hours. The caption for the graph states that "other tests show that milk loses even more of its vitamin A." Putting these two details together, it is logical to conclude (2). (1) is an opinion: to require dairies by law to add vitamins to their milk is a legal and political proposal that goes beyond a logical conclusion. The assumption that whole milk starts out with more riboflavin is not supported by any information in the graph, so the logic of (3) is faulty. Although the assumptions in both (4) and (5) are true, the generalizations based on them are too broad. There are other vitamins besides riboflavin which may be important for health, and other reasons why the different kinds of milk are more or less healthy. In fact, many doctors say adults and older children should avoid milk because of its high fat content.

3. **(5)** *Evaluation/ Chemistry.* This is the only generalization which follows logically from the evidence without being too broad. The loss was found in all milk studied, though each kind of milk varied in fat content. It logically follows that the same kind of loss would be found in 2 percent milk, which on the graph would appear between the 1% milk and whole milk. Reject choice (1), because the doctors hired to do this study are not necessarily objective. The ad was paid for by a group with a definite

interest in how the results came out. You cannot logically draw the conclusions in (2) and (4) from the information in the graph or the photo's caption. Fluorescent light and sunlight may be more similar than you think; riboflavin and vitamin A may be quite different from the other vitamins mentioned—and may be lost in smaller amounts, if at all. (3) is wrong because the graph gives no information to support the conclusion that the rate of vitamin loss depends on the size of the plastic milk container.

## Lesson 10 Exercise

1. **(2)** *Evaluation/Physics.* The main point of the article is *conservation of energy* by defrosting refrigerators manually. A science adviser (1) would not give homey advice; he or she also would probably NOT criticize a particular product as this author does; the President and his advisers value votes and do not want to offend particular groups. Eliminate (3) because it is in the manufacturer's best interest to praise his product, not criticize it. Although the article mentions an historical device (the icebox), the writer is primarily interested in energy-use by today's refrigerators; so reject (4). Defrosting by hand presumably takes more time than using the "automatic" defrost, so eliminate choice (5).

2. **(3)** *Evaluation/Physics.* It is conservation of electricity—not time-saving—that the writer stresses. Reject choices (1) and (2) because the writer does

not go so far as to say either that we should return to the past—nor that we should buy particular refrigerators. He merely offers advice on how to make the best of what we have. Reject (4) and (5) because they contradict the article. The expression "Time is money" implies "Don't waste time that could be used to earn money." Although the writer probably values saving money, it is saving electricity which he stresses, even at the expense of time. He stresses that automatic defrosters WASTE energy, not conserve it.

3. **(5)** *Evaluation/Physics.* The writer is interested in how the refrigerator functions, not in how it looks. Choices (1)-(4) are all consistent with his interest in conservation.

## Chapter 1: Nonfiction

### Lesson 1

1. **(3)** *Literal Comprehension/Nonfiction.* In line 9, the author states that "color has nothing to do with writing as such." The other choices are all incorrect because they're untrue. The author says, in lines 9–11, "in your mind don't be a *colored writer* . . . be a *writer* first."

2. **(5)** *Literal Comprehension/Nonfiction.* In line 1 and lines 7–8, the author states the importance of being a *consistent* writer. (1) and (3) are true statements but are not the main idea of the passage; they are details which help support the main idea. (2) and (4) are incorrect because they are not even mentioned in the passage.

3. **(4)** *Literal Comprehension/Nonfiction.* Choice (4) is the only statement among the answer choices that is large enough to cover the main ideas of all the paragraphs in the passage. It is a restatement of the first sentence in the passage, which is the topic sentence of the passage. (1) is the main idea only of the second paragraph and (5) is the main idea only of the first paragraph. The third paragraph is about what science has discovered about the dreaming of blind people and the fourth paragraph describes scientific discoveries about color in dreams. These discoveries, the main ideas of the remaining paragraphs of the passage, would also be covered by the statement in choice (4). Nothing in the passage supports the exaggerated statements in (2) and (3): because dreams have basic characteristics does not mean that all dreams are the same in every way; because science has discovered these basic characteristics does not mean it has explained everything about dreams.

### Lesson 2

1. **(4)** *Inferential Comprehension/Nonfiction.* All the details that follow the author's statement "The Great Plains which I cross in my sleep are bigger than any name people give them" (lines 15–16) suggest that the plains "extend beyond the frame of the photograph" (line 18) because they make the author feel and imagine things that no photograph could capture—such as his image of hills as sleeping women and his imagining that the great Native American chief Crazy Horse is still alive and free. He obviously experiences this region very intensely partly *because* of its size, so (2) is wrong. No detail suggests (1), (3), or (5).

2. **(5)** *Inferential Comprehension/Nonfiction.* The author's topic is the Great Plains and his main idea is that the Great Plains inspire him with dreams, emotions, and imaginings about them that "are bigger than any name people give them" (lines 15–16). Since they inspire him this way in the city as much as they do anywhere else, (3) cannot be true. He clearly prefers the country to city life, but (2) is too general since it doesn't mention the topic, the Great Plains. (4) is also vague because dreams of the plains don't make him want to travel *anywhere*. (1) is a detail, not the main idea, which is about what the plains make him feel and imagine.

3. **(3)** *Inferential Comprehension/Nonfiction.* The many details the author imagines seem to come from the memories of sounds, smells, and sights he has experienced; you can infer this from the vivid way he describes what he imagines. (1), (4), and (5) are incorrect because the author doesn't mention or suggest any of these as sources for the things he describes. (2) is also incorrect. In line 17, he says that the Great Plains are full of stories, but he doesn't state that he's heard any of them or that any particular story was the source of his imaginings.

## Lesson 3

1. **(5)** *Application/ Nonfiction.* In lines 6–7, the author says, "I resolved to tell them what I could, and hoped they would want to know as much as I could tell." This statement, combined with details about the father's gentleness toward his sons, allows you to conclude that the father would be both gentle and honest in telling his sons about their grandfather's death. (1), (2), and (3) are incorrect; the father's openness with his sons makes the reader think that he'll tell his sons directly, so none of these choices can be correct. (4) is also incorrect because lying to his children and avoiding telling them the truth are not in keeping with the father's openness.

2. **(1)** *Application/ Nonfiction.* The death of the author's father makes the father feel protective toward his sons, just as a defense attorney would feel protective of his or her client after damaging courtroom testimony. None of the other choices would inspire this reaction as they are either positive, like (2) or seemingly neutral, like (3).(4), and (5).

3. **(2)** *Application/ Nonfiction.* The details in the passage portray the author as a loving, protective father. Because his son Nicholas has nightmares about death and injured animals, the author would be *least* likely to take his sons to see a bull get injured and killed for sport. On the other hand, since he intends to be honest about death with his sons, he might very well take them to a funeral (4). (1), (3), and (5) are not correct because they are pleasurable events the author would probably enjoy taking his sons to.

## Lesson 4

1. **(4)** *Analysis/Nonfiction.* The tone of writing in this passage is straight-forward and somber and would be least appropriate for a wedding announcement, for which a joyful, light-hearted tone would be most appropriate. All the other answers could be written with the more serious tone used in this passage.

2. **(5)** *Analysis/Nonfiction.* (5) is the choice most closely linked with the girl's loss of happy memories about "the little plane" that flew over her village. Choices (1), (2), (3), and (4) were all tragic, sorrowful experiences for the girl, but it was the invading Russian gunship that made her formerly happy memories of "the little plane" seem like "something she once imagined, a childish dream" (line 19).

3. **(2)** *Analysis/Nonfiction.* By describing the girl's life before her village was bombed, the author shows how her life was changed by the invading gunships. The horrors of war the girl has experienced become more evident when compared with the peaceful life she knew before the Russian invasion. (1) and (3) are indirect effects of the author's describing the girl's life before the invasion; however, they are not the main reason he chose to include these details. (4) is incorrect because it's untrue. (5) is also not correct—it's too general an effect for this example.

## Chapter 2: Fiction

### Lesson 1

1. **(5)** *Literal Comprehension/Fiction.* All of the answers are part of the action of the passage, but choices (1) through (4) occur only briefly. Most of the action and dialogue center on the manager's and detective's accusations.

2. **(5)** *Literal Comprehension/Fiction.* The action of Michael's stealing the snakeskin box took place *just prior* to the action of this passage. So choices (1) and (4), which are part of the action of the passage, are incorrect. (2) is wrong because Michael's bet with his friends did not take place just before the action began but at some indefinite time in the past. (3) is incorrect because it is the detective, and not the clerk, who says that he saw Michael steal the box.

3. **(4)** *Literal Comprehension/Fiction.* We are told the manager and clerk "looked at Michael with a queer expression, in which astonishment and contempt were mixed with vague curiosity" (lines 5–6). When Michael tells them he can prove he stole the snakeskin box on a bet, "The three men looked at him in silence,

all three of them just faintly smiling, as if incredulously. 'Sure you can,' the detective said. . ." (lines 13–15). Even if you did not know "incredulous" means "disbelieving," you could tell that these details show the men to be mainly suspicious and contemptuous in their attitude toward Michael. Though the detective yanks Michael's hand from his pocket, nothing suggests all three men are cruel and brutal (2). No details indicate (1) and (3). The first sentence says "the events then happened with revolting and nauseating speed," not that the men's attitude was "disgusted and revolted" (5).

## Lesson 2

1. **(1)** *Inferential Comprehension/Fiction.* Don Anselmo's refusal of the extra money for the land suggests that he is a man of honor. You can infer this from his behavior at the end of the transaction: "But I do not care to be insulted. I have agreed to sell my house and land for twelve hundred dollars and that is the price" (lines 19–20). His departure also shows his pride and honor: "Then he shook hands all around, put on his ragged gloves, took his stick and walked out with the boy behind him" (lines 23–24). A man of his word, he will stick to the bargain that was struck, even if it costs his additional profit. (2) is wrong because it is clear that Don Anselmo understands the situation: "I know these Americans are good people, and that is why I agreed to sell to them . . . [but] I have

agreed to sell my house and land for twelve hundred dollars and that is the price" (lines 19–20). (3) is incorrect because his "ragged gloves" suggest that he is not wealthy at all. Eliminate (4) because there is nothing bitter about his actions; on the contrary, he is courteous and calm. Finally, (5) is wrong because he likes the Americans, agreeing with the narrator that they are "good people." That is why he agreed to sell to them originally.

2. **(5)** *Inferential Comprehension/Fiction.* The narrator tries to get Don Anselmo to accept the extra money. On line 21, the narrator says, "I argued with him but it was useless." Eliminate the other choices because they are not supported by the passage. (1) and (4) are wrong, because if the narrator wanted the land or some of the money, why would he argue with Don Anselmo to accept the Americans' offer? (2) is incorrect because the narrator feels the Americans' offer is generous: "These Americans are *buena gente*, they are good people, "he says, "and they are willing to pay you for the additional land as well, at the same rate per acre" (lines 10–12). (3) is plainly contradicted by the narrator's behavior.

3. **(3)** *Inferential Comprehension/Fiction.* You can infer the author's admiration for Don Anselmo by a number of details. First, the title of the story— "Gentleman of Río en Medio"— suggests the

author's admiration. This is echoed by Don Anselmo's actions at the end of the passage—he leaves with great pride. Eliminate (2) and (3) because they contradict the title and Don Anselmo's behavior. (4) is wrong because there is nothing to suggest that the author has sympathy for Don Anselmo's situation; the gentleman is in an admirable position, entitled to receive twice the money he had anticipated. Since Don Anselmo is not ignorant about the transaction, there is nothing for the author to criticize. Therefore, eliminate (5).

## Lesson 3

1. **(2)** *Application/Fiction.* The narrator believes, as he says in lines 10–11, that "the Lord aimed for [a man] to do and not to spend too much time thinking"; he compares the brain to a machine that shouldn't be used too much or it will break down. In applying this attitude to a situation where the narrator had a large problem, you could conclude that, most likely, he would only think about his problem a little bit and drop it. Therefore, he is unlikely to think a lot (1) or collect information to help him solve it (4). Nothing in the passage leads you to believe that he would ask anyone, so choices (3) and (5) are incorrect as well.

2. **(2)** *Application/Fiction.* Since the narrator thinks a man should not spend "too much time thinking" (lines 10–11) and compares the brain to a machine that should not be used any more than

necessary (lines 11–14), he most probably would think college a waste of time. With this attitude, he would not feel proud of his son (1) and would not think college would benefit women, either (3), even though he thinks a woman can help a man "know his own good" (lines 19–20). With this attitude he clearly would not believe college was the Lord's will (4). Since his attitude is definitely hostile to thinking more than necessary, he would not be simply indifferent (5).

3. **(1)** *Application/Fiction.* The narrator agrees with his wife when she says that all Darl needs "is a wife to straighten him out" (lines 15–16). Since this is Cora's opinion, he would not tell Darl to get Cora's opinion (3). Since he is hostile to "too much time thinking," he would not tell Darl to think a long time about his decision (2). (4) is clearly wrong. (5) is incorrect because the narrator would think the sooner Darl got married, the better.

## Lesson 4

1. **(1)** *Analysis/Fiction.* Much of the language used in this passage creates a menacing, or threatening, mood. We are told that there "was no joy in the brilliance of sunshine" and that the river "ran on, deserted, into the gloom" (lines 4–5) that this "strange world of plants, and water, and silence" "looked at you with a vengeful aspect" (lines 16–18). The author says that the "stillness of life did not in the least

resemble a peace" (line 17) so (4) is incorrect. No details suggest the narrator is angry (2) or sad (5). His main emotion is clearly fear, so he is not excited (3) in the usual sense of the word, which suggests positive feelings.

2. **(3)** *Analysis/Fiction.* In the first sentence the author describes "the earliest beginnings of the world" as a time "when vegetation rioted on the earth and the big trees were kings"—which further emphasizes that the river is a nonhuman world. Other details that stress this idea are the mention of hippopotami and alligators sunning on the river bank (lines 6–7), the narrator's sense of being "bewitched and cut off forever from everything you had known once" (lines 10–11) and his description of the river as "this strange world of plants, and water, and silence" (line 16). No detail suggests (1) or (2). The mention of hippopotami and alligators shows that the river includes animal as well as plant life, so (4) is wrong. The author emphasizes that the river is very old to stress that it is strange and nonhuman, not to suggest it is the most dangerous part of the world (5).

3. **(5)** *Analysis/Fiction.* All the details used to create the mood of menace (see the answer key for question 1) and to stress the strange, nonhuman character of the river (see the answer key for question 2) are used by the author to show the narrator's feeling that he is in a foreign and hostile world and therefore in danger.

For the narrator to say that he thinks the river and the jungle looked at him "with a vengeful aspect"—as if they wanted to take revenge on him for some unknown reason—brings to a climax the effect of menace and strangeness in the passage. No detail suggests the narrator is losing his sanity (1), that other humans are about to attack him (2), that the narrator is more lost now than earlier (3). The narrator calls the jungle along the river a "strange world of plants, and water, and silence," but when he says "It looked at you with a vengeful aspect," he does not seem to mean that jungle animals are looking at him (4).

## Chapter 3: Drama

### Lesson 1

1. **(2)** *Literal Comprehension/Drama.* Penny directly states: "The only trouble with dancing is, it takes so long. You've been studying such a long time" (lines 10–11). She does say that if new orders keep coming in, Essie might open a store (line 7), but her objection to Essie's dancing is not that she thinks Essie can make more money with a store than by dancing (1). None of her dialogue includes the statements in the other choices.

2. **(4)** *Literal Comprehension/Drama.* In line 5 Penny says, "Do you have to make candy today, Essie? It's such a hot day." Essie, not Penny, is the one who says the candy takes a

long time to cool (1), in the fourth line of the scene. No dialogue of Penny's includes the statements in the other choices.

3. **(3)** *Literal Comprehension/Drama.* A stage direction states "(*Bracing herself against the table, she manipulates her legs, ballet fashion.*)" Essie fans herself when she first enters the scene, before she starts dancing. She does none of the actions mentioned in the other choices.

## Lesson 2

1. **(2)** *Inferential Comprehension/Drama.* The stage directions at the beginning of the play say that Mary "*springs to her feet, as if she wanted to run away*" when she hears her son Edmund's fit of coughing. As he enters, she looks out the window, "*apparently calm,*" and then "*turns to him, her lips set in a welcoming, motherly smile.*" Her actions characterize her dramatically as a person who, when faced with any unpleasantness, such as her son's illness, wants to run away or to pretend that the unpleasantness does not exist. None of her actions suggests she is a calm person (4) or does not care for her son (5). Nothing suggests (3), and (1) is incorrect because her actions suggest that she wants not to charm everyone, but only to pretend to her son that she is not worried about his illness or about anything else.

2. **(3)** *Inferential Comprehension/Drama.* Mary speaks her first statement "(*almost resentfully*)" in line 9 and

her second statement "(*worriedly taking his arm*)" (line 12). This dialogue of hers shows that she has conflicting feelings about Edmund and his illness and therefore has a confused attitude toward him. For this reason she is not simply resentful (2). She is not simply encouraging (1) because she is partly resentful. She is not optimistic (5) because she is clearly worried. In fact, her second statement is more wishful thinking than sincerely encouraging or optimistic; it expresses her tendency to pretend everything is all right when she knows it isn't. Since she is worried, she cannot be detached (4).

3. **(4)** *Inferential Comprehension/Drama.* In her last portion of dialogue, Mary says several things that suggest she is ashamed that her family seems socially inferior to her neighbors. She speaks with some bitterness about their "second-hand" car, and even about the way her husband dresses in front of the neighbors. Nothing she says expresses any of the concerns mentioned in the other choices.

## Lesson 3

1. **(1)** *Application/Drama.* A man who uses his wife's temper as an excuse to stay at home each evening is most similar to Sibyl in the passage. Sibyl uses her mother's unwillingness to allow her to get a job as an excuse to stay home with her. Sibyl is someone who cannot make herself do what she needs to do to be happy (be more independent of

her mother) and therefore she is not like a woman who diets when she does not need to (2). (4) and (5) are incorrect because they are both examples of people who declare their independence from people who have authority over them, which is exactly what Sibyl cannot do with her mother. (5) is exactly what Miss Cooper wants Sibyl to do, not what Sibyl's situation is at present. (3) is another example of a person acting independently—of a partner—which is not like Sibyl's behavior, either.

2. **(3)** *Application/Drama.* You can tell from Miss Cooper's statement "To me all people are extraordinary" that she believes that every human being is a unique person; her encouraging Sibyl to strike out on her own indicates that she believes in the individuality of every person. In applying this attitude to Miss Cooper's situation as a teacher, it is clear that she would favor (3). All the other choices recommend either "doing as you are told"—(1) and (4) —or "following the crowd"—(2)—rather than individuality. (5) would express conformity to rules or majority taste, not individuality.

3. **(5)** *Application/Drama.* Sibyl tells Miss Cooper that she doesn't think her mother would agree with Miss Cooper's beliefs about the uniqueness of each individual. Miss Cooper says she's sure her mother wouldn't. It is the difference in the two women's attitudes—Miss Cooper's and Sibyl's mother's—that makes it very unlikely that the

playwright would include a scene in which they would be singing around the piano together. All the other choices are incorrect because the dialogue indicates that any of these situations would be possible.

Lesson 4

1. **(2)** *Analysis/Drama.* Babe says her mother killed the cat "'cause she was afraid of dying all alone" (line 19) and feels her mother was afraid to go to heaven alone because she imagined angels were frightening "and you don't want to meet 'em all alone" (line 24). The playwright gives Babe this speech to show that, from the fear and loneliness of her own suicide attempt, she has a sudden insight into her mother's motive for killing her cat along with herself; the speech suggests that she now understands how frightened and lonely her mother must have been. You may be able to find the correct answer best by eliminating the wrong answer choices. In line 17 Babe says "(with joy) Mama. I know why she hung that cat along with her." She would not say this "with joy" if (1) or (3) were true. No detail suggests (4) or (5)

2. **(4)** *Analysis/Drama.* Everything in Meg's dialogue and behavior suggests that she takes Babe's suicide attempt seriously. The scenes last line expresses a calm, detached attitude in Meg toward Babe's suicide attempt, which reveals a down-to-earth personality (3) and a gentleness toward this sister who has frightened her so badly (5). To say that sui-

cide "is getting to be a thing [a kind of fashion or fad] in our family" makes a link between Babe and their mother (1) and provides some dark comic relief (2) to a painful scene.

3. **(1)** *Analysis/Drama.* Meg is very shaken up by Babe's having attempted suicide. In comparison, Babe remains calm, almost neutral, about the episode, chalking it up to having had "a real bad day." (2), (3), (4), and (5) are incorrect because nothing in the stage directions or dialogue suggests these motives or actions for Meg.

## Chapter 4: Poetry

Lesson 1

1. **(3)** *Literal Comprehension/Poetry.* The key statement in the poem is the poet's comment that the poor immigrant "falls in love with wealth itself" (line 8). We are also told that with "his fingers he cheats." In a poem so full of images, you may want to find the correct answer by eliminating the wrong ones. Every line of the poem contains an image of the immigrant's unhappiness, so (1) cannot be true, although there are many images of his hard work. The second line says the immigrant "uses all his power to do evil," so (5) is incorrect. His "Heaven is like ironsides" (line 6) and therefore (4) is incorrect. The speaker says the immigrant "wishes he would have stayed home" (line 1) but nothing suggests the speaker hates the immigrant for leaving home (2).

2. **(1)** *Literal Comprehension/Poetry.* The third line tells us that the immigrant cheats and lies, and in line 8 we are told he fell in love with wealth itself, so dishonesty is the evil he commits. We are told he hates his life, but not other people, so (3) is wrong. No statement or image supports the other choices.

3. **(2)** *Literal Comprehension/Poetry.* The poet gives many images of sensations—the pricking of grain and crushing of grass by his feet, the wind on his bare head—and then he says, "I won't talk at all, I won't think about anything." Since the sensations he describes are experiences in nature, (5) cannot be correct. "Infinite love" is an emotion that arises from his sensations but nothing suggests that the poet thinks that it is better than the sensations he describes (3). Likewise, (4) is wrong because dreaming is an experience he has while feeling the cool grass on his feet, so it is not a cause (source) of sensations, but an effect of a sensation. (1) is too vague, since it does not refer to sensations at all.

Lesson 2

1. **(2)** *Inferential Comprehension/Poetry.* A dream that is deferred— that is, postponed or unrealized—may eventually produce violence; the last image of the poem expresses this idea by using the word "explode." None of the images in the poem suggests that unrealized dreams will just disappear (2). The poem is clearly not about destructive dreams (1) or

rotten dreams (4)—for instance, dreams of power and glory that are unreasonable or selfish; it is about the way in which the frustrating of people's good dreams can poison their lives. No details suggest the image in (5).

2. **(2)** *Inferential Comprehension/Poetry.* The use of the word "fester" in the phrase, "fester like a sore" (line 4) compares the deferred dream to a human wound that has become infected. All the other choices are incorrect because they are things that do not possess human qualities.

3. **(3)** *Inferential Comprehension/Poetry.* The poet suggests some of the possible negative things that might happen if a dream is deferred. This allows you to infer that the dream represents, or symbolizes, something positive. Disease (4), therefore, cannot be correct. Of the positive answers listed, (5) cannot be right because all the images, and the last line, are about the pain caused by having the dream deferred—postponed; if the dream was a symbol of patience, the people with the dream probably would not feel so much pain from having to wait indefinitely. Likewise, anger is clearly not the content of the dream but rather an emotion caused by the deferring of the dream; so (2) is wrong. Violence (1) is also a (possible) effect of the deferred dream, but not its content.

## Lesson 3

1. **(2)** *Application/Poetry.*

The attitude the poet expresses through all the images of the poem is that from the point of view of the entire universe, life on Earth is not important. With this attitude, he would consider a forest fire insignificant in the order of nature. None of the other choices expresses an attitude of the speaker of the poem.

2. **(1)** *Application/Poetry.* All the images of the poem combine to create the impression that no one form of life on Earth is any more important than any other. In the climax of the poem the speaker says that if the Earth were to fall into the sun, it might seem like nothing more than a shooting star to the inhabitant of another planet. The poet's point is not that the end of the world will make life on Earth insignificant (2), but that such life simply *is* insignificant. The theme of the poem focuses on the Earth's insignificance, not children's intelligence (3), or nuclear catastrophe (4). If the theme was how much more advanced life on other planets is (5), we would not be given the image of a child on another planet mistaking the end of the world for a shooting star.

3. **(4)** *Application/Poetry.* The child's response to seeing the Earth fall into the sun is pure excitement at how bright and pretty it is. This image of a completely unfeeling reaction to suffering is a very effective way to end a poem about the insignificance of life on Earth. All the other choices express alarm or concern for the victims of

the accident; the attitude of the child in the poem does not include these feelings.

## Lesson 4

1. **(5)** *Analysis/Poetry.* Since this poem communicates through a series of visual images, you may want to find the right answer by eliminating the choices that seem clearly to be wrong. Since the speaker keeps calling the sun "that brave man," his or her attitude is clearly one of admiration for what the sun represents: the sun is talked about as a fearless hero; it is a symbol of natural courage. (3) is therefore incorrect. The speaker does not express fear of the sun, only admiration, so (2) is wrong. No image suggests (1) or (4).

2. **(3)** *Analysis/Poetry.* This stanza describes how the sun causes the speaker's fears to run away. This imagery of a victory of light over darkness and—figuratively— of courage over fear gives the stanza its triumphant tone. The speaker's "fears of my bed" may refer either to nightmares, to fears that keep people awake in a state of insomnia, or to the fear some people have of going to sleep and never waking up. The lines also tell us that sun, as courage, chases away all the fears we may have of death or of dangers in life (line 11). Since the stanza describes fears running away, its tone cannot be frightened (2) or pessimistic (1) or sad (4). Nothing in the lines suggest a tone of anger (5).

3. **(1)** *Analysis/Poetry.* The most important detail in

the quoted lines is the description of the sun as walking "without meditation"—without thinking. All the images of the poem have shown the sun, as a symbol of courage, moving easily, without fear, past all dangers. None of the images in the poem suggests that the sun as a symbol of courage is unhappy (2), lonely (3), or cruel (5). (4) cannot be true because all the poem's images show the sun's actions. This suggests there is no difference between brave attitudes and brave actions because, as the last lines state, the brave person acts instinctively, without thinking.

## Chapter 5: Commentary on the Arts

### Lesson 1

1. **(3)** *Literal Comprehension/Commentary on the Arts.* The reviewer says that screenwriter Bruce Joel Rubin has "raided every genre to create this seductive, funny hybrid, but he's done his job with a witty, light touch" (lines 18–19). By saying that the screenwriter has "raided every genre" (genre means type of writing), the author reinforces his statement that *Ghost* is "built entirely out of borrowed parts" (line 17). (1) and (4) are wrong because the types of movie combined in *Ghost* are "comedy, romance and supernatural thriller" (line 15): (1) omits comedy and (4) leaves out romance. (2) and (5) express negative opinions about movies such as *Ghost*—movies based on other movies which use the supernatural—but these opinions are not opinions stated by the reviewer.

2. **(2)** *Literal Comprehension/Commentary on the Arts.* We are told that the Whoopi Goldberg character helps Patrick Swayze "track down the man who murdered him" (lines 13–14). None of the other choices restates facts used in the review.

3. **(1)** *Literal Comprehension/Commentary on the Arts.* In the first two sentences of the review, the author states that "ghostly love stories" are currently popular with audiences. (2) is wrong because the passage says that *Always* has a similar plot, not the same plot. (3) is not correct because it is not stated as a fact, or even as an opinion, in the passage. (4) is a statement of fact which neither supports nor contradicts the author's favorable opinion of the movie. (5) is an opinion which the critic states in the last sentence, but it doesn't support his main opinion of the movie, which is positive.

### Lesson 2

1. **(2)** *Inferential Comprehension/Commentary on the Arts.* The critic reveals that she thinks the painter is overrated by stating that she "hadn't noticed anyone waiting breathlessly" for another showing of his work (lines 6–7). (1) is not correct because this statement is just the opposite of what the critic expresses. (3) is incorrect because she calls

Bacon the "Grand Old Man of British painting," but makes no comparison between British and American painters. (4) and (5) are not correct because they are not even mentioned in the first paragraph.

2. **(1)** *Inferential Comprehension/Commentary on the Arts.* By including this phrase in her review, the critic indicates that her review contains personal opinion, and not just objective facts. Because the remaining choices all include facts, they can't be interpreted as simply being her opinion.

3. **(3)** *Inferential Comprehension/Commentary on the Arts.* The only choice which is supported by details in the commentary is (3). The critic states that Bacon was "one of those lucky painters who have had the consensus of history on their side" (lines 8–9) and goes on to state that one of his works "had no match in its time" (line 22) These statements, coupled with the opinion she expresses in the last sentence of the first paragraph, best summarize the main idea of the passage. (1) is a detail that can be inferred from the piece, but it doesn't express its main idea or even mention Bacon. (2) and (4) are neither mentioned nor suggested in the passage. (5) is also incorrect; Bacon's reputation, according to the commentary, has remained steady for decades.

### Lesson 3

1. **(4)** *Application/Commentary on the Arts.*

The author of the article clearly favors the breaking down of the prejudice against men being dancers, so it is logical to assume that he would be in favor of breaking down a prejudice against women working in a previously all-male profession. None of the other choices express attitudes that are in line with his basically favorable view of people who get past established opinions in order to do what they want to do in their professional lives.

2. **(3)** *Application/ Commentary on the Arts.* The author shows that Eddie Villella and Jacques d' Amboise did a lot to break down prejudice against men dancers by showing that they could be professional dancers and "regular guys" at the same time. The author nowhere mentions that Villella and d'Amboise changed prejudice by demanding new regulations (1), refusing to perform in major events (2), forming professional organizations (4), or criticizing the sexual attitudes of commentators on their field of performance (5).

3. **(2)** *Application/ Commentary on the Arts.* The author's basic attitude toward change in the arts is encouraging; logically, he would welcome a new dance-form just as he welcomes the new acceptance of men as dancers.

## Lesson 4

1. **(2)** *Analysis/ Commentary on the Arts.* The tone of the review is set in the first sentence by appealing to "all those women who wailed 'How could she do it?' when Gloria Steinem, the world's most famous feminist," started dating a real estate developer. The second paragraph ends with examples of women whose lives were changed or touched by Steinem, and the last lines of the essay appeal to all these women to make Steinem's book a best–seller. The essay is, therefore, not pitched toward active feminists (3) only. It does not try to persuade hostile or neutral audiences to like and admire Steinem and her book, so (1) and (5) cannot be correct. The review does have a gossip-column's interest in Steinem's social life, but its appeal is not primarily to a gossip interest because of its serious respect for Steinem as a leader. So (4) is incorrect.

2. **(1)** *Analysis/ Commentary on the Arts.* The reviewer finds fault with Steinem's book for not revealing enough of "what makes her tick" (line 16) and for citing too much popular, Eastern, and mystical philosophy (line 15), as well as literature that talks about nourishing your "inner child" (lines 18–19). However, the writer says no one is "more fascinating" or can combine "monastic commitment" and "glamour" (line 9) as she does, and that no one else has positively affected so many women's lives. None of the other choices correctly describes the reviewer's feelings.

3. **(4)** *Analysis/ Commentary on the Arts.* With its focus on the personal as well as the public life of Steinem, the essay has a style closest to that of a biography. (1) and (5) are types of books that would give step by step instructions. A political article (2) would concentrate on Steinem's public life and leave out her personal life. An historical study of feminism (3) would not focus exclusively on Steinem and probably would have even less interest in her personal life.

# Answer Key: Unit 5

## Chapter 1

### Level 1, Preview, pg. 403

1. 1,275,328

2. 1281
   323
   217
   + 89
   **1910**

3. 2196
   −328
   **1868**

4. 206
   ×38
   1648
   618
   **7828**

5.     **43**
   34⟌1462
     136
      102
      102

### Level 1, Lesson 1, pg. 404

1. **247 (hundreds)**
2. **4780 (tens)**
3. **846 (ones)**
4. **6750 (tens)**
5. **67,400 (thousands)**
6. **19,950 (ten thousands)**
7. **442 (tens)**
8. **750,000 (hundred thousands)**
9. **4,846,500 (millions)**
10. **8,200,000,000 (billions)**

### Level 1, Lesson 2, pg. 404

1. 8,432
   634
   + 13
   **9,079**

2. 1,589
   1,420
   + 1,222
   **4,231**

3. 45,931
   21,213
   6,708
   + 195
   **74,047**

4. 12,745,923
   + 252,189
   **12,998,112**

5. 1619
   419
   + 8
   **2046**

### Level 1, Lesson 3, pg. 405

1. 852
   − 361
   **491**

2. 23,538
   − 18,769
   **4,769**

3. 1059
   − 328
   **731**

4. 216
   − 98
   **118**

5. 1005
   − 426
   **579**

6. 13,328
   − 8,379
   **4,949**

7. 219
   − 37
   **182**

### Level 1, Lesson 4, pg. 406

1. 53
   × 4
   **212**

2. 321
   × 44
   1284
   1284
   **14,124**

3. 140
   × 2
   **280**

4. 532
   × 108
   4256
   5320
   **57,456**

5. 604
   × 79
   5436
   4228
   **47,716**

6. 397
   × 45
   1985
   1588
   **17,865**

7. 3028
   × 16
   18168
   3028
   **48,448**

8. 163
   × 129
   1467
   326
   163
   **21,027**

### Level 1, Lesson 5, pg. 408

1.     **23**
   20⟌460
     40
      60
      60

2.    **874**
   8⟌6992
    64
     59
     56
      32
      32

3.   **6589**
   5⟌32945
    30
     29
     25
      44
      40
       45
       45

**4.**
$$24\overline{)3504} = 146$$
$$\begin{array}{r} 24 \\ \hline 110 \\ 96 \\ \hline 144 \\ 144 \end{array}$$

**5.**
$$85\overline{)52445} = 617$$
$$\begin{array}{r} 510 \\ \hline 144 \\ 85 \\ \hline 595 \\ 595 \end{array}$$

**6.** **196 r 28**
$$36\overline{)7084}$$
$$\begin{array}{r} 36 \\ \hline 348 \\ 324 \\ \hline 244 \\ 216 \\ \hline 28 \end{array}$$

**7.**
$$204\overline{)19584} = 96$$
$$\begin{array}{r} 1836 \\ \hline 1224 \\ 1224 \end{array}$$

**8.**
$$196\overline{)5096} = 26$$
$$\begin{array}{r} 392 \\ \hline 1176 \\ 1176 \end{array}$$

## Level 2, Lesson 1, pg. 410

1. **260**
2. **1800**
3. **13,300**
4. **120,000**
5. **47,900**
6. **16,000**
7. **400,000**
8. **90,000**
9. **90,000**
10. **2,000,000**

## Level 2, Lesson 2, pg. 412

1. **90 miles**
$$\begin{array}{r} 15 \\ \times\ 6 \\ \hline 90 \end{array}$$

2. **$56**
$$\begin{array}{r} 28 \\ \times\ 2 \\ \hline 56 \end{array}$$

3. **95 miles**
$$6\overline{)570} = 95$$
$$\begin{array}{r} 54 \\ \hline 30 \\ 30 \end{array}$$

4. **7 pounds**
$$3\overline{)21} = 7$$
$$21$$

5. **$25**
$$40\overline{)1000} = 25$$
$$\begin{array}{r} 80 \\ \hline 200 \\ 200 \end{array}$$

6. **9 miles per hour**
$$12\overline{)108} = 9$$
$$108$$

## Level 2, Lesson 3, pg. 414

1. $8^2 = 8 \times 8 = $ **64**
2. $30^2 = 30 \times 30 = $ **900**
3. $7^3 = 7 \times 7 \times 7 = $ **343**
4. $10^3 = 10 \times 10 \times 10 = $ **1000**
5. $3^4 = 3 \times 3 \times 3 \times 3 = $ **81**
6. $\sqrt{36} = $ **6**
7. $\sqrt{64} = $ **8**
8. **(3) 4 and 5**
$$4 \times 4 = 16$$
$$5 \times 5 = 25$$
9. **(5) 19 and 20**
$$19 \times 19 = 361$$
$$20 \times 20 = 400$$

## Level 2, Lesson 4, pg. 417

1.

| | Perimeter | Area |
|---|---|---|
| *Fig.* 1-6 | **30 ft.** $P = 2(9) + 2(6)$ $P = 18 + 12$ $P = 30$ | **54 sq. ft.** $A = 9 \times 6$ $A = 54$ |
| *Fig.* 1-7 | **20 yds** $P = 4(5)$ $P = 20$ | **25 sq. yds** $A = 5^2$ $A = 25$ |
| *Fig.* 1-8 | **64 in.** $P = 30 + 17 + 17$ $P = 64$ in. | **120 sq. in.** $A = \frac{1}{2}(30 \times 8)$ $A = \frac{1}{2}(240)$ $A = 120$ sq. in. |

2. **180 feet**
$$P = 4(45)$$
$$= 180$$

3. **96 inches**
$$P = 2(36) + 2(12)$$
$$= 72 + 24$$
$$= 96$$

4. **16 feet**
$$P = 5 + 5 + 6$$
$$= 16$$

5. **192 square feet**
$$A = 16 \times 12$$
$$= 192$$

6. **180 square feet**
$$A = \frac{1}{2}(20 \times 18)$$
$$= \frac{1}{2}(360)$$
$$= 180$$

## Level 2, Lesson 5, pg. 419

1. **700 cubic inches**
$$V = 20 \times 7 \times 5$$
$$= 700$$

2. **980 cubic yards**
$$V = 14 \times 10 \times 7$$
$$= 980$$

3. **216 cubic inches**
$$V = 6^3$$
$$= 216$$

4. **1000 cubic feet**
$$V = 10^3$$
$$= 1000$$

5. **4096 cubic yards**
$$V = 16^3$$
$$= 4096$$

## Level 2, Lesson 6, pg. 421

1. **44**
$$\begin{array}{r} 43 \\ 42 \\ 30 \\ 50 \\ +\ 55 \\ \hline 220 \end{array}$$
$$5\overline{)220} = 44$$

2. **274**
$$\begin{array}{r} 123 \\ 421 \\ +\ 278 \\ \hline 822 \end{array}$$
$$3\overline{)822} = 274$$

**3. $54**

$$
\begin{array}{r}
58 \\
62 \\
63 \\
+\ 33 \\
\hline
216
\end{array}
$$

$$
\begin{array}{r}
54 \\
4\overline{)216}
\end{array}
$$

**4. 9 pounds**

$9 + 8 + 10 = 27$

$$
\begin{array}{r}
9 \\
3\overline{)27}
\end{array}
$$

**5. 5 feet 6 inches**

6 feet 1 inch
5 feet 9 inches
<u>5 feet 6 inches</u>
5 feet 4 inches
5 feet 1 inch

## Level 3, Lesson 1, pg. 423

**1. (4) 52(145 + 85)**

Number of weeks in a year multiplied by sum of weekly salaries.

**2. (3)** $\dfrac{(76 + 67 + 65 + 74 + 77 + 75 + 70)}{7}$

Sum of the temperatures divided by the number of temperatures added.

**3. (2) 48(252) – 8600**

Total payments less cash price.

**4. (2)** $\dfrac{(3 \times 2 \times 4)}{2}$

Formula for volume of a rectangle ($V = lwh$) divided by 2 to get $\frac{1}{2}$ cubic contents of container.

**5. (3) 4(2 × 3) × 12**

Cost of 1 square yard times area of one window times the number of windows.

## Level 3, Lesson 2, pg. 426

**1. $16**

$18 + 9 + 7 = 34$
$50 - 34 = 16$

**2. $1,200**

$$
\begin{array}{r}
16{,}500 \\
-\ 2{,}100 \\
\hline
14{,}400
\end{array}
$$

$$
\begin{array}{r}
1{,}200 \\
12\overline{)14{,}400}
\end{array}
$$

**3. $720**

$$
\begin{array}{r}
300 \\
\times\ \ \ 4 \\
\hline
1200
\end{array}
$$

$$
\begin{array}{r}
1200 \\
-\ 480 \\
\hline
720
\end{array}
$$

**4. $327**

$$
\begin{array}{r}
18 \\
\times\ \ 6 \\
\hline
108
\end{array}
$$

$435 - 108 = 327$

**5. 16**

$$
\begin{array}{r}
32 \\
\times\ 28 \\
\hline
896
\end{array}
$$
= how much she has saved so far

$$
\begin{array}{r}
1344 \\
-\ 896 \\
\hline
448
\end{array}
$$
= how much more she needs to save

$$
\begin{array}{r}
16 \\
28\overline{)448}
\end{array}
$$
= how many more weeks she needs to save

**6. 316 square yards**

*Large rectangle:*
$A = 13 \times 28$
$A = 364$

*Small rectangle:*
$A = 4 \times 12$
$A = 48$

*Shaded area:*
$364 - 48 = 316$

**7. 57 square feet**

*Square:*
$A = 9^2$
$A = 81$

*Rectangle:*
$A = 4 \times 6$
$A = 24$

*Shaded area:*
$81 - 24 = 57$

**8. 63 square inches**

*Rectangle:*
$A = 12 \times 6$
$A = 72$

*Triangle:*
$A = \frac{1}{2}(6 \times 3)$
$A = \frac{1}{2}(18)$
$A = 9$

*Shaded area:*
$72 - 9 = 63$

## Level 3, Lesson 3, pg. 428

**1. About 8000 passengers**

Round 398 to 400.

Round 22 to 20.
$400 \times 20 = 8000$

**2. (2) 90 shares**

Round 87,430 to 90,000.
Round 982 to 1,000.
$90{,}000 \div 1{,}000 = 90$

**3. (3) 30,000**

Round 33 to 30. Round 985 to 1,000. $1{,}000 \times 30 = 30{,}000$

**4. (2) $30**

Round $212 to $200. Divide 200 by 6: $200 \div 6 = 33.33$. Round $33.33 to $30.

**5. (5) 1800 sq. ft.**

Round 35 to 30. Round 65 to 60.

Multiply 30 times 60: $A = lw$; $A = 30 \times 60 = 1800$ square feet

## Level 3, Lesson 4, pg. 431

**1. $80**

$$
\begin{array}{ccc}
30 & 40 & 240 \\
\times\ 8 & \times\ 4 & -\ 160 \\
\hline
240 & 160 & 80
\end{array}
$$

**2. $9,200**

$$
\begin{array}{r}
40 \text{ hours per week} \\
\times\ \$4 \text{ per hour} \\
\hline
\$160 \text{ weekly pay}
\end{array}
$$

$$
\begin{array}{r}
\$160 \text{ weekly pay} \\
\times\ \ \ \ 50 \text{ weeks} \\
\hline
\$8000 \text{ work income}
\end{array}
$$

$$
\begin{array}{r}
\$40 \text{ cost per credit} \\
\times\ \ \ \ 30 \text{ credit hours} \\
\hline
\$1200 \text{ tuition total}
\end{array}
$$

$$
\begin{array}{r}
\$8000 \text{ work income} \\
+\ \$1200 \text{ tuition} \\
\hline
\$9200 \text{ annual income}
\end{array}
$$

**3. $4000**

*part-time job*
$8 per hour $\times$ 30 hours per week =
$240 per week
$\times$ 50 weeks per year
$12,000 per year

*work-study program*
$4 per hour $\times$ 40 hours per week =
$160 per week
$\times$ 50 weeks per year
$8000 per year

$$
\begin{array}{r}
\$12{,}000 \\
-\ \$\ 8{,}000 \\
\hline
\$\ 4{,}000
\end{array}
$$

**4. $6000**

$1500 \times 4 = 6000$

5. **45 feet**

$A = lw$

$2925 = 65 \times w$

$\frac{2925}{65} = w$

$45 = w$

6. **$377**

$\begin{array}{r} 1211 \\ \times\ \ \ 7 \\ \hline 8477 \end{array}$ $\quad$ $\begin{array}{r} 900 \\ \times\ \ \ 9 \\ \hline 8100 \end{array}$ $\quad$ $\begin{array}{r} 8477 \\ -\ 8100 \\ \hline 377 \end{array}$

## Chapter 1 Quiz, pg. 432

1. **1573 kilometers**

$\begin{array}{r} 385 \\ 255 \\ 305 \\ +\ 628 \\ \hline 1573 \end{array}$

2. **$7**

$40 - (28 + 5) = 7$

$28 + 5 = 33$

$40 - 33 = 7$

3. **600 people**

$40 \times 15 = 600$

4. **3750 hamburgers**

$75(30 + 20) =$

$75 \times 50 = 3750$

5. **2950 miles**

$(53 \times 42) + (66 \times 11) =$

$2226 + 726 = 2952$;

round to 2950.

6. **$24**

$c = 8 \times 3 = 24$

7. **125**

$5 \times 5 \times 5 = 125$

8. $\sqrt{841} = \mathbf{29}$

Estimate a number that, multiplied by itself, yields between 800 and 900.

$30 \times 30 = 900$

$25 \times 25 = 625$

This tells you the square root is between 25 and 30.

9. **122 yards**

$P = 2(18) + 2(43)$

$P = 36 + 86$

$P = 122$

10. **225 square feet**

$A = 15^2$

$A = 225$

11. **96 cubic feet**

$V = 8 \times 4 \times 3$

$V = 96$

12. **70 feet**

Add 4 feet to measures of inside rectangle.

$l = 15 + 2 + 2 = 19$

$w = 12 + 2 + 2 = 16$

$P = 2(19) + 2(16)$

$P = 38 + 32$

$P = 70$

13. **18 pounds**

$\frac{(15 \times 12)}{10} = 18$

$A = 15 \times 12$

$A = 180$ square feet

$180 \div 10 = 18$, *or*

$\frac{180}{10} = 18$

14. **$171**

*Larger rectangle area:*

$A = 11(22 - 8) = 11 \times 14$

*Smaller rectangle:*

$A = 8(11 - 9) = 8 \times 2 = 16$

*Total area:*

$11 \times 14 \times 16 = 170$ sq. ft.;

round off to 19 sq. yds.

$19 \times \$9 = \$171$

15. **$48,000**

$8(100 \times 60) = 48,000$

$A = 100 \times 60$

$A = 6,000$

$\begin{array}{r} 6,000 \\ \times\ \ \ \ \ \ 8 \\ \hline \$48,000 \end{array}$

16. **$40**

$\frac{(450 - 50)}{10} = 40$

$450 - 50 = 400$

$400 \div 10 = 40$

17. **$32**

$2 \times 4 = 8$

$8 \times 4 = 32$

18. **$1148**

$\begin{array}{r} 499 \\ 275 \\ 239 \\ 88 \\ +\ \ 47 \\ \hline 1148 \end{array}$

19. **21 minutes**

$(56 \div 2) - (56 \div 8)$, *or*

$\frac{56}{2} - \frac{56}{8} = 21$

$56 \div 2 = 28$

$56 \div 8 = 7$

$28 - 7 = 21$

20. **$(125 \times 52) + (350 \times 12)$**

Annual food expense plus annual rent expense.

## Chapter 2

### Level 1, Preview, pg. 435

1. $\begin{aligned} \frac{1}{4} &= \frac{6}{24} \\ \frac{4}{6} &= \frac{16}{24} \\ +\ \frac{7}{12} &= \frac{14}{24} \\ \hline \frac{36}{24} &= \frac{6}{4} = 1\frac{2}{4} = \mathbf{1\frac{1}{2}} \end{aligned}$

2. $\begin{aligned} \frac{14}{15} &= \frac{14}{15} \\ -\ \frac{3}{5} &= \frac{9}{15} \\ \hline \frac{5}{15} &= \mathbf{\frac{1}{3}} \end{aligned}$

3. $2\frac{5}{8} \times \frac{5}{9}$

$\frac{21}{8} \times \frac{5}{9}$

$\frac{7\ 21}{8} \times \frac{5}{9_{3}} = \frac{35}{24} = \mathbf{1\frac{11}{24}}$

4. $\frac{6}{11} \div \frac{21}{22}$

$\frac{6}{11} \times \frac{22}{21}$

$\frac{2\ 6}{1\ 11} \times \frac{22^2}{21_7} = \mathbf{\frac{4}{7}}$

5. $4\frac{1}{5} \div 1\frac{13}{15}$

$\frac{21}{5} \div \frac{28}{15}$

$\frac{21}{5} \times \frac{15}{28}$

$\frac{3\ 21}{1\ 5} \times \frac{15^3}{28_4} = \frac{9}{4} = \mathbf{2\frac{1}{4}}$

### Level 1, Lesson 1, pg. 436

1. $\frac{5 \div 5}{20 \div 5} = \mathbf{\frac{1}{4}}$

2. $\frac{6 \div 3}{9 \div 3} = \mathbf{\frac{2}{3}}$

3. $\frac{56 \div 7}{63 \div 7} = \mathbf{\frac{8}{9}}$

4. $\frac{15 \div 3}{21 \div 3} = \mathbf{\frac{5}{7}}$

5. $\frac{275 \div 25}{300 \div 25} = \mathbf{\frac{11}{12}}$

### Level 1, Lesson 2, pg. 437

1. $\frac{1 \times 3}{4 \times 3} = \mathbf{\frac{3}{12}}$

2. $\frac{1 \times 10}{2 \times 10} = \mathbf{\frac{10}{20}}$

3. $\frac{2 \times 3}{5 \times 3} = \mathbf{\frac{6}{15}}$

4. $\frac{2 \times 8}{3 \times 8} = \mathbf{\frac{16}{24}}$

5. $\frac{5 \times 5}{6 \times 5} = \mathbf{\frac{25}{30}}$

6. $\frac{3 \times 5}{7 \times 5} = \mathbf{\frac{15}{35}}$

## Level 1, Lesson 3, pg. 438

1. $7\overline{)7}$   $\mathbf{1}$

2. $4\overline{)28}$   $\mathbf{7}$

3. $10\overline{)22}$   $2\frac{2}{10} = \mathbf{2\frac{1}{5}}$

4. $9\overline{)66}$   $7\frac{3}{9} = \mathbf{7\frac{1}{3}}$

5. $8\overline{)54}$   $6\frac{6}{8} = \mathbf{6\frac{3}{4}}$

6. $1\frac{1}{2} = \frac{(1\times2)+1}{2} = \frac{3}{2}$

7. $2\frac{5}{6} = \frac{(2\times6)+5}{6} = \frac{17}{6}$

8. $8\frac{3}{7} = \frac{(8\times7)+3}{7} = \frac{59}{7}$

9. $4\frac{2}{5} = \frac{(4\times5)+2}{5} = \frac{22}{5}$

10. $5\frac{11}{12} = \frac{(5\times12)+11}{12} = \frac{71}{12}$

## Level 1, Lesson 4, pg. 438

1. $\frac{3}{5} + \frac{1}{5} = \mathbf{\frac{4}{5}}$

2. $\frac{7}{12} + \frac{11}{12} = \frac{18}{12} = 1\frac{6}{12} = \mathbf{1\frac{1}{2}}$

3. $6\frac{3}{8} + 7\frac{3}{8} = 13\frac{6}{8} = \mathbf{13\frac{3}{4}}$

4. $4\frac{7}{10} + 3\frac{3}{10} = 7\frac{10}{10} = \mathbf{8}$

5. $12\frac{3}{10} + 9\frac{8}{10} = 21\frac{11}{10} = \mathbf{22\frac{1}{10}}$

## Level 1, Lesson 5, pg. 440

1. $\frac{1\times3}{3\times3} = \mathbf{\frac{3}{9}}$   $\frac{2\times1}{9\times1} = \mathbf{\frac{2}{9}}$

2. $\frac{2\times8}{5\times8} = \mathbf{\frac{16}{40}}$   $\frac{3\times5}{8\times5} = \mathbf{\frac{15}{40}}$

3. $\frac{3\times3}{4\times3} = \mathbf{\frac{9}{12}}$   $\frac{5\times2}{6\times2} = \mathbf{\frac{10}{12}}$

4. $\frac{1\times5}{4\times5} = \mathbf{\frac{5}{20}}$   $\frac{7\times2}{10\times2} = \mathbf{\frac{14}{20}}$

5. $\frac{2\times10}{3\times10} = \mathbf{\frac{20}{30}}$   $\frac{9\times3}{10\times3} = \mathbf{\frac{27}{30}}$

6. $\frac{1\times8}{3\times8} = \mathbf{\frac{8}{24}}$   $\frac{5\times4}{6\times4} = \mathbf{\frac{20}{24}}$   $\frac{7\times3}{8\times3} = \mathbf{\frac{21}{24}}$

## Level 1, Lesson 6, pg. 441

1. $\frac{2}{3} = \frac{8}{12}$   $+ \frac{3}{4} = \frac{9}{12}$   $\frac{17}{12} = \mathbf{1\frac{5}{12}}$

2. $\frac{1}{2} = \frac{6}{12}$   $\frac{1}{4} = \frac{3}{12}$   $+ \frac{5}{6} = \frac{10}{12}$   $\frac{19}{12} = \mathbf{1\frac{7}{12}}$

3. $4\frac{1}{6} = 4\frac{4}{24}$   $+ 8\frac{3}{8} = 8\frac{9}{24}$   $\mathbf{12\frac{13}{24}}$

4. $7\frac{2}{3} = 7\frac{4}{6}$   $+ 6\frac{1}{2} = 6\frac{3}{6}$   $13\frac{7}{6} = \mathbf{14\frac{1}{6}}$

5. $3\frac{4}{5} = 3\frac{12}{15}$   $+ \frac{13}{15} = \frac{13}{15}$   $3\frac{25}{15} = 4\frac{10}{15} = \mathbf{4\frac{2}{3}}$

## Level 1, Lesson 7, pg. 443

1. $\frac{8}{9} - \frac{7}{9} = \frac{1}{9}$

2. $\frac{2}{3} = \frac{4}{6}$   $- \frac{1}{6} = \frac{1}{6}$   $\frac{3}{6} = \mathbf{\frac{1}{2}}$

3. $6\frac{4}{5} = 6\frac{8}{10}$   $- 2\frac{1}{2} = 2\frac{5}{10}$   $\mathbf{4\frac{3}{10}}$

4. $7\frac{2}{5}$   $- 5$   $\mathbf{2\frac{2}{5}}$

5. $11 = 10\frac{6}{6}$   $- 2\frac{5}{6} = 2\frac{5}{6}$   $\mathbf{8\frac{1}{6}}$

6. $8\frac{2}{5} = 7\frac{7}{5}$   $- 1\frac{4}{5} = 1\frac{4}{5}$   $\mathbf{6\frac{3}{5}}$

7. $12\frac{2}{3} = 12\frac{8}{12} = 11\frac{20}{12}$   $- 6\frac{3}{4} = 6\frac{9}{12} = 6\frac{9}{12}$   $\mathbf{5\frac{11}{12}}$

8. $13\frac{1}{8} = 13\frac{3}{24} = 12\frac{27}{24}$   $- 4\frac{7}{12} = 4\frac{14}{24} = 4\frac{14}{24}$   $\mathbf{8\frac{13}{24}}$

## Level 1, Lesson 8, pg. 444

1. $\frac{3}{4} \times \frac{1}{4} = \mathbf{\frac{3}{16}}$

2. $\frac{2}{3} \times \frac{5}{9} \times \frac{3}{8} = \mathbf{\frac{5}{36}}$

3. $\frac{3}{4} \times \frac{8}{1} = \frac{6}{1} = \mathbf{6}$

4. $2\frac{1}{2} \times \frac{4}{5} = \frac{5}{2} \times \frac{4}{5} = \frac{2}{1} = \mathbf{2}$

5. $2\frac{1}{4} \times 3\frac{1}{3} = \frac{9}{4} \times \frac{10}{3} = \frac{15}{2} = \mathbf{7\frac{1}{2}}$

6. $1\frac{2}{3} \times 9 = \frac{5}{3} \times \frac{9}{1} = \frac{15}{1} = \mathbf{15}$

7. $1\frac{1}{6} \times \frac{3}{7} \times 4\frac{2}{3} = \frac{7}{6} \times \frac{3}{7} \times \frac{14}{3}$   $= \frac{14}{6} = \frac{7}{3} = \mathbf{2\frac{1}{3}}$

8. $3\frac{1}{5} \times 6 \times 1\frac{1}{4} = \frac{16}{5} \times \frac{6}{1} \times \frac{5}{4}$   $= \frac{24}{1} = \mathbf{24}$

## Level 1, Lesson 9, pg. 446

1. $\frac{1}{3} \div \frac{3}{4}$

 $\frac{1}{3} \times \frac{4}{3} = \frac{4}{9}$

2. $8 \div \frac{1}{2}$

 $\frac{8}{1} \times \frac{2}{1} = \frac{16}{1} = \mathbf{16}$

3. $\frac{5}{6} \div 10$

 ${}^{1}\frac{5}{6} \times \frac{1}{10}{}_{2} = \frac{1}{12}$

4. $1\frac{2}{3} \div 3$

 $\frac{5}{3} \times \frac{1}{3} = \frac{5}{9}$

5. $\frac{3}{5} \div 5\frac{1}{4}$, or $\frac{3}{5} \div \frac{21}{4}$

 ${}^{1}\frac{3}{5} \times \frac{4}{21}{}_{7} = \frac{4}{35}$

6. $5\frac{1}{3} \div 4$, or $\frac{16}{3} \div \frac{4}{1}$

 ${}^{4}\frac{16}{3} \times \frac{1}{4}{}_{1} = \frac{4}{3} = \mathbf{1\frac{1}{3}}$

7. $5 \div 4\frac{1}{6}$, or $\frac{5}{1} \div \frac{25}{6}$

 ${}^{1}\frac{5}{1} \times \frac{6}{25}{}_{5} = \frac{6}{5} = \mathbf{1\frac{1}{5}}$

8. $3\frac{1}{2} \div 4\frac{5}{8}$, or $\frac{7}{2} \div \frac{37}{8}$

 ${}_{1}\frac{7}{2} \times \frac{8}{37}{}^{4} = \frac{28}{37}$

## Level 2, Lesson 1, pg. 448

1. $\frac{5}{11}$

 $\dfrac{\text{smaller tank}}{\text{larger tank}} = \dfrac{10 \div 2}{22 \div 2}$

 $= \frac{5}{11}$

2. $\frac{5}{3}$

 $\dfrac{\text{this year's speed}}{\text{last year's speed}} = \dfrac{10 \div 2}{6 \div 2}$

 $= \frac{5}{3}$

3. $\frac{2}{3}$

 $\dfrac{\text{not gym days}}{\text{gym days}} =$

 $\dfrac{2000 \div 1000 = 2}{3000 \div 1000 = 3}$

4. $\frac{1}{2}$

 Total parts in mixture =
 $2 + 1 + 1 = 4$

 $\dfrac{\text{topsoil}}{\text{total mix}} = \dfrac{2 \div 2 = 1}{4 \div 2 = 2}$

5. $\frac{4}{5}$

 Total correct answers =
 $100 - 20 = 80$

---

$\dfrac{\text{correct answers}}{\text{total questions}} = \dfrac{80 \div 20}{100 \div 20}$

$= \frac{4}{5}$

6. $\frac{3}{5}$

 $\dfrac{\text{engineers}}{\text{managers}} = \dfrac{150 \div 50}{250 \div 50}$

 $= \frac{3}{5}$

7. $\frac{1}{15}$

 $\dfrac{\text{employees}}{\text{population}} = \dfrac{3000 \div 3000}{45{,}000 \div 3000}$

 $= \frac{1}{15}$

8. $\frac{5}{1}$

| managers | 250 |
| engineers | 150 |
| office workers | +100 |
| | 500 |

 $3000 - 500 = 2500$ factory-floor workers

 $\dfrac{\text{factory-floor workers}}{\text{non-factory-floor workers}}$
 $= 2500 \div 500 = 5$
 $= 500 \div 500 = 1$

9. $\frac{4}{3}$

 $\dfrac{\text{warehouse workers}}{\text{maintenance workers}}$
 $= 400 \div 100 = 4$
 $= 300 \div 100 = 3$

10. $\frac{7}{60}$

 $\dfrac{\text{chassis assemblers}}{\text{total employees}}$
 $= 350 \div 50 = 7$
 $= 3000 \div 50 = 60$

## Level 2, Lesson 2, pg. 451

1. **13 gallons**

 $\dfrac{8}{120} = \dfrac{g}{195}$

 $120g = 1560$

 $g = \dfrac{1560}{120}$

 $g = 13$

2. **120 miles**

 $\dfrac{\frac{1}{2}}{20} = \dfrac{3}{m}$

 $\frac{1}{2}m = 60$

 $m = 60 \div \frac{1}{2}$

 $m = \frac{60}{1} \times \frac{2}{1} = \frac{120}{1} = 120$

---

3. $\mathbf{2\frac{2}{3}}$ **cups**

 $\dfrac{4}{3} = \dfrac{w}{2}$

 $3w = 8$

 $w = \frac{8}{3}$

 $w = 2\frac{2}{3}$ cups

4. **12 women**

 Use the ratio of women to total employees.
 $4{:}(4 + 7) = 4{:}11$

 $\dfrac{4}{11} = \dfrac{w}{33}$

 $11w = 132$

 $w = \dfrac{132}{11}$

 $w = 12$

5. **10,500 votes**

 $\dfrac{\text{Bill}}{\text{Dan}} = \dfrac{2}{5} = \dfrac{3{,}000}{n}$

 $15{,}000 = 2n$

 $\dfrac{15{,}000}{2} = n$

 $7{,}500 = n$

| Bill | 3,000 |
| Dan | 7,500 |
| Total | 10,500 |

6. **(4)** $\frac{1}{8}$ **of the apartment can be cleaned in 15 minutes.**

 $\dfrac{\text{part of apartment cleaned}}{\text{cleaning time}}$
 *(Change 2 hrs to 120 min.)*

 $= \dfrac{1}{120} = \dfrac{n}{15}$

 $120n = 15$

 $n = \dfrac{15}{120} = \dfrac{1}{8}$

7. **(1) 20 women**

 3 men
 + 1 woman
 4 total

 $\dfrac{\text{women}}{\text{total}} = \dfrac{1}{4} = \dfrac{n}{80}$

 $4n = 80$

 $n = \frac{80}{4}$

 $n = 20$

8. **(3) 9 yards**

 $\dfrac{\text{number of sets of curtains}}{\text{amount of fabric}}$

 $= \dfrac{1}{2\frac{1}{4}} = \dfrac{4}{n}$

 $n = 2\frac{1}{4} \times 4$

 $n = {}_{1}\frac{9}{4} \times \frac{4}{1}{}^{1} = 9$

9. **(4) 28 problems**

$$\begin{array}{r}7 \text{ right} \\ + 2 \text{ wrong} \\ \hline 9 \text{ total}\end{array}$$

$$\frac{\text{right}}{\text{total}} = \frac{7}{9} = \frac{n}{36}$$

$$9n = 252$$

$$n = \frac{252}{9}$$

$$n = 28 \text{ right}$$

10. **(1) 40 feet**

$$\frac{\text{length of shadow}}{\text{height of object}} =$$

$$\frac{15 \text{ (shadow of flagpole)}}{20 \text{ (height of flagpole)}} =$$

$$\frac{30 \text{ (shadow of house)}}{n \text{ (height of house)}}$$

$$15n = 20 \times 30 = 600$$

$$n = \frac{600}{15}$$

$$n = 40 \text{ feet}$$

## Level 2, Lesson 3, pg. 453

1. $\frac{1}{4}$

$$\frac{1}{(2 + 1 + 1)} = \frac{1}{4}$$

2. $\frac{1}{3}$

$$\frac{3}{(2 + 3 + 4)} = \frac{3}{9} = \frac{1}{3}$$

3. $\frac{3}{7}$

$$\frac{15}{(20 + 15)} = \frac{15}{35} = \frac{3}{7}$$

4. $\frac{2}{9}$

$$\frac{2}{(5 + 3 + 2 - 1)} = \frac{2}{9}$$

5. $\frac{17}{20}$

$$\frac{(20 - 3)}{20} = \frac{17}{20}$$

## Level 3, Lesson 1, pg. 455

1. **(4) 20 × 8 × 5**

First, find the number of lawn mowers made in one 8-hour day: multiply the number of lawn mowers made in 1 hour (20) times 8. Then multiply this total for 1 day times 5 (days). Once again, you can use a proportion if the whole number operations are not clear right away.

Step 1.

$$\frac{\text{number of lawn mowers}}{\text{number of hours}}$$

$$= \frac{20}{1} = \frac{n}{8}$$

Step 2. Cross-multiply.
$n = 20 \times 8 =$ number of lawn mowers made in one day

Step 3. Multiply total for one day times 5 (days):
$n = 20 \times 8 \times 5$

2. **(3)** $\frac{5}{7} = \frac{630}{n}$

Step 1. $\begin{array}{r}5 \text{ children} \\ + 2 \text{ adults} \\ \hline 7 \text{ total}\end{array}$

Step 2. $\frac{5}{7} = \frac{630}{n}$

(To solve the problem, you would cross-multiply to get $5n = 4410$, then solve $n = \frac{4410}{5}$ to get the answer: $n = 882$)

3. **(2)** $\frac{15}{(15 + 12 + 9)}$

$15 + 12 + 9 =$ total $= 36$

$\frac{15}{36} = \frac{5}{12}$ probability

4. **(3)** $\frac{(310 + 165)}{450}$

Step 1.

$$\frac{\text{number of calories}}{\text{number of hours}} =$$

$$\frac{450}{1} = \frac{(310 + 165)}{n}$$

Step 2. Cross-multiply.
$450n = (310 + 165)$

Step 3. Solve equation.

$$n = \frac{(310 + 165)}{450}$$

5. **(3)** $18(\frac{1}{6} \times 3\frac{1}{6} \times 6) + 25$

Volume (determined by numbers inside parentheses) is multiplied by the cost per square foot, $18, and this product is added to the delivery charge, $25.

## Level 3, Lesson 2, pg. 457

1. **36 tiles left.** The cost of the boxes is extraneous.

$5 \times 20 = 100$ total tiles

$3\frac{1}{5} \times 20 = \frac{16}{{}_1 5} \times \frac{\overset{4}{20}}{1} =$

64 tiles used

$$\begin{array}{r}100 \\ - 64 \\ \hline 36\end{array}$$

2. $\frac{2}{3}$ **pound.** The cost of the nails and anything to do with the 3-inch nails are extraneous.

$$1\frac{1}{2} = 1\frac{3}{6} = \frac{9}{6}$$

$$\begin{array}{r}- \ \frac{5}{6} = \frac{5}{6} = \frac{5}{6} \\ \hline \frac{4}{6} = \frac{2}{3} \text{ pound}\end{array}$$

3. **70 hours.** The number of employees and the minimum number of children at the center are extraneous.

$$\frac{\overset{2}{16}}{1} \times \frac{5}{{}_1 8} \times \frac{7}{1} = 70 \text{ hours per}$$

week at maximum capacity

4. $\frac{1}{11}$. The money she received for the bottles and the number of bottles are extraneous.

$$\frac{5}{55} = \frac{1}{11} \text{ coupon savings}$$

in relation to total bill

5. **6 cups.** The amounts of detergent and water conditioner he uses are extraneous.

$$\frac{1}{{}_1 2} \times \frac{3}{1} \times \frac{\overset{2}{4}}{1} = 6$$

## Chapter 2 Quiz, pg. 459

1. **5:8**

$$\frac{80}{128} = \frac{40}{64} = \frac{20}{32} = \frac{10}{16} = \frac{5}{8}$$

ratio is 5:8

2. **315 miles**

$$\frac{\text{inches}}{\text{miles}} = \frac{1}{90} = \frac{3\frac{1}{2}}{n}$$

$$n = \frac{90}{1} \times 3\frac{1}{2}$$

$$n = \frac{\overset{45}{90}}{1} \times \frac{7}{2_1}$$

$$n = \frac{(45 \times 7)}{1}$$

$$n = 315 \text{ miles}$$

3. **$82\frac{1}{2}$ miles**

$n =$ number of miles Rachel can drive on $\frac{1}{4}$ tank of gas

$$n = \tfrac{1}{4}(20 \times 16\tfrac{1}{2})$$
$$= \tfrac{1}{4}(20 \times \tfrac{33}{2})$$
$$n = \tfrac{1}{4} \times \tfrac{20}{1} \times \tfrac{33}{2}$$
$$= \tfrac{165}{2} = 82\tfrac{1}{2} \text{ miles}$$

4. **6 hours 30 minutes**

$$7\tfrac{1}{2} = 7\tfrac{2}{4}$$
$$6\tfrac{3}{4} = 6\tfrac{3}{4}$$
$$+ 9\tfrac{1}{4} = 9\tfrac{1}{4}$$
$$\overline{\phantom{xx}22\tfrac{6}{4} = 23\tfrac{1}{2}}$$

$$30 \;\; = 29\tfrac{2}{2}$$
$$- 23\tfrac{1}{2} = 23\tfrac{1}{2}$$
$$\overline{\phantom{xxx}6\tfrac{1}{2} \text{ hours}}$$

$$\tfrac{1}{2} \times 60 = 30 \text{ minutes}$$

5. **$500**

$$\tfrac{5}{\underset{1}{6}} \times \tfrac{\overset{500}{\cancel{3000}}}{1} = \tfrac{2500}{1}$$

$$3000$$
$$- 2500$$
$$\overline{\phantom{xx}500}$$

6. $\frac{5}{11}$

$$\tfrac{25}{(25 + 30)} = \tfrac{25}{55} = \tfrac{5}{11}$$

7. $14\tfrac{1}{2}:4$

$$\tfrac{14\tfrac{1}{2}}{(3 + 1)} = \tfrac{14\tfrac{1}{2}}{4}$$

8. **Whole-wheat cereal, by $\frac{1}{12}$ cup**

$$1\tfrac{3}{4} = 1\tfrac{9}{12}$$
$$1\tfrac{2}{3} = 1\tfrac{8}{12}$$
$$1\tfrac{9}{12} - 1\tfrac{8}{12} = \tfrac{1}{12}$$

9. **60**

| management | 3 |
|---|---|
| labor | + 14 |
| total | 17 |

$$\tfrac{\text{management}}{\text{total}} = \tfrac{3}{17} = \tfrac{x}{340}$$
$$17x = 1020$$
$$x = 60 \text{ people}$$

10. **189**

$$\tfrac{\text{boys}}{\text{total}} = \tfrac{4}{9} = \tfrac{84}{x}$$
$$4x = 756$$
$$x = 189 \text{ children}$$

---

11. **(1)** $\dfrac{(4 \times 11)}{16}$

$$11:16 = n:4$$
$$\tfrac{11}{16} = \tfrac{n}{4}$$
$$16n = 4 \times 11$$
$$n = \tfrac{(4 \times 11)}{16}$$

12. **(3)** $42 - (42 \times \tfrac{2}{7})$

Cost of health insurance less the amount paid by employee.

13. **(4)** $\dfrac{2000 - 1500}{2000}$

Difference between salary and take-home pay over his before-tax salary.

14. $\frac{9}{10}$. 8 is extraneous.

| right | 54 |
|---|---|
| wrong | + 6 |
| total | 60 |

$$\tfrac{\text{right}}{\text{total}} = \tfrac{54}{60} = \tfrac{9}{10}$$

15. **(1)** $\dfrac{(2500 + 4850 + 4200)}{5}$

The sum of all the receipts divided by the number of schools.

# Chapter 3

## Level 1, Preview, pg. 462

1. **.0007**

2. **1.761**

$$.431$$
$$.73$$
$$+ .6$$
$$\overline{1.761}$$

3. **.666**

$$.790$$
$$- .124$$
$$\overline{.666}$$

4. **1.075**

$$2.5$$
$$\times .43$$
$$\overline{\phantom{xx}75}$$
$$100$$
$$\overline{1.075}$$

---

5. **.13**

$$9.7\overline{)1.261} = 97\overline{)12.61}$$
$$\phantom{97)}\underline{9\,7}$$
$$\phantom{97)1}2\,9\,1$$
$$\phantom{97)}\underline{2\,9\,1}$$
$$\phantom{97)12910}0$$

answer: $.13$

6. $\frac{17}{25}$

$$.68 = \tfrac{68}{100} = \tfrac{17}{25}$$

7. **.25**

$$\tfrac{1}{2} = 4\overline{)1.00}$$
$$\phantom{4)}\underline{8}$$
$$\phantom{4)}20$$
$$\phantom{4)}\underline{20}$$

answer: $.25$

## Level 1, Lesson 1, pg. 463

1. **c. seventy-five ten-thousandths**

2. **e. seventy-five hun-dredths**

3. **d. one hundred and one hundredth**

4. **b. one hundred and one thousandth**

5. **a. seventy-five thou-sandths**

6. **7.013**

7. **.0027**

8. **10.000203**

9. **.13**

10. **300.7**

## Level 1, Lesson 2, pg. 464

1. $\phantom{xx}.190$
$$.800$$
$$+ .326$$
$$\overline{1.316}$$

2. $\phantom{x}$$.73
$$.26$$
$$+ .11$$
$$\overline{\$1.10}$$

3. $\phantom{xx}.0590$
$$.0700$$
$$+ .0694$$
$$\overline{.1984}$$

4. $\phantom{x}12.000$
$$.073$$
$$+ .380$$
$$\overline{12.453}$$

5. $\phantom{xx}.600$
$$.095$$
$$+ .450$$
$$\overline{1.145}$$

## Level 1, Lesson 3, pg. 465

1.  .700
    − .006
    **.694**

2.  30.0
    − .8
    **29.2**

3.  39.1
    − .2
    **38.9**

4.  $86.30
    − $23.00
    **$63.30**

5.  5.004
    − 1.999
    **3.005**

6.  9.04
    − 4.50
    **4.54**

7.  .800
    − .567
    **.233**

8.  189.11
    − 32.32
    **156.79**

9.  1.29530
    − .43701
    **.85829**

10. .64010
    − .39002
    **.25008**

## Level 1, Lesson 4, pg. 466

1.  9.6
    × 23
    288
    192
    **220.8**

2.  .72
    × .3
    **.216**

3.  .705
    × 5
    **3.525**

4.  1.029
    × .884
    4116
    8232
    8232
    **.909636**

5.  .678
    × .14
    2712
    678
    **.09492**

## Level 1, Lesson 5, pg. 468

1.  $$4\overline{)3.40} \quad \mathbf{.85}$$
    32
    20
    20

2.  $$6\overline{)1.26} \quad \mathbf{.21}$$
    12
    6
    6

3.  $$13\overline{)24.05} \quad \mathbf{1.85}$$
    13
    110
    104
    65
    65

4.  $$25\overline{)15{,}75} \quad \mathbf{.63}$$
    150
    75
    75

5.  $$5\overline{)75.40} \quad \mathbf{15.08}$$
    5
    25
    25
    40
    40

6.  $$.02\overline{)20} \quad \mathbf{10.} = \mathbf{10}$$
    2
    0

7.  $$5\overline{)6{,}15} \quad \mathbf{1.23}$$
    5
    11
    10
    15
    15

## Level 1, Lesson 6, pg. 469

1.  $\frac{9}{10}$

2.  $18.375 = 18\frac{375}{1000} = \mathbf{18\frac{3}{8}}$

3.  $7.08 = 7\frac{8}{100} = \mathbf{7\frac{2}{25}}$

4.  $6.4 = 6\frac{4}{10} = \mathbf{6\frac{2}{5}}$

5.  $.85 = \frac{85}{100} = \mathbf{\frac{17}{20}}$

6.  $$8\overline{)7.000} \quad \mathbf{.875}$$
    64
    60
    56
    40

7.  $$9\overline{)4.000} \quad \mathbf{.444}$$
    36
    40
    36
    40
    36

8.  $$10\overline{)8.0} \quad \mathbf{.8}$$
    8 0

9.  $$15\overline{)7.000} \quad \mathbf{.466}$$
    60
    100
    90
    100
    90

10. $$20\overline{)9.00} \quad \mathbf{.45}$$
    8 0
    1 00
    1 00

## Level 2, Lesson 1, pg. 471

1.  **.9**
2.  **.4**
3.  **1.5**
4.  **10.1**
5.  **78.4**
6.  **5.86**
7.  **.76**
8.  **23.71**
9.  **.6**
10. **8.11**

## Level 2, Lesson 2, pg. 472

1.  **$86.40**
    10.80
    × 8
    **$86.40**

2.  **$19.70**
    $$3{,}7\overline{)72{,}8{,}90} \quad 19.70$$
    37
    358
    333
    259
    259

3.  **$448,446.35**
    $119,583.54
    142,568.45
    + 186,294.36
    **$448,446.35**

4. **602.7 gallons**

$$
\begin{array}{r}
976.9 \\
-\ 374.2 \\
\hline
602.7
\end{array}
$$

5. **$173.55**

$$
\begin{array}{r}
195 \\
\times\ .89 \\
\hline
1755 \\
1560\phantom{0} \\
\hline
173.55
\end{array}
$$

## Level 2, Lesson 3, pg. 474

1. **1340**
2. **13.4**
3. **987,000**
4. **.0573**
5. **4.52214**
6. $17.21 \times 1000 =$ **17,210 mm**
7. $3764 \div 100 =$ **37.64 m**
8. $.7 \times 100 =$ **70 cl**
9. $17 \div 100 =$ **.17 g**
10. $1.85 \times 1000 =$ **1850 g**

## Level 2, Lesson 4, pg. 475

1. **3 inches**

   $r = \frac{6}{2}$

   $r = 3$
2. **18.84 inches**

   $C = 3.14 \times 6$

   $C = 18.84$
3. **28.26 square inches**

   $d = 6$, so $r = 3$

   $A = 3.14 \times 3^2$

   $A = 3.14 \times 9$

   $A = 28.26$
4. **62.8 inches**

   $d = 2 \times 10$

   $d = 20$

   $C = 3.14 \times 20$

   $C = 62.8$
5. **314 square inches**

   $A = 3.14 \times 10^2$

   $A = 3.14 \times 100$

   $A = 314$
6. **25.12 inches**

   $C = 3.14 \times 8$

   $C = 25.12$
7. **200.96 square inches**

   $A = 3.14 \times 8^2$

   $A = 3.14 \times 64$

   $A = 200.96$ square inches

8. **125.6 feet**

   $C = 3.14 \times 40$

   $C = 125.6$

## Level 2, Lesson 5, pg. 477

1. **678.24 cubic inches**

   $V = 3.14 \times 6^2 \times 6$

   $V = 3.14 \times 36 \times 6$

   $V = 678.24$
2. **150.72 cubic feet**

   $r = \frac{4}{2} = 2$

   $V = 3.14 \times 2^2 \times 12$

   $V = 3.14 \times 4 \times 12$

   $V = 150.72$
3. **2355 cubic meters**

   $V = 3.14 \times 10^2 \times 7.5$

   $V = 3.14 \times 100 \times 7.5$

   $V = 2355$
4. **.785 cubic yards**

   $V = 3.14 \times .5^2 \times 1$

   $V = 3.14 \times .25 \times 1$

   $V = .785$
5. **4019.2 cubic centimeters**

   $V = 3.14 \times 8^2 \times 20$

   $V = 3.14 \times 64 \times 20$

   $V = 4019.2$

## Level 2, Lesson 6, pg. 478

1. **.51**
2. **.901**
3. **.4**
4. **.791, .7901, .79, .7091**
5. **.631, .6301, .63, .6031**

## Level 3, Lesson, pg. 480

1. **Insufficient data.** You need to know for how many days the children saved their lunch money.
2. **$1.99 change**

   Total cost of purchases = $(3.99 + .24) + 3(1.19 + .07)$ = $4.23 + 3.78 = 8.01$

   $10.00 - 8.01 = 1.99$
3. **Insufficient data.** You need to know the number of feet per truckload. You could also have solved the problem if you had known the total cost of the shipments.
4. **Insufficient data.** You need to know the weight of all the items in the order.

5. **Insufficient data.** You need to know at what time Joe left and how long he rested.

## Chapter 3 Quiz, pg. 481

1. **185.212**

$$
\begin{array}{r}
114.682 \\
+\ 70.53\phantom{0} \\
\hline
185.212
\end{array}
$$

2. **51.419**

$$
\begin{array}{r}
60.010 \\
-\ 8.591 \\
\hline
51.419
\end{array}
$$

3. **1 min. 37.60 sec., 1 min. 37.52 sec., 1 min. 36.68 sec., 1 min. 13.36 sec.**
4. **1984, 1972, 1980, 1960, 1968, 1976, 1964**
5. **$71.64**

$$
\begin{array}{r}
125.35 \\
56.76 \\
14.60 \\
+\ 9.85 \\
\hline
206.56
\end{array}
$$

   $51.64 + 20 = 71.64$

   $4\overline{)206.56}$
6. **$42.71**

   $3.65 \times 3 \times 3.9 = 42.705$; round to 42.71
7. **$570**

   $22.40 \times 7.25 \times 5 = 812$

   $812 - 242 = 570$
8. **2.4 pages**

$$
\begin{array}{r}
2.4 \\
1375\overline{)3300.0} \\
2750\phantom{..} \\
\hline
5500 \\
5500 \\
\hline
\end{array}
$$

9. **$1726.06**

   $A = lw$

   $A = 14.25 \times 12.75$

   $A = 181.6875$ sq. ft.; round to 181.69

   $181.69 \times 9.50 = \$1726.06$
10. **Oil Tank A holds 48 cubic feet more than Oil Tank B**

    *Oil Tank A*

    $V = \pi r^2 h$

    $V = 3.14 \times 5^2 \times 6.2$

    $V = 3.14 \times 25 \times 6.2$

    $V = 486.7$

*Oil Tank B*
$V = \pi r^2 h$
$V = 3.14 \times (4.5)^2 \times 6.9$
$V = 3.14 \times 20.25 \times 6.9$
$V = 438.7365$; round to
   438.7

$\phantom{-}486.7$
$\underline{-438.7}$
$\phantom{-}48.0$

11. **C = 2.51 yards**
$C = \pi d$
$d = 2r = 2 \times .4 = .8$
$C = 3.14 \times .8$
$C = 2.512$; round to 2.51

12. **(3) $19.60**

| $2.75 | 6.5 | $13.75 |
|---|---|---|
| $\times \phantom{0}5$ | $\times \$.90$ | $+ \phantom{0}5.85$ |
| $13.75 | $5.85 | $19.60 |

13. **(5) Insufficient data is given to solve this problem.** We don't know how many walls in the room she will paint.

14. **(5) Insufficient data is given to solve this problem.** We are not told how much the beef cost per pound.

15. **(5) Insufficient data is given to solve this problem.** We are not told the width of the rectangle. The formula for area of a rectangle is $A = lw$.

## Chapter 4

### Level 1, Preview, pg. 484

1. $.137 = $ **13.7%**

2. **85%**
$$\frac{17}{{}_1 20} \times \frac{100\,^5}{1} = \frac{85}{1} = 85\%$$

3. **39**
$37.5\% = \frac{3}{8}$
$$\frac{{}^{13}104}{1} \times \frac{3}{8\,_1} = \frac{39}{1} = 39$$

4. **44%**
$$153\overline{)68.000}$$ 
quotient .444
$\phantom{153)}612$
$\phantom{153)}\phantom{0}680$
$\phantom{153)}\phantom{0}612$
$\phantom{153)}\phantom{00}680$
$\phantom{153)}\phantom{00}612$

5. **222**
$16\frac{2}{3}\% = \frac{1}{6}$
$37 \div \frac{1}{6} = 37 \times \frac{6}{1} = 222$

### Level 1, Lesson 1, pg. 485

1. $29\% = $ **.29**
2. $3\% = $ **.03**
3. $1\frac{7}{10}\% = 1.7\% = $ **.017**
4. $.07\% = $ **.0007**
5. $3.09\% = $ **.0309**
6. $.8 = $ **80%**
7. $.05 = $ **5%**
8. $.0396 = $ **3.96%**
9. $7.13 = $ **713%**
10. $30.001 = $ **3000.1%**

### Level 1, Lesson 2, pg. 487

1. $\frac{24}{25}$
$$96\% = \frac{96 \div 4}{100 \div 4} = \frac{24}{25}$$

2. $\frac{7}{50}$
$$14\% = \frac{14 \div 2}{100 \div 2} = \frac{7}{50}$$

3. $\frac{5}{8}$
$$62.5\% = \frac{62.5}{100} =$$
$$\frac{625 \div 125}{1000 \div 125} = \frac{5}{8}$$

4. $\frac{9}{16}$
$$56\frac{1}{4}\% = \frac{56.25}{100} =$$
$$\frac{5625 \div 625}{10000 \div 625} = \frac{9}{16}$$

5. $\frac{3}{16}$
$$18.75\% = \frac{18.75}{100} =$$
$$\frac{1875 \div 625}{10000 \div 625} = \frac{3}{16}$$

6. **$26\frac{2}{3}$%**
$$\frac{4}{{}_3 15} \times \frac{100\,^{20}}{1} = \frac{80}{3} = 26\frac{2}{3}\%$$

7. **$12\frac{1}{2}$%**
$$\frac{1}{{}_2 8} \times \frac{100\,^{25}}{1} = \frac{25}{2} = 12\frac{1}{2}\%$$

8. **$93\frac{3}{4}$%**
$$\frac{15}{{}_4 16} \times \frac{100\,^{25}}{1} = \frac{375}{4} = 93\frac{3}{4}\%$$

9. **$27\frac{1}{2}$%**
$$\frac{11}{{}_2 40} \times \frac{100\,^5}{1} = \frac{55}{2} = 27\frac{1}{2}\%$$

10. **80%**
$$\frac{4}{{}_1 5} \times \frac{100\,^{20}}{1} = 80\%$$

### Level 1, Lesson 3, pg. 487

(This exercise does not require an answer key.)

### Level 1, Lesson 4, pg. 488

| | part | rate | base |
|---|---|---|---|
| 1. | **12.5** | **5%** | **250** |
| 2. | **300** | **10%** | **3000** |
| 3. | **100** | **$33\frac{1}{3}$%** | **300** |
| 4. | **93.6** | **15%** | **624** |
| 5. | **33,180** | **175%** | **18,960** |
| 6. | **part** | | |
| 7. | **rate** | | |
| 8. | **base** | | |
| 9. | **part** | | |
| 10. | **rate** | | |

### Level 1, Lesson 5, pg. 490

1. **17**
$$\frac{1}{{}_1 6} \times \frac{102\,^{17}}{1} = 17$$

2. **72.9**
$81 \times .9 = 72.9$

3. **7.9**
$79 \times .1 = 7.9$

4. **679**
$$\frac{7}{{}_1 8} \times \frac{776\,^{97}}{1} = 679$$

5. **234**
$$\frac{2}{{}_1 3} \times \frac{351\,^{117}}{1} = 234$$

6. **9.36**
$234 \times .04 = 9.36$

### Level 1, Lesson 6, pg. 491

1. **80%**
$\frac{52}{65} = .8 = 80\%$

2. **$83\frac{1}{3}$%**
$\frac{85}{102} = .83\frac{1}{3} = 83\frac{1}{3}\%$

3. **87.5%**

$\frac{98}{112} = .875 = 87.5\%$

4. **20%**

$\frac{55}{275} = .2 = 20\%$

5. **700%**

$\frac{238}{34} = 7 = 700\%$

## Level 1, Lesson 7, pg. 492

1. **100**

$22\% = .22$

$b = 22 \div .22$

$.22\overline{)22.00}$ = 100.

2. **3600**

$37.5\% = .375$

$.375\overline{)1350.000}$ = 3600.

or

$37.5\% = \frac{3}{8}$

$1350 \div \frac{3}{8} =$

$\frac{\overset{450}{\cancel{1350}}}{1} \times \frac{8}{\cancel{3}_1} = 3600$

3. **3000**

$25\% = .25$

$.25\overline{)750.00}$ = 3000.

4. **296**

$87\frac{1}{2}\% = .875$

$.875\overline{)259.000}$ = 296.

or

$87\frac{1}{2}\% = \frac{7}{8}$

$259 \div \frac{7}{8} =$

$\frac{\overset{37}{\cancel{259}}}{1} \times \frac{8}{\cancel{7}_1} = 296$

5. **180**

$66\frac{2}{3}\% = \frac{2}{3}$

$120 \div \frac{2}{3} =$

$\frac{\overset{60}{\cancel{120}}}{1} \times \frac{3}{\cancel{2}_1} = 180$

## Level 2, Lesson 1, pg. 494

1. **1182 hinges**

$9850 \times .12 = 1182$

2. **60%**

$9 \div 15 = .6 = 60\%$

3. **$120,000**

$12,000 \div .1 = 120,000$

4. **90 assemblies**

$81 \div .9 = 90$

5. **$440**

$5500 \times .08 = 440$

6. **125%**

$65 \div 52 = 1.25 = 125\%$

7. **360,600**

$3,005,000 \times .12 = 360,600$

8. **1680 calories**

$2400 \times .7 = 1680$

9. **42 applications**

$35 \div \frac{5}{6} = 42$

10. **115%**

$341,550 \div 297,000 = 1.15 = 115\%$

## Level 2, Lesson 2, pg. 496

1. **$\frac{1}{6}$ year**

2. **$\frac{1}{4}$ or .25 year**

3. **$\frac{1}{3}$ year**

4. **5 years**

5. **4.5 or $4\frac{1}{2}$ years**

6. **$900**

$5000 \times .09 \times 2 = 900$

7. **$210**

$1750 \times .12 \times 1 = 210$

8. **$16.50**

$200 \times .11 \times .75 = 16.5$

9. **$337.50**

$750 \times .18 \times 2.5 = 337.5$

10. **$300**

$2000 \times .075 \times 2 = 300$

## Level 3, Lesson 1, pg. 499

1. **34%**

*First find the part:*

$50 - (23 + 10) = 17$

*Then find the rate:*

$r = p \div b$

$r = 17 \div 50 = .34 = 34\%$

2. **$180**

*First find the base:*

$b = p \div r$

$b = 220 \div .55 = 400$

*Subtract part from base:*

$400 - 220 = 180$

3. **$168**

*Find the part:*

$p = rb$

$p = .20 \times 200 = 40$

*Subtract part from base:*

$200 - 40 = 160$

*Find the part of the new base:*

5% of 160

$.05 \times 160 = 8$

*Add the part to the new base:*

$160 + 8 = 168$

4. **$2681.25**

*First find the base:*

$b = p \div r$

$b = 68.75 \div .025 = 2750$

*Subtract part from base:*

$2750 - 68.75 = 2681.25$

5. **97.2 pounds**

*Find the base (her former weight):*

$b = p \div r$

$b = 8 \div .08 = 100$

*Add the part to the base to get her new weight:*

$100 + 8 = 108$

*Find the part of the new weight:*

$p = rb$: $p = 10\%$ of 108 = $.10 \times 108 = 10.8$

*Subtract the part from the base to get her weight after the diet:*

$108 - 10.8 = 97.2$

## Level 3, Lesson 2, pg. 500

1. **15%**

$17,572 - 15,280 = 2292$

$2292 \div 15,280 = .15 = 15\%$

2. **7%**

$\begin{array}{r} 84,490.00 \\ - 78,575.70 \\ \hline 5,914.30 \end{array}$

$5,914.30 \div 84,490 = .07 = 7\%$

3. **20%**

$\begin{array}{r} 31,080 \\ - 25,900 \\ \hline 5,180 \end{array}$

$5{,}180 \div 25{,}900 = .2 = 20\%$

4. **40%**

$15 - 9 = 6$
$6 \div 15 = .4 = 40\%$

5. **150%**

$115 - 46 = 69$
$69 \div 46 = 1.5 = 150\%$

## Level 3, Lesson 3, pg. 502

1. **$64**

*Find the part:*

$\dfrac{20}{100} = \dfrac{p}{320}$

$100p = 6400$

$\dfrac{100p}{100} = \dfrac{6400}{100}$

$p = 64$

2. **$60**

*Find the part:*

$\dfrac{30}{100} = \dfrac{p}{200}$

$100p = 6000$

$\dfrac{100p}{100} = \dfrac{6000}{100}$

$p = 60$

3. **$50**

*Find the base:*

$\dfrac{60}{100} = \dfrac{30}{b}$

$60b = 3000$

$\dfrac{60b}{60} = \dfrac{3000}{60}$

$b = 50$

4. **$75**

*Find the base:*

$\dfrac{20}{100} = \dfrac{15}{b}$

$20b = 1500$

$\dfrac{20b}{20} = \dfrac{1500}{20}$

$b = 75$

5. **40%**

*Find the rate:*

$75 - 45 = 30$

$\dfrac{r}{100} = \dfrac{30}{75}$

$75r = 3000$

$\dfrac{75r}{75} = \dfrac{3000}{75}$

$r = 40$

## Chapter 4 Quiz, pg. 503

1. **(4)** $.05 = 5\%$

All the others are equivalents of 50%.

2. **(2)** $\frac{4}{5} = .8$ or 80%

All the others are equivalents of 40%.

3. **(3)** $.06 = 6\%$ or $\frac{6}{100}$

All the others are equivalents of 60%.

4. **567 customers**

$600 \times .055 = 33$
$600 - 33 = 567$

5. **$84.21**

$78.70 \times .07 = 5.509$;
round to 5.51
$78.70 + 5.51 = 84.21$

6. **(3) 24**

The other fast food choices total 76%:
$100\% - 76\% = 24\%$
24% of 100 students = 24

7. **1008 miles**

$392 \div .28 = 1400$
$1400 - 392 = 1008$

8. **$281.25**

$2500 \times .075 \times 1.5 = 281.25$

9. **37.5%**

$15 \div 100 = .15$ per pound
$.15 \div .40 = .375 = 37.5\%$

*or*

$100 \times .40 = \$40$ (price Kareen charges for 100 pounds)
$15 \div 40 = \frac{3}{8}$ or
$3 \div 8 = .375 = 37.5\%$

10. **85%**

$340 - 51 = 289$
$289 \div 340 = .85 = 85\%$

11. **6700 candidates**

$3819 \div .57 = 6700$

12. **(3)** $\frac{(100 \times 18)}{24}$

$24 is the whole or original amount, and $18 is the part. We are missing the percent.

$\dfrac{pc \text{ (percent)}}{100} = \dfrac{18}{24}$

$pc \times 24 = 100 \times 18$

$pc = \dfrac{(100 \times 18)}{24}$

$pc = \dfrac{1800}{24}$

$pc = 75$ or 75%

13. **(2)** $\dfrac{(100 \times 147)}{87.5}$

147 represents the part, and 87.5% is the rate or percent. The whole or total number of members is missing (the whole = b).

$\dfrac{87.5}{100} = \dfrac{147}{b}$

$87.5 \times b = 100 \times 147$

$b = \dfrac{(100 \times 147)}{87.5}$

$b = \dfrac{14700}{87.5} =$

$87.5 \overline{)14700.0}$

(Remember to move the decimal one place to the right in both the divisor and the dividend.)
$b = 168$

14. **(1)** $\dfrac{(6 \times 100)}{4}$

$4 is the original or base amount, and $6 is the part. We are missing the percent.

$\dfrac{pc}{100} = \dfrac{6}{4}$

$4 \times pc = 6 \times 100$

$pc = \dfrac{(6 \times 100)}{4}$

$pc = \dfrac{600}{4}$

$pc = 150$, or 150%

15. **(3)** $\dfrac{(100 \times 783)}{87}$

783 represents the part or number that attended, and 87% is the rate or percent. We are missing the whole, or total (the whole = b).

$\dfrac{87}{100} = \dfrac{783}{b}$

$87 \times b = 100 \times 783$

$b = \dfrac{(100 \times 783)}{87}$

$b = \dfrac{78300}{87} =$

$87\overline{)78300}$

$b = 900$

16. **(3) .10 (100 + 250 + 75) + 80**

Calculate total sales (figures inside parentheses); then find commission on total sales (.10 × total). Then add salary to that product.

17. **(2) $\dfrac{(10,000 \times 0.06)}{4}$**

Principal times the annual rate divided by 4 to get the quarterly rate.

18. **$76.50**

1.5(600 × .085)
1.5(51) = 76.5

19. **$8.50**

7.95 × .05 = .3975 = .40
 *or* .4
7.95 + .40 = 8.35
8.35 × .02 = .1670 = .17
8.35 + .17 = 8.52

20. **(1) 2(5000 × .055)**

Principal times the annual rate times 2 to get interest for 2 years.

## Chapter 5

### Preview, pg. 506

1. **John (55%), Elizabeth (50%), Roger (42%), Alberto (40%)**

2. $.10 machinery & vehicles
   .06 financial assets
   .05 livestock & poultry
   .03 household furnishings
   +.03 crops stored
   $\overline{\$.27}$

   $ \$ .73$ real estate
   $\underline{- .27}$
   $\overline{\$.46}$

3. 25,000,000 *1982*
   $\underline{- 5,000,000}$ *1970*
   20,000,000

   $r = p \div b$
   = 20,000,000 ÷
   5,000,000
   = 4 = **400%**

4. $35,000,000,000 *1984*
   $\underline{- 15,000,000,000}$ *1983*
   **$20,000,000,000**

5. $26,000,000,000
   20,000,000,000
   20,000,000,000
   27,000,000,000
   32,000,000,000
   20,000,000,000
   30,000,000,000
   25,000,000,000
   15,000,000,000
   $\underline{+ \ 35,000,000,000}$
   $250,000,000,000
   divided by 10 years =
   **$25,000,000,000 per year**

### Lesson 1, pg. 508

1. **4% higher**
   $\frac{32}{72}$ = 44%. Alberto's percentage is 40%.

2. **Elizabeth**
   She hit 35 out of 70 times for a percentage of 50%. Victoria's rate of hits to times at bat was $\frac{9}{24}$ or 37.5%.

3. **1 hour and 30 minutes for reserved buses (marked by **); 1 hour and 45 minutes for nonreserved buses**

4. **High Town and East Town**
   These towns are only 15 minutes apart.

5. **(5) 30**
   You would arrive at 5:15 p.m. for a 4:45 p.m. appointment.

### Lesson 2, pg. 509

1. **79%**
   $.73 + .06 = $.79
   100 × .79 = 79%

2. **Machinery and vehicles**
   10¢ = 2 × 5¢

3. **92%**
   $1.00 − ($.05 + $.03) =
   $1.00 − $.08 = $.92
   100 × .92 = 92%

4. **13%**
   $.10 + $.03 = $.13
   100 × .13 = 13%

5. **$980 billion**
   $b = p \div r$
   = $49,000,000,000 ÷ .05
   = $980,000,000,000, *or* $980 billion

### Lesson 3, pg. 511

1. **5 million**

2. **1981**

3. **1983 and 1984**
   34,000,000 *1984*
   $\underline{- 29,000,000}$ *1983*
   5,000,000

4. $\frac{1}{5}$
   $\dfrac{5,000,000}{25,000,000} = \dfrac{1}{5}$

5. **580%**
   34,000,000 *1984*
   $\underline{- 5,000,000}$ *1970*
   29,000,000
   $r = p \div b$
   = 29,000,000 ÷
   5,000,000
   = 5.8 = 580%

### Lesson 4, pg. 512

1. **30 oil wells**

2. **5 gas wells**

3. **55 wells**
   40 oil wells
   $\underline{+ \ 15}$ gas wells
   55 wells

4. **1982 and 1984**

5. 1974: 15 oil wells − 5 gas wells = 10 wells
   1976: 20 oil wells − 10 gas wells = 10 wells
   **1978:** 20 oil wells − 15 gas wells = 5 wells
   1980: 30 oil wells − 15 gas wells = 15 wells
   1982: 40 oil wells − 20 gas wells = 20 wells
   1984: 40 oil wells − 15 gas wells = 25 wells

### Chapter 5 Quiz, pg. 513

1. **56.1%**
   9.7% + 10 % + 18% + 18.4% = 56.1%

2. **Four or more children:** 9.7% − 3.2% = 6.5 point increase

no children: 49.9% – 43.9% = 6point increase

three children: 10% – 7.2% = 2.8 point decrease

two children: 19% – 18% = 1 point increase

one child: 20.7% – 18.4% = 2.3 point increase

3. no children: 49.9% – 43.9% = 6% increase

four or more children: 9.7% – 3.2% = 6.5 point decrease

three children: 10% – 7.2% = 2.8 point decrease

**two children:** 19% – 18% = 1 point increase

one child: 20.7% – 18.4% = 2.3 point increase

4. **9.3%**
1960: 10% + 9.7% = 19.7%
1984: 7.2% + 3.2% = 10.4%
19.7% – 10.4% = 9.3%

5. **30,938,000 families**
62,000,000 × .499 = 30,938,000

6. **1980**

7. **1965 and 1970**

8. **100,000**
460,000 – 320,000 = 140,000 →100,000

9. **100%**
400,000 – 200,000 = 200,000
$r = p \div b$
$r = 200,000 \div 200,000$
$r = 1 = 100\%$

10. **87%**
$\begin{array}{r} 100\% \text{ prison increase} \\ -\ 13\% \text{ general increase} \\ \hline 87\% \end{array}$

11. **millions of pounds**

12. **1979**

13. **1979 and 1983**

14. **300 million pounds**

$\begin{array}{r} 800 \text{ million pounds} \\ -\ 500 \text{ million pounds} \\ \hline 300 \text{ million pounds} \end{array}$

15. **1100 million pounds**
$\begin{array}{r} 600 \text{ million pounds} \\ 400 \text{ million pounds} \\ +\ 100 \text{ million pounds} \\ \hline 1100 \text{ million pounds} \end{array}$

## Chapter 6

### Level 1, Preview, pg. 516

1. **B**

2. **17**
$(+8) + (-4) - (-10) + (+3) =$
$(+8) - 4 + 10 + 3 = 17$

3. **$-2\frac{1}{4}$**
$\dfrac{\overset{-3}{\cancel{-6}}}{1} \times \dfrac{3}{\underset{4}{\cancel{8}}} = \dfrac{-9}{4} = 2\frac{1}{4}$

4. **$14ac^2$**

5. $+20a^5 \div -2a^3 =$ **$-10a^2$**

### Level 1, Lesson 1, pg. 518

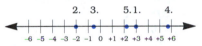

6. **D**

7. **A**

8. **E**

9. **B**

10. **C**

### Level 1, Lesson 2, pg. 521

1. $(+4) + (+8) =$ **$+12$**

2. $(-10) + (-20) =$ **$-30$**

3. $(+14) + (-16) =$ **$-2$**

4. $(-9) - (+13) = (-9) + (-13)$
$=$ **$-22$**

5. $(+4) - (-2) + (+6) = (+4) + (+2) + (+6) =$ **$+12$**

6. $(-15) + (+3) + (-6) + (+7)$
$= (-21) + (+10) =$ **$-11$**

7. $(+4) - (-8) = (+4) + (+8) =$ **$+12$**

8. $(-9) - (+6) = (-9) + (-6) =$ **$-15$**

9. $(-13) - (+3) + (-16) =$
$(-13) + (-3) + (-16) =$ **$-32$**

10. $(+3) - (-2) - (-20) = (+3) + (+2) + (+20) =$ **$+25$**

### Level 1, Lesson 3, pg. 522

1. $(+3)(-9) =$ **$-27$**

2. $-5(-5) =$ **$+25$**

3. $(+7) \times (+9) =$ **$+63$**

4. $\dfrac{(+50)}{(-5)} =$ **$-10$**

5. $(17)(-8) =$ **$-136$**

6. $\dfrac{(104)}{(-13)} =$ **$-8$**

7. $\dfrac{40}{10} =$ **$+4$**

8. $\dfrac{(-6)(-3)}{10} =$ **$+1.8$**

9. $(-2)(4)(-5)(-3) =$ **$-120$**

10. $\dfrac{(6)(+1)(-2)(-3)}{2} =$ **$+18$**

### Level 1, Lesson 4, pg. 523

1. $19x + 7x =$ **$26x$**

2. $(4b^2) + (13b^2) =$ **$17b^2$**

3. $(2abc) + (abc) =$ **$3abc$**

4. $(13n^2) - (4n^2) = (13n^2) + (-4n^2) =$ **$9n^2$**

5. $(-8s^3) - (+4s^3) = (-8s^3) + (-4s^3) =$ **$-12s^3$**

6. $(+13b^2c^2) - (-13b^2c^2) = (+13b^2c^2) + (+13b^2c^2) =$ **$+26b^2c^2$**

7. $(-9.5a) + (10.2a) - (a) = (10.2a) + (-9.5a) + (-a) =$ **$-.3a$**

8. $(8st) - (+3st) + (-14st) = (8st) + (-3st) + (-14st) =$ **$-9st$**

9. $c - (-4c) - 4c = c + (+4c) + (-4c) =$ **$c$**

10. $(10p^5q^7) + (p^5q^7) - (-9p^5q^7) = (10p^5q^7) + (p^5q^7) + (+9p^5q^7) =$ **$20p^5q^7$**

### Level 1, Lesson 5, pg. 525

1. $2t^3 \times 2t^2 =$ **$4t^5$**

2. $(3ab)(5ab^2) =$ **$15a^2b^3$**

3. $(-3x)(4xy)(-3y) =$ **$36x^2y^2$**

4. $y^4 \div y^2 =$ **$y^2$**

5. $-6s^6 \div 2s^2 =$ **$-3s^4$**

6. $(32x^5) \div (-8x^3) =$ **$-4x^2$**

7. $2a \times 2b \div 4ab = 4ab \div 4ab =$ **$1$**

8. $6(3x^6y^4z^6) \div 3(4x^4y^4z^3) =$
$(18x^6y^4z^6) \div (12x^4y^4z^3) =$
**$1.5x^2z^3$**

9. $(4 \times 5a^2b^3)(2 \times 7b^2c) =$
$(20a^2b^3)(14b^2c) =$
**$280a^2b^5c$**

10. $20x^2 \div -2x^3 = \mathbf{-10x^{-1}}$

## Level 2, Lesson 1, pg. 527

1. $9x = 72$
$\dfrac{9x}{9} = \dfrac{72}{9}$
**$x = 8$**

2. $g + 20 = 64$
$g + 20 - 20 = 64 - 20$
**$g = 44$**

3. $c - 14 = 39$
$c - 14 + 14 = 39 + 14$
**$c = 53$**

4. $\dfrac{b}{5} = 30$
$\dfrac{5}{1} \times \dfrac{b}{5} = \dfrac{30}{1} \times \dfrac{5}{1}$
**$b = 150$**

5. $32 = y + 7$
$32 - 7 = y + 7 - 7$
**$25 = y$**

6. $\dfrac{1x}{2} = 6$
$\dfrac{2}{1} \times \dfrac{1x}{2} = \dfrac{6}{1} \times \dfrac{2}{1}$
**$x = 12$**

7. $42 = x - 1$
$42 + 1 = x - 1 + 1$
**$43 = x$**

8. $x - 18 = 108$
$x - 18 + 18 = 108 + 18$
**$x = 126$**

## Level 2, Lesson 2, pg. 529

1. $3n + 5n = 40$
$8n = 40$
$\dfrac{8n}{8} = \dfrac{40}{8}$
**$n = 5$**

2. $8t + 12 = 2t - 6$
$8t + 12 - 2t = 2t - 6 - 2t$
$6t + 12 = -6$
$6t + 12 - 12 = -6 - 12$
$6t = -18$
$\dfrac{6t}{6} = \dfrac{-18}{6}$
**$t = -3$**

3. $2(y + 10) = 38$
$2y + 20 = 38$
$2y + 20 - 20 = 38 - 20$
$2y = 18$
$\dfrac{2y}{2} = \dfrac{18}{2}$
**$y = 9$**

4. $3x - 4 - x = 16$
$2x - 4 = 16$
$2x - 4 + 4 = 16 + 4$
$2x = 20$
$\dfrac{2x}{2} = \dfrac{20}{2}$
**$x = 10$**

5. $9s - 27 = 3s + 27$
$9s - 27 - 3s = 3s + 27 - 3s$
$6s - 27 = 27$
$6s - 27 + 27 = 27 + 27$
$6s = 54$
$\dfrac{6s}{6} = \dfrac{54}{6}$
**$s = 9$**

6. $p + 2(p + 5) = 22$
$p + 2p + 10 = 22$
$3p + 10 = 22$
$3p + 10 - 10 = 22 - 10$
$3p = 12$
$\dfrac{3p}{3} = \dfrac{12}{3}$
**$p = 4$**

7. $5b - 5 = 0$
$5b - 5 + 5 = 0 + 5$
$5b = 5$
$\dfrac{5b}{5} = \dfrac{5}{5}$
**$b = 1$**

8. $3(k + 7) + 7 = 80 + k$
$3k + 21 + 7 = 80 + k$
$3k + 28 = 80 + k$
$3k + 28 - k = 80 + k - k$
$2k + 28 = 80$
$2k + 28 - 28 = 80 - 28$
$2k = 52$
$\dfrac{2k}{2} = \dfrac{52}{2}$
**$k = 26$**

9. $2(3b - 15) = 3(11 - b)$
$6b - 30 = 33 - 3b$
$6b - 30 + 3b = 33 - 3b + 3b$
$9b - 30 = 33$
$9b - 30 + 30 = 33 + 30$
$9b = 63$
$\dfrac{9b}{9} = \dfrac{63}{9}$
**$b = 7$**

10. $25a - 193 = 17a + 71$
$25a - 193 - 17a = 17a + 71 - 17a$
$8a - 193 = 71$
$8a - 193 + 193 = 71 + 193$
$8a = 264$
$\dfrac{8a}{8} = \dfrac{264}{8}$
**$a = 33$**

## Level 2, Lesson 3, pg. 530

1. $4y - 10 \geq 14$
$4y - 10 + 10 \geq 14 + 10$
$4y \geq 24$
$\dfrac{4y}{4} \geq \dfrac{24}{4}$
**$y \geq 6$**

2. $5t + 2 > 12$
$5t + 2 - 2 > 12 - 2$
$5t > 10$
$\dfrac{5t}{5} > \dfrac{10}{5}$
**$t > 2$**

3. $9v - 2 \leq 25$
$9v - 2 + 2 \leq 25 + 2$
$9v \leq 27$
$\dfrac{9v}{9} \leq \dfrac{27}{9}$
**$v \leq 3$**

4. **The answer is "no."**
$13(1) - 4 > 22$
$13 - 4 > 22$
$9 > 22$
This expression is not true.
1 is not part of the set.

5. **The answer is "yes."**
$5(6) + 3 \geq 33$
$30 + 3 \geq 33$
$33 \geq 33$
This expression is true.
6 is part of the set.

## Level 2, Lesson 4, pg. 531

1.
$$
\begin{array}{r}
3t + 4 \\
\times \quad t - 6 \\
\hline
-18t - 24 \\
3t^2 + \ 4t \\
\hline
\mathbf{3t^2 - 14t - 24}
\end{array}
$$

2.
$$
\begin{array}{r}
x - 5 \\
\times \quad x + 5 \\
\hline
5x - 25 \\
x^2 - 5x \\
\hline
x^2 + 0 - 25 = \mathbf{x^2 - 25}
\end{array}
$$

**3.**

$$\begin{array}{r} 2b - 3 \\ \times \quad 3b - 4 \\ \hline - \; 8b + 12 \\ 6b^2 - 9b \quad\;\; \\ \hline \mathbf{6b^2 - 17b + 12} \end{array}$$

**4.**

$$\begin{array}{r} c + 3 \\ \times \quad c + 3 \\ \hline 3c + 9 \\ c^2 + 3c \quad\;\; \\ \hline \mathbf{c^2 + 6c + 9} \end{array}$$

**5.**

$$\begin{array}{r} 4a + 6 \\ \times \quad 2a - 3 \\ \hline - \; 12a - 18 \\ 8a^2 + 12a \quad\;\; \\ \hline 8a^2 + \; 0 \; - 18 = \mathbf{8a^2 - 18} \end{array}$$

## Level 2, Lesson 5, pg. 532

1. **$(a + 6)(a + 3)$**
   $6 \times 3 = 18$
   $6 + 3 = 9$

2. **$(b + 3)(b - 10)$**
   $3 \times -10 = -30$
   $3 + -10 = -7$

3. **$(c - 9)(c + 4)$**
   $-9 \times 4 = -36$
   $-9 + 4 = -5$

4. **$(d - 4)(d - 6)$**
   $-4 \times -6 = +24$
   $-4 + -6 = -10$

5. **$(e + 2)(e + 10)$**
   $2 \times 10 = 20$
   $2 + 10 = 12$

## Level 3, Lesson 1, pg. 534

1. **$6(x + 8)$**

2. $\dfrac{\mathbf{(x + 7)}}{\mathbf{3}}$

3. **$4r$**

4. **$.22g$**

5. **$3x + 5x = 24$**

6. **96**
   $\dfrac{x}{8} = 12$
   $x = 8 \times 12$
   $x = 96$

7. **(2) $3x = 87$**
   $x = \dfrac{87}{3}$
   $x = 29$

8. **\$12**
   $4x + 3 = 51$
   $4x + 3 - 3 = 51 - 3$
   $4x = 48$

$x = \dfrac{48}{4}$
$x = 12 = \$12$

9. **\$7,392**
   $\dfrac{x}{77} + 4 = 100$
   $\dfrac{x}{77} = 100 - 4$
   $\dfrac{x}{77} = 96$
   $x = 96 \times 77$
   $x = 7392 = \$7,392$

10. **297 miles**
    $3x + 364 = 1255$
    $3x + 364 - 364 = 1255 - 364$
    $3x = 891$
    $\dfrac{3x}{3} = \dfrac{891}{3}$
    $x = 297$

## Level 3, Lesson 2, pg. 536

1. **(3) $x + x + 15$**
   no. of men $= x$
   no. of women $= x + 15$
   $x + x + 15 = 47$

2. **(3) $\dfrac{(2x + 180)}{3}$**
   $x = $ Cindy's weight
   $x + 65 = $ Carl's weight
   $x + (x + 65) + 115 = $ total weight
   $2x + 180 = $ total weight
   $(2x + 180) \div 3$ *or* $(2x + 180)/3 = $ average weight

3. **(2) $2(x + 5)$**
   Jim's hours $= x$
   Carmen's hours $= x + 5$
   George's hours $= 2(x + 5)$
   The 40 hours each man worked at his regular job during the campaign is irrelevant information.

4. **(2) $5x - 118 = 357$**
   $x = $ the total number of tickets
   $5x = $ the total amount of money collected from ticket sales
   $5x - 118 = $ the total amount of money collected less expenses
   $5x - 118 = 357$ (the amount raised after expenses)

5. **(3) $265 + 15x = 375$**
   $x = $ the amount of money each player must pay
   $15x = $ the total to be paid by the team
   $265 + 15x = $ the cost of chartering the bus
   $265 + 15x = 375$ (the cost of chartering the bus)

## Chapter 6, Quiz, pg. 538

1. **C**

2. **+8**
   $(+14) - (-4) + (-8) - (+2) =$
   $(+14) + (+4) + (-8) + (-2) =$
   $(+18) + (-10) = +8$

3. **+72**
   $(+\tfrac{1}{3})(-18)(+4)(-3) = +72$

4. **$300m^6n^5$**
   $(-10m^2n^2)(+10mn)(-3m^3n^2)$
   $= +300m^{2+1+3} + n^{2+1+2}$
   $= 300m^6n^5$

5. **$b = 4$**
   $46 - 3b = 7b + 6$
   $46 - 3b + 3b = 7b + 6 + 3b$
   $46 = 10b + 6$
   $46 - 6 = 10b + 6 - 6$
   $40 = 10b$
   $\dfrac{40}{10} = \dfrac{10b}{10}$
   $4 = b$

6. **$x = -4$**
   $8x + 5 = 3(x - 5)$
   $8x + 5 = 3x - 15$
   $8x + 5 - 5 = 3x - 15 - 5$
   $8x = 3x - 20$
   $8x - 3x = 3x - 20 - 3x$
   $5x = -20$
   $\dfrac{5x}{5} = \dfrac{-20}{5}$
   $x = -4$

7. **$n \geq 2$**
   $12n + 3 \geq 2n + 23$
   $12n + 3 - 3 \geq 2n + 23 - 3$
   $12n \geq 2n + 20$
   $12n - 2n \geq 2n + 20 - 2n$
   $10n \geq 20$
   $\dfrac{10n}{10} \geq \dfrac{20}{10}$
   $n \geq 2$

8. **$w < 18$**

$$\frac{2w}{3} + 14 < 26$$

$$\frac{2w}{3} + 14 - 14 < 26 - 14$$

$$\frac{2w}{3} < 12$$

$$\frac{3}{2} \times \frac{2w}{3} < 12 \times \frac{3}{2}$$

$w < 18$

9. **$\frac{1}{2}n - 8$**

10. **9**

$5n - 16 = 3n + 2$
$5n - 16 + 16 = 3n + 2 + 16$
$5n = 3n + 18$
$5n - 3n = 3n + 18 - 3n$
$2n = 18$
$$\frac{2n}{2} = \frac{18}{2}$$
$n = 9$

11. **$8c^2 + 8c - 48$**

$$\begin{array}{r} 4c - 8 \\ \times \quad 2c + 6 \\ \hline 24c - 48 \\ 8c^2 - 16c \\ \hline 8c^2 + 8c - 48 \end{array}$$

12. **$k^2 - 121$**

$$\begin{array}{r} k - 11 \\ \times \quad k + 11 \\ \hline 11k - 121 \\ k^2 - 11k \\ \hline k^2 + 0 - 121 = k^2 - 121 \end{array}$$

13. **$(j - 5)(j + 4)$**

$4 \times -5 = -20$
$-5 + 4 = -1$

14. **Phil = 3 hours, Hal = 6 hours, Chris = 8 hours**

$p$ = hours Phil worked
$p + 3$ = hours Hal worked
$p + 3 + 2$ = hours Chris worked
$3p + 8 = 17$
$3p + 8 - 8 = 17 - 8$
$3p = 9$
$$\frac{3p}{3} = \frac{9}{3}$$
$p = 3$

15. **18 hours**

Mrs. Nash = $x$
Sally = $x + 3$
Mr. Nash = $2(x + 3)$
$x + x + 3 + 2(x + 3) = 33$
$2x + 3 + 2x + 6 = 33$

$4x + 9 = 33$
$4x + 9 - 9 = 33 - 9$
$4x = 24$
$$\frac{4x}{4} = \frac{24}{4}$$
$x = 6$
$2(x + 3) = 2(6 + 3) = 18$ hours

16. **(4) $b + 3b + 30$**

Company A = $3b + 30$
Company B = $b$
A + B = $3b + 30 + b$

17. **(4) $2g + 3 + 2(g + 3) = 246$**

Gail = $g$
Suzanne = $g + 3$
Ann = $2(g + 3)$
Total = $g + g + 3 + 2(g + 3)$

18. **(2) $10x + 10(x + 3) = 350$**

Phil's hourly wage = $x$
Joe's hourly wage = $x + 3$
$10x + 10(x + 3) = 350$

19. **(1) $x + 5x$**

deductions = $x$ (amount employer took out)
take-home pay = $5x$
$x + 5x = 324$

20. **Lisa = 12, Barbara = 36**

$x$ = Lisa's age
$3x$ = Barbara's age
$3x - x = 24$
$2x = 24$
$$\frac{2x}{2} = \frac{24}{2}$$
$x = 12$

21. **95 calories**

$3s + 105 + 130 = 520$
$3s + 235 = 520$
$3s + 235 - 235 = 520 - 235 = 285$
$$\frac{3s}{3} = \frac{285}{3}$$
$s = 95$

22. **14 pounds**

$x$ represents what she lost the first 3 months and $(x + 3)$ what she lost during the last 3 months. Add the two amounts together to equal 25:
$x + (x + 3) = 25$
$2x + 3 = 25$
$2x + 3 - 3 = 25 - 3$
$2x = 22$
$x = 11$
$x + 3 = 14$

23. **(2) $\dfrac{x + 125}{4}$**

$x$ represents their combined current rent. Add the increases for a studio and a one-bedroom apartment to their current rent: $75 + 50 = 125$, and then $125 + x$. Next, divide by 4 to calculate the weekly rent: $\dfrac{x + 125}{4}$.

24. **$12**

Ann's wages = $x$
Dorothy's wages = $x + 4$
$25x + 25(x + 4) = 500$
$25x + 25x + 100 = 500$
$50x + 100 = 500$
$50x + 100 - 100 = 500 - 100$
$50x = 400$
$$\frac{50x}{50} = \frac{400}{50}$$
$x = 8$
$x + 4 = 8 + 4 = 12$

25. **(1) $5c = 230$**

$c$ = Chan's typing speed. Giorgio's typing speed is 4 times faster than Chan's, or $4c$
$4c + c = 5c$ (their combined typing speeds)
$5c = 230$

## Chapter 7

Level 1, Preview, pg. 542

1. **Parallel lines**

2. **Right angle**

3. **$90°$**

4. **$70°$**
$180° - 110° = 70°$

5. **$\angle b, \angle g,$ and $\angle f$**

6. **$52°$**
$180° - 76° = 104°$
$104° \div 2 = 52°$

7. **$50°$**
$45° + 85° = 130°$
$180° - 130° = 50°$

Level 1, Lesson 1, pg. 543

1. **d**

2. **c**

3. **a**

4. **b**

5. **e**

## Level 1, Lesson 2, pg. 546

1. **65°**

   $\angle d$ and $\angle h$ are corresponding angles.

2. **115°**

   $\angle h$ and $\angle f$ are supplementary angles.
   $180° - 65° = 115°$

3. $\angle e$

4. $\angle d$

5. **25°**

   $\angle c$ and $\angle d$ are vertical angles.
   $\angle d = 65°$
   $\angle c = 65°$
   $\angle c$ and $\angle b$ are complementary angles.
   $90° - 65° = 25°$

## Level 1, Lesson 3, pg. 547

1. **50°**

   $\angle A = 90°$
   $90° + 40° + \angle C = 180°$
   $\angle C = 180° - 130°$
   $\angle C = 50°$

2. **100°**

   $45° + 35° + \angle E = 180°$
   $\angle E = 180° - 80°$
   $\angle E = 100°$

3. **54°**

   Base angles are $\angle G$ and $\angle I$. $\angle G = \angle I$
   $72° + \angle G + \angle I = 180°$
   $\angle I = \angle G = (180° - 72°) \div 2$
   $\angle I = \angle G = 108° \div 2 = 54°$

4. **60°**

   $\angle J = 55° + 10° = 65°$
   $55° + 65° + \angle L = 180°$
   $\angle L = 180° - 120°$
   $\angle L = 60°$

5. **34°**

   $120° + 26° + \angle N = 180°$
   $\angle N = 180° - 146°$
   $\angle N = 34°$

## Level 2, Lesson 1, pg. 551

1. $\angle E$

   $\angle A = \angle D$
   $\angle C = \angle F$

2. **7.5 feet**

   $\dfrac{\text{fence height}}{\text{fence shadow}} = \dfrac{\text{lamp post height}}{\text{lamp post shadow}}$

   $\dfrac{x}{9} = \dfrac{10}{12} = 12x = 10 \times 9$

   $12x = 90$

   $x = \dfrac{90}{12} = 7.5$

3. **18 feet**

   $\dfrac{\text{height of man}}{\text{shadow of man}} = \dfrac{\text{height of tree}}{\text{shadow of tree}}$

   $\dfrac{6}{24} = \dfrac{x}{72}$

   $6 \times 72 = 24x$

   $432 = 24x$

   $\dfrac{432}{24} = x$

   $18 = x$

4. **60 feet**

   $\dfrac{JK}{IK} = \dfrac{GH}{GI}$

   $\dfrac{JK}{100} = \dfrac{15}{25}$

   $25JK = 1500$

   $\dfrac{25JK}{100} = \dfrac{1500}{25}$

   $JK = 60$

5. **4 feet**

   $AC = AD + DC = 4 + 8 = 12$

   $\dfrac{DE}{DC} = \dfrac{AB}{AC}$

   $\dfrac{DE}{8} = \dfrac{6}{12}$

   $12DE = 48$

   $\dfrac{12DE}{12} = \dfrac{48}{12}$

   $DE = 4$

## Level 2, Lesson 2, pg. 553

1. **15 inches**

   $c^2 = 9^2 + 12^2$
   $c^2 = 81 + 144$
   $c^2 = 225$
   $c = \sqrt{225}$
   $c = 15$

2. **6 centimeters**

   $a^2 = c^2 - b^2$
   $a^2 = 10^2 - 8^2$
   $a^2 = 100 - 64$
   $a^2 = 36$

   $a = \sqrt{36}$
   $a = 6$ centimeters

3. **15 feet**

   $a^2 = 25^2 - 20^2$
   $a^2 = 625 - 400$
   $a^2 = 225$
   $a = \sqrt{225}$
   $a = 15$

4. **39 miles**

   $c^2 = 15^2 + 36^2$
   $c^2 = 225 + 1296$
   $c^2 = 1521$
   $c = \sqrt{1521}$
   $c = 39$

5. **20 feet**

   $c^2 = 16^2 + 12^2$
   $c^2 = 256 + 144$
   $c^2 = 400$
   $c = \sqrt{400}$
   $c = 20$

## Level 3, Lesson 1, pg. 556

1. **(+5, +4)**

2. **(+2, +3)**

3. **(−3, +5)**

4. **(−5, +2)**

5. **(−2, 0)**

6. **(−3, −3)**

7. **(+4, −2)**

8. **(+5, −6)**

9. **(0, +4)**

10. **(+4, 0)**

## Level 3, Lesson 2, pg. 557

1. $\dfrac{-2}{-5}$

   $m = \dfrac{+1 - (+3)}{0 - (+5)} = \dfrac{-2}{-5}$

2. **−4**

   $m = \dfrac{-2 - (+2)}{+3 - (+2)} = \dfrac{-4}{1} = -4$

3. $\dfrac{2}{3}$

   $m = \dfrac{+2 - (-2)}{+4 - (-2)} = \dfrac{4}{6} = \dfrac{2}{3}$

4. $-1\dfrac{2}{5}$

   $m = \dfrac{-5 - (+2)}{+2 - (-3)} = \dfrac{-7}{5} = -1\dfrac{2}{5}$

5. **−4**

   $m = \dfrac{0 - 4}{4 - 3} = \dfrac{-4}{1} = -4$

## Level 3, Lesson 3, pg. 560

1. **7**

   point $A = (-3, 5)$; point $B = (4, 5)$
   $A$ is 3 spaces from zero on the $x$-axis.
   $B$ is 4 spaces from zero on the $x$-axis.
   $3 + 4 = 7$

2. **9**

   point $C = (-5, -4)$; point $D = (4, -4)$
   $C$ is 5 spaces from zero on the $x$-axis.
   $D$ is 4 spaces from zero on the $x$-axis.
   $4 + 5 = 9$

3. **8**

   line $GH = -3$
   $y$ axis distance from point $A$ to $x$ axis $(0) = 5$
   $3 + 5 = 8$

4. **13**

   point $E = (-6, -2)$; point $F = (6, 3)$
   $d = \sqrt{(x_2 - x_1)^2 + (y_2 - y_1)^2}$
   $= \sqrt{(6 - (-6))^2 + (3 - (-2))^2}$
   $= \sqrt{12^2 + 5^2}$
   $= \sqrt{144 + 25}$
   $= \sqrt{169}$
   $= 13$

5. **$\sqrt{8}$**

   $d = \sqrt{(1 - (-1))^2 + (1 - (-1))^2}$
   $= \sqrt{2^2 + 2^2}$
   $= \sqrt{4 + 4}$
   $= \sqrt{8}$

## Chapter 7 Quiz, pg. 561

1. **complementary**

2. **supplementary**

3. **101°**

   $180 - 79 = 101$

4. **55°**

   $90° - 35° = 55°$

5. **65°**

   $\angle a$ is a corresponding angle to $\angle e$. $\angle e$ is a supplement to $\angle f$.
   $180° - 115° = 65°$

6. **45°**

   $180° - (80 + 55)° = 180° - 135° = 45°$

7. **35°**

   $180° - 110° = 70°$
   $\dfrac{70°}{2} = 35°$

8. **Similar**

   According to the information given, $\angle C = \angle F$ and $\angle B = \angle E$. Thus, all three angles are equal.

9. **5 miles**

   distance $= d$
   $d^2 = 3^2 + 4^2$
   $= 9 + 16$
   $= 25$
   $d = \sqrt{25}$
   $= 5$

10. **$D$**

11. **$\sqrt{61}$**

    $d = \sqrt{(4 - (-2))^2 + (-2 - 3)^2}$
    $= \sqrt{6^2 + -5^2}$
    $= \sqrt{36 + 25}$
    $= \sqrt{61}$

12. **$GH$**

13. **$-1\frac{2}{5}$**

    $m = \dfrac{2 - (-5)}{-3 - 2} = \dfrac{7}{-5} = -1\frac{2}{5}$

14. **54 feet**

    $\dfrac{6}{2} = \dfrac{b}{18}$
    $2b = 108$
    $b = 54$

15. **$-8$**

    $y = .5(-8) - 4$
    $= -4 - 4$
    $= -8$

16. **$\frac{1}{2}$**

    $m = \dfrac{-4 - 1}{-5 - 5} = \dfrac{-5}{-10} = \frac{1}{2}$

17. **26 miles**

    $d^2 = 10^2 + 24^2$
    $= 100 + 576$
    $d = \sqrt{676}$
    $= 26$

18. **20 inches**

    $d = $ length of $LK$
    $d^2 = 12^2 + 16^2$
    $= 144 + 256$
    $d = \sqrt{400}$
    $= 20$

19. **Yes**

    $\begin{array}{ll} \angle A = & 80° \\ \angle B = & 60° \\ \hline & 140° \end{array}$ $\begin{array}{l} 180° \\ -140° \\ \hline 40° = \angle C \end{array}$

$\begin{array}{ll} \angle D = & 80° \\ \angle F = & 40° \\ \hline & 120° \end{array}$ $\begin{array}{l} 180° \\ -120° \\ \hline 60° = \angle E \end{array}$

Since the angles in $\triangle ABC$ are the same as the angles in $\angle DEF$, the triangles are similar.

20. **15**

    $\begin{array}{l} \text{short leg} \\ \text{long leg} \end{array}$ $\dfrac{18}{30} = \dfrac{x}{25}$
    $30\, x = 450$
    $\dfrac{30\, x}{30} = \dfrac{450}{30}$
    $x = 15$

21. **120 feet**

    $\begin{array}{l} \text{height} \\ \text{shadow} \end{array}$ $\dfrac{5}{3} = \dfrac{x}{72}$
    $3\, x = 360$
    $\dfrac{3\, x}{3} = \dfrac{360}{3}$
    $x = 120$ feet

22. **80 feet**

    $\begin{array}{l} \text{long leg} \\ \text{short leg} \end{array}$ $\dfrac{10}{3} = \dfrac{x}{24}$
    $3\, x = 240$
    $\dfrac{3\, x}{3} = \dfrac{240}{3}$
    $x = 80$ feet

23. **60 inches**

    $c^2 = a^2 + b^2$
    $c^2 = 36^2 + 48^2$
    $c^2 = 1296 + 2304$
    $c^2 = 3600$
    $c = \sqrt{3600}$
    $c = 60$ in.

24. **16**

    $c^2 = a^2 + b^2$
    $34^2 = a^2 + 30^2$
    $1156 = a^2 + 900$
    $1156 - 900 = a^2 + 900 - 900$
    $256 = a^2$
    $\sqrt{256} = a$
    $16 = a$

25. **8 feet**

    $c^2 = a^2 + b^2$
    $17^2 = a^2 + 15^2$
    $289 = a^2 + 225$
    $289 - 225 = a^2 + 225 - 225$
    $64 = a^2$
    $\sqrt{64} = a$
    $8$ feet $= a$

# PRACTICE ITEMS ANSWER KEYS
## Writing Skills, Part I: Grammar

1. **(2)** *Usage/Ambiguous Pronoun Reference/ Sentence Revision.* By adding *the disabled* to the sentence, we eliminate the confusion as to whom the *they* refers to, *the skeptics* or *the disabled.*

2. **(4)** *Sentence Structure/ Parallel Construction/ Sentence Correction. To get more housing* is changed to one word to be consistent with the list of things.

3. **(3)** *Mechanics/Spelling /Sentence Correction. College* is capitalized when it is written as part of the name of a particular college.

4. **(1)** *Sentence Structure/ Subordination/Mechanics /Punctuation/Construction Shift.* The two sentences express opposite ideas, so *and* cannot be used to combine the sentences. *College* is singular, so its *is* correct. Only choice (1) has the correct punctuation. Choices (2) and (3) join two complete sentences; choice (2) needs a comma before the connecting word, and choice (3) needs a semicolon before *however.*

5. **(2)** *Usage/Verb Tense/Sentence Revision.* The past tense of *is* must be used because the sentence relates an incident that happened in the past, in 1988.

6. **(3)** *Usage/Pronoun Reference/Sentence Correction. Its* is a singular possessive pronoun that is used in this sentence to refer back to *Gallaudet,* which is singular, the name of one college.

7. **(5)** *Mechanics/ Sentence Correction.* No correction is needed within the sentence.

8. **(4)** *Usage/Subject-Verb Agreement/Sentence Revision. Block,* a plural verb, agrees with the plural subject *Barriers.*

9. **(5)** *Sentence Structure/ Sentence Coordination/ Sentence Correction.* The two sentences are joined together correctly; the second one adds related information, so *and* is the appropriate connecting word. *Braille* is capitalized because it is the name of a language.

10. **(4)** *Sentence Structure /Clarity—Dangling Modifier/Construction Shift.* "Someday you may be writing a business letter to accompany your application for a job." *Your letter,* not *you,* will accompany your application.

11. **(1)** *Sentence Structure /Sentence Fragment /Sentence Correction.* The insertion of a subject and verb, *You may not know,* corrects the fragment.

12. **(4)** *Sentence Structure/ Run-on Sentence/ Sentence Correction.* The period corrects the run-on by forming two sentences, each able to stand alone.

13. **(1)** *Sentence Structure/ Construction Shift.* "Research shows that, when in doubt about a choice of greeting, you should avoid the phrases *Dear Sirs* and *Gentlemen.*" The rewritten form reads more smoothly.

14. **(3)** *Usage/Subject-Verb Agreement/Sentence Correction.* The subject, *study,* and verb, *was done,* must agree despite the interrupting phrases between them.

15. **(4)** *Usage/Subject-Verb Agreement/Sentence Revision.* The singular subject, *none,* requires a singular verb, *was chosen.*

16. **(3)** *Usage/Verb Tense/ Sentence Correction.* To remain consistent with the rest of the paragraph, the past tense should be used to describe the study.

17. **(5)** *Mechanics /Spelling/Sentence Correction. Difference* is spelled correctly, and the sentence contains no errors in usage or punctuation.

18. **(1)** *Usage/Verb Form/Construction Shift.* "Perhaps masculine greetings annoy female employers." The rewritten form uses the active voice, *annoy,* rather than the passive

voice, *may be annoyed by* and *are read by.*

19. **(4)** *Sentence Structure /Improper Subordination /Sentence Revision.* It is incorrect to use *because of* before a subject-verb structure.

20. **(5)** *Mechanics/ Capitalization/Sentence Correction.* Here, *user group* is only the general name of a type of group. You would capitalize a proper name, such as *Kingston User Group.*

21. **(4)** *Mechanics/ Punctuation/Sentence Correction.* The comma only confuses the reader by separating *advantages* from the phrase essential to its meaning.

22. **(1)** *Sentence Structure/ Modification/Construction Shift.* "Having borrowed a program, you may be able to make and keep a copy." The rewritten form is simpler.

23. **(1)** *Mechanics/ Spelling/Sentence Correction. Another* is one word.

24. **(5)** *Sentence Structure/ Comma Splice/Sentence Revision.* The two sentences can stand alone and should be separated by a period.

25. **(4)** *Usage/Pronoun Shift/Sentence Revision.* The pronoun, *you,* has been used throughout the paragraph, and so should continue to be used.

26. **(5)** *Usage/Relative Pronoun/Sentence Revision.* The most effective version eliminates the awkward phrase, *that is nearest.*

27. **(5)** *Usage/Subject-Verb Agreement/Sentence Correction.* No correction is necessary.

28. **(5)** *Sentence Structure/ Parallelism/Sentence Correction.* Parallel ideas should be expressed in the same form: "the money you save, the knowledge you gain, the friends you make."

29. **(3)** *Mechanics/ Spelling/Sentence Correction.* Remember the silent *t* in often.

30. **(2)** *Sentence Structure/ Comma Splice/Sentence Revision.* A period is needed to separate the two independent clauses (*dealers add* and *dealers may charge*) into sentences.

31. **(4)** *Usage/Subject-Verb Agreement/Sentence Revision.* The singular subject, *it,* takes a singular verb, *makes.*

32. **(3)** *Sentence Structure/ Sentence Fragment/ Sentence Correction.* The fragment is corrected by insertion of a verb, *may come.*

33. **(3)** *Usage/Verb Tense/Sentence Correction.* The present tense is needed because ongoing tests are being described here and elsewhere in the paragraph.

34. **(2)** *Usage/Vague Pronoun Reference/ Construction Shift.* "After the car is driven at 35 miles per hour into a wall, the dummies' condition is examined." The rewritten version makes clear which condition is examined.

35. **(2)** *Mechanics/ Punctuation/Sentence Revision.* Do not use a comma to separate phrases joined by *or.*

36. **(4)** *Sentence Structure/ Run-on/Sentence Revision.* The semicolon corrects the run-on.

Each of the subject-verb structures, *you will travel* and *you do not want,* should stand alone.

37. **(5)** *Mechanics/ Capitalization/Sentence Correction. American* is a proper adjective referring to the United States, whereas *foreign* describes other countries generally.

38. **(2)** *Sentence Structure/ Sentence Fragment/ Sentence Correction.* The subject, *jobs,* requires a verb to correct the fragment. Changing *involving* to *involve* supplies the verb.

39. **(5)** *Sentence Structure/ Sentence Fragment/ Sentence Revision.* The fragment is corrected by supplying a verb, *is,* for *example,* which becomes the subject.

40. **(4)** *Mechanics/ Capitalization/Sentence Correction. U.S. Park Service* is the proper name of an organization and needs to be capitalized.

41. **(4)** *Sentence Structure/ Modification/Construction Shift.* "Since many applicants take the test, only those with excellent scores become finalists." The rewritten form avoids the awkward repetition of *finalists.*

42. **(2)** *Usage/Wrong Relative Pronoun/ Sentence Correction.* Few refers to people and requires the pronoun who.

43. **(5)** *Usage/Pronoun Shift/Sentence Revision.* Use of the pronoun *you* is inconsistent with the rest of the paragraph. There is no reference to the gender, male or female, of a ranger.

44. **(1)** *Mechanics/ Spelling/Sentence Correction.* Remember that *y* in *activity* is changed to *i* in the plural form and then add *es*.

45. **(3)** *Usage/Ambiguous Reference/Construction Shift.* "Rangers must relabel changing displays in park museums." The rewritten form clears up the ambiguous *they* and *them*.

46. **(4)** *Mechanics/ Punctuation/Sentence Revision.* Elements in a series are separated by commas: *writing comments, typing lists, filling out police reports.*

47. **(1)** *Mechanics/ Punctuation/Sentence Revision.* Put a comma before the word *but* when it separates two ideas that could stand alone.

48. **(4)** *Sentence Structure/ Coordination/Run-on/Sentence Revision.* There are two sentences that need to be joined with the correct punctuation and connecting word. The second sentence expresses an opposite idea from the first one; *nevertheless* is the appropriate word and has the correct punctuation.

49. **(2)** *Sentence Structure/ Fragment/Sentence Correction.* A past tense verb must be added for the subject, *movie house.*

50. **(4)** *Usage/ Subordination/Sentence Correction.* The verb *were* is incorrectly used. *Where* is a subordinator that refers back to *theaters*, a place.

51. **(1)** *Mechanics/ Commas/Nonessential Words/Construction Shift.* The new construction just turns the sentence around. A comma needs to go before and after *VCR* because it is not essential to the meaning of the sentence.

52. **(3)** *Sentence Structure/ Coordination/Sentence Correction.* The comma is unnecessary because there is only one sentence here. This sentence is an example of the overuse of the comma.

53. **(5)** *Mechanics/ Comma/Introductory Phrase/Sentence Revision.* A comma is needed at the end of the introductory group of words to show the reader where the subject of the sentence is.

54. **(5)** *Usage/Verb Tense/Sentence Correction. Sprang* is the past tense of the verb to *spring*. The entire paragraph is written in the past tense, so *sprang* is consistent with the other verbs.

55. **(2)** *Usage/Verb Tense/Sentence Revision.* The past tense, *grew*, of the verb *to grow* is used because the paragraph is written in the past tense.

# PRACTICE ITEMS ANSWER KEYS
# Writing Skills, Part II: Essay Writing

## How to Score Your Essay

To score your essay, compare it with the following model essays. These model essays received scores of 3 and 5 respectively.

Compare your essay with the 3 model essay. If it is as good as the 3 model essay, then assign your essay a score of 3. If it is not as good as the 3 model essay, refer back to the answer key for the Writing Skills Predictor Test and use the descriptions of the 1 and 2 model essays to evaluate your essay. It should be easy to assign a score to your essay if you compare your essay with these model essays and their character-trait analyses.

If your essay is better than the 3 model essay, compare it to the model essay that received a 5. If it is better than the 3, but not as good as the 5, score your essay a 4. Give your essay a 5 if it is as good as the second model. If your essay is better than the 5 model, score your essay a 6.

In addition, look at the notes and character-trait analyses that accompany the model essays. Those comments explain the strengths and weaknesses of the essays.

## Model Essay—Holistic Score 3

**States the point of view**

I don't think that forcing people to retire is a good idea. Many people are good at there work even if there really old. This is not a good law because a lot of people would not be treated right by this law.

**Elaborates on the point of view with a good example**
**Run-on sentences make this example less effective.**

Just because someone is older doesn't mean that they can't do a good job if they weren't doing a good job they would be fired for doing a bad job but this law would fire people just because of there age instead of because of the kind of job they were doing.

**Haphazard listing of ideas about the topic**

It is good to have older people on the job. Older people know lots of things that younger people don't know and they have lots of experiences too. Its unfair to make people retire when they don't want to. Maybe they could be good for there companys. Maybe they could help there companys. But if they retire they can't show what they can do. They can show that they can do a good job. Younger workers need jobs but older workers need jobs too. Maybe some day older people won't have to retire because of the law. Its not fair.

**Restates the point of view**

Character-Trait Analysis

1. The organization is poor. Better paragraphing would help this essay.
2. The point of view is clear in the opening, but the restated point of view in the conclusion is weak.
3. The supporting examples are too general. The example in the first paragraph is good, but the run-on sentence structure takes away from the impact of the underlying area. The examples in the third paragraph are simply a haphazard listing of ideas.
4. There are many problems with accepted English usage that interfere with the essay's effectiveness.

# Model Essay—Holistic Score 5

States the point of view and the reason the writer holds it

Restates one reason for point of view and supports the reason by explaining it

Restates the second reason for the point of view and supports it by explaining it with two examples

Summarizes and elaborates on the point of view.

First, presents possible reason behind contrasting opinion

Then suggests new alternatives for action based on the writer's point of view

I am opposed to requirements that employees retire when they reach a particular age. Such retirement rules are both unfair and unfounded.

In many cases, people are not ready to retire when the rules say they must. After having spent much of their adult lives working, these people find that their jobs are an important part of their daily lives. It is unfair to tell such loyal employees that they must give up their livelihood merely because they have reached a specific age.

Arguments for setting such a specified age are often unfounded. It is not necessarily true that younger workers can do a job better than older ones. For example, sometimes the best management decisions are made by people who have the advantage of long experience within a company. If eyesight or hearing is important on a job, let one's performance on vision or hearing tests, not one's date of birth, determine whether one keeps working.

I believe that the real reason many employers set a mandatory retirement age is that they find it cheaper to hire young employees at beginning wages than to continue paying higher salaries to older workers. If more money were spent hiring new personnel to retrain older employees, rather than to replace them, everyone would benefit. Older workers could share their valuable experience, younger workers could share their new job skills, and the company could benefit from the increased productivity of both groups. Hopefully, the day will soon come when more employers will recognize how unjust and unrealistic mandatory retirement is.

Character-Trait Analysis

1. The organization is very good.
2. The point of view is clear and consistent throughout the essay.
3. The point of view is supported by good examples, but the examples are not as specific as they could be. They do not paint a vivid picture for the reader in the way that a 6 essay would.
4. The essay is easy to read. It has a few problems with accepted English usage and flows smoothly.

1. **(4)** *Comprehension/ History.* The states were represented in Congress, and the executive consisted of a committee of states. Choice (1) is not discussed in the passage. Choices (2), (3), and (5) are all contradicted by the passage.

2. **(2)** *Comprehension/ History.* Congress lacked many powers, and the executive existed only as a committee of states. Choice (1) is incorrect, since it was the states themselves, and not the central government, that essentially held the power in the first place. Nothing is said about choice (3), choice (4), or choice (5). In fact, choice (3) is unlikely, since the executive was a weak committee of states, as is choice (4), since the national government did not have the power to tax.

3. **(1)** *Analysis/History.* Lacking the power to levy taxes, Congress found itself unable to pay off the Continental Army. Choice (3) is incorrect because the new government lacked the power to raise an army. When the rebellion in question (Shays's rebellion) occurred, the state of Massachusetts had to fend for itself. Choice (2) and choice (4) are wrong, since Congress couldn't regulate international trade. Choice (5) is not addressed in the passage.

4. **(2)** *Comprehension/ History.* Jackson's crown, sceptre and royal robe, the documents trampled beneath his feet, and the presidential veto clutched in his hand suggest that the cartoonist felt that Jackson was abusing his powers of office.

5. **(2)** *Analysis/History.* The passage states that there was distrust among the major powers. Therefore, it is logical that each wanted, by means of the veto, to protect its interests from possibly undesirable moves of the others that might be supported by a majority vote of the Security Council. Choice (1) and choice (5) are therefore incorrect. There is nothing in the passage to support choice (3) or choice (4) as an explanation for the veto.

6. **(2)** *Comprehension/ History.* Both plans imposed restrictions on certain former Confederates. And both required acceptance of the ban against slavery. (The congressional plan actually went much further, requiring acceptance of black citizenship and voting rights as well.) Choice (1) is not mentioned in the discussion of presidential Reconstruction. Choice (3) is incorrect because the only reference to blacks in the discussion of the presidential plan regards the abolition of slavery. The

return of property is mentioned only under the presidential plan and the assumption of debts is not discussed, so choice (4) is invalid. Choice (5) is not described in the passage.

7. **(3)** *Analysis/History.* The Ten Percent Plan did not require that blacks be given the vote and it restored the vote to most ex-Confederates. As the electorate was therefore essentially the same as before the Civil War, the passage of laws restricting black rights could be expected and did occur. For this same reason, choices (1) and (4) are unlikely. Choice (2) was specifically barred by the Ten Percent Plan. Choice (5) is not supported by the passage.

8. **(4)** *Analysis/History.* You cannot assume, or logically conclude, that because the congressional plan was more severe (5), and the president's or Ten Percent Plan was more lenient (3), that the Ten Percent Plan considered slavery less of a social evil than the congressional plan did; both plans for Reconstruction called for Southerners to accept the end of slavery—as (1) restates. Why one plan was more lenient than the other is not discussed in the passage. Therefore, the statement in (4) is an opinion, unsupported by

the information in the passage. All the other choices are restatements of factual information in the passage.

9. **(5)** *Evaluation/History.* The conclusion that America's neutrality policy would likely fail is justified by the fact that Uncle Sam is shown precariously walking a tightrope and having difficulty with his balancing act. The lack of cooperation from Britain and Germany also supports this conclusion. And a close examination of the goods Uncle Sam is trading suggests that the United States is already departing from strict neutrality: The allies are receiving war material (guns) while Germany is only receiving cotton. Choice (1) and choice (2) are neither confirmed nor denied by the cartoon. Choice (3) is not supported by this cartoon since Uncle Sam is shown bringing goods to Europe himself. Choice (4) is wrong because the John Bull figure representing Great Britain shouts his intention to search U.S. goods for contraband and suggests Britain's unwillingness to have the United States trade with Germany.

10. **(3)** *Analysis/History.* The main reason McKinley won was that all three groups mentioned in (3) opposed free silver for reasons of economic security, whereas only the farmers favored free silver. The three groups and their reasons are described in the last three sentences of the first paragraph. (2) is an inference you might

make because the passage states that workers wanted to be able to buy "life's necessities"—such as farm goods—with their fixed wages, and you are told that farmers wanted higher prices for their crops; but this would be only one of the three reasons given for Bryan's defeat. Being only one reason, (4) is also not the best explanation for McKinley's victory. (1) is wrong because nowhere does the passage say that free silver was actually put into circulation. Nothing suggests (5).

11. **(5)** *Analysis/History.* An inflationary policy is precisely what farmers wanted. They would benefit from such a policy in two ways. The prices of their crops would rise. And since the dollar would be worth less, while their debts would remain fixed, farmers would find it easier to repay these debts. Since inflation would have reduced the value of existing savings, thereby decreasing the number of potential investors, and would have raised prices of goods, those who were on fixed incomes, had savings, needed investors, or wanted lower-priced goods would all have been hurt. As a result, choices (1), (2), (3), and (4) are incorrect.

12. **(1)** *Analysis/History.* The introduction of more gold into the U.S. economy had the same effect the coinage of more silver would have had: It increased the money supply and thus had inflationary consequences. Note that the

passage says advocates of free silver were helped by the discovery of gold. Choice (2) is wrong since the cost of living increases during an inflationary period. Choice (4) is wrong since people on fixed incomes pay more during an inflationary period but do not earn more. Neither choice (3) nor choice (5) is discussed in the passage.

13. **(2)** *Comprehension/History.* The colonists felt that their hundred-year tradition of freedom to govern themselves was being denied by Parliament. They were not yet ready to declare independence. Thus choice (1) is incorrect. They were claiming their traditional rights as Englishmen, so choice (4) is wrong. Choices (3) and (5) are not discussed in the passage, nor can they be inferred from the material presented in it.

14. **(4)** *Comprehension/History.* The figures representing Soviet and American leaders are trying to put the cork of arms control back into the nuclear bottle; that is, they are trying to limit the arms race. The figure representing the Third World is trying to pull the cork from the bottle, in other words, to release nuclear power to be used for Third World armaments.

15. **(2)** *Evaluation/History.* As more Third World and other countries develop nuclear capabilities, the problem of arms control naturally becomes much more difficult. Choice (1) is contradicted by the car-

toon. There is nothing in the cartoon to support choices (3) or (4). Choice (5) is not supported because the figure on the right is merely a symbol used by the cartoonist in making his point; in fact, some Third World nations do have nuclear capabilities.

16. **(3)** *Analysis/History.* Guarantees of Cuban independence under the Teller Amendment were violated by provisions of the Platt Amendment, which gave the United States control over Cuban foreign policy, etc. For this reason, choice (1) is false. Choice (2) is incorrect since both amendments relate to the role of the United States in Cuba after the Spanish-American War. There is nothing in the passage to support choice (4) or choice (5), both of which are false.

17. **(2)** *Evaluation/History.* The provisions of the Platt Amendment, which gave the United States the right to intervene in Cuba and to have a naval base there, suggest that the United States was interested in exerting its influence in Cuba and the rest of the Caribbean. For this reason choice (1) is incorrect; the trend was toward imperialism. Choice (3) is not supported by the passage; in fact, Latin American nations generally opposed U.S. controls over the Cuban economy and government as inconsistent with Cuban independence. Neither choice (4) nor choice (5) is supported by the passage.

18. **(1)** *Analysis/Geography.* As the northwest is forest land that lacks any agriculture, it is likely to have a low population density. In fact, it is part of the Amazon Region, which is very thinly populated.

19. **(3)** *Evaluation/Geography.* Since the map shows that half of Brazil is chiefly forest and that only a small strip is intensively cultivated, it is possible to conclude that much of Brazil's land remains underused. None of the other choices can be supported by the map.

20. **(5)** *Application/Geography.* The statement in choice (5) described Chicago as linking two parts of the United States. All the other statements in one way or another involve a city linking a country with the outside world.

21. **(1)** *Comprehension/Geography.* All the cities within the same shaded area across the South of the United States from the East to the West coasts have temperatures in the 60's.

22. **(4)** *Analysis/Geography.* Since there is little snow activity in the Northern cities, and their temperatures fall in the 40's and 30's, the map is for March.

23. **(5)** *Evaluation/Geography.* San Francisco has temperatures in the 60's, which is not too hot or too cold for a marathon, and it is also free of precipitation. Both Houston and Memphis are at the edge of showers, and Kansas City's weather could become unstable because

it is on the edge of a cold front. Boston's temperature is cool, in the 40's.

24. **(4)** *Application/Geography.* A visitor in 1850 could not have seen Battery Park because it was not built until 1965.

25. **(2)** *Analysis/Geography.* The presence of mountains that break up regions and the absence of rivers that unify them result in the problem of geographic isolation. The regions in a country are isolated from one another, and this hinders development. Choice (4) is only part of the problem. None of the other choices is supported by the passage.

26. **(2)** *Application/Economics.* A situation in which three firms dominate the market for a product is an example of an oligopoly.

27. **(3)** *Application/Economics.* In combining to regulate production in order to increase prices, the oil-producing nations were acting as a cartel.

28. **(4)** *Application/Economics.* In formally combining the various firms into a single organization, John D. Rockefeller created a trust. (The Standard Oil Trust and similar organizations were soon eliminated by legislation.)

29. **(1)** *Application/Economics.* The situation described is a monopoly. For the reason mentioned in the description, utilities are the one kind of monopoly allowed.

30. **(3)** *Comprehension/ Economics.* Since 1979, women's earnings as a percentage of men's have increased steadily (note the generally upward direction of the graph's line), especially after 1990. Prior to 1980 (the graph goes back only to 1979), women's earnings were around 63 percent of men's. Choice (5) is incorrect because the graph provides information only up to the third quarter of 1991.

31. **(4)** *Application/ Economics.* The machine shop is a male-dominated work place where wages are determined according to a number of factors, such as training, experience, one's job classification, and the amount of overtime worked. A boss in this trade would likely pay a male machinist more than a female. Doctors and dentists are often self-employed, so answers (3) and (5) are incorrect. Letter carriers are on a set pay scale established by Civil Service, so it would be unlikely for men and women doing the same job for the same amount of time to receive unequal pay. Almost all receptionists are women; therefore, answer (1) is not the best choice.

32. **(3)** *Application/ Economics.* Since the number of service jobs is increasing, while the number of manufacturing jobs is decreasing, it should in general be more advisable to pursue a job in the service sector. With the exception of textile worker, all the careers mentioned are in the service sector.

33. **(4)** *Application/ Economics.* The passage states that U.S. manufacturing companies have been losing some of their market to foreign competitors. The clearest example of this is choice (4), which involves an American family selecting an imported car, rather than a domestic one. Note that choice (5) does not involve other countries, choice (2) does not involve the manufacturing sector, and choice (3), although perhaps bad for American workers, does not imply diminished competitiveness of the American manufacturer.

34. **(5)** *Analysis/Economics.* The passage points out that the new technologies allow manufacturers to make their operations more efficient. By being more efficient, they are able to produce more goods with fewer workers. This fact contradicts choice (1), as does the statement in the passage that the new technologies often require service workers. Choices (2), (3), and (4) are nowhere implied in the passage. Nothing is mentioned in the passage about cooperation between the U.S. companies and the companies of other countries.

35. **(4)** *Analysis/Economics.* The fact that U.S. companies compete with foreign companies means that economic developments overseas will likely affect the American work force. The passage indicates that developments in American society such as the growing number of old people, as well as technological changes,

have led to more service jobs. The passage also says that business decisions will have important repercussions for the health of manufacturing and, by implication, for the work force. Government legislation may or may not affect the number and kinds of jobs; nothing is said about it in the passage, however.

36. **(2)** *Comprehension/ Economics.* The sources in choice (1), choice (4), and choice (5) showed increases. The source in choice (3) showed a more moderate decrease than that in choice (2).

37. **(3)** *Analysis/Economics.* With fewer new houses under construction and more abandoned buildings, the property tax base would shrink. Choice (1) is incorrect since income taxes increased. In other words, unemployment may or may not have risen, but even if it did, this didn't lead to a decline in income tax as a source of revenue. Choice (2) would involve revenues from toll roads, which are not given as a separate category in this graph. Choice (4) is incorrect because the graph gives no information about an increase in sales taxes. Choice (5) is wrong because federal outlays increased.

38. **(2)** *Analysis/Political Science.* That bills become law when the president signs them is strongly suggested by the discussion of bills as proposed laws that the president may either sign or veto. Choice (1) is not

implied in the passage, especially since the one comparison of presidents and governors indicates that governors possess a power presidents lack. Choice (3) is incorrect; although presidents may propose laws, nothing is implied in the passage. Choice (4) is wrong since the president has the choice of signing bills or vetoing them. Choice (5) is contradicted by the discussion of the item veto, which the president lacks.

39. **(4)** *Analysis/Political Science.* (4) is a restatement of a factual statement in the passage and therefore cannot be a conclusion. All the other choices are conclusions that can be drawn from statements in the passage. If Congress tries to write bills acceptable to the president because a veto takes a two-thirds vote to override, you can conclude that it must be harder to override a veto than to write a bill the president will sign, as (1) states. If Congress adds riders to bills the president considers important and the president has no power to strike out these additions that he does not like, you can conclude that this is a way Congress tries to force the president to approve laws he dislikes, as (2) states. If many state governors have an "item veto" that allows them to strike out parts of bills that they dislike, you can conclude that in this way they have more veto power than the president, as (3)

states. If the president usually vetoes bills by sending them back to Congress, stating his reasons for rejecting them, whereas in a pocket veto he cancels a bill simply by doing nothing with it, you can conclude (5).

40. **(5)** *Evaluation/Political Science.* If the young, uneducated, poor, and minorities fail to vote, then a significant portion of the population is underrepresented in government. Choice (1) is incorrect since the poor, who presumably need the most help from government, are less likely than others to vote. Choice (2) and choice (3) are false because voting is related to education, income, etc. Choice (4) is an opinion, neither confirmed nor denied by the passage.

41. **(2)** *Comprehension/Political Science.* Public opinion is flexible and changing. Therefore, the statement in choice (2) is in direct contradiction to the strict constructionist perspective.

42. **(5)** *Application/Political Science.* Choice (5) is taken from McCulloch v. Maryland, the classic statement of the loose constructionist position. All the other choices are quotes from strict constructionists and express their philosophy, as defined in the passage.

43. **(2)** *Evaluation/Political Science.* Choice (2) is correct because the House conducts impeachment proceedings to determine whether there is enough evidence for a formal accusation against an

official, or grounds for a trial to be held. Thus choice (3) is incorrect. There is no evidence to support choice (1). Choice (4) is contradicted by the passage, which indicates that removal upon a verdict of guilty is obligatory. Choice (5) is also contradicted by the passage, as only a small number of individuals have been impeached in the nation's 200-year history.

44. **(5)** *Comprehension/Political Science.* The passage mentions that officials must be accused of "high crimes and misdemeanors." Thus, incompetency is not grounds for impeachment, nor are political opposition or "disloyalty" to Congress, as is also shown by the acquittal of President Johnson. Choices (1), (2), and (4) are therefore wrong. Choice (3) is also incorrect since the impeachment process does not apply to Congress.

45. **(5)** *Comprehension/Political Science.* PAC contributions tripled while contributions from other sources didn't even double. Therefore, the statement in choice (5) is inaccurate.

46. **(5)** *Evaluation/Political Science.* As of the last year in the graph, PAC contributions accounted for a far larger share of congressional campaign monies than they had in the past. Choice (1) cannot be determined from the graph, since even in the last year shown, three-quarters of contributions came from sources other than PACs. Choices (2) and (3) are opinions for

which the graph offers no information. Choice (4) is also an opinion that is not directly supported by the data.

47. **(2)** *Application/Political Science.* Choice (2) is correct, as it involves voting on a measure. Choice (1) describes the initiative, another form of participation, in which the voters can actually propose—rather than simply vote on—laws. Choice (3) illustrates recall, or removal of public officials by the electorate. Choice (4) is an example of a primary. Choice (5) is the act of a private citizen or pressure group, aimed at the national level.

48. **(1)** *Application/Political Science.* By prohibiting a member of Congress from holding any other position in government during his or her term of office, this article of the Constitution is ensuring that the legislative power is separated from other powers of government.

49. **(5)** *Application/Political Science.* Because the Senate has the right to support or reject the president's treaties and appointments, it is sharing—and limiting—an executive's power.

50. **(3)** *Application/Political Science.* The prohibition on creating noble titles is consistent with the principle of republicanism, which rejects an aristocracy.

51. **(2)** *Application/Political Science.* The process of constitutional amendment, as spelled out by the Constitution, involves a sharing of power between the national legislature and the state legislatures.

52. **(1)** *Application/Behavioral Science.* The passage emphasizes that each child is different and that parents' responses to these differences, from infancy on, will affect the way a child develops. Therefore, it is important that parents get to know their infants. There is nothing in the passage to support any of the other choices.

53. **(3)** *Evaluation/Behavioral Science.* The passage states that individuals have a certain temperament from the time they are infants (nature) but that the way they develop will also depend on parents' response (nurture).

54. **(4)** *Application/Behavioral Science.* The hypothesis in choice (4) would be tested by asking people for their opinions. None of the other hypotheses could be tested in this way. The hypotheses in choices (1) and (2), for example, could not be tested by a survey because they concern people's unconscious or undesired behavior.

55. **(2)** *Evaluation/Behavioral Science.* The right-hand side of the graph supports the idea that the decrease in household size is continuing. Choice (1) is therefore incorrect. Choice (3) is contradicted by the drop in household size during the 1930s. Neither choice (4) nor choice (5) can be supported on the basis of the information in the graph.

56. **(3)** *Analysis/Behavioral Science.* A decrease in immigration would *not* necessarily lead to a decrease in household size. And immigration has not steadily decreased over the period shown in the graph. All the other choices are demographic changes that would logically contribute to—and have in fact contributed to—the decline in household size.

57. **(5)** *Application/Behavioral Science.* As the average household size decreases, large economy packages become less appropriate for many households. All other choices may or may not be good advice, but they have nothing to do with the graph.

58. **(3)** *Analysis/Behavioral Science.* The decline in household size is in keeping with an emphasis on personal freedom, since such an emphasis might lead adults to decide to live alone, couples to have fewer or no children, etc. Emphasis on the values stated in the other choices would, if anything, contribute to increased household size.

59. **(4)** *Application/Behavioral Science.* The article indicates that television has contributed to the focus on personality by allowing voters to see the candidates and react to personal traits. Only choice (4) involves a personal trait.

60. **(3)** *Comprehension/Behavioral Science.* The conclusion of the research is essentially that in today's elections, the personality of the candidate, often revealed through television, is more important to voters than his/her political beliefs or party affiliation. (3) is the only choice that does not

support the conclusion of the research.

61. **(4)** *Evaluation/ Behavioral Science.* The surveys mentioned in the article document the decline in the number of voters who vote a straight ticket. The statement in choice (2) is presented as speculation by researchers, not as fact. None of the other choices is presented in the article.

62. **(3)** *Evaluation/ Behavioral Science.* It can be argued that by failing to focus on candidates' stands, their voting records, and their political philosophies, voters are not as informed as they should be, since a healthy democracy requires informed and knowledgeable voters. Choice (2) is incorrect because, although the article states that television has contributed to the focus on personality rather than issues, it does not claim that the media is exerting excessive influence. Choice (4) is incorrect because the declining importance of party affiliation is in no way equivalent to the failure of the two-party system. The statements in choice (1) and choice (5) are not discussed in the article.

63. **(2)** *Analysis/Behavioral Science.* Although advertising is often not thought of as propa- ganda, it in fact fits all aspects of the definition of "propaganda." Choices (1) and (4) are not necessarily true, and they are not supported by the passage. Choice (3) is contradicted by the passage. Choice (5) is a matter of opinion, and not a fact.

64. **(2)** *Analysis/Behavioral Science.* Sweden is known worldwide for its social programs, such as day care, which would enable more women to work without worrying about the shortage or high cost of day care.

# PRACTICE ITEMS ANSWER KEYS
## Science

1. **(3)** *Analysis/Biology.* Hemoglobin bonds with oxygen where oxygen is plentiful. Oxygen enters the blood through the lungs, so the lungs would be where the most hemoglobin would become bound to oxygen.

2. **(5)** *Analysis/Biology.* The passage states that once the capillaries are clogged with cells, the person becomes anemic and feels pain, which results in body fatigue (or tiredness) and discomfort. Only in severe cases of untreated sickle cell anemia would a person die, so choice (3) is incorrect. There is no mention of heart attacks, strokes, or high blood cholesterol in the passage, eliminating choices (1), (2), and (4).

3. **(1)** *Comprehension/ Biology.* Choice (1) is characteristic of sickle cell anemia hemoglobin, not healthy hemoglobin. The second paragraph states that in people with sickle cell anemia, the molecules "stick to one another, forming long, stiff rods or spirals."

4. **(2)** *Evaluation/Biology.* The passage states that sickle cell anemia was common in India, where many Hindus live; in central Africa, not South Africa; and in southern Italy, not northern. A second-generation Greek-American would not be likely to develop sickle cell anemia because his/her parents were born in the United States. The passage makes no mention of Native Americans.

5. **(3)** *Evaluation/Biology.* Only (3) is supported by the information in the diagram. For a male to be color blind, he must have color blind genes, which he receives from his mother. The diagram does not provide any information about when color blindness develops. Choice (2) states the opposite of the information provided in the diagram.

6. **(2)** *Application/Biology.* The other behaviors must all be learned. However, the ability to blink is inherited. It is a reflex behavior that people are born with.

7. **(5)** *Analysis/Biology.* The other choices were the same for both the front yard and the back yard. However, when the homeowner raked the front yard, she would have loosened the soil, increasing the erosion rate. The seeds were probably washed away in the sudden rainstorm.

8. **(4)** *Application/Biology.* By concentrating on growing food grains, a country with a limited amount of farmland could feed a large number of people more efficiently. Eating food grains instead of livestock would mean taking energy directly from the bottom of the food pyramid, eliminating the energy loss involved in raising livestock.

9. **(4)** *Comprehension/ Biology.* The results of the experiment indicate that a well-watered, well-lit, pinched-back marigold will yield the best results. None of the other choices include all three factors.

10. **(4)** *Application/Biology.* The fruit surrounds the seed and provides a food supply for the plant, just as we use the apple fruit for food.

11. **(1)** *Analysis/Biology.* Since the allergy is to pollen grains, and pollen is the plants' sperm, the allergy would most likely flare up during the plants' reproductive season.

12. **(2)** *Analysis/Biology.* Genetic variation tends to be an advantage in species survival, so pollen grains that help increase genetic variation give the species an advantage. Choices (1) and (4) would work against genetic variation. Choice (3) may or may not be true; it is difficult to assess. Choice (5) would be an advantage for a seed, but a pollen grain that traveled too far might not find another plant stigma to fertilize.

13. **(3)** *Evaluation/Biology.* Choices (1) and (2) are not covered in the passage. Choice (4) is false; the plants do not become seeds first. Choice (5) is also false; if the offspring are

genetic copies of the parent, they will grow into flowering plants like the parent. Choice (3) is correct because the plants are produced from a single parent, and are exact genetic copies of it.

14. **(2)** *Application/Biology.* The other choices are all possible uses. Choice (2) is not a possible use because the plants reproduce so quickly that they would clog up the waterways, making boating difficult.

15. **(4)** *Analysis/Biology.* The fact that the animal cannot move around during hibernation could decrease its chances for survival, since it is unable to escape from predators.

16. **(5)** *Comprehension/Biology.* Both hibernation and estivation are a response to extremes in temperature; in the first case, cold, in the second case, heat.

17. **(4)** *Application/Biology.* The ability to talk refers to a person's speech, which is controlled by the cerebrum. This diagram does not show the two sides or spheres of the brain.

18. **(5)** *Analysis/Biology.* Because food is brought to the animal, it can survive without moving. Choices (2) and (4) describe plant nutrition, not animal nutrition. There is no basis for choice (3) in the passage.

19. **(4)** *Comprehension/Biology.* The chart provides nutritional facts, not opinions, so (1) is incorrect. The chart does not provide the amounts of nutrients; therefore, (2) and (5) are incorrect. Soda is not included in the chart, so (3) is wrong. However, the chart lists bananas as a source of carbohydrates and simple units of simple sugars (4).

20. **(1)** *Evaluation/Biology.* Fruits and vegetables are listed as sources of all nutrient groups except fats. Fats, which may contribute to heart disease and certain types of cancers, should be kept to a minimum in our diet. They cannot be eliminated, however, so (3) is incorrect. Choice (2) is also incorrect because the chart does not show meat as an essential nutrient. It is shown only as a fat and as a source of minerals, and we can get minerals and fats from nonmeat sources. Furthermore, a balanced diet must include water. Choices (4) and (5) are both incorrect because the chart does not include information about either the Japanese or American diet.

21. **(3)** *Comprehension/Biology.* The peak of the graph for both years is between 20 to 24 years, indicating that the largest share of births are to women between these ages.

22. **(3)** *Evaluation/Biology.* In each year, the two age groups (15-19 and 30-31) each accounted for roughly 15 percent of total births. Therefore, whatever the total number of births in each year, the number for the younger age group was about the same as the number for the older group. If the younger mothers were more likely than the older ones to give birth to boys, the actual number of boys born to the younger mothers was most likely greater than the number born to the older mothers. None of the other conclusions is supported by the information.

23. **(5)** *Analysis/Biology.* The graphs from 1970 and 1980 are fairly close together, so the age group with the largest share of births was the same for both years. Some of the other choices may be true, but the graph does not offer enough information to confirm them. Choice (4) is probably not true; even though the share of births to women aged 20 to 24 was roughly the same for the two years, the actual number of births most likely was different.

24. **(1)** *Application/Biology.* Air-popped popcorn is high in fiber and low in fat. If unsalted, it is a good snack food. Choices (2), (4), and (5) all contain sugar and may contain high levels of fat. Choice (3) is usually high in both sodium and fat.

25. **(4)** *Application/Biology.* The best choice, per the guidelines, is a food high in protein, low in fat, and low in sodium. Six ounces of plain yogurt best fits that profile.

26. **(2)** *Application/Biology.* The best choice, per the guidelines, is a cereal that is a good source of protein and carbohydrates, and low in sugars. The other choices are all fairly high in sugars, although they are good sources of protein and carbohydrates.

27. **(2)** *Analysis/Biology.* The vegetarian group followed the second guideline, which suggests exercising several times a week. The guidelines do not include information about smoking or drugs. Choice (1) is incorrect because the amount of beer and wine consumed is not provided. Choice (5) is also incorrect because the question asks for the guidelines followed "in addition to" eating fruits and vegetables.

28. **(1)** *Evaluation/Biology.* You should advice your friend to quit this diet. Besides violating guidelines 1 and 4, it is also likely to be high in fat, since meat is generally high in fat. (In the extreme case, a diet that overemphasizes protein can lead to ketosis, a change in the body's chemical balance, which can cause death.)

29. **(3)** *Analysis/Biology.* The fact that the fox population becomes smaller and then larger in response to similar changes in the lemming population indicates that there is a natural balance between prey and predator.

30. **(3)** *Application/Biology.* In nature's predator/prey relationship, all animals live in balance with one another. Humans as predators have upset the balance by hunting, tearing down the forests, and fishing in oceans and fresh bodies of water. Establishing restrictions on when, what, and how much people can hunt could help to restore and maintain a balance

in nature. Therefore, (3) is the best answer. Choice (5) is incorrect because once a species is declared "endangered," the predator/prey relationship is already so seriously out of balance that the prey have nearly died out. Choice (1) helps raise money for cities and towns, and choice (2) helps protect national interests; neither attempts to protect the predator/prey relationship.

31. **(3)** *Comprehension/Biology.* Drugs, like nutrients and oxygens, diffuse across the placenta into the embryo's blood.

32. **(4)** *Application/Biology.* The other choices could be true of many different organisms. Choice (4) is specific enough to indicate a common ancestor.

33. **(4)** *Application/Biology.* A vaccine is taken to prevent a disease, not taken after the person already has the disease; therefore, choices (1) and (2) are incorrect. The prevention of the disease by vaccine also has nothing to do with whether the person has tested negative (3). Nothing suggests that a rabbit would be used in developing an AIDS vaccine, so (5) is incorrect. According to the passage and diagram, a person's body begins producing antibodies and, thus, an immunity or defense against the disease, after receiving the vaccine by injection (or by a special drink).

34. **(4)** *Comprehension/ Earth Science.* According to the passage, the moon's shadow affects

only a very small area of Earth. This area is on Earth's daylight side, so choice (1) is wrong. The moon is between the sun and Earth, so choice (3) is wrong.

35. **(4)** *Comprehension/ Earth Science.* Both North Carolina and Alabama are in a coastal plain region. Therefore, the answer is choice (4).

36. **(5)** *Application/Earth Science.* Colorado, Arizona, Nevada, and Idaho are all either mountains or plateaus, so a city in any of these states would not be likely to be suitable. Only Baton Rouge, in a state that is all coastal plains, would definitely be suitable.

37. **(2)** *Analysis/Earth Science.* Water coming off the western slopes of the Appalachian Mountains naturally flows from higher elevations to lower elevations. Some flows into the Great Lakes. The rest, blocked by mountains from the Atlantic Ocean and Pacific Ocean, flows into rivers that descend from the interior plains to the coastal plains and eventually enter the Gulf of Mexico.

38. **(3)** *Evaluation/Earth Science.* Both the Midwestern states and the Atlantic coast states are plains regions. If these states are noted for farming, then these plains regions must have large areas of rich soil.

39. **(3)** *Comprehension/ Earth Science.* Of the different types of stars, red stars are coolest, cooler even than red-orange stars. Our sun is

much cooler than the hottest stars, but hotter than the coolest ones, so choice (2) is wrong. Nothing in the chart supports choice (1).

40. **(3)** *Comprehension/ Earth Science.* Since Earth scientists use light-years to measure distances in space, the answer is choice (3). Despite the name, light-years are not used to measure time.

41. **(5)** *Comprehension/ Earth Science.* The article states that the star system closest to Earth is more than four light-years away. According to the definition of a light-year, the light from this star system would take more than four years to reach the Earth.

42. **(3)** *Analysis/Earth Science.* Since you are seeing light that left the star 1000 years ago, you are seeing the star as it appeared at that time. Choice (5) is wrong because the passage states that some distant stars are more than 12 billion light-years away.

43. **(4)** *Analysis/Earth Science.* In the last paragraph, the passage states that some distant star systems are more than 12 billion light-years away. This means that the light from those star systems would take more than 12 billion years to reach us. The passage goes on to say that the light from those star systems must have started traveling toward Earth long before Earth was even formed. Thus the age of Earth must be considerably less than 12 billion years.

44. **(4)** *Analysis/Earth Science.* Some scientists believe that the Earth's supply of petroleum will last until 2020; others, that it will last until 2330. Thus the statement that the world's petroleum will be gone by 2021 represents an opinion.

45. **(5)** *Analysis/Chemistry.* Water is produced as this peptide linkage is formed, so if the reaction is typical, water is always produced. Choices (1), (2), and (3) are not covered in the equation. Choice (4) is false, because the two amino acids have different numbers of atoms.

46. **(2)** *Analysis/Chemistry.* If an enzyme's shape is related to its function, then changing its shape will change its ability to bind with other molecules, thereby changing its function. Choices (1), (3), and (5) are false. Choice (4) is not covered in the passage.

47. **(4)** *Application/ Chemistry.* Adding the atoms on the left and right sides will show that for choice (1) there are one too many H (hydrogen) atoms on the right side. For choice (2) there are one too few of both O (oxygen) and hydrogen atoms on the right side. For choice (3) the right side lacks two H's and one O. Choice (4) has equal numbers on both sides. Choice (5) has one too few H's on the right side.

48. **(4)** *Application/ Chemistry.* The charge on the atom would be +2, since the loss of two electrons makes the total charge $+10 + (-8) = +2$.

49. **(5)** *Application/ Chemistry.* If the reaction proceeds as shown in the graph, the product, $CO_2$, will have less energy than the reactants, graphite and oxygen. This is because burning is a reaction that gives off energy; it is thus the opposite of endothermic, so choice (1) is wrong.

50. **(3)** *Analysis/Chemistry.* The change in energy level from point D to point B shows a loss in energy involved in the creation of the product XY. Since the reaction involves burning, this is the energy given off by the fire as heat and light.

51. **(2)** *Evaluation/ Chemistry.* In the experiment, the chemist took advantage of the different boiling temperatures to separate the substances in the mixture. The substances were not combined chemically, so choice (1) is wrong. Boiling is not a chemical reaction, so choice (4) is wrong. Nothing in the experiment supports choice (5).

52. **(1)** *Analysis/Chemistry.* Since carbon dioxide causes bread to rise, and since carbon dioxide is formed when sodium bicarbonate reacts with an acid, bread dough must contain at least one ingredient that is an acid.

53. **(1)** *Comprehension/ Chemistry.* Scientists use the decay of carbon-14 to date ancient organisms. If this decay did not take place at a constant rate, it could not be used as a standard of measurement.

54. **(1)** *Application/ Chemistry.* The half-life refers to one half, or 50 percent, of the substance. When a radioactive substance has a half-life, half of the substance is radioactive, and the other half is not. 20 is half of 40, so 40 grams of radioactive iodine after eight days contain 20 grams of a nonradioactive substance and 20 grams of radioactive iodine.

55. **(1)** *Analysis/Chemistry.* Because scientists compare the amount of carbon-14 present in the remains of an organism with the amount present in the living organism, it can be inferred that they know how much carbon-14 was present in the living organism.

56. **(4)** *Application/Physics.* Because of the property of light called refraction, objects under water look bent when viewed through the water's surface. The reason is that light rays bend as they pass through certain media.

57. **(4)** *Application/Physics.* (4) is the only answer that does not contain an object that is moving in a circle. The car is traveling downhill, not around.

58. **(4)** *Comprehension/ Physics.* The passage states that when popcorn is heated, the water in the kernel changes into steam, then the steam expands to pop the kernel.

59. **(5)** *Analysis/Physics.* It is the heating of the popcorn that makes the water change into steam and the steam expand. Raising the temperature would make the water turn to steam faster.

60. **(4)** *Analysis/Physics.* The article states that as the steam gets hotter, pressure builds up inside the kernel. Therefore, the relationship illustrated is that as temperature increases, pressure increases.

61. **(2)** *Analysis/Physics.* Since water in the kernels is what makes popcorn pop, it is most likely that the kernels will no longer pop because the water inside has dried up.

62. **(4)** *Application/Physics.* Rearranging the molecules in the bar will cause the magnetic domains to be arranged randomly, resulting in unmagnetized iron. Choices (1), (2), and (3) are incorrect because all would mean the bar is still a magnet, and it is unlikely the domains would retain an aligned arrangement after being heated and cooled. There is no evidence for choice (5).

63. **(2)** *Comprehension/ Physics.* Since pressure increases up the side of the graph and temperature increases from left to right across the graph, the straight diagonal line clearly shows that pressure steadily increases as temperature increases.

64. **(5)** *Analysis/Physics.* Pressure will increase as temperature increases only as long as the gas is kept at a constant volume—for example, inside the sealed container. If the sealed container were suddenly opened, some of the gas could escape, and the pressure of the gas would decrease.

65. **(2)** *Application/Physics.* Gas is easily compressed when pressure is added. As Boyle puts it: The more pressure is added to a gas, the smaller the volume it takes up.

66. **(1)** *Application/Physics.* Avogadro's hypothesis states that at the same temperature and volume, the number of molecules in a sample of gas—any gas—is constant. Chlorine molecules happen to be heavier than helium molecules, which explains the difference in the weight of the two samples.

1. **(2)** *Comprehension/ Nonfiction.* The author wonders if his high scores mean only that he is very good at answering the kinds of questions that writers of intelligence tests like to ask (lines 15-22). He also states that his intelligence "is not absolute but is a function of the society" in which he lives (lines 48-49). The adequacy of intelligence tests is called into question throughout the passage.

2. **(4)** *Comprehension/ Nonfiction.* The author is discussing tests that attempt to measure intelligence. Of his score on that aptitude test, he says that scores like that make him feel complacent about his intelligence (lines 11-15). It can be assumed that the aptitude test that he took in the army was an intelligence test.

3. **(1)** *Application/ Nonfiction.* In lines 23-35, the author compares his kind of "intelligence" with that of an auto-repair man. He states that in their respective fields, both are intelligent. He speculates that he would flunk a test written by "anyone but an academician." He seems to think that aptitude tests should measure intelligence in a given field, and one can assume that he would want to see such tests devised by those who are experienced in that field.

4. **(5)** *Analysis/Nonfiction.* The author's use of questions such as "What is intelligence, anyway?" (line 1) and his simple, straightforward sentences give the passage a conversational style.

5. **(3)** *Comprehension/ Nonfiction.* Throughout the passage, the author tells us that decisions should not be based on what others think or even on a person's own memories, but on each person's idea of what is best. The author makes statements that contradict choices (1), (4), and (5). The author does not discuss how to begin trusting oneself, choice (2).

6. **(4)** *Comprehension/ Nonfiction.* The author is trying to illustrate his belief that past events and deeds should remain, or be "buried," in the past.

7. **(2)** *Comprehension/ Nonfiction.* The author states that it is hard to follow your own ideas "because you will always find those who think they know what is your duty better than you know it" (lines 7-9). The author also says "The other terror that scares us from self-trust is our consistency; a reverence for our past act or word . . . " (lines 18-20).

8. **(3)** *Application/ Nonfiction.* The attitude presented in this essay would be appropriate for a drug and alcohol abuse workshop where participants are encouraged to ignore peer pressure. Young artists might also be helped by knowing that their own personal style is as valid as that of an existing art style.

9. **(4)** *Comprehension/ Nonfiction.* The authors are talking about eliminating farm-produced foods and creating all food products from chemicals.

10. **(3)** *Comprehension/ Nonfiction.* We are told that the synthetic foods of the future will have the normal amount of vitamins (line 48) and that they will be "infinitely better . . . than the best natural products" because their nutritional elements can be adapted to each person according to the person's needs (lines 55-59), but we have no reason to infer that people therefore will eat less of the synthetic foods than they eat of natural product foods. Besides, the question asks which of the choices is not a benefit mentioned—that is, stated, rather than implied—in the passage. All the other choices restate benefits mentioned by the authors.

11. **(2)** *Application/ Nonfiction.* These authors feel that agriculture is a costly, inefficient industry. They might wish to do away with natural fibers used in clothing and create a clothing indus-

try that uses only synthetic fibers.

12. **(2)** *Analysis/Nonfiction.* In the final paragraph, the authors state: "The society of the future gains on all fronts: economic, social and also moral. . . ." The preceding portion of the passage was spent illustrating this belief. The overall tone of the passage, therefore, is optimistic.

13. **(3)** *Comprehension/ Fiction.* There are specific references throughout the passage to indicate this answer: line 25—"Indian Curios"; line 42—"pseudo-Navajo"; line 75—"a fat Navajo."

14. **(5)** *Comprehension/ Fiction.* The paragraph states that Chee's "lips tightened," indicating that he became tense. Also, the phrase "bearing down on them, scowling" shows us the negative way in which Chee views Old Man Fat.

15. **(3)** *Analysis/Fiction.* Chee feels that Red Sands is an ugly place. The description of Red Sands as "sprawled in mushroom growth" highlights this feeling. "Sprawled" gives the reader a sense of disorganization and "mushroom growth" suggests the unpleasant characteristics of mushrooms (damp, moldy, etc.).

16. **(2)** *Application/Fiction.* Through the sympathetic portrayal of Chee, the authors present their love for the land and their respect for those who work the land. The authors most likely would want to help farmers keep their farms.

17. **(1)** *Comprehension/ Fiction.* We are told in lines 40-46 that the captain feels dejection and indifference because his ship went down. The whole paragraph about the injured captain describes the sinking of his ship to show that his memory of the ship's loss, not his injury (2), is what causes him to be dejected—that is, depressed and sad. The correspondent, not the captain, "wondered why he was there" (line 39)— as stated in choice (3). The captain cannot have lost his sense of direction (4) because he gives the oiler directions to steer the boat farther south in line 62. Though the captain probably is worried about the men in the boat (5), the passage nowhere says that he is and does not suggest that this is why he feels dejection and indifference.

18. **(4)** *Comprehension/ Fiction.* The sentence right after "None of them knew the color of the sky" (line 1) states: "Their eyes glanced level, and were fastened upon the waves that swept toward them." None of the other choices is supported by details in the first paragraph or in the rest of the passage.

19. **(5)** *Comprehension/ Fiction.* In lines 69-71 we are told that the boat "pranced and reared, and plunged like an animal" (which resembles a horse in these actions) and in lines 72-74 that the boat "seemed like a horse making at a fence outrageously high." In lines 66-67, we are told that "A seat in this boat

was not unlike a seat upon a bucking bronco"—that is, a wild horse used in cowboy riding contests—but it is the seat of the boat that is compared here to the seat on a bucking bronco, and therefore (2) is wrong. In lines 13-15 we are told "many a man ought to have a bathtub larger than the boat," but this does not describe the boat's action on the waves. (3) and (4) are details describing the sinking of the captain's ship.

20. **(3)** *Analysis/Fiction.* You may want to decide on the answer to this question by eliminating the wrong choices. Since the captain, probably the most closely described character, is shown lying in the boat, "buried" in "profound dejection and indifference," (1) does not seem an accurate statement of the theme. On the other hand, none of the characters is paralyzed by terror, so (2) cannot be correct. (4) cannot be right because all the characters react differently to the situation: The cook is active, noisy, and seems to react almost humorously to the situation; the oiler is silent, alert, and nervous; the correspondent is silent and detached; the captain is dejected and indifferent. Nothing in the behavior of these men suggests that hostile natural forces have reduced them to an animal level (5). Everything in the excerpt, however, suggests an image of life as a constant struggle

against unpredictable forces (3).

21. **(4)** *Comprehension/ Fiction.* Grandfather was telling his children and grandchildren not to sur- render, as he had done.

22. **(5)** *Comprehension/ Fiction.* Grandfather felt that he had betrayed his people by not fight- ing for his rights when he was younger.

23. **(3)** *Application/Fiction.* Because he was not one to oppose authority openly, Grandfather would not become an activitist of any kind, so (1), (2) and (3) are wrong. He also would not want his opinions publicly known, so (4) is correct. However, he would be likely to feel comfortable overcoming a boss "with yesses" in a service position.

24. **(5)** *Analysis/Fiction.* Death-bed scenes are often used to add drama to a situation. By using this setting, the author has created an addition- al sense of urgency about his grandfather's words.

25. **(5)** *Comprehension/ Drama.* Caligula already rules over a kingdom [choice (2)] but wants more. He wants to be "above the gods," have the moon in his hands (rule over nature), and give society "the gift of equality."

26. **(5)** *Analysis/Drama.* Caesonia disagrees with Caligula and is shown in the passage to become more and more upset by his remarks. The author's inclusion of the phrase "a man's heart from growing cold" emphasizes Caesonia's fear for Caligula's

increasing indifference to what the world is really like. She probably is also suggesting that his unnatural desires are making his own heart grow cold to nor- mal human emotions.

27. **(4)** *Analysis/Drama.* Caesonia disagrees with Caligula and knows that he is heading for trou- ble. By using the word "imploring" in the stage directions, the play- wright illustrates the urgency of her speech.

28. **(3)** *Comprehension/ Drama.* Although Ken's body is no longer func- tioning properly, his thinking processes are. Because so many machines keep him alive, he feels like the "thinking" part of a giant machine.

29. **(1)** *Comprehension/ Drama.* Ken believes that his moral atti- tudes about his own death are as impor- tant as Dr. Scott's attitudes about keep- ing him alive. He feels that Dr. Scott should respect his beliefs and allow him to die.

30. **(5)** *Comprehension/ Drama.* The characters disagree on a very basic point—a patient's right to die. At the end of this passage, Ken is still questioning Dr. Scott about this issue, which suggests that their con- flict will continue.

31. **(1)** *Comprehension/ Poetry.* In lines 20-21, the mother says "For I'se still goin', Honey,/I'se still climbin'." Although the mother has had a hard life, she wants her son to know that she is not going to stop struggling.

32. **(3)** *Comprehension/ Poetry.* In line 14, the mother tells her son not to turn back, which suggests that he had already begun his jour- ney through life and is finding the road diffi- cult. He might be tempt- ed to quit, but her words are intended to give him the encourage- ment he needs to continue.

33. **(3)** *Analysis/Poetry.* The mother wants to give her son the strength to continue his life by telling him that even though life has been dif- ficult for her, she still keeps trying and keeps on climbing.

34. **(5)** *Comprehension/ Poetry.* Line 7 states that the man was reading a book.

35. **(4)** *Comprehension/ Poetry.* The poet implies that the man was hun- gry for knowledge and that the words were nourishing to his spirit.

36. **(2)** *Analysis/Poetry.* We are told that the man reading "danced along the dingy days"–in other words, his reading enabled him to feel joy in spite of his gloomy and depressing daily life. The last two lines also tell us that his excitement over "The precious words" gave his spirit a wonderful feeling of freedom, None of the other choices describe the poem's tone accurately.

37. **(3)** *Comprehension/ Commentary.* The statis- tics given in lines 30-35 support this conclusion.

38. **(1)** *Comprehension/ Commentary.* Programs that would show "prosocial behavior" would be good role models.

39. **(5)** *Application/ Commentary.* The author quotes surveys of television-watching by children but nowhere raises the question of whether such surveys have any effect on the kinds of programs producers put on television.

40. **(5)** *Comprehension/ Commentary.* The last paragraph states that American parents rarely raise any of the questions the author asks in the third paragraph (lines 46-68) about the effect of television on children. (1) and (2) are therefore incorrect. Nothing suggests (3) or (4).

41. **(4)** *Analysis/ Commentary.* The use of statistics and a newspaper style of reporting would be inappropriate in a letter to a friend.

42. **(2)** *Comprehension/ Commentary.* Graham felt that classical ballet did not reflect the way people were living, so she created a style of dance that did.

43. **(3)** *Comprehension/ Commentary.* (3) restates Graham's statement in lines 51-53: "I had to find something to dance about, and the about was myself and the world around me." Lines 12-14 say that Graham has "dark eyes deep enough to hold the answers to all the questions of the universe," which does not mean that finding such answers was her motive for developing modern dance. In a similar way, lines 5-7 describe Graham as "a figure as monumental as the tragic heroines she portrayed"; again, her being monumental is not a motive for her creating modern dance, but an effect of her creating it. Likewise, her forming the taste of the twentieth century is an effect of her developing modern dance, not her motive for developing it, as (1) states. (4) is a detail about her development of modern dance.

44. **(3)** *Application/ Commentary.* Graham is quoted as saying (lines 40-43): "Life today [in 1929] is nervous, sharp, zigzag...That is what I aim for in my dances." Jazz, which also became popular in the 1920s, often has a "nervous, sharp, and zigzag" feel to it, and it is also uniquely American; it would be an appropriate type of music for Graham's choreography.

45. **(3)** *Comprehension/ Commentary.* In lines 15-20 the writer explicitly compares the carving of the Grand Canyon by the Colorado River to the reshaping of the art of dance by the power of Martha Graham's genius.

1. **(4)** *Arithmetic/Problem Solving.*

   $v = lwh$
   $v = (12)(16)(18)$

2. **(1)** *Arithmetic/Application.*

   $\frac{12,480}{52} = 240$ or $\frac{12,480}{52} = \frac{n}{1}$
   $12,480 = 52n$
   $240 = n$

3. **(5)** *Arithmetic/Application.*

   $1\frac{1}{2}$ x $24 = 36$ or $\frac{1}{1.5} = \frac{24}{n}$
   $n = 1.5$ x $24$
   $n = 36$

4. **(2)** *Arithmetic/Problem Solving.*

   $(.79 - .30)$ = cost per dozen
   To find unit cost, divide by 12.
   or
   Use a proportion.
   $\frac{79-.30}{12} = \frac{n}{1}$
   $.79 - .30 = 12n$
   $\frac{79-.30}{12} = n$

5. **(3)** *Arithmetic/Problem Solving.*

   Change minutes into hours, multiply each rate by its time, and add the two products together.

6. **(4)** *Arithmetic/Problem Solving.*

   $.12(795 + 550 + 340) = .12(1685) = 202.20$
   or
   $\frac{12}{100} = \frac{p}{795 + 550 + 340}$
   $12(795 + 550 + 340) = 100p$
   $20,220 = 100p$
   $202.20 = p$

7. **(4)** *Arithmetic/Problem Solving.*

   Sale price of sofa:
   $.2$ x $795 = 159$
   or $\frac{20}{100} = \frac{p}{795}$
   $20$ x $795 = 100p$
   $15,900 = 100p$
   $159 = p$
   $795 - 159 = 636$
   Total cost of items: $636 + 550 + 340 = 1526$

8. **(3)** *Arithmetic/Problem Solving.*

   $\frac{3}{4}$ = 45 minutes
   $\frac{45}{1} = \frac{20}{n}$
   $45n = 20$
   $n = \frac{20}{45} = \frac{4}{9}$

9. **(4)** *Arithmetic/Problem Solving.*

   $A = lw$
   $3328 = n$ x $52$
   $n = \frac{3328}{52}$

10. **(3)** *Arithmetic/Problem Solving.*

    Cost of the van plus tax = 107% of the cost of the van
    $1.07$ x $18,000 = 19,260$
    or
    $\frac{107}{100} = \frac{p}{18,000}$
    $107$ x $18,000 = 100p$
    $1,926,000 = 100p$
    $19,260 = p$

11. **(5)** *Arithmetic/Problem Solving.*

    The number of skirts is not given.

12. **(4)** *Arithmetic/Skills.*

    $-10 + 5 = -5$

13. **(2)** *Arithmetic/Problem Solving*

    $v = \pi r^2 h$
    Volume of one can: $(3.14)(1)^2(5)$
    Volume of six-pack: $(6)(3.14)(1)^2(5)$

14. **(4)** *Arithmetic/Problem Solving.*

    D $\frac{7}{8} = \frac{7}{8}$
    E $\frac{3}{4} = \frac{6}{8}$
    B $\frac{1}{2} = \frac{4}{8}$
    A $\frac{1}{4} = \frac{2}{8}$
    C $\frac{1}{8} = \frac{1}{8}$

15. **(2)** *Arithmetic/Problem Solving.*

$9 \times .05 = .45$
$13 \times .03 = .39$
$1 \times .40 = .40$
$7 \times .06 = .42$

16. **(3)** *Arithmetic/Problem Solving.*

Subtract the change in May from the change in June.

$.5 - .2 = .3$

17. **(3)** *Arithmetic/Application.*

$4 \times 4 \times 4 = 64$

18. **(4)** *Arithmetic/Application.*

$1.86 \times 10^5 = 186,000$

19. **(2)** *Arithmetic/Problem Solving.*

$\frac{624 + 547 + 763 + 436 + 925}{5} = \frac{3295}{5} = 659$

20. **(3)** *Arithmetic/Application.*

$\frac{\text{number of people who will win a prize}}{\text{number of people eligible to win a prize}} =$

$\frac{400}{2,000,000}$

21. **(1)** *Arithmetic/Problem Solving.*

6 months = $\frac{1}{2}$ year

$i = prt$

$i = 5000 \times .06 \times \frac{1}{2} = 150$

22. **(5)** *Arithmetic/Application.*

$d = rt$ or $\frac{4}{1} = \frac{n}{2 \times 7}$

$d = 4 \times 2 \times 7$  $\quad 4 \times 2 \times 7 = n$

$d = 56$  $\quad\quad\quad\quad 56 = n$

23. **(2)** *Arithmetic/Problem Solving.*

$45 \times 85 = 38.25$ or $\frac{45}{100} = \frac{p}{85}$

$45 \times 85 = 100p$

$3825 = 100p$

$38.25 = p$

24. **(1)** *Arithmetic/Problem Solving.*

$\frac{.06 \times 24,000}{5} = 288$

or

Total donation:

$\frac{6}{100} = \frac{p}{24,000}$

$6 \times 24,000 = 100p$

$144,000 = 100p$

$1440 = p$

Donation to each charity:

$\frac{1440}{5} = \frac{n}{1}$

$1440 = 5n$

$288 = n$

25. **(2)** *Arithmetic/Application.*

$A = s^2$
$30 = s^2$
$\sqrt{30} = s$

30 is between 25 and 36.

$\sqrt{25} = 5$ and $\sqrt{36} = 6$

26. **(2)** *Arithmetic/Problem Solving.*

$\frac{32}{11} = 3$, or $\frac{32}{11} = \frac{n}{1}$

$32 = 11n$

$3 = n$

27. **(5)** *Arithmetic/Problem Solving.*

Add to find the total number of cars serviced. Then divide by the number of days.

28. **(5)** *Arithmetic/Problem Solving.*

The cost of each type bag of food is not given.

29. **(4)** *Arithmetic/Problem Solving.*

$d = rt$ or $\frac{50}{1} = \frac{750}{n}$

$750 = 50t$  $\quad\quad 50n = 750$

$t = \frac{750}{50} = 15$  $\quad n = 15$

30. **(4)** *Algebra/Problem Solving.*

$\frac{25}{45} = \frac{5}{9}$

$\frac{5}{9} = \frac{4000}{n}$

$5n = 36,000$

$n = 7200$

31. **(2)** *Algebra/Application.*

$$P = a + b + c$$
$$300 = 75 + 100 + c$$
$$300 = 175 + c$$
$$c = 300 - 175 = 125$$

32. **(2)** *Algebra/Skills.*

$$8d - h + 3h + 2d = 8d + 2d + 3h - h = 10d + 2h$$

33. **(1)** *Algebra/Problem Solving.*

Four times the number of adults' tickets plus 2.5 times the number of children's tickets equals the total receipts.

$4a$ = number of adult tickets

$2.5c$ = number of children's tickets

$4a + 2.5c$ = total receipts

34. **(2)** *Algebra/Problem Solving.*

The insurance company will pay a percentage of the amount shown by the expression $(r - 200)$.

$.8(r - 200)$ equals 80% of that amount.

or

$$\frac{80}{100} = \frac{p}{r - 200}$$
$$80(r-200) = 100p$$
$$\frac{80(r - 200)}{100} = p$$
$$\frac{8(r - 200)}{10} = p$$
$$.8(r - 200) = p$$

35. **(4)** *Algebra/Skills.*

$$7(7 - 4) + 4 = 7(3) + 4 = 21 + 4 = 25$$

36. **(5)** *Algebra/Application.*

$$\frac{3}{1} = \frac{4.95}{c}$$
$$3c = 4.95$$
$$c = \frac{4.95}{3}$$

37. **(5)** *Algebra/Problem Solving.*

$s$ = cost of the dinette set at full price

$\frac{c}{2}$ = one-half the regular price of the couch

$s + \frac{c}{2}$ = total cost

Only the couch is at half price.

38. **(4)** *Algebra/Problem Solving.*

$w$ = time spent warming up and cooling down
$2w$ = time spent doing aerobics
1 hour = 60 minutes
$$w + 2w = 60$$
$$3w = 60$$
$$w = 20$$
$$2w = 40$$

or

$$\frac{2}{3} = \frac{n}{60}$$
$$2 \times 60 = 3n$$
$$120 = 3n$$
$$40 = n$$

39. **(5)** *Algebra/Problem Solving.*

$$\frac{4}{13} = \frac{24}{n}$$
$$4n = 13 \times 24$$
$$4n = 312$$
$$n = 78$$

40. **(3)** *Algebra/Problem Solving.*

$.3s = 480$ or $\frac{30}{100} = \frac{480}{s}$

$s = 1600$ $\quad 30s = 48,000$

$\quad\quad\quad\quad\quad s = 1600$

41. **(1)** *Algebra/Application.*

$$3k + 1 < 13$$
$$3k < 12$$
$$k < 4$$

42. **(2)** *Algebra/Problem Solving.*

Let $d$ = daughter's weight.
$$d - 20 + d = 70$$
$$2d - 20 = 70$$
$$2d = 90$$
$$d = 45$$
Son's weight: $d - 20$ or $45 - 20 = 25$

43. **(4)** *Algebra/Application.*

House A: $f = 30 \times 40 = 1200$ ; $1500 > 1200 > 950$

House D: $f = 45 \times 30 = 1350$ ; $1500 > 1350 > 950$

44. **(3)** *Algebra/Problem Solving.*

Let $c$ = cost.
$$\frac{29.61}{9} = \frac{c}{1}$$
$$29.61 = 9c$$
$$3.29 = c$$

**45. (3)** *Algebra/Problem Solving.*

$\frac{297}{33} = \frac{r}{45}$

$33r = 297 \times 45$

$\frac{297 \times 45}{33}$

**46. (3)** *Algebra/Application.*

Use the distributive property:
$(y + 9)(y - 5) = y^2 - 5y + 9y - 45$
Simplify to get $y^2 + 4y - 45$.

**47. (3)** *Geometry/Application.*

Both long sides are 8 feet long.
$P = 8 + 8 + 4$
$P = 20$

**48. (4)** *Geometry/Skills.*

Angle $a$ and angle $b$ are supplementary
  angles.
$180 - 54 = 126$

**49. (1)** *Geometry/Skills.*

The sum of the angles of a triangle equals
  $180°$.
$151 + 25 + 4 = 180$

**50. (1)** *Geometry/Problem Solving.*

$\frac{15}{12} = \frac{h}{20}$

**51. (2)** *Geometry/Application.*

$m = \frac{y^2 - y^1}{x^2 - x^1}$

$m = \frac{-1 - 2}{6 - (-3)} = \frac{-3}{9} = -\frac{1}{3}$

**52. (5)** *Geometry/Problem Solving.*

The radius of the cover would have to be
6 feet plus $\frac{1}{2}$ foot, or $6\frac{1}{2}$ feet. The
diameter is twice the radius.
$2 \times 6\frac{1}{2} = 13$

**53. (3)** *Geometry/Problem Solving.*

Use the Pythagorean relationship:
$c^2 = a^2 + b^2$
$c^2 = 9 \times 9 = 81; a = 9; b = 12; 12 \times 12 = 144$
$c^2 = 144 + 81 = 225$
$c = \sqrt{225} = 15$

**54. (2)** *Geometry/Problem Solving.*

$\frac{6}{8} = \frac{9}{w}$

$6w = 72$

$w = 12$

**55. (4)** *Geometry/Skills.*

The roof forms an isosceles triangle that
has equal base angles.
The sum of the three angles is $180°$.
$180 - 66 = 114$
$\frac{114}{2} = 57$

**56. (5)** *Geometry/Problem Solving.*

The distance equals the square root of the
difference between the Mt. Burn\
-Mt. Blue distance and the Mt. Burn\
-Mt. Green distance.

$a^2 + b^2 = c^2$

$a^2 + 75^2 = 125^2$

$a^2 = 125^2 - 75^2$

$a = \sqrt{225}$

1. **(5)** *Usage/Verb Tense/Sentence Revision.* Word clues in the rest of the paragraph indicate that present perfect tense should be used for consistency's sake.

2. **(4)** *Sentence Structure/ Parallelism/Sentence Correction.* Express equivalent ideas in the same form. You should think about two things, your choice and use of credit cards.

3. **(1)** *Usage/Pronoun Shift/Sentence Correction.* Don't shift pronouns within a sentence. *Before you apply for a card, (implied you) find out each company's charge.*

4. **(4)** *Sentence Structure/ Sentence Fragment/ Sentence Revision.* Correct the sentence fragment by providing a complete verb, *is added,* for the subject, *charge.*

5. **(2)** *Usage/Pronoun Reference/Sentence Correction. It* must be changed because there is no singular noun in the previous sentence to refer back to. Sentence 5 talks about *cards,* which is a plural noun; however, choice (3) is incorrect because the paragraph is written in the present tense.

6. **(3)** *Mechanics/ Capitalization/Sentence Correction. Sierra Club* is the proper name of an organization and needs to be capitalized.

7. **(2)** *Mechanics/Spelling/ Sentence Correction.* The final "y" becomes "ies" to make "company" plural correctly "companies."

8. **(5)** *Sentence Structure/ Sentence Coordination/ Construction Shift.* "Once you do choose one, put the account number and emergency phone number in a safe place, for the card may be lost or stolen." *For,* a connector which gives the reason, should be preceded by a comma to join the two sentences.

9. **(3)** *Mechanics/ Homonyms/Punctuation /Sentence Revision. It's* is the contraction for *it is.* Here *its* is a possessive pronoun referring back to *convenience.* A comma is needed after *plastic* to show the end of an introductory group of words.

10. **(1)** *Sentence Structure/ Subordination Coordination/Construction Shift.* "It may be inconvenient to write a thank-you note after a job interview, but the effort is worth the bother." The new construction preserves the meaning of the original.

11. **(5)** *Mechanics/ Spelling/Sentence Correction. Ability* is spelled correctly. Since *others* is a plural and not a possessive here, it requires no apostrophe.

12. **(4)** *Sentence Structure/ Modification, Dangling Modifier/Sentence Revision.* The thank-you note, not the interviewer, arrives in the mail. Make sure that the modifier stands close to the person or thing involved in the action.

13. **(3)** *Usage/Subject-Verb Agreement/Sentence Revision.* Singular nouns joined by *or* are considered a singular subject and require a singular verb: he or she thinks.

14. **(1)** *Sentence Structure/ Improper Subordination/ Sentence Correction.* The new construction is clearer and less awkward than the original. (The phrase *such that* usually modifies a noun: "Her temper was such that he didn't dare ask.")

15. **(4)** *Usage/Pronoun Shift/Sentence Correction. You,* not *one,* is the pronoun used throughout the paragraph.

16. **(2)** *Usage/Verb Tense/Sentence Correction.* The future tense, not the past, is consistent with the use in the rest of the paragraph. The writer is telling you what will happen if you write the note.

17. **(3)** *Sentence Structure/ Comma Splice/Sentence Correction.* Two complete ideas are incorrectly joined by a comma. The error is

corrected by forming two sentences.

18. **(5)** *Usage/Subject-Verb Agreement, Connectives Other Than And/Sentence Correction.* Despite the connecting phrase *like other agencies*, the subject is singular, *The Internal Revenue Service*, and requires a singular verb, *uses*.

19. **(4)** *Sentence Structure/ Run-on/Sentence Correction.* Two complete subject-verb structures are incorrectly joined without proper punctuation. The error is corrected by forming two separate sentences.

20. **(3)** *Mechanics/ Capitalization/Sentence Correction.* New York City is the complete name of a place and, as such, should be capitalized.

21. **(1)** *Mechanics/ Spelling/Sentence Correction. Service* contains a soft c.

22. **(2)** *Mechanics/ Punctuation/Sentence Correction.* Use commas to set off defining phrases. *Database* means not just computerized library but computerized library for storing large amounts of information.

23. **(2)** *Sentence Structure/ Parallelism/Sentence Revision.* The connector, and, joins sentence elements of equal importance. The elements should be expressed in similar form. "Your employer sends . . . and the Department of Motor Vehicles sends. . . "

24. **(2)** *Sentence Structure/ Subordination/Construction Shift.* "The computer searches the database for information that should be reported on your tax forms." The new construction effectively combines the two sentences, while stating clearly both the subject, *computer*, and the verb, *searches*.

25. **(4)** *Sentence Structure/ Sentence Fragment/ Sentence Revision.* The revised form corrects the sentence fragment by providing the singular subject with the singular verb, is processed, required by the either/or construction.

26. **(4)** *Sentence Structure/ Sentence Coordination/ Construction Shift.* "More people than ever are interested in higher education; as a result, the number of people taking the GED Tests has risen." Sentence 1 provides the cause, and sentence 2 provides the result. A semicolon precedes the connecting words and a comma follows them.

27. **(1)** *Mechanics/Overuse of Commas/Sentence Correction.* The comma confuses the reader by separating the subject, result, from the verb, has been.

28. **(2)** *Sentence Structure/ Sentence Fragment/ Sentence Correction.* The sentence fragment is corrected by supplying a verb, *reports*, which agrees with the subject, *American Council on Education.*

29. **(4)** *Usage/Verb Tense Errors/Sentence Revision.* The present tense of the verb, *advertise*, is consistent with the tense used throughout the paragraph.

30. **(1)** *Mechanics/ Spelling/Sentence Correction. Don't* is the contraction for *do not.* The apostrophe takes the place of the missing o.

31. **(3)** *Sentence Structure/ Comma Splice/Sentence Revision.* Two complete ideas are incorrectly joined by a comma. A semicolon—like the words and, *but, or, nor, for*, and yet—can be used to mark the dividing point between two such complete ideas.

32. **(3)** *Usage/Subject-Verb Agreement, Either-Or/Sentence Correction.* When the neither/nor construction is used, the verb agrees with the noun or pronoun closer to it: *anyone else needs.*

33. **(5)** *Mechanics/ Capitalization/Sentence Correction.* As part of an address, *Circle* is properly capitalized.

34. **(1)** *Sentence Structure/ Improper Subordination/ Sentence Correction.* Although the improper phrase, "something what" is used at times in speech, *that* is the connector required here.

35. **(3)** *Usage/Ambiguous, Vague Pronoun Reference/Construction Shift.* "Many workers change jobs, either by choice or necessity." The new construction eliminates the vague references to *they* and *it.* The revised version reads more smoothly.

36. **(4)** *Mechanics/ Punctuation/Sentence Revision.* Use a comma to set off the introductory clause from the subject, *many job hunters.*

37. **(5)** *Usage/Verb Tense Errors/Sentence Revision.* The present tense should be used to remain consistent with usage throughout the paragraph.

38. **(2)** *Sentence Structure/ Clarity, Modification/ Construction Shift.* "Although it may be fairly easy to get a service job, it is often difficult to find career ladders, steps for working up to higher wages, within service jobs." Meaning is made clearer by defining *career ladders* within the sentence.

39. **(2)** *Mechanics/ Capitalization/Sentence Correction.* Capitalize titles of people when they come before names; don't capitalize career names.

40. **(2)** *Usage/Subject-Verb Agreement, Interrupting Phrase/Sentence Correction.* Despite the subject and the verb, the singular subject, *problem*, requires a singular verb, *is*.

41. **(5)** *Sentence Structure/ Pronoun Shift/Sentence Revision.* Keep pronouns consistent within a sentence. The writer addressed the last two sentences of the paragraph to you, the reader.

42. **(1)** *Usage/Pronoun Agreement with Antecedent/Sentence Revision.* The sentence is correct as written.

43. **(2)** *Mechanics/ Punctuation/Sentence Correction.* Use a comma to separate the introductory element from the subject, *physicians*.

44. **(4)** *Mechanics/ Capitalization/Sentence Correction.* Capitalize a title when it comes before someone's name.

45. **(3)** *Sentence Structure/ Improper Subordination/ Sentence Revision.* Don't confuse *because of* (a preposition) with *because* (a conjunction). *Because of* precedes a noun, as in this sentence.

46. **(5)** *Sentence Structure/ Modification, Run-on/Sentence Correction.* The sentence is not a run-on. The phrase about people with similar symptoms modifies information and could not stand alone.

47. **(1)** *Usage/Subject-Verb Agreement, Inverted Structure/Sentence Correction.* Even if the usual order of subject followed by verb is reversed, the plural subject, *doctors*, requires a plural verb, *do*.

48. **(1)** *Sentence Structure/ Coordination, Subordination/Construc-tion Shift.* "Putting medical records into database is just one of many ways doctors can use computers to provide improved health care." The new construction effectively shows the relationship of ideas in the sentence, while the original simply strings ideas together with *and*.

49. **(1)** *Mechanics/ Punctuation/Usage/Verb Tense/Sentence Revision.* The sentence is correct as written. A comma is needed after an introductory group of words. The present perfect tense (*have* or *has* plus the past participle) is used when an action began in the past but continues into the present.

50. **(4)** *Usage/Verb Tense/ Sentence Revision. In 1988* tells you that the sentence should be written in the past tense.

51. **(4)** *Usage/Relative Pronoun/Sentence Revision. Which* is used to refer to things; use *who* for people. *Once* indicates simple past tense, an action completed. Names of specific national or ethnic groups such as "American" should be capitalized.

52. **(3)** *Mechanics/ Capitalization/Sentence Correction.* Since "Fair Share" is the name of a specific NAACP program, it should be capitalized.

53. **(5)** *Sentence Structure/ Usage/Subject-Verb Agreement/Construction Shift.* The increasing gap between the black middle class and the black "underclass" is what worries civil rights leaders most. The subject of the sentence is *gap*, a singular noun. The verb tense should be present.

54. **(1)** *Usage/Verb Tense/ Sentence Correction.* In the present perfect tense, the past participle follows *have* or *has. Percentage* is singular, so *has* is correct.

55. **(4)** *Mechanics/ Commas/Sentence Revision.* Commas should be placed before and after groups of words that are not essential to the meaning or understanding of the sentence. These words often provide additional descriptive information or interrupt the flow of the sentence.

**HOW TO SCORE YOUR ESSAY**

To score your essay, compare it with the following model essays. These model essays received scores of 3 and 5 respectively.

Compare your essay with the 3 model essay. If it is as good as the 3 model essay, then assign your essay a score of 3. If it is not as good as the 3 model essay, refer back to the answer key for the Writing Skills Predictor Test and use the descriptions of the 1 and 2 model essays to evaluate your essay. It should be easy to assign a score to your essay if you compare your essay with these model essays and their character-trait analyses.

If your essay is better than the 3 model essay, compare it to the model essay that received a 5. If it is better than the 3, but not as good as the 5, score your essay a 4. Give your essay a 5 if it is as good as the second model. If your essay is better than the 5 model, then score your essay a 6.

In addition, look at the notes and character-trait analyses that accompany the model essays. Those comments explain the strengths and weaknesses of the essays.

## Model Essay—Holistic Score 3

**Introduces the subject but point of view is not clearly stated**

**Repetitious statements, lists of ideas, and undeveloped examples on the subject do not provide an adequate explanation of the effect of technology on the writer's free-time activities. Point of view is stated in the conclusion.**

Technology affects how I spend my free time. Like when I come home from work, there are lots of things to do with it.

In the living room I have a video cassette recorder hooked up to the TV set. Near them is a small personal computer. On the other side of the room is a stereo. It sits between two bookcases.

After I eat if there is nothing on TV I'll go out and rent a movie and play it on the VCR. If its busy and I can't find anything to rent, I'll come home and play video games on the computer or listen to the stereo. Playing computer games is getting really boring. Ive got sports games like baseball games and space games and aliens games but once you figure them out their not fun to play anymore. I have to get more software if I want to play anything new on the computer but when I do the same thing will happen again and I'll have to buy more. That is how they get you.

New technology sounds good at first but it gets expensive to use and it keeps costing money all the time.

Character-Trait Analysis

1. The essay is not organized. It is a choppy account of the writer's activities after work. It lists the technological products used by the writer, but the essay does not explain how technology has affected the writer's choice of free-time activities. In the essay's conclusion, we are told that the writer does not enjoy the expense involved in using modern technology, but we are not told why the writer feels this way. A

more effective essay would explain how the writer feels about the effect of technology on his/her free time and why the writer feels this way.

2.  The essays listing of products and repetitious sentence structure make this composition less effective than it could be. An essay with specific examples, explanation of the writer's point of view, and varied sentence structure would be more interesting and effective.

3.  There are errors in spelling, punctuation, sentence structure, and accepted English usage that detract from the essay's effectiveness.

## Model Essay-Holistic Score 5

**Introduces subject and states point of view.**

**Elaborates on point of view with specific examples**

**Note contrasts between playing piano with and without modern technology.**

Technology has affected how I spend my free time in a number of ways. Primarily, it has enhanced my enjoyment in doing some, otherwise, old-fashioned activities.

For example, I have an electronic keyboard in addition to a regular piano. Whenever I have some free time, I like to practice playing the piano. This is not any different from what I did before I bought the electronic piano. What is different is that, now, I can use these skills on the electronic keyboard as well. The electronic keyboard can sound like a regular piano but it can also play rhythms and other special effects. With it I can sound like a one-man band! I really enjoy being able to play requests for different types of music whenever we have parties and family get-togethers.

In addition to playing the piano, during my leisure hours I relax watching television. The recent acquisition of a VCR has enabled me to watch many new movies in the comfort of my home. I no longer spend a lot of money on tickets or stand in long lines at the movie theater. With my VCR, I also have the opportunity to tape my favorite concerts, television specials, and movies for my friends and myself.

Technology has not really changed my choice of free time activities. I still enjoy the piano and watch television with my family. However, technology has provided me with different ways of enjoying those activities.

Character-Trait Analysis

1.  The essay is organized effectively.
2.  The point of view is clearly stated in the introduction and summarized in the conclusion.
3.  The first example supports the writer's stated point of view. The second example of watching new movies at home on the VCR is effective because the VCR vs. movie theater aspect is developed.
4.  The essay is easy to read. The sentence structure is awkward in places but it does not interfere with the essay's overall effectiveness.

# SIMULATED TEST ANSWER KEYS
## Social Studies

1. **(3)** *Evaluation/History.* The various inventions in choice (3) are examples of western resourcefulness and innovation. The developments in choices (1) and (4) are examples of interdependence and cooperation that would, if anything, contradict Turner's notion of individualism. The developments in choice (2) and choice (5) are essentially irrelevant to Turner's thesis.

2. **(4)** *Analysis/History.* Distrust of the East, while it may have existed, would not have promoted nationalism in the West. Quite the contrary, it would have encouraged regionalism. Choices (1), (2), (3), and (5) all offer reasons that historians frequently cite for western nationalism: In most instances, frontier people had not yet developed local traditions; they needed access to the rest of the nation, which only national funding and policies could provide; they required organized military defense from hostile Indians; and they resented the influence of faraway European powers and focused instead on their own country's virtues and power.

3. **(4)** *Evaluation/ Economics.* If there is a trade deficit and the amount of money earned from exports becomes closer to the amount of money spent on imports, then the trade deficit would be reduced. This is shown in the graph in 1981. Choice (1) is incorrect, as the graph shows imports increasing at the same time as exports. Choice (2) and choice (3) are incorrect because the deficit existed between 1981 and 1983, when imports decreased, and between 1983 and 1985, when exports increased. Choice (5) is incorrect because the difference between exports and imports would be a trade surplus if exports were higher than imports.

4. **(3)** *Application/ Behavioral Science.* The fact that Manifest Destiny included a concept of the United States as having a "civilizing" influence is indicative of the element of ethnocentrism involved in this policy. The other policies described either explicitly reject or do not involve ethnocentrism.

5. **(4)** *Comprehension/ Behavioral Science.* The passage centers on the evidently widespread feeling of alienation among the American public. The statements in choice (1) and choice (3) are necessary background. The statement in choice (2) provides an important detail; that in choice (5) an interpretation.

6. **(5)** *Comprehension/ behavioral Science.* The passage indicates that alienation had been fairly low, had climbed steadily and had reached high levels with Watergate, and had never really declined since. The graph in choice (5) most accurately describes this sequence.

7. **(3)** *Application/ Behavioral Science.* The passage ties the feeling of alienation to a sense of remoteness form decision-making processes. Regular meetings involving citizens and officials would be one way of attacking this sense of remoteness. None of the other alternatives suggested would serve the function. Failure to vote, for example, would proba bly stem from alienation, so that to get more of the public to vote it would be necessary to deal first with the alienation. A high-level commission would not involve the public, and press coverage, as suggested by the comment on Watergate, would just increase the feeling of alienation without dealing with it.

8. **(4)** *Evaluation/Political Science.* Choice (4) is supported by the comparison between bureaucracy in Jefferson's time, when the federal government did relatively little, and modern bureaucracy, and by the rapid growth of bureaucracy from the

mid-1920s to the mid-1970s, a period during which the federal government came to assume significantly more responsibility. None of the other choices is supported by the passage. If anything, Kaufman's finding that many new agencies were added in areas where agencies already existed might contradict the statements in choices (1) and (5) by suggesting that the bureaucracy is inefficient and that it involves extensive specialization of function.

9. **(2)** *Comprehension/History.* The passage states that the main causes of the fire and the deaths were unsafe working conditions: lint-filled air, eighth- and ninth-floor sewing rooms too high for the fire-fighters' ladders, and locked exit doors. (3) is therefore only one of the causes of the disaster. The panic of the workers (5) could not be the cause of the tragedy because the passage does not suggest any way the workers might have escaped if they had not panicked. Nothing suggests (1) or (4).

10. **(3)** *Evaluation/Political Science.* The passage states that the number of electors depends on the size of the congressional delegation. This, in turn, depends in large part on population. Therefore, the more populous states have more electors and more influence. The other choices are false and cannot be supported by the discussion in the passage.

11. **(5)** *Comprehension/Political Science.* Choice (5) is correct since the Electoral College is a two-state election system and therefore indirect. That is, the people vote for electors, who then cast their ballots for the candidates. Choice (1) refers to the mechanics of casting a vote. Choice (2) is the process of direct election, where voters' ballots directly determine the winner of an election. Choice (3) and choice (4) are part of the nominating process.

12. **(2)** *Analysis/Political Science.* The passage implies that the framers felt that selection of the president was too important to be entrusted to the people. They were also afraid to give too much power to Congress. They therefore created the Electoral College. The statements in the other choices are factually correct but are not supported by the material contained in the passage.

13. **(3)** *Application/Economics.* The passage emphasizes the importance of innovation, and research and development is the process through which innovations emerge. The fact that fewer patents are being applied for merely points to a lack of U.S. research and development activities. Therefore, the recommendations in choices (2), (4), and (5) may or may not make sense; however, they are not supported by the discussion in the passage.

14. **(5)** *Comprehension/History.* By consulting the map and the legend it can be seen that Hayes won the electoral vote (by one vote) while Tilden won the popular vote. The statements in all the other choices are contradicted by the map and legend.

15. **(2)** *Analysis/History.* Had even the contested state with the fewest votes (Oregon, with 3) been assigned to the Democrats, Tilden would have won the electoral, as well as the popular, vote. Therefore choice (1) is incorrect. Choice (4) is implicitly contradicted by the closeness of the election. Choice (3) is wrong since, as is indicated by the blank areas on the map, the territories did not participate in the election. The map does not support choice (5); note that Tilden won New York's 35 electoral votes.

16. **(3)** *Application/Geography.* In order to make room for large-scale farming, the Europeans cleared the land by cutting down the forests.

17. **(5)** *Application/Geography.* Because Manhattan is an island, and is already completely developed, the only way to make more land available is by creating it. Manhattan's shorelines have been extended by filling in parts of the rivers that surround it, thus creating extra land on which to build.

18. **(1)** *Application/Geography.* The Southeast Asian farmers' problem is one of keeping the water in

place to form ponds in which the rice can grow. This problem is solved by terracing the mountains in such a way that the water will remain on the slopes and not drain away.

19. **(2)** *Application/ Geography.* To solve the problem of seasonal drought, the Aswan Dam has been built on the Nile. This dam ensures that there will be a steady supply of water throughout the year, instead of too much at one time and not enough at another. Farmlands are connected to the artificial lake by a network of canals.

20. **(4)** *Application/ Geography.* Reformation is an attempt to restore an environment that has been damaged by human activities.

21. **(4)** *Comprehension/ Economics.* The figures for the country as a whole were 11.4 percent for small-business-dominated areas and 5.3 percent for large-business-dominated areas. The corresponding figures for service industries— 12.6 percent and 5.5 percent—come extremely close to these overall figures.

22. **(1)** *Evaluation/ Economics.* Despite variations, all industries with both small- and large-business-dominated areas show larger percent increases in job growth in the small-business-dominated areas. However, it is not possible to judge on the basis of the chart alone whether small businesses created more jobs than large businesses

(3), since the figures are not for small versus large businesses but for small-versus large-business-dominated areas. If large-business-dominated areas had more employees initially, a smaller percentage increase could in fact mean more jobs created than a larger percentage increase for small-business-dominated areas with fewer employees. Thus choice (3) is incorrect. The statement in choice (5) cannot be supported for the same reason: The 18.9 percent gain in small-business-dominated areas might actually mean fewer jobs created than were lost with the 10.2 percent decrease in the large-business-dominated areas. Choice (4) is incorrect, since no information is given about foreign competitors. Nothing in the chart supports choice (2), either.

23. **(4)** *Comprehension/ Political Science.* The passage discusses how the new testing and monitoring technology has made privacy in the workplace an important concern. Choices (1) and (3) are too general to accurately state the purpose of the passage. Since the passage is discussing the problems involved in the use of technology, choice (2) is wrong. Choice (5) is incorrect because the passage discusses employers, not the government, as using the technology.

24. **(4)** *Evaluation/Political Science.* As the opening sentences of the passage imply, breakthroughs in testing

and monitoring technology have positive as well as negative features. They may, for example, be useful for such purposes as the detection and apprehension of criminals. In addition, once technologies are available, it is difficult to ban their use. Thus choice (4) is the least appropriate and likely response to this threat to privacy. In contrast, the public can seek various ways to limit the technology's use and abuse, which is why choice (1), (2), (3), and (5) are more likely responses.

25. **(2)** *Application/Political Science.* Choice (2) is correct because these tests and monitoring devices may be seen as unauthorized searches and may yield incriminating evidence. The other choices are inappropriate to the situation described in the passage.

26. **(3)** *Comprehension/ Economics.* The passage treats advertising and packaging and labeling as psychological tools of competition; that is, as ways of attracting consumers' attention to a product and giving the product a "different" and desirable image. Thus choice (3) is correct. Choice (4) and choice (5), concerning advertising and differentiation, each refer to only one aspect of what is discussed.

27. **(5)** *Analysis/History.* If large businesses made deals with one another at the public's expense, this implies that there

was in all likelihood a lack of competition in many industries. Thus, government action came in the form of antitrust laws. Choice (1) is therefore incorrect. Choices (2), (3), and (4) would all promote, rather than regulate, business.

28. **(4)** *Comprehension/ Political Science.* The only reason suggested in the passage is the fact that the Arctic Ocean separates the Soviet Union from North America. Choice (1) is incorrect because the military bases are the result, not the cause, of the Arctic's perceived importance to national security.

29. **(5)** *Comprehension/ Economics.* The passage mentions that Japan has moved out of areas in which it can no longer realistically compete and has invested heavily in areas with potential for the future. The statements in choices (1), (2), and (3) are all explicitly contradicted by the passage. Nothing is said to support the statement in choice (4).

30. **(4)** *Evaluation/ Economics.* High prices for food result from middlemen, speculators, and monopolists who make profits from the farmers' crops, leaving farmers little to show for their efforts. There is little or no evidence in the cartoon to support the other choices.

31. **(2)** *Application/ Economics.* Monopolies, including railroad lines, which charge farmers high rates to ship their produce to markets in the East, are shown in the cartoon as the source of the farmers' misfortunes. Therefore, based on the cartoon, what farmers most need are laws to regulate the railroads and other large companies. None of the problems that the other choices would address are depicted in the cartoon.

32. **(4)** *Analysis/Political Science.* The Declaration of Independence says that it is the right and even duty of people "to throw off" a government that takes away their liberty and happiness and institute a new one.

33. **(1)** *Analysis/Political Science.* The passage states that Great Britain's or England's King had a "history of repeated injuries and usurpations." Choice (2) is incorrect because there were only 13 colonies at the time; the United States was not yet a country.

34. **(1)** *Evaluation/Political Science.* Choice (1) is the only example of a colony fighting for its independence from an oppressive government. All the other choices refer to movements within the same country with a long-established government.

35. **(3)** *Analysis/Geography.* Choice (1) is incorrect because 60 degrees refers not to temperature but to the number of degrees latitude, or distance north and south of the equator. Choices (4) and (5) are incorrect because the words "all," "exactly," and "never" make these statements too strong and, therefore, wrong.

Some people, mainly scientists, live in Antarctica in the southern Polar Zone, so (2) in also incorrect.

36. **(3)** *Application/ Geography.* Northern Brazil in a tropical zone, is the country closest to the equator, the hottest part of the Earth.

37. **(3)** *Analysis/History.* This explanation most closely draws together the information presented in the passage and shows how the economy embarked on a downward spiral. Choice (1) contradicts business decisions described in the passage. There is no information given to support either choice (2) or choice (4). The statement in choice (5), taken from the passage, is an effect of the Depression, not a cause.

38. **(4)** *Application/History.* The Works Progress Administration, which provided jobs for 8 million people, is the best example of a relief measure, although it may have also contributed to the goal of recovery. Choice (1) was a classic example of a muchneeded reform. Choice (2) was an example of a recovery act. Choices (3) and (5) were also examples of New Deal reforms.

39. **(1)** *Evaluation/History.* Only choice (1) is supported by the passage. President Roosevelt's New Deal was a federal or national program aimed at helping the unemployed, farmers and business people. You can infer that the author favors govern-

ment intervention in times of crisis because he/she states that the country was "in the throes of a severe economic depression" and that the government action was to "eliminate abuses in the economy" and "solve the nation's ills." No statements in the passage support the other choices.

40. **(4)** *Analysis/History.* Choices (1), (2), (3), and (5) are all facts, information that can be proven. The Gross National Product refers to the total value of everything bought and sold in a country in one year. In choice (4), the word "abuses" is an opinionated one. We are told in lines 4-9 that corporations went bankrupt because they could not sell their products or raise money for new production; nothing is said about "abuses" as a cause of these business failures.

41. **(5)** *Application/ Behavioral Science.* According to the chart, "Death of a close family member" has 63 Life-Change Units. (2) would come under "Personal injury or illness" and have 53 units; (1) would come under "Being fired at work (47 units); (4) would be under "Change in the health of a family member" (44 units); and (3) would come under "Gain of a new family member" (39 units).

42. **(2)** *Comprehension/ Behavioral Science.* The table lists "vacation" with only 13 life-change units, indicating a low level of stress. Choice (1) has 20 units; choice (3), 65 units; choice (4), 31 units; and choice (5),

63 units, because assault and battery can be classified as a major violation of the law.

43. **(2)** *Analysis/History.* The graph shows that both rural (countryside) and urban (city) areas were experiencing population growth; the urban areas were increasing at a faster rate. The graph therefore contradicts (1), (3), and (5). It provides no information on growth in different regions of the U.S., so (4) is wrong.

44. **(4)** *Analysis/History.* The passage states that the growth of the cities was fueled by industrial expansion and the establishment of manufacturing plants or factories. The factories created jobs, attracting people from rural to urban areas.

45. **(5)** *Analysis/History.* Choices (1) and (2) would be important reasons because newly arrived immigrants and the unemployed would provide a supply of labor. Choice (3), low taxes, would attract business people. Factories need to be near a source of transportation (4) to distribute and sell their products. Therefore, choice (5) is the least likely reason.

46. **(3)** *Application/History.* This selection from the Fourteen Points comes closest to restating Hay's goals since it also emphasizes territorial integrity and free trade. Choice (1) was an informal arrangement of spheres of influence, which Hay protested in China. Choice (2) also repre-

sents restraints on international trade that Hay would have opposed. Choice (5) treated Latin America as an American sphere of influence and thus also contradicted Hay's policy.

47. **(1)** *Comprehension/ Political Science.* Roosevelt's deal through an exchange of notes with British officials can only be described as an executive agreement, which the president, having primary responsibility for foreign affairs, may enter into. The other choices can all be eliminated. Choice (2) requires the advice and consent of the Senate. Choice (3) has no relevance to negotiations with another government. Choice (4) is wrong because no declaration of war was involved. Choice (5) is not the best answer because it does not explain where the president got the authority to make a trade with Britain. It only indicates that once made, an executive agreement is, like any other act of federal government, considered law.

48. **(2)** *Evaluation/ Behavioral Science.* The passage mentions that gift giving occurs between social groups in conjunction with social events and that a group that receives a gift must give something in return. From this it can be concluded that gift exchange serves largely to maintain relationships among groups. Thus, choice (5) is incorrect; although "showing off" may be a secondary purpose, it is

by no means the primary one. As the passage indicates that groups often deliberately attempt to return gifts of greater value than the gifts they receive, choice (1) and choice (3) must both be wrong. As gift giving occurs among all sorts of social groups and on all sorts of occasions, choice (4) is also wrong.

49. **(5)** *Application/ Behavioral Science.* Even those who do not agree with the particular rule believe it to be legitimate because it has been approved by a majority, as required by the Constitution.

50. **(3)** *Application/ Behavioral Science.* Public support from the law stems from support for the leader.

51. **(4)** *Application/ Behavioral Science.* The group members are actually breaking the rule of the larger society in obeying the rule of their group. They do so because the resolution is based on a value principle in which they believe, namely, nonviolence.

52. **(1)** *Application/ Behavioral Science.* The people support the proclamation naming the son king because this is the way it has always been done. The line of secession is established by tradition.

53. **(3)** *Application/ Behavioral Science.* The description focuses on the leader. Although choice (2)—emotion—may also be a factor, belief in the leader's vision would seem to stem ultimately from faith in the leader.

54. **(5)** *Application/History.* The example in choice (5) is the historical extension of Calhoun's doctrine, and it took a Civil War ultimately to deny this extremist states' rights position. The other choices are incorrect because in each case the entity rejecting the act, treaty, etc., is using powers it has been given. For example, the Constitution allows the Senate to reject treaties. Only the case of secession follows Calhoun's logic that a state has the right to overturn an act of the federal government.

55. **(2)** *Analysis/History.* Since poor housing and schools existed before the riots occurred, the Johnson Administration's efforts to improve housing and education through the War on Poverty and Great Society programs did not have a quick and significant impact. There is nothing in the cartoon to suggest the statement in choice (1). Choice (3) may or may not have contributed to the riots; however, it is not addressed in the cartoon. Neither choice (4) nor choice (5) is supported by the cartoon.

56. **(1)** *Analysis/Behavioral Science.* Although factually correct, choice (4) simply restates the pattern in the graphs. Choice (1) offers an explanation for this pattern: The reason children know more about their mother's parents than their father's parents is that they tend to be closer to, and talk more with, their mother

than their father. Choice (2) is incorrect as it would explain a pattern opposite to that found in the graphs. Choice (3) is an incorrect factual statement about the graphs; the graphs show that children do know about their grandparents. For this reason, choice (5) is also incorrect.

57. **(5)** *Comprehension/ Economics.* The chart shows that as the amount of the loan still outstanding goes down, interest paid during the year goes down as well. That is, yearly payments remain the same but an even greater share will consist of principal. Thus choice (2) and choice (3) are incorrect: The amount of total payments during a year is always the same, and very little principal is repaid during the early years of repayment. Choice (4) is also wrong because, as shown in the chart, total interest paid exceeds the principal (at $1,158 per year, payments at the end of 20 years total over $20,000 and the loan was for $10,000). Choice (1) is incorrect, because the chart shows that equity is calculated by adding payments of principal to date.

58. **(2)** *Evaluation/History.* White settlers, for sport and profit, killed off the buffalo, on which the Plains Indians depended for most of their life necessities. The settlers expected a nomadic people to live in a confined area and farm the land. It can therefore be concluded that the white settlers failed to understand or respect Indian culture. None of

the statements in the other choices can be confirmed on the basis of the passage.

59. **(3)** *Analysis/Economics.* Choice (3) is supported by the sharp increases in actual and projected Social Security payments, which are granted to people over the age of 65. Steep increases in Aid to Families with Dependent Children would not necessarily mean a high overall birth rate, and the increases in the graph are not steep, so choice (1) is incorrect. Choice (2) cannot be determined from any of the curves on the graph. Choice (4) is not supported by the military retirement data; data on enlistments is needed. Choice (5) is contradicted by the rise in Medicare costs. Note that the Medicare rise provides further support for choice (3), as Medicare is health insurance for retired people.

60. **(4)** *Evaluation/ Economics.* Choice (4) is consistent with the spending levels for Social Security and Medicare as compared to Aid to Families with Dependent Children. Although the aging of the population is one reason for the sharp increases in Social Security and Medicare spending, the budget is also affected by the relative strength of different constituencies and interest groups. Choices (1), (2), and (3) are not substantiated by the information in the graph. Choice (5) is an opinion that is not verified by the data.

61. **(4)** *Application/ Economics.* Only firefighters' services are a public consumer good/service. A car and a tax preparer's services are private consumer goods/services. A factory building is a private capital good. A highway system, although public, is a capital—not a consumer—good.

62. **(1)** *Application/ Economics.* GNP is a total figure; therefore, it does not indicate breakdown by kind of good or service. It provides no information about how goods and services are distributed.

63. **(4)** *Analysis/History.* As the passage indicates, Watergate badly shook the public's trust in government. Ford stated that in pardoning Nixon, he hoped to put the Watergate episode behind the nation so that the country might be able to move on. There is nothing in the passage to support any of the other choices.

64. **(4)** *Comprehension/ Political Science.* A summary of the graph must provide information about both types of elections; therefore, choices (2) and (3) are incorrect. Choice (1) is wrong because there is no information provided about congressional elections in 1964. Choice (5) is also incorrect because the line for congressional elections shows a decrease from 1966 to 1978, an increase until 1982, and then another decrease.

1. **(3)** *Application/Biology.* The facts that the amoeba consists of one cell and that it exhibits signs of independent life eliminate the other choices.

2. **(3)** *Application/Biology.* The fact that the heart is made up of tissues eliminates choices (1) and (2). The fact that it does not include any other organs eliminates choice (4). The fact that it does not function on its own eliminates choice (5). The heart is a group of different tissues that work together, so it is classified as an organ.

3. **(2)** *Application/Biology.* A chemical compound is nonliving matter composed of atoms.

4. **(5)** *Application/Biology.* The fact that a dog is an independent being eliminates choices (1), (2), and (3). The fact that it is composed of many cells eliminates choice (4), leaving multicellular organism as the only choice.

5. **(2)** *Application/Biology.* Little rain falls in the desert, so plants need to conserve whatever water they can. Since transpiration takes place through the leaves, having few leaves would decrease the rate of transpiration and thus conserve water for the cactus.

6. **(3)** *Comprehension/Biology.* Both plants and animals transpire, or give off moisture, so increasing the numbers of both would increase the relative humidity in a room.

7. **(1)** *Comprehension/Biology.* A low water level in the blood is an internal environment change that stimulates the hypothalamus to cause you to feel thirsty. The sun may be part of the stimulus that lowers your blood's water level, but it is not what actually causes you to feel thirsty.

8. **(5)** *Application/Earth Science.* Since Snowcap Mountain rises into the upper two-thirds of the troposphere, cold temperatures and noticeably less oxygen could be a problem.

9. **(3)** *Comprehension/Earth Science.* The correct response is (3) because it gives not only the correct order of events but also a logical sequence in which one step leads to another. Choice (1) is incorrect because it is water heated by the sun, not the heat alone, that is circulated through the house. Choice (2) and (5) lack a logical link between the heating of the water and the obtainment of warm air. Choice (4) by-passes the whole idea of heating the house.

10. **(1)** *Application/Earth Science.* A solar collector should be painted black on the inside to absorb maximum sunlight; it should have a clear covering to prevent heat loss while allowing the rays to pass through; and it should be surrounded on the sides by an insulating material. White or shiny metal containers would reflect too much sunlight; a clear glass container would transmit, rather than absorb, the light. Lack of a cover or insulating material would allow too much heat to be lost to the surroundings.

11. **(5)** *Analysis/Earth Science.* Water is heated in a boiler and also in a solar collector. If you answered choice (2), you confused the idea of a heating device with the fuel that runs it. The sun is to a solar heating system as fuel for the boiler is to a hot-water heating system.

12. **(4)** *Evaluation/Chemistry.* The passage states that "In times of great physical exertion, additional leaves were chewed to increases stamina." The effect of coca consumption in (1) is to create a passive rather than an active condition. The effect in (2) is to give the coca-consumer special intellectual powers rather than to stimulate the person's energy. (3) and (5) clearly do not relate to the idea of coca as a stimulant.

13. **(1)** *Analysis/Biology.* If the orange and yellow colors are visible only

after the chlorophyll decays, and the chlorophyll is necessary for photosynthesis, then the tree is not carrying on photosynthesis after its leaves change color.

14. **(2)** *Comprehension/Biology.* The passage is about the pros and cons of a particular program to manage a wolf population. There is disagreement between backers and opponents of the program, which indicates controversy.

15. **(1)** *Evaluation/Biology.* The fact that the prey populations decreased in large numbers in those years supports the argument that these populations are headed for extinction. Choice (4) is irrelevant to the argument. Choices (2), (3), and (5) support the position of the program's opponents.

16. **(4)** *Comprehension/Biology.* One of Darwin's conclusions was that individuals with favorable variations are more likely to survive and reproduce than others of their species.

17. **(5)** *Comprehension/Biology.* Darwin did not know about the existence of genes and thus could not have known that natural selection acts on genetic variations.

18. **(5)** *Analysis/Biology.* The passage states that Darwin's "theory was incomplete" because he couldn't explain how traits were inherited. In each generation, different combinations of genes from parents produce new traits in their offspring. No statements in the passage support (2), (3), and (4). (1) is a

true restatement of a basic part of Darwin's theory, but it does not explain why his theory ``did not go far enough in its explanation of how species develop.''

19. **(1)** *Analysis/Biology.* Since natural selection operates through reproduction, the speed at which the species reproduces would most determine the speed at which evolution takes place. The other choices describe conditions that may affect evolution, but not necessarily the speed with which it occurs.

20. **(5)** *Evaluation/Biology.* Nowhere does the passage say that according to Darwin's theory a trait acquired by the efforts of some members of a species may be passed on to their offspring. If a father lifts weights and a mother runs regularly, their child will not inherit better muscle tone or added strength in its arms and legs. If a parent develops skills in math or music, the parents' offspring will not be born with skills in math or music. If the child does inherit such abilities, they will come from the parent's genes. Darwin "suggested that certain traits might make some individuals more successful than others in the struggle for existence" because they would "be more likely to survive and reproduce, thus passing the traits on to the next generation." Such favorable traits may help individuals survive by adapting to new conditions that favor them rather than most of

their species; therefore, (1) and (2) support Darwin's theory. (3) restates Darwin's observation that "not all members of a species survive to reproduce" and that the "size of the population of a given species tends to remain the same over long periods of time". (4) summarizes the last seven lines of the passage, which describe how modern genetic research supports Darwin's theory.

21. **(2)** *Application/Physics.* The correct response is (2) because the gain and loss of magnetism with electric current would be very useful in picking up and dropping pieces of metal.

22. **(3)** *Comprehension/Biology.* The evidence supports the generalization that inhaling the smoke of others is a health hazard. Choice (2) is false. Choices (1), (4), and (5) are true but are not concerned with passive smoking.

23. **(4)** *Analysis/Earth Science.* Statements (1) and (5) are opinions. Statements (2) and (3) are presented in the passage as facts. The idea that ozone can cause cancer is a hypothesis that is currently being tested.

24. **(2)** *Application/Chemistry.* Of all the elements listed, sodium has the lowest atomic number (11) and atomic mass (22.9897). Therefore, if a relatively heavy metallic substance is needed, of the elements listed, sodium is the least likely choice.

25. **(4)** *Evaluation/Chemistry.* The elements listed are all located in the same vertical column ("group") in the table. Similarity of chemical and physical properties is clearly one of the principles determining the structure of the table, so choice (5) is wrong. Choices (1), (2), and (3) can be seen to be wrong by examination of the table.

26 **(4)** *Application/Physics.* The arrow flies upward in a straight line until gravity, an outside force, causes it to change direction and fall back to the ground. Choice (1) describes an object at rest that is set in motion. Choice (2) describes an object that changes speed but not direction. Choice (5) illustrates another law of motion: For every action there is an equal and opposite reaction.

27. **(3)** *Application/Earth Science.* Since carbonated water consists of carbon dioxide dissolved in water, it would have the same effect on limestone as rainwater mixed with carbon dioxide, Dissolving sulfur dioxide gas in rainwater is similar to dissolving carbon dioxide in rainwater, but no mention is made in choice (4) of the sulfuric acid's having a corrosive effect on an object.

28. **(5)** *Analysis/Chemistry.* Cleaning the silver immediately would remove any sulfur-containing foods such as egg yolk. Keeping it in an airtight container would prevent contact with the hydrogen sulfide in the atmosphere.

29. **(3)** *Comprehension/Physics* The idea that heat is a fluid was part of the caloric theory. Heat is a form of energy. Like all forms of energy, it is invisible: only the results it produces are visible.

30. **(2)** *Application/Physics.* Choice (2) is the only answer that describes an object, not a person, in motion or moving. The tires are producing heat as they rub against the ground.

31. **(2)** *Analysis/Physics.* The correct response is (2) because motion produces heat as kinetic energy is converted into heat energy. Choice (4) is incorrect because the rope is not in motion. Choices (1), (3), and (5) are incorrect because the rope is not the source of the heat.

32. **(4)** *Evaluation/Physics.* If energy of motion can be converted into heat, then energy must be able to change from one form to another. Choices (3) and (5) relate to the misconceptions of heat that were part of the caloric theory. Choices (1) and (2) are incorrect because the passage included no quantitative discussion of molecular energy.

33. **(2)** *Application/Biology.* The muscles of the body enable a person to walk, sit, talk, and chew.

34. **(3)** *Application/Biology.* The adrenal glands secrete the hormone adrenaline, which is a chemical that gives the body a rush of temporary energy.

35. **(4)** *Application/Biology.* The mouth and intestine are two major organs in the digestive system, which breaks down food into smaller and smaller particles until it is finally absorbed into the bloodstream.

36. **(1)** *Evaluation/Chemistry.* The graphic shows that some substances, like saliva and human blood, are neutral, neither acidic nor basic. (3) is wrong because tomato juice, with a pH of 4, is only moderately acidic, being in the middle of the acidic portion of the scale. The passage states the opposite of (5). Nothing supports (2) or (4).

37. **(2)** *Evaluation/Physics.* The passage explains that people use levers, such as crowbars, bottle openers, and wheelbarrows, to do work more easily. Choices (1), (3), (4), and (5) are incorrect because they are too strongly worded. Neither the passage nor the graphic provides enough information about gears, levers, and pulleys to explain the uses of simple machines mentioned in these choices.

38. **(4)** *Comprehension/Biology.* Having a smooth coat is determined by recessive genes. The passage states that for a recessive trait to be visible, the offspring must inherit two recessive genes. In the diagram, there is only one smooth-coated guinea pig out of four, which is 25%.

39. **(5)** *Analysis/Biology.* Since the rough-coated guinea pig can only give an "R" and the smooth-

coated guinea pig an "r," Rr is the only possible combination.

40. **(1)** *Evaluation/Biology.* If either gene was dominant, one would determine the trait when crossed with the other. However, a flower with one red gene and one white gene is neither red nor white but pink.

41. **(5)** *Evaluation/Biology.* If skin color is inherited in a way similar to that for flower color, then dark skin color may be considered analogous to a red flower, and light skin color to a white flower. Thus neither the gene for dark skin color nor the one for light skin color is dominant. If one parent has dark-colored skin and one has light-colored skin, all the children will have skin colors between dark and light.

42. **(3)** *Comprehension/ Earth Science.* Although one paragraph of the passage discusses possible reasons for Earth's magnetism, the main purpose of the passage is to discuss the magnetic properties of Earth in general. Use of an iron bar magnet simply provides an opening illustration.

43. **(1)** *Comprehension/ Earth Science.* The fact that the magnetosphere contains charged particles, and the idea that Earth's magnetism may be caused by bands of electric current, suggest that a relationship exists between electricity and magnetism.

44. **(2)** *Analysis/Earth Science.* A compass would point to Earth's magnetic, not geographic, north pole. Thus a person using a compass must take into account the "error" of the compass in locating true north.

45. **(4)** *Analysis/ Earth Science.* The idea that Earth's magnetism is caused by bands of electric current is presented as a possible explanation for Earth's magnetic behavior. Therefore, it is a hypothesis. The other choices all represent statements that can be verified as fact or established theory.

46. **(4)** *Evaluation/Earth Science.* Statements about the locations of the poles are backed up by geographic data. Choices (2) and (3) are supported by the opening demonstration of the bar magnet, as well as by detailed information about the magnetosphere. Recent ideas about the cause of Earth's magnetism are stated but not supported by data.

47. **(4)** *Application/ Chemistry.* In this reaction, the sodium and hydrogen exchange places: HCl + NaOH Nacl + HOH. Thus the procedure is a double replacement reaction.

48. **(2)** *Application/ Chemistry.* Water is broken down into oxygen and hydrogen: $H_2O$ O + $H_2$.

49. **(3)** *Application/ Chemistry.* The zinc replaces the hydrogen in sulfuric acid to form zinc sulfate: Zn + $H_2SO_4$ $ZnSO_4$ + $H_2$.

50. **(5)** *Application/ Chemistry.* Because sodium is less active than lithium, it cannot replace lithium in lithium chloride. Thus, no reaction occurs.

51. **(3)** *Analysis/Biology.* Statements A and C could be chemically proven. B and D are the opinions of the author of the article.

52. **(5)** *Comprehension/ Physics.* As the train passed by, you would hear sound waves that were less compressed. As a result, the whistle would sound lower in pitch than it did before the train passed by.

53. **(1)** *Application/Biology.* The red blood cell is the only substance of this group that is not a foreign substance and thus will not provoke an attack by the immune system.

54. **(4)** *Comprehension/ Biology.* The rat is the smallest animal listed, so it has the shortest life expectancy.

55. **(5)** *Evaluation/Biology.* If you are exercising in an intense way, it would be unlikely for you to have recently eaten a big meal. When the body is digesting food, other body functions slow down. That is why you often feel tired after eating a big meal. Digestion, the breaking down of food, would interfere with the release of energy needed to power the body.

56. **(1)** *Analysis/Biology.* There is nothing in the passage about a difference in reuse of ADP, speed of energy release, type of carbohydrates, or individual differences among cells regarding anaerobic versus aerobic respiration, which eliminates choices (2),

(3), (4), and (5). The presence of free oxygen is a difference between aerobic and anaerobic respiration, and thus seems likely to have something to do with the greater yield of energy.

57. **(5)** *Analysis/Biology.* The passage is concerned with biology in that it discusses how cells obtain energy; it is concerned with chemistry in that it discusses how certain molecules and atoms change and combine; and it is concerned with physics in that it discusses changes in energy. There is no mention of the concerns of Earth science.

58. **(2)** *Analysis/Biology.* If the first living organisms evolved in an atmosphere without oxygen, then it is likely that anaerobic respiration evolved earlier than aerobic respiration, since these organisms would have needed to obtain energy in the absence of oxygen. This eliminates choice (1). Choices (3), (4), and (5) are irrelevant information.

59. **(5)** *Analysis/Biology.* There is no information contained in the graph regarding the brain location or the size of the two cortexes, so choices (1), (2), and (4) are eliminated. Choice (3) is false because the cortexes each receive signals from the same body parts. Thus choice (5) is correct because a body part such as the lips, which are moved often, has more space devoted to it in both cortexes than the trunk, which is used less often.

60. **(4)** *Comprehension/ Physics.* The passage and the graphic provide information about both refraction and reflection.

61. **(1)** *Analysis/Physics.* The apparent bending of the straw is caused by the bending of light waves as they pass from air to water. This is the only choice that correctly relates to the information provided.

62. **(5)** *Analysis/Chemistry.* Choice (1) is a statement of fact. Choice (2) is incorrect because the author does not imply that the industries are careless in the burning of fuels. Choices (3) and (4) are facts that can be verified by measurement and analysis.

63. **(1)** *Comprehension/ Biology.* As the diagrams show, a plant cell and a bacterium both have a cell wall, a cell membrane, and at least one chromosome, which eliminates choices (2), (3), and (4). Only a plant cell has chloroplasts, so choice (5) would not tell you that your cell is a bacterium. However, a plant cell has a nucleus and a bacterium does not, so choice (1) would immediately tell you that the cell is a bacterium.

64. **(3)** *Analysis/Chemistry.* Depending upon the structure of the molecule, the formula $C_2H_6O$ can represent either ethanol or ethyl ether—two very different compounds. Thus a structural formula, rather than a molecular formula, is needed to determine the arrangement of atoms in a molecule.

65. **(4)** *Evaluation/Biology.* Choice (4) would indicate that the female cowbird listens to the dialect in choosing her mate. Her rejection of newcomers and young cowbirds could be based on other reasons, such as smell or appearance, eliminating choices (1) and (3). Choices (2) and (5) do not support the hypothesis because learning the dialect could serve other biological purposes, such as communicating the location of food.

66. **(3)** *Evaluation/Physics.* In a rainbow, the white light from the sun is split apart into its many component wavelengths, each of which appears as a different color. Choice (4) is incorrect because infrared and other normally invisible types of light are not visible in a rainbow. Choice (5) is incorrect because the rainbow effect is created not by the bending of light but by the separation of the different wavelengths. Choices (1) and (2) are not addressed by the passage.

1. **(5)** *Comprehension/ Fiction.* The Evertons have left their home in San Francisco for a place that they have never seen and know little about. The author explains that they have done this to "weave chance and hope into a fabric that would clothe them as long as they lived" (lines 44-46). Their motive is not to find adventure (choices [1] and [3]), nor to get away from the sadness of society (choices [2] and [4]), but to pursue a rather unrealistic goal.

2. **(3)** *Comprehension/ Fiction.* Ibarra is described as lacking telegram services (lines 50-51). Also, when the Evertons are asked about airport facilities and lighting for the house, they avoid answering (lines 51-53).

3. **(2)** *Comprehension/ Fiction.* Memories can be compared to corks left out of bottles because, after a while, they "swell" and "no longer fit" reality (lines 68-71). The Evertons base their vision of Ibarra on a great-aunt's memories of it, never imagining that those memories may have been exaggerated or otherwise distorted.

4. **(3)** *Analysis/Fiction.* A story told in the present tense expresses the immediacy of the here and now. The author's choice of the present tense makes the Evertons' travels unfold before the reader's eyes as though they happen at the moment of reading.

5. **(5)** *Comprehension/ Poetry.* If the fog acts like a cat, then its movements are slow and stealthy. The fog "moves on" (line 6) rather than stays (choice [2]). It also is not described as swift (choice [1]) or dark (choice [3]). The feet (line 2) and haunches (line 5) are figurative rather than literal (choice [4]).

6. **(3)** *Comprehension/ Poetry.* The "little cat feet" can be interpreted in several ways, but the fog would not hold soot (choice [4]). Pedestrians (choice [1]) are not mentioned. The wisps of mist are probably the "feet."

7. **(4)** *Analysis/Poetry.* The poet concentrates on the image of the moving fog, not on the way the fog feels. The fog moves silently and slowly, as a cat walks.

8. **(5)** *Comprehension/ Drama.* In lines 2-3 Blanche asks, "What are you doing in a place like this?" and in lines 7-11 she says, "Never, never, never in my worst dreams could I picture—Only Poe! Only Mr. Edgar Allan Poe—could do it justice! Out there"—she means outside the apartment—"I suppose is the ghoul-haunted woodland of Weir! (*She laughs.*)" If you do not know that Poe was famous for his stories of supernatural horror, you probably do recognize the word "ghoul," which means "demon" or "evil spirit." A ghoul is usually represented in horror movies as an ugly monster that eats human beings or human corpses. Blanche says to Stella in lines 18-20, "why didn't you write me, honey, why didn't you let me know?"; so (1) is wrong. Since Blanche does not mention other cities, (2) is wrong. She specifically says that the apartment's condition "has got nothing to do with New Orleans," and therefore (3) and (4) are wrong.

9. **(5)** *Analysis/Drama.* In lines 62-65 Blanche says, "my—nerves broke . . . I was on the verge of—lunacy, almost!" She explains that therefore the high school superintendent gave her a leave of absence. In lines 57-58 she asks Stella, "You thought I'd been fired?"—which may make you suspect that she was fired—but she does not say that she was; so (4) is wrong. Blanche does say to Stella in lines 38-39, "You're all I've got in the world," but she does not give this as an explanation of why she has come to visit her at this specific time; therefore, (3) is not correct.

Nothing Blanche says supports (1) or (2).

10. **(5)** *Comprehension/Drama.* In lines 45-46 Stella says, "You never did give me a chance to say much, Blanche. So I just got in the habit of being quiet around you." Stella says she has not asked Blanche why she is visiting her because she thought Blanche would tell her if she wanted to (lines 54-56); that is not the same thing as saying that she is waiting for Blanche to tell her why she has come, and it is not the reason Stella gives Blanche for being quiet. Therefore, (4) is wrong. In line 41-42 Stella ("sincerely") denies that she is not glad to see Blanche (3). Nothing suggests (1) or (2).

11. **(4)** *Analysis/Drama.* In lines 25-28 Stella says, in replay to Blanche's comments about her apartment, "Aren't you being a little intense about it? It's not that bad at all! New Orleans isn't like other cities." Stella's comment does not indicate that she thinks Blanche fails to notice enough about her apartment—that she is unobservant (2); in fact, her comment indicates that Blanche is observing too many of the unattractive features of her lifestyle (for example, the L & N railroad tracks nearby) and is exaggerating them (for example, by comparing the L & N tracks to a forest full of monsters—"the ghoul-haunted woodland of Weir"). Blanche's remarks obviously do not express envy of Stella's lifestyle (1), and nothing sug-

gests she does not mean what she says—that she is insincere (5). Blanche's hostile comments express shock and disgust but not fear, so (3) is wrong.

12. **(4)** *Analysis/Commentary.* In lines 34-40 of the third paragraph, Oates is quoted as saying that the referee "makes boxing possible," that unsupervised boxing would be "hellish, if not obscene." (1) refers to the attitude of people in Oates's working-class background, who thought a man who would not fight was a coward (lines 20-23). The other choices are contradicted by the information in the passage.

13. **(4)** *Comprehension/Commentary.* (4) is not one of Oates's arguments in defense of boxing but is her early "feminist preconception" of boxing as socially accepted "masculine violence," that is, her early negative idea that boxing was a kind of social disorder, like organized crime or violence against women. (1), (2), and (5) all restate arguments of Oates in lines 48-55. (3) restates an argument in lines 15-16.

14. **(4)** *Comprehension/Commentary.* In lines 44-48, Oates is quoted as saying that as a political parable, boxing is an "image of the political impotence of most (men")) "impotence" means lack of power or powerlessness). (1) restates a description of boxing as "theater" in lines 40-43. (2) restates a description in lines 38-39 of what boxing

would be without a referee. Lines 45-48 directly contradict (3). (5) is an incomplete and misleading restatement of lines 45-48: Boxing is called an image of most men's anger at their lack of power, not an image of most men in every way.

15. **(1)** *Analysis/Commentary.* Oates first compares boxing to the arts in her discussion of the role of the referee (lines 33-39). She then considers boxing as theater (lines 40-43). Her quotation of Emily Dickinson (lines 67-69) implies a comparison between the impact of great art and of a great boxing match.

16. **(4)** *Comprehension/Commentary.* The term is used to refer to the Greco-Roman origins of boxing, which Oates mentions as part of the "history lesson" in "On Boxing."

17. **(5)** *Application/Commentary.* Oates expresses her belief that boxing is an outlet for aggression that cannot be directed toward any "legitimate objects" in society (line 47-48). However, she also views aggression as "inevitable and quite natural" (lines 54-55). It is likely that Oates believes that competitive instincts are natural and that school sports provide a healthy outlet for these instincts.

18. **(5)** *Comprehension/Poetry.* The poem begins with "I think it must be lonely to be God" (line 1) and ends with "Perhaps sometimes He tires of being great/In solitude" (lines 27-29).

Throughout the poem, consideration is given to the thought that God and humans cannot feel close to each other.

19. **(3)** *Comprehension/ Poetry.* The poet says that despite these seeming shows of worship, "Nobody loves a master" (line 2).

20. **(4)** *Application/Poetry.* Nothing is said in the poem about social programs (choice [2]), about church involvement in political matters (choice [3]), or about missionary work (choice [5]). What is said concerns the great separation between people and God. A church that offered elaborate, dignified services (choice [1]) probably would only widen the gap. A church whose members were "friends of God," however, might keep God from feeling "lonely."

21. **(5)** *Comprehension/ Fiction.* In repeating the story of his offer to buy the horse, the rancher explains that Joe's answer was "Ain't my horse" (line 60).

22. **(1)** *Comprehension/ Fiction.* The Indians want to keep secret the reason for the killing of the horse. Although the mission priest believes that the event has "dark, pagan significance" (choice [3]), there is no evidence in the passage to support his view.

23. **(2)** *Application/Fiction.* The cultural ritual of killing the horse is similar to the cultural ritual of a bullfight. To someone outside the tradition, the event may seem to be distasteful. (Choice [3] is the only other event that might arouse distaste, but it does not produce nearly as strong a reaction as bullfighting does for most people.) Like Joe's killing of the horse, the killing of the bull and the entire bullfight have great cultural significance.

24. **(2)** *Analysis/Fiction.* It is ironic that a character with the name of Joe Walking Wolf should be lame. The fact is revealed in line 31. None of the other choices is supported in the passage.

25. **(3)** *Analysis/Fiction.* In lines 65-67, we are told that the Indian agent "knew more about Indians than The Federal Government required him to know." Therefore, if he "did not investigate, figuring it was none of his business" (lines 71-72), we can conclude that is because he understood that the shooting of the horse was a natural expression of the Native American way of life, and that the laws of the white world he was supposed to enforce were irrelevant to this situation.

26. **(5)** *Comprehension/ Nonfiction.* The speaker explains the term by saying that Estebita's voice "could be heard by everyone" (lines 6-7).

27. **(1)** *Comprehension/ Nonfiction.* The speaker specifically mentions his "will to survive" and his "determination" (lines 14-15). The passage as a whole focuses on how he found ways to cope with the ordeal of his imprisonment.

28. **(4)** *Application/ Nonfiction.* The passage shows that the speaker is able to adapt to a harsh environment; he is not the kind of person to give up (choice [2]). Just as he figured out ways to preserve his physical fitness and his mental concentration in prison, so would he probably figure out how to feed and shelter himself on a desert island.

29. **(3)** *Analysis/Nonfiction.* Although the speaker may have felt some anger and frustration over his situation (choice [5]), he gives the reader a picture of prison life through the use of concrete, descriptive details. These details include a mention of Estebita's story-telling, descriptions of the physical and mental exercises the speaker performed, and information about the physical appearance of the prison.

30. **(4)** *Comprehension/ Fiction.* Elena's deepest wish is to do something meaningful with her life. As she explains when speaking of "one's proper place," "Each of you .-.. knows what he is working for." Her "proper place" is not necessarily in her social class (choice [1]) or with a respectable family (choice [3]), but in a productive task that would give her life a purpose.

31. **(5)** *Analysis/Fiction.* Elena sees the benefits of being healthy and productive. Concerning her own situation, she states, "I should prefer the hardest labor to such a condition" (lines 16-18). She does not despise wealth in general (choice [1]); she merely states that wealth

does not guarantee happiness. She is not embarrassed by her own wealth (choice [3]). If she resents her husband (choice [4]), it is for caring too much for the in-laws who have refused to forgive them for marrying.

32. **(5)** *Comprehension/ Fiction.* Elena says of her "illness," "I get no sleep; a continual headache gives me no peace ... I am weak all over" (lines 12-14).

33. **(4)** *Analysis/Fiction.* The author mentions young and old, male and female in the group of peasants. All hear what Elena speaks of as a lesson that not everyone who looks wealthy is satisfied with life (lines 56-59).

34. **(1)** *Comprehension/ Fiction.* In the first sentence of the passage, the narrator says that when you are eleven you are also all the ages you have ever been, back to year one; this idea is repeated in the third paragraph and the last paragraph. When she is forced to put on the sweater, she says, "all the years inside me—ten, nine, eight, seven, six, five, four, three, two, and one—are pushing at the back of my eyes" (lines 130-133)—meaning that younger parts of herself are hurting and are about to make her cry. When she does cry, she says, "I'm eleven and it's my birthday today and I'm crying like I'm three in front of everybody." Since her main point is that people suffer because they remain children even as they grow older, (2) and (5) cannot be correct. (3)

and (4) are details that are part of the author's main idea: The reason she is helpless against the authority figure and has a painful birthday is that younger parts of herself are still alive inside her and cause her to suffer.

35. **(3)** *Comprehension/ Fiction.* In the narrator's first reaction to the sweater in lines 61-65, she says, "It's an ugly sweater" and "It's maybe a thousand years old." In lines 71-73 she again says it is ugly, "all raggedy and old," and in lines 139-141 she says, "the sweater hurts me... all itchy and full of germs that aren't even mine." She has all these reactions before she learns it belongs to "stupid Phyllis Lopez," so (1) cannot be correct. It is the fact that the sweater is ugly and old that makes her feel ashamed to have the teacher say it belongs to her (see lines 66-67: "even if it belonged to me I wouldn't say so"); this is more important than the fact it has been in the coatroom a month (2) or that "stupid Sylvia Saldivar" said it was hers (4). Nowhere does the narrator say the sweater was made for a three year old (5), only that being forced to take it made her feel like a three–year–old.

36 **(5)** *Analysis/Fiction.* The narrator says she wants to be "far away like a runaway balloon" because "I wish I was anything but eleven, because I want today to be far away already." The image of the balloon "like a tiny o in the sky, so tiny-tiny you have to

close your eyes to see it" expresses her desire to escape the pain of her experience, like a balloon breaking free of the Earth and disappearing, or going to heaven in some sense. Her desire to be one hundred and two years old (2) in the next-to-last sentence is only part of her desire to be "anything but eleven" and to escape the pain of her experience. Since her suffering comes from the three-year-old part of herself that is still alive inside her, (3) is obviously wrong. Nothing suggests (1) or (4).

37. **(2)** *Comprehension/ Commentary.* The critic points out that the Beatles were quite concerned with melody, harmony, and poetry (lines 6-10). Heavy metal, on the other hand, seems to care more "about sound, not music" (line 22). Although some of the other choices may be true, only choice (2) is the focus of the passage as a whole.

38. **(3)** *Comprehension/ Commentary.* The comment appears immediately after the critic comments, "And in most pop rock, synthesized handclaps and artificial impulses ... take the place of melody and harmony" (lines 56-60). The reference to a "barren landscape" (line 64) is his prediction that current trends in pop music probably will not change. Society still may be interested in music (choice [2]), but it will be music of a different order.

39. **(5)** *Comprehension/ Commentary.* In lines 45-48, the critic says the American public loved the Beatles because they "had a natural grace and charm, and they were obviously enjoying themselves and hoping that the fun would last." It is true that earlier, in line 36, the critic says that "they were good," meaning that they were musically talented; but in the lines referred to in the question, he does not say the public loved the Beatles because they were musically talented (1) or musically original (3), but because they were natural and entertaining. In lines 47-48, we are told that they seemed to hope "that the fun would last," but that does not mean that they were funny (2), as a comedian would be. The critic nowhere says that the Beatles were "musically natural" (4).

40. **(1)** *Analysis/ Commentary.* The critic does not attempt to support his view by referring to authorities on music or by arguing against those who may like heavy metal. Rather, he uses historical references to recall nostalgically the impact that the Beatles originally made. He also gives frequent examples—especially of the aspects of heavy metal that he finds distasteful.

41. **(5)** *Application/ Commentary.* The recent dominance of special-effects technology in movies can be compared to the increasing importance of musical-effects technology in pop songs. It could be argued that both kinds of technologies replace natural "effects" with something artificial and thus hurt the media in which they are used.

42. **(5)** *Comprehension/ Nonfiction.* The poacher's reason for hunting rhinos is summed up in the statement "The prize is the rhino's horn" (lines 45-56) and explained in the rest of that paragraph.

43. **(3)** *Comprehension/ Nonfiction.* The threats to the African wildlife population are discussed throughout the passage. Given the problems of poaching (lines 25-34) and takeover of wilderness areas for human use (line 1), the future looks grim for African wildlife. The author seems to side with the "pes- simists [who] predict that wild Africa will soon become little more than a string of glorified safari parks as the true wilderness shrivels and the animals die out" (lines 15-18).

44. **(3)** *Application/ Nonfiction.* The author's main concern is that "wild Africa will soon become little more than a string of glorified safari parks as the true wilderness shrivels and the animals die out" (lines 13-18). Therefore, he clearly would not recommend more zoos (1)—where wild animals would be caged—or more safari parks (2). Since in lines 53-54 he says that game laws do not stop the poaching, he would not recommend (4) or (5).

45. **(5)** *Comprehension/ Nonfiction.* In line 37, we are told that rhinos have "a keen sense of smell." Choices (2) and (4) restate information in lines 41-44. (3) restates information in lines 38-41. Lines 37-38 tell us rhinos "have poor eyesight" (1).

# SIMULATED TEST ANSWER KEYS
## Mathematics

1. **(4)** *Arithmetic/Application.*
$$V = \pi r^2 h$$
$$V = (3.14)(1.5)^2(4)$$

2. **(2)** *Arithmetic/Problem Solving.*
50 minutes = $\frac{5}{6}$ hour

$d = rt$     or     $\frac{90}{1} = \frac{n}{\frac{5}{6}}$

$d = 90 \times \frac{5}{6}$       $90 \times \frac{5}{6} = n$

$d = 75$        $75 = n$

3. **(2)** *Arithmetic/Problem Solving.*
$$\frac{15 + 22 + 19 + 8 = 39}{5} = \frac{103}{5} = 20.6$$

4. **(5)** *Algebra/Problem Solving.*
$.65u$ gives 65% of the units.

5. **(2)** *Algebra/Problem Solving.*
If $a$ = size of apartment:
$$3a + 75 = 1500$$
$$3a = 1425$$
$$a = 475$$

6. **(2)** *Geometry/Application.*
Angles $a$ and $c$ are equal, and angles $b$ and $c$ are supplementary.
$180° - 100° = 80°$

7. **(5)** *Arithmetic/Application.*
The total length of the deck is not given and cannot be found from the measurements given.

8. **(5)** *Arithmetic/Problem Solving.*
Add the profits made from trains and the profits made from puzzles. Then divide by the number of people.

9. **(1)** *Arithmetic/Application.*
$$\frac{1}{24} = \frac{n}{180}$$

10. **(3)** *Arithmetic/Application.*
$i = prt$
$= 588 \times .15 \times 1$
$= 88.20$
or
$\frac{15}{100} = \frac{p}{588}$
$15 \times 588 = 100p$
$8820 = 100p$
$88.20 = p$

11. **(4)** *Arithmetic/Problem Solving.*
Interest:
3 mo. = $\frac{1}{4}$ yr.
$i = prt$
$i = (29 + 84) \times .18 \times \frac{1}{4} = 5.085$
5.085 rounds to 5.09
Balance: $29 + 84 + 5.09 = 118.09$

12. **(4)** *Arithmetic/Problem Solving.*
$700 - 200 = 500$

13. **(1)** *Arithmetic/Skills.*

14. **(3)** *Arithmetic/Problem Solving.*
Discount:
$.2 \times 150 = 30$    or    $\frac{20}{100} = \frac{p}{150}$
$20 \times 150 = 100p$
$3000 = 100p$
$30 = p$
Sale price: $150 - 30 = 120$

15. **(4)** *Geometry/Application.*
Use points $E$ (-2, -8) and $F$ (1, 4):
$$m = \frac{y_2 - y_1}{x_2 - x_1}$$
$m -= \frac{4 - (-8)}{1 - (-2)}$
$m = \frac{12}{3}$
$m = 4$

16. **(4)** *Geometry/Application.*

(0, 0) and (9, -3)

$$d = \sqrt{(x_2 - x_1)^2 + (y_2 - y_1)^2}$$
$$= \sqrt{(9 - 0)^2 + (-3 - 0)^2}$$
$$= \sqrt{(9)^2 + (-3)^2}$$
$$= \sqrt{81 + 9}$$
$$= \sqrt{90}$$

17. **(4)** *Arithmetic/Problem Solving.*

.08 x (20,000 + 25,000) = .08 x 45,000 = 3600

or

$$\frac{8}{100} = \frac{p}{20,000 + 25,000}$$

8 x (20,000 + 25,000) = 100$p$

360,000 = 100$p$

3600 = $p$

18. **(3)** *Algebra/Comprehension.*

$(z + 7)(z - 1) = z^2 - z + 7z - 7$

Simplify to $z^2 + 6z - 7$

19. **(3)** *Algebra/Problem Solving.*

Let $c$ = cost.

$$\frac{12}{3.00} = \frac{50}{c}$$

12$c$ = 3.00 x 50

12$c$ = 150.00

$c$ = 12.50

20. **(2)** *Geometry/Problem Solving.*

Using the Pythagorean relationship:

$c^2 = a^2 + b^2$

$c^2 = 4^2 + 3^2$

$c = \sqrt{4^2 + 3^2}$

21. **(5)** *Arithmetic/Problem Solving.*

No correlation can be made between the amount of coal mined and the amount used.

22. **(1)** *Arithmetic/Problem Solving.*

12.7% produced by hydroelectric power.
2,310,000 x .127 = 293,370

23. **(4)** *Arithmetic/Problem Solving.*

$$\frac{7\frac{1}{2}}{1} = \frac{5}{n}$$

$$n = \frac{5}{15\!/_{2}} = \frac{5}{1} \div \frac{15}{2}$$

$$n = \frac{{}^1\cancel{5}}{1} \times \frac{2}{\cancel{15}_3} = \frac{2}{3}$$

24. **(2)** *Arithmetic/Application.*

$C = \pi d$
  = 3.14 x 24
  = 75.36

25. **(3)** *Algebra/Problem Solving.*

If $f$ = people who work in the office, then
   4$f$ = people who work in the factory.

4$f$ + $f$ = 60

5$f$ = 60

$f$ = 12

4$f$ = 4(12) = 48

26. **(1)** *Algebra/Application.* Find the factors of 18, using pairs of negative numbers that add up to the negative 9.

-3 x -6 = 18

-3 + (-6) = -9

The factors of the trinomial are: (s-3) (s-6)

27. **(5)** *Algebra/Problem Solving.*

The cost of mailing the packages would be 10p. Her change would equal $20 minus the mailing cost.

28. **(3)** *Arithmetic/Application.*

53 is between 49 and 64.
$\sqrt{49}$ = 7 and $\sqrt{64}$ = 8

29. **(1)** *Geometry/Problem Solving.*

$$\frac{6}{4} = \frac{21}{s}$$

6$s$ = 84

$s$ = 14

30. **(4)** *Algebra/Skills.*

$$\frac{10(10 - 4)}{4} = \frac{10(6)}{4} = \frac{60}{4} = 15$$

31. **(5)** *Arithmetic/Application.*

Add to find the total commission. Then divide by 4, the number of weeks.

32. **(3)** *Algebra/Problem Solving.*

2$r$ + 5 = 45

33. **(1)** *Algebra/Problem Solving.*

$\frac{3s}{7} = \frac{3}{7}$ of the salary

Rent is (-25) that amount.

34. **(1)** *Arithmetic/Skills.*

36 Million = 36,000,000 = $3.6 \times 10^6$

35. **(5)** *Arithmetic/Problem Solving.*

This summer's daily adult attendance = 115% of last summer's adult attendance.

$1.15 \times 460 = 529$ or $\quad \frac{115}{100} = \frac{p}{460}$

$$115 \times 460 = 100p$$
$$52,900 = 100p$$
$$529 = p$$

Total daily attendance this summer:

$$542 + 529 + 315 = 1386$$

36. **(4)** *Arithmetic/Problem Solving.*

Find the areas of both the triangular part and the rectangular part of the wall, then add.

Triangular area:

$A = \frac{1}{2}\, bh$

$= .5 \times 15 \times 5$

$= 37.5$

Rectangular area:

$A = lw$

$= 15 \times 12$

$= 180$

$180 + 37.5 = 217.5$

37. **(4)** *Arithmetic/Problem Solving.*

1 square yard = 9 square feet

38. **(4)** *Arithmetic/Problem Solving.*

.045 = the amount of sales tax charged
1.045(5.78) = the total cost
Divide by 48 to get the unit cost.

39. **(2)** *Geometry/Skills.*

The triangle formed by the rake is an isosceles triangle. Angle $b$ is the second base angle and measures 55 degrees.

$55 + 55 = 110$

$180 - 110 = 70$

40. **(1)** *Geometry/Problem Solving.*

$P = 2l = 2w$

$100 = 2(30) + 2w$

$100 = 60 + 2w$

$40 = 2w$

$20 = w$

41. **(2)** *Algebra/Skills.*

Divide coefficients; subtract exponents.

$$\frac{32\, a^8\, b^7\, c^6}{8\, a^2\, b^7\, c^3}$$

Divide coefficients: $32 \div 8 = 4$

$a^8 \div a^2 = a^{8-2} = a^6$

$b^7 \div b^7 = b^{7-7} = b^0$

$c^6 \div c^3 = c^{6-3} = c^3$

Therefore: $\quad \dfrac{32\, a^8\, b^7\, c^6}{8\, a^2\, b^7\, c^3} = 4\, a^6\, c^3$

42. **(4)** *Algebra/Problem Solving.*

Let $w$ = water

$\frac{1}{3} = \frac{18}{w}$

$w = 3 \times 18 = 54$

43. **(4)** *Arithmetic/Problem Solving.*

$V = lwh$

$V = 4 \times 4 \times 8$

$V = 128$

44. **(3)** *Algebra/Problem Solving.*

Multiply the rate, 50, by the time, $m$, to find the distance.

45. **(1)** *Arithmetic/Problem Solving.*

45 minutes = .75 hour

$d = rt$

$= 11 \times .75 \times 5$

$= 41.25$

or

$\frac{11}{1} = \frac{n}{.75 \times 5}$

$11 \times .75 \times 5 = n$

$41.25 = n$

46. **(4)** *Arithmetic/Application.*

$80 \times 23 = 1840$

47. **(1)** *Algebra/Skills.*

$-7g + 2h - (-4g) - 3h = -7g + 4g + 2h - 3h = 3g - h$

48. **(5)** *Geometry/Application.*

The measure of the angle formed by the line extended through the fishing pole and the pier is not given.

49. **(2)** *Algebra/Problem Solving.*

$\frac{15}{6} = y$

$15 = 6y$

So, 6 times the number of yards for each vest must be less than or equal to 15.

50. **(1)** *Geometry/Problem Solving.*

$\frac{6}{8} = \frac{n}{39}$

51. **(1)** *Algebra/Problem Solving.*

$q + b$ = total of amount of money she made.
Dividing the total by 52 gives the average weekly salary.

52. **(5)** *Arithmetic/Problem Solving.*

Since the problem does not give the number of people who left early, the chances for those people who stayed cannot be calculated.

53. **(3)** *Arithmetic/Problem Solving.*

**A.** 4 x 8.99 = 35.96   or   $\frac{8.99}{1} = \frac{n}{4}$
$\qquad\qquad\qquad\qquad$ 8.99 x 4 = $n$
$\qquad\qquad\qquad\qquad$ 35.96 = $n$

**B.** 3 x 15 = 45   or   $\frac{15}{1} = \frac{n}{3}$
$\qquad\qquad\qquad\qquad$ 15 x 3 = $n$
$\qquad\qquad\qquad\qquad$ 45 = $n$

**C.** 12 x 4 = 48   or   $\frac{4}{1} = \frac{n}{12}$
$\qquad\qquad\qquad\qquad$ 4 x 12 = $n$
$\qquad\qquad\qquad\qquad$ 48 = $n$

**D.** 2 x 19 = 38   or   $\frac{19}{1} = \frac{n}{2}$
$\qquad\qquad\qquad\qquad$ 19 x 2 = $n$
$\qquad\qquad\qquad\qquad$ 38 = $n$

54. **(1)** *Geometry/Skills.*

The sum of the angles in a triangle is 180°.
180 - (88 + 60) = 180 - 148 = 32

55. **(2)** *Geometry/Problem Solving.*

The diameter of each can is 6 inches. The cans could be placed in 2 rows of 3. 2 x 6 = 12 and 3 x 6 = 18. The cans could also be placed in 1 row of 6. 1 x 6 = 6 and 6 x 6 = 36. 6 inches by 36 inches is not given as a choice.

56. **(3)** *Arithmetic/Problem Solving.*

3 x 8 = 24

$\frac{15,000,000}{24} = 625,000$

$\qquad\qquad$ or

$\frac{15,000,000}{24} = \frac{n}{1}$

$24n = 15,000,000$

$n = 625,000$